THE CAMBRIDGE HISTORY OF
FRENCH LITERATURE

From Occitan poetry to francophone writing produced in the Caribbean and North Africa, from intellectual history to current films, and from medieval manuscripts to *bandes dessinées*, this History covers French literature from its beginnings to the present day. With equal attention to all genres, historical periods, and registers, this is the most comprehensive guide to literature written in French ever produced in English, and the first in decades to offer such an array of topics and perspectives. Contributors attend to issues of orality, history, peripheries, visual culture, alterity, sexuality, religion, politics, autobiography, and testimony. The result is a collection that, despite the wide variety of topics and perspectives, presents a unified view of the richness of French-speaking cultures and gives support to the idea that French writing will continue to prosper in the twenty-first century as it adapts, adds to, and refocuses the rich legacy of its past.

WILLIAM BURGWINKLE is a Reader in Old French and Occitan at the University of Cambridge and a Fellow of King's College, Cambridge.

NICHOLAS HAMMOND is a Reader in Early Modern French Theatre and Thought at the University of Cambridge.

EMMA WILSON is Professor of French Literature and the Visual Arts at the University of Cambridge.

THE CAMBRIDGE
HISTORY OF
FRENCH LITERATURE

⋆

Edited by
WILLIAM BURGWINKLE, NICHOLAS HAMMOND,
and
EMMA WILSON

CAMBRIDGE
UNIVERSITY PRESS

CAMBRIDGE UNIVERSITY PRESS
Cambridge, New York, Melbourne, Madrid, Cape Town,
Singapore, São Paulo, Delhi, Tokyo, Mexico City

Cambridge University Press
The Edinburgh Building, Cambridge CB2 8RU, UK

Published in the United States of America by Cambridge University Press, New York

www.cambridge.org
Information on this title: www.cambridge.org/9780521897860

© Cambridge University Press 2011

This publication is in copyright. Subject to statutory exception
and to the provisions of relevant collective licensing agreements,
no reproduction of any part may take place without the written
permission of Cambridge University Press.

First published 2011

Printed in the United Kingdom at the University Press, Cambridge

A catalogue record for this publication is available from the British Library

Library of Congress Cataloguing in Publication data
The Cambridge history of French literature / edited by William Burgwinkle,
Nicholas Hammond, Emma Wilson.
p.   cm.
Includes bibliographical references and index.
ISBN 978-0-521-89786-0 (hardback)
1. French literature – History and criticism.   I. Burgwinkle, William E., 1951–
II. Hammond, Nicholas, 1963–   III. Wilson, Emma.
PQ103.C26   2011
840.9 – dc22   2010051863

ISBN 978-0-521-89786-0 Hardback

Cambridge University Press has no responsibility for the persistence or
accuracy of URLs for external or third-party internet websites referred to
in this publication, and does not guarantee that any content on such
websites is, or will remain, accurate or appropriate.

Contents

Contents

Contents

Contents

Notes on contributors

BARBARA K. ALTMANN is director of the Oregon Humanities Center at the University of Oregon. Her research area is late medieval French narrative and lyric poetry, and her publications include *The Love Debate Poems of Christine de Pizan* (1998) and *An Anthology of Medieval Love Debate Poetry* (with R. Barton Palmer, 2006). She has also co-edited (with Deborah McGrady) *Christine de Pizan: A Casebook* (2002).

WILDA ANDERSON is Professor of French in the Department of Romance Languages and Literatures at Johns Hopkins University. She is the author of *Between the Library and the Laboratory: The Language of Chemistry in Eighteenth-Century France* (1984) and *Diderot's Dream* (1990).

ROGER ARIEW is Professor and Chair of the Philosophy Department at the University of South Florida. He is the author of *Descartes and the Last Scholastics* (1999) and co-author, with Dennis Des Chene, Douglas Jesseph, Tad Schmaltz, and Theo Verbeek, of the *Historical Dictionary of Descartes and Cartesian Philosophy* (2003); he is also editor and translator of such works as Descartes, *Philosophical Essays* (2000), Montaigne, *Apology for Raymond Sebond* (with Marjorie Grene, 2003), and Pascal, *Pensées* (2005).

NADINE BÉRENGUIER is Associate Professor of French at the University of New Hampshire. Her first book was *L'Infortune des alliances: contrat, mariage et fiction au dix-huitième siècle*, and she has published articles on Anne-Thérèse de Lambert, Madeleine de Puisieux, Françoise de Graffigny, Isabelle de Charrière, and Suzanne Curchod Necker. In her forthcoming book, *Conduct Books for Girls in Enlightenment France* (2011), she examines the challenges posed by books targeting young female readers and outlines their reception in the eighteenth century as well as their editorial fortunes in the nineteenth century.

CLAIRE BOYLE is Lecturer in French at the University of Edinburgh and the author of *Consuming Autobiographies: Reading and Writing the Self in Post-War France* (2007). Her published research focuses on issues of identity, marginality, gender, and sexuality and the work of Hélène Cixous, Jean Genet, Georges Perec, and Nathalie Sarraute. Current research is on (especially queer) identities and testimonies and contemporary French cinema. Claire Boyle is an affiliate of the Centre for the Interdisciplinary Study of Sexuality and Gender in Europe at the University of Exeter.

DAVID BRADBY is Professor Emeritus of Royal Holloway, University of London. His books include *The Theater of Michel Vinaver* (1993), *Beckett: Waiting for Godot* (2001), and *Le Théâtre en France de 1968 à 2000* (2007). He has translated works by Jacques Lecoq, Michel Vinaver, and Bernard-Marie Koltès. With Maria M. Delgado, he edits *Contemporary Theatre Review*.

CELIA BRITTON is Professor of French and Francophone Literature at University College London and a Fellow of the British Academy. She has published widely on French Caribbean literature and thought, particularly on the work of Edouard Glissant. Her books include *Édouard Glissant and Postcolonial Theory* (1999), *Race and the Unconscious: Freudianism in French Caribbean Thought* (2002), and *The Sense of Community in French Caribbean Fiction* (2008). She has also co-edited an issue of *Paragraph* on 'Francophone Texts and Postcolonial Theory' (2001), and edited a special number of *L'Esprit créateur* entitled 'France's Colonies and the Second World War' (2007).

WILLIAM BURGWINKLE is a Reader in Medieval French and Occitan at Cambridge and a Fellow of King's College. His publications include *Sodomy, Masculinity and Law, 1150–1230* (2004), *Love for Sale* (1997), *Razos and Troubadour Songs* (1990), a co-edited volume entitled *Significant Others: Gender and Culture in Film and Literature, East and West* (1992), and the co-authored volume (with Cary Howie), *Sanctity and Pornography in Medieval Culture: On the Verge* (2010).

EMILY BUTTERWORTH is Senior Lecturer in French at King's College, London. Her publications include *Poisoned Words: Slander and Satire in Early Modern France* (2006), and she is currently engaged in a project on forms of excessive speech in the early modern period.

EMMA CAMPBELL is Associate Professor of French at the University of Warwick. She is the author of *Medieval Saints' Lives: The Gift, Kinship and Community in Old French Hagiography* (2008) and is currently working on a book-length project on translation and the untranslatable in medieval French literature.

KATHARINE CONLEY is Professor of French and Comparative Literature and Associate Dean for the Arts and Humanities at Dartmouth College. She is the author of books and articles on surrealist writers and artists including 'A Swimmer between Two Worlds: Francesca Woodman's Maps of Interior Space' in the *Journal of Surrealism and the Americas* (December 2008), *Robert Desnos, Surrealism, and the Marvelous in Everyday Life* (2003), *Automatic Woman: The Representation of Woman in Surrealism* (1996), and the forthcoming *Surrealist Ghostliness*.

MARTIN CROWLEY teaches French at the University of Cambridge. He is the author of *L'Homme sans: politiques de la finitude* (2009), *The New Pornographies: Explicit Sex in Recent French Fiction and Film* (with Victoria Best, 2007), *Robert Antelme: l'humanité irréductible* (2004), *Robert Antelme: Humanity, Community, Testimony* (2003), and *Duras, Writing, and the Ethical: Making the Broken Whole* (2000). He edited 'Contact! The Art of Touch/L'Art du toucher', special issue of *L'Esprit créateur* (Fall 2007), and *Dying Words: The Last Moments of Writers and Philosophers* (2000).

COLIN DAVIS is Professor of French at Royal Holloway, University of London. His research falls principally in the area of post-war French fiction and thought, with a particular interest in the connections between philosophy, literature, and film. His principal publications are *Michel Tournier: Philosophy and Fiction* (1988), *Elie Wiesel's Secretive Texts* (1994), *Levinas: An Introduction* (1996), *Ethical Issues in Twentieth-Century French Fiction: Killing the Other* (2000), *French Fiction in the Mitterrand Years* (co-authored with Elizabeth Fallaize, 2000), *After Poststructuralism* (2003), *Haunted Subjects: Deconstruction, Psychoanalysis and the Return of the Dead* (2007), and *Scenes of Love and Murder: Renoir, Film and Philosophy* (2009).

MARILYNN DESMOND is Distinguished Professor of English and Comparative Literature at Binghamton University. Her publications include *Reading Dido: Gender, Textuality and the Medieval Aeneid* (1994) and *Ovid's Art and the Wife of Bath: The Ethics of Erotic Violence* (2006), and she is co-author (with Pamela Sheingorn) of *Myth, Montage and Visuality: Christine de Pizan's Othea* (2003).

WILLIAM EDMISTON is Professor of French at the University of South Carolina. His publications include *Diderot and the Family* (1985), *Hindsight and Insight: Focalization in Four Eighteenth-Century French Novels* (1991), and, as co-author, *La France contemporaine* (3rd edition 2005).

JODY ENDERS is Professor of French and Theatre at the University of California, Santa Barbara. She is the author of numerous articles and four books on the interplay of rhetoric, law, and the theatrical culture of the European Middle Ages, among them *Death by Drama and Other Medieval Urban Legends* (2002) and *Murder by Accident: Medieval Theater, Modern Media, Critical Intentions* (2009).

GARY FERGUSON is Professor of French at the University of Delaware. He has published numerous studies on sixteenth-century literature and culture, dealing in particular with the history of religion, devotional poetry, women's writing, and questions of gender and sexuality. In 2008, he authored *Queer (Re)Readings in the French Renaissance: Homosexuality, Gender, Culture* and edited *L'Homme en tous genres: masculinités, textes et contextes*.

PHILIP FORD is Professor of French and Neo-Latin Literature at the University of Cambridge. His interests focus on the relationship between humanism and writing, particularly poetry. Publications include a book on Ronsard's *Hymnes* (1997), proceedings of nine conferences on the French Renaissance organised in Cambridge, and a work on the reception of Homer: *De Troie à Ithaque: réception des épopées homériques à la Renaissance* (2007).

CHARLES FORSDICK is James Barrow Professor of French at the University of Liverpool. His books include *Victor Segalen and the Aesthetics of Diversity* (2000), *Travel in Twentieth-Century French and Francophone Cultures* (2005), and *Ella Maillart, 'Oasis interdites'* (2008). He is co-editor of *Francophone Postcolonial Studies: A Critical Introduction* (2003) and *Postcolonial Thought in the French-Speaking World* (2009).

SIMON GAUNT is Professor of French Language and Literature at King's College London. His publications include *Love and Death in Medieval French and Occitan Courtly Literature* (2006), *Retelling the Tale* (2001), *Gender and Genre* (1995), and the co-edited volumes *The Troubadours: An Introduction* and *The Cambridge Companion to Medieval French Literature* (1999 and 2008, both with Sarah Kay). He is currently working on medieval travel writing.

ALAIN GÉNETIOT is Professor of French Literature at the University of Nancy and General Editor of the journal *XVIIe Siècle*. His interests focus on French Classicism and seventeenth-century poetry. He has published *Les Genres lyriques mondains* (1990), *Poétique du loisir mondain, de Voiture à La Fontaine* (1997) and *Le Classicisme* (2005), and edited *L'Éloge lyrique* (2008).

MIRANDA GILL is Lecturer in French at the University of Cambridge and a Fellow of Jesus College. Her research focuses on the history of psychological concepts in post-revolutionary French culture from the perspective of intellectual history and rhetorical analysis. She has worked extensively on the concept of eccentricity in relation to the cultural history of nineteenth-century Paris, publishing various articles on this subject. A full-length study entitled *Eccentricity and the Cultural Imagination in Nineteenth-Century Paris* was published in 2009.

ELIZABETH C. GOLDSMITH is Professor of French at Boston University. Her books include *Lettres de femmes* (co-edited with Colette Winn, 2005), *Publishing Women's Life Stories in France, 1647–1720* (2001), *Going Public: Women and Publishing in Early Modern France* (co-edited with Dena Goodman, 1996), *Writing the Female Voice: Essays on Epistolary Literature* (1989), and *Exclusive Conversations: The Art of Interaction in Seventeenth-Century France* (1988). She has also co-edited the memoirs of Marie Mancini with Patricia Cholakian (1998).

RUSSELL GOULBOURNE is Professor of Early Modern French Literature at the University of Leeds. His research focuses in part on seventeenth- and eighteenth-century French drama. He has published critical editions of a number of Voltaire's plays and is the author of *Voltaire Comic Dramatist* (2006).

MIRANDA GRIFFIN is College Lecturer in French at St Catharine's College, Cambridge. She has published articles on the *lais*, the *fabliaux*, Christine de Pizan, and the Vulgate Cycle. Her book, *The Object and the Cause in the Vulgate Cycle*, was published in 2005. She is currently working on a book about transformation and rewriting, entitled *Transforming Narratives*.

WENDELIN GUENTNER is Professor of French and International Studies at the University of Iowa and has published widely on nineteenth-century French literature and culture. The author of *Stendhal et son lecteur: essai sur les 'Promenades dans Rome'* (1989) *and Esquisses littéraires: rhétorique du spontané et récit de voyage au XIXe siècle* (1997), she has also published on women art critics, and her edition of essays on this topic, *Vanishing Acts: Women Art Critics in Nineteenth-Century France*, is forthcoming. She is currently working on two books, one on the sketch in nineteenth-century cultural discourse in France and another on Jules Claretie's *La Vie à Paris* (1881–1913).

SUZANNE GUERLAC is Professor of Modern French Studies at the University of California, Berkeley. Her interests include the examination of cultural ideologies and articulations between literature and philosophy, and literature and the visual arts. She is the author of *The Impersonal Sublime: Hugo, Baudelaire, Lautréamont* (1990), *Literary Polemics: Bataille, Sartre, Valéry, Breton* (2000), and *Thinking in Time: An Introduction to Henri Bergson* (2006); and she is co-editor (with Pheng Cheah) of *Derrida and the Time of the Political* (2009).

NOAH D. GUYNN is Associate Professor of French at the University of California, Davis, and author of *Allegory and Sexual Ethics in the High Middle Ages* (2007). He is currently working on a new book: *The Many Faces of Farce: Ethics, Politics, and Urban Culture in Late Medieval and Early Modern France*.

NICHOLAS HAMMOND is a Reader in Early Modern French Theatre and Thought at Cambridge University and is the author of *Playing with Truth: Language and the Human Condition in Pascal's Pensées* (1994), *Creative Tensions: An Introduction to Seventeenth-Century French Literature* (1997), *Fragmentary Voices: Memory and Education at Port-Royal* (2004) and *Gossip, Sexuality and Scandal in France (1610–1715)* (2011). He is also the editor of *The Cambridge Companion to Pascal* (2003), and of the series *New Readings: Introductions to European Literature and Culture*.

MICHÈLE HANNOOSH is Professor of French at the University of Michigan, Ann Arbor. She has published widely on nineteenth-century French literature, art, and society, including *Parody and Decadence: Laforgue's Moralités légendaires* (1989), *Baudelaire and Caricature: From the Comic to an Art of Modernity* (1992), and *Painting and the Journal of Eugène Delacroix* (1995). She has recently brought out a major new edition of Delacroix's *Journal* (2009).

NIGEL HARKNESS is Senior Lecturer in French at Queen's University Belfast, and has published widely on women's writing in nineteenth-century France. He is the author of *Men of their Words: The Poetics of Masculinity in George Sand's Fiction* (2007), and is currently working on a project on literary–sculptural intersections in nineteenth-century French literature.

JOSEPH HARRIS is Senior Lecturer in French at Royal Holloway, University of London, specialising in early modern French theatre and spectatorship. He is the author of *Hidden Agendas: Cross-Dressing in Seventeenth-Century France* (2005) and editor of a special issue of *Nottingham French Studies* entitled 'Identification before Freud: French Perspectives' (Autumn 2008).

NICHOLAS HARRISON is Professor of French and Postcolonial Studies at King's College London. His main publications are two books, *Circles of Censorship* (1995) and *Postcolonial Criticism: History, Theory and the Work of Fiction* (2003), and two edited collections of essays, 'The Idea of the Literary', a special issue of *Paragraph* (28.2, 2005) and 'Gillo Pontecorvo's *Battle of Algiers*, 40 Years On', a special issue of *Interventions* (9.3, 2007).

MICHAEL HAWCROFT is Fellow and Tutor in French at Keble College, Oxford, and the author of *Word as Action: Racine, Rhetoric and Theatrical Language* (1992), *Rhetoric: Readings in French Literature* (1999), and *Molière: Reasoning with Fools* (2007).

JAMES HELGESON is a Lecturer in French at the University of Nottingham and has previously taught at Columbia University and Cambridge University. He is the author of *Harmonie divine et subjectivité poétique chez Maurice Scève* (2001) and is currently working on subjectivity in the early modern period.

NICHOLAS HEWITT is Professor of French at the University of Nottingham and editor of *French Cultural Studies*. He has worked extensively on French literary and cultural history in the first half of the twentieth century, and is the author of books on Troyat, interwar intellectual malaise, Céline, and the 'Hussards'. He is the editor of *The Cambridge Companion to Modern French Culture*.

ROBIN HOWELLS is Professor Emeritus of French at Birkbeck, University of London. He is the author notably of *Disabled Powers: A Reading of Voltaire's 'Contes'* (1993), *Playing Simplicity: Polemical Stupidity in the Writing of the French Enlightenment* (2002), and *Regressive Fictions: Graffigny, Rousseau, Bernardin* (2007), along with numerous articles principally in the field of the French eighteenth century.

CARY HOWIE is Assistant Professor of Romance Studies at Cornell University. He is the author of *Claustrophilia: The Erotics of Enclosure in Medieval Literature* (2007) and co-author, with William Burgwinkle, of *Sanctity and Pornography in Medieval Culture: On the Verge* (2010).

DAVID F. HULT is Professor of French at the University of California, Berkeley. He is the author of *Self-Fulfilling Prophecies: Readership and Authority in the First Romance of the Rose* (1986) and editor and translator of Chrétien de Troyes's *Le Chevalier au lion (Yvain)* (1994), the *Cycle de la Belle Dame sans Mercy* (2003), and *La Mort du Roi Artu* (2009). He has also translated into English the documents known as *The Debate of the Romance of the Rose* (2010), and has published widely on Alain Chartier, Christine de Pizan, Jean de Meun, medieval theatre, textual traditions and manuscript traditions of literary texts.

CAROLINE JEWERS is an Associate Professor at the University of Kansas. She has published widely on medieval romance, including *Chivalric Fiction and the History of the Novel* (2000), on the troubadours, and on diverse topics involving medievalism, popular culture, and film.

GILLIAN JONDORF is Fellow of Girton College, Cambridge, and was formerly Senior Lecturer in the Department of French at Cambridge University. She is the author of *Robert Garnier and the Themes of Political Tragedy in the Sixteenth Century* (1969) and *French Renaissance Tragedy: The Dramatic Word* (1990).

NEIL KENNY is Reader in Early Modern French Literature and Thought at Cambridge University. He is the author of *An Introduction to Sixteenth-Century French Literature and Thought: Other Times, Other Places* (2008), *The Uses of Curiosity in Early Modern France and Germany* (2004), *Curiosity in Early Modern Europe: Word Histories* (1998), and *The Palace of Secrets: Béroalde de Verville and Renaissance Conceptions of Knowledge* (1991).

SHARON KINOSHITA teaches World Literature and Cultural Studies at the University of California, Santa Cruz. She is the author of *Medieval Boundaries: Rethinking Difference in Old French Literature* (2006) and co-director of several projects in Mediterranean Studies. Her current project is *Medieval Literature and the Eastern Culture of Empire*.

T. JEFFERSON KLINE is Professor of French in the Department of Romance Studies at Boston University. His publications include *André Malraux and the Metamorphosis of Death* (1973), *Bertolucci's Dream Loom: A Psychoanalytic Study of Cinema* (1987), *I film di Bertolucci* (1992), and *Screening the Text: Intertextuality in New Wave French Film* (1992). He is co-editor of *Bernardo Bertolucci: Interviews* (2000), *Unraveling French Cinema* (2009) and, with the late Naomi Schor, *Decadent Subjects* (2002) by Charles Bernheimer. Kline currently serves on the editorial board of *Studies in French Cinema* (UK).

ANDREW LEAK is Professor of French at University College London. His publications include *Sartre* (2006), *Barthes: Mythologies* (1994), and *The Perverted Consciousness: Sexuality and Sartre* (1989); and he has co-edited *Sartre Today* (with Adrian van den Hoven, 2005) and *The Holocaust and the Text: Speaking the Unspeakable* (with George Paizis, 1999).

JOHN LEIGH is a Lecturer in Eighteenth-Century French Thought and Literature at Cambridge University. He is the author of *The Search for Enlightenment* (1999) and *Voltaire's Sense of History* (2004). He is also the editor of *Beaumarchais, the Figaro Plays* (1998) and *Voltaire, Letters upon the English Nation* (2007). He is currently writing a biography of Voltaire.

ROBERT LETHBRIDGE is Honorary Professor of Nineteenth-Century French Literature at the University of Cambridge and Professor Emeritus of French Language and Literature in the University of London. His publications include *Maupassant: 'Pierre et Jean'* (1984), *Artistic Relations: Literature and the Visual Arts in Nineteenth-Century France* (co-edited with Peter Collier, 1994), and editions of Maupassant's *Bel-Ami* and Zola's *L'Assommoir, Pot-Bouille, and La Débâcle*, as well as some fifty essays, in scholarly journals and collective volumes, on French naturalism, late nineteenth-century French painting, Bourget, Mérimée, and Fromentin.

ROSEMARY LLOYD did a PhD and taught at Cambridge, then moved to Indiana University, from where she retired in 2007 to return to South Australia. Her main interests are in nineteenth- and twentieth-century poetry and prose, especially their relationships with painting. Her publications include *The Cambridge Companion to Baudelaire* (2005) and *Baudelaire's Literary Criticism* (1986), *Closer and Closer Apart: Jealousy in Literature* (1995), *The Land of Lost Content: Children and Childhood in Nineteenth-Century French Literature* (1992), and many translations, essays, and introductions.

MICHAEL LUCEY is Professor of French and Comparative Literature at the University of California, Berkeley, and the author of *Gide's Bent: Sexuality, Politics, Writing* (1995), *The Misfit of the Family: Balzac and the Social Forms of Sexuality* (2003), and *Never Say I: Sexuality and the First Person in Colette, Gide, and Proust* (2006).

JOHN D. LYONS is Commonwealth Professor of French at the University of Virginia. He is the author of *Exemplum: The Rhetoric of Example in Early Modern France and Italy* (1989), *The Tragedy of Origins: Pierre Corneille and Historical Perspective* (1996), *Kingdom of Disorder: The Theory of Tragedy in Seventeenth-Century France* (1999), and *Before Imagination: Embodied Thought From Montaigne to Rousseau* (2005).

JENNY MANDER is a Senior Lecturer in French at Cambridge University and Director of Studies at Newnham College. She is the author of *Circles of Learning: Narratology and the Eighteenth-Century French Novel* (1999) and editor of *Remapping the Rise of the European Novel* (2007). She is currently working on eighteenth-century colonialism, islands, and the abbé Raynal's *Histoire philosophique des Deux Indes*.

DEBORAH MCGRADY is Associate Professor at the University of Virginia. She is the author of *Controlling Readers: Guillaume de Machaut and his Late Medieval Audience* (2006) and co-editor (with Barbara Altmann) of *Christine de Pizan: A Casebook* (2002). She is currently writing a study entitled *The Gift of Literature: Reinventing Patronage during the Hundred Years War*.

PATRICK MCGUINNESS teaches French at Oxford University and is a Fellow of St Anne's Oxford. His books include *Maurice Maeterlinck and the Making of Modern Theatre* (2000), a translation of Mallarmé's *For Anatole's Tomb*, and two collections of poems. In addition, he has co-edited many volumes, including: *Belgique entre deux siècles* (2007), *From Art-Nouveau to Surrealism* (2007), and *Selected Writings of T. E. Hulme* (1998).

ISABELLE MCNEILL is an Affiliated Lecturer in the Department of French, University of Cambridge and a Fellow of Trinity Hall. Her publications include *Memory and the Moving Image: French Film in the Digital Era* (2010), and essays on theories of memory, Godard, film and new media, and Agnès Varda's exhibition *L'Île et Elle*. She co-edited *Transmission: Essays in French Literature, Thought and Cinema* (2007) and is currently working on the postcolonial journey in cinema. She is a co-founder and trustee of the Cambridge Film Trust, which runs the Cambridge Film Festival.

WENDY MICHALLAT is Lecturer in French at the University of Sheffield and co-editor of *Lesbian Inscriptions in Francophone Society and Culture* (with Renate Günther, 2007). She has published essays on French queer cinema, *bandes dessinées*, pop culture, and media.

CRAIG MOYES is a lecturer in the French Department at King's College London, specialising in seventeenth- and eighteenth-century French and comparative literature. He has most recently edited a special issue of *Études françaises*, entitled 'L'Échelle des valeurs au XVIIe siècle: le commensurable et l'incommensurable' (45.2, 2009) and is currently completing a book on Furetière's *Roman bourgeois*.

LARRY F. NORMAN is Associate Professor in the Department of Romance Languages at the University of Chicago. He is the author of *The Public Mirror: Molière and the Social Commerce of Depiction* (1999) and *The Shock of the Ancient: Literature and History in Early Modern France*

(2011). Among the volumes he has co-edited are *Du spectateur au lecteur: imprimer la scène aux XVIe et XVIIe siècles* (2002) and *Révolutions homériques* (2009). He is currently completing a book on the Quarrel of the Ancients and the Moderns.

JOHN O'BRIEN is Professor of French Renaissance Literature at Royal Holloway, University of London. He is the author of *Anacreon redivivus* (1995) and of '*La Chaleur de la narration': le cas Martin Guerre entre histoire et récit* (forthcoming). He is the editor of Rémy Belleau's *Les Odes d'Anacréon* (1995), *Distant Voices Still Heard* (2000), and *The Cambridge Companion to Rabelais* (2010).

RICHARD PARISH is a Professor of French at Oxford University. His work on religious polemic includes Pascal's *Lettres provinciales: A Study in Polemic* (1989), and editions of La Bruyère's *Dialogues posthumes sur le quiétisme* (2005) and of Voltaire's annotations of Condorcet, *Éloge et Pensées de Pascal* (2008). In 2009 he delivered the Bampton Lectures in Oxford, with the title: '*Le christianisme est étrange*: Christian particularity in Writing of the French Seventeenth Century'.

ELIZABETH W. POE is a Professor at Tulane University, New Orleans, and is the author of *Compilatio: Lyric Texts and Prose Commentaries in Troubadour Manuscript H (Vat Lat 3207)* (2000) and *From Poetry to Prose in Old Provençal: The Emergence of the Vidas, the Razos, and the Razos de Trobar* (1984). She has written numerous articles on texts of disputed attribution, lexical items of uncertain meaning, and the reception of troubadour poetry in medieval and Renaissance Italy.

CHRISTOPHER PRENDERGAST is a Fellow of King's College, Cambridge and a Professor Emeritus of the University of Cambridge. His publications include *The Classic: Sainte-Beuve and the Nineteenth-Century Culture Wars* (2007), *For the People by the People?: Eugène Sue's* Les Mystères de Paris; *a Hypothesis in the Sociology of Literature* (2003), *The Triangle of Representation* (2000), *Napoleon and History Painting* (1997), *Paris and the Nineteenth Century* (1992), *The Order of Mimesis* (1986), and numerous edited volumes.

RICHARD L. REGOSIN is Professor of French and Italian at the University of California, Irvine. His publications include *Montaigne's Unruly Brood: Textual Engendering and the Challenge to Paternal Authority* (1996), *The Matter of My Book: Montaigne's 'Essais' as the Book of the Self* (1977), and *Agrippa d'Aubigné's 'Les Tragiques': The Poetry of Inspiration* (1970).

PIERRE SAINT-AMAND is Francis Wayland Professor and Professor of French Studies and Comparative Literature at Brown University. His publications include: *Diderot: le labyrinthe de la relation* (1984), *Les Lois de l'hostilité* (1992), and *The Libertine's Progress* (1994). He is the editor of *Thérèse philosophe* (2000) and *Confession d'une jeune fille* in *Romanciers libertins du XVIIIe siècle* (2005). He has completed a new book, *Idle Enlightenment: The Pursuit of Laziness in Eighteenth-Century France*.

LIBBY SAXTON is Senior Lecturer in French and Film Studies at Queen Mary University of London. She is author of *Haunted Images: Film, Ethics, Testimony and the Holocaust* (2008), co-author, with Lisa Downing, of *Film and Ethics: Foreclosed Encounters* (2009), and co-editor, with Simon Kemp, of *Seeing Things: Vision, Perception and Interpretation in French Studies* (2002).

RICHARD SCHOLAR is University Lecturer in French and a Fellow of Oriel College, Oxford. He is the author of *Montaigne and the Art of Free-Thinking* (2010) and *The Je-Ne-Sais-Quoi in Early Modern Europe: Encounters with a Certain Something* (2005), and the co-editor of several volumes, including *Thinking with Shakespeare: Comparative and Interdisciplinary Essays* (2007), *Pre-Histories and Afterlives: Studies in Critical Method* (2009), and *Fiction and the Frontiers of Knowledge in Europe, 1500–1800* (2010).

MICHAEL SHERINGHAM is Marshal Foch Professor of French Literature, University of Oxford. He has been President of the UK Society of French Studies, General Editor of *Cambridge Studies in French*, Visiting Professor at Paris VII, Paris IV, and Bordeaux III, and Pagus Distinguished French Visitor at the University of California, Berkeley. His publications include *Everyday Life: Theories and Practices from Surrealism to the Present* (2006), *Beckett: Molloy* (1986), and *French Autobiography: Devices and Desires* (1993); and he has edited *Parisian Fields* (1996), and *The Art of the Project* (with J. Gratton, 2005).

JAMES R. SIMPSON is a Senior Lecturer in French at the University of Glasgow. He is the author of *Animal Body, Literary Corpus: The Old French 'Roman de Renart'* (1996), *Fantasy, Identity and Misrecognition in Medieval French Narrative* (2000), and *Troubling Arthurian Histories: Court Culture, Performance and Scandal in Chrétien de Troyes's 'Erec et Enide'* (2007).

FINN E. SINCLAIR is a Fellow of Girton College, Cambridge, and Affiliated Lecturer in the Department of French. She is the author of *Milk and Blood: Gender and Genealogy in the 'Chansons de geste'* (2003) and the co-editor (with Rebecca Dixon) of the volume, *Poetry, Knowledge and Community in Late Medieval France* (2008). She is currently working on a book about the interrelation of history and fiction in the later Middle Ages.

ZRINKA STAHULJAK is Associate Professor of French and Comparative Literature at the University of California, Los Angeles. She is the author of *Bloodless Genealogies of the French Middle Ages* (2005), co-editor of *Minima Memoria: Essays in the Wake of Jean-François Lyotard* (2007), and co-author of *Thinking through Chrétien de Troyes* (2010). She is currently completing a book, *'Pornographic Archeology': Medieval Sexuality in Nineteenth-Century France*.

RICHARD STAMELMAN is the former William R. Kenan, Jr., Professor of the Humanities at Wesleyan University and is Professor of Romance Languages and Comparative Literature Emeritus at Williams College. He now serves as the Executive Director of the Montgomery Endowment, Dartmouth College. His publications include *The Drama of Self in Guillaume Apollinaire's 'Alcools'* (1976), *Lost Beyond Telling: Representations of Death and Absence in Modern French Poetry* (1990), *Perfume: Joy, Obsession, Scandal, Sin* (2008), and (co-edited with Mary Ann Caws) *Écrire le livre: autour d'Edmond Jabès* (1989).

KAREN SULLIVAN is Professor of Literature at Bard College in Annandale-on-Hudson, New York. She is the author of *Truth and the Heretic: Crises of Knowledge in Medieval French Literature* (2005), *The Interrogation of Joan of Arc* (1999), and *The Inner Lives of Medieval*

Inquisitors (2011). She has published widely on medieval French and Occitan literature, heresy, and inquisition, and is currently working on a project entitled *The Danger of Romance*.

HANNAH THOMPSON is a Senior Lecturer in French at Royal Holloway, University of London. She has published widely on nineteenth-century French prose fiction and is the author of *Naturalism Redressed: Identity and Clothing in the Novels of Emile Zola* (2004). She is currently completing a study of hitherto unnoticed references to female sexual pleasure, disability, weakened masculinity, torture, cruelty, murder, illness, and childbirth in works by Hugo, Sand, Zola, Rachilde, Mirbeau, and Barbey d'Aurevilly, amongst others.

MICHELLE R. WARREN is Professor of Comparative Literature at Dartmouth College. She is the author of *History on the Edge: Excalibur and the Borders of Britain (1100–1300)* (2000) and *Creole Medievalism: Colonial France and Joseph Bédier's Middle Ages* (2011), and co-editor of *Postcolonial Moves: Medieval through Modern* (2003) and *Arts of Calculation: Quantifying Thought in Early Modern Europe* (2004).

NICHOLAS WHITE teaches French at the University of Cambridge and is a Fellow of Emmanuel College. He is the author of *The Family in Crisis in Late Nineteenth-Century French Fiction* (1999). In addition to a range of articles and chapters in this domain, he has edited translations of Zola's *L'Assommoir* (1995) and Huysmans's *À Rebours* and co-edited the journal *Dix-Neuf* (since its inception in 2003), in addition to three volumes of essays: *Scarlet Letters: Fictions of Adultery from Antiquity to the 1990s* (with Naomi Segal, 1997), *Currencies: Fiscal Fortunes and Cultural Capital in Nineteenth-Century France* (2005), and *After Intimacy: The Culture of Divorce in the West since 1789* (with Karl Leydecker, 2007).

WES WILLIAMS is a University Lecturer in French at Oxford University and a Fellow of St Edmund Hall. His research concerns travel writing, critical theory, and monsters. Publications include: *Pilgrimage and Narrative in the French Renaissance* (1998) *and Mighty Magic: Monsters and their Meanings in Early Modern Culture* (forthcoming).

EMMA WILSON is Professor of French Literature and the Visual Arts at the University of Cambridge and a Fellow of Corpus Christi College. Her publications include *Sexuality and the Reading Encounter* (1996), *French Cinema since 1950: Personal Histories* (1999), *Memory and Survival: The French Cinema of Krzysztof Kieslowski* (2000), *Cinema's Missing Children* (2003), *Alain Resnais* (2006), and *Atom Egoyan* (2009).

THOMAS WYNN is Senior Lecturer in French at Durham University. His research focuses on eighteenth-century theatre and libertinage, and his publications include *Sade's Theatre: Pleasure, Vision, Masochism* (2007). He is editor of C. J. F. Hénault, *François II, roi de France* (2006) and several contributions to the *Complete Works of Voltaire*.

Acknowledgements

The editors would like to thank the following: Esther Palmer for her invaluable administrative help; Chantal Hamill for preparing the index; Linda Bree and Maartje Scheltens of Cambridge University Press for overseeing the project at its various stages; Tom O'Reilly for shepherding us through the final steps; and all the contributors to this volume.

Introduction

WILLIAM BURGWINKLE, NICHOLAS HAMMOND,
AND EMMA WILSON

This volume combines the expertise of a large number of distinguished academics and promising younger scholars, from Europe and North America, writing about their specialisations from a variety of literary, historical, and theoretical perspectives. It is intended to serve as an introduction to the major writings in French and also to the literary, cultural, and intellectual history of France over the centuries and of the French-speaking world. It should be of use to undergraduates, graduate students, and researchers alike.

Although most major French and francophone authors are covered in the course of the volume and can be easily referenced in the index, *The Cambridge History of French Literature* is inspired not only by period and historical concerns but also by topical and theoretical points of view. The topics outlined in this introduction, and addressed variously through the contributions to this history, were selected on the basis of their continuing interest to current and future researchers, their relevance to the place of French-language writing in European and world cultural production, and as a way of distinguishing this volume from other such volumes produced in the past. Contributors were encouraged to address one or more of the following topics in their essays, not necessarily as the focus of the essay but as a way of suggesting how the subject of their discussion is informed by one or more of these issues.

The oral and the written

While the earliest vernacular texts composed in French (from the late eleventh century to the early twelfth century) are marked by signs of orality in composition, rhetoric, and even manuscript presentation, what we read today as the signifiers of an oral or written text are imprecise and were often deliberately blurred in the Middle Ages. Far from indicating an evolution of mentalities, in which a culture would move from a period of primitive delivery into some superior form of written transmission, the oral and written are both exploited contemporaneously throughout the Middle Ages and the two modes emerge as interdependent. Signs of oral composition continued to be exploited into the later Middle Ages, long after manuscript compilation had become commonplace, and questions raised about the truth value of speech and written communication extend, even by the thirteenth century, into intense debates about the proper language and format for discussions of theology, poetry, and history – prose or verse. Is oral communication to be trusted as more spontaneous and unmediated or distrusted as more likely to deceive? Arguments about the truth value of verse and prose, of rhetoric v. 'natural' communication, extend well into the early modern period and far beyond. Literary salons of the seventeenth century, often derided as spaces of artifice and rhetoric in which the veneer and sheen of sophistication overwhelmed any possibility of sincerity, could also be championed as sites of rhetorical inventiveness, in which a new language – often a language associated with women – presented an alternative, and some resistance, to patriarchal and hackneyed norms. And in the modern period, orality has re-emerged as central to an understanding of postcolonial writings, both because of the competing voices and languages that are highlighted by authors from nations subjected to colonial domination (as in internalised oral and written sources) and because the study of testimony and oral traditions – traditions that might challenge the terms of colonialist and imperialist languages – is currently being revitalised and revalorised. As the questions of literary value, and what constitutes a text, have been rethought in the second half of the twentieth century, in the twenty-first century texting, blogging, recorded interviews, and DVD commentaries – the spoken word as privileged indicator of subjective identity, critique and resistance – have emerged as critical to an understanding of literary and cultural production in the age of new media, in which quick oral transmission sometimes appears to be winning out over the written word.

Writing in/from the periphery

Following on from the issue of oral transmission is the question of the place and space of writing and speaking. Where are modes of communication produced and for whom are they destined? These are essential questions for understanding twenty-first-century issues about culture, especially global culture, but they are by no means new. From the late eleventh century, contact between Western Christendom and 'the East' (the Byzantine Empire and the Levant) had become ever more frequent with the development of new trade routes and frequent travel, often in the form of Crusades. By the mid-twelfth century there were four prospering Latin centres surrounding Jerusalem and these inhabitants traded in culture and language as well as in goods. This early contact with the East influenced almost every aspect of French medieval literature – genres, themes, manuscripts – but the French language also absorbed influences from these encounters, as it coexisted with and slowly replaced Latin, moving into a dominant position as a sort of lingua franca across Western Europe. By the early modern period, a buoyant tradition of travel literature had developed that demonstrated an interest both in other peoples and cultures and in justifying a Western and Christian presence around the world. Texts that highlight contact between France and (the) new world(s) figure prominently in the period of the Enlightenment, at which time other peoples and cultures are often seen not as inferior to the European but as mirror images that can offer up correctives to Western Christian corruption. Anxieties persisted throughout the nineteenth century regarding religious and cultural adaptation: how far should Christianity go in adapting to other cultures' norms, including linguistic norms? Fascination with the 'Orient' and fantasised forms of 'Oriental exoticism' accompany the colonial aspirations of France through the nineteenth century into the first part of the twentieth century. The modern period has also seen, however, the development of an extraordinary range of writings from the French-speaking world that challenge the dominance of metropolitan France and Parisian intellectual authority. Questions of identity and belonging, covering the construction of community, language use, imperialism and indigenous subordination, become major thematic elements in literary and historiographical writings in the post-World War II era, while questions of geography and boundaries, literal and metaphorical, play a burning role in political and historical rhetoric into the twenty-first century.

Alterity and alienation

The Middle Ages, relatively free from the rigidity of nationalist thinking, are nonetheless marked by a particular meditation on otherness in all its forms, including religious, sexual, and ethnic. Madness, disease, sodomy, heresy – all of these haunt the borders of medieval texts and tell us more about the construction of medieval norms than they do about medieval tolerance. In the early modern period, a particular sort of alienation from the self, such that 'le moi', the sense of self as self, can be seen as quite separate not only from the body but from the social group as well. The self-confidence of seventeenth-century political and religious thought gives way to a greater questioning in the eighteenth century. Issues of intimacy/privacy became the focus of much early modern writing, precisely at a time when notions of the private and public were changing, sometimes radically. These questions are central to the thought of social theorists by the mid-nineteenth century, and they are transmitted as well to the modern period, sometimes most memorably in literary form. The distinction between self and other, the other as untouchable and alien, the other inside ourselves – all of these are subjected to the scrutiny of psychoanalytical and philosophical investigation and the introspective attention of authors such as Proust, Beauvoir or NDiaye. These questions cut across literature and theory, and have opened new perspectives on madness, mourning, race, ethics and sexuality that continue to challenge the validity of fixed identity categories.

Literature and history

History as a discipline is already practised during the Middle Ages, though not always in recognisable form. Fiction and history can scarcely be distinguished one from the other but medieval 'historical' texts tend to be supplemented by a combination of chronicles, memoirs, and eyewitness accounts, with the aim of presenting some notion of verifiable truth. For the same reason, medieval authors often refer obsessively to a source text, real or imagined, to which they owe their material and their fidelity. From the Crusaders' chronicles to the *Grandes Chroniques de France* and the narratives of Joinville, Villehardouin, and Froissart, authors traced and constructed the genealogies and myths of a French, Christian identity and its shaping through the interpretation of historical events. The explosion of memoirs and the reutilisation of inherited themes and plots in the early modern period give evidence of a continued interest in the past but also accentuate, once again, the often uneasy division between history and fiction. History and the rewriting of history reaches a particularly crucial point at the time of the Revolution, during which politically opposed points of view were put forward to explain the same supposedly verifiable event. France's involvement in the two World Wars and the wars of colonial independence in the twentieth century further calls into question the relation of literature to history and the necessity of considering the individual point of view as well as the global. Literary texts are increasingly seen as essential to constructing and questioning a historical perspective. Modernity's yoking of literature to commemoration, personal and national, has led to an expansion of the definition of literature to include testimony, archival investigations, verbal and photographic evidence and oral history.

Popular culture

Medieval literature often defies scholarly attempts to categorise it with reference to audience or genre. Bawdy tales include frequent religious references; sex and transgressive themes share centre-stage in romance and song with moralising denunciations of that very material; pious epics include all the barbarity and gore of twenty-first-century action films, and all seem to have been equally appreciated. For some, the popular might be distinguished from the learned by considerations of language, references and register, but actual audiences' consumption of genres and themes is difficult to determine, even to the point that the distinction between clerical and secular remains muddled. Popular culture is therefore everywhere in the Middle Ages and most literature seems to appeal to most people, regardless of social class. The question of popular culture manifests itself in increasingly interesting ways in the early modern period, from the bawdy tales of Rabelais, to satirical and revolutionary street songs, to newspaper editorials and the political theatre of the eighteenth and nineteenth centuries. In the modern period, in particular, popular culture has been increasingly recognised as an essential component of cultural analysis, and literary scholars have shown an increased interest in visual media of all sorts, from *bandes dessinées* to digital video and the internet. Film studies has developed sometimes in inter-relation with literary studies and the two fields increasingly overlap, offering new attention to reception and spectatorship, to authorship, and to genre.

Visual culture

While visual culture has exploded in the twentieth and twenty-first centuries, the taste for and emphasis on visual material goes much further back in French history. Manuscript culture is inseparable from medieval literature, and a full understanding of medieval texts is impossible without some consideration of the forms in which they were transmitted. In sacred books and romance, illustration plays a major role as miniatures comment on and disrupt the texts they pretend to be explicating. Knowing where a text figures in a manuscript can be as enlightening to a reader as understanding its commentary; it can tell us what associations were being made between one text and another at the time of its inscription, as well as the occasions on which it might have played a role. The increasing prominence of visual material in the early modern period is demonstrated not only in paintings and sculptures and the return to Classical models, but in the attention paid to architecture, theatre of all types, and political pageants. This is a period when a building can speak not only to its predecessors and its own ambitions to rival ancient splendour, but can also portray its patron in all his/her ambition and desire to be associated with grandeur, reason, or clever play. Painting and photography in the nineteenth century, and cinema in the twentieth century, became dominant modes of artistic expression and the recording of reality, and challenged literary modes of representation. Poets and novelists engaged in writing art criticism, drawing the fields of the verbal and the visual more closely together, while the questioning of relations between the different senses and different media, through synaesthesia and the *transposition d'art*, allowed new exchanges to be developed. From Romanticism to realism, Symbolism, and surrealism, and equally through both literary adaptation and auteurism in cinema, the inter-relation between literature and visual culture is opened out in new ways with divergent results.

Sexualities

The medieval period has often been described as the moment when Western Christian sexualities developed rhetorically and were set in place through law and religious orthodoxy. Yet neither homosexuality nor heterosexuality appear as firmly established discursive entities in medieval genres: both are ever-present as competing modalities and attract throughout the period the kind of polarised polemics that marked the close of the twentieth century. Discussions of alternative sexualities and cross-dressing abound in the early modern period, not only in the 'libertin' writings of the eighteenth century but also in writers such as Montaigne and the rage for memoirs, letters, and anecdotes that characterise their literary production. By the late nineteenth and early twentieth centuries, new explorations of sexual pathologies and perversion intersect with a flowering of 'decadent' writing. While the autobiographical and questions of eroticism and exposure dominate some twentieth-century writings on sexuality and intimacy, the latter part of the century witnesses a newly politicised (and differently embodied) engagement with sexuality in the wake of HIV/AIDS. Contemporary writing in French today shows increased attention to the reshaping of societal structures to incorporate alternative forms of family, shifting identity politics, and transgression as an end in itself.

Women writers

While largely a domain limited to men, writing in the Middle Ages was not exclusively masculine. From the *trobairitz* to Marie de France and Christine de Pizan, women often fired the first shots of discontent with the status quo and offered witty corrections to patriarchal modes of social organisation. In spite of the many restrictions imposed on women in the early modern period, each century produced writers of subtlety and distinction. Women increasingly engaged in literary work during the Renaissance period, following the royal model of Marguérite de Navarre, and the emergence of the literary salon in the seventeenth and eighteenth centuries coincided with a greater emancipation for women's writing and an increase of control over their production. From questions about the value and status of women's writing in the nineteenth century, to questions about the senses, sensuality, the intimate, and the melancholic in the twentieth and twenty-first centuries, writing by women has come to the fore in France and the French-speaking world in the modern period, and has presented a challenge to traditional notions of genre and stable categories of identity. While much feminist scholarship of the twentieth century was occupied with excavating women's writing and bringing it to a wider public, the twenty-first century has seen a remarkable expansion of women into important positions in all modes of literary and artistic production, including film-making, photography and installation art.

Literature and religion

Much of medieval literature is touched by an encounter with religious thought. Clerics, both as patrons and authors, left their mark on contemporary literary production, but not always in ways that would receive an ecclesiastical imprimatur. Although it is clear that some texts were composed for monastic audiences, for religious propaganda, or as philosophical/theological apologiae, this would hardly account for those texts that are the most popular and well known amongst a modern audience. Nor would it indicate that medieval literature is subject to monologic interpretation. Many of the age's texts are subversive of religious dogma even when they were produced for what would seem to be a church audience; and many of the lyrics and romances take on topics that would have been anathema to orthodox church figures. Religion in the early modern period is no less present in the literary texts, though again not from any one point of view, but it cannot be interpreted without understanding its link to the religious struggles that left such a mark on the period, from the Wars of Religion to the Edict of Nantes. The sixteenth century could even be termed a golden age for religious poetry, philosophy and theatre, despite the sometimes polarised presentation. Yet the seventeenth and especially the eighteenth century are equally marked by religious questions, particularly in the rise of secularisation and the critique of religion that followed on from Enlightenment thought. The confrontation between religious dogma and reason becomes more politicised and increasingly central to philosophy throughout the eighteenth and nineteenth centuries; and in the modern period, questions of personal faith and doubt give way to broader questioning of the relation between religion, nation, culture and prejudice. The tumultuous events of the twentieth century reinstated religion as a major issue in the construction and analysis of culture, from the after-effects of the Dreyfus Affair and representations of the Shoah and the Occupation in France, through to contemporary engagement with the importance of Islam in French and francophone writing.

Literature and politics

Medieval subjectivity was not constructed entirely through religious discourse, despite what some scholars have argued, and many of the most influential texts from the period concentrate precisely on the contested borderline between philosophy, theology and politics. Vernacular saints' lives, to take just one example, offer a privileged view of how religion constructs communities as well as controls them, and how it serves to validate and question notions of sovereignty and servitude. An imagined politics dominates in the early *chansons de geste*, as rebellious noblemen wage war against their legitimate lords and feudal models of reciprocal duties and protections come in for critical examination. The Inquisition and the uneasy journey towards a unified French identity in the late fifteenth century produced a mass of political documentation in which both truth and Christian values are shown as contingent and malleable. With increased royal patronage of the arts and literature, it is difficult to separate politics and writing in the early modern period. For the first time, the theatre, for example, became a symbol of national prestige, and playwrights were expected to produce works depicting the heroism of great leaders. This politicisation of literature (or rather open admission of politicisation) comes to the fore in the late nineteenth century, when authors openly use their works to address political issues and influence political opinions. This tendency continues in the first half of the twentieth century, as writers return with due obsession to the relation between literature and politics, the problem and challenge of committed writing, culminating in the events of 1968. This inter-relation of politics and literature, never absent from the history of French writing, evolves nonetheless in the twenty-first century into a more theoretical questioning of politics itself and of the politics of writing. The development of new modes of transmission and commentary in the form of shared internet sites and blogs has further destabilised the boundaries between political and artistic production and opened the door to new understandings of the literary.

Memory and testimony

The earliest text of vernacular French literature deals with a virgin martyr and the need to memorialise her and others' sacrifices as constitutive of Christian communities. From the bloody wars of religion, including the Crusades, to the struggles for a centralised kingship, medieval literature struggles with how language communities construct a shared past and process profound losses and a sense of shame. These problems plague the early modern period as well, as religious massacres and natural disasters are celebrated, bemoaned and commemorated in diverse ways, depending on religious and political affiliation. Memory acquires a particular significance and fragility in the period, not least in the part played by antiquity in early modern culture and the impetus to recreate and better the past. Modern texts have found new strategies to represent ungraspable impressions: memories of events whose magnitude and violence threaten to collapse conventional literary forms. New modes, new forms, new temporalities of writing emerge from such experience and have been particularly innovative in the period post-World War II.

Autobiography

Though largely an early modern invention, autobiography exists in the interstices between medieval genres. The *Confessions* of Saint Augustine carried enormous weight throughout the Middle Ages and prompted a host of authors to tell their own autobiographical tales of conversion and salvation. Lyric poetry also flirted with autobiographical revelations, especially in the fourteenth and fifteenth centuries; and the first biographical texts in the vernacular tradition, the *razos* of the troubadours, explicitly linked biography and autobiography to history, as bricks in the construction of cultural capital. Augustine continued to be immensely influential in the early modern period, as witnessed by the *Essais* of Montaigne, and at the same time, as new theories of the self were developing, so too interest in autobiographical writing was growing, culminating in the extraordinary confessional writings of Rousseau. The genre of autobiography, upheld within nineteenth-century analysis, and the foregrounding of the modern self in isolation, is effectively parodied and dismantled in the subsequent century in a range of texts which put on display authors' doubts about truth, the transparency of the literary text, and the coherence of the identity produced by an 'I' in writing. This deconstructive approach to autobiographical writing is more than matched, however, by an outpouring of do-it-yourself video practitioners, bloggers, and social networking sites, for whom the expression of the self in writing, pictures, images and music becomes the dominant mode of expression – popular and literary – in the first decade of the twenty-first century.

It is our hope that through the essays that follow you will not only get to know the present better by visiting the past, but also be illuminated by that past through encountering its continual rewriting, forgetting, inscription, and reinscription within the dominant paradigms of the ages that followed. We do not expect a linear reading of the material any more than we expect a linear development of the literature that is being cited. French literary history circles back upon itself through time and advances across what Michel Foucault called *epistèmes* by denying its debts to the past and reconstructing a present from its detritus. Writing in French is as healthy and productive as it has ever been, and it is our hope that in celebrating the diversity of that production we can contribute to its continued vitality.

Manuscripts and manuscript culture

DAVID F. HULT

The study and interpretation of medieval literature is inseparable from the conditions of its circulation in handwritten copies. In Paris, the first printing press was installed in 1470, some twenty years after Gutenberg started mechanically reproducing copies of his Bible in Germany. Prior to that time, the production of books was a labour-intensive process that resulted in individual, not multiple, copies. Technologies developed gradually in the period extending from the Roman Empire to the beginning of the Renaissance. The most common material support for written documents in ancient times in the Eastern Mediterranean had been papyrus, typically in the form of scrolls, but it was replaced starting in late antiquity by prepared animal skins, parchment or vellum, and began to be arranged in the format which is still the standard for books, that of the codex. The codex presented a text as separate pages bound together as opposed to the continuous format of the scroll: separate gatherings of folios, known as quires, were stitched together to form the finished book. Advantages of this innovative new format included the ability to use both sides of the page for text and much greater ease of consultation. Though the moves towards parchment and the codex format developed separately, they both seem to have become more or less the norm by the fourth century CE. Paper, a considerably cheaper alternative to parchment, was introduced into Europe in the twelfth century, but only became common in France in the course of the fourteenth century.

The preparation of books was a group project. Scribes and artists joined ranks, often working separately, to produce manuscript copies of theological, classical and vernacular works. Until the early twelfth century, nearly all manuscripts were copied in the *scriptoria* (rooms devoted to the copying of texts) in monasteries. These manuscripts were predominantly for the use of these communities, either Bibles, theological works, commentaries and prayer books, or classical Latin works for educational purposes. Indeed, most of the classical Latin works that have survived in manuscript were copied during the Middle Ages. In the period extending from the ninth to the early twelfth century, when the first evidence of writing in the vernacular appears, there was little likelihood that copyists in monasteries would be interested in, or even familiar with, these works. Furthermore, the likely oral nature of the composition and transmission of early epic and lyric explains how it would happen that their remnants prior to the end of the twelfth century are limited in number (epic) or non-existent (lyric poetry).

The early part of the twelfth century brings the first evidence of significant manuscript production outside the monastery, as the growth of cities and the appearance of schools, and later universities, created increasing demand in non-monastic communities for religious, theological and possibly secular works. However, the combination of a paucity of lay readers and the great expense of manuscript production (due to both the cost of the materials, particularly parchment, and the length of time – counted in months – one copyist would take to produce a single manuscript book) undoubtedly explains why the bulk of manuscripts produced during the century were intended for students and teachers working in Latin. In their comprehensive list of vernacular manuscripts dating with considerable certainty to the twelfth century or to the turn of the century, Brian Woledge and Ian Short list scarcely 125 items;[1] they include predominantly religious and didactic texts (including one of the important early narrative genres, the saint's life), chronicles and historical or pseudo-historical narratives (such as the *Roman de Troie* by Benoît de Sainte-Maure and Wace's history of the dukes of Normandy, the *Roman de Rou* [*Rollo*]), and a couple of early epic poems, including one of the monuments of French literature, the Oxford manuscript containing an early version of the *Chanson de Roland (Song of Roland)*. As far as courtly romance and lyric are concerned, only one set of fragments of Thomas's *Tristan* romance can be dated to the twelfth century, while one set of fragments of four of Chrétien de Troyes's romances is dated to the turn of the century. So while the latter half of the twelfth century is widely recognised to be a golden age of literary production, with the likes of Chrétien de Troyes, Thomas d'Angleterre, Béroul, Marie de France, Benoît de Sainte-Maure, Wace, and dozens of less well-known writers, somewhat paradoxically virtually no copies of their works contemporary to their activity have survived. It can only be assumed that in this early period secular workshops were only exceptionally commissioned to reproduce vernacular texts and that the aristocratic patrons for most writers

---

1 Brian Woledge and Ian Short, 'Liste provisoire de manuscrits du xiie siècle contenant des textes en langue française', *Romania* 102 (1981), pp. 1–17.

of the time had secular clergy working for them as secretaries and scribes who would have executed single copies of these works. But, as Ian Short has suggested, there was undoubtedly increasing competition among literate nobles to acquire books, as a mark of prestige, which fuelled the infrastructure necessary to increase vernacular book production.[2]

The thirteenth century sees a major upswing in the composition of vernacular works of all types, including adaptations of works originally written in Latin, and an accompanying boom in manuscript production. Whereas manuscripts of the earlier period tended to be of modest format and design, frequently containing a single work with one column to a page and with little or no decoration, they become increasingly larger and more elaborate starting early in the thirteenth century. Ian Short lists only six surviving twelfth-century manuscripts, all comparatively small, containing more than one French text (two to a maximum of five).[3] The early thirteenth century sees the appearance of much more expansive literary and didactic anthologies, volumes containing upwards of a dozen texts, frequently related by genre or by theme, with larger pages having a layout of two or even three columns. One very well-known example dating probably to 1230 is the so-called Guiot manuscript of the romances of Chrétien de Troyes, ms. 794 of the Bibliothèque Nationale de France in Paris, named after the scribe, who identifies himself at one point. It contains, in addition to Chrétien's five romances, a handful of other works, including Wace's *Roman de Brut*, which was the principal vernacular source for the historical version of King Arthur's reign, and the *Roman de Troie*. Thematically, it associates the courtly romances with a historical context provided by these latter two works, suggesting that, rather than frivolous fictions, they participate in that history. At 433 folio leaves written on both sides, each holding three columns of text, forty-four lines apiece, this was a massive undertaking, but not unusual for thirteenth-century productions.

Up until the fourteenth century, there is typically a considerable lapse between the time of the work's composition and that of its transcription, due at least in part to the fact that during these early centuries it does not appear for the most part that authors were themselves responsible for the transcription of their own manuscripts, a task which was handled by professional scribes; many authors from the earliest periods were possibly even illiterate and needed to recite their text to a copyist. Furthermore, it is not uncommon for works not even to be attached to an authorial name, either because of an accident

---

2 Ian Short, 'L'Avènement du texte vernaculaire: la mise en recueil', in 'Théories et pratiques de l'écriture au Moyen Age', special issue of *Littérales* 4 (1988), pp. 11–24.
3 Ibid., p. 20.

of transmission, or simply because the author did not care to be identified. Sometimes the identity is given as a first name, scarcely sufficient to provide an individual identification. The name 'Marie de France' that we use to identify one of the earliest female authors is for instance itself a modern creation, a rewriting of the statement she makes: 'I am Marie and I am from France.'[4] It is also undoubtedly the case that many of the material links in the transmission of these texts have simply been lost due to wars, revolutions and other events that have destroyed books and libraries over the centuries. But what made manuscripts extremely expensive to produce, and therefore limited their ownership, also played a role in their preservation, for as luxury items they were carefully guarded and passed down from generation to generation. Many of the modest and unattractive twelfth-century manuscripts have perhaps disappeared precisely because they did not measure up as valuable artefacts. One example of the fate of such a manuscript was discovered quite recently: a scrap of parchment, found to be used as a binding for a set of charters in England, turned out to be a precious fragment of Thomas's *Romance of Tristan*. The original book was simply dismembered in order for the parchment, deemed more valuable than the text it contained, to be used for other purposes.

It is not known exactly how manuscripts were used during this period, and there are numerous theories to account for the reception of literary works either through or alongside their manuscript transmission. Many assume that the oral transmission of vernacular literature continued well into the thirteenth century, either through the performance of minstrels or the reading aloud of works from a codex. One of the most famous 'scenes' of literary consumption in the twelfth century comes from Chrétien de Troyes's romance *Le Chevalier au lion* (*The Knight of the Lion* [c. 1180]), in which a girl is reading a romance out loud from a book to her parents. Some of the anthologies mentioned above contain large numbers of short works, satirical, comic and religious, that might have served as a source for live performances. The physical preparation of the codex was increasingly developed with a view towards visually guiding readers, either for an oral reading in performance to a group or perhaps for an individual reading: rubrics (introductory or ending identifications of the text and/or author, occasionally containing other extra-textual information, written usually in red ink), enlarged illuminated initial letters, and miniatures of various sizes depicting episodes from the texts, become increasingly common features of the more elaborate manuscripts. All of these features assist in detecting the beginnings of texts (especially

---

4 Marie de France, *Lais*, ed. Alfred Ewert (Oxford: Blackwell, 1944), p. v.

important in a codex that might contain dozens of short texts) and their identification, as well as their segmentation, which would be especially useful for finding one's place in longer works.

The consequences of this situation are significant and suggest not only that texts, and textuality itself, were viewed differently from those in print culture, but that numerous of our most common paradigms regarding the creation, publication and transmission of literary works need to be revised. In a modern context, a published text is under the ownership of its author or producer, that ownership being protected by copyright laws. The production of books represents a contract between this author/owner and a publisher, who takes care of all the material aspects of book production. It is also a common assumption that a given work of literature is relatively fixed, stable, invariable. If I take a book out of my local library in San Francisco and tell a friend in Cincinnati about it, she can consult it in her own library and be assured of having the identical text that I am reading. This situation is more or less guaranteed by the nature of print reproduction and the ownership rights of the author, which prevent pirated editions.

No such system exists in the manuscript context of textual transmission. Works are anonymous or attributed to an author, but in either case their circulation occurs freely. The business part of the transaction takes place on two distinct fronts: between the (usually aristocratic) patron who requests from an author either a work or a translation from Latin into French; and between the client who makes a request for a copy of a book (which might contain one large work, such as the *Roman de la Rose* or the Prose *Lancelot*, or a collection of thematically related shorter works) and the copyist or workshop that undertakes to get a copy of the work desired and to transcribe it, with more or less decoration depending upon the patron's wishes. Once an author produces a work and is paid by his or her patron, there ends any sense of ownership or authorial control in the modern sense. Furthermore, authors freely lift passages from previous texts, with or without acknowledgement; when they do mention their source, it is typically due to the prestige a well-known name (such as Cicero or Virgil) might add to their own product. One example from the twelfth century provides an intriguing case: in 1174 Guernes de Pont-Sainte-Maxence completed a verse life of Saint Thomas Beckett, including an account of his murder in Canterbury Cathedral in 1170. In the version that has come down to us, Guernes tells us that this version is the revision of a prior one, which was based upon hearsay and contained erroneous material. The second version is based upon his on-site interviews at Canterbury. He claims that unfortunately the first version has been stolen from him by copyists who in turn sold copies of it to many rich men, adding that the scribes are to be blamed for this. Somewhat ironically, we know that Guernes's own French text contains unacknowledged translations from previous Latin biographies of Beckett. It is undoubtedly the case that Guernes's disapproval of those who were reproducing his first version has more to do with his desire to have the definitive revised version in circulation under his name, than with his outrage that they were making profit illegally (as would be our reaction).

Now, the problem for the modern consumer of these works is as follows: there are by and large no autograph manuscripts of literary works prior to the mid-fourteenth century. The manuscripts that have survived were copied by professionals, as we have already mentioned, some considerable time after the author composed the work(s) in question. Many texts have survived in only one manuscript copy and a large number in anywhere from a handful to some fifty or so copies (fifty surviving manuscripts of any medieval work would indicate a significant circulation). Extraordinarily successful and widely read works, such as the *Roman de la Rose*, have survived in more than a hundred. The nature of individual handwritten copies is such that no two copies of the 'same' text can possibly be identical. Copyists make mistakes; furthermore, spelling was not fixed and therefore scribes would silently (and perhaps unconsciously) convert individual words into their own dialect. If a scribe does not understand a passage, he or she might rewrite it according to the way it is construed. Faced with a potential multiplicity of different versions of the same 'text', and with no guarantee of what the author intended, how do we determine what that text is? This is essentially the question that editors of texts have asked for more than a century in their attempt to produce readable and reliable versions of these medieval works.

But, in a certain way, the very notion of an edition of a medieval work runs counter to the nature of medieval textuality. The essential variability of manuscript copies is analogous to, but less dramatic than, the variability of texts produced by oral tellers of tales who, individually, recount a different version of a given story at each performance and, collectively, through tales being passed down through generations of storytellers, produce radically different versions that can scarcely be considered the same 'text'. Scholars have recently made use of a term coined in French by Paul Zumthor nearly forty years ago to refer to the essential instability and dynamism of medieval oral *and* written production: *mouvance*. According to his definition, *mouvance* is the 'nature of a work that, as such, before the age of the [printed] book, takes shape from a quasi-abstraction, since the concrete texts in which it is realised present, through a play of variants and reworkings, something like a ceaseless vibration and a fundamental instability'.[5] A significant example that combines the remnants of oral *mouvance* (which itself arises from somewhat of a paradox, since medieval oral culture is only available to us through written documents) with those due to scribal culture comes from the foundational epic text known as the *Chanson de Roland* (*Song of Roland*). The work to which we usually give this name is in fact the earliest extant version of this text found in the earliest dated manuscript, known as the Oxford Manuscript because it is housed in the Bodleian Library (ms. Digby 23). But there exist a half-dozen discrete versions copied in the following two centuries that provide significantly different accounts of the story, both formally and narratively. The Oxford *Roland* contains just over 4,000 lines of assonanced decasyllabic verse; several of the other versions are hundreds to thousands of lines longer, one totalling double that number; many are in rhymed verse; one uses alexandrines (twelve-syllable verse); and the dialects are quite diverse, including Franco-Italian.[6] One of the major differences in content of some of the versions is the greatly expanded role of Aude, the betrothed of Roland, who receives only brief mention in the Oxford text. One needs at the very least to consider the *Songs of Roland* that are irreducible to a single version, but also appreciate the dynamism of a tradition that freely rewrites texts according to local preoccupations and interests.

Another instance of rewriting or reconception of previous works is related to the not unusual practice of 'continuation' of previously written texts. A text that an author did not finish is left open for a later author to bring to completion. The most spectacular example of this phenomenon is Chrétien de Troyes's last romance, *Le Conte du Graal* (*The Story of the Grail*), which recounts the knight Perceval's quest for the not-yet-holy Grail. Chrétien appears not to have brought this romance to a conclusion, leaving it off in mid-sentence, and no fewer than four successive continuators, working over a period of some thirty to forty years, added an additional 60,000-odd lines of narrative verse to Chrétien's approximately 9,000. A writer named Guillaume de Lorris composed a poetic fragment of some 4,000 lines which he entitled *Le Roman de la rose* (*Romance of the Rose*), recounting an allegorical quest of a young man in love for the object of his desire, a rose. Some forty years later, a learned author with a highly satirical and misogynistic bent, Jean de Meun,

---

5 Paul Zumthor, *Essai de poétique médiévale* (Paris: Seuil, 1972), p. 507. Translation mine.
6 *La Chanson de Roland/The Song of Roland: The French Corpus*, 3 vols., Joseph J. Duggan (general ed.), with Karen Akiyama, Ian Short, Robert F. Cook, Annalee C. Rejhon, Wolfgang van Emden, and William W. Kibler (eds.) (Turnhout: Brepols, 2005).

added a continuation of over four times the original's length that more or less deconstructs the sentimental original, and it is the combined version of this work that is found in nearly every manuscript produced of this best-seller. Is it a work of one author or two? How do we deal with the issue of authorial intention in this case?

Still another example of the ways in which manuscript collections force us to reconceive individual works is the tendency for some genres to be conceived as cycles of previous works written at different times by different authors. This is particularly visible in some of the epic traditions, most notably the manuscripts containing the so-called 'Cycle de Guillaume d'Orange'. To an early text known as the *Chanson de Guillaume*, dating to the mid-twelfth century, there accrued over twenty different works written over the following century, in which Guillaume's previous exploits as well as subsequent ones, in addition to works celebrating exploits of other family members, are recounted. The huge cyclical manuscripts contain as many as two dozen distinct epic texts copied together as a semi-continuous super-epic. Prose Arthurian romance provides another example. To the Prose *Lancelot-Grail*, a vast early thirteenth-century version of the story of Lancelot and Guinevere, connecting it to the quest for the Holy Grail, later writers added what we would call 'prequels', works preceding the *Lancelot* that tell of the holy origins of the Grail, the story of Merlin and the birth and early reign of King Arthur. In many manuscripts of this lengthy cycle these 'prequels' are copied as part of the cycle and not as later additions.

To a lesser degree, manuscript versions of what one would agree to be the 'same' text display huge numbers of different (called 'variant') readings, ranging from the scribal alterations and errors already mentioned to deliberate word choice and portions of text either skipped over or excised (by accident or by design) and the converse phenomenon, more or less lengthy interpolations. In a romance by Chrétien de Troyes, for instance, one manuscript might contain the word *amor* (love) while another might have in the same place *enor* (honour), the two terms being metrically interchangeable with each other. One's most basic interpretation could be radically changed depending upon which of these words the editor has decided to print as the definitive text. In thinking of medieval textuality, therefore, it is necessary to modify two of our most basic modern notions of literary creation: those of the all-powerful, unmediated authorial voice and of the stable text. We can and do of course speak of medieval authors, but one must consider that the product that has come down to us, the 'concrete texts' referred to by Zumthor, are the result of a series of interventions frequently undetectable as such: the original author (who perhaps composed more than one version, as the example of Guernes de Pont-Sainte-Maxence shows), a potential sequence of scribal copies that have not even survived, an organiser of the manuscript who would decide not only what texts would be included, what order they would be copied in, and what sort of decoration or illustration to provide, but also a scribe who could potentially be so proactive as to have significantly altered the text being copied – not to mention the modern editor of these texts, who adds an additional layer of mediation.

A number of recent scholars, including most notably Sylvia Huot and Keith Busby, have concentrated upon the manuscript collection or anthology itself as a context that has been too often overlooked in our appreciation of the literary works that are frequently presented as unproblematic creations emanating directly from an author's pen. Sylvia Huot has shown how a number of anthologies from the thirteenth and fourteenth centuries contain, along with the poetic narratives they transmit, visual and verbal reflections on oral versus written culture, authorial creation and performance, and the relation between love and song.[7] She has likewise shown how many of the fascinating manuscripts of the *Romance of the Rose* demonstrate sophisticated reactions to, and interpretations of, this omnipresent work in the second half of the Middle Ages, on the part of scribes, but also on the part of readers, who not infrequently added marginal commentary and doodles.[8] More recently, Keith Busby has produced a massive study of verse manuscript production in France in the thirteenth and fourteenth centuries, including discussions of their physical preparation and organisation, illustrations, circulation and ownership, in which he argues for the centrality of the manuscript context for an understanding of medieval literature.[9] Indeed, one might go further and suggest that literary history, if the expression has any meaning, can only make sense for the medieval period if we foreground the unavoidable enumeration of individual authors and discrete works with a solid understanding of the material means by which they were transmitted, associated, deformed, supplemented, dis-membered, re-membered, and understood.

---

7 Sylvia Huot, *From Song to Book: The Poetics of Writing in Old French Lyric and Lyrical Narrative Poetry* (Ithaca, NY: Cornell University Press, 1987).
8 Sylvia Huot, *The* Romance of the Rose *and its Medieval Readers: Interpretation, Reception, Manuscript Transmission* (Cambridge: Cambridge University Press, 1993).
9 Keith Busby, *Codex and Context: Reading Old French Verse Narrative in Manuscript*, 2 vols. (Amsterdam: Rodopi, 2002).

2

The troubadours: the Occitan model

WILLIAM BURGWINKLE

For much of the twentieth century, French literary scholars interpreted the word 'French' in 'medieval French literature' in the narrowest possible manner – as a linguistic rather than political or geographical marker. Despite the conquest of Occitan lands in the thirteenth century and the gradual incorporation of those lands into the French state in the centuries that followed, the appellation 'French' has rarely been applied to the languages or literary texts from the South. Individuals were, of course, understood to belong to the political collective known as France but they retained their local appellations (Gascon, Rouergais, Toulousain, Provençal, etc.). Because they did not write or speak primarily in French, they and their culture were largely excluded from national cultural history. Yet it was already clear in the twelfth century that some portion of the Occitan population was bilingual and certainly by the time of the Ordonnances de Villers-Cotterets (1535), which mandated its use in all legal and judicial documents, French had made significant headway amongst the educated classes in the South. It had also long been used as a lingua franca around the Mediterranean and was written and spoken in dialects that dominated commerce along the major trading routes throughout northern Italy and on to the Levant. Yet in writing the cultural history of France, in producing a coherent post-1789 narrative in which the power and prestige of the French people is said to emerge from this first republican identity, varieties of French, and the regional languages that nourished its early literary production, were conveniently overlooked. This changed somewhat in the Romantic period, when French and German scholars rediscovered the bounty of Occitan manuscripts, but since then Occitania has largely been reduced to a footnote or swept aside entirely as being of regional interest only.

Even the late twentieth century's change in nomenclature, from 'Provençal' to 'Occitan', has had a deleterious effect on efforts to reintegrate the north and the south within a larger and more inclusive concept of French literature. This renaming, reflecting a legitimate move away from Mistral's noble nineteenth-century initiative to celebrate the local dialects and literary culture of Provence and move towards a more inclusive term that would incorporate the centre and south-west as well, has been almost too successful. While shifting the attention to the actual regions where much troubadour poetry was produced, scholars also inadvertently reinforced the marginalisation of Occitania as somehow foreign or backward. Southern literature was, in essence, seen as someone else's heritage – an excision from the French canon that has benefited Italian and Catalan scholars.

Rightly claiming the legacy of the troubadours as their own, and recognising in its rich cultural foundations the earliest manifestation of their linguistic and literary heritage, early Italian and Catalan scholars were actually following in the footsteps of their own prescient medieval masters. Dante Alighieri most famously celebrated Occitan (*langue d'oc*) as the perfect language for verse (until the advent of Tuscan, that is); and the Catalans, especially Raimon Vidal de Besalù and Jofre de Foixà, contributed enormously to the prestige of troubadour traditions by composing theoretical treatises on the art of composition and praise for the culture that supported it. Occitan is commonly taught in the universities of both areas and remains a necessary step in the acquisition of philological expertise. The northern French academy, on the other hand, has gradually backed away from medieval Occitan studies, especially since May '68, as something that either does not really concern it, or as a phenomenon that can simply be alluded to – a stepping stone to something better that replaced it.[1] Needless to say, a genuine history of French literature, i.e. the writings and languages of the lands that have comprised 'France' since the Middle Ages, can no longer afford that oversight, any more than it can overlook the francophone contributions of authors from the colonial and postcolonial periods.

A list of Occitan 'firsts' is therefore necessary, however boastful it might sound. Troubadour song represents the earliest rhyming verse known in a vernacular 'European' language (*c.* 1100); and the sophistication of its versification, from the earliest songs of Guilhem IX, has been taken as a sign that it sprang forth, fully formed, from its first appearance. Marrou claimed that the astonishing complexity of troubadour rhyme schemes produced 'an original technical vocabulary, the likes of which the West hadn't matched

---

1 Oddly enough, Jacques Lacan is one of the few intellectuals to have considered the troubadours outside of their Occitan box. His seventh (1959–60) and twentieth seminars (1972–3) include important consideration of the implications of *fin'amor* for psychoanalysis, and it is from his understanding of troubadour erotics (via Aristotle and Hegel) that he formulated his influential notion of desire.

since the good old days of Greek rhetoric, some time between Gorgias and Aristotle'.[2] It is also the first lyric poetry to celebrate a love that elevates, rather than denigrates or ridicules, the individual. While many of its themes are familiar from Ovid, Catullus, or even religious material such as the Song of Songs, troubadour *cansos* are presented as first-person narratives, dramatisations of the struggle to be and have what one can normally only aspire to; and from which the poet/narrator will be either bettered (morally or socially), cured (the topos of the *domna* [lady] as medical doctor), refined (through endless suffering) or killed (voluntarily, of course). It presents the first evidence of a collective literary identity, secular and regional rather than clerical, which fuses or replaces entirely divine devotion with praise of beauty, power, wealth, youth, and erotic love. This collective identity emerges through a quite amazing degree of intertextuality that characterises the corpus of some 2,500 extant songs. Singers and poets clearly knew the works of other poets like them and imitated or alluded to their rivals/models frequently – melodically, metrically, and thematically. Such songs mix clerical registers with secular references, skirting blasphemy freely, and often assert that there is continuity between religious devotion and erotic obsession. Devotion to the *domna* takes on the mythic and ritualistic character of the sacred, though it often springs back to reveal scabrous and cynical subtexts as well.[3]

Generic distinctions that might seem to have existed forever are particularly flexible in Occitan verse, and the organisation of many of the manuscripts by genre tells us that while these distinctions might have provided a pretext for a good deal of play – one of the prime characteristics of the poetry and the manuscripts themselves – they also provided a way to organise thought and discipline form. The mixing of genres in troubadour poetry, and the invention of others, can still seem shocking: how can love songs both praise and condemn the beloved or allude to their own absolute truth at the same time as they exploit their status as constructed objects? Such postmodern game playing is nonetheless pretty much standard in the troubadour bag of tricks. Arnaut Daniel's famous sestina, in which a series of six rhyme words are used over six stanzas to create an intertextual puzzle, is probably the best example of this self-conscious doubling and destabilisation of word and meaning. Dante wrote his own, in imitation; Petrarch wrote another six; and

---

2 Henri-Irénée Marrou, *Les Troubadours* (Paris: Seuil, 1971), p. 69 (translation mine); István Frank's *Répertoire métrique de la poésie des troubadours*, 2 vols. (Paris: Champion, 1966).
3 See Arnaut Daniel's composition, 'Pus Raimons e Truc Malecx' or Uc de Saint Circ's 'Ma dompna cuit fasa sen' as examples. Elizabeth Poe, 'Unraveling a Woolly Text: "Ma dompna cuit fasa sen"', *Neophilologus* 74.4 (October 1990), pp. 527–35.

the mid-twentieth-century Oulipo movement emulated this constriction and creation of rules, paying close attention to Arnaut's twelfth-century model. Classical mythology and stories borrowed from it also figure prominently in troubadour song, earlier than, or contemporary with, the French *romans d'antiquité*. These references are not, however, limited to Greek, Roman and Celtic material; they often sit beside similar references borrowed freely from other cultural traditions – Iberian/Arabic/Jewish and motifs from traditional song.

Perhaps most importantly, or at least it is this innovation that has most appealed to modern readers, troubadour lyric poetry grounds literary inspiration and individual suffering in the material conditions from which they spring – the courts, patrons and bodies that allowed for their enunciation. Poets love ladies but give these ladies secret names (*senhals*) that mask their identity except to those in the know; the allure that springs from this secretive status becomes almost indistinguishable from what it is that the poet claims to love about the *domnas* in the first place. Shadowy figures, often indistinguishable one from the other, who are simultaneously silent, haughty, and disdainful, these women are ciphers, markers for masculine desire, and mirrors for the poets who see in them their only hope for advancement. In this sense, the songs lay bare the dependence of high art on low commerce, of poetic inspiration on the exchange of precious metals and the booty of warfare. Poets need patrons, objects to love, props for their own vainglory; and ladies do quite nicely to fit that bill, especially when they represent something bigger and more extensive than their proper selves. Patrons, for their part, need poets to sing their praises in order to maintain their own exalted reputations and status. While singing to his lady, whom he calls 'Bel Cavalier', Raimbaut de Vaqueiras is hitting several targets: he is addressing his patron, Bonifaccio, the brother or father of this lady (according to the *razo*); the noble family that produced her (the lady often stands as a synecdoche for a court or political faction); and alluding as well to the noble knight (the Bel Cavalier) that he aspires one day to be.

In the *canso*, the most highly valued of the poetic genres, the *domna* serves almost always as the desired object, the requisite to masculine identity; but in a move that is unique to the troubadour corpus, some of these women are also objects that actively desire and live to write about it. Like the male poets who celebrate them, these women poets (called *trobairitz* in modern scholarship), or their poetic alter egos, speak out, often in dialogue and discussion with other women and with men who seek their help (*tensos* and *joc-partits*). But they also compose love songs in which they refer frankly to their lovers' failings and allude to their shared erotic history. The refusal of early critics to consider these poets as women or these particular women as poets has been silenced in recent years by rising interest in this earliest known phenomenon of vernacular poetry in Europe, penned by learned women in imitation of, and in outright challenge to, the conventions of their male models and interlocutors. Their presence among the poets accorded *vidas* and *razos* (supposedly biographical), especially in a section of manuscript H (an early collection of verse songs) given over to women poets, indicates that even their contemporaries were aware of their accomplishments and sought to celebrate them in essentially the same way that they honoured the men. If for no other reason than having celebrated these first female vernacular poets (roughly contemporary with the Anglo-Norman Marie de France), troubadour poetry deserves pride of place in the pantheon of innovative and revolutionary French literary texts.

Parody and self-conscious reference to one's predecessors and models are fundamental from the second generation of the known poets (early 1140s). Self-promotion is widespread among them; braggadocio is common; erotic wordplay is popular and paranoia even more so.[4] Obscenity sits easily beside courtly customs (all common features in Arnaut Daniel's songs) and vituperation against abuses can itself be abusive (as in the case of the poet Marcabru). Political satire and attacks on enemies make up some 25–30 per cent of the some 2,500 extant songs; and dialogues between poets are common enough to be seen as an early endorsement, as well as reflection, of the poets' embrace of dialectics, even as the practice was moving into the schools. Finally, the whole phenomenon of 150 years of rapid composition, exchange and promulgation of poetic texts in the Occitan *koiné*, a standardised form of the language, was quickly taken up by Occitan-speaking intellectual historians who provided a self-conscious mythologisation of the greatness of the tradition, its language, courts and poetics, through the compilation of a collection of 'biographical' accounts of its primary practitioners (*vidas*), a set of glosses on the poetic texts themselves (*razos*) that seek to link the imaginary (the poetry) and the real (the lived experience of the poets)· plus a series of poetic treatises, word lists, and grammars that codified the tradition for future practitioners and non-native, would-be followers.[5] The *vidas* and *razos* present the first contemporary

---

4 The *lausengier*, the rival and ubiquitous opponent of the poet who undermines his work and cheapens his art, features far more commonly in the songs than a jealous husband.
5 These texts include Uc Faidit's *Donatz proensals*, Raimon Vidal de Besalu's *Razos de trobar*, and Guilhem Molinier's *Leys d'amor*.

history of a vernacular literary phenomenon, a 'who's-who-and-here's-why' that documented a culture under siege, an evolving economy, and a constellation of exemplary figures for whom poetry, language, and regional affiliation conspired to form a collective identity, built upon artistic practice, and the value of giving and exchange.

Let us step back for a moment from this slightly rebarbative list of innovations to examine some of the factors that went into making Occitan literature of the twelfth and thirteenth centuries a primary reference for the medieval literatures of what we now call France, Spain, Italy and Germany. The appeal of the language, closer to Catalan and some varieties of Italian than to modern French, might well have been its harmonious compatibility with new music, the sweet vocalic tone and multiple rhyming possibilities it afforded; but it was clearly the new thematics that appealed on a wider level. There is almost no theme that appears in later French medieval literature that did not get a first hearing in Occitan verse or narrative, and some thirteenth-century French texts overtly incorporate Occitan material into their stories or simply adapt it.[6] Principal amongst these themes was, of course, carnal desire expressed in ethereal, quasi-allegorical form. The bringing together of what some would have thought antithetical themes and images was part of what established the tradition's staying power. Loving a lady as one loves God, asking God to help you seduce your lover, proffering prayers to the lady on bended knee, head bowed and hands raised in supplication, are signs just ambiguous enough to ensure a sacrilegious thrill. The northern French *trouvères* and the German *Minnesänger* were quick to enact similar scenarios, focusing almost exclusively on the poetic sensibility of the narrator rather than his engagement with the object of desire. Sticking with a model, varying little if at all from its essential traits, and moderating it only in terms of melody, versification, and dedicatee, ensured that the tradition would remain intact, however widespread its practitioners. The roots of this snapshot of erotic devotion have been studied endlessly but to no particularly satisfactory end. Clearly the troubadour tradition shares elements with early Latin poetry (Fortunatus, Baudri de Bourgueil), musical forms with versus, tropes, and laudes from Saint Martial de Limoges, and themes with Andalucian Arabic poetry of earlier centuries (similarly exquisite gems, often addressing a boy and varying only in detail from a unifying model template), but no satisfactory narrative has been assembled to explain how these strands came together to produce the highly refined work of a single poet, Guilhem IX, by the year 1120.

---

6 *The Roman de la rose de Guillaume de Dole*, the *Roman de la Violette*, and the *Roman de Fauvel* all cite Occitan material (sometimes in translation).

The songs of Arnaut Daniel provide a rich illustration of much of what I have been saying. Arnaut is one of the more experimental and daring of the poets, well educated, interested in innovation, self-referential, a wordsmith, a pioneer in versification, using vocabulary that Dante, who emulated his work, called 'shaggy' or 'hairy'.[7]

> Sols sui qui sai lo sobrafan que.m sortz / al cor, d'amor sofren per sobramar, / car mos volers es tant ferms et entiers / c'anc no s'esduis de celliei ni s'estors.
>
> (I alone know the torment that weighs on my heart, suffering from love through over-loving; for my will is so firm and complete within itself that I have never pulled away nor abandoned her.
>
> ['Sols sui', lines 1–2, translation mine])

The opening lines of Arnaut's song play out through anaphoric homophony the excessive and obsessive quality of the poet's love and craftsmanship.[8] Stuttering through an initial series of sibilants that overflow through enjambment, the narrator brags that his desire is both 'ferm' and 'entier', an odd statement about abstract qualities that can only metaphorically, and with some transformative powers of imagination, be considered 'firm' and 'whole'.

This is typical of Arnaut's poetic world – one in which metaphors actualise and de-actualise before our eyes, where the real and imaginary (or signifier and signified) are both solid and refractory and no one seems to be able to tell the difference. The opening to another of his songs, 'En breu brisara.l temps braus, / e.ill bias busina els brancs' enacts the same sort of obsessively repetitive opening, this time in order to suggest the cracking of branches as wind whistles through them; and in another, 'L'aura amara / fa.ls bruoills brancutz / clarzir / que.l doutz espeissa ab fuoills / e.ls letz / becs / dels auzels ramencs / ten balps e mutz', Arnaut gives full rein to his 'shagginess' – that insistence on the materiality of language and its ability to shake off nature's restrictions, then reformulate itself through solipsistic vision and acoustic acuity. The wind blasts through the trees, denuding their branches and silencing the birds, while at the same time Arnaut's song cracks the syllables and form of the *canso*, making us hear what has been silenced, and feel in those crackling consonants the effects of his bitter wind.

'Sols sui . . .' emphasises language that is uniquely capable of performing its own significance. The song constructs a pattern of oxymoronic encounters and suggested impasses that imply that desire is inscribed within the spaces

---

7 Dante Alighieri, *De vulgari eloquentia*, ed. Steven Botterill (Cambridge: Cambridge University Press, 1996), pp. 68–9.
8 Arnaut Daniel, *Canzoni*, ed. Gianluigi Toja (Florence: Sansoni, 1960).

between such antithetical poles. 'D'autras vezer sui secs e d'auzir sortz' (line 8) ('In seeing others, I am blind and in hearing them, I am deaf'); 'que mais la vol non ditz la boca.l cors' (line 11) ('for I love her more than my mouth can speak for my heart'); 'que ies Rozers, per aiga qe l'engrois, / non a tal briu c'al cor plus larga dotz / no.m fassa estanc d'amor, qan la remire' (lines 26–8) ('for not even the Rhone, with all the water that swells it, has such power that it can quench my love, when I gaze at her'); 'pero l'afans m'es deportz, ris e iois, / car en pensan sui de lieis lecs e glotz' (lines 34–5) ('but the torment is pleasure, laughter and joy, for in thinking of her I am ravenous and insatiable'). He concludes in typical fashion, addressing the *domna* directly in the *tornada* (closing stanza) as he sends her his song: 'Ma chanssos prec que no.us sia enois / car si voletz grazir lo son e.ls motz / pauc prez' Arnautz cui que plass' o que tire' ('I pray that my song will not displease you for if only you would grace the tune and lyrics with your blessing, little would it matter to Arnaut who else was pleased or drawn to it'). Highlighting his own creation and fusing together song, lady, and self, Arnaut leaves us with a plea that he and his song will find favour, that his words will have their desired effect on the one interpreter who matters, and that all of this will redound on him as the ultimate lover and craftsman. Here, the personal is political; the theological is amorous; the material is metaphysical; and the poet is the supreme master of a language in which begging and bragging emerge from the same semantic field.

3

The *chanson de geste*

FINN E. SINCLAIR

The *chanson de geste* represents the first manifestation of a French literary tradition, with its oldest extant written text dating from around 1098. This is the *Chanson de Roland*, preserved in the Oxford Manuscript Digby 23. These *chansons*, and the *Chanson de Roland* in particular, have been the focus of critical attention from the nineteenth century onwards, as theories of their origins, the means of their composition and dissemination, their relation to history, and their function as ideological and literary models have been repeatedly constructed and deconstructed. Whether we take the view expressed by Gaston Paris in the late nineteenth century and see the *chansons de geste* as works of the collective imagination that grew and evolved as part of a nascent national consciousness (traditionalism), or whether we espouse the view of Joseph Bédier, who in the early years of the twentieth century suggested that the *chansons de geste* were consciously and spontaneously created by individual poets (individualism), seems to matter relatively little nowadays. The essential point to note here is that epic texts, by their very nature as texts spanning the oral/literary divide, were subject to *mouvance* – that is, to reinvention, renewal and rewriting. Even if they were composed as integral poems, their subsequent dissemination through singing and performance, and through repeated copying over the years, produced living texts, open to transformation and regeneration in response to their changing context.

Despite this openness to reinvention, there is an essential coherence to the *chanson de geste* as a genre: the content and form of the majority of Old French and Occitan epics have much in common. Content focuses predominantly on conflict, either between the Christian and his pagan other, or between the king and his barons. The genre has thus often been viewed as masculine in focus, a poetic celebration of heroic deeds (*chanson de geste* means 'song of deeds'). Yet, as we shall see below, this is not exactly the case, as women play an integral and important role in the genre, even if this is at times simply to provide a foil against which the male protagonists may be defined. As for the formal shape of the poems, this is stylistically formulaic, 'composed from a public fund of pre-existent narrative schemes, motifs, and a stock of adaptable hemistichs or "formulae"'.[1] The poems were composed in decasyllabic *laisses* (stanzas of irregular length), although towards the end of the twelfth century the popular alexandrine line (twelve syllables) was sometimes used instead. The earliest poems were assonanced, rather than rhymed. *Chansons de geste* were often grouped in 'cycles', which brought together a range of tales that either focused on a particular hero and his lineage, as in the case of Guillaume d'Orange (*Cycle de Guillaume d'Orange*), or on a particular theme. The two main themed cycles are the *Cycle du roi*, which includes the *Chanson de Roland* and poems featuring Charlemagne; and the *Cycle des barons révoltés*, the most famous of which is *Raoul de Cambrai*.

Both content (the semantic) and form (the syntactic) serve to define a genre, although there is inevitably a range of variations among a genre's individual works. Definition by genre helps to give context to a particular text and points to the way in which it may be read and interpreted. The semantic and syntactic markers of the *chanson de geste* indicate its oral origins, with repetition, intertextual borrowing, and allusion being key elements in both areas. The fact that a text may be classed as a *chanson de geste* places it within a matrix of similar texts that dialogue with each other and which can be seen as responding to a particular cultural desire or need. Two recent studies are especially illuminating in their discussion of the way in which genres arise in response to cultural tensions, and how these tensions are then played out in the literary forum. Simon Gaunt suggests that different genres may simultaneously present different types of imaginary resolution to historical and cultural problems, while Sarah Kay focuses on the dialogic relationship between the *chansons de geste* and the romance.[2] Each of these genres, suggests Kay, illuminates the 'political unconscious' of the other, as their narratives are bound by assumptions about 'the personal and the social, the licit and the illicit, the ethical and the unethical, the representable and the unrepresentable'.[3]

1 Sarah Kay, *The Chansons de Geste in the Age of Romance: Political Fictions* (Oxford: Clarendon Press, 1995), p. 2.
2 Simon Gaunt, *Gender and Genre in Medieval French Literature* (Cambridge: Cambridge University Press, 1995); see in particular the introduction. Kay, *Chansons de Geste*.
3 Kay, *Chansons de Geste*, p. 5.

History and memory

Epics are not historical documents, but works of literature that nonetheless testify to certain modes of thought prevalent at a particular point in time. They both disseminate and help to shape an ideological social narrative. Although the *chansons de geste* can be seen as tied into a certain cultural and historical context, the narrative and chronological space in which the action of many epics unfolds is not that of the eleventh, twelfth, or thirteenth centuries, when the majority of these tales were transcribed. Instead, they look backwards to the 'Golden Age' of Charlemagne and to the somewhat less gilded era of his son Louis. The *Chanson de Roland*, often seen as the French 'national epic', and as a symbol of French collective identity, commemorates events that took place in 778, when the rearguard of Charlemagne's army was massacred in the Pyrenees during their return to France from Spain. Various accounts written in the ninth century testify to the historical reality of this event, but none gives a clear indication of what actually occurred, nor of who was involved. Roland himself is mentioned briefly by Einhard in his *Vita Caroli magni* (*Life of Charlemagne*), written around 830, but he is obviously not viewed as a major protagonist. It is only in the Oxford *Roland* that the eponymous character becomes the focus of a heroic tale that weaves together the feudal, the 'nationalistic' and the religious to create a commemorative narrative that transcends history.

Eugene Vance suggests that the *Chanson de Roland* is 'as much a drama of memory as it is a memory of a historical drama'.[4] Memory and history interlink, as a historical event and the collective memory of this event are reshaped and renewed to produce a narrative of desire in poetic form. Rather than serving as the commemoration of Charlemagne's military loss at the pass of Roncevaux in 778, the *Roland* commemorates its composition as an ideological myth. The *chanson* reflects the era of the First Crusade (1098), with the primary conflict of the text being between Christians and Saracens. If the Crusades were a form of geographic territorialisation, the *chanson de geste* can be seen as a textual and linguistic one. The cultural impetus outwards, towards conquest and colonisation, had as its corollary the creation of a nascent sense of nationhood in which the notion of coherent identity played a key role. The *chanson de geste* was the first literary form to be widely composed in the vernacular, the use of French, rather than Latin, creating a space for the exploration

---

4 Eugene Vance, *Mervelous Signs: Poetics and Sign Theory in the Middle Ages* (Lincoln and London: University of Nebraska Press, 1986), p. 57.

and establishment of Frankish or 'French' identity. In the historical, cultural context, the idea of a unified Christian community was problematic, as the linguistic and cultural diversity within different regions of Europe, and indeed within the boundaries of what we now call 'France', produced a multiplicity of Christian 'selves'. The Christian body represented in the *Chanson de Roland* is that of the Franks – a term which here designates the armies of Charlemagne, but which nonetheless appears amorphous, as sections of the army retain a strong regional identity.[5] The Frankish community is imaginary rather than real, tied together ideologically, rather than geographically, by the poem's nostalgic evocation of 'la douce France'. 'France' as we know it now did not exist as a coherent geographical entity in the early Middle Ages, but was generally used to refer to the Île-de-France, the area ruled directly by the monarchy. The poem, however, creates and perpetuates a vision of geographical, cultural, and religious unity across all regions, which is shored up by its composition in the French language and by the existence of the text itself as an act of collective memorialisation.

Self and other

In the *Chanson de Roland*, as in many other epics that pit the Christian against his pagan other, Western Christian identity is partly defined in relation to difference. The ethnic, cultural, and religious difference of the Saracen helps to shape the parameters of the Western self, providing a repository for all that the Christian is not, or at least is not according to the genre's idealised vision of Western collective identity. Although the text affords a privileged space for the construction of an ideal, the depiction of the Christian and his pagan other does not function as a straightforward binary opposition. In a manner that foreshadows the instability of constructs of racial and ethnic otherness revealed by modern postcolonial theory, the boundaries between the two are blurred, as the representation of the pagan shifts to underscore either his similarity or his difference.

Cultural and religious otherness is not a monologic, unvarying construct in the *chanson de geste*, although two predominant tropes can be discerned: the other as alien and threatening, and the other as recognisable and open to assimilation. Both of these appear in the *Chanson de Roland*, as the Saracen is constructed either as mirror to the Christian, or as his stark opposite. Christianity provides the model for the depiction of the Muslim religion,

---

5 *La Chanson de Roland*, ed. I. Short (Paris: Livre de Poche, 1990), laisses 218–25.

with its anomalous trinity of Mahomet, Tervagant and Apollyon; Marsile, the Saracen king, is practically Charlemagne's double in the early court scenes, and the Western chivalric system operates in both realms. Yet throughout the battle scenes the radical difference between Christian and non-Christian is clear, from Roland's unequivocal statement: 'Paien unt tort e chrestiens unt dreit' (line 1015) ('The pagans are in the wrong and the Christians in the right'), to the symbolic depiction of the opposing foreigners as darkly sub-human: 'Cil d'Ociant i braient e henissent, / E cil d'Arguille si cume chen glatissent' (lines 3526–7) ('Those from Ociant bray and whinny, while those from Arguille yap like dogs'). This type of split depiction presents the Saracen world as one open to a colonisation that functions not only through physical conquest but also through literary appropriation. The mediating gaze of the Western text appropriates, redefines and rewrites the image of the non-Christian in a way that either assimilates it to the hegemonic Christian norm or allocates it to a space that lies beyond, and which is ultimately indefinable. The instability of the image of the other impacts, however, on the definition of the Christian self. Without a clear-cut model of opposition, the Western self-image is inevitably partial and fragmented, open to a similar shift and play.

The discontinuities and slippages inherent in the Western vision of the East appear in the shifting perspective of the *Roland* and in the narratives of difference explored by other epic texts. Religion provides a fundamental source of otherness in Crusade narratives, yet it is not the sole point of cultural difference recognised and explored by *chansons de geste*. The *Voyage de Charlemagne à Jérusalem et à Constantinople* (early twelfth century) describes a fictional journey taken by Charlemagne and his knights. The principal focus of the narrative lies on Charlemagne's exploits in the city of Constantinople; the Frankish army is thus read against the Christian world of the Greeks, rather than against that of a culture more immediately perceived as alien, such as that of the Saracens. Yet despite this apparent similarity, the text reveals a fundamental ambivalence in its depiction of a people at once same and yet unavoidably other. This reflects the Western attitude towards Greek Orthodoxy in the twelfth century, when the Greeks were perceived as Christian heretics. Constantinople becomes a liminal space in which Frankish identity is both destabilised and reaffirmed through the encounter with a foreign world that must be negotiated, but which cannot truly be either rationalised or categorised. The physical riches and moral worth of Constantinople present an alternative vision of the world that contrasts with the lack inherent in the Frankish community. Measured against the Byzantine king Hugo, Charlemagne is not slow to recognise his own inferiority: 'Karle vit le paleis e la richesce grant; / La sue manantise ne priset mie un guant' (lines 363–4) ('Charles saw the palace and the splendour of it. He held his own possessions as not worth a jot').[6] The superiority of Charlemagne and his entourage is finally affirmed, but this only takes place with the help of God, and is continuously undercut by the narrative's tongue-in-cheek tone.

Gender and difference

Ethnic, cultural and religious differences were significant in shaping a sense of cultural identity in early medieval France. In the *chanson de geste*, this cultural identity appears, however, predominantly masculine in focus. Much has been written on the male homosocial networks of both medieval feudal society and its literary reflection: Gaunt sees the ethical system of the *chanson de geste* as 'exclusively masculine', yet, as Kay points out: 'Men are the architects of social structure, women the mortar used to hold it together.'[7] In the epic, the narrative focus often lies on a masculine duo – Roland and Olivier in the *Chanson de Roland*, Ami and Amile in the poem of that name (*c.* 1200), Raoul and Bernier in *Raoul de Cambrai* (*c.* 1200) – yet this core masculine relationship is open to the influence of the text's female characters, who may play either a supportive or a subversive role in relation to it. Although women may be minor characters in the *chanson de geste*, they are integral to its narrative structure and its imaginary community, and thus significant to the genre's exploration and creation of social and cultural identity.

Female alterity was recognised and affirmed by medieval society in general – in religious, medical, didactic and literary discourses – but in the *chanson de geste* this difference functions in a similar way to that of the foreign other. Women can either be assimilated to a text's ethical discourse (Aude in the *Roland*, Belissant in *Ami et Amile*), or opposed to it, breaking apart the masculine relationships that structure feudal society (Lubias in *Ami* is a clear example of this). If Western Christian identity can be mapped against its external, foreign other, masculine identity finds a figure of internal difference in its feminine other. Yet neither the external nor the internal representative of difference provides a clear and unambiguous image against which medieval masculinity may be defined.

---

6 *Le Voyage de Charlemagne à Jérusalem et à Constantinople*, ed. P. Aebischer (Geneva: Droz, 1965).
7 Gaunt, *Gender and Genre*, p. 22; Kay, *The Chansons de Geste*, p. 15.

Those women who are doubly other – both female and Saracen – often function as the site of a discourse of assimilation, as the Saraceness converts to Christianity, changes her name, and marries into Western Christian society. Bramimonde is wife to the pagan king Marsile in the *Chanson de Roland*, but following the defeat of the Saracen army she is taken back to France, where she converts and is baptised 'Juliane'. This is a conversion through love, not for a new husband, but for the Christian religion itself and for the society that upholds it. Bramimonde's absorption into Western Christian society marks its religious and ethical supremacy, and the failing of Saracen religious and military power. The Saracen queen functions as a forceful critic of her native regime prior to her conversion, but is silenced by her transfer to the Christian context: from being a source of disruption, she becomes a symbolic possession conquered by right, rather than might.

This assimilation of Saracen women into Christian society is not always seamless, however. In the *chansons de geste*, a feature of female portrayal in general is women's ability to voice criticism of the masculine social order (Christian as well as Saracen) – a power that has the potential to destabilise the gender balance and undercut the genre's ideological framework. In the *Prise d'Orange* (late twelfth/early thirteenth century), Guillaume d'Orange conquers the city of Orange, which is held by the Saracens. In so doing, Guillaume gains land, wealth and wife, 'commodities' often inexorably linked in the epic. Orable is originally wife to a Saracen emir, but converts to Christianity, marries Guillaume instead, and changes her name to Guiborc, a shift that separates her linguistically from the otherness of a foreign city, Orange, and allies her metonymically with her new husband, Guillaume. As in the case of Bramimonde, Guiborc's assimilation to Western society implicitly underscores the 'rightness' of Christianity when measured against the inherent 'lack' of other religions and shores up the ethical system of the *chanson de geste*. Guillaume d'Orange's status as an epic hero is affirmed by his conquest and by Guiborc's evident wifely worth as supporter of her husband and of the system he represents. However, in the *Chanson de Guillaume* (late eleventh/early twelfth century; reworked as *Aliscans* [1150–1200]) Guiborc's zeal paradoxically undercuts Guillaume's heroic depiction, as she becomes more dedicated to sustaining inter-religious warfare and upholding the epic ideal than her husband. The definition of epic masculinity is destabilised through the blurring of gender boundaries; ethnic and religious difference may be subsumed into Western Christian identity, yet gender difference proves more complex and potentially subversive in relation to the epic masculine norm.

Conflict and resolution

As mentioned above, the impetus of many *chansons de geste* is outwards, towards Crusade and conquest, but the *Prise d'Orange* points to a further source of conflict – that between the king and his barons. Guillaume's conquest of Orange resolves an internal problem: King Louis fails to compensate his faithful knight for services rendered, so Guillaume is forced to seek lands and wealth elsewhere. The theme of the failure of the feudal system, which should theoretically provide a framework of reciprocal duty and allegiance between king, knights and vassals, is taken up by later epics, in particular those of the *Cycle des barons révoltés*.

By the early thirteenth century, the power of the French monarchy had increased, and a strong power base had been consolidated in the area around the Île-de-France. This was in direct contrast to the situation a hundred years earlier, when the French king wielded less power and influence than some of his dukes (especially those of Aquitaine and Normandy). As the power of the monarch increased (notably that of Philippe-Auguste, who ruled 1180–1223), that of his knights and the lesser nobility waned. The epic's shift towards depicting an inverse power relationship, with a weak king and powerful, authoritative barons, can be seen as an attempt to mediate social reality and to fulfil a perceived lack. The epic's nostalgia for an imaginary 'Golden Age' also comes into play here, linking past and present in an idealised vision of homosocial loyalty and comradeship between knights. The text provides an imaginary space for the exploration of issues of power and conflict, yet the notion of a shared ideology structuring male–male relationships is revealed as inherently flawed, as is the feudal system that theoretically provided their frame.

Kay sees a shift in the epic's focus from an external enemy to an internal one by the 1160s and 1170s and she reads this as a response to the internal problems of feudal society.[8] Even in the earlier *Chanson de Roland*, however, the traitor Ganelon appears a greater threat to Roland than the Saracens. Roland may be killed in conflict with the pagan army, but he is brought to his death by the machinations and disloyalty of his stepfather, who becomes the archetypal villain who spawns a whole lineage of traitors that appear in later *chansons de geste*. Like the figure of the weak and vacillating king, that of the traitor signals the failing of the feudal order, in imaginary as well as historical terms.

---

8 Kay, *Chansons de Geste*, p. 234.

Different *chansons* struggle in different ways with the problem of the fragmentation of the feudal and epic ideal. In *Ami et Amile*, which forms part of the *Cycle du roi*, the narrative revolves around the physical and moral sameness of the two companions. Their identical appearance functions as a metaphor for the ideal of masculine companionship and loyalty; Ami and Amile's oneness is, however, broken apart by women (the subversive female other) and by the traitor Hardré (of Ganelon's lineage). Masculine unity cannot function in the context of the real, social world, which is plagued by difference. It can only be restored through God's intervention and maintained through the companions' retreat to a monastery. The model of masculine bonding constructed by the *chanson* is inherently imaginary and is increasingly recognised as such by the text.

Raoul de Cambrai explores the problem quite differently. Raoul is the epitome of the 'baron in revolt' and the poem has been described as the bloodiest and most murderous of *chansons de geste*, the one that marks the disintegration of the epic ideal. The two companions here are Raoul and Bernier, but there is an original disparity between them, as Bernier is vassal to Raoul and is illegitimate. There is little sense of masculine unity even at the beginning of this poem, and the feudal bonds between Raoul and Bernier become increasingly strained until Raoul's unpardonable violence against Bernier's mother (whom he burns alive in her nunnery) breaks all allegiance between them. The narrative is long and complex, but it is significant that the original seed of discord is sown by King Louis (son of Charlemagne and traditionally depicted as weak in the epic). Louis fails to fulfil his duties as monarch: on the death of Raoul's father, Louis gives away the lands that should have been inherited by his son. He promises Raoul the first alternative parcel of land that becomes available, but again this leads to a disinheritance, as the death of Bernier's grandfather sees possession of his fief disputed between Bernier's father and uncles on one side and Raoul on the other. The concentrated violence and conflict of *Raoul de Cambrai* springs from this misuse of regal power. The text reveals the late twelfth– and early thirteenth-century preoccupation with the changing structure of feudal society, but in this case it provides no imaginary solution, only a fearsome destruction of the bounded world of both text and society.

Epic diasporas

The *chanson de geste* has traditionally been viewed as an early medieval genre, yet epics continued to be produced until the fourteenth century. This is not to say, however, that the genre did not change and evolve. Texts tended to become longer and more complex during the thirteenth century, with a greater space allocated to love interest and the marvellous. The traditional notion of an increasing romance influence on the epic has been questioned by Kay, but narrative content certainly diversified away from a general focus on Crusade and conflict. *Chansons* such as *Florence de Rome* (early thirteenth century), *Parise la Duchesse* (c. 1225–50), and *Berte aus grans piés* (c. 1274–8) mark a shift towards depicting female characters and their role in society. The *Crusade Cycle*, which originated at the end of the twelfth century with poems focusing (not surprisingly) on Crusade – *La Chanson d'Antioche*, *Les Chétifs*, and *La Conquête de Jérusalem* – saw the later addition of texts reworking the legend of the mythical Swan Knight and extending the genealogy of the crusading hero Godefroy de Bouillon.

The *chanson de geste* may have originated in northern France, but there are a few Occitan and hybrid Franco-Occitan examples of the genre, which testify to its social and ideological relevance in the south. *Daurel et Beton* (c. 1150–68) and *Girart de Roussillon* (c. 1150s), composed in a mixture of Occitan and Old French, are important texts which share the syntactic and semantic features of Old French epics while reflecting their southern context. The chronological and geographical reach of the *chanson de geste* reveals it to be a vibrant literary form open to shift and change in response to the social realities and the collective imaginary of the French Middle Ages.

4

Saints' lives, violence, and community

EMMA CAMPBELL

Violence in medieval literature is often codified and formulaic. This is well known to students of medieval literature from genres such as epic and romance, where the depiction of violence is frequently repetitive and highly stylised. Critics have sometimes pointed out the ideological value of such depictions for the formation of community and identity both within and beyond such texts.[1] In a technical sense, medieval saints' lives offer comparable representations of violence to those found in so-called 'secular' literature: where violence is represented, it is bound by certain conventions and is ideologically significant. Indeed, on a formal level, vernacular saints' lives have much in common with epic and frequently depict violence in terms of feudal relations; the widespread notion of the saint as a soldier of Christ, or *miles Christi*, is just one example of this. Saints' lives in the high and late Middle Ages also borrow substantially from romance literature, though not always in ways that flatter romance: one occasionally finds in saints' lives a derogatory layering of recognisable scenarios of romance seduction with more explicit forms of violence and coercion. Certain commentators have seen this as an exposure of what is really at stake in romance plots, which tend instead to euphemise and romanticise sexual violence.[2] Yet, despite such formal similarities, the representation of violence in saints' lives is worked into what is in many respects a different textual framework from that underlying either epic or romance. Saints' lives are first and foremost religious texts, and their representation of violence therefore serves their religious aims.

Though modern readers are often less familiar with saints' lives than they are with epic or romance, it is worth remembering that in terms of extant

---

1 Peter Haidu, *The Subject of Violence: The Song of Roland and the Birth of the State* (Bloomington: Indiana University Press, 1993) and Sharon Kinoshita, *Medieval Boundaries: Rethinking Difference in Old French Literature* (Philadelphia: University of Pennsylvania Press, 2006), pp. 15–45.
2 Notably Kathryn Gravdal, *Ravishing Maidens: Writing Rape in Medieval French Literature and Law* (Philadelphia: University of Pennsylvania Press, 1991).

manuscripts saints' lives pre-date most other vernacular genres. Despite the relative lack of attention currently paid to hagiography (or writing about saints) by literary scholars, this literature constitutes an important corpus that almost equals romance in volume. Martyrdom is perhaps the most obvious example of how saints' lives represent violence. Typically in accounts of martyrdom, the saint's Christian faith is discovered by the pagan authorities and attempts are made to persuade him/her to convert; this process usually involves a mixture of bribery and threats which rapidly translates into torture. After being sustained by God through the punishments imposed by pagan law, the saint eventually dies with God's consent and is transported directly to heaven. The earliest extant saints' lives in French – the *Vie de Sainte Eulalie* and the *Vie de Saint Léger* – are both accounts of martyrdom; though this is not the only type of saint's life copied in the Middle Ages, accounts of martyrdom continue to be popular into later periods. These later texts often amplify the violence of earlier models: whereas the violence of the earliest texts is almost incidental, texts from the twelfth century onwards represent torture in more comprehensive and brutal levels of detail, and frequently expand the number of torments that martyrs have to endure. The stylised violence of accounts of martyrdom thus seems to become more rather than less important as saints' lives evolve over the course of the high and late Middle Ages.

Even if one accepts that violence in medieval texts sometimes had mnemonic or pedagogical functions that may have informed the way it oper-ated in hagiographic literature, the violence of accounts of martyrdom poses a number of problems related to the way it features in such texts.[3] First, the graphic, repetitive nature of depictions of violence raises issues of interpre-tation: does the formulaic nature of violence result in an almost cartoon-like evacuation of the horrific content of what is being represented, or does it cumulatively underline its most disturbing qualities? Is this part of a sublima-tion of violence that transforms brutality into religious experience or does it simply result in a thinly veiled sado-masochistic poetics? Second, unlike romance, or to a large extent epic, the violence of saints' lives is directed at men and women in ways that are broadly equivalent, while being expressed in different ways. In their roles as soldiers of Christ, male and female martyrs are all subjected to horrific physical violence, yet this violence occasionally takes what are often considered to be more explicitly eroticised forms in female saints' lives. This, in turn, raises the question of the sexualisation of violence

---

3 On violence, mnemonics, and pedagogy, see Jody Enders, *The Medieval Theater of Cruelty: Rhetoric, Memory, Violence* (Ithaca, NY: Cornell University Press, 1999).

in hagiography and whether or not it can be considered pornographic or sexually enjoyable, especially when the victim is female.

The problematic nature of hagiographic violence for modern readers might be seen in the larger perspective of how violence signifies in these texts and the ways it serves ideological and communal ends. The relationship between violence and community in accounts of martyrdom is arguably as pronounced as it is in epic. Yet, whereas epic community is almost exclusively male, the type of community that saints' lives promote is intended to apply to all, regardless of gender or social status. Women's involvement in hagiographic violence might thus be seen as part of an attempt to include them in a model of Christian community as well as forming part of a violently sexualising aesthetic. This does not close down problems relating to the interpretation of violence in medieval hagiography, but it does mean that violence in female saints' lives can be seen on a continuum with that found in male saints' lives. It also suggests that such violence has an important ideological value that demands our attention as readers of such texts. My aim here is to consider how violence serves a narrative purpose in hagiography and, more specifically, how it is related to the communal function of the texts themselves. What might be the relationship between violence and community in saints' lives? Is this violence a purely gratuitous – possibly even quasi-pornographic – filler? Or does it in fact serve some other ideological purpose related to how those texts attempt to influence the communities that read them? Addressing such questions does not of course mean that saints' lives cannot do both: that they cannot be gratuitously violent while also using that violence to certain ideological ends. However, we are missing something rather important if we regard such violence as peripheral to the purpose of this literature as a focus for community formation.

Violence, power, and ideology

Though it should be noted that martyrdom was not the only – or even the most popular – model of sanctity in medieval saints' lives, the Lives of martyrs were copied throughout the Middle Ages and constitute an important part of the hagiographic corpus. Violence is integral to martyrdom, which is a form of sanctity that demands suffering for one's faith. Accounts of martyrdom depict violence in a way that makes it part of the political and ideological conflict that opposes pagan and Christian, earthly and divine authority in these texts. The polarisation of these different elements can often seem crude and caricatural to modern sensibilities, placing blustering, irrational pagans on one side and composed, logically persuasive Christian martyrs on the other. Violence – or the threat of violence – is usually associated with a pagan authority attempting to impose itself on Christians who disobey the religious and civic obligations attached to that authority. As such, it is most frequently a mark of desperation: having failed to win the ideological argument, the last resort of pagan law is to inflict itself on Christian dissenters through violent punishments. Paradoxically, pagan violence is thus a sign of ideological weakness. What is more, the violence that pagan authorities attempt to do to the martyr is usually forestalled or counteracted by God, thereby providing opportunities for saints' lives to illustrate God's superior control over the created world.

An example of how such a dynamic operates in vernacular texts can be found in the late twelfth-century *Vie de Saint Georges* by Simund de Freine.[4] Having outspokenly rejected pagan religion, Georges is tortured in a wide variety of ways by the pagan persecutor Dacien, and dies no fewer than three times during his ordeal. These sufferings are anticipated in some detail from the outset: towards the beginning of the *Vie*, Georges receives a message from God while in prison telling him he will die and be resurrected for him three times (lines 483–94). The ordeal Georges undertakes in God's name is presented as a means of defending Christian religion (*lei*) as well as guaranteeing him a place in heaven. Suffering and death, though visited on the martyr by the pagan tyrant, are thus ultimately represented as proof of God's power. Georges's agreement with God means that the violence to which he is subject is a predictable part of a divine scheme that demonstrates God's control over the martyr's life. Moreover, in being subjected to violence and death, the martyr indicates his own faith in God's power, submitting to punishment in the belief that God will relieve or reward his suffering. This is implicitly how the martyr defends *divine lei*: Georges's acceptance of his punishment is an affirmation (as well as a proof) of the faith he professes and, as such, provides a model for other believers both within and outside the text.

Sex and violence

Critics have pointed out for some time that the violence visited upon the martyr often takes a sexualised form in the case of female saints. An illustration of this can be found in the thirteenth-century *Vie de Sainte Agnes*, where the

---

4 *Les Œuvres de Simund de Freine publiées d'après tous les manuscrits connus* (Paris: Firmin-Didot, 1909), pp. 61–117.

saint's refusal to marry on account of her faith leads to her being stripped and thrown into a brothel by the pagan provost of Rome.[5] If there were any ambiguity in the provost's actions, this is quickly resolved when he states that any young men in the vicinity are welcome to have their way with her (lines 353–6). Despite these threats to Agnes's virginity, the sexual violence with which she is menaced is never actualised. While in the brothel, she is visited by an angel, who clothes her and tells her she is called upon to serve God (lines 361–71). Then, when the young man who has previously proposed to Agnes attempts to take her by force, God strikes him down dead (lines 401–20). At the request of the youth's father, Agnes prays for and obtains his resuscitation – a miracle that converts many spectators to Christianity (lines 437–540). Thus, though the punishment of the female saint mirrors that seen in the *Vie de Saint Georges*, pagan violence threatens both her life and her sexual integrity, which are taken to be synonymous. Furthermore, as an additional illustration of God's superior power, the violence with which the saint is threatened here redoubles on its perpetrator, leaving her spiritually and physically intact.

The protection of the martyr's body in the brothel is later echoed in her immunity to the flames of the pyre onto which she is placed in a later pagan attempt on her life. The Old French poem here alters or elaborates upon the Latin *Gesta* in a number of ways.[6] The violence of this scene is immediately offset by the assertion that he who protected Agnes in the brothel can do so during this torment as well (lines 661–4). In a subtle departure from the Latin source, where the flames divide and destroy those who lit the fire, the flames in the Old French text protectively encircle Agnes like a secret chamber (*cambre celee*) but cannot touch or hurt her (lines 665–72). On seeing the miracle, Agnes again implicitly refers to the earlier scene in the brothel by giving thanks to God for protecting her from the 'pollutions' of her persecutors (lines 685–7).[7] The changes made in the vernacular text thus link the two episodes in a way that associates the protection of the martyr's sexual body and the protection of her body from the flames, as each transforms the destructive potential of pagan violence into a demonstration of God's superior power.

The martyr's immunity to violence is thus, in the case of both male and female saints, attributed to God's greater sovereignty and serves dramatically

5 A. J. Denomy (ed.), *The Old French Lives of Saint Agnes and Other Vernacular Versions of the Middle Ages* (Cambridge, MA: Harvard University Press, 1938). I refer throughout to the A text.
6 Ibid., pp. 129–30.
7 This term implies general spiritual corruption as well as having sexual connotations. On the etymology of the term, see Adolf Tobler and Erhard Lommatzsch (eds.), *Altfranzösisches Wörterbuch*, 10 vols. to date (Berlin: Weidmann, 1925–), VII, col. 1381, lines 20–33.

to expose that sovereignty both to characters within the text and to the text's medieval readers. It follows from this that the representation of violence in accounts of martyrdom has a number of effects. First, insofar as the threat of torture is associated with worldly, pagan authority, violence is used as a device that distinguishes that authority from the sovereignty of a Christian God. Whereas pagan violence is the largely ineffectual product of a continually frustrated worldly power, divine authority is shown to be based on a more solid, all-encompassing mastery of human life and the natural world. When God is associated with violence in saints' lives it is, as illustrated by the *Vie de Sainte Agnes*, often presented as a deflection of pagan violence back onto its perpetrator, or as an effective punishment of those who refuse to believe what seems to be staring them in the face. Second, the depiction of violence in saints' lives often takes gender-specific forms, depending on whether a saint is male or female. Yet, despite such differences, the ultimate ideological aims of such depictions remain the same.

Community

The Life of St Agnes examined above can also be used to illustrate how martyrdom acts as a focus for community in hagiographic texts – a feature common to the Lives of male and female martyrs. As with other accounts of martyrdom, Agnes's suffering and death provide focal points for the profession of Christian faith by other characters in the text and generate further tales of martyrdom. After Agnes's death and burial, Christians often congregate at her tomb to pray. On discovering this, however, the pagans take to attacking those who come to worship and the Christians flee in fear of their lives. Esmeree (Emerentiana) – a Christian woman who knew the saint when she was alive – takes the pagans to task and receives martyrdom by being stoned to death. The storm that follows so frightens the pagans that they leave the Christians to worship in peace (lines 741–804).

Esmeree's martyrdom thus not only emerges from the persecution of the Christian community within the text, but also facilitates the re-establishment of that community as it forms itself through worshipping Agnes. What is more, Esmeree provides an important link between the saint and the community that pray to her: on the one hand, Esmeree is aligned with the saint insofar as her martyrdom echoes that of Agnes, yet, on the other, Esmeree also belongs to the community that prays to the saint, and indeed dies in the process of defending her right to do so. Esmeree's role in forging connections between the Christian community and Agnes thus potentially extends beyond the community depicted in the text to the Christian faithful who make up the audience of the *Vie* in the medieval present.

Agnes's protection from pagan violence also translates into other forms of divine agency with which she is associated in the miracles following her death. Primary among these is a miracle involving Constance (daughter of Emperor Constantine) who is afflicted with leprosy but cured by Agnes when she visits the saint's shrine (lines 849–920). Appearing to Constance in a dream, Agnes informs the girl that God will cure her:

> 'Tu n'auras mais enfrete ne dolour,
> Or soies virgene jamais por soie amour.
> Or soies lie, jamais n'auras torment,
> En Diu hounour reçoif baptisement.
> Il t'a bien fait; bon gerredon l'en rent,
> Dorenavant a lui servir entent.
> Retien de cuer chou que je te conseille,
> De baptisier le matin t'apareille.'
> Li nuis s'en va, li puciele s'esveille;
> Sainne se trueve, si en a grant merveille.
>
> (lines 895–904)

('You shall no longer have infirmity or pain; now forever remain a virgin for his love. Now be happy, you shall never again be tormented. In God's honour, receive baptism. He made you well; offer him a good recompense, henceforth strive to serve him. Keep in your heart that which I advise you, ready yourself to be baptised in the morning.' The night comes to an end, the maiden awakes; she finds herself healthy and wonders greatly at this.)

The connections between God's protection of Agnes and his restoration of Constance's health are apparent here; indeed, the Old French poem emphasises these connections more than its Latin source, by stressing Constance's dedication of her virginity to God.[8] Constance, like Agnes, is to offer her virginity to God in return for his protection of her body from pain (*dolour*) and torment (*torment*). The poem thus suggests that the preservation of the saint's body under torture and the protection of Constance's body from disease are on a continuum.

Constance's miraculous recovery leads to the foundation of an abbey and the formation of a community of female religious (lines 935–64) – details which again are not features of the Old French poem's Latin source.[9] This is directly followed in the vernacular text by an exhortation to prayer that

8 Denomy, *Agnes*, p. 132.   9 Ibid., pp. 131–2.

re-adopts the themes of service and protection and makes them accessible to the community as a whole through their reading of the Life (lines 965–84):

> Proions li tout, li grant, et li millor,
> K'ensi nous daigne aqueillir a s'amor,
> K'ele nous soit a nostre darrain jor
> Bonne plaidive envers nostre Signor.
>
> . . .
>
> Qu'ele nous prenge en sa protection,
> Si nous recuevre de nos pechies pardon.
>
> . . .
>
> Ki la joie de lassus velt avoir,
> De tout sen cuer, de trestout son pooir,
> Doit Diu servir, et en memoire avoir,
> (por Diu) doit tout laissier, et le monde, et avoir.
>
> (lines 965–8, 971–2, 981–4)

(Let us all pray to [Agnes], the great and the best, that she deign to gather us to his love, that she be on our final day a good advocate for us with our Lord . . . May she take us into her protection, so that we might receive pardon for our sins . . . Whoever wants to have the joy of heaven must, with all his heart and all his power, serve God and keep him in mind; he must relinquish everything (for God), both the world and possessions.)

God's protection of the martyr's body from pain and torture thus exemplifies a form of divine agency also exercised through miracles performed after her death. What is more, this agency gives rise to and confirms faith in the Christian community both within and outside the text. Auxiliary figures potentially play an important role in this process. The forms of emulation and identification represented by accounts of martyrdom through figures such as Esmeree and Constance provide the basis for the confirmation of Christian community. Yet the saint's Life itself also plays a part in enabling the community to access the divine protection that she enjoyed, and exhorts its listeners to emulate her example through service to God.

The depiction of violence in medieval saints' lives can quite easily be associated with sexist, orientalist, even racist perspectives that modern readers justifiably find uncomfortable and even offensive; in exploring the relationship between violence and community it has not been my intention to suggest that we should excuse or cease to interrogate these associations. What I hope instead to have demonstrated is that, however objectionable it may be, the representation of violence in saints' lives is part of the ideological fabric of such texts, and reinforces their consolidation of Christian community. The female saint's implication in the violence of martyrdom has often been seen as especially problematic by modern critics. Though these critics are not wrong, the female martyr's exposure to sexualised, gender-specific forms of aggression is – as demonstrated by the Life of St Agnes – part of her participation in a formulaic narrative of violence that also applies to male martyrs. Moreover, the ideological work that violence performs in hagiographic texts such as these means that the forms of aggression to which saints are subject are intimately bound to the communal purposes of this literature. Violence ultimately exposes a relationship to God that others – within the text as well as outside it – are encouraged to adopt in emulation of the saint. Thus, if we can be justifiably shocked by the violence of martyrdom, this should not blind us to the fact that it also possesses an expository power in hagiography that makes it integral both to the communication of a religious message and to the text's function within the Christian community that reads it.

5

Myth and the *matière de Bretagne*

CAROLINE JEWERS

By the late twelfth century, when Jean Bodel describes contemporary literature as comprising 'trois materes ... de France de Bretaigne et de Ronme la grant', the 'matter of Britain' had clearly distinguished itself from the *chansons de geste* and *romans d'antiquité* that he finds more authentic and didactic.[1] He contrasts the *matière de Bretagne* as pure entertainment, delineating in a stroke the widely disseminated and influential works that take Brittany (construed as Britain as well as the French province) as their inspiration. This includes those that use the blurred geography of *Bretagne* for local colour (as in the short narrative *lais*, or quick shorthand allusions in lyric poetry), and romances that evoke such figures as King Arthur, his knights, and Tristan and Iseult. This broad category burgeoned rapidly into a complex metafiction enfolding some of the most memorable literature of the High Middle Ages, beginning in the second half of the twelfth century with Wace's *Roman de Brut*, the works of Chrétien de Troyes, Marie de France's *Lais*, and the *Tristan* romances of Thomas and Béroul. From the late twelfth through the thirteenth century, verse romances proliferate, accompanied by the adaptation and vast expansion of central narratives into prose, principally in the *Didot-Perceval*, the monumental *Vulgate* and *Post-Vulgate Cycles*, and the Prose *Tristan*. In addition, a host of named and anonymous authors propagate the individual and collective adventures of key characters at Arthur's court, chiefly Gawain (*La Mule sans frein*; *Le Chevalier à l'épée*; *Hunbaut*; *La Vengeance Raguidel*; *L'Âtre périlleux*), Perceval (the *Continuations*; *Perlesvaus*) and Tristan (*La Folie de Berne* and *La Folie d'Oxford*, and in more episodic form embedded in the *Donnei des amanz* and Gerbert de Montreuil's *Continuation* of *Perceval*).

Some romances feature new heroes deriving their pedigree from a primary association with Arthur's court (Renaut de Beaujeu's *Le Bel Inconnu*; *Gliglois*;

---

1 Jean Bodel, *La Chanson des saisnes*, ed. Annette Brasseur, 2 vols. (Geneva: Droz, 1989), I, lines 6–7.

Yder; Meraugis de Portlesguez; Durmart le gallois; Beaudous; Floriant et Florete; Les Merveilles de Rigomer; Le Chevalier aux deux épées; Claris et Laris; Escanor). Others exploit a more distant, or even tangential, connection (*Fergus*, Heldris de Cornuälle's *Roman de Silence*, the Occitan romances *Jaufre, Flamenca* and *Blandín de Cornualla, Le Tournoiement Antéchrist, Le Roman du Hem*, and the fanciful epic cycle of *Huon de Bordeaux*).

Epitomised by Chrétien's *romans*, the love stories of Lancelot and Tristan, and the Grail texts, the exciting multiple-quest narratives of Arthurian romance ensured its appeal to authors and aristocratic audiences. Primarily the vehicle for a richly woven fantasy projection of the feudal order, the Arthurian romance combines the kind of memorable battle scenes and compelling adversaries found in the feudal epic, the sublime love of courtly lyric, and the colourful *merveilleux*, conjured from a background of Celtic myth and folklore. The concatenated adventures of these romances blend action and emotion, and place an engaging spectrum of characters in a realm slightly suspended in time and place above the literal and mundane, in settings ranging from the verisimilar to the exotic and otherworldly, settings that could easily shift to a symbolic plane.

Through the elaboration and iteration of formulae expressing core codes of chivalry and courtly love, the *matière de Bretagne* plays a crucial part in the development of romance in poetry and prose, establishing a literary fashion that spread not only in France, but also inspired adaptations all over Europe; and while a wealth of material survives, extant fragments of romances (*Les Enfances Gauvain, Gogulor, Ilas et Solvas*, and *Le Valet à la cote mal tailliee*) serve as a reminder that many other works have been lost.

Almost all known Arthurian authors of the Middle Ages privilege the masculine perspective of their sex, except Marie de France, who probably wrote her *Lais* at the Plantagenet court of Henry II (1154–89). She claims the Breton oral tradition as her inspiration, using *Bretagne* as a backdrop for her stories, one of which (*Lanval*) is devoted to an unflattering depiction of Arthur's court. She also combines folklore with more contemporary themes in her triangular love stories so as to foreground the role of women in courtly narrative, while exploring the effects of the emerging conventions of desire, love, and *aventure* on both genders. Most of the small corpus of anonymous Breton *lais* share common traits, or even a direct connection with her work (*Graelent, Guingamor, Desiré, Espine, Doon*, and *Lecheor*), as do two romances, *Ille et Galeron* (from *Fresne*) and *Galeran de Bretagne* (*Eliduc*). Other unconnected examples, both Breton (*Tydorel* and *Nabaret*) and Arthurian (*Tyolet, Melion, Trot*, and the *fabliau*-like

Lai du cor and *Le Mantel mal taillé*), attest to a broader experimentation with the form.

What became the highly diversified *matière de Bretagne* was a confection of the court cultures of France and England that created a picturesque model owing more to contemporary aesthetics and *mores* than to a distant past. This apparent burst of vernacular literary activity was immediately preceded by a wave of Latin chronicles that renewed interest in reshaping the early history of Britain, the most famous of which, Geoffrey of Monmouth's *History of the Kings of Britain* (*c.* 1138), fabricates an account of Arthur's life and exemplary kingship. Part history and mostly fiction, Geoffrey's expansion and consolidation of Arthurian myth laid the foundation for subsequent literary works. He and other medieval authors based their reinventions of the realm of Celtic myth, Arthur, and Tristan on much earlier Celtic traditions that had filtered through oral and learned cultures in the intervening centuries.

Myth and history

The myth of Arthur became synonymous with the *matière de Bretagne* in two phases. The first spans the post-Roman period to the twelfth century, when isolated fragments of a legendary figure emerge from Latin chronicles, hagiography, and Welsh poetry and prose. Together they constitute the suggestive written evidence for what was undoubtedly a much broader oral tradition (Gildas, *On the Ruin of Britain*, *c.* 540s; *Y Gododdin*, sixth-century elegiac poems ascribed to Aneurin; Bede, *The Ecclesiastical History of the English People*, *c.* 731; the early ninth-century *The History of the Britons* and *Marvels*, probably by Nennius; the tenth-century *The Annals of Wales*).[2]

In the sixth century, a Christian warlord like Arthur, if not the legendary king himself, seems to have lived in the general area of the west of England and Wales, and in a series of battles (the most famous being Badon) resisted the Saxon invaders who were in the process of pushing Britain's indigenous peoples to their geographical margins. The Breton *Legend of Saint Goeznovius* (1019) describes Arthur as successful not only in his campaigns against the Saxons in Britain, but also in Gaul, possibly linking him with the hazy figure of Riothamus (his name is a Latinised British title denoting 'supreme ruler'). Such a leader was also alluded to in early Latin sources in Gaul, where

2 Nicholas J. Higham, *King Arthur: Myth-Making and History* (London and New York: Routledge, 2002).

he is said to have taken a large army in the late fifth century. Evidence is tantalisingly inconclusive regarding the historical existence of Arthur, or a composite figure he represents, though such traces indicate he was more than a myth.

The Arthur of Welsh hagiography displays a more folkloric character: a handful of anecdotal Latin texts portray him as quick-tempered, covetous, and tyrannical, unlike the saints whose paths he crosses (Lifris of Llancarfan's *Life of St Cadoc*, c. 1090; the *Life of St Carantoc* and the *Life of St Illtud*, c. 1100; the twelfth-century *Life of St Padarn*, and Caradoc of Llancarfan's *Life of St Gildas*, which includes the story of Guinevere's abduction to Glastonbury, later developed by Chrétien in *Le Chevalier de la charrette*).[3]

In a similar vein, the rich corpus of medieval Welsh literature reinforces a strong early British Arthurian mythography, but it is a frustrating consequence of manuscript transmission that although internal evidence points to earlier dates for some important works, the oldest surviving manuscript anthology is from the thirteenth century, postdating Geoffrey of Monmouth and the rise of the *matière de Bretagne*. Of particular value are *Spoils of Annwfn* (early tenth century), where a magic cauldron may provide an early analogue for the Grail quest, and the poem *The Stanzas of the Graves*, which mentions Arthur's wondrous resting-place, as well as the tombs of some key warriors. The tales known collectively as the *Mabinogi* (particularly branch two) are a storehouse of Arthurian motifs, while *The Dream of Rhonabwy* provides an oneiric and surreal vision of the heroic age of Arthur. Most illustrative is *Culhwch and Olwen* (c. 1100), which draws on a wealth of folk motifs to relate how the eponymous hero wins his bride by accomplishing a series of Herculean tasks with the aid of his cousin Arthur and his super-heroic band. Debate continues over the relationship of three thirteenth-century Welsh romances (*Geraint, Owain*, and *Peredur*) that provide analogues to Chrétien's *Erec et Enide*, *Le Chevalier au lion*, and *Le Conte du Graal*. Though it is overwhelmingly likely that Chrétien came first, their inter-relation and possible derivation remain unresolved.

Finally, the fifth- or sixth-century examples from *The Triads of the Island of Britain* preserve Arthur as a powerful ruler with multiple courts, and also refer to a conflict with Mordred. The triads were designed to preserve the bardic repertory through quick allusion to many now-forgotten stories, and include several cryptic references to Drystan/Tristan (whose name is originally of

3 On the Welsh saints' lives and legends of Arthur see Rachel Bromwich, A. O. H. Jarman, and Brynley F. Roberts (eds.), *The Arthur of the Welsh: The Arthurian Legend in Medieval Welsh Literature* (Cardiff: University of Wales Press, 1991).

Pictish origin) as a legendary warrior whose orbit and fame seem akin to Arthur's. The Tristan legends no doubt had a similarly broad circulation in oral culture, further suggested by some parallel plotlines in early Irish stories (*The Wooing of Emer* and *The Pursuit of Diarmaid and Gráinne*, for example), but he is otherwise unattested in written works until Thomas and Béroul, and Marie's *lai, Chèvrefeuille*. Relating only a part of the story, Béroul's romance is extant in one incomplete manuscript, while a series of fragments preserve Thomas's complementary text, allowing reasonable speculation that an earlier more complete mid-twelfth-century version has been lost. *Chèvrefeuille* focuses on a tiny, insignificant parenthesis in the tangled love-life of Tristan and Iseult, suggesting that Marie expected her audience to know their complete dramatic tale already. Chrétien de Troyes also claims to have written a Tristan romance, now lost, and it seems likely that others have shared the same fate. In the early romances Tristan has only a distant connection to Arthur's court, and only in the later prose versions is he inducted as one of the king's foremost knights.

The saturated colours of Celtic myth tint the Welsh narratives of Arthur and his companions: their exploits, supernatural combats, monsters, and mysterious journeys seem to foreshadow the *merveilleux* of later romances.

Myth and fiction

The second period of development begins in the first half of the twelfth century, with Arthur's historiographical rebirth in Latin chronicles, most notably in Geoffrey's *History*, with its much fuller, fictitious, biography. In Geoffrey's wake, the 'matter of Britain' first enters the French courtly canon in Wace's *Roman de Brut* (c. 1155).

Arthur's time had clearly come, and many historians contribute material to his revival, principally William of Malmesbury (*The Deeds of the English Kings*, c. 1125), Geoffrey (who also penned *The Prophecies of Merlin*, c. 1130s and *The Life of Merlin*, c. 1150), Henry of Huntingdon (*The History of the English*, c. 1129; the *Letter to Warin*, c. 1139), and later Giraldus Cambrensis (*On the Instruction of Princes*, 1193). With over two hundred extant manuscripts, Geoffrey's *History* became one of the most widely read medieval works for centuries afterwards. A cleric later named as bishop of St Asaph, Geoffrey taught in Oxford (c. 1129–51/2), and besides his presumed Welsh connections was perhaps of Norman, or even Breton, ancestry. Whatever his motivations, his foregrounding of the links between the Britons and the Bretons and the unifying myth of Arthur provided convenient political justifications for Anglo-Norman, and then Anglo-Angevin, territorial ambitions on both sides of the

Channel. Geoffrey wrote during the period of conflict following the death of Henry I (1135), and the bitter dispute between the king's daughter Matilda (whom Henry had named as heir) and nephew Stephen (who took the crown). The day-residue of contemporary events must have influenced the construction of the reborn Arthur as well: from the nebulous Celtic twilight, Geoffrey plucks the vague outline of a national hero and forges a flattering wish-fulfilment fantasy of strong, indigenous kingship; of particular utility to this mythic reinscription is the great literary and ideological potential of Arthur's open-ended, possible return.

Geoffrey distils early sources and claims the use of an ancient British book (probably invented), all of which he embroiders with great creativity in filling the gaps in Arthur's legend and the historical record. In an astounding opening, Brutus, Aeneas' great-grandson, arrives in Albion with a group of Trojans rescued from Greece. The island is renamed Britain, and so begins a fanciful account of events until the seventh century; in between, Geoffrey never lets facts spoil a good story. The Arthurian sections (Books 6–11) begin with the introduction of Merlin and his enigmatic prophecies, before the now familiar story of how he and Uther Pendragon deceive Igerna of Cornwall, and Arthur is conceived. Crowned at fifteen, and with the aid of his sword Caliburnus/Excalibur, Arthur achieves many British conquests, subduing the Saxons and Scots, then marrying the Roman Ganhumara/Guinevere before undertaking further campaigns in Ireland and Iceland, Scandinavia and Gaul. Arthur's fame, charm and largesse draw the best men and most virtuous ladies to join his rich court at Caerleon, with its tournaments and lavish feasts, anticipating later descriptions of Camelot. Peace reigns until problems arise concerning Gaul. Leaving his wife and his nephew in charge, Arthur undertakes another expedition against the Romans, his further ambitions checked only by news of Ganhumara's adultery and the treachery of his incestuous son Mordred. Arthur is mortally wounded as he battles for his crown, and is spirited away to Avalon and his mysterious fate.

Myth and literary model

If Geoffrey expanded and codified a now pseudo-historical myth, then Wace vulgarises it in his adaptation of the *Historia* into vernacular poetry. He dedicates the *Roman de Brut* to Eleanor of Aquitaine, while his patron for the unfinished *Roman de Rou* (c. 1160, about the dukes of Normandy) was Henry II, at whose court Benoît de Sainte-Maure composed the *Roman de Troie* (c. 1165), also dedicated to Henry's queen. These works together provide useful prequels to the dynastic history of those they served, and are by no means alone in exemplifying the ideological move to forge an imperial myth for contemporary rulers.[4] Henry II became more powerful than the king of France, thanks to his wife, and consolidated an empire that stretched from England to the Pyrenees; so while the French Capetian kings could encourage the resurrection of the myth of Charlemagne and his twelve peers, Arthur and his knights provided a perfect foil. Wace prepares the way for subsequent romances by imbuing Arthur's court with even more chivalry and *courtoisie*, and is the first to mention the Round Table, fusing idealised leadership with a sense of fraternity and equality among his principal knights. So pervasive was the cult of Arthur that in 1191, during the reign of Richard Coeur de Lion, monks at Glastonbury conveniently 'discovered' Arthur's and Guinevere's remains.

Eleanor's fondness for troubadour lyric and courtly love inspired the poets and *romanciers* at Henry's court (among them should probably be counted Thomas and Marie de France), and contemporary tastes in England and France found a natural outlet in the *matière de Bretagne*. In Occitania it did not take hold: besides *Jaufre* and the lacklustre *Blandín*, nothing remains, except a few passing allusions. This could be an accident of transmission, or a sign that the northern romances needed no translation. However, given the Plantagenet domination of the south lands, it is an anomaly that may indicate that their politically stubborn courts also harboured some aesthetic or cultural resistance to the genre.

Otherwise, the Arthurian romance's diffusion at the courts of Eleanor's children played a key role, especially Marie de Champagne (Eleanor's daughter by her first husband, King Louis VII of France), mentioned by Chrétien de Troyes in the prologue to *Le Chevalier de la charrette*. Her court was also a haven for lyric poets, debates on love casuistry (*cours d'amour*), and perhaps Andreas Capellanus, author of the Ovid-inspired treatise *On Love* (c. 1185), which includes a fashionable light-hearted episode in which one of Arthur's knights ('the Breton') braves danger to win a hawk for his lady. With it come the rules of love, summarised on a piece of parchment attached to its perch by a little gold chain.

From its emergence into the vernacular, the *matière de Bretagne* fused with the ethos of courtly love, and while cultural politics acted as a catalyst for its rebirth, an inherent irresistible charm plays the overwhelming role in its

---

4 Martin Aurell, *L'Empire des Plantagenêt 1154–1224* (Paris: Perrin, 2003), and Amaury Chauou, *L'Idéologie Plantagenêt: royauté arthurienne et monarchie politique dans l'espace Plantagenêt (xiie–xiiie siècles)* (Rennes: Presses Universitaires de Rennes, 2001).

pan-European rise. There must have been much more of an oral and textual tradition for the *matière* than can be measured, since in the earliest remaining extant works so many conventions and stories seem to spring fully formed. Myth now became a flexible literary model, and a simple evocation sufficed for authors to be able to engage audiences in a familiar world, and explore limitless narrative possibilities. As knightly adventures multiply, Arthur himself takes a secondary role, and is mostly portrayed as much older: he offers stable chivalric values, metes out justice, and ennobles incoming knights, and his court provides a point of departure and return. The nature of the romance is thus both conservative and innovative, constantly recycling fundamental themes, patterns, and characters into new variations, such that the genre that appears to generate sameness is, in fact, engaged in its own literary quest for difference through constant self-renewal and re-creation.

No one realised its potential better than Chrétien de Troyes (*fl. c.* 1160–90), the finest exponent of the verse romance, whose poetic narratives redefine the 'matter of Britain' as a conscious space for literary experiment (*Erec et Enide, Cligès, Le Chevalier au lion, Le Chevalier de la charrette, Le Conte du Graal*). Critical posterity often contrasts the novel and the romance, privileging the former for its sense of contingency to reality, and lack of closure. And yet the *roman* deserves so much more recognition as an antecedent of the novel, since it was never newer than in the Middle Ages, when it is the most plastic and protean of genres.

In his prologues, Chrétien reveals a playful awareness of literary technique, and how *matiere et san* (content and meaning) and well-ordered composition (*bele conjointure*) are vital elements in the romance. In the *Conte du Graal*, he compares writing to sowing good seed to ensure a fruitful yield. His harvest is rich: Roger Middleton concludes that it is no accident that 'over half the surviving copies of Arthurian texts in Old French verse are of Chrétien's five romances and the *Perceval* additions (108 out of the total 217)'.[5] Chrétien casts a long artistic shadow over the romances of the many writers who sought to continue or emulate him in their reformulations of knightly adventure. Ironically, his success is partly due to the lack of closure of two of his works. In the *Conte du Graal*, Perceval witnesses a strange candlelit ritual at the Fisher King's castle and sees what is described first as 'a Grail', and a bleeding lance. He fails to ask what all this means, leading him on a path of chivalry and penitence, during which 'the' Grail takes on an ever greater moral and

---

5 Roger Middleton, 'The Manuscripts', in Glyn S. Burgess and Karen Pratt's excellent essay collection, *The Arthur of the French: The Arthurian Legend in Medieval French and Occitan Literature* (Cardiff: University of Wales Press, 2006), pp. 8–92.

spiritual significance, inspiring continuations that created tension between earthly and spiritual knighthood. Similarly, Chrétien did not finish *Le Chevalier de la charrette*: Lancelot and Guinevere become lovers during her rescue, and where Chrétien would have had to resolve the conflict of duty and adultery posed by their mutual fidelity to Arthur, Godefroi de Lagny's tacked-on conclusion avoids the central questions that launched the Prose *Lancelot*.

Le Chevalier au lion is a perfect example of what the virtual reality of Arthurian romance became: the knight Yvain leaves the court in pursuit of adventures that take place in settings oscillating between culture (castle, chapel and *bourg*) and nature (an otherworldly fountain, the forest, agricultural lands, gardens). Aided by a friendly lion, his quest involves the marginal (a herdsman, some impoverished noblewomen) and the monstrous (a giant and a dwarf), violent challengers, odd customs that govern instead of the rule of law, and supernatural forces. On the way he endures a series of combats, falls in love, goads his wife beyond his reason and hers, takes part in tournaments, sees the good and bad side of enchantment, rescues many distressed damsels, and helps to solve an inheritance dispute. Yvain's journey entails losing his identity the better to rediscover it, and evaluate what it means to be a man, a knight, and an individual in a broader collective. Though the social construction of femininity also becomes a frequent theme in romance, it is never better explored than in Heldris de Cornuälle's *Roman de silence*, in which a girl is raised as a boy and quests for the meaning of her sexuality, Chrétien concentrates largely on male heroes and their quests for glory and identity, though his many female protagonists are rich and memorable.

Generally, in the romance's decentred narratives, the displaced self is more the ultimate object of the quest than justice, the acquisition of worldly success, material gain, or unexpected noble lineage (though all are, of course, welcome). Serious and playful by turns, it is essentially a didactic model of social and personal crisis and reward that operates in romance, one that sublimates chivalry and love into fantasy, inscribing it within a symbolic order that creates rich interpretive layers. If the semiotics of romance posit norms, deviancy from them is equally important, most often expressed in the use of the monstrous 'other' confronting the hero, whether in the form of a supernatural animal or demon, a cultural 'other', or a variety of emblematical incarnations of primal human fears, such as giants who exaggerate man's capacity for violence, or dwarves whose stature indicates too little humanity.

The advent of the prose romance (*c.* 1210) in vast cycles and collections (such as the *Compilation* of Rusticiano da Pisa) further enlarged the *matière de Bretagne* by elaborating familiar stories and inventing new ones (*Perceforest*). Extant prose works far outnumber and outweigh their verse counterparts, taking full advantage of the freedoms of the novelistic form in terms of description, character development, dialogue, and emotional and psychological depth. They guaranteed the longevity and re-exploration of the Arthurian material until the late Middle Ages (*Meliador*; *Le Chevalier au papegau*) and into the sixteenth century (with the works of Pierre Sala, Jean Maugin, and Claude Platin). Interest in Arthurian literature then waned, though no century has been without its reconsideration. Its revival in the nineteenth mirrors the coeval reinvention of the Middle Ages, while the twentieth century was perhaps the richest since the thirteenth in its re-adaptation of the myth in a variety of media, a sure sign that its enchantments will endure.

6

Sexuality, shame, and the genesis of romance

ZRINKA STAHULJAK

What is the relationship between courtly love discourse, sexuality and shame in the earliest Old French romances, the romances of antiquity?[1] In the *Roman d'Eneas* (c. 1156–60), the anti-sodomitical invective weaves in and out of the lengthy courtly love monologues of Eneas and Lavinia, an invention of the Eneas poet. In the *Roman de Troie* (c. 1165), Achilles, once inconsolable over the death of his lover Patroclus, killed by Hector, is later tortured for over 3,000 lines by his love for Hector's sister Polyxena, a major development of Benoît de Sainte-Maure. In the *Roman de Thebes* (c. 1150), courtly love discourse is an attempt to attenuate, albeit on a small scale, the venomous hatred of Oedipus' incestuous offspring; and in Alexandre de Paris's *Roman d'Alexandre* (c. 1180), the scarcity of such discourse highlights the ambiguity of Alexander's sexual practices and even his legitimacy. Although courtly love discourse is used to reject sodomy and incest in these romances, the terms 'hontos' or 'vergondos' are not used to qualify these sexual behaviours. Shame does describe inappropriate love behaviour but not along our modern line of division between 'heteronormative' and 'non-normative' sexualities. In view of the recent debate over the use of categories of 'homosexuality', 'heterosexuality' and 'heteronormativity' to describe sexual acts or identities in medieval literature and culture, this particular angle of 'shame' sheds another light on the issue.[2] First, even though it has been argued that courtly love discourse emerges and is constructed in opposition to sodomy, with courtly

---

1 I warmly thank Virginie Greene, James Schultz, and Carla Freccero, for their help and generosity in thinking through this chapter. *Eneas: roman du xiie siècle*, ed. J. J. Saverda de Grave (Paris: Champion, 1983–5), henceforth *Eneas*; Benoît de Sainte-Maure, *Le Roman de Troie*, ed. E. Baumgartner and F. Vielliard (Paris: Livre de Poche, 1998), henceforth *Troie*; *Le Roman de Thebes*, ed. F. Mora-Lebrun (Paris: Livre de Poche, 1995), henceforth *Thebes*; Alexandre de Paris, *Le Roman d'Alexandre*, ed. E. C. Armstrong *et al.* (Paris: Livre de Poche, 1994), henceforth *Alexandre*. All translations from Old French throughout are my own.
2 Karma Lochrie, *Heterosyncrasies: Female Sexuality When Normal Wasn't* (Minneapolis: University of Minnesota Press, 2005), pp. xi–xxi, 1–25; James A. Schultz, *Courtly Love, the Love of Courtliness, and the History of Sexuality* (Chicago: University of Chicago Press, 2006), ch. 4.

love monologues (Eneas–Lavinia; Achilles–Polyxena) developing on the heels of accusations of sodomy or the manifestations of male love (Eneas–Pallas; Achilles–Patroclus), what looks like a clear-cut line of separation between 'heterosexuality' and sodomy disappears when looked at through the prism of shame.[3] Second, medieval sodomy, like male–male or male–female love, is not simply a sexual act, but a behaviour inherently linked to the larger politico-social order in which 'sexual' acts are understood to resonate.[4] Finally, if shame blurs a neat division between 'courtly love' ('heterosexuality') and 'sodomy' ('homosexuality'), then generic distinctions based on shame between the epic (shame as affront, insult) and romance (shame as a progressively internalised feeling) may also have to be reconsidered.

The dialectic of honour and shame acts as one of the organising principles of the romances of antiquity, which, in the traditional view, provide the transition between the epic and the full-fledged romance: the epic grounded in the collective honour/shame culture and the romance transitioning to an ethics of a more individuated knightly honour.[5] *Thebes*, the most epic of the romances of antiquity, is all about 'honor', 'deshonor', and 'tort'. The infrequent expressions 'vengier sa honte' and 'a grant honte' occur only in a military, feudal, or non-sexual context in the epic. The sexual offence of incest, on the other hand, is systematically characterised as 'pechié' and not once as 'honte'. It is fratricidal war not incest that is 'countre nature' (lines 503, 12058). In the *Alexandre*, 'honte' and 'vergoigne' express an act (an affront) and a feeling (embarrassment, being ill at ease) respectively. Alexandre's father's repudiation of his mother is a 'honte' (branche I: lines 1831–2), but the allegation of Alexander's illegitimacy is a 'vergoigne' (branche I: lines 1816–17). The almost complete absence of courtly love discourse and its imbrication with the feudal context means that there is little consideration of sexual acts in this romance. The term 'drus/drue' for Alexander's companions, both male and female, conflates feudal homage with the homage of courtly love; but the courtship of Alexander by both Queen Candace (branche III: lines 4445–8) and the queen of the Amazons, though couched in terms of courtly love

3 Susan Crane, *Gender and Romance in Chaucer's 'Canterbury Tales'* (Princeton, NJ: Princeton University Press, 1994), pp. 39–54; Simon Gaunt, *Gender and Genre in Medieval French Literature* (Cambridge: Cambridge University Press, 1995), pp. 75–85; Noah Guynn, *Allegory and Sexual Ethics in the High Middle Ages* (New York: Palgrave Macmillan, 2007), pp. 51–92.

4 Mark D. Jordan, *The Invention of Sodomy in Christian Theology* (Chicago: University of Chicago Press, 1997).

5 I do not discuss the guilt culture here, nor maintain the sharp distinction between shame and guilt cultures as a product of Christianity. Cf. Virginia Burrus, *Saving Shame: Martyrs, Saints, and Other Abject Subjects* (Philadelphia: University of Pennsylvania Press, 2008).

(branche III: lines 7585–6, 7597–8), is initiated simply to ensure against military aggression. Penetration into a foreign kingdom is a form of 'honte', during which not only female but also male rulers are subjugated (Amazon queen, branche III: lines 7625–8; Porus, the king of India, branche III: lines 3925–4265). Alexander is told that he could touch the prophetic trees, 'A vallet n'a meschine se tu geü nen as' (branche III: line 3793) ('provided you have not slept with a young man or woman'). Even though the door to sexual ambiguity is left wide open in the romance, it is never condemned as shameful; and though pervasive, it is hardly ever acknowledged.

In the *Eneas* and *Troie*, however, the mention of shame can be found regularly in sexual contexts but in full defiance of our contemporary expectations. In general, the *Eneas* uses shame sparsely. Sodomy is never called shameful, even when the practice is 'maldite' (line 9165) and 'contre nature' (line 8660). When courtly love discourse and anti-sodomitical diatribe are inserted by the medieval poet into the original Virgilian narrative, their ideological aim is to ensure integration into the social order through marriage and procreation (lines 8596–602). If to 'love' is to procreate, then sodomitical love is a 'malvés mestier' (lines 8764, 9168), or a 'deduit' (line 9133) and a 'jués' (*Troie*, line 13185), a simple diversion. Sodomy may be the opposite of reason, the antithesis of the serious 'business' of procreation (*Eneas*, lines 9169, 8676), yet it is never claimed as inherently shameful. Eneas experiences shame only when he abandons his compatriots in burning Troy ('et anvers ols se vergondot' [line 2682, also 3365]); yet when the sodomite is said to neglect his wife, another form of abandonment (lines 9145–6), this is not characterised as shameful. In contrast, Dido's fatal love for Eneas is referred to as an 'hontage' (line 1529), but it is only when she breaks the vows she made to her (dead) husband that she can be said to feel shame ('por son forfet se vergondot' [line 2662]).

Just as Dido's behaviour shamed her and left her 'sor lo lit . . . honie' (line 2050), Lavinia's choice of Eneas as her love interest will beget more of the same (lines 3304–6). It is the neglect and the abandonment that Lavinia might have to endure at the hands of her husband-to-be – his treason – that are subject to condemnation, not any sexual act. In the *Troie*, it is again Eneas' treason and cowardice that are characterised as shameful: 'Cuiverz, fet ele, Satanas, / vils e hontos e reneiez' (*Troie*, lines 26164–5; also 26176–7). It is the change of loyalty, the diversion that becomes an inversion, that Lavinia's mother is objecting to when she says: 'Sez tu *vers cui* tu t'es donee? / Cil *cuiverz* est de tel nature / qu'il n'a gaires de femmes cure' (*Eneas*, lines 8566–8). In both cases, there is an easy slippage from traitor to sodomite, a turning to the 'other' side, 'vers cui' / 'cui-verz', that goes against political and social norms.

Shameful behaviour is thus defined within the larger politico-social context and in that context shame is more characteristic of male–female relationships than of *sexuality per se* or of male–male relationships in particular.

Of all the romances of antiquity, the *Troie* is the only one that is truly about shame, but it is also the first to introduce the notion that 'honte' is linked to internal emotional suffering (cf. 'vergoigne'), rather than just a reaction to an affront or outrage. Hesiona's dishonourable enslavement by the Greeks ('ceste honte' [line 3670]), is the cause of an illness in the social body (lines 3686–9); and Menelaus lives immobilised in a state of melancholia (lines 4950–6), 'por le hontage de sa femme' (line 4943). Internalised shame is all the more striking when contrasted with the one instance in which sodomitical practice is qualified, externally, as shameful:

> e la dolor del cumpaignon
> dont j'ai fet la desevreison,
> que tante nuit avez sentu
> entre vos braz tot nu a nu.
> Icist jués est vils e hontos,
> dont li plusor sunt haïnos
> as deus, quin prenent la venjance
> par la lor devine poissance.
>
> (Troie, lines 13181–8)

(the sorrow that I caused you in separating you from the one you held naked in your arms for so many nights. This is a vile and shameful practice (game), whose practitioners are offensive to the Gods, who take vengeance through their divine power.)

Here Hector speaks from a clerical stance, posing as the divine avenger of this 'jués . . . vils e hontos'.[6] Yet his condemnation of these sexual practices falls on deaf ears; it occurs in the highly masculinised context of a provocation to duel during battle. If Achilles does experience shame, it is not because of Hector's invective, but because of the implication that he is not willing to confront him (lines 13195–9). Indeed, the sodomitical 'game' never compromises Achilles' warrior prowess (lines 10878–80). Achilles' and Patroclus' committment to each other is exemplary and embodies the very foundation of the feudal order: 'Onc chevalier plus ne s'amerent / ne greignor fei ne se porterent' (lines 8175–6); 'e a la mort e a la vie / li fus amis sans tricherie' (lines 10397–8).[7]

---

6 Benoît de Sainte-Maure washes the Trojans of their reputation as sodomites (*Eneas*, lines 8567–77), assigning it to the Greeks.

7 There is no shame for the sexual crime of Paris and Helen either (*Troie*, lines 23077–8, 23088).

Though virile military fellowship is the medieval epic norm, Patroclus' case nevertheless appears more ambiguous:

> Biaus fu mout, ce puet hon bien dire . . .
> mais mout par esteit *vergoindos*.
>
> (lines 5176, 5178)

(He was beautiful, any man would admit it; but he was also shameful.)

This 'shamefulness' cannot, however, be singled out as linked with same-sex acts, since one hundred lines later Briseida is described in the very same terms: 'si iert el mout *vergoindose*, / simplë, aumosniere e pietose' (lines 5287–8), as is Medea, when she offers herself to Jason, 's'en vint a euz, mout vergoindose' (line 1309). If both Briseida and Medea are said to be shamed like Patroclus, then a different reading must be proposed. Indeed, what Benoît may be condemning is not sodomy, but the fact of being subdued or submissive to another. This is what links Patroclus to the two women and distinguishes him from Achilles. In every other way, the two men's portraits follow and mirror each other: they are both beautiful and 'larges' (lines 5165, 5177) (generous), but while Achilles is an angry foe (line 5164), Patroclus is not (line 5175); and, unlike Achilles, who was neither 'pensis ne mornes' (line 5142), he is 'vergondos' (line 5178). In short, Patroclus could be seen as 'embarrassed' (timid and subdued), 'vergondos', and by implication 'pensis', 'morne' and easily shamed. This is a character flaw, an impediment for a warrior, not the qualification of a sexual act.

Achilles' subsequent behaviour in the Trojan War, his refusal to fight because of his love for Polyxena, is condemned far more severely and consistently than his sodomitical 'game'. His efforts to convince the Greek army to lift the siege are refused as 'trop hontous' (line 18366), and his subsequent decision not to fight and to withhold his men from battle also creates feelings of blame and shame (lines 18462, 18467). Warriors, including Diomedes, try in vain to make Achilles feel shame: 'Recreanz e coarz e feus, / quel vergoigne devez aveir!' (lines 19032–3; also 19720–1). Achilles is thus subject to the charge of being 'hontos' in his love relationships with both men and women, and 'vergoindos' is used to describe both a man, Patroclus, and two women, Briseida and Medea. In this sense, the *Troie* confirms the case of the *Eneas*, where shame appears tied to love and sexual acts that are simply inappropriate in the larger politico-social context.

It is crucial, nonetheless, to observe that the shame imposed on Achilles and, more ambiguously, on Patroclus comes from an external point of view:

in Achilles' case, Hector justifies his position by invoking divine hatred and punishment, while in Patroclus' case the accusation comes from the narrator. Yet neither Achilles nor Patroclus feels the shame. In the case of Briseida, on the other hand, the internalisation and subjectivisation of shame, observed earlier in the case of Menelaus, is confirmed in the context of her betrayal of the Trojan Troilus in favour of the Greek Diomedes: 'Honte i ai feit' (lines 20259, 20324–6). Dereliction of duty is a far more serious reason for shame on the part of Achilles than Hector's condemnation of the 'jués . . . vils e hontos': one is a game, the other a war. Sodomitical relationships, then, are not in themselves shameful in the romances of antiquity, but dishonourable comportment in love is, especially when male–female love provokes dishonourable or treasonous comportment on the battlefield or in government. This is not just a question of analogy or metaphor – war being like love and vice versa – but of how one form of comportment, love, directly affects the other, war. Most significantly, as male warrior fellowship is still seen as an ideal, there is no internalised shame for male–male love: that is reserved for the male–female relationship.

By the time prose romance appears, however, dishonourable comportment in battle and government becomes the province of the sodomite. Even if Galehaut in the Prose *Lancelot* (*c.* 1215–20) is a great warrior and a perfectly courtly character, once he falls in love with Lancelot, his love shames him.[8] In the romances of antiquity, male–male love could be the source of the highest warrior achievements, as in the case of Eneas and Pallas, or Nisus and Euryalus. In the Prose *Lancelot*, love for another man no longer increases one's determination and prowess, as it did for Achilles after the death of Patroclus (*Troie,* lines 11079–82). Instead, love brings Galehaut down:

> si sui ge li chevaliers al monde qui de greignor chaance a esté . . . et ge sui en la perte entrez.   (*Guenièvre*, p. 66; also *Lancelot*, p. 584)

> (I am the knight who has been most blessed in this world . . . and now begins my downfall.)

Male–male love becomes shameful because it makes this great knight commit acts that detract from his honour. Love changes honour into shame:

> Mais de totes iceles choses qu'il avoit enprises le traist Lanceloth arieres et il li mostra bien, la ou il li fist de sa grant honor sa honte, quant il estoit a[u]

---

8 *Lancelot du Lac*, vol. ii, ed. E. Kennedy (Paris: Livre de Poche, 1993), henceforth *Lancelot*; *Lancelot du Lac*, vol. iii: *La Fausse Guenièvre*, ed. F. Mosès (Paris: Livre de Poche, 1998), henceforth *Guenièvre*. *Lancelot* belongs to the earlier non-cyclical version, *Guenièvre* to the later *Lancelot-Grail* Cycle.

desus del roi Artu et il li ala merci crier; et aprés ice grant tans, la ou dui home de son lingnage . . . li reprocherent la honteuse pes a conseil qu'il avoit [fete] *por un seul home.* *(Guenièvre,* p. 60; also 62)

(But it was Lancelot who led him astray such that he gave up his gains; and he made this clear the day that he turned his honour into shame by going to King Arthur, a man he had vanquished, to beg for his mercy; and after that date, two men of his lineage reproached him for peace he made with Arthur and all for just one man.)

Galehaut knows that the cause of his fall is his love of Lancelot – 'lo grant meschief que ge fis por sa compaignie avoir' *(Lancelot,* p. 584) – and even Lancelot recognises this truth: 'Si [ai] fait del plus vigerous home del mont le plus pereceus et tot ce li est avenu por moi' *(Guenièvre,* pp. 72–4; also *Lancelot,* p. 586). This knowledge of having committed dishonourable acts for love is a source of emotional distress that signals the ongoing process of internalisation of shame: Galehaut is tortured by this realisation *(Guenièvre,* p. 68) and Lancelot sheds bitter tears because of it *(Guenièvre,* p. 74; also p. 66). Sodomitical love is shameful because it makes one the worst knight: i.e. it remains linked to military prowess and is not yet condemned as *inherently* shameful. Male–male love is opposed to and supersedes in gravity male–female adultery: Lancelot's love quest for Guinevere is honourable, Galehaut's for Lancelot, dishonourable.

The process through which shame enters into male–male relationships is particularly marked in the straightening out of the romances of antiquity by Chrétien de Troyes's *Cligés (c.* 1176) and the privileging of adultery as a form of shameless behaviour over sodomy in *Le Chevalier de la charrete (c.* 1177–81). David Hult has successfully argued that 'we see in the *Charrette* a movement toward its [shame's] internalization as a personal recognition of disgrace, while not yet as a full-fledged emotion originating from within the individual'.[9] Shame is well on its way to becoming an internal affect; it is no longer limited to an act of verbal or physical affront linked only to the larger politico-social context. Lancelot is not shamed for his adulterous love but for failing to accomplish the greatest knightly exploits because of it. In other words, male–female love also remains shameful but now only if it causes dishonourable comportment on the field.

The evolution of this process is already visible in *Cligés. Cligés* is a romance that speaks to the whole tradition – the epic, the *matière de Bretagne,* and

9 David F. Hult, 'Lancelot's Shame', *Romance Philology* 42.1 (1988), pp. 30–50, at p. 33.

the *matière de Rome* – and it foreshadows Guinevere and Lancelot.[10] In the marriage of the East and the West, of Greece with the Arthurian kingdom, the romances of antiquity undergo a thorough disciplining. Although Soredamors is disdainful of love, like Lavinia, and decides once in love that 'ja autres m'amor n'avra' ('never will another have my love', line 987), *Cligés* is also a criticism of the gender roles found in the *Eneas*. *Cligés* sets out to correct the bad habits that brought about the destruction of Thebes and Troy. First Alis, the brother of Alexander who took the Byzantine crown, is reminded of the fatal internecine war of Etycolés and Polinicés (lines 2494–8); and when Cligés later proposes that he and Fenice imitate Paris and Helen by escaping from Constantinople to the Arthurian court (lines 5228–38), Fenice rebukes him, saying that this would only attract criticism (lines 5244, 5250–2). Finally and most importantly, the romance rejects any ambiguity or confusion with the Narcissus myth; it replaces Narcissus outright with Cligés, whose sexuality is anything but ambiguous:

> Plus biaus estoit et avenanz
> que Narcisus qui desouz l'orme
> vit en la fonteinne sa forme,
> si l'ama tant quant il la vit
> qu'il en fu morz si com en dit
> por ce qu'il ne la pot avoir.
> Molt ot biauté et pou savoir,
> mes Cligés en ot plus grant masse,
> tant com fins ors le coivre passe,
> et plus que je ne di encor.
>
> (lines 2720–9)

(He was more beautiful and attractive than Narcissus who, beneath the elm, saw his face in the fountain and so loved what he saw that he died for it since he couldn't have it, at least that's what they say. His beauty was great but his wisdom small. Cligés, on the other hand, had much more of the latter, to the degree that gold is more worthy than tin.)

Cligés is simply better, 'plus biaus . . . et avenanz'; there is not a hint of Cligés loving his own reflection or making the mistake of thinking the image is that of another boy. Whereas in the *Troie*, the invocation of Narcissus produces Achilles' admission that he *is* Narcissus ('Narcisus sui, ce sai e vei, / qui tant ama l'umbre de sei / qu'il en morut sor la funteine' [lines 17691–93]), in *Cligés* male–male love is completely written out.

---

10 This process began with the 'straightening out' of the *Eneas* in *Erec et Enide*. Chrétien de Troyes, *Cligès*, ed. C. Méla and O. Collet (Paris: Livre de Poche, 1994); henceforth *Cligès*.

One could therefore conclude that courtly love between men is impossible. The ideology of *Cligés*, albeit without an explicit moralising purpose, straightens out Greek male–male love, using both father and son, Alexander and Cligés. It replaces the dyadic model of male–male bonding and military fellowship, such as the love of Nisus and Euryalus (*Eneas*, line 4945), or of Achilles and Patroclus (*Troie*, line 10356), with an exclusively male–female dyad: Fenice is hidden and sealed away in the tower, putting the tradition of the sealed tombs of the romances of antiquity to a splendid new use (*Cligés*, lines 5510–14). She refuses to share her body, thus nullifying the analogy with the adulterous triangulation of Tristan, Yseut and Marc (lines 3099–118, 5196–7, 5244–7). Male–female relationships in the fictional universe of Chrétien will tend to strive towards straight, upright love: 'Ceste amors fust laiaus et droite' (line 537). Adultery is privileged over sodomitical love: Lancelot will feel no shame for taking a ride in the cart in order to get to Guinevere, but Galehaut will internalise shame in accepting his destiny: 'et il est des or mes bien resons qu'il me meschie' (*Guenièvre*, p. 66; also *Lancelot*, p. 584). The previously inseparable male–male couple must part:

> Et je criem que je vos perde par tans et que nos soiens departi par mort ou par altre dessevrance.
> (Guenièvre, p. 76)

> (And I fear that I will soon lose you, that we will be parted by death or some other forced separation.)

While the romances of antiquity had earlier argued that male–female love was shameful only if it caused dishonourable comportment on the field, male–male love now causes such dishonourable comportment as a necessary component of its own make-up. Hult has suggested in 'Lancelot's Shame' that 'the lexical development of *honte* from 1180 to 1225–30 evinces a marked shift away from its predominantly social application and toward an individual, private sense'.[11] I have suggested that the confrontation of the two modalities, external v. internal, is already at work in the *Roman de Troie* (*c.* 1165), thus blurring the traditional division between epic and romance. Furthermore, despite our contemporary expectations, shame does not delimit 'heterosexual' from 'homosexual' behaviour in the romances of antiquity. If these romances define shameful behaviour within the larger politico-social context and not solely on the grounds of the kind of sexual acts that are performed, then we must question whether sexuality, as a modern category, exists at all in the Middle Ages. Should not medieval 'sexuality' be defined otherwise

---

11 Hult, 'Lancelot's Shame', p. 45.

than through what we consider to be sexual acts? Should we speak, not of 'medieval sexuality', but of 'political sexualities'? Should we consider treason, cowardice and bad government categories of medieval sexuality, since any violation of the politico-social order can give rise to the accusation of sodomy, without sodomitical acts having been committed? Is this what gave rise to the famously reversible formula of heretic/sodomite? We also must question Simon Gaunt's powerful argument in *Gender and Genre* that the division between the 'homo' and the 'hetero' is at least in part an effect of the passage from epic to romance.[12]

When the larger politico-social context that the romances bring into play is considered, these modern 'genres' and the discourses that they may represent are fuzzier than our classifications would have us believe. In questioning our politics of 'genre', we can also question our politics of (sexual) shame, one that has reduced the reading of shame to a binary of honour/dishonour and to the opposition of external (social, collective) v. internal (individual, subjective) controls. What the romances of antiquity show is that while there is no internal without the external, and vice versa, the real difference lies in how shame is articulated. The new stance of prose romance – that sodomitical love results by definition in ignominious acts of dishonour – leads inevitably to the idea that sodomitical love is incompatible with the status of warrior-knight. Those who commit shameful acts on the military, social and political fields will see themselves assimilated to the status of sodomite, thereby making sodomy shameful as a sexual act per se. This generic move, however subtle, will ultimately enable the formulation of the familiar modern narrative of (gay) shame internalised.

12 Gaunt, *Gender and Genre*.

7

Medieval lyric: the *trouvères*

ELIZABETH W. POE

The first Old French love songs to which we can assign an approximate date are those of Chrétien de Troyes.[1] They were produced in all likelihood around 1160 at the court of Marie de Champagne, or perhaps at that of her mother, Eleanor of Aquitaine.[2] Modelled on the repertory of the troubadours, which was already well established and quite diverse, the earliest *trouvère* pieces were little more than '*cansos* in French garb'.[3] From such slavish beginnings, however, would emerge a lively and independent tradition of song, which distinguished itself from that of the Midi not only by its language but also by its eclecticism. Boundaries between aristocratic and popular, borrowed and indigenous, new and old, sacred and secular were crossed and re-crossed with apparent abandon. Women were given a voice. Refrains, vestiges of a more primitive, less pretentious kind of song, came to disrupt the solemn dignity of the *grand chant courtois*. Literate bourgeois joined the ranks of the *trouvères*, engaging in spirited debates, or *jeux-partis*, about the proper behaviour of courtly lovers. The locus of performance gradually shifted from the great hall of a castle to the town square. As time went on, the occasion for song was less frequently a lavish dinner party than a local fair or a professionally sponsored contest known as a *puy*. The ultimate achievement of the Old French lyric – and arguably the cause of its demise – was the polyphonic motet. The complexity of simultaneously competing melodies, each equipped with its own text, was probably more than a *trouvère* without specialised musical training could master and certainly more than most audiences could readily comprehend. By the early fourteenth century, French poetry and music were

---

1 Rita Lejeune, 'Le Rôle littéraire de la famille d'Aliénor d'Aquitaine', in *Littérature et société occitane au moyen-âge* (Liège: Marche Romane, 1979), p. 456; Reto R. Bezzola, *Les Origines et la formation de la littérature courtoise en Occident (500–1200)* (Paris: Champion, 1963), p. 310.
2 Bezzola, *Les Origines*, pp. 310–11.
3 Samuel N. Rosenberg, Margaret Switten, and Gérard Le Vot (eds.), *Songs of the Troubadours and Trouvères: An Anthology of Poems and Melodies* (New York and London: Garland, 1998), p. 2.

no longer inextricably intertwined, thus ending a long and fruitful marriage, which had lasted 150 years and produced over 2,000 songs.

While it may have been Eleanor of Aquitaine, queen of France, who introduced troubadour song to the French court and either Eleanor or her daughter Marie de Champagne who commissioned the composition of the first French songs in the style of the troubadours, it was one of Eleanor's sons by her marriage to Henry II, Richard the Lionheart, who deserves particular credit for bridging the cultural and linguistic gap between the troubadours and the *trouvères*. As the great-grandson of the first troubadour, William IX, and Eleanor's favourite child, Richard always felt a strong attachment to Aquitaine, which he understood from an early age would some day be his. Even as king of England, he remained passionately involved in the politics of the region that was home to him, devoting much of his considerable energy to the subjugation of his rebellious vassals there. Like his parents before him, Richard received at his court many of the major troubadours of his generation. He was especially close to Bertran de Born, who became his outspoken defender, and he took Giraut de Bornelh and Peire Vidal with him in 1190 when he set out on the Crusade that for him at least would end in imprisonment in Austria.[4]

Richard was a patron also of the *trouvères*. His friendship with Blondel de Nesle is legendary. It was Blondel who, according to one thirteenth-century account, discovered Richard's whereabouts in prison, when nobody else had a clue, by recognising that the song the forlorn captive was singing one day as the *trouvère* happened by was one that the two of them had composed together.[5] Although none of Richard's collaborative ventures with Blondel has survived, two songs that Richard composed on his own are still in existence. The first, written in 1193 during his second year in prison, is a plea to his friends to collect the huge ransom being demanded by the German emperor for his release. In order to appeal to as many of his vassals as possible, Richard prepared two redactions of this piece, one in French, the other in Occitan. Both versions are dedicated to his half-sister, Marie de Champagne.[6]

The second of Richard's extant songs is a *sirventes* (poem of blame, whether personal, political, or moralising), reproaching Dalfi d'Alvernhe for not having supported him in his struggles against Philip Augustus. Surprisingly, this song

---

4 Bezzola, *Les Origines*, pp. 220–7; Lejeune, 'Le Rôle', pp. 451–3.
5 Natalis de Wailly (ed.), *Récits d'un ménestrel de Reims au treizième siècle* (Paris: Renouard, 1876), pp. 41–5.
6 Bezzola, *Les Origines*, p. 227; Martin de Riquer, *Los trovadores: historia literaria y textos*, 2 vols. (Barcelona: Planeta, 1975), II, lines 751–4.

is written in French.[7] In choosing not to address Dalfi in his native Occitan, Richard distances himself from the man who has turned his back on him, lords it over him linguistically, and issues a pointed reminder that he and the king of France speak the same language. Chastened, Dalfi responds with a *sirventes* of apology, in Occitan.

Richard's death was eloquently mourned by the troubadour Gaucelm Faidit, who saw him as the embodiment of the courtly ideal: 'Never will there be another like him, so expansive, so noble, so bold, so generous.' Indeed, Richard's demise was viewed as a threat to the whole value system on which the troubadours depended: 'Alas! My lord, valiant king, what will become now of arms and hard-fought tournaments, of rich courts and fine gifts, since you are no longer among us, you who were the master and leader of them all?'[8] With Richard gone and with political and religious tensions mounting between the north and the south, tensions that would culminate in the Albigensian Crusade (1209–29), troubadours and *trouvères* took divergent paths.[9] The thirteenth century was to be a period of innovation and rejuvenation for the French lyric.

Paradoxically, one of the ways in which the *trouvères* moved forward was by reaching back into their indigenous lyric past. Long before the Occitan *canso* was introduced to the French court, people in France were singing. Shepherds, watchmen, peasant girls, ladies, knights and clerics sang to pass the time and to express their heartfelt emotions. Such songs were never written down, and yet they were not completely forgotten. An oral tradition kept them alive, and eventually so did the *trouvères*. Appropriating refrains, rhythms, and motifs from pre-existent folkloric songs and using archaic language and primitive rhymes or mere assonance, professional *langue d'oïl* poets produced new songs that gave the semblance of being old.[10] Certain of these *genres popularisants*, as they have been called, are defined by their metrical form and musical structure, e.g. the *ballette*, the *rondet de carole*, and the *estampie*; others by their theme, e.g. the *pastourelle*, in which a knight tries to seduce a shepherdess, the *chanson d'ami*, in which a young girl yearns for true love, the *chanson de mal mariée*, in which a married woman complains about her jealous husband, and the *chanson de toile*, in which a lady is distracted from her handwork by

---

7 Prosper Tarbé (ed.), *Les Œuvres de Blondel de Néele* (Reims: Dubois, 1862), pp. 119–21.
8 Jean Mouzat (ed.), *Les Poèmes de Gaucelm Faidit* (Paris: Nizet, 1965), pp. 415–24.
9 Pierre Bec, 'Troubadours, trouvères et espace Plantagenêt', *Cahiers de Civilisation Médiévale* 29 (1986), pp. 9–11.
10 Michel Zink, *Le Moyen Âge et ses chansons ou un passé en trompe-l'œil* (Paris: Fallois, 1996), pp. 141–7.

reflecting on an often tragic love affair. Some of these compositions are so convincing in their simplicity that they could be mistaken for genuine folk songs; others, like the *chanson de toile* in which la Bele Doete is sitting near a window in her castle, reading a book, reveal their courtly imprint.[11] Their anachronisms notwithstanding, these songs preserve precious relics, whether real or imagined, of a preliterate lyric past.

The *chanson d'ami*, the *chanson de mal mariée*, and the *chanson de toile* are all varieties of the *chanson de femme*, or woman's song. This means at the very least that they represent a woman's perspective (*féminité textuelle*), even though they were probably written by men, and at the most that they were actually written by women (*féminité génétique*). Because the *chansons de femmes* were typically recorded without attribution by the medieval scribes who included them in their *chansonniers*, we will never know who the authors of these pieces really were. But we should remember that Anonymous was not necessarily a man, and that anonymity itself could be an indication of female authorship.[12]

Recent scholarship on the women *trouvères* has exposed the inadequacies of the conventional division of medieval French lyric into two registers, popular and aristocratic, or, to use Pierre Bec's more nuanced but equally polarising terms, *popularisant* and *aristocratisant*.[13] The perceived dichotomy between the *pastourelle*, *chanson de toile*, and *chanson de mal mariée* on the one hand and the *grand chant courtois*, *tenson*, *jeu-parti*, and *chanson de croisade* on the other was essentially, though no one dared state it so bluntly, an opposition between women's songs and men's songs. It was understood that men could be, and often were, authors of women's songs, but it was assumed that women could never be authors of men's songs. Maintaining this masculine fiction has required wilfully neglecting or discrediting manuscript rubrics that assign certain songs of the noble register to women of names as plausible as Maroie de Diergnau and as well-documented as Blanche de Castille, and arguing that, in the case of a *jeu-parti* involving a man and a woman, not only was the male speaker a man but the female speaker was a man as well.

Historical documents, notably tax records from Paris and a necrology of the guild of jongleurs at Arras, confirm that there were women performers, or

11 Edmond E. Faral, 'Les Chansons de toile ou chansons d'histoire', *Romania* 69 (1946–7), p. 447.
12 Eglal Doss-Quinby, Joan Tasker Grimbert, Wendy Pfeffer, and Elizabeth Aubrey (eds.), *Songs of the Women Trouvères* (New Haven, CT and London: Yale University Press, 2001), pp. 7–14.
13 Pierre Bec, *La Lyrique française au moyen-âge (XIIe–XIIIe siècles): contribution à une typologie des genres poétiques médiévaux*, vol. I: *Études* (Paris: Picard, 1977), pp. 57–119; Doss-Quinby *et al.*, *Songs*, p. 9.

jongleresses, in northern France in the thirteenth century, and the literary record of the period (e.g. the Prose *Tristan*) contains references to women composing songs.[14] Still, some modern scholars resist the idea that any of the pieces in the extant *trouvère* repertoire were produced by women. Curiously, there is much less scepticism about the active role of women in the *langue d'oc* lyric. That the women *trouvères* have fared worse than the women troubadours, or *trobairitz*, may result in part from the fact that, instead of carving out a niche for themselves within the dominant (masculine) tradition of the *chanson* (as the *trobairitz* had done with the *canso*), they apparently preferred to work in ancillary genres, which were less likely to earn them fame in their lifetime or to ensure them a place in one of the major *chansonniers*. Among these genres were the *jeu-parti*, Crusade song, religious song, and the various types of *chanson de femme*, an ancillary genre being anything other than the *grand chant courtois*.

The *grand chant courtois*, or *chanson d'amour*, was the premier genre of the *trouvères*: premier in terms of both age and nobility. It was the genre with respect to which all the other Old French lyric genres were defined, arguably even the songs of the *registre popularisant*.[15] The *grand chant courtois* itself was defined with respect to the Occitan *canso*, from which it derived. Like the *canso*, the *chanson (d'amour)* was strophic, typically consisting of five or six stanzas of equal length and concluding with a shorter stanza of dedication, or *envoi*, which was the equivalent of the Occitan *tornada*. Metrically, the *chanson* displayed more uniformity than the *canso*, with individual verses most commonly of seven, eight or ten syllables. Musically, the *chanson* resembled the *canso* in its tendency to repeat the first two lines of melody before moving into the coda, but differed from its Occitan counterpart in its more sparing use of melisma. Stylistically, the *chanson* showed greater restraint than the *canso*, eschewing intentional obscurity (*trobar clus*) and rare rhymes (*trobar ric*).[16] Thematically, the *chanson* emulated the *canso* in its unique preoccupation with love, that particular kind of love which the troubadours called *fin'amors* ('perfect love') and which modern scholars since Gaston Paris have referred to conveniently as *amour courtois* ('courtly love').

The *fin'amors* of the troubadours was a love based on choice. The troubadour loved his lady because of her social and moral superiority. He placed himself voluntarily in her service in the hope of bettering himself and of receiving some kind of reward. Given that the lady whose praises he sang

14 Doss-Quinby *et al.*, *Songs*, pp. 14–26.   15 Zink, *Le Moyen Âge*, p. 147.
16 Samuel N. Rosenberg and Hans Tischler (eds.), *Chansons des trouvères: Chanter m'estuet* (Paris: Livre de Poche, 1995), p. 10.

was in the typical instance the wife of his patron, the troubadour had to conceal her identity under a nickname, or *senhal*, which, in principle, only she would recognise. Secrecy was of the utmost importance because exposure could not only tarnish the lady's reputation, thus making her less desirable, but also jeopardise the troubadour's standing (not to mention his earnings) at court. The greatest threat to the *fins amants* resided, oddly enough, not in the jealous husband, who played a minimal role in the lyrics of the troubadours, but rather in the gossips, or *lauzengiers*, who were often rival poets. The feudal terms in which *fin'amors* is cast betray the only thinly veiled pragmatism of the majority of troubadours, petty noblemen who counted on the success of their songs to advance them in society. In general, the love celebrated by the troubadours was opportunistic. It was also highly erotic. On the lips of the troubadours neutral words like *joven* ('youth') and *joi* ('joy') carried a sexual charge.

At the hands of the *trouvères*, *fin'amors* became less carnal and more metaphysical. The concrete imagery of the *canso* was replaced in the *grand chant courtois* by abstract, quasi-allegorical language. The courtly lover in the *langue d'oïl* lyric is passive, having been struck by Love's arrow. He feels powerless, not because of any inferiority in his social position but rather because he finds himself caught in the prison of Love. The troubadour's obsession with future *joi* is overshadowed in the lyrics of the *trouvères* by a preoccupation with present suffering. The *trouvère*, whose heart has left him to reside with his lady, sustains himself as best he can on bittersweet memories. For the *trouvères*, as for the troubadours before them, to love is to sing.[17] But the *trouvères* place greater emphasis on the necessity of singing: *chanter m'estuet* ('I have to sing').[18] This phrase, which emerges as the exordium par excellence of the *grand chant courtois*, suggests a fundamental difference in motivation between the troubadours and the *trouvères*. While the former sang for profit, the latter sang out of existential need.

The French courtly love song reached its apogee in the mid-thirteenth century with Thibaut IV, count of Champagne and king of Navarre, as its most prolific and most illustrious practitioner. Grandson of Marie de Champagne, Thibaut descended from a long line of literati stretching back to the first troubadour, William IX. His father having died shortly before his birth, Thibaut spent his early years at the royal court of Philip Augustus, where he received his first education. Though generally loyal to the French crown, he

17 Paul Zumthor, 'De la circularité du chant (à propos des trouvères des xiie et xiiie siècles)', *Poétique* 2 (1970), pp. 129–40.
18 Rosenberg and Tischler, *Chansons*, p. 7.

occasionally acted erratically. After agreeing to assist King Louis VIII in his campaign against the Albigensians, Thibaut left this monarch in the lurch, right in the midst of the royal siege of Avignon in 1226. When the king died unexpectedly several months later, Thibaut was suspected of having murdered him. In disrepute at the French court, Thibaut joined forces with other feudal lords in an effort to dethrone Louis's widow, Blanche de Castille, who was serving as regent on behalf of their son Louis IX. But somehow the queen persuaded Thibaut to dissociate himself from the rebels and to become her defender. The mysterious circumstances surrounding the death of the king in combination with Thibaut's inconsistent behaviour toward the queen spawned rumours as persistent as they were unfounded that she was the great love of his life.[19] Whether inspired by Blanche de Castille or by an unidentified lady of lesser renown, Thibaut produced over sixty songs, which cover the gamut of medieval lyric types: from *pastourelles* to devotional songs, from debate poems (*tensons* and *jeux-partis*) to *chansons de croisade*. He even composed one political song, or *sirventois* (Occitan *sirventes*), a relatively uncommon genre among the trouvères. His *jeux-partis* are among the earliest known, but his glory both then and now rests on his love songs, of which approximately three dozen have survived.

The crowning achievement of Thibaut's poetic career was the *chanson* beginning *Ausi comme unicorne sui*, in which the poet compares himself to a unicorn that swoons when it gazes upon a virgin and in that vulnerable state is then traitorously slain. The poet has been killed by his lady and Love, who have taken his heart from him. The first time that he saw his lady, his heart leapt out of his body and stayed with her when he took leave from her. It is being held captive in the sweet Prison of Love, whose columns are of Desire, whose doors are of Beautiful Sight and whose chains are of Good Hope. The assault upon the heart by the three wardens, Fair Seeming, Beauty, and Rejection, is similar to the relentless attacks on Roland and Olivier, the difference being that the epic heroes were able to prevail by fighting back, while the heart can only suffer and wait for mercy to bring deliverance. Nevertheless, the poet remains steadfast in his love; nothing can erase the memory of his lady. Thibaut's song is replete with literary allusions. The initial metaphor recalls the *canso* of the troubadour Rigaut de Berbezilh in which he likens himself to an elephant (*Atressi com l'orifanz*) and the bestiary of Philippe de Thaon, in which the characteristics of the unicorn are described. The reference to Roland

19 Rosenberg *et al.*, *Songs*, p. 305; Kathleen J. Brahney (ed.), *The Lyrics of Thibaut de Champagne* (New York and London: Garland, 1989), pp. xiii–xxii.

and Olivier is taken from the *Chanson de Roland*, and the little allegory of the lover surrounded by personified abstractions is reminiscent of Guillaume de Lorris's *Roman de la Rose*. *Ausi comme unicorne sui* illustrates well one of the chief distinctions between the Occitan *canso* and the French *chanson*, in that the former never lost sight of its own performance and of the presence of an audience, while the latter was more introspective, more meditative. In contrast to the troubadour Rigaut, who turns immediately from his analogy with the elephant to address the lords at the court of Puy-en-Velay, the *trouvère* Thibaut allows the unicorn to lead him deeper and deeper into an imaginary realm that he alone inhabits.[20]

Ausi comme unicorne sui was singled out by Johannes de Grocheio in his treatise *De musica* (c. 1300) as a *cantus coronatus* ('crowned song') exemplary of the best in secular monophonic composition.[21] And Thibaut de Champagne was the only *trouvère* to be cited by Dante among the 'illustrious poets' in his *De vulgari eloquentia*.[22] Moreover, Thibaut was regularly granted privilege of place by the scribes of Old French lyric *chansonniers* who put his songs first.[23]

Thibaut de Champagne's contribution to the *langue d'oïl* literary legacy may have extended beyond composing excellent songs. He may also have overseen their compilation. According to the *Grandes Chroniques de France*, 'He had [his songs] written in his room at Provins and in that at Troyes, and they are called the Songs of the King of Navarre.' Whether Thibaut set up a private scriptorium for the purpose of editing, organising, and copying his own songs may never be confirmed; however, the consistency in the ordering of his songs from one *chansonnier* to the next suggests that they were assembled early and that they circulated as a unit.[24]

Thibaut de Champagne was, of course, not the only *trouvère* to make a lasting name for himself as a lyric poet. There were also Conon de Béthune, Gace Brulé, Colin Muset, Châtelain de Couci and a few others. But the list is remarkably short. Indeed, what is striking is how many of the *trouvères* are remembered primarily for something besides their love songs: Chrétien de Troyes for his romances, Richard de Fournival for his bestiary, Jean Bodel for

20 Frederick Goldin, *Lyrics of the Troubadours and Trouvères* (New York: Anchor/Doubleday, 1973), pp. 443–53.
21 Christopher Page, 'Johannes de Grocheio on Secular Music: A Corrected Text and a New Translation', *Plainsong and Medieval Music* 2 (1993), pp. 23–4.
22 Dante Alighieri, *De vulgari eloquentia*, ed. S. Botterill (Cambridge: Cambridge University Press, 1996), pp. 19, 61, 65, 92 n. 32.
23 Sylvia Huot, *From Song to Book: The Poetics of Writing in Old French Lyric and Lyrical Narrative Poetry* (Ithaca, NY: Cornell University Press, 1987), p. 47.
24 Ibid., pp. 64–6.

his *fabliaux* and his epic poem, Adam de la Halle for his plays, Philippe de Rémy for his customary law, Rutebeuf for his saints' lives, Guiot de Provins for his Bible. It would appear that the majority of *langue d'oïl* poets, many of whom had clerical training, never felt entirely at home with the *grand chant courtois* and the values associated with *fin'amors*, which were so blatantly incompatible with the teachings of the church.

8

The Grail

MIRANDA GRIFFIN

The Grail is one of the most compelling and paradoxical objects in Western literature, as well as one of the best known. Uniting chivalric romance and mystical writing inspired by the Gospels, it wounds and heals; it is the object of a quest which is a foregone conclusion and of a question which is not asked. It magically distributes food, but also serves a man who is nourished solely by the Eucharistic host, and is associated with the famine of a wasteland. As it occurs in a succession of twelfth- and thirteenth-century romances in French, the medium of the Grail's description changes from verse to prose. The Grail itself changes shape and significance, and its quester changes his name and genealogy. It is also the centre of a constellation of supernatural objects (a special seat at Round Table, an enchanted castle, broken swords, a lance that bleeds), and is attended by extraordinary people (wounded kings who live for hundreds of years, virginal female guardians, omniscient hermits and chaste knights).

The noun *graal* derives from the Latin *gradalis*, a large platter which could hold a selection of different foods. Later texts, in which the Grail has become 'le Saint Graal', offer an alternative etymology for *graal*, based on *graer/greer* to grant, to fulfil. The image of a dish or cup which has supernatural powers has been traced to Celtic folkloric roots. The Grail and the tales that surround it may also have been influenced by artefacts and stories encountered by crusaders in the Holy Land. Indeed, the Grail's journey, portrayed in the romances which explain its origins, from the Holy Land to Western Europe, can be interpreted as a kind of reverse Crusade.

Chrétien de Troyes's *Conte du Graal* (c. 1180) is the text in which the Grail is first portrayed in an Arthurian context. The *Conte* is the last Arthurian romance by Chrétien, who names Count Philip of Flanders as the patron of this romance. In this work, the naïve young knight, Perceval, visits the castle of the wounded Roi Pêcheur (Fisher King) – so called because he fishes rather than hunts as a pastime, his wound making it impossible for him to ride.

There Perceval witnesses a mysterious procession, in which 'un graal' and a silver *tailleor* (trencher, platter) are carried by two beautiful damsels, and a bleeding lance is carried by a young man. Having recently been advised that knights should not be too talkative, Perceval refrains from asking about this mysterious vision; specifically, he wants to know whom the Grail serves, but he remains silent. This proves to be a mistake, however, since the next morning, he finds himself alone in the castle, and discovers that the King would have been healed had he asked about the Grail and the lance. Perceval vows not to spend more than one night in the same place, nor to fear any danger, until he has learned whom the Grail serves and why the lance bleeds. Much later in Chrétien's text, a hermit tells Perceval that the Fisher King's father is served by the Grail. The Grail is 'Tant sainte chose' (such a holy thing),[1] and the king it serves so pious, that he needs no other nourishment than the host served to him daily by the Grail. The hermit who reveals this to Perceval is the brother of both the king served by the Grail, and of Perceval's mother, making both the hermit and the Grail King Perceval's uncles.

Chrétien's romance is unfinished, possibly due to the death of its author; ever since, modern and medieval readers have been asking the questions that Perceval suppressed, about the Grail's purpose, signification and ontology. Some medieval authors responded to Chrétien's unfinished text by continuing (although not necessarily finishing) it; others took the notion of a holy artefact at the heart of chivalric romance and explored its implications.

Four of the fifteen manuscripts that transmit Chrétien's *Conte du Graal* contain the *Conte* on its own. The others, however, append continuations to Chrétien's romance, which extend the *Conte* by many times its original length. In the manuscripts that transmit the continuations there is little or no obvious demarcation between the end of Chrétien's text and the beginning of the work of other authors, implying that medieval audiences may not have made the same distinctions as modern readers between the *Conte* and its continuations. The first continuation is also known as the *Continuation-Gauvain*, since it relates the adventures of Gauvain, with whom the *Conte du Graal* ends.

The *Conte du Graal*'s second continuation or *Continuation-Perceval* is attributed in the text to Wauchier de Denain. As its alternative title suggests, it shifts attention back to Perceval's adventures on the quest. This

---

1 Chrétien de Troyes, *Le Conte du Graal*, ed. and trans. Charles Méla (Paris: Livre de Poche, 1990), verse 6351.

continuation ends with Perceval's attempt to join the broken sword which Gauvain had failed to mend at the end of the first continuation. A tiny crack remains in the sword, however, which can only be mended once Perceval has proved himself to be a worthy knight and has atoned for his sins. This lack of completion in the sword, then, signals Perceval's own incompleteness, as well as the incompleteness of his story.

Consequently, yet another continuation is called for: in the majority of manuscripts, this is a text attributed to Manessier, in which Perceval's questions are answered: he learns that Joseph of Arimathea used the Grail to collect blood from the crucified Christ; the *tailleor* was used to cover the Grail after the blood had been collected; the lance is that of the soldier Longinus, with which he stabbed the crucified Christ; and the blood that flows from it is Christ's blood. The Fisher King is healed, and then dies; Perceval becomes the Grail King. He rules in peace for seven years, before retiring to a hermitage where he is ordained, and spends ten years sustained only by the Grail; when he dies the lance, *tailleor* and Grail ascend to heaven. In two manuscripts, however, Gerbert de Montreuil's continuation, probably composed later than Manessier's, is inserted between the second continuation and Manessier's. It is in Gerbert's continuation that Perceval mends the sword completely.

Although Perceval learns in the *Conte* itself whom the Grail serves, the continuators adapt and rework the question Perceval is expected to ask, and the conditions of the answers he gets. What is at stake in asking the question is therefore not the acquisition of new information in the shape of the answer, but what the question can achieve and signify beyond its lexical content. As well as a potentially powerful speech act which can heal the Fisher King, the question Perceval should ask or does ask in the *Conte* and its continuations is a means of prolonging the tale, of deepening the mystery of the Grail, rather than explaining it.

Many episodes in the later continuations were influenced by Robert de Boron's Grail Cycle, which expands on the Christian origins of the Grail, and turns Chrétien's 'tant sainte chose' into 'le Saint Graal'. Robert's *Estoire dou Graal*, also known as *Joseph d'Arimathie*, and the first 504 lines of his *Merlin* are preserved in one manuscript, Paris, BNF f.fr 20047. In this manuscript the texts are in verse form, and are dated to the turn of the thirteenth century. A prose version of the texts, along with a Prose *Perceval* (known as the *Didot-Perceval* after Ambroise Firmin Didot, who once owned one of the two manuscripts that transmit it), date from around the same time. Despite the usual practice of verse texts being 'dérimés', a convincing case has been formulated by Linda

Gowans for Robert de Boron's texts originally being composed in prose and then rhymed.[2] There is no firm evidence that Robert is responsible for the *Perceval*.

Robert's *Joseph* is the first to construct the Grail sought by Arthurian knights as the cup from which Christ drank at the Last Supper, and in which Joseph of Arimathea collected the blood of the crucified Christ. Joseph, a knight in the service of Pilate, is mentioned briefly in the Gospels, but would have been familiar to a medieval readership from the popular but apocryphal *Gospel of Nicodemus*. Pilate grants Joseph the crucified Christ's body to inter in his own tomb; as Joseph prepares the body for burial, he collects Christ's blood in a dish or 'veissel' taken from the house of Simon, where Christ performed the sacrament at the Last Supper. Joseph is arrested and imprisoned, but is sustained for many years by visitations from Christ and the holy vessel. Upon his release, Joseph leads a small band of believers into the desert, where the vessel is named the Grail.

The Grail's association with the Last Supper is figured through the establishment, at Christ's instigation, of a Grail table in the *Joseph*. Christ appears to Joseph and tells him that only the faithful will be able to sit at the table. Joseph is to sit in the seat corresponding to Christ's place at the table of the Last Supper; one seat will remain empty, figuring the seat of Judas. This seat will only be filled, Christ tells Joseph, by the child, as yet unborn, of Joseph's sister and her husband, Bron. With the Grail placed in the middle of the table, the faithful take their seats, while the sinners depart in shame. At the end of the *Joseph*, Robert announces his intention of continuing his story in five more parts, the first of which is the *Merlin*.

In its turn, the Grail table is commemorated in the *Merlin* by the Round Table, established by Merlin at the court of Uther Pendragon, who later becomes the father of Arthur. The fifty best knights of the realm sit at the table, but one place, the *Siege Perilleux* (Perilous Seat), is empty, reserved for the knight who will accomplish the adventures of the Holy Grail. Unworthy knights who attempt to sit in the Perilous Seat meet a nasty end. This representation of the Round Table as a space of the elite knights awaiting a knight greater than them all contradicts the notion of the Round Table as a means of eradicating rivalry between Arthur's knights. In Wace's *Roman de Brut*, the first text to mention the Round Table, no knight at the table can boast that

---

2 Linda Gowans, 'What Did Robert de Boron Really Write?', in Bonnie Wheeler (ed.), *Arthurian Studies in Honour of P. J. C. Field* (Cambridge: D. S. Brewer, 2004), pp. 15–28.

he sits higher than any of his peers;[3] yet the introduction of the Grail into the Arthurian romance world ushers in a new hierarchy.

The knight anticipated by the empty seat at the Round Table is, initially at least, Perceval. In the *Didot-Perceval*, Perceval is son of Alain, to whom Joseph entrusted the Grail, and the grandson of Bron, the Fisher King. In similar terms to Chrétien's *Conte du Graal*, Perceval at first fails to ask whom the Grail serves, but after eight years of wandering, he returns to the castle, and asks the correct question, healing his grandfather, and becoming himself the guardian of the Grail.

Such was the success of Robert de Boron's Cycle that his name becomes associated with Grail romance for the rest of the thirteenth century. In the Vulgate Cycle and in later Grail romance texts, his name and names associated with him were invoked as authors of texts that he did not compose. Whether or not it was originally composed in verse, the Robert Cycle of Grail texts is widely transmitted in prose, although prose does not replace verse as the means of writing about the Grail. In the early thirteenth century, prose was explicitly deployed in French historiography as a means of telling the unvarnished truth, without the inevitable distortion brought about by the rhyme and metre imposed by verse narrative. The adoption of prose by authors of Arthurian Grail romances reflects a desire to present material on the same plane as historical truth, and a concomitant aspiration to record and transmit the corpus of Arthurian material in its entirety.

The *Perlesvaus*, also known as *Le Haut Livre du Graal*, is a fascinatingly anomalous prose romance which refocuses many of the principal pre-existing ideas and figures surrounding the Grail in a dark and unique work. The hero of this text, like Perceval of the Robert de Boron Cycle, is the son of Alain, but owes his name to his father's loss of the Vales of Camalot: 'Perd-les-vaux'. As well as Perlesvaus, Arthur, Lancelot and Gauvain all undertake the Grail quest. A work suffused with the violent confrontation between allegorical manifestations of the Christian Old Law and New Law, composed in the first half of the thirteenth century, the *Perlesvaus* is different in tone to, yet most likely contemporaneous with, *La Queste del Saint Graal*: critics have thus far failed to agree about the relative dating of the two texts.

The *Vulgate Cycle*, or *Lancelot-Grail Cycle*, comprises five separate prose texts or 'branches': *L'Estoire dou Saint Graal* traces the story of the Grail from its inception at the Crucifixion, and its arrival in Britain with Josephus, the son

---

3 Wace, *Le Roman de Brut: A History of the British*, ed. and trans. Judith Weiss (Exeter: University of Exeter Press, 1999), verses 9747–58.

of Joseph of Arimathea. The *Merlin*, incorporated from the Robert de Boron Cycle, is followed by a *Suite* peculiar to the Vulgate Cycle, which narrates the early years of Arthur's kingship. The focus shifts in the *Lancelot*, by far the longest text in the Cycle, to the biography of the eponymous hero, kidnapped as a baby by the Lady of the Lake and brought by her to Arthur's court, where he becomes both the best knight and the lover of Queen Guenevere. At a visit to the Grail castle, Lancelot sleeps with Amide, the daughter of Pellès, the maimed Fisher King (he has been given a potion which makes him believe he is sleeping with Guenevere), and Galahad is conceived. The Grail knight's genealogy now links him to the Grail family of the Fisher King through his mother; while Lancelot in the Vulgate Cycle is the descendant of Nascien, the brother-in-law of Mordrain, king of Sarras converted by Joseph of Arimathea. Because of the sin he has committed with Guenevere, Lancelot is unable to play a significant part in the Grail quest.

Elspeth Kennedy has argued convincingly that the earliest versions of the *Lancelot* were not conceived as part of a larger romance cycle, and references to the Grail anticipate Perceval as the Grail knight.[4] References to Galahad were integrated once the *Queste* had been composed and joined to the *Lancelot*. Certainly, the predictions concerning the Grail knight, specifically Merlin's prophecies as he establishes the Round Table, had to be reworked as Robert de Boron's *Merlin* was assimilated into the Vulgate Cycle. As the *Lancelot* progresses, the earthly, adulterous love and *chevalerie terrienne* which inspires Lancelot is contrasted unfavourably with the divine *chevalerie celestielle* which will characterise the long-awaited Grail knight. At the beginning of the *Queste*, Galahad arrives at Camelot, pulls from a stone a sword destined for the best knight in the world (Lancelot has not dared to attempt to release it) and sits in the *Siege Perilleux*. The Grail appears at court, moving mysteriously through the assembled throng and dispensing everyone's favourite food.

Attention is shifted in the *Queste* from the question to the quest as a means of understanding the Grail. Perceval's compulsion in the *Conte* and its continuations to discover what the Grail is and whom it serves is replaced in the *Queste* by a desire in those who undertake to Grail quest to 'voir apertement' ('see clearly') the secrets of the Grail. The Grail in this romance is infused with enigmatic agency: it can appear, disappear and travel of its own accord, and is not a fixed end-point to the quest, awaiting the first knight to find it. The Grail quest should therefore be understood less as a geographical journey towards a fixed endpoint and more as a manifestation of divine predestination.

4 See Elspeth Kennedy, *Lancelot and the Grail* (Oxford: Clarendon Press, 1986).

Critics have detected Cistercian influence in the *Queste*'s composition, although it is unlikely to have been composed by a Cistercian monk. Women and the temptation they represent are banned from the quest, and earthly chivalric prowess counts for little in the new moral hierarchy of the Grail quest. Lancelot discovers this to his cost, and repents of his adultery with Guenevere. Gauvain is spectacularly unsuccessful in any adventure pertaining to the Grail. He ends up riding in a cart as a sign of his ineptitude in the *Lancelot*; is indignant at his failure to encounter adventure during the *Queste*; and at the beginning of the *Mort* has to confess to Arthur that he killed eighteen of his companions during the quest.

As the *Queste* draws to a close, Galahad, aided by Perceval and Bohort, the only other two knights pure enough, is united with the Grail. Galahad uses the blood from the bleeding lance to cure the *Roi Mehaignié* (Wounded King), mends the broken sword, and then looks inside the Grail, declaring that he has seen that which tongue cannot describe nor heart conceive. Having achieved his heart's desire, Galahad asks God for his own death. The Grail and the lance ascend to heaven, and the adventures in Logres are brought to an end. Nevertheless, there is one more *branche* of the Vulgate Cycle to come: in *La Mort le roi Artu*, Lancelot and Guenevere fall back into their adultery, putting into motion a chain of tragic events which result in Arthur's death and the end of the Arthurian world.

Although the *Mort* closes with the declaration that to add any more to the story would be a lie, prose romance's compulsion to complete is such that the story of the Arthurian kingdom and the Grail is elaborated in the Prose *Tristan* and other later prose romance texts. Fanni Bognadow has postulated the existence of a post-Vulgate Cycle, suggested by surviving manuscripts, and in translations from the French into Spanish and Portuguese.[5] The post-Vulgate *Suite du Merlin* reworks many of the prophecies that anticipate Galahad as the Grail knight. Merlin takes a sword from the body of the knight Balain and sticks it into a stone, which then mystically sails on the river to Camelot, to arrive on the same day as Galahad. Before he dies, Balain strikes King Pellehan through the thighs with the lance which accompanies the Grail. This is the Dolorous Stroke, which not only makes Pellehan the *Roi Mehaignié*, but also lays waste to his kingdom, the barren land reflecting the mutilation of its king.

In these texts, the Fisher King and his wounded father often merge, or at least have confusingly similar names (Pellehan, Parlan, Pellès). *Rois Mehaigniés*

---

5 See Fanni Bogdanow, *The Romance of the Grail: A Study of the Structure and Genesis of a Thirteenth-Century Arthurian Prose Romance* (Manchester: Manchester University Press, 1966).

proliferate in Grail romance, and they can be harmed or healed by the Grail. In the Vulgate *Estoire*, Mordrain is wounded and blinded when he comes too near to the Grail, but remains in this near-death limbo for 400 years until Galahad cures him; Mordrain then dies a pious and grateful death. The Fisher King in the *Perlesvaus* is afflicted *because* Perlesvaus did not ask the question about the Grail before the beginning of the narrative of the *Perlesvaus*.

The preoccupation with blood, the wounded and the whole body is reflected in the Grail's close association with the Crucifixion and the Eucharist, although it is important to note that the Grail never forms part of official Christian doctrine. The Eucharist was one of the issues debated and pronounced upon by the Fourth Lateran Council in 1215, an assembly of bishops, abbots, priors and chapters of churches and of religious orders, which produced a series of canons on doctrine and practice. The Council's pronouncement seems to respond to contemporary anxiety about the exact nature of transubstantiation as it occurs in the Mass. The Grail participates in several Eucharistic Masses in the French texts that tell its story, including what is ostensibly the first ever Eucharist. In this Mass in the Vulgate *Estoire*, and in the Grail Mass celebrated at the end of the Vulgate *Queste*, faith is supplemented by proof, in rather disturbingly graphic representations of the corporeal reality present in the ceremony of the Eucharist. In the *Estoire*, Josephus tearfully and fearfully follows commands to tear up and eat what sometimes looks like bread and sometimes like the body of a child; in the *Queste*, the crucified Christ emerges from the Grail and conducts the ceremony himself.

The Grail therefore raises questions about visibility and the truth. In the *Perlesvaus*, King Arthur witnesses the Grail going through five different manifestations, although only the last – a chalice – can be described.[6] In the Vulgate *Estoire*, the Grail is described as a dish, but in the *Lancelot* it is a chalice. The Grail is surprisingly rarely depicted in early manuscripts, and in the elaborate fifteenth-century manuscripts of the Vulgate Cycle, it is often represented in illuminations as a ciborium.

Just as it is difficult to see or to picture, the Grail is also recurrently represented as defying expression in language. Perhaps the ultimate paradox embodied by the Grail is that it provokes a search for the truth and significance, in the forms of quests and questions, and yet is characterised by ineffability, in a story that is difficult to conclude.

6 *Le Haut Livre du Graal [Perlesvaus]*, ed. and trans. Armand Strubel (Paris: Livre de Poche, 2007), p. 790.

9

Women authors of the Middle Ages

BARBARA K. ALTMANN

There is much to be gleaned on the topic of women writers of the Middle Ages simply from the existence of such an entry in a literary history. The reader will note immediately that there is no parallel article on male authors, a category so big as to be unthinkable as a single unit. On the one hand, it is reasonable to assume that the topic of women authors is small and circumscribed enough to fit comfortably into relatively few words. On the other hand, however, the inclusion of such an article implies that even if limited in scope, the topic is important enough in our current understanding of the Middle Ages to merit its own discussion.

We can never know how many of the anonymous authors of the Middle Ages might, in fact, have been 'anonyma'. All we know for certain is that the list of women authors of that era to whom we can reliably attach a name, a biography, and a list of works is very small indeed. The spectrum broadens somewhat when we consider women authors of lyric poetry whose names we do not know, poetry written in a woman's voice that may or may not be authored by women, and the existence of women authors in the fictional realm, all of which we will consider briefly here.

Whether for fictional or historically verifiable women authors, the sine qua non for participation in literary culture was access to education and to the necessary means of production. For women as well as men, those advantages were available primarily in two milieux: the court and the church. Not surprisingly, then, most of the women authors we know of were noble by birth, wrote courtly and/or devotional literature, and lived in or on the periphery of religious institutions and aristocratic, even royal, households. In those environments, one might expect the confluence of gender, class, and resources that would have made it possible for a woman to compose literary texts.

The earliest known woman writing in Old French was Marie de France, who produced her works between approximately 1160 and 1190. Marie is an example of an author whose identity we determine based largely on who she must have been rather than on any historical fact. Her name is known from an often quoted phrase in one of her works: 'Marie ai num, si sui de France', meaning, 'My name is Marie and I am from France.' Taken from the epilogue of her *Fables* (line 4), this statement is one of the few bits of evidence on which to hang her identity.[1] Apart from the name, we can deduce some information from the Anglo-Norman traits of the French in which her tales are preserved in manuscript. That, combined with contextual and intertextual clues, leads scholars to posit that 'Marie' most likely wrote at or in connection with the English court of Eleanor of Aquitaine and King Henry II (1113–89), a great centre of learning and culture in its day. There is further speculation that Marie might have been an abbess in a religious order, given her erudition.

The literary texts attributed to Marie de France are *Les Fables* mentioned above, which consist of about one hundred short moralising fables in the tradition of Aesop; *Les Lais*, a collection of twelve short tales on romance themes; and *L'Espurgatoire Seint Patriz* (*Purgatory of St. Patrick*), a work of approximately 2,300 octosyllabic lines that describes a journey through the Other World.

Marie's *Lais*, her earliest, best-known, and most appreciated work, is named for the genre to which her tales belong. The dozen *Lais* are short narratives on the topic of love – tales inspired, the authorial voice tells us, by the Breton 'lais' she has heard recounted orally. To that subject matter, which has its origins in Celtic culture and which is called the 'matière de Bretagne' ('matter of Britain'), she adds elements borrowed from Ovid, from the romances of antiquity of a few decades earlier, and from existing tales of the hero Tristan. Marie weaves together this diverse set of sources into stories of happy and unhappy lovers, the emotions they share, and the help and hindrances they encounter from human and otherworldly figures alike. The story 'Chevrefoil', shortest of the twelve 'lais', is of particular interest because it relates a brief episode from the romance of Tristan and Iseut. The tale 'Lanval' is generally considered to be the jewel of the collection. Along with the other tales, it illustrates the social and feudal hierarchies of the late twelfth century while freely mixing in agents and locations known from Celtic mythology.

In the *Prologue* that precedes the *Lais*, Marie states that the person to whom God has given skill and wisdom must not hesitate to disseminate good stories for the benefit of both author and audience. Her erudition and mastery of a

---

1 *Lais de Marie de France*, ed. K. Warnke, trans. L. Harf-Lancner (Paris: Livre de Poche, 1990), and *Marie de France: Fables*, ed. H. Spiegel (Toronto: University of Toronto Press, 1995).

broad range of sources place her in the tradition of the learned authorities she refers to in her *Prologue*. Marie, whoever she was, deserves a place among the leading writers of the French Middle Ages, and, along with her contemporary Chrétien de Troyes, marks the first great flowering of medieval romance.

The intriguing ambiguities and lacunae in information regarding Marie's identity and works raise the issue of whether one can, or should, seek to define a feminine subjectivity behind and in her narratives. Especially in light of the paucity of medieval women writers, it is appealing to try to see in Marie's work, and in the *Lais* in particular, an example of 'écriture féminine', to use the term pioneered by Hélène Cixous in 1975. Can we say that Marie's writing indeed uses language and the elements of romance in a distinctively gendered way? Critics vary in their opinion, but ultimately it is difficult to substantiate such an argument, despite the desire to distinguish the poetics of the few women writers we can identify from those of the great many male authors alongside whom they take their place. No author of the Middle Ages, whether male or female, could write entirely outside the referential framework of the mainstream, in part because the rhetorical authority and credibility of the author depended to some extent on the use of references to other authorities who in some way define the subject matter.

There is more scholarly discussion concerning the issue of a distinctive female voice in the case of women authors of lyric poetry. Much more than narrative, medieval lyric poetry, of which the predominant subject is love, puts the first-person voice on display and thus invites examination of subjectivity, subject position and the psychology of human relationships. The *trobairitz*, meaning women troubadours, are a group of women poets who composed poetry in the Occitan language in southern France. We can identify approximately twenty *trobairitz*, as compared with more than 400 known male troubadours, and their work dates from the mid-twelfth to the mid-thirteenth centuries.[2] There is little to go on beyond the names that emerge from *razos* and *vidas* (respectively, commentaries on the poems and biographies written in the thirteenth century, often fictitious).[3] We can be certain these poets were noblewomen, some related to renowned troubadours, and some identified as participating with male contemporaries in poetic dialogue.

Obviously well schooled in the brilliant literary Provençal culture of their day, the *trobairitz* wrote in several poetic forms, including the *tenso* and

---

2 M. Bruckner, L. Shepard, and S. White, *Songs of the Women Troubadours* (New York and London: Garland, 2000).
3 M. Egan, *The Vidas of the Troubadours* (New York: Garland, 1984), and W. E. Burgwinkle, *Razos and Troubadour Songs* (New York: Garland, 1990).

partimen (examples of debate poems involving exchanges between poets), the *sirventes* (poems of blame, whether personal, political, or moralising), the *planh* (a lament), and the *canso*, or love song, which was the most elevated of genres. The comtessa de Dia is the best known of the *trobairitz*. Manuscripts preserve several portraits of her, as well as four *cansos* considered virtuosic examples of the genre. We have manuscript portraits of the poet Na Castelloza as well, who, like the comtessa, is singled out for the quality of the three, or possibly four, *cansos* attributed to her. We have even less preserved work for the other known *trobairitz*, and some, like Gaudairenca, are mentioned in texts by other authors, but none of their work survives. A good deal of commentary on these poets concerns their creative reworking of standard vocabulary and themes to represent the woman's side in matters of love. Some scholars posit that there were women *trouvères*, analogues in northern France to the *trobairitz* in the south, who were composing in Old French by the thirteenth century, although the historical and manuscript evidence of authorship is even less substantial in their case than for their southern sisters (see Chapter 7).[4]

Much depends on how one reads poetry written in a woman's voice but without a definite author attribution. Can we equate the presence of a first-person female voice in poetry with a woman poet? Such is the question for a small corpus of poetry considered women's songs, among which are a few *chansons de malmariée* and some *chansons de toile*, of which most of the extant examples are anonymous. *Chansons de malmariée* (songs of the unhappily married wife) are songs in which a young woman laments that she has been married to an unsuitable husband, usually an old and jealous man unattractive to his bride. The *chanson de toile* is named for the kind of textile work (weaving, spinning, embroidery) that was a traditional occupation for women, and in these thirteenth-century poems, which combine narrative and love lyric, the woman telling the story is sometimes depicted as singing the song while she sits at her work. The subject matter is usually a tale of love, in which, unlike much of the male-authored corpus of love poetry, the woman is an active and vocal participant. The assumption of agency on the part of the female voice is no doubt one of the factors that has encouraged literary historians to conjecture that the authors of such *chansons de toile* must also be women.

Despite the uncertainties regarding questions of female authorship, we have ample proof in romance that the notion of women writing and performing

---

4 E. Doss-Quinby, J. Tasker Grimbert, W. Pfeffer, and E. Aubrey, *Songs of the Women Trouvères* (New Haven, CT: Yale University Press, 2001).

literary work was plausible in the medieval imagination. For example, in Jean Renart's early thirteenth-century romance, *Le Roman de la rose ou de Guillaume de Dole*, the heroine Lienor is much admired for her graceful singing.[5] Jean Renart obviously considered the *chansons de toile* she performs worthy of inclusion alongside the more courtly forms of lyric he also showcases as insertions into his plot. The anonymous *Roman de silence* (*The Romance of Silence*) recounts the adventures of a heroine named Silence who has to disguise herself as a man in order to circumvent an unjust ruling that forbids women to inherit.[6] The story explores at considerable length the relative advantages and disadvantages of men's and women's roles. Ironically, the need to hide her female identity opens many spheres of action to Silence, who excels as a knight but also as a 'jongleur', a public performer of poetry and song. In the fourteenth-century *Voir dit* (*The True Tale*) by Guillaume de Machaut, the aging poet–author attracts a young and cultivated woman as his lover by virtue of his mastery as a poet. The lady, 'Toute Belle', replies in kind, and her lyric poems find their way along with his into the poetic exchange that traces the evolution of their relationship.

In a realm far removed from the secular preoccupation with courtly love, another type of medieval writing often associated with women authors is mysticism, a discursive field in which women's voices were countenanced (see Chapter 16). We know few medieval women mystics in France, and none as renowned as Hildegard of Bingen, Mechtild of Magdeburg, and Mechtild of Hackeborn in Germany, Margery Kemp and Julian of Norwich in England, Birgitta of Sweden, or Catherine of Sienna, to name some of the most widely read and appreciated. The two French writers we know who worked in this tradition are Marguerite d'Oingt and Marguerite Porete, both of whom died in 1310. Marguerite d'Oingt, daughter of a powerful family in the Beaujolais region, became the prioress of a Benedictine convent near Lyon. She was a learned woman who wrote in standard French, Franco-Provençal and Latin. Her works are the *Pagina meditationum* (*Page of Meditations*); the *Speculum*, her major book; and a biography of another woman religious entitled *Li Via seiti Biatrix, virgina de Ornaciu* (*La Vie de Sainte Beatrix d'Ornacieux*).[7]

The other French woman mystic who left us a significant work is Marguerite Porete. Porete is associated with the Beguine movement, a lay religious

5 *Le Roman de la rose ou de Guillaume de Dole*, ed. J. Dufournet (Paris: Champion, 2008).
6 Le Roman de silence: *A Thirteenth-Century Arthurian Verse-Romance*, ed. L. Thorpe (Cambridge: Heffer, 1972).
7 *Les Œuvres de Marguerite d'Oingt*, ed. A. Duraffour, P. Gardette, and P. Durdilly (Paris: Les Belles Lettres, 1965).

movement within the Catholic church. Porete was a preacher of sorts who provoked the ire of ecclesiastical authorities initially for reading aloud in public rather than for the content of her work. Her book, *Le Mirouer des simples ames* (*The Mirror of Simple Souls*), is the oldest known mystical work written in French, and the only surviving medieval text by a woman writer executed as a heretic.[8] Marguerite's theology was suspect in the eyes of the Catholic church, although she had the support of a number of highly placed churchmen. One of the objections against her was that rather than addressing her work exclusively to theologians, she insisted on communicating her teachings to the common people, which included composing her work in the vernacular Old French instead of Latin.

Marguerite's book describes the progress of the 'simple soul' through a series of seven stages towards ecstatic union with God. Her vision angered the church because she considered the soul, once united with God, no longer subject to the dictates of morality or the intervention of the clergy. Porete's writing is learned and elegant, using vocabulary and imagery belonging to the themes of secular courtly love to make sense of the soul's love for God. The text consists mainly of dialogue between the allegorical figures Amour (Love) and Raison (Reason) and contains poetic passages that are highly rhymed and rhythmic. Despite the efforts to suppress it, the *Mirouer* had a considerable afterlife. It spread across Europe, was translated into several other languages (including Latin) and the existence of numerous manuscripts attests to its popularity and influence. Its wide passage may well have been aided by the removal of the controversial author's name. After Porete's death, her book circulated as an anonymous work until well into the twentieth century.

With the appearance of Christine de Pizan (1365 – c. 1430) in the late fourteenth century, all the elements identified above as hallmarks of medieval women's writing come together. She was associated with the two milieux – court and convent – that were the centres of medieval intellectual culture: for the first part of her life she lived at or in the shadow of the royal French court under kings Charles V and Charles VI. When forced to flee Paris in 1418 because of civil unrest, she moved to the abbey at Poissy, where her daughter had become a nun and where she herself lived until her death. She also had immediate access to scholarly circles through both her father and her husband. The former, Tommaso da Pizzano (or, Thomas de Pizan in French),

---

8 Marguerite Porete, *Le Miroir des âmes simples et anéanties et qui seulement demeurent en vouloir et désir d'amour* (Paris: Albin Michel, 1997), and *The Mirror of Simple Souls*, trans. E. Babinsky (Mahwah, NJ: Paulist Press, 1993).

was an Italian astrologer whom Charles V invited to his court in 1368 as a councillor. Tommaso moved his family to Paris, and Christine tells us that he encouraged her to pursue her studies. The latter, Étienne du Castel, was a notary in the royal chancellery and Christine describes her marriage to him as a love match rather than the pragmatic sort of union much more common in her day.

In recent years, a phrase often used with regard to Christine describes her as the first French 'woman of letters'. That formulation is based on the notion of writing as a profession, a way to earn one's livelihood. When the death of her father and husband left her responsible for the upkeep of her family, Christine began to write for a living. She had an extensive network of patrons thanks to her close ties to the court. As a result, she could dedicate and send her works to noblemen and women of the highest rank, as we see, for example, in the presentation manuscripts of collected works she prepared for the duke of Orleans and Queen Isabeau de Bavière (Isabel of Bavaria), wife of Charles VI. Her many writings were her stock in trade. She supervised closely the production of her manuscripts and was herself a scribe.

Christine was prolific and worked in a surprisingly large range of genres. She composed hundreds of lyric poems in the fixed-form models of the day, primarily the *ballade*, the *rondeau*, and the *virelai*. She experimented most with the *ballade*, producing, along with many incidental poems, two collections of one hundred *ballades* each – the *Cent ballades* (*Hundred Ballades*) and the *Cent ballades d'amant et de dame* (*Hundred Ballades of a Lover and a Lady*) – in which storylines build from one poem to the next.[9] Her early writings, in the last years of the fourteenth century, comprised exclusively courtly work, with love as its theme. In the first decade of the fifteenth century, she turned her hand to more sustained works on more serious themes. That period of production includes a biography of Charles V, which she was commissioned to write by the duke of Burgundy; several moral treatises; and a book on military strategy. The *Avision* of 1405 contains considerable autobiographical detail. She also wrote devotional works, and bold, overtly political and polemical works exhorting the king, queen, and nobility to rally and reverse the tide of the Hundred Years War, which was going badly for France.[10] Most striking to a modern reader's eye, perhaps, is her book the *Livre de la Cité des dames*

9 Christine de Pizan, *Cent ballades d'amant et de dame*, ed. J. Cerquiglini (Paris: Union Générale d'Éditions, 1982).
10 Christine de Pizan, *Le Livre de l'advision Cristine*, ed. C. Reno and L. Dulac (Paris: Champion, 2001). Trans. G. McLeod and C. Cannon Willard, notes by G. McLeod, as *The Vision of Christine de Pizan* (Cambridge: D. S. Brewer, 2005).

(*The Book of the City of Ladies*), written in 1404–5.[11] In the *City of Ladies*, she reflects on her own experiential knowledge in face of the misogyny she reads in male authors and she willingly becomes the handmaid to three allegorical goddesses, Ladies Reason, Rectitude, and Justice, who instruct her to build a refuge for all honourable women.

In all her writing, Christine demonstrates a strong authorial consciousness and creates a distinct authorial persona. Her author figure is a learned, chaste widow, writing out of necessity and sometimes against her will. Whether she can be labelled a feminist writer is a topic of hot debate. The term is anachronistic when discussing a medieval author and needs to be used with due allowance for different societal norms and expectations. Christine's work is, however, undeniably pro-feminine. She portrays and actively promotes an image of women as inherently good and capable. Her last known work, the *Ditié de Jeanne d'Arc* (*Tale of Joan of Arc*), is a remarkable conjunction of a powerful woman author who wielded considerable influence with her quill and an extraordinary woman soldier and visionary who led the dauphin to his coronation as Charles VII and led France out of a period of dire crisis.[12]

It is a recent development in the field of medieval studies that a literary history should include a chapter such as this one. Even reference works from the middle of the twentieth century have no overarching discussion of the social conditions that allowed for or precluded the existence of medieval women writers, and many have no entries for individual women authors or the genres associated with women writing.

The recovery project of second-wave feminism in the 1960s and 70s focused medieval scholarship on bringing to light the women's names, biographies, and works we can still retrieve from the pre-modern period. It was the era of finding 'her story' in 'history'. Building on that groundwork, medievalists began to publish the critical editions of primary sources that allow new generations to discover the work of women authors. The existence of critical editions, in turn, makes possible the translation of those texts into modern languages accessible to a broader readership. Once both reliable editions and translations are available, scholars can analyse these works and update

---

11 *La città delle dame*, ed. P. Caraffi and E. J. Richards (Milan: Luni Editrice, 1998). Translated by R. Brown-Grant as *The Book of the City of Ladies* (London and New York: Penguin, 1999).
12 *Le Ditié de Jehanne d'Arc* ed. A. J. Kennedy and K. Varty (Oxford: Society for the Study of Mediaeval Languages and Literature, 1977); and Christine de Pizan, *Ditie de Jehanne d'Arc*, in R. Blumenfeld-Kosinski and K. Brownlee (eds.), *The Selected Writings of Christine de Pizan: New Translations, Criticism* (New York: W. W. Norton, 1997).

an older, somewhat myopic understanding of the cultural production of the Middle Ages. Given the impossibility of knowing what has been lost, we cannot assess the number of women writing or how they were circulating their work in the French Middle Ages. What has survived demonstrates that at least a few women overcame the sizeable odds against their participation in literary culture. Their works, which rival the achievements of their male counterparts, provide at least a small corrective to an otherwise overwhelmingly masculine literary tradition.

10

Crusades and identity

SHARON KINOSHITA

In a much-quoted passage from his *History of the Expedition to Jerusalem*, Fulcher of Chartres, chaplain to the second king of Jerusalem, wrote:

> Consider, I pray, and reflect how in our time God has transferred the West into the East. For we who were Occidentals now have been made Orientals. He who was a Roman or a Frank is now a Galilaean, or an inhabitant of Palestine. One who was a citizen of Rheims or of Chartres now has been made a citizen of Tyre or of Antioch. We have already forgotten the places of our birth; already they have become unknown to many of us, or, at least, are unmentioned. Some already possess here homes and servants which they have received through inheritance. Some have taken wives not merely of their own people, but Syrians, or Armenians, or even Saracens who have received the grace of baptism . . . The one and the other use mutually the speech and the idioms of the different languages. Different languages, now made common, become known to both races, and faith unites those whose forefathers were strangers. As it is written, 'The lion and the ox shall eat straw together.' Those who were strangers are now natives; and he who was a sojourner now has become a resident. Our parents and relatives from day to day come to join us, abandoning, even though reluctantly, all that they possess. For those who were poor there, here God makes rich. Those who had few coins, here possess countless *besants*; and those who had not had a villa, here, by the gift of God, already possess a city. Therefore, why should one who has found the East so favourable return to the West?[1]

Though composed in Latin rather than in Old French, this passage evokes several of this volume's themes: history, of course; memory and testimony; writing from the periphery; alterity, in the interface between Latin Christians and their religious, ethnic, and linguistic others; and sexuality, in crusader marriage practices and the hybrid populations they produced. From Pope

---

1 Edward Peters (ed.), *The First Crusade: The Chronicle of Fulcher of Chartres and Other Source Materials* (Philadelphia: University of Pennsylvania Press, 1971), pp. 220–1.

Urban II's call for an 'armed pilgrimage' to the East in 1095 to the fall of the last crusader outpost at Acre in 1291, the experience of the Crusades brought new identities into being even while disrupting others. This chapter examines the effect of that experience and its afterlife on medieval Western notions of identity, particularly as refracted in the Old French vernacular tradition running from the *Chanson de Roland* (*c.* 1100) to Jean de Joinville's *Vie de Saint Louis* (1309).

In modern minds, the term 'Crusades' conjures up an originary moment in the 'clash of civilisations', a violent world of 'Christians' versus 'Saracens' where identities were poured into religiously based categories of self and other. In the *Chanson de Roland*, the eponymous hero's memorable line, 'Paien unt tort e crestïens unt dreit' ('Pagans are wrong and Christians are right') readily confirms modern presuppositions of medieval rigidity and prejudice;[2] though (like numerous *chansons de geste*) set in Spain rather than in the Holy Land, the *Roland* seems clearly to illustrate Edward Said's claim of the long history of Europe's demonisation of the Islamic East.[3] In fact, from their inception, the Crusades set identities in motion: unforeseen situations, arising with what must have seemed a bewildering speed, challenged conventional understanding and called for the formation of new identities and practices. In Fulcher's exuberant rendition, we get a taste of the spectrum of religious, ethnic, linguistic, place- and class-based elements available for recombination in the ever-shifting construction of crusader identity.

The Crusades were part of a larger movement of expansionism formative in the making of 'Europe'. Between the years 950 and 1350, conquerors, settlers, and other adventurers from the heartland of the old Carolingian Empire fanned out in what the historian Robert Bartlett has described as an 'aristocratic diaspora'. Recognisable by a cluster of shared institutions and practices (including the use of a standardised Roman liturgy and a military technology centred around heavily armoured cavalry, castles, and siegecraft), these foreigners came to be identified as 'Franks' – originally an ethnic designation now recoded to signify 'aggressive westerner . . . far from home'.[4] In northern and north-eastern Europe, 'Frankish' culture – comprising features as disparate as coins and charters, universities, and onomastic patterns based on the cult of

---

2 *La Chanson de Roland*, 2nd edn, ed. and trans. Ian Short (Paris: Livre de Poche, 1990), line 1015.
3 Edward W. Said, *Orientalism* (New York: Random House, 1978). For an opposing view, see Sharon Kinoshita, 'Deprovincializing the Middle Ages', in Rob Wilson and Christopher Leigh Connery (eds.), *The Worlding Project: Doing Cultural Studies in the Era of Globalization* (Santa Cruz, CA: New Pacific Press, 2007), pp. 61–75.
4 Robert Bartlett, *The Making of Europe: Conquest, Colonization and Cultural Change 950–1350* (Princeton, NJ: Princeton University Press, 1993), pp. 18–21, 70, 101–5.

the universal saints – carried connotations of modernity and power, enticing pagan rulers (and their subjects) to embrace Latin Christianity through acculturation rather than conquest.[5] In the Mediterranean, on the other hand, the emerging culture of Western Europe had little to offer Muslims and Eastern Orthodox Christians with more advanced cultures of their own.

The Crusades were decisive in the Westerners' self-identification as Franks. Urban II's call for an armed expedition to come to the assistance of beleaguered Christians in the East gathered knights from different parts of Latin Europe, speaking a multiplicity of languages and acknowledging the overlordship of different feudal masters. As they made their way toward Jerusalem, this experience of diversity was intensified by their encounters with their Eastern coreligionists. Fulcher of Chartres retrospectively registers this heterogeneity in a passage that conveys a mixed sense of bewilderment and exuberance:

> Who ever heard of such a mixture of languages in one army, since there were French, Flemings, Frisians, Gauls, Allogroges, Lotharingians, Allemani, Bavarians, Normans, English, Scots, Aquitainians, Italians, Dacians, Apulians, Iberians, Bretons, Greeks, and Armenians? If any Breton or Teuton wished to question me, I could neither understand nor answer.[6]

For Fulcher, this serves as an opportunity to highlight the pilgrims' singularity of inspiration and purpose: 'we who were diverse in languages, nevertheless seemed to be brothers in the love of God and very close to being of one mind'.[7] *E pluribus unum*. A similar transformation takes place in the *Chanson de Roland*, where the Frenchmen, Bavarians, Alemans, Normans, Bretons, Poitevins, Auvergnats, Flemings, Frisians, Lorrainers, and Burgundians comprising the battalions of Charlemagne's army (laisses 218–24), even while maintaining their feudal-linguistic identities, are simultaneously sublated in the imagined community of 'douce France'. In the idealised homology of the *Roland*'s religious and political imaginary, to be Christian is inseparable from being Charlemagne's man.[8]

It was in the eastern Mediterranean that Western Europeans came to think of themselves as Franks. Eleventh-century Byzantine writers already used the term to refer to Norman mercenaries; soon both Greeks and Muslims had extended its meaning to include all Western Christians. 'It was this "broad sense" that westerners on the First Crusade came to be willing to apply to

---

5 Ibid., pp. 269–91.   6 Peters, *The First Crusade*, p. 49.   7 Ibid., p. 49.
8 For the internal complexities of this transformation, see Sharon Kinoshita, *Medieval Boundaries: Rethinking Difference in Old French Literature* (Philadelphia: University of Pennsylvania Press, 2006), pp. 29–31.

themselves . . . The name symbolized the desired transcendence of local and ethnic rivalries and rang down the years as the rallying cry to western Christian unity.'[9]

In the long passage with which we began, on the other hand, Fulcher of Chartres focuses less on the emergence of Western Christian unity than on the transformation of 'Occidentals' into 'Orientals'. If the term 'Frank' served to distinguish Latin Christians from their Eastern coreligionists as much as from their Muslim foes, Fulcher, in contrast, underscores their easy and speedy integration through intermarriage (taking wives among Syrians, Armenians, and 'even Saracens who have received the grace of baptism'), linguistic exchange, acculturation, and the irresistible attraction of vast estates and 'countless besants'.

How accurate is this image? What are we to make of the claim of the whole-sale transformation of immigrants from Rheims or Chartres into Galilaeans and Palestinians? Epistemologically speaking, one of the greatest challenges the crusaders faced was their encounter with the indigenous Christians of the eastern Mediterranean. At least at first, the newcomers 'were alarmed by the religious diversity of the Christian world of the Middle East. Turks and Muslims they were prepared for, but for Armenians, Greeks, and Jacobites they were not'.[10] The early stages of contact between crusaders and the 'Eastern brethren' that Pope Urban II had called upon them to support resulted in what one historian has called 'close encounters of the ambiguous kind'.[11] The first such challenge came from crusader contact with Byzantine Greece. The First Crusade had been launched in response to an appeal for military assistance made by Emperor Alexios I in the wake of Byzantine losses to the Seljuk Turks – a request Urban had transmogrified into the call to aid Christian 'brothers living in the Orient'.[12] Once the first waves of armed pilgrims reached Constantinople, however, any feeling of common cause linking Eastern and Western Christians began to splinter in the face of political rivalries and cultural difference. Latin leaders bristled at Alexios's assertion of lordship over any territories they might reconquer and at Byzantine willingness to negotiate with the Saracen foe. By the time of the Second Crusade (1147–8), a French bishop accompanying the forces of King Louis VII could vituperate against their Byzantine allies, condemning Constantinople as 'Christian

9 Bartlett, *The Making of Europe*, p. 104.
10 Christopher MacEvitt, *The Crusades and the Christian World of the East: Rough Tolerance* (Philadelphia: University of Pennsylvania Press, 2008), pp. 22–3.
11 This is the title of chapter 2 of MacEvitt's *Rough Tolerance*.
12 Peters, *The First Crusade*, 30.

only in name' and calling for its conquest.[13] Old French literature renders this undercurrent of hostility in the mid-twelfth-century parodic epic *Le Pèlerinage de Charlemagne*. In this text, a comic prequel to the *Chanson de Roland*, the Frankish emperor undertakes a pilgrimage to the East expressly to take the measure, literally, of the Greek king, Hugh the Strong; after suffering a series of humiliations, the Franks flood Constantinople and wreak havoc in the royal palace – with Charlemagne standing a full foot and three inches taller than his chastened rival. In Chrétien de Troyes's 'Byzantine' romance, *Cligés*, the half-Greek, half-Arthurian titular protagonist cuckolds his paternal uncle, Alis, before eventually replacing him as emperor of Constantinople.

Latin ambivalence toward the Byzantine Greeks reached a breaking point in 1204 when the forces of the Fourth Crusade, originally intended to recover Jerusalem (lost to Saladin in 1187), sacked the city of Constantinople instead. This extraordinary turn of events was recounted in vernacular French prose by two eyewitness participants: Geoffrey of Villehardouin, *maréchal* of Champagne and one of the Crusade's central organisers; and Robert de Clari, a simple Picard knight in the retinue of Pierre of Amiens. Modern historians have long dismissed Clari's account as 'naïve' and therefore of little historical interest, preferring Villehardouin's version as the more authoritative.[14] But however apparently credulous, Robert's text reveals the fissures the Fourth Crusade provoked in the feudal imaginary; in the course of his narrative, the powerful betray the poor, and traditional values such as lineage, chivalry, and lord–vassal relations break down or are challenged.[15]

Equally disconcerting, if in different ways, was crusader contact with the other indigenous eastern Mediterranean Christians. Such ambivalence is understandable: the *Chanson de Roland*, for example, places the Armenians (Ermines) – together with the Moors (Mors) – in the sixth of the pagan emir Baligant's thirty battalions (line 3227). Yet, reversing received notions on the segregation of crusader society, recent historiography has begun to build a case for the extent of the Latins' 'religious and cultural interaction' with Eastern Christians such as the Jacobites, Armenians, and Copts.[16] The Frankish Levant was 'a world in which religious and social identities were flexible'.[17] In contrast to a 'clash of civilisations' or an Orientalist model opposing a

---

13 Odo of Deuil, *De Profectione Ludovici VII in Orientem / The Journey of Louis VII to the East*, ed. and trans. Virginia Gingerick Berry (New York: Columbia University Press, 1948), pp. 68–9.
14 See Chapter 11, pp. 102–10.   15 Kinoshita, *Medieval Boundaries*, pp. 139–75.
16 Benjamin Z. Kedar, 'Latins and Oriental Christians in the Frankish Levant, 1099–1291', in *Franks, Muslims and Oriental Christians in the Latin Levant* (Aldershot: Ashgate, 2006), selection v (esp. p. 220).
17 MacEvitt, *Rough Tolerance*, p. 14.

Western self to an Eastern other, interactions between crusaders and indigenous Christians were local and ad hoc; neither side developed a rhetoric
of 'us' and 'them' or attributed 'lasting symbolic significance [to] inci-
dences of conflict'.[18] The result was a permeability that 'allowed a Frankish . . . count . . . to have an Armenian priest as his confessor without either
having converted, a Latin family to build a shrine to a Jacobite saint who
healed their child, or a Melkite bishop to request that he be buried as a Latin
Hospitaller' – a mode of coexistence the historian Christopher MacEvitt has
termed 'rough tolerance'.[19]

To a certain extent, a similar kind of 'rough tolerance' shaped crusader
relations with local Muslims, particularly at higher social levels. 'Both on
the Christian and on the Muslim side an appreciation of the enemies' ability as combatants and their merits as human beings took shape and certain
enemy leaders, notably Richard I and Saladin, acquired reputations for laud-
able behaviour that persisted for generations'.[20] In a famous passage from his
memoirs, the twelfth-century Syrian prince Usamah ibn Munqidh records his
relationship with a Frankish knight in the army of King Fulk of Jerusalem:
'He was of my intimate fellowship and kept such constant company with me
that he began to call me "my brother". Between us were mutual bonds of
amity and friendship.'[21] Coming from opposite sides of the Christian–Muslim
divide, the two are nevertheless linked in a brotherhood of shared attitudes,
values, and forms of life. A literary example occurs in the late twelfth-century
'rebel baron' epic, *Raoul de Cambrai*. Taken prisoner in a Saracen raid on the
pilgrimage town of Saint-Gilles, the northern French knight Bernier de Ver-
mandois finds himself on the receiving end of a remarkable offer: now at war
with a rival pagan king, his captor, Corsuble, turns to Bernier and, addressing
him as 'Crestiie[n]s, frere', offers him gold, silver, and silk in return for his
military assistance.[22] After Bernier fights and kills the attacker, a delighted
Corsuble offers him half his kingdom to remain in his permanent service.
(Bernier declines, returning to northern France instead.) Such interconfes-
sional exchange had its limits: when his Frankish 'brother' offers to take
his son 'into the land of the Franks' to 'see the knights and learn wisdom
and chivalry', Usamah is horrified, judging that captivity would be less of a

---

18 Ibid., p. 22.   19 Ibid., pp. 22–3.
20 Norman Housley, *Contesting the Crusades* (Malden, MA: Blackwell, 2006), p. 159.
21 *An Arab-Syrian Gentleman and Warrior in the Period of the Crusades: Memoirs of Usamah ibn-Munqidh*, trans. Philip K. Hitti (Princeton, NJ: Princeton University Press, 1987), p. 161.
22 *Raoul de Cambrai*, ed. Sarah Kay (Oxford: Clarendon Press, 1992), lines 6733 and 7507. For historical examples of such alliances, see Kinoshita, *Medieval Boundaries*, pp. 19 and 242 n. 18.

misfortune; he gracefully declines the offer by saying he has sworn an oath to the boy's grandmother that they should never be parted from him – an explanation the Frank readily understands and accepts.[23]

A fascinating sequel to Villehardouin's and Clari's chronicles of the Fourth Crusade is Jean de Joinville's *Vie de Saint Louis*, a secular hagiography of the saint-king Louis IX (ruled 1226–70). Begun at the behest of the French queen (Louis's granddaughter-in-law) Jeanne de Navarre and dedicated to her son, the future Louis X of France, the *Vie* focuses primarily on the king's long sojourn in the eastern Mediterranean during the Seventh Crusade and its aftermath (1248–54). The intervening years had brought not only Louis's death (on the disastrous Eighth Crusade to Tunis in 1270) and canonisation (1297), but the fall of Acre – the last crusader outpost in the Holy Land – to the Mamluks in 1291, bringing nearly two hundred years of Western presence in the territories collectively known as 'Outremer' to an end.[24] Thus when an aging Jean de Joinville presented his reminiscences of his old friend and master to the young king of Navarre in 1309, he was evoking a world that must already have been tinged with nostalgia.

In the dedicatory preface to the *Vie de Saint Louis*, Joinville divides his work into two parts: the first devoted to the king's piety ('how he lived his whole life according to God and the church' ['comment il se gouverna tout son tens selonc Dieu et selonc l'Eglise']), the second to his chivalry – that is, to his exploits in Outremer. For Joinville, one particular aspect of the king's 'granz chevaleries' stands out: 'four times I saw him risk his life in order to save his people from harm' ('je li vi quatre foiz mettre son cors en aventure de mort . . . pour espargnier le doumage de son peuple').[25] Of all the adventures Joinville witnessed in his many years at Louis's side, this for him is the purest summation of the king's valour and character.

The extraordinary thing about the four incidents he goes on to describe, however, is that in each case Louis risks his life in direct defiance of the advice of his vassals. As the royal fleet first nears the Egyptian coast at Damietta, for example, 'his entire council advised him' ('tout son conseil li loa') to remain on board ship, pending the outcome of the initial skirmish; but the king 'wouldn't listen to anyone' ('ne voult nullui croire'), and, jumping into the water with sword in hand, leads the charge to shore.[26] On the one hand, this dramatic act

---

23 *An Arab-Syrian Gentleman*, p. 159.
24 On the effects of the fall of Acre, see Housley, 'Crusading after 1291', in *Contesting the Crusades*, pp. 122–43.
25 Jean de Joinville, *Vie de Saint Louis*, ed. and trans. Jacques Monfrin (Paris: Livre de Poche, 1995), p. 146.
26 Ibid., pp. 146–8.

seems just the sort of heroic gesture one would want from a Crusade leader. Yet the fact that the king 'ne voult nullui croire' would surely have caught the attention of a contemporary audience, for *consilium* – though cast, along with *auxilium* (military aid), as one of the obligations a vassal owed his overlord – was, reciprocally, a kind of feudal prerogative ensuring that the lord would act only with the consensus of his vassals. Before taking the cross, Louis had behaved like a conventional king: in preparing a campaign against the English, he had dutifully followed 'his good mother's counsel and that of the worthy men of the time of his father and grandfather' ('le conseil de la bone mere . . . et des preudeshomes . . . du tens son pere et du temps son ayoul').[27] (Joinville's language is vaguely reminiscent of the opening scene of Chrétien de Troyes's *Erec et Enide*, with King Arthur's insistence on 'keeping and maintaining' the 'custom and practices' of his father, Uther Pendragon, and lineage.[28]) Now he begins openly to disregard the advice of his council, repeatedly disdaining his barons' advice and counsel. In Joinville's retrospective account, Louis's saintliness and good kingship (in contrast to Charlemagne's in the *Chanson de Roland*) are made to reside precisely in his *trespass* of feudal identities and institutions.

A curious reversal, on the other hand, attends King Louis's relations with the Mongols, who had burst into Latin Europe's consciousness with their lightning raids into eastern Europe in 1238–40. Accounts of their conquests evoked terror – tempered by rumours of the invaders' (sympathy towards) Christianity, which raised tantalising prospects of an anti-Saracen Latin–'Tartar' alliance. During his stay in Cyprus, King Louis receives messengers from 'the great king of the Tartars' (presumably Möngke) who, with 'many good and gracious words', offer Mongol assistance in conquering the Holy Land and liberating Jerusalem. In return, the king dispatches two 'Saracen'-speaking Dominicans bearing a lavishly decorated tent meant to serve as a chapel. When the Dominicans return many months later, the king is horrified to learn the use that has been made of his offering:

> [Q]uant le grant roy des Tartarins ot receu les messages et les presens, il envoia querre . . . pluseurs roys qui n'estoient pas encore venus a sa merci, et leur fist tendre la chapelle et leur dit en tel maniere: 'Seigneur, le roy de France est venu en nostre sugestion, et vez ci le treü que il nous envoie; et se vous ne venez en nostre merci, nous l'envoierons querre pour vous confondre.'

27 Ibid., p. 210.
28 Chrétien de Troyes, *Romans*, ed. Michel Zink (Paris: Livre de Poche, 1994), p. 117, lines 1800–10.

Assés en y ot de ceulz qui, pour la poour du roy de France, se mistrent en la merci de celi roy.[29]

([W]hen the great king of the Tartars had received the envoys and gifts, he summoned . . . several kings who had not yet submitted to him. For their benefit, he had the tent pitched and said: 'Lords, the king of France has subjected himself to us; see here the tent he sends us. And if you do not submit to us, we'll send for him to destroy you.' There were many who, out of fear of the king of France, submitted to this king.)

If crusading had inspired Louis to suspend the traditional practice of *consilium*, he is here recast as a tributary subject whose *auxilium* (military aid) the Great Khan uses to threaten recalcitrant kings. Worse still are the letters brought by the Mongols accompanying the Western envoys, explicitly interpellating the French king as Möngke's vassal:

Avec les messages le roy vindrent li leur, si aporterent lettres de leur grant roy au roy de France qui disoient ainsi: 'Bone chose est de pez, quar en terre de pez manguent cil qui vont a quatre piez l'erbe paissant, cil qui vont a deus labrourent la terre, dont les biens viennent, passiblement. Et ceste chose te mandons nous pour toy aviser car tu ne peus avoir pez se tu ne l'as a nous . . . Se te mandons que tu nous envoies tant de ton or et de ton argent chascun an que tu nous retieignes a amis, et se tu ne le fais, nous destruirons toy et ta gent aussi comme nous avons fait ceulz que nous avons devant nommer.'[30]

(The king's messengers were accompanied by theirs, bringing the king of France letters from their Great King that said: 'Peace is a good thing, for in a land at peace, four-legged creatures graze peacefully; two-legged creatures peacefully till the earth, from which all goods come. We send you this to warn you that you can have no peace if you are not at peace with us . . . We order you to send us as much gold and silver as it takes to keep us as your friends; if you don't, we'll destroy you and your people, just as we have destroyed those [kings] previously mentioned.')

No wonder that, as Joinville tersely concludes, Louis 'strongly repented of having made contact with him' ('se repenti fort quant yl y envoia').[31]

---

29 Joinville, *Vie de Saint Louis*, pp. 434, 436.   30 Ibid., p. 436.   31 Ibid.

11

Rhetoric and historiography: Villehardouin's *La Conquête de Constantinople*

NOAH D. GUYNN

Like their modern counterparts, medieval historians operated under epistemological and methodological constraints governing evidence. They perceived critical differences between real events (*res factae*) and fictional narratives (*fabulae*), and deemed certain forms of testimony and modes of representation more appropriate to historiography than others. Nevertheless, a wide gulf separates medieval *scriptores rerum* from modern documentary historians. Whereas the latter are concerned with verifiable, referential propositions about the past and hope to restrict as much as possible the 'distortions' of aesthetics and style, the former would have been baffled by the notion of a strictly factual presentation of events and emphasised instead rhetorical techniques of figuration, persuasion, and moralisation. In this respect, they take their lead from Roman predecessors, especially Sallust, whose speeches, though attributed to historical actors, were legitimately understood by medieval readers as models of oratorical invention. Cicero justifies rhetorical history in the *De oratore*, arguing that historians must be 'exornatores rerum' (ornamenters of things done), rather than 'tantummodo narratores' (mere relaters of facts) (*De oratore*, 2.12.54). Quintilian likewise argues that historians should alleviate the tediousness of factual reporting with a liberal, vivid use of figures (*Institutio oratoria*, 10.1.31). The seventh-century encyclopaedist Isidore of Seville augurs a change in Western historiography when he argues for the priority of eyewitness testimony over second-hand sources, content over form. Yet like all medieval thinkers, he also believes that sublime truth (*veritas*) takes precedence over the merely true (*verus*), metaphysical beliefs over empirical observation.[1] History in the Middle Ages is thus not a factual, evenemential

---

1 See J. Beer, *Narrative Conventions of Truth in the Middle Ages* (Geneva: Droz, 1981), pp. 9–11, citing Isidore of Seville, *Etymologiae*, line 41, 10.v.274.

chronology valued for its own sake, rather a rhetorical disposition in which facts and testimonies have been sifted, altered, and reorganised in order to illuminate providential design and naturalise prevailing ideologies. Medieval historians – like *all* historians – not only translated experience into narrative but also translated narrative into power by controlling the ways in which the past was remembered. They could be unusually flexible in the first instance, since they understood worldly events as subsumed to, and determined by, otherworldly essences. As a result, they were remarkably successful in the second instance, creating stylised narratives of the past that efficiently served the ideological needs of the present.

Taking medieval historiographical theory as a point of departure, I will present here a rhetorical and ideological analysis of the earliest original Old French prose history: Geoffroi de Villehardouin's *La Conquête de Constantinople*, an eyewitness account of the Fourth Crusade written after the death of its leader, Boniface de Montferrat, in 1207. Scholars have long recognised the importance of this work, and have nearly always preferred it to another eyewitness history of the same events by Robert de Clari.[2] Whereas Villehardouin was a high-ranking officer with an insider's perspective on operations and diplomacy, Clari was a petty knight who witnessed the Crusade from the standpoint of the rank and file. Clari's style is usually described as naïve, subjective, and digressive, and therefore as impeding a factual reconstruction of events. By contrast, modern readers typically revere Villehardouin for his reputed plainspokenness, sobriety, and sincerity, and for the light they believe he sheds on the unusually murky historical problems of the Fourth Crusade. Sometimes referred to as the 'ungodly' or 'unholy' Crusade (though one wonders which were the godly, holy ones!), the Fourth failed in its original goal, to retake Jerusalem, and instead devastated two Christian cities, Zara and Constantinople, and established an ill-fated Latin Empire in Byzantium. Seeking explanations for this astonishing outcome, many scholars have embraced a modified version of what they take to be Villehardouin's thesis: that the Crusade's trajectory was the result of accident and circumstance rather than conspiracy and design. Those scholars who are attuned to rhetorical techniques in the *Conquête* often dismiss them as extrinsic rather than intrinsic, or as insignificant with respect to the factual information the text contains.[3] Those who are unconcerned with structure and style often assume that the

2 S. Kinoshita offers a corrective in *Medieval Boundaries: Rethinking Difference in Old French Literature* (Philadelphia: University of Pennsylvania Press, 2006), pp. 139–75.
3 A crucial exception is J. Beer's still-unsurpassed *Villehardouin: Epic Historian* (Geneva: Droz, 1968).

Conquête rests upon a bedrock of fact that is virtually undisturbed by rhetorical or ideological manoeuvring.

My own approach to the *Conquête* is quite different and embraces two principal claims. First, I argue that though Villehardouin's history is indeed sparing in its use of figures, it is hardly uninflected, in particular where the use of providential explanation, direct discourse, and prose narration are concerned. My second argument is based on an axiom derived from cultural materialism, namely that aesthetic forms and modes of domination are inextricably linked. I believe the rhetorical and structural design of the *Conquête* works not only to justify the actions of the crusading army retroactively but also to bolster aristocratic ideologies in a period of destabilising change. In other words, Villehardouin's stylistic choices have less to do with transparency than with transferring historical knowledge and political power into the hands of his readers: northern French and Flemish lords whose traditional rights were eroding under pressure from Philip Augustus's proto-nationalist rule. Gabrielle Spiegel argues that anti-royalist ideologies motivate both form and content in early thirteenth-century vernacular histories, especially six Old French translations of the *Pseudo-Turpin Chronicle*.[4] The original Latin text, purportedly Bishop Turpin's eyewitness account of Charlemagne's expedition to Spain, represents an attempt by the clergy to moralise and restrain chivalric literature. French translators turn the *Pseudo-Turpin* history to different purposes: celebrating aristocratic virtue, reclaiming Charlemagne as forebear and peer, and laying claim to prose as a privileged medium for depicting historical truths. Spiegel views this defence of prose as ideological rather than merely stylistic – as an appropriation of the discursive and intellectual authority of *clergie* on behalf of an embattled aristocracy. I will advance a similar claim regarding the *Conquête*, in which Villehardouin uses prose history to commemorate and justify a Crusade spearheaded by the same aristocratic families who commissioned the *Pseudo-Turpin* translations. In my view, Villehardouin is invested less in the supposed lucidity of prose than in the ideological, mystifying power of ecclesiastical rhetoric and historiography.

Let me begin by summarising Villehardouin's version of the 'accidental' conquest of Constantinople.[5] Lacking ships, the crusaders (with Villehardouin

---

4 G. Spiegel, *Romancing the Past: The Rise of Vernacular Prose Historiography in Thirteenth-Century France* (Berkeley: University of California Press, 1993), esp. pp. 55–98.
5 The parenthetical citations that follow refer to paragraph numbers in *La Conquête de Constantinople*, ed. E. Faral, 2 vols. (Paris: Les Belles Lettres, 1973), and page numbers in *Memoirs of the Crusades*, trans. F. T. Marzials (New York: Dutton, 1958).

serving as one of six envoys) negotiate a contract with Enrico Dandolo, Doge of Venice, to build them a fleet. As it happens, the number of ships requested is vastly too high given how many crusaders assemble in the Veneto. Here and throughout the *Conquête*, Villehardouin bitterly denounces those who betray feudal and religious obligations by travelling to Jerusalem 'by other ways, and from other ports' (¶ 51, p. 14). Unable to meet the terms of the contract, the crusaders are obliged to compensate the Venetians by helping them reclaim the city of Zara, which has rebelled against their dominion. After sacking Zara, the crusaders receive envoys from Philip of Swabia and his brother-in-law Alexius, an exiled Byzantine prince whose father, Isaac II, has had his throne usurped by his younger brother, Alexius III. The crusaders are told that if they are willing to help Prince Alexius claim the throne, he will reward them with money and supplies, an ally in the East, and reconciliation between the Greek and Roman churches. Fearful that the expedition will fail without this alliance, many crusaders promote an attack on Constantinople as a temporary, just, and tactically necessary diversion; ultimately, they prevail over their opponents. After sacking Constantinople a first time and installing the exiled prince as Alexius IV, a series of unanticipated events (including Alexius's failure to fulfil the terms of the treaty) lead to a second sacking of the city and the establishment of a Latin Empire in Byzantium under the rule of Baudouin de Flandres. The new empire is swiftly overwhelmed by Greek rebellions, foreign assaults, and territorial conflicts between Baudouin and Boniface de Montferrat. The second half of the *Conquête* reports a succession of victories and defeats for the Franks, culminating in the death of Boniface in a battle against the Bulgarians.

Despite intense suspicion of Villehardouin by nineteenth- and early twentieth-century treason theorists, most scholars today accept a modified version of the 'theory of accidents' as an explanation for the course of the Crusade: there was no conspiracy to divert the Franks; rather they were caught up in a web of events they could not have predicted and over which they had little control. These scholars argue, moreover, that Villehardouin's history is in general factually accurate and lacks only an awareness of deeper historical causes leading to conflict between Venice and Byzantium. Indeed, many have claimed that Villehardouin anticipates modern documentary history by avoiding stylistic embellishments and presenting a strictly chronological progression from event to event. Jean Frappier's reading is typical. He argues that the 'quality' of Villehardouin's information is beyond doubt, as are his 'sincerity' and 'good faith'. Villehardouin provides 'a clear idea of the causes and effects that, by virtue of internal necessity, led the crusaders to seize

Constantinople and remain there'. And though this emphasis on a 'logical and chronological succession of acts' may not constitute 'a solid guarantee of impartiality', the *Conquête* nevertheless represents a 'victory of history over rhetoric'.[6]

Much recent scholarship leaves Frappier's thesis unchallenged. Literary critic Peter Noble cites Villehardouin's claim that he has not lied 'by one word to his knowledge' and adds, 'there is no reason to doubt this assertion'.[7] Though Villehardouin occasionally suppresses information in order to shield the crusaders from censure, his 'facts are, as far as they can be checked, accurate', and 'his style is sober and undramatic'. Ultimately, then, the *Conquête* presents 'the truth' if not 'the whole truth'.[8] The most respected contemporary historians of the Fourth Crusade, Donald Queller and Thomas Madden, likewise consider Villehardouin's history to be 'relatively accurate and quite specific'. Though Villehardouin is not a 'trained historian', his 'mind' is 'well-organized and clear', his narrative linear and straightforward; and there is even reason to believe he used official documents and a private journal in reconstructing events after the fact. Indeed, Queller and Madden's history reads very much like a vindication of Villehardouin: they adopt the *Conquête*'s narrative sequence, quote passages of direct discourse as if they were transcriptions of actual speeches (often with nothing more than an endnote to indicate provenance), and present their study as a meticulous recreation of the Crusade from the crusaders' own perspective: 'We have tried, as far as possible, to march along with [them], to become observers in their councils, to view events as they saw them.'[9]

It would be difficult to describe this statement as evidence of intellectual neutrality, and a good deal might be said about Queller and Madden's tendentious approach to documentary history. More to the point, construing the *Conquête* as a relatively uninflected record of lived experience means disregarding medieval conceptions of the nature and function of historical narrative. For medieval chroniclers (including Villehardouin), the truth of temporal events derives not from factual reporting but from the instantiation

---

6 J. Frappier, *Histoire, mythes, et symboles: études de littérature française* (Geneva: Droz, 1976), pp. 57, 69, 83.
7 Peter Noble, 'The Importance of Old French Chronicles as Historical Sources of the Fourth Crusade and the Early Latin Empire of Constantinople', *Journal of Medieval History* 27 (2001), pp. 399–416 at pp. 409, 410, citing Villehardouin (¶ 20, pp. 29–30).
8 Ibid., pp. 409, 410.
9 D. E. Queller and T. F. Madden, *The Fourth Crusade: The Conquest of Constantinople*, 2nd edn (Philadelphia: University of Pennsylvania Press, 1997), pp. 18, ix.

of universal, theological paradigms. In the *Conquête*, this is made clear by the Crusade envoys' description of their expedition as a divinely ordained mission 'to avenge the shame done to Jesus Christ' (¶ 18, p. 5; see also ¶ 27, p. 7) and by Villehardouin's frequent references to God's foresight and protective care over the crusaders. Having arrived in Venice, the Franks despair that 'the host must fail and go to pieces'; but Villehardouin and God know better: 'God, who advises those who have been ill-advised, would not so suffer it' (¶ 61, p. 16). The Almighty subsequently facilitates the capture of Zara (¶ 86, p. 21), with apparent disregard for a papal interdiction barring the attack, as well as both assaults on Constantinople (¶¶ 181, 242; pp. 44, 61). Villehardouin's conviction that Yahweh is on his side remains unshaken even when the crusaders suffer devastating losses at Adrianople and Rusium (¶¶ 360, 408; pp. 94, 108). Whatever accidental events may befall the host, the course of history finds its ultimate significance in providential teleology; and even if the Crusade leaders did not anticipate the end of their mission at its beginning, they certainly believed God would illuminate the righteousness and inevitability of their actions in the fullness of time. Put another way, providence is not merely a theological doctrine but also a historiographical method. Far from being a simple chronology of events recorded as they transpired, the *Conquête* was written retrospectively and with a specific audience in mind. It is not an artless, unbiased transcription of fact, but a stylised, naturalistic narrative in which events betoken divine intentions and God serves as guarantor of baronial achievement and virtue.

Villehardouin's extensive use of direct and collective discourse can also be linked to a rhetorical and ideological vindication of the Crusade. The passages describing negotiations between Franks and Venetians are particularly rich in dramatic, calculated, efficacious oratory. During the initial negotiations, when Villehardouin exhorts the Venetians to 'take pity on Jerusalem' and the envoys kneel at their feet weeping, 'the Doge and all the others burst into tears of pity and compassion, and cried with one voice, and lifted up their hands, saying: "We consent, we consent!" Then was there so great a noise and tumult that it seemed as if the earth itself were falling to pieces' (¶¶ 27–8, pp. 7–8). During the second set of negotiations, after the crusaders have agreed to attack Zara, Dandolo attends Mass at San Marco's and grandly proposes that he take part in 'the highest enterprise ever undertaken' (¶ 65, p. 16) and lead the Venetian troops into battle. 'When [his people] had heard him, they cried with one voice: "We pray you by God that you consent, and do it, and that you come with us!"' (¶ 66, p. 17). The image of Dandolo (who was blind and in his nineties) kneeling before the altar as a cross is sewn on to his hat evokes strong feelings and is used to inspire new faith in a faltering, diverted Crusade:

> Very great was then the pity and compassion on the part of the people of the land and of the pilgrims; and many were the tears shed, because that worthy and good man would have had so much reason to remain behind, for he was an old man, and albeit his eyes were unclouded, yet he saw naught having lost his sight through a wound in the head. He was of great heart. Ah! how little like him were those who had gone to other ports to escape the danger.
>
> (¶ 67, p. 17)

> (Mult ot illuec grant pitié del pueple de la terre et des pelerins et mainte lerme plorée, porce que cil prodom aüst si grant ochoison de remanoir; car viels hom ere; et si avoit les iaulç en la teste biaus et si n'en veoit gote, que perdue avoit la veüe par une plaie qu'il ot el chief. Mult par ere de grant cuer. Ha! Cum mal le sembloient cil qui a autres porz estoient alé por eschiver le peril!)

In these instances, the merging of multiple voices into a *vox populi* and the expression of fellow feeling are direct responses to oratory and have unmistakable tactical goals: to signify the reunification of the host and condemn defections; to incorporate the diversion to Zara into the crusaders' sacred mission; and to construct a highly potent, earth-shaking consensus consonant with feudal and religious values. Dramatic oratory is used to mitigate the fundamental problem of the Crusade (the army's failure to coalesce) and to justify the course of events; it should not be mistaken for verbatim transcription.

This conclusion is borne out by Villehardouin's use of direct discourse at moments when the military and moral integrity of the crusade is most seriously in doubt. God's sanctioning of the sack of Zara is established proleptically through the voice of the crusaders, who marvel at the city's fortifications and wonder aloud, 'How could such a city be taken by force, save by the help of God himself?' (¶ 77, p. 19). Those Franks who purportedly wish to disband the Crusade encourage the Zarans to resist (¶ 81, p. 20) and are supported in this by the abbot of Vaux: 'Lords, I forbid you, on the part of the Pope of Rome, to attack this city; for those within it are Christians, and you are pilgrims' (¶ 83, pp. 20–1). Dandolo, however, terminates the debate by reminding the Franks, 'You have convenanted to help me . . . and I summon you to do so' (¶ 83, p. 21). Before initiating the assault, the counts and barons jointly deplore 'the outrage of those who have caused this agreement to be broken' and condemn them along with those who from the beginning have 'tried to break up the host' (¶ 84, p. 21). Predictably enough, the messengers who subsequently travel to Rome to request absolution from the pope also speak as one, successfully justifying the assault on Zara as the result of earlier defections: 'The barons cry mercy to you for the capture of Zara, for they acted as people who could do no better, owing to the default of those who had gone to other ports, and because, had they not acted as they did, they could not have held the host together' (¶ 106, p. 26). Though Villehardouin could not have witnessed this speech, it contains his trademark phrase 'other ports'; it is plainly his invention, and it evinces the rhetorical and ideological force of verbal and thematic repetition.

Villehardouin shares his predilection for direct discourse with the *Pseudo-Turpin* translators, who, according to Spiegel, 'replaced the indirect discourse of the Latin text with direct speech, in an obvious attempt to enliven the narrative'.[10] This kind of rhetorical elaboration belies the claim, articulated by the translators themselves, that prose is less contorted and more truthful than verse. Spiegel ably demonstrates that we cannot take these truth claims at face value; after all, the *Pseudo-Turpin* translations are larded with material cribbed from sources such as the *Roland*, and therefore could not have been mistaken for unembellished eyewitness testimony. More to the point, prose is not *actually* more transparent than verse, and the claim that it is should be interpreted as yet another rhetorical tactic. In the Middle Ages, historiography centred more on the historian's skills and the circumstances of his writing than events themselves; indeed, *res factae* were understood not as raw facts but as opportunities for embroidery and edification. Rather than construing the *Pseudo-Turpin* translations as transparent and unbiased history, then, medieval readers probably read them much as Spiegel does: as 'a verbal substitute for a social past irretrievably lost' and 'a partisan record intended to serve the interest of a particular social group'.[11]

Given the many links between the *Pseudo-Turpin* and the *Conquête*, it seems reasonable to conclude that Villehardouin, too, used prose less as an instrument of clarity than as a rhetorically and ideologically inflected signifying practice. Indeed, the choice of prose may have implicitly suggested what Villehardouin never fully articulates in his history: that Pope Innocent's call for a new Crusade was addressed to four kings, none of whom took part in military actions. Twice, Villehardouin has sovereign figures (Dandolo and Alexius III) refer to the Crusade leaders as the 'greatest' of 'men uncrowned' (¶¶ 16, 143; pp. 5, 34–5). Might this phrase signal not just the valour and piety of those leaders but also the oppressive rule of *crowned* men, including Philip Augustus himself? Might Villehardouin's obsession with keeping the

10 Spiegel, *Romancing the Past*, pp. 95–6.   11 Ibid., pp. 81, 96.

host together serve as a rallying cry to secure baronial power against a tyrant? Might we understand the power struggle between Emperor Baudouin and Boniface de Montferrat as mirroring conflicts between the French monarch and aristocratic rivals? It is certainly difficult to imagine that Villehardouin's status as a member of a beleaguered elite writing for and about members of that elite did not somehow shape his account of the Fourth Crusade. My argument is less that he falsified evidence in order to mislead his readers than that he used stylistic devices to bring about cohesion among them: 'Now be it known to you, lords, that if God had not loved the host, it could never have held together, seeing how many people wished evil to it!' (¶ 104, p. 25). He was powerless to halt the project of royal consolidation that famously culminated in a victory for the monarchy at Bouvines in 1214, or the eventual demise of the Latin Empire, which fell in 1261. Still, Villehardouin evidently understood, as would royal historians at Chantilly and Saint-Denis several decades later, that rhetorical, providential history was a potent tool for narrating the past and imagining, if not actually securing, the future.

12

Humour and the obscene

JAMES R. SIMPSON

'Et scis tu qualiter fuit factus Deus?' et dictus Raimundus respondit: 'Ego dicam tibi: factus fuit *foten e mardan*', et hoc dicens percutens unam manum suam cum alia, et ipse, ut dixit, respondit dicto Raimundo quod male dicebat, et quod propter predicta verba deberet occidi.[1]

[Raymond Segui of Tignac asked] 'And do you know how God was made?' and the aforementioned Raymond [de l'Aire] answered, 'I will tell you: he was made *fucking and shitting*', and when he said this he struck one hand against the other. And [Raymond Segui] answered that he spoke ill and should be killed for saying these things.[2]

If only to judge from its influence on later periods, the Middle Ages clearly produced a striking wealth of both comic and obscene material. Some measure of the power and impact of these traditions can be gleaned from Geoffrey Chaucer's clear sense that the *Canterbury Tales* would be incomplete without either tortuously contrived, French-inspired arse-kissing or episodes lifted wholesale from the *Roman de Renart*.[3] Likewise, Molière clearly regarded French *fabliaux* (verse comic narratives) and their medieval stage cousins, the *farces* and *sotties*, as sure-fire plotline blueprints (*Le Médecin malgré lui*, for example, deriving from 'Le Vilain mire'), these texts also forming the basis of compilations such as *Les Cent Nouvelles Nouvelles* and the *Decameron*. In addition, there survive parody love lyrics, whether in the *langue d'oc* or *d'oïl*, alongside more extended works. Among these figure the prosimetric idyll, *Aucassin et Nicolette*, along with irreverent views of the Arthurian court

---

1 Jean Duvernoy (ed.), *Le Registre d'inquisition de Jacques Fournier, évêque de Pamiers (1318–1325): manuscrit Vat. Latin 4030 de la Bibliothèque Vaticane*, 3 vols. (Toulouse: Privat, 1972), II, p. 120.
2 Translation after Emmanuel Le Roy Ladurie, *Montaillou: Cathars and Catholics in a French Village 1294–1324*, trans. Barbara Bray (Harmondsworth: Penguin, 1980), p. 144.
3 The *Nun's Priest's Tale* is a translation of *Le Roman de Renart*, branche II's tale of the fox playing on the cockerel's vanity to snatch him in his jaws, only to be fooled in turn when Chantecler reveals the fox to be prone to the same vice, suggesting to his captor that it would damage his reputation for wit if he failed to taunt the hounds pursuing him.

and its ways, such as *Le Chevalier à l'épée*, in which Gauvain is derided and humiliated to no edifying end, or *Le Mantel mautaillé*, an obscene Cinderella story of the ladies at Arthur's court trying on a magical coat that only fits the chaste and faithful, with only a minor courtier – Galeta, beloved of Carados – fitting the bill. Similarly, the sprawling textual tradition of *Le Roman de la rose*, a modulating synthesis of love themes into an encyclopaedic allegorical reflection, can be seen as evidence of not just intellectual and creative verve but also an inability to take itself anything like seriously, unleashing perhaps the greatest literary quarrel of the later Middle Ages in France. Among the mock epic material we might cite the comic and burlesque episodes of the William Cycle: *La Chanson de Guillaume*'s proto-Rabelaisian portrait of the mighty giant kitchen-boy, Rainouart, or William himself bursting his borrowed merchant boots in *Le Charroi de Nîmes*. More extreme is the scatological mock epic, *Audigier*, where hero and heroine meet while squatting in a ditch. Beyond this, parodic revisionings and refashionings proliferate: mock 'wisdom literature' (e.g. parodic proverbs and pedagogical dialogues) and religious parodies (e.g. rewritings of the *paternoster*, or *Les Quinze Joies du mariage*, a parody of the meditation on the fifteen joys of the Virgin). A final striking example here is the mock testamentary tradition, notably represented in François Villon's *Testament*, a rich tapestry of comic crudity, whether drunks walking smack into lampposts, flatulence in bed or homosexual innuendo. In short, any genre or discourse in the Middle Ages has a comic double. It is therefore no accident that medieval sources or prototypes exist for almost every gag in *Monty Python and the Holy Grail*. To take a more serious example, the three manuscript families of the *Roman de Renart* playfully re-use and echo the prologue attributed to the putative originator, Pierre de St Cloud, as a springboard into a range of genres and discourses. Pierre's burlesque opening announces Renart's 'great fornication' with Hersent the she-wolf and the 'great war' that resulted between him and Isengrin the wolf, a tale to rival *chansons de geste*, stories of Paris and Helen or of 'Yvain and that animal of his'.[4] *Le Jugement de Renart*, which opens manuscripts from the α and β families in the tradition, slyly upstages Pierre by pointing out that he actually omitted the war he had promised, a narrative it then proceeds to supply.[5] Raising the stakes further still, the opening of the youngest group of manuscripts (γ) uses Pierre's 'original' prologue to herald a story derived from an even older 'source', attributed to a mysterious 'Aucupre' in which Adam and Eve

4 See *Renart et Chantecler*, lines 1–10 in *Le Roman de Renart*, ed. and trans. Jean Dufournet, 2 vols. (Paris: Garnier Flammarion, 1985).
5 Ibid.

accidentally create Renart as they bicker over a God-given magic staff.[6] In what emerges as a 'chicken-or-egg' history of origins and subversions, the *Renart*'s mock filial debt to the noble discourse of epic takes its place in a larger genealogy traceable back to Eden's own 'domestic comedy'. Such a plentiful, diverse and creative production belies any view of the comic or obscene as marginal to either a 'serious' literary mainstream or indeed medieval culture as a whole.

For all this, as any academic teaching such material can attest, readers and students of medieval literature sometimes confess astonishment that such works were written in the Middle Ages and that obscenity or humour are not fundamentally modern phenomena. Naïve as such comments may appear at first glance, they reveal an important insight: since our attitudes to the comic and the obscene are so often demonstrably products of specific historical and cultural contexts, it is often extremely difficult to understand not only *what* other cultures find offensive or funny but *why* they do so. A major problem here is that humour is supremely elusive and evanescent. While it seems every culture enjoys straightforward physical comedy, laughter is as likely to derive from oblique references and leaps of intuition, from the delight of nudges and winks caught on the fly: as Sigmund Freud cites from Theodor Lipps, 'A joke says what it has to say not always in few words but in *too* few words . . . It may even actually say what it has to say by not saying it.'[7] There is thus every danger that our reactions to medieval texts could spring either from well-founded intuitive sympathy or entire misunderstanding, our laughter glossing over complex issues of cultural difference. Moreover, just as audiences will laugh collectively at things they do not consider funny individually, for all modern audiences can find Chaucer hilarious, it is unclear how genuinely in tune with medieval sensibilities we would admit ourselves to be – were such quasi-telepathic understanding possible. In the *fabliau Les Tresces*, the cuckold who savagely revenges himself on a woman he mistakes for his wife arguably loses the sympathy of medieval audiences not out of revulsion at his violently abusive act but because of his stupidity. Obscenity presents similar problems: the nature of taboos can vary as much as the measure of

---

6 *Les Enfances Renart*, line 29 in *Le Roman de Renart*, ed. and trans. Naoyuki Fukumoto *et al.* (Paris: Livre de Poche 2005).
7 Sigmund Freud, *Jokes and their Relation to the Unconscious*, ed. Angela Richards, trans. James Strachey (London: Penguin, 1991), p. 44, original emphasis. For a recent examination of the history of theories of laughter, see John Morreall, 'Humour and the Conduct of Politics', in Sharon Lockyer and Michael Pickering (eds.), *Beyond a Joke: The Limits of Humour* (Basingstoke and New York: Palgrave Macmillan, 2005), pp. 63–78.

licence accorded to individuals to play with them.[8] Issues of cultural understanding are further complicated by the linguistic divide between Latin and the vernacular, reflected in the extract cited above from inquisitional records made famous in Emmanuel le Roy Ladurie's *Montaillou*. The crux of Raymond de l'Aire's obscene and heretical speech, for which Raymond Segui comments he deserves to be killed, is not translated into the pedestrian, sometimes pidgin, Latin of the record but is rather left in the original Occitan dialect, beyond the verbal pale in the manner of the gesture that accompanies them, thus implying that, in their vernacular profanity, the f-word and the s-word are more akin to physical signs than verbal ones. Such anecdotes not only highlight the vernacular's power to shock, they bear witness to what seems to be a glaring paradox. For all the Cathars were persecuted for their dualist view of the physical world as the sullied domain of the devil, the transcript's linguistic policing points to what seems to be a view of the vernacular as irremediably fallen. It is in this reflection on the problems, dangers and pleasures of contact and transgression that the connection between the two terms lies. Humour is said to bring together seemingly disparate items, revealing previously hidden affinities. In this view, both comedian and humorous text profit from their marginal vantage to '[articulate and express] linguistically the moral sentiments, attitudes opinions etc. which [its audience] perceives as meaningful or recognisable and which they are inhibited from saying or cannot articulate or express so readily or so well'.[9] Likewise, obscenity brings an audience into uncomfortable proximity with the repellent or fascinating beyond of taste and decency – an energy that drives the rich tradition of grotesque and humorous illustration and carving, with its fascination with transgression and hybridity of all kinds.

A principal intersection here is the body and the bodily: humour and obscenity often spring from carnavalesque reassertions of the corporeal in the cultural domains of language and socialised behaviour. As Umberto Eco's novel *The Name of the Rose* reminds us, some medieval commentators argued that since Jesus never laughed, comedy was obscenely incompatible with Christian belief and thought. And yet the body naked, desiring, shitting, eating, fucking or dying is source not merely of humour and profanity but also of more serious reflections. Central here is the emphasis on the transience and

---

8 See Jerry Palmer, 'Parody and Decorum: Permission to Mock', in Lockyer and Pickering, *Beyond a Joke*, pp. 79–97.
9 George E. C. Paton, 'The Comedian as Portrayer of Social Morality', in Chris Powell and G. E. C. Paton (eds.), *Humour and Society: Resistance and Control* (Houndmills: Macmillan, 1988), pp. 206–33, at p. 207.

fragility of the flesh – notably in the poignant and macabre humour of Villon's *Testament*, whether it be the evocation of the poet straddled by 'la grosse Margot' or 'la belle héaumière's' wry lament for her own wizened breasts. This proliferation of images, both of the erotic and of corruption and mortality, transforms all of Villon's glances at the body into an intimately obscene 'playing with the dead'. A potentially more troubling domain is that of the derisive and malicious caricature of bodies deformed, foreign or monstrous, their perceived obscenity a cue for mockery, persecution and exclusion.[10] One might cite here the descriptions of Baligant's army in the Oxford version of the *Chanson de Roland*, a moment of fearful drama readable as the obverse of a tradition of xenophobic caricature and insult; or the moment in the *Couronnement de Louis* when William of Orange taunts the pagan champion Corsolt with the information that Mohammed went to Mecca, but got drunk and was eaten by pigs.[11] In other texts, that gaze is inverted: in the parody epic *Le Voyage de Charlemagne à Jerusalem et à Constantinople*, it is the turn of Charles and his peers to be sent up as crass, thuggish bumpkins.

In all this, the body seems to exceed and flaunt the hygienic limits imposed on it by language and social proprieties, medieval audiences clearly finding much both to amuse and appal in the shame, embarrassment and shock value attaching to parts, functions and acts, as well as the words used to denote them. Texts show medieval people acutely alive to the body's capacity to butt in and upend cultural decorum, hence perhaps the popularity of humour relating to animals and peasants, creatures somehow more 'of the body' than aristocratic audiences saw themselves as being. Indeed, embodiment and the return of the bodily are presented as literally degrading. In *Le Chevalier qui fist parler les cons* a knight fallen on hard times finds unexpected renown through his magical ability to make orifices speak. The tale culminates with our hero risking all in a bet with a tricky countess who has stuffed her vagina with cotton. In the nick of time, Huet ('wee Hughie'), his squire and the ancestor of *Blackadder*'s Baldrick, cunningly reminds his master of his other gift, with the result that the lady is denounced as a cheat before the court by her own arse. The resulting blokeish delight at a haughty lady of the palace effectively breaking wind in public takes its place in a tradition that includes Elizabeth I's reputed welcome to a courtier returning from self-imposed exile: 'Fear not, my good lord – we have forgotten the fart.'

10 On which see especially Debra Higgs Strickland, *Saracens, Demons and Jews: Making Monsters in Medieval Art* (Princeton, NJ: Princeton University Press, 2003).
11 *Le Couronnement de Louis*, version C, lines 593–94 in *Les Rédactions en vers du 'Couronnement de Louis'*, ed. Yvan Lepage (Geneva: Droz, 1978).

Indeed, flatulence generally, female especially, functions recurringly as an audible corporeal sign of hidden sexual improprieties, part of a tradition of court 'noise', hubbub and rumour manifest in works from the *Roland* to Shakespeare.[12] Yet, though a fart might appear no more than the body's brouhaha, it may also say something by allusion: as the audience of *Le Chevalier* already knows by this point, the countess is also an adulteress who would have slept with the knight herself but – inconveniently preoccupied with her husband – she sent her maid instead. Likewise, in *Trubert*, the disguised trickster-hero blasts prodigiously at the duke's table and then blames it on the duchess's handmaid – much to her embarrassment.[13] Such a denunciation allusively bespeaks Trubert's disruption of the regulated sexual economy of the household, as he has his way in disguise with the duchess, her daughter, and the maid. This reading of the fart as whiffily pregnant suspension in court discourse fits with other literary practices. As Simon Gaunt argues, William of Poitiers's mock lament at having to choose between two mistresses may well feature a deliberately hypometric first line: 'My friends, I'll sing you a . . . seemly song' ('Companho, farai un vers . . . covinen').[14] Filling the bubble of this missing syllable is a collective recognition and celebration of the song's subversive and slanderous intent. Continuing with things that are both paradoxically void and full, meaningless and meaningful, critics have read both French and Occitan lyric poetry and narrative romance as delighting in the striptease revelation of *le con* as the obscure object of desire underpinning its sublimely elevated strivings, thus allusively contesting court culture's attempts to contain either the bodily fact or verbal rumour of misbehaviour – in effect, to stop the cunt 'farting' in public. But, of course, court slander in the Middle Ages did not stop there, delighting in rumours of same-sex relations (e.g. Richard the Lionheart) and incest (e.g. Eleanor of Aquitaine).[15] Indeed, as I have argued elsewhere, Chrétien de Troyes's seemingly serious *Erec et Enide* may bristle with mischievous allusions to the accusations of sodomy and sexual impropriety that dogged the hero of the *Roman d'Eneas*, one of Erec's

12 On which see Valerie Allen, *On Farting: Language and Laughter in the Middle Ages* (New York: Palgrave Macmillan, 2007) and, on later material, Kenneth Gross, *Shakespeare's Noise* (Chicago: University of Chicago Press, 2001).
13 'Trubert', in Luciano Rossi and Richard Straub (eds. and trans.), *Fabliaux érotiques: textes de jongleurs des xiie et xiiie siècles* (Paris: Livre de Poche, 1992), lines 532–3.
14 Simon Gaunt, *Troubadours and Irony* (Cambridge: Cambridge University Press, 1989), p. 19.
15 On Richard and the rumours of sodomy, see William Burgwinkle, *Sodomy, Masculinity and Law* (Cambridge: Cambridge University Press), pp. 73–85. On Eleanor and rumours of incest with her uncle Raymond, see B. Wheeler and J. Carmi Parsons (eds.), *Eleanor of Aquitaine: Lord and Lady* (New York: Palgrave Macmillan, 2003).

key prototypes in the literary cultures of the courts of Anjou and Champagne. Similarly, other texts attest to the power of the obscene and comic to irrupt onto the stage. In the *fabliau La Demoisele qui ne pouvait oïr parler de foutre*, the comedy revolves around precisely all that *cannot* be said. Just as the father has had to sack all his workers on account of his daughter's seemingly pathological intolerance of vulgar language, so the text appears emptied of everyone except the happy few able to conduct their business – including flirtation, foreplay and intercourse sufficiently vigorous to make the young woman initiating it fart uncontrollably – without recourse to profanity. Such materials paint a picture of medieval culture caught between hypocrisy (do it, but just don't say it) and the implantation of a mischievous perversity (it's more fun to do it *because* you mustn't say it).

Such a divorce between what the mouth says and the body does is central to medieval reflections on licence, prohibition and the clandestine. The recurrent representation of monks and priests hypocritically happy to engage in what they denounce is the most immediate sign of the church as a suspect agent in a culture of repression characterised by a very grey terrain separating extremes of severity and tolerance. For example, the hidden recesses of thought, desire or practice may have been of greater concern than the ribald but potentially self-policing communality of frank speech. Indeed, bawdy as their language and scenarios may appear, works often flirt teasingly with other suggestions from a vanilla 'soft-core'. While texts joke about variations of position in intercourse (not encouraged by the church), overt jocular references to same-sex acts, masturbation, bestiality or incest (all of which led to directly to hell) are either rare or lacking altogether. For example, in one version of *Le Jugement de Renart*, the mock epic list of peasants attacking the unfortunate bear, Brun, who has just lost the skin from his muzzle and paws in a trap, includes 'Baudouïn Porteciviere, who fucks his wife from behind' ('qui fout sa feme par derrieres').[16] However, this echo of collective hilarity presumably indicates vaginal intercourse 'doggy-style' rather than any alternative from the pages of Sade's *Justine*. By contrast, the analogous character in the γ tradition is celebrated as having strangled his wife, leaving us slightly uncertain as regards the relative weighting of sexual peccadillos and domestic brutality.[17] Likewise, in *Les Tresces*, a silent implication of the wife's running-gag substitution of her husband's animals (the calf) and

16 'Le Jugement de Renart', line 660, in *Le Roman de Renart édité d'après le manuscrit de Cangé*, ed. Mario Roques (Paris: Champion, 1948–63).
17 *Les Enfances et al., Renart*, lines 659–60.

parts thereof (the palfrey's tail) for people is that the husband himself cannot distinguish one category of chattels from another: to him his horse is
as his wife. One exception is *La Confession Renart*, in which the fox admits
to having his way with all the household – not merely mother and daughter, but also father and son.[18] However, here the fox is deliberately trying
to shock the kite acting as his confessor and to distract him long enough to
eat him.

Where evidence is glimpsed or inferred rather than found in plain view,
getting a representative picture of practices and attitudes is very difficult. Here
the problem may sometimes be of our making: for example, for all their merits,
generic definitions and the anthologisation of comic works can obscure our
sense of their literary and cultural horizon. Emphasis on genre and on the
narrative character of the *fabliau* has led to canonical examples being abstracted
from the texts accompanying them in manuscript compendia. These squibs
often state things more crudely than the *fabliaux* themselves, luxuriating in
filth where the economy of action characteristic of *fabliau* comedy moves
things on more smartly. (For example, in *Les Tresces*, the laugh lies partly in
the sheer speed with which the wife performs her tricks – this in hilarious
contrast to her stumbling dolt of a husband.) A case in point is Bibliothèque
Nationale ms. français 837, a sizeable compilation containing lyric, religious,
moral and satirical material alongside a number of well-known *fabliaux*.[19] One
text, the parody dream allegory, 'Le Débat du cul et du con' (fos. 183v–84),
offers an intriguingly messy reflection on the body specifically and culture
generally. The two orifices debate who owes the other rent: the *cul* claims
the *con* owes it payment for 'blowing its horn' to entertain it, while the *con*
argues that the debt is paid by its liberal sharing of the 'food' it receives. The
cul objects: 'I never got any of the sausage you had last night.' 'Oh yes you
did', responds *le con*, going on – before we infer anything else – to explain
that its partner got its fair share of the accompanying juices. In response, the
con complains that, were the vile *cul* further away, it would be able to subdue
'counts, castellans and viscounts, bishops and abbots'. Getting the last word
in, the *cul* objects that without it no one could ever eat. The soiling but fertile
proximity of these two interlocutors allegorises the relation of the obscene
and humorous to other discourses, mirroring this text's dialogue with other

---

18 *Renart et Chatecler*, lines 707–9.
19 In addition to the manuscript itself and the various editions of texts from it, the compilation
can also be accessed through Henri Omont's facsimile edition (*Fabliaux, dits et contes en vers
français du xiiie siècle: fac-similé du manuscrit français 837 de la Bibliothèque Nationale* (Paris: Leroux,
1932; reprinted Geneva: Slatkine, 1973).

genres represented in the codex. The dream frame derives from lyric (ms. 837 contains a number of poetic addresses and complaints to the lady), the conceit of the warring parts from fable traditions. Likewise, the *con*'s vision of world domination echoes comments in other works on the levelling power of fortune (e.g. 'La Roue de Fortune', fos. 219v–20v; 'Le Dit de Fortune', fos. 247v–48v; 'Les Vers du monde', fos. 208–9), as well as social satires by authors such as Rutebeuf, a number of whose works also feature in ms. 837. 'Le Débat' also notably counterpoints the version of the life of Mary of Egypt (fos. 316v–23), who in her wild years laid entire cities to waste by her sexual wiles: the voice of the *con* is thus the displaced jubilation of Mary the triumphant sinner.

Telling of the havoc wreaked in the Arthurian court by a young lad who brings the king a magical coat that only fits faithful women, *Le Mantel mautaillé* (fos. 27r–31r) also reprises themes elaborated elsewhere, a key interlocutor being ms. 837's version of *La Chastelaine de Vergi* (fos. 6–11), a poignantly tragic tale of two lovers destroyed by the machinations of the duchess of Burgundy, jealous of the eponymous *chastelaine*'s relation with a knight. *Le Mantel* shows a comparable – if more playful – mastery of the motifs and poetic conventions of romance (descriptions of physical beauty, evocations of court protocol and splendour, the importance of *aventure*). Although no orifice murmurs in *La Chastelaine*, both works depict scandals unfolding through a chain of unfortunate events as the comic or tragic machine dictates. *Le Mantel*'s exploration of the fateful pull of narrative mechanisms begins with the tricky issue of getting the women to try the garment on in the first place. For whatever reason (a silence perhaps as pregnant as those in serious works such as *La Mort le roi Artu*), Gauvain does not tell the queen the whole truth when sent to summon her and her household before the king. Once revealed as false, Guinevere is quick to cajole others into taking their turn so as to deflect attention from her own embarrassment, setting the tone for an unfolding debacle of social suicides in which vanity and malice play key roles. True to type, Kay foolishly insists his *amie* try on the garment and is inevitably mortified as a result. His revenge is then to force others to expose themselves to collective ridicule. He is especially delighted when Gauvain's *amie* is revealed as even worse and when the coat leaves Ydier's lady's backside bare, a detail interpreted as a sign of the manner of her infidelity. However, for all the levity, the tale's conclusion, highlighting the absolute distraction of Carados as he desperately tries to dissuade Galeta from trying on the coat, arguing that he would prefer the torment of doubt about her fidelity to the stinging certainty of proof, reads as an uneasy and far from comic counterpoint to the actual suicide of the knight–lover in reaction to the death of his mistress in *La Chastelaine*. Such a contrast speaks volumes about the sometimes deadly serious play associated with comic reflection: what is a laughing matter at Arthur's court is elsewhere a mechanism of destruction and damnation. The obscene and scandalous speech of the body is clearly sometimes far beyond a joke.

13

Travel and orientalism

SIMON GAUNT

In the spring of 1271 three Venetians set out for Acre, the last Christian stronghold in Palestine: Marco Polo, just seventeen, his father, and his uncle. Venetian merchants frequently travelled around the Mediterranean and Black Sea, for Venice's international trade was already highly organised: in addition to trading convoys, Venetians had their own quarters in numerous foreign ports. Extended Venetian merchant families would thus often have several households around the Mediterranean, and with a house in Constantinople the Polos were one such family. Their journey in 1271 would have been banal had they not intended to go much further than Acre, to the Far East, for just two years earlier the two elder Polos had returned from an extended trip, commissioned as ambassadors to the pope by none other than the Great Khan, Kubilai, ruler of the vast Mongol Empire that stretched across Asia to the edges of Europe. The Polos were to spend twenty-four years in Asia. If his own account is to be believed, Marco learned to speak several non-European languages, was employed as an administrator by Kubilai, and visited places virtually unknown to Europeans, notably Cathay (China), Indochina, Sumatra, Java, Ceylon, and India. Several years after his return, in 1298 – again according to his own account – Marco was imprisoned in Genoa following one of its sporadic naval skirmishes with Venice. There, helped by one Rustichello da Pisa, author of a compilation of Arthurian tales, he composed possibly the most famous travel book ever written, still frequently adapted into English as Marco Polo's *Travels*.[1]

This much is well known. It is perhaps less well known that this text – originally called *Le Divisament dou monde* – was composed in French, as was the other resoundingly popular medieval travel narrative, John Mandeville's

---

1 The best historical account is J. Larner, *Marco Polo and the Discovery of the World* (New Haven, CT and London: Yale University Press, 1999).

Le Livre des merveilles du monde (1356–7). Among the most successful vernacular texts of the Middle Ages, they were frequently reworked, and translated into an exceptional number of other languages. They have usually been studied as marginal chapters in the literary histories of Italy and England, but they are nonetheless an important, if neglected, element of French literary history. Indeed, they raise the crucial question of what we mean by 'French literary history' in the Middle Ages. Their use of French is usually attributed to the prestige of French as the language of courtly culture. This may be sufficient explanation of the use of French as a literary language in England after the Norman conquest (since French was the language of the ruling elite), but by the thirteenth century and further afield the role of French was more complex: following the Crusades and Norman expansion in the Mediterranean, French was embedded in a network of multilingual, multicultural communities in the Near East.[2] By writing in French, Marco Polo and Mandeville made their texts available to a wide international readership outside Western Europe. French did not belong to the French in the Middle Ages: it was widely spoken and written in a variety of forms, including the so-called Franco-Italian of Marco Polo, or the Anglo-French of John Mandeville.

Apart from French and their popularity, *Le Divisament* and *Le Livre des merveilles* share other traits of medieval travel narratives: they are generically hybrid; they inscribe themselves in a quasi-encyclopaedic tradition of descriptions of the world and taxonomies of its peoples (*divisament* means both 'description' and 'division'); finally, the knowledge they transmit is implicitly (sometimes explicitly) intended for evaluation in relation to other texts about distant lands. Medieval travel narratives, in other words, are not just vehicles for knowledge; they engage an intertextual debate about this knowledge. Since for the most part their object of knowledge is 'the Orient', it is not inappropriate to speak of medieval Orientalism, even if the modern relation between knowledge of the Orient and imperialism, charted influentially by Edward Said,[3] did not pertain in the Middle Ages. Indeed, as medieval Europe became more conscious of Asia, there could be little doubt that Asian cultures were more advanced technologically, with formidably more military muscle. But modern Orientalism has an important medieval prehistory in Marco

---

2 See C. Aslanov, *Le Français au levant, jadis et naguère: à la recherche d'une langue perdue* (Paris: Champion, 2006).

3 E. Said, *Orientalism*, 3rd edn (London: Penguin, 2003).

Polo and Mandeville, with a key pre-text for both being the so-called *Roman d'Alexandre*.

Le Roman d'Alexandre

The earliest narrative poem in French devoted to Alexander the Great dates from the early twelfth century, but it was followed by a flood of other versions, including those of Lambert le Tort (*c.* 1170), Thomas de Kent (also known as *Le Roman de toute chevalerie, c.* 1175–85), and Alexandre de Paris (*c.* 1180–5).[4] If Lambert's poem pioneered the dodecasyllabic line in French (whence the alexandrine, the twelve-syllable line of subsequent French verse), and Thomas's offered the first complete biography of Alexander in French, Alexandre de Paris's became the most enduringly popular (spawning numerous adaptations and *mises en prose*). I focus here on Thomas de Kent partly because his is a fine poem, but also because it is yet another illustration of the richness of literary activity in French outside France.

Le Roman de toute chevalerie narrates the birth of Alexander, his education at the hands of Aristotle, his many battles, particularly those against the Persian and Indian kings Darius and Porrus, his exploration of Asia and Africa, and finally his premature death from poisoning.[5] Thomas de Kent was part of the important wave of literary activity in French among English clerics under Henry II. He makes no bones about his *clergie*, repeatedly drawing attention to his sources and discussing his own work as a writer. For example, when apologising for not being able to include a description of everything Alexander saw (line 6643), he insists upon the veracity of his account, attributing this to his comprehensive survey of written sources (line 6646: *autorité*):

> Quant Solin e Trege averez tot reversé
> E Ysidre, qe fu de langage estoré,
> Jerome e Ethike, Orosye l'escrié,
> E Dyonis de Inde, Magesten le barbé,
> E l'espistre Alisandre qu'il tramist par chereté
> E mestre Aristotle qui l'out endoctriné,
> E les autres liveres a cestui assemblé,
> Donc saverez [vous] pur voir qe n'est pas contrové.
>
> (lines 6657–64)

---

4 For an overview of the tradition see M. Gosman, *La Légende d'Alexandre le Grand dans la littérature française du 12e siècle* (Amsterdam: Rodopi, 1997), pp. 25–45.
5 C. Gaullier-Bougassas and L. Harf-Lancner (eds.), *Thomas de Kent: Le Roman d'Alexandre ou Le Roman de toute chevalerie* (Paris: Champion Classique, 2003).

(But when you have combed all of Solinus and Trogus, eloquent Isidore, Jerome and Aethicus, renowned Orosius, Denis of India, bearded Megasthenes, and the letter Alexander affectionately wrote to master Aristotle, who educated him, and all the other books that go with this, then you will know truly that nothing here is false.)

Thomas may have added stylistic embellishment, as befits a vernacular versifier (lines 6647–8), but substantively everything he narrates – the knowledge of the world he transmits – is derived from written sources, which he invites his reader to check. He maintains, with false modesty, that he is clumsy and scarcely educated (line 6652), but he lists a comprehensive range of sources that belie the latter claim at least. Immediately before this, Alexander leads his army towards Ethiopia (line 6639), having searched throughout the entire world (line 6630); immediately after this, Thomas also turns his poem towards Ethiopia (line 6665). Whereas the stress in many Alexander romances is on his drive to conquer the world, his quest here is as much to *know* the world as to conquer it, and in this the poet is his bookish double, searching obsessively through books for new knowledge, just as Alexander searches the world obsessively for new wonders to behold. Alexander desires, as his men reproachfully tell him, to know all God's secrets (line 5799).

Though Alexander's desire to know drives the narrative, knowledge of the world in *Le Roman de toute chevalerie* is nonetheless purely textual, since the author's account derives explicitly from texts, and most of the Asian and African locations described were way beyond the experience of his readership. Thus, as Thomas himself says, his aim is not just to entertain, but also to organise knowledge (line 6653) and he opens with a synopsis of the classic medieval understanding of the topography of the world:

> Ancienement ly sage mesurerent le monde,
> Cum le firmament torne e cum la terre est ronde.
> En trois la departirent sanz compas e desponde:
> L'une est Aufrike, Asye est la seconde,
> Europe est la tierce, de toz biens est feconde.
>
> (lines 32–6)

(In olden times wise men surveyed the world, how the sky rotates and how the earth is round. They divided it into three, without compass or ruler: one part is Africa, the second is Asia, Europe, which is teeming with good things, is the third.)

The so-called medieval T/O map or schema is clearly evoked here. This represents the world as a circle divided into three unequal parts by a 'T' (a semi-circle over two quarters); the arms and crux of the 'T' represent the Mediterranean (situated, as its etymology suggests, at the centre of the world, with Jerusalem at its centre); above the Mediterranean, occupying fully half of the world, is Asia, below it Europe and Africa. Now maps (including modern maps) are always symbolic representations of space and what this tripartite schema shows is the pre-eminence of Asia in the medieval imaginary. Twice the size of Europe, it sits literally above it. And if Thomas defensively describes Europe as 'teeming with good things', Asia emerges from his account as so vast, so full of wonders, that no text may describe it in its entirety.

Alexander romances are part of a larger body of twelfth-century texts based on Latin sources, the so-called *romans antiques*. But whereas these other texts adopt the form of courtly romance and rework their sources to make love more central, most Alexander romances use the strophic form (the *laisse*) and style of the *chansons de geste*. Thomas exploits this to invoke a vernacular intertext alongside his Latin sources. Thus Alexander is implicitly an epic hero in Old French, which is to say the hero of a tale of military exploits; and, tellingly, no sword is better than his save Durendal, Roland's sword (line 4150). But if this comparison helps contemporary audiences identify with Alexander's thirst for glory and conquest, *Le Roman de toute chevalerie* is not a *chanson de geste*. Ultimately, the style is exploited to facilitate Thomas's transmission of knowledge to a vernacular audience; and at key moments the text loses narrative momentum, and the *laisses* become shorter and disjointed, as he starts to catalogue, in encyclopaedic fashion, the legendary monstrous races and wonders of Asia (for example, lines 4690–751, 6714–882): peoples with odd diets, people who kill their parents, cynocephali, sciapods (creatures with only one large foot used for shade), dragons, giant mice and so on. In these passages, Thomas lapses into direct translation of his sources (usually Solinus, though the indirect source is Pliny) and, if the popularity of this exotica with illustrators is anything to go by,[6] the change of mode should not be regarded as a flaw. On the contrary, the body of knowledge Thomas transmits was crucial to the text's appeal. So did contemporary audiences believe in this fantastic account of the world beyond Europe?

Le Divisament dou monde

By medieval standards *Le Divisament* was a sensation: by *c.* 1310 it had been adapted from its original Franco-Italian literary idiom into standard French,

---

6 On which see D. H. Strickland, *Saracens, Demons and Jews: Making Monsters in Medieval Art* (Princeton, NJ: Princeton University Press, 2003).

translated into two Italian dialects and Latin. The wide dissemination of this last version indicates that the authority of Marco Polo's account of Asia quickly rivalled that of the Latin texts used by Thomas de Kent, but Marco offered a different image of the Far East, one that explicitly corrected earlier versions. The success of *Le Divisament* indicates that at the very least the nature of the rest of the world was a matter of debate.

As with *Le Roman de toute chevalerie*, the rhetoric of truth looms large:[7]

> Seignors enperaor et rois, dux et marquois, cuens, chevaliers et borgiois, et toutes gens que volés savoir les deverses jenerasions des homes et les deversités des deverses region dou monde, si prennés cestui livre et le feites lire. Et qui trouvererés toutes les grandismes mervoilles et les grant diversités de la grande Harminie et de Persie et des Tartars et de Indie, et de maintes autres provinces, sicom nostre livre voç contera por ordre apertemant, sicome meisser Marc Pol, sajes et noble citaiens de Venece, raconte por ce que a seç iaus meisme il le voit. Mes auques hi n'i a qu'il ne vit pas, mes il l'entendi da homes citables et de verité; et por ce metreron les chouse veue por veue et l'entendue por entandue, por ce que notre livre soit droit et vertables sanç nulle mansonge. (I, 1–3)

> (My lords, emperors and kings, dukes and marquises, counts, knights, and burghers, and all people who wish to know about the various races of men and the diversity of the various parts of the world, take this book and have it read. And here you will find all the great wonders and curiosities of Greater Armenia, of Persia and the Tartars and India, and many other provinces, just as our book will relate clearly and in order, just as Messer Marco Polo, noble citizen of Venice, recounts, since he saw them with his own eyes. But some he did not see, rather he heard about them from trustworthy and truthful men; and so we will set down the things he saw as witnessed and hearsay as hearsay, because our book is straight and truthful, with no falsehood.)

This stress on eyewitness is constant, suggesting an implicit contrast with previous texts, but the conception of the world is also different. Whereas Alexander romances frequently use the generic term Orient to designate the non-European world (*Roman de toute chevalerie*, line 327 and *passim*), Marco never does so. Instead, he stresses the world's great internal diversity. The adjective *diverse* certainly figures in earlier texts (for example, *Roman de toute chevalerie*, lines 6702–4), but in the twelfth century at least it had moral overtones, meaning not just 'diverse', but also 'strange' and 'terrifying'. Marco's

---

7 G. Ronchi (ed.), *Marco Polo: Milione. Le Divisament dou monde. Il milione delle redazioni toscana e franco-italiana* (Milan: Mondadori, 1982), Franco-Italian redaction; references are to chapter and sentence number.

use of the noun *diversités* in the plural seems tautological alongside *deverses jenerasions* and *deverses region*, but it strikingly sets the tone for his drive to chart a seemingly infinite gradation of differences between human beings and places.

A frequent touchstone of Marco's implicit contrast between his and earlier accounts is Alexander (mentioned first XXIII, 6–9). Significantly, his description of the world arrives relatively early on at the edge of civilisation as famously defined by Alexander: somewhere on the fringes of India, Alexander is said to have enclosed the legendary biblical peoples of Gog Magog – evil beyond measure (*Roman de toute chevalerie*, lines 5974–6590) – a feat that enhances his status as a worthy pre-Christian hero. This is the point at which Alexander turns back, realising nothing good can come from going on. For Marco, in contrast, this is but a staging-post on the way to China (LXXIV, 11–12), noted almost in passing. Thus *Le Divisament* knowingly pushes back the frontiers of the known world and corrects earlier texts. One amusing example of this is when a description of a rhinoceros concludes with the remark that unicorns are thus not as we think (CLXVI, 16). The world – at least as described in European texts – can never be the same again. Earlier accounts emerge as incomplete and fictional.

There was some urgency to this revisionism in the late thirteenth century. It had been apparent for some time that Christendom was not winning its battle against Islam in the Middle East and the Balkans, while Europeans had become painfully aware of the dauntingly ferocious, vast new Mongol Empire. In 1241–2, Mongol troops had brutally swept all before them on the eastern fringes of Christendom – Kiev, Hungary, Poland, even Germany – turning back only at the news that Ogodei Khan, successor to Genghis, had died; in subsequent decades, they took cities uncomfortably close to home (notably Damascus). But European powers were uncertain about the threat the Mongols posed: they were, after all, also at war with Muslims, while rumours had been circulating for some time about a great Christian potentate in the East, Prester John. Were the Mongols somehow connected to him? Several papal emissaries had been sent to the Great Khan, including John of Pian Ciarpino (in 1246) and William of Rubruck (in 1253–4), whose written accounts survive.[8] From these it is clear the West already knew how vast and wealthy the Mongol Empire had become. Certainly it was strange, but intriguingly it was tolerant of different religions, with substantial Christian communities in some places, while the so-called *pax mongolica* made it relatively safe to travel the length of

---

8 C. Dawson, *Mission to Asia* (Toronto: University of Toronto Press, 1980).

Asia, offering enticing opportunities for trade, opportunities a few Westerners were already exploiting.

The Polos were not pioneers, though they were in the vanguard of contact between Europe and Asia. *Le Divisament* presents much of Asia as a land of opportunity and promise, which for some medieval Europeans in the late thirteenth century it clearly was. But for this promise to be exploited, information was crucial. The text's success is due not just to Marco's drive to impart this information, but also to its readers' apparently insatiable appetite for it: *Le Divisament* is often tidied up and abridged in transmission, but the lengthy lists of cities and provinces, accounts of what they produce, how they are governed, whether they pay tribute to the Great Khan, how to get there, whether it is safe, and so on, are always substantially retained. The dominant mode is again encyclopaedic and much of the text is descriptive, not narrative. Indeed, the story of the Polos' travels is dispatched in a nineteen-chapter prologue, with the bulk of the text then devoted to a seemingly objective description of places, roughly following the trajectory of a journey. The underlying style is that of prose romance (particularly in the excurses that offer historical background), but this is subordinate to the drive to impart information. Marco himself is often absent from the text and although the narrative voicing of the text is complex, the narrating 'je' is usually that of Marco's collaborator, Rustichello, for whom Marco is the eyewitness authority for what is described.

Certain types of knowledge are of greater interest than others. Constantly attention is focused on the economy, government and religion. Marco was particularly impressed by paper money (as yet unknown in Europe), the Mongols' administrative infrastructure and their religious tolerance, which possibly leads him to a markedly open-minded consideration of other religions (not so much Islam, but certainly Buddhism and Hinduism). Above all he is mesmerised by Kubilai Khan: his court's opulence and rituals, his regime's grandeur and sophistication, his personality. Although he frequently uses the word *mervoille* and its cognates, he does so with the etymological sense of that which is to be gazed upon with admiration, largely to describe unfamiliar or strange human customs and artefacts. Supernatural creatures or events, together with the legendary monstrous races, are conspicuously absent. On the odd occasion they do appear (on the fringes of Asia, or in Africa, for example, which Marco may have visited on the way home), the text notes Marco did not see them for himself. Significantly barbaric practices, such as cannibalism, are relegated to the new edges of civilisation (as defined by Marco): Japan, Java, Sumatra, and the Andaman Islands.

Le Divisament's description of the world is thus radically different from previous accounts, but while his representation of Asia seems more realistic, it remains nonetheless a textual fantasy. For one thing, its representation of Kubilai Khan's regime verges on the utopian; for another, everything in Asia – wealth, war, sex, human diversity, distances, mountains – is bathed in hyperbolic excess. The world according to Marco Polo, at least the non-European world, is larger than life, incredible not because it is fantastic, but because it is so vast and various.

Le Livre des merveilles du monde

Many medieval readers found Marco's account incredible. They mistrusted the self-aggrandising self-presentation of the narrator as the purveyor of amazing knowledge, while his rhetoric of truth is so insistent it seems almost to challenge the reader to disbelieve. Indeed, Marco Polo's undertaking is inherently risky: any text that seeks to displace and usurp the authority of previous texts is open to similar manoeuvres. Historical circumstances did not help Marco's reputation: by the 1350s, the Mongol Empire had largely disintegrated, closing down the overland routes to the Far East, while the Black Death devastated the world's economies. European trade with the Far East did not cease, but it was once again mediated through Middle Eastern merchants, as it had been before the Mongol Empire. The Far East Marco Polo described so vividly became not so much a closed book, as a world that could only be experienced through books.

The principal interest of Mandeville's *Livre des merveilles*, which proved even more popular than *Le Divisament*, is precisely that it falls back on familiar textual culture.[9] It is now generally agreed that Mandeville went no further than a library, in that there is virtually nothing in his text without an identifiable source. Although he never mentions Marco Polo, essentially what he offers is a riposte, one concerned to put Christianity centre-stage. Whereas *Le Divisament* pays the Holy Land scant attention, a detailed, biblical topography of the Middle East sits squarely at the centre of *Le Livre des merveilles*. The monstrous races of India are reinstated and the Great Khan is no longer a ubiquitous authority in Asia, but a curiosity on the way to the edge of the known world: the enticing legendary realm of Prester John and the frustratingly inaccessible earthly paradise. The popularity of Mandeville, in other words,

---

9 C. Deluz (ed.), *Jean de Mandeville: Le Livre des merveilles du monde* (Paris: CNRS, 2000) is an edition of the earliest version, in Anglo-Norman French.

may be due to the fact that the textual fantasy he offered was a more familiar one.[10]

Yet, *Le Divisament* had opened the world up in a way Mandeville could not quite ignore. First, he cannot avoid the commonplace of medieval travel narratives that his own account is incomplete, so vast and complex is the world, but he adds the twist that he does not wish to foreclose the possibility that another will explore distant lands and return to write about it, thereby acknowledging that he may not have the last word (pp. 478–9). Second, in one intriguing episode he describes an encounter with the 'Saracen sultan', whose vast knowledge of Christendom surprises him (chapter xv): the Sultan's curiosity about Christians echoes Kubilai Khan's curiosity about Europeans in *Le Divisament*, raising the tantalising possibility of a non-European subject of knowledge, of Europe as the object of knowledge. Third, like many medieval writers Mandeville believed the world to be round, evoking the possibility of circumnavigation at some length (chapter xx). Armed with this belief and a heavily annotated copy of Marco Polo's book, one late medieval traveller, Christopher Columbus, famously sailed west in 1492, looking for the riches of the East described therein. And initially he believed he had found Marco's Cathay when he reached his destination. People like to believe what they read in books, but as Columbus eventually realised, if you travel with one eye on a guidebook, you may not fully realise where you are going; on the other hand, without the book you might not set out at all.

10 See M. Gosman, 'Marco Polo's Voyages: The Conflict between Confirmation and Observation', in Z. von Martels (ed.), *Travel Fact and Travel Fiction: Literary Tradition, Scholarly Discovery and Observation in Travel Writing* (Leiden: Brill, 1994), pp. 72–84; also I. M. Higgins, *Writing East: The 'Travels' of Sir John Mandeville* (Philadelphia: University of Pennsylvania Press, 1997).

14

Allegory and interpretation

KAREN SULLIVAN

If the Middle Ages might rightly be considered the Age of Allegory, it may well be because its authors were fascinated by the relation between abstract qualities and concrete human beings, a topic that allegory explores more fully than any other trope. In his prologue to the *Chevalier de la charrette* (composed between 1177 and 1181), Chrétien de Troyes refers to 'la dame qui passe / totes celes qui sont vivanz' ('the lady who surpasses all those living' [lines 10–11]), but he makes clear that this lady is 'ma dame de Chanpaigne', that is, Marie, countess of Champagne, daughter of King Louis VII and Eleanor of Aquitaine, and one of the most important patronesses of her day.[1] Marie may epitomise a universal value, but, as Chrétien establishes, she has done so through her own particular excellence. As the story opens, Chrétien represents Queen Guinevere, similarly, as at once the incarnation of Love and an actual, historical woman, whom Lancelot both worships and honours. In contrast, in the beginning of the *Roman de la rose* (composed around 1230), Guillaume de Lorris alludes obliquely to 'cele qui tant a de pris / et tant est digne d'estre amee / qu'el doit estre Rose clamee' ('she who has so much value and is so worthy of being loved that she should be called "Rose"' [lines 42–4]).[2] The poet portrays his beloved, not as an actual historical woman, like Marie of Champagne, but as a rose, whose identity derives from her allegorical status. Far from incarnating Love, as Guinevere does, the Rose who appears in the poem serves merely, as we shall see, as the arbitrary object of the Lover's displaced desires. While, for Chrétien, abstract qualities can be incarnated in concrete human beings, just as God is incarnated in one man, for Guillaume, abstract qualities are inevitably separate from concrete human beings and even opposed to them. And while, for Chrétien, allegory is something that

1 Chrétien de Troyes, *Les Romans de Chrétien de Troyes*, vol. III: *Le Chevalier de la charrette*, ed. Mario Roques (Paris: Champion, 1990).
2 Guillaume de Lorris, *Le Roman de la rose*, ed. Félix Lecoy, 3 vols. (Paris: Champion, 1973–82), vol. I.

can possibly intersect with our own world, for Guillaume it is something that necessarily runs parallel to it. The conflict between this incarnational and this metaphysical model of allegory plays out in these two romances and, to a large extent, in medieval literature as a whole.

Chrétien de Troyes

Throughout Chrétien's *Chevalier de la charrette*, Love is identified with the loss of the sense of self in the contemplation of the other. At one point, when Lancelot is riding his horse, we are told:

> de rien nule ne li sovient
> fors d'une seule, et por celi
> a mis les autres en obli;
> a cele seule panse tant
> qu'il n'ot, ne voit, ne rien n'antant.

(nothing did he remember except a single woman, and for this one he had forgotten all the others. Of this single one, he thought so much that he did not hear, nor see, nor pay attention to anything [lines 720–4].)

At another point, he is said to be so immersed in such thoughts that he does not at first notice that his maiden escort has led him astray. So intense are these meditations that, Chrétien tells us, 'ne set ou va, ne set don vient' ('he did not know where he was going nor did he know whence he was coming' [line 719]) and, even, 'ne set s'il est, ou s'il n'est mie, / ne ne li manbre de son non' ('he did not know if he existed or not, nor did he remember his name' [lines 716–17]). With no past or future, no origin or destination, Lancelot no longer situates himself in time or place, and hence no longer experiences himself as existing. Chrétien states, 'ses pansers est de tel guise / que lui meïsmes en oblie' ('his thought was of such a kind that he forgot himself' [lines 714–15]). So absolute is the loss of the self in the other that Lancelot experiences that it cannot but recall Cistercian accounts of the loss of the self in the otherness of God. In his *Liber de diligendo deo*, Bernard of Clairvaux describes the fourth and highest degree of love as one where, 'quasi enim miro quodam modo oblitus sui, et a se penitus velut deficiens, totus perget in Deum' ('in some wonderful way, one forgets oneself, and, ceasing to remain inside oneself, proceeds entirely into God').[3] If you attain this degree of love, Bernard writes, you become like

---

3 Bernard of Clairvaux, *Liber de diligendo deo*, in *S. Bernardi Opera*, vol. III, *Tractatus et opuscula*, ed. J. Leclercq and H. M. Rochais (Rome: Editiones Cistercienses, 1963), pp. 119–54, at chap. XV, section 39, p. 153.

someone 'qui non sis, et omnino non sentire teipsum, et a temetipso exinaniri, et paene annullari' ('who does not exist, as if you do not experience yourself at all, you are emptied of yourself, and you are nearly annihilated' [x, 27, p. 142]). If Lancelot loses himself in the contemplation of the other, it is because, as in mystical experience, this other is so overwhelmingly present to him that it annihilates the self.

The experience of the loss of self is, for Lancelot, a pleasurable one because the other he encounters proves so real to him that it compensates for the loss of self. In his reverie, Lancelot is so abstracted from the world that he repeatedly disregards the dangers that threaten him. He does not feel his horse galloping toward a ford; he does not hear the knight who guards the ford repeatedly challenge him; he does not see this knight charge at him with his lance. Only the impact of the cold water into which he falls awakens him from his meditations. Chrétien does not disclose to us the content of Lancelot's meditations or the nature of the pleasure they afford him, but, in the *Conte du Graal*, he does give us some insight into his hero Perceval's similar reveries.[4] When Perceval sees a falcon attacking a goose, the three drops of the goose's red blood that fall on the white snow remind him of the blush on his lady's cheek:

> An l'esgarder que il feisoit
> li ert avis, tant li pleisoit,
> qu'il veïst la color novele
> de la face s'amie bele.

(As he gazed upon this sight, it seemed to him – so much did it please him – that he was seeing the fresh colour of his fair lady's face [vol. v, line 4249]).

Absorbed in apparently similar visual images of his beloved, Lancelot is so content that he does not demand, let alone expect, to obtain any reward from her. When he finally defeats the queen's abductor Meleagant in battle and, by doing so, frees her from captivity, she denies that she feels any gratitude toward him, yet he merely states 'Dame, certes ce poise moi / ne je n'os demander por coi' ('My lady, indeed this grieves me. I dare not ask your reason' [lines 3963–4]). He no more feels that his feats of arms should entitle him to her favour than a Christian would feel that his merits should entitle him to God's grace. Distinguishing between 'affectus' (affection) and a 'contractus' (transaction), Bernard of Clairvaux notes, 'Verus amor praemium non requirit'

---

4 Chrétien de Troyes, *Les Romans de Chrétien de Troyes*, vols. v and vi, *Le Conte du Graal (Perceval)*, ed. Félix Lecoy (Paris: Champion, 1972–5).

('True love does not require a reward').[5] Instead, he explains, 'Verus amor seipso contentus est. . . . Nam quidquid propter aliud amare videaris, id plane amas' ('True love is content with itself . . . For whatever you seem to love on account of something else, that thing is what you really love').[6] If Lancelot is content to lose himself in contemplation of the other, without any hope, let alone expectation, of obtaining anything from her, it is because, again, as in a mystical experience, that other is so overwhelmingly present to him as to obviate a desire for anything beyond her.

In the first part of the romance, it seems that Love might be separate from the other Lancelot loves and even in opposition to her. In the queen's absence, it is Love that Lancelot obeys, even, it appears, against his beloved's wishes. A passing dwarf offers to give Lancelot a ride on his cart with the promise that, if he accepts, he will learn what has become of the queen. At this time, Chrétien informs us, carts were reserved for criminals and other malefactors, so that whoever rode in one would forever suffer shame and ignominy, but Lancelot climbs in anyway, having been commanded to do so by Love (lines 372–3). Despite the disgrace he incurs as a result of this ride, Lancelot later justifies his action and establishes that it was an act of humility (lines 4354–96). He also establishes that he is chaste enough to share the bed of a beautiful maiden without touching her and devoted enough to travel to the kingdom of Gorre, a land typically identified with the Celtic underworld, in order to rescue his beloved. What seem to be objective trials, imposed by Fortune and testing his outer strength, are thus revealed to be subjective trials, imposed by Love and testing his inner passion. As Chrétien writes, 'Amors ensi les suens essaie, / ensi conuist ele les suens' ('Thus does Love test her own; thus does she know her own' [lines 4374–5]). Though Lancelot believes that everything he does is for Love, he suspects that the queen does not share this belief when she acts coldly towards him. It is simply incomprehensible to Lancelot that there should be any contradiction between Love and the queen, between the abstract quality and the concrete manifestation of that quality. Faced with such an apparent contradiction, and hence with a breakdown in the incarnational logic that undergirds his existence, he succumbs to despair.

Yet in the second part of the romance, when Lancelot rejoins the queen, Love is revealed to be identifiable with the other he loves. Now it is the queen who commands Lancelot. During his first battle with Meleagant, she

---

5 Bernard de Clairvaux, *Liber de diligendo*, chap. VII, section 17, p. 134.
6 Ibid.

says that she wants him to hold back (line 3794). Hearing her words, Lancelot immediately ceases fighting, though Meleagant continues to attack him. Later, at a tournament, she repeatedly sends him messages that she wishes him to fight his worst. Receiving these orders, he immediately starts flailing at his opponents and running from their blows. Now it is the queen who, through these commands, is testing him in order to know who he truly is. When she is informed that Lancelot seems as happy to be told to do badly in the tournament as to do his best, she rejoices 'por ce c'or set ele sanz dote / que ce est cil cui ele est tote / et il toz suens' ('because now she knew, without doubt, that this was the one whose she was entirely and that he was entirely hers' [lines 5873–5]). In the end, the queen reveals herself, not only to understand Love, but to understand it far better than Lancelot himself. She was cold to him, she explains, not because he rode in the cart, but because he hesitated for two steps before climbing into the cart. After Lancelot repents of this moment of hesitation and receives her absolution, he finally receives permission to spend the night in her bed. While Lancelot loves the queen spontaneously, without demanding, expecting, or even hoping for such a reward, the queen nevertheless recognises that he has merited this reward and grants it. As Bernard explains, 'Non enim sine praemio diligitur Deus, etsi absque praemii sit intuitu diligendus' ('God is not loved without a reward, although he should be loved without regard for a reward').[7] The high point of the romance lies precisely in the moment when Lancelot and the reader are reassured that Love is to be identified with the queen, that the abstract quality is to be identified with the concrete realisation, and that, whatever doubts we might have about it, divinity can indeed be found in our world, loving us as much as we love it.

Guillaume de Lorris

As in Chrétien's *Chevalier de la charrette*, in Guillaume's *Roman de la rose* Love is identified with the loss of the self before the other; yet, unlike in Chrétien's romance, this loss of the self is due, not to the contemplation of the other, but to the contemplation of the self. Having entered the Garden of Delight, the Lover gazes into the Fountain of Narcissus and perceives two marvellous crystals in which, when the sunlight strikes them, more than a hundred colours become visible. Like a mirror, the crystals represent everything before them. While C. S. Lewis interprets these crystals as the lady's eyes, it seems more

---

7 Ibid., p. 133.

likely that they constitute the Lover's own eyes:[8] gazing into this dangerous pool, like Narcissus, he sees the self, but believes it to be another. Unlike Lancelot, who loses the self because he so fully perceives the other, as other, the Lover loses the self because he so fully perceives the self as the other.

It is only after the Lover has looked into the Fountain of Narcissus and has mistaken the self for an other that he catches sight of the rosebushes also reflected in the fountain and that he is filled with desire for them. Having looked into the fountain 'por folie' ('foolishly' [line 1520]), mistaking the self for the other, the Lover demonstrated calm deliberation as he 'well considered' the numerous rosebuds ('je . . . oi bien avisé' [line 1658]) and 'selected' ('eslui' [line 1655]) her, from among the numerous rosebuds, as the object of his desire. He loves, not because a woman has come into his life, and through her excellence has compelled him to love, but rather because, feeling a lack within himself, he can say, with Augustine, 'amare amabam, et . . . quaerebam quid amarem' ('I loved to love, and . . . I sought that which to love').[9]

The experience of the loss of self is, for the Lover, a painful one because there is no genuine other there to compensate him for that loss. Guillaume writes of Narcissus:

> Quant il vit qu'il ne porroit
> acomplir ce qu'il desiroit,
> et qu'il estoit si pris par fort
> qu'il ne porroit avoir confort
>
> . . .
>
> il perdi d'ire tot le sen
> et fu mors en poi de termine.

(When he saw that he could not accomplish what he desired and that he was captured so strongly that he could not have any consolation . . . he lost his senses from frustration and died shortly thereafter [lines 1495–1501].)

Because Narcissus believed that he loved another, when he really loved himself, he could not 'accomplish what he desired': true happiness would lie in being able to love the self, not as the self, not as what one *is*, but as the other, as what one *has*. The inability to have what one is, and hence to possess what one desires, is a trait of all true lovers, Guillaume suggests. The God of Love informs the Lover, 'Amanz n'avra ja ce qu'i quiert, / tot jors i faut' ('A lover will never have what he seeks all the days that there may be' [lines 2407–8]). It is because one cannot possess the self as an other that one seeks an other

8 C. S. Lewis, *The Allegory of Love: A Study in Medieval Tradition* (Oxford: Oxford University Press, 1936; reprinted 1995), p. 125.
9 Augustine, *Confessiones* (Turnhout: Brepols, 1983), bk III, section 1, p. 27.

(or, as Jacques Lacan might put it, the *objet petit a*) to stand in for that self; throughout this romance, it is the Rose, or rather what the Lover hopes to attain from the Rose, that plays this role of substitute. It is because the Lover is not content to think about his beloved, as Lancelot was, that he seeks a reward from her. He relates of the roses in general, 'j'en cueillisse / au moins une que je tenisse / en ma main por l'odor sentir' ('I would pluck at least one of them, which I would hold in my hand to smell the odour' [lines 1630–2]). Reaching out with his hand, he strives to 'coillir' (to pluck), 'tenir' and 'prendre' this flower. Despite the God of Love's warning that 'A lover will never have what he seeks', the Lover concretises 'what he seeks' in the physical possession of the Rose. If the Lover is not content to lose himself in the contemplation of the other, without hope or expectation of obtaining anything from her; if, on the contrary, he demands what he calls 'riche deserte / de la poine que j'ai souferte' ('a very rich desert for the pain I have suffered' [lines 2465–6]), it is because the Rose is not what he truly wants, but only a supplement for that true desideratum.

The God of Love, who is separate from and in opposition to the Rose throughout the romance, promises to grant the Lover this flower, yet it is not clear that, even if he were able to fulfil this bequest, he would satisfy the Lover's desire. When the Lover sees the Rose, which he does on two occasions, her odour spreads throughout the surrounding atmosphere; her shape and colour prove subject to transformation; her multiple, feminine petals conceal her seed from his view. Diffused, mutable, folded in upon herself, the Rose is not some phallic, self-contained entity that, once seized and plucked, could truly be possessed. When the Lover goes on to kiss the Rose, the pleasure this contact affords him is not experienced in the present, but rather projected, proleptically, into the future. He tells himself, 'Je ne serai ja si dolenz, / s'i m'en sovient, que je ne saie / toz plains de delit et de joie' ('I shall never be so sorrowful that, if I remember it, I will not be filled with delight and joy' [lines 3488–90]). Though Guillaume leaves his section of the romance unfinished, he makes it clear that, even at the moment the Lover would be plucking the Rose, the pleasure he would be taking in doing so would vanish. Fair Welcoming refuses to give the Lover the Rose because, he insists, 'n'est pas droiture / que l'en l'oste de sa nature' ('It is not just for one to remove it from its nature' [lines 2897–8]). Because the Rose constitutes, not what the Lover truly wants, but a displacement of that desire, because what the Rose stands to give him would vanish the instant he grasped it, the lack within the Lover, which he associates with this flower, will never be filled.

Can an individual human being ever incarnate an abstract quality, or must this human being, however exemplary, necessarily serve as a mere screen for our projections? Could Heloïse be right when she declares that Peter Abelard constitutes the epitome of what a man can be? Could Dante Alighieri be telling the truth when he declares that Beatrice is a miracle? Or, rather, should we trust Abelard when he attempts to redirect Heloïse's idolatrous attentions from himself to God? Should we believe Guido Cavalcanti, when he identifies love, not, like Dante, with a particular lady, but with the universal excellence the lady (falsely) seems to possess? In the Middle Ages, the disagreement over the relation between abstract qualities and concrete human beings provided the fertile ground out of which allegory grew.

15

History and fiction: the narrativity and historiography of the matter of Troy

MARILYNN DESMOND

If Aristotle classified history as a branch of literature, it was the vernacular French cultures of the late Middle Ages that most fully develop what Hayden White calls the 'narrativity' of historical discourse. In his *De vulgari eloquentia* (*c.* 1305), Dante refers to the supple and pleasing features of French prose as the qualities that make the *langue d'oïl* the most appropriate language for the compilations of history (Book 1, chapter 10). From its emergence in the eleventh century, the literary tradition of Old French is dominated by narrative genres. When vernacular chronicles begin to appear in the twelfth century, they draw on this highly developed narrative tradition. As the lingua franca that enabled some form of linguistic and cultural exchange for a broad swathe of Western Europe from Norman England to the Frankish settlements of the Latin East, as well as francophone courts from Angevin Naples to Bohemia, French was the vernacular language in which the *historia* of Western Europe could be written. Since the narrative imperatives of *historia* require that a temporal awareness of the past be represented through emplotment, the historiographical traditions of medieval French rely on the narrative and rhetorical conventions of literary traditions. Nothing better illustrates this dynamic interplay between history and fiction – or historiography and narrativity – than the matter of Troy.

The plot of history requires an origin, and the medieval West located its origins in the city of Troy in Asia Minor. Juxtaposed to the story of Genesis from the Hebrew Bible, the narratives surrounding the Trojan War provided an originary myth that allowed for the conflation of sacred and pagan time. According to ancient legend, the Greek conquest of Troy precipitated the migration of Trojan heroes who settled in the West and became the progenitors of the people of Western Christendom. This legend derives from a geopolitical paradigm centred on the Mediterranean basin whereby the East was superseded by the West. In the seventh century CE, Fredegarius claimed Trojan ancestry for the Franks in the first book of his *Chronicle*; from that point on, Western European chroniclers routinely celebrate the Trojan ancestry of noble and royal figures by opening their narratives with a description of the fall of Troy and an account of the Trojan diaspora. Such a programmatic use of the Troy story in chronicles testifies to its status as a historical event in medieval textual cultures.

Until the twelfth century, texts that treated historical events – annals or chronicles such as the *Gesta gentis Francorum* (1120–31) – appear exclusively in Latin. The Crusades, a predominantly Frankish enterprise undertaken in the name of Western Christendom, stimulated the production of vernacular chronicles, initially in verse in the twelfth century, followed by prose in the thirteenth. Verse chronicles were also composed to articulate noble and royal lineage: the tradition of the *Grandes Chroniques de France* illustrates the trajectory of historical discourse – even in monastic houses – from Latin to vernacular. Produced at the abbey of Saint-Denis, the *Grandes Chroniques* were composed in Latin prose until the thirteenth century as a narrative record of the Capetian dynasty. In 1274, however, Hugh (Primas) of Orléans translated these Latin records into French in order to compile a vernacular history of the monarchy up until the reign of Philip II Augustus (1179–1223). In following his Latin sources, Primas locates the origin of the Capetian line with the fall of Troy and the Trojan diaspora. In his prologue he asserts: 'Certaine chose est donques que li roi de France, par les quex li roiaumes est glorieus et renommez, descendirent de la noble lignie de Troie.' ('Thus it is a certainty that the king of France, through whom the realm is glorious and renowned, descended from the noble lineage of Troy.')[1] The first chapter of Primas's *Grandes Chroniques* briefly narrates the rape of Helen, the siege and fall of Troy and the consequent westward migration of the Trojan heroes. Primat's chronicle initiated a tradition of vernacular history that was continuously produced at Saint-Denis until the late fifteenth century, thereby assuring the historicity of the Troy story in vernacular narratives.

Medieval French literary traditions are likewise shaped by the historiographical possibilities of the Troy story. While early genres such as hagiography or the *chanson de geste* implicitly evoke the truth claims of history as a means of performing contemporary ideologies and identities, the emergence of the *romans antiques* in the twelfth century depended on a historical vision inherited from ancient Roman constructs that subsumed classical legends drawn from the Troy story into a paradigm of universal history. Virgil's *Aeneid*, for instance, enabled a medieval appropriation of classical legend as

---

1 *Les Grandes Chroniques de France*, vol. 1, ed. Jules Viard (Paris: Société de l'Histoire de France, 1920), p. 4.

history in the earliest verse romances: the anonymous *Roman de Enéas* (c. 1155) and *Roman de Thèbes* (1150–5), as well as Benoît de Sainte-Maure's *Roman de Troie* (c. 1165). Although the generic classification of these texts as romances in modern scholarship would suggest that they do not lay claim to any historical foundation, the narratives of the *romans antiques* authorise themselves by reference to ancient history. Benoît sets up an elaborate framework for the process of *translatio studii* that argues for the authenticity of his account of the Troy story; he further argues that the veracity of the Troy story is important: 'En maint sen avra l'om retrait, / Saveir com Troie fu perie, / Mais la verté est poi oïe.' ('One often hears recounted how Troy perished, but the truth is difficult to hear.')[2] Benoît establishes his poetic authority by identifying his source as the Latin text of Dares, a fifth-century prose account of the destruction of Troy, which circulated widely in the medieval West in place of Homer's *Iliad*, for which there was no complete Latin translation. Benoît reiterates in detail the fictional credentials of Dares as they were outlined in the prologue to the Latin text: that Homer lived more than a hundred years after the siege of Troy and consequently wrote a fictional account of the destruction of that city. Dares' account, by contrast, presents itself as an eyewitness record, since the Latin text purports to be a translation of a Greek account supposedly written by a Trojan who lived through the war and preserved an eyewitness account of it. Benoît fleshes out his source slightly to emphasise the materiality of Dares' book, supposedly found in Athens and translated from Greek into Latin by Cornelius Nepos, whom Benoît designates as the nephew of Sallust. Benoît argues for the truth of Dares' account as an accurate record of the truth of the Trojan War. In his emphasis on his own faithful word-for-word translation of Dares, Benoît claims that his *Roman de Troie* provides the vernacular reader with a historically accurate account of the fall of Troy.

The *Roman de Troie* was produced in the court of Henry II (1133–89), the Norman/Angevin king whose patronage of vernacular clerks was intended to support his claim to the re-conquered throne of England. The significance of the Troy matter for the Angevin/Plantagenet ideology is evident in the *Roman de Brut* by Wace (c. 1100–74), a text composed in 1155 and dedicated, like the *Roman de Troie*, to Henry's wife, Eleanor of Aquitaine. An adaptation of Geoffrey of Monmouth's *Historia regum Britanniae* (c. 1135), the *Roman de Brut* is a verse chronicle that narrates the legendary past of the Britons. In translating Geoffrey's brief account of the Trojan diaspora from the introduction of the

---

2 Benoît de Sainte-Maure, *Le Roman de Troie*, ed. Léopold Constans (Paris: Société des anciens textes français, 1904), lines 42–4.

Historia regum Britanniae, Wace greatly expands Geoffrey's narrative to relate the travels of Brutus, the grandson of Aeneas, up until his arrival in Britain, where he founds a city he calls New Troy, which, Wace explains, came to be called London. The *Roman de Brut* appears to have prompted Henry II to commission Wace to compose another vernacular chronicle on the history of the Normans, the *Roman de Rou* (1160–74). When Wace failed to complete the chronicle, Henry turned to Benoît with the same commission. Benoît's *Chronique des ducs de Normandie* (c. 1180), composed in the same octosyllabic metre as the *Roman de Troie*, establishes Trojan descent for the Normans through their Danish heritage by positing Antenor as the founder of the Danish race. Benoît's historical vision uses the Trojan past to recuperate the Danes despite the well-known atrocities of their earlier campaigns in England. Through his Danish heritage, the Norman king Henry II could appeal to a Trojan ancestry as a counterclaim to the Trojan heritage represented by Brutus in the *Roman de Rou*. While the modern scholar might seek to make generic distinctions between the *Roman de Troie* and the *Chronique des ducs de Normandie* in order to classify one as fiction and the other as history, the texts themselves allow no such distinctions. Like Wace's *Roman de Brut* and *Roman de Rou*, Benoît's two texts share the same discourse of historical authenticity suggested by their historiographical rhetoric.

The story of the Trojan diaspora was fluid enough to enable the Capetians, the Britons, and the Normans to identify their respective Trojan ancestors, and thereby appeal to the authority of history in support of their competing dynasties.[3] But the Trojan past could also be used to buttress aristocratic claims to autonomy in the face of encroaching monarchical power, as the production of the *Histoire ancienne jusqu'à César* illustrates. In the first few decades of the thirteenth century, Roger IV, castellan of Lille, commissioned this extensive compilation of universal history, the first such text to appear in the vernacular rather than Latin. The *Histoire ancienne* follows a chronology that incorporates Genesis and biblical history, and the history of Assyria, Greece, Thebes, the Amazons, the fall of Troy, and the founding of Rome by Aeneas. The narrative includes the story of Alexander the Great and the early history of Rome before it abruptly breaks off. As Gabrielle Spiegel has shown, this text functions as a statement of aristocratic resistance to the consolidation of royal power by Philip II Augustus (1165–1223).[4] Like the *Faits des Romains*

---

3 Colette Beaune, *The Birth of an Ideology: Myths and Symbols of Nation in Late-Medieval France* (Berkeley: University of California Press, 1991), pp. 226–44.
4 Gabrielle M. Spiegel, *Romancing the Past: The Rise of Vernacular Prose Historiography in Thirteenth-Century France* (Berkeley: University of California Press, 1993), pp. 107–18.

(1213–14), a contemporary vernacular compendium of Roman history drawn from Sallust, Caesar, Suetonius and Lucan, the *Histoire ancienne* was composed in prose. The choice of prose emphasised the historical veracity claimed for these narratives, since by the thirteenth century verse narrative had become associated with fiction and prose with historical truth. The ancient legends gathered together in the *Histoire ancienne* all derive from the Mediterranean basin; in that spatial and temporal context, the fall of Troy marks a pivotal moment since it precipitates the founding of Rome, and by extension Western Christendom. In the context of universal history as constructed in medieval cultures, the Trojan diaspora not only unites East and West but simultaneously links the pagan past to the medieval Christian present. For the aristocracy of Flanders, the initial patrons of the *Histoire ancienne*, the narrative of the Trojan diaspora allowed them to locate for themselves a place in history.

Over the next three centuries the *Histoire ancienne* was copied and extensively revised throughout the francophone West, most noticeably in the colonial outposts of the Latin East as well as the Angevin court in fourteenth-century Naples. The Angevin dynasty, which had gained dominion in southern Italy in the thirteenth century, was a branch of the Valois dynasty. In the 1330s, Robert of Anjou, who ruled the kingdom of Naples from 1309 to 1343, commissioned a new redaction of the *Histoire ancienne*; this version omits the segment on Genesis and begins its historical narrative with Thebes. The most significant alteration in the second redaction is the expansive narrative of the Troy story; in the first redaction, this is a brief French translation of Dares's account of the fall of Troy. The first redaction consequently deploys the Troy story only for the sake of the Trojan diaspora in order to choreograph the Trojan genealogy leading up to the settlement of Flanders. By contrast, the second redaction, the Angevin/Neapolitan version of the *Histoire ancienne*, greatly expands the Troy segment of the text by adding a lengthy prose rendition of Benoît de Saint-Maure's *Roman de Troie*. Benoît's twelfth-century verse narrative had extensively developed the plot of events related to siege warfare, such as the twenty-three battles that took place outside the walls of Troy; such a detailed heroic plot becomes the basis for a prose history of the fall of Troy in the *Histoire ancienne*. The importation of the *Roman de Troie* results in a historical paradigm that emphasises the story of the destruction of Troy rather than the Trojan diaspora. The Troy story is more than a vehicle for articulating the Trojan foundations of European history. Since the narrative possibilities of siege warfare are vast, the story from Benoît's text offers a compelling and dramatic plot, one dense with heroes and battles in place of the schematic description of destruction and defeat represented by the first redaction of the *Histoire ancienne*. The conventions of romance narrative have become the plot of historical narrative.

Throughout the medieval period, the Troy matter enjoyed considerable currency as a historical event that could be put to a variety of literary, political or ideological uses, all of which depend on a cultural acceptance of the historicity of the Trojan War as well as the Trojan diaspora. Perhaps the most vivid example of the rhetorical applications of the Troy story is found in Robert de Clari's account of the Fourth Crusade, the *Conquête de Constantinople* (1207). Towards the end of this prose narrative, Robert de Clari reports that one of the crusaders, Pierre of Bracheux, was questioned about the purpose of their expedition by Jehans li Blaks, the leader of the Vlachs: "'De n'avés vous", fisent il, "teres en vos païs dont vous vous puissiés warir?'" ('"Have you not got", they said, "lands in your country from which you can support yourself?"')[5] Given the problematics of accounting for the goals and intentions that led to the conquest of Constantinople by the crusaders and their Venetian allies, this question could be taken programmatically (see Guynn, Chapter 11). Pierre responds by asking if Jehans has heard the story of how the great city of Troy was destroyed; when Jehans replies that they do indeed know the ancient tale, Pierre explains: 'Troies fu a nos anchiseurs. [E]t chil qui en escaperent si s'en vinrent manoir la dont nous sommes venu. [E]t pour che que fu a nos anchisieurs, sommes nous chi venu conquerre tere.' ('Troy belonged to our ancestors. And the ones who escaped from it came to stay where we are now. And because it belonged to our ancestors, we have come here to conquer the land' [pp. 124–5]). In conflating Troy and Constantinople, this fanciful anecdote illustrates the figurality of Troy as a city that might represent a contemporary city in the eastern Mediterranean such as Jerusalem or Constantinople. The rhetorical shape of Robert of Clari's *Conquête* treats the legend of Troy as a well-known historical fact. With this anecdote, Robert of Clari manages to collapse the past and the present in order to claim a truth value for his own account of the Fourth Crusade. The conventional quality of the ideology suggested by this rhetorical set piece on the fall of Troy and the Trojan diaspora demonstrates how well the fictions of Trojan origin served the historiographical imperatives of Old French narratives.

5 Text and translation from Robert of Clari, *La Conquête de Constantinople*, ed. Peter Noble (Edinburgh: Société Rencesvals British Branch, 2005), pp. 124–5.

16

Mysticism

CARY HOWIE

Mysticism, like literature, is an invention of modernity. This may be more than a coincidence. Like literature, mysticism coheres around an absence, an evanescent quality that its defenders can never concretely summon; like literature, it owes its coherence to institutional structures that have built canons around it and made it the object of critical scrutiny since the rise of the human sciences in the nineteenth century. Mysticism is nothing if not written: it is crucially, if paradoxically, a textual practice that documents, constructs, and frequently seeks to produce other lived or 'experienced' practices. In other words, mysticism is not just like literature; mysticism *is* literary.

Georges Bataille implicitly says as much in his later writings, in which mystical 'eroticism' (think, paradigmatically, of the swooning Saint Teresa) and literature are bound up with death and sacrifice, which is to say, with the limits of experience in every sense. This is not unimportant for medieval French mysticism, given that its pre-eminent figure, Marguerite Porete, was ultimately burned at the stake. Still, the fact remains that none of the so-called medieval mystics described themselves as such: as we shall see below, Marguerite d'Oingt calls herself, charmingly and tellingly, 'una persona': a person but also a character and, etymologically, a mask. Marguerite Porete's text, an allegorical dialogue, refuses to speak in a single voice. Their grouping under the rubric of mysticism is as foreign to them as their grouping under the rubric of literature; or, for that matter, of France. Bataille may have been more faithful to the Middle Ages than we are in his insistence that these sorts of texts are – before mysticism and before literature – engagements with excess and flirtations with the limits of language and life.

Scholars may be inclined these days to speak of 'visionary literature' or, in Nicholas Watson's phrase, 'vernacular theology', but these, too, are approximations, even less adequate to what they designate than generic descriptors typically are.[1] On the one hand, theology does not do justice to these texts' profound equivocations about whether God (*theos*) even concedes himself to speech (*logos*); it also inevitably, if unintentionally, attempts to recuperate mysticism for orthodoxy. On the other hand, Bernard McGinn will observe that Marguerite Porete's *Mirror of Simple Souls*, far from constituting an example of visionary literature, is downright 'hostile to visions'.[2] Amy Hollywood, in a similar vein, eloquently cautions against reading mystical texts as transparent to the lives – frequently lay and frequently female – behind them: 'While all creative thought and writing may be grounded in personal experience, the current danger in reading women's texts is to deny the highly mediated nature of this relationship and subsequently to denigrate the philosophical, theological, or literary profundity of the writer in favor of claims to spontaneity . . . naturalness, or subjective force.'[3] Mystical texts constitute such a large number of the texts written by women in the Western European vernaculars that 'medieval women writers' can often, through only a slight stretch of synecdoche, come to mean 'medieval mystical writers'. Resisting the temptation to draw conclusions about the lives of actual medieval women from so-called mystical texts is, as a result, no small task. It is, however, a crucial one, especially given the alternative: Marguerite Porete was after all burned because her accusers conflated her body with her book.

Medieval mysticism is more generally characterised in terms of two sets of distinctions: between bridal mysticism and essential mysticism, on the one hand; and between affirmative and negative theology, on the other. Bridal mysticism is a blatant euphemism for an entire tradition of writing inspired by the Song of Songs. It is, in other words, shorthand for erotic mysticism, generally replete with bedroom imagery and amorous anticipation. Essential mysticism is, in its way, a euphemism as well, since what it wishes to pare down and struggle towards is no less than the blank space at the heart of the human, the blank space where the created proceeds from the uncreated – and where, still more crucially, the uncreated God might persist within his creatures. It is indebted more to syllogism and logical paradox than so-called bridal mysticism, and it is, accordingly, less obviously indebted to figurative language and concrete metaphor. Nonetheless, it is worth insisting, with

1 Nicholas Watson, 'Censorship and Cultural Change in Late-Medieval England: Vernacular Theology, the Oxford Translation Debate, and Arundel's Constitutions of 1409', *Speculum* 70 (1995), pp. 822–64.
2 Bernard McGinn, *The Flowering of Mysticism* (New York: Crossroad, 1998, p. 247).
3 Amy Hollywood, *The Soul As Virgin Wife: Mechtild of Magdeburg, Marguerite Porete, and Meister Eckhart* (Notre Dame, IN: University of Notre Dame Press, 1995), p. 96.

Denys Turner, that there is still an enormous difference between 'negative' imagery and negating the image altogether. That is to say, philosophical rhetoric is still rhetoric; metaphors in which God is 'nothing' are still, in the end, metaphors.[4] Not surprisingly, 'affirmative' theology – based upon what can be said about God – is more frequently aligned with the 'bridal' tradition and 'negative' theology with the 'essential'. All the caveats from Turner still pertain, however: the proliferation of images in certain mystical texts is oriented precisely towards the moment when the images will exhaust themselves; likewise, for any creature, any being obliged to deal in and with language, there is no purely 'negative' theology.

Mysticism also provides crucial evidence for how the modern literary disciplines fail to do justice to medieval textual production. This is an article in a history of French literature, but mystical texts are famously pre- and trans-national. There is, to put it bluntly, nothing particularly French about them. Marguerite Porete is more frequently, and plausibly, discussed in relation to her Flemish and Germanic contemporaries – e.g. Hadewijch, Meister Eckhart and Mechtild of Magdeburg – than she is considered a part of the French medieval canon. (For a crucial exception to this, however, see Barbara Newman's recent consideration of Porete in relation to the *Romance of the Rose*.[5]) Furthermore, as Laurie Finke and others have shown, the many vernacular and Latin translations of Marguerite Porete's *Mirror* are as famous as, or even more famous than, the original French. It is, moreover, important to recognise that Marguerite's authorship was first argued by an Italian scholar in an Italian newspaper – Romana Guarnieri in *L'Osservatore Romano* in June 1946 – and the first critical edition, again by Guarnieri, appeared in Italy in 1965. Marguerite's text is thus as much a product of Italian modernity – the same modernity as, say, Roberto Rossellini and Pier Paolo Pasolini – as it is a document of medieval France.

The history of vernacular French mysticism in the Middle Ages is, however, a history of not just one Marguerite but two: Marguerite Porete, the northern heretic, finds her complement and foil in the Carthusian from Lyon, Marguerite d'Oingt, her strict contemporary. Both women would, in fact, die in 1310: Marguerite d'Oingt, on 11 February, presumably in her priory outside

---

4 Denys Turner, *The Darkness of God: Negativity in Christian Mysticism* (Cambridge: Cambridge University Press, 1995).
5 Barbara Newman, 'The Mirror and the Rose: Marguerite Porete's Encounter with the *Dieu d'Amours*', in R. Blumenfeld-Kosinksi, D. Robertson, and N. Bradley Warren (eds.), *The Vernacular Spirit: Essays on Medieval Religious Literature* (New York and Basingstoke: Palgrave Macmillan, 2002), pp. 105–23.

Lyon; four months later, on 1 June, Marguerite Porete would be burned at the stake in Paris for heresy. There is also, of course, a long tradition of Latin devotional writing in what is now called France, from at least Bernard of Clairvaux in the twelfth century to the thirteenth-century Occitan heretic Na Prous Bonheta and, arguably, the transplanted Italian theologian Bonaventure. Still, the only major vernacular authors of so-called mystical treatises are these two women with their uncannily shared name.

The symmetrical points of convergence and divergence between these Marguerites are numerous. Marguerite Porete was most likely a northern beguine, Marguerite d'Oingt a southern Carthusian prioress. 'Beguine' is a term used to designate holy women of varying orthodoxy, generally thought to have sprung out of the Franciscan tradition, most famously in the Rhineland and the Low Countries. They frequently lived in houses – *beguinages*, characterised, in Ellen Babinsky's words, by 'moderate enclosure' – but the dissemination of Marguerite Porete's text gives the impression that her life was at least partly an itinerant one, not unlike that of the mendicant orders. Marguerite does, in fact, speak in chapter 96, and with an intriguing gender equivocation, of 'une mendiant creature' (a mendicant creature), although she does not, elsewhere, have particularly good things to say about mendicancy. When, in chapter 16 of the *Mirror*, Reason interrogates Love about one of her more incendiary affirmations, namely that the Unencumbered Soul 'ne desire ne messes ne sermons, ne jeunes ne oraisons' ('desires neither masses nor sermons, nor fasts, nor prayers'), Love says that those things are nourishing only 'pour celles qui mendient; mais ceste ne mandie neant' ('for those who go begging; but this soul does not beg at all').

Carthusian monks and nuns, on the other hand, lived a life of greater enclosure than most of their contemporaries: the Carthusian order, founded in the eleventh century, privileged solitude as much as, if not more than, community, and thus struck a kind of compromise between the eremitic (i.e. solitary) tradition of the desert fathers and the cenobitic (i.e. communal) tradition of Benedict and his successors. Guibert of Nogent, as cited by Renate Blumenfeld-Kosinski, gives a succinct twelfth-century description of the Carthusian paradox when he observes, 'in [the original charterhouse] are thirteen monks who have a cloister quite suitable for common use but who do not live together in cloister fashion like other monks'.[6] In Carthusian practice the very commonplaces of monastic life – what could be more common than

6 Renata Blumenfeld-Kosinski, *The Writings of Margaret of Oingt* (Newburyport, MA: Focus Library of Medieval Women, 1990), pp. 2–3.

a cloister? – literally take on new meaning. It should not be surprising, then, that Marguerite d'Oingt, much like Marguerite Porete, was a deft interrogator of received terms and ideas; however, unlike Porete – and perhaps, I would like to speculate, in part because of her commitment to enclosure – she knew where to stop. It is, nevertheless, true that Marguerite Porete's anglophone afterlife is largely the result of a fifteenth-century Carthusian translator, whose commentary attempts to tame the less orthodox passages in the *Mirror* but ultimately, as Finke argues, fails to do so: 'because he is so clearly enamoured of the text's performative dimensions, it resists appropriation and disputes his intentions'.[7]

But what are these 'performative dimensions'? Marguerite Porete's *Mirror of Simple Souls* – whose full French title is *Le mirouer des simples ames anienties et qui seulement demourent en vouloir et desir d'amour* (*The Mirror of simple, annihilated souls who solely dwell in will and desire of love*) – is, in Catherine Müller's felicitous phrase, 'an unclassifiable work' ('une œuvre inclassable'): an allegorical dialogue in 139 chapters (or 140, or 122, depending on who is counting), with a prefatory poem and occasional lyric interludes, written under the sign of the *speculum*.[8] As Giovanna Fozzer notes, a medieval *speculum*, or mirror, indicates in the first place a text 'in cui il lettore-spettatore vede riflessi aspetti della realtà' ('in which the reader-spectator sees aspects of reality reflected').[9] It is, therefore, a subjective as well as an objective genre: one in which received data (historical, political, scientific, spiritual) are collected so as to transform their observer, who will inevitably also be observing herself. The transformation at stake in Marguerite's text is that of the created, 'encumbered' soul into its unencumbered and ultimately uncreated ground, namely God. To the extent that an allegorical debate among characters such as Soul, Love, and Reason – not to mention less common (and more colourful) figures such as Stupefaction and Holy Church the Little – can be said to constitute a straightforward account of anything, here it is an account of how the soul may pass through a series of stages and 'deaths' to reach a state of union with and transparency to God. In the process, and crucially for Marguerite's inquisitors, the soul takes leave of good works, the virtues, reason, the church – anything, in short, that comes between her and God.

---

7 Laurie A. Finke, '"More Than I Fynde Written": Dialogue and Power in the English Translation of *The Mirror of Simple Souls*', in M. Suydam and J. Ziegler (eds.), *Performance and Transformation* (New York: St Martin's, 1999), pp. 47–67, at p. 63.
8 C. Müller, *Marguerite Porete et Marguerite d'Oingt de l'autre côté du miroir* (New York: Peter Lang, 1999).
9 G. Fozzer (intro. and trans.), *Lo specchio delle anime semplici* (Milan: San Paolo, 1994), p. 59.

Marguerite d'Oingt's *Mirror* is much shorter than Porete's – three chapters that amount to thirteen pages in the bilingual critical edition – and is accompanied, in her oeuvre, by a saint's life and a series of letters, all in the vernacular. (Marguerite is also the author of a Latin devotional text, the *Page of Meditations*.) Its departure from Porete in tone and style is evident from the opening paragraph. Porete begins her text twice – once, in the prefatory poem, with 'Vous qui en ce livre lirez' ('You who will read in this book') and once, in the first chapter, with 'Ame de Dieu touchee, et denuee de peché' ('Soul touched by God, and stripped of sin') – and thereby establishes the ambivalence of her text, caught between 'you' and 'Soul', the book's insides and God's denuding touch. Marguerite d'Oingt, in contrast, enfolds her audience more thoroughly and capaciously into her text. Like Porete, she addresses a 'vous' – or, in fact, a 'vos' – but does so in relationship to an authorial 'I' altogether lacking in the *Mirror of Simple Souls*.

Compare Porete's opening lines with this declaration from the beginning of Marguerite d'Oingt's *Mirror*:

> Oy me semble que jo vos ay huy dire que quant vos aves huy reconter alcuna graci que Nostre Sires a fayt a acuns de ses amis, que vos en vales meuz grant tens. Et por co que jo desirro vostra salut assi come jo foy la min, je vos diroy, al plus briament que jo porroi, una grant cortesi que Nostre Sires a fait a una persona que je connoisso non a pas mout de tens.

> (Now it seems to me that I heard you say that, when you have heard some of the favours that Our Lord has done to some of his friends, you become, for a long time afterwards, more worthy on their account. And because I desire your salvation as much as I do my own, I will tell you, as briefly as possible, about a great courtesy that Our Lord granted, not long ago, to a person I know.)

Marguerite d'Oingt's text begins, crucially, with the casual inscription of the narrator as the horizon against which even the demand for the text's production must take place: 'Now it seems to me' says, among other things, that this text did not come out of nowhere. Along these lines, characteristic of Marguerite's text – and also of its more orthodox and traditional commitments – is the emphasis that 'your salvation' is somehow intimately connected to 'my own'. Divine favour – literally grace – is something unthinkable in isolation. Marguerite also, and again more traditionally, stresses that she will speak briefly, following a tradition of mystical 'abbreviation' with contemporary echoes in, for example, the Italian Franciscan Iacopone da Todi.

Marguerite d'Oingt's *Mirror* explicates a vision of a book. She thus shares Marguerite Porete's emphasis on the 'livre', whose heuristic status is taken for granted by both women, while nonetheless being put to radically different uses, for when Marguerite Porete says 'ce livre', this book, she means *her* book, although this book is never unequivocal; Marguerite d'Oingt, on the other hand, uses the 'book' as a visual metaphor: it is something she sees, the book of Christ, and therefore (among other things) another iteration of *logos* as word and person, body and Bible. Jesus, in her vision, holds 'un livre clos' ('a closed book') in his hand; the book is inscribed with red, white, black and gold letters. Each kind of letter teaches Marguerite – or, more accurately, teaches the third-person, gender-ambiguous 'illi' (s/he) – a different kind of response to the life of Christ: self-correction, endurance, enjoyment, desire. The *Mirror* then becomes effectively a treatise on sanctity, showing the extent to which mysticism is never easily separated from hagiography and hagiology. If, for Marguerite Porete, the soul loses her name in God like a river flowing into the sea, here the saints 'serant dedenz lor creatour tot assy com li peysson qui sont dedenz la mar' ('will be in their creator just like the fish in the sea'). In fact, this shift from soul to saint, from self-abandon to trinitarian incorporation, marks most vividly the point where these Marguerites' *specula* throw back different images – different watery reflections – to their readers.

In closing, it is worth emphasising the frequency with which medieval mysticism appears in modern and contemporary French thought. Deconstruction has had a long and vexed history of being considered in relation to negative theology, as Jacques Derrida makes clear in a series of essays, including but not limited to 'Comment ne pas parler: Dénégations' ('How Not to Speak: Denials') and 'Sauf le nom' ('Save [except for] the Name'). Georges Bataille and E. M. Cioran both devote entire books to the vertiginous excess with which so-called mystics are entranced; Jacques Lacan invokes medieval holy women in his twentieth seminar, *Encore*. Michel de Certeau's account of the possessed women in seventeenth-century Loudun, together with his more explicitly theoretical engagements with the baroque 'mystique', show the fragile and porous boundaries between the demonic and the sacred, sex and sanctity, self-authorised speech and speech generated by something wholly other.[10]

10 Jacques Derrida, 'Comment ne pas parler: dénégations', in *Psyché: inventions de l'autre* (Paris: Galilée, 1987), pp. 535–95; Jacques Derrida, *Sauf le nom* (Paris: Galilée, 1993), translated as *On the Name*, ed. D. Dutoit (Stanford, CA: Stanford University Press, 1995); Georges Bataille, *L'Expérience intérieure* (Paris: Gallimard, 1986), and *Guilty*, trans. B. Boone, intro. D. Hollier (Venice, CA: Lapis Press, 1988); E. M. Cioran, *Tears and Saints*, trans I. Zarifopol-Johnston (Chicago: University of

What mysticism insists upon, then, is that the Middle Ages are always already modern. More importantly, mysticism – understood in the most capacious sense, with everything that passes under that name at one time or another – insists that there is something unspeakable, then and now, that prompts us to speak. Anne Carson cites a sentence of Marguerite Porete's – 'His farness is more near' – and observes, 'I have no idea what this sentence means but it gives me a thrill. It fills me with wonder.'[11] I would propose, then, that mysticism is nothing if not a word we use to designate texts, medieval and modern, whose primary effect is to fill us with wonder.

Chicago Press, 1995); Michel de Certeau, *La Possession de Loudon* (Paris: Gallimard, 1980) and *La Fable mystique* (Paris: Gallimard, 1987), trans. as *The Mystic Fable*, trans. M. B. Smith (Chicago: University of Chicago Press, 1992); and Jacques Lacan, *Le Séminaire, livre xx: Encore* (Paris: Seuil, 1975), translated as *Encore: The Seminar of Jacques Lacan, Book xx*, ed. J.-A. Miller, trans. B. Fink (New York and London: Norton, 1999).
11 Anne Carson, *Decreation: Poetry, Essays, Opera* (New York: Knopf, 2005), p. 177.

17

Prose romance

MICHELLE R. WARREN

The history of medieval French prose romance has often been told in stereo-typical 'romance' style: the form rose suddenly to great heights in the early thirteenth century only to decline sadly in the course of the fourteenth and fifteenth centuries. This narrative, however, presupposes understandings of genre and aesthetics that derive more from modern definitions of style than from medieval literary practice. We can learn much more about medieval cul-ture (about literacy, memory, patronage, etc.) by setting aside the 'romance of romance', in which even the thirteenth century is something of a disap-pointment compared to the verse arts of the twelfth. Comparisons between prose romances, prose compositions that are not romances, and romances not in prose, for example, can illuminate some of the varied attractions and functions of prose romance for medieval writers and readers.

Texts

The earliest prose romances tell stories of the Grail and its eventual relations with King Arthur's court. Derived partly from verse romances composed by Robert de Boron (*Roman de lestoire dou Graal, Merlin, Perceval*), these narra-tives coincide with French prose accounts of the Fourth Crusade (Robert de Clari, Geoffroi de Villehardouin, Henri de Valenciennes) and translations from Latin histories of more distant events (*Pseudo-Turpin, Histoire ancienne jusqu'à César, Li fet des Romains*). These conjunctions illustrate two enduring characteristics of prose romance: its association with 'truthful' historiography, and its engagement with various forms of re-writing (translation, *dérimage* or *mise en prose*, continuation, interpolation, abridgement, cyclical expansion, etc.). Of course, twelfth-century verse-romance narrators also claim to tell true stories and to base them on pre-existing sources. From the beginning, then, prose romance operates in dialogue with multiple forms and genres. It both continues and departs from established narrative modes.

The best-known and most widely studied prose romances are the 'second generation' of Arthurian tales, referred to collectively as the *Lancelot-Grail* or *Vulgate Cycle*. The cycle includes (in order of the fictional chronology): *Estoire del Graal*, *Estoire de Merlin*, *Lancelot du lac*, *Queste del Saint Graal*, and *La Mort le roi Artu*. Critics have long posited that the cycle's composition began with *Lancelot*, and that the first two parts were composed last. Recent editorial and art historical work, however, suggests that the entire question of dating and ordering merits reconsideration.[1] Different parts of the cycle exist in several distinct forms (short and long, 'cyclic' and 'non-cyclic') with numerous variations even within related versions; the complete sequence survives in only a very few manuscripts.

The prevalence of spiritualised representations of the Grail in early prose romance suggests strong connections with existing forms of religious prose. The *Lancelot-Grail*, and even the romances derived from Robert de Boron's verse trilogy, of course go far beyond the Grail material to encompass a full range of 'romance' themes – chivalry, love, adventures, marvels, exoticism, etc. Other contemporary prose compositions do the same. The *Tristan* (composed in several versions during the thirteenth century), for example, is integrated into the world of the *Lancelot-Grail*, including a fictive author, Hélie de Boron, presented as a relative of Robert de Boron. *Guiron le Courtois* extends the adventures of the *Lancelot-Graal* to the previous generation, developing the exploits of the fathers of Tristan, Erec, Perceval, and Arthur. Finally, *Perlesvaus*, *haut livre du Graal*, linked to Glastonbury Abbey in Britain, presents a prose continuation of Chrétien de Troyes's *Conte du Graal*. Numerous versions, continuations, and compilations of the *Lancelot-Grail-Tristan* materials were elaborated from the thirteenth century to the fifteenth (including one by Rustichello da Pisa, who composed Marco Polo's adventures). Beyond the nexus of the Arthurian world, prose romance in the thirteenth century includes many other important compositions, from *La Fille du comte de Pontieu* to the *Sept sages de Rome* (both also rewritten in the fifteenth century).

Fourteenth-century romances continue many of the methods of composition initiated in the thirteenth century: recombinations of Arthurian material (*Roman de Perceforest*, *c.* 1340, itself reworked by David Aubert more than a century later), new compositions inspired by Arthurian forms (*Chevalier au papegau*, *Petit Artus de Bretagne*), romance-inflected genealogies (*Baudouin de Flandres*, Jean d'Arras's *Mélusine*), translations (Philippe de Mézière's *Griseldis*),

1 J.-P. Ponceau, *Lestoire del Saint Graal* (Paris, Champion, 1997), pp. xi–xiv; M. Meuwese, 'Crossing Borders: Text and Image in Arthurian Manuscripts', *Arthurian Literature* 24 (2007), pp. 157–77 and 27 figures, dating discussion at pp. 168–9.

and prosifications of verse sources (*Apollonius de Tyr, Bérinus, Girart de Rous-sillon*). Fifteenth-century compositions continue all of these trends, with new inflections. Genealogical romances proliferate (*Histoire des seigneurs de Gavre*, 1456; *Roman du comte d'Artois*, after 1487; *L'Histoire de Jason et de Médée* by Raoul Lefèvre for Philippe le Bon; *Jehan d'Avesnes*) alongside 'biographical' romances featuring a single hero, sometimes a contemporary figure (*Livre des faits du bon chevalier messier Jacques de Lalaing*), while the very sources of vernacular romance are given new forms (*Erec et Enide*).

Court patronage drove much of the demand for these kinds of works. In Burgundy, Phillip the Good (1419–67) was especially influential in commissioning books of all sorts, including romances. The courts of Berry and Anjou were also active centres of patronage (especially under René d'Anjou, himself a prolific writer, including the allegorical romance *Le Livre du cœur d'amour espris*, 1457, explicitly modelled on Arthurian Grail romances[2]). The well-documented political and social interests of literary patrons make fifteenth-century prose romances particularly rich sites for analyses of cultural history and ideology. Courtly performance, moreover, beginning already in the thirteenth century, often draws on the texts of prose romance, conflating fiction and social action.[3] Chivalric social events such as tournaments and banquets took inspiration from narrative, and in turn inspired narratives of courtly life.

Fifteenth-century prose romance involves a number of identifiable individual writers, including Jean de Wavrin, David Aubert, Philippe Camus, Raoul Le Fèvre, Olivier de la Marche and the prolific Jean Wauquelin (*Manekine*; *Livre des conquestes et faits d'Alexandre le Grand*; *Roman de la Belle Hélène de Constantinople*; *Girart de Roussillon*; *Histoire des rois de Bretagne*). Wauquelin's production illustrates how prose could bring together seemingly disparate genres in the unified project of illustrating heroic chivalry. The last 'medieval prose romance' is often identified as *Petit Jehan de Saintré* by Antoine de la Sale (1456), a narrative steeped in the ethos of crusade that concludes in 'fabliau' fashion. This *terminus*, however, marks only the last 'original' composition. There is in fact no need to terminate prose romance so abruptly, since copying, rewriting, and translating continued uninterrupted into the sixteenth century and beyond. Rewriting confronts linguistic changes that made thirteenth-century texts difficult to read; it also works through the aesthetics

2 René d'Anjou, *Le Livre du cœur d'amour espris*, ed. F. Bouchet (Paris: Librairie générale française, 2003), p. 92.
3 Cf. J. H. M. Taylor, 'The Fourteenth Century: Context, Text and Intertext', in Norris J. Lacy, Douglas Kelly, and Keith Busby (eds.), *The Legacy of Chrétien de Troyes* (Amsterdam: Rodopi, 1987), I, pp. 267–332.

of 'renewal' and 'embellishment'.[4] The continuities of the prose romance tradition, traversed by numerous discontinuities, challenge some of the standard periodisations of literary history, including the division between manuscript and print, medieval and modern.

From the thirteenth to the fifteenth century, many of these 'romances' draw on a number of different kinds of narrative and prose forms – epic, chronicle, hagiography, legal briefs, encyclopaedias, sermons, etc. The very vocabulary of textual identity underscores convergences between seemingly disparate forms. The word *estoire*, for example, designates both historical and romance narrative (in verse and prose). The earliest prose histories include some of the same stories as the twelfth-century *romans antiques* – adventures related to Trojans, Thebans, and Romans. Some of these same adventures also survive as independent *romans*, some derived from Latin sources, others from French verse romances. Individual heroes, many of whom remain readily recognisable today (Lancelot, Perceval, Tristan, etc.), recur as both characters and intertextual references. Romances continue to make truth claims, while histories include fantastical events. In the fourteenth century, for example, romance chivalry appears throughout Froissart's *Chroniques*, while numerous manuscript collections mix discursive forms (placing moralising tales alongside epic conquests and erotic romances). When an epic in verse, which includes 'romance' elements in the first place,[5] is transformed into prose, the difference between a 'prosified epic' and a prose romance seems almost beside the point. The formations of 'prose fiction' both highlight and sideline the utility of generic thinking. Ultimately, the prose form both does and does not matter significantly to the themes and meanings of romance.

This semi-chronological sketch – cursory and lacunary as it is – reveals some of the hazards of linear histories of prose romance.[6] Not only are many dates of composition unknown or uncertain, many works survive in manuscripts copied decades apart, many texts were rewritten in multiple different versions, and many later texts derive from earlier ones (sometimes in other languages or forms, some surviving and some not). In some cases,

---

4 E.g., Jean Wauquelin, *Le Roman en prose de Manekine*, ed. H. Suchier, in *Œuvres poétiques de Philippe de Remi, sire de Beaumanoir* (Paris: Firmin Didot, 1884), I, pp. 267–366, at pp. 267–8.

5 S. Kay, *The Chansons de Geste in the Age of Romance* (Oxford: Clarendon Press, 1995).

6 Bibliographical resources include: B. Woledge and H. P. Clive, *Répertoire des plus anciens textes en prose française depuis 842 jusqu'aux premières années du xiiie siècle* (Geneva: Droz, 1964), pp. 9–24; B. Woledge, *Bibliographie des romans et nouvelles en prose française antérieurs à 1500* (Geneva: Droz, 1954 [*Supplément 1954–1973*, Geneva: Droz, 1975]); G. Doutrepont, *Les Mises en proses des épopées et des romans chevaleresques du xive au xvi siècle* (Geneva: Slatkine, 1969); *La Littérature française aux xive et xve siècles*, ed. D. Poirion (Heidelberg: Carl Winter, 1988); *Splendeurs de la cour de Bourgogne: récits et chroniques*, ed. D. Régnier-Bohler (Paris: Robert Laffont, 1995).

individual manuscripts that seem to 'repeat' established narratives actually represent new creative interventions.[7] Whether recopied or revised, the prose romance corpus represents a relatively consistent form of narrative production across several centuries. Already in the thirteenth century, and with few changes in a core canon of references by the fifteenth, prose romance attests to medieval theories of literary value, cultural heritage and language change. Collectively, prose romances (both individual texts and their multiple copies) contain a repository of medieval thought on the nature of literary history and aesthetic norms.

Forms

A number of elusive factors must have contributed to the initial formation of prose romance, and to its enduring appeal in later centuries – such that the European 'novel' became almost unthinkable in any other form. Early prose romance certainly owed as much to established forms of prose narration in Latin and French (hagiography, sermons, historiography) as it did to established forms of French romance (*romans antiques*, Chrétien de Troyes).[8] In the early decades of the thirteenth century, courtly patrons' interest in vernacular history (pressed by assertions of royal authority) also contributed to the social and imaginative weight of long-form vernacular narration.[9] Meanwhile, increases in vernacular literacy expanded the ranks of the reading public and thus the practice of private reading that prose romances seemed to encourage. Changes within the structure of Old French language forms, especially the weakening of the case system, also favoured the syntactic development of prose while challenging the habitual patterns of octosyllabic verse.[10]

Whatever the initial inspirations and motives for prose romance composition, its effects repositioned established relations between literature and

7 E. Baumgartner, *Le Tristan en prose: essai d'interprétation d'un roman médiéval* (Geneva: Droz, 1975); C. E. Pickford, *L'Évolution du roman arthurien en prose vers la fin du moyen âge d'après le manuscrit 112 du fonds français de la Bibliothèque nationale* (Paris: Nizet, 1960); F. Bogdanow and R. Trachsler, 'Rewriting Prose Romance: The Post-Vulgate *Roman du Graal* and Related Texts', in G. S. Burgess and K. Pratt (eds.), *The Arthur of the French* (Cardiff: University of Wales Press, 2006), pp. 342–92.

8 Woledge and Clive, *Répertoire*, pp. 9–24; J. Beer, *Early Prose in France: Contexts of Bilingualism and Authority* (Kalamazoo: Western Michigan University Medieval Institute, 1992); M. Zink, *Littérature française du moyen âge* (Paris: Presses Universitaires de France, 2004), p. 59.

9 G. Spiegel, *Romancing the Past: The Rise of Vernacular Prose Historiography in Thirteenth-Century France* (Berkeley: University of California Press, 1993).

10 C. Galderisi, 'Vers et prose au Moyen Age', in F. Lestringant and M. Zink (eds.), *Histoire de la France littéraire: naissances, renaissances* (Paris: Presses Universitaires de France, 2006), pp. 745–66, at p. 749.

orality. If verse romance animates a single narrative voice (*je*), usually embodied in the physical performance of a *jongleur* before an audience, prose romance crowds the narrative space with many other voices (*contes, estoires*, character-narrators, character-scribes, etc.) usually disconnected from declamatory performance.[11] If the literal presence of a *jongleur* narrator stabilises and singularises narration, the virtual presence of multiple and conflicting disembodied sources endlessly defers audiences' perceptions of narrative origins. In the *Lancelot-Grail* Cycle, for example, narrative reference refracts in recursive ways that point in multiple directions at once. Since all paths lead to other paths, the overall effect is one of self-referential enclosure.[12] And yet, through reading aloud as well as through the representation of oral transmission within their fictive worlds, prose romances maintain intimate and complex relations with oral performance.

Prose has often been understood to enjoy a closer relation with everyday speech (quotidian orality) than verse since it is not constrained by the laws of versification (syllable counts and rhymes). Brunetto Latini expressed an early form of this view, characterising the 'wide and open' path of prose as akin to 'common speech' ('la voie de prose est large & pleniere, si come est hore la comune parleure des jens'). And yet Brunetto also states that the laws of rhetoric apply equally to prose and verse, and that in both cases one must take care to apply the appropriate colours of rhetoric ('Mais coment que ta parleure soit, ou por rime ou por prose, esgarde de que tes dis ne soient maigres ne sec, mais soient raenpli de jus & de sanc').[13] Thus even when writers do not follow the 'narrow' confines of versification, they must compose their texts artfully. And indeed, prose narration works within its own formal constraints, demanding a deliberate and recursive rhythm as sentences accumulate information and extend away from their putative subjects.[14] The materiality of length tests memory, structuring a literary experience that directly challenges habits of thought formed by the relatively short lines of

11 M. Perret, 'De l'espace romanesque à la matérialité du livre: l'espace énonciatif des premiers romans en prose', *Poétique* 50 (1982), 173–82; J. Kittay and W. Godzich, *The Emergence of Prose: An Essay in Prosaics* (Minneapolis: University of Minnesota Press, 1987), pp. 17–18.
12 E. J. Burns, *Arthurian Fictions: Rereading the Vulgate Cycle* (Columbus: Ohio State University Press, 1985); S. Marnette, *Narrateur et points de vue dans la littérature française médiévale: une approche linguistique* (Berne: Peter Lang, 1998), pp. 185–200.
13 Brunetto Latini, *Li livres dou Tresor*, ed. S. Brown and P. Barrette (Tempe, AZ: Arizona Center for Medieval and Renaissance Studies, 2003), pp. 300–1.
14 B. Cerquiglini, *La Parole médiévale: discourse, syntaxe, texte* (Paris: Minuit, 1981); E. Baumgartner, 'Remarques sur la prose du *Lancelot*', *Romania* 105 (1984), 1–15; M. T. Bruckner, 'Redefining the Center: Verse and Prose *Charrette*', in Carol Dover (ed.), *Companion to the Lancelot-Grail Cycle* (Cambridge, D. S. Brewer, 2003), pp. 95–105, at pp. 98–9.

octosyllabic and decasyllabic verse, whose units of meaning rarely exceed the rhymed couplet.

By repositioning relations between literature and orality, prose romance both responded to and promoted the idea that 'books' rather than *jongleurs* purveyed narrative fictions. The terminology of narrative communication remains multiple and variable through to the fifteenth century. The fourteenth-century *Perceforest* seems to express a distinctly material idea of narrative when the narrator divides the work into numbered *volumes* (rather than, say, the topical *branches* of the thirteenth-century *Lancelot-Grail*). At the same time, the explanation of the volumes reveals an enduring sense of narrative 'speech': 'il est de necessité de faire aucunes fois plus d'un ou deux volumes parlans d'une mesme matiere' ('it is necessary sometimes to make one or two volumes talking about the same topic').[15] The book here 'speaks', much like the talking *estoire* and *conte* of the *Lancelot-Grail*. Similarly, one version of the fifteenth-century *Bérinus* equivocates repeatedly between speaking and reading: the narrator begins by requesting that those 'who will hear or read' the book not blame him if they do not like what he has 'said or put' into it.[16] Here, the book (*livre*) occupies a double status as material object and embodied voice, illustrating the unresolved and mobile status of prose romance narrative.

The mechanics of prose narration structure a number of complex relations within the physical and metaphoric space of the text. The issue is not so much that prose is better suited than verse to lengthy narration (the *Perceval* continuations and Froissart's *Meliador* clearly illustrate narrative dilation in verse) but that the surviving prose romances do indeed deploy a relatively limited set of narrative and transitional strategies that structure a distinct narrative space and vocabulary.[17] The poetics of prose are easily identified, for example, in the use of conjunctions and transitional phrases. *Et, puis, après*, and *tandis que* extend the narrative without subordinating one scene to another, repeatedly placing incommensurable events in more or less the same place and time. These expressions form the basis of the characteristic

---

15 *Perceforest*, ed. G. Roussineau, 8 vols. (Geneva: Droz, 1988), I, p. 1.

16 *Bérinus, roman en prose du XIVe siècle*, ed. R. Bossuat (Paris: Société des anciens textes français, 1931), p. 1.

17 I have explored some specific instances of these issues in *History on the Edge: Excalibur and the Borders of Britain, 1100–1300* (Minneapolis: University of Minnesota Press, 2000), pp. 173–6, and 'Take the World by Prose: Modes of Possession in the *Roman d'Alexandre*', in D. Maddox and S. Sturm-Maddox (eds.), *The Medieval French Alexander* (Albany: State University of New York Press, 2002), pp. 143–60. Some of the paragraphs that follow are adapted from these discussions.

of 'interlace' (*entrelacement*), or the weaving together of multiple strands of action. They give prose romance its open potential for continued narration, limited ultimately only by material constraints (e.g. supplies for making books, length of a writer's life, etc.).

The powers of interlace lie as much with the 'seams' that connect one 'thread' of the story to another as with the threads themselves. Jeffrey Kittay and Wlad Godzich emphasise the primacy of the seam following an analysis of *tandis que*: 'Conjunction and disjunction work formally together: they are both seams.'[18] In the seam, which joins while separating, all references point to the narrative space itself. The dominant seam of many prose romances takes various forms of 'se test ore atant li contes de . . . Or dit li contes que . . . ' ('the *conte* now at this point stops talking about . . . Now the *conte* says that . . . '). This phrase encloses reference grammatically in the reflexive verb (*se test*), whose subject and object are the narrative itself (*conte*). In the seam, disparate times, places and discourses converge on the 'here and now' of narration. Prose is thus simultaneously expansive and restricted: it can extend infinitely within a domain firmly circumscribed by self-reference. As such, medieval prose performs, in its very structures, desires for autonomy, totalisation and transcendence. The prose-literate reader occupies multiple disconnected positions, repeatedly shifting perspectives and identifications.

The potentially endless chain of substitutions afforded by prose literacy (or what Mikhail Bakhtin called 'prose consciousness'[19]) disrupts hegemonic discourse – hence the medium's attractiveness as a mode of aristocratic resistance. Yet this same chain of substitutions can also subsume resistance itself: no boundary is off limits. Indeed, Kittay and Godzich conclude that the prose literacy that enjoins border subjectivity also serves the demands of centralised authority.[20] The prose medium thus contributes to the ironies that Gabrielle Spiegel and R. Howard Bloch both identify in prose patronage: aristocratic readers helped refine a form that served the ideological goals of the monarchy that eventually disempowered them. The defence of chivalric ideals (such as individualism), for example, ultimately proved their impossibility; the monarchy itself adopted prose for its own chronicles.[21] The verse prologue of a prose history of Philip II inflects royal appropriation directly: the author explains

18 Kittay and Godzich, *The Emergence of Prose*, p. 124.
19 M. Bakhtin, *The Dialogic Imagination: Four Essays*, ed. M. Holquist, trans. C. Emerson and M. Holquist (Austin: University of Texas Press, 1981), p. 324.
20 Kittay and Godzich, *The Emergence of Prose*, pp. 202–7.
21 Spiegel, *Romancing the Past*, pp. 158–9, 269ff; R. H. Bloch, *Medieval French Literature and Law* (Chicago: University of Chicago Press, 1977), pp. 224–58.

that he will not write in rhyme, 'Si con li livres Lancelot / Ou il n'a de rime un seul mot, / Pour mielz dire la verité' ('like the book of Lancelot, where there is not a single word of rhyme, in order to better tell the truth').[22] Here, the prose romance form justifies a royal genealogy at odds with the values of romance itself.

Prologues such as this one, which decry the mendacity of verse, were composed in both prose and verse, usually to introduce historiographic or spiritual texts.[23] They nonetheless serve as a vital reminder that prose and verse cohabited many narrative spaces, and that romances in both forms developed together. Indeed, the complaints of historiographers against the lies and deformations of verse sound similar to those of Chrétien de Troyes against his predecessors (*Erec et Enide*) and potential continuators (*Le Chevalier au lion*). And Philippe de Rémi opens his thirteenth-century *Roman de la Manekine* with the claim that, despite never having rhymed before, the truth of his material compels him to write in verse; he also promises not to lie 'Se n'est pour ma rime alongier' ('except to draw out my rhyme').[24] The claims of both truth and 'mere translation' that seem to define vernacular prose are thus themselves partly literary topoi shared with verse romance.[25] In Philippe's case, the admission that verse may lead him to lie derives more from his proclaimed lack of skill than from verse itself.

The prologues of Jean d'Arras's *Mélusine* (in prose) and Coudrette's *Mélusine* (in verse) illustrate some of the commonalities and differences between the forms. Both narrators express interest in truth, identify authenticating sources, and proclaim the limits of their talent as writers while beseeching God for help. Jean gives the precise date on which he began to write – 'mettre en prose' – without attributing any particular value to the medium itself.[26] Coudrette, meanwhile, represents his patron asking for a versified text to speed the story's diffusion: 'Je vueil qu'elle soit rimoÿe, / Elle sera plus tost ouye' ('I want it to be rhymed, it will be heard sooner'); Coudrette replies by protesting

22 Woledge and Clive, *Répertoire*, p. 30.
23 C. Galderisi, 'Vers et prose au Moyen Age', in F. Lestringant and M. Zink (eds.), *Histoire de la France littéraire: naissances, renaissances* (Paris: Presses Universitaires de France, 2006), pp. 754–5; M. Stanesco, 'Les Romans en prose au moyen âge', ibid., pp. 970–83, at pp. 972–3; Woledge and Clive, *Répertoire*, pp. 27–31.
24 Philippe de Rémi, *Le Roman de la Manekine*, ed. and trans. B. N. Sargeant-Baur (Amsterdam: Rodopi, 1999), lines 33–6, 47.
25 E. Baumgartner, 'Le Choix de la prose', *Cahiers des recherches médiévales* 5 (1998), pp. 7–13; R. W. Hanning, 'Arthurian Evangelists: The Language of Truth in Thirteenth-Century French Prose Romances', *Philological Quarterly* 63 (1985), pp. 347–65.
26 Jean d'Arras, *Mélusine ou la noble histoire de Lusignan*, ed. and trans. J.-J. Vincensini (Paris: Librairie Générale Française, 2003), p. 112.

that a rhymed version already exists.[27] These prologues reveal competing assumptions about appropriate narrative form, although not necessarily in the terms most commonly attributed to 'prose' and 'verse'. Coudrette's prologue, moreover, shows verse replacing verse and prose at the same time, as well as a utilitarian approach to verse that might be more expected for prose. Together, these prologues resist generalisations about the development of verse–prose relations (especially since both survive in about the same number of copies, if one includes printed texts of the sixteenth century).

The example of *Mélusine* illustrates succinctly the ongoing production of new and revised texts in both verse and prose from the thirteenth to the fifteenth century. Verse and prose interact throughout their literary history. Indeed, a number of verse histories date from the same period as the early prose histories (Ambroise's *Histoire de la guerre sainte*, *Histoire de Guillaume le Maréchal*, Calendre's *Les Empereors de Rome*); the *Histoire ancienne jusqu'à César* includes regular verse commentaries;[28] verse encyclopaedias appear throughout the thirteenth century; Froissart composed his *Meliador* in verse; Philippe Mousket wrote 30,000 lines of octosyllabic verse to recount French history from Troy to the year 1243 (drawing on both romance and epic sources in both verse and prose). Transfers between verse and prose, moreover, happened in both directions, with some of the earliest and latest prose romances deriving from verse originals – and prose originals providing the basis for some versifications.[29] Verse also appears within prose romance compositions, from mixed-form narratives (*Aucassin et Nicolette*, *Le Livre du cœur d'amour espris*) to lyric insertions (*Tristan en prose*).[30] While prose romance titles from the thirteenth century survive in proportionally more manuscripts, verse romances evidence a greater number of discretely different narratives.[31] All of these formal variants and innovations belie the notion of any simple 'evolution' from verse to prose, even if it is true that long-form narration in verse became increasingly rare in the modern centuries.

Prose romances attracted some of the most elaborate pictorial cycles that survive from the medieval period. They thus sustain a major form of visual

---

27 Coudrette, *Le Roman de Mélusine ou Histoire de Lusignan*, ed. E. Roach (Paris: Klincksieck, 1982), lines 81–2.

28 C. Croizy-Naquet, *Écrire l'histoire romaine au début du XIIIᵉ siècle* (Paris: Champion, 1999), pp. 189–218; *Histoire ancienne jusqu'à César (Estoires Rogier)*, ed. M. de Visser-van Terwisga (Orléans: Paradigme, 1999).

29 Woledge and Clive, *Répertoire*, pp. 35–9.

30 D. Poirion, 'Romans en vers et romans en prose', in J. Frappier and R. Grimm (eds.), *Le roman jusqu'à la fin du XIIIᵉ siècle* (Heidelberg: Carl Winter, 1978), pp. 74–81; Galderisi, 'Vers et prose'; Stanesco, 'Les Romans en prose', p. 971.

31 Galderisi, 'Vers et prose', pp. 758–61.

art that engaged artists and designers from throughout Europe. As such, they articulate a transcultural language of visual narrative while furnishing resources to an active commerce in portable luxury goods.[32] The broadly European nature of illustrated manuscript production serves as a useful reminder that the texts of French prose romance were also adapted in many other European languages, making them a vital node for a comparative understanding of linguistic and cultural interactions from the medieval to the modern period.[33]

At present, critics have many reasons to shift their criticism away from approaches that privilege individual authorship and originality. As such, the study of prose romance has no reason to follow the narrative of 'decline' that has often shaped medieval literary history – tracing a genre that began with such promise in the twelfth century to the deep 'senility' of the fifteenth. Instead, translations and rewritings work within rich dynamics of patronage, language change, social practices of reading, scribal culture, and intercultural and transhistorical communications. The relative influence or critical importance of a work in later centuries, moreover, need not frame its place in literary history. Incomplete, prolix, repetitive, and idiosyncratic survivals always bear witness to something: it is the challenge of literary historians to seek what that something might be, and to find the questions that those survivals might answer.

32 R. Middleton, 'The Manuscripts', in G. S. Burgess and K. Pratt (eds.), *The Arthur of the French* (Cardiff: University of Wales Press, 2006), pp. 8–92; Meuwese, 'Crossing Borders'.
33 M. Stanesco and M. Zink, *Histoire européenne du roman médiéval* (Paris: Presses Universitaires de France, 1992), pp. 63–6, 129–52.

18

Rhetoric and theatre

JODY ENDERS

Its intuitive yet detailed formulae have structured oral traditions from *Beowulf* to modern Yugoslavia. Numerous medieval literary genres bore its imprint in moments as varied as the complicated ratiocinations of Chrétien's *Cligés*, Christine de Pizan's mnemotechnical prologue to the *Cité des dames*, and the divine or all too earthly allegories of Guillaume de Deguileville's *Pelerinaige de la vie humaine*, Alain Chartier's *Quadrilogue invectif* or the ubiquitous *Roman de la rose*. Moreover, given its influence in the medieval university's trivium, where it cohabitated with grammar and dialectic, it informed both pre-modern literary criticism and satires about the excesses of scholasticism. It was rhetoric, the art and science of persuasion which, whether school-taught or instinctive, was especially influential in the theatre.

The subject of countless legal, ethical, moral and aesthetic debates from Plato onward, *rhetorica* was largely Ciceronian in medieval France, where it constituted a bona fide habit of thought and where its five parts or canons were just as adaptable to literary communication as they had been long ago to the usually forensic contexts in which Graeco-Roman theorists had codified its principles.[1] *Invention* (*heuresis* or *inventio*) referred to the authorial act of *finding* (*invenire*) one's subject along with the arguments liable to assist in its reception; and its considerable literary resonances are just as clear in the Old Provençal poets who sought to *trobar* as they would be in the twelfth-century *Poetria nova*, where Geoffrey of Vinsauf describes a painful, even torturous, self-reflexive wresting of the subject from his own mind.[2] *Arrangement* (*taxis*

---

1 The canonical work on the subject is J. Murphy, *Rhetoric in the Middle Ages: A History of Rhetorical Theory from Saint Augustine to the Renaissance* (Berkeley: University of California Press, 1974; reprinted 1981); and, more generally, G. A. Kennedy, *Classical Rhetoric and its Christian and Secular Tradition from Ancient to Modern Times* (Chapel Hill: University of North Carolina Press, 1980).

2 Geoffrey of Vinsauf, *Poetria nova*, in *The* Poetria Nova *and its Sources in Early Rhetorical Doctrine*, trans. E. Gallo (The Hague: Mouton, 1971), lines 1754–62; 109; and J. Enders, *The Medieval Theater of Cruelty: Rhetoric, Memory, Violence* (Ithaca, NY: Cornell University Press, 1998), pp. 25–7.

or *dispositio*) supplied the building blocks for the order of both spoken and written discourse as that canon proffered variations on the theme of the fundamental oratorical sequence of Introduction, Statement, Proof, Confirmation, Refutation and Conclusion. *Style* (*lexis* or *elocutio*) enabled speakers and writers to render beautiful (or memorably ugly) the language that they had thus *found* and *arranged* – allegedly, but impossibly, in that order. *Memory* (*mneme* or *memoria*) consigned language, visions, and voices to a mental dwelling place, complete with columns, backgrounds, and lighting whose function was to safeguard the speaking, writing, imaging, imagining, and acting to come – all by placing *imagines agentes* on a psychodramatic but presciently physical stage whose patently theatrical ramifications were outlined in the 1960s by Frances Yates.[3] And, with its emphasis on voice, volume, intonation, gesture, and even pantomime as semiotic systems, *delivery* (*hypokrisis*, *pronuntiatio*, or *actio*) hosted the transformation of thought and words into acts of performance – and, occasionally, into what the ordinary language philosopher J. L. Austin would later term bona fide performative acts: *doing things with words*. Indeed, in the eighth century, Alcuin seconded Cicero in granting the palm to delivery, the 'last and highest' stage of rhetoric whose power:

> surpasses the other powers of the speaker to such a degree that, in the opinion of the peerless Tully, a speech devoid of skill may nevertheless achieve merit by virtue of a speaker's excellence in Delivery, while on the other hand a speech excellent beyond description may meet contempt and mockery if it is pronounced inappropriately.[4]

Apparently that was all too true of medieval French practice, such that Thomas Basin found himself proposing (albeit unsuccessfully) a massive juridical reform in the mid-fifteenth century in which he recommended the abolition of the histrionic oral trial in favour of written pleas alone. 'It will be very difficult and burdensome, in my opinion', he argued, 'for our colleagues to strip the pomp from their oral trials and forensic oratory, which clearly puts on display a certain splendour and the magnificence of the courts.'[5]

Thus, while rhetoric was paramount to any oral tradition and, for purposes of this volume, to any medieval French literary tradition, it is in the spectacular dimensions of theatre, an artistic medium literally foreshown by the two most

---

3 On the *imagines agentes*, see the Pseudo-Ciceronian *Ad C. Herennium*, ed. and trans. H. Caplan (Cambridge, MA: Harvard University Press, 1954; reprinted 1977), 3.37.
4 Alcuin, *The Rhetoric of Alcuin and Charlemagne*, ed. and trans. W. S. Howell (Princeton, NJ: Princeton University Press, 1941), lines 81–2; 1093–8.
5 T. Basin, 'Projet de réforme en matière de procédure', in J. Quicherat (ed.), *Histoire des règnes de Charles VII et de Louis XI*, 4 vols. (Paris: Renouard, 1859), IV, p. 50.

neglected rhetorical canons of memory and delivery, that medieval France reveals its unbroken connections with both a classical past and a present theatricality, especially in a society that, as Jacques Le Goff has famously noted, had a tendency to play itself out.[6] Given the often repeated Ciceronian observation that 'orators are the players who act real life', rhetorical discourses underwent a long history of 'aestheticisation' or what George Kennedy calls a *letteraturizzazione* 'from persuasion to narration, from civic to personal contexts, and from discourse to literature, including poetry'.[7] Equally productive, equally generative was the *letteraturizzazione* from the enacted discourses of law, politics, and praise or blame – that is, of forensic, deliberative and epideictic rhetoric – to theatre, all suggesting that Paul Zumthor's celebrated *mouvance* was as capital to textual instability as it was to the countless instabilities of the ephemera of performance.[8] Although memory and delivery were neglected even by Roland Barthes (who presented only a tripartite schema of rhetoric based on invention, arrangement, and style), analysis of the extant French dramatic corpus – largely of the fourteenth and fifteenth centuries as painstakingly catalogued by L. Petit de Julleville in his signature study, *Les Mystères* – bears out Ernst Robert Curtius's earlier insight that, like antiquity, the Middle Ages 'had rhetoric for a general theory of literature'.[9] That is the case, moreover, despite the initial literary emphasis by such scholars as F. Douglas Kelly and R. Howard Bloch on the rhetorical structures of the *roman*, and despite a longstanding distrust of literary rhetoric, as evidenced by such early dismissals of that art by Gaston Paris and Gaston Raynaud in their own edition of Arnoul Gréban's *procès de paradis*; by Howard Graham Harvey's complaint that the so-called fathers of French comedy, the Basochiens (the legal apprentices and frequent playwrights who belonged to the society known as the Basoche), had written morality plays 'as dull as any a cleric had produced'; and by Allardyce Nicoll's more general objection that, in the mystery cycles,

6 On orality and literacy in medieval France, see P. Zumthor, *La Lettre et la voix: la 'Littérature médiévale'* (Paris: Seuil, 1987); on the proto-dramatic status of memory and delivery, see J. Enders, *Rhetoric and the Origins of Medieval Drama* (Ithaca, NY: Cornell University Press, 1992), chaps. 1 and 2; and for J. Le Goff, see *Medieval Civilization, 400–1500*, trans. J. Barrow (Oxford: Blackwell, 1995), pp. 360–1; C. Symes, *A Common Stage: Theater and Public Life in Medieval Arras* (Ithaca, NY: Cornell University Press, 2007); and G. Olson, 'The Medieval Fortunes of "Theatrica"', *Traditio* 4 (1986), pp. 265–86.
7 See Cicero, *De oratore and De partitione oratoria*, ed. and trans. H. Rackham, 2 vols. (Cambridge MA: Harvard University Press, 1942; reprinted 1976), 3.215; and Kennedy, *Classical Rhetoric*, p. 5.
8 P. Zumthor, *Essai de poétique médiévale* (Paris: Seuil, 1972), pp. 65–72.
9 See Barthes, 'L'Ancienne Rhétorique', *Communications* 16 (1970), pp. 172–229; L. Petit de Julleville, *Les Mystères*, vols. I and II of *Histoire du théâtre en France* (Geneva: Slatkine, 1880; reprinted 1968), II, pp. 175–85; and E. R. Curtius, *European Literature and the Latin Middle Ages*, trans. W. R. Trask (Princeton, NJ: Princeton University Press, 1953, reprinted 1973), p. 71.

'rhetoric and intellectual argument' were only too often 'substituted . . . for dramatic passion'.[10] Thanks to the important recuperative efforts of James J. Murphy, George Kennedy, F. Douglas Kelly, Aron Kibédi Varga, and Marc Fumaroli, it is clear to any historian of rhetoric that there need be no divide between intellect and passion, nor between rhetoric and theatre.[11] Rhetoric was not antagonistic to creative expression: quite the contrary, it nurtured artistry. Beyond that, however, rhetoric completes the picture once outlined by E. K. Chambers, Karl Young, and O. B. Hardison for the ontological and proto-dramatic commingling of ritual and representation, be it on the streets in processions and parades or in the Christian liturgy.[12]

Rhetoric in the French Middle Ages was performance art, an important site of precisely the sort of theatrical activity that has attracted the attention of so many medievalists attending to the liminal spaces in which ritual oscillates generically with representation, undergoing its own anthropological version of *mouvance*, and in which thought oscillates with action.[13] Indeed, numerous medieval theorists described a generic and epistemological passage according to which any orator moved from 'reading' the psychodramatic language of the *ars memorandi* to speaking theatrically the words of delivery. The most striking accounts of that progression occur in such staples of the medieval intellectual diet as Saint Augustine, Geoffrey of Vinsauf, and John of Garland. Augustine, for instance, had once practised mnemonics in a dimly lit room by 'singing' silently and meditatively within the memory palaces of his mind: 'I can sing as much as I want, even though my tongue does not move and my throat utters no sound.'[14] Geoffrey later observed that 'the voice is as it were the image (*imago*) of the thing . . . As the

10 D. Kelly, *Medieval Imagination: Rhetoric and the Poetry of Courtly Love* (Madison: University of Wisconsin Press, 1978); R. H. Bloch, *Medieval French Literature and Law* (Berkeley: University of California Press, 1977); A. Gréban, *Mystère de la Passion*, ed. G. Paris and G. Raynaud (Geneva: Slatkine, 1878; reprinted 1970), p. xvi; H. G. Harvey, *The Theatre of the Basoche* (Cambridge, MA: Harvard University Press, 1941), p. 13; and A. Nicoll, *World Drama from Aeschylus to Anouilh*, 2nd edn (New York: Harper and Row, 1976), p. 116.

11 Aron Kibédi Varga, *Rhétorique et littérature: études de structures classiques* (Paris: Didier, 1970); Marc Fumaroli, *L'Âge de l'éloquence: rhétorique et 'res literaria' de la Renaissance au seuil de l'époque classique* (Geneva: Droz, 1980).

12 E. K. Chambers, *The Mediaeval Stage*, 2 vols. (Oxford: Oxford University Press, 1903); K. Young, *The Drama of the Medieval Church*, 2 vols. (Oxford: Clarendon Press, 1933); O. B. Hardison, Jr, *Christian Rite and Christian Drama in the Middle Ages: Essays in the Origin and Early History of Modern Drama* (Baltimore, MD: Johns Hopkins University Press, 1965).

13 See esp. K. A. Ashley and W. Hüsken (eds.), *Moving Subjects: Processional Performance in the Middle Ages and the Renaissance* (Amsterdam: Rodopi, 2001).

14 Augustine of Hippo, *Confessions*, trans. W. Watts, 2 vols. (Cambridge, MA: Harvard University Press, 1950), bk 10, chap. 8.

subject exhibits itself (*recitator*), so the speaker exhibits his voice';[15] while John rearticulated the classical concept of the memory background in his *Parisiana poetica* (c. 1220), complete with 'three main sections and columns', one of which was to house, synaesthetically, 'all kinds of languages, sounds, and voices of the various living creatures'.[16] Since the process of mnemonic imaging anticipated the oral regeneration of the referents of those images during delivery, the *ars memorandi* might thus have helped to bridge the gulf, not only between image and performance, but between rhetoric and a nascent drama as well.

So it was that other medieval theorists such as Isidore of Seville, Hugh of Saint Victor and many others identified within the art of rhetoric such crucial protodramatic components as privileged or sacred space, costume, staging, ritual conflict, audience participation, spectacle, dialogue, imitation, and, above all, impersonation (as evidenced in frequent medieval attention to prosopopoeia, probably the single most important element in the critical establishment of the so-called origins of medieval liturgical drama in such extant documents as the *Regularis concordia*, the *Winchester Troper* and the *De tragoediis* by Honorius Augustodunensis).[17] As described, for example, in the widely circulated *Rhetorica ad Herennium*, and reprised by such medieval authors as Bede, William of St Thierry, and Origen, prosopopoeia appears in what William describes as the *modus dramatis et stylus comicus* of the Song of Songs, which is 'written in the mode of a drama and in theatrical style, as if to be recited by characters and with action'; and, for Origen, once those characters were speaking and acting for themselves, they became veritable *dramatis personae*: 'For we call a thing a drama, such as the enaction of a story on the stage, when different characters are introduced and the whole structure of the narrative consists in their comings and goings among themselves.'[18] In ways excitingly anticipatory of the modern school of acting known as 'the method' (as derived from the writings of Constantin Stanislavski), Geoffrey of Vinsauf even went so far as to urge that 'Outer motion follows the inner, and the outer and inner man are equally moved. If you play this part (*quid recitator ages*), what shall you, the speaker, do?' His answer was as oxymoronic

15 Geoffrey of Vinsauf, *Poetria nova*, lines 2060–4, 2044–5.
16 John of Garland, *The Parisiana Poetria of John of Garland*, ed. T. Lawler (New Haven, CT: Yale University Press, 1974), bk 2, pp. 94–110.
17 See Honorius *et al.* in D. Bevington, (ed.), *The Medieval Drama* (Boston: Houghton Mifflin, 1975), pp. 9, 27–9; and re-explored by D. Dox, *The Idea of the Theater in Latin Christian Thought* (Ann Arbor: University of Michigan Press, 2004).
18 Both authors are cited by A. J. Minnis, *Medieval Theory of Authorship: Scholastic Literary Attitudes in the Later Middle Ages* (London: Scholar Press, 1984), pp. 57–8.

as any verisimilitude enacted by any Faux Semblant: 'Imitate (*imitare*) genuine fury.'[19]

Once the rhetorical focus on both *showing* and *telling* stories has been reintegrated into the literary life of medieval France, a number of false binaries collapse between learned v. popular, sacred v. profane, tragic v. comic, musical v. non-musical, and, above all, dramatic v. non-dramatic, which includes, à la D. W. Robertson, the *caritas*- v. *concupiscientia*-driven symbolism at such a key site of the alleged 'origins' of liturgical drama in the *quem quaeritis* trope or *Visitatio sepulchri*.[20] A revitalised focus on that theatricality is highly beneficial to a great variety of orphaned medieval art forms that have defied traditional generic classification: forensic debate and the *tenso*, romance dialogues and interior monologues, the *ars praedicandi* and the *sermon joyeux*, the quodlibetal disputation at the Sorbonne and the royal entry – all in ways that herald a discipline that is now much in vogue: performance studies.[21]

Thanks to exciting scholarship in that ever-expanding interdiscipline (inspired, in many ways, by the work of Erving Goffman, Victor Turner, and Richard Schechner), we now find, occupying the same intellectual home, numerous non-canonical, theatrical, and ritual activities, many of which had already been identified by Isidore of Seville as early as the seventh century in his discussion of 'War and Play' (*De bello et ludis*).[22] Where Isidore grouped together warfare, courtroom, classroom, judgement, sport, circus, theatre, music, the gladiatorial amphitheatre, spectacle, and gambling, contemporary performance theorists would do the same, classifying under the same ritual rubric such entities as medieval processions, tournaments, public executions, dubbing ceremonies, royal entries, and the Mass itself alongside modern parades, rugby matches, work sites, cocktail parties, parlour games, political rallies, funerals, and even reality TV.[23] But the mere multiplication of our objects of inquiry neither addresses nor resolves the complicated ontological

---

19 Geoffrey of Vinsauf, *Poetria nova*, lines 2051–3. Faux Semblant is the infamous figure of hypocrisy and double-talk in the *Roman de la rose*.
20 D. W. Robertson, *A Preface to Chaucer: Studies in Medieval Perspectives* (Princeton, NJ: Princeton University Press, 1962); and A. E. Knight, *Aspects of Genre in Late Medieval French Drama* (Manchester: Manchester University Press, 1983).
21 On preaching, the masterwork is M. Zink, *La Prédication en langue romane* (Paris: Champion, 1976); and, for the *quodlibet*, see P. Glorieux, *La Littérature quodlibétique de 1260–1320*, vol. I (Kain: Belgium, 1925); vol. II (Paris: Vrin, 1935).
22 For Isidore, see *Isidori Hispalensis Episcopi Etymologiarum sive Originum Libri XX*, ed. W. M. Lindsay, 2 vols. (1911; reprinted London: Oxford University Press, 1962), II: bk 18; discussed in Enders, *Rhetoric and the Origins*, 74–89.
23 For a superb introduction to performance studies, see Henry Bial's anthology, *The Performance Studies Reader*, 2nd edn (London and New York: Routledge, 2007).

issues that have always characterised a literary form such as drama or a performance medium such as theatre, as hospitable to the canonical as it is to the marginal, as apt to moral, ethical, and aesthetic critique as it is receptive to Goffman's 'frame analysis' or Turner's concept of liminality.[24] Indeed, given that scholars of medieval England continue to launch exciting, performance-oriented analyses of a much more limited corpus of extant works, one of the great ironies of current trends in medieval theatricality is that the vast theatrical resources of medieval France are still largely untapped.

Ultimately, by restoring memory and delivery in particular to our readings of medieval French literary events, we enhance our understanding not only of the generic interplay between early forms of ritual and representation but of theatre itself, which we may appreciate, at long last, in the full literary, socio-historical, and communicative scope that it once enjoyed in a pan-European performance continuum. Rhetoric was no bully pulpit; at least, it was not necessarily that, despite modern and postmodern feminist insistence that the mere invocation of hegemonic logico-rhetorical structures constitutes a complicit reinforcement of that hegemony. Instead, it is helpful to think of a pulpit itself as a locus of persuasion, as both a performance setting and a fantastic or realistic image of such a setting which nurtures and hosts all manner of events: the legal struggles of the Ciceronian courtroom, the medieval French disputational warfare of the Sorbonne, the Châtelet, the rue du Fouarre, or the Pré-aux-Clercs; the 'theatre of the church' as described by Honorius;[25] or the countless sermons advocating the interpretational richness of parables, the imperialism of the Crusades, or even – both on stage and off – the Second Coming. After all, Isidore himself had noted that, etymologically speaking, the term *pulpitum* denotes simultaneously the scaffolding and platforms of the actor's stage as well as the 'pulpit' of preaching, public representations, lectures, and post-Senecan *controversiae*: 'Moreover, the stage-building was a place below the theatre proper, the size of a house built with a platform in front, the "pulpit", which pulpit used to be called the "orchestra", where the comic and tragic poets sang, and actors and mimes danced. Moreover, it is also called the *skene* in Greek, because it was constructed to look like a house.'[26] In the house of rhetoric there are many rooms, some of which are not rooms at all, some of which fade away as quickly as they are built in performance, only to endure as mnemonic traces as powerful as anything Stephen Greenblatt

---

24 See Goffman, *Frame Analysis: An Essay on the Organization of Experience* (Cambridge, MA: Harvard University Press, 1974); Victor W. Turner, *From Ritual to Theatre: The Human Seriousness of Play* (New York: Performing Arts Journal Publications, 1982; reprinted 1992), pp. 20–60.
25 Bevington, *Medieval Drama*, p. 9.   26 Isidore of Seville bk 18, chap. 43.

ever imagined when he began his negotiations with Shakespeare as a dialogue with the dead.[27] Such dialogue means speaking, preaching, acting and emoting with the full affective power long associated with delivery, and especially with its energetic use (as *enargaeia*) of two emotions that were considered to be the most powerful of all and which are of no small consequence in matters theatrical: pity and fear.

Martianus Cappella once wrote that 'the audience is to be moved by pity or hatred or envy or fear or hope or anger or the like. With pity, when we respond to someone's calamity with great sorrow, or when we recall the wickedness of the age or the greatness of the danger... Fear, however, is aroused by dangers, either personal ones or those common to all.'[28] Although curiously neglected by Henry Ansgar Kelly in his work on Aristotelian tragedy, pity and fear represent, of course, the very emotions that characterise catharsis, as in such Latin translations of *Poetics* 1449b as these: 'non per enarrationem rei, sed *per misericordiam, metumque* factis expressum, eius modi vehementes animorum perturbationes unasquasque purgans expiansque' ('not through narrating the thing, but through pity and fear expressed by the deeds, in that way purging and relieving all such violent disturbances of the soul'); or 'aequat passiones per misericordiam et metum et purgat illos qui patiuntur' ('through pity and fear, it both regularises the passions and also purges those who suffer from them').[29] Theatre has always been a socio-cultural conduit of and to thought and emotion, its verisimilitude not always a *faux semblant* but a rehearsal for history and social change, a visionary future that rhetoric foregrounds, enables and changes in the literary imaginary and on the stage of the world.

27 Stephen Greenblatt, *Shakespearean Negotiations: The Circulation of Social Energy in Renaissance England* (Berkeley: University of California Press, 1988), p. 1.
28 Martianus Capella, *De nuptiis Philologiae et Mercurii*, ed. A. Dick (Leipzig: Teubner, 1925), p. 163.
29 The Latin appears in these editions of Aristotle respectively: *De poetica liber Graece et Latine*, ed. T. C. Harles (Leipzig: Siegfried Lebrecht Crusius, 1780); and *The Poetics of Aristotle: Translated from Greek into English and from Arabic into Latin*, ed. and trans. D. S. Margouliouth (London: Hodder and Stoughton, 1911). See H. A. Kelly, *Ideas and Forms of Tragedy from Aristotle to the Middle Ages* (Cambridge: Cambridge University Press, 1993), pp. 1–5 and 111–25.

19

The rise of metafiction in the late Middle Ages

DEBORAH McGRADY

When Guillaume de Machaut's *Voir dit* (*c.* 1363–5) and Jean Froissart's *Prison amoureuse* (*c.* 1371–2) document the experience of writing the very book we read; when Christine de Pizan transforms the literary process into an allegorical adventure; and when the *Belle dame sans mercy* (1424) codices present reader confrontation as an integral part of the text, we as readers are coaxed into a metafictional world where writing is not simply the process of telling stories but the story itself. If the principal subject matter of these late medieval texts becomes the book in process, the author figure emerges as the main protagonist and readers function as characters in their own right. As representative examples, these late medieval authors and texts signal a singular preoccupation with shaping literary production as an adventure equal in interest to the wanderings of knights and the longings of lovelorn princes.

That the term 'metafiction' was not coined until the late 1960s by William Gass, and then only to define self-reflective modern fiction, should not obscure the fact that the late medieval French corpus introduces many of the characteristics associated with this genre. Indeed, more recent critical inquiry, while still ignoring medieval precursors of metafiction, invites comparison with important early examples. Specifically Patricia Waugh defines metafictional texts by their intent to 'explore a *theory* of fiction through the *practice* of writing fiction', and Mark Currie goes further when speaking of a 'borderline discourse' that exists 'between fiction and criticism, and which takes that border as its subject'.[1] Reflecting similar preoccupations, late medieval metafictions often dramatise the literary process from creative inception through composition, fabrication, distribution, and reception. Concerning subjects of critical inquiry, medieval metafictions pursued the most pressing issues facing contemporary literature. Not simply self-referential, this literature looked

---

1 P. Waugh, *Metafiction: The Theory and Practice of Self-Conscious Fiction* (London and New York: Routledge, 1984), p. 2; and Mark Currie (ed. and intro.), *Metafiction* (New York: Longman, 1995), p. 2.

back on antecedents and confronted anticipated audience expectations. Thus it established intertextuality and reader response as necessary tools for exploring the place and status of fiction. Late medieval examples consciously blurred boundaries between fact and fiction, form and content, poetry and prose, reader and author, and story and response, all of which invited reassessment of the status of vernacular literature in society.

R. Barton Palmer has already called attention to the metafictional nature of Machaut's corpus and the quintessential role he plays in the subsequent development of this literature.[2] It is, however, important to acknowledge Machaut's debt to his thirteenth-century predecessors who exhibited early manifestations of self-reflective literary discourse. Sylvia Huot speaks of the 'lyrico-writerly poetics' that emerge in the thirteenth century in which the 'process of writing is thematized' as a phenomenon announcing a shift in poetic as well as book culture; bookmakers and poets alike approached literature as a tangible material artefact intricately linked with the author figure.[3] The increased use of author portraits in manuscripts from this period in which the poet holds pen in hand before the artefact displayed on his lectern provided a visual reminder to the viewing audience that they were reading a *written* text. This technique of inscribing within a work references to the writing process shaped thirteenth-century manuscript anthologies of troubadour poetry, where the addition of *vidas* and *razos* provided pseudo-biographical information on the author and worked to flesh out a literary corpus. Similarly, thirteenth-century hybrid literature incorporated into love narratives well-known refrains, songs, and lyrics alongside newly composed poems and letters, not simply to enhance the love story but to draw attention to the love narrative as a continuum that spanned engaged reception, as witnessed by the narrator's citing of past texts, and the final writerly act of the author. Thus when Nicole de Margival cites Adam de la Halle throughout his *Dit de la panthere* (written between 1290 and 1328), he both anchors his text in an established literary tradition and models ideal reader engagement that culminates in poetic production. Here Adam's poetry inspires the text we read while shaping the behaviour of its fictional reader, as seen when the narrator refers to the lessons drawn from Adam's writings: 'D'Adam ay je oÿ retraire / .I. ver encore qui moult retraire / M'a fait de requerre asprement' ('One of Adam's verses that I heard made me hold back on aggressive pursuit' [lines

---

2 R. B. Palmer, 'The Metafictional Machaut: Self-Reflexivity and Self-Mediation in the Two Judgment Poems', *Studies in the Literary Imagination* 20 (1987), pp. 23–39.
3 Sylvia Huot, *From Song to Book: The Poetics of Writing in Old French Lyric and Lyrical Narrative Poetry* (Ithaca, NY and London: Cornell University Press, 1987).

1081–3]).[4] Greater insistence on the potential impact of the physical book on future readers is expressed in the *Roman de la poire* (c. 1250), in which the narrator assigns the written artefact an important role in the game of seduction between the narrator and his lady: 'cist romanz que ge ci voi / savra molt bien parler por moi / et mostrer pleinement a l'ueill / que ge demant et que je veil' ('this romance that I see here will know how to speak well on my behalf and to show clearly to the eye what I request and what I desire' [lines 2221–4]).[5] In these examples, we see early literature already revealing a preoccupation with the literary process that anticipates late medieval metafictions, where traditional love narratives will give way to the poetic adventure.

Scholars have singled out the *dit* as a distinctive late medieval genre known for its fascination with the literary event. Jacqueline Cerquiglini defines this elusive genre as a literature *au second degré* because of the tendency to narrate its own existence.[6] Machaut's corpus serves as an especially fertile site since the 'metafictional impulse' drives both *dits* and debates.[7] The *Voir dit* stands out as a particularly accomplished and complex metafiction. If it first promises to provide a detailed and intimate account of an amorous correspondence between the aged poet Guillaume and the young, vibrant Toute-Belle, it quickly reveals the couple's equally intense commitment to poetry. After all, the affair begins with Toute-Belle expressing her love for the poet *and* for lyric. Her first letter details her sentiments in prose and lyric form, and then requests that besides answering her amorous pleas, the poet correct her poem and send her samples from his musical repertoire. For the narrator Guillaume, Toute-Belle's letter heals him of an illness that left him 'assourdis, arudis, mus et impotens' ('deaf, stupid, mute, and impotent', lettre II) and generally incapable of writing.[8] Now, with Toute-Belle as his lady, Guillaume enthusiastically returns to what he knows best – composing – while he does his utmost to avoid engaging in a true amorous affair. Nevertheless the affair does advance through the expected stages that move us from the first kiss to the evening spent together, through separation, jealousy, intrigue, and break-up, only to return to the final reconciliation of the couple. Alongside the account of the affair, the *Voir*

---

4 Nicole de Margival, *Le Dit de la panthère*, ed. B. Ribémont (Paris: Champion, 2000). All translations are the author's.
5 Tibaut, *Le Roman de la poire*, ed. Christiane Marchello-Nizia (Paris: SATF, 1984), lines 2221–4.
6 Jacqueline Cerquiglini, 'Le Clerc et l'écriture: le *Voir dit* de Guillaume de Machaut et la définition du dit', in Hans Ulrich Gumbrecht (ed.), *Literatur in der Gesellschaft des Spätmittelalters* (Heidelberg: Carl Winter, 1980), pp. 151–68.
7 Palmer, *Machaut*, p. 27.
8 Guillaume de Machaut, *Le Livre du voir dit*, ed. P. Imbs and intro. J. Cerquilini-Toulet (Paris: Livre de Poche, 1999).

dit audience enjoys a detailed account of the making of the book it reads. Guillaume interrupts his story early on to address the audience and explain the contents of the book, the editorial liberties adopted, and where readers might find additional supporting materials within the larger codex he presumes will contain the text we read (lines 490–525). Here form and content converge to define the text. At regular intervals, the narrator reminds his readers that they are engaging with a material reproduction of the affair through deictic references that point to letters, poems and illustrations inserted in the text.[9] At the same time, the readers of the *Voir dit* are privy to the reactions of an inscribed audience. Toute-Belle marvels over Guillaume's poetic talents, applies lessons learned from his writings to interpret her dreams, and sometimes protests at the unfair portrait of her provided by the poet. At yet another level, the reactions of a larger audience to the poet's writings are recorded in the form of mocking remarks made by lords and city folk. In spite of repeated attacks on his story by an internal audience that questions the veracity of his 'True Story', the narrator doggedly records his writing experience, including comments on the number of verses he produces each night, the adventure of organising an undated and unruly correspondence, and the frustration of filling in when he lacks 'matère' due to the faltering relationship. Given that the narrator spends more time in his study writing the book we read than in the presence of his lady, it is easy to conclude that the love affair becomes a mere pretext to speak about book production. But the *Voir dit* is not simply unique because it represents one of the most elaborate early manifestations of metafiction. While the love affair remains predictable, Machaut uses the book adventure to engage in a number of important debates of the period, thereby participating in Currie's borderline discourse between literature and criticism. For the *Voir dit* pushes beyond an account of writing to address issues of audience participation, the impact of forms of delivery on reception, the ability of text to capture lived events, the function of literature in shaping lives, and the thorny question of the ownership of literature – from creation to material reproductions of text.

The *Voir dit* represents the apex of medieval metafiction and inspired several later works. Whereas most of these imitations privilege love over the writing process, Froissart's *Prison amoureuse* adopts the hybrid format of the *Voir dit* by incorporating lyrics, short tales and epistolary exchange to celebrate the collaborative process of poetic creation, a process that Guillaume repeatedly identified as threatening and problematic given the poet's progressive loss of

---

9 For further development of these ideas, see D. McGrady, *Controlling Readers: Guillaume de Machaut and his Late Medieval Audience* (Toronto: University of Toronto Press, 2006).

control over his work as his audience grew to doubt his capacity to record the truth. For Froissart, metafiction allows him to argue against Machaut's negative portrait of readers. Over the course of the story, Flos, the narrator, comes to appreciate reader involvement and he eventually identifies literary collaboration between poets and audience as vital to poetic creation.[10]

The *Prison amoureuse* opens with a timid lover–poet who circulates anonymously a poem in honour of his lady, only to be publicly humiliated when she responds with a public performance of her own song in which she mocks his suffering. Running from the scene as Guillaume had done when readers openly mocked his naïvety, Flos threatens to write a new *virelai* that will be 'si entendable et si commun' ('so understandable and so common' [line 529]) that no one can misunderstand (as in reinterpret) its meaning.[11] Yet soon after the narrator receives a letter from an esteemed prince who speaks of the poet's reputation as an advisor to lovers. He seeks the narrator's guidance in his own affairs. This first request leads to an epistolary exchange between the two men, an adventure that quickly replaces the narrator's tale of his failed attempts in love. Initially the conversation sticks to love advice, but when the prince sends an account of a troubling dream and invites the narrator to interpret the work, the two embark on a literary collaboration that will eventually include the prince's lady. The prince's dream with the poet's commentary and the lady's remarks on the combined product will culminate in the commissioning by the lady of the book we read. We observe the various stages of writing, including Flos's first attempts at glossing the dream, the reaction to his gloss by both the prince and his lady, and, finally, the incorporation of revisions as proposed by his readers. Framing this account of literary collaboration between poet and audience is the acknowledgement by the narrator that a new work must circulate and stimulate audience response, whether negative, as in the case of his lady, or positive, as in the case of the prince:

> Nouveleté gaires ne gist
> Ne ne sejourne ne repose:
> Elle est tel que par tout s'ose
> Hardiement mettre ou embatre
> Pour gens couroucier ou esbatre

(New works hardly sit still or rest. They are such that they dare impose or introduce themselves everywhere to either anger or entertain people [lines 327–36])

---

10 *Ibid.*, pp. 185–7.
11 Jean Froissart, *La Prison amoureuse*, ed. A. Fourrier (Paris: Klincksieck, 1974).

Here again metafiction moves beyond self-absorption to engage with pressing theoretical questions concerning reader involvement, specifically in regard to literary partnership and freedom of interpretation in the spirit of Roland Barthes' writerly text. For Froissart, foregrounding book production leads to re-imagining the literary process as an activity that continues long after the author has said his piece.

The investigation of the combined reading–writing process in Machaut and Froissart continues in fifteenth-century metafictional works. Christine de Pizan's frequent accounts of her authorial experience are key examples. The metacommentary provided in prologues to her commissioned works, where she expresses her disinterest in the imposed project, gives way to fuller accounts of the writing experience in her lengthier texts. In the *Chemin de longue etude, Mutacion de Fortune*, and the *Advision Christine*, Christine-the-narrator pairs accounts of past and future events as well as conduct advice with a detailed description of her development as a writer. In the *Livre de la cité des dames* (c. 1405), the writer becomes the leading character, and the story line retraces her own experience of coming to the present topic and the various struggles faced in treating her subject. Opening with an intimate account of her study habits, Christine the narrator records the self-doubt experienced when reading what 'philosophes, pouettes, tous orateurs' ('philosophers, poets, and rhetoricians' [i.i.ia]) have to say about women.[12] Questioning her own status as a woman, the narrator is visited by three allegorical figures who will aid her in building a city where women can be protected. The construction of that city entails retelling and reworking the misogynous literary tradition encountered in the narrator's studies. Each brick of the city wall doubles as a chapter in which a new account of a famous woman takes shape. Interlaced throughout these new biographies, the reader participates in the lively dialogue between Christine and the three allegorical women, a conversation that typically stems from Christine-the-narrator's readings and then proceeds to document the important transformation in her way of thinking about women's contributions to society as well as her own role as a writer. The opening illumination to this work in the extant copy she offered the queen of France (British Library, ms. Harley 4431) prepares the audience for a metafictional reading. The famous two-part frontispiece depicts twice the creative enterprise: first the narrator adopts a conventional authorial pose behind a lectern, and in the second frame a link between

---

12 Christine de Pizan, 'Le Livre de la cité des dames de Christine de Pizan: A Critical Edition', 2 vols., ed. M. Curnow, PhD Dissertation Vanderbilt University, 1975.

writing the book we read and the city constructed within the book is made explicit as we see the narrator now applying mortar to the brick she holds.[13]

To appreciate fully the impact of late medieval metafiction on vernacular literature, one need only consider the fascinating history of Alain Chartier's *Belle dame sans mercy*. The metafictional content of this work appears in the frame narrative surrounding the troubling dialogue between a suffering lover and his indifferent lady. The tale begins with the narrator threatening to abandon amorous literature that would please others. He dramatises this decision by turning away from minstrels he hears playing in a nearby garden and pursuing instead a solitary path where he will overhear the antithesis of the courtly song in the heated dialogue between a suffering lover and an indifferent lady. Although modelled on debate poetry, Chartier's work fails to include an invitation by the characters to write the work so a third party can judge the exchange. Instead the narrator records what he overhears, stopping only when the two characters cease to speak. The narrator concludes his tale by mentioning rumours that the lover died from sorrow, thereby seemingly sealing the fate of the text. And yet the unexpected conclusion was received as a blatant attack on courtly ideals and ostensibly ignited a lively and robust debate, first expressed through a supposed exchange of letters between court readers and Alain Chartier concerning the text. This initial exchange includes a letter from the men of the court to ladies urging them not to read Chartier's work, a letter from the ladies to Chartier requesting that he appear at court to defend his work, and Chartier's *Excusacion*, in which he confronts his external readers' complaints by recording a dream narrative in which the God of Love accuses him of similar transgressions. Through these inscribed paratextual responses, Chartier's text, while initially only containing marginal metafictional gestures, becomes a metafictional site, meaning a work that inspired reflection on the writing and reading process which was then integrated into the body of the text. These additions blur the boundaries between fiction and reality, authors and readers, as well as courtly texts and metacommentary on court literature. Here, regardless of whether the audience's letters represent a real correspondence or a fictional hoax, reader responses and the author's defence form a borderline discourse that centres on questions concerning the fictionality of the text. Similar to Machaut's *Jugement de Navarre* in which the poet was urged to alter his earlier recorded judgement, Chartier's readers demand revisions to the outcome of the *Belle dame* dialogue. Chartier's

---

13 Digitised reproduction of this image and entire manuscript is available online on 'Christine de Pizan and the Making of the Queen's Manuscript' at www.pizan.lib.ed.ac.uk/.

Excusacion, however, redirects the conversation by introducing a new metafictional layer. Where his (fictional?) audience demanded that he acknowledge his creation of a fictional event, then assume responsibility for his harsh treatment of an established courtly discourse, and rewrite the work according to their expectations, the *Excusacion* stages an encounter between the poet and an angry God of Love who accuses him of writing a fictional work that challenges his authority. But the narrator protests by citing the work's original metafictional gestures to the 'facts' and reasserts that he did not create the work but simply recorded what he heard. In the process, Chartier moves the subject of debate beyond an author's responsibility to uphold readers' expectations to challenge metafiction itself. Through this newly added metafictional farce, Chartier disrupts grievances related to the love story with complaints of the powerlessness of writers to control their texts. That the God of Love, a fictional creation, demurs in judging the poet and defers judgement to the 'real' court who treats the work as a fiction pushes to the extreme the instabilities metafiction seeks to spotlight – where does fiction begin and reality end? What role in literature is to be attributed to tradition, authorial freedom, and readers' expectations? The multiple continuations of Chartier's work, known as the *Belle dame sans mercy* Cycle, produced over the next 100 years, while rarely engaging with Chartier's larger theoretical questions, confirm the malleability of the fictional work, the powerlessness of the author to dictate content, and the authority of readers to transform texts. If modern metafiction is a response to realism in that it refuses to allow readers to forget that they are participating in a fictional world, Chartier's text with these additions reverses the dynamic to the same effect. Here the poet protests the 'reality' of the dialogue while his readers insist on its fictionality and falseness, both of which justify, according to them, demands for altering the text. Here fiction and reality are blurred, and for Chartier's external reader the ensuing discomfort is no less troubling than the complaints of the narrator of that quintessential metafiction, *The French Lieutenant's Woman*, on the difficulties of writing his story.

As postmodern metafiction attacks the pretensions of realist literature, so late medieval metafiction from Machaut to Chartier challenged established contemporary traditions, from the links between past and present literature to the relationship between authors and their audience. These medieval metafictions challenged period expectations by imagining new narratives and new roles for vernacular writers, lay literature and audience. In the process, they established metafictional literature as a genre defined by its relentless engagement with contemporary theoretical and critical issues surrounding artistic production.

20

What does 'Renaissance' mean?

PHILIP FORD

In reading early sixteenth-century French texts, it does not take long to realise that writers were aware of a break with the medieval past. If they do not quite use the word 'Renaissance', they come close to it in many of the expressions they adopt to describe the educational and cultural changes in which they are participating. While Vasari may have been the first to use the term 'rinascita' in the Preface to his *Lives of the Artists* to refer to the recovery of the beauty and purity of the visual arts along classical principles, in northern Europe it was the world of education that was more directly affected by the rediscovery of the classical heritage. In some senses, then, when scholars talk about the Renaissance, there are two connected but distinct phenomena: the Italian Renaissance, celebrated and defined in the nineteenth century by the Swiss historian Jakob Burckhardt, and the northern Renaissance, accompanied by a move to religious as well as cultural reform. Occupying geographically and culturally an intermediate space between the two domains, France was able to benefit from both of them, to produce its own version of the Renaissance.

It is unsurprising that the term 'rebirth' should first have been applied in the field of the visual arts rather than of literature: the difference in kind between, say, Michelangelo's *tondo* of the 'Holy Family' in the Uffizi, with its emphasis on the human form, the dramatic pose of the central figures, the classically inspired ephebes in the middle ground, and a medieval painting of the Virgin and child is obvious even to the untutored eye. However, in literature such a comparison can be less clear, and an architectural analogy may be more revealing. Many large-scale buildings are the result of development through time: a Romanesque chancel in a church may give way to a Gothic nave and be completed by a Renaissance facade. Sixteenth-century French literature, with its elements of continuity and change, may be viewed as a similarly composite building.

Nevertheless, writers at the time were aware of an important transformation going on, and Rabelais's letter from Gargantua to his son Pantagruel

(*Pantagruel* chap. 8, first printed *c.* 1532) is often cited as evidence of this. Speaking of the changes that have taken place since his youth, the fictional giant claims:

> Le temps estoit encores tenebreux et sentant l'infelicité et calamité des Gothz, qui avoient mis à destruction toute bonne literature. Mais, par la bonté divine, la lumiere et dignité a esté de mon eage rendue es lettres, et y voy tel amendement que de present à difficulté seroys je receu en la premiere classe des petitz grimaulx . . . Maintenant toutes disciplines sont restituées, les langues instaurées, Grecque sans laquelle c'est honte que une personne se die sçavant, Hebraicque, Caldaicque, Latine. Les impressions tant elegantes et correctes en usance, qui ont esté inventées de mon eage par inspiration divine . . . [1]

> (This was still a dark age, redolent of the wretchedness and misery of the Goths, who had destroyed all good literature. But, through God's goodness, light and honour have in my lifetime been restored to literature, and I can see such an improvement that now I would scarcely be accepted in the first class of a primary school . . . Now all branches of learning have been reinstituted, and languages restored: Greek, without which it is shameful for a person to claim to be learned, Hebrew, Chaldaic, Latin. Printed works, which are so elegant and correct, are in common use, invented in my lifetime through divine inspiration.)

To some extent, this can be seen as (sincere) flattery of François I's initiatives to turn France into a country that could rival both Italy, whose wonders he had witnessed during his incursions into Piedmont and Lombardy in the early years of his reign (1515–25), and northern Europe, where scholars such as Erasmus (*c.* 1469–1536) had been inspiring their readers to embrace Greek culture as well as to extend their knowledge of the Roman classical tradition. In the area of the visual arts, the king did his best to bring the foremost Italian artists to work for him at the French court: Benvenuto Cellini (1500–71), Rosso Fiorentino (1494–1540), Francesco Primaticcio (*c.* 1504–70). Between them, they helped to develop the French Mannerist style, centred on the château of Fontainebleau, François's favourite residence. However, establishing a suitable level of scholarship would require more than simply buying in a number of international stars.

To achieve this, François was aided by the greatest of the first generation of French scholars, Guillaume Budé (1467–1540). Highly learned in Greek as well as Latin literature, in 1530 he persuaded the king to found the Collège

---

1 François Rabelais, *Œuvres complètes*, ed. Mirelle Huchon, in collaboration with François Moreau (Paris: Gallimard, 1994), p. 243.

des lecteurs royaux, on the model of the Collegium trilingue at Louvain (founded 1517), dedicated to the teaching of the three ancient languages, Latin, Greek, and Hebrew. Rabelais appears to be marking this important event in the Gargantua letter. The foundation of the Collège Royal is all the more significant in that the existing university institutions, particularly the theological faculty of the University of Paris, the Sorbonne, had set their face against the study of the ancient biblical languages. Rabelais himself had suffered from this attitude when, as a young Franciscan, his Greek books had been confiscated in 1523. In the mind of the established Church, Greek and Hebrew were both associated with the rebellious attitudes of Protestantism, which called the authority of the Church into question and considered reading the Scriptures to be the only way to attain religious truth. The new educational movement, centred on the study and imitation of the classical tradition, is known as humanism, and its central ideas, particularly the importance of returning *ad fontes*, to the foundational texts of the ancient world, lie at the heart of the literary Renaissance in France as well as that of the Reformation.

The other development that Rabelais highlights in his letter is the invention of printing, the technology that had the same kind of democratising effect on the dissemination of knowledge as the internet has had in recent years. Thanks to printing, the texts of the ancient world were becoming available in cheap editions, instead of remaining in the hands of a small ecclesiastical or noble elite. By 1500 virtually all the major works of Roman literature had been printed, and a significant number of Greek texts. The French book trade flourished in Paris and Lyon in particular, once again with royal patronage and encouragement. François introduced into France the *privilège* system, which gave printers exclusive rights to print their books for a fixed number of years; he established the Imprimerie royale in 1539, and his collection of books and manuscripts, the Bibliothèque royale, formed the core of what would become the Bibliothèque nationale. The Greek characters developed by the printer Claude Garamond (1499–1561) were known as *les grecs du roi*.

François I's role, then, in establishing a Renaissance in France should not be underestimated. But what exactly was being reborn? We have already referred to the desire on the part of Italian artists to return to the purity and beauty of the classical past, and to a large extent this too was the goal of Italian humanists, whose aims involved the recuperation of Greek as well as Latin literature. While the Roman tradition continued throughout the Middle Ages, albeit with a smaller corpus of extant texts than we have today, Greek essentially disappeared, not just the texts, but the ability even to read the language. When around 1353 Petrarch finally achieved his youthful ambition of obtaining, from the Greek ambassador to Venice, a manuscript of Homer, he had to admit that 'your Homer is dumb to me, or rather I am deaf to him'.[2] A century later, in 1453, the Turks sacked the intellectual centre of the Greek-speaking world, Constantinople, driving out its scholars and their books. They headed west, to Italy, where many of them made a living teaching Greek, publishing Greek texts, and disseminating Greek literature and culture to an avid humanist audience. Byzantium's disaster was the West's good fortune.

The humanist Renaissance, then, was more about the recovery of Greek than the rebirth of Latin. Latin had remained the intellectual language of Western Europe throughout the Middle Ages, a lingua franca that allowed an easy interchange between scholars and churchmen wherever they lived. Medieval Latin may not have been what it was in the time of Cicero and Virgil, but many of the ancient texts continued to be read and studied, and what was known of Greek authors such as Aristotle was also in Latin (not infrequently translated from Arabic versions of the original). It is true that early Italian humanists such as Lorenzo Valla (c. 1407–57) worked towards the restoration of Latin to its classical purity, and lost texts were being rediscovered (e.g. the complete text of Quintilian in 1416, Statius' *Silvae* in 1417, Valerius Flaccus) thanks to the searching or good luck of philologists such as Poggio Bracciolini (1380–1459), who discovered the three authors mentioned here in St Gallen. As Ann Moss has shown,[3] there was a deliberate move from the precise but jargon-filled Latin of medieval scholasticism to a more elegant, though sometimes less precise, humanist Latin, and France certainly shared in this. The reforms of the University of Paris carried out by Cardinal D'Estouteville in 1452 were aimed inter alia at improving students' knowledge of Latin, with verse composition as one of the principal means chosen to achieve this.

However, it was the rediscovery of Greek that had the most dramatic impact on Renaissance writers and thinkers. Italy again played an important part in this. For example, it was in fifteenth-century Florence that the most important philosophical development of the Renaissance took place. When in 1462 Cosimo de' Medici handed over to Marsilio Ficino (1433–99) his recently acquired manuscripts of Plato for translation, he could not have imagined that he was initiating a philosophical movement that would have widespread implications for how people would view the world for the next 150 years. Ficino did more than translate Plato into Latin; he also wrote a commentary

2 See Francesco Petrarca, *Rerum familiarum libri xvii–xxiv*, trans. Aldo S. Bernardo (Baltimore, MD: Johns Hopkins University Press, 1985), pp. 45–6.
3 See Ann Moss, *Renaissance Truth and the Latin Language Turn* (Oxford: Oxford University Press, 2003).

on the Platonic works and other sources of ancient wisdom (including the *Corpus Hermeticum*), demonstrating their consonance with Christian thought. Although his commentary on the *Symposium* is undoubtedly the work which had the most popular appeal, especially in the area of love poetry, many other aspects of Platonism also came through, notably the theory of the divine frenzies and the parallels they presented with the Christian notion of grace. Early French humanists such as Jacques Lefèvre d'Etaples (*c.* 1450–1536) visited members of the Florentine Academy on more than one occasion, and helped introduce Neoplatonism to France. François I's sister, Marguerite de Navarre, proved to be a more than enthusiastic audience for the particular blend of Neoplatonism and evangelical Christianity that marked the followers of Lefèvre, and syncretism in general, the blending of pagan and Christian ideas, became a central aspect of French Renaissance thought.

In the realm of poetry, the great (many people believed divinely inspired) Greek bards such as Homer, Hesiod, and Orpheus were being read in the West for the first time in centuries. (Humanists believed the works attributed to Orpheus, including the *Hymns*, were authentic.) To start with, in France scholars such as Budé had to rely for a knowledge of the language on Greek speakers such as George Hermonymus who had made their way to the West earning a living from teaching.[4] On a rather higher plain was Janus Lascaris (1445–1535), a frequent visitor to the French court who edited Greek texts and was the principal of the Ginnasio Mediceo in Rome. Although the early Greek poets could sometimes appear primitive in comparison to the elegance of Virgil, humanists began to realise for the first time the debt Roman writers owed to their Greek predecessors. This in itself helped to validate the notion of imitation as a principle of literary creation. Such poets were also seen as presenting important truths about the world, often in allegorical form, which had been revealed by divine means, a view advanced by one of the main aids to reading Homer at the time, Pseudo-Plutarch's *Life and Works of Homer*. Greek poetry was not merely an amusing form of entertainment for a courtly elite, it was, like the Psalms of David, a conduit to divine truth.

There were other, nationalistic reasons why Greek should be considered more influential than Roman literature in sixteenth-century France. The Italians saw themselves very much as the spiritual and cultural descendants of the Romans: Virgil and Cicero were part of their national tradition. In their emulation of Italian culture, the French came to see Greece as their principal

---

4 Gerald Sandy, 'Resources for the Study of Ancient Greek in France', in Sandy (ed.), *The Classical Heritage in France* (Leiden: Brill, 2002), pp. 47–8, at pp. 50–2.

source of inspiration. Humanists such as Henri Estienne (1531–98) set out to demonstrate that the French language had more in common with Greek than with Latin, and it was frequently to Greek models that the Pléiade poets, inspired by their mentor Jean Dorat (1508–88), turned for inspiration. In the sixteenth century France was the only country to produce a vernacular version of the *Iliad* in verse form, started by Hugues Salel for the benefit of François I in the 1540s, and completed by Amadis Jamyn in 1577.

If Italy was one of the main influences as well as the main cultural rival of France, northern Europe also had much to offer in the area of humanism and religion. The influence of Erasmus has already been mentioned. Through his publications and his correspondence with humanists throughout Europe, he helped disseminate a radically new approach to the classics, which had important ramifications in vernacular as well as neo-Latin literature. He set out to reform the pronunciation of both Greek and Latin along what are still considered to be sound principles; he introduced Greek culture to a general audience through his enormously popular *Adages*; he popularised the use of the commonplace book, in which young students were to inscribe quotations from their reading of classical writers under headings which would allow their re-use in their own writing; and he was responsible for disseminating the idea of *copia*, abundance of style, which might be seen to reach its height in the writings of Rabelais.[5] But in addition to all this, Erasmus was a moderate in an increasingly polarised world. His authorial ethos was just as influential on the development of humanism as his literary and philological writing, and many of his adages are as much diatribes against cruelty and tyranny as they are commentaries on classical writing.

Although Erasmus remained a champion of the idea that the Catholic Church could be reformed from within, many of his ideas were not so far removed from moderate reformers such as the other great northern European humanist, Philipp Melanchthon. A staunch supporter of the importance of the language arts in education, his works were widely read in France as well as Germany, where he helped educate a whole generation of scholars at the University of Wittenberg. His awareness of the importance of rhetoric as a life skill, and the role of the works of the Greeks and Romans in developing this, helped to validate the shift in emphasis which took place in the sixteenth century in the teaching of the *trivium*. While the world of education had

---

5 See, for example, Jean-Claude Margolin, 'Erasme de Rotterdam (Désiré) (1467?–1536)', in Colette Nativel (ed.), *Centuriae Latinae: cent une figures humanistes de la Renaissance aux Lumières offertes à Jacques Chomarat* (Geneva: Droz, 1997), pp. 341–9; and Terence Cave, *The Cornucopian Text: Problems of Writing in the French Renaissance* (Oxford: Clarendon Press, 1979).

inherited the medieval division of knowledge into the seven liberal arts (grammar, rhetoric, and dialectic, known as the *trivium*; arithmetic, geometry, astronomy, and music, the *quadrivium*), the more progressive humanist colleges in France emphasised rhetoric as opposed to dialectic as the most important element in education. This reflected the shift that was taking place in career prospects for the educated young in an increasingly urban and centralised society: while logic may have had the upper hand in medieval theological, philosophical, and legal circles, an ability to manipulate language was becoming vital for success in the new world of improved communications, where a theological or political tract could change the fate of nations.

Progressive humanist colleges, such as Sainte-Barbe in Paris or the Collège de Guyenne in Bordeaux, set out to educate the new generation of teachers, lawyers, diplomats, and administrators in what they considered to be essential skills, the foremost of which was a firm grasp of classical Latin. But what place did women have in this system? Although it is really only in the seventeenth century that public education for girls becomes any sort of priority, female education was less neglected in the Renaissance than has sometimes been claimed. Private tutors, often young men travelling around Europe, found employment in upper-middle-class families, teaching both sons and daughters in Latin, Greek, and even Hebrew. Despite the unfavourable legal status of women, widows often found themselves running printing businesses or factories. And women writers such as Pernette du Guillet or (the possibly fictional) Louise Labé were seen in cities such as Lyon as a source of pride, evidence of France's cultural equality to Italy.

French society underwent a vast change in the sixteenth century. In some cases, notably in the poetry of the Pléiade and their followers, the change was explicitly based on classical principles and the desire, through imitation, to rival and even outstrip the works of the Ancients.[6] In other cases, such as Montaigne, assimilation of the classical tradition was a more personal, though no less thorough-going, process, in which not only the writers but the historical figures of ancient Greece and Rome became privileged interlocutors, informing and inspiring the radically new way of thinking which the essayist developed, and which was capable of embracing the discovery of the New World in just the same way as it took in the Old World.[7]

---

6 On the aesthetic principles of the Pléiade, the name given to a group of classicising poets whose members included Ronsard, Du Bellay, Baïf, Belleau, Jodelle, and Pontus de Tyard, and who were strongly influenced by the Hellenist Jean Dorat, see Grahame Castor, *Pléiade Poetics: A Study in Sixteenth-Century Thought and Terminology* (Cambridge: Cambridge University Press, 1963).
7 On Montaigne see below, Chapter 26.

In many ways, France's Renaissance was unique in Europe. The product of both Italian and northern European, of Catholic and Protestant influences, embracing enthusiastically Hellenism without discarding the Roman tradition, in the first half of the century it benefited from the patronage and enthusiasm of one of Europe's more enlightened monarchs. Sadly, his son, Henri II, had little interest in his father's vision, and the Wars of Religion, which plagued the country from 1562 to 1598, are largely his legacy. The enlightened humanist virtues of scholarship and tolerance, of the unifying ethics of the *res publica litterarum*, had little chance of surviving the partisan attitudes and religious bigotry of the last years of the Valois dynasty, whose emblematic event must surely be the Saint Bartholomew's Day massacre of 1572.

21

Sixteenth-century religious writing

GARY FERGUSON

The importance of religion is evident in almost all aspects of the literature of sixteenth-century France and in particular in writers' engagement with two major, complexly inter-related phenomena: first, the Reformations, Protestant and Catholic (or Counter-Reformation), in which were involved theological issues such as the relationship between grace and human nature, the value of good works versus faith alone, the constitution of the Church, the Bible and its interpretation, the intercession of the saints, and the sacraments (notably the Eucharist and confession), and which, in the second half of the century, gave rise to a long series of civil wars; and, second, the humanist movement's revalorisation of ancient culture, including philosophical ideas more or less susceptible to syncretic reconciliation with Christianity (most notably in the form of Neoplatonism), and its development of new historical and philological methodologies, along with an emphasis on the study of Greek and Hebrew, applied within the fields of biblical translation and commentary. While this essay will focus on Christian religious culture, the study of Hebrew by scholars such as François Vatable entailed an engagement with some aspects of Jewish thought, although this was often regarded with suspicion. An interest in the cabbala, related to the enthusiasm in certain quarters for esoteric traditions, was developed notably by Guillaume Postel, a student of Vatable, and passed on to Guy Le Fèvre de la Boderie (see below) among others.

In the early decades of the sixteenth century, medieval literary traditions continued to flourish, with poetic competitions or *puys*, often organised around liturgical and particularly Marian feasts, continuing to be celebrated regularly in numerous towns. Similarly, poets such as Pierre Gringore composed prayers and meditations using traditional lyric forms (*rondeaux, chants royaux, noëls*), as well as verse paraphrases of parts of the Divine Office (notably that of the Virgin Mary). From the 1520s and 1530s on, reformist ideas were increasingly developed and began to circulate. While Erasmus and Luther did not publish in French, their works had a wide influence, for example the 1524–5 exchange on free will (Erasmus's *De libero arbitrio*; Luther's *De servo arbitrio*), and some of their more didactic and devotional works, including the former's *Enchiridion* (1503/4), were translated by Louis de Berquin (burned at the stake in 1529). In France, these years were also marked by the influence of moderate reform-minded Evangelical thinkers such as Jacques Lefèvre d'Etaples and Guillaume Briçonnet, the latter being remembered mostly for his spiritual correspondence with Marguerite de Navarre, the sister of François I. Some of those associated with this group, such as Briçonnet and Gérard Roussel, remained Catholics; others, such as Guillaume Farel, joined the Protestant Church in Geneva; yet others, such as Pierre Caroli, moved back and forth between the two confessions several times. Evangelism had a marked influence on a number of the foremost writers of the time. Clément Marot's most influential and lasting contribution to religious verse was his translation of fifty-two psalms that appeared in a series of publications in the early 1540s. As completed by Théodore de Bèze and set to music by Claude Goudimel, this would become the official Calvinist Psalter. Marguerite de Navarre's first published work, the long meditative poem *Le Miroir de l'âme pécheresse* (1531), was initially condemned by the Sorbonne, yet the queen continued to give voice to religious beliefs of an Evangelical character in almost all her writings, up to and including her great unfinished collection of short stories, *L'Heptaméron* (posthumously edited 1558–9). The promotion of Evangelical ideas, along with satire of the Catholic Church, is also strongly present throughout the novels of François Rabelais. The second of these, moreover, *Gargantua* (1534), concludes with an enigma by Mellin de Saint-Gelais offering a description of a tennis match in bellicose language that is also presented as an account of the persecution of believers in the Gospel, an eventuality that did indeed befall religious dissidents with the hardening of royal policy following the *affaire des placards* that very same year.

Among the Evangelical and breakaway Christians who left France at this time, a number benefited from the protection of Marguerite de Navarre, including not only Marot but Jean Calvin. In exile initially in Basle, Calvin drafted the single most influential text for French-speaking Protestants, the *Institution de la religion chrétienne*, the earliest versions of which appeared in Latin in 1536–9 and in French in 1541. Augmented in a series of editions, the definitive text was published in 1559–60. The *Institution* represents not only the first work of comprehensive theology in the vernacular, important for the ideas it expounds; it also stands as a monument of French prose that, on account of its systematic exposition and the clarity and sobriety of its language, is often seen as a forerunner of the classical style and the great prose works of Montaigne, Descartes, and Pascal. Dedicating his theological *summa* to François I, Calvin also pursued the political aim of persuading the French king that Huguenots, falsely portrayed as fomenters of dissent and sedition, desired to remain his loyal subjects and constituted no threat to his authority or the stability of his kingdom. Protestantism itself, however, was marked by divisions, both more and less serious in nature, and Calvin, having settled in Geneva in 1536, found himself exiled by the city council only two years later. It was in this context that the former Augustinian nun Marie Dentière addressed her *Épître très utile* to Marguerite de Navarre. In addition to denouncing the current leaders in Geneva, Dentière offers a bold and tightly argued exposition of central Protestant doctrines. Her epistle is also of interest today since it raises the issue of the role of women in the Church. If Protestantism might initially have seemed to offer its female adherents greater possibilities of participation in religious affairs, the reality was that both Protestant and Catholic ecclesiastical authorities tended to work to curb women's activities and to channel their efforts into officially sanctioned forms.

The first half of the sixteenth century was also marked by the influence of Neoplatonism, as developed by thinkers such as Marsilio Ficino, whose commentary on the *Symposium* was published in Latin in 1484 and subsequently in a French translation by Symon Silvius, dedicated to Marguerite de Navarre, in 1546. Neoplatonic ideas had a profound influence not only on the queen herself and those in her immediate circle, but also on the poets of the Pléiade, offering them a set of tropes through which to describe both the passion of love (notably the figure of the androgyne) and the 'poetic fury' (*furor poeticus*) that constituted the basis of their claim to be privileged interpreters of truths both physical and metaphysical. Beyond Neoplatonic thinking, other ancient philosophical or mythical currents were also explored by Pierre de Ronsard and his companions – the figure of Orpheus, for example, or of Dionysus/Bacchus, who represents both the poetic faculty of fantasy and the principle of the holding in equilibrium of the totality of the contrasting passions and forces of life. Nor should we assume that these audacious and ambitious writers were drawn by Dionysian ideas in an abstract way alone. The atmosphere prevailing at the property of Jean de Brinon in Médan, frequented by Jean Dorat and the members of the Pléiade in 1551–2, was distinctly Epicurean. After the relaunching of classical tragedy with the successful performance in 1553 of Étienne Jodelle's *Cléopâtre captive*, a ceremony was held at Arcueil in imitation of a Bacchic orgy that was to become a source of considerable controversy. Just how far did the young poets go in their imitation of ancient religious rites? There is evidence to suggest that a goat might have been sacrificed to the god. Such issues are clearly fundamental for understanding Ronsard's religious world; they also intersect forcefully with currents of reform, since accusations of paganism came principally, though not exclusively, from Protestants, readily growing out of and in turn feeding a vision according to which all Catholics were idolatrous, superstitious, given to sexual perversion, and simply godless to one degree or another. Despite repeated and strenuous denials, moreover, Ronsard remained dogged by a reputation for paganism, a situation not altogether surprising when we consider some startling verses from the 'Remonstrance au peuple de France', written in 1562 at the very beginning of the Wars of Religion. The poem offers a defence of the Catholic faith, in the course of which the poet nonetheless imagines himself, outside Christian revelation, as a pagan worshipping the sun. In a brilliant reading of the passage, Terence Cave describes what he terms Ronsard's 'croyance au conditionnel' ('belief in the conditional tense').[1]

Before the outbreak of civil war in the early 1560s, attempts were made at reconciling religious divisions and finding common theological ground, notably at the Colloquy of Poissy in 1561; however, each party was interested primarily in defending its own doctrines, and Catholic participants were anxious not to pre-empt the deliberations of the ongoing but currently suspended Council of Trent (1545–63), officially charged with the reform of discipline and affirmation of doctrine within the Catholic Church. Secondarily, the Colloquy had the effect of launching the poetic career of Anne de Marquets, a Dominican nun at the priory that hosted the event. Best known for her meditative *Sonnets spirituels* (published posthumously in 1605), Marquets's first collection of verse, *Sonnets, prières et devises en forme de pasquins* (1562), represents a rare intervention by a woman (comparable to that of Dentière in her epistle to Marguerite de Navarre) in the domain of religious polemic.

The decades of the 1560s to the 1580s, and especially following the Saint Bartholomew's Day massacre in 1572, saw an outpouring of engaged confessional and polemical writing. Reading the work of a memorialist such as Pierre de L'Estoile, who collected and recorded in his *Registre-Journal* all kinds of occasional verse, pamphlets, posters, and so on, one has the impression that a city such as Paris was awash in a veritable sea of such ephemera attacking or defending one religious or related political position or another. In the later years of the reign of Henri III, the propaganda war reached dizzying heights, driven mostly by the polemicists of the ultra-Catholic League, when, as a result of the king's failure to produce a male heir and after the death of

---

1 T. Cave, *Pré-histoires: textes troublés au seuil de la modernité* (Geneva: Droz, 1999), pp. 53–9.

his younger brother in 1584, the Huguenot Henri de Navarre stood next in line to the throne. The reigning couple's sterility was a major factor in the satirising of Henri III's relationship with his young favourites or *mignons* as involving 'unnatural' sexual relations; accusations of effeminacy were also fed by the king's numerous penitential activities – processions, retreats, private and public devotions – which he saw as being in line with Tridentine piety and to which he increasingly turned as he became convinced of the futility of force in the battle for souls and of the necessity of promoting himself as a sacred monarch, God's anointed, chosen to rule over France. Henri's policy convinced few. Protestants considered him a corrupt tyrant, despotic and morally degenerate in every way; fervent Catholics saw him at best as weak, cowardly, and lacking conviction. Both sides united in levelling against him accusations of effeminacy and sexual deviance. Court poets, of course, such as Philippe Desportes and Jacques Davy Du Perron, wrote verse in praise of the king, but often in terms that served only to fan the flames of the fires lit by his enemies. Much of this polemical religio-political literature is little read today, with the magnificent exception of the Protestant Agrippa d'Aubigné's *Les Tragiques* (composed mostly between 1577 and 1579; published 1616–23). Epic verse constituted an important part of this literary production, and *Les Tragiques* forms an epic fresco of such compelling ferocity that it can be seen as the ultimate illustration of the thesis whereby force of conviction was productive of particularly powerful and innovative poetry. In addition to cataloguing the miseries of a war-torn France, d'Aubigné's text mercilessly satirises the king, the royal family, the court, and the Catholic Church, memorialises the sacrifice of the Huguenot martyrs, and looks forward to divine judgement in apocalyptic terms.

From the 1570s onwards, there was also an abundant production of devotional literature, especially poetry, frequently meditative and penitential in character. In some of this, confessional differences are apparent, principally in relation to subjects such as the Eucharist, the Virgin Mary, and the saints. Nonetheless, this writing is decidedly less divisive than that discussed so far, in particular the many works that express general penitential sentiments or constitute paraphrases of the Scriptures, and notably of the psalms. Conscious of the power of biblically inspired poetry, especially when set to music and sung, Catholic writers such as Jean-Antoine de Baïf, Desportes, and Blaise de Vigenère were anxious to provide their Church with a vernacular Psalter to stand over and against that of Marot and Bèze. Much of this devotional verse is of a high quality, representing the work of some of the finest poets of the day, including, in addition to those mentioned already, Guillaume de

Salluste Du Bartas (for example, *La Muse chrétienne* [1574], containing *Judith, Le Triomphe de la foi*, and other works; see also below), Rémy Belleau (paraphrases of Job [in *La Bergerie*, 1572] and Ecclesiastes and the Song of Songs [in *Les Amours et nouveaux échanges*, 1575]), Guy Le Fèvre de La Boderie (*Hymnes ecclésiastiques* [1578]; see also below), François de Malherbe (*Les Larmes de saint Pierre* [1587]), and Jean de Sponde (*Méditations sur les psaumes ... avec un Essai de quelques poèmes chrétiens*, including the 'Sonnets de la mort' [1588]). Numerous lesser-known figures also published devotional verse: for example, Jacques de Billy (two collections of *Sonnets spirituels* [1573 and 1578]), Jean de Boyssières (*Œuvres spirituelles* [1582], etc.), Isaac Habert (*Œuvres chrétiennes* [1585]), Jean-Baptiste Chassignet (*Le Mépris de la vie* [1594]), and Antoine Favre (*Centurie première* [1595]). This rich tradition carried on well into the following century with poets such as César de Nostredame (*Les Perles, ou les larmes de la Magdeleine* [1601], *Dymas, ou le bon larron* [1606], etc.), Pierre de Croix (*Le Miroir de l'amour divin* [1608]), Lazare de Selve (*Œuvres spirituelles* [1620]), and Jean de La Ceppède (*Les Théorèmes* [1613–21]). Religious and devotional poetry was also an area in which women made a significant contribution. Georgette de Montenay published a series of Christian emblems (1571), and substantial collections of verse were also composed by Gabrielle de Coignard (*Œuvres chrétiennes* [1594]) and Anne de Marquets (see also above). The latter wrote poetry inspired principally by the Catholic liturgy in the form of 480 spiritual sonnets, a lyric cycle without precedent in the 1570s and 80s and equalled in scope only decades later by La Ceppède's *Théorèmes*. The style of much of this writing, moreover, is characterised by an abundance of feminine imagery and an emphasis on devotional sweetness that found its most influential expression, again in the following century, in the writings of François de Sales, notably the highly influential *Introduction à la vie dévote* (1608/9–19).

A less bellicose religious stance was also adopted by those who came to be known as *politiques*, mostly Catholic moderates who put national interests before religious adherence in order to argue for the necessity of finding a political solution to the civil wars, and whose views would prepare the way for the acceptance of Henri de Navarre as Henri IV following his definitive conversion to Catholicism, the eventual pacification of the kingdom, and the promulgation of the Edict of Nantes (1598). One such was the neo-Stoic moralist Guillaume Du Vair, initially a supporter of the League, best known today for his treatises *De l'éloquence française* (1594) and *La Philosophie morale des Stoïques* (1598), but also the author of a series of meditations on the psalms (1580) and of *La Sainte Philosophie* (1600). The last decades of the century also saw the composition of a number of long encyclopaedic poems, generally non-polemical in tone, such as Le Fèvre de La Boderie's eclectic *Encyclie des secrets de l'éternité* (1571) and Du Bartas's highly successful *Semaine, ou Création du monde* (1578). The *Semaine* sets out to offer, at one and the same time, an epic paraphrase of the story of creation, as recounted in the first two chapters of Genesis, and a vast *summa* of current scientific knowledge relating to the whole of the natural order, accompanied by moral and theological reflection on this and on the place of man within it. Du Bartas subsequently began work on a *Seconde Semaine*, intended to cover human history from Eden to the Apocalypse: only the first two days were completed and published, however (1584), with two more appearing posthumously in preliminary form (1591–1603).

The later years of the century also saw the development of a strongly sceptical current of thought, fed equally by the intractable doctrinal disputes between competing Christian confessions and by the renewed influence of ancient philosophical schools, each offering its own different vision of the human condition and corresponding ethical values. Such a current is evident in the *Essais* (1580–95) of Michel de Montaigne, whose religious convictions have been the subject of considerable scholarly debate. What is clear is that a work such as the 'Apologie de Raimond Sebond' (*Essais*, II.12), even if it is presented ostensibly as a defence of Catholic natural theology (as exemplified by Sebond's *Theologia naturalis*), is one so paradoxical in character as to raise more questions than it settles. Moreover, if it has been possible to argue that the tenor of the *Essais* is not in conflict with late sixteenth-century Catholic ideology in general, there is also little evidence of a convinced endorsement of Catholic doctrine or moral teaching and much that promotes a profoundly sceptical and relative vision of all knowledge and a secular humanist ethics based on personal experience. In this light, it is not difficult to understand why Montaigne was often seen in the seventeenth century as the principal source of a vein of sceptical thought culminating in the *Dialogues faits à l'imitation des anciens* (1630–1) of François de La Mothe Le Vayer and the works of such radical free-thinkers as Théophile de Viau. At its close, then, the sixteenth century bequeathed to its heirs the materials they would develop in the areas of piety as well as of doubt to make of their age both the century of saints and the century of the *libertins*.

The utter centrality of religious concerns to the literature of the sixteenth century is apparent from the fact that the names of so many of the foremost writers of the period have figured in these pages. While clearly not all of the century's literature was equally engaged with theological, spiritual, or polemical questions, little of it remained untouched by them. Not only was literature inextricably bound up with religion, but both intersected also, as we have seen, with politics, with concepts of gender and sexuality, and with issues of alterity and marginality, memory, and testimony. The vitality and range of penetration of religious questions bear witness to a century in turmoil and discovery, as well as to one in which the establishment of the medium of print meant that censorship became more and more difficult to exercise and a single orthodoxy more and more difficult, if not impossible, to impose. A final illustration of how these multiple elements might coalesce in striking and fundamental ways finds expression in the French encounter with the recently discovered American continent, the 'New World'. Religious divisions and the civil strife they engendered significantly undermined early exploratory and colonial enterprises, in which Protestants were particularly active. They also gave rise to understandings of the alterity of American Indian cultures inflected in national but also in more specifically confessional ways, profoundly marked in the case of Huguenot writers such as Jean de Léry by their own collective experience of marginalisation and persecution. The long-lived myth of the 'noble savage' was developed in this context, whose particularities constituted a set of determining factors not only for the development of travel writing, but also, much more widely, for the writing of cosmographies (geography, ethnography) and even history.

22

Sixteenth-century poetry

JAMES HELGESON

Poets come and go; generally this is a matter of taste, occasionally it is a matter of ontology. For example, Louise Labé, the most famous female poet of the French sixteenth century, possessed many qualities but not – or at least so Mireille Huchon has argued – that of existence.[1] More precisely, someone called Louise Labé (c. 1524–66) seems to have existed, but may not have been the author of the much read *Evvres* (1555) attributed to her: a fiery dedication in defence of women's writing; an erudite and witty 'Debat de Folie et d'Amour'; three elegies; and twenty-four sonnets. The consternation that, in many quarters, has greeted Huchon's theory – that Labé's work is a cynical *supercherie* with comic intent – would seem to indicate that 'the author' has not been permanently put to rest. Indeed, his or her 'death' has never been entirely convincing for readers for whom the particulars of identity or social position (such as being a woman, or not being one) are significant.

The guiding questions of this chapter will be the following: what were poets doing by means of writing and publishing poetry in the sixteenth century? How did poetry relate to the individuals, or in some cases perhaps collectives of individuals, who wrote it?

Like many familiar distinctions, the division of poetry into the three genres – epic, dramatic, and lyric – may seem timeless. Yet the partition does not map neatly onto, for example, Aristotle's; it gained its familiar modern form in the nineteenth century, in the second volume of G. W. F. Hegel's *Aesthetics*. The distinctions made by Plato and Aristotle, familiar especially in the later Renaissance, bear rather on varieties of poetic mimesis or imitation. A tripartite division of poetry is also often attributed to Horace (*Ars poetica*, lines 73–98), although his taxonomy is not as clearly threefold as is sometimes assumed. In the sixteenth century, the *Poetices libri septem* (pub. 1561) of J. C. Scaliger (1484–1558), to take an important example, does not reproduce

---

1 Mireille Huchon, *Louise Labé, une créature de papier* (Geneva: Droz, 2006).

this familiar structure either, but a Platonic and Aristotelian one, founded on mimesis and the separation of modes dominated by (a) narrative, (b) dialogue, and (c) the mixture of these two (i, iii). Unlike Aristotle, Scaliger does not equate these modes directly with the genres of poetry.

I will speak of 'epic' and 'lyric' in turn, as sixteenth-century writers did use these terms, although their fields of application cannot be neatly delineated. More information on sixteenth-century drama can be found in Chapter 23 in this volume.

'Epic'

In his 1549 polemic, the *Deffence et illustration de la langue françoyse*, Joachim du Bellay (1525–60) enjoined his compatriots to cultivate 'long poems' in French through the imitation of prestigious models: 'choysi moy quelque un de ces beaux vieux Romans Françoys, comme un *Lancelot*, un *Tristan*, ou autres; et en fay renaitre au monde une admirable *Iliade*, et laborieuse *Enéide*' ('choose me one of these beautiful old French romances, a *Lancelot* or *Tristan*, or others, and bring into the world again an admirable *Iliad*, or carefully crafted *Aeneid*').[2] Du Bellay's goal is glory for the poet and the nation ('immortelle gloire, honneur de la France' ['immortal glory, honour to France']) although he does not call here specifically for the composition of 'epics'. There seems to be no rigorous distinction between 'romance' and 'epic'; and although du Bellay generally devalues older poetry in French, the *romans* of Lancelot and Tristan are appropriate material for a new French national poem. The medieval *roman* has not disappeared; the republication of *Le Roman de la rose*, reworked in prose by the Burgundian court poet Jean Molinet (1435–1507), 'moralisé cler et net' ('clearly and plainly moralised'), and published in 1503 – updated in verse as well, possibly by Clément Marot (1496–1544) in an edition reprinted several times after 1526 – testifies to readers' continued interest in the form, alongside their fascination with the more recent developments of the Italian *romanzo* as exemplified by the *Orlando furioso* (1516 / 32) of Ludovico Ariosto (1474–1533).

Most important to the history of sixteenth-century French epic is the pseudo-historiographical tradition surrounding the mythical 'Francus'. In his *Les Illustrations de Gaule et singularitez de Troie* (published 1511–13), Jean Lemaire de Belges (1473–1525) tells of a putative son of Hector and Andromache, sometimes identified with the infant Astyanax generally thought murdered by

---

2 Joachim du Bellay, *La Deffence et illustration de la langue françoyse & l'Olive*, ed. J.-C. Monferran and E. Caldarini (Geneva: Droz, 2007) pp. 139–40.

Achilles. The story of Francus is first attested in the seventh-century chronicle of Fregedarius. The wanderings of Francus link Troy to France, or rather Gaul, just as Aeneas' odyssey ties Priam's lost city to Rome. (Francus, it should be noted, has, e.g., British, German, and Portuguese analogues.) Guillaume Cretin (1460–1525) also exploits the story in an unfinished *Chronique françoise*.

Epic is most strongly represented after 1560. It falls to Pierre de Ronsard (1524–85), unquestionably sixteenth-century France's most prominent and influential poet, to attempt the composition of a national epic that might rival Greek and Roman exemplars. Born near Vendôme to a noble family, he served several kings of France and was much appreciated by both the Scots queen Mary Stuart and Elizabeth I of England. For his national epic Ronsard chose not one of the romances recommended by du Bellay, but the story of Francus already exploited by Lemaire and Cretin. His epic is unfinished (and, for most, unsuccessful) although it strives to establish primacy in French historical mythmaking and to mark the origins of the new, great French political and literary empire. In the posthumous 1587 preface to the *Franciade* (1572), the poet, or perhaps his publisher, reworked a verse from Virgil (*Aeneid*, IV, 49) to the effect that 'through words, how much will France increase in glory' – replacing Virgil's 'Carthage' with 'Gaul' and 'arms' with 'words'.

Charles IX had insisted that Ronsard's Francus epic should contain a complete genealogy of the royal house, although the truth value of epic – like all poetry – has long been doubtful. Most scholars in Ronsard's time thought the Francus story fictional; indeed, the 1587 preface situates the epic in the realm of the 'vraisemblable' (plausible) rather than the 'vrai' (true), following Aristotle, for whom 'the distinction between historian and poet' is that 'the one describes the thing that has been, and the other a kind of thing that might be' (*Poetics* 1451a38–1451b5). Truth is the province of the historian; before Aristotle, Herodotus had already begun his *Histories* with a harsh dismissal of Homer's account of the Trojan War.

By contrast, Guy Le Fèvre de la Boderie (1541–98) asserts in the 'advertissement' to his monumental pseudo-historical summa *La Galliade, ou de la révolution des arts et sciences* (1578, expanded 1582) that he values 'l'utilité & la vérité' ('usefulness and truth') over 'la vraysemblance' ('plausibility'). Indeed, the Platonic–Hermetic tradition underlying the cosmological and 'scientific' poetry that flourished in the second half of the century privileges the true over the possible. Maurice Scève's (*c.* 1511 – *c.* 1564) *Microcosme* (1562), Guillaume de Sallustre du Bartas's (1544–90) *La Semaine: ou, Creation du monde* (1578), and *Seconde Semaine* (1584) are important works in the encyclopaedic vein. Although Du Bartas's work is perhaps the best known (he influenced Milton), Le Fèvre's

Galliade exhibits the archaeological and universalising tendencies of the knowledge epics of late sixteenth-century France in perhaps their most exaggerated form. Le Fèvre's subject, like Ronsard's, is the origins and primacy of 'Gaul'. Le Fèvre derives his title from the Hebrew *Galal* ('return, revolution'): wisdom had emanated from the nation in ancient times and had returned full circle to France under the stewardship of the Valois kings. Renaissance Neoplatonists, in particular the admirers of the Florentine Marsilio Ficino (1433–99), of whom Le Fèvre is an important late sixteenth-century French example, are theoreticians of an efficacious metaphysical poetry that imitates the harmony of the cosmos. Claiming a metaphysical poetic birthright can of course be self-interested, as the poet becomes a privileged mouthpiece for divine truth. Indeed, the elastic character of these doctrines, as presented by poets such as Ronsard, exemplifies the often puzzling nature of early modern belief.

Another important epic, *Les Tragiques*, an account by Agrippa d'Aubigné (1552–1630) of the persecution of Protestants (begun *c.* 1577, published anonymously 1616), values truth over likelihood, though for different reasons. D'Aubigné's seven-book poem gives a partisan account of the religious wars. His historical account occasionally relies on cosmological tropes – for example on the disturbance and restoration of cosmic order (end of books I and VII) – but also on the urgency of bearing witness to the brutality visited on his coreligionists. D'Aubigné, intensely committed to the truth of his poetic vision, was also devoted to the Catholic Ronsard's poetry. As in Ronsard's great broadsides from the 1560s against the Protestants (the 'Discours sur les misères de ce temps', and its 'Continuation'), d'Aubigné relies heavily on the apparent character, or *ethos*, of the poetic 'I'. Like Ronsard, d'Aubigné lays claim to the fire of divine truth; his pseudonym is 'le larron Promethée'. Yet d'Aubigné's unnamed poetic fire-carrier is not punished; rather, in the end he disappears, fused with his god. In this apotheosis d'Aubigné seeks to secure glory and immortality as an heir to the poet whom Le Fèvre had called 'le Pindare Français'.

'Lyric'

Pindar was not an epic poet, but a lyric one. Yet the word 'lyric' was sufficiently rare in 1550 that Barthélémy Aneau (*c.* 1505–61) made a caustic riposte to du Bellay about the younger poet's use of the term in his *Deffence*. In his *Quintil horatien*, Aneau sharply criticises du Bellay – the author of a collection of *Vers lyriques* (1550) – for taking up the 'lyre' with less practical knowledge of music than a village fiddler or flute-player.

A 'lyric' poem is often thought of as a text intended for music. The term is also often associated, from the eighteenth century, with 'personal' verse in the first person that expresses, or simulates, felt emotion. 'Lyrique' was not a medieval term, nor was it common in the early sixteenth century. It is strongly associated with humanist circles. Early attestations in French are from the 1490s, for example in Octavien de Saint-Gelais (1468–1502). In the *Art de rhétorique vulgaire* of 1493, Jean Molinet evokes various precursors to his patron's eloquence, mythical musicians, although his subject is not yet 'lyric' poetry. Nor is the term featured in the *Grant et vray art de rhetorique* of Pierre Fabri (*c.* 1450 – *c.* 1535). When 'lyric' becomes familiar, the term is still far from perspicuous. Scaliger's definition is exceedingly broad; brevity is the common denominator in the quasi-Rabelaisian list of types of poems defined as 'lyric'. As for du Bellay, lyric poetry can be about everything from the most exalted subjects to 'la solicitude des jeunes hommes, comme l'amour, les vins libres, et toute bonne chere' (230–1) ('the cares of young men, such as love, free-flowing wine, and great merriment'). The 'lyric' is not necessarily personal: it flourishes through *imitatio*, and particularly the imitation of prestigious classical examples.

Yet the idea that poetry and music go together was common, and thus the question of what we might call the 'lyric' was contentious. Amongst Franco-Flemish and French composers the traditional fixed forms, especially the *ballade* and *rondeau*, were disappearing by the end of the fifteenth century. Although these forms would have an afterlife in printed poetry collections until the 1530s (when they are largely supplanted by the epigram, the chanson, and later the sonnet) it was the new and freer poetic forms, short *chanson* texts and epigrams cultivated by Clément Marot and his followers, that were generally set to music in the early sixteenth century.

The *Grands Rhétoriqueurs*, including Jean Meschinot (*c.* 1415 – *c.* 1491), Jean Molinet (1433–1507), Guillaume Cretin, Jean Marot (*c.* 1450–1526) and Jean Lemaire de Belges, develop a sophisticated poetics characterised by complex formal devices and rhyme schemes. The *Rhétoriqueurs* remake the traditional fixed forms, the *rondeau* in particular, reinventing them in ways that distance them from traditional musical structures (e.g. the *rondeau à rentrement*). They tend, like Eustache Deschamps (1346–1406), to define verse as a type of music. For example, in 1493, Molinet writes that 'vernacular rhetoric is a kind of music called '*richmique*'. Although the term 'musica rhythmica' is familiar in late antique and medieval music theory, Molinet appears here to be reproducing a common conflation between 'rhyme' and 'rhythm'. For the *Rhétoriqueurs*, the writing of music and the writing of poetry are nonetheless distinct activities.

Yet the sense of a link between the two was strong, and music would later represent a problem for humanist poetics. Poets who believed, as Jean-Antoine de Baïf put it in 1570, that 'Jadis, Musiciens, Poètes et Sages / furent mesmes auteurs' ('Long ago, musicians, poets, and wise men / were the self-same authors')[3] chose self-consciously 'musical' genres such as *chansons*, restyled as 'odes' by the Pléiade (the elite septemvirate of poets centred around Pierre de Ronsard after 1556).

The *Rhétoriqueurs'* poetry is often a sophisticated synthesis of late medieval formal experimentation, philosophical speculation, and playful self-reference. Early sixteenth-century poets are also highly conscious of the problems besetting the poet obliged to earn a living by his pen, within the traditional context of courtly culture and the new one of printers and publishing. Clément Marot (1496–1544) built on the *Rhétoriqueur* tradition, navigating between the traditional forms that dominate in his *Adolescence clémentine* of 1532, classically inspired formal choices, notably the epigram, of which he was a great master, and erotic forms such as the *blason*. Marot's contempories set many of his poems to music. Perhaps Marot's crowning achievement is in sacred lyricism: his late verse translations from the psalms were enormously popular among Protestant (and Catholic) readers throughout the century. Like his predecessors, Marot also excels in non-lyric short forms such as the epistle; his letter poems are among the most subtle examples of poetry as action in the sixteenth century, playing on the relationship between the 'I' of poetry and the action carried out by poems written to powerful patrons, often as requests for intercession, although the problem of poetic action is often suggested by the 'lyric' forms as well.

Marot's poetry strongly shaped that of his serious-minded contemporary Maurice Scève, whose 1544 *Délie, object de plus haulte vertu*, is often called the first Petrarchan poetic sequence in French. This collection – an opening *huitain* and 449 *dizains* interspersed with fifty emblems – has fascinated and puzzled readers since Scève's time. Mireille Huchon has suggested in her work on Labé that Scève may have been a major actor in the elaboration and publication of her works in 1555, and if she is right, Scève is an impressive poetic ventriloquist, manipulating multiple poetic personae with the virtuosity of a sixteenth-century Pessoa. Yet Scève's other production, although diverse, does not entirely suggest such protean talent. The 'discoverer' of the false tomb of Petrarch's Laura in Avignon in 1533 adapted a Spanish novel and

---

3 Jean-Antoine de Baïf, *Euvres en rime*, ed. C. Marty-Lavaux, 4 vols. (Paris: Lemerre, 1881–90), IV, p. 244.

published several short pieces as well as the *Microcosme* of 1562, mentioned above. He is also responsible for a pamphlet describing the royal entry of Henri II into Lyon in 1548, and probably much of its iconographical content. Many contemporaries of Scève (e.g. Antoine Héroet [*c.* 1492–1558]) were, as he was, fascinated by Ficinian Neoplatonism, with its emphasis on idealised love and its valorisation of poetry.

The double influence of Marot and Scève can be perceived in the subtle *Rymes* (1545) of Pernette du Guillet (*c.* 1520–45). The young Lyonnais noble-woman, perhaps the model for 'Délie' herself, assimilates and twists the Petrarchan and Neoplatonic topoi dear to Scève, gently mocking the poet whose name is included as an anagram in several poems. Their poetic conversation has analogues among the *Grands Rhétoriqueurs*, and poetic 'networking' will be an important ingredient in Pléiade poetics.

Montaigne, in the *Essais* (1.26), mentions Ronsard and du Bellay as the most influential French poets, followed by a host of imitators (of whom Philippe Desportes [1546–1606] is probably the most noted), and indeed their lyric production is among the richest in the French tradition. In a series of important collections, constantly revised throughout his career, notably the *Amours* (1552), their *Continuations* (1555–6), *Le Second Livre des Amours* (1560) and the *Sonnets pour Helene* (1578), Ronsard explores and develops the possibilities of the sonnet, still a novel form, imported in the 1530s, that he did more than any other poet to naturalise in France. Ronsard's *Amours* of 1552 appeared with a musical supplement. Du Bellay, the author of an early Petrarchan collection, *L'Olive* (1549), would distance the sonnet sequence from its origins in Italian love poetry in the *Regrets* (1558), and provide a melancholy meditation on *Les Antiquitez de Rome* (1558), presented to the king as the first of its kind and, oddly, as a 'good omen' for his reign. Edmund Spenser (1552–99) translated this latter collection into English. For Ronsard, however, lyric was not limited to the 'elegant low style' of many of the sonnets, but underlay the grandiloquence and metaphysical import of his innovative *Odes* (1550) and *Hymnes* (1556). In the 1550 preface to the *Odes*, Ronsard insists on his primacy in poetry, describing his project with a quotation from Horace about the first footsteps in a virgin field.

Neoplatonic ideas about music and poetry underlie much of the lyric production after 1549. Pontus de Tyard (1521–1605) is probably the most important link in the chain of transmission of Neoplatonism from Italy to France; a friend of Scève, he was later included in the Pléiade. The polymath Jacques Peletier du Mans (1517–82) was also added; this poet and mathematician fused the concerns of encyclopaedic poetry with lyric form. Neoplatonic ideas, which

Ronsard seems to have regarded with a certain ambivalence, are strikingly expressed in the founding, by Jean-Antoine de Baïf (1532–89) and Thibault de Courville (d. 1581), of a royal 'Academy of Poetry and Music' conceived 'for the establishment and advancement of measured poetry and music joined together in imitation of the Greeks and the Romans'.[4] Baïf wished to reinvent French prosody as 'measured verse' in line with Greek and Latin metrics, in the hope that the pacifying 'effects of music' exemplified by Orpheus' lyre might stem from an accurate reproduction of ancient song. Proper poetry would manipulate and tune the spirit of its listener through the metaphysical conformity of cosmos and poem. The poet, like the Thracian bard, stands at the centre of a ring of musical power.

Although one might in the end argue that since poetic texts are primarily instances of imitation – both Platonic, metaphysically significant *mimesis* and rhetorical *imitatio* – and that the question of the first person in 'lyric' is superfluous, such a thesis is an oversimplification. Readers could and did sometimes make an equation between poetic persona and the writer, especially in situations where such an equation might be convenient. Such identification is more common than we post-Romantics, preoccupied with the 'elocutionary disappearance of the poet', might expect. Indeed, the notion that lyric poetry spoke non-mimetically 'pro persona sua' was one of the reasons the genre was difficult to reconcile with an Aristotelian theory of mimesis in the later Renaissance. The French verse of Queen Mary Stuart (1542–87) was, for example, used against her as evidence at her trial. The important current of religious poetry, for example the works of Marguerite de Navarre (1492–1549) and later Jean de Sponde (1557–95) and Anne de Marquets (1533 – c. 1598), also occupies a boundary position between the exemplary first person and the particulars of individual devotion. Nevertheless, since poetry accomplishes actions and has effects that are not necessarily 'expressions' of first-person sentiment, the question of first-person expression is better addressed if verse is considered less as a representation of the inner affections of the soul and more as a form of worldly action. The remarkable afterlife, for example, of Louise Labé's *Evvres*, with which I began, is indeed a testament to this peculiarity of poetic expression: poetry makes something happen, although what 'happens' is often unexpected.

---

4 Frances A. Yates, *The French Academies of the Sixteenth Century* (London: Warburg Institute, 1947), p. 323.

23

Sixteenth-century theatre

GILLIAN JONDORF

The most striking innovation in French dramatic literature in the sixteenth century is the humanist theatre: tragedies and comedies drawing on classical (mainly Latin) and Italian models, allied to the Pléiade enterprise, and appealing to an educated audience or readership. These plays (particularly the tragedies) are the best-known dramatic works of the period.[1] However, other more popular forms preceded and to some extent coexisted with this learned output. Mystery plays, for example, continued to be performed in Paris until banned by the Parlement in 1548, and in the provinces for some time thereafter. The morality plays, farces, and *soties* of the medieval period also survived well into the sixteenth century, but need no separate account here.

A link or hybrid between the older type of play and the humanist theatre may be seen in some Protestant plays, which are given the designation of 'tragédie' but do not fully adopt the humanist model. Théodore de Bèze was an eminent Calvinist theologian and pastor. His play *Abraham sacrifiant* was performed in Lausanne in 1550 and published in Geneva the same year.[2] The title page identifies the play as a *Tragedie Françoise* and in an introductory note to readers Bèze discusses his use of this word, but only in terms of whether it should be called 'Comedy' or 'Tragedy' (as it has elements of both), not whether it could have been called a 'Mystery'. It is divided by *Pauses* into three episodes of different lengths, the first preceded by a Prologue and the last completed by an Epilogue, so that the structure approximates to that of a five-act play, although unlike the chorus of a humanist play the *Troupe* of Abraham's shepherds performs its *cantiques* (the term still used for hymns in

---

1 Most of these plays are most conveniently available in the series Théâtre français de la Renaissance, ed. E. Balmas *et al.* (Florence: Leo S. Olschki; Paris: Presses Universitaires de France). References to texts in this series will be in the form TFR followed by series number and volume number.
2 Théodore de Bèze, *Abraham sacrifiant*, ed. Patrizia De Capitani, TFR I, I, 1986.

French Protestantism) during rather than at the end of the episodes. The play urges obedience to God however harsh his command; this alone would not necessarily characterise it as a Protestant work, but the comic anachronism of having the character of Satan appear in a monk's habit makes the confessional loyalty plain. Bèze's title echoes the form used for classical plays such as Seneca's *Hercules furens* ('Hercules Mad'), and the same style is adopted by another Protestant playwright, Louis Des Masures, for his trilogy of plays about David and Saul, *David combattant*, *David triomphant*, and *David fugitif*.[3] His plays have many similarities to Bèze's, including the use of Satan as a character.

These works are plainly intended to be edifying. They are closely based on supposedly 'historical' texts. Both these things are also true of many humanist tragedies. The first of these was the *Cléopâtre captive* of Étienne Jodelle, performed in the winter of 1552–3; it can be seen as a response to the advice in the Pléiade manifesto, Du Bellay's *Deffence et illustration de la langue françoyse*.[4] Du Bellay, addressing an ideal French poet, says:

> Quand aux comedies & tragedies . . . je seroy' bien d'opinion que tu t'y employasses, & si tu le veux faire pour l'ornement de ta Langue, tu sçais ou tu en doibs trouver les archetypes.[5]

> (As for comedies and tragedies . . . I certainly think you should turn your hand to these, and if you want to do it to enhance your language, you know where you must find models.)

The models are to be found in Italy, where there was already a genre of regular tragedy written in Italian, and in classical antiquity. The most accessible classical models were Latin – the tragedies of Seneca and the comedies of Terence and Plautus, for all educated French writers could read Latin. Although fewer knew Greek, several Greek tragedies were accessible in Latin translations. In accordance with these models, almost all humanist plays are in verse, contain five acts, and have a chorus (or more than one).

In the absence of a professional theatre, the homes of humanist drama were the library (for many plays were probably never performed), the school or college, or the great house, including royal residences; *Cléopâtre captive* was first performed before the king in the house of the cardinal de Reims, and then

---

3 Louis Des Masures, *Tragédies saintes*, ed. Michel Dassonville, TFR I, 2, 1989.
4 Étienne Jodelle, *Cléopâtre captive*, ed. Enea Balmas, TFR I, 1, 1986.
5 Joachim du Bellay, *La Deffence et illustration de la langue françoyse*, ed. H. Chamard, 3rd edn (Paris: Librairie Marcel Didier, 1996), 125–6. (The *Deffence* was first published in 1549; Chamard's edition was first published in 1970.)

in the Collège de Boncourt. It is partly because of this amateur status that we know very little about the staging of these plays. If there was no theatre, there was also no profession of playwright. Many humanist plays were written by young men who later went on to other activities in law or the church. Robert Garnier, the most prolific and best known of humanist dramatists, was atypical in that he wrote plays for over twenty years, but he did this alongside a successful career as a lawyer.

The humanist playwrights found theoretical guidance for their endeavours principally in the Roman poet Horace's *Ars poetica* ('The Art of Poetry'). His precepts include: violent or shocking action to be narrated, not represented; plays to consist of five acts; no more than three speaking characters to be on the stage at once; no supernatural intervention to resolve the plot 'unless a knot occur, worthy of such a champion' (191–2); the chorus to take part in the action, and to sing nothing between the acts which is not relevant to the plot; the chorus should favour virtue and moderation; the playwright should hurry his listeners into the middle of the story (*in medias res*); in order to sway the emotions of his audience, he must choose his words appropriately, making them fit the personality and situation of the character.

Sixteenth-century playwrights, including Jodelle, usually respect these principles; sometimes they re-express or enlarge upon them. Thus Jean de La Taille, who wrote two biblical tragedies (1572 and 1573) and two comedies (1573), prefaced his published work with an essay 'De l'art de la tragedie' in which he offers a series of contrastive definitions of tragedy and comedy, and emphasises the emotional appeal of tragedy.[6]

One difference between Senecan tragedy and its Greek precursors is that the Senecan corpus includes a play about very recent Roman history, whereas Greek tragedy dealt with the remote legendary past. *Octavia*, not now thought to be by Seneca but regarded as his by sixteenth-century readers, deals with a passage in the life of the emperor Nero only three years before Seneca's death, and Seneca himself appears in it as a character. The example of this play justified both the use of ancient history as material for humanist tragedy (as in *Cléopâtre captive*, based mainly on Plutarch's life of Antony), and the use of recent French history. The use of biblical material could be justified on the same basis.

The language of humanist drama reflects its models and the education of its writers. The plays of Seneca are highly rhetorical, and rhetoric formed a

---

6 Jean de La Taille, *Dramatic Works*, ed. Kathleen Hall and C. N. Smith (London: University of London Athlone Press, 1972).

prominent part of the French educational curriculum. Not surprisingly, then, the language of humanist tragedy (but not comedy) is elaborate. Speeches are often very long, interspersed with passages of clashing single lines (stichomythia) to convey the polarities of an argument. Metre is generally decasyllabic or dodecasyllabic (i.e. alexandrine) for the body of the play, in rhyming couplets usually observing alternation of masculine and feminine rhymes. Choric passages are stanzaic, except where the chorus engages in dialogue with another character, and in a variety of metres. Rhetoric by definition has a purpose, and its purpose in most of these plays seems to be to promote a moral or political message of some kind, and, as one of the means of doing this, to provoke pity for the protagonists and for others whose sufferings are caused directly or indirectly by the protagonists' actions.

While many sixteenth-century tragedies deal with the same legendary subject matter as Greek tragedy, it is perhaps in its treatment of historical subjects that the humanist enterprise best displays its characteristic features. Comedy, too, can contain a historical element, but of a different kind, which I shall discuss first. There were comparatively few regular comedies in French, and many of these were translations or adaptations from Italian. Comedy is less rule-bound than tragedy, presumably because ancient theorists had less to say about it; most sixteenth-century theorists describe it by contrasting it with tragedy: tragedy deals with characters of high rank, comedy with ordinary people; tragedies are in verse, and their language is elevated, comedies may be in verse or prose (most are in verse) but in either case their language is close to everyday speech; tragedy characteristically ends with death and disaster, comedy with a marriage.

Jean de La Taille, the playwright and theorist mentioned above, wrote two comedies, *Les Corrivaux* ('The Rivals') and *Le Négromant* ('The Necromancer').[7] *Le Négromant* is a prose translation of a verse comedy of 1520 by the Italian poet Ariosto, and La Taille has made no attempt to 'naturalise' it into a French context. Indeed he translates Ariosto's prologue, which jokes about Cremona (the setting of the play) having been magically brought to Rome (the place of performance of Ariosto's work), and refers flatteringly to the qualities of Pope Leo X. In *Les Corrivaux*, however, although the material is derived partly from Italian sources (Boccaccio and possibly Ariosto) and partly from the Roman dramatist Terence, La Taille has taken some pains to Frenchify it. In a lengthy prologue, which is also an essay 'de l'art de la comedie', forming

---

7 Jean de La Taille, *Les Corrivaux*, ed. Monica Barsi; *Le Négromant*, ed. François Rigolot; both in TFR I, 9, 1997.

a companion piece to his earlier piece on tragedy, La Taille gives a detailed back-story, which involves a reference to Henri II's campaign against Charles V, when in April 1551 the French army occupied Metz and Toul (where one of the female characters was abandoned as a small child). In Étienne Jodelle's comedy *Eugène* (published 1574 but probably written in late 1552; TFR I, 6, 1994) two of the characters have taken part in Henri II's expedition to Germany in summer 1552. In the case of these comedies, then, references to current events place the play in a world known to the audience.

Some plays labelled as tragedy do this too – there are plays dealing with recent events, such as the Saint Bartholomew's Day massacre (August 1572) or the killing on Henri III's orders of the duc de Guise and his brother (December 1588), where the historical reference is the whole point of the play. Such plays are fiercely, even viciously, partisan – one might adapt Baudelaire's comment on *Tartuffe* and say they are not tragedies, but pamphlets. Writers using material from older history have various ways of suggesting or stating the contemporary relevance of remote events. Robert Garnier's career falls within the period of the French Wars of Religion, and many of his plays contain harrowing descriptions of the sufferings caused by war, especially civil war. The relevance of these descriptions to the contemporary plight of France is plain enough, but he emphasises it in prefatory writings. Thus, three of his plays are set during the Roman Civil Wars, and in the dedication of one of them, *Cornélie* (1574; TFR I, 5, 1993), he mentions 'les cris et horreurs de mes Tragedies (poeme à mon regret trop propre aux malheurs de nostre siecle)' ('the lamentations and horrors of my Tragedies (a poetic genre unfortunately all too suited to the miseries of our age)'). Even a play on mythical material may have contemporary relevance, and this is true of Garnier's *Antigone* (1580; TFR II, 2, 2000) where the fight for the Theban throne between Oedipus' sons provides an image of the fratricidal horror of civil war. Conversely, it is of course possible to write a play on a historical subject where the main focus is not historical: this is true of Jacques de La Taille's *Alexandre* (published posthumously in 1573; TFR I, 4, 1992), where the hero is concerned with questions about his own nature and his chance of immortality, and finally wins that immortality by his courage in facing death. However, there are contemporary resonances in other aspects of that play, promoted by an element of the structure of humanist tragedy. History is not only the story of the deeds of great men and women and their part in shaping events, but also the story of the societies participating in and affected by those events, and humanist tragedy can show both these aspects. The heroes of humanist tragedies include many of the prominent figures of ancient history, but the presence of a chorus allows these great figures to be balanced by representatives of the ordinary people whose lives will be shaped by their actions. In *Alexandre* the chorus consists of Alexandre's soldiers, proud of their exploits but now weary of fighting, and longing to go home to boast of their prowess. In Garnier's *Les Juives* (1583; TFR II, 3, 2002) the chorus of Jewish women expresses the pain of defeat and exile in poems based in part on the psalms of exile. There may even be more than one chorus so that the views of different groups can be represented (Garnier's *Antigone* has three), and this is possibly the case in the last play I shall look at, the *Regulus* of Jean de Beaubreuil (1582).[8] Marcus Atilius Regulus was a Roman consul and general in the First Punic War who after several victories was defeated and captured by the Carthaginians in 255 BCE. History or legend relates that he went to Rome on parole to arrange an exchange of prisoners or offer peace terms, which he urged the Senate to reject. To honour his parole he returned to Carthage where he died in captivity, possibly under torture.

I have chosen this play because it is typical of humanist tragedy in some respects but not others, and so illustrates the flexibility as well as the norms of the genre. It is typical in being in verse and having five acts; its subject is from Roman history; there is a chorus (possibly more than one); like the Senecan *Octavia* and many of Garnier's plays, it contains a debate about the relative merits of mercy or severity towards a defeated enemy. It is, however, unusual in several respects and I suggest that these oddities make sense if we think of the play as having a historical focus rather than being primarily concerned with heroism or the development of a Stoic sage.

Perhaps the most startling feature of the play is its extended time-scale and the way the action shifts several times between Rome and Carthage (most humanist plays conform to Jean de La Taille's recommendation that the action take place in one day and in one place). This irregularity could be provoked by a wish to show the spread and duration of a historical subject, rather than focusing on one climactic or catastrophic day. Violent action (a battle) is apparently intended to be shown on stage. Again, this could reflect a concern to give the historical facts fully, in spite of the difficulty of making such a scene convincing. An odd change is made to the historical record, whereby the Spartan mercenary general Xanthippus who defeated Regulus is elevated to 'Roi de Lacédémone' (king of Sparta). Perhaps Beaubreuil wanted to give more weight to his views about power and loyalty, which are important issues for Regulus as a Roman citizen. In typical *clémence / rigueur* (mercy / harshness) debates, *rigueur* is defended by a tyrant or ruthless commander ('It is weak

---

8 Jean de Beaubreuil, *Regulus, Tragedie*, ed. Jole Morgante, TFR II, 2, 2000.

to show mercy to rebels or defeated enemies; power gives freedom to act as one pleases'). The case for *clémence* is argued by a virtuous subordinate or colleague ('It is noble to forgive; better to be loved than feared; the suffering of war should not be prolonged beyond need; spare the innocent'). In *Regulus* a Carthaginian ambassador promises Carthaginian devotion to Rome in return for mercy, while the proponent of *rigueur* is the hero (after he has defeated the Carthaginians), whom at all other times we are invited to admire. Although this scene seems perverse in terms of characterisation, perhaps it is meant to cast doubt on the honesty of the Carthaginians (and they do indeed turn out to be liars) or to show that war forces people to make difficult decisions and act in ways that seem alien to their natures. The chorus is notably ambivalent in this act: after praising the merciful heart, it comments that Romans know the arrogance of the Carthaginians too well to trust their expressions of contrition.

The modern editor suggests that the chorus represents Roman citizens in the first two acts, Roman soldiers in the second two, and perhaps 'tous ceux qui voient dans Regulus un modèle' ('all those who find a model in Regulus') in the last. Alternatively we might hear in the chorus of *Regulus* the voice of the historian, able to admire heroism and yet see its shadowy side, the complexity of its motivations and the difficult decisions heroes have to make. Humanist tragedy can be much more than an exercise in verse composition, and its treatment of historical subjects illustrates this.

24

Women writers in the sixteenth century

EMILY BUTTERWORTH

'[I]l y a bien assez d'hommes qui escrivent, mais peu de filles se meslent à un tel exercice' ('There are certainly enough men who write, but very few girls involved in this type of exercise'), noted the Poitiers writer Catherine Des Roches, defending her first venture into print in 1578.[1] On the face of it, she was right: of over 2,000 literary figures in La Croix du Maine's 1584 guide to French writers, the *Bibliothèque françoise*, only fifty-four are women (forty-eight active in the sixteenth century); obstructed by a lack of education, expectation, leisure, or funding, women were responsible for less than 1 per cent of editions from sixteenth-century French presses.[2] And yet La Croix du Maine himself offers a different understanding of the female literary field: he mentions not only printed authors (eleven, including two translators) and women with pieces in miscellanies (five), but also women whose works circulated in manuscript (another way of publishing texts), and those who had works dedicated to them. Women were patrons and commissioners of all sorts of writing, the creators of literary and scientific salons, and the writers of letters. Their plays were performed, often for closed family circles, but also in public: Catherine de Parthenay's *Tragédie d'Holoferne* was shown in La Rochelle around 1574.[3] They wrote (and sometimes signed) family histories on the flyleaves of family bibles; nuns in convents produced accounts and histories of their orders. Alongside these forgotten writers, women were involved in the book trade in other capacities: as printers (some of whom commissioned works), editors, copy-editors, and investors. Women would also read women: female-authored texts would often address an explicitly female reader, either in personal (to a named dedicatee) or in generic terms. Small formats were

---

1 Madeleine and Catherine Des Roches, *Les Œuvres*, ed. Anne R. Larsen (Geneva: Droz, 1993), p. 183.
2 *Les Bibliothèques françoises de La Croix du Maine et de Du Verdier*, 6 vols. (Austria: Druck, 1969), I–II.
3 *La Croix du Maine*, I, p. 100.

often marketed to women, for domestic and private use; cheap and quick to produce, they could reach their market in growing numbers. Women, then, were becoming visible both as writers and as readers.

Prose narrative

Throughout the first half of the sixteenth century, stories that commented on contemporary mores known as *nouvelles* became increasingly popular. Jeanne Flore's *Comptes amoureux* (*Amorous Tales, c.* 1537), ostensibly written by a woman for women, recount the disasters that befall those who refuse their lovers; it is now generally considered a collective work, making the author's female name a kind of marketing tool. Hélisenne de Crenne also addresses a female readership, particularly in *Les Angoysses douloureuses qui precedent d'amours* (*The Painful Torments which Come from Love*, 1538), offering her story of an impatient lover and a jealous, violent husband as a warning against adulterous love. Like Flore and Crenne, Marguerite de Navarre's *Heptaméron* stages a confrontation between clichés of female behaviour and women's reactions to them. Published after her death, the *Heptaméron*'s frame narrative and the roles of the storytellers suggest an origin in a project patronised by women. Inspired by the success of Boccaccio's *Decameron* (Marguerite commissioned a French translation from Antoine Le Maçon in 1545), the *Heptaméron* establishes an equality between the sexes that is absent in Boccaccio: five men and five women are marooned in a monastery, and must devise pastimes in order to stave off melancholy. Parlamente, defender of women's virtue and constancy, suggests that they produce a French *Decameron* and present their gift to the queen on their return to civilisation: both the fictional motivation and instigator of the project are female. The female network is something that returns in Marguerite's work: she addresses a large number of the pieces in her selected works, *Les Marguerites de la Marguerite des princesses* (*Pearls from the Pearl of Princesses*, 1547), to individual women or to generic honourable ladies. While this appeal to a female readership played an important role in the defence of women's writing, it also helped create a female precedent that endorsed and supported other women going public with their works.

In the *Heptaméron*, Marguerite's narrator does not adopt a specifically female persona, unlike Crenne's; there is thus less of an explicit engagement with the difficulties and particularities of women's writing, but the presence of the five women as storytellers as well as listeners sketches out a position for women in literary and cultural creation, and a number of the stories feature women as readers and authors of their own narrative. Marguerite herself was depicted in many contemporary accounts as surrounded by literate and cultured women who would pass books between themselves; she combined her literary pursuits with her political duties as sister of the king. If the stories themselves do not offer a radical revision of patriarchal social structures and women's enforced dependency, they do insist on the cultural nature of these structures and the difference between men's and women's experience of love, family, and honour.

Lyonnais love lyric

The intense cultural activity and rapidly increasing prosperity of Lyon at the mid-century produced two women poets who directly tackled the contradictions and problems of writing in a male tradition. Both Pernette du Guillet (*Rymes*, 1545) and Louise Labé (*Evvres*, 1555) transformed the Neoplatonic and Petrarchan tradition of love lyric, writing as a desiring subject rather than the object of desire. Both had their work packaged as an address to the circles that had nurtured them: the literary salons of Lyon and the community of Lyon women.

Pernette du Guillet's *Rymes* were published after her death and offered as an example of virtuous literary activity by her first editor, Antoine du Moulin. Guillet's work is a response to (and a struggle with) that of Maurice Scève, whose sonnet sequence *Délie* (1544) is believed to represent her. She responds to his poetry in her own voice, writing explicitly as the female beloved. Offering a Neoplatonic vocabulary of transcendence and virtue, she is able to express an ideal of equality, a 'commun bien' ('common possession/good') that their poetic bond produces.[4]

Louise Labé's poetic voice differs from Guillet's in the collection of poetry and prose she published in 1555: three elegies, twenty-four sonnets, a prose debate between love and folly, and twenty-four eulogising poems by a number of anonymous poets. The authorship of Labé's works has recently been called into question, with a male poetic collective (led by Maurice Scève) proposed as the most likely candidate; but the distinctive irony of her poetry remains unchallenged.[5] She nods to her own status as love object, lamenting how she was taken in by her lover's words: 'Las! que me sert, que si parfaitement / Louas jadis et ma tresse doree' ('Alas! What good does it do me if you once praised my golden hair'). But her usual mode of address is as desiring

---

4 Pernette du Guillet, *Rymes*, ed. Victor E. Graham (Geneva: Droz, 1968), epigram 26, p. 35.
5 Mireille Huchon, *Louise Labé: une créature de papier* (Geneva: Droz, 2006).

subject, prizing her male love object for his beauty and grace: 'O dous regars, o yeus pleins de beauté' ('O sweet glances, o eyes full of beauty').[6] Her preface, addressed to Lyonnaise Clémence de Bourges, is a militant statement of female aspiration: it begins with the famous and rousing call, 'Estant le tems venu, Madamoiselle, que les severes loix des hommes n'empeschent plus les femmes de s'apliquer aus sciences et disciplines: il me semble que celles qui ont la commodité, doivent employer cette honneste liberté que notre sexe ha autrefois tant desiree, à icelles aprendre' ('Since the time has come, Mademoiselle, that men's severe laws no longer forbid women to apply themselves to knowledge and other disciplines, it seems to me that those who have the leisure should use this honourable liberty that our sex has so much desired to learn them' [p. 17]). Both a reflection of humanist optimism and a recognition that women had long been deprived of literary freedom and opportunity, Labé's preface is a performative call to action. Indeed, what is striking in the sixteenth-century presentation of Pernette du Guillet and Louise Labé is the insistence on a privileged female audience of Lyon women who defend and authorise the publications, acting as both instigators and beneficiaries of the move into the public sphere.

Devotional and confessional literature

Female networks provided support for other women too. The literary and humanist circles that gathered at the workshop of her printer, Denys Janot, may have fulfilled this supportive role for Hélisenne de Crenne; for Marie Le Gendre and Marie de Gournay, the bookshop of the celebrated Abel L'Angelier may have provided both books and community. Another supportive sphere for the production of women's writing was religious. Women's voices emerged from both Catholic convents and Protestant proselytising as well as within personal devotion throughout the sixteenth century. Half of Marguerite de Navarre's *Marguerites de la Marguerite des princesses* was devotional in inspiration (including her *Miroir de l'ame pecheresse* – *Mirror of the Sinful Soul* – which featured temporarily in the Sorbonne's list of subversive books when it was first published in 1531, for its evangelical orientation). Marguerite also provided protection and patronage for many evangelical writers such as Étienne Dolet, Clément Marot, Antoine Héroët, and Bonaventure des Périers. One who sought her patronage was the Protestant convert and

6 Louise Labé, *Œuvres completes*, ed. Enzo Giudici (Geneva: Droz, 1981), sonnets 23 and 11 (pp. 151, 163).

preacher Marie Dentière, who addressed an *Epistle tres-utile* (*Very Useful Epistle*), in part a defence of women's pastoral and theological work, to her in 1539. One of Dentière's first 'missions' was to bring the truth of the Reformation to the convent of Poor Clares in Geneva, described in an account by the convent's memorialist, Jeanne de Jussie, in her chronicle of the Clares' eventual expulsion from Geneva.

While Jussie's chronicle was written for the convent which she served and was only printed after her death, a Dominican nun found herself a reluctant celebrity after the publication of the sonnets she composed in response to the famous debate between Protestant and Catholic advocates in the town of her convent, Poissy, in 1561. Anne de Marquets's *Sonets, prieres et devises* (*Sonnets, Prayers and Mottos*, 1562) brought her a productive literary friendship and collaboration with Claude d'Espence; a second, more developed collection of sonnets was published after her death, edited by a novice from her convent. The *Sonets spirituels* (*Spiritual Sonnets*, 1605) elaborate an art of religious poetry, rewriting the practices of the Pléiade for devotional purposes: a series of meditations for the major celebrations of the Catholic calendar, they, like Jussie's chronicle, reflect a life of devotional practice and the support of a female network. This network includes not just the nuns in Marquets's convent, but an ahistorical group of women who played a crucial role in sacred history, with Mary at its centre. The community of Christian women have a clear and recurrent presence in Marquets's poetry, her own endeavours in her devotional and poetic life assisted by 'l'admirable vertu d'innumerables femmes' ('the admirable virtue of innumerable women').[7] Her defence of women, written for Easter, addresses men directly, insisting on the role women played in the resurrection story as the first to see and proclaim the truth about the risen Christ, an honour extended to all women in Marquets's theology.

If Marquets and Jussie wrote in the supportive and protected environment of the convent, other sixteenth-century women expressed their faith in the world. Georgette de Montenay's *Emblemes ou devises chrestiennes* (*Emblems, or Christian Mottos*, 1571) was produced in the Protestant court of Jeanne d'Albret, to whom it is dedicated, and addressed to a female audience who would draw comfort from its message, and perhaps even write emblems of their own. Marie Le Gendre's popular *Cabinet des saines affections* (*Cabinet of Pure Affections*, 1584) and *Exercice de l'ame vertueuse* (*Exercise for a Virtuous Soul*, 1596) devotes its rhetorical skills to the praise of virtue and the condemnation of vice. Gabrielle

---

7 Anne de Marquets, *Sonets spirituels*, ed. Gary Ferguson (Geneva: Droz, 1997), sonnet 442, p. 347.

de Coignard's religious poetry was published after her death by her daughters, Jane and Catherine, in 1594, and addressed to 'dames devotieuses' ('devout ladies').[8] Coignard's work was written during the Catholic spiritual renewal of late sixteenth-century France that was considerably driven by women. Widowed young, she refused to remarry, and struggled in her poetry with the conflicting obligations of raising her daughters, keeping her house, and her growing religious sensibility. The poetic subject that emerges from Coignard's writing is an insistent, very present, yet conflicted one; in sonnet 73, she expresses the tension between devotion and writing: 'Je ne puis plus chanter, je ne puis plus escrire . . . Je vois le Sainct des Saincts sur la terre eslever' ('I can no longer sing, I can no longer write . . . I see the Holy of Holies rise up over the earth' [pp. 228–9]). What comes across in Coignard's poetry is a sense of the tension that writing produces in a lived life; and a deliberate fashioning of a poetic self through confessional and meditative practice.

Memoirs, miscellanies and the *querelle des femmes*

Coignard's poetry could on one level be read as a spiritual autobiography. Other women were also writing their political and historical life stories in greater numbers than ever before: royal women, with the education to write and the events to write about. Writing and a literary sensibility became a necessary part of court sociability; and if the memoirs of many royal women were never meant to be printed, they were nevertheless circulated and read. Louise de Savoie, mother of François I, left behind a *Journal* that describes and justifies her methods in raising her son. Louise's grand-daughter, Jeanne d'Albret, wrote similarly self-justifying chronicles of her energetic engagement with the political struggles of her time. A recently converted Protestant at the height of the Wars of Religion, she allowed her letters and memoirs to be printed in 1570 as part of a recent history of the conflict, demonstrating deft and efficacious rhetoric in defending her actions as ruler and educator of her son. Although she traditionally excuses her 'style de femme' ('woman's style'), she insists on its veracity and the intrinsic worth of her narrative, and rejects any criticism of her governance.[9] Louise's great-grand-daughter Marguerite de Valois's *Mémoires*, careful not to betray any personal secrets, are another skilful self-justification in the wake of such events as the St Bartholomew's

---

8 Gabrielle de Coignard, *Œuvres chrestiennes*, ed. Colette H. Winn (Geneva: Droz, 1995), p. 129.
9 *Mémoires et poésies de Jeanne d'Albret*, ed. Baron de Ruble (Paris: Em. Paul, Huart, and Guillemin, 1893), pp. 120–1.

Day massacre, offering a personal, subjective account of events that would previously have been chronicled by a male historian. Like Guillet and Labé, Louise and her female relatives in their own way demand the right to be heard in a historical discourse that would normally discuss them as its object.

In Poitiers in the 1570s and 80s a mother and daughter, Madeleine Neveu and Catherine Fradonnet, more commonly known as the Dames Des Roches, were also establishing a literary reputation in a male domain. Their literary and learned salon was one of many that grew up around this time, and attracted Poitiers humanists such as Éstienne Pasquier and Marc-Antoine Muret. Often directed by wealthy noblewomen such as Madeleine de L'Aubespine or Catherine de Clermont, salon life put women at the centre of the culture of patronage that drove literary production in these years, leading to the commissioning of works by men and women that were circulated in manuscript. Printed miscellanies were another possible platform for women's writing, and work by celebrated learned women such as Camille de Morel and her mother, Antoinette de Loynes, appeared in collections of poetry and as prefatory matter. Women also broke into the translation market, with Marguerite de Cambis's Boccaccio and Marie de Costeblanche's Pedro Mexía.

The Dames Des Roches came from the emerging educated bourgeoisie. The reciprocity and support between mother and daughter are clear in their published works, as is an awareness of their uniqueness. Madeleine consciously rejects the familiar female path; but aware that this might draw blame, she defends herself in her liminary 'Epistre aux dames' ('Epistle to ladies') that if silence is a fitting ornament for women, it brings them no honour.[10] Catherine's preoccupation with how to reconcile her writing with more typically female obligations is expressed in her sonnet 'A ma quenoille' ('To my distaff'), which ends with a desire to keep both 'le fuzeau, et la plume' ('the spindle, and the quill' [p. 293]). Her passionate advocacy of education for women, having benefited from her mother's example and teaching herself, is expressed in her 'Dialogue de Placide, et de Severe' in which the merits of educating daughters are put forward. Its sequel, 'Dialogue d'Iris, et de Pasithée', puts the daughters themselves on stage to debate the question, where Pasithée speaks eloquently for women's education.[11]

Catherine's 'Dialogue', focusing on women's learning, illustrates the sixteenth-century educational turn of the Quarrel of Women. Towards the end of the century, women's voices were increasingly heard in this debate,

10 Des Roches, Les Œuvres, pp. 79–80.
11 Madeleine and Catherine Des Roches, Les Secondes Œuvres, ed. Anne R. Larsen (Geneva: Droz, 1998), pp. 187–222 and 223–61 (p. 237).

following the example of Christine de Pizan. Marie de Romieu's 'Brief discours que l'excellence de la femme surpasse celle de l'homme' ('Brief argument that the excellence of women is greater than that of men') names Hélisenne de Crenne, the Morel sisters, the Dames Des Roches, Marguerite de Navarre, and Catherine de' Medici as support for her cause. If Romieu's response was a humanist one, calling on examples to structure and authorise her discourse, Nicole Liébault, daughter of the famous printer Charles Estienne, eschewed the exemplum in Les Miseres de la femme mariée (Misfortunes of the Married Woman, 1587), concentrating instead on the social inequalities that women suffer through men's 'loix trompeurs' ('treacherous laws').[12] There is nothing natural or inevitable in women's inferior status for Liébault; it is strictly social, and unjust.

A woman who experienced this injustice keenly throughout her long writing career was Marie de Gournay, literary executrix of Michel de Montaigne and posthumous editor of the Essais, who wrote moral essays herself alongside treatises, polemic, a novella, and poetry. By the close of the sixteenth century she had already published two editions of the Essais, for which she wrote the prefaces (1595 and 1599), and a novella, Le Proumenoir de Monsieur de Montaigne (Monsieur de Montaigne's Walk, 1594). The Proumenoir is a violent, fantastical story which already contains the germ of fierce polemic that Gournay made her own. She is unapologetic about women's independence of mind and action: 'C'est gloire de faire reprouver sa maniere de vivre en un temps de mauvais exemple' ('It is glorious to have one's way of life reproached in a time of such bad example').[13]

The preface to the 1595 edition of Montaigne's Essais is even more uncompromising. The male reader of the Essais would have found himself addressed in this manner: 'Bien heureux es-tu, Lecteur, si tu n'ez pas d'un sexe, qu'on ait interdit de tous les biens, l'interdisant de la liberté' ('Happy are you, Reader, if you are not of that sex, for whom all benefits are forbidden, since freedom is forbidden' [p. 283 variant]). Women, Gournay argues, are unable to fulfil their potential because of the restrictions on their freedom of movement, education, and speech. Her staging of an educated gathering where any woman attempting to join the debate can be dismissed with the simple observation, 'C'est une femme qui parle' ('It's a woman talking' [p. 284]), acquires a painfully personal edge: 'eussé-je les arguemens, de Carneades,

---

12 Ilana Zinguer (ed.), Misères et grandeur de la femme au XVIe siècle (Geneva: Slatkine, 1982), p. 32.
13 Marie de Gournay, Œuvres complètes, ed. Jean-Claude Arnould and others, 2 vols. (Paris: Champion, 2002), II, pp. 1355–6.

il n'y a chetif qui ne me rembarre avec solenne approbation de la compagnie assistante' ('Even if I had the arguments of a Carneades, there is no one
too inferior to dismiss me, with the solemn approbation of all the company'
[pp. 283–4]). Gournay became more expert in conversation, holding her own
salon in Paris in the 1620s where she was involved in the establishment of the
Académie Française. Self-taught in humanist method and in the salon arts of
conversation, she represented a new breed that would develop throughout
the seventeenth century: neither an amateur noblewoman nor a cloistered
nun, she was a professional woman of letters. These women would build on
the ground marked out by their sixteenth-century predecessors, contributing to debates on women's education and spirituality, and developing a new
genre: the novel.

25

Sixteenth-century prose narrative

JOHN O'BRIEN

The vogue for prose narrative in the Renaissance derives from some established and some imported forms of literature that are not dissimilar in nature. Established forms included primarily the prose romance (*roman de chevalerie*), a late-medieval expansion and rendering into prose of earlier chivalric epic. Arthurian material, Tristan and Iseut, the epic adventures of Fierabras, Huon de Bordeaux and others, all fuelled interest in a heroic storyline, often combined with love interest, with a strong central character or characters and a recognisable plot, albeit one that might be convoluted on the way to resolution and contain supernatural as well as realistic elements. This trend was reinforced by the popularity of translated works such as *L'Histoire palladienne*, Juan de Flores's *Flamete* (translated by Scève in 1535) or Diego de San Pedro's *Prison d'Amors* (1526), and *Arnalte et Lucenda* (1539). The translator of this last work, Herberay des Essarts, went on to even greater success with *Amadis de Gaule*, which achieved very wide circulation. It was not approved of in all circles: Montaigne speaks slightingly of it,[1] and it provokes outright condemnation in La Noue, along with other Protestant writers.[2] The gradual 'disgrâce d'Amadis' has been well studied by Michel Simonin, but the very vehemence of the attacks against it should alert us to its obstinate popularity and enduring appeal: the eight books translated by Des Essarts between 1540 and 1548 initiated a series of twenty-four books in their entirety; and although the series had been published by 1613, editions of individual books were frequently re-printed throughout the period.

---

1 *Essais de Michel de Montaigne*, ed. Pierre Villey and V.-L. Saulnier (Paris: Presses Universitaires de France, 1965), I.26, p. 175.
2 François de La Noue, *Discours politiques et militaires* (1587) (Geneva: Chouët, 1614), sixième discours, pp. 189–209, including Lancelot of the Lake, Perceforest, Tristan, and Giron le Courtois; François Grandin, *Destruction de l'orgueil mondain* (1558), has a longer list that includes Poggio's *Facéties* alongside Lancelot, *Le Roman de la rose*, Tristan, Artus de Bretagne, Huon de Bordeaux, and Ogier le Danois, among others.

Among early works that blend this indigenous and this foreign tradition, *Jehan de Paris*, which appeared in 1533, can be mentioned. A combination of romance and *féerie*, this self-proclaimed 'histoire joyeuse' (joyful story) and 'passetemps' (pastime) has an eponymous hero of superhuman valour who implicitly symbolises the superiority of France and the French king. The work is written to a popular formula, but the inflection towards France suggests some consciousness of adapting a successful model to localised interests. Elsewhere, experimentation is bolder and firmer. The prime example among early works is Hélisenne de Crenne's *Les Angoysses douloureuses qui procedent d'amours* (1538), which makes use of the *roman de chevalerie* in its second and third parts, but critical attention is usually concentrated on the 'tesmoignage' (testimony) that comprises the first part of the work. Making use of an ornate Latinate style and extensive classical allusions, its content evokes openly Lancelot and Gueneviere and Tristan and Iseut in its picture of love as obsession. A married woman named Hélisenne falls for Guenelic, a younger man of a lower social class. The torture she suffers is intensified by the small cast of characters and especially the restricted spaces in which the action takes place, with their claustrophobic atmosphere and the ever-present threat of verbal and physical violence towards the heroine. Of special interest is the scene of writing connected with Hélisenne's bedroom and later a tower in which she is imprisoned by her husband. By a neat twist, the bedroom and the tower become places of self-expression, as she writes down the story we are reading, re-conceptualising physical and psychological space through the medium of writing. In its graphic portrayal of the lot of women caught up in the transgression of male prescriptions in a heavily patriarchal society, Hélisenne's work prefigures Marguerite de Navarre's *Heptaméron*. In its reflexive dimension, it gives eloquent voice to the pressures and tensions that are the seedbed of women's writing.

Rabelais's own experiments with prose narrative stretch over a period of twenty years. The nature of his relationship to the *roman de chevalerie* is visible in *Gargantua* and *Pantagruel*, where the broad division into 'enfances' (childhood), 'épreuves' (testing-time) and 'prouesses' (valiant deeds) in both books mirrors the development and growth of the chivalric hero, recognisable from medieval models. Thus Gargantua's education is followed by his war against Picrochole and the founding of the abbey of Thélème after the victory over Picrochole. *Pantagruel* offers a similar structure: after his education, the young Pantagruel wages war against Loup-Garou in which he is the victor, before setting off with Panurge on the quest that will occupy the remainder of Rabelais's works. The early works are moreover billed, initially, as 'chronicque(s)' (chronicle(s) – a term that appear in both historical accounts proper and romance), but later 'tant veritables contes' (such veritable tales), or more straightforwardly, 'ceste histoire tant veridique' (this so very truthful history / story), with assertions of truth-telling that one finds standardly in prose narrative, often in direct proportion to its fictionality.[3]

Yet this bald characterisation scarcely does justice to the multilayered, richly polyphonic texture that Rabelais creates. A breadth of reference to politics, religion, education, law, medicine, and the classics is fused with a comic vision that plays ambiguously on drink as a source of laughter and of serious inspiration and makes use of features such as *gigantisme* as a focus for both bawdy humour and quiet reflection. A comedy of the outsize and the grotesque rubs shoulders with humanist values; Erasmian perspectives sit side-by-side with Lucianic mockery. The reader is expected to be sufficiently versatile not to lose sight of the constant shifts in register, theme or idea and to understand that the comic outlook is one that embraces the whole of Rabelais's work, not one that sees laughter as a mask for seriousness or seriousness as an intellectual palliative for vulgarity. Equally, while a plotline is broadly clear across the four authentic books, it permits of digressions that add little or nothing to the onward dynamic of the narrative. Asides and pauses, discontinuities and non sequiturs, stories and embedded tales crowd in, offering diversion and *divertissement* and showing us, in the process, that digression or even stasis has a particular role in the overall comic design. The text delays, drags its feet, as a supposedly epic and heroic narrative in the first books and a quest narrative in the third and fourth books linger to embrace comedy of character, of situation or of words – the best episodes combine all three: Janotus and Picrochole in *Gargantua*, the 'écolier limousin' in *Pantagruel*, Her Trippa in the *Tiers Livre*, the storm scene in the *Quart Livre*.

Such traits are permanent, not incidental, narrative features. Thus Panurge is presented on his first appearance in *Pantagruel* as one who is alienated from ordinary human communication, a Tower of Babel fluent in all languages except the very one that will bring him what he wants – food and drink. A traveller of the known world, he echoes through his polyglot languages the expansive designs of a Picrochole, except that Panurge returns to France and French at the close. Yet the very plethora of languages used by Panurge reminds us that excess is his mode of being; in that light, his adventures with the 'haulte dame de Paris' (high-born lady of Paris), while not amusing

3 F. Rabelais, *Œuvres complètes*, ed. M. Huchon with F. Moreau (Paris: Gallimard, 1994), pp. 7, 9, 330, 315, 505.

to us, are entirely in character, as is his praise of debts, a mock encomium that makes debt the centre of the world. And it is also via Panurge that questions of stasis and repetition recur, in the form of his marriage quest as it is projected in the *Tiers Livre*. His indecision about whether to marry provides the thread for the whole book. Each consultation prolongs his own uncertainty and encapsulates the dilemma of the man who does not know his own will or his own mind, faced with the task of interpeting signs; and each consultation also betokens a general failure of communication, leaving characters trapped within a supposedly shared language. Of Panurge's many encounters, possibly the deepest irony is reserved for that with Trouillogan, which holds historical significance as an early instance of sceptical formulae in French literature. One fool encounters another – and Trouillogan is at least a fool by profession who is able to articulate (in paradoxes) what Panurge, blinded by *philautia* (self-love), cannot. In this book, Rabelais abandons the chronicle and romance structure that had provided at least a framework for his previous works and moves towards something less definable in generic terms, more loosely woven.

The *Quart Livre* is the corresponding panel of the diptych that begins with the *Tiers Livre*. Prefigured by the narrator's excursus into Pantagruel's mouth in Chapter 32 of that work, it now imagines Panurge's quest as an itinerary without a foreseeable pattern (unlike therefore the *roman de chevalerie*), amid a disconnected archipelago where the travellers will find not only the strange, but the familiar made strange through distortion and monstrosity of various kinds. From Quaresmeprenant to Homenaz, from the whale to Gaster, the *Quart Livre* deploys its 'mythologies Pantagruelicques',[4] a self-description that is glossed by a more modern commentator as 'récits fabuleux à visée pédagogique' ('fabulous narratives that aim at imparting a lesson').[5] That fabulous, mythological dimension is signalled from the outset: the voyage first reaches Medamothi, 'Nowhere', a variant on the Utopia where the giants live, but by setting the book's remaining episodes *beyond* Nowhere, Rabelais is able to appeal to the non-realistic settings common in other Renaissance prose narratives, while taking aim at the various dystopias his travellers encounter. Part of the 'visée pédagogique' of the *Quart Livre* is the increased threat of violence – actual physical harm in the case of the Seigneur de Basché and the Chicquanous, or implicit future harm, as with the host of monks hurrying off to the Council of Chesnil with the intention of repressing heresy.

4 Ibid., p. 517.
5 P. Mousnier, *Le Roman humaniste: un genre novateur français, 1532–1564* (Paris: Champion, 2007), p. 222.

Rabelais portrays an unpredictable world ruled by personal and sectarian obsessions, against the background of which Panurge's quest has become more hazardous and which contrasts sharply with the implicit optimism of an episode such as Thélème in *Gargantua*. And if the *Quart Livre* does not provide a solution to Panurge's enquiry, neither does the largely spurious *Cinquiesme Livre*: the final injunction of the Dive Bouteille – 'Trinch' – throws him back on the bitter-sweet comedy of his own impossible self-knowledge, and the double-edged nature of laughter.

Rabelais's use of deferral in respect of Panurge's dilemma has a particular echo in Barthélemy Aneau's *Alector* of 1560. Its subtitle, 'Histoire fabuleuse' ('Fabulous History/Story'), is a mark of its distancing from the *roman de chevalerie*,[6] while also being one of the 'substituts du [mot] *roman*' (substitutes for [the word] *novel*).[7] The structure of the work is intricate, divided into five days, with the complex embedding of time and place paralleled by the counterpointed adventures of the dual heroes, Alector and his father, Franc-Gal, which are themselves organised by the principle of simultaneity. Such precisely calibrated literary techniques are counterbalanced by features that point in another, less settled direction. The preface provides the hint: this work is 'un fragment d'une diverse et estrange narration' ('fragment of a diverse and strange narrative'), 'une piece rompue d'un ouvrage' ('a piece broken off from a work') (p. 10) which has happened to fall into Aneau's hands. Common in Renaissance literature, this device holds a particular resonance here and is reinforced by three examples of such 'propos rompus', expressly entitled such, and, more importantly, by the technique of *in medias res* with which the book begins. Research on the *ordo artificialis* – as the *in medias res* technique is known, by contrast with *ordo naturalis* – has rightly underlined its role in the history of narrative suspense in the Renaissance and has aligned *Alector* with Heliodorus, whose *Ethiopian History*, published in French translation by Amyot in 1547, offers an outstanding instance of the theory and practice of narrative suspense. *Alector* displays some features in common with Heliodorus' work: the counterpointed adventures of Alector and Franc-Gal, for example, clearly rely for their effect on punctual forms of suspense, while Alector's search for his father is announced and undertaken from the earliest chapters but its completion is suspended until the closing section of the work.

---

6 B. Aneau, *Alector ou Le Coq: histoire fabuleuse*, ed. Marie-Madeleine Fontaine, 2 vols. (Geneva: Droz, 1996), I, p. XL.
7 P. Mousnier, 'Quelques substituts du *roman* au XVIe siècle: innovation romanesque et prudence lexicale', in M. Clément and P. Mousnier (eds.), *Le Roman au XVIe siècle* (Strasbourg: Presses Universitaires de Strasbourg, 2005), pp. 33–49.

Other combinations of these features are tried out elsewhere. Nicolas Denisot's *L'Amant ressuscité de la mort d'amour* (published under a pseudonym, Théodose Valentinian) expands lovesickness into actual illness from which a 'malade' is dying. Its five books, set in England, are notable for the adaptation of the Dido and Aeneas story in Book 3, an instance of 'folle amour' (wild love) which contrasts with the praise of Christian marriage expounded in Book 2 by the countess, Margaret Meyssour (i.e. Seymour?). The novel also involves techniques of delay – the patient's own account of his ailment being deferred until the lengthy Book 4 – and *peripeteia* – his unexpected recovery in the closing pages of Book 5. In this connection, one should also mention Guillaume des Autelz's *Mitistoire Barragouyne de Fanfreluche et Gaudichon*. Probably published in 1550 or so, but known only through surviving editions of 1574 and 1578, it displays its Rabelaisian allegiance in its title and its linguistic usage, as well as a more general debt to Lucian's *True History*. Criticism has seen in it, and in its outright attack on *Amadis*, a critique of contemporary novelistic themes such as love interest and techniques such as suspense and contrived *dénouement*, providing a wry commentary on a writer such as Denisot and on the activity, generally, of prose narrative in the 1550s and 1560s.

The *nouvelle* tradition

Rabelais shows a liking for virtually self-contained tales in his later writing – one thinks of the marriage of the Seigneur de Basché or Panurge's encounter with Dindenault, both in the *Quart Livre* – and the tradition of *nouvelles* and *contes* as a medium for prose fiction is a strong vein of Renaissance writing. As with romance, the development of the *nouvelle* owes part of its impetus to foreign models, notably the availability of Boccaccio's *Decameron*, especially in the French translation by Antoine Le Maçon, which first appeared in 1545. Its influence makes itself felt on Marguerite de Navarre's *Heptaméron*, as discussed in Chapter 24 in this volume, but it also feeds into an indigenous tradition of *nouvelle* writing represented by Philippe de Vigneulles's *Les Cent Nouvelles Nouvelles*, Nicolas de Troyes's *Parangon des nouvelles nouvelles* of 1531 and La Motte Roullant's *Les Facetieux Devis de cent et six nouvelles nouvelles* of 1550. Marguerite herself is the best known of a current of women's writing that starts with Jeanne Flore's *Comptes amoureux* of around 1530. This collection of seven stories told by a group of ladies shares with the *Heptaméron* the technique of *devisants* who provide the links between the different narratives. In each case, the emphasis is on defending love in its most extreme form, with each tale a sort of case study of 'folle amour'. Jeanne's work has aroused conflicting interpretations, with one critic (Gray)[8] arguing that it may have been written by a man. It is, at any rate, one of number of productions throughout the period that use the *nouvelle* format for an exploration of love. Taillemont's *Discours des champs faëz* (1553) and the anonymous *Comptes du monde aventureux* (1555), for example, form contrasting tableaux in their treatment of amorous themes. The former develops a Platonic defence of women within a chivalric romance framework, with three knights journeying to the *Champs faëz* of which the heroine becomes queen; whereas the latter emphasises once again the 'intolerable ardeur' (intolerable heat) of love in tales told by a party travelling to Savoy. The author, moreover, regards his work as competing with Boccaccio.

A central issue affecting interpretation of the *nouvelle* is the question of its realism. Pérouse led the way in scouring *nouvelles* for *realia* (real-life situations or events). In more recent years, however, critics have shifted the focus to foreground the critical relation between 'verisimilitude and fable, mimesis and parody, history and story, realism and fantasy'.[9] On that view, *nouvelles* do not so much reflect reality as put it into question; and the claims to truth-telling they standardly employ are not to be taken as an automatic index of a realist fiction (they occur, after all, among the authors of romance). Context rather than genre determines the issue. Thus the large number of stories about lecherous priests that fill the pages of Henri Estienne's *Apologie pour Herodote* (1566) have significance because they are intended as evidence of ecclesiastical corruption; even here, their source is often other writers (Marguerite de Navarre and Des Périers, for example) rather than first-hand experience. Similarly, Jacques Yver's *Le Printemps* (1572), despite its references to contemporary issues, really uses its manorial setting as a prop for the *châtelaine* to lead a debate about the disordered, tragic nature of love, with five stories spread over five days. Again, the sequence of three works by Noël du Fail is memorable for its evocation of country life and, in the *Propos rustiques* (1547), the learned re-creation of rustic speech. But the author's real strength lies in projecting on to village life the values he cherishes, as demonstrated by the 1585 *Contes et discours d'Eutrapel*: a more stable society, a fairer system of justice, a more socially responsible nobility and a less rapacious clergy. In all these cases, the prevalence of certain types of setting and plot certainly tells us something about how sixteenth-century society saw itself, but the imperatives that shape these narratives are not those of a transparent realism.

8 F. Gray, 'Jeanne Flore and Erotic Desire: Feminism or Male Fantasy?', in D. LaGuardia and G. Ferguson (eds.), *Narrative Worlds: Essays on the 'Nouvelle' in 15th- and 16th-Century France* (Tempe: Arizona State University Press, 2005), pp. 77–95.
9 D. LaGuardia and G. Ferguson (eds.), *Narrative Worlds: Essays on the 'Nouvelle' in 15th and 16th Century France* (Tempe: Arizona State University, 2005), introduction, p. 8.

Bonaventure des Périers has no qualms about dismissing the issue of realism, urging readers of his *Nouuelles Recreations*, 'ne vous souciez point si ce fut à Tours en Berry, ou à Bourges en Touraine: vous vous tourmenteriez pour neant . . . les noms ne sont que pour faire debattre les hommes' ('do not concern yourself whether it was in Tours en Berry or Bourges en Touraine: you would be tormenting yourself for nothing . . . the names are only to get a discussion going').[10] In his writings, he declares, 'il n'y a point de sens allegorique, ny mystique, fantastique' (fo. 4r) ('there is no allegorical nor mystical, fantastical meaning'); his only motto is 'Bien viure, & se resiouyr' (fo. 3v) ('to live well and enjoy oneself'). Des Périers bases his work loosely around the clown Triboulet (actually the court jester of François I and the model on whom Rabelais's Trouillogan is based). This alter ego of the comic author appears as a framing device at the beginning and near the end of the collection, which celebrates his passing by remarking approvingly that he was 'plus heureux que sage' (fo. 242v) ('more happy than wise'). The tone throughout the work is light-hearted, relying on comedy of language (puns, misunderstandings) or of situation (relations between the sexes, ignorant or fumbling clerics, although without the censoriousness that is often found elsewhere in the *nouvelle* tradition). There is little of the violence or cruelty common in the *Heptaméron* and the author is happy to call himself and his readers fools and place us all on the same level as Triboulet (fo. 10r–v).

Traditionally but not conclusively ascribed to Des Périers, *Cymbalum mundi* (1537) is arguably one of the most intriguing of prose narratives and a teasing example of the problem of seeking *realia*. The diversity of interpretations that have been offered of it should warn us that we are in the presence of a particularly powerful and hermeneutically obdurate fiction, whose very title, with its references to Pliny's preface to Book 25 of the *Natural History*, and possibly to I Corinthians 13:1, points to a world of self-aggrandisement and chatter, devoid of charity. That the work's target may, at least in part, be religious is hinted at by the obvious anagrams and near-anagrams in the opening epistle: Thomas du Clevier (Thomas Incrédule; Doubting Thomas) and Pierre Tryocan (Pierre Croyant; the Apostle Peter). This is carried through into the second dialogue where Rhetulus, it is agreed, is a straightforward anagram of Luther, and Cubercus of Bucer (the leader of the Reformation in Strasbourg and South Germany), while Drarig is either Erasmus (Girard being Erasmus's father's name) or Girard Roussel, a leading evangelical in the

---

10 Bonaventure des Périers, *Les Nouuelles Recreations et ioyeux devis* (Paris: Galiot du Pré, n.d.), fos. 4v–5r. Subsequent references are inserted in the text.

circle of Marguerite de Navarre. The first and second dialogues have often been held to be Lucianic attacks on the Catholic church and Reformed church respectively; Mercure, who is the link character in the first three dialogues, is portrayed in them as both deceiver and deceived. With the second part of dialogue 3 and the whole of dialogue 4, the focus shifts to the notions of word and silence, news, novelty and curiosity; these ideas, which had occurred earlier, are now given special prominence. The closing words of the book as a whole, uttered by the dog Pamphagus, offer a summary of these motifs: 'tant sont les hommes curieux, & devisans voluntiers des choses nouvelles & estrangeres' ('men are so very inquisitive, and discourse willingly about new and unknown things').[11] This sentence ostensibly looks back to recurrent ideas in *Cymbalum mundi*, but it points outwards as well, inasmuch as it is not only gods, humans and animals that come under attack for their inquisitiveness and loquacity: the reader too is implicitly targeted by the same pervasive irony, because curiosity and the desire for novelty are equally features of the act of reading that is driven on by the search for an (inconclusive) answer to the riddles the book poses. *Cymbalum* is both novelty and evidence of the lust for novelty in others, which it mockingly ridicules.

The uncomfortable feeling that *Cymbalum* gives one no solid place to stand from which to appraise it is equally part of the larger problem of exegetical extensibility this work poses: how far should we push our analysis of the data it provides? Does the philosopher's stone represent specifically religious truth, or any truth whatsoever? Is Mercure merely a parody of the classical patron of alchemy, or is he an attack on the Christian Son of God, under the guise of a deceiver? And in that the work reflects on the fallibility of words, written or spoken, are we to take that as a reflection on the divine promises of Christian revelation? It is characteristic of *Cymbalum* to encourage our thinking on such issues, but not to answer fully the questions it raises. The only criterion it holds to is provided in its title: 'quatre Dialogues Poetiques . . . ioyeux, & facetieux' ('four poetic dialogues . . . joyful and wittily conceitful'). It mocks and plays, tricks and teases; like poetry, it leads us to speculate on what seems hidden under its allegorical veil; and all the while, it emmeshes us inexorably in the trammels of curiosity. With its gestures towards a *conjoncture* and its invitation to decipher, without indicating where the limits of deciphering might be, *Cymbalum* encapsulates in succinctly potent form the problems and pleasures of prose narrative.

11 Bonaventure des Périers, *Cymbalum mundi*, ed. Y. Delègue (Paris: Champion, 1995), p. 85.

26

Sixteenth-century thought

NEIL KENNY

Thought about thought

Sixteenth-century high culture involved much thinking about what thought *is*. This reflexivity was propelled by a particular historical factor – humanism.

Although earlier Italian humanism had mostly focused on recovering the ancient Roman and Greek 'pursuits of humanity' (*studia humanitatis*) – usually considered to be grammar, rhetoric, poetry (roughly what we now call 'literature'), and moral philosophy – by the sixteenth century the attempted restoration of antiquity included in principle the whole range of ancient philosophy. Therefore, various ancient theories about the nature of thought now vied with each other. The default model of mind continued to be Aristotelian. Indeed in most areas of philosophical inquiry Aristotle continued to be more influential than any other ancient (including even his teacher Plato), following the late medieval synthesis between Christianity and Aristotelianism known nowadays as scholasticism. Humanists famously attacked scholasticism, but they still often shared some of its assumptions.

One of these (outlined in Aristotle's treatise on the soul, *De anima*) was that we are animated by three kinds of soul (vegetative, sensitive, intellective) and do our most advanced, abstract thinking through the intellective soul. Although the intellect is (in scholasticism's Christianised version) immortal and so separable from the body, its knowledge depends on the body, since the intellect produces knowledge by analysing the data that originates in the five external senses. The intellect transforms the particulars of sensory experience into universals. True knowledge – *scientia* in the period's Latin, *science* in its French – is of universals, not of particulars (Aristotle, *Metaphysics*, A.1). But thought can also be half-baked, in which case it is not knowledge at all but mere opinion. Especially in the later part of the period, thinkers such as Montaigne and his follower the sceptic Pierre Charron wondered whether virtually all knowledge is mere opinion. Yet even this more pessimistic epistemology was often couched in the same framework of Aristotelian faculty psychology:

> En ceste partie [*sc.* l'imagination] se tient et loge l'opinion, qui est un vain et leger, crud et imparfait jugement des choses, tiré et puisé des sens exterieurs, et du bruict commun et vulgaire, s'arrestant et tenant bon en l'imagination, et n'arrivant jamais jusques à l'entendement, pour y estre examiné, cuict et elaboré, et en estre faict raison.

> (Within this part of the soul (the imagination), there sits opinion, which is a vain, flighty, crude, and imperfect judgement of things. Opinion, derived from the external senses and from the rumble of popularly held beliefs, comes to a standstill in the imagination, where it holds firm, never proceeding from there to the mind, where it would be examined, 'cooked', developed, and turned into reason.)[1]

In this Aristotelian tradition, the imagination (*phantasia* in Latin, often *fantaisie* in French) is a faculty of the sensitive soul and turns our sense perceptions into would-be likenesses of things. Those likenesses can mislead us, but (as Charron indicates here) they have the potential to become knowledge if our intellect works on them. So imagination was widely considered crucial to standard thought processes, as was memory, both in the sensitive soul, where memory stores images, and in the intellective soul, where it stores the concepts forged by reason.

Although this Aristotelian theory of mind remained dominant, it was now challenged afresh by its ancient competitors, most obviously in French high culture by Platonism and its offshoot in late antiquity and the Renaissance – Neoplatonism. Whereas for Aristotle thought is an inductive process of generating abstract universals from sense-based particulars and gradually inscribing knowledge on the soul's clean slate, in Neoplatonism true 'thought' already exists out there in the great world of the cosmos (the macrocosm). We can capture a fragment of it within ourselves (the microcosm) under certain conditions. Pure thought or mind is thus more 'other' to our current human state, more emphatically divine, than in Aristotelianism.

The Neoplatonic cosmos is structured as a hierarchy. As it descends, thought gets bogged down in matter: 'Quant aux quatre degrez de la descente, le premier, et plus haut, est l'Angelique entendement, le second la Raison intellectuelle, le tiers l'Opinion, et le quart la Nature' ('As for the four descending steps, the first and highest is Angelic Mind, the second is Intellectual

---

1 Pierre Charron, *De la sagesse* (Bordeaux: Simon Millanges, 1601), pp. 150–1. All translations are my own.

Reason, the third is Opinion, and the fourth is Nature').[2] Our soul descended in this way from the realm of Being into that of Becoming when it was born into our body and so forgot the true reality it had previously known (the Ideas and Forms). So in this tradition memory is even more central to knowing. Whereas in Aristotelianism memory stores reason's conclusions, in Neoplatonism to remember *is* to know. Corresponding to the four-fold descent are four ways for our soul to rise up temporarily through the cosmos and do some recollecting. These are the frenzies (*fureurs* in French) of poetry, religion, prophecy, and love, all described in Tyard's *Solitaire premier*, for example (pp. 17–18). Whereas in Aristotelianism the body grounds knowledge, with which it has a relationship of considerable continuity, in Neoplatonism the body is more of an impediment to knowledge or at least a veil over it.

Such Neoplatonic thought was widely reworked in France, whether by Latin-writing philosophers and theologians such as Charles de Bouvelles (*c.* 1480–1533) and Jacques Lefèvre d'Etaples (?–1536) – in characteristically eclectic humanistic mode they combined it with traditions such as mysticism and even Aristotelianism – or by Pléiade poets (Ronsard, Pontus de Tyard), or by Lyon writers, such as the polymath Symphorien Champier (1471–1537/9) and the poets Pernette du Guillet and Maurice Scève. The lines quoted above are from a 1552 prose work in which Tyard – who also spent much time in Lyon – paraphrases the most influential Neoplatonist since late antiquity, the Italian Marsilio Ficino (1433–99). Although Ficino emphasised that the exercise of human reason is crucial to the soul's participation in divine intelligence, another strand of Neoplatonism diagnosed not just the senses but even discursive reason as severely limited in its capacity to apprehend true knowledge (of God). This mystical strand went back to thinkers such as pseudo-Dionysius the Areopagite in the sixth century CE and the German Nicolas of Cusa (1401–64). It particularly attracted the French religious reformers of the first half of the sixteenth century known as *évangéliques*, such as Marguerite de Navarre, Guillaume Briçonnet, and indeed Rabelais (for example in the madman episode of the *Tiers livre*).

Humanism also unleashed another ancient philosophy – scepticism – which questioned even more any equation between human thought and knowledge. Scepticism had two main strands. One, Pyrrhonism argued that we do not know whether knowledge is possible and so should suspend judgement on

---

2 Pontus de Tyard, *Le Solitaire premier*, ed. Silvio Baridon (Lille: Giard; Geneva: Droz, 1950), p. 13.

all questions. The other, Academic scepticism, argued that knowledge is definitely *not* possible but that some claims look more plausible (for example because believed by the wise). Humanists rediscovered in some cases and relaunched in others the main surviving sources regarding ancient scepticism – the life of Pyrrho of Elis written by Diogenes Laertius; the works of Sextus Empiricus; Cicero's *Academica*. The years 1562 and 1569 were watersheds as Latin translations of first Sextus' *Outlines of Pyrrhonism* and then his *Against the Mathematicians* were printed in Geneva and Paris respectively. There soon followed the extraordinary exploration of scepticism by Montaigne. But scepticism had already seeped into earlier writing in France: as a stick with which to beat scholasticism in Omer Talon's Latin *Academica* (1547); as a threat to be countered in Guy de Bruès's *Dialogues . . . contre les nouveaux académiciens* (1557); as a baffling pyrrhonist philosopher (Trouillogan) in Rabelais's 1546 *Tiers livre*.

Montaigne and others used pyrrhonism to doubt among other things the three traditional routes to knowledge which still dominated sixteenth-century epistemology: reason, experience, authority. Texts transmitting knowledge appealed constantly to one or more of these. Montaigne himself, whose relation to pyrrhonism is not uniform, presents reason and experience more positively at the start of the chapter of his *Essais*, 'De l'expérience', which begins by paraphrasing the famous opening of Aristotle's *Metaphysics*: 'Il n'est désir plus naturel que le désir de connaissance. Nous essayons tous les moyens qui nous y peuvent mener. Quand la raison nous faut, nous y employons expérience' ('No desire is more natural than the desire for knowledge. We try out all means which might lead us to it. If reason is lacking, we use experience instead').[3] Although these sentences revise Aristotle by showing that knowledge can be of particulars (supplied by our bodily experience of the world) as well as of universals (reached by reason), again Aristotelian sense epistemology remains the background framework.

The third traditional route to knowledge is authority: that is, the best authors, especially ancient, but often modern. Even someone like the barber–surgeon Ambroise Paré, well known for empirical medical discoveries, often included proof by authority ('Preuve faite par autorité'), for example when denying that a unicorn's horn has therapeutic properties: 'Quant à l'autorité, il se trouvera la plupart des doctes, gens de bien et expérimentés médecins qui assureront cette corne n'avoir aucune des vertus qu'on lui attribue'

---

3 Michel de Montaigne, *Les Essais*, ed. Jean Céard *et al.* (Paris: Librairie Générale Française, 2001), II.13, p. 1655.

('As for authority: most learned people, respectable people, and experienced physicians insist that this horn has none of the powers attributed to it').[4] The mention of 'experienced physicians' shows that the three routes to knowledge were interconnected: experience is written up in authoritative texts which become a collective memory. Yet Montaigne's pyrrhonism-dominated 'Apologie de Raimond de Sebonde' (*Essais*, II.12) argues that it is impossible to trust authorities given the hopeless disagreements between them, that experience is unreliable because the senses mislead us, and that human reason is weak.

Women and thought

Humanism's unsettling impact on thought about thought was not uniformly felt. For example, among the educated it would be interesting to investigate whether pyrrhonism dented male epistemological confidence more often than female, given that women had in any case mostly been told all their lives that their reason was weaker than men's and so left them particularly prone to believe their imagination's half-baked products. Despite the works (by men such as François de Billon) which comprised the pro-feminist half of a mid-sixteenth-century reprise of the late medieval debate about women's capacities (the *Querelle des femmes*), it remained unusual and very controversial for a woman to argue, as did Marie de Gournay in her *Égalité des hommes et des femmes*, that differences between male and female intellectual achievement were down to education rather than nature.[5]

Even women of the nobility and upper bourgeoisie were excluded from the apprenticeship in formal, institutionalised thought that was provided by humanist colleges or by the university philosophy or arts faculty to which their brothers and fathers went before progressing to one or more of the three higher faculties – theology, medicine, law. Philosophy in this university sense was predominantly Aristotelian and consisted of logic, metaphysics, natural philosophy (the rough equivalent of our 'science'), and ethics. A few women did gain some training in these and other kinds of formal thought, whether through a brother's tutor, a father, or self-education. The latter was Gournay's route. She takes pains to present her radical *Égalité* as following the rules of formal argumentation, in particular the tripartite epistemology

---

4 A. Paré, *Textes choisis*, ed. Louis Delaruelle and Marcel Sendrail (Paris: Société des Belles Lettres, 1953), p. 134 (*Discours*, 1582, chap. 16).
5 Initially part of her *Proumenoir de Monsieur de Montaigne* (1594), then revised and published as a separate work in 1622.

of reason, experience, and authority.[6] Her voluminous writings focus on grammar, poetry, and moral philosophy, which was indeed the branch of philosophy with which women engaged most, another example being Marie Le Gendre's best-selling treatise *Des saines affections* (1584). Yet, since formal thought was gendered as masculine, it is perhaps not surprising that some of the most searching female thought is found not in treatises but in outgrowths of other genres, for example in the extensive, unresolved ethical debates between interlocutors in Marguerite de Navarre's collection of novellas, the *Heptaméron* (composed in the 1540s).

However, one barrier separating women from formal thought did totter: the medieval assumption that formal thought is largely confined to Latin. One effect of humanist philological interest in ancient Greek and indeed Hebrew was to dispel any notion that one language, Latin, had a monopoly of abstract complex thought. Outlined in theory in 1549 by Du Bellay's *Deffence et illustration de la langue françoyse* (1.10), this conclusion was implemented by Calvin's French translations of his Protestant theological summa, the *Institution de la religion chrestienne*, and was indeed boosted by Protestantism's concern to explain doctrine in the vernacular. Although a few upper-class women did learn Latin, the large-scale translating into French of ancient Greek and Latin philosophical texts made philosophy more accessible to some women (as well as to non-Latinate men). Louis Le Roy translated works by Plato, Aristotle, and Xenophon into French (from 1551 onwards); Philippe Canaye paraphrased Aristotle's works on logic, the *Organon* (1589); Jacques Amyot translated Plutarch's *Moralia* (1572), and so on.

Language and thought

Humanist translators also sought to make ancient philosophy as *eloquent* as they believed the original to have been, especially in the case of a Plato or a Cicero. Although philosophy was dominated by an Aristotelian assumption that language, reality, and thought about reality are all distinct from each other, on the other hand the humanist focus on the language arts (grammar, rhetoric, and probabilistic reasoning known as dialectic) promoted a view that thought about human and natural reality is virtually inseparable from the language in which that thought is communicated: true philosophy is inseparable from eloquence. This view served especially to denigrate scholasticism,

---

6 M. de Gournay, *Égalité des hommes et des femmes*, in *Œuvres complètes*, ed. Jean-Claude Arnould et al., 2 vols. (Paris: Champion, 2002), I, p. 987.

which prized formal syllogistic logic (as distinct from probabilistic reasoning) over eloquence.

This humanistic rapprochement between rhetoric and thought was widely pursued by French writers who experimented with ways of inserting much philosophy into prose fiction (Rabelais), into dialogues (Tyard, Pierre de La Primaudaye), into long poems (Du Bartas and others who imitated ancient philosophical poets like Lucretius), or into all of these genres (François Béroalde de Verville).

Thought and action

Part of the point of making philosophy more eloquent was to enable it to move people's will and passions as well as their intellect, and so influence their behaviour. Although humanist thought was sometimes characterised by a contemplative ideal (in Bouvelles, for example), it was more often geared towards action. Indeed, if we extend the scope of 'thought' beyond systematic philosophy to include the kinds of pragmatic deliberations, oral and written, that took place in everyday social, political, and moral life, then what is distinctive about humanistic culture is less a fixed worldview than a set of thinking tools. As Ann Moss has shown, one of these was the commonplace book – a vast, ordered compendium of ancient textual fragments, a selection of which the user could string together according to the procedures of dialectic and rhetoric when deciding upon and advocating a course of action.[7]

But broader systems of thought too were commonly used for pragmatic ends. Here are four examples. First, pyrrhonism, which from our modern standpoint we might expect to have attacked religion, mostly served the fideist view that only religious knowledge is secure, since it comes from revelation and is sustained by faith not reason. Thus, Gentian Hervet's 1569 translation of Sextus Empiricus' *Against the Mathematicians* was intended to protect Catholic orthodoxy against Protestant attempts to *reason* against its doctrines. Second, Stoicism was advocated by Guillaume du Vair (in the 1580s and 1590s) and others as a way of remaining steadfast in reason and will during the French Wars of Religion rather than succumbing to the passions provoked by the prevailing horrors. Third, the aim of treatises on political philosophy varied from uniting France around an absolute monarchy strong enough to withstand the factionalism that had battered it during those wars (Jean

7 A. Moss, *Printed Commonplace-Books and the Structuring of Renaissance Thought* (Oxford: Clarendon Press, 1996).

Bodin's *Six livres de la République*, 1576) to limiting royal power by restoring what were argued to be ancient popular controls over it (a 'constitutionalist' argument made by Protestants such as François Hotman in his *Francogallia*, 1573). Fourth, occult philosophy (magic, divination, alchemy, the cabala, and so on) was quite widely pursued in France (by Jacques Gohory, Guillaume Postel, and others) with numerous aims, ranging from medical (the production of cures) to financial (the production of gold) to more intangible (the universal toleration and concord which Postel promoted).

The insistence that thought should have pragmatic outcomes served as a further constraint on female thought, since it was often argued that people should only learn what was useful to their vocation in life, and so that few women needed the kinds of knowledge necessary for action in the public sphere.

Calvin

Theological writing too had a range of pragmatic aims. The fundamental aim of the most extensive theological work that had ever been put into French – Jean Calvin's *Institution de la religion chrestienne* (1541–60) – was the characteristically Protestant one of teaching people how to read the Bible.

Inspired by Martin Luther and others, Calvin advocated reform of the Catholic church, went into exile in 1535 when the French monarchy's initial toleration of reform evaporated, and settled in Geneva – first temporarily, then permanently from 1541 – where he founded a French-speaking church dominated by refugees. Although the Wars of Religion (1562–98) left France largely Catholic, Calvinism evolved into a major international strand within the Protestant Reformation.

The *Institution* was not intended to help people increase their chances of salvation. Calvin abhorred the traditional Catholic belief that good works (including participation in the sacraments) could help one acquire 'merit' in God's eyes and so reduce the penalty that our sins deserve. For according to Calvin (developing Luther's ideas), God has predestined us to salvation or damnation. This doctrine of double predestination occupied only a few pages of the *Institution* (III.21–4 in the final version). But it was crucial, and his Calvinist successors such as Théodore de Bèze emphasised it still more. It had the potential to make people despair, which is why the Lutheran leader Philipp Melanchthon became less keen on it. Why indeed did Calvin bother writing the *Institution* and countless sermons, letters, and Bible commentaries to teach people how to find Christ if it was already a foregone conclusion whether they would? In fact Calvin turns the doctrine into a motivating one. For, although no one knows who will be saved, virtuous living and membership of the visible, Geneva-based church are signs that one probably belongs to the invisible church of the elect: 'Car il a préordonné ceux qu'il avoit précognus, pour estre conformes à l'image de son Fils' ('For He has pre-ordained that those whom he has known in advance will conform to the image of his Son').[8] Why then read the *Institution*? Because the elect are not instant saints: they need to go through the process of having their corrupt nature renewed. That will then free them from the Law, since in its terms *all* humans deserve to be damned (III.19). This Christian freedom is nothing to do with free will, which is a heretical Catholic invention according to Calvin (II.2). His view of the radical discontinuity between God and humans was inspired especially by the Church Father St Augustine (354–430).

Montaigne

By contrast, the *Essais* which Michel de Montaigne first published in 1580 and continued augmenting until his death in 1592 mention God surprisingly little, even for a secular work of the period. Indeed they contributed to a growing separation of secular from religious thought. This does not seem to have been due to any closet atheism on the Catholic Montaigne's part. Rather, his attitude sometimes resembles fideism, emphasising faith in God rather than our ability to say anything true about him.[9] This leaves open for analysis the vast field of human affairs, not because one can say anything about *them* that is definitely true, but because one's discourse can roam freely in it without being sacrilegious. Why, then, does Montaigne occasionally stretch that freedom of thought to question Catholic doctrines and practices, relating to prayer and repentance for example (I.56, III.2)? He justifies this by expressing his willingness to have any erroneous views censored by the church.[10]

It would be simplistic to read such moments of withdrawal to orthodox positions as insincere. Rather, as Terence Cave has shown, the *Essais* rebound from radical views to orthodox ones, from doubt to dogma, on a range of topics.[11] This makes them something other than a straightforward 'application' of pyrrhonism. Their ultimate aim is neither to outline a philosophy nor to question the possibility of philosophy (although they often do the latter),

---

8 Jean Calvin, *Institution de la religion chrestienne*, ed. Jean-Daniel Benoît, 5 vols. (Paris: Vrin, 1957–63), III.24, p. 450.
9 Montaigne, *Essais*, II.12, pp. 931–2.   10 Ibid., I.56, p. 513.
11 T. Cave, *Pré-histoires: textes troublés au seuil de la modernité* (Geneva: Droz, 1999), pp. 39–50.

but rather to register in language the unfolding of Montaigne's own personal thought over time – in its experimental encounters (= *essais*) with philosophies, books, people, alien cultures – and in a way that flaunts the twists, turns, layers, and inconsistencies of that thought. The humanistic rapprochement between language and thought produces here a digressive, quasi-oral mode of writing ('the same on paper as in the mouth')[12] modelled not on Cicero's smooth style but on the choppier rhythms of Seneca and Tacitus. The faculty of memory which was crucial to thought in sixteenth-century theories of soul is now deprecated as a chaotic interrupter of trains of thought.[13]

Montaigne's statements that he is portraying himself, his discussions of his eating habits and ailments (III.13), sexuality (III.5), and so on have led to a common view that he founded the modern genre of intimate autobiography and its corollary, the self, in contrast to memoirs of public deeds. Yet the *Essais* do not even claim to represent *le moi* – a conceptual category which, as Cave has shown, emerged just after Montaigne and is at most dimly heralded by the ways in which he experiments with the first-person pronoun.[14] He tends to emphasise the difference and alterity that lies within his *je* more than any solid identity, but both possibilities emerge, and they too rebound off each other.

Even the attempt to record faithfully the mind's antics is not an end in itself. Although Montaigne partly undermines humanism, he retains its overriding pragmatism by making reflexive thought an aid to living, in both the public and the private sphere. For example, in an age of genocide in the 'New World' (III.6), witch-hunts (III.11), and religious wars in France, Montaigne questions people's desire to destroy the other, and he does so by unpicking individual or collective claims to be united, consistent, rational, infallible, whole. Studying one's own thought leads not to a theory of humanity but to better living: 'Il a passé sa vie en oisiveté, disons-nous: je n'ai rien fait d'aujourd'hui. Quoi? avez-vous pas vécu?' ('He idled away his life, we say; I haven't done anything today. What? Haven't you been living?').[15] Montaigne stretches his contemporaries' understandings of both 'thought' and 'action' to include dimensions of consciousness and life which had previously been marginalised.

---

12 Montaigne, *Essais*, 1.26, p. 265.   13 Ibid., 1.9, pp. 88–9.   14 Cave, *Pré-histoires*, chap. 4.
15 Montaigne, *Essais*, III.13, p. 1727.

27

Sixteenth-century travel writing

WES WILLIAMS

The Renaissance is often characterised as the golden age of exploration: new worlds were discovered both due west and within the self. Montaigne serves as an exemplary witness to this process, as his *Essais* (like the *Journal de Voyage* he left unpublished at his death) record both the incessant 'vagabondage' of his restless mind, and the experience gained from his own travels, whether on diplomatic business, pilgrimage, or in search of relief and perhaps even a cure. The argument in favour of travel which he presents in the essay on the education of children begins and ends positively:[1]

> Le commerce des hommes y est merveilleusement propre, et la visite des pays estrangers, non pour en rapporter seulement, à la mode de nostre noblesse Françoise, combien de pas a Santa Rotonda, ou la richesse des calessons de la Signora Livia, ou, comme d'autres, combien le visage de Neron, de quelque vieille ruyne de là, est plus long ou plus large que celuy de quelque pareille medaille, mais pour en rapporter principalement les humeurs de ces nations et leurs façons, et pour frotter et limer nostre cervelle contre celle d'autruy.

> (Mixing with men is in this respect wonderfully useful, as is visiting foreign countries, not merely to bring back, in the manner of our French noblemen, knowledge of the measurements of the Santa Rotunda, or the richness of Signora Livia's drawers, or how much longer or wider is Nero's face on some old ruin there than on some similar medallion, but more importantly to bring back with us the moods and the customs of these nations, and to rub and polish our brains by contact with those of others.)[1]

Contributing to the history of the peculiarly French notion of *formation*, Montaigne represents travel as an activity at once artisanal and somatic: mixing, rubbing, and polishing are the verbs that serve, not so much (as the English phrase has it) to broaden, as to shape the mind. That these are positively charged verbs of *praxis* is made clear still by the main body – extending from 'not merely' to 'but more importantly' – of the argument. Here the essayist

---

1 Michel de Montaigne, *Essais*, ed. A. Thibaudet and M. Rat (Paris: Gallimard, 1962), p. 153.

details the negative aspects of (early modern) travel, and in particular of *travel writing*. Outlining three of its dominant modes – architectural, sexual, and antiquarian tourism – he dismisses them all as being worse than worthless, not so much in themselves, as in the kinds of experiential return that they generate. Measurement, size, length, width: such notation of objects seen on the journey (whether modern places or antique faces) supports the new sciences of quantification and accumulation, promoting knowledge, learning, and wealth. But none of this has any value, Montaigne suggests, compared to that peculiar kind of self-undoing generated by (writing about: *rapporter* has this sense too) contact with other people, body and soul; this alone makes of travel a genuinely transformative experience.

Generic crossroads: scope and form

The travel writing of the French Renaissance takes on many forms and takes in many places. Italy remained, throughout the period, the most common destination of those who ventured abroad. Of course not all those who made the journey wrote about it, but the French encounter with Italy finds itself transformed into lyric poetry, pilgrimage journals, and descriptions (often illustrated) of the splendour and the corruption that was Renaissance Rome. Some French travellers passed through Italy on their way to the French embassy at Constantinople, which, flourishing in the 1540s and 1550s, represents an important moment both in the history of French relations with the Ottoman court and in the development of the genres in which the experience of travel comes to be narrated in the vernacular. Establishing modes of enquiry into the natural world that were not bound by the conventions of inherited sacred and generic forms, several of the travellers who benefitted from this embassy moved, with relative ease, beyond the borders of Christendom, without making of that move either a pilgrimage or a Crusade.

Only very few French travellers wrote of places still further east: India, Cathay, and Japan. But the great majority of early modern travel accounts – twice as many as those that concern America – are pilgrimages to the Holy Land. We return to them in more detail below. Those who travelled west were initially largely ignored by contemporaries, and not until 1608 did Champlain found, in Québec, a lasting French settlement in what eventually became Canada. Efforts to establish colonies in Brazil (1555) and Florida (1562–5) foundered almost as soon as they began. But failure provides rich material for writers, and, as we shall see, the disaster that was 'Antarctic France' generated some of the most powerful and persuasive polemical travel writing of the time.

Writers and readers

There exist a number of important poetic vernacular meditations on travel, most notably those of du Bellay on Rome; there are also many prefatory poems in praise of this or that account. But most early modern travel writing was narrated in prose. While no single generic or titular marker unites these diverse texts, all are bound together by the politics and poetics of polemic and of mediation. Under these combined pressures the travellers-become-writers – nobles, sailors, cosmographers, pilgrims, diplomats, guides, captives, and interpreters – find that their efforts to translate the particularities of their experiences to readers at home oblige them to speak not only in the first person, but also (and indeed more often) in borrowed terms and voices. This is partly a function of the rhetorical practice of imitation, but it is also due to the fact that (almost) none of these travellers were writers by profession. Some – such as André Thevet, Jean de Léry, and Henri de Castela – became so through force of circumstance, as they engaged in sustained religious argument arising out of readers' (and rival travellers') responses to their accounts. But few had committed themselves to paper, let alone print, before, nor did so again.

For many years scholars made this fact the basis for a clear distinction between on the one hand accounts of actual journeys and on the other 'imaginative' travel. It was the writing of a metaphorical journey that made for a proper travel writer. Travel accounts were, from this perspective, read (if at all) as historical 'background', providing a rather dull contrast to the lively literary games played by authors, who either wrote verse and/or sent their characters off to Utopia, the moon, the many and strange islands of Rabelais's *Quart Livre*, or that 'other world' which was to be found within Pantagruel's mouth. Recent approaches have transformed the critical landscape, both by demonstrating the generic complexity of travel writing across the period, and by illuminating the ways in which our understanding of early modern culture is enriched and complicated by histories of encounter. Yet most French travel writers of the period still remain relatively unknown, and their texts are little read, except insofar as they bear direct relation to the writings of more generally recognised literary authors.

France and its neighbours: linguistic and literary borders

The invention of print brought about the codification and dissemination of a wide range of practical arts, including those related to travel. Phrase books for use in foreign travel developed alongside cheap format guides to the roads, rivers, and principal towns of France (and eventually beyond). Rabelais's fictions form part of this cartographic process. Moving out from the closely defined and defended territory around Chinon, his texts map both the external and the internal borders of a nation in the process of linguistic and cultural (trans)formation. Figures for inept and old-fashioned forms of travel, whether in pursuit of learning (the Limousin scholar) or of power (Picrochole) alternate, as if programmatically, with others skilled in the modern arts of displacement; none more so than the polyglot and polytropic Panurge, whose arrival marks the point at which Pantagruel's educational journey is diverted into one of the period's most digressive, comic, and savagely satirical travel romances.

Montaigne's questioning of the value of travel writing as a mode of mere accumulation echoes that of earlier Reformers both within and without the church. Marguerite de Navarre and Calvin are (like Rabelais) among those of an earlier generation who carried the forms of Latin argument (conducted most persuasively by Erasmus) across into the French vernacular. The border-crossing stories of the *Heptaméron* (composed in the 1540s), from the prologue to the very last tale, present a powerful set of meditations on the pleasures and dangers of travel, as of its narration. For his part, Calvin moves away from the gentler critique of his precursors by presenting in his treatise on relics a breakneck tour of the sites of European pilgrimage, the better to argue, insistently, that the accumulation and worship of bones and body parts which grounds pilgrimage is, and is only, an invention of the corrupt church; an idolatrous trade, it serves only to commodify the body and the word.[2]

Pilgrimage: witness and the sacred

Christian pilgrimage, whether to a local shrine, to Rome, or to the Holy Sepulchre, is a practice central to early modern travel. Nicole Huen, one of the earliest printed French pilgrims, writes in 1517 of having been moved to leave home by the force of 'la saincte curiosité (pour ainsi parler)' ('holy curiosity (in a manner of speaking)'). Just as curiosity can be sanctified by pilgrimage, so too can the worst kind of sinner: on seeing Jerusalem, Huen insists, 'possible n'est qu'il ne change . . . *pour veoir*' ('he cannot but be changed'). The last two

---

2 Jean Calvin, 'Advertissement tresutile du grand proffit qui reviendroit à la Chrestienté, s'il se faisoit inventoire de tous les corps sainctz, et reliques' [1543], in F. Higman (ed.), *Three French Treatises* (London: Athlone Press, 1970), pp. 47–97.

words of witness here amount to a telling pun; *pour veoir*: on seeing, and in truth.[3]

Faith of this order has direct narrative consequences. Renaissance pilgrims rarely write about things they have done on their own, and the structure of the sentences in which they bear witness is scrupulously plural, communitarian. The final quarter of the century saw this practice codified as a set of rules. Appropriating developing Protestant and secular humanist arguments that the worth of a journey lay not so much in the destination, as in the cultivation of the traveller's character, the Counter-Reformation church re-invented pilgrimage in two distinct ways. The first was to make of it a metaphorical progress, instantiated in the stations of the cross, and so to alleviate the need for movement beyond the parish bounds, let alone those of Europe. The second was to transform even the journey proper into a spiritual exercise in the avoidance of others met on the road.

Not rubbing up against others – not only non-Christian locals, but also fellow, non-pilgrim, travellers – the pilgrim was required to travel always in the protection of priestly guides. Avoiding above all the temptation posed by narrative curiosity, he (for it is always he) was urged not to make of himself a travel writer: 'God does not inspire us to undertake the Holy Pilgrimage so that we can prattle and boast afterwards about having seen many rare or singular things, but to give added confirmation to the Christian character.'[4] These are not new arguments. Indeed their very lack of novelty ensures their value, insofar as they assert the force of a long and still living tradition. Having acknowledged adherence to this tradition in their prefaces, most pilgrim narrators then went on to recount the incidents and accidents of travel – especially its perils and dangers, from which their faith repeatedly preserved them – in often richly accented detail.

As noted above, not all travellers due east subscribed to this tradition. Some, such as Pierre Gilles and Nicolas de Nicolay, steered clear of Jerusalem altogether, offering their readers instead a historical topography of Constantinople, an account of the recent dissection of the ambassador's pet elephant, and the lavishly illustrated *Navigations, peregrinations and travels, made into the land of Turkey*.[5] Others made of Jerusalem just another destination. Of these the most

---

3 Nicole Huen, *Le Grant Voyage de Jherusalem* (Paris, 1517), fo. 5v (italics added).
4 Henri de Castela, *La Guide et adresse pour ceux qui veulent faire le S. Voyage de Hierusalem* (Paris, 1604), fo. 4v. The final phrase here reads: 'la personne Chrestienne'. See also Castela's prolix account of his own journey, *Le Sainct Voyage de Hierusalem et Mont Sinay* (Bordeaux, 1603).
5 Nicolas de Nicolay, *Quatres premiers livres des navigations et peregrinations en la Turquie* (Lyons, 1567), and Pierre Gilles, *De Topographia Constantinopoleos* (Lyons, 1561) and *Descriptio nova elephanti* (Hamburg, 1614).

important are André Thevet, who transformed pilgrimage into *Cosmographie* (a means to narrating all manner of things, all supposedly witnessed by himself), and the naturalist Pierre Belon, who trademarked the genre of the *Observations*. Each of the elements of the title of Belon's account – *several, singularities, memorable things*, and even *Judea* (as opposed to *the Holy Land*) – draws on that lexicon of fetish objects, which underscores the developing discourses of early modern curiosity and wonder.[6] For all that he travels along ancient pilgrim paths, Belon promises his readers not the unique experience of a glimpse of the sacred, but rather the purview of that 'wondrous variety of things' which goes to make up the new world still waiting to be found due east (fo. 2r).

New worlds: cannibals, monsters, and home

Montaigne's famous chapter on cannibals (I, 30), concluding with his imperfectly translated conversation with the three Tupinambá he met in Rouen in 1562, is probably the best-known example of early modern French travel writing. His exploration of the impact of the European encounter with the Americas, further pursued in the far bleaker companion essay, 'Des Coches' (III.6), constitutes an experiment in thinking about the limits of community, both elsewhere and in what he calls 'our world'. Both essays draw on a rich body of contestatory sources – gestural, oral, written, and printed – including one of the period's most remarkable accounts: Jean de Léry's *Histoire d'un voyage faict en la terre du Brésil*, a narrative which gives vivid expression to the force of the *novelty* of the New World, and to the consequent transformation of long-cherished cultural conventions. Not least of these, Léry suggests, are those which govern the writing of travel:

> Si quelqu'un, di-je, trouve mauvais que, quand ci-apres je parleray de la façon de faire des sauvages (comme si je me voulois faire valoir), j'use si souvent de ceste façon de parler, Je vis, je me trouvay, cela m'advint, et choses semblables, je respon . . . qu'ils trouveront les choses par moy proposées en ceste histoire non seulement veritables, mais aussi aucunes, pour avoir esté cachées à ceux qui ont precedé nostre siecle, dignes d'admiration.

> If someone, as I say, finds it ill that hereafter, when I speak of savage customs, I often use this kind of expression – 'I saw', 'I found', 'this happened to me' and so on (as if I wanted to show myself off) – I reply that . . . the things put

---

6 André Thevet, *La Cosmographie de Levant* (1554), ed. F. Lestringant (Geneva: Droz, 1985), and *La Cosmographie universelle* (Paris, 1575); Pierre Belon, *Observations de plusieurs singularitez, & choses memorables, trouvées en Grece, Asie, Iudée, Egypte, Arabie & autres pays estranges* (Paris, 1553).

forth by me in this history are not only true, but also, since they have been hidden to those who lived before our age, worthy of wonder.[7]

But the *Histoire* is also – indeed principally – an argument with the Old World, a Jeremiad for a now lost France, torn apart by the recent civil wars. A Calvinist, Léry was pressed into print by rage against the 'lies' concerning the failed attempt to found a cross-confessional colony in Brazil propagated by the Catholic Cosmographer Royal, André Thevet, both in his *Singularitez de la France antarctique* (1557) and in the compendious *Cosmographie universelle* (1575). The 'extreme dangers' that Léry and his coreligionist fellow travellers faced both within Brazil, and – indeed especially – on their journey home, find their narrative significance in relation to the travails endured by his readers at home. The contemporary force, and the enduring impact, of the *Histoire* is that time and again it turns the anthropologist's eye back on to itself, making the traveller (and his readers) see for the first time the strangeness, the barbarism, and the monstrosity of his own culture. Having described in detail a cannibal feast which he had witnessed, he cannot help but recall the trauma of the St Bartholomew's Day massacre, noting that 'one need not go beyond one's own country, nor yet as far as America, to see such monstrous and prodigious things'.[8] It is these recursive moves, as much as the quality of his observations in the field, that led to Léry's account being dubbed the 'anthropologist's breviary' by Lévi-Strauss in that revisiting of it which is *Tristes Tropiques*.

Léry's *Histoire* exemplifies the two central claims of early modern travel writing in its many forms. First, that to write is to write *against*; this is above all a contestatory mode. And, second, that travelling, listening to others' stories, writing one's own, and then reading still more, are part of one and the same collective continuum. It is from the tension generated by these claims that early modern travel writing derives its peculiar and engaging energy. For in all of these texts, and to varying degrees, arguments heralding the advent of emergent cultural forms (the subject, the nation state, Protestantism, the vernacular, the author, and even 'literature' itself) rub shoulders with those which assert the value of enduring networks, practices, and oppositions (iconography and myth, communities of belief and confessional conflict, diplomacy and warfare, the encounter with alterity and the stain of colonisation). It is in the detail and the differences of these arguments, woven into the texture of the writing itself, that the force of encounter can most powerfully be felt by readers today.

---

7 Jean de Léry, *Histoire d'un voyage faict en la terre du Brésil (1578) [précedé d'un entretien avec Claude Lévi-Strauss]*, ed. F. Lestringant (Paris: Livre de Poche, 1994), pp. 98–9; *History of a Voyage to the Land of Brazil*, trans. J. Whatley (Berkeley: University of California Press, 1990), p. 6.
8 Léry, *Histoire d'un voyage*, p. 377; translation, p. 132.

28

Sixteenth-century margins

RICHARD REGOSIN

From the borders of Montaigne's *Essais* to the edges of Christian Europe, from peripheries marked by gender and sexuality to those delineated by ethnicity – borders, edges, and peripheries that are literary and philosophical, geographical, cultural, social, or religious, and that can be literal, figurative, or symbolic – the concept of the 'margin' provides a valuable hermeneutic perspective for considering French thought and literary production in the sixteenth century. Margin is not, of course, an absolute term but a relational one whose precise location can only be plotted by association with a centre. Although one could argue that it is the margin that frames and thus produces the centre, in this binary structure the margin has tended traditionally to be subordinated, plotted spatially as the outside of a privileged inside, dependent on what for all intents and purposes Western culture has traditionally consecrated as the point from which all else radiates and derives meaning and value.

If we were to begin our discussion with Montaigne's *Essais* (1580, 1582, 1595) we could plot a specific disposition of centre and margin both physically within the space of the written page and mentally in the emergence of a distinctive sense of self. Montaigne opens the well-known essay 'De l'amitié' (1.28) with a vivid metaphor of the origin and the development of his work in just these terms, depicting himself emulating a painter who selects the finest place in the middle of the wall for a picture elaborated with all his skill and who then fills up the empty space all around with *grotesques* and fantastical paintings. The marginal design he can carry out, he claims, but since he is incapable of creating a polished and artful centrepiece of his own, he will borrow one from his great friend Étienne de la Boétie (1530–63). In fact Montaigne does not carry out this project: the text of *La Servitude volontaire* does not occupy the centre of the *Essais* although La Boétie himself remains central to Montaigne's writing. Positing La Boétie at the centre, as a centre, allows Montaigne to conceive of himself, and to conceive of himself as marginal: that is, like his writing, as varied, diverse, changing, having no order or proportion other than accidental – in a word, as monstrous other and alien to himself. From the margins Montaigne comes into being through the writing, through alterity he writes himself into and as the centre of his own text, and constitutes himself as the centre of his being.

Montaigne's own manner of reading and composition mirrors this complex relation of centre to margin in multiple ways. The possessor of an impressive library of over a thousand volumes, he marked and annotated his books on the flyleaves and in the margins. When he composed his own book, he wrote, in a profound way, a book of commentary on his readings, as if composing in the margins of other texts, around centres that inspire thought, that invite query, response, and commentary. But as in the case of La Boétie, what begins in or as the margins of the 'other' transgresses or spills over into the centre, and displaces, replaces, but never effaces the 'other'. The self, we might say, cannot be conceived without reference to the other; like centre and margin, they are relational terms, and differential terms, although difference in this case also admits of the same, and is as much an opening as a closing off.

In a third iteration of the relation of centre to margin in the *Essais*, Montaigne reads his own writing and himself writes in the margins. Taking up their successive editions, he rereads and then reworks his essays, occasionally deleting, sometimes revising between the lines, but primarily adding text around the body of his writing. In each succeeding edition, the marginal, handwritten additions are absorbed into the printed centre, which, with its justified lines, resembles a polished, artful, and framed centrepiece. But once again the empty frame calls out to be filled. Enclosure, or closure, is not possible because the centre is never self-contained or self-sufficient; it is always to some extent a product of its inevitable margins. The centre continues to push out into the margins and the margins continue to spill back into the centre in an endless dynamic that ultimately constitutes both the book and the self.

Paradoxically Montaigne represents one of the strongest sixteenth-century voices raised against what he considered the excesses of the marginal activity we call commentary, figuratively marginal because it derives from a central, primary text but often literally written in the margins. In his work as a magistrate, as well as in his general reading, Montaigne encountered the traditional commentary, gloss, scholium, and annotation that for him inevitably fractured meaning and gave rise to doubt. Although like his contemporaries he himself read and wrote this way, he railed against the proliferation of commentary and the interpretation of interpretation: 'Qui ne diroit que les gloses augmentent les doubtes et l'ignorance, puisqu'il ne se vit aucun livre, soit humain, soit divin, auquel le monde s'embesongne, duquel l'interpretation face tarir la difficulté . . . Nous ne faisons que nous entregloser' (III.13) ('Can anyone deny that glosses increase doubts and ignorance, when there can be found no book, whether human or divine which men toil over whose difficulties are cleared up by interpretation . . . All we do is gloss each other'). For Montaigne, we might say, the margins had spiralled out of control, and in their accumulation had obfuscated and perhaps even obliterated the centre.

In the passage from manuscript culture to that of the book, sixteenth-century humanism inherited from the Middle Ages a rich and widespread tradition of erudite commentary that endured long after the invention of movable type. Often the primary text was surrounded by its gloss in smaller type or a different font: we have examples in the Bible and in theological writings, in editions of Aristotle's philosophy, in legal writing on the Pandectes or the Decretals, in editions of the literary texts of Cicero, Ovid, and Virgil, and in scientific writing. Interpretation, translation, explanation, exposition, gloss, scholia, annotation, observation were just some of the terms used to define this widespread genre, diverse and sprawling, characterised by different ends, different forms, different relationships between the commentator and the commented work, and different sites. The pedagogue, for example, made philological and historical notations to help his students read, glossing for rhetorical, stylistic, and moral ends; students made notes in their texts and scribbled the teacher's remarks in the margins. The early literary critic Marc-Antoine Muret (1526–85) provided commentaries of Ronsard's *Amours* (1553) following each poem: he clarified stylistic and lexical obscurities, explained mythological allusions, identified the poet's sources of inspiration, and offered the reader privileged insight given to him by Ronsard himself.

The biblical commentator, in his turn, addressed the correctness of his text and the restoration of what he took to be the authentic meaning of the Divine Word. The margins of the Catholic Bible commonly included direct quotations of interpretations from earlier glossators and condensed versions or summaries of patristic and medieval exegetical material. Although generally condemning gloss as duplicitous and obfuscating, Reform-minded humanists such as Lefèvre d'Étaples (c. 1455–1536) did include explanatory notes and paraphrase and Robert Estienne inserted marginal verse numbers, and in his 1555 Bible added marginal concordance references to them. The legal scholar engaged with the tradition of secular and canon law in an effort to capture the historical significance of jurisprudential writing and to understand its contemporary import. Early in the century, for example, Guillaume Budé in *Les Annotations aux Pandectes* (1508) addressed the broad issue of Roman law from a philological and historiographic perspective although his concerns were also broadly literary, philosophical, and social as well as legal and lex-icographical. Later in the century Jean de Coras, doctor of laws and author of Latin commentaries on Roman and canon law, wrote his *Arrest memorable* (1561) recounting the trial of the supposed Martin Guerre where he was an acting magistrate. Into his narrative of the evidence, the formal arguments, and the judgements of the case he inserted his personal 'annotations', printed in smaller type as a form of marginalia, and he supplemented these reflections with further references to source material in the literal margins of his text (references, for example, to the Decretals and to Bartolus, to Scripture, and to classical authors such as Cicero, Seneca, and Plutarch).

In its various forms, commentary appears to be ubiquitous in the sixteenth century. Apparently as old as writing itself, it represents one of many kinds of writing generated inevitably by other writing, which seems to suggest that writing itself is never self-sufficient or self-evident, that it is always in need of supplementation, of explicitation, of 'margins' to compensate for what it does not or cannot say clearly or transparently enough to foreclose further writing. But because the relation between centre and margin is a complex and unstable one, a relation whose boundaries are constantly blurred and easily transgressed, the marginal commentary outside can appear to speak from within the text itself, to be the privileged discourse that gives voice to the 'truth' of the text at the centre. However much centre and margin appear to be complementary and mutually reinforcing, however much they appear to dialogue with each other, there is always a latent tension between them, each always threatening to displace or to overwhelm the other. That is the lesson of those printed pages where the text shares its space with parallel columns of commentary or where it shrinks to a small, almost insignificant centre dwarfed by the massive weight of gloss all around, or in other instances where it gets pushed out into the margins by the commentary at the centre. And it is also the lesson of the opposing tendency to reassert the centre that operated over the course of the sixteenth century, a tendency expressed by Melanchthon (1497–1522) in his early admonition to avoid 'the petty, frigid gloss'. Marginal writing does not entirely disappear in that period (nor will it ever) but pressure is put on restraining interpretive commentary and on providing less intrusive, more practical reading aids instead.

At the heart of the unsettled relation between centre and margin lie issues of power, whether we are talking about the scene occurring on the pages of the book, on the stage of society, or on contemporaneous world maps. Biblical gloss, for example, was intended not only to elucidate the true mean-ing at the centre of Scripture but also to assert the authority of theological tradition. Even for the Protestants who attempted to disencumber the Bible from the long presence of biblical exegesis, the purpose of their more minimalist Protestant commentary and marginal reader's aids was still to guide and control interpretation and understanding. The same could be said for the glosses on legal texts or on the literary works of the Ancients. Those who cited and referenced 'auctoritatis' invoked powerful names and voices from the past to bring their weight to bear on how readers read and the ways meaning was shaped. Those who advocated the reduction or elimination of marginal commentary sought to restore the dominance of the primary text. The relationship between the central text and the marginal gloss played out differently on the site of different texts, but what was always at stake was the question of power, the degree to which the one dominated, interfered with, or supported and subordinated itself to the other.

If we were to examine the social fabric of sixteenth-century France from this same perspective, we would see that ethnicity, gender, religious affiliation, and sexual orientation were used then (as they have been historically) to configure society in terms of those who occupy the centre and those whom we now refer to as marginalised. Jews, Muslims, Protestants, women, and homosexuals were among those who could be said to have existed on the margins of white, Catholic, patriarchal, heterosexual France. There were individual exceptions, of course: women of broad influence such as Marguerite de Navarre (1492–1549) or Louise Labé (c. 1520–66) and Pernette du Guillet (c. 1520–45) who gained prominence as poets in Lyon. There were also individual Protestants, well-known writers such as Du Bartas (1544–90) and d'Aubigné (1552–1630) or political figures such as Admiral Gaspar de Coligny (1519–72), and of course, Henri de Navarre (1553–1610) whose crossing from margin to centre is legendary. But these were exceptions that prove the rule by which the dominant social forces excised alterity by relegating it to the margins. The centre, in fact, could only constitute itself by constructing the margins as the site of difference; it could only claim to be identical to itself in contradistinction to an 'other', to an 'outside' of itself. The history of the sixteenth century is replete with what we might take as accepted forms of misogyny, anti-Semitism, ethnic and religious hatred, and sexual prejudice emanating from the 'inside' as both the expression of power and its source.

The marginalising of the 'other' within France in the sixteenth century was one element in the early development of a national French identity. Equally important were the efforts to centre France in relation to a European 'outside' located on its topographical margins, a centring that the cultural productions of the period both mirrored and helped create. From the mythic genealogy constructed by Lemaire de Belges (1473–1525) to the critical research of Étienne Pasquier (1529–1615) historians attempted to endow France with a past that could rival the Roman (and Trojan) heritage claimed by the Italians. The *Arts poétiques* of the period that debated the status of the French language and its literary accomplishments also reflected the concern with France's place. Sébillet's *art poétique* (1548) and Aneau's *Quintil horatien* (1551), for example, argued that France and the French language already occupied a cultural centre; du Bellay's *Deffense et illustration de la langue françoyse* (1549) contended, on the contrary, that the language was still marginal compared to Greek, Latin, and Italian and urged the enrichment of its aesthetic capabilities. In its attempt to be the epic that finally fulfilled the promise of the language and rivalled those of the Ancients, Ronsard's *Franciade* (1572) sought to confirm France's aspiration to be the literary, historical, and political centre of Europe.

On the geographical margins of Renaissance Europe itself lay the Ottoman Empire to the east and the New World to the west, the first an old, sophisticated, and powerful Muslim society, the second pagan tribes taken to represent the infancy of man. The 'Turk' and the 'cannibal' could also be said to have occupied the margins of French consciousness, imaginary constructions due as much to borrowed learning as to first-hand experience, phantasmic figures within a distant space of profound alterity that was as much cause as effect of France's sense of itself and of its place. In his *Navigations et peregrinations orientales* (1567), Nicolas de Nicolay projected on the East both Europe's scorn and the expression of its inadmissible desire – its fascination with the seraglio. Guillaume Postel's *De la Republique des Turcs* (1560) represented the Muslim Turk as the avatar of both the barbarous Scythe and the cultured Roman, a brutal and devious enemy and a valuable military ally against the Christian Charles V. Although Postel invents a 'bon Turc' to teach moral lessons to Christian France, the figures of the lubricious, lying 'Turk' of the harem and the barbarous Moor allow him the necessary condemnation and rejection of Islam. However much the 'other' may appear to be the same, or to be like the same, the 'other' of the East always remains inalterably 'other'. The 'other' of the West shares the same fate, whether we encounter the Brazilian that Thevet depicts in his *Singularités de la France antarctique* (1557) who is a composite of what he had seen, heard, or mostly read or the Tupinamba represented in Léry's *Histoire d'un voyage au terre du Brésil* (1578) who is the object of direct observation. The alien figure of the cannibal haunts a discourse that remains profoundly ethnocentric, like the parallel discourse about the East, and which marks the boundaries between the Christian European communities and their others relegated to its margins.

One might argue that the history of sixteenth-century France is marked by cultural, political, intellectual, religious, literary, and social developments that reveal a centripetal bias – movement from the peripheries towards consolidation and affirmation of axes of government, religion, learning, language, and national identity. At the same time, in these same realms, we have recognised centrifugal motion exerting opposing pressure towards the margins – pressure that not only strengthens the centre but also always threatens at the same time to weaken or disperse it. In the interdependence of centre and margin in Renaissance France we observe that the history of each can only be written in relation to the other. Perhaps it is always so.

29

Tragedy: early to
mid seventeenth century

JOHN D. LYONS

Looking back on his first thirty years as a playwright, Pierre Corneille wrote in 1660 that 'la poésie dramatique a pour but le seul plaisir du spectateur' ('the objective of dramatic writing is simply the spectator's pleasure').[1] Though unusually emphatic, Corneille expressed a view that increasingly became the bedrock of dramatic theory during the first half of the seventeenth century: writers of tragedy should create a certain type of theatrical experience for the audience. Even Corneille's critics and rivals, such as Georges de Scudéry, the Abbé d'Aubignac, and Jean Chapelain did not dispute the importance of the spectator, but merely emphasised different aspects of audience require-ments.

With the spectator in mind, we can see why seventeenth-century tragedy evolved towards an illusionistic spectacle with lively dialogue in contemporary diction, concentrated in time and space, and centring on protagonists whom the audience could like. This shift can be seen in the radical changes in tragedy between Antoine de Montchrestien's *Hector* (1607) and the dominant model of Corneille's tragedies from 1637 until at least mid-century.

The eclipse and return of tragedy

In the first decades of the century, tragedy was shaped by the ideal of recreating Greek and Latin models in French, in an often ornate and learned style but very highly wrought emotionally, with subjects from biblical and classical sources, and with much more pathos than action – that is to say that the characters spend a good deal of time deploring their misfortune. This is quite clear in Montchrestien's *Hector*. The simple, straightforward story consists of the Trojan hero Hector's farewell to his father, mother, and wife, and his

---

1 P. Corneille, *Œuvres complètes*, ed. Georges Couton, 3 vols. (Paris: Gallimard, 1980–8), III, p. 817.

departure from the royal palace to face the Greek army. His father Priam recounts Hector's heroic off-stage combat to Hector's wife Andromaque in act IV, but then in act V further accounts of the battle reveal that Hector has died and that the Greeks are victorious. The atmosphere of gloom and foreboding is amplified by a chorus of Trojan women. The chorus, a mark of Montchrestien's deep attachment to the models of antiquity, links *Hector* more closely to sixteenth-century humanist tragedy than to most works of the new century.

Yet while the chorus disappeared quickly, tragedy for the first two decades of the century resembles *Hector* both in style and in the general emotive tone. Sadness, foreboding, and lamentation sometimes pass over into the frankly horrible, as in Alexandre Hardy's *Scédase* (performed sometime between 1605 and 1615, but printed in 1624) in which two young sisters are raped and murdered by their father's guests. When the father, Scédase, is unable to persuade the Spartan authorities to punish the murderers, he commits suicide on his daughters' tomb. These horrifying events are conveyed in dense, highly stylised alexandrine verses, filled with allusions to classical myths and in a word order that distinguishes the declamatory, oratorical discourse of the characters from the colloquial French of the day. There are great tragedies of this early seventeenth-century form, with its great lyric force, such as Théophile de Viau's *Les Amours tragiques de Pyrame et Thisbé* (1623), but by the mid-1620s a new genre became dominant, tragi-comedy.

Although it often kept the ornate language and the horrifying subject matter of the earliest French tragedies, tragi-comedies conclude with some form of happy outcome for the more appealing of the dramatic characters. Hardy recognised the shift, and found a way to reconcile one of his preferred subjects, rape, with what passed for a happy ending: the raped woman marries the man who violated her (*La Force du sang, tragi-comédie*, performed between 1614 and 1625). In the decade preceding Corneille's epochal *Le Cid*, tragi-comedies far outnumbered tragedies (*Le Cid* itself was performed and printed as a tragi-comedy in 1637, and later revised and republished in 1648 as a tragedy). Their dominance shows that audiences expected complex dramatic works with several intricate plots (often loosely related), many surprises, events that come about by the most improbable chance, disguises and other forms of mistaken identity, staged violence, extreme highs and lows of emotion, and finally punishment for the 'wicked' and a happy outcome for the 'good' characters.

Corneille's *Clitandre, ou l'Innocence délivrée* (performed 1632) shows all of these characteristics, which can be delightful (somewhat reminiscent of

Shakespearean comedies such as *A Midsummer-Night's Dream*) if the play is not judged by the standards of later in the century. In *Clitandre* there is a core couple of happy lovers, Caliste and Rosidor, each of whom is loved by at least one other character. Dorise attempts to kill Caliste in order to have Rosidor to herself, while Pymante plots to kill Rosidor out of jealousy over Dorise. Meanwhile, Clitandre is in love with Caliste, although he foments no violent plots to obtain her. Much of the action occurs in a forest, where the various plots cross at key moments. Dorise, having failed to kill Caliste, disguises herself as a man, but is recognised by Pymante, whose attempt to rape her Dorise repels by putting out one of his eyes with a hair pin. The eponymous character, Clitandre, is falsely accused of the attempt to kill Rosidor and pines away in prison, although he is finally released.

Suspense and the unities

In the mid-1630s a shift took place, even within tragi-comedy, towards plays that were easier to understand and more tightly plotted – that is, depended less obviously on chance, and that attached the spectator more strongly to events affecting the protagonist. In a tragi-comedy such as *Clitandre*, surprise dominates at the cost of suspense. This distinction – surprise versus suspense – is a major demarcation between tragi-comedy and the more familiar tragedies of the 1640s and beyond. It comes from a recognition that an important affective resource of drama is anticipation; indeed, this had been the core of tragedies such as *Hector* and *Pyrame et Thisbé*. What playwrights attempted to do in the 1630s was keep the dynamism of tragi-comedy without straining the attention of the audience to the point at which it was difficult to foresee what might happen to the leading characters. Jean de Mairet's preface to *La Silvanire* (1631) is the major theoretical text on drama prior to the debate that followed *Le Cid* and is the first to proclaim the importance of four principal 'conditions' for a proper tragedy: a historically true subject, a single action, a duration of twenty-four hours or less, and a maximum spatial dimension equivalent to the distance that a character could actually travel in the time of the dramatic action. Although on the first point (the requirement of a true historic subject) the subsequent critical consensus differed from Mairet in preferring a plausible (*vraisemblable*) subject to a true one, the preface to *La Silvanire* essentially outlines the dramatic aesthetic of the rest of the seventeenth century.

Mairet's most important point, however, is often overlooked. The conditions of a proper tragedy all derive from the playwright's goal, which is to construct tragedy on the basis of the spectator's imaginative capacity. In regard to the one-day rule, he writes that the playwrights of antiquity 'established this rule in deference to the spectator's imagination, since he has much more pleasure (experience has shown this), at the performance of a plot arranged in this way rather than another; because without any strain or distraction he sees things as if they were happening before his eyes'.[2] Mairet admits that a reader's imagination can follow an epic character for long distances and periods of time but argues that this requires a strain on the spectator that defeats the playwright's aim to 'satisfy the spectator's imagination' (p. 485). While presenting this argument for a spectator-centred aesthetic, Mairet introduces another key concept for most of the tragedies in the following decades: the idea of theatrical illusion; things should *really* seem to be happening in front of the spectator. Tragedy, on this view, is thus not a ritual or a display of eloquence or an elegiac reference towards an event that the audience can reconstruct mentally; rather, tragedy appears to be a real event witnessed by the spectator. Consequently, anything that strains the imagination of the audience and that creates a distance between the apparent reality of the event and the spectator will be considered bad. One outcome of this logic is that the complex and literary language of much tragi-comedy is unacceptable because no character in the grip of strong emotion could be expected to have the presence of mind to speak so ornately. And, of course, a plethora of complex plots would prevent the audience from being truly caught up in emotional anticipation of the repercussions of events for the protagonists.

Le Cid, its quarrel, and Corneille's poetics of history

Corneille's *Le Cid* is recognised as a pivotal event not only in French dramatic literature but in the historical formation of French cultural institutions that have lasted until today. This play was one of the biggest popular successes of the century and had both direct and indirect effects on all subsequent French tragedy. Its direct effect was to provide a model of a highly concentrated, relatively realistic plot with dialogue in language close to contemporary French. Performed as a tragi-comedy, *Le Cid* borrowed from that genre its 'happy end' (though some critics contest this description) and subsequently freed tragedy from the expectation that all such plays should end in unhappiness (or, as Mairet wrote, with 'kings and princes reduced to despair'[3]). Corneille

---

2 J. Mairet, 'Préface', *La Silvanire*, in J. Scherer and J. Truchet (eds.), *Théâtre du xviie siècle*, 2 vols. (Paris: Gallimard, 1975–86), I, p. 484.
3 Mairet, 'Préface', p. 482.

managed, in *Le Cid*, to combine a certain illusionistic realism with a plot concept so paradoxical that it is truly astonishing. Stated in two steps: first, Rodrigue kills the father of his lover Chimène, and she, as a consequence, loves him all the more; second, she in return demands the death of the man she loves. This seems, on the face of it, implausible. Writing the play as a tragi-comedy, Corneille might be excused for including implausible events, but right from the start his critics decided to judge *Le Cid* by the standards of tragedy, with many invocations of Aristotle's *Poetics*. In the critical skirmishing that followed, Corneille found a crucial insight about tragedy that he stated in 1660 in his *Discours*: great tragic subjects are necessarily implausible. Even though Corneille, in practice, had constructed *Le Cid* as a tragi-comedy, with its taste for unbelievable action, the play created the occasion for a subsequent theoretical breakthrough in regard to tragedy itself. It is implausible, he argued, that Medea kills her children, that Clytemnestra kills her husband, and that Orestes kills his mother – yet these are among the canons of ancient tragedy. What Corneille achieved in *Le Cid* was to take something apparently implausible and then show, quite convincingly, how it might happen.

Indirectly, *Le Cid* provided the occasion for an outpouring of critical and theoretical writing on the theatre (with emphasis on tragedy) that endowed playwrighting with a new social and intellectual status. The newly formed Académie Française was asked by Cardinal Richelieu to give its views on the merits of this very popular play. The resulting document, the *Sentiments de l'Académie Française sur la tragi-comédie du Cid*, written by Jean Chapelain, found much to blame, primarily the implausibility (and immorality) of the heroine's continued love for Rodrigue. Significantly, however, Chapelain and his fellow academicians based their arguments against the play on the same core principle: that all critical reasoning about drama should be based on the capacity and expectations of the audience. The two major points of disagreement between Corneille and the Academy concern plausibility (*le vraisemblable*). First, Chapelain conflated plausibility with morality (in the sense of what people *should* do) and judged that Chimène's continued love for Rodrigue and her apparent consent to the royal decree that she marry him after a period of mourning marked her as a deeply immoral character. As a consequence, the tragi-comedy as a whole constituted a danger to public morality (it is worth noting that the Academy did not find Rodrigue's duel with Chimène's father similarly dangerous to public order). Second, Chapelain insisted that playwrights should eliminate the implausible, thus defined, from tragedy altogether, and thus avoid subjects that are grounded in history when the historical event itself is implausible. Corneille's riposte to this double attack was, first, to promote history as the major source and warranty of transgressive, implausible subjects, and, second, to argue that playwrights need not write with the didactic purpose of showing evil punished and good rewarded. Again, with reference to a spectator-centred aesthetic, Corneille considers it sufficient that an event be grounded in history in order to persuade the audience that the tragic plot is worthy of belief. Although Corneille's practice of locating obscure historical figures, often from the late Roman Empire, as he did for *Héraclius, empereur d'Orient* (1647), was far from unique – Mairet's *Sophonisbe* (1635) and Rotrou's last great tragedy *Cosroès* (1648) are representative – Corneille made a highly original theoretical argument for the value of history as foil to the proponents of tamer, more plausible, and less transgressive subjects. As for the possible moral influence of tragedy upon the audience, Corneille declared that the 'naïve depiction' of conduct sufficed – it was up to the spectators or readers to draw the appropriate conclusions. The playwright's work was to give the public something extraordinary, to stretch the situation until it became almost – but not entirely – unbelievable.

In *Le Cid*, as far as the general public was concerned, Corneille achieved this aim. Both Chimène and Rodrigue are rather simple characters. They are strong, good-looking, energetic, and extremely devoted to a shared set of ethical standards. Otherwise, there is little we know about them, or need to, for they find themselves in a situation in which their agreed-upon ethic dictates what follows. This form of dramatic construction depends on what Corneille called the *acheminements*: the tight, step-by-step plotting that could lead the audience to believe in a predicament that, in its rough outline, seems absurd.

Tragedy and the emotions

Seventeenth-century audiences left moving accounts of the emotional impact of tragedy. The critic René Rapin reminisced that performances of Tristan L'Hermite's *La Mariane*, with the actor Mondory playing the role of Hérode, 'made such a strong and violent impression on people that they left the theatre . . . possessed by this play'.[4] Marie de Sévigné, in her letters, wrote that some of Corneille's dialogue made the audience shiver.[5] Despite a modern tendency to view French culture as highly intellectual, audiences, playwrights, and theorists of the day insist that tragedy was meant to provoke an emotional

---

4 R. Rapin, *Réflexions sur la poétique de ce temps*, ed. E. T. Dubois (Geneva: Droz, 1970), p. 102.
5 Marie de Sévigné, *Correspondance*, ed. R. Duchêne, 3 vols. (Paris: Gallimard, 1972–8), I, p. 459.

response in the audience, both during a performance on stage and upon simple reading of the text. La Mesnardière, in his *La Poétique* (1640), declared, 'I believe, like Aristotle, that a work is lacking if reading it does not stir the audience's passions and move them to the point of trembling or weeping.'[6] Similar references to pity and fear, those core tragic affects mentioned in Aristotle's *Poetics*, are ubiquitous. But these two emotions alone do not account for the experience of French tragedy. Rapin wrote that 'our nation's creative inclination could not easily sustain a plot on the stage through fear and pity alone'.[7] Rapin pointed to the importance of love in French tragedy, contrasting the violence of English tragedy with French amorous gallantry, and the austere moralist Blaise Pascal, no great friend of theatre, needing an illustration of the arbitrary but irresistible force of love, pointed to Corneille's work.[8] But beyond fear, pity, and love there are other powerful, yet often overlooked emotional effects characteristic of early seventeenth-century tragedy. Suspense itself – which Corneille calls the 'agréable suspension dans l'esprit de l'auditeur' ('agreeable suspense in the spectator's mind')[9] – a mixture of fear, curiosity, and desire (desire, at least, to see the good prevail) was clearly a major goal of playwrights in this period, and they used many devices to create and maintain it. Such ploys include the oracular pronouncement or the dream retold at the beginning of a play, such as Herod's frightening dream in Tristan L'Hermite's *La Mariane* (1637), or heroine Pauline's dream in the first act of Corneille's *Polyeucte martyr* (1643), which give the audience, as well as the characters, something to worry about right from the start. Another technique consists of interrupting events at the end of acts so that the intermission itself could generate suspense. At the end of the first act of Corneille's *Cinna* (1642), the titular hero, who has just told his lover Emilie the details of his plot to assassinate the emperor Octave, is summoned to the emperor's chambers. He leaves for this meeting with the fear that his conspiracy has been discovered, and the suspense about this issue lingers until act II begins. Most of all, the playwrights of the 1640s aim to keep the action going up to the very last scenes of the fifth and final act, trying to avoid a denouement that consists entirely of grieving or deliberating. The disconcertingly sudden conversion of the conspirators at the end of *Cinna* illustrates this desire to keep the audience hooked until the very end.

---

6 J.-H. La Mesnardière, *La Poétique* (Geneva: Slatkine Reprints, 1972; 1st edn 1639), p. 102.
7 R. Rapin, *Réflexions*, p. 103.
8 B. Pascal, *Pensées* fragment 32, in *Les Provinciales: Pensées et opuscules divers*, ed. G. Ferreyrolles and P. Sellier (Paris: Classiques Garnier, 2004).
9 Corneille, *Œuvres complètes*, iii, p. 158.

The most innovative dramatic emotion of seventeenth-century tragedy as it reached the mid-century was, however, something for which the historical name is misleading for the modern reader: 'admiration'. Descartes, writing in 1649, called admiration 'first among all the passions', but for him this term did not signify great respect or esteem but rather a strong perception of something as new, unusual, and astonishing. Corneille used the term in his tragedies sometimes in the Cartesian sense of astonishment and recognition of something amazing or marvellous and sometimes in the sense of esteem. In both senses, admiration is a powerful component of the spectator's experience as created by playwrights in the 1630s and later. Sometimes the protagonists of a play are astonished at their own circumstances, as in *Horace* at the moment when the protagonist Horace finds that he will soon be fighting in combat directly against his best friend and brother-in-law, Curiace. Horace declares to Curiace, 'je ne vous connais plus' ('I no longer know you'), thus depersonalising the combat. Curiace is unwilling or unable to imitate this 'virtue' and he tells Horace, 'Souffrez que je l'admire et ne l'imite point' ('Permit me to admire yet not imitate it', line 506). This verse can be read in two ways: as expressing great esteem for Horace's resolve or as expressing a more ambiguous amazement at his inhumanity. Jean Rotrou's *Le Véritable Saint Genest* (1645) provides another example of admiration, this time in an ambivalent (that is, having two distinct points of view), rather than an ambiguous, form. Rotrou's play is about a Roman actor and playwright who performs for the Emperor Diocletian at the time of the emperor's rigorous persecution of Christians. Genest performs the role of Adrian, a Christian martyr, for the imperial court, and all agree that Genest excels at portraying this character type. All the characters in the play, both the imperial audience and the other actors, are amazed and dismayed to see Genest stop speaking the lines of the martyr Adrian and insist that he, Genest, has in fact become a Christian by dint of playing the role. In one sense Genest is admirable (that is, worthy of esteem) as an actor because he has achieved perfection within the illusionistic aesthetic, in which the spectators are confronted with what seems like reality, but in another sense what happens is simply astonishing. The most paradoxical cases of dramatic 'admiration' are those of the frankly evil characters, such as the queen-regent Cléopâtre in Corneille's *Rodogune, princesse des Parthes* (1644–5) who is so enamoured of her power that she decides to kill both her sons to keep them from the throne. The playwright wrote in 1660 that *Rodogune* was his favourite tragedy, and it is hard to imagine that this preference could be unrelated to the astounding energy, ambition, resourcefulness, and evil of its most powerful character, Cléopâtre, who dies in the last few seconds of the play, having killed one son and cursing the other who has survived her attempt to poison him on his wedding day. For Corneille, Cléopâtre is an example of a desirable quality in dramatic personages: that they be pushed to the maximum intensity of their defining traits. In his *Discours*, commenting on Aristotle's term *chrestos* or 'good' in regard to character, Corneille did not give a moral interpretation but rather an aesthetic or representative one, saying that that what matters

> is the brilliant and exalted quality of a virtuous or criminal habit, in accordance with its suitability to the person one is presenting. Cléopâtre in *Rodogune* is very wicked; no parricide horrifies her . . . but all her crimes are accompanied by a greatness of spirit that has something so lofty, that even while one abhors her actions, one admires their source.[10]

Later in the century La Rochefoucauld noted in his *Maximes* (1664) that there were heroes of evil as well as heroes of good (maxim 185), capturing the ambivalence of tragic emotion in Corneille's vision. A well-known instance of 'admiration' is the verse from *Le Cid*, so often quoted by the earliest spectators of the play. The protagonists Rodrigue and Chimène are amazed at the improbability of their own situation, she feeling obliged to demand that he be put to death for killing her father in a duel and he being urged by her to defend himself against the punishment she seeks. They exclaim, one to the other: 'Rodrigue, qui l'eût cru? Chimène, qui l'eût dit?' ('Rodrigue, who would have believed it? Chimène, who would have said it?', line 988). In this single verse, Corneille exemplified a model of tragedy that lasted for decades, one that expressed, in simple language, both the importance of love and amazement at unbelievable results that can arise from the contradictory demands of social values.

10 Corneille, *Œuvres complètes*, III, p. 129; emphasis added.

30

Tragedy: mid to late seventeenth century

MICHAEL HAWCROFT

In *Les Caractères*, first published in 1688, Jean de La Bruyère (1645–96) pays eloquent tribute to the effects of tragic drama in performance:

> Le poème tragique vous serre le cœur dès son commencement, vous laisse à peine dans tout son progrès la liberté de respirer et le temps de vous remettre, ou s'il vous donne quelque relâche, c'est pour vous replonger dans de nouveaux abîmes et dans de nouvelles alarmes. Il vous conduit à la terreur par la pitié, ou réciproquement à la pitié par le terrible, vous mène par les larmes, par les sanglots, par l'incertitude, par l'espérance, par la crainte, par les surprises et par l'horreur jusqu'à la catastrophe. (1.51)[1]

> (The tragic play takes hold of your heart from the very beginning and throughout its whole length hardly leaves you time to breathe and recover, or if it offers you some respite, it is in order to plunge you once again into new abysses and new alarms. It leads you through pity to terror or alternatively through terror to pity, and takes you on a journey of tears, sobbing, uncertainty, hope, anxiety, surprise, and horror right up to the catastrophe.)

For La Bruyère, these are the qualities that characterise the genre to which the ancient Greeks gave birth and which Pierre Corneille (1606–84) and Jean Racine (1639–99) had recently restored to the French stage. He adds the subtle distinction that Corneille, more noble and more intellectual, resembles Sophocles, whilst Racine, more passionate and more moving, is closer to Euripides (1.54). The court of Louis XIV and the public theatres in Paris, which the king's better-off subjects patronised, are thus the arena for the French conquest of a genre whose importance was traditionally thought to be second only to that of the verse epic. School textbooks and literary histories since the eighteenth century have offered an image of tragic drama as an elegant, refined genre, worthy of its status as a national monument, characteristic of

---

1 Jean de La Bruyère, *Les Caractères,* ed. R. Garapon (Paris: Garnier, 1962), p. 86.

the cultural achievements of the Sun King's reign, and summed up above all in the work of Racine.

Taking stock: dramatic theory

This image of seventeenth-century tragedy is of course mythical, although it is not entirely unrelated to reality. Prompted by the plea of the poet Joachim du Bellay (c. 1522–60) in his *Deffence et illustration de la langue françoyse* (1549) for the enrichment of the French language, writers such as Étienne Jodelle (1532–73) and Robert Garnier (1545–90) had consciously tried to recreate something of ancient tragedy in French. Subsequently, the likes of Corneille and Jean Rotrou (1609–50) had taken over the baton in the 1630s and adapted this new style of serious French drama for a modern theatre-going public. Then the mid-seventeenth century became a time for taking stock of the achievement to date and capitalising on it.

Two major publications towards the end of the 1650s might be said to constitute the stocktake: *La Pratique du théâtre* (1657) by the abbé d'Aubignac (1604–76); and *Le Théâtre de Pierre Corneille* (1660), in three volumes, each one prefaced by a theoretical *Discours* on the art of theatre and every play accompanied by a critical analysis by the dramatist himself. In one sense, these are backward-looking works. D'Aubignac's book, largely composed in the 1640s, takes many of its examples of dramatic practice from that earlier period, and Corneille's edition of his plays to date appears as the summa of a career essentially carved out in the 1630s and 1640s, with the author's mature reflections on it. What both these works do, however, regardless of major differences in theoretical approach between the two writers, is to identify the main features of a form of drama that had taken shape over the three preceding decades of bustling theatrical activity.

Plays in the new mould had to be constructed so as to grip audiences and engage their emotions. It was thought that the best way of doing this was to conjure up an illusion of reality for the theatre audience (*vraisemblance*): 'Voici le fondement de toutes les Pièces du Théâtre', says d'Aubignac ('Here is the foundation of every play').[2] This aim would be facilitated if dramatists observed a number of so-called rules, including the unities of time, place, and action. Spectators would be more likely to suspend their disbelief if the action was clearly focused, if it evolved in a single stage setting (as opposed to the multiple sets simultaneously present on stage, typical of plays earlier

---

2 Abbé d'aubignac, *La Pratique du théâtre,* ed. H. Baby (Paris: Champion, 2001), p. 123.

in the century), and if it could be plausibly thought to elapse within at most twenty-four hours (after all, the watching time was barely three hours).

Whereas d'Aubignac believed that *vraisemblance* had to govern all aspects of dramatic composition and, above all, the choice of a believable subject for a play, Corneille believed passionately that the dramatist should have the right to choose an extraordinary subject. Both agreed on the basic form of the play, however, and if they disagreed on the criteria governing the choice of subject, they were both motivated by the desire to maximise audience engagement and excitement. La Bruyère's views, already cited, bear witness to the success of the best tragedies in achieving this aim. The form of play identified in these two works set the pattern not only for the remainder of the seventeenth century, but for much of the eighteenth, and even into the nineteenth.

Renewal: modern sex and ancient learning

The publication of these two important works by d'Aubignac and Corneille was accompanied by a particular phenomenon that allowed the second half of the seventeenth century to capitalise on the achievements in tragic drama in the first half: namely the demands of a contemporary French audience in which the opinion of women spectators was playing an increasingly important role. After the troubled years of the virtual civil war known as the Fronde (1648–53), cultural life in Paris resumed and women exercised considerable influence through the activities of the salons. When Corneille was enticed out of the retirement he had imposed on himself in 1652 in order to write *Œdipe* (1659), he faced the problem of adapting one of the best-known Greek tragedies for a modern audience, in particular for an audience of ladies, 'qui composent la plus belle partie de notre auditoire' ('who constitute the finest part of the audience') ('Au lecteur').[3] The difficulty was that the Greek play is about a monarch's discovery of his acts of parricide and incest, and ends when he returns to the stage, having dashed out his eyes by way of self-punishment. Corneille thought that this subject was 'dénué des principaux ornements qui nous gagnent d'ordinaire la voix publique' ('devoid of the main attractions that usually earn us the public's favour') (p. 19). He was explicit about his remedy. He decided not to bring Œdipe back on stage after his self-mutilation, thus sparing his modern audience the bloody spectacle; and he

3 Pierre Corneille, *Œuvres complètes,* ed. Georges Couton, 3 vols. (Paris: Gallimard, 1980–7), III, pp. 18–19.

decided to complicate and enrich the plot of the source play by inventing two new roles, those of Thésée, prince of Athens, and Dircé, princess of Thebes and sister of Œdipe, whose mutual love offers the audience a romantic interest that goes a long way towards tempering the raw horror of the Sophoclean original. The success of Œdipe encouraged Corneille to resume his theatrical career, and between 1659 and 1674 he wrote eleven plays, mostly tragedies, eventually competing explicitly with those of Racine, the upstart dramatist of the 1660s, whose first performed play La Thébaïde (1664) is clearly an attempt to outdo the success of his older rival's Œdipe.

The example of Œdipe is instructive for the course that tragedy took in the second half of the seventeenth century. As a serious genre with an ancient pedigree and extensive theoretical underpinning that derives ultimately from Aristotle's Poetics, tragedy aimed to arouse the emotions of pity and fear in audiences by engaging them in the life-endangering political tribulations of great rulers. French dramatists tried to advertise their seriousness of purpose and scholarly credentials (as well as to bolster the audience's belief in the events they depicted) by demonstrating their allegiance to the great exemplars of Greek and Latin tragedy and, in prefaces, citing their alleged ancient source material, whether dramatic or historical.

Racine was the master of self-publicity in this respect. In the prefaces to his plays he repeatedly and deftly fights off his jealous critics (unnamed, though it is often clearly Corneille whom he has in his sights) with some ancient citation. When critics find King Pyrrhus in Andromaque (1667) a less than perfect lover and too given to threats of violence, Racine parries by citing first Horace on the need to paint characters as they really were and then Aristotle on the need to make tragic heroes neither wholly good nor wholly bad (First Preface). When he publishes Iphigénie, he boasts (and simultaneously flatters his French audiences) by claiming that 'mes spectateurs ont été émus des mêmes choses qui ont mis autrefois en larmes le plus savant peuple de la Grèce' ('my spectators have been moved by the same things that in times past reduced to tears the most learned people of Greece') (Preface). And when he published his complete Œuvres to date in two volumes in 1675–6, he prefaced his text with an illustration by Charles Lebrun depicting an allegory of tragedy above the impressive-looking Greek legend 'phobos kai eleos' ('fear and pity'), making crystal clear the traditions of Graeco-Roman antiquity which he wants his plays to be seen to maintain.[4]

4 Jean Racine, Théâtre. Poésie, ed. Georges Forestier (Paris: Gallimard, 1999), p. 197 (Andromaque preface); p. 699 (Iphigénie preface); p. xcix (illustration).

And yet the amorous intrigues of Corneille's *Œdipe* are an even more significant pointer to tragedy's new directions. French tragedy to some extent softens the political seriousness and even horror of its ancient predecessors and extends the emotional range by depicting romantic love. Theorists and churchmen were not always happy with the depiction of sexual love on stage. In his *Art poétique* (1674) Boileau notes its new predominance, and tries to draw a line:

> Bientôt l'amour, fertile en tendres sentiments,
> S'empara du théâtre ainsi que des romans.
> De cette passion la sensible peinture
> Est pour aller au coeur la route la plus sûre.
> Peignez donc, j'y consens, les héros amoureux,
> Mais ne m'en formez pas des bergers doucereux:
> Qu'Achille aime autrement que Tircis et Philène;
> N'allez pas d'un Cyrus nous faire un Artamène;
> Et que l'amour, souvent de remords combattu,
> Paraisse une faiblesse et non une vertu.
> (Chant 3, lines 93–102)[5]

(Soon love, fertile in tender feelings, took hold of the theatre as it had of novels. The sensitive portrayal of this passion is the surest route to the spectator's heart. So by all means depict amorous heroes, but I do not want to see any sugary shepherds. Let Achilles love differently from Tircis and Philène; do not turn Cyrus into an Artamène; and let love, often with remorse battling against it, look like a weakness and not a virtue.)

Cyrus was the historical hero of Madeleine de Scudéry's multi-volume novel *Le Grand Cyrus* (1648–53), who, to Boileau's chagrin, often puts love before heroism and, for convenience, assumes the name of Artamène. Boileau's double-edged attitude to love in the theatre is shared by Racine in the preface to *Phèdre* (1677), the last play he wrote for the public theatre, before devoting himself full-time, with Boileau, to writing the history of Louis XIV and reconciling himself with his former teachers, the Jansenists of Port-Royal, for whom the lasciviousness of the theatre was especially obnoxious. Racine is unable to spirit away the romantic love that subtends the dramatic action of his play, but he claims that the play presents it as a real weakness: 'Les faiblesses de l'amour y passent pour de vraies faiblesses. Les passions n'y sont présentées aux yeux que pour montrer tout le désordre dont elles sont

---

5 Nicolas Boileau, *Œuvres*, vol. II, ed. Sylvain Menant (Paris: Garnier-Flammarion, 1969), pp. 100–1.

cause' ('The weaknesses of love are seen as real weaknesses. The passions are presented only in order to reveal all the disorder that they cause') (Preface, p. 819).

Despite the claims to ancient pedigree and despite the caution with which theorists and dramatists tackled the notion of romantic love, the subject and the effects of tragedy in the second half of the seventeenth century depend crucially on the depiction of such love. Corneille and Racine are following a trend that had been set by others in the 1650s. The tragedies of the prolific Claude Boyer (1618–98), those of Thomas Corneille (1625–1709), Pierre's younger brother, whose career took off in the 1650s (when Pierre was in retirement), and those of Philippe Quinault (1635–88) all exhibit the fondness for adapting ancient historical or mythological material to the romantic tastes of their French audiences. Some felt that the enthusiasm for *galanterie* in tragedy went too far. Boileau lampooned Quinault for the unrelievedly amorous tones in which his tragic heroes speak: 'Les héros chez Quinault parlent bien autrement, / Et jusqu'à *Je vous hais*, tout s'y dit tendrement' ('Quinault's heroes speak very differently. They say everything tenderly – even *I hate you*') (*Satire III*).[6]

Boileau's criticism was formulated in 1665, the same year in which *Astrate*, one of Quinault's most successful tragedies, was performed at one of the major Parisian theatres, the Hôtel de Bourgogne. At the beginning of the printed text, Quinault cites four historical sources beginning with the Jewish historian Josephus. The relationship of the dramatic action to historical events is, however, tenuous. History does not mention Quinault's leading woman, the usurping queen Elise, whose role amply justifies Boileau's quip. Whilst she wants to hold on to power for the benefit of Astrate, the man she loves, her love for him is so great that she prefers to relinquish power and commit suicide in order to save his endangered life:

> J'aime encore moins que lui la vie et la couronne
> Et le danger qu'il court est le seul qui m'étonne.
> Il faut qu'un prompt trépas qui soit tout de ma main
> Luy sauve des forfaits qu'il pourrait faire en vain.
>
> (v.i, lines 1435–8)

(I love life and the crown much less than I love him, and the danger he faces is the only one that alarms me. With a prompt death by my own hand I must spare him the crimes which he might commit in vain.)

---

6 Nicolas Boileau, *Œuvres*, vol. I, ed. Jérôme Vercruysse (Paris: Garnier-Flammarion, 1969), p. 64.

The predominance of romantic love is similarly visible in the plays written by the few women dramatists of the period. Marie-Catherine Desjardins (c. 1640–83), otherwise known as the novelist Mme de Villedieu, had her most successful play *Manlius* staged at the Hôtel de Bourgogne just three years before *Astrate* in 1662. It draws on an episode of Roman history as recounted by Livy, but the ancient material is significantly reworked to allow for the incorporation of a strong dose of *galanterie*. Desjardins invents the role of the captive Latin princess Omphale and makes the Roman consul Torquatus and his son Manlius rivals for her affections. And she ends her play, feeding her audience's appetite for romance, by making Torquatus spare his son's life and by marrying Manlius to Omphale at a point at which, in history, Manlius died.

Racine learnt the lessons of his elders and contemporaries. We know, for instance, that he owned and annotated a copy of *La Pratique du théâtre*. He perfected the art of bolstering his literary reputation with learned references to his ancient source material, whilst deftly adapting that material for his modern audiences, and in particular inventing roles for young female characters, who then become instrumental in establishing the emotional tenor of the play. What Racine adds to his tragedies by doing this is an emotional range that is particularly characteristic of his plays.

Racine delights in presenting, as his audiences must have delighted in watching, the display of sexual jealousy with all its aches, torments, and perils. *Britannicus* (1669) is on one level a play depicting an episode in Roman history as recounted by Tacitus: the Emperor Néron's assassination by poison of his half-brother Britannicus whom Agrippine, Néron's mother, was threatening to make emperor in his place. It is a drama of political intrigue in an imperial palace. But it is much more than that, thanks to Racine's additions. He has invented the character of Junie and created a mutual love between her and Britannicus. Crucially, he has also made Néron fall in love with Junie and, as Néron is all-powerful and a monster in embryo, Racine makes him kidnap Junie, so ensuring that political intrigue mixes potently with sexual rivalry. Néron is driven not only by the desire to assert his political authority but also, simultaneously, by a jealous desire for Junie. Racine attempts, in his preface, to justify her existence with reference to a Junia Calvina in Tacitus' history. This is a smokescreen. Junie is entirely Racine's invention and one which allows the dramatist to paint the chilling sadism of his powerful and lustful emperor: 'J'aimais jusques aux pleurs que je faisais couler' ('I loved even the tears that I caused to flow') (II.2, line 402).

Racine's tragedies often derive their power from the portrayal of the dark side of human sexual urges when these are combined with the exercise of political authority. In *Phèdre* the eponymous heroine has a wrongful accusation made against her stepson Hippolyte, whom she desperately desires. Her conscience leads her to want to clear his name. But when she learns of his and Aricie's mutual love, she is stricken with sexual jealousy and allows her false accusation to stand. This is the emotional climax of the tragedy (iv.5–6), and it owes nothing to Racine's illustrious predecessors, Euripides and Seneca. Like Junie, Aricie is the dramatist's own invention and she allows him to maximise his appeal to the audience's emotions of pity and fear, which tragedy properly seeks to arouse. Racine certainly participates in his contemporaries' desire to depict amorous love on the stage, but he explores its more terrifying facets and relates it, far more than Quinault or Thomas Corneille ever did, to the heart-rending emotions of tragedy.

Plot, poetry, and performance

Writing plays like this was very much an art that depended on constructing a plot in such a way as to play off suspense and surprise so as to keep delivering the emotional blows that La Bruyère's description of the experience so evocatively conjures up. In terms of plot construction, Racine's *Bérénice* (1670) is a masterpiece. With the most minimal material – the Roman Emperor Titus and queen of Judea Bérénice love each other, but Bérénice has to leave Titus because the Romans will not allow their emperor to marry a foreign queen; and Antiochus, who loves her, but is not loved in return, has to leave empty-handed too – the dramatist piles up suspense, uncertainty, dilemma, and surprise until it looks as if all three characters are on the point of committing suicide, before Bérénice's sudden and surprising grasp of the reality of their predicament and her concluding acceptance of the sad separation that all three of them must now suffer.

This skilful construction of the plays' macrostructure is matched by a similarly skilful construction of their microstructure. For all that plays were supposed to create an illusion of reality for audiences, they were, by convention, written in verse, mostly in rhyming couplets of alexandrines. Prompted no doubt by a frequent seventeenth-century term for a tragedy, 'poème tragique', as well as by the verse form, much subsequent admiration for the genre has dwelt on its poetic as opposed to its theatrical qualities. All too frequently in the hands of the less skilful dramatic poet, the verses labour along their weary and monotonous path. Racine's rival Nicolas Pradon (1632–98), who in the spirit of the times wrote a *Phèdre et Hippolyte* to compete against Racine's play on the same subject (Racine's at the Hôtel de Bourgogne, Pradon's at the Hôtel Guénégaud), makes his heroine, shortly after first entering, draw attention to her distress in one sentence contained in two rhyming couplets. The third line deploys a neat (but too often used) antithesis, and the third and fourth lines are padded with relative clauses of increasing banality:

> Princesse, vous voyez une Reyne affligée
> Dans les plus noirs chagrins mortellement plongée,
> Qui ne peut plus se taire, & qui n'ose parler,
> Et qui cherche par tout qui peut la consoler.
>
> (1.3, lines 217–20)

(Princess, you see an afflicted queen, mortally plunged into the blackest despair, who can no longer remain silent, and who dares not speak, and who looks everywhere for someone who might console her.)

This is lazy and undramatic writing, and quite different from Racine's varied sentence structure and contrasting rhetorical devices in the equivalent four lines he writes for his own heroine:

> Que ces vains ornements, que ces voiles me pèsent!
> Quelle importune main, en formant tous ces nœuds,
> A pris soin sur mon front d'assembler mes cheveux?
> Tout m'afflige et me nuit, et conspire à me nuire.
>
> (1.3, lines 158–61)

(How these vain ornaments, how these veils weigh me down! What importunate hand has created these knots and carefully arranged my hair above my brow? Everything afflicts me and hurts me and conspires to hurt me.)

Both rhythmically and phonetically Racine helps the actress to speak in a way that will convey her derangement and despair for the audience. The best writers of seventeenth-century tragedy can, therefore, make their poetry contribute to the arousal of the emotions of a theatre audience.

The way in which these lines were delivered at the time is, to some extent, lost to us. A long tradition has told us that seventeenth-century tragedies were declaimed in an extremely pompous way and that the comic dramatist and actor Molière (1622–73) tried to revolutionise tragic performance styles in his theatre, the Palais-Royal. It is true that Molière, in addition to starring in comedies, put on and sometimes acted in tragedies and that, in *L'Impromptu de Versailles* (1663), he seems to have ridiculed the performance style of the Hôtel de Bourgogne for being too bombastic. Molière's troupe first performed Racine's first two plays *La Thébaïde* and *Alexandre le grand* (1665), and the two dramatists fell out spectacularly when Racine offered *Alexandre* to the Hôtel de Bourgogne while it was still being performed by Molière. The usual explanation is that Racine, with high ambitions, seized the opportunity to have his play performed by the troupe most renowned for tragic acting. The truth is, however, that all acting in the seventeenth century, including Molière's comic performances, was declamatory, that is to say it made use of a special kind of pronunciation and intonation and a highly visual gestural code, the better to communicate with audiences in testing performance conditions, and less conducive to concentrated listening than those of theatres today.

French tragedy of the period was not the disembodied abstract poetry that posterity (especially Anglo-Saxon posterity, accustomed to the effervescent rumbustiousness of Shakespearian theatre) has sometimes believed it to be. Dramatists had direct dealings with troupes of actors when trying to sell them their scripts. Racine was allegedly very keen on coaching his leading actresses. Even if the action of tragedies at this date takes place before a single unchanging decor, dramatists can be aware of the decor and exploit it for dramatic effects. The Emperor Titus' agonising dilemma is emotionally intensified for the audience when he has to choose between Bérénice and the Roman Empire by exiting through either the door to her apartment or the door that will take him to meet the tribunes, consuls, and senate (IV.8). Any sense that these tragedies are staidly decorous is countered by the image of Phèdre inviting the astonished Hippolyte to plunge his sword into her breast, then wresting it herself from its sheath (II.4).

Tragedy and music

It is true that such visual excitements are subdued in comparison with the spectacular extravaganza of tragic opera. This genre, new in the 1670s, is an amalgam of tragedy, machine plays (spoken plays with complex sets and much machinery, such as Pierre Corneille's *Andromède* of 1650), court ballet, and the so-called *comédie-ballet* as practised in the 1660s by Molière and court musician Jean-Baptiste Lully (1632–87). The ambitious Lully broke away from Molière and acquired the monopoly on musical entertainments in Paris. He persuaded Quinault to turn from spoken tragedy and write, between 1673 and 1686, eleven libretti for Lully to orchestrate. Performed at phenomenal expense first at court, then on the stage of the Palais-Royal (after Molière's death in 1673), with huge casts, hosts of singers and dancers, numerous changes of set, river scenes, and deities flying through the air, *tragédies en musique* such as *Alceste* (1674) and *Atys* (1676) appeared to offer the public much more than spoken tragedy. And it is possible to interpret Racine's choice of *Iphigénie* in 1674, with its subtly supernatural dimension and its polemical preface, both as a gesture towards the kind of material that the new opera might favour and a vigorous assertion of the superiority (in his eyes) of spoken drama with its challenging mixture of *vraisemblance* (so blatantly flouted in opera) and the pursuit of the true tragic passions of pity and fear.

Racine's last answer to his musical rivals was to come, unexpectedly, in the form of two tragedies on biblical subjects, *Esther* (1689) and *Athalie* (1691), written for performance by the schoolgirls of Saint-Cyr at the request of Louis XIV's wife Mme de Maintenon, some years after his abandonment of the public theatre in 1677. Spoken tragedies continued to be written and performed in the 1680s and 1690s by dramatists such as Jean-Galbert de Campistron (1656–1723), whose plays, such as *Arminius* (1684), aim at effects of pathos by showing characters in situations of entrapment, but have none of the dramatic poetry of Racine's earlier successes. With *Esther* and *Athalie*, Racine was breaking new ground. Although the theme is biblical, the religious dimension creates a link with the supposed religious origins of Greek tragedy. And like Greek tragedy, these plays deploy both a dramatic action in the Aristotelian mould that aims to arouse pity and fear, and sung choruses between the acts. They therefore constitute Racine's ultimate response to tragic opera and, by his lights, his most successful re-creation of Greek-style tragedy. As he says in the preface to *Esther* (p. 946):

> Je m'aperçus qu'en travaillant sur le plan qu'on m'avait donné, j'exécutais en quelque sorte un dessein qui m'avait souvent passé par l'esprit, qui était de lier, comme dans les anciennes tragédies grecques, le chœur et le chant avec l'action, et d'employer à chanter les louanges du vrai Dieu cette partie du chœur que les païens employaient à chanter les louanges de leurs fausses divinités.

> (I noticed that, whilst working from the plan I had been given, I was in a sense bringing to fruition an idea that had often passed through my mind, which was to join together, as in ancient Greek tragedy, chorus and singing with the action, and to employ for the purpose of singing the praise of the true God that part of the chorus which the pagans used to sing the praise of their false gods.)

These unusual plays can be seen as the climax of Racine's (and his century's) experimentations with tragic form. But the unusual circumstances for which they were composed and the increasingly austere nature of Louis XIV's court ensured that they had no immediate successors. If the courtiers and theatre-goers of the late seventeenth century were swayed by the glittering charms of musical opera, it is the spoken tragedy of the period, and most notably Racine's profane plays, that best mirrored those intense passions that are common to all humanity, but that provide a peculiarly compelling and moving spectacle when they are seen to govern the behaviour of people in positions of power and authority.

31

Seventeenth-century comedy

LARRY F. NORMAN

Comedy and French Classicism

The full view of seventeenth-century comedy and its wide array of playwrights has sometimes been obstructed in literary history by the pre-eminence of its single greatest representative, Molière. This is something of an exception. If we turn to tragedy, the parity of Corneille and Racine levels the field for broader considerations of the genre; as for the *moralistes*, the traditional grouping together of authors such as Pascal, La Rochefoucauld and La Bruyère allows no single figure to obscure the whole; and the stark absence at the time of a great French epic poet opens that genre to the widest, if most purely theoretical, accounts. Fortunately for comedy, the experimental genius of Molière managed to assemble in a single corpus a remarkable range of the comic forms that flourished around him. High literary comedy or physical farce, biting social satire or gently elegant pastoral, modern setting or ancient, verse or prose or musically interspersed *comédie-ballet*, one-act or three-act or five-act, the playwright's work would seem to exceed even the exhaustive generic catalogue detailed by *Hamlet*'s Polonius. Beyond questions of theatrical form, Molière's subject matter similarly spans a vast spectrum, from the courtiers that surrounded the Sun King (*Les Fâcheux*, *L'Impromptu de Versailles*) to the beggar in the forest (*Dom Juan*), from Latin-spouting university professors and pedantic poets (*Le Mariage forcé*, *Les Femmes savantes*) to the most education-deprived servant or sequestered girl (*L'École des femmes*).

If Molière overshadows his contemporaries, his expansive approach to comedy nevertheless perfectly demonstrates the formidable capaciousness possessed at the time by the genre as a whole. In an age dubbed 'Classical', where literary and theatrical works were subject to strict rules of formal order (the dramatic unities, regular alexandrine verse), decorum, and moral propriety, comedy seems to resist such constraints. Given that the neo-Aristotelian poetics of the day placed comedy high on the literary pyramid as one of the three great genres (with tragedy and epic), those constraints could certainly be strict. But unlike the elevated genres of tragedy and epic, set according to convention in the aggrandising haze of distant times or lands, comedy has as one of its poetic requirements a powerfully liberating mandate: to portray faithfully the daily life of its own time. This adherence to the here and now of contemporary society poses a real challenge to certain ideals of Classical aesthetics and culture. The close resemblance between the subject matter depicted on stage and the audience viewing it, indeed the possible confusion of the two, allows for little of the hermetically sealed perfection, universalised abstraction, and reflective distance that the century so often valued in art. Furthermore, the realistic representation of widely disparate classes, of high and low culture – seen in conflict, or perhaps more troubling, in surprising equality – disturbs the period's conceptions of fixed social hierarchies and of a unified cultural elite.

There is also the troubling matter of laughter. Tragedy provokes its own visceral response in the form of tears; but these, as Racine observed in his preface to *Bérénice*, may be decorously experienced as a seemly 'majestic sadness' (*tristesse majestueuse*). Comedy less easily accommodates social form. As Molière remarked, 'c'est une étrange entreprise que celle de faire rire les honnêtes gens' ('it is a strange business to make respectable people laugh').[1] That he and his fellow playwrights accomplished this unlikely feat, and to such applause, may suggest that comic theatre thrived at the margins of Classical culture; that, as Erich Auerbach remarked, it 'staked out the limits of what was possible at the time.'[2] Or perhaps the supple reach of comedy simply reveals the surprisingly broad latitude allowed to literature and drama at the time, effectively illustrating what has been called the paradoxical 'freedom of French Classicism'.[3] Before further consideration, though, we might ask to what degree a genre of such wide-ranging scope may even be accounted a coherent subject for study.

An evolving genre?

The early seventeenth century, arriving after the decline of Renaissance humanist comedy, left little mark on the history of the genre. But by 1630

---

1 *La Critique de L'École de Femmes*, scene vi, in Molière, *Œuvres complètes*, 2 vols., ed. G. Forestier (Paris: Pléiade, 2010), vol. i, p. 505.
2 E. Auerbach, *Mimesis*, trans. W. Trask (Princeton, NJ: Princeton University Press, 1953), p. 365.
3 E. B. O. Borgerhoff, *The Freedom of French Classicism* (Princeton, NJ: Princeton University Press, 1950).

a dramatic change was underway. The coming decade saw the tripling of permanent Paris theatres (albeit from just one to three), the growth of an elite theatre public, and the conferral of state-sponsored prestige on dramatic works and on their authors by Richelieu and the newly founded Académie Française (1635). Comedy was integral to this spectacular rise of theatre. Indeed, the name most associated with France's new drama, Pierre Corneille, began his career in 1629 with a comedy, *Mélite*, which the playwright dubbed revolutionary in its modernity. The radical newness of the play, which, according to the typically immodest Corneille in his 1660 'Examen', had no precedent in any language, lay in its adherence to the manners and speech of his elegantly gallant audience, in its 'natural style, which created a picture of the conversation of cultivated people'. Although in the following six years Corneille pursued this new style of comedy with a series of plays exploring the nuanced psychology of love in a realistic and elite Parisian setting, his approach was not to dominate the rest of the century; indeed he rapidly abandoned the project himself.

The decades that follow have often been divided into three identifiable periods. First, the 1640s and 50s saw a taste for plot-based comedies rich in the intrigues and adventures typical of prose romances, pastorals, and tragicomedies. Although the models for these works were sometimes Classical or Italian (as in the case of Jean Rotrou), Spanish Golden Age theatre exercised a powerful sway, most notably on Corneille (with his 1643 *Le Menteur* adapted from Alarcón) and on Paul Scarron, whose burlesque master/valet reversals in plays such as *Jodelet ou le maître valet* (1645) proved powerfully influential. A new period opens around 1660. Molière's first Parisian comedies, from the 1659 *Les Précieuses ridicules* to the 1662 *École des femmes*, firmly established the predominance of his trademark character-based comedy (*comédie de caractère*), featuring keenly satirical but artfully generalised types drawn from contemporary society. After Molière's death in 1673, the genre is often seen as struggling in the shadow of past glory, and tending towards a final phase of post-Classical cynicism in the sometimes biting, sometimes fanciful comedy of manners of Baron (*L'Homme à bonne fortune*, 1686), Dancourt (*Le Chevalier à la mode*, 1687) and Regnard (*Le Joueur*, 1696).

But such a rigid periodisation can hardly account for the untidy mix of productions ranging throughout the century. Although differing decades see shifts in tastes, the comic toolbox available to playwrights remains relatively stable. Thus, while Molière's career may represent the apogee of the comedy of character, the form was pioneered in France much earlier with Desmarets de Saint-Sorlin's 1637 *Les Visionnaires*, a comic menagerie of monomaniacal types from which Molière later borrowed. Likewise, the acid satire of contemporary life can hardly be considered the invention of the latter part of the century: Charles de Saint-Évremond's cruel mockery of the French Academy in 1643 (*La Comédie des académistes*), published belatedly and anonymously owing to its libellous use of real names, proves the contrary. And although we may think of Molière as a master satirist, his repeated recourse to pastoral and gallantly romantic comedies (e.g. *La Princesse d'Elide* [1664], *Mélicerte* [1666]) demonstrates that forms rooted in the earlier century continued to please later. Finally, thriving throughout the period, although decidedly outside generic norms, were two vital forces: French farce, inherited from the Middle Ages and performed both in one-act form on stage and in improvised routines on the streets (most notably by Tabarin in the 1630s), and the Italian *commedia dell'arte*, whose stock characters and conventional comic tricks (*lazzi*) were particularly influential on Molière.

Turning from practice to theory, certain cohesive strands can also be identified throughout the century. Commentators and critics almost universally defined comedy in relation to tragedy; the two genres were generally subject to the same rules, such as those of unity of time, place, and action. Comedy was therefore largely conceived as something of a mere variation on tragic form. Indeed, the very element we might most closely associate with comedy, laughter itself, played a relatively minor role in critical treatises. Likewise, the denouement of the comedy, its traditional happy ending, did not by itself distinguish it from tragedy. Some of the most successful tragic works of the period, after all, concluded with surprisingly felicitous reconciliations (e.g. Corneille's 1640 *Cinna*). Comedy, in parallel, did not always finish as convention dictates. Although Molière faced sharp criticism for the bitterly unhappy end suffered by his leading character, Arnolphe, in *L'École des femmes*, it did not prevent him from pursuing the same dark path with *Dom Juan* (1665) and *Le Misanthrope* (1666).

Despite the porous border between tragedy and comedy, commentators did of course differentiate the two. The key distinction to emerge can be summed up as follows: tragedy depicts elevated, extraordinary characters and events whose believability is guaranteed by history or myth; comedy, in contrast, depicts quotidian and lifelike characters and events that are invented by the author. As the learned playwright Jean Mairet remarked in the 1631 preface to his *La Sylvanire*, the plot of comedy is 'entirely made up, and yet entirely verisimilar'. This definition, however, is not uncontested. Later in his career, for example, Corneille experimented with the *comédie héroïque*, a dramatic form inherited in part from tragi-comedy and depicting the private lives of noble figures, sometimes including those drawn directly from ancient history (*Don Sanche d'Aragon* [1649], *Tite et Bérénice* [1670]). *Comédie héroïque* is distinguished from tragedy simply by the crucial absence of what Corneille called *péril de mort*, a life-threatening crisis that would inspire tragic pathos. This subgenre, in which 'comedy' suggests merely a lessening of tragic tension, encountered some success, although Molière famously failed in his 1661 attempt (*Dom Garcie de Navarre*) at this loftier form.

Such depictions of characters defined as noble (in terms of both social rank and moral virtue) demonstrate how far French seventeenth-century criticism had veered from Aristotle's definition of comedy as depicting humans 'as worse . . . than in actual life' (*Poetics*, ch. 2). Corneille set his sights considerably higher in *Mélite*, already noted, where he claimed in his later 'Examen' to have rid comedy of 'ridiculous characters' and depicted 'people of a condition above those found in the comedies of Plautus and Terence'. What Corneille proclaimed as radical innovation, however, soon became conventional wisdom. By the second half of the century, even the most impassioned defenders of antiquity during the Quarrel of the Ancients and Moderns embraced this modern approach, significantly raising the reach of comic representation: Boileau's 1674 *Art poétique* urges the depiction of a variety of social conditions from both the aristocratic 'court' and the more bourgeois 'town'; even the great Classical philologist Anne Dacier manages artfully to cite Aristotle while actually contradicting him in a passage where she defines good comedy as 'painting' humans not as 'worse', but instead exactly 'as they are' in real life.[4]

Comic realism from high to low

This taste for wide-ranging comic realism most often expressed itself, as Dacier's remarks show, through the metaphor of pictorial representation, considered more direct and transparent than other media. We have already seen the analogy at work in Corneille's vaunted 'picture' of real conversation, a visual immediacy characterised by an unadorned, frank (*naïf*) style. (It should be noted that the seventeenth-century forerunner of the realistic novel, the *roman comique*, also defined itself by the 'naïve' freshness of its depictions of daily life.[5]) By the second half of the century, this naturalist aesthetic tended towards an idealised elimination of art itself: the 'public mirrors' of comedy, as Molière phrased it, were most effective when mistaken for life.[6] When,

4 A. Dacier, Preface to *Les Comédies de Térence* (Paris, 1688), p. 6.
5 E.g. Charles Sorel, *Histoire comique de Françion* (Paris, 1633), bk 10, pp. 486–7.
6 *La Critique*, scene vi, in Molière, *Œuvres complètes*, vol. I, p. 503.

for example, the influential critic René Rapin defined comedy as 'an image of common life', he identified the artistic 'image' so strongly with its model in reality that the spectator should no longer be able to distinguish one from the other: 'comedy is as it should be when one believes oneself to be in a group of neighbours or at a family gathering when one is viewing a play, and when one sees nothing there but what one sees in the real world'.[7] Or as Boileau said of good comedy in his *Art poétique*: 'Ce n'est pas un portrait, une image semblable; / C'est un amant, un fils, un père véritable' ('It is no longer a portrait, a lifelike image; / It is a lover, a son, a real father'). The perceived fluidity between stage and life was further accentuated by the tremendous interest that the leisured public displayed in all things theatrical. Playwrights such as Corneille (*L'Illusion comique* [1636]) and Georges de Scudéry (*La Comédie des comédiens* [1634]) responded to this passion by crafting comedies about theatre itself. Beyond such metatheatrical experiments, many other comedies, reflecting the fashions of the day, portrayed their characters as impassioned theatre-goers. Thus Corneille's 1632 *Galerie du palais* features a scene in which the characters not only discuss contemporary drama, but also allude, as one would expect at the time, to the rising star of Corneille himself (I, vii). Molière made such self-references a staple of his comedy; his characters, well abreast of the playwright's success and correctly sensing themselves to be ripe targets for mockery, frequently rail at the satirist's punch. Indeed, in the wake of *L'École des femmes*, Molière penned two plays entirely about the public reaction to his comedies: one portrays a typical Parisian salon debating his work (*La Critique de l'École des femmes*); the other presents the playwright himself directing his troupe while interacting with passing courtiers (*L'Impromptu de Versailles*). It is important to note that aside from the reflexivity of such plays, the dizzying interplay of representation and reality was also facilitated at the time by the relatively informal state of theatrical productions. Indeed, with minimal decor and lighting, and with audience members seated on stage next to the performing actors – who were frequently all dressed in the same fashion – it is no surprise that there were reports of spectators being mistaken for characters in comedies.

This blurring of art and life naturally alarmed those wishing to keep comedy on its poetic pedestal. The author of the century's most influential critical treatise on theatre, the abbé d'Aubignac, went so far in his defence of proper aesthetic distance as to recommend that comedy represent only times and places safely distanced from those of the audience, thus allowing no such

---

7 R. Rapin, *Réflexions sur la poétique de ce temps* (Paris, 1674), ch. 25, pp. 114–15.

confusion.[8] The ancient demon of direct, libellous satire – and of Old Comedy, infamous for Aristophanes' ridiculing of Socrates – threatened to return with its dangerously topical reflection of contemporary society and politics. Comedy struck some as less an artful portrait of the times than an artless transcription of the day. Critics accused Molière of travelling about town copying word-for-word overheard conversations and then constructing his plays from nothing but these scribbled records (*mémoires*). Orality appeared to vanquish textuality. Furthermore, the emphasis on physical imitation, on the actors' tone of voice, gestures, and expressions, threatened to drag comedy from timeless literature to fleeting performance. The theatrical intensity of the genre reached a new pitch with one of Molière's most influential innovations, the *comedie-ballet*, a form he pioneered with the leading composers of his day (first Lully, then Charpentier) and which ingeniously wove into the play's plot and character development musical and dance interludes. It is indicative of comedy's capaciousness that it could so seamlessly incorporate other performing arts; in contrast, the emerging form of French opera (elevated by the same composers) faced ferocious opposition from the defenders of traditional verse tragedy. Given the gamut of the theatrical devices employed by comedy, however, it was easy to dismiss its literary status. Did not Molière himself (despite his likely ambitions as a published author) belittle the printing and reading of his plays, insisting that 'comedies are made only to be performed'?[9]

By the end of the century, La Bruyère was left decrying comedy for abandoning the high poetic mission of mimesis, its careful selection and correction of subject matter, for what he deemed a mere stage rehearsal of realistic ephemera, a performance as transitory as life itself. To those who demanded only 'natural' characters, he responded:

> According to this rule, the audience would soon be amused with a lackey whistling, or an invalid sleeping or vomiting: is there anything more natural? It is the nature of an effeminate man to rise late, to spend part of his day at his *toilette*, to look in the mirror, to perfume himself . . . Put this role on stage. The longer you make it last, one act, two acts, the more it will be natural and resemble its model; but also the more it will be dull and insipid.[10]

La Bruyère's list of unfit topics suggests that comic portrayals anywhere on the social spectrum, from low (the idle lackey) to high (courtly fop), could

---

8 Abbé d'Aubignac, *La Pratique du théâtre* (1657) (Amsterdam, 1715), bk 1, ch. 7, p. 40.
9 Preface ('Au lecteur') to *L'Amour médecin* (1665), in Molière, *Œuvres complètes*, vol. 1, p. 603.
10 'Des ouvrages de l'esprit', no. 52, in Jean de la Bruyère, *Les Charactères*, ed. E. Bury (Paris: Classiques de Poche, 1995), pp. 146–7.

disturb. As for the lower end, the critics were principally concerned with questions of propriety. Boileau's *Art poétique* typifies the period's criticism in repeatedly blaming indecency on the tastes of the 'masses' ('le peuple' and 'la populace'). Aside from matters of decorum, however, few seemed troubled by the social or political implications of comedy's depiction, for example, of the searing class resentments expressed by characters of lower rank, from Corneille's waiting-maid in *La Suivante* (c. 1634), to the more colourful railing against aristocratic privilege in Molière's *George Dandin* (1668), a play that was performed at Versailles with no controversy. That servants often got the better of their masters provoked little of the kind of excitement Beaumarchais's Figaro would in the coming century.

When, on the other hand, we move up the social ladder to comic portrayals of the powerful, there could be considerably more consternation. The lower aristocracy, if not specifically named, were nevertheless fair game under the absolutist regime. As Montesquieu later remarked, satire best flourishes under monarchy: few but the king have the power to punish its audacity.[11] Mocking the royal family itself, on the other hand, was a very dangerous business, as the Italian troupe learned in 1697 after performing what was viewed as a veiled lampoon (*La Fausse Prude*) of the king's second wife, Madame de Maintenon. As for the bourgeoisie, the established professions were rich targets for comedy: Molière made a business of mocking medicine; Racine devoted his sole comedy, *Les Plaideurs* (1668), to a merciless parody of the law courts; and university professors and professional writers were universally deemed fit fodder for ridicule. One institution, however, effectively claimed exemption: the church – as Molière learned with the censorship of his two plays mocking religious hypocrisy, *Tartuffe* (banned 1664–9) and *Dom Juan* (banned in 1665 and never published in his lifetime). In the end, comedy's reach was not boundless.

Laughter and its effects

In his preface to *Tartuffe*, Molière blamed the censoring of the play not on any heterodox philosophy it might appear to espouse, but instead on the uncomfortable laugher it produced. Religious zealots, he contended, simply could not bear to laugh at themselves, and would not allow others to do so. But just who laughed at comedy? Why and to what end? We have seen

---

11 Montesquieu, *De l'Esprit des lois* (1748), in *Œuvres complètes*, ed. A. Masson, 3 vols. (Paris: Nagel, 1950), I, bk 12, ch. 13, p. 267.

that critical treatises gave little attention to laughter; even a dramatist like Corneille insisted that comedy could be effective without it. Nevertheless, most playwrights, being pragmatists at heart, embraced hilarity as essential to a comedy's success; the decorous Racine, for example, even while roundly condemning improper and suggestive humour, declared in his preface to *Les Plaideurs* that 'the aim of my comedy was to make people laugh', and congratulated himself on brilliantly succeeding in the task. One way to accommodate laughter to the higher aims of comedy was to reduce its raucousness. Boileau's *Art poétique* recommended a 'laughter without bile' ('rire sans aigreur'), and prefers the 'pleasant and subtle' ('l'agréable et le fin') to jovial buffoonery ('le bouffon'). Molière included a preface to his *Le Misanthrope* (penned by Donneau de Visé) conceding that 'one laughs less loudly' at the comedy's subtleties, but boasting that one laughs more philosophically, with a 'laughter of the mind' ('rire dans l'âme').

Philosophy and laughter, then, need not contend. The age, after all, was fond of the ancient adage *castigat ridendo mores*, encapsulating the punitive power of laughter to correct manners and morals. But according to what mysterious criterion did laughter choose its targets? The anonymous 1667 'Lettre sur la comédie de l'Imposteur', a defence of *Tartuffe* that was likely indicative of Molière's thinking, offered a response in perfect keeping with the rationalist spirit of the age. The risible (*ridicule*) is nothing but the exterior, visible sign of the unreasonable or the inappropriate; the laughter it produces providentially reveals a logical fault that might otherwise go unnoticed and unpunished. Molière's comedies, however, sometimes suggest that the most reliable standard against which the laughable was measured was in fact based not on abstract universal reason, but instead on arbitrary societal norms. So it is that Alceste, the eponymous hero of *Le Misanthrope*, bemoans the haughty laughter of the social insiders around him who mock the absent for their oddities (II, iv). He makes a charge against the amorality and unjustness of laughter that Rousseau would take up in the next century, aiming it in turn against Molière himself and his successors. According to the philosopher's 1758 *Lettre à d'Alembert*, Molière aimed to please the prevailing tastes and to comfort the collective prejudices of his elite audience; the applause he sought thus depended on mocking the marginalised and ridiculing the alienated, even if it meant flattering popular vice at the expense of lonely virtue.

In retrospect, though, we have little evidence demonstrating the social or moral effects produced on the audience by comedy, be it in the service of idealised reason or of mere social convention. Some claimed that Molière's mockery of the literary mannerisms of the day (*préciosité*) helped end a cultural fad. This has been contested. In any case, one could certainly argue that the end of the century offered no signs of a marked decline of pedantry, hypocrisy, or miserliness, despite being the targets of countless comedies. The debate over the corrective power of comedy may never be resolved. But even if we admit such limitations, the genre proves resilient. In the face of comedy's perceived social inefficacy, a number of other, non-prescriptive functions of laughter have been elucidated over the years. Some critics view comic laughter as an eruptive force of intellectual play, a carnivalesque reversal of reason and norms, as intense as it is artfully self-contained. This perspective places the seventeenth century in a continuous line from Rabelais to Ionesco. Others regard comedy as a pure form of artistic pleasure, an ingenious theatrical mechanism for producing laughter. This school of thought certainly accords with the pragmatic approach of French Classical writers and their attachment to the audience. Finally, comedy's supposed ineffectuality may serve to expose the weaknesses of the audience itself, revealing a certain human incapacity for self-correction even when presented with the most spectacular evidence of ridiculous faults. Comedy's apparent failure thus proves paradoxically illuminating. This last view of comedy, and its somewhat perverse utility, would have no doubt pleased the century of the *moralistes* and their piercing, if pessimistic, lucidity.

32

Seventeenth-century poetry

ALAIN GÉNETIOT

In his verse comedy *Clymène* (published in 1671), La Fontaine (1621–95) portrays a Mount Parnassus plagued by boredom: Apollo deplores that no one knows how to compose good love poems anymore, while the Muse Urania bluntly announces the death of poetry, a divine language that has fallen into the hands of rhymesters. Reflecting a satirical commonplace, this scene nonetheless has symptomatic value in the age of Classicism insofar as it manifests the feeling that the Orphic poetry which was the dream of the Renaissance has been lost.

La Fontaine's *Avertissement* to his *Songe de Vaux* (1671) similarly diagnoses the rapid degradation of the grand genres during the decade that has passed since Fouquet commissioned the work: 'lyric and heroic poetry . . . are no longer in vogue now as they were then'.[1] But at the same time *Clymène* proves by example the abundance and variety of poetic genres and forms, illustrating the subject assigned by Apollo with an eclogue, a ballad, a dizain, and a verse narrative.

Likewise, Boileau (1636–1711) devotes the second canto of his *Art poétique* (1674), which imitates Horace, to a catalogue of the lyric genres of the time, including some minor ones, thus documenting the diversity of the forms, both fixed and open, which poets have at their disposal to address all kinds of subjects in a wide range of tones. From the cheerful eclogue to the touching elegy and the noble encomiastic ode, Boileau adopts the rhetorical distinction known as the 'wheel of Virgil', formalised in the fourth century by Donatus. On the basis of the three works of Virgil, Donatus had identified for each of the three styles (simple, moderate, and elevated) the respective dramatis personae (from the shepherds of pastoral to the heroes of epic), symbolic imaginary universes (the *locus amoenus* of amorous bliss or the *locus horribilis* of despair), requisite themes (love, death, glory) and more generally a set of topoi, i.e. commonplaces which correspond to the public's horizon of

---

1 Jean de La Fontaine, *Œuvres diverses*, ed. Pierre Clarac (Paris: Gallimard, 1958), p. 78.

expectations and fuel the inspiration of the poet who modulates them in his variations.

Such a formal definition is all the more necessary as non-epic, non-dramatic poetry is completely absent from Aristotle's *Poetics* and presents itself in the seventeenth century in a great variety of forms, some of them inherited and revived from antiquity (ode, eclogue, elegy, epistle, satire, epigram), others the products of medieval France (*rondeau*, ballad, *chanson*) or Italy (sonnet), or more recent creations (*stances*, madrigal), and all open to manifold variants.

Taking over from the definitional endeavours of the Renaissance (Sébillet in 1548, Peletier du Mans in 1555, Laudun d'Aigaliers in 1597), the *arts poétiques* of the seventeenth century are characterised by a taxonomical effort which is indicative of the wish to rationalise the creative act, and to subject it to training and precise rules of fabrication. The list of authors in this field ranges from Vauquelin de La Fresnaye in 1605 and Deimier in 1610 to Phérotée de La Croix in 1675–94; in the middle of the century, Guillaume Colletet (1598–1659) published the manual *L'École des Muses* (1652) as well as *L'Art poétique* (1658), which includes a *Traité de l'épigramme* and a *Traité du sonnet*. With the exception of certain specialists of the sonnet and the epigram such as Gombauld (1590?–1666), poets not only practise simultaneously a multitude of forms and genres which are sometimes quite different, with Jean Auvray (1580?–1630?), for example, switching from violent satire to devotional verse; lyric poets also excel in other genres, such as Tristan L'Hermite (1601–55) and Georges de Scudéry (1601–67), both renowned playwrights and novelists, whereas still others, conversely, write poetry only occasionally: thus the dramatists Jean Racine (1639–99), who moves from the encomiastic verse of his youth to the sublime *Cantiques spirituels* (1694), or Pierre Corneille (1606–84) who paraphrases in verse the *Imitation de Jésus-Christ* (1656).

Far from retreating into the isolation of an exclusive and hermetic practice, seventeenth-century poetry engages instead in constant dialogue with other genres and goes to meet the public of *honnêtes gens*, not only through *mondain* (worldly, urbane) poetry but also through religious verse written in the vernacular for the conversion of these very same *mondains*.

The Malherbian reform

Before surveying the poetry of the baroque and Classical age in its diversity and contrasts, it is important to define the common foundation that distinguishes it from that of the Renaissance. The poetic reform of which literary history, following Boileau, 'Enfin Malherbe vint' ('Finally Malherbe arrived'), in *L'Art poétique* (1.131), attributes the paternity to François de Malherbe (1555–1628) consists in a process of modernisation that was latent in the principles stated in Du Bellay's *Deffence*, with its emphasis on the need for nature to be polished by art.

Whereas Ronsard himself had continually revised his own works and while, among his heirs, the gently flowing style of Desportes had prevailed over the boldness of Du Bartas, Malherbe covers an entire copy of Desportes's *Œuvres* with his stylistic corrections, claiming to be an iconoclastic innovator when in fact he simply radicalises and appropriates an evolution already apparent in his contemporaries Bertaut (1552–1611) and Du Perron (1556–1618). In the midst of the baroque, the 'modern' Malherbe invents Classical language by holding poetry to standards of clarity and order, under the rational watch of critical judgement. Through his example and the lessons he imparts to his disciples Racan (1589–1670) and Maynard (1582–1646), he precipitates the decline of the Neoplatonic and Orphic theories of enthusiasm which presented the poet as an inspired prophet and legitimated the audacities of a poetry full of fury and mystery. From this moment on, critical judgement doused the flames of inspired genius; poetry ceased to be an obscure language saturated with hermetic references, especially erudite mythology, in order to become a vehicle for the direct expression of human emotions.

The language of the gods became that of men – and even women – whose native French had not been corrupted by the Latin of the pedants, learned in school. Forty years before the grammarian Vaugelas (1585–1650) published his *Remarques* (1647) on the *bel usage* of polite society, Malherbe, in the name of clarity and propriety, banished archaic and dialectal expressions and above all vulgar and equivocal terms, thus providing French poetry with a tool better suited for the expression of the nuances of sentiment than the realistic description of objects.

This precise and abstract language puts the finishing touches to the image of poetry as a subtle technique whose rules govern metre and stanza, and of poets as 'excellent arrangers of syllables', as Malherbe himself quipped.

This concern for sober elegance, typical of French Classicism, would be further refined in the maxims of Boileau's *Art poétique* before becoming a source of misunderstanding in the international reception of Classicism, and even more so in post-Rimbaud modernity. Following Malherbe, whose example remains valid for the entire century, poetry seeks the (hidden) art of pleasing the public of *honnêtes gens*, the worldly public under construction whose polite and refined taste will from now on influence artistic creation. After the Wars of Religion, which had exacerbated a baroque aesthetic of shocking the senses, the return to political stability was accompanied by an evolution toward the syntactic order and euphonic harmony of a poetry which is oratorical in the best sense of the term, that is to say capable of stirring the passions of the soul in order to please and move.

Heroic and epic poetry

But it is, paradoxically, in the grand Ronsardian genre of the encomiastic ode that Malherbe asserted his mastery, with poetry written in the service of royal grandeur which confers immortality on the hero as well as on the poet who celebrates him. From the *stances* 'Prière pour le roi partant en Limousin' (1605) to the ode 'Pour le roi allant châtier la rébellion des Rochelais' (1627), Malherbe extols the king who crushes the rebels to restore peace, prefacing a new golden age proclaimed in the ode 'À la reine sur les heureux succès de sa régence' (1610).

This political discourse, expressing the need for order at the end of the civil wars, resonates throughout a troubled century in which France was to be involved, first, in the Thirty Years War on account of its rivalry with the Habsburgs, then, under Louis XIV, against the northern powers Holland and England. Yet the seventeenth century, during which absolute monarchy was established, from the ministry of Richelieu to the personal government of Louis XIV, witnessed a decline in grandiloquent ceremonial poetry, despite the still numerous eulogists of the regime such as Boisrobert (1592–1662), a founder of the Académie Française, Chapelain (1595–1674), Desmarets (1595–1676) or Charles Perrault (1628–1703).

The 'beau désordre' ('beautiful disorder') of the Pindaric ode, which Boileau continued to long for, is hardly compatible with the well-ordered composition and oratorical style of Classicism, as exemplified by the failure of his own 'Ode sur la prise de Namur' (1693). Nonetheless, the high poetry of praise, practised by the most prominent writers such as Théophile de Viau (1590–1626) and Tristan L'Hermite, and less and less tied to the formal framework of the ode, remains a must for poets, whose precarious social situation forces them to serve a king, a grandee, or a patron of the arts, the most brilliant of whom is Fouquet, the mid-century Minister of Finance.

Even more patent is the failure of epic poetry. Since antiquity the epic had been at the top of the hierarchy of genres and a touchstone of poetic excellence, but it did not produce in France the equivalent of Tasso or Milton. Commissioned by Richelieu to display the magnificence of France at the time of her entry into the war against Spain (1635), the epic poems which appear in quick succession twenty years later are the works of writers close to the crown. They either celebrate, in Counter-Reformation vein, Christian heroes battling against the infidels, as in *Saint Louis* (1653) by Le Moyne (1602–71), *Saint Paul* (1654) by Godeau (1605–72), and *Alaric* (1654) by Scudéry, or they exalt national history as in Chapelain's *La Pucelle* (1656) or Desmarets's *Clovis* (1657), in accordance with the project of dynastic glorification inherent in epic poetry. The boom would continue under Louis XIV with *Charlemagne* (1664) by Le Laboureur (?–1679) or the biblical epics of Coras (1630–77), whereas Charles Perrault, having already composed *Saint Paulin* (1686), revives the cosmological perspectives of the Renaissance with *Adam ou la création de l'homme* (1697), inspired by Tasso.

An attempt to renew the genre is made by Saint-Amant (1594–1661) whose sacred poem *Moïse sauvé* (1653) borrows from Marino the mixed genre of the 'heroic idyll'; it displays a tension between the aspiration toward the sublime and the realistic description of details which Boileau would condemn as dissonance. La Fontaine himself tried his hand at these various genres: the heroic idyll with *Adonis* (1658), the Christian poem with *La Captivité de saint Malc* (1673), and the medical poem with *Le Quinquina* (1682), a vestige of the humanist tradition of scientific poetry.

Despite these numerous endeavours, the failure of the epic in France is due less to the development of the small *galant* genres than to the rejection of the *romanesque* and to the difficulty of mixing the pagan and the Christian 'merveilleux', as illustrated in 1674 by the quarrel between Desmarets and Boileau, who insists on the exclusion of Christian references from epic poetry.

Religious poetry

The seventeenth century was an age of devotion and produced an important body of religious poetry. At the end of the sixteenth century, the Wars of Religion with their physical horrors and metaphysical upheavals, had exacerbated the sense of precariousness and vanity of human life, fostering a baroque taste for the macabre and funereal. Following the example of Sponde and Chassignet, seventeenth-century poets continued in the tradition of the *memento mori* derived from meditation upon Ecclesiastes, and penitential poetry inspired by the seven penitential psalms.

Enacting a meditative approach similar to the spiritual exercises of Ignatius of Loyola, the *Théorèmes* (1613–22) of La Ceppède (1550?–1623) invite the reader to experience through prayer the stages of the Passion of Christ, paraphrased in a series of 520 sonnets. Representing in every detail the executioners' cruelty, these formally brilliant tragic sonnets aim to rattle the soul of the meditating reader and enjoin him to walk in the steps of Christ and ensure his own salvation. The Recollect friar Zacharie de Vitré adopts the same formula in his *Essais de méditations poétiques* (1659). This 'age of saints' is also marked by great mystical verse influenced by the Spaniards Teresa of Avila and John of the Cross; the poems of the latter are rendered in French verse as part of his *Œuvres spirituelles* (1641) by Cyprien de la Nativité de la Vierge (1605–80). But it is Claude Hopil (1580–1633) who best represents the mystical flight of the spirit by which the poet loses himself in the union with God whom he adores and whose praises he sings in *Les Douces Extases de l'âme spirituelle* (1627) and *Les Divins Élancements d'amour* (1629), in the vein of the Song of Songs.

Similarly, Le Moyne celebrates the mystical wedding between the soul and its creator in his *Hymnes de la sagesse divine et de l'amour divin* (1641), highlighting in his prefatory *Discours* the enthusiasm (or divine possession) of a poetry inspired by the Holy Spirit. During Louis XIV's reign, the *Sonnets chrétiens* (1677) of the Protestant pastor Drelincourt (1626–80) and the *Poésies spirituelles* (1671) of the quietist Malaval (1627–1719) perpetuate the poetry of contemplation.

After the *mondains* are reprimanded an attempt is made to charm them into seeking their salvation in God. Faced with the trials of this world, the stoic consolation of Malherbe gives way to the longing for retreat expressed in Racan's *stances* 'Tircis il faut songer à faire la retraite' (1620), away from the lies and turpitude of the court and the false values of the world.

In the solitude of his final years, Brébeuf (1617–61) likewise devotes his *Entretiens solitaires* (1660) to God. At the same time as the *mondains* are increasingly attracted to the spiritual austerity of Port-Royal, whose Augustinianism was also a source of poetry as in the case of Arnauld d'Andilly (1589–1674), there develops a kind of heroic poetry which takes as its special emblem Mary Magdalene, the converted sinner and mystical bride of Christ, thus combining penitential concern and mystical devotion, in the works of writers like Godeau, Cotin (1604–82), Le Laboureur and Saint-Louis (1626–84).

But it is in the final analysis through liturgy that devotional poetry attains its widest diffusion, striving to reconquer the faithful in the wake of the Counter-Reformation. In the manner of the Huguenot psalm book, Bishop Godeau paraphrases in his *Œuvres chrétiennes* (1633–60) the psalms and then St Paul's epistles for a Catholic audience. Tristan L'Hermite put into verse the *Office de la Sainte Vierge* (1646), as did Corneille the *Imitation de Jésus-Christ* (1656) and the *Office de la Sainte Vierge* (1670), and Racine the *Cantiques spirituels* (1694).

That the greatest writers thus personally appropriate the songs and prayers of liturgy attests to the period's high spiritual consciousness, which has as its most marked anthology Port-Royal's *Recueil de poésies chrétiennes et diverses* (1671), edited by La Fontaine.

Satirical and comic poetry

But not all the poetry of the *grand siècle* is uniformly elevated, noble, or serious. The same concern for truth that underlies the praise of God or the king can motivate a discourse of blame censuring falsehood and vice in vehement or ironic tones. Since antiquity the task of noble satire, in the tradition of Horace, had been to propose a type of comic moral poetry which mocked vice without directly attacking individuals; Juvenal offered a more mordant version of this. Following in their footsteps, Mathurin Régnier (1573–1613) composed 'regular' satires, in rhymed couplets of alexandrines, on conventional situations (the *poète crotté*, the *fâcheux*, the ridiculous banquet) but adapted to the mores of the day.

Illustrious satirists include Du Lorens (1580–1655), Furetière (1619–88), and Boileau, who made an eminently personal use of the genre, including even *ad hominem* attacks on those that he denounces (for the attention of posterity) as bad writers. But there is another, more violent type of satire, inspired by the Italian pasquinades, which rails against the corruption of the times in forceful images: it is exemplified by Sigogne (1560?–1611), Motin (1566?–1612?), d'Esternod (1592–1640), or the 'Norman Satirists' Sonnet de Courval (1577–1627), Angot de l'Eperonnière (1581–1637), and Auvray. A favourite motif is the hatred heaped upon the figure of the old crone, on the model of the counter-blazon; this misogynistic poetry resurfaces in Boileau's satire X against women.

The years 1610–20 see a flurry of obscene poetry, full of vigour and vitality, which flourished in printed collections of 'free' and cabaret verse; this rebellious poetry ceased, however, after the trial of the *Parnasse des poètes satyriques* (1622), attributed to Théophile de Viau who was persecuted, burned in effigy and imprisoned in 1623 for alleged 'libertinage'.

But comic verve in the wake of Rabelais's linguistic invention persists in Saint-Amant, whose baroque aesthetic of *caprice* injects diversity, fantasy, and the motley manner of Montaigne (proceeding 'by leaps and gambols') into a carefree poetry of self-amusement, tuned to the motifs of idleness, the pleasures of the table, and wine. On the occasion of his *Passage de Gibraltar* (1643), a 'caprice héroï-comique' that blends epic with comedy, Saint-Amant launched the word 'burlesque' to designate a motley mix which exploits the clash between different stylistic registers.

But it is Scarron (1610–60) who fixed the identity of the burlesque by restricting it to epic parody. His *Virgile travesti* (1648–52) caricatures the *Aeneid* and sparks off other parodies of ancient epics, such as *L'Ovide en belle humeur* (1650) by D'Assoucy (1605–77), *Les Murs de Troie* (1653) by the brothers Perrault, or Brébeuf's *Lucain travesti* (1656); these parodies are thus contemporaneous with the serious epics mentioned above. Reacting to Malherbian *douceur* and to the weakening of language under the impact of *bienséances*, Scarron reintegrates the archaic, dialectal, and popular expressions that had been eliminated from literary language; his comic verve even allows him to joke about the misery of his own paralysed body, as in the 'épîtres chagrines' and the *stances* in which he proclaims himself 'the Queen's invalid' and solicits a pension for his infirmities.

But on the eve of the Fronde, what was just a witty game reveals its subversive potential: the burlesque takes a seditious political turn with *Le Ministre d'État flambé* (1649) by Cyrano (1619–55) and Scarron's *Mazarinade* (1651), two parodic poems whose crude vehemence is commensurate with the general hatred felt for Cardinal Mazarin, France's chief minister, whose rule was widely reviled.

This subversive violence was, however, no longer appropriate once political order returned after the failure of the Fronde, putting a stop to such burlesque deluge at the same time as the *douceur* of *galant* taste became widespread. Burlesque survives among the libertines and, in the attenuated and amusing form of 'fine raillery', in *mondain* poetry.

A light, gentle form of comedy also characterises the entire œuvre of La Fontaine, moving from the wonder and amazement of the *Songe de Vaux* and the 'gaiety' of the *Fables* (1668–94) to the bawdiness of the *Contes* (1665–85). Boileau meanwhile reactivates in *Le Lutrin* (1674) the heroic-comic style and defines it, on the model of the *Batrachomyomachia*, as the epicisation of little things, a definition which also applies to the project of La Fontaine's *Fables* and the speaking animals that populate them.

Mondain *and* galant *poetry*

Once it was rid of its subversive charge, this comic mixing of styles and tones, based on the permutation of literary codes, converged with the playful practice of the *mondain* and *galant* poets for whom verse must be above all an art of pleasing and a source of enjoyment. The 1650s saw the triumph of this *galant* poetry, which had been initiated at the Hôtel de Rambouillet in the 1630s by Voiture (1597–1648). His *Œuvres*, published in 1650, serve as a reference point for the new taste marked by badinage, the subtle art of gallant compliment and piquant raillery which puts a light spin on even the most serious topics. More seductive than passionate, this poetry plays off the serious, Petrarchist code of amorous praise, which it pushes to its extremes; the traditional theme of woman idolised and adored by a bashful lover thus becomes the subject of numerous variations by Malherbe, Malleville (1596–1647), Scudéry, or Tristan.

Serious encomium is exemplified by *La Guirlande de Julie* (1641), Montausier's homage to Julie d'Angennes, in which the poets of the Hôtel de Rambouillet, with the intentional exception of Voiture, laud the marquise de Rambouillet's daughter by speaking through various flowers. Voiture's innovation, on the other hand, consists of maintaining a jovial, natural tone, inspired by the badinage of Marot, which enlivens and spices up the conversation of *honnêtes gens*. It expresses itself in small genres (sonnets, epigrams, madrigals), but also through the supple form of the discursive epistle which mimics the casual manner of conversation to report and embellish the smallest trifles of everyday life.

After Voiture, the *mondain* and *galant* aesthetic continued with Sarasin (1614–54), Benserade (1612–91), Pellisson (1624–93), and the famous or anonymous poets included in the printed collections of the 1650s and 1660s (Sercy, Pellisson-La Suze), then in the *Mercure galant* from 1672 onwards. But the games of *bel esprit* also fostered a serial poetry marked by brilliance and ingenuity; this aesthetic, sometimes improperly labelled *précieux*, is represented by the successive and ephemeral vogues of *énigmes*, *rondeaux*, *métamorphoses en vers*, or *sonnets en bouts-rimés* whose formal sophistication appears as an end in itself. These poetic games, which may seem to us today rather artificial, take on meaning as part of a collective practice aiming to create in the select surroundings of *ruelles* (salons) and *hôtels* an atmosphere of leisure and enchantment in which the *mondains* dream of a new Arcadia.

The poetry of sentiment and nature

The seventeenth century was deeply influenced by the ancient tradition of pastoral, revived in the sixteenth century by the Italian novel and tragi-comedy which were then naturalised in Honoré d'Urfé's *L'Astrée* (1607–27) or Racan's *Les Bergeries* (1625). The genre of the eclogue was cultivated throughout the century, from Lingendes (1580–1615?), Racan, Sarasin, and Segrais (1624–1701), who dedicated his long pastoral poem *Athis* to Mademoiselle de Montpensier, to the philosophical idylls of Mme Deshoulières (1637–94) which combine quietist thought with an epicurean ideal of retreat 'far from crowds and noise', to quote La Fontaine's expression.

Since Virgil and Petrarch, the *locus amoenus* had indeed been the traditional site of literate leisure to which Boileau reaffirms his attachment in his epistle VI. Adopting the aristocratic dream in shepherds' clothing, the idyll also serves to express sentiment in a natural setting governed by abstract convention and not by a realistic concern for the depiction of landscape; at the end of the century, the eclogues of the 'modern' Fontenelle (1657–1757) no longer even mention flocks or herds.

But the simple enchantment of the pastoral setting can also blossom in a more refined, ingenious, and 'pointed' poetry, inspired by Marino's *concettismo* and aesthetic of *meraviglia*, as in Tristan's *Les Plaintes d'Acante* (1633) and *La Lyre* (1641) or in the *Idylles* (1648) of Rampalle (1603–60); for this poetry of nature is above all a poetry of imagination in which description yields to the marvellous vision of a world transfigured by art and strives to surpass painting through its power of enchantment.

From Théophile to La Fontaine, poetry thus endows Ovidian mythology with all its evocative force, whereas the iconographic programme of the gardens of Versailles and the *Métamorphoses d'Ovide en rondeaux* (1676) by Benserade reduces it to mere conventional allegory. Through the pointillistic description of a landscape and its denizens, the great baroque descriptive poetry of Théophile, Saint-Amant, and Tristan presents nature as the poet's confidante and refuge, the mirror of his alternately exalted and tormented soul.

Indeed, the pastoral can also express the tortures of passions and the anguish of death, in funereal visions and hallucinations typical of a dark neo-Petrarchism which is in tune with this tragic era permeated by a diffuse anxiety. This melancholy flourishes in the genre of the elegy, illustrated by Théophile, Malleville, La Fontaine, and Marie-Catherine de Villedieu (1640–83), in which the poets confide their despair and loneliness to a consolatory nature. Although confined within certain limits codified by the genre, and displaying a lyric 'I' that is in part fictional, the elegy's open form thus tends towards a more personal expression of sentiment, in accordance with a dictum by Boileau which will resonate in the eighteenth century: 'Il faut que le cœur seul parle dans l'élégie' ('In elegy only the heart must speak') (*L'Art poétique*, II.27).

At the end of this rapid overview, let us return to La Fontaine, whose *Fables* remain today the most widely read poetry collection of the seventeenth century. A 'miracle of culture', in the words of Gide, the *Fables* are indeed highly complex poems that go far beyond the didactic dryness of Aesop's apologue and need to be read in response to the poetry of their time of which they are the synthesis. La Fontaine fuses all the genres, from pastoral to epic, and all the tones, from the comic to the pathetic; all lyric forms, from the extended epigram to the epistle and the verse tale, are mixed together, while the *vers mêlés* with their lines of variable length, impart to the noble language of the gods the fluidity of urbane conversation.

The *Fables* are anything but simple children's tales, but neither can they be reduced to brilliant exercises and variations of humanist erudition under a surface of worldly badinage: even in his most humble narratives, the poet speaks as a *moraliste*, giving a personal, nuanced description of the depths of human nature and the perils of life in society, rather than prescribing which behaviour to adopt. La Fontaine thus invites reflection on major ethical, political, and philosophical issues, which are both anchored in their original context and capable of being reinterpreted by successive generations, and proposes an open plurality of responses, from Epicureanism to Augustinianism, leaving it up to the diligent reader to choose.

The example of the Classical synthesis realised by the moral poetry of La Fontaine and Boileau thus enables us to re-evaluate seventeenth-century poetry as a whole, characterised by the 'just temperament' of a supple and adaptable middle style allowing for subtle transitions between the sublimity of the high style and the gentle *douceur* of the simple style. Indeed, this is not the least of paradoxes: that a poetry so fundamentally learned, dominated by codes and topoi, is finally not at all abstract and disembodied but rather the locus of a personal voice which animates it well beyond the expected postures of the lyric persona. Far from being detrimental to its lyric character, the promotion of poetry as discourse rather than incantation confers upon it a more human tone and function.

Translated by Volker Schröder

33

Seventeenth-century philosophy

ROGER ARIEW

It would be no great exaggeration to state that seventeenth-century philosophy came to be dominated by René Descartes (1596–1650) and the Cartesians. The century opened with a generally dominant scholasticism, in many flavours, encountering some opposition from various humanists. Although there were scholastics and humanists throughout the era, the ascendancy of Cartesian philosophy in mid-century changed the equation, and the battle became defined as Cartesians versus anti-Cartesians, or perhaps rather more broadly as Moderns versus Ancients. Even the neo-Epicurean humanist Pierre Gassendi (1592–1655) and the theologically minded Augustinians from Port-Royal came to be characterised in relation to Cartesianism.

Renaissance humanism used history and the study of languages to revive and rediscover much of Classical antiquity: its science, philosophy, art, and poetry. When we think of its accomplishments, we remember the works of Rabelais, Montaigne, and Charron, among others. Although one does not find the term 'humanist' used by the circle around Descartes, Descartes's principal correspondent Marin Mersenne (1588–1648), in his *L'Impiété des Deistes* (1624), refers to a distinct set of opponents in which we can find several scholars we would consider as such. After having discussed such 'despicable authors' as Charron, Cardano, Machiavelli, Bruno, the 'accursed' Vanini, 'and similar rogues', Mersenne talks about the work he is writing against them: 'I do not want to spend much time on this subject, since I expect to refute everything these authors stated so inappropriately in the Encyclopaedia I am preparing in the defence of all truths and against all sorts of lies, in which I will examine more diligently what has been advanced by Gorlaeus, Charpentier, Basso, Hill, Campanella, Bruno, Vanini, and a few others.'[1] Mersenne proceeds to give examples of the 'impertinence' of these authors. According to him, 'ultimately, they are all heretics, which is why we should not be surprised that they agree,

---

1 M. Mersenne, *L'Impiété des Deistes* (Paris, 1624), pp. 237–8.

being all as thick as thieves' (p. 238). A year later, in *La Vérité des sciences* (1625), Mersenne refers again to the same group, but this time as anti-Aristotelians:

> Franciscus Patrizi has tried to discredit Aristotle's philosophy, but he made no more progress than Basso, Gorlaeus, Bodin, Charpentier, Hill, Olive, and several others, who raise monuments to Aristotle's fame through their writing, since they are not able to strive high enough to bring down the flight and glory of the Peripatetic Philosopher, for he transcends everything relating to the senses and imagination, and they grovel on the ground like little worms: Aristotle is an eagle in philosophy and the others are like small chicks who wish to fly before they have wings.[2]

The group of atheists and rogues referred to by Mersenne are also mentioned by Descartes, who designates them by the term *novatores*. Descartes once asserted: 'Plato says one thing, Aristotle another, Epicurus another, Telesio, Campanella, Bruno, Basso, Vanini, and all the *novatores* all say something different. Of all these people, I ask you, who is it who has anything to teach me, or indeed anyone who loves wisdom?'[3] Descartes's reference is all too brief, but in another context one can see that he thinks of them as anti-Aristotelians. In particular, he makes additional comments about Sébastien Basso (*c.* 1577 – post-1625). Constantijn Huygens (1596–1678) had sent Descartes a copy of Basso's *Philosophiae Naturalis adversus Aristotelem* (1621). Descartes, in his reply, thanks Huygens and makes a characteristic Cartesian pronouncement:

> The book which you did the favour of sending me yesterday is truly a recent blessing, for which I very humbly thank you. I do not know whether I dare say this to you, since you have had the patience to read it, but I am persuaded that my reveries will not be insufferable to you, for, if I remember, it is only good for destroying the opinions of Aristotle, and I seek only to establish something, so simple and manifest, that the opinions of all others would agree with it.　　　　　　　　　　　　　　　　　　　　　(AT I, 602–3)

Thus some of the scholars we think of as humanists are classed by Descartes as innovators and by Mersenne as heretics and by both as anti-Aristotelians. Of course, we might consider that Descartes himself seems to fit the mould. So, thinking of 'humanism' as our term, and using it from our perspective, we can ask about Descartes's relation to it.

Descartes, the philosopher who so famously excommunicates the past to start anew from stable foundations, is also the gentlemanly sceptic who, in his

---

2 M. Mersenne, *La Vérité des sciences* (Paris, 1625), pp. 109–10.
3 R. Descartes, *To Beeckman*, 17 October 1630, in *Œuvres de Descartes*, ed. C. Adam and P. Tannery, 11 vols. (Paris: Vrin, 1974–86), I, p. 158. Henceforth AT, vol., page.

Discours de la méthode (1637), gives solid advice about the advantages of history. He famously said:

> reading good books is like having a conversation with the most distinguished people of past ages – indeed, a rehearsed conversation in which these authors reveal to us only the best of their thoughts . . . Conversing with those of past centuries is much the same as travelling. It is good to know something of the customs of various peoples, so that we may judge our own more soundly and not think that everything contrary to our own ways is ridiculous and irrational, as those who have seen nothing of the world ordinarily do.
>
> (AT vi, 6)

Descartes also writes eloquently about some of the disadvantages of history: 'But one who spends too much time travelling eventually becomes a stranger in his own country; and one who is too curious about the practices of past ages usually remains quite ignorant about those of the present' (AT vi, 6). However, Descartes's advice about history does not fully originate with him; he is just repeating some commonplaces.

The analogy between reading and travelling belongs to the concept of erudition and history acclaimed by Renaissance humanists such as Montaigne and Charron (1541–1603). For example, Charron, whose *De la sagesse* (1601) Descartes is known to have owned and read, writes:

> The ways of profiting through speech and exemplar are dual, since they are exercised and derived from excellent people, whether alive, in the course of meeting them and conferring with them physically and externally, or dead, as a result of reading their books . . . The former can be accomplished by . . . travelling and visiting foreign lands . . . The latter commerce with the dead, using books, is much more secure, more our own, more regular, and costs the least.[4]

Descartes's thoughts about the disadvantages of history, on the other hand, are part of his own general critique of humanist methods. Erudition and history give us the experience of the world; Descartes wishes to establish knowledge on reason, not on experience. There is a strong echo of this critique in his unfinished dialogue *Recherche de la vérité* (1641?–9?), one of whose main themes is that the desire for knowledge, which is common to all people, is an illness that cannot be cured, 'for curiosity increases with learning' (AT x, 495); Descartes proposes instead the search for truth by the light of reason, because 'This light alone . . . determines the opinions a gentleman should have about

---

4 P. Charron, *De la sagesse* (Paris, 1601), III.14.26.

all matters that may occupy his thoughts and penetrate into the secrets of the most curious sciences'. According to Descartes, 'A gentleman does not need to have read every book, nor to have carefully learned everything taught in the Schools; it would even be a kind of defect in his education if he had devoted too much of his time to the study of letters' (AT x, 495). And, in case we did not fully understand the point, he reinforces it by directly associating science with reason and history with experience:

> But to give you a more distinct conception of the sort of doctrine I propose to teach, I should like you to notice how the sciences differ from those simple forms of knowledge that can be acquired without any process of reasoning, such as languages, history, geography, and in general any subject that rests on experience alone.
> (AT x, 502)

As is clear, although Descartes prefers reason and science, he does not altogether eliminate history and experience as constituents of knowledge. Still, Descartes's thoughts about the historical method are abstract pronouncements he does not usually put into practice; but there is one aspect of Renaissance method Descartes does espouse, namely its critique of logic and syllogism. According to many humanists, formal logic – that is, syllogism – is useless; it may even be harmful. For example, we see Pierre de la Ramée (1515–72) argue in his *Dialectique* (1555) that only method, not dialectics, can usefully order known precepts:

> Let us suppose that all the definitions, distributions, and rules of grammar are discovered and each correctly judged, and that all of these teachings are written on different tablets, which are thrown together and jumbled up out of order and put in a jug, as in the game of blank. What branch of dialectic could teach me to deal with such confused precepts and restore them to order?[5]

In his 'Apologie de Raymond Sebond' Montaigne reports that logic has no practical use, that its inventors must have been playing a game.[6] Similarly, Francisco Sanchez (1551–1623), in *Quod nihil scitur* (1581), attacks the barrenness of conventional uses of the syllogism and the emptiness of elaborate definitions. On standard accounts, knowledge is a disposition acquired by demonstration, but Sanchez says he does not understand what a disposition is and, worst of all, demonstration amounts to explaining something obscure by something even more obscure. 'How subtle, how long, and how difficult

---

5 Petrus Ramus, *La Dialectique* (Paris, 1555), pp. 138–9.
6 Michel de Montaigne, *Essais* (Bordeaux, 1580), II.12 (Paris: Gallimard, 1962), p. 488; see also p. 466.

is the science of syllogism! In fact it is *futile*, long, and difficult, and there is *no* science of syllogism!'[7] Sanchez even argues that syllogism destroys and obscures the sciences: 'So what use have all these syllogisms been? Why did Aristotle spend so much effort on teaching them? And why do all his successors still expend their labour on them? When it comes to writing, we do not make any use of syllogisms, nor did Aristotle. No science has ever emerged from them; indeed, they have led many sciences into error and confusion' (p. 11).

Descartes, famous for his method, was clearly sympathetic to this sort of criticism, producing similar arguments in the *Regulae* (1618?–28?). He begins by asserting: 'I find of little use those bonds by which the dialecticians seek to rule human reason' (Rule 2, AT x, 365). He continues, 'as to the other operations of the mind, moreover, which dialectic struggles to direct with the aid of these prior ones, they are useless here – or rather they may be counted as obstructions, since nothing can be added to the pure light of reason without in some way obscuring it' (Rule 4, AT x, 372–3). So he rejects syllogisms as contrary to his ends. According to Descartes,

> Dialecticians can find by their art no syllogism that yields a true conclusion unless they first have the material for it, that is, unless they have already learned the truth itself they are deducing in their syllogism. Hence it is clear that they themselves learn nothing new from such a form, and that vulgar dialectic is therefore entirely useless for those who wish to investigate the truth of things. (Rule 10, AT x, 406)

The only positive thing Descartes can say about syllogism or dialectics is that there is a distant resemblance between syllogism and his method, which, in the fashion of Ramus and others, is all that he thinks is useful. Descartes describes what he calls 'deduction' as a procedure that finds something unknown from what is already known; he specifies that the procedure can be achieved through a simple comparison of two or more objects with one another by means of a common idea. He insists, however, that:

> since the forms of the syllogisms are of no help in perceiving the truth of things, it will be of advantage to the reader, if, after he has completely rejected them, he grasps the fact that every cognition whatsoever which is not obtained by a simple and pure intuition of one isolated object, is obtained by the comparison of two or more objects with one another. (Rule 14, AT x, 439–40)

---

7 Francisco Sanchez, *Quod nihil scitur* (Lyon, 1581), p. 7.

So deduction, one of the basic elements of Descartes's method (along with intuition), has little to do with the application of the laws of logic. What Descartes has in mind is the type of ampliative inference used in mathematics, when we 'perceive' how different propositions relate to each other and how an unknown truth follows from truths already known.

Descartes repeats many of the same points from the *Regulae* in the *Discours de la méthode*, Part II, when he gives his famous four rules of method. He also refers to these passages from the *Discours* in the preface to the French translation of the *Principia* (1647), where he talks about the order of teaching and the tree of philosophy. According to Descartes, before applying himself to true philosophy a person who has only common and imperfect knowledge should form a code of morals sufficient to regulate the actions of his life and should likewise study 'logic', but not the logic of the Schools:

> for this is strictly speaking nothing but a dialectic which teaches ways of expounding to others what one already knows or even of holding forth without judgement about things one does not know. Such logic corrupts good sense rather than increasing it. I mean instead the kind of logic that teaches us to direct our reason with a view to discovering the truths of which we are ignorant. (AT IXb, 14–15)

So again, the logic of the Schools is a dialectic that corrupts rather than improves good sense, but this time we also have Descartes's method as 'another logic' recommended as a good practical exercise to improve one's mind.

These more positive pronouncements allow Cartesians to construct a logic that blends scholastic syllogism and Cartesian method – *Logica vetus et nova* (1654), as Johannes Clauberg (1622–65) calls it. In the same way as with history, Descartes begins in general sympathy with humanistic method, as an anti-Aristotelian, but, in practice, moves away from his initial position. Ultimately Descartes shares little with the humanists except anti-scholasticism.

Traditional accounts of the seventeenth century treat the systematic philosophy of Descartes as a comprehensive rejection of scholasticism, of scholastic substantial form and the qualitative account of change. Descartes wished to capitalise on an increasing awareness that philosophy was in a state of disrepair – an old building that needed to be torn down, instead of being repaired – and to posit a novel system for its replacement. However his rhetoric usually reflected a more cautious approach; he frequently denied the novelty of his philosophical principles and seems not to have believed that he would be seen as mounting a direct frontal assault on the old philosophy. He revealed in a letter: 'I hope that readers will gradually get used to my principles, and recognise their truth, before they notice that they destroy those of Aristotle' (AT III, 298). In general Cartesians were 'mechanists': they limited their explanations of the material world to the motion, shape, and size of particles, although they advocated a plenum of material extension and vehemently denied the possibility of the void. In contrast, followers of Gassendi propounded a different kind of mechanism, holding an atomistic worldview in which material corpuscles moved within a void. Critics, however, did not always fully distinguish Gassendism from Cartesianism. The Jesuit Louis Le Valois (1639–1700) attacked both Descartes and the Gassendist François Bernier (1620–88) on the incompatibility between their mechanical philosophy and the explanation of the Eucharist.[8] And the Oratorian Jean-Baptiste de la Grange (c. 1641 – post-1680) wrote a critique of the 'new philosophers' in which he lumped Gassendi and the Minim Emmanuel Maignan (1601–76) in the Cartesian camp: Descartes, Jacques Rohault (1620–72), Henricus Régius (1598–1679).[9] De la Grange's target was the allegedly corrupting influence of Cartesianism within his own order, given the then recently published work of Nicholas Malebranche (1638–1715).

Although many considered themselves Cartesian, the latitude represented by Cartesian doctrines was remarkable. For instance, Gérauld de Cordemoy (1626–84), an active participant in several Cartesian academies and salons, published his first work anonymously as an appendix to Descartes's (posthumous 1664) edition of *Le Monde*. His quite popular *Le Discernement du corps et de l'ame* (1666) expounded Cartesian physics, including an occasionalist answer to Descartes's notorious mind–body problem. Cordemoy followed Descartes by defining body as 'extended substance', but he proceeded to distinguish between body (as a substance) and matter as an aggregate of bodies. Thus, for Cordemoy, body is indivisible, yet matter is divisible. He also accepted the possibility of void space. Upholding indivisible atoms and the void would seem to be following the fundamentals of Gassendi's neo-Epicureanism; nevertheless, Cordemoy was considered a good Cartesian.

Other 'Cartesians' attempted to synthesise the old and new doctrines of matter, form, and void. René Le Bossu (c. 1635–80) published a 'parallel' of

8 Louis de la Ville (Louis le Valois), *Sentimens de Monsieur Descartes touchant l'essence et les proprietez du corps opposez à la Doctrine de l'Église, et conforme aux erreurs de Calvin sur le sujet de l'Eucharistie* (Caen, 1680).
9 Jean-Baptiste de la Grange, *Les principes de la philosophie contre les nouveaux philosophes, Descartes, Rohault, Régius, Gassendi, le p. Maignan, etc.* (Paris, 1675–9).

the principles of physics of Aristotle and Descartes and argued for consistency between the two. Le Bossu maintained that Aristotle analysed matter in terms of what was knowable around him: for instance, the bronze in a statue. Descartes, with the advantage of a more sophisticated science, considered matter common to everything – extended substance. According to Le Bossu, Aristotle had been teaching beginners, and so started with what was obvious to everyone; Descartes, at a more advanced stage of science, thought that every particular is given a form by the way general matter is shaped. Thus Descartes needed only two principles: 'form' and matter. Basically Le Bossu believed that Descartes and Aristotle accepted the same form–matter universe, considered from different stages of the development of scientific knowledge.

Aristotle and Descartes could be harmonised in other ways. Johannes de Raey (1622–1702), among others, blamed Aristotle's commentators and later scholastics for distorting his works, then proceeded to reconcile the two by reading passages of Aristotle in Cartesian terms and out of context. Within the academies Descartes's views could be incorporated into traditional formats. Several late seventeenth-century textbook authors taught the Cartesian doctrines of matter and form under properly scholastic protocol.

In spite of the attempts at harmony, condemnations of various Cartesian propositions were issued and reissued throughout the second half of the seventeenth century. The Catholic church put Descartes's works on the *Index Librorum Prohibitorum* in 1663. Louis XIV forbade the teaching of Cartesianism in France in the 1670s. The authorities of the Oratorian College of Angers declared, in 1679, that they were 'fighting at once the two greatest enemies that the Catholic Church had at the time: the Jansenists and the Cartesians'.[10] These two 'heresies' intersected in the person of Antoine Arnauld (1612–94), one of the theologians associated with Port-Royal who, after writing one of the more critical set of *Objections* to Descartes's *Meditations* (1641), became known as a staunch defender of Descartes.

The other significant Port-Royal figure, Blaise Pascal (1623–62), was more equivocal in his relations with Descartes. Pascal, of course, is famous for his epithet 'Descartes, useless and uncertain'.[11] This unusual and doubly negative

10 François Babin, *Journal ou relation fidèle de tout ce qui s'est passé dans l'université d'Angers au sujet de la philosophie de Des Carthes en l'execution des ordres du Roy pendant les années 1675, 1676, 1677, et 1678* (Angers, 1679), Avis au Lecteur.

11 Blaise Pascal, *Pensées*, trans. Roger Ariew (Indianapolis: Hackett, 2005), p. 133. *Pensées*, ed. L. Lafuma (Paris: Seuil, 1962) and *Pensées*, ed. P. Sellier (Paris: Garnier, 2004). Henceforth Sellier ed. numbering/Lafuma ed. numbering; i.e., in this case: S445/L888.

assessment is generally taken to be Pascal's wholesale indictment of Descartes's irreligious philosophy and deeply flawed science. But do we really understand the fragment? Descartes is both useless and uncertain: is he useless in all respects and uncertain in all domains? Useless because uncertain? The 'palaeographic' edition of the *Pensées* (1942) indicates that one of the versions of the fragment was originally 'Descartes, inutile et certain', the negative particle having been added. 'Descartes, useless and certain' might have made more sense, if read as 'Descartes though certain, is useless'. Fortunately, Pascal repeats 'Descartes, useless and uncertain' in another, slightly longer *pensée*:

Descartes

We must say in general: 'This happens through shape and motion', because it is true. But to say which shapes and motions and to constitute the machine is ridiculous, for it is *useless* [and] *uncertain*, and laborious. And if it were true, we do not believe all of philosophy to be worth an hour of labour.

(S118/L84, emphasis mine)

Here Pascal is clearly supporting the reductive aspects of Cartesian philosophy – the behaviour of bodies is to be explained through 'shape and motion' – against scholastic opponents. What is useless and uncertain (and laborious) is only the extension of Cartesian metaphysics to particular physical phenomena – 'saying which shapes and motions' – what Pascal calls 'constituting the machine'. It is useless because Pascal thinks *all* such activities to be useless, as they do not lead to salvation: they are not worth an hour of labour. This is consistent with another of Pascal's fragments: 'Write against those who delve too deeply in the sciences. Descartes' (S462/L553). It allows one to relate what Pascal says about Descartes with what he says about Copernicus:

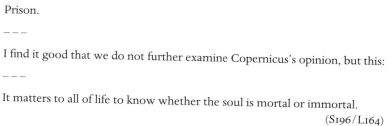

Prison.

– – –

I find it good that we do not further examine Copernicus's opinion, but this:

– – –

It matters to all of life to know whether the soul is mortal or immortal.

(S196/L164)

'Prison' in the fragment refers to Pascal's previous *pensée* about how one should spend an hour of life: 'A man is in prison, not knowing whether his sentence has been passed, with only an hour to find out, this hour being sufficient to obtain its repeal if he knew that it had been passed. It would be unnatural if he spent the hour not finding out whether his sentence had been passed, but playing piquet' (S195/L163). Our situation is like that of the man in prison: when we are delving too deeply into the sciences or further examining Copernicus's opinion, we are not dealing with what is crucial; we are just playing games. This is useless behaviour. Thus Descartes's science is useless, whether certain or uncertain – but so is all science. And Descartes's science is uncertain to boot. Descartes would have agreed that his science was not absolutely certain, although he would have preferred to call it morally certain. This is enough for Pascal to call it uncertain.

Pascal's criticism of Descartes's science should not obscure for us his acceptance of Descartes's metaphysics: we must say in general: 'This happens through shape and motion', because it is true. To constitute the machine may be ridiculous, but what needs to be constituted is a machine. Following Descartes, Pascal thinks of human bodies as machines:

> The custom of seeing kings accompanied by guards, drums, officers, and all the things that direct the *machine* to yield respect and fear, makes their faces, when they are sometimes seen alone without these trappings, impress respect and fear in their subjects, because we cannot separate in thought their persons from what usually accompanies them. (S59/L25)

Similarly, for Pascal, animals are machines whose behaviour is explained as responses to stimuli, or 'instinct':

> If an animal did with a mind what it does by instinct, and if it spoke with a mind what it speaks by instinct when hunting and warning its mates that the prey is found or lost, it would certainly also speak about things that affect it more, as for example, 'Gnaw on this cord which is hurting me and I cannot reach'. (S137/L105; see also S139/L107, S617/L738, and elsewhere)

As for humans, their nature transcends mere mechanism:

> Man's greatness lies in his knowing himself to be wretched.
>
> A tree does not know itself to be wretched.
>
> So it is wretched to know you are wretched, but it is great to know you are wretched. (S146/L114; see also S143/L111, S 140/L108, and elsewhere)

Thus even Pascal accepts two crucial aspects of Descartes's philosophy: that is, mechanism, entailing the denial of real qualities and substantial forms, and dualism, requiring the clean separation of soul as immaterial thinking substance and body as material extended substance.

In the 1690s Edmond Pourchot (1651–1734) famously taught Cartesian philosophy at the University of Paris – a first. Condemnations of Cartesianism continued to be issued in various quarters – one by the Jesuits as late as 1705 – but the war had already been lost. Cartesianism supplanted scholasticism in France and eclipsed all other philosophies. The victory was brief, however, because of the advent of Newtonian thought.

34

Seventeenth-century women writers

ELIZABETH C. GOLDSMITH

In 1598, Marie Le Jars de Gournay, a friend of Montaigne and the editor of his *Essais*, moved to Paris and embarked on her own career as a woman of letters. The story of her struggle, and her own published reflections on the subject of 'she who writes', anticipate many of the issues that would concern women writers throughout the seventeenth century. Although initially intending to follow in the footsteps of her mentor, Gournay became progressively more interested in the particular challenges faced by women who chose a public voice. Her treatise *Egalité des hommes et des femmes* (1622) focused on the importance of education for women. Her essay *Grief des dames* (1626) describes the experience of speaking with a woman's voice to a male public that is reluctant to listen. The many editions of her single work of fiction, *Le Proumenoir de Montaigne*, in itself constitutes a record of a woman writer's struggle with editors and censors. In the last edition that she published of *Le Proumenoir*, Gournay appended an essay entitled *Apologie pour celle qui escrit*, defending herself against the slanders that had plagued her life and threatened her livelihood. The hostility and derision that plagued Marie de Gournay's career may have contributed to a more ambivalent approach to publishing expressed by writers later in the century. Anne-Thérèse de Lambert's treatises on women's education and equality, composed in the 1690s, were circulated privately and only published, without her knowledge, over thirty years later.

Gournay's vocation as a writer was given strong impetus by her patrons: first Montaigne, and later, in her early years in Paris, by Marguerite de Valois, who gave her a small pension and included her in the company of her learned court 'salon', where Gournay met other writers including Honoré d'Urfé and François Maynard. She was also able to cultivate the society of influential people who would later become her benefactors. By the 1620s she was adept at hosting her own gatherings of scholars and writers, in her modest quarters in Paris, away from the court.

Salons, usually conducted by women, were an important locus of French elite culture, and a social space that was crucial to the participation of women writers in the literary sphere. From the first decades of the seventeenth century, the project of cultivating social interaction in a place that was sheltered from the distractions of courtly politics, while still committed to cultivating ideal behaviour in the courtly tradition, was one in which women played a leading role. The prototypical salon, or *ruelle* as it was most commonly called until the eighteenth century, was one that was established by 1610 by Catherine de Vivonne, marquise de Rambouillet, in her famous *chambre bleue*, where gatherings were held until her death in 1665. Salon habitués cultivated the idea that they constituted an ideal elite, which could always close ranks and create a separate reality even when surrounded by a heterogeneous crowd of courtiers. Salon society, self-consciously apart from the court, came to define itself not so much by a concrete space as by the principal activity that occurred there, conversation.

Commentators on politeness, sociability, and conversation agreed on the 'natural' superiority of the conversation of women. This view was linked to the notion that conversation should be organised so as to exclude social hierarchy as much as possible. The essentially democratic nature of ideal sociability (in contrast to the rigid ceremony of the court) would be a fundamental organising principle of salon society throughout the seventeenth and eighteenth centuries, and women would continue to play a central role in defining the culture of the republic of letters.

Some literary genres, such as the maxim and the portrait, were often produced and first circulated in salon circles. Marguerite de La Sablière held a salon famous for the philosophical discussions hosted there and she authored a collection of maxims that were published along with those of her friend La Rochefoucauld. The Jansenist salon of Madeleine de Souvré, marquise de Sablé also fostered the production of maxims, including those authored by Sablé and published after her death.

Of the many seventeenth-century women who achieved recognition in their lifetimes as writers, two were particularly influenced by the evolving cultural practice of conversation and the challenge of transposing conversational style into written form: Madeleine de Scudéry and Marie de Rabutin Chantal, marquise de Sévigné. The novel that established Scudéry's celebrity was written as a roman à clef whose characters were based on the habitués of salons that Scudéry had frequented and hosted. *Artamène ou Le Grand Cyrus*, published in ten volumes between 1649 and 1653, was translated into English, German, Italian, and Arabic. In her novel *Clélie*, published between 1654 and

1660, Scudéry inserted an allegorical map of the human heart, called the 'Carte du pays de Tendre'. The conversations generated by the map elaborate a theory of love that values reason over passion and discourages marriage. Scudéry's shorter works of fiction, *Célinte* (1661), *Mathilde* (1667), and *La Promenade de Versailles* (1669), are more realistic than her novels, are situated in modern times, and take place in locations that would have been familiar to her readers. But Scudéry continued to portray characters who themselves were captivated by the epic plots of heroic novels, thus drawing on the strong influence of the genre on the collective imagination of her own social world.

In her later works Scudéry focused increasingly on the philosophical discussions of salon society. She produced ten volumes of collected conversations, many of them excerpted from her novels. Many of her contemporary readers viewed these collections as representing the best of her writing. Unlike her earlier works, they were published under her own name. They reflect the efforts of Scudéry's milieu to cultivate the art of talk and develop a new aesthetic and practice of conversation. Translated almost immediately into English, they contributed to a body of literature describing new 'French' styles of living that were imitated by elite circles in England, Germany, Italy, and Spain.

Sévigné occupies a special position in the history of French literature. She is one of the best-known writers in the language, but she never wrote anything intended for publication. Her fame derives exclusively from her correspondence, made up of thousands of letters that were first published after her death. She enjoyed a lifetime of close friendships with many of the principal figures on the French literary, cultural, and political scene: Lafayette, Scudéry, La Rochefoucauld, Retz, La Fontaine. Sévigné's close ties with the circle patronised by Nicolas Fouquet, minister of finance in the first years of Louis XIV's reign, drew her into the debates that polarised Parisian high society during Fouquet's trial for treason in 1664. Her letters written during the trial, and circulated among her friends, offer a subtle interpretation of political events and a lively, dramatic narrative.

As time went on, Sévigné became an expert observer of the experience of displacement, disgrace, and exile. Her letters invite her scattered circle of correspondents to continue their engagement in social conversations and remain, at least through writing, on the 'inside'. Letters addressed to exiled aristocrats such as her cousin, Roger de Rabutin, comte de Bussy, reassured their addressees that their voices would still be heard in Paris and at court. Epistolary conversations could be read aloud, absorbed into social dialogue, and prized for the insights they offered from a distance. Likewise, Sévigné's own letters were circulated, read and admired by her correspondents, who cited her witty and conversational style and praised her for her abilities as a writer and a kind of gazeteer. Ultimately, Sévigné's principal correspondent was to be her daughter Françoise-Marguerite, who in 1671 moved to Provence with her new husband the comte de Grignan. Seventy-five per cent of the letters of Madame de Sévigné that we know today were written from mother to daughter. They reveal an intense, often contradictory relationship. Mother and daughter visited each other for lengthy periods, but their repeated experience of separation and reunion inspired Sévigné's ongoing struggle as a writer to find words to express her affection. In these letters, Sévigné's mastery of a conversational style at times becomes itself the subject of scepticism, as she finds language to be inadequate for communicating intense passion.

Sévigné's friend Marie-Madeleine Pioche de la Vergne, comtesse de Lafayette, has been traditionally designated by literary history as the originator of the modern psychological novel. In her works sociability and conversation are always problematised, strongly counterbalanced by the appeal of retreat from the world and the urge to turn inwards. She received a broad education in the classics and languages, was an enthusiastic reader of the popular new novels of her day, and from an early age was close to prominent figures including La Rochefoucauld, Retz, and the writer Gilles Ménage. After her marriage in 1655, she moved to her husband's property in the Auvergne, but after three years in the provinces Marie-Madeleine moved back to Paris, leaving her husband behind to manage his country estates. She lived independently in Paris for the rest of her life in her home next to the Luxembourg Palace, where she remained closely involved with the intellectual and political life at court and in the salons of the capital.

In her most important and influential novel, *La Princesse de Clèves* (1678), she designed a plot drawn from events at the French court of the sixteenth century. Into a group of characters including Catherine de Medici, the duke of Guise and the young Mary Stuart, she placed a central figure of her own invention and wove a plot focused on the psychological development of this young woman maturing in the oppressive atmosphere of courtly intrigue. The book precipitated a major literary quarrel, conducted in print via a popular gazette of the day, *Le Mercure galant*. Readers argued passionately about the novel's realism, the plausibility of the heroine's behaviour, and the moral implications of her story. The controversy extended to Lafayette's readers in England, where each of her novels was published in translation within a year of its appearance in France.

Themes central to *La Princesse de Clèves* are examined in all of Lafayette's fiction: the difficulty of sincere communication, the fugitive quality of love, the tensions between religious principles and worldly demands, the constraints of marriage. Retreat from the world is the solution that holds the strongest appeal for her female characters. But the difficulty of decisions such as these, and their slow maturation in the minds of the protagonists, is what most fascinates Lafayette. Exemplary behaviour is achieved at a great cost. In the darkest of Lafayette's scenarios, as in the posthumously published *La Comtesse de Tende* (1724), the heroine's urge for escape is suicidal. In *La Princesse de Clèves*, retreat is a solution that is closer to a form of religious devotion. Lafayette's interest in the tension between public and private space and the difficulty of sincere communication may have also been reflected in her ambivalent attitude toward her own status as an author and her strategic use of the practice of anonymous publication.

Religious writing

Women played an important role in the development of new religious practices that emerged in the wake of the Reformation. Conduct books and books of piety such as *Introduction à la vie dévote* by François de Sales encouraged women to record their spiritual growth, and writers such as Jeanne de Schomberg, duchesse de Liancourt, circulated and sometimes published autobiographical works inspired by this tradition. Schomberg's *Règlement que cette Dame avait dressé pour elle même* appeared in 1698 and was reprinted numerous times. Some of the earliest published diaries and personal memoirs were religious testimonials. Seventeenth-century France saw the practice of the written confession, or 'life story', become common. Women's life narratives in this tradition provided readers with models of female self-expression and contributed to an aesthetic of artlessness, spontaneity, and simplicity that was particularly admired in women's writing. Autobiographical texts of a more mystical bent, such as Jeanne Guyon's *Vie* (1720), made a public display of a personal mystical journey and would be severely criticised by Enlightenment thinkers such as Rousseau, who advocated a more sheltered and domestic practice of female piety.

The range of written forms that were developed to accommodate this new turn toward 'interiority' was broad. Women who were active in the formation of new religious orders and the expansion of French missions around the world established a vast web of epistolary conversations with their followers and patrons. Jeanne-Françoise Frémyot de Chantal, who founded the order of the Visitation with François de Sales and presided over its rapid expansion, produced a huge correspondence documenting the central place she occupied in a complex network of discussions relating to religious culture and pastoral practice. Women authored, with increasing frequency, religious biographies. Jacqueline Bouette de Blémur, historian of the Benedictines, wrote biographies of Benedictine nuns and also a *Vie des saints* that modernised the rhetorical style traditionally used in the genre. Other writers whose oeuvre grew out of the religious upheavals of the period include Anne-Marguerite du Noyer, a Huguenot who founded a gazette and published memoirs and letters recounting her life as an exile in Holland, Anne de La Roche-Guilhen, a Huguenot who moved to London in 1675 and supported herself writing novels, and Marie de l'Incarnation, an Ursuline nun and one of the first women to join the missions in New France. Like other secular women of her generation, Marie de l'Incarnation joined the Ursuline order as a widow, abandoning her children to the care of her extended family. Her son, Claude Martin, who as a boy had beseeched her not to sacrifice her family to religion, was eventually reconciled with her and devoted himself to circulating and eventually publishing her correspondence, in 1677. Gabrielle Suchon fled the convent and won her struggle to lead an independent life as an unmarried but not cloistered woman, publishing two treatises dealing with the question of women's engagement with the world, *Traité de la morale et de la politique* (1693) and *Du célibat volontaire ou la vie sans engagement* (1700). The Port-Royal prioress Angélique de Saint-Jean, and other nuns who were exiled after their refusal to sign a formulary repudiating Jansenism, produced writings that were published under the title *Relations de captivité*. Marie-Eléonore de Rohan, abbess in the more worldly convents of La Trinité in Normandy and Notre Dame de la Consolation in Paris, wrote occasional pieces for salon gatherings and corresponded with prominent literary figures.

Memoirs and life-writing

Memoirs, letters, travel journals, diaries, and confessional narratives were adopted as writing practices by educated women of letters. In France, the memoir genre was highly developed by the seventeenth century and was usually considered to be an aristocratic form, written by individuals concerned with recording public history and their family's role in it. Towards the end of the century some intimate memoirs began to be published by women, some of them arguing for a revision of history through a look at the behind-the-scenes, private actions of public figures. The memoirs of Marie-Catherine d'Aulnoy, Anne-Marguerite du Noyer, Catherine de La Guette, Hortense Mancini Mazarin and Marie Mancini Colonna, all published before 1700, are examples of memoirs that highlight the private lives of their writers and of other public figures who would have been known to their readers. This new type of autobiographical writing reflected the growing belief in the truth value of intimate reflection. Confession and private revelation were viewed as marks of authenticity, and to tell the truth about oneself was to tell what was hidden.

Historical memoirs such as those authored by Françoise de Motteville and Mademoiselle de Montpensier, inspired by the memoirs of Marguerite de Valois, first published in 1628, asserted the more traditional purpose of serving as personal testimony to historically significant figures and events. As part of the wave of aristocratic memoirs published after the death of Louis XIV in 1715, historical memoirs became popular with French readers for their revelations about the conduct and ideas of the elite. Marie d'Orléans-Longueville, duchesse de Nemours, wrote memoirs of the Fronde years and was an important patron of women of letters, including the Comtesse de la Suze, Madame de Villedieu, Marie-Jeanne L'Héritier de Villandon, and Madame de Pringy. Lafayette wrote historical memoirs of the court of Louis XIV, *Mémoires de la cour de France* (1731). She also used the memoir genre to dramatise the inevitable confrontation with death in her more personal historical memoir, *Histoire de Madame Henriette d'Angleterre*, begun as a biography at the request of her friend Henriette d'Angleterre and transformed by the princess's abrupt death in 1670.

Many of the women who published or circulated their life stories express a clear understanding of the risky choice they were making. Whether or not they try to justify this choice as an effort to defend their reputations, they are aware that their stories, once launched into the world, would take their place in a network of discussions that extended beyond the control of any one participant. The novelist and playwright Marie-Catherine Desjardins de Villedieu, whose collection of stories entitled *Les Désordres de l'amour* defined the emerging genre of the historical novella, was an important innovator in new literary forms blending fact and fiction. The experience of going public with one's life is a central theme of her pseudo-memoir *Histoire de la vie de Henriette-Sylvie de Molière*, a work merging fictional descriptions of the adventures of a picaresque heroine with real accounts of the lives of contemporary women who had left their families and were living 'on the road'. Three of these women, Marie-Sidonie de Courcelles, Hortense Mancini Mazarin, and Marie Mancini Colonna, also published their own memoirs even as their adventures were unfolding. Various accounts of their movements were reported in gazettes and circulated in letter correspondence, making of their lives a kind of media spectacle.

Other women, with similar awareness, seemed to engage in the risky but exhilarating practice of going public without committing their voices to print. Ninon de Lenclos was renowned as a libertine whose wit and wisdom were often quoted, but she wrote little outside of her correspondence with Saint-Evremond and other free-thinkers. Charlotte Saumaise de Chazan, comtesse de Brégy, was an influential figure in salon culture who published some poems and portraits, but her most influential oeuvre may have been in the form of the lawsuits surrounding her divorce case in the 1650s and 1660s, which fuelled contemporary debates about women's obligation to marry and bear children. Henriette de Coligny, comtesse de La Suze, who was one of the first women to publish a collection of her own poetry, also drew public attention via a court battle to end her marriage, which she eventually won in 1661, providing a compelling model of female independence to those who followed her struggles. The publicised real adventures of women who had fled their family and households influenced fictional narratives such as Antoinette de Salvan's historical novel about a runaway noblewoman *La Comtesse d'Isembourg*, and the accounts of itinerant women by Marie-Catherine Le Jumel de Barnville, comtesse d'Aulnoy in her *Mémoires de la cour d'Angleterre*. Writers also drew inspiration from engagement with a generation of dominant female actors on the political scene, women such as Françoise d'Aubigné, marquise de Maintenon, mistress and eventual wife of Louis XIV, who founded a school for girls, authored pedagogical texts, model conversations, and a lifetime of letters. One woman who came to France from abroad, Elisabeth-Charlotte d'Orléans, wife of Louis XIV's brother Philippe d'Orléans, left an enormous literary legacy in the form of her epistolary exchanges throughout Europe. Louis XIV's first cousin Mademoiselle de Montpensier played an active role in the Fronde and documented her life in her memoirs, which she composed with the participation of her friends. Montpensier's entourage of artists, writers, and architects, drawn to her provincial chateau in the years following the Fronde, served as a model for other coteries that strove to create elite social and artistic communities at a distance from Versailles.

Fairytales

The genre that, perhaps surprisingly, incorporates the largest number of themes that seem to traverse the corpus of seventeenth-century writing by women is the literary fairytale. A genre that in France was developed and authored predominantly by women, it emerged from salon culture and first flourished in the last decades of the reign of Louis XIV. Tales that began as stories told in society games gradually appeared in print, and were often framed as collectively produced works. Drawing more on Italian literary traditions than French folklore, the tales written by d'Aulnoy, L'Héritier, Henriette-Julie de Castelnau, comtesse de Murat, and Charlotte-Rose Caumont de la Force, as opposed to the more familiar tales by Perrault, appeal more to adults than children, and reflect the values of elite culture while also confronting some of the more violent costs of female agency.

D'Aulnoy is credited with having published the first French literary fairytale in her novel *Histoire d'Hypolite, comte de Duglas*. She coined the term 'conte de fées' with the publication of her two collections of fairytales published in 1697 and 1698. D'Aulnoy also travelled widely and authored novels and travel narratives. De la Force published a narrative describing salon society, *Les jeux de l'esprit*, along with her collection of fairytales, and Henriette-Julie de Castelnau, comtesse de Murat authored two collections of fairytales along with a novel, *Voyage de campagne*, depicting the world of the salon. L'Héritier, niece of Charles Perrault, who published poetry, novellas, and fairytales, also wrote responses to Boileau's attack on women in his *Satire X* and was a defender of women's education.

The figure of the 'fairy', a term used to refer to salon habitués as well as mythical creatures, was also familiar to opera, a musical form that emerged in the baroque period. Literary fairytales blend references to new forms of spectacle such as opera with references to myth. In the fairytales, spaces and theatrical productions that were recognisable to contemporary readers were transformed into utopian places. D'Aulnoy's fairytales sometimes seem to be defending modern, worldly culture against critics hostile to both modernity and to women's active role in it. Several women writers produced operas and machine plays (spoken plays with complex sets and varied machinery) in this period. Françoise Pascal was one of the first women to have her plays produced by a professional acting company. Her works include the machine play *Endymion*. Louise-Geneviève Gillot de Saintonge was the first French woman to write opera libretti. Catherine Bernard, best known for her historical novels and poetry, also authored plays, one of which, *Laodamie* (1689), was the first by a woman to be performed at the Comédie-Française. The poet, philosopher, and dramatist Antoinette Deshouilères also published an opera libretto, *Zoroastre*. Deshouilères was a woman who earned the rare honour of membership in several intellectual academies, including the Arles Academy and the Académie des belles-lettres in Paris.

The contributions of women to the literature of seventeenth-century France are numerous and varied, and cannot be adequately accounted for in the scope of this short essay. There is ample evidence that seventeenth-century women writers, from Marie de Gournay to the Marquise de Lambert, were widely read and admired, exerted influence and engaged fully in the literary and philosophical discussions of their day. However, official recognition from cultural and political authorities and, later, academic ones, was only reluctantly granted to them. Forms of dissent that were fostered in salon society, particularly the challenge to traditional gender roles and the institution of marriage, did not easily earn the approval of authorities. Very few women received royal pensions and the Académie Française, along with most other intellectual societies, excluded them. A notable exception to this institutional indifference was the Accademia dei Riccovrati of Padua, which bestowed prizes and granted memberships to many French women writers including Scudéry, Deshouilères, Salvan, L'Héritier, Murat, and Bernard.

35

Moraliste writing in the
seventeenth century

RICHARD SCHOLAR

Moraliste writing of the seventeenth century deserves the name not because it is moralising in intention but in so far as it examines *mœurs* ('morals') in the sense of human manners or behaviour. It typically makes that behaviour the object of disenchanted reflections delivered in short, fragmented forms. The period's most prominent examples of writing in this vein – the *Pensées* (*Thoughts*) (first published in 1670) of Blaise Pascal (1623–62), the *Maximes* (*Maxims*) (1665–78) of François de La Rochefoucauld (1613–80), the *Fables* (1668–94) of Jean de La Fontaine (1622–95), and the *Caractères* (*Characters*) (1688–96) of Jean de La Bruyère (1645–96) – all combine moral dissection with pithiness. Influenced by the Augustinian pessimism of the so-called Jansenist movement, but generally secular in perspective, they reveal something of the shifting frontier between religion and literature in the period. Like their most important precursor, the *Essais* (*Essays*) (1580–95) of Michel de Montaigne (1533–92), they reflect on important questions by experimenting with literary form. Each of the texts has come, as a result of its success, to lend the short title by which it is commonly known – *pensées*, maxims, and so on – to a distinct form of *moraliste* writing.

The term *moraliste* needs, however, to be handled with caution when applied to writing of the seventeenth century. A later invention, one that becomes an established feature of critical discourse only in the first half of the nineteenth century, it risks imposing a false coherence on the texts of the period and masking the differences between them. It is best seen as a category with blurred edges, a provisional as well as a belated one, containing texts that are marked by various important family resemblances and connections. These connections can in part be traced to the intertextual play that goes on within and between them, for each *moraliste* text rewrites its predecessors, and – as the work of La Fontaine and La Bruyère shows – it does so with an ever more acute sense of working within a tradition. In that sense, the later invention of the umbrella term *moraliste* merely confirms a perception found in the texts.

The first collected volume of such texts to appear was published by Pierre Mortier in Amsterdam in 1705. It includes, alongside the work of La Rochefoucauld, the *Maximes* (*Maxims*) of his friend Madame (Madeleine) de Sablé (1599–1678), the *Pensées diverses* (*Various Thoughts*) of her protégé Nicolas d'Ailly (*fl.* 1670–1700), and the *Maximes chrétiennes* (*Christian Maxims*) of Madame (Marguerite) de la Sablière (1640–93), to whom La Fontaine dedicated the important closing poem of his ninth book of *Fables*. Mortier's collection reveals various features of *moraliste* writing in the period as a whole: the coexistence of religious and secular moral themes; the importance of women as well as men in this kind of literary production; the networks of friendship and patronage connecting different *moralistes*; and the salon culture in which the work of all the *moralistes*, great and lesser, is embedded. That culture promoted conversation between members of both sexes from the social and cultural elite as the ideal means of mixing wit with learning in the elaboration of new ideas. Madame de Sablé, having frequented the influential salon of Madame de Rambouillet in the middle decades of the century, then established her own of which La Rochefoucauld, a regular visitor, reported in a letter: 'L'envie des sentences se gagne comme le rhume' ('The desire for *sententiae* is spreading like a cold').[1]

That infection is ever-present in *moraliste* writing of the second half of the seventeenth century, which marks its moment of greatest vigour in French literary history, and further names of lesser practitioners could be added to those in Mortier's collection. It is difficult to know why this period should have produced what now looks like a *moraliste* moment. The work of La Rochefoucauld and his contemporaries certainly reflects, in elliptical form, not only the legacy of humanism but the preoccupations of court society under Louis XIV: the constant need for prudence and politeness in the search for grace and favour, the frequent discrepancy between appearance and reality in relations between people, and the obscure depths of human motivation. *Moraliste* writing pursues, at the same time, the epigrammatic ideal of salon orality by displaying polished fragments of the purest language suspended above the sparkling conversations from which they first emerged. The drama of *moraliste* writing is to be found in the resistance of its dark materials to the lucidity of its formulations.

---

1 Quoted in J. Lafond (ed.), *Moralistes du xviie siècle* (Paris: Robert Laffont, 1992), p. 110. This and all subsequent references to the work of the *moralistes* are, unless otherwise indicated, taken from this edition. All subsequent references are incorporated in the text. All translations are mine.

Contexts

The themes that *moraliste* writing explores are, in themselves, nothing new. Questions of prudence and politeness are the focus of a sequence of French seventeenth-century texts dealing with the untranslatable courtly virtue of *honnêteté*. These include the treatises of Nicolas Faret (1596–1646) and his imitators Jacques Du Bosc (d. 1660) and François de Grenaille (1616–80?), all published in the second quarter of the century, and, a generation later, work by two of Pascal's interlocutors, Antoine Gombault, Chevalier de Méré (1610–84) and Damien Mitton (1618–90). Ideally, *honnêteté* is a form of behaviour that combines prudence with politeness, the morally correct with the socially pleasing. The tension between those two principles often comes to the surface, however, accompanied by the suspicion that *honnêteté* is no more than a self-interested aesthetics – the art of winning friends and influencing people – disguised as a disinterested ethics. The obscurities of human motivation and relationships are examined by the authors of treatises on the passions. The genre is dominated in the first half of the century by men of the church such as Pierre Charron (1541–1603), Jean-Pierre Camus (1584–1652), Nicolas Coëffeteau (1574–1623), and Jean-François Senault (1601–72). Their treatises, systematic in presentation, owe much to scholastic faculty psychology and to the revived stoic moral tradition which attempts to 'heal' the passions by treating them as errors of judgement. In his *Les Passions de l'âme* (*The Passions of the Soul*) (1649), the philosopher René Descartes (1596–1650) breaks with the traditional psychology of his predecessors in the treatise genre, attempting to apply the principles of his new mechanical philosophy to a physiological study of the passions. Pascal's complaint against the same authors has above all to do with their chosen method of presentation: the systematic divisions that Charron uses in his philosophical treatise *De la sagesse* (*On Wisdom*) (1601), Pascal says, 'attristent et ennuient' ('sadden and bore') the reader (*Pensées*, no. 644).

Pascal goes on in the same fragment to praise, by contrast, the winningly anti-systematic style of Montaigne. Montaigne constitutes the single most important precursor of the *moraliste* tradition in the seventeenth century pre-cisely because he creates, in the course of his *Essais*, a discontinuous conver-sational mode of writing that makes the most important questions accessible to his readers. Whatever the *moralistes* make of the approach that Montaigne takes to those questions – and Pascal, along with his Jansenist friends Antoine Arnauld (1612–94) and Pierre Nicole (1625–95), considers it to be unpardon-ably lax – they nonetheless admire the quality of his sentences. Montaigne's constant recourse to quotations and examples from ancient sources makes his text, like the many collections of adages, commonplaces, and proverbs produced earlier in the sixteenth century, a treasure-house of sayings upon which his inheritors draw. However, the *Essais* represent more than just another textual repository to the *moralistes*, for the process of appropriation and rewriting to which Montaigne subjects the materials he borrows foreshadows their own literary practice. *Moraliste* writing, in that sense, shows its greatest debt to Montaigne when it appears to write him out of the story. Pascal puts the point most succinctly: 'Ce n'est pas dans Montaigne mais dans moi que je trouve tout ce que j'y vois' ('It is not in Montaigne but in myself that I find everything I see there') (*Pensées*, no. 568).

The texts

Moraliste writing exists only in collections of discontinuous fragments. Like the treatise, it attempts to redefine and refine thinking about human behaviour, but where the treatise sets out an argument in continuous discursive prose, it offers flashes of insight in one assertion after another. The speaker in the *moraliste* text, a discreet but unmistakable presence, may choose to adopt any one of a number of postures, playing at different moments the judge who lays down the law about our behaviour, the observer who simply describes the facts, and the analyst who dissects the illusions we hold dear. It is the text's discontinuous form that makes it so difficult to tease out a coherent narrative or perspective. At one extreme, an individual fragment may be consumed in isolation, since it is a self-sufficient text of its own. At the other extreme, a collection of fragments may be read as a whole, with the gaps between them inviting the making of connections as much as they frustrate it. Each island of text on the page appears close to, but cut off from, a whole string of other islands in a kind of puzzling textual archipelago. How do you get from one to the other? And in what order?

The text of the *Pensées* raises these interpretative questions in their most acute form. Most of its eight hundred or so fragments relate to Pascal's projected apology of the Christian religion, but that project remained incomplete at his death in 1662, leaving readers to puzzle over individual fragments and their role within the broader argument. It is not even safe to assume that the text is discontinuous simply because it is unfinished, since Pascal eschews the technical arguments and methodical divisions of writers like Charron, preferring instead to introduce shorter forms such as the dialogue and the letter form into his apology. His ultimate aim is to bring his implied readers to belief by persuading them, in a language they can understand, to take two steps: first, to recognise that life in this world, when lived out with no sense of deeper purpose, is shot through with contradiction and self-delusion; and, second, to see that Christianity alone explains why this is so and offers the possibility of salvation. Many of Pascal's most celebrated and haunting fragments – those that reveal the weakness of human reason, the power that our imagination and habits of mind hold over us, our constant need for *divertissement* (diversion), and our monstrous capacity for *amour-propre* (self-love) and vanity – seem broadly designed to bring the reader to take the first of those two steps. Those fragments tend, however, to lack any explicit apologetic dimension. What this means is that they can be, and indeed often have been, read as isolated expressions of a disenchanted secular worldview. Take, for example, the sentence that asserts vanity to be an inescapable fact of human behaviour: 'Qui ne voit pas la vanité du monde est bien vain lui-même' ('Whoever is unable to see the vanity of the world is truly vain') (no. 70). The sentence owes its coercive rhetorical impact to its brevity and self-sufficiency, the qualities that make it a fragment, and yet those very qualities also mean that it can be read according to different moral perspectives. One might choose to see in this an intrinsic consequence of the fragment as a literary form. Pascal, however, prefers to stress the interpretative challenge that this kind of writing poses for its readers: 'Toutes les bonnes maximes sont dans le monde; on ne manque qu'à les appliquer' ('All the right maxims are abroad in the world; we fall short only in applying them') (no. 458). Our inability to 'apply' maxims as we should reveals, for Pascal, our failure to recognise the truth of the story they tell about us.

The *Maximes* of La Rochefoucauld share with the *Pensées* a deep pessimism about the powers and motivations of humans in a fallen world. In the *Pensées*, that pessimism is clearly Augustinian in inspiration, and it thus connects Pascal's projected apology to the Jansenist movement based at Port-Royal (on this, see Chapter 37 below). If there is a religious dimension to the pessimism of the *Maximes*, it constitutes the text's hinterland rather than its horizon, and is counterbalanced by the text's interest in the secular values of prudence and politeness. The world that the *Maximes* describe is governed by *amour-propre* and hypocrisy, but it is the only world on offer, and it rewards scrutiny even as it passes complete understanding. The epigraph to the entire collection sets the tone: 'Nos vertus ne sont, le plus souvent, que des vices déguisés' ('Our virtues are most often only vices in disguise'). The maxim takes the form of a definition here, as it often does in La Rochefoucauld's collection, which resembles in this respect the monolingual French dictionaries that first appear in the same period. Three key features, however, distinguish this maxim from a dictionary-style definition. Its use of the first-person plural possessive adjective 'nos' instantly implicates the reader and the *moraliste* alike in the observation that is to follow; its vertiginous redescription of the term 'vertus' by means of its antonym 'vices' does not so much define the former as threaten to unmask it as a snare and a delusion; and the qualification 'le plus souvent', by allowing for rare instances of true virtue to be found, leaves one wondering how to tell true from false in a world of disguise and dissimulation. Lucid but not omniscient, the *moraliste* merely raises the question, leaving the rest to the reader. The ordering of the maxims, too, seems designed to offer its readers pleasure and profit but no overarching synthesis: from the second (1666) edition of the *Maximes* onwards, a short preface indicates that while the fragments have been left in a state of disorder, an index has been provided so that readers may pursue a particular theme through the collection. The discontinuous internal organisation of the *Maximes* is not, as it was in part at least in the *Pensées*, an accident of history. It reflects a strategy of literary ambiguity.

The two last major *moralistes* of the seventeenth century, La Fontaine and La Bruyère, show the influence of Pascal and La Rochefoucauld even as they invent – or reinvent – new short forms of *moraliste* writing. La Fontaine dedicates one of his early fables, 'L'Homme et son image' ('The Man and his Image') (1.11), to La Rochefoucauld, describing the *Maximes* as a stream in which everyone sees reflected the follies of self-love.[2] In the 'Discours sur Théophrastus' ('Discourse on Theophrastus') that serves as a general preface to his *Caractères*, La Bruyère describes his own work as less sublime than the *Pensées* and less subtle than the *Maximes*: a middling text that aims simply to make humankind 'reasonable'. Unlike their predecessors in the *moraliste* tradition, but like certain of their contemporaries in other areas of literary activity, La Fontaine and La Bruyère initially present themselves as translators of ancient writers: La Fontaine of Aesop's *Fables* into French verse, and La Bruyère of Theophrastus' *Characters* into the idiom of a new age. The long-running tension in France between those writers who revered ancient models and those who claimed the freedom to innovate had sparked a full-blown Quarrel of the Ancients and Moderns which, from the 1670s onwards, divided the literary and cultural establishment. The self-presentation of La Fontaine and La Bruyère needs to be understood in this context: it puts them on the side of the Ancients. The first six books of La Fontaine's

2 Jean de La Fontaine, *Fables*, ed. M. Fumaroli (Paris: Imprimerie Nationale, 1985), pp. 55–6.

Fables are indeed predominantly Aesopic in inspiration: they introduce the reader to the bestiary of that tradition and to the knowing observations on human nature, offered here in true *moraliste* style, that their animal encounters occasion. Already visible in the opening poem of Book 2, however, is perhaps La Fontaine's greatest achievement: his sly reinvention of the fable as a remarkably supple and capacious poetic form, a kind of literary Trojan horse, capable of carrying within its flanks a cohort of other forms and genres. La Bruyère brings a similar diversity of invention to his prose *Caractères*, which contain short reflections reminiscent of Pascal and La Rochefoucauld alongside society portraits, caricatures, and sketches. But where La Fontaine stresses the gaiety of his inventions, La Bruyère emphasises the belatedness of his, as in the famous first line of the *Caractères*: 'Tout est dit, et l'on vient trop tard' ('Everything has already been said, and we come too late') (1.1). La Bruyère's opening expresses the position in which *moraliste* writing finds itself at the end of the seventeenth century: belated, certainly, but – faced with the continuing spectacle of human behaviour – with everything still to do.

Moraliste writing itself has continued to play a part in the French literary tradition since the age of La Fontaine and La Bruyère: more recent practitioners include, among others, the marquis de Vauvenargues (1715–47), Nicolas Chamfort (1740–94), Joseph Joubert (1754–1824), Alain (1868–1951), and Pascal Quignard (1948–). But the second half of the seventeenth century is the *moraliste* moment. It witnesses the rise to prominence of a kind of writing that can sometimes seem all-pervasive. Plays and prose fiction of the same period reveal the potential of maxims to frame or intervene in narrative situations. In the plays of Molière (1622–73) and Jean Racine (1639–99), for example, characters often trade sentences worthy of La Rochefoucauld or La Bruyère: the drama unfolds through the clash of maxims. The novels of Madeleine de Scudéry (1608–1701) contain within them extractable set-piece maxims that reflect on the implications of the narrative. In the fictions of Madame de Lafayette (1634–93), particularly her historical novel *La Princesse de Clèves* (1678), *moraliste* reflection is fully integrated into the narrative. The novel portrays a court society in which people use the elliptical form of the maxim to tell one another what cannot decently be expressed by any other means. Survival at court signifies, for the novel's eponymous heroine, learning both how to interpret the maxims of others and to use her own maxims in such a way as to exercise linguistic control. It is a *roman d'apprentissage* in the art of 'applying' maxims, as Pascal puts it, to everyday life.

36

Seventeenth-century prose narrative

CRAIG MOYES

Not so very long ago, a chapter like this in a history of French literature would probably have been called 'The seventeenth-century novel', or 'Seventeenth-century prose fiction'. It would have doubtless discussed the major variants of narrative fiction in chronological order, beginning with the pastoral and heroic romances of the first half of the century, moving through the comic novels of Sorel, Scarron, and Furetière, the proto-realist novellas of Segrais and Saint-Réal, as well as the early experiments with the epistolary novel (notably Guilleragues's *Les Lettres portugaises*, 1669), before giving pride of place to the single undisputed masterpiece of the century, Lafayette's *La Princesse de Clèves* (1678). For those readers wishing such an overview, they could do much worse than to turn to Henri Coulet's admirable survey, which more than forty years on still stands as one of the most succinct and subtle tableaux of the variants and changes in French narrative fiction over the course of the *ancien régime*.[1]

As indicated by its broader title, this chapter hopes to accomplish something slightly different. While clearly the novel must remain an important part of the seventeenth-century literary landscape, a renewed critical interest in other, formerly minor, genres has moved the emphasis away from *narrative fiction* to the more general category of *prose narrative*. At this point, one may well be struck with a M. Jourdainesque astonishment – *Quoi!... tout ce qui n'est point vers?* – and yet, the philosopher's cod definition notwithstanding, the broad category of 'not verse' is for many reasons a better starting point than the as yet uncodified generic distinctions of the *roman* or the *nouvelle*. If verse is well represented in this volume with three chapters on theatre and one on poetry, the space devoted to prose reflects its importance to the seventeenth-century reading public. Of course, a long tradition of French Classicism had, long before Boileau, privileged poetry and dramatic verse, verse (especially

---

1 H. Coulet, *Le Roman jusqu'à la Révolution* (Paris: Colin, 1967).

alexandrine verse) being, at least in theory, the noblest form of expression. Even such obviously prosaic forms as the novel and history were elevated by their association with poetry. Be that as it may, this *theoretical* superiority of verse is at odds with the extraordinary expansion and unprecedented popularity of prose throughout the seventeeth century. One need only look at the sheer volume published to see that it is far and away the dominant literary category of the age. The explosion of narrative fiction (from just two or three novels published in France from 1560 to 1590, to 118 from 1600 to 1610, to a total of well over 1,200 by the end of the century)[2]; the vogue for history, for memoirs, for the curious genre made up of collections of anecdotes known as *les anas*, with titles named after the authors concerned; the rise of 'familiar' forms such as conversations, dialogues, and correspondence – forms which, when joined with the ideology of *honnêteté*, were able to bring such formerly rebarbative and pedantic genres as philosophy and religion within the sphere of 'polite' learning; and, in the last half of the century, the moralists' fragmentary and apophthegmatic approach to the world: the popularity of all of these forms *qui ne sont point vers* point to the unequivocal centrality of prose to seventeenth-century society. Despite Boileau placing poetry at the mythical foundation of civilisation in *L'Art poétique*,[3] in the seventeenth century it is prose – and more precisely everyday, unaffected prose (albeit 'polished' and 'cultivated') – which becomes, as Marc Fumaroli puts it, 'both a social bond and a matter of State, irrigating the connective tissue of the French nation . . . This triumph of prose without the affectation of art is definitive, and continues today.'[4]

A further reason for displacing the centre of interest away from fiction has to do with the fact that what we understand as a 'novel' – that is, a more or less realistic narrative of mostly or entirely fictional events centred around one or more convincingly drawn characters – is of relatively recent conceptual invention. Despite many works which may be retrospectively read in terms of a genre that was to flourish in the eighteenth and especially the nineteenth centuries, the varied state of prose fiction in the seventeenth century sits uneasily within such an essentially teleological definition. Behind the sober veneer of its Classical style, we may be able to recognise the *Princesse de Clèves* as a novel, but in what way can we claim that the endless pastoral conversations of

2 Maurice Lever, *Romanciers du Grand Siècle* (Paris: Fayard, 1996), pp. 11–12.
3 *L'Art poétique*, chant iv, in *Œuvres complètes de Boileau*, ed. Antoine Adam (Paris: Gallimard, 1966), pp. 183–4.
4 Marc Fumaroli, *La Diplomatie de l'esprit: de Montaigne à La Fontaine* (Paris: Hermann, 1994), 'Préface', pp. viii, xiii.

d'Urfé's *L'Astrée* (1607–27) or the twelve volumes of La Calprenède's sprawling adventure tale *Cléopâtre* (1647–58) or that the disjointed satire of Furetière's *Roman bourgeois* (1666) are examples of the same genre? For many (including, as we shall see, Madame de Lafayette herself) they are not. From a modern perspective, the former seem little more than exercises in an inflated and wordy formlessness from which the novel would eventually – and inevitably – detach itself whilst the latter's low vulgarity would only be redeemed much later by its incipient realism. The delicate modal qualifications of one late twentieth-century scholar betray precisely this teleological bias:

> Although the seventeenth century produced a large number of works of fiction and though they appear to have been widely read and apparently enjoyed, it is clear that in many respects the French novel could not yet be regarded as a true literary form. The writers were not without talent but their works, as we can see from the practice of Honoré d'Urfé and Madeleine de Scudéry, often consisted of a lengthy collection of adventure and love stories which today are found unreadable and a serious burden for literary historians.[5]

Now such peremptory exclusion may seem to be a congenitally English vice, where the modernity of the *novel* foregrounds a dual reality which the continuity of the French term *roman* tends to hide. In England the novel – i.e. this new, or 'novel' form of realist narrative – famously arose at the beginning of the eighteenth century (or at the end of the seventeenth, depending on which history you read), clearly marking itself off as something different from the *romances* which came before. Yet in France too, despite the persistence of a term that seemingly stretches unbroken from *Le Roman de Renart* to the *nouveau roman*, a similar change occurred. The *roman* – understood as a long (sometimes exceedingly long: La Calprenède's three novels run to a total of over 17,000 pages) tale full of fabulous deeds and impossibly heroic and *galant* characters – fell out of favour in the 1660s in the face of a new vogue for shorter, simpler and more personal tales variously known as *nouvelles*, *mémoires*, or *histoires secrètes*. Thus Mme de Lafayette, writing (anonymously) about the *Princesse de Clèves*, saw it as something essentially different from a *roman*: not a fabulous tale, but 'une parfaite imitation du monde de la Cour et de la manière dont on y vit. Il n'y a rien de romanesque ni de grimpé; aussi n'est-ce pas un roman, c'est probablement des Mémoires, et c'estoit à ce que l'on m'a dit, le titre du livre, mais on l'a changé' ('a perfect imitation of Court and its way of life. There is nothing romantic or pompous about it; therefore

5 Martin Turnell, *The Rise of the French Novel* (London: Hamish Hamilton, 1979), p. 3.

it is not a novel, but probably memoirs. I heard that was to be the title of the book, but it was changed').[6] It is an irony of literary history that these works we now consider the most 'novelistic' (i.e. realistic) were often written in opposition to novels. From Charles Sorel's *Berger extravagant* (1627) and Jean-Pierre Camus's *Tapisseries historiques* (1644), both of whom called their (very different) works *anti-romans* (in Sorel's case, the subtitle being added to the 1633 edition), to Mme de Lafayette's refusal to call the *Princesse de Clèves* a romance, this turn away from a poetically inflected understanding of narrative representation goes no small way towards making these novels *novels* for later generations of readers.

If these 'secret histories' and 'anti-novels' would lay the groundwork for the (*nouveau*) *roman* of the eighteenth and nineteenth centuries, relegating the older romances to the status of 'unreadability', they also point to the importance of an approach to prose narrative which is not restricted by genre, and especially by a genre such as the novel which had not yet been fully explored or codified. Not only might we be led to exclude tremendously important writers such as Honoré d'Urfé and Madeleine de Scudéry, restricting our object to *fiction* also leaves far too much out of the picture, including precisely those sorts of prose narratives pointed up by the nomenclature of the new 'anti-romance'. Where else, for example, are we to place history, both the grand narrative of royal history (which was to be written under Louis XIV by none other than the two most prominent poets of the age, Racine and Boileau) or the many 'secret histories', or memoirs, produced in the margins of Bourbon absolutism? Fumaroli, who has usefully focused much work on the intersection between genres, remarks that in the seventeenth century historiography was in an analagous position to epic poetry: despite both genres boasting long and illustrious pedigrees, neither had yet produced practioners of any merit.[7] No writer had managed, in either genre, to adequately fulfil the narrative function entrusted to him by the Aristotelian separation of the *vrai* from the *vraisemblable*, the historically true from the poetically plausible, the genuine account of what *did* happen from the fictional tale of what *might* have happened. But if both history and the epic were, in the seventeenth century, narrative genres awaiting their Herodotus and their Homer, the *vrai* and the *vraisemblable* nonetheless found expression elsewhere, in two very unregulated literary arenas: on the one hand in 'the heavy and misshapen

6 Madame de Lafayette, Letter to the Chevalier de Lescheraine, 13 April 1678, in Madame de La Fayette, *Correspondance*, ed. A. Beaunier, 2 vols. (Paris: Gallimard, 1942), II, p. 63.
7 Fumaroli, *La Diplomatie de l'esprit*, p. 183.

mass' of aristocratic memoirs (as Marguerite de Valois called hers)[8] and on the other in the unruly, often inflated, occasionally undignified and in any case widely varied production of prose fiction.

These types of narrative might seem at first glance to have little in common beyond their status as prose, or even to be fundamentally opposed to one another, as truth is contrary to fiction. Be that as it may, over the course of the century they would gravitate towards a common ground which was, in terms of both its style and its public, essentially *mondain*. It is here, on the rhetorical 'commonplace' of polite society, that the stylistic virtues of conversation – characterised by a 'familiar' style, proper to the language of leisure (as opposed to the 'high' style of political, religious, or scholarly discourse, or the 'low' Rabelaisian style of burlesque and comedy) – and the social virtues of *honnêteté* formed a background which allowed for the interpenetration of theoretically incompatible genres. For conversation in the seventeenth century was more than a simple pastime for an idle aristocracy; it was a refined art of linguistic complicity and social conformity. Because this conformity is not given by nature, it requires work, in this case the rhetorical elaboration of a dedicated *ars convivia* which allowed for the polishing of rough edges and the reconciliation of conflict.

The first major novel of the seventeenth century, *L'Astrée*, is emblematic in this regard. A four-volume romance, published over two decades (a posthumous fifth volume was written by d'Urfé's secretary in 1628), it recounts the amorous trials and tribulations of a young shepherd and his shepherdess in an idealised pastoral setting placed against the historical backdrop of fifth-century Gaul. It is impossible to summarise the scores of intrigues and hundreds of characters that people its more than 5,000 pages, but suffice it to say that before it became a 'burden for literary historians' it held several generations of readers in thrall (including La Fontaine and Rousseau, who in the *Confessions* warmly recalls his father reading it to him as a young boy). In the aftermath of the Wars of Religion, a terrible and bloody civil war which had literally rent the body politic of France, *L'Astrée* offers a civilised and civilising solution, providing a literary alternative to violence and discord (embodied in the novel by the machinations of the villainous Polémas) based on a theoretical ideal of love, itself embedded within a practical ideal of polite conversation. That the narrative representation of the these things should involve shepherds discoursing eloquently about the rarefied nature of Neoplatonic love would only trouble later generations of readers (for

8 Ibid.

example, because 'shepherds are normally coarse and stupid'[9] or because the entire plot hangs on 'a misunderstanding which could have been cleared up in four words'[10]). For the readers of the first half of the century, d'Urfé's novel was nothing short of a model of *vraisemblance*, which is to say, following Aristotle, that it was 'more philosophical and more excellent'[11] than the mere recounting of events would allow, for it prefered the general truths of social interaction (the theory and practice of love and conversation) to the particular facts of history (Merovingian politics or the practice of ovine husbandry).

Indeed, it is the meaning of this vexed term *vraisemblance* (verisimilitude, plausibility) that will change over the century and that will make prose, despite falling by its nature outside the sphere of poetics proper, the site of an important aesthetic shift. Insofar as *vraisemblance* is grounded in the public, elevating those truths admissible according to received opinion (i.e. those accepted amongst the greater part of the audience) over the narrow truth of historical event (known to a more restricted group of specialists) – or as Boileau puts it in a pithy and oft-cited couplet: 'Jamais au spectateur n'offrez rien d'incroyable, / Le vrai peut quelquefois n'estre pas vraisemblable' ('Never, to the spectator, present anything unbelievable / The [historically] true may sometimes be implausible')[12] – the privileging of the *vraisemblable* could in many ways be considered as the literary and theoretical pendant to what Fumaroli calls the 'generalised rhetoric' of conversation which shaped both social interaction and much of the literature of the period. And if Boileau could also say that the famous rules that guaranteed *vraisemblance* in the theatre may be dispensed with in 'frivolous romances', it is nevertheless remarkable that, at least in the early part of the seventeenth century, romance novelists – and their readers – understood this same essentially moral and social definition of literary verisimilitude as grounding their works.

But what will remain true for poetry and dramatic verse throughout the period (and indeed well into the following century) will, by the 1670s, no longer obtain for prose. If René Rapin – now little known, but in his time an important critic – can define poetic *vraisemblance* quite classically as that which is both 'consonant with public opinion' and which represents things not as they are but 'as they ought to be',[13] he will place historical *vraisemblance*

---

9 Charles Sorel, *La Bibliothèque françoise* (Paris: La Compagnie des Libraires du Palais, 1664), p. 158.
10 *Grand dictionnaire universel du XIXe siècle*, 15 vols. (Paris: Librairie Classique Larousse et Boyer, 1866), art. 'Astrée', I, p. 829b.
11 Aristotle, *Poetics*, 51b5–6.   12 Boileau, *L'Art poétique*, chant III, p. 170.
13 René Rapin, *Les Réflexions sur la poétique de ce temps* (1675), quoted in Aron Kibédi-Varga, *Les Poétiques du classicisme* (Paris: Aux Amateurs de Livres, 1990), pp. 196–7.

on a different footing altogether. And tellingly for Rapin, it is the public's changed attitude to the novel which has become the clearest indicator of the fundamental change in the relationship between public opinion and narrative representation:

> Il semble que le goust du siècle commence enfin à se perfectionner; qu'en toutes choses nous allons assez au bon sens; que nous estimons ce qui est réel & solide, & que nous ne pouvons presque plus rien souffrir ou de faux ou de frivole. C'est le sentiment de tous les gens raisonnables, qui est la plus saine partie de ceux qui se meslent de juger, quoy que ce soit peut-estre la plus petite. Mais rien ne marque plus ce discernement que le dégoust qu'on a pour les Romans, & pour tout ce qui en approche. Ainsi comme cet amour de la vérité & du bon sens est une disposition à aimer l'Histoire, profitons d'une si favorable conjoncture, pour servir le public selon son esprit.

> (It seems that the taste of our age is at last beginning to improve, that in all things we tend towards what is reasonable, that we prize what is solid and real, and that it is now almost impossible to suffer anything either false or frivolous. This is the feeling of all reasonable people, which is to say the soundest, if perhaps the smallest part of those who concern themselves with judgement. But nothing demonstrates this discernment more than the distaste we have for romances and everything resembling them. So, as this love of truth and reason predisposes us to love History, let us take advantage of such a propitious conjuncture in order to serve the public according to its spirit.)[14]

The poetics of *vraisemblance* is here turned on its head. Public opinion is no longer that which demands the correction of history in favour of higher poetic truths informed by an idealised – and socialised – notion of reason; it is reason, or *bon sens*, now modelled on the public's essentially Cartesian faculty of 'distinguishing the true from the false',[15] that requires writers to forgo fiction and to embrace history.

Not only is the 'frivolousness' of earlier romance writers taken to task, the 'something of the poet' which had traditionally been seen to animate the writing of history[16] – at least history in its public and usually royal incarnation – is also seen to be defective. Increasingly, writers began to look to the private and indeed 'prosaic' observations of memoir writers whose self-interest

---

14 René Rapin, *Instructions pour l'histoire* (Paris: Chez Sébastien Marbre-Cramoisy, 1677), pp. 1–2.
15 René Descartes, *Discours de la méthode* (1637), §1 in *Discourse on the Method and Meditations on First Philosophy*, trans. E. S. Haldane (London and New Haven, CT: Yale University Press, 1996), p. 3.
16 Lucian, *De historia conscribenda*, trans. J. Racine, 'Fragments historiques', in *Œuvres complètes* (Paris: Seuil, 1962), p. 369.

offered a singular prism and whose style, moreover, found itself implicitly pitched as much against the 'romantic' excesses of novels as the pomp and grandeur of royal history. Both types of narrator met at this intersection and mutually benefited from the exchange, bringing to it on the one hand the frankness of the memoir writer (the narrative *je* which says 'this is what actually happened') and on the other the psychological penetration which would come to characterise the narrator of the (modern) novel ('this is *why* these things happened'). Rapin continues:

> Ce n'est pas écrire l'Histoire que de conter les actions des hommes, sans parler de leurs motifs; c'est faire le Gazetier, qui se contente de dire les évenemens des choses, sans remonter à leur source . . . rien ne plaist davantage dans une narration, que l'explication de ce qu'il y a de secret & d'important dans les intentions & dans les desseins de ceux dont elle raconte les actions . . . Car rien ne touche davantage la curiosité des hommes, que quand on découvre ce qui est le plus caché dans le cœur humain, c'est à dire, les ressorts secrets qui le font agir dans les entreprises qui luy sont ordinaires.

> (Simply recounting the actions of men without speaking of their motives is not History writing; it is journalism, being content to talk of events without returning to their source . . . nothing in a narrative delights so much as the explanation of what is secret and important in the intentions and designs of those whose actions are being recounted . . . For nothing touches the curiosity of men more than discovering what is most hidden in the human heart, which is to say the secret springs which make it act in the ordinary course of events.)[17]

It should come as no surprise that Madame de Lafayette – who, perhaps more carefully than any other writer in the seventeenth century, focused the narrative of her novel on the 'secret springs' of her protagonist's heart – also wrote, near the beginning and end of her career, two works of history relating to the court of Louis XIV.[18] Nor should it come as a surprise that the highly developed art of conversation in the society she describes depended on a set of hermeneutic and rhetorical skills very similar to those required for the narrator of 'memoirs' and 'secret histories'. As one of the seventeenth century's most celebrated *honnêtes hommes*, the chevalier de Méré, writes in his 'Discours de la conversation' (1677): 'Il faut observer tout ce qui se passe dans le cœur et dans l'esprit des personnes qu'on entretient, et s'accoutumer de bonne heure à connaître les sentiments et les pensées, par les signes presque

---

17 R. Rapin, *Instructions pour l'histoire*, pp. 63, 65.
18 Mme de Lafayette, *Histoire de Madame Henriette d'Angleterre* [c. 1664] *et Mémoires de la Cour de France pour les années 1688 et 1689*, ed. Gilbert Sigaux (Paris: Mercure de France, 1965).

imperceptibles' ('It is necessary to observe everything that happens in the hearts and minds of those one converses with, and to quickly get used to knowing their thoughts and feelings through almost imperceptible signs').[19]

La Princesse de Clèves is an important novel for many reasons, but perhaps its first claim to fame is that it touched off a heated public debate on the nature of narrative *vraisemblance*. As one of its first readers observed, the confession that Mme de Clèves makes to her husband is 'extraordinary', '*invraisemblable*', and could only be the sort of thing that could happen in real life, which is to say in the world of 'extravagancies' uncorrected by reason. As such, it has no place in a novel. 'L'auteur . . . a plus songé à ne pas ressembler aux autres romans qu'à suivre le bon sens' ('The author . . . has cared more for not resembling other novels [*sic*] than in following reason').[20] Of course, Bussy Rabutin did not understand what René Rapin – at least the Rapin *historiographe* – clearly saw. Bussy judged the work according to the dictates of poetics (where, as the etymology of *extravagant* suggests, events must not stray from the path of reason) when he should have looked to the judgement and to the (revised) *bon sens* of the historian, or indeed the *honnête homme*.

Twelve years previously, another writer attempted a novel which would set itself off from the romance tradition. Unlike the *Princesse de Clèves*, however, *Le Roman bourgeois* was not a success. Taking the opposite tack from the narrative strategy of Mme de Lafayette, who carefully follows the chiaroscuro of her protagonist's heart through the subtle use of indirect style, the voice of Furetière's author/publisher argues directly against the poetics of the romance in order to claim that the content of his tale is all the more genuine and sincere for its limited point of view and for the disorder of its telling. 'Pour le soin de la liaison', he jokes, 'je laisse à celui qui reliera le livre' ('As for the task of putting it all together, I leave that to the bookbinder/[reader]').[21] Antoine Adam, in his magisterial history of seventeenth-century literature, thought such puns little more than poor excuses for an unstructured work of 'myopic' realism.[22] But whether we accept his judgement or not, amongst Furetière's *bons mots* there is one regarding the novel in general which literary historians

19 C. de Méré, *Des agréments: discours de Monsieur Le Chevalier de Méré à Madame* *** (Paris: Chez Denis Thierry, 1677), quoted in J. Hellegouarc'h, *L'Art de la conversation* (Paris: Dunod, 1997), p. 66.
20 Bussy Rabutin to Mme de Sévigné, 29 June 1678, quoted in Gérard Genette, 'Vraisemblance et motivation', *Figures II* (Paris: Seuil, 1969), pp. 71–2.
21 Antoine Furetière, *Le Roman bourgeois* (1666), ed. M. Roy-Garibal (Paris: Flammarion, 2001), p. 225.
22 Antoine Adam, *Histoire de la littérature française au XVIIe siècle*, 4 vols. (Paris: Éditions Mondiales, 1948–56), IV, pp. 194–8.

should consider carefully, and upon which this chapter might well conclude: 'si vous y vouliez rechercher cette grande régularité que vous n'y trouverez pas, sachez seulement que la faute ne serait pas dans l'ouvrage, mais dans le titre: ne l'appelez plus roman et il ne vous choquera point' ('if you do not find here that lofty order which you were looking for, know only that the fault lies not within the work, but in the title: don't call it a novel and it will no longer shock you').[23]

23 Furetière, *Le Roman bourgeois*, p. 226.

37

Seventeenth-century religious writing

RICHARD PARISH

Religious writing in the French seventeenth century is, to all intents and purposes, Christian and Catholic. Islam is accorded no more than a cursory treatment in the domain of apologetics; and Judaism tends to be viewed above all as a precursor of Christianity. It is presented as the flawed channel that makes way for, and by its very opposition affords additional credibility to, the revealed truth of the Incarnation. Even Protestant writing is scarce: the Revocation of the Edict of Nantes by Louis XIV (1638–1715) in 1685 (denying the freedom of conscience to members of the 'Religion Prétendue Réformée' [the 'so-called reformed religion'] granted by Henri IV in 1598) resulted in the exile of many of its adherents; and the single most celebrated Protestant text to be published earlier in the century, in the form of the epic account of the Huguenot cause during the Wars of Religion by Agrippa d'Aubigné (1552–1630) (*Les Tragiques* [1616–23]), shares more of the characteristics of the previous century by virtue both of its ethos and of its aesthetic.

Yet the written legacy of Catholic Christianity in the seventeenth century is of itself, perhaps surprisingly in view of the Roman church's authoritarian and monolithic reputation, a complex phenomenon, replete with argument, paradox, and dissent from ecclesial authority. Looking back to its origins in the narratives of the Incarnation and Redemption, historically recorded in the Gospels yet in many respects unclear as to their nature and implications (an ambiguity to which the early Christian councils bore witness in their painstaking formulation of orthodoxy), it could well be argued that some element of doctrinal controversy is likely to endure; but it is in a later event, the Council of Trent (1545–63), that the coexistence of conformity and plurality has its more immediate origins. This reply to the Protestant Reformation gave definitive expression to the teaching of what is commonly known as the Counter-Reformation (and more correctly as the Catholic Reformation), yet stood, probably unwittingly and certainly unintentionally, at the origin of a fertile and not always compatible diversity of traditions and practices. Indeed the greatest single difficulty in understanding the religious climate of the period in France arises from the fact that its best-known manifestation, and the origin of much of its greatest writing, is a movement (for which Jansenism is the commonest shorthand term) that was in many respects at odds with Catholic orthodoxy.

If we start at the centre, so to speak, we find that the major corpus of writing from within the Catholic hierarchy is due to three prelates: François de Sales (1567–1622), bishop of Geneva (resident in Annecy, in exile from his titular see in Calvinist Switzerland); Jacques-Bénigne Bossuet (1627–1704), bishop of Meaux, and preceptor to the Dauphin; and François de Salignac de la Mothe Fénelon (1651–1715), archbishop of Cambrai and preceptor to the king's grandson. However, although all three figures held episcopal appointments, their contributions to the Catholic conspectus of the age was significantly different. François de Sales typically attracts the label of Christian humanism: in both of his major works, the *Introduction à la vie dévote* (*Introduction to the Devout Life*) (1609) and the *Traité de l'amour de Dieu* (*Treatise on the Love of God*) (1616), the dominant impression is one of tolerance and pragmatism. The first seeks to find a path which, whilst not denying scriptural imperatives and the life of the spirit, recognises at the same time the legitimacy of the (explicitly) female addressee's secular concerns; whereas the second, while retaining a tonality of patient encouragement, moves in all respects more ambitiously and indeed at times lyrically into the world of the cloister. The impact of both texts, as well as of François's copious correspondence in his capacity as spiritual director, was extensive, as was manifest in his exceptionally rapid canonisation in 1665. From a literary point of view, his writing is marked by a methodical precision allied with a mastery of the pertinent image, often drawn from the natural world.

Bossuet's vast output includes historical and political works, in which the government and destiny of both past and present regimes are interpreted in the Christian perspective, as well as a significant corpus of polemical writing. But it is above all as a preacher that he is remembered. His sermons (usually given as autonomous homilies rather than within the context of the Mass), panegyrics of the saints and above all *Oraisons funèbres* (*Funeral Orations*), delivered in honour of members of the royal family and of the highest dignitaries of his age, display an unparalleled capacity for triumphalist rhetoric, in which all transitory values are superseded by a providential understanding of the immanent, when viewed from a transcendent perspective. They are characterised by a rigorous overarching structure and by an interweaving of biblical texts to the greatest affective purpose. Fénelon undoubtedly eclipses Bossuet in terms of his spiritual finesse, and yet is doomed to be remembered above all for his involvement in the quietist controversy in the last years of the century. If Bossuet is the disciple of François de Sales by virtue of his rigour and pragmatism, Fénelon is above all indebted to his precursor's subtle taxonomy of the higher forms of prayerful communion with God, as manifested in the *Explication des maximes des saints* (*Explanation of the Sayings of the Saints*) (1697), even though the sheer sophistication of the spiritual distinctions proposed in this work militates against its more strictly literary qualities. Fénelon's best-known work, *Les Aventures de Télémaque* (*The Adventures of Telemachus*) (1699), written as a pedagogical exercise for his royal pupil, adapts a classical fable into an enlightened allegory of good monarchical government informed, unsurprisingly if at the time controversially, by a Christian ethic of justice and moderation.

Moving into two traditionally more imaginative genres, we have to consider lyric poetry and stage drama. Despite efforts at rehabilitation of a wider range of writers, however, it is difficult to claim enduring significance for more than a handful of Christian poets, mostly in the early part of the century, and of these only one or two command any attention that is wider than antiquarian. The *Théorèmes* (1613–21) of Jean de La Ceppède (*c.* 1548–1623) are a sequence of sonnets that view the specifics of Christ's Passion, death and resurrection through a closely focused prism. As such they foreground the sheer physicality of the Incarnation and, as an inevitable corollary, draw the reader into an intimate relationship with the suffering victim. Their poetic idiom exploits all the compression of which the highly wrought form of the sonnet is capable, notably in its capacity for the dramatic use of repetition and contrast; and the intense christocentrism that informs them is entirely characteristic of much devotional writing of the period. Claude Hopil (*c.* 1585–*c.* 1633), representing perhaps the complementary poetic challenge afforded by Christian theology, writes in *Les Divins Élancements d'amour* (*Exclamations of Divine Love*) (1629) on the mystery of the Holy Trinity. This sequence takes the most intractable of orthodox dogmas as its starting point for an often vertiginous exploration, in a freer metrical tradition and with occasional use of the telling neologism, of the logically inexpressible coexistence of three persons (Father, Son, and Holy Spirit) in a single triune godhead.

The dramatic spectrum is equally varied and has proved more enduring. In the first half of the century a range of plays on strictly Christian subjects – most predictably, given its inherent dramatic potential, the call to martyrdom – were written and performed. These include the seminal *Polyeucte martyr* (1641–2) of Pierre Corneille (1606–84), his lesser-known and dramatically somewhat weaker *Théodore* (1646), and *Le Véritable Saint-Genest, comédien et martyr* (*The True Saint Genesius, Actor and Martyr*) (1645) of Jean Rotrou (1609–50). What the first and last of these pieces convincingly achieve is a thoroughgoing conflation of episodes from the Christian martyrology with the exploration of dramatic aesthetics. In the case of Corneille, the compatibility is exploited between an unquestioning iconoclastic zeal and the rewards (or heroic *gloire*) that, in Polyeucte's case posthumously, it carries, giving rise thereby to one possible understanding of the necessarily complex notion of a Christian tragedy. In that of Rotrou, the troubling overlap between a staged (and therefore feigned) and authentic experience of conversion is portrayed, affording in the process a powerful example of the theatre within the theatre. Both pieces rely heavily for their dramatic (and arguably didactic) impact on an epiphanic understanding of the workings of divine grace.

Before further dramatic works were to be staged in a religious idiom, however, a major dispute was to break out concerning the legitimacy of the theatre in a Christian state, commonly referred to as the *querelle du théâtre*. Writers in the authoritative mainstream, such as Bossuet, joined figures of a yet more zealous tendency, above all the moralist Pierre Nicole (1625–95) and the highly influential prince de Conti (1629–68), in a condemnation of the theatre per se, at best as a waste of time, and at worst as an ungodly activity susceptible of inflaming unhealthy and sinful passions (albeit sometimes, in the process, coming paradoxically closer to grasping the power of the stage than was the case for certain of their more secularly minded Aristotelian contemporaries). Although there were timid attempts from within the clergy to oppose such an outpouring of opprobrium, it remains that the church and the theatre spent much of the second half of the century in an essentially conflictual relationship. The salient exception to this tension is afforded by Jean Racine (1639–99) who, having written a magnificent series of tragedies drawn from classical antiquity, returned, after a break, to the genre with two pieces based on Old Testament subjects, conceived for performance by the pupils of the influential girls' school of Saint-Cyr, which enjoyed the patronage of Louis XIV's morganatic wife, Madame de Maintenon (1635–1719). The heavily didactic *Esther* (1689) is a three-act dramatisation of substantial parts of the eponymous biblical book; *Athalie* (1691), a work of far greater scope and complexity, turns to the Jewish queen of the books of Kings and Chronicles, and makes of her a figure poised between her traditional biblical status (as an evil ruler who stands by her actions as an impediment to Jehovah's designs for the redemption of humankind), and that of a more ambiguous and vulnerable woman, endowed with certain of the key features of Racine's secular tragic heroines. Both plays employ a chorus (to enunciate the Judaeo-Christian perspective), as well as an orchestra, and it is against this musical backdrop that the psychological dramas unfold. Corneille and Racine were also responsible for non-dramatic poetry, notably, in the former's case, for a verse paraphrase of the *Imitation of Christ* (1656); and in the latter's for the lyrical *Cantiques spirituels* (*Spiritual Canticles*) (1694).

If the church was divided over questions of stage performance, however, these were as nothing alongside the doctrinal controversies that raged in the second half of the century; and the movement known as Jansenism undoubt-edly marked the French church in the period more strongly than any other. In a paradoxical sequence of reaction and counter-reaction, an austere tendency had grown up in the aftermath of the Council of Trent that came to believe that the Catholic Reformation had, above all in its countering of Calvinist teachings on grace and free will, lost sight of the predominantly Augus-tinian emphasis on the Fall and its consequences. Taking as its base text the posthumous *Augustinus* (1640) of Corneille Jansen, bishop of Ypres, the adher-ents of this tendency gained in influence over the following decades, finding spokesmen in such figures as the abbé de Saint-Cyran (1581–1643), Nicole, and members of the influential Arnauld family, especially Antoine, known as Le Grand Arnauld (1612–94), whose name was initially associated with his treatise on (that is, against) the frequent reception of the Blessed Sacrament (*De la fréquente communion* [1643]). Partisans of the movement were associated with communities of both women and men on two sites: at Port-Royal, in Paris, and at Port-Royal-des-Champs, nearby, where the male *solitaires* founded a school, of which Racine was a pupil. The Christian pessimism that marked its adherents extended far beyond such confines, however, and served as a powerful counterbalance to the influence of the more tolerant ethos of the Society of Jesus (founded by St Ignatius Loyola in 1540), that had tended to prevail at court, as manifested in the person of the king's confessors. Jansenism was at the same time repeatedly condemned by both the Sorbonne (the Paris Faculty of Theology) and the papacy, in an intricate sequence of attacks and rebuttals. These reached their literary apogee in the brilliantly scathing attack launched by the Port-Royal sympathiser Blaise Pascal (1623–62) and known as the *Lettres provinciales* (*Provincial Letters*), originally published in pamphlet form, and then as a collection in 1656. This series of fictitious letters shifts from a defence of the condemned Jansenist, Arnauld, to an assault on the perceived laxism of the Jesuits in both their penitential and devotional practices, and deploys wit, irony, and satirical deformation in the process (although the later letters predictably shift into a tonality of evangelical indignation). Even if the Jansenists won the literary battle, in that the Jesuits never rose to the challenge of producing an equivalently readable reply, it was nonetheless Port-Royal that, in the early years of the eighteenth century, lost the war, when the papal condemnation known as the Bull *Unigenitus* was promulgated in 1713. Several members of both communities left memoirs.

It was, however, the tradition of Port-Royal that fostered the single most important manifestation of Catholic writing in the seventeenth century, a work that is in many other respects a bewildering puzzle. Pascal, scientist, mathematician, and polemicist, is also the most influential apologist for Christianity to write in French. The powerful and often elliptical writing, combined with the provision of a broad scheme of chapters, a rhetorical programme devised to lead the reader to belief, and a sketchily identified dramatis personae, have resulted in the huge prestige that the *Pensées* (*Thoughts*) (first published in 1670), as they are inaccurately but now unalterably known, have enjoyed ever since. Some part of the impact and notoriety of his text undoubtedly stems from the unfinished and fragmentary state in which Pascal left it at his death and, although there are now accurate and authentic editions available, there remain major, and in the end probably insoluble, areas of hypothesis and speculation. The principal burden of his argument is that the unbeliever needs to recognise in the first instance that there is a question about the purpose of his life on earth that urgently needs to be addressed and answered, and one furthermore to which indifference is not an available reply (a proposal contained in the fragment notoriously know as the wager argument, but more correctly described by its own title of 'Infini: Rien' ['Infinity: Nothing']). The previously unconcerned libertine, now prepared at least to accept that he has nothing to lose by wagering on the existence of a divine being, will then begin his enquiry into religious practices and beliefs, and will find that Christianity, given the state of frustration and bewilderment in which he finds himself (as a result both of his aspirations and his failure to live up to them), affords the most credible explanation of and remedy for his dilemma; and that it does so by the twin dogmas of the Fall and the Redemption. (The deistic riposte to such a conjunction, as articulated by Voltaire [1694–1778] in his reply to Pascal in the 25th *Lettre philosophique* [*Philosophical Letter* (1734)], positing the harmonious coexistence of a supreme being and his creation, is conversely bound to start from the premise that humankind is not in a state of despair in the first place.) The writing is remarkable for its relentlessness, for its imagery (in some cases taken from the *Essais* of Michel de Montaigne

[1533–92], who furnishes Pascal with some of his most powerful illustrations of the weakness of human reason), for its provision of epistemological categories (the 'three orders' of body, mind, and heart), and for its readiness to take material on board that points superficially away from the apologist's ultimate purpose. But if Pascal is at pains to demonstrate the appropriateness of Christian doctrine to the human predicament (while conceding that in many respects it constitutes an unimaginable paradox to do so), he is also concerned to prove the rationality and historicity of Christianity, in which process he accords a major role to Judaism and to the fulfilment of biblical prophecies. Pascal is an adamantly anti-fideistic Christian thinker, who insists, despite his emphasis on personal inspiration, that a simple statement of unfounded belief has no intellectual value or persuasive capacity, and therefore that reason has a central if self-denying role to play in the recognition of its own limitations. It nonetheless remains that his own religious conviction was sealed by an experience of a supernatural order (recorded in the exuberant document known as the *Mémorial* [Memoir]), placing him firmly in the tradition of Saints Paul and Augustine, as borne out in such devotional sequences as the *Mystère de Jésus* (*Mystery of Jesus*); and that his tortuous *Ecrits sur la grâce* (*Writings on Grace*) leave the reader unsure as to the degree of free will he can or should expect to exercise on his journey to salvation.

The second dispute to arise, now at the very end of the century, concerned the promotion of the individual practice of higher forms of prayer, and was known, in the first instance pejoratively, as quietism. The writings and influence of Madame Guyon (1648–1717) were at the epicentre of a fierce debate concerning the degree to which the aspiration to a state of spiritual union with God could be both orthodox and popular (as she had taught in the *Moyen court et très facile de faire oraison* [*Short and Very Easy Method of Prayer*, 1685]), alongside her questionably scholarly commentaries on biblical texts. Quietism undoubtedly answered a widely felt need by the laity to aspire to a form of unmediated communion with God that was less predicated on verbal prayer, as its supporters and practitioners proposed; what its opponents held against it was a tendency to underplay the revealed dogmas of the Christian faith (so, for example, reducing the role of meditation on the life of Christ or the mystery of the Trinity), and to give rise to the kinds of expression of individual piety that carried the potential for doctrinal error (pejoratively known in this context as 'enthusiasm'). Accounts of the practices advocated, of the ecclesiastical conflict that they initiated, and of the theology that underlies it, are found, respectively, in the posthumous *Vie* of Madame Guyon (many of whose later years were spent in various forms of incarceration), and in the drearily self-perpetuating sequence of polemical exchanges between Bossuet and Fénelon.

Further evidence of the central role of discernment in the interpretation of individual inspiration is present in a number of other spiritual autobiographies in the period. These range from the narratives of diabolic possession by members of the clergy and religious life (above all the inter-related lives of the Jesuit Père Surin [1600–65] and Mère Jeanne des Anges [1602–65] at Loudun), through the self-destructive account of an individual who believed she had a vocation to reform the church (Antoinette Bourignon [1610–80]), to the autobiography of the Visitandine nun Marguerite-Marie Alacoque (1647–90), canonised only in the twentieth century, whose intimate devotion to Christ led her to promote the adoption by the church of what was to become the Feast of the Sacred Heart of Jesus. These often stylistically eccentric documents are both revelatory and disconcerting, by virtue of the unyielding intensity of personal conviction they display, by the extremes of behaviour they record, and by their uneasy relationship to all forms of ecclesiastical authority. They carry as a result the potential for a wide diversity of interpretations, in particular in the light of insights afforded by more recent psychological research.

Two other complementary remarks need to be made in conclusion. The first is to mention the existence of a massive corpus of writing that, in the loose sense of the word, does not comfortably figure in a literary survey: catechisms, doctrinal polemics, devotional treatises, manuals of confessional practice, or letters of spiritual direction, to select the most obvious. The founder of the French Oratory, Pierre de Bérulle (1575–1629), and the founder of the Trappist order, Armand Jean le Bouthillier, abbé de Rancé (1626–1700), both merit a place in religious history for their reforming achievements, as do Madame Acarie (1566–1618) and St Jeanne Chantal (1572–1641) for their contribution to devotional practice and individual (especially female) piety. In a different area again, Nicolas Malebranche (1638–1715) contributed much to the reconciliation of Cartesian rationalism with Christian orthodoxy, above all in his *De la recherche de la vérité* (*On the Search for Truth*) (1674–5); and in 1678 Richard Simon (1638–1712) published a controversial *Histoire critique du Vieux Testament* (*Critical History of the Old Testament*), considered to be a pioneering work in biblical exegesis. But the strictly literary impact of such figures is slight.

The counterpoint to this dimension is afforded by the omnipresence of a Christian perspective in writing that is not first and foremost 'religious'. The most obvious area of the impact of Christian belief in a domain that throws it into question lies in the realm of parody, such as is present in the comic theatre of Molière (1622–73), and in particular in *Le Tartuffe* (1664/69) and *Dom Juan* (1665). *Le Tartuffe* concerns the attempt by a religious impostor to infiltrate the family of a bourgeois believer in order to seduce his wife and lay claim to his property. It has been seen as an attack on the intrusive practices of the lay organisation known as the Compagnie du Saint-Sacrement (Society of the Blessed Sacrament) (pejoratively referred to as the Cabale des dévots [Plot of the pious]), as well as on Jansenism and on the Society of Jesus. It is most likely to be all those things at once, as well as containing dangerously blasphemous parodies of biblical injunctions and Marian devotions. *Dom Juan* too presents the audience with a superficially attractive free-thinker, pitted more often than not against an intellectually challenged supporter of conventional beliefs in the figure of his valet Sganarelle. Less contentious, because less apparent, is the whole postlapsarian subtext present in the bitterly cynical aphorisms known as the *Maximes* (1678) of the duc de La Rochefoucauld (1613–80) – post-Fall certainly, but equally certainly not pre-Redemption; or in the more derivative *Caractères* (1688–94) of Jean de La Bruyère (1645–96), that combine in their concluding chapters an unconvincing amalgamation of Cartesian, Pascalian, and downright fideistic apologetics with an unyielding attack on the superficialities of the contemporary church and on certain of its practices. Further away again from doctrinal engagement is the quiet underpinning of the year's calendar by its feasts and fasts, such as we encounter for example in the *Correspondance* of Madame de Sévigné (1626–96); or the robust treatment of religious concerns that are more often than not the subject of comic narratives in the *Mémoires* of the duc de Saint-Simon (1675–1755). Such documents, within their different idioms, tell us much about the religious Zeitgeist as it was experienced by the laity of the time.

What the religious writing of the century most obviously shows is an explosion of activity in a range of genres (homiletic, poetic, dramatic, polemical, didactic, or autobiographical), accompanied by a need rationally to account for Christian belief, and to do so by argument and evidence – in reply, it might logically be inferred, to the whole spectrum of currents of thought that were beginning to throw the hegemony of Catholic Christianity into question. Such writing often revitalises as a result the reader's awareness of the specificity and physicality of Christian dogmas and practices. It is often characterised by its fervour, its christocentrism and its theological sophistication, but also by the potential for polemic that arises from each of these features. As such, it allows later readers to chart the limits and parameters of orthodoxy as it was perceived in the period and, at least in part by so doing, to evaluate the role played by human acts of discernment in the problematic business of interpreting the revealed will of God. Above all, it reminds readers of all ages, from whatever background they approach it, that, in Pascal's phrase, 'le christianisme est étrange' ('Christianity is strange'), and it charts that strangeness on the printed page.

38

Seventeenth-century margins

NICHOLAS HAMMOND

To write about margins in any period might immediately imply a sense of relegation to the sidelines or mere tokenism. Yet in the seventeenth century, the centralising impetus of both Louis XIII's chief minister, Cardinal Richelieu, and, after him, Louis XIV, inevitably marginalised those who did not fit the mould which the figures of authority fashioned for literature, the arts, politics, and even lifestyle.

For the publication of books, a system of censorship had existed since the sixteenth century in granting 'privileges', even though on the whole they had not been applied in a systematic way. However, such censorship became more effective from 1635, when the chancellor Pierre Séguier (1588–1672) set up a system whereby manuscripts were secretly reviewed by a panel of readers. It is even possible that the Académie Française, founded by Richelieu in the same year, was set up as one way of censoring books; certainly one of its founding members Valentin Conrart (1603–75) is known to have been involved in the vetting of manuscripts. Such a role for the Académie, however, was scuppered by the Paris Parlement when its statutes were published. Under the personal rule of Louis XIV, the printing and distribution of books became even more tightly controlled.

Although the publication of works, and most particularly theatre, which emanated from the founding of the Académie Française and Louis XIV's subsequent enthusiastic support of the arts, led to what can safely be called a golden age of literature, the very fact that certain genres were given precedence over others means that a wide range of writings which stood outside the official boundaries tended to be ignored or belittled. It is extraordinary how even in subsequent centuries scholars have tended to concentrate on this 'official' canon of works at the expense of the other texts, both published and unpublished, which make the seventeenth century so fascinatingly diverse. Closer attention has since been paid to the small corpus of works which were written outside the aristocratic elite, such as memoirs by valets or the role played by popular song, but there still remains much work to be done in this area.

Another factor that needs to be taken into account is the seventeenth-century attitude towards authorship and publication. There has been much debate about what exactly constituted the status of the author. Michel Foucault, for example, in a famous piece entitled 'What Is an Author?',[1] contends that, whereas in the Middle Ages scientific texts were assigned names, literary texts tended towards anonymity. He argues that, by contrast, in the seventeenth or eighteenth centuries, scientific authors lapsed into anonymity and creative writers started to be named. Roger Chartier countered Foucault's analysis of the term 'auteur' in both medieval and early modern periods, maintaining that the author's role in the seventeenth and eighteenth centuries is not so clearly delineated as Foucault suggests.[2] Whatever the case may be, it is evident that those who saw themselves as civilised beings (honnêtes gens) often equated publication with vulgarity: one should only write for the pleasure of writing and not for circulation beyond one's close circle of family and friends. The comment which Molière's Alceste makes to Oronte in Le Misanthrope, 'What pressing need do you have to write rhymes / And what on earth compels you to have your work published?' (lines 363–4), is therefore not as outlandish as it might at first appear. As a result of this prevailing attitude, there was a culture of able writers, many of them women, who either did not write with publication in mind, like Marie de Rabutin-Chantal, marquise de Sévigné, whose letters to her daughter are creative tours de force, or published anonymously, like Marie-Madeleine Pioche de La Vergne, comtesse de Lafayette, whose novel La Princesse de Clèves is discussed elsewhere in this book.

Other works were published anonymously, not because they were written by women but because of their delicate sexual, political, or religious subject matter. Throughout the century, texts were published which either led directly to censorship or appeared in clandestine editions. In the early years of the century, for example, many collections of mostly erotic and pornographic poems had enormous success. La Muse folastre (The Playful Muse), which first appeared in 1600, was reprinted eighteen times by 1624. Perhaps the most famous of these collections, Le Parnasse des poëtes satiriques (The Parnassus of Satirical Poets, 1622), comprised a number of signed and unsigned pieces, including an opening poem on the subject of syphilis, sodomy, and masturbation, purported to be by the free-thinking poet Théophile de Viau (1590–1626), which led to his trial between 1623 and 1625. After escaping, being condemned

---

1 Michel Foucault, 'What Is an Author?', in Vassilis Lambropoulos and David Neal Miller (eds.), Twentieth-Century Literary Theory (Albany: State University Press of New York, 1987), pp. 124–42.
2 R. Chartier, L'Ordre des livres: lecteurs, auteurs, bibliothèques en Europe entre xive et xviiie siècle (Aix-en-Provence: Alinéa, 1992).

to death by burning and then reimprisoned, eventually he was sent into exile, but the experience of prison destroyed him, and he died soon afterwards, at the age of thirty-six. Although Théophile's trial and tighter censorship led to the suppression of many works, a number of erotic works still appeared later in the century, none more groundbreaking than the anonymously published *L'École des filles* (*The School for Girls*, 1655), which celebrates feminine sexuality in a series of dialogues between women. Although most of the first print-run was seized and burnt, clandestine editions were published in Holland in 1667 and 1668 and distributed throughout France. Anonymous political tracts were also widespread, most notably those pamphlets (*mazarinades*) that satirised and attacked the rule of the Italian-born first minister Cardinal Mazarin during the various civil uprisings known as the Fronde (1648–53). Religious dissent was also most safely expressed through anonymous tracts; this was how Pascal's *Lettres provinciales* (*Provincial Letters*) and the vigorous counter-polemic that they engendered first appeared to the general public.

Other free-thinkers (subsequently known as *libertins érudits*), such as Pierre Gassendi (1592–1655), François La Mothe le Vayer (1588–1672), Gabriel Naudé (1600–53), and Gassendi's pupil Cyrano de Bergerac (1619–65), used to meet secretly to discuss recent trends in science and philosophy, often questioning moral and religious orthodoxies of the day.

The need to hide under the veil of anonymity was exacerbated by the fact that during the seventeenth century people's opinions and private lives began to be surveyed as never before. A police force under a lieutenant-general, the first of whom was Gabriel Nicolas De la Reynie (1625–1709), was eventually created by Louis XIV in 1667. Its prime purpose was to place informers in various public spaces in order to listen to private conversations about the king and events. These informers (known as 'mouches' by the people) would transcribe these conversations and then transmit them to the lieutenant-general, who in turn would communicate them in a weekly audience with the king. Notwithstanding the dangers associated with such talk, gossip was often the only medium through which taboo subjects could be articulated.

Gossip

Although gossip is by its nature transient and mediated largely through oral communication, it is not through the spoken word alone that rumours are spread or that gossip gathers momentum. Gossip, even more than rumour, thrives through the written word. Indeed, the dangers associated with written gossip were deemed even greater than those attached to spoken gossip.

Madeleine de Scudéry (1607–1701), in 'De la médisance' ('On Gossip'), makes just such a distinction through her speaker Almedor, who argues that 'written and printed gossip is even more dangerous and criminal than the other kind, because it does not die with conversation and is not confined to the place where the gossip is indulged in'. And the seventeenth century is particularly ripe for various written forms of gossip which both augment spoken forms of gossip and constitute gossip in themselves: journals, memoirs, letters, songs, collections of conversations, stories or sayings, and gazettes all proliferated during the period.

Through these channels, different kinds of orthodoxy could be questioned more freely than in any more official medium. Street songs or anonymous poems were therefore an appropriate medium to counter the very successfully propagated image of Louis XIV as all-conquering, especially in the later years of his reign, or to gossip about his infatuation with various women. The personal failings of both the famous and not so famous were celebrated in collections of anecdotes. The *Historiettes* of Gédéon Tallemant des Réaux (1619–92), for example, which constitute the most lively and scurrilous tales about various figures of his time, were distributed in manuscript form amongst Tallemant's friends and only published for the first time, in expurgated form, in the nineteenth century.

Same-sex desire

One subject that does not appear openly in official literature of the time but which can be found frequently in Tallemant's writings as well as in letters, journals, memoirs, and songs, is that of same-sex desire.

Foucault's notion of homosexuality in the early modern period as being conceived in terms of 'acts' and not 'identities' does hold true generally, but it should not be forgotten that certain people did define themselves through their sexual attraction to the same sex. Even if the word 'homosexual' does not feature at that time, there does indeed exist a vocabulary to denote people attracted to their own sex. In the case of men and boys, for example, we have 'bardaches' (signifying the passive partner) and 'bougres' (denoting the active partner); 'sodomites' was also used but not exclusively for same-sex desire. Women who preferred their own sex were sometimes referred to as 'tribades'.

Within the writings of the time which deal with the subject, a clear disparity can be discerned between the Christian standpoint (where same-sex love is not accepted at all) and the social standpoint (where it is certainly tolerated to some degree). A few printed sermons and religious discourses of the time refer to the sin of sodomy, but more often than not the dangers of even mentioning such an abomination are signalled rather than the abomination itself. On the other hand, many memoir- and letter-writers of the time refer to its widespread acceptance, especially in court circles. The Princesse Palatine (1652–1722), who was the second wife of Louis XIV's brother Philippe d'Orléans (1640–1701), himself well known for his preference for men, is especially eloquent on the subject in her correspondence. Other writers, such as Roger de Bussy-Rabutin (1618–93) in his scurrilous *Histoire amoureuse des Gaules* (*Tale of the Loves of the Gauls*, 1665), a thinly disguised satirical portrait of court life which led to his imprisonment and then exile, treat the subject with an amused tolerance. Other works, such as Cyrano de Bergerac's prose narratives, have been read as containing coded references to same-sex desire.

In the field of poetry, Denis Sanguin de Saint-Pavin (1595–1670) openly celebrates love for and sex with men in his poems, but it is perhaps significant that in his lifetime much of his poetry was only distributed in manuscript form. Another poet, Théophile de Viau, was known for his sexual preferences and obscene poetry, and (as we have seen) these factors in all probability led to his condemnation. There are many other mostly anonymous poems and songs which circulated at the time and which consider same-sex sexuality with a direct and earthy openness. The multi-volume manuscript collection of pieces known as the *Chansonnier Maurepas* (some of which were only published for the first time in the nineteenth century and many of which remain unpublished), for example, contains hundreds of such songs dealing directly with same-sex desire.

Lesbianism, while being referred to less openly in these kinds of pieces, receives greater coverage than male homosexuality in the theatre of the time, usually through the medium of cross-dressing, perhaps most daringly in Benserade's *Iphis et Iante* (1634), where two women end up in bed together. Indeed, the subject of cross-dressing is one which deserves attention in considering literature of the period.

Cross-dressing

In seventeenth-century France, cross-dressing was officially censured by ecclesiastic, legal, and royal authorities. The church, in accordance with the Book of Deuteronomy (22:5), was unequivocal in its condemnation of the practice, especially since a papal interdiction had been issued in 1522. Moralistic treatises, such as Alexis Trousset's *Alphabet de l'imperfection et malice des femmes* (*Alphabet of the Imperfection and Malice of Women*, 1617) and Isaac Le Maître de Sacy's 1686 commentary on Deuteronomy, where female to male and particularly male to female cross-dressing was severely criticised, were symptomatic of this disapproval. In civil and military courts, action was taken against transvestites, and Louis XIV is known also on occasion to have condemned and even banished certain cross-dressers.

Yet such official condemnation in no way reflects both the reality and the fascination for cross-dressing which manifested itself in so much literature of the period. Louis XIV himself danced a number of ballet roles cast as a woman, ranging from the wine-loving Bacchante in the 'Ballet des Fêtes de Bacchus' ('Ballet of the Festival of Bacchus', 1651) when he was twelve to the part of a village girl in *Les Noces de village* (*Village Weddings*, 1663), culminating in the role of a nymph in the 'Ballet des Muses' ('Ballet of the Muses', 1666). Moreover, his brother Philippe d'Orléans, who also danced female roles, was a notorious cross-dresser. Other establishment figures, such as the infamous François-Timoléon, abbé de Choisy (1644–1724), who was a member of the Académie Française and whose scandalous activities are recorded in his *Memoirs* (written in the early years of the eighteenth century), and Queen Christina of Sweden (1626–89), who entered the French court in 1656, often flaunted their taste for transvestism. Throughout early modern Europe, carnival time temporarily allowed people to cross-dress with legitimacy, even if certain practices, such as priests dressing as women during the 'Feast of Fools', were censured.

Choisy has left the most colourful accounts of his cross-dressing. As Joseph Harris puts it in his study of cross-dressing in seventeenth-century France, 'Choisy's writings blend the narcissistic and the self-effacing, the confessional and the ironic, the factual and the fantasized, in such a way that it is impossible to tell how sincere he is being at any one time'.[3] Choisy describes his transvestism variously as a 'bizarre pleasure' and as a practice to which anybody might be susceptible. In one passage of extraordinary self-justification, he argues that men enjoy dressing in women's clothes because 'they feel the inexpressible pleasure of being loved'. That said, much of his account is devoted to his seduction of young women while cross-dressed.

Even given the fact that there are a number of historical examples of cross-dressing in the seventeenth century, its omnipresence in theatre and prose narrative in particular shows the extent to which it dominates the wider literary imagination of the time. Perhaps the most influential prose narrative

---

3 Joseph Harris, *Hidden Agendas: Cross-Dressing in 17th-Century France* (Tübingen: Biblio 17, 2005), p. 212.

of the century, D'Urfé's monumental *L'Astrée*, is largely sustained by the hero Céladon's continuing disguise as the druidess 'Alexis'. Resolution to this disguise is constantly deferred, as Céladon's lover Astrée believes him to be dead. There includes even a fetishistic scene where Céladon, already dressed as 'Alexis', dons the clothes of Astrée, which leads him to decide to wear her clothes regularly on future occasions. In Charles Sorel's *Berger extravagant* (*Extravagant Shepherd*, 1627), the character Lysis's decision to dress as a woman is directly informed by his reading of romances like *L'Astrée*.

However, most dramatic and narrative works in which cross-dressing features tend to be resolved by a moment of recognition, where the cross-dresser's true sex is revealed, thereby indicating that rarely is cross-dressing performed without motivation.

Conclusion

The second half of the seventeenth century and the early years of the eighteenth century are justifiably dominated by the figure of Louis XIV and his political and cultural dominance. The many works which were inspired or encouraged by him testify to his influence. Yet there remains a significant underbelly of writings which question the received wisdom of the day, including poems and songs contradicting the overwhelming praise of Louis in the official literature of the age. One such song, written at the time of his death in 1715, and found in the *Chansonnier Maurepas*, effectively sums up the spirit of dissent to be found in so many of the 'marginal', hitherto silent texts which have been discussed in this section:

> Pour paroître au grand Tribunal,
> Enfin Louis déloge,
> Bien des gens en disent du mal,
> Et peu font son éloge;
> Pour laisser ses mannes en paix
> Je ne veux rien escrire,
> L'honneste homme ne doit jamais
> Ni mentir ni médire.

(Finally Louis is moving to join the great Judgement Seat; many people are speaking ill of him and few are praising him; in order to leave his manna in peace, I do not wish to write anything; the civilised man must never lie or gossip.)

39

What is Enlightenment?

JOHN LEIGH

In 1784, Immanuel Kant published a short essay under the title, *What is Enlightenment?* Kant's answer to his own question was stated, seemingly without hesitation, at the very outset of the work:

> Enlightenment is man's release from his self-incurred tutelage. Tutelage is man's inability to make use of his understanding without direction from another. *Sapere aude!* Have courage to use your own reason! – that is the motto of enlightenment.

While the placing of this definition both guaranteed its prominence and, to an extent, exemplified the author's own bold self-reliance, it also allowed Kant to go on, in the remainder of the essay, to complicate his prompt answer to the initial question. Indeed, the definition duly makes way for somewhat looser, less definite conclusions. Kant ultimately provided a delicately balanced assessment by arguing that eighteenth-century men and women were living in an age of Enlightenment, but not an enlightened age.

Many of Kant's intellectual contemporaries and his immediate antecedents in France, of whom he was highly aware, were, however, inclined to think, or at least write, that theirs *was* an enlightened age – 'un' or 'ce siècle éclairé'. Indeed, such was the frequency with which these words came together that by the 1750s the happy designation had already hardened into a cliché. The antiquarian and art historian, the Comte de Caylus observed that these magical words were bandied about at the drop of a hat: 'Quoiqu'on dise à tout propos, *dans un siècle aussi éclairé que le nôtre*, on peut assurer que la race des barbares n'est pas encore éteinte'[1] ('Although at every juncture people say *in a century as enlightened as ours*, you can be assured that the barbarians are still with us'). Voltaire was one of those figures who described the eighteenth century as a 'siècle éclairé' in a number of places, but, in common with Caylus's rather

---

1 Comte de Caylus, *Recueil d'antiquités*, 7 vols. (Paris: Desaint and Saillant, 1752–), I, p. 286.

weary observation, the formula seems to surface in his writings only when something distinctly unedifying and unworthy of the century has occurred: 'Ces horreurs', he writes in 1765 (lamenting the terrible miscarriages of justice that were to lead to the Sirven and Calas affairs when Protestants suffered terrible persecution), 'sont d'autant plus effrayantes qu'elles se passent dans un siècle plus éclairé' ('these horrors are all the more frightening given that they are occurring in a more enlightened century').[2] Yet these atrocities did not disqualify the century from being described as enlightened. Voltaire comes close to anticipating the hesitant quality of Kant's characterisation of the age in a statement he makes in a letter to the duke de Saint-Megrin, whom he tells: 'Vous êtes né dans un siècle éclairé; mais la lumière qui s'est étendue depuis quelques années n'a encore servi qu'à nous faire voir nos abus et non pas à les corriger' ('You were born in an enlightened century; but the light which has spread over the last few years has still only served us to show us our failings and not enabled us to correct them').[3] In other words, even in the late 1760s, enlightenment remained an aspiration, rather than a description, of the age. Although Voltaire's remarks (even, or rather especially, in his letters) need to be weighed carefully as evidence of a prevailing state of mind or affairs, this comment seems typical of the age's mixture of self-satisfaction and frustration.

Kant was therefore not alone in detecting the ambivalence of an age which saw itself as having enlightenment, without yet being enlightened. Either way, it should be clear that these labels were already bestowed on the age by itself. This precociously developed self-awareness may seem complacent. It is certainly rather unusual. Other labels which continue to designate characteristic or recognisably eighteenth-century movements – such as 'baroque' or 'rococo', for instance – were imposed retrospectively (and pejoratively at first) on the tendencies they purported to circumscribe. But integral to the ambition of Enlightenment was an intense curiosity, which could become an anxiety, about the proper scope and scale of the movement itself and the capacities of the individuals who were associated with it. There was also a perhaps unprecedented excitement and optimism about the possibilities that the present and the immediate future seemed to promise. Some authors were persuaded that a state of Enlightenment would dawn, only not before their eyes. The fact that it seemed to shimmer on the horizon just beyond their lifetime could on occasion lend the works and words of these writers a vatic,

---

2 Voltaire, *Correspondence and Related Documents*, ed. T. Besterman (Geneva and Oxford: Voltaire Foundation, 1968–77), D12618. All letters will henceforth be referred to by their number.
3 Ibid., D15294.

even rather sorrowful quality. As Frederick the Great wrote in a letter to Voltaire, 'je ne verrai pas ces beaux jours de ma patrie, mais j'en prévois la possibilité' ('I will not see such beautiful days in my country, but I foresee the possibility').[4]

However, in practice, the death of Louis XIV in 1715 and the French Revolution provide the convenient, if highly approximate, opening and closing brackets by which we can circumscribe the movement – if indeed it is a movement. The 'age of Enlightenment' may be characterised as an era in which thinkers worked on assumptions about the world (and man's place in it) that were radically different from those of previous thinkers. But, less glamorously, the thinkers of the Enlightenment may simply have turned out to be bolder, better organised, and more numerous than their counterparts from the past. Each view seems admissible, to an extent. Some critics, such as Lionel Gossman,[5] have tended to emphasise the essentially diffuse character of the Enlightenment, an assemblage of individuals who speak a common language rather than sharing one philosophy or the same ideas and values. The Enlightenment, then, is more like a language whose accents and expressions vary according to the particularities and circumstances of its speakers at any given time.

This language could be heard with increasing force across eighteenth-century Europe and its colonies. Kant's injunction, *sapere aude*, voiced in Latin, diplomatically acknowledges the pan-European nature of the Enlightenment. Indeed, it had branches across Europe, from Scotland to the Swiss cantons. London was a capital of tolerance; Dutch cities such as Rotterdam and Amsterdam had a tradition of offering asylum to dissidents and publishing their works; Berlin, under Frederick the Great, became another refuge. However, this list risks making the Enlightenment sound like an exclusively Protestant phenomenon, a secular reprise of the Reformation perhaps. It was in France that the *philosophe*, the harbinger of the Enlightenment, came to mean someone other than just a philosopher from or in France. This term denoted not only a propensity to thought and abstraction, as usual, but a distinctive and modern type of attitude to authority. Owing in part to the continuing stranglehold of Catholicism, and in part to the highly centralised monarchical structure in place, the business of Enlightenment in France was more urgent and dangerous and, as a consequence, its vehicles and ruses perhaps more subtle and risqué. As Kant said, Enlightenment required courage – the

---

4 Ibid., D19571.
5 L. Gossman, *Medievalism and the Ideologies of the Enlightenment* (Baltimore, MD: Johns Hopkins University Press, 1968).

courage to think for oneself, when it would always be easier to let others think for you. But in France that courage consisted not only in rejecting a supine approach to life, but in endangering life by running considerable risks. Rousseau, who like the other chief figures of the Enlightenment, was hounded and exiled by intolerant, often uncomprehending authorities, commemorated the burden of this privilege in a Latin dictum of his own: *Vitam impendere vero* ('To risk one's life for truth'). Particularly after the expulsion of the Huguenots in 1685, France was confirmed as an aggressively Catholic nation. Yet French wás the lingua franca of Europe, the language of politeness, the ideal vehicle for the expression of clear ideas and arguments. If her free-thinking writers were threatened and marginalised, they were no less confident and visible on the European stage.

Whether French or not, the thinkers of the Enlightenment did have a list of non-negotiable convictions and a corresponding set of goals to which more or less any of its exponents would reliably subscribe. There is, unfortunately, nothing as trite as a mission statement for the Enlightenment in French writing, but a résumé of what might now be called the 'aims and objectives' of the French Enlightenment may be found in Beaumarchais's comic play, *Le Barbier de Séville* (1776). Bartholo, who is holding a young woman, Rosine, against her will with the intention of marrying her is soon confirmed as an enemy of modernity and progress by professing hatred of the vaunted enlightened age which, like Caylus, he calls a 'siècle barbare' ('barbaric century'):

> Qu'a-t-il produit pour qu'on le loue? Sottises de toute espèce: la liberté de penser, l'attraction, l'électricité, le tolérantisme, l'inoculation, le quinquina, l'Encyclopédie et les drames.
>
> (What has it produced to earn such praise? Follies of all kinds: free thought, gravitation, electricity, arguments in favour of tolerance, inoculation, quinine, the Encyclopaedia and plays.)

An ancestor of the Monty Python 'What did the Romans do for us?' sketch, this speech catalogues the latest reforms and accomplishments. We may be assured that these achievements are worthwhile if only because the man deploring them is himself so deplorable. Perhaps this coincidence hints at a continuing lack of confidence on the part of the Enlightenment. Bartholo, a doctor who seems to have strayed from a Molière comedy onto the eighteenth-century stage, evidently does not care for Enlightenment science. But the scientific breakthroughs of which he disapproves are interspersed with artistic and moralistic concerns. The sense that these different endeavours might be complementary is a key feature of the Enlightenment. Its authors took pleasure in such *mélanges* – fast-moving and wide-ranging forms worthy of the century's boundless polymath curiosity. It was this restlessness that recommended Voltaire's *Lettres philosophiques* (first published in the 1730s), a text that moves rather unpredictably from considerations of Quakers to Newton and inoculation, though perhaps in the interests of suggesting that improved scientific precision might authorise moral certainties. It is also one of the pleasures of the *Encyclopédie*, a collaborative multi-volume enterprise edited by Diderot and d'Alembert (1750–65), which Bartholo berates towards the end of his rant. Readers are to negotiate its entries as they wish, leafing or cross-referencing at will.

As the preface to the *Encyclopédie* made clear, knowledge might lead to greater virtue and in turn to greater happiness, all three reconciled in a mutually supporting equilateral triangle. This now not only does not seem controversial but may look self-evident. But then the presumptuousness of such wishes earned the *Encyclopédie* a ban and copies were housed in the Bastille.

Another of Bartholo's 'sottises' is 'attraction' – the eighteenth-century French term for gravitation. Indeed, there is something ironically apposite about this repulsive character's dislike of attraction. Isaac Newton, the man responsible for these revelations, became a demi-god, even in France. The deification of this Englishman became a double blasphemy. And Bartholo also deplores inoculation, which continued to be opposed by the Catholic church in the eighteenth century. This shibboleth was revered by Enlightenment thinkers as a sacrament, a second baptismal rite. More generally though, there was something dangerously Promethean about arrogating the vocabulary of light, especially in its French variant (*les lumières*), for purely human and secular purposes. 'God said let Newton be and all was light'. Pope still left God some power and agency, but, from Newton's work on optics and prisms and the spectrum of colours to Franklin's feat in taming lightning, the ability to understand and exploit the world around man was developed ever more stridently. That this was possible, defensible, and even desirable only seemed obvious to the post-Enlightenment world.

Just as Beaumarchais's tribute to the Enlightenment was paid by one of its fictional enemies, so another telling description of its ambitions and achievements comes from a real adversary, even though he had earlier written for the *Encyclopédie*. Jean-Jacques Rousseau's controversial, even tragic, career as a thinker outside the mainstream of the Enlightenment was launched by his *Discours sur les sciences et les arts*, an essay set by the Academy of Dijon in 1750. It begins in this way:

C'est un grand et beau spectacle de voir l'homme sortir en quelque manière du néant par ses propres efforts; dissiper, par les lumières de sa raison les ténèbres dans lesquelles la nature l'avait enveloppé; s'élever au-dessus de lui-même; s'élancer par l'esprit jusque dans les régions célestes; parcourir à pas de géant, ainsi que le soleil, la vaste étendue de l'univers; et, ce qui est encore plus grand et plus difficile, rentrer en soi pour y étudier l'homme et connaître sa nature, ses devoirs et sa fin. Toutes ces merveilles se sont renouvelées depuis peu de générations.

(It is a great and wonderful sight to see man emerging in some ways from nothing thanks to his own efforts; banishing, thanks to the light shed by his reason, the darkness in which nature had enveloped him; rising above himself; scaling celestial heights thanks to his intelligence; moving, as does the sun, across the whole universe, with the strides of a giant; and, what is even greater and harder still, turning in on oneself to study man and to know his nature, his duties and his purpose. It is only a few generations since all these marvels have taken place.)[6]

With the *chiaroscuro* imagery, its faith in man's capacity for self-renewal, and above all the celebration of the ability of humans to explore not only the world and the universe around them but also previously unknown regions of the inner self, this is a hymn to the might of the Enlightenment. However, with his allusions to celestial realms, giants, and marvels, Rousseau over-inflates the terminology just a little to hint that this argument may be self-satisfied and misconstrued. And so it proves in the essay that follows, as Rousseau provides the first potent arguments against the fundamental assumptions and convictions of the Enlightenment. All its attempts to alleviate injustice through intellectual progress were, Rousseau argued, vain and ill-conceived.

Rousseau was concerned about the damage that the Enlightenment would do to the capacity of individuals to feel, and therefore to judge, for themselves. Nevertheless, as he realised, it would be wrong to assume that this was therefore an era devoted exclusively to abstraction and axioms. Eighteenth-century thinkers were in many ways glorified spectators. They travelled widely and collected ardently. Nothing was beyond or beneath the curiosity of such figures, the last credible polymaths. Illumination and inspiration could be vouchsafed by dreams, as Diderot's unconventional *Rêve de d'Alembert* (1769) suggested. As Voltaire declared: 'N'importe d'où vienne la lumière, pourvu qu'elle éclaire' ('It does not matter where the light comes from, as long as it

---

6 Jean-Jacques Rousseau, *Discours sur les sciences et les arts*, in *Œuvres complètes*, ed. M. Launay, 3 vols. (Paris: Seuil, 1967), II, p. 53.

illuminates').[7] Similarly, Enlightenment writers swerved between discursive, theoretical texts and fictional works in which the reader is confronted head on by some of the epistemological problems merely discussed or entertained by those other texts. In fiction such as Voltaire's *Candide* (1759), Rousseau's *Julie ou la nouvelle Héloïse* (1761) and Diderot's *Jacques le fataliste* (1771), the reader is set a common challenge: what can we believe? What, if anything, should we take seriously? What do we really know for sure? All these questions can be bracketed under one simple, yet wider question: how should we read these books? All of them advance claims about their status as real documents, while exhibiting their fictional forms in a contradictory fashion. While Enlightenment ideas naturally found expression in voluminous works, dictionaries, and encyclopaedia that ordered knowledge, shorter, fictional forms proved instrumental too. Montesquieu provides a good example of the way Enlightenment thinkers diversified their output. On the one hand, the *Esprit des lois* (1748) is Montesquieu's and perhaps, along with Rousseau's *Du contrat social* (1761), the eighteenth century's seminal theoretical text, linking facts and observations about the natural world and man to legislative possibilities and theories. But his *Lettres persanes* (1725), a humbler work of fiction, is more daring and dangerous. There is perhaps no more economical and pungent statement of the values of the Enlightenment than in the words of Roxane, who pens the text's final letter to her despotic husband, Usbek:

> Comment as-tu cru que je fusse assez crédule pour m'imaginer que je ne fusse dans le monde que pour adorer tes caprices? Que, pendant que tu te permets tout, tu eusses le droit d'affliger tous mes désirs? Non! J'ai pu vivre dans la servitude, mais j'ai toujours été libre: j'ai réformé tes lois sur celles de la nature, et mon esprit s'est toujours tenu dans l'indépendance.[8]

> (How could you possibly think that I would be credulous enough to imagine that I existed only in order to worship your whims? That, while you allow yourself anything, you have the right to thwart all my desires? No! I have been able to live in captivity, but I have always been free: I have reformed your laws on the basis of those of nature and my mind has always maintained its independence.)

The rash of first-person imperfect subjunctives, already rather unusual by the eighteenth century, helps to prepare the way for the simple majesty of the statement that follows and eclipses them. Hers is a triumphant 'Non!', that

---

7 Voltaire, *Correspondence*, D13014.
8 C.-L. de Secondat, baron de Montesquieu, *Œuvres complètes*, 2 vols. (Paris: Gallimard, 1949), I, p. 372.

curiously positive word (perhaps in part thanks to the palindrome – so it is no, whichever way you look at it), which has resonated with particular force through French culture all the way up to Victor Hugo's defiance ('Je serai, sous le sac de cendre qui me couvre, / La voix qui dit: malheur! La bouche qui dit: non!' ('I shall be, beneath the sack of ashes that covers me, the voice that says, misfortune! The mouth that says no!') and Edith Piaf's lack of regret.

This one paragraph already encompasses the major questions that animate the thinkers of the Enlightenment, and it outlines many of the terms of subsequent debates: the wish to ground arguments in credible explanations rather than resting on blind faith or 'credulity'; to eliminate 'caprices' – arbitrary, often irrational, unjustifed practices; to give voice to 'desires' and the right to pursue happiness; to predicate rights, and the laws that enshrine them, in nature. It is an affirmation of the life of the mind, undiminished in its independence even when its owner is subjugated. Above all, this Islamic woman provides a supreme example of courage, both intellectual and physical. It is therefore a particular shame that this wonderful statement should be a suicide note, for Roxane explains in the sentences that follow that she has poisoned herself. And the letter ends with her death. If the Enlightenment celebrated self-made, self-determining individuals, it was also particularly concerned with those who chose to kill themselves, the ultimate proof of sovereignty over oneself and defiance of the laws.

Sometimes the curve traced by a particular narrative did not meet an Enlightenment trajectory unproblematically. The very titles of a number of eighteenth-century texts announce the Enlightenment's enjoyment of bifocal views of the world. These dual titles, pivoted on the 'ou', suggest plural ways of interpreting them and this world: Voltaire, *Candide ou de l'optimisme*; Rousseau, *Émile ou de l'éducation* (1762); Diderot, *Supplément au Voyage de Bougainville ou dialogue entre A et B* (1772). Typically, the promise of a high-minded exploration of a philosophical issue is accompanied by an intractably individualistic account. The unprecedented popularity of such dual titles points to the readiness of eighteenth-century writers to wrap ideas up in stories but perhaps also their sense that there is more than one way of seeing the same thing.

Nevertheless, the optimism of eighteenth-century thinkers and their desire for clarity came to look not just quaint and misplaced but egregious by the sophisticated standards of postmodern thought and theory, with the sorry retrospection afforded by successive twentieth-century disasters that occurred in the very homelands of the Enlightenment. If the makings of the modern world could be traced back to the Enlightenment, then so too could the horrors of the recent past. Foucault saw in the desire to collect knowledge a sinister urge to control. Barthes saw in the plates illustrating the *Encyclopédie* a new and alienating relationship between people and the modern technological world they created. Horkheimer and Adorno, writing in 1944, saw the origins of the disasters around them in the worldviews promoted and sanctioned by the Enlightenment.[9]

But if the direction taken in the twentieth century alerted thinkers to the fatal dangers of some of the Enlightenment's assumptions, a sensitivity to the fallibilities and dangers of the age and a downright impatience with its tastes and habits can be seen, in a more frivolous light, well before this in the nineteenth century, especially in the aftermath of Napoleon's rise and fall. When in Thackeray's *Vanity Fair* (set in the teens of the nineteenth century), Becky Sharp hurls Johnson's dictionary out of the window of her carriage, an act of rebellion against the controlling intelligence promoted by the previous age has already occurred.

Ultimately, if the Enlightenment has been held indirectly responsible for attitudes to the world which subsequent ages have come to suspect and resent, that critical disposition is itself also indebted to the restlessly questioning spirit of the Enlightenment. It was the French Enlightenment that supplied the only fictional figure who still makes headlines every day. Figaro, Beaumarchais's ill-born, self-made hero, is quoted on the masthead of the newspaper to which he has lent his name: 'Sans la liberté de blâmer, il n'est point d'éloge flatteur' ('Without the freedom to criticise, there can be no meaningful praise').[10] His dictum, first heard in the 1780s, is surely still worth recalling and respecting, every day of the week.

---

9 Roland Barthes, 'Les Planches de l'*Encyclopédie*', in *Nouveaux essais critiques*, in *Le Degré zéro de l'écriture* (Paris: Seuil, 1972), pp. 89–105; Michel Foucault, 'What is Enlightenment?', in P. Rabinow (ed.), *The Foucault Reader* (New York: Pantheon Books, 1984), pp. 32–50; T. W. Adorno and Max Horkheimer, *Dialectic of Enlightenment*, trans. Edmund Jephcott (Stanford, CA: Stanford University Press, 2002).
10 P.-A. Caron de Beaumarchais, *Le Mariage de Figaro*, Act V, scene III.

40

The eighteenth-century novel

WILLIAM EDMISTON

Over the course of the eighteenth century the novel rose from a minor literary genre to the dominant one in France, eclipsing all others in popularity. It was a free form, without rules, as it had never been defined by the theorists of Graeco-Roman antiquity nor by their French neo-classical imitators. It afforded a subjective presentation of a life, of an individual consciousness within a social context, and thus offered an open-ended opportunity to express sentiment and to explore contemporary questions of morality, gender, and class. For many writers, it served as a polemical vehicle for social satire and criticism. Novels were attractive to many readers. Reading for pleasure was increasingly becoming a form of entertainment. The growth in size and in wealth of the reading public – especially middle-class readership – meant that more people could afford to buy and read books. In private libraries, books of history and theology were gradually replaced by novels. While there is a persistent myth that novels in the period were written largely by and for women, it is true that a proportionately larger number of women began writing novels during the period. By mid-century there was a steady current of literary production by women, and by the 1770s the idea of women writing novels had become commonplace. In *De l'usage des romans* (1734), Nicolas Lenglet-Dufresnoy pointed out that while everyone seemed to agree about denouncing the novel, novels were nonetheless written and read. Numbers of new titles are instructive. Approximately 1,050 new French works of fiction were published during the seventeenth century. By comparison, 2,900 new works of fiction written in French were published during the eighteenth century, nearly triple the number, while another 600 or so foreign novels were translated into French.

While the novel saw its fortunes rise during the eighteenth century, it was not a new genre. Whereas *novel* became a new generic term for prose fiction in England during this period, replacing the term *romance*, the word *roman* already had a long history in French, dating back to the verse narratives (*romans courtois*) of the Middle Ages. The word *nouvelle* first appeared in the Middle Ages as well and competed with *roman* for a time, but usage finally reserved *nouvelle* for shorter works of fiction. Fictional narratives in prose specifically designated as *romans* began to appear in the baroque period (early seventeenth century) in various subgenres: the pastoral novel, the heroic novel, and the comic novel. In the classical period (latter part of the seventeenth century) a new kind of novel began to appear, the *nouvelle historique* (a term doubtless used to distance the new form from the much-disparaged *roman*), which was less fanciful than earlier novels and more representational of French social life. The *nouvelle historique* was bound only by the rules of *vraisemblance* (verisimilitude) and *bienséance* (social propriety). Its best-known practitioners were women: Marie-Madeleine de Lafayette and Marie-Catherine de Villedieu. This turn towards the historical novel was much criticised because it blurred the distinction between archival histories of great figures and events, on the one hand, and fictional invention on the other. Novelists would eventually abandon the famous and illustrious characters and instead create imaginary and unknown protagonists, as they would abandon the obviously fictional third-person narrator (the tradition of third-person narration was kept alive in shorter fiction, especially the fairytale, the philosophical tale, and the moral tale). It was on the personal stories of unknown protagonists, told in their own words, that most early eighteenth-century novelists would set their sights.

Novelists in France could not earn a satisfactory living with their pens. Writers such as Alain-René Lesage, Antoine-François Prévost, and Pierre de Marivaux were often in desperate financial straits and needed to depend on patronage or on other activities such as journalism during their careers. The growth of the reading public required increasingly larger editions and therefore better payments from booksellers, but until the Revolution most writers continued to depend on literary patronage to supplement their incomes. In the 1780s royal pensions were still being awarded to a variety of writers, including Jacques-Henri Bernardin de Saint-Pierre. For most of the century, French legislation favoured the booksellers while authors had almost no legal rights. The commercial interests of the booksellers were served by the royal system of *privilèges* (a kind of copyright for the bookseller). There was no established principle of royalties. Authors normally sold their manuscripts to a bookseller for a fixed sum. Until Malesherbes replaced Daguesseau as chancellor at mid-century, novels seldom obtained a *privilège*, which meant they were at the mercy of pirates. Like all manuscripts submitted for publication in France, novels were subject to both royal and ecclesiastical censorship. This lack of freedom of expression led many novelists to have their works published abroad, especially in Holland, and then smuggled into France. Under Turgot's reforms (1777–8), the author was allowed to retain the *privilège* for a work, and fines were imposed on French publishers who produced pirated editions. The Revolution produced the first modern copyright law, which protected the rights of authors.

One of the earliest novels of the century, Lesage's *Gil Blas*, was published in three instalments over three decades. Serial publication of novels became popular by the 1730s and the procedure was adopted by the great novelists of that decade (Prévost, Marivaux, and Claude-Prosper Jolyot de Crébillon). If the first instalment was popular, novelists could ask booksellers for more money for the sequels. Later in the century, Nicolas Restif de La Bretonne frequently published novels in instalments. When works were left unfinished by their creators, other writers would at times step in to publish sequels, knowing that the public would be avid to read them even if the author had changed. Both of Marivaux's memoir-novels were finished by other writers.

By the beginning of the eighteenth century, the French and English literary worlds were beginning to influence each other significantly for the first time. Beginning in the middle of the seventeenth century, dozens of French novels were almost immediately translated into English, and vice versa. French men and women of letters of the eighteenth century knew the novels of Defoe, Swift, Fielding, Burney, and especially Richardson, to whom Denis Diderot devoted a passionate essay in the 1760s.

Despite the novel's popularity, the genre suffered from a bad reputation. Critics created what Georges May famously labelled *le dilemme du roman*, a dilemma that its practitioners could never escape. The novel owed a duty to morality but also to the representation of reality. The more novelists turned towards a believable imitation of contemporary reality, the more their work was condemned on moral grounds. Many writers felt the need to affirm the moral value of their text in its preface. Moralists condemned the genre as lies, falsehoods, and tainted with sentiment and eroticism. Aestheticians condemned its illegitimacy, calling it an ill-defined genre without classical ancestry. Should the novel be realistic and descriptive of society, including sentimental and erotic relationships? Or should it be didactic and morally prescriptive? Such was the dilemma of the novelist. As a result of the poor reputation of the novel on both moral and aesthetic grounds, its practition-ers were often reluctant to be identified as such. Like the word *roman*, the author's name was usually absent from the title page, but by the end of the eighteenth century the number of new novels bearing the author's name was at last exceeding the number of works published anonymously or under a pseudonym.

According to the aesthetic theory enshrined by Horace and endorsed by French neo-classical theorists, literature was supposed to be both useful and pleasing. On the one hand, its purpose was to instruct and edify morally (a didactic function). It was widely believed that readers could be edified only if their emotions were touched, and that this could be accomplished only if they believed in the truth of the story. The other purpose of literature was to amuse (an entertainment function). Many were convinced that readers' enjoyment was enhanced if they believed in the truth of the story. In short, both theories led novelists to create a convincing illusion of truth.

The last years of the reign of Louis XIV saw the publication of a best-seller that would have a determining influence on French fiction of the eighteenth century. In 1704 Antoine Galland began to publish *Les Mille et Une Nuits*. More than a translation, Galland's work is a talented recording of oriental tales that had existed only in oral form and that he learned in Arabic. For many years Europeans knew these tales only through the French version. This work opened up an entire new mythology previously unknown to the West, and it introduced into France an oriental vogue, an exoticism that appealed to French curiosity about 'otherness'. Much of the shorter fiction of the century would be characterised by Orientalism and other forms of exoticism. Charles-Louis Secondat, baron de Montesquieu saw the potential for social satire in the French public's infatuation with exoticism. Through his Persian visitors to Paris in *Lettres persanes* (1721), he turned a critical eye towards religion, government, social class, and gender relations. The literary device of the foreign observer of French mores, used for lessons of cultural relativism, would often be seen again, most notably in Françoise de Graffigny's Peruvian princess in *Lettres d'une Péruvienne* (1747) and in Voltaire's Huron in *L'Ingénu* (1767).

The development of first-person narration was the major innovation of the French novel of the eighteenth century. The first-person narrator was a quasi-historical voice, objective (in that it was 'historical', not obviously fictional) and subjective in its ability to express sentiment and to explore a personal consciousness. Eighteenth-century novelists tried to escape the morality/reality dilemma by pretending to write something other than fiction – an autobiography, a memoir, or a collection of letters. For this reason they turned overwhelmingly to the first-person form of narration, the form used by an individual telling his or her own story or writing letters to one or more correspondents. Readers of the classical period were already familiar with first-person narratives. Many Spanish picaresque novels had been translated into French during the baroque period, although the tradition found no French imitators before Lesage. Autobiographical narration in fiction was very rare in French, although the picaresque tradition did inspire a few comic first-person novels. But authentic historical memoirs, letters, and real and fictional travelogues were all written in the first person and encouraged the use of this form in the novel. What had changed between Lafayette's *La Princesse de Clèves* (1674) and Gatien de Courtilz's *Mémoires de M. d'Artagnan* (1700), to choose one example, was the introduction of the first-person narrator. The latter novel tells the life story of a well-known name in a recognisable socio-historical context, but it is narrated by the protagonist and appears to be (and was often judged to be) an authentic memoir. Courtilz's memoir-novels were very popular at the turn of the century and doubtless gave impetus to the genre in the early eighteenth century. Two early best-sellers of the period were also instrumental in setting the direction toward first-person narration. Robert Challe's *Les Illustres françaises* (1713) renewed and strengthened the tradition of the 'histoire' in which narrators are involved in their stories. The first six books of Lesage's *Histoire de Gil Blas de Santillane* were published in 1715 (the last instalment appeared in 1735). This was the first French novel to draw heavily on the tradition of the picaresque romance of Spain. It is a novel of manners and social conditions that satirises contemporary French society (later instalments would satirise the society of the regency).

Many an author guaranteed the authenticity of his text in its preface, affirming that what readers were about to consume was a true account of someone's life, a translation of an authentic correspondence, and so on. Novelists often posed as editors of the memoirs or letters, explaining how the manuscript had fallen into their hands, or how it had been found among the papers of a deceased person, and admitting perhaps to making corrections of style or suppressing less interesting passages. Did eighteenth-century readers believe these claims of authenticity? The answer is probably no and yes. It is likely that many readers accepted the claims as a necessary convention at a time when novels were not viewed favourably in official circles. Yet the fact that many readers of Jean-Jacques Rousseau's *Julie* wrote to the author with questions about the fate of Saint-Preux forces us to consider that some readers, at least, did believe in the truth of the texts they were reading.

The two first-person forms most commonly adopted were the memoir-novel and the epistolary novel. The memoir-novel was very popular until about 1740. Its ancestors were the Spanish picaresque novel and, in French, Villedieu's *Mémoires de la vie d'Henriette-Sylvie de Molière* (1671), a fictional autobiography. It was a form adopted mostly by male writers, even when the protagonists were women. In Philip Stewart's corpus of forty-six memoir-novels from the first half of the century, only three bear the name of a woman, although a number are still anonymous today. In this form, typically, the mature narrator writes the story of his own youthful amorous adventures and often of his initiation into society or his social ascension. It has too often been said that the memoir-novel offers no focal freedom to the novelist, as the information presented is restricted to the knowledge and point of view of one individual, the narrator-hero. Such is not the case, however. Theoretically, the memoir-novelist has at least two focalisations at his disposal. The limited 'internal' focalisation of the protagonist is restricted to the knowledge/ perspective of the experiencing self, whereas all subsequent knowledge is suppressed – a technique used at times by all storytellers in order to build suspense and keep the reader or listener guessing. The far less limited 'external' focalisation is only restricted to what the narrator knows and understands now, at the moment of narration perhaps many years later. This outer limit of the memoir-novelist's focal possibilities can be used to flash forward, to anticipate later developments and to fill in understandings that the protagonist did not possess at the moment when the events took place. In practice, however, there were few restrictions and certain eighteenth-century memoir-novelists – Crébillon, Prévost, Marivaux, and Diderot – were experimental and innovative in developing narrative technique while remaining more or less credibly within the limitations of the first-person form.

The decade of the 1730s is the golden age of the memoir-novel. These years witnessed publication of the great memoir-novels that are best known today: Prévost's *Mémoires et aventures d'un homme de qualité* (1728–31), *Histoire du chevalier des Grieux et de Manon Lescaut* (1731), *Le Philosophe anglais ou Histoire de M. Cleveland* (1731–5), *Le Doyen de Killerine* (1735–40), and *Histoire d'une Grecque moderne* (1740); Marivaux's *La Vie de Marianne* (1731–42) and *Le Paysan parvenu* (1734–5); Crébillon's *Les Égarements du cœur et de l'esprit* (1736); and Claudine Guérin de Tencin's *Mémoires du comte de Comminge* (1735). These novels are remarkable in their creation of an illusion of contemporary society, in their psychological observation, and in their expression of sentiment. The popularity of these novels drew increased hostility from the government. In 1736 the Jesuit scholar Charles Porée published a diatribe against the novel, calling upon government officials to put a stop to the publication of such works in the name of good taste and good morals. Subsequently, the Jansenist chancellor Daguesseau pronounced an official proscription of the novel, an event which seems to have had little impact on the book trade.

A common feature of the memoir-novel, inherited from the picaresque novel, is the *tiroir* (literally, 'drawer'), an interpolated narrative within the main narrative, often told by a character whom the narrator meets. Lesage makes frequent use of this technique in *Gil Blas*. Prévost's *Histoire du chevalier des Grieux et de Manon Lescaut*, published separately since 1731, is really a *tiroir* of the larger *Mémoires et aventures d'un homme de qualité*, and the Man of Quality admits, in his preface to Des Grieux's story, that it is too long to have been inserted into his own memoirs in its chronological place. But the length of the *tiroir* was not an issue for many writers. In Marivaux's *La Vie de Marianne*, the heroine meets the nun Tervire, whose story is certainly long enough to be its own novel. The device of the *tiroir* also appeared in works that were not memoir-novels. In Diderot's *Jacques le fataliste* (written in the 1770s but not published until the Revolution), the *hôtesse* at the inn tells Jacques and his master the very long interpolated story of Madame de La Pommeraye. In Donatien-Alphonse-François, marquis de Sade's epistolary novel, *Aline et Valcour* (1795), two of the letters contain long narrations that go on for hundreds of pages.

The 1740s and 1750s saw the development of the licentious or libertine novel, which was very successful in the upper levels of society. The memoir-novels of Charles Pinot Duclos, *Histoire de Madame de Luz* (1740) and *Les Confessions du comte de **** (1741), are often included in this group. A better-known example is Diderot's *Les Bijoux indiscrets* (1748), the only one of his novels published during his lifetime. Also dating from this mid-century period are three well-known pornographic novels: *Histoire de Dom B*** ou Le Portier des Chartreux* (1745) by Gervaise de Latouche, *Thérèse philosophe* (1748) attributed to Boyer d'Argens, and *Margot la ravaudeuse* (1748) by Fougeret de Monbron.

The publication of the epistolary novels of Richardson in French, beginning in the 1740s, corresponded with the waning of the memoir-novel. Richardson's novels brought with them a wave of sentimentality and an increased predilection for the epistolary form, soon viewed by many writers as richer and more creative than the memoir-novel. Its ancestor was the anonymous seventeenth-century success, *Lettres portugaises* (1669, sometimes attributed to Guilleragues), still widely read during the following century. There had been two hugely popular successes of the epistolary form in the first half of the century – Montesquieu's *Lettres persanes* (1721) and Graffigny's *Lettres d'une Péruvienne* (1747) – but the letter-novel grew more prevalent in the second half of the century. The monophonic version of the epistolary novel, in which all letters are written by the same narrator, was modelled on the *Lettres portugaises* and was adopted by many women writers (Graffigny, Marie-Jeanne

Riccoboni, and Isabelle de Charrière, for example) although Crébillon also used this form in his *Lettres de la marquise de M**** (1732). The polyphonic version of the letter-novel, in which various characters correspond with one another, was adopted by Montesquieu, Crébillon, Rousseau, Restif, Pierre Choderlos de Laclos, and Sade, among others.

The letter-novel was a form that appealed to women writers, who were less likely to write about the social success or amorous conquests of a male protagonist than about the sense and sensibility of female ones. The subjects treated by these writers are those that most affected women in contemporary French society: compulsory internment in convents, forced and loveless marriages, abandonment by a lover, solitude. Graffigny ended her *Lettres d'une Péruvienne* with a remarkable declaration of autonomy on the part of the heroine, but sequels were published nonetheless by writers who did not approve of her open-ended conclusion in which a woman remained alive, unmarried, and uncloistered. Riccoboni wrote some of her best novels in the wake of Richardson and before the watershed of Rousseau's *Julie*: *Lettres de mistriss Fanni Butlerd* (1757) and *Lettres de mylady Juliette Catesby* (1759).

Rousseau's *Julie, ou la Nouvelle Héloïse* (1761) capitalised on both the themes and form used by Richardson and was probably the best-selling novel of the French eighteenth century. It catapulted Rousseau to fame and spawned numerous imitations. *Julie*'s opening themes are those of the struggle between passion and virtue and of the sufferings of young love, but the novel also contains long philosophical discussions and reflections on the household and the estate of Julie and her husband. The novel's gushing sentimentality and obvious edifying purpose seem dated today, but it was a huge success at the time. Even Sade, in his preface to *Les Crimes de l'amour* (1800), asserted that Rousseau's sublime novel would never have any imitators, but then paradoxically called for an end to the crowd of forgotten writers who had been publishing poor imitations of *Julie* for thirty years.

The epistolary form continued to dominate the genre throughout the 1770s and 1780s. Some well-known authors include Restif, who gave vivid portraits of contemporary manners in *Le Paysan perverti* (1775) and *La Paysanne pervertie* (1784); Charrière, who has been compared to Jane Austen and who wrote about woman's marginality and vulnerability in *Lettres neuchâteloises* (1784), *Lettres de mistress Henley* (1784), *Lettres écrites de Lausanne* (1785), and *Caliste* (1787); and Choderlos de Laclos, whose only novel, *Les Liaisons dangereuses* (1782), portrayed two depraved and unscrupulous aristocrats – the memorable marquise de Merteuil and the vicomte de Valmont – engaged in a battle of the sexes for power and domination. Laclos's novel is unequalled in its technical perfection. Its letters are not merely the vehicle of narration but actions that advance the plot. With its complex structure, differentiation of styles, and brilliant juxtaposition of letters creating dramatic irony, it is hailed by most critics as the masterpiece of the letter-novel in French.

Another famous novel from the 1780s, although not in epistolary form, is Bernardin de Saint-Pierre's *Paul et Virginie* (1788), a tribute to Rousseauist views of nature and virtue. The novel was an enormous success and influenced a generation of Romantic writers. Its first-person narrator quickly turns the account over to an old man, who tells the story of Paul and Virginie largely in the third person, a tradition that would re-emerge in the great novels of the nineteenth century.

Perhaps the most brilliant French writer of his century, Diderot wrote two experimental novels that had no influence on the eighteenth-century novel, as they were not published until 1796, after the author's death and, more importantly, after the end of censorship. *La Religieuse* (composition begun in 1760) is a curious amalgam of the memoir-novel and the letter-novel, with interesting incursions of one form into the other on numerous occasions, straining against their limitations as if to stress the inadequacy of both forms. *Jacques le fataliste* (composition probably begun in the early 1770s) has often been described as an anti-novel and a modernist novel as it foregrounds and subverts every convention of the contemporary novel, forcing readers to confront the very nature of fiction. Inspired by Sterne's *Tristram Shandy*, its most remarkable (and to some readers, frustrating) feature is the insistent dialogue between the first-person (but extradiegetic) narrator and the virtual reader (a fictional character), constantly interrupting Jacques's narration of his loves to his master. Henri Coulet concludes his monumental study of the French novel before the Revolution by calling Diderot the first French modern novelist.

The best-known writer of the revolutionary decade is Sade, who probably exploited the third-person narrative form more than any other writer of the period. In his longest and most infamous novel, *La Nouvelle Justine ou les malheurs de la vertu, suivie de l'Histoire de Juliette ou les prospérités du vice* (1799–1801), Juliette narrates her own story of vice in the first person as a six-volume *tiroir*, while the story of her virtuous sister Justine is told in the third person (although two earlier versions of Justine's story had been written in the first person). Sade's sprawling ten-volume novel is framed by a third-person narrator who claims no historical authenticity.

It was the eighteenth century's first-person forms that prepared the way for the great third-person novels of the following century. By adopting a 'historical' voice, or voices, writers had demonstrated that the novel could be a serious literary genre, one capable of analysing the sentiments and psychology of individuals in a familiar social context. It is not possible to pinpoint exactly when, but certainly by the end of the eighteenth century the novel had found its own voice. Once fiction was accepted on its own status as fiction, it could be recognised as such and the pretence of historical illusion was no longer necessary. Nineteenth-century novelists would be free to write their stories using omniscient third-person narrators, in an established and recognisable form of art.

41

The eighteenth-century *conte*

ROBIN HOWELLS

The *conte* is in some ways the perfect literary form for the French eighteenth century. The tale is among the most ancient of genres, which endows it with a received if modest status within the French classical hierarchy inherited by the Enlightenment. It is also associated, though less specifically than the fable, with exemplarity and the conveying of wisdom. Its popular origins and its simplicity, transmuted by literary treatment, allow for a variety of registers; its openness will admit a variety of content. Its brevity too is admirably suited to the mode of the rococo and the age of wit. A tale can be included within a longer narrative, or appear freestanding in the elite monthly *Mercure*, or be collected with other pieces in a volume. But it may first circulate sociably through salon performance or manuscript transmission. It would tend to be published anonymously, and if a little improper then illegally or abroad. For these reasons, the literary folktale (*conte gaulois*, *conte de fées*, *conte oriental*) is often in this period less 'itself' than an ironic or double-voiced version of itself. Offered playfully, it can be enjoyed in the same way, authorising a sophisticated culture to take pleasure from its mock naïvety, while hinting perhaps at a certain scepticism towards grander narratives. Frivolity would increasingly serve as a cover for material which is indecent, vulgar or polemical (combined variously in the *conte libertin*, *conte poissard*, and *conte philosophique*). The 1760s, however, will see the rise of the *conte moral*, alongside that of didactic tales for children. As foreign literatures impinge and other places attract, Paris becomes anti-Paris. Pastoral innocence and moral pathos are to prompt our natural feelings in the interests of reform. But 'nature' is becoming an active force, which may be embodied in the collectivity, or separate the individual from society.

To understand what is new in the eighteenth-century tale, we need to glance first at what precedes it. If there is a traditional or 'received' mode, it is represented by La Fontaine's *Contes et nouvelles en vers* (1665–85). This title itself tells us two things. First, it implies the considerable generic overlap between the *conte* or tale (dealing perhaps in more general truth) and the *nouvelle* or novella (more located and particularised). Second, we are reminded that the tale could still be (like most ancient literary forms) in verse. The printed sources of La Fontaine's tales are often Italian, notably Boccaccio, as well as Latin and French. Their subject matter is usually trickery and the gratification of sexual appetite, their tone roguish and popular. In form too they are relatively free. La Fontaine's *contes* elevate traditional material through literary refinement, while retaining its old-fashioned charm by means of studied naïveties.

The 1690s see the sudden rise of the *conte de fées* (fairytale). Again, traditional material is given literary treatment. But the result is rather different, marking a new era. The basic matter is more primitive – closer to oral folklore and legend. The treatment is more sophisticated and ludic. Instead of the *gaulois* mode of comic realism we have something more feminised, imaginative, and ironic. Exchanging such stories seems to have been a society amusement, and at least half the fairytales published at this time are by titled ladies. The rise of the marvellous tale reflects the shift from high classical stability to rococo play, with its politics and poetics of gender and genre, its cult of *mondanité* (worldliness), its mild subversiveness and codified liberation of desire.

Perrault's *Histoires ou contes du temps passé, avec des moralités* (1697) is the masterpiece of this fairytale corpus, but far from typical. Perrault's eight prose tales are all short. Narration is rapid, *personae* simple and story central. The protagonists may be children (Little Red Riding Hood, Tom Thumb) or adolescents (Sleeping Beauty, Cinderella, the master of Puss-in-Boots). Four of the eight are of peasant stock (the first two and the last, plus the hero-ine of *Les Fées*), including two in extreme poverty. Only two protagonists are royal (Belle and Riquet à la houppe), though two more will marry roy-als. These appellations themselves are 'popular' in their familiar particularity (Red Hood, Thumb, Boots, Riquet's curl; likewise Bluebeard). Within the stories, the particular will serve to establish concrete situations, anchoring the extraordinary events (talking animals, fairies, or ogres, spells and trans-formations) which are recounted in the same matter-of-fact way. The tales are very varied in kind. But almost all begin with 'Il était une fois . . . ' ('Once upon a time . . . '), establishing our generic expectations. These are confirmed by the occasional use of other traditional features: oral narrative style, dated locutions, onomatopoeia, formulae, and repetitions (the last of a threesome; 'What big arms/legs/ears/eyes/teeth you have!'). But they are also gently subverted by dissonant elements: ironic narratorial interventions, arbitrary details, and anachronisms (festivities include the opera; the ogress wants the child cooked with a special sauce). The versified 'moral' at the end is often playfully doubled, and in the earlier tales tends to be more satirical (of modern and especially female behaviour) than improving.

In the same year of 1697, and with the same fashionable printer-publisher (Barbin), appeared the first of two collections by Mme d'Aulnoy. This is the most considerable and systematic body of work in the genre. Her *Contes des fées* in four volumes were soon followed by another four appropriately subtitled *les fées à la mode*. In contrast with Perrault, d'Aulnoy deals in royal protagonists, enchanted luxury and romantic love. Her stories are lengthy, but follow the basic structure of the folktale. One or both of a beautiful young couple seek happiness (quest). Persecuted by malevolent fairies or bad queens (misdeed/lack), but protected by other forces and their own qualities, they overcome obstacles (ordeal/struggle). Finally they marry and reign happily ever after (reparation, reward). Perhaps the most notable feature of d'Aulnoy's tales is the frequency of animal metamorphosis, sometimes soothing (doe-woman, sheep-man), but sometimes in a more sexually disturbing form (furry cat-woman, scaly serpent-man, or tusked boar-boy). A notable reflexive feature of the two collections is the insertion, part-way through each, of 'nouvelles' whose characters tell the subsequent tales. These characters also declare what a fairytale should be: a 'bagatelle' but requiring 'art'; naïve, 'enjoué' (playful), and 'délicat'. The 'nouvelles' as frame narratives also fictionalise (ideally, then more satirically) the conditions of social production and reception of the genre.

Recent criticism, often feminist, has given much attention to d'Aulnoy, but less to other *conteuses*. They too tend to expansiveness (as do some *conteurs* such as Préchac, though not Mailly), and to ideal love. Psychological subtlety and moral pessimism are offered by Catherine Bernard (in two tales within her novel *Inès de Cordoue*), and to some extent by Mme de Murat. Probably the most interestingly multivalent tales are those of Mlle L'Héritier de Villandon, a woman of letters in the *précieuse* tradition. Her stories, which develop the allegorical tendency of the genre, valorise virtue, self-cultivation, and the arts. In paratexts she affirms that her tales are drawn from the old French troubadours, preserved but also contaminated by popular transmission, which she has refined and expanded for today. The elaborated fairytale, established around 1700, will be the norm throughout the eighteenth century. Only with Romanticism does preference shift decisively towards the apparently simple 'folk' mode.

The fairytale is soon joined by its cousin in the marvellous, the *conte oriental*. Here, however, the new subgenre is created by the genius of one man. Antoine Galland, a scholar acquainted with the Middle East, puts into print *Les Mille et Une Nuits: contes arabes* (1704–17). Galland draws his material from early Arabic manuscript collections under this title, but also from other sources. The latter category in fact embraces the three stories which will remain best known in the West: 'Sindbad', 'Aladdin', and 'Ali Baba'. Equally famous, however, is the frame situation. Scheherazade, the accomplished daughter of the Vizir, has volunteered to be the next of the virgins whom the Sultan has vowed (in unending revenge for the debaucheries of his previous spouse) to wed each evening and execute in the morning. Abetted by her little sister Dinarzade, each dawn she will distract him with surprising tales. Thus Scheherazade narrates for her life. Each night joins sex with the prospect of death postponed by storytelling. This 'nocturnal poetics' embraces the tales themselves. They too are marked by sexuality, by violence (death, grotesque disablement, cruel punishments), by the serial but also the arbitrary and the oneiric (genies, astonishing events, terror, and wish-fulfilment). They too contain stories, some also told in order to assuage the wrath of the powerful, which are then recorded in their turn in the royal annals. The tales are of varied provenance (cycles notably from China, Egypt, and Baghdad) depicting the lives of porters and ladies, merchants or princes, and heterogeneous in tone. But all are drawn together by their previous assimilation to medieval Arab culture, by their extraordinary internal nesting and interweaving, by the frame narrative, and then by Galland's French treatment. Galland 'classicises' the material (abstraction, clarification, propriety) without ironising it.

Les Mille et Une Nuits (promptly translated as *The Arabian Nights*) was hugely influential. Today's cultural criticism frowns on such 'Orientalism', but we should see it in the terms of the time. The work must have appealed to Galland's public (largely privileged and female) by taking them further than the fairytales. To exoticism were added the particular forms of another culture, allowing more embodied expressions of desire. That specific otherness is then increasingly lost through absorption and diffusion. The allusively-titled *Mille et Un Jours: contes persans* (1710–12) by Galland's colleague Pétis de la Croix assembles what seem to be genuine materials within a reversed and palliated frame situation (stories persuade Princess Farukhnaz that men can be faithful). The gentleman amateur Gueulette will add *Les Mille et Un Quarts d'heure: contes tartares* (1715), and other variants. But Bignon's *Abdalla* (1712–14) may be the first collection which can clearly be read as self-ironic. Galland is evoked in the preliminaries of all three of the delicately burlesque fairytales of Hamilton – known and admired even before their belated publication in 1730. The marvellous story will be practised, at least in passing, by most major writers of the Enlightenment. Tales from the classic corpus of 1690–1715, with later additions, are selectively anthologised throughout the century, culminating in the famous forty-one-volume *Cabinet des fées . . . et autres contes merveilleux* of 1785–9.

Hamiltonian whimsy becomes aggressive fantasy in the *conte libertin*. The founding text of this new male mode is Crébillon's extraordinary *Tanzaï et Néadarné* (1734) also called *L'Écumoire*. A nominally 'oriental' setting, and a parodic version of the fairy romance, are redeployed in the service of an indecent satire of French religious politics and of ideal love. The titular 'skimmer' seems to represent papal authority. But it is also the object which the titular prince and princess on their wedding night find in place of his genital organ (Book 2). To recover the means to consummate their passion, each in turn must be sexually unfaithful – he repeatedly with the disgusting old *fée* Concombre, she once with the charming genie Jonquille. The work is occasionally brutal and sometimes obscene. But most consistently it is witty: by its multiple allusions, its preposterous events, its oneiric ambiguities, suggestive circumlocutions, and generic play. Dwelling pruriently on the young lovers' discovery together of the stages of erotic pleasure, it also reveals quite tenderly their moral ambivalence faced with infidelity as the price of possession. Reinforcing gender roles (men besiege, Néadarné defends), it nevertheless recognises women's desire, and the hypocrisies imposed on them by men and social mores. Cynically complaisant, it is also coolly analytical. The work was much admired for its stylishness, while its scandalous content (prompting an official ban and the brief jailing of its author) further aided its great success.

The 1740s sees the apogee of the *conte libertin*, including Crébillon's *Le Sopha* (1742), a more orderly review of sexual dissemblance among the privileged. Soon after appeared notably Duclos's *Acajou et Zirphile* (1744), Voisenon's *Sultan Misapouf* (1746), La Morlière's *Angola* (1746), and Diderot's *Bijoux indiscrets* (1748). These works share many elements. First there may be a paratext which derides the text or its readership. Several works begin with a debased version of the *Mille et Une* frame situation, featuring a bullying sultan who will repeatedly intervene during the main narrative (disruption, reflexivity), prompting his favourites into debates about content or form (hermeneutics, poetics) which are left unresolved. The marvellous tale, parodied, depicts quite transparently the 'real' world of fashionable Paris, satirised. The latter is usually reviewed through the adventures of the naïve protagonist(s), sometimes in serial episodes. The former allows metamorphosis, by which a desiring human being is identified with a small animal (mole, bird, rabbit) or a base object (sofa, bathtub, chamber-pot, bidet – a recent invention) and its low perspective. Or magical power gives human body parts independent life (hands that pinch, female genitals that talk, or bite). Alongside these implicit male fears (enclosure, ingestion) are explicit episodes of impotence. Erotic encounter is a principal focus in these narratives. But their *libertinisme* is also *philosophique*. The body and sexuality are central to the new Enlightenment understanding of humankind. So is learning through sensual experience and what we would call socialisation. These tales use fairyland to exhibit ambivalently the sexual mores of the Parisian *beau monde*, magic to foreground mutability, and fantasy to explore – lewdly, morally, and sometimes ruefully – the relations between the old ideal of sentimental love and the new fact of corporeal pleasure.

Improper tales also embrace, for the first time, less privileged urban life. Most of these stories are appropriately devoid of magic. One category is that of the female libertine, who is usually a commoner (matching and expos-ing her to vulgar realities) and tells her own story (sufficiently generalised nevertheless to call a tale). The two most notable examples at this time are *Thérèse philosophe*, attributed to d'Argens (1748), and *Margot la ravaudeuse* by Fougeret de Montbron (1750). Thérèse's 'philosophy' begins with her child-hood discovery of self-pleasuring. It develops via her observation of sexual intercourse (abusive monk and 'pénitente', then enlightened abbé and lady), and an interpolated *histoire*. It is completed by the rational cohabitation that Thérèse agrees with a count (no marriage, *coitus interruptus* to prevent preg-nancy). Their philosophy – also thematised earlier – is a deistic determinism, their motto utility which includes maintaining the existing social order. *Margot la ravaudeuse* (the seamstress) is baser and sourer. The memoirs of a Parisian whore present to us a social range of clients and a sexual range of practices. We are told that the prostitute's life is squalid and humiliating, its imperative money. Margot finally loses her looks and falls ill, but she recovers through a healthy diet and regular exercise. Thus libertine materialism, 'picaresque' as well as philosophical, ends in a very modern way with a programme of self-control.

The *colporteur* ([book-]pedlar), hawking publications which may be unau-thorised, is another marginal figure pleasuring and punished by society. *Col-portage* as a social practice centres on the Paris of this period, but as literary subject matter it moves us towards the *poissard*. The ironically titled *Mémoires de l'académie des colporteurs* (1748), a mixed bag assembled by Caylus, includes several short fictional memoirs. Some (such as 'Catherine Cuisson' and 'Jean Longcuart') recount not just a *colporteur*'s rise and fall (jail) but the secrets of the trade. Piron's 'La Malle-bosse' is a more highly coloured story of trickery. *Poissard* as a term is defined for the first time in the *Dictionnaire de l'Académie*

Française of 1762 as 'qui imite le langage, les mœurs, du bas peuple' ('imitating the language, the mores, of the lowest ranks'). Thus, however, it exhibits to us not rogues at the margin but a broad, albeit base, social class. Urban picaresque, one might say, becomes picturesque. Verse tales by the alleged founder of the genre, Jean-Joseph Vadé (d. 1757), seem closer to traditional burlesque. More interesting are Caylus and his circle. The *Colporteurs* eschews the essential *poissard* characteristic of popular language. But demotic registers are assigned to the first-person narrators of *Guillaume cocher* (*William the Coachman*), the *Écosseuses* (*Pea-Shelling Gossips*) and the *Bals de bois* (*Dance-Halls*). In these informal works we find the main elements of the carnivalesque: collective work and festivity; a royal wedding and the public street; consumption and exchange; disorderly life and embodied language. But the treatment is mainly patronising, if not ironic. The literary representation of popular mores and language is notable, but its legitimation is as *facétie* or comic amusement.

The *conte philosophique* is a category that we associate primarily with Voltaire. Voltaire's earliest tales, dating from around 1715, were elite entertainments with a lighter *gaulois* vein in verse. In prose the mock oriental mode predominates up to *Zadig* (1748). Added then are rapid narrative tours of the modern world (*Scarmentado*, 1756; *Candide*, 1759), and finally an increasing focus on France and England (*L'Ingénu*, 1767; *Jenni*, 1775). The 'classic' prose tales offer a witty review, a scathing critique and a joyous demolition of most forms of human ideal: romantic, social, cultural, political, religious, intellectual, and – reflexively – literary. Voltaire's *contes* are *philosophiques* essentially in using the naïve protagonist to test an idea against 'reality', so that the usual lover's quest is subordinated to the quest for truth. Thus in his masterpiece Candide is assigned the theory of Optimism, and then sent out into the world. His experiences, amply demonstrating the mismatch, are serial, mainly painful (for him) and comic (for us). Candide cannot learn, because his role is to keep on being surprised and shocked by the real world; but also because it is to keep on keeping on – like the motley band which gather around him – in the indomitable folly of humanity. The truth will not be found, until it comes home in the more sentimental and reformist late tales. These accordingly move away from ironically omniscient narration towards more immediate forms: first-person witness, theatrical dialogue. Such forms characterise the later 'contes' of Diderot, which can also be called philosophical, though they are – typically of their author – multivalent and unclassifiable. Most were unpublished, only circulating semi-privately, like his longer fictions such as *Jacques le fataliste* in which tales of more roguish inclination are organically embedded. The exception (published in 1773) is *Les Deux Amis de*

Bourbonne. Provincial, 'realist' (to draw in the reader, as the important 'post-face' explains), socially critical, exalting simple lives and sublime feelings, it reflects a new era.

The chief index of the new is a kind of tale which proposes to improve us through feeling: the *conte moral*. This category was established around 1760 by Marmontel. His tales usually centre on a 'cœur sensible' ('sensitive heart') seeking within privileged society its own happiness. Natural moral sentiments and worldly *mores* (the two senses of *moral*) are increasingly shown to be in conflict. Appearing initially in the monthly *Mercure* from 1755, Marmontel's tales move from mild libertinism and disenchantment (*Alcibiade*, *Le Scrupule*) to a positive teaching of family values (*La Bonne Mère*, *Le Bon Mari*). The social world depicted remains largely Parisian and aristocratic (with occasional 'ancient', rural, or mercantile excursions), and the focus feminine; the writing is still decorous, and the narrative neatly structured. But the ethos becomes more affective and bourgeois. The huge success of Marmontel's collected *Contes moraux* (1761) is reflected in the subsequent publication of a dozen other collections with similar titles. These include Mercier's volume of 1769, which points to the future by promising to expose not just 'le ridicule' but the real scourge of society which is 'le vice'. The same undertaking is proclaimed by Baculard d'Arnaud, the author of increasingly overheated *nouvelles* and (like Mercier) of *drames* (melodramas). The writer's vocation is to depict distress which will move the wicked to tears, *bienfaisance* (charitable deeds) and virtue (*Les Épreuves du sentiment*, 1770). Mme Le Prince de Beaumont, a more circumspect author of moral tales (1773, 1776), had come to fame earlier as the founder of an allied genre: improving tales for children. These (including a notable version of *La Belle et la bête*) first appear in her highly successful *Magasin des enfants* of 1756. Berquin's twenty-four-part *Ami des enfants* (1782–3) is another best-seller. As the children's tale addresses a new market, so the *conte moral* reflects a widening and less sophisticated readership. The two tend to come together, and feed into the didactic stories of the revolutionary period.

But while the 1760s in France see the rise of reformism, they also show us a culture long centred on Paris opening up to multiple outside forces. Some *conteurs* use British models (Baculard, Saint-Lambert), others adapt German material (Mercier, Berquin). Provincial life is no longer necessarily ridiculous, nor the exotic just playful. Tales begin to be set in Savoy or Scotland, America or India. There indeed the French reader, turning away from metropolitan corruption, will find natural simplicity and true feeling. The great success of Gessner's *Idylles* (translated in 1761) announces a cult of rural innocence.

Imagination seeks the ideal, and stories are presented as dreams. Even *libertin* tales tend to contain pastoral elements (Boufflers, *Aline, reine de Golconde*), or enchanting events (Denon, *Point de lendemain*). But, obversely, the 'moral' exhibition of criminal acts and ravished victims may arouse not so much our remorse as our own desires. Nature is becoming not only a refuge but a principle of energy and power. Tales laud virtue and celebrate the people, but are increasingly drawn to extreme passions and alienated individuals.

42

Eighteenth-century comic theatre

RUSSELL GOULBOURNE

Two received ideas beset our vision of eighteenth-century French comedy. The first is that the comic stage was so haunted by the ghost of Molière that dramatists had little or no room for creative manoeuvre. Frequently performed and constantly cited, Molière's plays put eighteenth-century comic dramatists in an impossible situation, as the poet figure suggests in the prologue to Dufresny's three-act prose comedy *Le Négligent*, first performed at the Comédie-Française in February 1692, less than twenty years after Molière's death: 'Molière a bien gâté le théâtre. Si l'on donne dans son goût: Bon, dit aussitôt le critique, cela est pillé, c'est Molière tout pur; s'en écarte-t-on un peu: Oh! ce n'est pas là Molière' ('Molière has really spoilt the theatre. If you write like him: Right, says the critic straightaway, that's borrowed, it's pure Molière; and if you try to be a little different: Oh! that's not Molière') (Scene 3). And the second received idea – the first notwithstanding – is that the only comic dramatists of any lasting interest and significance in eighteenth-century France, and therefore the only worthy successors to Molière, were Marivaux and Beaumarchais. However, neither of these received ideas, on closer inspection, holds good, since eighteenth-century French comedy, encompassing plays performed at public theatres in Paris (the Comédie-Française, the Théâtre Italien, the fairground theatres) and in the provinces, as well as on innumerable private stages, or *théâtres de société*, across the country, was a site of enormous creativity and experimentation as well as a space of significant contestation in the context of the Enlightenment.

Molière excelled at making audiences laugh at themselves, and many of his successors strove to do exactly the same thing, albeit, if anything, with increased emphasis on what might be termed, not unproblematically, 'social realism'. At the turn of the century, comic dramatists such as Regnard, Dancourt, Dufresny, and Lesage wrote cynical comedies of social observation. For example, Regnard's five-act verse comedy *Le Joueur*, first performed at the Comédie-Française in December 1696, satirises the contemporary vogue for gambling through the character of Valère, who comically wavers between gambling when he has money and paying attention to his unfortunate mistress, Angélique, when he does not; and Lesage's *Turcaret*, first performed at the Comédie-Française in February 1709, despite the actors' reluctance to offend the targets of the play's satire, recalls Molière's *Le Bourgeois Gentilhomme* in satirising a corrupt tax farmer of low birth with pretensions far above his station.

These comedies were followed by theatrical satires which focused more explicitly still on recognisable contemporaries. For example, Palissot's one-act prose comedy *Le Cercle ou Les Originaux*, set in Paris and first performed at the new theatre in Nancy in November 1755, recalls Molière's *Les Fâcheux* in satirising a string of foolish characters, but goes further than the earlier play in presenting these characters in such a way as to ensure that audiences would recognise famous contemporaries: M. Volcan, an affected poet, can be none other than Voltaire; Araminte, a learned lady who has fallen in love with M. Volcan, represents Mme Du Châtelet; and Blaise-Gille-Antoine, a moody and reclusive philosopher, distinctly recalls Jean-Jacques Rousseau. Five years later, in May 1760, Palissot returned to the fray with his controversial three-act verse comedy *Les Philosophes*, staged at the Comédie-Française, in which he lampooned Diderot, presenting him, via the Latinised anagram 'Dortidius', as pompous and wicked, and Rousseau, embodied in the character of Crispin, who appears on stage on all fours, munching a lettuce. Voltaire was spared, although he responded with his five-act prose comedy *L'Écossaise*, first performed at the Comédie-Française two months later, in July 1760, in which he satirises Fréron, the staunchly Catholic and monarchist journalist, enthusiastic supporter of Palissot and general thorn in the side of the *philosophes*, under the thin but meaningful guise of 'Frélon' (the French word for wasp), a ridiculously envious hack writer. These three comedies, written and performed at precisely the time when the free-thinking *philosophes* started to be seen as a distinct party, provide evidence of the way in which comic theatre could become involved in broader intellectual debates of the period.

What these different brands of satirical comedy – from Regnard's *Le Joueur* to Voltaire's *L'Écossaise* – have in common is that, like their seventeenth-century models, they focus on character types who are satirised for their absurd unwillingness to change their foolish ways. By contrast, a number of dramatists, particularly from the 1730s onwards, wrote more serious, even moralising comedies about flawed characters who see the error of their ways by the end of the play. One such play is Destouches's five-act verse comedy *Le Glorieux*, first performed at the Comédie-Française in January 1732, about a poor but obsessively rank-conscious nobleman, which ends with the central character, the comte de Tufière, movingly resolving to mend his ways. Destouches's preface to his play is particularly revealing of the way in which comedy was developing at this time:

> Qu'y a-t-il de plus glorieux pour notre nation, si fameuse d'ailleurs pour tant de qualités, que de faire aujourd'hui connaître à tout l'univers, que les comédies, à qui l'ancien préjugé ne donne pour objet que celui de plaire et de divertir, ne peuvent la divertir et lui plaire longtemps, que lorsqu'elle trouve dans cet agréable spectacle, non seulement ce qui peut le rendre innocent et permis, mais même ce qui peut contribuer à l'instruire et à la corriger?

> (What greater glory can we bring to our nation, which is already so well known for so many qualities, than to show the whole world today that comedies, which have always been thought of as intended simply to please and to entertain, can only ever really succeed in entertaining and pleasing our nation when we find in this enjoyable spectacle not only that which can make us innocent and blameless, but also that which can serve to instruct and correct us?)

Destouches's serious comedy paved the way for Nivelle de la Chaussée's *comédies larmoyantes*, or tearful comedies, the best example of which is *Mélanide*, in five acts and in verse, which was first performed at the Comédie-Française in May 1741 and in which, like other contemporary tragic dramatists, La Chaussée appeals to the audience's finer feelings through the spectacle of virtue in distress: he takes the familiar comic structure of an older man in love with a younger woman and drains it of its comic potential. Going further still than Destouches and La Chaussée, first Mme de Graffigny and then Diderot break new ground in abandoning verse in favour of prose for their serious dramas, though with varying degrees of popular success: Graffigny's *Cénie*, first staged at the Comédie-Française in June 1750, enjoyed a remarkable first run of twenty-five performances, but neither of Diderot's two *drames bourgeois*, or serious plays in prose about bourgeois families, *Le Fils naturel* (1757) and *Le Père de famille* (1758), were box-office hits, with the former having to wait until 1771 for its first performance at the Comédie-Française.

If increasingly sombre *drames* enjoyed a certain vogue in the 1760s and 1770s, at least amongst dramatists if not with spectators, as suggested by plays such as Baculard d'Arnaud's *Les Amants malheureux* (1764), which is set in a catacomb, and Mercier's *L'Indigent* (1772), about a poor weaver, they also found themselves, like the tragedies with which they had much in common, becoming the subject of parodies, an enormously popular subgenre in the eighteenth century. In the 1770s, for example, Cubières-Palmézeaux wrote a series of comedies parodying the *drames sombres*, including the three-act verse comedy *La Lacrymanie ou Manie des drames*, published in 1775, and *Le Dramaturge ou la Manie des drames sombres*, first performed at Fontainebleau in October 1776. But by far the century's most successful parody was Biancolelli's one-act verse comedy *Agnès de Chaillot*, first performed by the Italian actors at the Foire Saint-Laurent in July 1723. It parodies Houdar de La Motte's equally successful tragedy *Inès de Castro*, which had been staged at the Comédie-Française three months earlier: Alfonse, the king of Portugal, becomes Trivelin, the bailiff of Chaillot; his son, Don Pèdre, becomes Pierrot, who has just won the musket-shooting prize; and the lady-in-waiting, Inès, becomes the servant girl, Agnès.

These parodies point to an important feature of eighteenth-century French comedy: the taste for the burlesque, the carnivalesque, even the subversive. Indeed, it was precisely this scope for playfulness that, paradoxically perhaps, furnished comedy with the potential to engage with serious issues of the day; for another way of reacting against the seventeenth-century Molièresque model of comedy consisted in depicting a broader social canvas and, in so doing, in dealing with a wider range of social, political, and sexual issues than earlier comedies, and often, crucially, under the guise of exoticism, fantasy, and irreality. One particularly popular comic device in this respect was the figure of the outsider.

In some plays, straightforward fun could be had at the expense of 'the other'. Such is the case, for instance, in Louis de Boissy's *La Surprise de la haine*, first performed at the Théâtre Italien in February 1734, which includes a caricature of a wealthy English gentleman in Paris, appropriately called Milord Guinée, who is satirised for writing and speaking appallingly bad French and for being outrageously blunt in his attempts to find a French bride. But in other plays, the figure of the outsider, and with it the stance of ironical false naïvety, offered an ideal literary vehicle for the critical spirit of the Enlightenment: fictional visitors could interrogate France and its customs, making the familiar appear strange and exposing the humbug of the humdrum. A good example of this is Louis-François Delisle de La Drevetière's enormously successful three-act prose comedy *Arlequin sauvage*, first performed at the Théâtre Italien in June 1721. Contemporaneous with Montesquieu's *Lettres persanes* and the first French translation of Daniel Defoe's *Robinson Crusoe*, the play sets Arlequin in the role of a young Huron from Canada who is transported by the young French sailor Lélio to Marseille, where he soon begins to criticise, to great comic effect, the follies of French society in the manner of Montesquieu's Persians. His views on laws, reason, money, property, and relations between the sexes and between masters and servants are cleverly integrated into the traditional comic structure of two men (Lélio and Mario) falling in love with the same woman (Flaminia), culminating in his mockery of the men for wanting to fight a duel over their beloved rather than simply asking her which of them she prefers. As Lélio observes to Arlequin at the end of Act II: 'Nous t'avons obligation d'être devenus plus sages' ('It is thanks to you that we have become wiser').

Like Delisle de La Drevetière before him, Marivaux, in a number of his comedies written for the Théâtre Italien, exploits the irreality and fantasy of that theatre's dramatic conventions in order to interrogate such issues as power structures and social difference and to offer topical, satirical insights into contemporary French society. *La Double Inconstance*, for example, first performed at the Théâtre Italien in April 1723, is Marivaux's first play to contain elements of social criticism: it satirises court morals by playing on the contrast between the authentic simplicity of the rustic existence enjoyed by Arlequin and Silvia, and the sometimes cynical tricks of the aristocratic world, represented by the prince, in whose palace the action unfolds and who has fallen in love with Silvia and is determined to possess her, and the scheming Flaminia, who plays on Silvia's vanity to make her abandon Arlequin in favour of the prince. In Marivaux's play world, the powerful oppress the weak. But this is not the stuff of revolution, for the play ends with two seemingly happy marriages: the Prince wins Silvia, and Arlequin is consoled by marriage to Flaminia. Similarly, Marivaux's *L'Île des esclaves*, first staged by the Italian actors in March 1725, is a satirical allegory in which masters and servants change places when they are shipwrecked on an island. The master and mistress are forced to listen to satirical portraits of themselves: correction comes through ridicule. The play offers a satirical analysis of institutionalised social structures. But Marivaux, again, is no revolutionary: everything turns out well in the end, as the servants take pity on their masters and the social order is reinstituted, although attitudes within it, the dramatic action suggests, have been changed forever – and for the better.

The kind of comic distancing effected by dramatists like Delisle de La Drevetière and Marivaux is at a far remove from the kind of moral uplift sought by dramatists such as Destouches, La Chaussée, Graffigny, Diderot, Baculard d'Arnaud, Mercier, and even Beaumarchais, who experimented with the sentimental *drame bourgeois* in *Eugénie*, first performed at the Comédie-Française in January 1767, *Les Deux Amis*, first performed at the Comédie-Française in January 1770, and *La Mère coupable*, first staged at the Théâtre du Marais in Paris in June 1792. *La Mère coupable* is in fact the third in Beaumarchais's trilogy of plays about Figaro, the first two being *Le Barbier de Séville*, first performed at the Comédie-Française in February 1775, and *Le Mariage de Figaro*, begun in 1778 but not staged at the Comédie-Française until April 1784, after the dramatist's long fight against political and royal opposition. It is for these last two plays that Beaumarchais is best remembered today. And what is perhaps most remarkable about them, at least in the context of the development of French comic drama in the eighteenth century, is that they work precisely as reactions against, or even parodies of, the kind of serious comedy that had become prevalent in the 1760s and 1770s and that even Beaumarchais himself had dabbled in. Significantly, in the preface to *Le Mariage de Figaro*, Beaumarchais defines his aim as being to 'ramener au théâtre l'ancienne et franche gaieté, en l'alliant avec le ton léger de notre plaisanterie actuelle' ('bring back to the stage good old jollity, linked to the lightness of our humour today').

What does Beaumarchais mean by 'notre plaisanterie actuelle'? This could refer to the plays' satirical thrust, which is one aspect of the dramatist's return to an earlier comic tradition. *Le Barbier de Séville*, for instance, contains a number of stingingly satirical one-liners, including Figaro's jibes to the comte: 'Un grand nous fait assez de bien quand il ne nous fait pas de mal' ('A superior treats us well enough when he doesn't do us any harm') and 'Aux vertus qu'on exige dans un domestique, Votre Excellence connaît-elle beaucoup de maîtres qui fussent dignes d'être valets?' ('Given the virtues expected of a servant, does Your Excellency know many masters worthy of being valets?') (I.2). The dramatic action also gives scope for satirising medicine (II.13) and the legal profession (IV.8). But, like Marivaux's Arlequin, Figaro is no revolutionary: his satirical jibes do not coalesce into a rounded philosophical stance. In their context, they are witty rejoinders, satirical insights, but nothing more. The comic structure of *Le Barbier de Séville* is conventional: a servant and his aristocratic master join forces to outwit Bartholo, a bumbling bourgeois conservative, and win the girl. Figaro's social satire is limited in scope.

Much the same can be said of the sequel, *La Folle Journée, ou Le Mariage de Figaro*. The revolutionary potential of the play is partly veiled by the exoticism of the setting: Almaviva is a Spanish *corregidor*, not a French aristocrat; like *Le Barbier*, *Le Mariage* exudes an air of cheerful unreality. Yet the play bristles with satirical jibes: there is some conventional satire of the legal system in Act III, but more importantly there is an attack on social inequalities and a critique of noble pretensions as Almaviva tries to claim his feudal right to sleep with Figaro's fiancée, Suzanne. But throughout the context is comic: justice is denounced as arbitrary, but only when Figaro faces the grotesque prospect of being forced to marry his own mother; Almaviva abuses his privilege not for political ends, but for his own sexual gratification; and the servant Figaro may go against his master Almaviva, but the same social divide is breached by the women, the countess and Suzanne, who join forces in outwitting the count, who ends the play by coming to his senses. After all the topsy-turvy events of the 'folle journée', or the crazy day, to which the play's title refers, order is restored. Beaumarchais is, after all, the author of great comedies, not political manifestos.

If Beaumarchais's first two Figaro plays are perhaps the most enduring of eighteenth-century French comedies, they are nonetheless only two instances of a genre that underwent huge evolution in the course of that century. Indeed, the well-known works of Marivaux and Beaumarchais only properly make sense when seen in the broader context of the many developments in non-tragic drama in the period. Moreover, within these developments are a number of works which, for their sheer comic value and theatrical verve, deserve still to command our attention as readers and play-goers today. Comic dramatists who might be considered as candidates for such rediscovery include Regnard, whose *Le Légataire universel*, for instance, first performed at the Comédie-Française in January 1708, is a witty comedy about the attempts of young lovers to secure the estate of the elderly Géronte; Boissy, whose *Le Français à Londres*, performed more than 200 times at the Comédie-Française between its premiere in July 1727 and the Revolution, anticipates Voltaire's *Lettres philosophiques* (1734) by transporting the French audience to England and showing them the relativism of character and customs; and Voltaire himself, author of eighteen comedies, a number of which are starting to attract theatre directors and audiences alike, including *L'Écossaise*, staged at the Théâtre du Lucernaire in Paris in 2007 by Vincent Colin, and *Le Droit du seigneur* (1760), a comedy which anticipates *Le Mariage de Figaro* and which was successfully staged at the theatre in Metz in 2003 by Didier Doumergue. Eighteenth-century French comedy, it seems, can lay claim to a longevity that is unrivalled by the tragedy of the period.

43

Eighteenth-century theatrical tragedy

JOSEPH HARRIS

The eighteenth century was the last period in France in which tragedy could be said to exist as a genre in any meaningful sense. In various respects, the spirit of the Enlightenment was fundamentally untragic; the period's increasing optimism in reason, progress, bourgeois values, natural religion, and later republicanism, sat increasingly uneasily alongside the traditional demands of tragedy. But while the spirit of 'the tragic' dwindled, tragedy as a genre proved surprisingly robust, with average audience numbers being some 50 per cent higher than for comedy.[1] If, because of the overall expense required, the theatre has to reflect popular tastes and beliefs more than any other medium, then eighteenth-century tragedy can be seen as a gauge of the progression of Enlightenment ideas and ideals. Yet, as dramatists, theoreticians, and politicians alike increasingly recognised, tragedy can not only reflect public tastes, beliefs, and morality, but also play an active role in shaping them.

The eighteenth century was a period of both experimentation and conservatism. Setting the benchmark for eighteenth-century tragedy even as their popularity fluctuated, Racine and Corneille were a source of both pride and anxiety for France's new generations of tragedians. While few dramatic conventions went unchallenged, the broad formal framework of tragedy remained relatively constant; indeed, in certain formal and stylistic respects, a typical tragedy from the final decades of the eighteenth century differs relatively little from one from Racine's time. The tenacity of these conventions is particularly apparent in the evident compromises placed on Jean-François Ducis's verse and stagecraft in his attempts to reconcile Shakespeare to eighteenth-century French tastes in plays from *Hamlet* (1769) to *Othello* (1792). Yet even these basic rules and conventions came under attack in both theory and practice as the century progressed. Some writers took liberties with the five-act structure, producing plays in four acts (Mailhol's

---

1 J.-P. Perchellet, *L'Héritage classique: la tragédie entre 1680 et 1814* (Paris: Champion, 2004), p. 13.

Ramire, 1757), three (Randon de Boisset's *Zamir*, 1761) or even one (Landois, *Sylvie*, 1741). Verse was increasingly regarded as an inappropriate means of representing real life, and was typically rejected in more naturalistic genres such as bourgeois tragedy and the *drame*; Landois explains in his prologue to his domestic tragedy *Sylvie* how he rejected 'le pompeux galimathias tragique' ('the pompous gibberish of tragedy') as being a poor way to express one's sentiments.[2] Yet those few writers who attempted non-bourgeois prose tragedies (including La Motte, Hénault, and Sedaine) had little success and faced influential opponents, not least Voltaire.

Alongside these formal literary experimentations came a greater awareness of, and willingness to engage with, the theatre's potential as a performance able to affect spectators in a variety of ways. The early decades of the century saw a darker, more sombre streak enter tragedy. Although his bloodiest and most melodramatic plays (*Atrée et Thyeste*, 1707; *Rhadamiste et Zénobie*, 1711) were written in the final years of Louis XIV's reign, Prosper Jolyot de Crébillon (Crébillon *père*) continued to exploit the dramatic potential of horror and violence throughout his career, culminating in the shocking conclusion to his final play, *Le Triumvirat* (1748), in which Tullie uncovers the decapitated head of her father Cicéron and commits suicide on stage. Yet Crébillon was only the most famous exponent of this brand of tragedy, and other writers throughout the century were not averse to similar appeals to horror; in de Belloy's *Gabrielle de Vergy* (1777), for example, the Comte de Faïel, believing his wife unfaithful, presents her with a vase containing the heart of her supposed lover Raoul.

Even when the intended effect was not to shock or horrify, the eighteenth century was, in the words of one contemporary, 'avide de Spectacles' ('hungry for spectacle'),[3] and tragedians took increasing advantage of – and liberties with – the theatrical potential of the stage. The expulsion of spectators from the stage in 1759 crucially freed up enough on-stage space for the actor playing Ninus's ghost in Voltaire's *Sémiramis* (1748) to now move freely without attracting incongruous cries amongst the spectators of 'Place à l'ombre!' ('Make way for the ghost!'). Actions, events, and props that had previously been consigned to the off-stage realm for reasons of good taste or theatrical practicability were now increasingly exposed to the public view; these include cannons (Voltaire's *Adélaïde du Guesclin*, 1734), funeral pyres (Lemierre's *La Veuve du Malabar*, 1770), archery scenes (Lemierre's *Guillaume Tell*, 1766), and

2 P. Landois, *Sylvie* (Paris: Prault, 1741), p. 7.
3 P. J. B. Nougaret, *De l'art du théâtre*, 2 vols. (Paris: Cailleau, 1769), II, p. 337.

even (mechanical) scorpions (Marmontel, *Cléopâtre*, 1750). Guymond de La Touche's *Iphigénie en Tauride* (1757) features a very dramatic scene in which Pylade tries to break the door down as Iphigénie is about to be sacrificed; Oreste forces the victim out of harm's way and offers himself up to the blow, before being rescued by Pylade's arrival.

The theatre was also quick to cater for the period's developing taste for refined sentiment known as sensibility. The exact role of sensibility in tragedy was a matter of critical debate; while some, such as Marmontel, regarded it as tragedy's very basis, others, including Beaumarchais, starkly opposed the brutal and unpleasant tears of tragedy with the poignant emotions of new genres. Yet tragedies exploited the appeal of touching emotion decades before bourgeois tragedy and the *drame* even surfaced. In a famously moving episode from the end of La Motte's *Inès de Castro* (1723), the heroine begs the king to approve of the clandestine marriage she has conducted with his son Dom Pèdre; as a final attempt to tug at his heart-strings, Inès has her two young children brought on stage and goads him to sacrifice them alongside her. Finally won over by a surge of familial affection, the king spares them all, before he and his son discover that Inès has been fatally poisoned by the queen.

The ending of *Inès de Castro* is an early example of a more general tendency within eighteenth-century theatre to invest the family unit with a particular emotional and ideological power. The recognition scene between long-separated or unwitting family members became a frequent resource for evoking sensibility; the stock device known as the *cri du sang* ('the call of blood') gained a particular significance as the cult of nature came to prominence over the period. One of the most famous scenes of Voltaire's *Zaïre* (1732) occurs when the old man Lusignan recognises Nérestan and Zaïre as his son and daughter, and numerous other plays offer variants on the same theme. Yet *Inès de Castro*, in taking a married heroine as its subject, also reflects the period's growing distaste for plots concerning young love. Romantic love was still, of course, a potent source of sentimental emotion, but Enlightenment tragedians focused increasingly on married heroes and heroines; for writers such as Lemierre, this new focus allowed a more serious exploration of the political and domestic duties of married life.

The period's taste for sentimentality and its ideological attachment to the family unit often invites works to end on a note of reconciliation and forgiveness that sits uneasily with traditional tragedy and opens the way towards more bourgeois genres such as the *drame*. While some writers opted to write 'domestic' or 'bourgeois' tragedy, France, unlike Germany, was generally content with more sentimental or melodramatic plots. In many respects, the *drame* offered a haven from the violence and near-compulsory deaths of tragedy; revealingly, when Sauvigny rewrote his tragedy *Gabrielle d'Estrées* (1778) so that his heroine survived, he rebranded the play as a 'pièce dramatique'. Yet the typically poignant, conciliatory spirit of the *drame* does not exclude the possibility of more traditionally tragic conclusions. Indeed, the expectation that *drames* would end happily could be exploited to powerful effect by writers prepared to break with convention; La Harpe's verse *drame Mélanie* (1778) ends with the heroine's tragic suicide by poison in order to escape being sent to a convent – a conclusion all the more striking for being atypical of the genre.

Yet the period's taste for happy, or at least touching rather than distressing, endings was also reflected in more regular tragedy. While few eighteenth-century tragedies ended with no bloodshed at all – Crébillon's *Pyrrhus* (1726) being a notable exception – many chose not to inflict death and suffering on the virtuous heroes but rather to mete out punishment to characters clearly painted as villainous (Lemierre's Gessler, Crébillon's Sémiramis, de Belloy's Edouard III). Some works, such as La Motte's *Romulus* (1722), combine the antagonist's downfall with a (traditionally comic) marriage between the more sympathetic heroes. Rare indeed are works which end, like Crébillon's *Atrée et Thyeste*, with the unconditional triumph of the wicked. Even Voltaire's Mahomet, a cynical and manipulative fraudster who exploits the religious fanaticism of his followers, is finally tormented by guilt, exclaiming in surprise that:

> Il est donc des remords! ô fureur! ô justice!
> Mes forfaits dans mon cœur ont donc mis mon supplice!

(So remorse does exist! O fury! O justice! My crimes have put my punishment in my own heart!)[4]

Yet eighteenth-century tragedians were not content simply to impress, shock, move, or delight their audiences. Exploiting the theatre's capacity to reach a large number of people, eighteenth-century tragedy raised and explored many issues that would become fundamental to the Revolution – politics, religion, justice, pacifism, feminism, and so forth – and, starting in the 1730s and 1740s, looked beyond the relatively limited pool of Graeco-Roman mythology and history for new settings and subject matter. Voltaire was one

---

4 Voltaire, *Le Fanatisme ou Mahomet le prophète*, in *Zaïre – Le Fanatisme – Nanine – Le Café*, ed. Jean Goldzink (Paris: Garnier-Flammarion, 2004), v.4, lines 1465–6.

of the pioneers, setting plays in places as far away as Jerusalem (*Zaïre*), Peru (*Alzire*, 1736), Mecca (*Mahomet*), and China (*L'Orphelin de la Chine*, 1755). Besides allowing pompous and visually impressive displays of costume and decor, these settings allowed writers to deal with a range of political and philosophical issues. By presenting audiences with unfamiliar locations and cultures, plays such as Anne-Marie Du Boccage's *Les Amazones* (1749) and Lemierre's *La Veuve du Malabar* could shake audiences out of established expectations and viewing practices, compelling them to take a more critical stance towards the morals and values depicted. Exoticism allowed writers the freedom to criticise aspects of European culture through an appeal to other cultures. The Islamic setting of *Mahomet*, for example, allowed Voltaire to explore religious fanaticism while not explicitly criticising Christianity, while his *Alzire* is markedly sympathetic to the invaded Peruvians and heavily critical of European colonial practices. Not that the clash of different value systems always works to the Europeans' discredit; in *La Veuve du Malabar*, for example, traditional Indian customs lose out to enlightened Western values (although even here the West does not escape criticism, particularly in its continued tolerance of duelling).

Yet while opening up tragedy as a vehicle for social and philosophical debate, such culture clashes also promote a sense of moral and religious relativity that runs counter to traditional tragedy. While the role of the divine had always been ambivalent even in conventional tragedy, the Enlightenment's renewed critical focus on established belief and its growing optimistic faith in natural religion sat uneasily with the inherited tragic form. Several plays expose how religion can be manipulated by its self-appointed representatives; like Voltaire's Mahomet, La Motte's Muréna (*Romulus*) and Lemierre's Danaüs (*Hypermnestre*, 1758) consciously manipulate others' religious belief to serve their own ends. These villains are not superstitious fanatics, but clear-sighted tricksters who, sharing but abusing the Enlightenment's suspicion of superstitious belief, exploit others' gullibility in order to preserve their jealously guarded political power.

While some French tragedians scoured the globe in search of new subject matter, others looked closer to home. De Belloy's *Le Siège de Calais* (1765) offered a stirring example of patriotic stoicism that met with a phenomenal success at a time when France was recovering from heavy losses during the Seven Years War. While it was not, as de Belloy suggested, the first French national tragedy – Voltaire's *Adélaïde du Guesclin* had taken place in medieval Lille – it opened the way for various later dramatists to draw similarly from France's history for their sources. Unashamedly nationalistic, de Belloy's play vigorously defends the French monarchy as a symbolic reflection of the fatherland. Such an idealised view of the monarchy, unsurprisingly, became less and less common in the following decades, and by the Revolution national tragedy in general had become controversial. Most notably, Marie-Joseph Chénier's vastly successful *Charles IX* (written *c.* 1787) was banned from the stage until late 1789 because of its depiction of the French king, understood to represent Louis XVI, as a cruel tyrant. Plays not drawn from French history were granted far greater freedom in expressing republican ideals; La Harpe's Roman tragedy *Virginie* (1786), for example, offered a searing critique of tyranny and a stark contrast between the duties of citizen and subject:

> Un sujet a tout fait quand il sait obéir;
> Il suffit d'être vil pour savoir être esclave;
> Le citoyen doit être et vigilant et brave. (III.2)

(A subject has no more to do than obey; to be a slave, it is enough to be vile; the citizen must be both vigilant and brave.)[5]

With their introduction of large crowds of commoners onto the stage, plays such as *Le Siège de Calais* and Saurin's *Spartacus* (1760) also rehabilitated the vast masses who had formerly been all but excluded from tragedy. A precursor to these plays had been Voltaire's *La Mort de César* (1731) in which, as in its Shakespearean model, Antoine's eulogy of the murdered emperor is punctuated by the remarks of the Roman crowd whom he progressively wins over. Not unlike ancient choruses, the on-stage public helped to create a continuity between the fictional action and the world of the spectators, thus heightening the plays' political import. Some tragedies went still further, drawing their heroes from the bourgeoisie or even the lower classes. Lemierre's *Guillaume Tell* was the first tragedy to take its hero from the common people, and the following year, Voltaire's *Les Scythes* (1767) took a group of farmers as its heroes. Tragedy was no longer a private, personal affair, a struggle between the individual and fate, but a social, political, and philosophical one.

For all its nascent ideals of social equality, however, French tragedy remained reluctant to extend such principles to women. While the period is dominated by a succession of famous tragic actresses, female tragedians did not feature highly on the period's radar. Tragedies written by women were often either limited to private performances – such as Charlotte-Jeanne de Montesson's *La Comtesse de Bar* (1783) and *Agnès de Méranie* (1784) – or went unpublished, such as much of the output of Marie-Anne de Marron. While the early century produced two notable women tragedians, Marie-Anne Barbier

5 J.-F. de La Harpe, *Virginie* (Paris: n.p., 1793).

and Madeleine-Angélique Poisson (Madame de Gomez), later female play-wrights achieved greater success in more domestic genres, such as Madeleine Bouillé's domestic tragedy, *Repsima* (1767). Towards the end of the century, Olympe de Gouges would adopt the *drame* for a number of political pur-poses, criticising slavery in *Zamore et Mirza* (1784) and women's banishment to convents in *Le Couvent* (1790). Many female tragedians addressed issues of women's emancipation in a very muted fashion, without advocating a radical upheaval of the gender hierarchy. One of the most explicit plays to deal with gender relations, Anne-Marie Du Boccage's *Les Amazones*, positively assesses women's capacities in government and high office while ultimately dismissing the Amazons' militarism and misanthropy. Love, which threatens the care-fully policed borders of the all-female Amazon society, eventually triumphs, but at a cost; the lovers have to leave the society to be together, and with the queen's suicide the throne falls to the bellicose Ménalippe, who vows to avenge womankind for their betrayal.

Male writers could often afford to be more outspoken in their pleas for female emancipation. In Lemierre's *Guillaume Tell*, Tell's wife Cléofé draws an explicit parallel between the twin tyrannies of class and of sex, just as the eponymous heroine of Colardeau's *Caliste* (1764) vigorously challenges men's social position of superiority, revealing how the revered roles of father and husband conceal 'des tyrans ou des maîtres jaloux' ('tyrants or jealous masters').[6] That said, active heroines are rare in even those works that advo-cate women's rights. In *La Veuve du Malabar* – an extended critique of the practice of self-immolation – the main arguments against the practice are assigned not to the play's heroine, who is nobly resigned to her death, but rather to her confidant and to other characters. Figures such as Lemierre's anonymous widow, like Arrie in Barbier's *Arrie et Pétus* (1702), are often self-abnegating and, often literally, self-sacrificing; unwilling to speak out, they welcome their subjugation with a sense of duty and honour.

In terms of tragedy, the eighteenth century is a period of developments and contradictions, in which experimentation constantly jostles with conser-vatism. This complexity stems largely from the period's relationship to its predecessor. If we measure eighteenth-century tragedy according to the stan-dards and expectations of the previous century, we are bound to be dissatisfied; indeed, a recent critic claims that the period is so stuck, formally speaking, in 'la réproduction stérile de stéréotypes convenus' ('the sterile reproduc-tion of accepted stereotypes') that its tragedies are at best 'pseudo-classical'

6 C.-P. Colardeau, *Caliste* (Avignon: n.p., 1764), III.2.

rather than genuinely 'neo-classical'.[7] In terms of subject matter, dramaturgy, philosophical engagement, and audience response, however, it is precisely the period's drive for innovation that flouts accepted notions of tragedy and the tragic. While neither of these criticisms is entirely unjustified, both implicitly rely on an outmoded and ultimately anachronistic conception of tragedy, one inherited above all from the seventeenth century. The (perhaps tragic) irony is that, with its own fraught but decisive relationship to the theatre of Corneille and Racine, the eighteenth century holds more than a little responsibility for the tenacity of the norms by which its own tragedy continues to be judged.

7 C. Delmas, *La Tragédie de l'âge classique (1553–1770)* (Paris: Seuil, 1994), p. 9.

44

Eighteenth-century women writers

NADINE BÉRENGUIER

The obstacles that eighteenth-century women writers had to surmount were constant reminders of the 'place' they held in the literary world of their time. Although they were not denied participation – in addition to their publications, there are records of their personal interactions with male writers in salons, academies, and correspondence – they could not forget that they were women. Pursuing such an activity also made them eminently aware of not conforming to the generally accepted 'norm' of female behaviour. Women's uneasy position affected their relationship to writing and, most importantly, to the decisive step of going public with what they wrote.

The anxiety of publicity

Writing – that is, taking notes and reflecting on readings for one's own edification or pleasure – was deemed an appropriate activity for elite women. In Madeleine de Puisieux's *Conseils à une amie* (1749) the mentor recommended writing to her young friend: 'Écrivez beaucoup: en écrivant on se forme le style; l'on apprend sa Langue, qu'il est honteux de ne pas savoir pour une fille de condition. Écrivez donc: faites des remarques sur vos lectures; on s'en imprime mieux dans la mémoire ce que l'on a lu' ('Write as much as possible: by writing you will develop your style, learn your own language because a young woman of your rank should be ashamed not to know it well. Write: make comments on your readings; it will help you better remember what you have read').[1] Writing, as this passage shows, was perceived as an auxiliary to reading and as a tool to master one's language, not as a way to express personal and original ideas, and even less as a means to publicise them.

Women writers belonged to the upper ranks of French society (from the bourgeoisie to the high aristocracy) and, within this elite group, were among

---

1 M. de Puisieux, *Conseils à une amie* (Oxford: Voltaire Foundation, 1995), p. 427. Translation mine.

the happy few who had benefited from a comprehensive education, even if it did not match the rigorous intellectual training of their male counterparts. This made them vulnerable to attacks pointing to their pretentiousness. When Anne-Thérèse de Lambert (1647–1733) was 'betrayed' by a friend who published the manuscripts of *Avis d'une mère à sa fille* and *Avis d'une mère à son fils* (1727), she famously attempted to prevent their dissemination by buying the whole edition. The fear of being branded a 'femme savante' explained, according to Roger Marchal, the marquise's decision.[2] Many years later, such a fear was clearly articulated by Marie-Jeanne Roland de la Platière, known as Manon Roland (1754–93), in her posthumous *Mémoires* (1795):

> Jamais je n'eus la plus légère tentation de devenir auteur un jour; je vis de très bonne heure qu'une femme qui gagnait ce titre, perdait beaucoup plus qu'elle n'avait acquis. Les hommes ne l'aiment point et son sexe la critique; si les ouvrages sont mauvais, on se moque d'elle, et l'on fait bien; s'ils sont bons, on les lui ôte.[3]

> (I never had the slightest intention of becoming an authoress. I realised very early on that a woman who becomes known as a writer loses much more than she gains. Men do not like it and her own sex are always critical. If her works are bad she is jeered at and rightly so. If they are good, then everybody says she cannot have written them herself.)[4]

Another woman for whom writing was a passion that was not supposed to see the light of day was Suzanne Necker (1737–94). She was mainly known for the brilliant *salon* over which she presided. Unwilling to let her be a published writer during her lifetime, her husband, Jacques Necker (1732–1804), waited until she was dead to reveal how productive a writer she had been. In addition to letters to a myriad of distinguished friends, the five-volume *Mélanges* (1798) and *Nouveaux mélanges de Madame Necker* (1801) contained a combination of diaries, intimate thoughts, aphorisms, and reflections on social, moral, and literary issues. Whether self-imposed or required by marital authority, these women's reluctance to go public and be labelled 'women writers' was symptomatic of the problematic status that such a pursuit entailed.

Publishing anonymously was common practice at the time, for both men and women, but the fear of derogatory labels such as 'femme bel esprit' was one of the chief reasons why women preferred to hide their identity. Even when their anonymity was 'transparent', the sheer unwillingness to disclose one's name displayed enough modesty to defuse the negative impact

---

2 Roger Marchal, *Madame de Lambert et son milieu* (Oxford: Voltaire Foundation, 1991), pp. 186–9.
3 M. Roland, *Mémoires* (Paris: Henri Plon, 1864), p. 135.
4 M. Roland, *Memoirs*, trans. Evelyn Shuckburgh (London: Barrie and Jenkins, 1989), p. 218.

of publishing. The recent reinterpretation of anonymity (by Joan DeJean and Carla Hesse) as a woman's control over publishing rather than a mere display of reticence certainly nuances the perception of this practice but does not completely obliterate the unease that surrounded women's participation in the public discourse.[5]

If the anxiety surrounding publishing certainly hampered the literary ambitions of some, it did not stifle all women's desire to go public through print. Since books were already at the time objects of economic exchange and publishing was a business, earning a living could be an incentive. Literature was a 'suitable' occupation for financially needy women who did not belong to the working class, as Marie-Laure Girou-Giwerski has argued. But pursuing such a career did not mean that women could count on it to make a comfortable living or amass much wealth. The less affluent needed other sources of income, as was the case for Marie-Jeanne Leprince de Beaumont (1711–80) who also worked as a governess in London. Even literary success did not guarantee a sustained source of income. Publishing the best-seller *Lettres d'une Péruvienne* (1747) and having her plays *Cénie* (1750) and *La fille d'Aristide* (1758) performed at the Comédie-Française did not prevent Françoise de Graffigny (1695–1758) from leaving a huge debt at the time of her death. Similarly, the financial security that the novelist Marie-Jeanne Riccoboni (1714–92) finally secured did not last forever: she experienced poverty after the revolutionary regime deprived her of the royal pension that her literary fame had warranted her. Even for the most acclaimed women writers, the financial rewards could be quite precarious.

Another motivation to go public was the desire to draw attention to women's role and status in the society of the time as well as targeting a female readership. Scrutinising the conditions in which they lived, exposing the double standards that ruled gender relations, and condemning the many restrictions imposed on women were at the centre of their preoccupations, even though they used different genres to different ends. This attitude was not unique to the eighteenth century. Women had a long record of publishing in order to provide accounts of their lives and express their discontent, and it had gained in urgency in the late seventeenth century. But by the middle of the eighteenth century, the demands for change had become pervasive enough in general literary discourse to give women's longstanding aspirations

5 Joan DeJean, 'Lafayette's Ellipses: The Privileges of Anonymity', *PMLA*, 99.5 (1984), pp. 884–902; Carla Hesse, 'Reading Signatures: Female Authorship and Revolutionary Law in France, 1750–1850', in 'The French Revolution in Culture', special issue of *Eighteenth-Century Studies* 22.3 (Spring 1989), pp. 469–87.

a renewed relevance. Quite a number of them shared with many of their male counterparts a fervent resolve to challenge the status quo, even if they had their own set of frustrations and demands.

Gender and genres

Like the men who embraced Enlightenment ideas, women used a variety of genres to state their beliefs and perspectives: novels, essays, plays, political and social pamphlets, tales, journalistic pieces, and educational works. Even if being a novelist was a literary career of choice, few limited themselves to one genre. Novelists could also be playwrights, political essayists, journalists, and educators. Different genres were more or less conducive to the expression of feminist claims, and the level of 'activism' also varied from author to author.

Undoubtedly, the genre in which women published most consistently during the eighteenth century was the novel. Raymond Trousson found no less than forty names of female novelists while preparing his volume *Romans de femmes du dix-huitième siècle* (1996).[6] As Georges May convincingly argued in *Dilemme du roman* (1963), during the eighteenth century the novel was a despised and criticised genre in need of legitimacy, but also unencumbered by a strict set of rules.[7] To fend off the various attacks to which their works were subjected, novelists focused on the depiction of a social world that they strove to present as 'realistically' as possible. As a genre that had the observation of social 'reality' at its core, it became a conduit for social commentary in general and a fitting tool for a discussion of women's experiences in particular.

Jean Larnac and those who have labelled women's novels as 'sentimental' argued that love was their dominant preoccupation. But plots revolving around young women entering the world, courtship, arranged marriages, and gender relations in general, however conventional they may appear, allowed novelists to address social issues of a more general nature.[8] We find topics such as girls' education and their preparedness for adult responsibilities, the economics of the marriage market, the parents' role in this economy, and the ramifications of women's legal status. Countless variations of these themes as well as the moral implications of female behaviour and virtue can be found

6 Raymond Trousson (ed.), *Romans de femmes du dix-huitième siècle: Mme de Tencin, Mme de Graffigny, Mme Riccoboni, Mme de Charrière, Olympes de Gouges, Mme de Souza, Mme Cottin, Mme de Genlis, Mme de Krüdener, Mme de Duras* (Paris: Robert Laffont, 1996).
7 Georges May, *Le Dilemme du roman au xviiie siècle: étude sur les rapports du roman et de la critique, 1715–1761* (New Haven, CT: Yale University Press, 1963).
8 Jean Larnac, *Histoire de la littérature féminine en France* (Paris: Éditions Kra, 1929).

in the novels of Claudine de Tencin (1682–1749), Françoise de Graffigny, Marie-Jeanne Leprince de Beaumont, Marie-Jeanne Riccoboni, Madeleine de Puisieux (1720–98), Anne-Louise Elie de Beaumont (1729–83), Isabelle de Charrière (1740–1805), Françoise-Albine Benoist (1724–1809), Stéphanie-Félicité de Genlis (1746–1830), Adélaïde de Souza (1761–1836), Germaine de Staël (1766–1817), and Sophie Cottin (1770–1807) to name only a few. Whether these women's views were overall conservative or progressive has been a question for debate. It is safe to assume that the range of opinions in such a diverse group makes a cursory generalisation impossible. But as Nancy Miller, Joan Hinde Stewart, Jacqueline Letzter, Lesley Walker, and other feminist critics have argued, these women walked a fine line between the urge to denounce some aspects of their situation and the need to fit into a mould of acceptability.[9] Quite typical of such a balancing act was Graffigny's *Lettres d'une Péruvienne*, in which a 'sentimental' plot and socio-political considerations were intimately intertwined, allowing its author to embed contention into convention.

Writing for the theatre entailed a different set of challenges that were experienced by both men and women, but to different degrees. Not only did the theatre enjoy the highest standing in the hierarchy of genres prevalent at the time but it was also subjected to strict rules that needed to be obeyed to satisfy a demanding public. Women who wrote for the theatre, precisely because of its more prestigious status, were easily perceived as displaying too much hubris and ridiculed for their literary ambitions.

Women did not limit themselves to a particular genre. The most prestige went to full-length tragedies, a genre practised by Marie-Anne Barbier (1670–1745), Madeleine de Gomez (1684–1770), and Anne-Marie Du Boccage (1710–1802). They also wrote comedies (Marie-Anne Barbier, Isabelle de Charrière, Stéphanie de Genlis), *drames bourgeois* (Françoise de Graffigny), dramas (Olympe de Gouges), and opera libretti (Marie-Anne Barbier, Isabelle de Charrière). In the early part of the century, strong feminist sentiments were not pervasive in most women's plays, with the exception of Marie-Anne Barbier who introduced examples of female heroism into some of her tragedies. When women questioned the status quo – Barbier was the most outspoken – they did so in their prefaces rather than in the dramatic works

9 Nancy K. Miller, *French Dressing: Women, Men, and Ancien Régime Fiction* (New York: Routledge, 1995); Joan Hinde Stewart, *Gynographs: French Novels by Women of the Late Eighteenth Century* (Lincoln: University of Nebraska Press, 1993); Jacqueline Letzter, *Intellectual Tacking: Questions of Education in the Works of Isabelle de Charrière* (Amsterdam: Rodopi, 1998); Lesley Walker, *A Mother's Love: Crafting Feminine Virtue in Enlightenment France* (Lewisburg, PA: Bucknell University Press, 2008).

themselves. An exception was Anne-Marie Du Boccage's *Les Amazones* (1749) that pleaded openly for women's superiority. A more militant tone came to characterise later dramatic productions, especially Olympe de Gouges's *L'Esclavage des noirs*, which evolved into an abolitionist manifesto between its original 1784 version, entitled *Zamore et Mirza, ou L'Heureux naufrage*, and its 1789–90 performance and 1792 reprinting.

Enlisting the help of a mentor to bring a dramatic piece to the stage – a common practice for both male and female playwrights – frequently led to suspicions that women's plays had actually been written by men. Marie-Anne Barbier's plays, for example, were attributed to the abbé Pellegrin, who served as her guide and counsellor. A man's intercession was usually necessary, because the theatre world – actors and actresses in particular – was not deemed reputable and there was concern about an association that could taint a woman's reputation. Moreover, the logistics of a stage production were daunting: Anne-Marie Du Boccage, author of *Les Amazones*, complained in a private letter about the difficulties of staging her tragedy and discussed her husband's active involvement. Access to the most prestigious stages had to be secured through well-connected acquaintances: Graffigny enrolled the help of the comte de Clermont who used his status and influence to have her plays *Cénie* (1750) and *La Fille d'Aristide* (1758) performed at the Comédie-Française. Success was in no way guaranteed and theatrical careers tended to be short.

It should come as no surprise to see some women avoid these challenges and present their plays in a more private setting, such as Stéphanie de Genlis who first brought out *Théâtre à l'usage des jeunes personnes* (1779), a collection of didactic plays to be performed by young amateurs, before publishing two volumes of *Théâtre de société* (1781). Entire dramatic productions remained unperformed, as was the case with Isabelle de Charrière's twenty-six comedies, operas, and lyric tragedies. Living far from urban centres, unable to find professional theatre troupes favourably disposed to perform her plays, and unwilling to settle for private performances, she could not bring her theatrical ambitions to fruition. Being an outsider was not easy for any playwright, whether male or female, but that was the reality for most women. During the century only twenty-six women's plays were performed at either the Comédie-Française or the Comédie-Italienne out of hundreds. This did not prevent women from actively writing for the theatre, as Jeffrey Ravel has shown in his groundbreaking research on eighteenth-century play publishing.[10] The

---

10 Jeffrey Ravel, 'Theater beyond Privilege: Changes in French Play Publication, 1700–1789', *Studies on Voltaire and the Eighteenth Century* 12 (2001), pp. 299–347.

explosion in the number of women's plays published between 1770 and 1789 was a sign that they did not give up and also used the print media to disseminate their works.

The press provided another kind of outlet for women who wanted to go public with their writing. The twenty-five female journalists involved in periodical publications as owners, editors, owner-editors, or contributors, according to the *Dictionnaire des journaux, 1660–1789*, constituted a small but significant level of participation and displayed a keen awareness of female readers' needs.[11] Some periodicals were short-lived, such as Marie-Jeanne L'Héritier de Villandon's (1664–1734) *L'Érudition enjouée* (1703) and Jeanne Vaucher's satirical *Nouvelliste universel* (1724). A few were published over longer time periods: Anne-Marguerite Dunoyer's (1663–1719) political *La Quintessence des nouvelles* (1710–19), Marie-Anne Barbier's *Saisons littéraires* (1714–22), and Adélaïde Dufresnoy's (1765–1825) *Courrier lyrique et amusant* (1785–8). Three of the nine editors of the *Journal des dames*, during the nearly twenty years of its tumultuous existence (1759–78), were women (Madame de Beaumer [d. 1766], Catherine de Maisonneuve [d. 1774?], and Marie de Montanclos [1736–1812]) and it had a number of female contributors. The early years of the Revolution also saw women's attempts at launching newspapers, such as the short-lived *Annales de l'éducation du sexe* (1790) by Madame Mouret. Most of these periodicals struggled financially, including Marie-Jeanne Leprince de Beaumont's wide-ranging *Nouveau Magasin français* (1750–2) with its sequels *La Suite du Magasin français* (1758) and *Lettres curieuses, instructives et amusantes* (1759), which brought their editor renown but no monetary rewards. The women who participated in journalistic endeavours assessed the potential of this relatively new form of communication. They were aware of the specific needs of a female readership that could benefit from a discussion of literary, cultural, as well as moral issues. They did not consider these journals, however, as a tribune for extensive political commentaries.

Whether women exerted a significant political influence behind the scenes through the men with whom they were acquainted or whether they were excluded from the political realm has been an object of debate since the eighteenth century. Montesquieu in *Lettres persanes* (1721) had his characters argue for an indirect influencing while Laclos in 'Des femmes et de leur éducation' and Condorcet in 'Sur l'admission des femmes au droit de cité' deplored their powerlessness. Published contributions by women to a public

---

11 Jean Sgard (ed.), *Dictionnaire des journaux, 1600–1789*, 2 vols. (Paris: Universitas; Oxford: Voltaire Foundation, 1991).

political debate were not extensive until the Revolution. The approach of this momentous event unleashed a more tangible desire to take a stand in the political realm. Carla Hesse's statistical investigation has shown a noticeable increase in the number of women's publications, many of them short political pamphlets, during the Revolution.[12]

Engaged in such a debate was Isabelle de Charrière, who lived – except for a twenty-month stay in Paris in 1786–7 – in Switzerland. The geographical distance did not prevent the Paris publication of a series of seventeen anonymous political pamphlets, *Observations et conjectures politiques* in 1787 and 1788, followed by her 1789 *Lettres d'un évêque français à la nation*, a denunciation of abuses perpetrated under the monarchy. It did not take her long, however, to be disappointed by the revolutionary turn of events, which she deplored with wit and irony in the *Epigrammes de la mouche du coche* in the autumn of 1789. She continued her critique in *Lettres d'un Anglais à un député de l'assemblée nationale de France* (1790). Manon Roland, for her part, experienced the Revolution first-hand and preferred not to publicise her political views, even anonymously, convinced that women should seek satisfaction in the domestic sphere rather than the public one. She used private letters as a forum in which she displayed her deep interest in political issues and familiarity with political theory. Her sympathies led her to favour a regime change, but a moderate one. The extreme regime change introduced by Robespierre led her to become a primarily political author: she wrote her memoirs in jail, where she was sent after the Jacobins took power in 1793. Those memoirs were addressed, however, not to her contemporaries, but to future generations, as the title *Appel à l'impartiale postérité* attests. Even though Olympe de Gouges (1748–93), like Manon Roland, was guillotined in 1793, her political participation could not have been more different. She was a very prolific political writer who published no fewer than sixty-three pamphlets on a great variety of topics, such as taxation (*Lettre au Peuple*, 1788), social and societal issues (*Remarques patriotiques*, 1788), and, most famously, the rights of slaves (*Réflexions sur les hommes nègres*, 1788) and of women (*Déclaration des droits de la femme et de la citoyenne*, 1791). In all of them she called for extensive reforms, even if she remained faithful to the monarchy. She was a real activist, who frequently petitioned the legislature, sending them her pamphlets. Unlike Olympe de Gouges and

---

12 Carla Hesse, *The Other Enlightenment: How French Women Became Modern* (Princeton, NJ: Princeton University Press, 2001).

Manon Roland, Germaine de Staël did not die prematurely under the guillotine and she was able to leave France during the Terror. Like them, she was a believer in the Enlightenment values of justice and tolerance, and this conviction coloured the political pamphlets she published during the French Revolution. *Réflexions sur le procès de la reine* (1793) was a call for compassion on behalf of Marie-Antoinette and *Réflexions sur la paix adressées à Mr. Pitt et aux Français* (1794) and *Réflexions sur la paix intérieure* (1795) promoted peace. Written during the Terror, *De l'influence des passions sur le bonheur des individus et des nations* (1796) offered reflections on the political consequences of fanaticism. An advocate of political moderation and conciliation and rallying against violence, she was later exiled by Napoleon who feared her outspokenness. In spite of their different social background, education, connections, and in some cases personal animosity, Isabelle de Charrière, Manon Roland, Olympe de Gouges, and Germaine de Staël responded similarly to the development of the revolutionary situation. They welcomed the Revolution in the hope that it would bring the reforms to which Enlightenment thinkers had drawn attention. In their writings, they expressed both hope and disappointment about the abuses that came with the desired changes.

Perhaps less directly political but with definite political ramifications was the field of education. After all, the debate over the need to educate larger proportions of the population was eminently political. Some women participated in it, including Madeleine de Puisieux. In her *Prospectus sur un ouvrage important* (1772), she proposed a plan for reforming the education of boys and implementing a more rigorous education for girls. She also expressed the hope of eradicating the abject ignorance of the lower classes in the *Prospectus relatif à l'éducation des enfants du peuple* (1772). There was no question that education was of central concern to all in a period that emphasised reform and progress, and was perceived as the foundation without which social changes could not be accomplished. Like men, women deplored the dismal state of education in general and of women's education in particular. They set out to improve both women's moral standing and their level of instruction.

To that end women produced both general treatises and 'applied' manuals seeking to improve educational practices. In so doing, they contributed enormously to the educational production of the period, and pioneered the domain of children's and adolescents' literature. Focused on moral education and social conduct were Anne-Thérèse de Lambert with the *Avis d'une mère à sa fille* and, about twenty years later, the more cynical Madeleine de Puisieux with *Conseils à une amie*. In this pre-Rousseauian period, these women underscored social rules more than domestic responsibilities, but they already faced the challenge of reconciling their desire for change with the obligation to tone down their demands in order to make their books acceptable.

The women who wrote theoretical treatises – rather than prescriptive conduct manuals – faced a similar dilemma when they extolled the benefits of a more solid intellectual formation not as a way to change women's social roles but in order to bolster their moral grounding. Such was the case of Adélaïde d'Espinassy's (d. 1777) *Essai sur l'éducation des demoiselles* (1764) and Marie-Joséphine de Monbart's (1750–1800) *Sophie, ou L'Éducation des filles* (1777). A few years later, the formidable Stéphanie de Genlis, whose influential pedagogical treatise took the form of the novel *Adèle et Théodore* (1782), joined the ranks of those who adopted Rousseau's views on the dependence and domestic role of women, but she refused to consider such duties as a justification of ignorance and lack of intellectual stimulation.

A similar logic lay behind the more 'applied' manuals that acquainted their young readers with specific subjects. This was Anne de Miremont's (1735–1811) project in her seven-volume *Traité de l'éducation des femmes et cours complet d'instruction* (1779–89), in which she introduced girls to a variety of disciplines, including physics, and Marie-Jeanne Leprince de Beaumont who mixed instruction, religious education, and tales in the three *Magasins* she published between 1758 and 1764 (*des enfants, des adolescentes, Instructions des jeunes dames*). The recognition of girls' intellectual aptitude also motivated Louise d'Épinay (1726–83) to write *Conversations d'Émilie* (1774; 1781), a project that showcased a young girl's ability to think and reason and provided other educators with a model relationship. While all those books confirmed the heightened awareness of young women's educational needs and pointed to their authors' faith in the power of print to reform and improve the conditions and content of this education, they also offered a dramatic insight into the dilemmas women faced when they set out to change the social role of their peers without overstepping the boundaries of propriety. They walked a fine line, crafting a new ideal of womanhood that could fit into the social mould they were simultaneously calling into question.

For women in the eighteenth century, going public with their opinions and experiences took courage, since publishing was perceived as an activity that strayed from the social norms and expectations of the period. Recently, scholars have discussed the significance of women's contributions to Enlightenment culture. In this debate, Robert Darnton and Carla Hesse have argued for a less significant contribution than feminist scholars such as Dena Goodman and

Nancy K. Miller have proposed.[13] The participants in this conversation would certainly agree, however, that in the eighteenth century, the role and status of women writers was still precarious. They were tolerated, occasionally admired, yet never completely assimilated into a male writers' world.

13 Robert Darnton, 'Two Paths through the Social History of Ideas', in Haydn T. Mason (ed.), *The Darnton Debate: Books and Revolution in the Eighteenth Century* (Oxford: Voltaire Foundation, 1998), pp. 251–94; Carla Hesse, 'French Women in Print, 1750–1800: An Essay in Historical Bibliography', ibid., pp. 65–82; Dena Goodman, *The Republic of Letters: A Cultural History of the French Enlightenment* (Ithaca, NY: Cornell University Press, 1994); Miller, *French Dressing.*

45

Eighteenth-century philosophy

WILDA ANDERSON

Philosophy in eighteenth-century France was not a subject matter. It was rather, to judge by the texts of the *philosophes*, a form of action; it was not a noun, but a verb. The classical Enlightenment historians (Peter Gay, Ernst Cassirer, etc.) reflect a rereading of the French Enlightenment from the point of view of the very different German idealist philosophical tradition, but this point of view hides its distinctive character. The French Enlightenment was in effect a plurivocal debate, a long and convoluted conversation, a descendant of the Republic of Letters, a proof that literacy is not a state, but an activity creating culturally dense communities.

In the French Enlightenment philosophical activity was neither homogeneous nor monolithic. There are two complementary ways to cut across the dozens if not hundreds of authors and voices throughout nearly a hundred years: a chronological one – they sort rather cleanly into three generations; and a conceptual one – they separate into three strains of conceptualising the activity and consequences of knowing.

First, the question of generations. Voltaire lived through almost the entire period that we now consider the Enlightenment. How can we attribute him to a single generation? Because what is determining is what the members of each generation had in common with each other and the relationship that each generation understood itself to have to the others – an identity explicitly and consciously assumed by each, an attribution whose consequences were strategic: each generation served with respect to its successor as its conceptual foundation, but also as the source of its philosophical authority. Enlightenment philosophising was not only about how you go about knowing, but, especially, about what the consequences of different forms of knowing are and how to manage these consequences. One example provides a characterisation of what we mean by a generation.

Montesquieu theorised a hydraulics of the passions produced by the circulation of and consequent pressures, balances, and imbalances of the glandular secretions. In the *Essai sur les causes qui peuvent affecter les esprits et les car-actères* (n.d.; written prior to *L'Esprit de lois*), the *Considérations sur la grandeur et décadence de l'empire romain* (1734), or especially the *Lettres persanes* (1721), Montesquieu systematised – gave a more 'modern' basis to – the conventional physiology of the passions so well known to the seventeenth century, and not only as it was embodied in Descartes's *Traité des passions* (1649) and mecha-nised by analogy with Harvey's treatise on the circulation of the blood (1628).[1] For the encyclopedists, and also for Condillac and Rousseau, all members of the second generation of the Enlightenment, Montesquieu was the Newton of human behaviour, the philosopher who naturalised history by revealing the underlying causes of human interactions, the thinker whose authority produced theirs. Naturalising the study of the invalidity of the perceptual activity of the physiological body, and showing the contingency of observa-tion of the outside world as a result of modifications of the observer's internal physiological balance, shifted the focus from celestial laws to laws of human behaviour – those laws of history and social structure embodied in *L'Esprit des lois* (1748). Yet each group of the second generation understood him differently and used his work to justify very different epistemological practices. In fact, it is the activity of recognising and exploring the consequences of their different uses of the same primordial Enlightenment thinkers (mostly Montesquieu and Voltaire) that characterised the second generation. The third generation, authors as different as Condorcet and Robespierre, continued and deepened this divergence and, as we shall see, as a result concluded by eliminating the very discipline of philosophy as the French Enlightenment understood it.

The complementary structure to characterise the Enlightenment philoso-phers is to consider them not across time, but from within the practice of literate community-building. Characteristic of the French Enlightenment, especially if compared to English or German contemporaries, was the process, across these three generations, of making visible three different epistemolog-ical strains initially thought to be one. These tendencies had in common first that each defined itself with respect to the problem posed by the nature of knowledge. But each adopted a different definition of what knowing is. Sec-ond, these ways of knowing authorised and determined ways of philosophis-ing which led to, third, divergent programmes of social behaviour. It is the productive tension between the strains that is the most revealing of the

---

1 C.-L. de Montesquieu, *Essai sur les causes qui peuvent affecter les esprits et les caractères*, in *Œuvres complètes*, ed. R. Caillous, 2 vols. (Paris: Gallimard, 1949 and 1951), II, pp. 39–68; *Considérations sur la grandeur et décadence de l'empire romain*, ibid., II, pp. 69–225; *L'Esprit des lois*, ibid., II, pp. 227–995 and *Les Lettres persanes*, ibid., I, pp. 129–373.

specificity of the French case: we can only speak with validity of the plurality of French Enlightenments, or of the French Enlightenment as existing only in the dynamic space between the three.

The first strain defined the stakes of knowledge in terms of knowledge itself. It included many of the authors routinely recognised as Enlightenment but can be typified by the *Logique*[2] of Condillac. Let us call it the Enlightenment of being. The second defined the practices of knowing in terms of the creation of new types both of knowledge and of beings, and was characterised by its most famous proponent, Diderot, as poetic; I call it the Enlightenment of becoming. The third tendency defined itself in terms of what knowledge does to structure interpersonal actions. Its principal concern was not to determine what one knows, but to analyse the conditions under which a person's knowledge combines with a quasi-psychological process to create the moral status of the subject of knowledge through the ways in which it causes him to perceive himself as an agent. We might, therefore, call this the Enlightenment of action. The exemplary author for this tendency was Jean-Jacques Rousseau.

Strain one. Condillac's principal goal throughout the *Cours d'instruction pour le Prince de Parme* (1775) was to reconcile Descartes and Locke in order to produce a synthesis of the 'natural' Cartesian method of reasoning with Locke's definition of thought as produced by sensations. In so doing, Condillac thought he had rendered congruent the 'naturalness' of intellectual processes with the naturalness of the material world. He proposed that logical analysis is structured the same way in which the material world is structured.

He argued that the proper method to describe the world is to enumerate facts and then to specify their interrelationships. The same type of analysis can be applied to the phenomena of the mental domain which reveal themselves to be the ideas of perceived objects. Combining the analysis of mental and material objects produced the *Logique* (1780) which, through its multiple portrayals of varied acts of analysis, incarnated the ultimate analytic exercise, the analytic description of analysis. This multifaceted analysis depended on one thing: the world must be unchanging, both in its various forms of substance and the laws that rule the behaviour of substance. If this condition holds, then analysis designates the perceived structures of the material and the mental worlds, as well as the processes involved in obtaining these perceptions and in putting them into linguistic form: the analyst links each idea to a word to create a group of denotative signs and their interrelationships. The goal and structure of all natural philosophy is then a perfect language – what

2 É. de Condillac, *Logique; ou, les premiers développemens de l'Art de Penser* (Geneva: n.p., 1785).

Condillac defined as a science: an ordered body of knowledge in which no poetic figures of similarity or invention are allowed to impede the clear perception of the natural world by introducing analogical error. To carry out scientific work then becomes to speak the truth about the world. The scientist does not invent these truths: Nature 'speaks' through him to uncover them, to dis-cover them.

D'Alembert's 'Discours préliminaire' (1751) depended on this type of analysis to justify the *Encyclopédie*.[3] For d'Alembert, science generates its own progress, but this progress is anti-historical. Each philosopher, bent over the writings of his predecessors, should through the activity of reading be drawn into completing the description of nature they began; he will incorporate more of the world into the digestive analytic structure so that it will eventually become a single, totalising universal and transhistorical truth, a primordial scientific law that explains all phenomena. He says, indeed, that 'nature is always the same' (p. ix). But history, the very phenomenon of change, whether as innovation or catastrophe, interrupts or deforms progress towards the discovery of the unique natural law defining a world that cannot evolve, can only always have been. The role of the scientist is to resist such change so that the singular truth about nature can be obtained and preserved. To do so, he adopts an external universal point of view from which historical events can be revealed as nothing other than manifestations of natural laws, analogical to the laws of physics, that generate human comportments. The *Encyclopédie*, then, for d'Alembert, was the continuation of the historical project of Montesquieu, but understood as anti-historical: the only acceptable kind of change does not involve becoming. Good change is the accumulation of knowledge that allows the scientist to reveal that behind the contingent lies the unchanging essential. This is why I call this strain of the Enlightenment the Enlightenment of being. If the scientists' words are by definition true, they acquire a natural authority that can be used to control, in both senses of the word, the speech of those who do not speak science.

The second strain. The most typical examples were the materialists, many of them atheists, of the 1750s and 1760s. Like d'Alembert, Denis Diderot considered the philosopher's task to be the investigation of the material world. But his material world does not work in the same way; his philosopher is not a scientist for whom the world is made up of eternal material essences or universal laws. He is the historian of nature because nature is always

---

3 J. d'Alembert, 'Discours préliminaire', in *Encyclopédie; ou, Dictionnaire raisonné des sciences, des arts et des métiers, par une société de gens de lettres*, 5 vols. (Paris: Briasson, David, Le Breton and Durand, 1751–67; repr. Elmsford Park, NY: Pergamon, 1969), I, pp. i–xxv.

changing, possibly to the level of the laws that determine its functioning. A natural historian must, through direct interventions in the world, enter into communication with the material world so that he can intuit never-before-understood relationships between himself and a world in continual transformation. The result will still be a form of knowledge privileged to manipulate the material and human worlds, but the definition of knowledge must be adapted to this perception of nature as essentially dynamic. The natural historian's knowledge must be as contingent, as changeable, as the world it designates. So how can he know this world? Not through decompositional and recompositional analysis of unchanging essences. As Diderot argued in the *Interprétation de la nature* (1754),[4] valid knowledge can only be derived from a continual 'tâtonnement' – a groping, tentative touch, a form of exchange that causes the historian to become increasingly sensitised to the operation of the material world as it reacts to him. In a curiously Montesquieuan mechanics of material interaction, the historian and his subject become attuned to each other. This harmony provokes a writing or speaking event that embodies the ideal natural historical style. In Diderot's article 'Encyclopédie' (1753)[5] (his rebuttal to the 'Discours préliminaire'), or, as Buffon argued in his 'Discours sur le style',[6] style is a conversation between the philosopher and his environment. The *Rêve de d'Alembert* (1769)[7] (the challenge to the first strain was explicit) uses a multi-character conversation to demonstrate this creative interaction between structure and content, style and message, author and reader, mind and matter, at the very moment when the characters are discussing it. Through a battery of literary figures, the reader is obliged to perceive text as process and him or herself as an engaged participant. The reader must question the status of the text, to 'sniff out' the functioning of the intellect in its interaction with the material world. The natural historians foregrounded their works as poetic, as one force among many creating the new. But newness was not the source of error that it was for the positivists. On the contrary, such provocative conversation was a continual interchange of mutual modifications, of changes, that were what the natural philosopher, as historian, was principally interested in understanding. This is why I call this strain of the Enlightenment the Enlightenment of becoming. Nothing more unlike d'Alembert's single universal law of nature could be imagined. Yet, for

---

4 D. Diderot, *Interprétation de la nature* (1753) in *Œuvres complètes*, ed. H. Dieckmann, J. Proust and J. Varloot, 24 vols. (Paris: Hermann, 1975–), IX, pp. 25–111.   5 *Encyclopédie*, v, pp. 635–48.
6 G. Leclerc, comte de Buffon, *Discours sur le style, suivi de l'art d'écrire du même et de Visite à Buffon d'Hérault de Séchelles* (Castelnau-le-Lez: Climats, 1992).
7 D. Diderot, *Le Rêve de d'Alembert*, in *Œuvres complètes*, XVII, pp. 25–209.

Diderot, a privileged relationship to history was obtained through the poetic that paralleled what the analysts obtained with respect to nature from their perfected language. It resulted in a complementary authority for the speech acts of the philosopher: rather than speaking through him, Nature watches itself create through him. The second-strain philosophers did not sit back and observe the world. They provoked it to generate new meanings, and in so doing became agents who create and judge.

The third strain. The theoreticians of action also drew on Montesquieu as a precursor. Rousseau was the acknowledged emblem of this strain. The philosophical origin of his work lay in his 'Discours sur les Sciences et les Arts' (1750) which posits that all sciences not necessary to minimal survival lead infallibly to moral decadence.[8] This is often characterised as an anti-Enlightenment position. But much as Diderot argued against the positivist sciences yet accepted the primordial importance of knowing, Rousseau understood action as an extension of an epistemological gesture in his major work, the *Contrat social* (1762). He presented man in his infamous 'state of nature' – a state of isolation in which a man matures without ever meeting one of his contemporaries. Like the statue in Condillac's *Traité des sensations* (written at about the same time),[9] Rousseau's natural man was a thought experiment, the familiar *tabula rasa* – an abstraction embodying only the epistemological characteristics needed for the demonstration. He is not only a psychological *tabula rasa*: he is a social *tabula rasa*, emptied not so much of ideas as of social contact. Never having seen anyone but himself, he does not conceive of himself as a man, but passively receives the 'gifts of nature', like Condillac's statue which at first only 'is' the rose that it smells. Once he meets another human being, his consciousness of himself as other than this other is born. He then becomes aware of his own knowledge of otherness, and in so doing understands two things at once: his own existence as a thinking subject, and finally the abstract idea of knowledge.

Once natural man can sense his own knowing, he can feel curiosity (the desire to know more). Knowledge is the paradigm, then, for desire: by analogy, natural man realises that desire can be felt for things other than knowledge. Vice was defined by the Rousseauists as acting on this primitive desire, above all as the expropriation of the other's goods, his knowledge or himself. Until this moment, natural man had been virtuous, but only because, having no

---

8 J.-J. Rousseau, 'Discours sur les sciences et les arts' (1750), in *Œuvres complètes*, ed. Bernard Gagnebin and Marcel Raymond, 5 vols. (Paris: Gallimard, 1964), III, pp. 3–110; *Du contrat social ou principes du droit politique* (1762), III, pp. 349–472.
9 É. de Condillac, *Traité des sensations* (1754) (Paris: Fayard, 1984).

notion of otherness, he could not conceive of exploitation. Once the other and he himself are conceptualised as desiring subjects, exploitation can begin. The social contract for mutual support that will form the first communities becomes necessary to ensure the freedom of each person to dispose of his own being as he sees fit.[10]

But this freedom makes possible a perverted form of knowledge. Some people will have more time than necessary to produce what they need to survive. With idleness returns curiosity. The pleasure provided by the satisfaction of curiosity allows one to conceive of oneself as an individual no longer defined only in terms of minimal physical needs, but also of pleasure. Perverted knowledge leads to luxury: the excess knowledge gained in satisfying his curiosity allows the *savant* to invent tools to produce more than he needs and to sell the surplus to those who covet products they do not have time to make. The process is self-accelerating: riches create even more leisure time to invent; inventing creates more riches, leading directly to vice: our *savant* can accumulate enough money to hire others to do the work necessary to his survival, thus leaving him splendidly isolated to continue to experience pleasure for its own sake. This hyper-individual, whose individuality is the product of his drive to inequality, in his distortion of the natural economy of the circulation of the goods produced to satisfy a society's needs, is strikingly like Montesquieu's eunuchs whose internal imbalance (here read as moral rather than glandular) produces social disfunction.

For Rousseau, it was impossible to regain the state of nature because it is impossible to forget the experience of having knowledge and the sense of one's self as a desiring self. A historical society (one founded on the knowledge embedded in memories) can only slow the growth of inequality. If the problem is to be found in an initial moment of knowing, then what Rousseau seemed to be calling for was the abolition of knowledge. Yet Rousseau was the proponent of a civil education founded on knowledge that undermines knowledge: it destroys the awareness the student has of himself as a desiring subject, so he becomes incapable of willing individuality. He instead defines his interest as the group interest, the general will that writes the social contract. Education in this model focuses no longer on knowledge of the world that exists or for the creation of the new, but on the habilitation of a functioning social agent. It is the enabling condition for valid political action, where the *polis* and the *civis* are in perfect harmony.

10 Rousseau, *Du contrat social*, Bk II, Chap. 3, pp. 371–2.

The members of the three strains of French Enlightenment philosophy initially thought that they were discussing the same subjects. What they actually had in common was to take thinking and knowing as the basis for human culture, and as the only acceptable warrant for social and political behaviour. They initially neither abolished nor disproved each other's work. The activity of their disputes created the essence of the literate space itself. But what happened in the third generation? The later years of the second generation hardened this initially productive interaction into a divisive separation of disciplines: they were no longer *doing philosophy*. The Enlightenment of being led to the hard sciences (the chemistry of Lavoisier, the mathematical sociology of Condorcet) and to the economics of the Physiocrats, although it did lead, in the nineteenth century, to the only French philosophical figure worthy of the name, the positivist Auguste Comte. The Enlightenment of becoming of Diderot and Buffon had no third-generation figures at all, and their last works (Diderot's *Essai sur les règnes de Claude et de Néron* [1778] and Buffon's *Époques de la nature* [1779]) were rejected by a literate community that had moved on. Instead, their work resurfaced in the programmatic literature of Stendhal or Zola or the anti-scientific musings of Geoffroy de Saint-Hilaire. The Enlightenment of action led to a splitting off of political science from philosophy commonly understood: the activity of politics, while embedded within the conceptual matrix of the general will, turned to the creation of institutions (Turgot, Necker, Robespierre, eventually even Napoleon Bonaparte) and abandoned the questioning of philosophical principles.

It is a commonplace that the French Revolution brought about the end of the French Enlightenment, the children devouring their parents. Yet it is just as plausible to argue that the internal stresses of the intellectual debate necessarily led to the dissolution of this knowledge-based project, resulting inevitably in the creation of the modern disciplines as they would be embodied in the university structures and the aesthetic programmes of the nineteenth century.

46

Libertinage

THOMAS WYNN

'It is strange that of the many writers who, in their novels, have wished to paint their century, so few have stepped beyond the circle of libertinage.'[1] Jean-François Marmontel's observation in his *Essai sur les romans* (1787) points to the paradox of eighteenth-century French libertine writing. A defining feature of the period, libertinage is essentially exclusive and oppositional in nature. On the one hand, it is a common subject of novels, plays, memoirs, dialogues, poetry, and songs. On the other, it is characterised by an aspiration to singularity, opposing as it does religious, moral, and political orthodoxy. Concerning above all the theorisation, practice, and expression of sexual pleasure (not love), libertinage is an affront to conventional behaviour. The apparent permanence of libertinage in eighteenth-century French letters might imply that this is a movement whose definition remains fixed from the regency until the Revolution. Yet, as this chapter will attempt to show, libertinage is a fluid concept, encompassing literature, philosophy, and politics. Elite and vulgar, disruptive and restrictive, erotic and cerebral, spontaneous and rehearsed, libertinage is a protean and contradictory practice.

The term *libertin* derives from the Latin *libertinus* meaning freedman, and its usage in early modern France suggests both emancipation and degradation. It was first employed in French by Calvin in 1544 to condemn dissident Anabaptist sects in the Low Countries primarily for their religious heresy, and for their apparent moral depravation. The early and mid-seventeenth century sees such writers as Théophile de Viau (1590–1626), Cyrano de Bergerac (1619–55), and François La Mothe Le Vayer (1588–1672) elaborate a materialist philosophy (inspired by Epicurus and Gassendi) to challenge orthodox religious doctrine. Though distant relatives of literary characters such as Versac, Valmont, and Juliette, these *libertins érudits* demonstrate that dissident behaviour may be founded on philosophical principles rather than driven by lust. In the second

---

1 In J.-F. Marmontel, *Œuvres*, 6 vols. (Paris: A. Belin, 1819), III, p. 572.

half of the century, libertinage was a term of reproach suggesting freethinking impiety, and consequently moral dissoluteness. Molière's use of the term illustrates this link between religious and moral laxness. Consider how Orgon expresses his distaste for Valère in Le Tartuffe (1662): 'Je le soupçonne encor d'être un peu libertin; / Je ne remarque point qu'il hante les églises' (II.2) ('I still suspect him of being somewhat of a libertine; / I have not observed him frequenting churches'). The link is made with greater force in Molière's next play, Dom Juan (1663), where the title character's nonchalant atheism and cynical sexual promiscuity make him the first great libertine hero of French literature. Despite Pierre Bayle's attempt to separate faith and morality in the Pensées diverses sur la comète (1682), the first edition of the Académie Française dictionary (1694) confirms that libertinage concerns impiety before immorality: 'L'état d'une personne qui témoigne peu de respect pour les choses de la religion... Il se prend quelquefois pour débauche et mauvaise conduite' ('The state of a person who signals little respect for religious matters... It is sometimes used for debauchery and wicked conduct'). But within a decade the irreligious element of libertinage gives way to a more secular sense of autonomy and depravation. The Trévoux dictionary defines libertinage primarily as 'débauche, désordre, dérèglement dans les mœurs' (debauchery, disorder, unruliness in matters of morality), and secondarily as an insufficient respect for the mysteries of religion. It is certainly how Diderot (1713–84) understands the term when he 'translates' the Earl of Shaftesbury's Inquiry concerning Virtue, or Merit in 1743: 'La débauche, qui n'est autre chose qu'un goût trop vif pour les plaisirs des sens, emporte avec elle l'idée de société. Celui qui s'enferme pour s'enivrer, passera pour un sot, mais non pas pour un débauché. On traitera ses excès de crapule, mais non de libertinage' ('Debauchery, which is nothing more than too keen a taste for pleasures of the senses, implies the idea of society. He who hides himself away to get drunk, will pass for a fool, but not for a debauched man. His excesses will be treated as villainy, but not as libertinage').[2] Libertinage, here synonymous with debauchery, is a matter of bodily satisfaction, but crucially it is not antithetical to social pleasures. Diderot here accords significant importance to sociability, whereas other examples of libertinage will require this social world precisely in order to assert the independence of the libertine individual. The effacement of antireligious aspects from libertinage and its consolidation as social practice in the eighteenth century is confirmed in Grimod de La Reynière's remark of 1783: 'Today people glory in libertinage as much as in unbelief, and they would

2 D. Diderot, Œuvres complètes, ed. J. Varloot et al., 24 vols. (Paris: Hermann, 1975–), I, p. 397.

seem to blush for being virtuous, just as they have long done so for showing faith.' A fashionable habit by this time, libertinage is considered as distinct from atheism. Libertinage and anti-clerical sentiment will be casual bedfellows throughout the century, in such texts as the novel *Dom Bougre, ou Le Portier des Chartreux* (1741, attributed to Gervaise de Latouche, 1715–82) or the anonymous obscene play *La Bougie de Noël* (late 1790s), but libertinage only rediscovers its radical, foundational atheism in the works of Sade (1740–1814).

The regency of Philippe d'Orléans (1715–23) marks a crucial phase in the development of libertinage in France. Following the austerity of the final years of Louis XIV's reign, the regency represents a period of sexual licentiousness, moral irreverence, and financial speculation (epitomised by John Law's catastrophic attempts to reform the French banking system). For all that the memorialist Saint-Simon (1675–1755) criticises Philippe's court, now firmly established not at Versailles but at the Palais-Royal in Paris, the regency set up an urban and urbane model of libertinage. Even Marmontel recognises that 'libertinage was of a better tone there'.[3] Although no significant libertine works were produced during the regency, its combination of society, sophistication, and sexuality, embodied by the duc de Richelieu (1696–1788, great-nephew of the cardinal, and subject of apocryphal memoirs), was to prove appealing to writers such as Crébillon *fils* (1707–77), Laclos (1741–1803) and Sade. Certainly there are numerous libertine texts that stray out of the *hôtel particulier* and into the street or brothel (such as Andréa de Nerciat's *Félicia ou mes fredaines*, 1775, and the *Correspondance de Madame Gourdan*, attributed to Théveneau de Morande, 1784), but eighteenth-century libertinage tends to be an aristocratic phenomenon. Closed in upon itself, this ritualistic world is governed by strict rules of behaviour whose very existence invites infringement, and where private actions are played out before an audience adept at the shared code. Reduced by royal absolutism to a parody of the warrior, the aristocratic libertine achieves renown through the conquest of women, as Mirabeau (1749–91) confirms in *La Morale des sens* (1781): 'Une femme que poursuit un amant ressemble à une ville que l'on assiège' ('A woman pursued by a lover resembles a besieged town').[4] In this respect, libertinage is not simply a matter of mindless debauchery, it is a strategy of seduction, domination, and glory. Though we no longer speak of 'libertinism', that is not to say that libertinage is not in some ways a system. A key exposition of libertine principles occurs when Versac instructs Meilcour in Crébillon *fils*'s *Les Égarements*

---

3 Marmontel, *Œuvres*, III, p. 571.
4 H. R. Mirabeau, *La Morale des sens, ou l'homme du siècle* (Paris: Phébus, 2000), p. 109.

du cœur et de l'esprit (1736). Attentive to maintaining one's rank in society, he insists upon the singularity of the libertine enterprise:

> De quelle finesse n'avez-vous pas besoin pour conduire tout à la fois plusieurs intrigues que pour votre honneur vous ne devez pas cacher au public, et qu'il faut cependant que vous dérobiez à chacune des femmes avec qui vous êtes lié! . . . Être passionné sans sentiment, pleurer sans être attendri, tourmenter sans être jaloux: voilà tous les rôles que vous devez jouer, voilà ce que vous devez être.

> (What dexterity you must have in order to manage several intrigues simultaneously, which your honour demands you must not hide from the public, but which you must hide from each of the women with whom you are involved . . . To be passionate without feeling, to weep without being moved, to torment without being jealous: those are the roles you must play, that is who you must be.)[5]

The same disciplined attention to principles is what distinguishes Valmont from other men in Laclos's *Les Liaisons dangereuses* (1782): 'sa conduite est le résultat de ses principes. Il sait calculer tout ce qu'un homme peut se permettre d'horreurs, sans se compromettre; et pour être cruel et méchant sans danger, il a choisi les femmes pour victimes' ('his behaviour is the result of his principles. He knows just what wickedness a man may allow himself without compromising himself; and to be cruel and vicious without danger, he has chosen women for his victims').[6] Unlike the *petit-maître* who poses no threat to women, this dangerously apathetic libertine engineers scenarios to humiliate and ruin women, and thereby publicise his own glory. Libertinage almost always involves triangulation. The libertine must understand, profit from, and maintain the social conventions by which he achieves renown; his tactical sexual aggression does not intentionally overturn the ideology that underpins his noble caste. This form of libertinage is an essentially conservative strategy of hypocrisy and subversion, and is typified by the four heroes of Sade's *Les 120 journées de Sodome* (written in the Bastille in 1785). In the face of bourgeois virtue, such behaviour saps the aristocracy's claim to moral superiority, but libertine literature avoids moralising. In Laclos's novel the 'avertissement de l'éditeur' punctures the moral claims of the 'préface du rédacteur', and Vivant Denon's *Point de lendemain* (first version, 1777; second version, 1812) ends with the hero's bemused ignorance: 'Je cherchai bien la

5 P. J. de Crébillon, *Les Égarements du cœur et de l'esprit*, ed. R. Etiemble (Paris: Colin, 1961), p. 176.
6 P. Choderlos de Laclos, *Les Liaisons dangereuses*, ed. R. Pomeau (Paris: Garnier-Flammarion, 1996), p. 96.

morale de cette aventure, et . . . je n'en trouvai point' ('I sought the moral of this adventure and . . . I did not find one').[7]

Libertinage in all its forms is connected with the acquisition and transmission of knowledge. Many early modern erotic works present scenarios of education, from *L'Académie des dames* (originally published in Latin in 1660), to Mirabeau's *Le Rideau levé, ou l'éducation de Laure* (1786), and Sade's *La Philosophie dans le boudoir* (1795). More generally, the libertine novel takes the form of the *Bildungsroman*, whereby the young hero or heroine is educated to the realities of the world. This education is primarily of an erotic nature, and it is one of the eighteenth century's key lessons that sexual pleasure, devoid of the stain of sin, can liberate the mind as well as the body. As Diderot writes in *Le Neveu de Rameau* (written 1762–73): 'on tire parti de la mauvaise compagnie, comme du libertinage. On est dédommagé de la perte de son innocence par celle de ses préjugés' ('one benefits from wicked company, as one does from libertinage. The loss of one's prejudices compensates for the loss of one's innocence').[8] The eighteenth-century book trade's conception of clandestine 'philosophical books' illustrates that libertinage may be philosophical, transgressive, and disruptive. Robert Darnton cites a bookseller in Poitiers who, writing about 'un petit catalogue de livres philosophiques' to his Swiss distributor in 1772, requests the following works: '*La Religieuse en chemise, Le Christianisme dévoilé, Fausseté des miracles des deux Testaments, Mémoires de Mme la marquise de Pompadour, Recherches sur l'origine du despotisme oriental, Système de la nature, Thérèse philosophe, Margot la ravaudeuse*'.[9] This list would seem to encourage links between categories that modern scholarship has tended to separate into 'high' and 'low' Enlightenment. One might thus consider how Boyer d'Argens's *Thérèse philosophe* (1748) and Fougeret de Monbron's *Margot la ravaudeuse* (1748) resemble the abbé du Prat's *Vénus dans le cloître, ou la religieuse en chemise* (1692) in their description of sexuality, but also how these works are as free-thinking as Boulanger's political and historical enquiry (*Recherches sur l'origine du despotisme oriental*, 1761), and the baron d'Holbach's landmark work of materialist and atheist philosophy (*Système de la nature*, 1770).

Influenced by the English philosopher John Locke (1632–1704), materialist thinkers such as Helvétius (1715–71), Condillac (1715–80), and Buffon (1707–88) argue that knowledge comes through sensory perception, and that the natural world is characterised by energy and change. Linking materialism and

---

7 V. Denon, *Point de lendemain*, ed. M. Delon (Paris: Gallimard, 1995), p. 69.

8 D. Diderot, *Le Neveu de Rameau*, in *Œuvres*, XII, p. 137.

9 R. Darnton, *Bohème littéraire et révolution* (Paris: Gallimard, 1983), p. 7.

libertinage is La Mettrie (1709–51), whose *L'Homme-machine* (1748) insists upon the natural movement within man: 'The human body is a machine which winds its own springs: it is the living image of perpetual movement.'[10] He was also a theorist of pleasure in such works as *L'École de la volupté* (1746). Without relying on religious explanations, this mechanistic view of human nature privileges the accumulation of diverse sensory experiences, and appeals to many libertine writers who locate human happiness in the physical satisfaction of desires in this world. Thus *Thérèse philosophe* combines graphic sex scenes and discussions of masturbation, dildos, and sodomy with materialist philosophy supported by empirical evidence. Sade rather esteemed this text, proposing that it gave the idea of a 'livre immoral'. His own works theorise extreme sexual liberty in terms of materialism. As a character declares in the *Histoire de Juliette* (1797): 'Il doit y avoir une théorie sur cela comme sur tout, il doit y avoir des principes, des règles' ('There must be a theory to this as there is to everything, there must be principles, rules').[11] Fougeret de Monbron's Margot may be less philosophical than Thérèse or Sade's heroines, but her story – a whore's progress in the vein of John Cleland's *Fanny Hill* (1749) – similarly emphasises that human behaviour may be perceived authentically through erotic acts; thus the ruling classes, represented in the novel by debauched clergymen, magistrates, and financiers, sexually and financially exploit the poor.

Despite the philosophical centrality of nature in many libertine works, few take place in the natural world; Sade is a notable exception, sending his characters into forests and up (and indeed into) volcanoes. When libertines find themselves in the countryside, it is normally to recover from a sexually transmitted disease or to enjoy their retirement, as in Duclos's *Les Confessions du comte de **** (1741); otherwise, like Valmont, they long to return to the city, and that city is usually Paris. Whether the salons of Crébillon, the Opéra and Comédie-Française of Chévrier's *Le Colporteur* (1761), or the modest apartments of Rétif de La Bretonne's *L'Anti-Justine* (1798), Paris is the principal sphere of libertine activity. The classic libertine space is the boudoir, described by Mirabeau in *Ma conversion* (1783):

> [Il y avait des] panneaux placés avec art réfléchissant en mille manières tous les objets, et des amours dont les torches enflammées éclairaient ce lieu charmant. Un sofa large et bas exprimait l'espérance pour les coussins vert

---

10 J. O. de la Mettrie, *L'Homme machine*, ed. J. Vérain (Paris: Mille et Une Nuits, 2000), p. 25.
11 D. A. F. Sade, *Histoire de Juliette*, in *Œuvres*, ed M. Delon, 3 vols. (Paris: Gallimard, 1990–8), III, pp. 591 and 747.

anglais dont il était couvert; la vue se perdait dans les lointains formés par
les glaces, et n'était arrêtée que par des peintures lascives que mille attitudes
variées rendaient plus intéressantes; des parfums doux faisaient respirer à
longs traits la volupté. Déjà mon imagination s'échauffe, mon cœur palpite;
il délire; le feu qui coule dans mes veines, rend mes sens plus actifs.

([There were] artfully positioned panels reflecting all the objects in a thousand
different ways, and cupids whose flaming torches lit up this charming place.
A large and low sofa promised much for the deep green cushions with which
it was covered; one's gaze was lost in the far-off distances created by the
mirrors, it was only halted by the lascivious paintings that a thousand varied
postures made more interesting; sweet scents made one breathe this pleasure
in deeply. Already my imagination becomes excited, my heart beats fast; it
is in a frenzy; the blood running through my veins makes my senses more
alert.)[12]

Erotic decoration saturates the boudoir with desire, stimulates the senses, and
creates an impression of dynamism. Luxury is rehabilitated in this enclosed
and aestheticised space, preparing the libertine for more carnal pleasures. The
boudoir encourages the libertine's self-regard and passion for accumulation,
gradation, and novelty: 'La singularité d'une liaison en fait quelquefois tout
le mérite' ('The singularity of an affair is sometimes all its merit').[13]

The contradictory aspect of libertinage is perhaps clearest in its depiction of
women. Despite no significant libertine works being written by women, such
texts abound with heroines who spurn the Rousseauian model of virtuous,
maternal, and domestic womanhood, and enjoy their own and others' bodies.
Yet generally the female libertine must operate within strict boundaries of
decorum. As a character declares in the anonymous *Histoire de Mademoiselle
Brion, dite Comtesse de Launay* (1754): 'Un joli homme se fait une espèce de
point d'honneur d'avoir été libertin; on ne veut point nous permettre qu'on
puisse l'être' ('For a handsome man it is a point of honour to have been a
libertine; we are not allowed even to be so').[14] Madame de Merteuil in *Les
Liaisons dangereuses* epitomises one type of libertine heroine in her quest for
knowledge, power, and sexual pleasure. She reveals in Letter 81 her technique
of discipline and deceit, differentiating herself from other women by her
attention to her principles. Such singularity prevents solidarity with other
women, and Sade's Juliette similarly aspires to total autonomy, murdering

---

12 Mirabeau, *Ma conversion*, ed. J.-P. Dubost, in P. Wald Lasowski (ed.), *Romanciers libertins du
XVIIIe siècle*, 2 vols. (Paris: Gallimard, 2000–5), II, p. 990.
13 *Vie privée du maréchal de Richelieu*, ed. B. Craveri (Paris: Desjonquères, 1993), p. 115.
14 *L'Espion libertin, ou le calendrier du plaisir*, ed. P. Wald Lasowski (Paris: Éditions Philippe
Picquier, 2000), p. 96.

her female acquaintances when necessary. Unlike these determined heroines, many libertine texts present women as passive commodities, as demonstrated in titillating semi-fictional works such as *Les Bordels de Paris avec les noms, demeures et prix* (1790). Furthermore, any potential threat to patriarchy that lesbianism might pose is neutralised when a good man arrives on the scene to channel the woman's sexuality appropriately, as in Pidansat de Mairobert's *Confession d'une jeune fille* (1784). Male homosexuality is almost non-existent, except for in *Le Portier des Chartreux* and in unexpurgated editions of the memoirs of Casanova (1725–98). Again the principal exception here is Sade, who dismantles conventional sexual categories to maximise the number of positions and pleasures.

Libertinage does not long outlast the Revolution, and arguably culminates with Sade. Many texts from the end of the century use erotic material as a vehicle to criticise orthodoxy and power; for instance, Marie-Antoinette was the subject of numerous obscene images, pamphlets, and plays, such as *L'Autrichienne en goguettes, ou l'orgie royale* (1789). But the ideology on which libertinage depends, that which allows private acts to be judiciously performed or revealed in public, collapsed under the revolutionary imperative of exposure and transparency. The insistent politicisation of erotic activity proved fatal to libertinage.

47

Eighteenth-century travel

JENNY MANDER

The Enlightenment adopted the classical figure of travel to express and explore its own relationship to knowledge, which in turn influenced and was influenced by its relations with peoples from other societies with different manners or, to use the *philosophes'* own term, *mœurs*.

The centrality of this particular trope can been seen in the vignette adorning the opening page of Denis Diderot and Jean le Rond d'Alembert's *Encyclopédie, ou dictionnaire raisonné des sciences, des arts et des métiers* (1751–72). In the middle of the engraving is a ship in full sail; to the right is a printing press; in the foreground are a number of figures representing the various arts and sciences. In the ship can be seen an allusion to the work of Francis Bacon, hailed by d'Alembert in his 'Discours préliminaire' as one of the precursors to the *philosophes*. For it was a ship that had been chosen as the emblem for the frontispiece of the English philosopher's *Instauratio Magna* (1620), sailing between the Pillars of Hercules that marked the boundaries of the classical world. In his writing, in which voyaging and the progress of knowledge are constantly equated, Bacon recharged this classical image with all the excitement and prestige associated with the voyages of discovery, which, beginning with Columbus in 1492, had quite literally opened up a New World to Europeans. Transferring the term of 'discovery' from the sphere of geography, where it referred to the exploration for and finding of new lands and oceans, to the domain of the empirical sciences, where it was used to speak of what had until then been called 'inventions', he was perhaps the first to compare the scientist to the intrepid, pioneering explorer.

The eighteenth-century *philosophes* understood themselves to be building on the foundations laid by Bacon. Rejecting traditional authorities, above all Scripture, as the basis of knowledge, they turned instead to nature. Nature, they believed, was a book that could be read by direct observation; it could then be brought within the mastery of reason and this knowledge could then be further disseminated through their own writings, as suggested in the vignette by the printing press leading directly down to the shore – an image which also evokes the belief, following John Locke and Étienne Bonnot de Condillac, that it is through our senses and our experience of the world that our ideas are engraved onto the blank slate of our mind.

Travel, however, was not just a metaphor for Enlightenment thought. Voyages that brought contact with foreign cultures were integral in a much more literal sense to the cosmopolitan outlook of the period and to its embryonic anthropology. In the words of Jean-Jacques Rousseau: 'Quiconque n'a vu qu'un peuple, au lieu de connaître les hommes, ne connaît que les gens avec lesquels il a vécu' ('Whoever has seen only one people does not know men; he only knows the people with whom he has lived').[1] It was by looking beyond its own frontiers to the social and political organisation, religion and manners of other peoples, as documented by travellers, early colonists, and missionaries, that the Enlightenment sought, through the study of differences, to construct a truly universal science of man. It was a science in which geographical variation was used to articulate a *historical* narrative of progress through distinct stages in which the so-called 'savage' living in what were deemed to be more primitive societies could be regarded as the ancestor of more civilised societies such as those found in Europe.

In this narrative of progressive civilisation that fundamentally underpins Enlightenment thought, exchange between peoples was given a crucial role. As the historian of the *Histoire philosophique des deux Indes* asks in the opening pages of this monumental history of European colonialism to which Diderot, amongst other *philosophes*, contributed in significant ways: 'What has led nations out of the shadows of barbarism . . . and dug the canals, drained the plains, built the towns, clothed and civilized the inhabitants?' The voices of the enlightened, he says, all tell him that all this has been achieved through commerce.[2]

By the turn of the eighteenth century, commerce had knitted together distant points on the globe. Notwithstanding the immense distances and the ever–real dangers during ocean voyages of pirates, disease, and shipwreck, there was a steady influx of foreign goods into French ports. With the growing consumption in the new cafés of coffee and chocolate, sweetened with sugar, all imported from the *îles françaises*, it could be said that the exotic had in certain very tangible ways become part of the domestic landscape. The sense

---

1 J.-J. Rousseau, 'Des Voyages', in *Émile, or On Education*, trans. Allan Bloom (New York: Basic Books, 1979), p. 451.
2 G.-T. Raynal, *Histoire philosophique et politique des établissements et du commerce des Européens dans les deux Indes* (Ferney-Voltaire: Centre International d'étude du XVIIIe siècle, 2010), p. 24.

of increasing familiarity with the foreign is further suggested by the large sales of travel literature relating to both past and more recent expeditions. These not only became the focus of popular discussion; they also spawned further texts. Two examples of this process of dissemination that took travel literature into the heart of both popular and philosophical thought can be found in Voltaire's *Micromégas* and Diderot's *Supplément au Voyage de Bougainville*.

Micromégas (published 1752, probably written around 1739) is, in part, a celebratory response to an expedition to Lapland, undertaken in 1735 by an international team of scientists and geographers led by the French mathematician, Pierre Louis Maupertuis, to determine the shape of the Earth. Under Voltaire's pen, this historical journey is, however, explored from the perspective of a *voyage extraordinaire* belonging to a long literary tradition, which had gained huge popularity over the previous century with utopian works from Bacon's *Nova Atlantis* (1627) to the *Histoire des Sévarambes* by the Huguenot exile Denis Veiras (published in English, 1675, in French 1677–79) and Simon Tyssot de Patot's *Voyages et aventures de Jacques Massé* (1710), and which, stimulated by developments in scientific research in astronomy and cosmography, had taken the specific form of an interplanetary journey in Cyrano de Bergerac's *États et empires de la lune* (1635) and, more recently, in Jonathan Swift's *Gulliver's Travels* (1726). Furthermore, Voltaire combines this tradition of the extraordinary voyage with a newer tradition, illustrated supremely by the baron de Montesquieu's *Lettres persanes* (1721) and imitated by Mme de Graffigny in her *Lettres d'une Péruvienne* (1747), of a journey to France undertaken by a foreign visitor who observes and judges what he or she sees.

In the case of *Micromégas*, the visitors in question are the eponymous character, some eight leagues tall, exiled from Sirius for having written a treatise on insects, and his somewhat shorter companion from Saturn, where (clearly evoking Bernard le Bouyer de Fontenelle) he was the secretary of the Academy. By means of sunbeams, comets, and finally with the aid of an aurora borealis, they make their way through the solar system and alight on Earth by the northern shore of the Baltic Sea, 5 July 1737, exactly the same day that Maupertuis's expedition had been shipwrecked on its return from the pole. Ingeniously fabricating a monstrous pair of ear trumpets, Micromégas and the Saturnian are able to enter into conversation with the men who appear to be almost invisible insects. What they hear is impressive. The scientists display their prodigious ability to calculate the measurements of things that are much larger than themselves (skills that to Voltaire's immense satisfaction had enabled them, while at the pole, to prove the Newtonian model of the world to be right), and the visitors are forced to recognise the undeniable intelligence of these 'invisible insects' who had initially seemed so despicable: 'I see more clearly than ever', Micromégas exclaims, 'that we should judge nothing by its apparent importance.'

Yet the visitors are horrified in equal measure by what they go on to learn of the war and bigotry on Earth, and, in contrast to the philosophers' impressive understanding of what lies outside themselves, by their ignorance of what lies within them. The only words of wisdom are offered by a little student of Locke, who is unable to explain how he thinks, but knows at least that 'I have never thought except on the suggestion of my senses'.

At the end of the *conte*, we are told that inspired by great kindness yet tinged also with feelings of disgust at seeing these infinitely insignificant creatures so puffed up with pride, Micromégas presents the group of men with a handsome book of philosophy, written in minute characters for their use, in which he promises that 'ils verraient le bout des choses' ('they will see the ends of all things'). The book is carried to Paris and laid before the Academy of Sciences, but when the secretary opens it 'il ne vit rien qu'un livre tout blanc' ('he saw nothing but a blank book').

In the empty pages of this book, Voltaire no doubt offers his readers a symbol of the book of destiny, which, should it exist at all, cannot be read by dwellers on Earth, limited in their perspective by their temporality. However, there is perhaps rather more to this enigmatic image. The unreadable book does not just mark the limits of those to whom it is given; it also foregrounds the failure of those travellers of supposedly superior intelligence to pass on their greater knowledge of the world of nature to those they meet. The empty book thus exposes the problematic nature of what is now referred to as 'knowledge transfer' between different peoples, and as such it constitutes, in displaced form, an ironic negation of the Enlightenment's own pretensions to educate and civilise more primitive peoples – pretensions that were often used to legitimate its colonial activities. Micromégas and his companion ultimately leave little of value behind them. If what they offer to the 'animacules' is to be considered as a gift in any sense of the word, it is ultimately as one of corrective vision: the unwritten pages, ironically reminiscent of the Lockean blank slate of the mind at birth, comment wryly on the relatively limited extent of man's progress and provide a space for humble self-scrutiny.

Diderot's *Supplément au Voyage de Bougainville* (which first appeared in Grimm's *Correspondance littéraire* in 1773, although it was frequently revised over the period in which Diderot was also working on Raynal's *Histoire philosophique des deux Indes*) began as a review of Louis-Antoine de

Bougainville's account of his voyage around the world, the first French circumnavigation of the globe (1766–9), undertaken to bolster France's pride
after its defeats during the Seven Years War (1756–63). Like *Micromégas*, it provides its readers with another reflection – this time more explicitly critical –
on the Enlightenment's belief in the positive value of contact and exchange
between distant peoples.

The extracts from the supposed supplement to Bougainville's *Voyage autour
du monde* – the publication of which in 1771 had caused a European sensation –
are framed within a discussion between two male figures, referred to anonymously as A and B, which dramatises, not without irony, the way in which
travel literature and scientific debate became the topics of conversation in
polite society. Towards the end of the opening discussion, A prompts B to
turn his attention away from things that Bougainville had seen on his voyage and to reflect briefly instead on the journey undertaken by a Tahitian,
named Aotourou, who returned with Bougainville to France where he was
presented at court and became the darling of the whole of Paris. After some
eleven months, at his own request, he was returned to his homeland, unfortunately contracting smallpox on the way and dying at sea. A wonders what the
Tahitian traveller would have told his fellow countrymen about his sojourn in
Paris. Would he have taken back the gift of greater knowledge to his 'savage'
society 'qui touche à l'origine du monde' ('which is close to the origins of
the world')? B suggests not. He points out that Aotourou was never able to
learn French – something which, drawing on prevailing linguistic theories,
he accounts for in terms of the deficiencies of the Tahitian's own primitive
language which lacked so many of the letters used in French, thereby pre-
venting him from mastering the new sounds. B speculates that, as a result, he
would have understood little of what he saw in France and have been even
less able to translate what he had understood of the French way of life into his
own tongue. Any sense of superiority that might be enjoyed by the French
reader with respect to Tahiti is, however, quickly overturned: B intimates that
there would have been very little *worth* taking back by Aotourou to his Pacific
island. In French customs and laws, his people would have only seen 'des
entraves déguisées sous cent formes diverses' ('fetters disguised in a hundred
different ways').

Calling into question the trajectory from savage to civilised on which
Enlightenment thought is predicated, the story of Aotourou's voyage thus
prefaces Diderot's *Supplément* with a powerful negation of the figure of travel
as a universal metaphor and means for translating progress. At the same time,
the dense fog to which A and B periodically refer and which, they say, conceals

even the neighbouring trees, ironically sets their discussion of Bougainville's global voyage within a context of limited vision.

Diderot's *Supplément* does not deny the potential value of intercultural contact; what the multifaceted text does do, however, is to hold up such contact to critical scrutiny. This is achieved not least through the intermediary of Orou who welcomes the French visitors and offers hospitality to the French chaplain in the belief that he has something far more valuable to give in return, namely children. As Orou confides to his guest after the chaplain has slept with his youngest daughter, Thia: 'Nous avons tiré de toi et des tiens le seul parti que nous en pouvions tirer' ('We've drawn from you and yours the only part which we could take'). The Tahitians need additional hands to till the soil, more soldiers to defend themselves against nearby enemies, and, should the sons left behind by the French prove to be less hardy than their own, they will use them to pay off a debt to a neighbouring oppressor. Orou's hope, however, is that the children who issue from this mixed parentage will form a better race: 'Plus robustes, plus sains que vous, nous nous sommes aperçus au premier coup d'œil que vous nous surpassiez en intelligence, et sur-le-champ nous vous avons destiné quelques-unes de nos femmes et de nos filles les plus belles à recueillir la semence d'une race meilleure que la nôtre' ('We saw at once that you surpassed us in intelligence, and we immediately marked out for you some of our most beautiful women and girls to receive the seed of a race superior to ours').

Reflecting eugenic ideas circulating in eighteenth-century French thought to which Diderot himself gave some support, Orou's experiment, which brings sexual relations within crudely commercial calculations, exposes the concept of cultural exchange built upon commerce – as extolled in Raynal's *Histoire philosophique des deux Indes* – in a less attractive light. Furthermore, by putting the Enlightenment's own ideology into the mouth of a fictional 'savage', Orou's positive interpretation of 'commerce', in all senses of the word, is deliberately made to sound naïve: all the more so since his dialogues with the chaplain have been preceded and virtually pre-empted by the vehement monologue of the Old Man who calls upon his countrymen to lament the coming of Bougainville and his crew – 'ces hommes ambitieux et méchants' ('these ambitious and wicked men'). Bearing the full force of Diderot's anger and outrage against colonial attitudes and behaviour, the chieftain portrays their arrival as a fateful moment, marking the transition from a state of innocence and independence to one of oppression and servitude. The Europeans have not brought progress, but disease, corruption, jealousy, and folly.

In the Old Man's harangue, A thinks he can detect ideas and turns of phrase that sound distinctly European. By way of response, B asks him to bear in mind that the words have been translated from Tahitian into Spanish, and from Spanish into French. With this so-called explanation, Diderot not only flags playfully the inauthenticity of his 'supplement' to Bougainville's *Voyage*; he also deliberately draws attention to a fundamental problem afflicting travel literature and one that would continue to haunt anthropology as it emerged as a recognised discipline. Even while travellers emphasised that they had been eyewitnesses to what they described, reports of foreign peoples and places were mediated through the structures of European thought and contained much that was fictional or false.

This was an issue that had greatly exercised Rousseau and, writing in 'Des voyages', he declared that he had been reading travel reports all his life but that he now regretted the time he had wasted trying to learn from such reading, for in it the truth is invariably tinged with false colours and it is difficult to disentangle what is factual from the web of lies and bad faith. To travel well, the traveller needs to know how to look. But for Rousseau, while the French may be able to pride themselves on the fact that they travel more than any other nation, they are so preoccupied with their own systems of thought and customs that they are unable to see clearly. Furthermore, if commercial interests are the basis for contact, he argues, there is very little need to acquire any real understanding of the foreign culture:

> L'instruction qu'on retire des voyages se rapporte à l'objet qui les fait entreprendre. Quand cet objet est un système de philosophie, le voyageur ne voit jamais que ce qu'il veut voir; quand cet objet est l'intérêt, il absorbe toute l'attention de ceux qui s'y livrent. Le commerce et les arts, qui mêlent et confondent les peuples, les empêchent aussi de s'étudier. Quand ils savent le profit qu'ils peuvent faire l'un avec l'autre, qu'ont-ils de plus à savoir?

> (The information acquired by travel depends upon the object of the journey. If this object is a system of philosophy, the traveller only sees what he desires to see; if it is self-interest, it engrosses the whole attention of those concerned. Commerce and the arts which blend and mingle the nations at the same time prevent them from studying each other. If they know how to make a profit out of their neighbours, what more do they need to know?)

Rousseau acknowledges that it is illogical to conclude that travel is useless because we travel badly; but the fact that we travel badly, he says, is another reason for the limited success of research into the natural history of the human race.

Thus, in 'Des voyages', Rousseau, like Diderot in the *Supplément* and Voltaire in *Micromégas*, takes up the figure of travel negatively to measure the lack of progress made by empirical exploration of the globe. However, it is not just in the philosophical writing of the eighteenth century that this *mise en question* of the Enlightenment's science of man is to be found. It is arguably in the genre of the novel that the epistemological fault lines of travel writing are most comprehensively explored.

From the voyages of classical heroes such as Odysseus and Aeneas, the figure of travel has been at the heart of the European narrative tradition. With the advent of the Age of Exploration, the journeys of fictional protagonists became inflected by the accounts of travellers to the New World and to the East. These accounts borrowed from the language and methods of familiar fiction; they, in turn, stimulated further tales of fictional voyages.

Seeing the hallmark of the novel as its heteroglossia or propensity to display varied and opposing languages, Mikhail Bakhtin defined the genre as one that has always developed on the boundary between cultures and languages, stimulated by international and interlinguistic contacts.[3] Others have since gone on to show the extent to which the rise of the modern novel in the seventeenth and eighteenth centuries was shaped by the European experience of colonialism. Certainly, the figure of travel, connecting distant peoples and places, is inscribed into the warp and weft of the novel. In the eighteenth century there is a marked tendency to restrict the rangy geographies so characteristic of the 'baroque' novel of the previous century and still a feature, for example, of Antoine-François, abbé Prévost d'Exiles's *Cleveland* (1731–9), and the object of parody in Voltaire's *Candide* (1759). Nonetheless, travel – undertaken by choice or by force – remains the essential premise in very many of the major and also more minor narrative fictions. Persians, Peruvians, and Tahitians travel to France, as in Montesquieu's *Lettres persanes* (1721), Mme de Graffigny's *Lettres d'une Péruvienne* (1747), and Marie-Joséphine de Monbart's *Lettres taïtiennes* (1784); Parisians travel to the New World, as in Prévost's *Manon Lescaut* (1731), or to the East, as in his *Histoire d'une Grecque moderne* (1740) or they roam the high seas, as in his *Histoire de la jeunesse du commandeur de Malte* (1741); in other novels, protagonists might just walk and talk, as in Diderot's *Jacques le fataliste* (published posthumously, 1796), which self-consciously exploits the novelistic topos of travel as a means to explore the philosophies of fatalism and determinism.

---

3 M. Bakhtin, *The Dialogic Imagination: Four Essays*, ed. Michael Holquist, trans. Caryl Emerson and Michael Holquist (Austin: University of Texas Press, 1981), pp. xxvi–xxvii.

But the figure of travel does not only inform the plot in this way; just as crucially, it also typically structures the narration, embedding the fictional tale within a chain of mediation, like that which is invoked by B with respect to the multiple translation of the Old Man's speech in Diderot's *Supplément*. Numerous titles gesture to a real or fictional source by presenting the text as a translation from another tongue, and the story of the text's journey in either oral or manuscript form, from person to person, place to place, and language to language, is often expanded on in the prefatory discourse that is such a characteristic feature of the eighteenth-century French novel, especially in the earlier decades of the century. This familiar paratextual rhetoric captures and capitalises on the generic identity of the novel, widely understood at this time to be a narrative prose form that was inherently foreign. Typical in this respect is the view, for example, expressed by Pierre-Daniel Huet in his frequently cited treatise on the origins of the novel, in which he argues that it is not in Provence or in Spain that the beginnings of the form are to be found; they must be sought in the Orient with the Egyptians, Arabs, Persians, and Syrians.[4]

The historical conception of the novel as a genre originating from outside the boundaries of France continues to associate it with discourse that is in some way new – that is to say, novel – and potentially heterodoxal. But the same preface in which this 'exotic' dimension is so frequently underscored also typically acts as a gateway, explaining how the potentially dangerous differences between the foreign and the domestic have been bridged. Thus the fictional translator of Montesquieu's *Lettres persanes* informs his reader:

> Je ne fais donc que l'office du traducteur: toute ma peine a été de mettre l'ouvrage à nos mœurs. J'ai soulagé le lecteur du langage asiatique, autant que je l'ai pu, et je l'ai sauvé d'une infinité d'expressions sublimes qui l'auraient ennuyé jusque dans les nues.

> (My role, therefore, has been merely that of a translator; all I have taken the trouble to do is adapt the work to our own manners. I have relieved the reader of oriental turns of phrase as far as I have been able, and I have saved him from innumerable sublime expressions, which would have bored him to death.)

The *Avertissement* to Prévost's *Histoire d'une Grecque moderne* points to a very similar redemptive process of translation:

4 P.-D. Huet, *Lettre de monsieur Huet, à monsieur de Segrais: de l'origine des romans*, in *Zayde, Histoire espagnole par Monsieur de Segrais avec un traité de l'origine des romans par Monsieur Huet*, 2 vols. (Paris: Claude Barbin, 1670), I, pp. 3–99.

On a retranché un étalage d'érudition turque qui aurait appesanti la narration, et l'on a rendu par des termes français tous les noms étrangers qui pouvaient recevoir de changement.

(We have cut out displays of Turkish erudition which would have weighed down the narration and we have replaced as far as possible all foreign names with French terms.)

These sorts of changes that profess to have accommodated 'foreign' tales to the expectations, manners, and morals of a French readership have often attracted from modern critics the charge of Eurocentrism, a charge that has also been increasingly levelled at the nascent anthropology and ethnography of the Enlightenment. These charges are certainly not without foundation. What is more often overlooked, however, is how the French novel dramatises this problem, almost to the point of making the problems of understanding difference into its defining subject matter.

This can be seen perhaps nowhere better than in the novels of the abbé Prévost, an author who was steeped in travel literature and who would spend over a decade preparing a monumental *Histoire générale des voyages* (1746–59), which would become a major reference tool for the *philosophes*. Beginning with the chevalier des Grieux, the narrator of *Manon Lescaut*, which first appeared as the final volume of the *Mémoires d'un homme de qualité*, Prévost's narrators experience increasing difficulties in seeing others for who they really are, and they struggle to accommodate what they self-consciously see as the 'foreigner' (be this on account of sex, class, or nationality) within the structures of their own texts.

These limits, which help Prévost to enclose his first-person narratives within the subjective contours of the narrating subject perhaps to a greater degree than any previous novelist, are particularly marked in the case of the *Histoire d'une Grecque moderne*. Having freed a Greek slave, named Théophé, from a Turkish harem, the male narrator, who portrays himself as a former French ambassador to Constantinople, tries to educate her to be worthy of him. To do this, he uses a carefully chosen selection of French books to try to shape her behaviour. Slowly and painfully, however, he is forced to recognise that his civilising mission has been a sham and what he really wants is to possess her as his lover. But she eludes his strategies of control and refuses to respond to his amorous advances, leaving him in a state of jealous torment. What brings him to the verge of madness, following her death, is his uncertainty as to whether her rejection of him really stemmed from her moral determination to live a virtuous life, influenced by his lessons of conduct, or, conversely, from a secret love affair with another man, which she had concealed from him. She remains an enigmatic sign that he is unable to read, an inscrutable blank space at the heart of a narrative that professes to tell *her* story. It is a narrative that conspicuously achieves no enlightenment, forcing the narrator to abdicate control, leaving the reader to be master and to draw whatever conclusions he or she chooses: 'J'abandonne absolument le jugement de mes peines au lecteur, et . . . je le rends maître de tout ce qui lui a pu paraître obscur et incertain dans le caractère et la conduite de Théophé' ('I completely abandon the judgement of my sufferings to my reader and I leave him master of everything that might have struck him as enigmatic or uncertain in the character and behaviour of Théophé'). In the figure of an ambassador, that is to say someone whose professional role is one of intercultural negotiation, Prévost thus constructs a disturbing symbol of the failure of patriarchal Western European civilisation to mediate successfully between different ways of seeing and being.

Novels such as the *Histoire d'une Grecque moderne* do not just reflect the interest in other cultures that was stimulated by travel reports and would, in turn, stimulate the nascent ethnography of the Enlightenment. They also reflect *on* the problem that, as we have seen, would be identified by Rousseau as being the central stumbling block to the Enlightenment's natural history of the human race, namely the problem for the traveller of truly understanding what is seen en route. In so doing, these narratives help shape the modern novel as a form of discourse in which the individual is characterised as a limited point of view whose representations are inherently partial.

The progress that is confidently expressed in the form of travel in the vignette to the *Encyclopédie* is thus qualified within the eighteenth-century novel just as it is in the philosophical writings of Voltaire, Diderot, and Rousseau. Despite the physical distances that may be covered, the traveller, imbued with prejudice and guided by self-interest, often scarcely seems to leave home behind him. With this trivialisation of the topos of the voyage, the positive equation between travel and knowledge can only be figured negatively in terms of exile. At least this would seem to be the lesson to be drawn from the *Lettres persanes*, *Micromégas* – and indeed, Choderlos de Laclos's *Les Liaisons dangereuses* (1782), which ostensibly has little to do with the issues of travel writing and anthropology. With the publication of Merteuil's correspondence to Valmont, which exposes her radical critique of and nonconformity to the manners and morals of her century, she can no longer be countenanced by polite society and must leave, alone, for Holland – the place of refuge for so many Huguenots and other free-thinkers, and the place of publication for so many unauthorised French texts, including, it can be noted, the *Histoire d'une Grecque moderne*. Merteuil is just one in a series of semi-caricatural self-representations of Enlightenment progressive thinkers whose journey is configured as one of exile. It is a list that includes Usbek in the *Lettres persanes*, whose efforts to speak a language that is critical of court life – 'un langage jusqu'alors inconnu' ('a language hitherto unknown') – result in his exile. It also includes Micromégas, whose scientific writing is deemed to contain 'des propositions suspectes, malsonnantes, téméraires, hérétiques' ('suspicious, offensive, rash, and heretical statements'), resulting in him being ordered not to appear at court for 800 years. It is finally a list to which we might also add Montesquieu's Roxane, whose revelations in her final letter to Usbek, written in an assertive politicised language which, she says, 'sans doute, te paraît nouveau' ('will probably strike you as new'), necessitates that she undertake what the *Encyclopédie* refers to as 'le grand voyage' to her death. New knowledge, afforded by new or 'foreign' voices, could bring social progress. The Enlightenment was not unaware, however, that this progress that would necessarily question the status quo would be fiercely resisted, at least in certain powerful quarters. Yet, even without such resistance, it recognised that empirical science promised to yield up only part of the truth of human existence. For Voltaire, this was the Enlightenment of the blank book; for Diderot the lesson to be learnt from the fog; and for Laclos, the real wisdom to be found in Merteuil's bout of smallpox that leaves her with only one eye intact: not blind, yet her sight *clearly* limited.

48

Eighteenth-century margins

PIERRE SAINT-AMAND

Exploring 'margins' in the eighteenth century entails searching the places where the century overflows its bounds, and refuses to be contained or corralled by any monolithic notion. In a book published several decades ago, Georges Benrekassa reopened this question, with a view to re-examining the screen of rationality that veiled the century, a rationality conceived as 'faith'.[1] For Benrekassa, the margins of the Enlightenment are to be found above all through a process of ideological tunnelling, in order to uncover the spaces eccentric to the age of reason understood as a 'thought of ordering' (p. 12). In clarifying his approach, his effort to avoid the trap of concentricity, he wrote that 'the question we are faced with is how to break these circles within which the ideology of the Enlightenment contemplates itself' (p. 13). In effect, Benrekassa's critique belongs to a genealogy that began with the work of Horkheimer and Adorno in their *Dialectic of Enlightenment* (1947), a critique of Enlightenment reason as a force of domination, and that was continued by Foucault in *Discipline and Punish* (1977). Foucault lays bare, behind the positivity of the contract and the idealisation of law promoted by the *philosophes*, a series of disciplinary devices, technologies of coercion. This essay will explore the question of margins in a less ideological fashion by repositioning the literature of the eighteenth century in the context of certain works of history with a sociological dimension. A reversion to concentricity tends to circumscribe the period's major writers, the *philosophes*. It is no secret that the century teems with a whole host of other writers, all seeking a place in the sun. The first historian of this abundance of other kinds of writer was Robert Darnton, whose book *The Literary Underground of the Old Regime* (1982) will remain a pre-eminent treatment of the subject.

---

1 G. Benrekassa, *Le Concentrique et l'excentrique: Marges des Lumières* (Paris: Payot, 1980), p. 12. All future page references to this work will appear in the text.

Dimming the lights

Darnton's approach radically revised the intellectual history of the century of Voltaire. His aim, as he so succinctly put it, was to 'get to the bottom of the Enlightenment'.[2] Alongside the highbrow Enlightenment, Darnton pointed to the existence of a prolific alternative literary culture attempting to rival the established writers, Voltaire in particular. Next to the 'noble' stratum of great authors there appeared a parallel world of minor writers. The history of these scribblers echoes the narratives of social mobility that were common at the time, often centred around provincials who moved to Paris to seek literary fortune. Voltaire is known for being highly critical of these writers. He coined numerous epithets for them, one of the most patent being 'la canaille de la littérature' ('the riff-raff of literature').

Voltaire was clearly the most powerful symbol among those men of letters who attained success in a literary career. Institutions also played a role in promoting the success of this class: the Académie Française and numerous aristocratic salons of Paris offered protection to celebrated writers. Great writers mixed easily with the grand nobility, with whom they shared common cultural ambitions. Breaking down this hierarchy, Darnton is interested in the existence of that other world, that of the lesser writers, during the last quarter-century of the *ancien régime*.

Darnton, responding to criticisms of his hierarchical vision, readily cites his literary sources. This is the world of scribblers that Denis Diderot (1713–84) portrays in *Le Neveu de Rameau*, a text that exploits marginality from several vantage points. On the one hand, he creates the portrait of a failed musician, Jean-François Rameau (1716–77), a habitué of the seedier locales of Paris who is unable to accede to the cultural establishment in the manner of his uncle Jean-Philippe Rameau (1683–1764), the celebrated musician and author of numerous operas. Rameau kept company with the enemies of the *philosophes* to whom Diderot's dialogue gives voice – hacks of all stripes such as those who flock around the minister Choiseul and the financier Bertin.

It is no accident that the scene where Diderot sets his dialogue is the Café de la Régence. This place, actually frequented by the band of scribblers whom Darnton studies, was granted a rare literary immortality by Diderot's depiction, which consecrates in literary fiction one of the new institutions of the public sphere of the *ancien régime*. The periodicals in which these

2 R. Darnton, *The Literary Underground of the Old Regime* (Cambridge, MA: Harvard University Press, 1982), p. 1.

writer-journalists express themselves are also mentioned in *Le Neveu de Rameau*: 'Et j'oubliais . . . les grands critiques de la littérature. *L'Avant-Coureur, Les Petites-Affiches, L'Année littéraire, L'Observateur littéraire, Le Censeur hebdomadaire*, toute la clique des feuillistes'[3] ('And I was forgetting . . . the great literary critics . . . in fact all the gang of columnists').[4] Diderot's text serves as an echo-chamber for the quarrel between these divergent classes of writers: on one side, the tenors of the High Enlightenment (in the dialogue, Voltaire is presented as a genius), and, on the other, their adversaries, all the writers who envy them. Among the latter were Charles Palissot (1730–1814), Antoine-Henri Poinsinet (1735–69), Elie-Catherine Fréron (1719–76), Abraham Chaumeix (1730–90), abbé Joseph de La Porte (1714–79), and Sabatier de Castres (1742–1817), whose famous text *Trois siècles de la littérature française* (1772) Diderot mentions.

In this context, Jean-Jacques Rousseau (1712–78) occupies an unusual position. His name is even used to refer to this troupe of literary gypsies, in the coinage 'Rousseau du ruisseau' ('Rousseau of the gutter'). But Rousseau's own work reflects a constant struggle over his own ambiguous case: a celebrity who, since the publication of his *Discours sur les sciences et les arts* (1750), enjoyed access to the best Parisian salons, he was at the same time a writer dogged by censorship and marginalised by institutions. Rousseau's autobiographical work, notably his *Confessions* (1782), embarks on the narrative exploit of marginality: from a wretched state of vagabondage to the alienating fame of his final years. But the *Dialogues de Rousseau juge de Jean-Jacques* (1780, 1782) bear the most dramatic, and the strangest, witness to the complex case of Rousseau. The portrait of 'Jean-Jacques' that we are left with is a figure of alterity in the extreme. Accumulating the stigmata of marginality, the writer is a beggar and an exile. Rousseau famously ends up describing his situation as that of a conspiracy mounted against him. In the second of these dialogues, he summarises his situation of extra-territoriality with regard to philosophical space: 'Cet esprit cruel et méchant se fait sentir dans toutes les sociétés, dans toutes les affaires publiques, il suffit seul pour mettre à la mode et faire briller dans le monde ceux qui se distinguent par là. L'orgueilleux despotisme de la philosophie moderne a porté l'égoïsme de l'amour propre à son dernier terme'[5] ('This cruel and wicked spirit makes itself felt in every

3 D. Diderot, *Le Neveu de Rameau* (Paris: Flammarion, 1983), p. 92. All future references to this text will appear in the main text.
4 D. Diderot, *Rameau's Nephew* and *D'Alembert's Dream*, trans. L. Tancock (Harmondsworth: Penguin, 1984), p. 84. All future references to this translation will appear in the main text.
5 J.-J. Rousseau, *Dialogues de Rousseau juge de Jean-Jacques* (Paris: Flammarion, 1999), p. 315. Future references to this edition will be in the main text.

group, in all public affairs; it is sufficient by itself to make those who stand out in that way fashionable and brilliant in society. The proud despotism of modern philosophy has carried the egoism of amour-propre to its furthest extreme').[6]

These texts of marginality, moreover, challenge the ideology of the Enlightenment in another way. Not only does *Le Neveu de Rameau* dramatise the conflict with the literary underclass, but the social crisis perceived by Diderot takes on broader proportions. In discussing the quarrel against the *philosophes*, Diderot generalises the social conflict, the hostility opposing different groups, the squabbling among various factions. This is the idea put forth in the *Neveu* of the famous 'pacte tacite' ('tacit agreement'). The concept is telling in its echo of the progressive idea of the contract promoted by the century. It is in the mouth of the Nephew that the *philosophe*, his interlocutor, places the following remarks on the negativity of the social bond, the breaking and shattering of reciprocity: 'Il y a un pacte tacite qu'on nous fera du bien, et que tôt ou tard, nous rendrons le mal pour le bien qu'on nous aura fait' (p. 97) ('there is a tacit agreement that they will do us good and that sooner or later we shall return evil for the good they have done us' [p. 89]).

Likewise, in Rousseau's *Dialogues*, we see the positivity of the social contract come spectacularly undone. It is inverted into a 'plot', the 'concours unanime de tout le monde à l'exécution d'un complot abominable' (p. 319) ('unanimous collaboration in the execution of an abominable plot' [p. 181]). What unfolds in Rousseau's text is the obverse face of the general will, which disintegrates into factions and cabals. Rousseau describes the collective bodies of hatred that victimise him – none other than the fractious France, which he analyses in the Third Dialogue, where we see the city and the *philosophes* entrenched in opposite camps: 'les Français n'ont point d'existence personnelle; ils ne pensent et n'agissent que par masses, chacun d'eux par lui seul n'est rien. Or il n'y a jamais dans ces corps collectifs nul amour désintéressé pour la justice: la nature ne l'a gravé que dans les cœurs des individus, où il est bientôt éteint par l'esprit de ligue' (p. 397n) ('The French have no personal existence. They think and act only in groups; each one of them by himself is nothing. Now there is never any disinterested love of justice in these collective

---

6 J.-J. Rousseau, *Rousseau, Judge of Jean-Jacques: Dialogues*, ed. R. D. Masters and C. Kelly, trans. J. R. Bush, C. Kelly, and R. D. Masters, vol. 1 of *The Collected Writings of Rousseau* (Hanover, NH: University Press of New England, 1990), p. 179. All future references will be to this translation in the main text.

bodies. Nature engraved it only in the hearts of individuals where it is soon extinguished by the spirit of conspiracy' [pp. 237–8n]). The century of 'reason' reverts to a 'haineux et malveillant' (p. 315) ('hateful and malevolent' [p. 179]) era, into 'ténèbres' (p. 109) ('darkness' [p. 36]), a gloom that clouds the entire perspective of the *Dialogues*. Rousseau emphasises how 'passions irascibles' ('irascible passions' [ibid.]) have taken over the body politic. Such is the despotic degeneracy that prevails – the tyranny of the wicked, the despotism of hatred, universal contagion. Rousseau's diagnosis of the ultimate pathology of the state of society is this: 'on ne sait plus que haïr, et l'on ne tient point à son propre parti par attachement, encore moins par estime, mais uniquement par haine du parti contraire' (p. 316) ('Everyone hates everything that is not himself more readily than he loves himself. People pay too much attention to others to know how to pay attention to themselves. The only thing still known is hating, and no one stays with his own side because of attachment or still less because of esteem, but uniquely because of hatred for the other side' [p. 179]).

Import / export

If marginality can be distributed along the axis of high and low, Paris and province, as in the context of Enlightenment literary production discussed above, there exists another axis which makes it possible to open an eccentric breach in the bastion of the Enlightenment: this is the axis of metropole and periphery. Certain Enlightenment texts, distancing themselves from the vogue of Orientalism, were quick to criticise Enlightenment ideology from within, but by pursuing the political and cultural debate over French colonial and imperial expansion.

Such is the case with a novel that has achieved practically the status of a classic, having been rediscovered by feminist criticism in the late 1980s. The novel in question is *Lettres d'une Péruvienne* (1747) by Françoise de Graffigny (1695–1752). The story follows the destiny of an Inca heroine, abducted from her native temple, tossed from ocean to ocean, and traded as booty after a naval battle between the Spanish and the French. The New World heroine ends up in France where she is introduced into the world of Parisian bigotry. Graffigny structures Zilia's story as an original pedagogical experiment in affirmation and emancipation. As the story progresses, Zilia abandons her heliocentric universe to seek other lights, but she is always guided by her native reason. With subtle irony, the narrator recounts her aesthetic experience of nightfall:

un astre moins brillant s'élève, reçoit et répand une lumière moins vive sur les objets, qui, perdant leur activité par l'absence du Soleil, ne frappent plus nos sens que d'une manière douce, paisible, et parfaitement harmonique avec le silence qui règne sur la terre.[7]

(a less brilliant star rises, receiving and spreading a less vivid light on objects that, losing their activity in the absence of the Sun, now strike our senses in a manner that is but sweet, peaceful, and in perfect harmony with the silence reigning upon the earth.)[8]

Forgetting the beauties of the Inca temple where she was originally confined, the virgin of the Sun becomes receptive to cosmological diversity. In this process of emancipation, she applies herself to learning French and other subjects, all the while criticising the lack of education suffered by the women of France. Recognising these limits, the constraints imposed by marriage obligations, and other social customs, Zilia proudly proclaims her difference. In particular, she demonstrates the superiority of her education compared with that of French women: 'Elles ignorent jusqu'à l'usage de leur langue naturelle; il est rare qu'elles la parlent correctement, et je ne m'aperçois pas sans une extrême surprise que je suis à présent plus savante qu'elles à cet égard' (p. 141) ('They do not even know the proper usage of their native language. Rarely do they speak it correctly, and I have noticed not without great surprise that I am now more expert than they in that regard' [p. 146]). The revenge of the 'savage'.

Graffigny also organises the end of the narrative around a process of reparations for colonial injustices and the return of plundered property. In Zilia's house, a shrine to self-improvement (the library becomes her favourite location), a golden chair looted from the Inca temple is restored to the heroine after being transformed into various forms of property: 'en maison, en jardins, en terres' (p. 152) ('a house, gardens, and land' [p. 157]) and 'pièces d'or à l'usage de France' (p. 153) ('gold pieces used in France' [p. 158]). No effort is spared so that the former Sun virgin can find familiar objects from her native culture in a cabinet whose rococo style handily echoes Peruvian decorative motifs: 'Les ornements du temple que j'avais laissés dans la maison religieuse, soutenus par des pyramides dorées, ornaient tous les coins de ce magnifique cabinet. La figure du Soleil . . . achevait par son éclat d'embellir cette charmante solitude' (p. 152) ('Supported by golden pyramids, the decorations from the temple that

---

7 F. de Graffigny, *Lettres d'une Péruvienne* (New York: MLA, 1993), p. 59. Future references to this edition will be in the main text.
8 F. de Graffigny, *Letters from a Peruvian Woman*, trans. D. Kornacker (New York: MLA, 1993), pp. 60–1. Future references to this translation will appear in the main text.

I had left in the convent adorned every corner of this magnificent study. The brilliance of the figure of the Sun, hanging from the middle of a ceiling painted the most beautiful colours of the heavens, put the finishing touches on the embellishment of this charming place of solitude, and comfortable furnishings that matched the paintings made it thoroughly delightful' [p. 157]).

As for Diderot, he turns towards the Pacific Ocean, the frontier opened up by the Indian Ocean. He gives us a text in the margins of travel literature, a dialogue conceived as a commentary on the voyage of the navigator Louis-Antoine de Bougainville (1729–1811). Diderot's *Supplément au Voyage de Bougainville* (first published in 1772) is a forum for his reflections on French colonial exploitation at the far end of the Earth. The elderly man whom Diderot portrays at the beginning of the text manifests the violence of the colonial encounter; he displays the weapons of conquest carried by the European conquerors: 'le morceau de bois que vous voyez attaché à la ceinture de celui-ci, et le fer qui pend au côté de celui-là, dans l'autre'[9] ('that piece of wood you see suspended from this one's belt and in the other that piece of steel that hangs at the side of his companion')[10] – the missionary's crucifix and the soldier's sword. Later in the book, Western Enlightenment is relativised, and Tahiti generates a series of alternative values.

The people of Tahiti remain close to their origins, removed from concerns of property, from pressing need and other moral preconceptions. The clash of civilisations is thrown into relief in Orou's speech to the ship's chaplain. Through the two protagonists, representing different cultures, Diderot sums up the absurdity of European prejudices. The vision of the island put forth by Orou reconciles the civil code with the code of nature. Tahiti is indeed free from many of the taboos of European society, notably that of incest.

Pornographic literature is another realm where the dream of harmonising civil and natural codes is explored, not in the utopian register of Diderot's distant peoples, but in fictions of emancipated, enlightened society. Here at last reason is in harmony with nature. This is the case with one of the period's most widely circulated works of pornography, *Thérèse philosophe* (1748?), attributed to Jean-Baptiste de Boyer d'Argens (1704–71). In this text the author proposes a positive materialism which gives precedence to the action of bodies upon one another. As in Diderot's *Supplément*, anarchy is absent from *Thérèse philosophe*. Control mechanisms in the form of self-regulation allow the participating subjects to master their pleasure. If the *Supplément* portrays

9 D. Diderot, *Supplément au voyage de Bougainville* (Paris: Flammarion, 1972), p. 147.
10 *Supplement to Bougainville's 'Voyage'*, in *Rameau's Nephew and Other Works*, trans. Jacques Barzun and Ralph Bowen (Indianapolis, IN: Bobbs-Merrill, 1964).

a world centred around population, around the urgency of increasing birth rates – the economic, cultural, and symbolic motor of Tahitian society – the subjects in *Thérèse*, by contrast, devote themselves to pleasure while avoiding reproduction, preserving their precious seed. In *La Philosophie dans le boudoir* (1795), the marquis de Sade (1740–1814) takes to its extreme this visionary exploration of a society whose laws are modelled upon nature. Dolmancé, reading the pamphlet 'Français, encore un effort si vous voulez être républicains' ('Yet another effort, Frenchmen, if you wish to be Republicans'), declaims a series of utopian proposals relating to incest and murder.

Inside / outside

Diderot's *Supplément* treats the voyagers circumnavigating the world on their 'wooden floor' in an ironic mode. At the end of the century, another writer in the margins of the travel narrative composes a true 'armchair' voyage, an exploration of the study. This is the final frontier exploited by the eighteenth century, that of interiority – not the guilt-ridden religious interiority of old, but a euphoric confinement, on a scale with the individual's own measure. In his *Voyage autour de ma chambre* (1795), Xavier de Maistre (1763–1852) describes the arrogant and voluptuous leisure of a protagonist who has chosen immobility, expelling history out of doors. Ironically outstripping all the travel narratives of the century by inverting his own and immobilising it in snug interiority, Maistre glues his character to his bed, his most precious furniture, a shell dedicated to pleasure. The author also swaddles him in a dressing gown, an intimate accessory that swallows up the narrator in his chosen retreat.

Another text that can be included in this series is a brief essay by Diderot, a sort of guided tour of the philosophical study cum moral commentary on the bad taste of luxury, which illustrates the relations between the *philosophe* and his patrons (in this instance, Madame Geoffrin). The essay *Regrets sur ma vieille robe de chambre* (1769) belongs in a sense to this literature of bourgeois confinement. The *philosophe*'s work space is idealised as a space of contemplation, a museum conducive to creativity (the study contains works by great painters such as Vernet). In the midst of his books and papers, the *philosophe* nostalgically reflects upon his condition.

Of course the most radical return to profound interiority was to be realised, paradoxically, in the work of a writer who transported the subject out of doors, into nature. In his *Rêveries du promeneur solitaire* (1782), Rousseau shows us his outdoor 'study'. Philosophical contemplation no longer takes place within the narrow confines of the library, among books. Rousseau draws us into nature, which offers the walker the sole possibility of self-realisation. This outdoor journal, which Rousseau completes in the margins of his autobiographical writings, flies in the face of eighteenth-century rationalism: 'Plus un contemplateur a l'âme sensible plus il se livre aux extases qu'excite en lui cet accord. Une rêverie douce et profonde s'empare alors de ses sens, et il se perd avec une délicieuse ivresse dans l'immensité de ce beau système avec lequel il s'est identifié' (p. 135) ('The more sensitive a soul a contemplator has, the more he gives himself up to the ecstasies this harmony arouses in him. A sweet and deep reverie takes possession of his senses then, and through a delightful intoxication he loses himself in the immensity of this beautiful system with which he feels himself one' [p 59]). This book of solitude runs against the grain of the collective text that Rousseau conceives elsewhere in his political writings: 'Me voici donc seul sur la terre, n'ayant plus de frère, de prochain, d'ami, de société que moi-même. Le plus sociable et le plus aimant des humains en a été proscrit par un accord unanime' (p. 55) ('I am now alone on earth, no longer having any brother, neighbour, friend, or society other than myself. The most sociable and the most loving of humans has been proscribed from society by a unanimous agreement' [p. 3]). In the end the general will is contradicted by a singular will, actually a non-will, a refusal to act in which the subject discovers the pleasure of its autonomy.

Translated by Jennifer Curtiss Gage

49

The *roman personnel*

NIGEL HARKNESS

While the origins of the term *roman personnel* may be traced back to at least the late nineteenth century, and while it continues to enjoy largely unproblematic critical currency as a shorthand designating a subset of the French Romantic novel, there is little agreement amongst literary commentators as to what constitute the defining characteristics of the genre. The broad-brush definition of the personal novel as the fictional transposition of the lived experience of the author, and the general acknowledgement of the centrality of Rousseau's influence, which are common to most accounts, conceal significant divergences regarding the genre's thematic or formal attributes. Must a *roman personnel* be narrated in the first person? Is the *roman personnel* primarily autobiographical or fictional? Is the introspection of the *roman personnel* compatible with (realist) plot development? Depending on one's critical position in relation to these questions, the corpus of novels considered to be representative of the genre will vary, but will normally be drawn from the following long-list: Chateaubriand, *Atala* (1801) and *René* (1802); Staël, *Delphine* (1802) and *Corinne* (1807); Krüdener, *Valérie* (1803); Senancour, *Obermann* (1804); Constant, *Adolphe* (1816); Duras, *Ourika* (1824) and *Édouard* (1825); Sand, *Lélia* (1833); Sainte-Beuve, *Volupté* (1834); Musset, *La Confession d'un enfant du siècle* (1836); Balzac, *Le Lys dans la vallée* (1836); Nerval, *Sylvie* (1854); and Fromentin, *Dominique* (1862).

Whatever one's definition of the *roman personnel*, this list of titles highlights its concentration in two main periods: the very first years of the nineteenth century, and the early 1830s. This second period of the *roman personnel's* development in fact coincided with the rediscovery of texts from the earlier period. While a novel such as *Atala* was an instant best-seller (within a year there were five editions of the novel, and it had been translated into all the major European languages), others, such as *René*, went almost unnoticed on publication. By 1830, however, *René* had displaced *Atala* and attained canonical status: the novel's themes and form were widely imitated, and René himself was seen as the embodiment of the alienated and superior Romantic hero. The year 1833 also witnessed the rediscovery of another text from the early part of the century: Senancour's *Obermann*. In two important essays, which would subsequently serve as prefaces to the 1833 and 1840 editions of the novel, Sainte-Beuve and Sand established *Obermann* as a significant precursor to contemporary literary trends, and placed the novel alongside – even above – *René* as the perfect manifestation of the metaphysical malaise afflicting the Romantic hero.

Sainte-Beuve's and Sand's essays, now regularly published in editions of the novel, highlight two of the original features of the *roman personnel*. The first of these is the absence of major events in the plot: these were, in Sand's pithy formulation, novels 'parlant peu aux yeux, mais à l'âme constamment' ('speaking little to the eyes, but constantly to the soul').[1] This focus on the intimate suffering of the human soul rather than the twists and turns of plot would be a recurring feature of the *roman personnel*, stressed by authors and characters alike. Constant, for instance, in his preface to the third edition of *Adolphe*, described the work as exploring 'la possibilité de donner une sorte d'intérêt à un roman dont les personnages se réduiraient à deux, et dont la situation serait toujours la même' ('whether it was feasible to give some sort of interest to a story in which the characters would be restricted to two, and in which the situation would always remain the same').[2] The second feature of the *roman personnel* revealed by Sand's and Sainte-Beuve's analyses is the melancholy suffering of the hero, his 'ennui', which Sainte-Beuve linked to a more widespread condition afflicting a whole generation, and which he named 'le mal du siècle' ('the malady of the century').[3] Senancour's solitary hero, beset with spiritual questioning and a paralysing self-analysis, comes to represent the disproportion between desire and reality leading to a chronic inability to act, and a debilitating sense of the individual's powerlessness vis-à-vis the world. While the first recorded use of this term occurs in relation to *Obermann*, it is Chateaubriand's hero René who has become synonymous with this metaphysical malaise. Obermann and René together provide the template for the protagonist of the *roman personnel*, characterised by sensitivity, melancholy, vague desires (René is representative of what, in *Le Génie du christianisme*, Chateaubriand termed 'le vague des passions' ['the imprecision of passions']), powerlessness, disenchantment, and marginalisation from society. Their suffering is also that of a whole generation, as the title

---

1 É. P. de Senancour, *Obermann* (1804) (Paris: Flammarion, 2003), p. 526. Translations are mine.
2 B. Constant, *Adolphe* (1816) (Paris: Classiques Garnier, 1955), p. 9.
3 Senancour, *Obermann*, p. 511.

of Musset's *Confession d'un enfant du siècle* implies, and as Sand's heroine Lélia indicates when, in more self-deprecating mode than her male counterparts, she describes herself as 'un type si trivial et si commun de la souffrance de toute une génération maladive et faible' ('such an ordinary and unexceptional representative of the suffering of a sickly and weak generation').[4]

Acting as a unifying – and hence perhaps necessarily imprecise – concept, the *roman personnel* overlaps with and subsumes the categories of the *roman intime*, the Romantic confession novel, and the *roman autobiographique*. It shares with the *roman intime* a focus on the trials and tribulations of love, but can be distinguished from the excesses of the sentimental novel by its pared-down plot in which the spiritual searching of solitary characters is foregrounded. The heightened subjectivity of the *roman personnel*, and its depiction of marginalised protagonists afflicted by the *mal du siècle*, bring it thematically and stylistically within the ambit of the Romantic confession novel. However, the personal novel is often more formally heterogeneous than the confessional form adopted in *René* and Fromentin's *Dominique* (both framed narratives, in which an older – if not always wiser – self narrates his story, allowing scope for distanced reflection on past events and behaviours). The category of the *roman personnel* can thus include epistolary novels (*Obermann*, *Delphine*), third-person narratives (*Corinne*), and the narratologically unclassifiable *Lélia* (a combination of extended dialogues, letters, monologues, confessions, and intermittent passages of third-person narrative).

The genre's links to autobiography are equally complex. In one of the first recorded uses of the term in literary criticism, Ferdinand Brunetière in his *Questions de critique* (1889) identified the primary feature of 'la littérature personnelle' as a focus on the personality of the poet to the exclusion of all else, and situated the contemporary proliferation of this form of writing in a literary heritage reaching back to Musset, Lamartine, Rousseau, and Prévost. Joachim Merlant, in *Le Roman personnel de Rousseau à Fromentin* (1905), placed even greater emphasis on the links between author and protagonist when he made the *roman personnel* synonymous with the 'roman autobiographique', and argued that it is thematic features, rather than any common formal attributes, that define the *roman personnel*. Recent theories of autobiography similarly include the *roman personnel* within a broad spectrum of autobiographical texts, but are more formally restrictive in that they include only first-person narratives. Thus in Philippe Lejeune's *Le Pacte autobiographique*, the *roman personnel* complies with the autobiographical model in terms of

4 G. Sand, *Lélia* (1833) (Paris: Classiques Garnier, 1985), p. 164.

form (it is a retrospective account in prose), subject (it is the story of one person's life), and narrative structure (the narrator is also the main character); what distinguishes it from autobiography is the fact that a direct equivalence between the identities of the author and the narrator-protagonist is never established, even if the reader may suspect similarities.

The autobiographical pact underpinning the *roman personnel* is consequently an ambiguous one. Authors exploit the tensions between the generic designation of the work as a novel and the chain of identification linking author, narrator, and main character. They deploy a range of techniques which give the impression that their works contain autobiographical revelations: for instance, concealing dates and names of people and places, thus creating the impression that sensitive information is deliberately being withheld to protect the individuals concerned; incorporating 'real' documents such as private diaries or re-discovered letters; and even engaging in more or less explicit nameplay, most famously in François-René de Chateaubriand's 1802 tale, *René*. But they also frequently insist on the fictional nature of the story told and deny any autobiographical intent. Constant's preface to the second edition of *Adolphe* contains this blanket denial: 'aucun des caractères tracés dans *Adolphe* n'a de rapport avec aucun des individus que je connais' ('none of the characters depicted in *Adolphe* bears any relation to any individual I know');[5] and Balzac's preface to *Le Lys dans la vallée* includes a similar disclaimer. Unlike contemporary forms of writing which similarly blur the boundaries between fiction and autobiography, but in which the autobiographical dimension is explicit – as the definition of 'autofiction' which Serge Doubrovsky gives in his 1977 novel *Fils* makes clear: 'fiction, d'événements et de faits *strictement réels*' ('a fiction made up of events and facts which are *plainly real*') (my emphasis)[6] – the *roman personnel* generally avoids the conflation of author's and narrator's/hero's identities which Doubrovsky's work stages explicitly (even *René* remains somewhat elusive in this regard). While the ambiguous pact which they proposed to readers was an important element of their popularity, in that it left readers guessing as to whether the secrets divulged were those of the author or not, it is not their quasi-autobiographical content that has ensured their enduring interest, and criticism has long since given up seeking out the autobiographical facts concealed within the fictional narratives.

Romans personnels are in fact first and foremost novels, and highly self-conscious ones at that. Their intense awareness of their place on a

5 Constant, *Adolphe*, p. 4.   6 S. Doubrovsky, *Fils* (Paris: Éditions Galilée, 1977).

fictional map and as part of a network of other texts frequently manifests itself in prefaces. The 'Note de l'Éditeur' included in the 1837 edition of Krüdener's *Valérie*, declares that the novel 'enrichi[t] cette famille de livres intimes' ('adds to this body of intimate writing'),[7] and goes on to list *Werther, René, Adolphe, Édouard, Obermann,* and *Volupté* as the key exemplars of the form. We find a similar strategy in Constant's preface to the second edition of *Adolphe*, which sets the novel alongside *René, Delphine,* and *Corinne*, whereas Balzac writes *Le Lys dans la vallée* with the express desire to rewrite (and improve on) *Volupté* following Sainte-Beuve's negative review of his *La Recherche de l'Absolu*. Such intertextual references also proliferate in the narratives themselves. In *Volupté*, the protagonist, Amaury, confesses to the influence *René* had on him: 'J'ai lu *René* et j'ai frémi; je m'y suis reconnu tout entier' ('I read *René* and shuddered; I recognised myself completely in it');[8] *Lélia* evokes Senancour and Rousseau as examples of suffering and passion;[9] and the title of Musset's *La Confession d'un enfant du siècle* alludes indirectly to Sand's novel, for it is here that the expression 'enfant du siècle' is first used in a description of Lélia's would-be lover, Sténio.[10] It is also worth noting the number of protagonists who are also writers: Corinne and Sténio are poets, Dominique has published poetry and political works, and, in an important addition to the second edition of Obermann, the protagonist announces his decision to write not the story of his own life, but a philosophical treatise (Lettre xc). Finally, the literary self-awareness of the *roman personnel* also translates into the thematic structure of these novels by way of a heightened interest in linguistic and discursive power. Allusions to the inadequacy of language pepper René's confession, and a comparable mistrust of language's ability to give form and meaning to feelings is articulated at the beginning of *Adolphe* (Chapter ii). This is to be contrasted with the deft rhetorical strategies deployed in these first-person narratives, in which language is manipulated for maximum effect on the reader/listener. Thus while Adolphe affirms his aversion to maxims and aphorisms, he is not above using them himself as part of a strategy that aims to deny personal responsibility by reference to generalisations on human behaviour (whose choice is always motivated by self-interest on the part of the narrator-protagonist). Adolphe's linguistic performance not only compensates for personal and moral failings evident in the story recounted, but also problematises a mimetic conceptualisation of representation whereby language is understood to copy or mirror the real.

7 J. de Krüdener, *Valérie* (1803) (Paris: Ollivier, 1837), p. ix.
8 C.-A. Sainte-Beuve, *Volupté*, 2 vols. (Paris: Imprimerie Nationale, 1984), I, p. 243.
9 Sand, *Lélia*, p. 68.   10 Ibid., pp. 277 and 303.

Women writers frequently diverged from the dominant model of the narrating male 'je', though it is striking that there is no corresponding shift in their work towards a female 'je'. None, in fact, writes a novel conforming to the model of either *René* or *Adolphe* in which the 'je' of the author might be seen to overlap with the 'je' of the text. This can largely be explained by the autobiographical underpinnings of the *roman personnel*, and by the fact that when it came to confessions of a personal nature, the stakes were very different for women writers compared to their male counterparts. As a result, they deploy a range of additional distancing techniques in their fictional transposition of lived experience: Staël's *Corinne* is written in the third person and *Delphine* is an epistolary novel; Duras's *Édouard* and Krüdener's *Valérie* are written from the point of view of the male character, the latter in the form of an epistolary exchange between the male protagonists in which the heroine's voice – and desires – are barely heard; and in *Ourika*, Duras writes from the point of view of a heroine whose social situation and racial identity distance her from the author. While Sand deploys a polyphonic narrative form in *Lélia* thereby disrupting the dominance of a single voice, this was insufficient to prevent the heroine's frank confession of sexual frigidity from being read as a less than veiled reference to the author's own sexual pathology. But Sand gave a new edition of the novel in 1839, in which the heroine's physiological frigidity was transformed into a metaphysical malaise. Thus while the *mal du siècle* is indeed a predominantly male malady, the *Lélia* of 1839 constitutes an important exception to this rule.

In light of the dominance of the male voice in the *roman personnel*, feminist criticism has highlighted the concomitant silencing of the female characters, and the role these novels play in the promotion of an ideal of non-desiring femininity. Naomi Schor has argued for the exemplary status of *Atala* in this regard. Chateaubriand's novel celebrates not the desiring and unfettered heroine, who in the early part of the novel liberates the imprisoned Chactas, but the sexually pure Atala who commits suicide to avoid breaking the vow of chastity which she swore to her mother. For Schor, then, Atala 'puts into place a cultural construction of femininity adequate to the reactionary sexual regime brought into being by the French Revolution'.[11]

However, insofar as gender is at the core of the *roman personnel*'s preoccupations, it is with masculinity rather than femininity that it is principally concerned. Marginalised from the social, economic, and conjugal contexts in

---

11 S. Melzer and L. Rabine, *Rebel Daughters: Women and the French Revolution* (Oxford: Oxford University Press, 1992), p. 144.

which manhood is both constructed and affirmed, the heroes of these novels embody a deficient masculinity, though, as Margaret Waller has argued, one that achieves 'compensatory empowerment' through the act of narration.[12] This is made manifest in these novels through the narrator's isolation from a father figure, when he is not – as is the case in *Volupté* and *Valérie* – the surrogate father's rival in love. René's marginalisation from patriarchal society and its root cause are encapsulated in the statement: 'je fus élevé loin du toit paternel' ('I was brought up far from my father's house').[13] But it is in *Adolphe* that the processes of patriarchal self-perpetuation are most insistently challenged in the failure of the son to replicate the model of masculinity embodied by the father. This expectation is articulated in the opening pages of Adolphe's narrative when he exposes his father's project as one in which, after a period spent travelling, he would return to take up a position in his father's ministerial cabinet. He speaks not of his own ambitions, but subsumes his destiny entirely within the phrase 'l'intention de mon père' ('my father's intention').[14] The hero, however, sets himself on a collision course with the path charted by the father when he falls in love with Ellénore, and allows his life choices to be dominated by this relationship. The implications of this in terms of the hero's failure to conform to masculine codes of behaviour, and his consequent feminisation, are reinforced lexically as his and Ellénore's personalities are established as mirror images of the other, in which the terms 'rêverie', 'taciturnité', and 'impressions fougueuses' ('reverie', 'silence', and 'passionate feelings') apply to both characters. The father's voice is constantly heard by way of the letters which act as reminders to Adolphe of his masculine duty. Thus, when he flees with Ellénore, his father's letter reminds him that his destiny is to be fulfilled in the public rather than the private sphere: 'votre naissance, vos talents, votre fortune, vous assignaient dans le monde une autre place que celle de compagnon d'une femme' ('your place in the world, by your birth, talents and fortune, should be a very different one from that of companion to a woman').[15] The novel concludes on Adolphe's failure to return to the patriarchal fold after Ellénore's death: we are told in one of the postfaces that 'il n'a suivi aucune route fixe, rempli aucune carrière utile' ('he followed no set path, had no productive career').[16]

In *Adolphe*, the father's presence, as well as the three prefatory chapters and the two letters included as a coda to the novel, draw our attention to the homosocial framework that structures the exchange of narrative in these

12 M. Waller, *The Male Malady* (New Brunswick, NJ: Rutgers University Press, 1993), p. 8.
13 F.-R. de Chateaubriand, *René* (1802) (Paris: Flammarion, 1994), p. 169.
14 Constant, *Adolphe*, p. 19.   15 Ibid., p. 85.   16 Ibid., p. 150.

novels, for these are stories that are traded between men, often over the body of the heroine. When Chactas agrees to tell René the story of his past and his love for Atala, this functions symbolically as a sign of René's integration into the Indian tribe, and cements his bond to Chactas who has adopted him as his son and given him a wife (the exchange of narrative thus mirrors and consolidates this earlier exchange of a woman). These narrative frames also ensure that the hero's story is contained within a clear ideological framework in which his failure to align himself with the norms of patriarchal masculinity is highlighted. This is the function of the uncompromising judgement, which Père Souël offers at the conclusion of René's narrative, and in which he dismisses René as a young man whose head is full of wild fantasies, condemns his nonconformity, narcissism, and self-indulgent melancholy, and reminds the hero of his social and conjugal responsibilities. In Fromentin's *Dominique*, such voices are, however, absent, though the silence of Dominique's interlocutor at the conclusion of the narrative may be read as a natural consequence of the gendered order which reigns at the end of this novel and which requires no corrective. While it is true that Dominique's urge to tell his story suggests that his Romantic past still has a hold over him, his rejection of Romantic chimera means that as a narrator he embodies the values of bourgeois masculinity, and his status as husband, father, landowner, and mayor confirms him as a fully (re-)productive member of society.

This focus on questions of gender highlights the significant social dimension to the *roman personnel*. In his preface to *René*, Chateaubriand links the deficiencies of the contemporary male to the corrupting influence of feminine qualities in post-revolutionary society, and thus points to the importance of socio-historical context for understanding this individual malaise. It soon becomes clear that while the historical allusions in the novel suggest that *René* is set in the early eighteenth century, its plot resonates in significant ways with more contemporary events. The anxiety, instability, and transience that typify the hero's condition, not to mention the theme of exile common to both *René* and *Atala*, evoke the situation of the French aristocracy in the wake of the Revolution. Later novels will look back to the Empire as a period that offered men the opportunity to affirm their manhood by seeking military glory. In *Volupté*, Amaury idealises the army as the means to 'conquérir nations et femmes' ('conquer nations and women'),[17] the formulation tellingly linking public and private performances of masculinity. Musset's *Confession d'un enfant du siècle* offers a lengthy contrast between the opportunities for action and glory

17 Sainte-Beuve, *Volupté*, II, p. 45.

during Napoleon's reign, and the fossilisation of society under the Restoration Monarchy, and expresses the disorientation of a generation of men, 'nés au sein de la guerre, pour la guerre' ('born in the midst of war and for war'),[18] and who find no outlets for their energy in a moribund post-Empire society. Women writers also used the *roman personnel* as a vehicle for social commentary and criticism. *Lélia* has much to say about the marriage laws of the early nineteenth century and the ways they affected women. And in *Ourika*, the story of an African slave brought up in a French aristocratic family, Duras uses the structures of the romance plot to expose racial prejudices, for it is only when the question of marriage is raised that the social reality of Ourika's position as a black woman in white aristocratic society comes into sharp focus. As these examples demonstrate, the scope of the *roman personnel*, born from the social and political instability of post-revolutionary France, ultimately extends well beyond the portrayal of individual experience, and bears witness to the trauma of a whole generation.

18 A. de Musset, *La Confession d'un enfant du siècle* (Paris: Gallimard, 1973), p. 22.

50

Romanticism: art, literature, and history

MICHÈLE HANNOOSH

Qu'est-ce que le romantisme? (*What Is Romanticism?*) When the young Baude-laire posed this question in a chapter-heading of his first major publication, the *Salon de 1846*, French Romanticism was at least a quarter-century old. Indeed, he was reopening a question which had already been debated in some highly celebrated works by Hugo, Stendhal, and Musset, and which Stendhal in particular had seemingly answered: a famous chapter of the latter's *Racine et Shakespeare* of 1823 was entitled 'Ce que c'est que le romanticisme' ('What Romanticism Is'). Baudelaire's return to this question long after the fact sug-gests to what extent Romanticism designated more than a group of individuals devoted to particular artistic practices or even to particular conceptions of art. As Charles Rosen and Henri Zerner observe, the history of Romanticism is a history of redefinitions.[1] Many scholars have referred to 'Romanticisms': different conceptions of the term according to period, nationality, art form, or discipline.[2] Not least is the problem of defining a movement which was based on a *refusal* to establish and apply norms.[3]

Yet, as Baudelaire's *Salon* shows, debates about Romanticism continued, well into the nineteenth century, to concentrate and define the terms of a *modern* art and aesthetics. 'To say Romanticism is to say modern art', he wrote: 'that is, intimacy, spirituality, colour, aspiration toward the infinite, expressed by all the means that the arts possess'.[4] However much this retro-spective view may have given to Romanticism more definite contours than

---

1 C. Rosen and H. Zerner, *Romanticism and Realism: The Mythology of Nineteenth-Century Art* (London: Faber and Faber, 1984), p. 16.
2 G. Gusdorf, *Le Romantisme* (1982–4), 2 vols. (Paris: Payot, 1993), I, pp. 160–2; J.-C. Caron, 'Aux âmes bien nées . . . ou romantisme et génération(s)', in S. Allard (ed.), *Paris 1820: l'affirmation de la génération romantique* (Berne: Peter Lang, 2005), p. 41; H. Honour, *Romanticism* (New York: Harper and Row, 1979), pp. 11–20; P. Wat, *Naissance de l'art romantique: peinture et théorie de l'imitation* (Paris: Flammarion, 1998), pp. 5–8.
3 Rosen and Zerner, *Romanticism and Realism*, p. 23; Wat, *Naissance de l'art romantique*, pp. 8–9.
4 C. Baudelaire, *Salon de 1846*, in *Œuvres complètes*, ed. Claude Pichois, 4 vols. (Paris: Gallimard, 1976), II, p. 421. Translations are mine.

it had had in its 1820s heyday, the emphasis on the modern was not a mere imposition, on an earlier moment, of current aesthetic concerns. Stendhal had already affirmed the crucial association between Romanticism and the modern with typical comic impudence: 'Romanticism is the art of presenting to the peoples of the world those literary works which, in the current state of their practices and their beliefs, are likely to give them the most pleasure possible'; 'Classicism . . . presents to them that literature which gave the most pleasure possible to their great-grandfathers'.[5]

'The current state of their practices and their beliefs': in the plethora of features, often contradictory, which characterised those works to which the term 'Romantic' was applied, this 'appropriateness to the times' is a constant. 'A new art for a new people', wrote Hugo in the preface to his 1830 play, *Hernani*, the opening night of which came to be considered a founding moment of Romanticism.[6] This did not mean a rejection of the past; for many, Sophocles, Euripides, Dante, and most of all Shakespeare, were Romantic because they created works that reflected the 'spirit' of their age – what Baudelaire called 'la morale du siècle'.[7] The Romantic programme formulated by Stendhal involved imitating Shakespeare on this one point: 'The Romantics do not urge anyone to imitate Shakespeare's dramas directly. What should be imitated in this great man is his way of studying the world in which we live, and the art of giving to our contemporaries . . . the kind of tragedy that they need', a tragedy 'called for by their mores'.[8] Racine himself, Stendhal asserts, was Romantic in his time, depicting passion tempered by a 'dignity' which spoke to the public of the court of Louis XIV. Baudelaire goes a step further, mocking those who 'blaspheme the Greeks and Romans in the name of Romanticism', and stating: 'Romanticism lies not specifically in the choice of subjects, nor in exact truth, but in a way of feeling . . . For me, Romanticism is the most recent, the most current expression of the beautiful.'[9]

In this regard, Romanticism was a coming to terms with the fact of history, a recognition of the historical nature of the nonetheless enduring idea of the beautiful. This would later define the Baudelairean concept of modernity – 'the transitory, fleeting, and contingent', that half of the beautiful of which the other half is the eternal and invariable.[10] The relation between contemporary

---

5 Stendhal, *Racine et Shakespeare*, ed. P. Martino, 2 vols. (Paris: Champion, 1925), I, p. 39.
6 Victor Hugo, *Hernani, ou L'Honneur Castillan: drame* (Paris: Mame, Delaunay-Vallee, 1830), p. iii. In the Preface to *Cromwell* (1827) he had similarly asserted that a new society demanded a new poetry.
7 Baudelaire, *Salon de 1846*, II, p. 421.   8 Stendhal, *Racine et Shakespeare*, I, p. 40.
9 Baudelaire, *Salon de 1846*, II, p. 420.
10 C. Baudelaire, *Le Peintre de la vie moderne*, in *Œuvres complètes*, II, p. 695.

mores and particular art forms had been often affirmed before, notably in connection with ancient art;[11] but the *necessity* of this relationship, and thus of artistic change, was a fundamental tenet of Romanticism. Mme de Staël had argued for the relationship between literature and social institutions in her *De la littérature* of 1800, which sought to analyse the moral and political forces which brought about artistic change. In his essay, 'Des variations du beau' (1857), Eugène Delacroix asserted both the vicissitudes of the beautiful in its diverse historical and cultural circumstances, and its stability as the beautiful:

> [The beautiful] undergoes, absolutely, like habits and ideas, all sorts of meta-morphoses. I am not saying...that it can vary in its essence, since then it would not be the beautiful, but only whim or fancy; its character, however, can change. A certain face of the beautiful which captivated a distant civilisa-tion does not surprise or please us as much as does the one which responds to our sentiments or, if you like, to our prejudices.[12]

For the 1820s, the period when French Romanticism was named, theorised, and associated with a literary and a pictorial practice, the present required a dramatically new artistic approach consistent with the magnitude of the historical change which had taken place in the preceding three decades: 'Never in history has a people gone through a more rapid and total change, in its mores and its pleasures, than in the period 1780 to 1823; and they still want us to have the same literature!' exclaims Stendhal indignantly. 'The same literature' was that of Classicism, the rules of which, established primarily in connection with seventeenth-century tragedy, still dominated the literary genres until the late eighteenth century. The existential 'changes' evoked by Stendhal were seen to have their historical counterparts in the Revolution and, to a lesser extent, the Empire. 'While admiring the literature of the age of Louis XIV, so well adapted to monarchy, contemporary France will be able to have its own literature... the France of the nineteenth century to which Mirabeau gave liberty and Napoleon power', wrote Hugo in the preface to *Hernani*. The association had already been made by Mme de Staël in *De la littérature*, where she sought to define the changes which the new institutions of liberty and political equality would bring about in the character of French

---

11 Winckelmann's *History of the Art of Antiquity* (1764) was a notable example. Numerous Enlight-enment writers (Voltaire, Marmontel) followed the same principle of relating works of art to the civilisation in which they were produced.
12 E. Delacroix, *Écrits sur l'art*, ed. Francois-Marie Deyrolle and Christophe Denissel (Paris: Séguier, 1988), p. 39.

writing.[13] Although painting followed a somewhat different historical course – Classicism in painting took hold *during* the Revolution, in opposition to the rococo style of the eighteenth century, and as an expression of republican ideals of virtue, valour, and citizenship – Romanticism in painting was nevertheless seen to express the 'spirit' of revolution and the changes in attitude, as in real circumstances, initiated by the Revolution itself. And the alliance of painting and literature around these same values and models was seen to be a feature of Romanticism.[14]

Romanticism was deeply embedded in history in another sense, too: its alliance with a specifically revolutionary history was forged in an era which by definition denied that same history, the Restoration. Romanticism was the child of the deliberate anachronism that was Restoration France, and some of its chief features corresponded to the equivocal situation of an official ideology of reaction in a post-revolutionary and post-Napoleonic society. The importance of exile as a psychological state, a social mode of being, or a political and personal fact, so prominent in the Romantic imaginary, bears a close relation to the ambiguous status of a movement that took shape within a political and social reality in which its very basis was disavowed. In turn, the Revolution of 1830 was perceived to be the manifestation, and perhaps the consequence, of Romanticism itself.[15]

The 'new' consciousness represented by Romanticism was built on these two foundations: it defined itself in *opposition* to a 'Classicism' identified with a pre-revolutionary existence and mentality, and in *accordance* with the political, philosophical, and social values associated with the newly formed nation. In this respect, French Romanticism arose in a period of crisis, much as early German Romanticism had in the last few years of the eighteenth century: the social and moral crisis of a bourgeoisie which came to power and acquired wealth but within a social structure restored to its pre-revolutionary state, and complicated by the return of an aristocracy which had been absent for a quarter of a century; a political crisis associated with the Restoration's repudiation and repression of the Revolution and Empire; a philosophical crisis linked to Kantian philosophy, transmitted through Mme de Staël's *De l'Allemagne* (1810), which complicated Classical distinctions between subject and object, sense and spirit, real and ideal. As with the early German Romantic movement studied by Jean-Luc Nancy and Philippe Lacoue-Labarthe, literature and theory were, for

---

13 G. de Staël, *De la littérature*, ed. Axel Blaeschke (Paris: Classiques Garnier, 1998), Part II, chap. 1, p. 286. Stendhal, *Racine et Shakespeare*, 1, p. 45; Hugo, *Hernani*, p. iii.
14 T. Gautier, 'Eugène Delacroix', in *Écrivains et artistes romantiques* (Paris: Plon, 1933), p. 232.
15 Gusdorf, *Le Romantisme*, 1, p. 145.

French Romanticism too, the privileged expression of a more general critique – social, moral, and political.[16] Literature as critique and, conversely, critique as literature: French Romanticism shared in this conception of a 'literary absolute', variously called Poetry, Art, or the Ideal, which had ramifications well beyond aesthetics. While it did not generate a discourse of metaphysics, French Romantic literature was itself a kind of philosophy, and was thus all the more, not less, connected to a social function and a historical mission: expressing the particular character of the post-revolutionary present.

Not that there was any easy correlation between aesthetics and political allegiances: many Romantics began – and some remained – monarchists. But the values of the two systems were deeply political. Classicism had belonged to a social order guaranteed by an absolute monarch, and Classical values in art and literature reflected the social and ideological values (if not the realities) of the *ancien régime* – hierarchy and proportion, order, regularity and stability, moderation, discipline and restraint, harmony, wholeness and unity, good taste and appropriateness, symmetry and balance. Romanticism was associated with the post-revolutionary, democratic age, with its emphasis on freedom, equality and the individual. It was a discourse of spontaneity and freedom, passion, drama and theatricality, multiplicity, variety and difference, the disproportionate and fragmentary, excess and extravagance, deformity and distortion, sublime and grotesque.

Romantic writers and artists thus rejected the strict, and in their view restrictive and constraining, rules which had governed Classical art: fixed forms and conventions; the unities of time and place, according to which the action had to happen in a single place, within a space of twenty-four hours (only the unity of action was retained); the 'tyranny' of the alexandrine, the twelve-syllable line of French Classical tragedy; an allusive and formulaic 'literary' language; a proscription on represented violence and excess; plausibility, wholeness, and consistency; adherence to the norms of acceptable behaviour; in painting, symmetrical composition, linear perspective, sobriety and austerity of form, linear drawing, finish. Romanticism instead advocated formal freedom, a mixture of high and low language, spontaneous expression, hybridity, abundance, colour, movement, and sketchiness. Shakespeare was the model of the Romantic writer precisely because of his 'shocking' manner of mingling

---

16 J.-L. Nancy and P. Lacoue-Labarthe, *L'Absolu littéraire: théorie de la littérature du romantisme allemand* (Paris: Seuil, 1978). Paul Bénichou concentrates on the religious character of this new role accorded to art, in which poetry becomes the highest value and the writer becomes a successor to the philosopher of the preceding age. *Le Sacre de l'écrivain 1750–1830: essai sur l'avènement d'un pouvoir spirituel laïque dans la France moderne* (Paris: Corti, 1973), p. 275.

within a single work both comedy and tragedy, obscenity and nobility, high poetic language and popular dialect, vulgar puns and polished rhetoric, fantasy and realism. That Hamlet could be joking with the gravediggers at one moment, and deliver his famous monologue on the finality of death – 'Alas, poor Yorick' – in the next, was, from a French perspective, outlandish. His violent and abusive treatment of Ophelia, with its explicit sexual accusations, was excluded from the domain of the French Classical writer. The performances of Shakespeare by an English troupe in Paris in 1827 provided a rallying-point: Hector Berlioz, who attended them, wrote in his *Mémoires* that Shakespeare 'struck him like a thunderbolt', and made him see 'true dramatic grandeur, beauty, and truth . . . and the pitiful paltriness of our old poetics of pedagogues and friars'.[17] Hugo's *Hernani*, so emblematic of Romantic theatre, is eminently Shakespearean, something of a cross between *Hamlet*, in the hero, and *Romeo and Juliet*, in the plot, veering between comedy, by the end of Act IV, and the most excruciating tragedy, in Act V. 'Shakespearean' was the term by which the art critic Étienne-Jean Delécluze first designated the Romantic painters at the 1824 Salon, comparing Delacroix's *Massacres at Chios* to the final act of a Shakespearean tragedy.[18]

Romanticism represented not only a rejection of Classical values, but an inversion of them. The commonplace and trivial became sources of the beautiful and worthy subjects of art, which was no longer limited to the exploits of gods and heroes. As in a revolutionary ideology, in art too the great were dethroned and the lowly raised up. What had been considered inappropriate for high art was now privileged, notably everyday life, contemporary history, the ugly and grotesque. Hugo set out this principle in the *Préface de Cromwell*: in life, he argued, ugliness exists alongside beauty, the deformed alongside the graceful, the grotesque with the sublime, evil with good, darkness with light, and art should be likewise. For Hugo, this union of opposites characterises the modern spirit, as opposed to the 'uniform simplicity' of Classicism. Quasimodo, the grotesque hunchback who is the hero of his novel, *Notre-Dame de Paris* (1831), represents the principle of beauty in ugliness: 'in all this deformity, some imposing air of vigour, agility and courage; making a strange exception to the eternal rule by which strength, like beauty, comes from harmony'.[19] The

---

17 H. Berlioz, *Mémoires*, ed. Pierre Citron (Paris: Flammarion, 1991), chap. XVIII, p. 112.
18 E.-J. Delécluze, *Journal des débats*, 5 October 1824 and 19 January 1825. See M. C. Chaudonneret, *L'État et les artistes: de la Restauration à la monarchie de Juillet (1815–1833)* (Paris: Flammarion, 1999), pp. 80–6.
19 V. Hugo, *Notre-Dame de Paris*, ed. Jacques Seebacher and Yves Gohin (Paris: Gallimard, 1975), Part I, chap. 5, p. 52.

'lowly' included all that had been considered marginal and unworthy of representation formerly: the people, women, peasants, criminals, and prostitutes, now recognised as historical agents (as in Michelet's histories of witchcraft, of Joan of Arc, of the people), and as literary and artistic subjects too.

The same refusal of Classical hierarchies is evident in the settings of Romantic works. In painting, the traditional hierarchy of genres, with history painting at the top, followed by genre, portraiture, landscape, and still-life, was dismantled. Whereas Classicism had required subjects drawn from the exemplary realm of ancient history, Romanticism privileged other eras, especially the Middle Ages, the Renaissance, and the present. From the Gothic fantasy of Hugo's *Notre-Dame de Paris*, set in fifteenth-century Paris, to the 'chronicle of 1830' which, as the subtitle to Stendhal's *Le Rouge et le noir*, identifies the story as contemporary with its publication; from 'troubadour' painting on anecdotal medieval and Renaissance subjects to Géricault's *Radeau de la Méduse* (1818) and Delacroix's *Le 28 juillet: la Liberté guidant le peuple* (1831), both based on contemporary events, painting and literature drew on a broad spectrum of historical periods previously excluded from the domain of serious art. Delacroix reported with incredulity Jacques-Louis David's reproach of his former pupil Antoine-Jean Gros, already the painter of *Napoleon visiting the plague house at Jaffa*, *The Battle of Aboukir*, *Napoléon on the battlefield of Eylau*, and other major history paintings, for producing only 'incidental paintings' based on 'trivial subjects', rather than 'a true history painting', that is, on a subject from Greek or Roman history.[20]

The historical novel, which emerged in this period, is symptomatic of Romanticism's relation to, and treatment of, the past. Inspired by Walter Scott, whose novels had enormous success in France in the 1820s, Chateaubriand, Hugo, Balzac, Dumas, and Vigny all wrote in this genre. The historical novel not only recreated the past to illuminate the present, it established a past for a nation which had ostensibly overthrown it, defining a new national and social identity after the old one had been seemingly swept away. Moreover depicting the powerful figures of history as common characters, and locating true heroism in courage, cleverness, and intelligence, the historical novel reflected democratic ideals of equality and opportunity, as opposed to the privileges of birth.

The democratic emphasis on the individual which characterised the political developments of the late eighteenth century marked Romantic philosophy and art as well. The self had been the starting point for all knowledge even in the

---

20 Delacroix, 'Gros', in *Écrits sur l'art*, p. 201.

Classical tradition of Descartes. But a *focus* on the self was a feature of Romanticism: inspired by German philosophy, notably that of Kant and Schlegel, the Romantics asked what constituted the self, how it could be known and what could be apprehended beyond it. Self-analysis, self-interrogation, and self-discovery thus became common themes; first-person narration was used commonly in both poetry and prose; autobiographical forms such as diaries, memoirs, and 'testimonial' genres came to the fore, as writers sought, fictitiously or not, to create or affirm a self through writing; to control, or simply to follow, through writing, the mobility of a self set loose by – and into – history.

Isolation and solitude accompanied this emphasis on individualism. The Romantic hero or heroine often stands apart and alone, on the margins of society, in physical or spiritual exile. The heroic outcasts of the Western literary tradition – those who rejected received ideas and values, and dared to act accordingly – serve as recurrent Romantic models: Faust, Satan, Cain, Don Juan, the quintessential non-conformists, the great, unrepentant transgressors. In a society in which responsibility was sometimes brutally conferred upon the individual, the sense of limitless possibility was matched by a kind of despair. The individual's search for happiness, peace, and inner tranquillity sometimes brought instead a restless agitation, unsatisfied desire, melancholy, and lassitude – what the Romantics called *ennui* or *spleen*. Chateaubriand's *René* is perhaps the most extreme example of this, as the hero wanders the Earth in search of knowledge, happiness, and community, but continually feels himself in a desert or a tomb. Much Romantic literature takes pleasure in this ennui, a depth and intensity of feeling which rivals the sublime – Baudelaire's 'delicate monster' which forms the fraternal bond between poet and reader in 'Au lecteur', the liminal poem of *Les Fleurs du Mal*.

The alienation of the modern individual was both realised and overcome in Nature, which provided a mythical refuge from the ills of society and civilisation. Nature mirrored the soul or revealed the divine; oneness with Nature became an ideal. Chateaubriand's *Atala* takes place in the New World, a kind of garden of Eden where people seem to live in a golden-age simplicity and happiness; paintings by Delacroix and Ary Scheffer inspired by this work won great acclaim. George Sand's novel *Indiana* (1832) is partly set on an exotic island, a place of authenticity and genuine feeling in contrast to the corruption, falsehood, and deceit of European society. Nature also inspired the awe and wonder of the sublime, a crucial Romantic concept. The sublime was defined as the sudden perception of transcendent greatness, of something markedly superior to the perceiving subject. In Romantic art it is associated with stunning natural scenery, such as the Alps or the sea. It is incalculable and immeasurable, undefinable and inexpressible. It can be represented only through *creating* the experience in art.

As the intuition of something beyond the individual, the sublime constitutes an antidote to the Romantic problem of solipsism, of the individual's otherwise inescapable enclosure in the self, with no possibility of communication with others, divorced from humanity and the absolute alike. This predicament, and the individual's awareness of it, constitutes Romantic irony: the individual's imprisonment in the self while conscious of existences beyond it. The Romantic self comes to the unsettling realisation that identity depends on alterity, and is defined as a relation to others, but realises equally the impossibility of transcending the self to know those 'others'. Much Romantic literature is concerned with the individual's capacity, or incapacity, to escape the confines of the self. The imagination was Romanticism's answer to this problem; the experience of the sublime was its immediate proof; and the function of art was to create the conditions by which such self-transcendence could come about. The 'ironic' position which might otherwise be intolerable – the dual condition of being aware of a beyond but limited to ourselves – becomes the means by which we overcome the problem, taking on, through art, an alternative self or many alternative selves, which give us perspectives on ourselves. In his prose poem, 'Les Foules', Baudelaire calls this the privilege of the poet, which applies to the reader as well: 'The poet enjoys the incomparable privilege of being able, at will, to be himself and another.'

The emphasis on the self brought the work of creation into the realm of the individual imagination. The 'queen of faculties', as Baudelaire called it in his *Salon de 1859*, the imagination had the creative power formerly associated only with the Almighty. It decomposed the impressions the mind received from the external world and refashioned them into something new. Baudelaire quotes Delacroix's analogy between the external world and a dictionary: the Romantic artist does not copy the 'dictionary', i.e. imitate external reality, but takes from it 'words and phrases' to formulate a new and different idea. Thus the traditional metaphor of art as a mirror – of life, of nature, of society – took on a special twist, for the Romantic mirror was one that altered the reflection, sending back an image that was an 'interpretation', a 'translation', of the subject – a revelatory image, which could show something unknown about the known, the truth behind the appearance, or the possibilities beyond the given. The creative and revelatory power of the imagination accounts for the Romantic interest in the fantastic, the supernatural, the occult, the irrational, the mysterious, the world of dreams, and the unconscious. This visionary spirit was an attempt to penetrate the facade of reason, science, and logic by which we attempt to control an unwieldy and confusing experience; for many Romantics, truth lay behind this, in realms as yet unexplored. Nerval's *Aurélia* recounts the narrator's terrifying and exhilarating journey into the world of his own dreams and ultimately his own madness. Mérimée, Gautier, and Balzac mingled the highly realistic with the fantastic and bizarre, suggesting the extent to which these existed in our everyday lives, within the most believable situations, in the heart of modern Paris itself.

The means of Romantic representation, concentrated in sensuality and powerful feeling – extravagance, exaggeration, materiality, an evocative language, colourism in painting – were consistent with the idea that the representation was a creation in itself, not a derivative image of a superior original. On a theoretical level, this effort to create and affirm real presence in the representation may be taken as nostalgic, an attempt to fill a void, to respond to a sense of loss, to an apprehension, unconscious perhaps, of isolation and separateness. Nostalgia, and the feelings associated with it, indeed figure among the more prominent themes of Romantic art: the emphasis on melancholy and ennui, on memory and the past, on absence and death, on crumbling ruins and bygone glory certainly suggests a regret for something that can never be recovered. The nature and causes of this void were multiple – the loss of authority and security involved in the weakening of political regimes, the loss of philosophical certainty which the Enlightenment provoked, an increasing anxiety about individual responsibility in the face of newly won liberties. Yet by affirming reality and presence, Romantic art can be seen to create the 'absent' ideal through the representation. Thus the superior, transcendent phenomenon which is the sublime is apprehended from within the 'inferior', phenomenal world; it is unrepresentable, but is discovered through the representation. Through the material poem or painting, the imagination conceives of the absolute which lies beyond its limits.

To sum up, if Classicism implies discipline, moderation, and order, Romanticism evokes spontaneity, extravagance, and freedom; Classicism involves invention within convention, Romanticism the creative imagination; if Classicism goes with absolute monarchy, a hierarchy of power and value, a stable authority, Romanticism goes with revolution, democracy, egalitarianism; Classicism is good taste and appropriateness, Romanticism is passion, drama, and theatricality, sublime and grotesque; Classicism is normative, positing a standard behaviour to which all should aspire, whilst Romanticism delights in eccentricity, the unusual, and the strange; Classicism privileges the public order, Romanticism individualism and the self; Classicism is reason,

Romanticism the fantastic, supernatural, and irrational; Classicism is proportion and symmetry, Romanticism disproportion and irregularity; the Classical ideal was unity, harmony, and wholeness, the Romantic ideal multiplicity, variety, difference, and the fragment. For all the distinctions between the arts, or among works, genres, periods, and individual practitioners, a loosely adequate image of Romanticism emerges from these oppositions. At its foundation was an engagement with history as a new mode of being, and with the particular history subsequent upon the Revolution.

Although the term 'Romantic' came to be replaced by others, notably 'modern', as the century progressed, the key role played by Baudelaire as a theorist of both Romanticism and modernity suggests to what extent the two concepts were linked. All the features of Romanticism discussed above recur in Baudelaire's conception of *modernité* and its realisation in his work. From the beauty inherent in the ugliness and freakishness of the modern city, to the fragmented 'unity' of the prose poems; from the poetry of the everyday to the transitory, contingent element of the beautiful dependent on 'the times, fashion, mores, passion';[21] from ironic dualism to its transcendence in the form of imaginative ironic doubling; from alienation from nature to the perception of *correspondances* among nature's diverse elements, and between objects and ideas; from otherworldly dream to the violent, excessive experience of 'flowers of evil' or 'Parisian spleen', *modernité* inherits most of the features which Baudelaire attributes to Romanticism. There is perhaps no better expression of the Romantic individual's insertion in history than Baudelaire's description of the *flâneur*, that quintessential modern urban subject cast 'into the throng, the ebb and flow, movement, the fleeting and infinite' in his iconic essay on modernity, *Le Peintre de la vie moderne*. Through this genealogy, one might concur with the assertion by Nancy and Lacoue-Labarthe that 'a veritable Romantic unconscious' is still today 'detectable in most of the main motifs of our modernity'.[22]

21 Baudelaire, *Le Peintre de la vie moderne*, ii, p. 683.
22 Nancy and Lacoue-Labarthe, *L'Absolu littéraire*, p. 26.

51

Realism

MICHAEL LUCEY

'The word *realism*', wrote Champfleury (pen-name of the minor French novelist and art critic Jules-François-Félix Fleury-Husson) in 1857, 'a transitional term that isn't likely to last more than thirty years, is one of those ambiguous words that lend themselves to all kinds of uses.' He notes that at the moment he is writing critics wield the term mainly as an insult. 'Doubtless a moment will come', he predicts, 'when critics will begin trying to divide writers into *good* realists and *bad* ones.'[1] Champfleury's comments suggest that the word *realism* did not gain widespread use in France as a term for describing or classifying literary texts until the 1850s, well after the two novelists often taken to be the founders of French realism, Balzac and Stendhal, had ceased writing. Its usage in relation to literature has in fact been traced back at least to 1826, when an article in the *Mercure français* suggests that *le réalisme* is likely to be 'the dominant literature of the nineteenth century'. At least one critic, Gustave Planche, used the term in relation to literature several times in the 1830s.[2] Bernard Weinberg confirms that the term starts picking up momentum in relation to literature around 1846 (when Hippolyte Castille refers to Balzac and Mérimée as members of the *École réaliste*), finally gaining 'real currency' in 1851.[3] (The term was at the centre of a polemic in French painting in the 1840s and 1850s as well.)

Champfleury's remarks also reveal that in mid-nineteenth-century contexts *realism* or *realist* were often negative aesthetic evaluations. Associated with the ugliness of empirical observation, *realism* would commonly be juxtaposed to the positively valued term, *idealism*. Idealist art or literature set itself the task of revealing the unchanging ideas or essences providing an abstract basis

1 Champfleury, *Le Réalisme* (Paris: Michel Lévy, 1857), p. 5.
2 See E. B. O. Borgerhoff, '*Réalisme* and Kindred Words: Their Use as Terms of Literary Criticism in the First Half of the Nineteenth Century', *PMLA* 53.3 (1938), pp. 839–42.
3 B. Weinberg, *French Realism: The Critical Reaction, 1830–1870* (New York: Modern Language Association of America, 1937), pp. 118–19.

for the material world.[4] As is the case with many sets of paired terms, the opposition between real and ideal turns out to be a fuzzy one. When in 1842 Balzac composes the 'Avant-propos' for his *Human Comedy*, on the one hand he refers to himself as a secretary taking an inventory of features of the social world around him, thereby emphasising the empirical side of his project; on the other, he foregrounds the abstract or analytical work of creating *types*.[5] Elsewhere he defines a type as 'a character who collects together all the characteristic traits of those who resemble him more or less . . . the model of his genre'.[6] The *type*, a central notion in many discussions of realism, thus involves elements that in their abstraction could be thought of as ideal or essential rather than empirical.

Champfleury's prediction that the term *realism* would last only thirty years was not a good one. The term has been remarkably durable, and some might argue that realist novels continue to be written today. Others assert that the realist novel was a specific historical phenomenon confined to a particular historical period, say the 100 years from Balzac to Céline.[7] Realism – both as writing practice and as critical term – is, in many ways, a problem of labels and categories and the role they play in producing intelligibility. Labelling and categorisation as forms of social and critical action are central both to practices of realism and to critical discussions of it. Realist novels are seen as offering the promise of a certain kind of intelligibility to the world by the way they portray it; critical discussions of realism work to make the term itself distinctive, thereby providing certain kinds of intelligibility to the universe of literary objects. There have been endless discussions of realism's defining characteristics or, in related fashion, of the term's extension. (Does the category *realist novel* extend to Stendhal's *Armance*, Sand's *Indiana*, Flaubert's *Salammbô*, Hugo's *Les Misérables*, Céline's *Voyage au bout de la nuit*, or Simone de Beauvoir's *Les Mandarins*?)

At the conclusion of his study of mid-nineteenth-century writings that employed the term *realism*, Weinberg assembles a list of the features that came to be associated with the emerging category of the realist novel. They include truthful representation of the real world, a newly expanded range of subjects deemed appropriate for novelistic treatment (including subjects previously deemed inappropriately ugly or trivial), a focus on contemporary

4 See N. Schor, *George Sand and Idealism* (New York: Columbia University Press, 1993), pp. 35–47.
5 H. de Balzac, 'Avant-Propos', in *La Comédie humaine*, ed. P.-G. Castex, 12 vols. (Paris: Gallimard, 1976–81), I, p. 11.
6 Balzac, 'Préface' to *Une Ténébreuse Affaire*, in *La Comédie humaine*, VII, p. 493.
7 See J. Dubois, *Les Romanciers du réel de Balzac à Simenon* (Paris: Seuil, 2000).

life and manners, attention to the details of the material world, an analytical approach to the characters portrayed, and a relatively impersonal attitude on the part of the author.[8] Many of these very characteristics are taken up and elaborated in later critical discussions of realism as well. For example, in the conclusion to his classic study, *Mimesis* (1946), Erich Auerbach writes:

> When Stendhal and Balzac took random individuals from daily life in their dependence upon current historical circumstances and made them the subjects of serious, problematic, and even tragic representation, they broke with the classical rule of distinct levels of style, for according to this rule, everyday practical reality could find a place in literature only within the frame of a low or intermediate kind of style, that is to say, as either grotesquely comic or pleasant, light, colorful, and elegant entertainment... And they opened the way for modern realism, which has ever since developed in increasingly rich forms, in keeping with the constantly changing and expanding reality of modern life.[9]

For Auerbach, the 'basic attitude' that characterises modern realism assumes that 'man' cannot be represented 'otherwise than as embedded in a total reality, political, social, and economic, which is concrete and constantly evolving'; realists posit, contrary to previous aesthetic traditions, that 'there are no high and low subjects'.[10] The 'mixture of seriousness and everyday reality' that characterises realism builds on the 'agitation for the mixture of styles' carried out by French Romantics in their polemic against classical aesthetics.[11] Auerbach ties the emergence of realism in France to historical changes revealed and accomplished in events such as the French Revolution and the Revolution of 1830; he seems himself to advocate the realist attitude in literature as part of a democratic ethos: it was realism that 'made it possible for characters of any station, with all the practical everyday complications of their lives – Julien Sorel as well as old Goriot or Madame Vauquer – to become the subject of serious literary representation'.[12]

Auerbach's *Mimesis* offers a systematised approach to realism across all of Western literary history, transforming the loose list of features early critics had collectively identified into a synthetic view of a specific attitude towards the social and material world. Key to Auerbach's synthesis is the notion of a 'total

8 Weinberg, *French Realism*, pp. 193–5.
9 E. Auerbach, *Mimesis: The Representation of Reality in Western Literature*, trans. W. R. Trask (Princeton, NJ: Princeton University Press, 1953), p. 554.
10 Auerbach, *Mimesis*, pp. 555, 463, 487.   11 Ibid., p. 481.
12 Ibid., p. 474. For a more recent approach to realism and democracy, see J. Rancière, 'Why Emma Bovary Had to Be Killed', *Critical Inquiry*, 34.2 (2008), pp. 233–48.

reality' that realism strives to make intelligible. The notion of *totality*, drawn from Hegel's philosophy of history, is also crucial in the writings of György Lukács, another influential critic of French realism. In *The Order of Mimesis*, Christopher Prendergast describes the sense and significance of totality for Lukács and Auerbach as follows:

> The term 'totality' . . . is not to be confused with a purely empirical or quantitative notion; it does not designate the ambition of an exhaustive transcription of contingent particulars . . . it aims at a maximum differentiation of the contingent and the essential . . . The authentic mimetic work thus selects and arranges the essential or representative patterns of experience, and, in so doing, grasps the underlying laws of reality and history, reveals the world in its inner principle of intelligibility.[13]

Auerbach's commentary on the description of the Vauquer *pension* that comes towards the beginning of Balzac's *Père Goriot* provides an instance of this understanding of totality. 'Balzac feels his milieux', Auerbach writes, 'as organic and indeed demonic unities, and seeks to convey this feeling to the reader. He not only . . . places the human beings whose destiny he is seriously relating, in their precisely defined historical and social setting, but also conceives this connection as a necessary one.'[14] Settings are not described for the sake of description; rather the description of the material world has an analytic purpose, carrying explanatory force in relation to both the characters and the action. The abstract unity implied between character, action, setting, and historical moment is crucial to the realist novel's approach to the intelligibility of the world.

The protocols for the construction of a character are another key element in certain visions of the realist novel. In this regard, Lukács is particularly famous for the way he mobilises the notion of the *type*:

> The central category and criterion of realist literature is the type, a peculiar synthesis which organically binds together the general and the particular both in characters and situations. What makes a type a type is not its average quality, not its mere individual being, however profoundly conceived; what makes it a type is that in it all the humanly and socially essential determinants are present on their highest level of development, in the ultimate unfolding of the possibilities latent in them, in extreme presentation of their extremes, rendering concrete the peaks and limits of men and epochs.[15]

13 C. Prendergast, *The Order of Mimesis: Balzac, Stendhal, Nerval, Flaubert* (Cambridge: Cambridge University Press, 1986), p. 26.
14 Auerbach, *Mimesis*, p. 473.
15 G. Lukács, *Studies in European Realism*, trans. E. Bone (London: Merlin, 1972), p. 6.

As a Marxist critic, Lukács more or less limits the range of social determinants he is willing to consider to those related to economic class. For Lukács, the nineteenth-century realist novel, through the use of typical characters, essentially analyses the ways in which the spread of capitalism produces the dominance of the bourgeoisie. About Balzac, whose use of types he takes to be exemplary, Lukács comments that 'the unfolding of material problems is always indissolubly bound up with the consequences arising from the personal passions of his characters', but 'the relationship between the individual and the social setting of which it is the product and in which – or against which – it acts, is always clearly discernible, however intricate this relationship may be'.[16]

From the earliest attempts to discern the defining features of realism, critics have also focused on its relationship to setting – in particular to the detailed description of settings often found in texts subsumed into the realist category. Baudelaire, in the article he wrote about Flaubert's *Madame Bovary* in 1857, refers to *realism* as a 'disgusting insult, tossed in the face of those given to clear concepts, a vague and elastic word, which for the common herd signifies not a new method of creation, but a minute description of what is superfluous'.[17] The relationship between what is superfluous and what is essential, both as regards a novel's general subject, and as regards particular passages of description, is much debated by critics committed to establishing realism's boundaries. Both Auerbach and Lukács find superfluity of subject or descriptions to be grounds either to limit the extension of the realist category, or to characterise 'pathological' instances of it. Auerbach sees the writings of the Goncourt brothers, for instance, as caught up with accessory, rather than essential subjects: 'Whatever the milieu, the subjects treated are always strange and unusual, often pathological . . . They were collectors and depicters of sensory impressions, especially of sensory impressions valuable for their strangeness or novelty.'[18] The consequence is that 'the subject treated is not one which concerns the center of the social structure; it is a strange and individual marginal phenomenon'.[19] Lukács is even more explicit about the ways in which certain practices of description produce a perversion of what is essentially realist. Of the famous description of an agricultural fair in *Madame Bovary*, he notes:

16 Ibid., pp. 51, 55.
17 C. Baudelaire, 'Madame Bovary by Gustave Flaubert', in *Selected Writings on Art and Literature*, trans. P. E. Charvet (London: Penguin, 2006), p. 248.
18 Auerbach, *Mimesis*, p. 498.   19 Ibid., p. 505.

Flaubert presents only a 'setting'. For him the fair is merely background for the decisive love scene between Rudolf and Emma Bovary . . . [who] are nothing but observers of this setting. To the reader they seem undifferentiated, additional elements of the environment Flaubert is describing. They become dabs of colour in a painting which rises above a lifeless level only insofar as it is elevated to an ironic symbol of philistinism. The painting assumes an importance which does not arise out of the subjective importance of the events, to which it is scarcely related, but from the artifice in the formal stylization.[20]

In an article from 1968, 'The Reality Effect', Roland Barthes would attempt to restructure the understanding and the value assigned to description in realist texts as part of a larger project of challenging the preference for novels by Stendhal and Balzac that one finds in critics such as Auerbach and Lukács. Barthes argues for a different kind of value of the aesthetic enterprise of a novelist such as Flaubert. Taking Flaubert to challenge certain facile or naïve approaches to referentiality that he considers to have governed many previous readings of the realist novel, Barthes makes a case both for the superior sophistication of Flaubert's writing and for the superior sophistication of a certain rhetorical way of approaching the reading of any realist text. He analyses how a belief that words on a page represent objects in the real world discourages us from studying the textual, rhetorical relations of the words themselves. Discussing a description from Flaubert's story, 'A Simple Heart', that includes a piano and a barometer, Barthes suggests that whereas the piano might serve as 'an indication of its owner's bourgeois standing', the barometer is 'an object neither incongruous nor insignificant', which seems to serve 'no purpose'.[21] Yet its purpose, for Barthes, is precisely to say 'we are the real'. That is, the word barometer is not present to refer to an actual barometer, but to refer to the referential promise of the realist novel.[22] Barthes's essay itself is an example of the rhetorical reading which he was advocating, a kind of reading he pursued in S/Z, his book-length study of Balzac's short story, 'Sarrasine', where he again insists on the rhetorical, rather than simply the mimetic, underpinnings of any realist representation. Such representation depends, in order to be intelligible, on the successful imitation not of reality, but of previous depictions of reality: 'thus, realism (badly named, at any rate often badly interpreted) consists not in copying the real but in copying a

---

20 G. Lukács, 'Narrate or Describe?', in *Writer and Critic*, trans. A. Kahn (London: Merlin, 1978), p. 115.
21 R. Barthes, 'The Reality Effect', in *The Rustle of Language*, trans. R. Howard (Berkeley: University of California Press, 1989), pp. 141–2.
22 Ibid., p. 148.

(depicted) copy of the real... This is why realism cannot be designated a "copier" but rather a "pasticheur" (through secondary mimesis, it copies what is already a copy)'.[23]

Flaubert has often had a troubling effect on the category of realism. If Balzac and Stendhal were regularly assigned the role of foundational figures of the French realist novel, after the publication of *Madame Bovary* in 1857 Flaubert was frequently named as the head of the realist group of his time. 'Everyone thinks I am in love with reality', Flaubert would write, 'whereas actually I detest it. It was in hatred of realism that I undertook this book. But I equally despise the false brand of idealism which is such a hollow mockery in the present age.'[24] He would write in another context, 'I wrote *Madame Bovary* to annoy Champfleury. I wanted to show that bourgeois dreariness and mediocre sentiments could sustain beautiful language.'[25] Pierre Bourdieu cites these passages in his remarkable study, *The Rules of Art*, stressing the importance of understanding the system of social relations that organises a particular literary field in order to grasp how different labels functioned for the writers who defended or rejected them as they staked out positions in that field, and as they strove to establish themselves and their aesthetic achievements. To what end would Flaubert distance himself from someone like Champfleury, a cheerleader for the realist school whom Flaubert found of meagre interest? What would Flaubert do to differentiate his literary achievement from the monumental achievement of an earlier writer such as Balzac? How do multiple strategic moves such as these being made by multiple writers affect the direction of the literary field as a whole?

In a passage from the preface to his novel *Pierre et Jean*, Maupassant recounts some advice he tells us he received from Flaubert that might be seen to draw a distinction between Balzac's approach to observation and typicality and Flaubert's approach to observation and style:

> 'When', he said, 'you pass by a shopkeeper sitting on his doorstep, or a concierge smoking his pipe, next to a rank of carriages, show me everything about that shopkeeper or concierge (how they look, how they're sitting, and in those outward physical details – thanks to the acuteness of your images – their inner character), and in such a way that I never confuse them with any other shopkeeper or concierge and, with a single word, how one cab horse is different from the fifty others in front of it and behind it.'[26]

---

23 R. Barthes, *S/Z*, trans. R. Miller (New York: Hill and Wang, 1974), p. 55.
24 Cited in P. Bourdieu, *The Rules of Art: Genesis and Structure of the Literary Field*, trans. S. Emanuel (Stanford, CA: Stanford University Press, 1995), p. 92.
25 Cited ibid., p. 93.
26 G. de Maupassant, *Pierre et Jean*, trans. J. Mead (Oxford: Oxford University Press, 2001), p. 13.

Flaubert rethinks the roles of typicality and referentiality in his pursuit of writing itself, famously claiming in an 1852 letter that his dream was to write 'a book about nothing... which would hold itself together by the internal strength of its style'.[27]

The question of typicality returns in some recent reflections on realist fiction. In her work on the historical elaboration of the mode of *fictionality* upon which realist novels depend, Catherine Gallagher notes that 'the *fictionality* defining the novel inhered in the creation of instances, rather than their mere selection, to illustrate a class of persons. A general referent was thus indicated through a particular, but explicitly nonreferential, fictional individual.' She continues, 'the referential claim of the novel, its stake in the world outside the text, therefore attaches to classes of persons, whereas the fictionality of the novel, its disavowal of personal reference, defines the individual characters'.[28] Yet, as any experienced reader of novels knows, 'individuated fictional characters... can never efficiently refer to types that, in turn, organize individuals in the world'.[29] Gallagher suggests that this predicament is what defines realism:

> A novel's realism is often assumed to be a matter of referential fidelity. When we analyze the nature of the gap between the general and the particular, however, reference and realization appear to be quite distinct, whereas fictionality and realization appear to be identical. Fictional characters may *refer* to people in the world by conforming to type, but they only *resemble* people in their *non*conformity. The impulse toward reference and the impulse toward realization are thus not only separate but also deeply opposed, and their tension, rather than cooperation, might be said to define realism.[30]

The tension Gallagher identifies here, present in the novels and the critical reflections of both Balzac and Flaubert, seems closely linked to the kinds of pleasure or excitement testified to by early readers of realist novels, who enjoyed recognising themselves and their world in the novels they read, and felt compelled to write to the novelists in question to pursue discussions about the world they seemed to share. 'Readers who wrote to Balzac and to Sue', Judith Lyon-Caen notes, 'express in a variety of ways a single certainty: the novel permits one to formulate the truth of the contemporary social world... [Readers] treat fiction as an important instrument for the revelation

---

27 G. Flaubert, *Correspondance*, ed. J. Bruneau, 5 vols. (Paris: Gallimard, 1973–2007), II, pp. 345–6.
28 C. Gallagher, 'George Eliot: Immanent Victorian', *Representations*, 90 (Spring 2005), pp. 61–2.
29 Ibid., p. 65.   30 Ibid., p. 66.

of social reality.'[31] Such readers transformed themselves into what Prendergast has called the 'subject of mimesis': 'an intersubjective entity, a socially constructed subject issuing from the "cultural codes" which . . . are held to underlie the whole organization of the mimetic text'.[32] The realist novel was immediately experienced by such contemporary readers as helping to make their personal experience and their social world intelligible. The nature and the consequences of the particular form of intelligibility those readers came upon have been a critical problem ever since. As Prendergast sums it up:

> Mimesis as a matter for the police, a regulative symbolic system for keeping a check on our collective *carte d'identité* or, alternatively, as one of the crucial symbolic forms through which collective sense is forged, and without which there is always the risk of collapse into trivial individualism or a sliding off the map of intelligibility altogether? Collective paranoia or collective wisdom?[33]

Recent critics have suggested other ways of reading that somewhat qualify this sharp dichotomy. In the case of Balzac, for instance, the novels themselves might be seen not as producing or composing collective forms of intelligibility, but revealing struggles between different forms of intelligibility and the social interests they represent. The novels themselves might be taken as fields of epistemological contestation: 'the works . . . are not ideologically consistent or coherent, but rather are arenas in which ideological conflicts are being played out. The voice of the narrator, for instance, is never ideologically trustworthy – it cannot be said that the narrator speaks for anyone or anything other than the narrator. Other aspects of the work may not share the narrator's ideological predispositions.'[34] 'Reality' itself might be redeployed to refer to different phenomena altogether. Bourdieu finds in Flaubert's *Sentimental Education*, for instance, not an attempt to offer any kind of simple reflection of the material world, but an attempt to objectify the immanent structures of the social world, the structures that produce our sense of the material world even as they shape our strategies and life histories within it.[35] In a feminist extension of Bourdieu's framework, Margaret Cohen analyses the gendered social relations hidden behind the intervention of a realist poetics into a literary field that also included other kinds of (now less well-remembered) novels: 'Realist codes are one powerful way writers seek to renew the French novel starting in

---

31 J. Lyon-Caen, *La Lecture et la vie: les usages du roman au temps de Balzac* (Paris: Tallandier, 2006), pp. 144–5.
32 Prendergast, *The Order of Mimesis*, p. 30.   33 Ibid., p. 217.
34 M. Lucey, *The Misfit of the Family: Balzac and the Social Forms of Sexuality* (Durham, NC: Duke University Press, 2003), p. 28.
35 Bourdieu, *The Rules of Art*, pp. 3–34.

1830. The sentimental social novel is the primary alternative solution writers employ throughout the 1830s and 1840s.'[36] Cohen notes that many of the most successful sentimental novelists were women, and that 'from their emergence, realist works assert their claims to literary importance by identifying the novel with men, by forging a poetics associated with masculine forms of knowledge, and by undercutting the authority of the woman writer along with sentimental codes'.[37] We see again in all these instances how studying realism returns us to a consideration of the ways in which both critical and literary acts of labelling, categorising, and typifying, with their concomitant construction of patterns of intelligibility, reveal themselves as forms of critical position taking, forms of social action that make active claims on what is or should be real.

36 M. Cohen, *The Sentimental Education of the Novel* (Princeton, NJ: Princeton University Press, 1999), p. 18.
37 Ibid., p. 195.

52

French poetry, 1793–1863

ROSEMARY LLOYD

The French Revolution brought in its wake not merely a far more fluid society than that which preceded it, but also a radically different image of the self. Under the pervasive influence of Enlightenment thinkers on the one hand, and Rousseau on the other, individuals began to define themselves not so much in terms of national or social position but with regard to smaller family units, emphasising less inherited class than acquired wealth and position. Poetry reflected that radical swing towards the appreciation of individual values, resulting in an outpouring of highly personal poetry, which explored feelings and emphasised the importance and uniqueness of each human being. But the Revolution transformed poetry in other more formal ways. The concept of what language was fitting for poetry had gradually led to a stultification of the genre, a highly limited vocabulary, and forms of speech that were now held to be inadequate, not merely to express the range of emotions that were central to individual experience, but also to convey the unprecedented changes in material life, as the Industrial Revolution began to transform what had been until then a largely rural society. The red beret that revolutionaries had sported was now to be placed on the dictionary, with poets enhancing their word hoards from a wide variety of sources, and bringing together, in clashing but liberating juxtaposition, high and low registers, the language of the universities and that of the streets. Where in England Wordsworth was promoting the use of the common language instead of the lofty forms that had become associated with poetry, the French Romantics ranged widely in seeking out a richer language, more appropriate to the growing complexity of modern life. Despite those changes, and the increasingly urban realities of contemporary life, nature would continue to play a predominant role in poetry until the middle of the nineteenth century. Nevertheless, this is not the nature of the English Lake poets, admired, appreciated, and feared for its own sake, but a far more humanised, even anthropocentric, poetry, where the natural world was assumed to correspond to elements of human experience, or to reflect aspects of human emotions, for it is humankind that stands at the centre of the Romantics' universe. The centrality of the individual also exercised an effect on the forms of French verse, forcing the polished and frequently restrictive forms of the alexandrine into a far more flexible rhythm, responding more to the needs of the particular poet and what he or she was eager to express. Among other changes, the classical bipartite balance of the alexandrine was now frequently replaced by the more mobile partition into three. Forms that had been abandoned or that had become devalued were dusted off and brought back into fashion, with the endless variety of the ode vying with the formal constraints of the rondo, villanelle, and sonnet.

The Terror, witnessing the guillotining of King Louis XVI in 1793, and that of the great poet André Chénier in 1794, brought an abrupt if temporary halt to the production of mainstream poetry. Many of those with poetic talents turned to the form of political songs and satires to voice their emotions. Most popular among these was Pierre-Jean de Béranger, a highly productive and very popular songwriter, whose witty satirical attacks on those in power forced him at various times out of a job and into prison. Songs on war, love, political events, or simply items of clothing (his old coat, for example, presented as the faithful friend of his last decade) were widely disseminated, and earned him the reputation of speaking for the people. Nevertheless, despite their popular appeal, his poems reveal considerable sophistication in their form, and already reflect that shift in poetic language that would become so marked later in the nineteenth century.

While Béranger offered above all the image of the independent songwriter, less concerned with achieving literary fame than with responding to the political and social needs of the moment, a generation of poets born around the turn of the century and coming of age in the 1820s were beginning to produce poetry that was at once more polished and more inward-looking. The first volume of poetry that can be regarded as representative of the French Romantic movement is that of Marceline Desbordes-Valmore, who in 1818 published the typically titled *Élégies et romances*. For the next four decades she would continue to produce volumes of intensely personal verse that nevertheless offers universal appeal. Her subjects were primarily those of woman's experience, of female erotic love and loss, of maternal affection, of the dynamics of the family. The raw intensity of much of her verse disconcerted some stylistic purists, but what her work may lack in polish and sophistication it gains in its sense of immediacy, the impression it gives us of coming directly into contact with a unique individual who grants us access to her deepest emotions. Less intensely personal but more technically accomplished, Amable

Tastu published several volumes of poetry between 1826 and 1858. Drawing on the themes of nature, patriotism ('La France et l'industrie' for instance), and on the matter of history, she created finely crafted poems, which were well received during her lifetime, although her works fell into oblivion after her death. Feminist critics have recently focused attention on this forgotten Romantic writer, whose poems have a particular charm and originality.

A very different but also strongly personal voice is heard in the work of Alphonse de Lamartine, whose *Méditations poétiques* of 1820 presented its readers with a new poetic sensibility, one in which the natural landscape of rural France was imbued with emotions, sometimes offering a metaphorical equivalent to the poet's own feelings, and sometimes enigmatically suggesting a divine meaning which the poet struggled in vain to decipher. The gentle melancholy that pervades his writing, together with his mastery of the alexandrine verse, left an indelible mark on the generation of poets that followed him. The highly personal tone adopted by both Desbordes-Valmore and Lamartine contrasts sharply with another great poet of the first decades of the century, Alfred de Vigny, whose *Poèmes antiques et modernes* of 1826 offer a meditation on stories from ancient and more recent history, attempting to trace through them a sense of the continuity of human experience. While the primacy of the individual is still paramount in his writing, the tone is no longer one of personal reminiscence but rather a search for a universal morality. The easy movement between the sound of a horn at evening in the woods and the historical memory of Roland dying at Roncesvaux, while the horn rang out in a desperate attempt to recall Charlemagne and the main army, offers one example of the historical thickness of Vigny's imagination and his desire to make use of history and legend rather than personal experience. Equally typical of him is his determination to extract a philosophical and primarily stoic message from the world around him. He sought above all to present himself, not as a lover or as an admirer of natural beauty, but as a thinker, and in so doing both continues and inspires a rich vein of philosophical poetry in French.

Victor Hugo, born in 1802 and thus slightly younger than these first Romantics, had been writing and publishing poetry from a very early age, but it was his 1829 volume *Les Orientales*, inspired by exotic images of the Middle East, that first really established him as a force that all subsequent poets would have to take into account. A virtuoso display of rhythms and rhymes, of shimmering, colourful images and unfamiliar landscapes, *Les Orientales* also carried a political message, turning attention to the plight of suffering civilians in the war between Greece and Turkey. This is typical of Hugo's belief that poetry was an adequate vehicle for transforming opinion and bringing about changes in social values. A charismatic figure, Hugo gathered around him a dynamic group of artists, musicians, and writers, the inner circle of the Romantic movement. Until his exile after Louis Napoleon's *coup d'état* in 1850 he would occupy a leading role in French literature, and even after he left France, to live abroad throughout the Second Empire, he continued to exercise an inescapable domination. A writer of exceptional virtuosity, he explored all the poetic forms, shunning only the sonnet, which he despised (but even then he wrote several of these, just to show he could). His poems sing of the domestic and the exotic, of personal love and political ambition, offering meditations on the dreams of childhood as easily as they enter into vast cogitations on the meaning of the cosmos. He could turn his hand to bitter satire, as he does not only in his virulent attack on Napoleon III but also in his condemnation of dull teachers or brutal warmongers, or to extended reflections on nature or the human condition. His most ambitious work, published in several volumes, was a highly imaginative retelling of the earth's history, *La Légende des siècles*, but his best-known and most moving collection of poems was his *Contemplations* of 1856. In this volume, divided into two eloquent parts, 'Autrefois' and 'Aujourd'hui', he responds in deeply emotional terms to the death of his elder daughter, Léopoldine, in a boating accident that happened during her honeymoon. His attempts to enter into the mind of children, already attempted in *Les Feuilles d'automne*, his long questioning of a divine purpose, and his eventual painful acceptance of her loss give this volume a momentum and a magnitude that have rarely been equalled. A poet who worked largely by the accumulation of images and epithets, gradually building up to resounding climaxes, he is the master of the extended poem, demanding of his readers a willingness to read at his rhythm, but rewarding them by the cumulative power of many of his works.

It was Hugo's friend Sainte-Beuve, who was later to become such a powerful presence as a critic, who did much to reintroduce the sonnet to French literature, after teaching himself enough English to be able to read and translate the English Romantics. The Lake poets, Sainte-Beuve proclaimed, offer countless poems in a moral, familiar, domestic genre that he was determined to see become naturalised in France, and that he did his utmost to introduce. He not only translated Wordsworth's sonnets, but also wrote many himself in exploring his alter ego, Joseph Delorme, the poet whose life, poetry, and thoughts as well as whose death, 'd'une affection de cœur', he chronicles in his *Vie de Joseph Delorme*, which came out in the same year as Hugo's *Orientales*. He was also to find in the Lake poets a form of impressionism, of suggestion rather than statement, a sense of the correspondences existing between outer and inner worlds, that he took up in his own poetry in ways that Baudelaire recognised and acknowledged when he referred to *Joseph Delorme* as a precursor of *Les Fleurs du Mal*.

Other writers took up the challenge laid down by Sainte-Beuve to reinvigorate the sonnet. Gérard de Nerval in particular, in a group of highly wrought, enigmatic sonnets, *Les chimères*, presented a model of the kind of writing the younger Romantics were convinced was needed. We wanted, he proclaimed in his autobiographical work, *Petits châteaux de Bohème*, to rejuvenate the old French versification, which had been weakened by the languor of the eighteenth century and muddied by the brutality of overly ardent innovators. Drawing on antiquity as well as on folklore, Nerval's sonnets are hauntingly beautiful, even when they are so intensely personal as to remain opaque.

Among the generation of poets born around 1810 Alfred de Musset, while better known to modern readers as a playwright and novelist, produced several volumes of poetry. A brilliant rather than a profound writer, his work is full of laments for lost love, the joys of youth, and the beauty of nature. His technical virtuosity, which is considerable, and the variety of forms he deploys are perhaps the most remarkable features of his poetry. In a poem written in answer to the question 'What is poetry?', he sums up his task in the following revealing terms: sing, laugh, weep, alone, aimless, at random, and from a smile, a word, a sigh, a glance, create exquisite work, transforming a tear into a pearl.

Despite Hugo's close friendships with artists, his poetry bears little trace of any interest in the plastic arts. It was left to some of his younger friends to tap into the rich vein of ekphrastic poetry: verse that sets out to offer a verbal equivalent of the visual arts, responding to the challenge of conveying shape and colour in an entirely different medium. Théophile Gautier, for instance, devoted some of his finest poetry to revealing the affinities between the sister arts. His first ambition had been to be a great painter, and throughout his adult life he was an influential critic of the visual arts at a time when readers relied on a critic's power of description to convey to them works of art which they might never see. His 'Symphonie en blanc mineur', for example, not only plays with the musicality of verse, but attempts to evoke, in a series of meticulously wrought stanzas, a panoply of different shades of white. Turning away from the exuberance and the Gothic nature of his early verse, his later work is marked by a determined sparseness, taking as his models the enamels and cameos whose small scale does not preclude intensity of colour and whose hardness, he proclaims in his influential poem 'L'Art poétique', guarantees they will live long after softer materials have faded away.

Gautier declares in the prefatory poem to his best-known collection, *Émaux et camées*, that when the 1848 Revolution came, he closed his shutters and concentrated on art. In fact many poets, most notably Lamartine, who for a brief time led the fledgling and doomed Republic, were filled with enthusiasm for the changes that they believed would follow. The brutal repression of the workers, followed by Napoleon III's *coup d'état* and proclamation of the Empire, led many of them to turn away from politics altogether and insist that poetry had no political role but should be written purely for its own sake. These proponents of art for art's sake included Leconte de Lisle, a highly erudite poet who drew on classical mythology, Indian legends, and Scandinavian sagas to carry out what he saw as the poet's principal aim of 'educating souls', as he put it in the preface to his first volume, *Les Poèmes antiques* of 1852. For him the dominant role of poetry was to create beauty, and particularly in his second anthology, *Poèmes barbares* of 1862, he drew not merely on his vast reading but on personal memories of growing up on the island of Réunion to create poems that blend together in striking ways evocations of exotic scenery, a rich, precise vocabulary, and immaculate control of verse forms. 'Le Manchy', for instance, conveys through its rhythms and its delicate descriptions the rocking of the palanquin carrying a lovely young woman to Mass.

Very different from the aristocratic austerity of Leconte de Lisle, Théodore de Banville, whose first collection of poems appeared when he was not yet twenty, was a virtuoso rhymester, constantly experimenting, playing with possibilities, and expanding the repertory of poetic forms and techniques. Of the mid-nineteenth-century poets, he is among the most open to change, the least locked into the thematic and prosodic rigidity of the group that have become known as the Parnassian poets. His influential treatise on French verse is often witty and tongue-in-cheek, as he appears to lay down the law on prosody, but his contemporary audience, especially the poets among them, would have realised how often he himself had broken or bent or manipulated those laws. A prolific poet, his best collection is probably the 1857 *Sang de la coupe*, although *Odes funambulesques*, which came out in the same year, is his wittiest, playing on the names and characteristics of contemporaries to produce a series of playful poems. As the title suggests, Banville uses this book to walk a verbal tightrope, constantly playing with sounds and images. A poet who delighted in finding witty and unusual rhymes and in exploiting forgotten forms of verse, Banville was also a master of parody and pastiche, moving beyond his models to create works of amusing originality.

The poet who was to have the profoundest influence on subsequent poets was, however, Charles Baudelaire, to whom we owe two radical transformations of French poetry. The first of these is associated with his verse poetry, most of which is included in the volume entitled *Les Fleurs du Mal*. A determined individualist, who had resolved from an early stage to astonish his readers, as he put it in a letter to his mother, he rejected the familiar themes and modes of Romanticism, turning instead to the topics of modernity. Acutely aware of the rapid changes in society that were finding a physical analogy in the city of Paris, he devoted much of his poetry to society's outcasts, the ragpickers, drunkards, and prostitutes, and to the accretions of time reflected in the multiple physical layers of a great city. Refusing to gloss over the harsher realities of life, his erotic poems have an earthiness that his contemporaries found hard to accept and his desire to astonish occasionally leads to a determination to shock or even offend that can still make his work abrasive for modern readers. A masterful manipulator of the sonnet (because the form is restrictive, he would argue, the idea bursts forth all the more intensely), he offers a sharp contrast to Hugo, rejecting the accumulation of words and images for the minimalist's choice of the single most powerful metaphor or most appropriate term. Like Gautier, Baudelaire was deeply influenced by the visual arts. A gifted art critic, he extended the possibilities of art criticism by insisting that the best response to a painting or a statue might be an elegy or an ode. Several of the poems in *Les Fleurs du Mal* are imaginative reactions to contemporary works of the plastic arts, in which, like Gautier, he relishes the challenge of making language do the work of a painter's colours and contours. Unlike most of the poets of his time, Hugo being as so often a striking exception, he organised his poems into a coherent whole, insisting that his volume had an architecture which allowed each poem to gain in resonance by its position within the book.

Baudelaire's second great revolution, in addition to his transformation of the themes and lexicon of verse poetry, drew on a genre which had been explored by various writers over the century but to which he gave an unstoppable impetus and a highly recognisable form. This was the prose poem, a genre which, or so he argued, by setting aside conventional rhythm and rhyme became supple and abrupt enough to adapt itself to the lyrical movements of the soul, the undulations of reverie, and the leaps of conscience. His acknowledged predecessor in this genre was Aloysius Bertrand, whose collection of prose poems, *Gaspard de la nuit*, draws on the picturesque and the uncanny, as well as the earthy, to create brief prose pieces owing their form in large measure to the traditional structures of the ballad. Where Bertrand remains deeply imbued with the romantic fascination with the past, however, Baudelaire's prose poetry is very much anchored in the present. Ranging from brief passages that are little more than extended epigrams to longer works that resemble concise short stories, *Le Spleen de Paris* offers evocations of exotic landscapes, portraits of dreamers and schemers, analyses of eccentrics and those on the edge of society, and scathing attacks on the greed of Second Empire materialism. Where *Les Fleurs du Mal* is a complex depiction of a poet's journey through life, *Le Spleen de Paris* is a multilayered evocation of a modern urban society.

The seventy years from the Revolution to the 1860s had thus seen enormous changes in the structures, language, and themes of poetry, and the development of the prose poem, as well as changes within fixed verse forms, were preparing the ground for an even greater transformation, which would be the invention of free verse.

53

Symbolism

PATRICK McGUINNESS

French Symbolism is perhaps the most influential poetic movement of the late nineteenth and early twentieth centuries, leaving its mark not just on all subsequent poetry and poetic thought (as well as prose, literary criticism and, importantly, theatre and dramatic practice) in French-speaking countries, but on European literature and on the literatures of South and North America. Symbolist ideas and influences can be found in poets as diverse as Yeats, Rilke, D'Annunzio, Ungaretti, and Akhmatova, in the Hungarian Endre Ady, the Romanian Ion Barbu, not to mention in British and American 'modernism', and especially in the work of Pound, Eliot, and Wallace Stevens. Its importance is difficult to overstate, and though it is often explained in terms of a few 'buzzwords' such as 'suggestion', 'musicality', 'free verse' (though it was also a formalist movement), its poetry and critical principles are more complicated, more various and less coherent than is often allowed. It was commonplace, even among Symbolist poets themselves, to claim that there were as many Symbolisms as there were Symbolists, and the critic looking for a stable literary doctrine, or even a set of agreed principles, would be disappointed. In terms of the poetry the movement produced, this is undoubtedly a good thing: the Symbolists emitted plenty of literary formulae, but few ever wrote according to them.

The poets we usually associate with the school are Mallarmé, often seen as its leader, and Verlaine (a sort of louche absentee father who, when interviewed, always claimed not to know what 'Symbolisme' meant). Both of them were well into the second half of their careers when the movement was 'launched' in September 1886 with Jean Moréas's 'Le Symbolisme', a document published in *Le Figaro littéraire* that has come to be known as the Symbolist 'manifesto', despite the word 'manifeste' not actually appearing in the text. Two other poets associated with the movement have an equally problematic place in Symbolism, despite being included in its rosters: Arthur Rimbaud, who abandoned poetry sometime in 1874, and Jules Laforgue, who died a year after the 'manifesto' appeared. One might reflect that these four poets, ironically enough the best-known 'Symbolists', are also those whose writing was least affected by the movement *as* a movement, though they all influenced its development in different ways, and all benefited (in terms of fame and critical standing) from it. Mallarmé enjoyed an extraordinary level of affection and prestige from the younger poets (admiration for Mallarmé was one thing they could all agree on), while Verlaine was kept financially and reputationally afloat by them. Rimbaud and Laforgue were published by Symbolist presses such as Léon Vanier, and their work promoted and reviewed by their contemporaries at a time when it could easily have been forgotten or consigned to the 'prehistory' of twentieth-century poetry. The Symbolists created their own canon too, and it is in large measure one that has survived – not just in terms of works but in terms of values. Behind the movement lurk the ghosts of three predecessors, Victor Hugo, Baudelaire and Villiers de l'Isle Adam, along with two respected senior practitioners, Théodore de Banville and Théophile Gautier. Another profound influence on the Symbolists, as he was on Baudelaire, was Edgar Allan Poe, whose impact on French literature of the nineteenth and early twentieth centuries constitutes one of the greatest examples in literary history of cross-cultural reception.

Of the younger generation, among those who would have called themselves 'Symbolists' we may count Paul Valéry, Edouard Dujardin, Gustave Kahn, Henri de Régnier, Jean Moréas, René Ghil, Paul Claudel, Saint-Paul-Roux, the Belgians Émile Verhaeren, Georges Rodenbach and Maurice Maeterlinck, and two Americans who were close confidants of Mallarmé, Stuart Merrill, and Francis Vielé-Griffin. The movement was also aided by perceptive and open-minded critics: Albert Mockel, another Belgian; Téodor de Wyzewa, a Polish polymath; and, perhaps the greatest critic of his time, and certainly the most influential on British and American poetry, Rémy de Gourmont. In the margins of the literary movement are the art critics Fénéon and Albert Aurier, who provided an important bridge between the literary and artistic worlds and who helped discern common ground between the different arts. While Symbolism remains a predominantly poetic movement, it had important things to contribute to drama and to prose fiction. In prose Georges Rodenbach's *Bruges la morte* was the most successful novel to emerge from Symbolism (his short stories are also important), along with Gourmont's *Sixtine*, and the experimental but undeservedly forgotten Francis Poictevin, whose novels have been claimed as forerunners of the French *nouveau roman*. Apart from Maeterlinck, whose one-act plays gave Symbolism its most authentic and durable theatrical pieces, the drama and dramatic thought of Claudel, Saint-Pol-Roux, and Dujardin (whose novel *Les Lauriers sont coupés* was so important to James Joyce) were also innovative and ambitious in scope. Jarry, a capable poet in the Symbolist mould, may be said to have brought Symbolist theatre to its absurd and violent fruition in *Ubu Roi*, while the Symbolist theatre director Aurélien Lugné-Poë (he added the Poë to his name to give it a specifically poetic aura) created Symbolist staging, acting, and set design that had important repercussions on the theatrical practice of the twentieth century.

When we consider that painters such as Fernand Khnopff, Odilon Redon, Georges Minne, and others illustrated Symbolist books, that Vuillard and members of the Nabis group painted stage designs for Symbolist plays, that Debussy and Satie set Symbolist poems to music, we see that it was in many ways a movement of all the arts, a nexus of collaborations. It was also a cosmopolitan movement, whose writers nurtured links with foreign countries, and whose outlook on the world was profoundly international. Symbolist theatres put on Ibsen and Strindberg, Eastern dramas, and English Elizabethan plays; Symbolist poets translated Whitman, Poe, Emerson, and others. Literature from the Dutch, the German, the Russian, and Polish appeared in the many Symbolist magazines such as *La Revue blanche*, *Entretiens politiques et littéraires*, *La Vogue*, *Mercure de France*, and *La Plume*, along with reviews of foreign plays and books, and an often forgotten (by literary critics) quantity of radical political material from France and abroad: Marx, Herzen, Proudhon, Jean Grave, and Elisée Reclus (hero of the Commune who was invited to write the editorial for one issue of Vielé-Griffin's *Entretiens politiques et littéraires*). When the reactionaries of Action française, the radical nationalist group founded in 1899 in the wake of the 'Dreyfus affair', turned on the Symbolist writers, it was not only for their artistic experimentation, but for their 'Germanity', their 'Jewishness', their un-Frenchness, and their allegedly anarcho-leftist Romanticism. When Jean Moréas turned his back on the Symbolist movement in order to found, in 1891, the 'école romane', it was to effect a return to the supposedly 'classical' values of an authentically 'French' poetry. Moréas's *école romane* needs to be seen not so much as a break from Symbolism as a reactionary secession from a movement that many writers believed had strayed too far towards artistic liberty and rootless cosmopolitanism, and which had, as Moréas claimed, abandoned the clarities of thought and language of the 'esprit français'. Among the *école romane*'s earliest adherents was Charles Maurras, one of the leaders of Action française, who showed himself adept at connecting (Maurras would have called it 'prolonging') these apparently literary or artistic debates to greater – and more consequential – cultural and political issues.

The first problem – and it is a problem the so-called 'Symbolists' were acutely conscious of – is the name. As one of the movement's first historians, Tancrède de Visan, observed in 1904, 'Symbolisme' was a confusing label, perhaps an outright misnomer. The Symbolists knew this, spending much of their time and critical energy explaining exactly what they meant by 'symbole', and producing, ironically enough for a group of poets supposedly interested in 'pure' poetry and in the poem's self-sufficiency, a large corpus of 'theory'. They argued out their theoretical differences in a range of publications, from specialised 'petites revues' to mainstream newspapers, and made sure that their ideas attracted interest beyond the usual limited poetry readership. What we tend to forget about the Symbolist poets is that they were noisy, media-savvy and good at promoting themselves; their poems might be quiet and reflective, but their prose was not – it sought attention, and often drew on political, military, or outrightly revolutionary metaphors to do so. One way in which the Symbolists might be said to have influenced even those literary movements that owe little to them aesthetically, is in their understanding of the press, and their ability to orchestrate media interest through manifestos, declarations, and well-engineered public spats. It can even be argued that Symbolism (and its predecessor, Decadence) helped inaugurate what we might call the 'era of manifestos', where no aesthetic product (play, poem, painting, novel or musical composition) was complete without an accompanying fanfare of promotion and explanation. These were tumultuous political times, and it is thus no surprise that its literature – even when, like Symbolism, it claims to ignore worldly concerns – should register that tumult at the level of literary group formation, in the issuing of manifestos and 'prises de position', and in the factionalism, leadership rivalries, and secessionism we associate with politics. In addition, much of what is called Symbolist 'theory' is amateur philosophy, linguistics, occultism, or politics, and is more interesting as such – for what it tells us about the literary culture of the time, the different discourses on which literature drew, and the interpenetration of those discourses – than as a tool for explaining particular poems or authors.

Visan, writing when the major Symbolists were still alive and active, and when Symbolism remained influential though the movement itself had dispersed, reminds us of some basic but important opening distinctions. 'Symbolism' in its ordinary usage refers to the system of associations whereby something concrete 'stands for' something abstract. Thus the dove 'symbolises' peace. The process by which the mind converts the concrete image, the dove, into the larger, numinous idea of peace is not an issue. On the contrary, the mark of a successful symbol in the ordinary sense is that this process should be instantaneous, even automatic, and that it should go unnoticed. The point is to get from one to the other without tarrying over what connects them, or wondering how that connection works upon us. Symbolism as traditionally understood is thus a kind of shorthand, and depends on accepted (through usage or imposition) codes and values. Symbol*ist* writing is a different matter. Indeed Visan suggests that it is the opposite: cryptic, elusive, suggestive, the poetry, prose, and theatre produced under the aegis of the Symbolist movement strives to be anything but an automatic transaction between writer and reader, or between playwright and spectator. Instead, that space opened up in the poem between its words and images and the way they are interpreted is where what we might call the 'poetry' takes place. Visan is writing under the influence of Bergson, and it is not surprising that Visan's appreciation of Symbolism should bear the imprints of his own intellectual formation: he sees the Symbolist poem not as a representation of an outside reality, nor even (in a loosely Romantic sense) a mood or state of mind, but instead as a means of disrupting our ordinary or automatic consciousness and liberating something analogous to what Bergson called the *moi profond*. It is significant in this respect that much of the poetry Visan most prizes comes from what we might call Symbolism's violent wing: Rimbaud, Laforgue, Maeterlinck, Verhaeren, and other poets often held to be precursors of surrealism. Visan is conscious of Symbolism's contemplative side, and of what it owes to the tradition (notably Parnassianism), but for him Symbolism as a movement is not only modern but modern*ist*, ready to adapt and radically alter the rules of art to attain its effects, and to bring about a corresponding change in the way we read or interpret the work.

Visan's essays on Symbolism and the Symbolist legacy are often slanted in Bergsonian directions (such as his discussion of how 'images successives' open the reader to the excitement and uncertainty of a consciousness face to face with its own sense-making process), but they remain valuable because they show what the early twentieth-century avant-gardes were doing with Symbolism, and how they were adapting it to their own developing priorities in the movement's immediate aftermath. From Apollinaire to Francis Jammes, from Valéry Larbaud to Jean Cocteau, from Paul-Jean Toulet and Léon-Paul Fargue to Breton and the surrealists, the influence of Symbolism is as pervasive as it is formative. Meanwhile, its critical or theoretical perspectives have become so much a part of how we read that we forget how hard-won many of their values at first were.

The Symbolists may not have agreed on much, but they were agreed that ambiguity was not the same as confusion, that a poem should open up meanings and engineer their simultaneous coexistence, and that the reader should have as much of a role in the creation of the poem as the poet. These may not seem like radical ideas to us, attuned as we are to these very standards as markers of poetic success, but they were by no means universally accepted. 'Un esprit ouvert à la compréhension multiple' is how Mallarmé described his ideal reader – 'a mind open to multiple comprehension' – and it is a good definition of what all the Symbolist poets sought.[1]

Despite their talk of an intellectual elite (and their belief that they were that elite), the Symbolists agree on the need to involve the reader in the creation process, and on the reader's active engagement in reading. A poet such as Mallarmé and his immediate intellectual successor, Valéry, attaches almost as much prestige to reading as to writing – in Mallarmé especially we find frequent references to reading as an active and creative process: not the passive consumption of literature but a share in the creation of meaning, a share in the poem – in fact, joint creative ownership not just of the product (the poem), but, we might say, the means of production (the process of creating and interpreting meaning). Corresponding to the writer / reader relationship is another one, which both Mallarmé and Valéry insist on: the play-off between chance and organisation, between what the poet can control and what he cannot. On the one hand the poet's job is to 'céder l'initiative aux mots' ('to cede the initiative to words'), yet he must also be 'l'ordonnateur de fête' ('the master of ceremonies of words').[2] In the face of language, the poet is playing off exertion against abdication, contingency against agency. Related to this is the state of language itself: some Symbolists (Laforgue, Rimbaud, Moréas) used recondite vocabulary, neologisms, or disused ancient words, while others such as Mallarmé, Rodenbach, or Valéry did not. Obscurity (with its suggestion of shadow, darkness, of something needing to be brought into the light) was not the same as difficulty (suggesting a puzzle, or a crossword, or something to which there is an answer, provided one knows where to look for it). Nor is indecisive the same as undecidable: a poem by Verlaine, with its mellifluous lines and pastel shades ('où le précis à l'indécis se joint', as he writes in 'Art

---

1 S. Mallarmé, 'La Déclaration foraine', in *Œuvres complètes*, ed. Bertrand Marchal, 2 vols. (Paris: Gallimard, 2003), II, p. 98.
2 S. Mallarmé, 'Planches et feuillets', in *Crayonné au théâtre*, ibid., p. 197.

Poétique', often taken as a poem-manifesto of Symbolist values)[3] is not the same as a poem by Mallarmé, multifaceted, crystalline, not so much 'obscure' as full of competing clarities.

This is why that catch-all term 'suggestion', used by all the Symbolists (and by the critics who explain them), is so slippery: it can cover a range of effects from the delicate half-tones of a poem by Rodenbach or Henri de Régnier to the arch ironies of Laforgue, from the violent clashes of image and narrative of a Rimbaud prose poem to the polysemic, imbricated syntactical play of a text (poem, prose or even, to use his term for many of the pieces collected in *Divagations*, 'poème critique') by Mallarmé. The reader who investigates the spectrum of Symbolist 'suggestion' on a poet-by poet – or better still a poem-by-poem – basis will get further in terms of understanding and enjoyment than one who stays satisfied with the idea of 'suggestion' as an abstract category for Symbolism as a whole.

For Mallarmé, who took pride in using words that could be found in the newspaper every day, the issue was not creating new words; it was creating new effects. When he was told that people could not understand his poems because the words were difficult, he replied that the words were the same as the bourgeois read every day in the newspaper: the difference was that in his poems the same words had been *re*written by a poet. Poetry, as Valéry later said, may have been a 'language within a language',[4] but it was above all an operation performed on the language that we all use every day – and the technical, almost scientific term 'operation' is appropriate for Valéry, who admired the skill of the surgeon and once addressed a group of surgeons by discussing the similarities between their art and his.

This is important, because it reminds us that Mallarméan 'difficulty' is not a product of diction, of specialised lexis, or neologistic vocabulary, but a result of arrangement. The dictionary does not help (except if we are searching for etymology, which Mallarmé often draws on), but a different way of reading may: if one thinks of a poem's difficulty not as a problem that needs to be resolved but as a part of the experience of reading (just as, Tancrède de Visan would say, following Bergson, obscurity and confusion are not by-products of consciousness but part of its processes, and thus need to be rendered, evaluated, and given status), then the poem becomes less a puzzle than an exploration in miniature of how we make sense of the world, how we process information, assess uncertainty, and keep different possibilities simultaneously

3 P. Verlaine, 'Art poétique', in *Jadis et naguère* (Paris: Vanier, 1884).
4 P. Valéry, 'Situation de Baudelaire', in *Œuvres*, ed. Jean Hytier, 2 vols. (Paris: Gallimard, Pléiade, 1957), I, p. 611.

open. That is why, when we read Mallarmé, we are often struck by the almost existential timbre of the way he describes reading and writing: they are both arts, but also acts; they involve choices and they have consequences. Mallarmé insisted on writing as an act in a semi-existential sense too: it was an act of confirmation, a struggle, defining and definitive in its commitment, though always provisional in its result.

It is thus hardly surprising that poets like Mallarmé and Valéry should have exerted such fascination on French literary thought – not only are their poems polysemic, but their theories and ideas about what happens when we read, where meaning comes from, how meaning can be sustained, are also concerns they share with philosophy and modern literary theory. Rather than read the Symbolists' theories of poetry as clues to the poems, it is far more productive to read them as a separate enterprise, or at least a parallel one: not so much a reinvention of reading as an extension of its scope, and a recalibration of its principles, undertaken with a sense, not always articulated, that reading should stand for something altogether more central to our experience of the world.

Symbolism's most penetrating critics were also emphatic in promoting the reader to a place of near-parity with the writer. For Mockel:

> The Poet seeks less to conclude than to provoke thought, so that the reader, collaborating through his own guessing process, finishes what is written. The diverse forms that make up the work are thus oriented like an *ensemble* of lines which, without quite reaching the precise point of their unity, nonetheless gesture towards that unity.[5]

The construction of the Symbolist reader was a key critical enterprise, and the various manifestos and poetic battle-cries of the period are concerned as much with how to read a poem as with how to write one: hence Symbolism's fondness for the unfinished, the half-seen, and the half-heard (among favourite Symbolist verbs are 'entrevoir' and 'sous-entendre'). The Symbolist poem exists to set in motion the adventure of reading, and one of the best, because most permissive, definitions of Symbolism, comes from Emile Verhaeren:

> First of all, no confusion between Symbolism and Allegory . . . Symbolism today, unlike the Symbolism of ancient times, which was the concretisation of the abstract, is rather concerned with the abstraction of the concrete . . .

---

5 Albert Mockel, *Propos de littérature* (Paris: Librairie de l'Art indépendant, 1894; reprinted Brussels: Palais des Académies, 1962), p. 33.

Formerly, Jupiter, incarnated in a statue, represented domination; Venus, love; Hercules, strength; Minerva, wisdom.

Today?

We start with the thing seen, heard, smelled, touched, tasted, in order to bring out the evocation and the sum through its idea. A poet looks at Paris crawling with nighttime lights, scattered into an infinity of fires and colossal with shadow and depth. If we give a direct view of it, as Zola might do, by describing its streets, squares, monuments, gas lamps, nocturnal seas of ink, feverish agitations beneath the still stars, he would of course present a very artistic image but nothing would be less Symbolist. If conversely he presents the mind with an indirect, evocative vision, if he says: 'an immense algebra whose key has been lost', this phrase alone will conjure up, far from all description and notation of facts, the luminous, shadowy and extraordinary Paris.[6]

Few Symbolists would have objected to this, not least because it focuses on how to communicate an effect rather than on how make a statement. It uses the real, what is 'there' (in this case Paris), as a means to an evocative end, rather than an end in itself, in such a way that the real always gestures beyond its own bounds. Verhaeren is careful too to say that 'modern' Symbolism is the opposite of what was formerly understood by the term: the Symbolism he celebrates is a process by which what is concrete is turned into something mysterious.

It does not deliberately escape the real (though escapism is often the result of much Symbolist poetry); instead it promises us that what is 'real' or 'true' (and the 'réel' and the 'vrai' are not synonymous) will be more essentially evoked elliptically, obliquely, ambiguously than in any exhaustive realist or naturalist descriptions. In short, poetry deciphers the world by first of all encrypting it once more. What is also interesting in Verhaeren's definition is the way it stresses the essential *economy* of the Symbolist mode, and his revealing use of algebraic images to denote a process at once precise and mathematically exact, and something magical, cabbalistic, occult. The thought of Paul Valéry will bring this particular paradox of Symbolist poetic theory – the relationship between mystery and deliberation, between magic and technique – to its fullest (and most frequently reiterated) point. Behind Verhaeren, and behind Valéry, is Poe, who to the French nineteenth-century writer represented the ultimate poet, able to demystify the craft (and the *graft*) of writing a poem without tarnishing the mystery of Poetry.

6 É. Verhaeren, 'Le Symbolisme' (1887), in *Impressions*, 3 vols. (Paris: Mercure de France, 1926–8), III, pp. 114–15.

54

Madness and writing

MIRANDA GILL

Nineteenth-century French culture had an uneasy preoccupation with madness (*la folie*) and the new concept of mental illness (*l'aliénation mentale*). Both were defined in opposition to a normative model of good health, implicitly identified with the perspective of male bourgeois rationality. Yet it remained unclear whether, or how, the normal and the pathological could be definitively separated. Writers and doctors were well aware of an ambiguous intermediary zone encompassing nervous disorders, eccentricity, and 'perverse' desires as well as dreams, mystical ecstasy, and intoxication – in short, any deviant or oppositional behaviour, as well as the entire realm now known as the unconscious.

Post-revolutionary French culture has played an important role in research on the histories of madness and psychiatry since the publication of Michel Foucault's *Folie et déraison* in 1961. His study outlines different stages in the treatment of madness in France from the medieval period, culminating in Philippe Pinel's establishment of the psychiatric profession after the 1789 Revolution. The ostensibly humanitarian aims of Pinel's new 'moral treatment' were mythologised in paintings of the era, which portray him removing the chains of the insane in the Bicêtre asylum. Foucault famously proposes, instead, that Pinel's paternalistic and moralising methods merely replaced visible chains with the no less oppressive internalised chains of guilt (pharmacological constraints would follow in the twentieth century). Whilst aspects of Foucault's account are questionable, it powerfully critiques the psychiatric profession's normalising drive, like other works of the period. The rich vein of social and medical history that they have inspired has only quite recently begun to be integrated with literary studies, though the centrality of madness to nineteenth-century French writing has also been explored by critics. In the wake of poststructuralist theories of the 'other side of reason', an influential strand of criticism has suggested that madness was integral to many writers' anti-bourgeois oppositional strategies, particularly after 1848. Madness and neurosis are indeed central themes for key figures of early French modernism, including Gérard de Nerval, Charles Baudelaire, Gustave Flaubert, and Arthur Rimbaud. There were also many significant historical intersections between medical and literary discourse on madness, which this essay explores after outlining the rise of psychiatry in France.

Psychiatric approaches to madness

Philippe Pinel and his successor Étienne Esquirol sought to establish French psychiatry (known during the nineteenth century as *aliénisme* or *la médecine mentale*) as an independent profession. Some stages of this process, which involved contesting the authority of the church, were highly visible: in 1838, a new law established a network of state asylums in France. Others were more subtly ideological: the emergence of specialised taxonomies and terminology – for example, substituting 'aliénation' for the more popular 'folie' – helped foster perceptions of the alienist's professional expertise. In line with their expansionist ambitions, alienists pathologised ever more borderline forms of behaviour. The first step in this process was the success of the doctrine of monomania as a form of partial insanity in the 1820s and 30s. Monomaniacs, startlingly depicted in paintings by Théodore Géricault, were held to be dominated by a single fixed obsession, though were otherwise disconcertingly lucid. The alienist styled himself as an expert witness or *médecin légiste* in court, proposing that many criminals were undiagnosed victims of maladies such as homicidal monomania. These debates, which raised complex issues of free will and agency, threatened the dogma of the unified bourgeois self. Later in the century the odd, rebellious, and eccentric were targeted by alienists, in their efforts to map the allegedly vast 'territory' of *névroses, neurasthénies*, and *névropathies*.

During the early part of the century it was believed that 'moral treatment' could cure the mentally ill; it certainly allowed for some rhetorical engagement between doctors and patients. In the more pessimistic cultural climate that followed the failed Revolution of 1848, degeneration theory rose to prominence under the influence of the alienist Bénédict-Auguste Morel. By the 1860s, the asylum system was overcrowded, becoming a dumping-ground for socially undesirable individuals who were judged incurable. Anxieties about morbid heredity were exacerbated after defeat in the Franco-Prussian war of 1870–1, and evolved into a full-blown medical doctrine of national decline. In frequently moralising language, degeneration theorists attacked the socially disruptive consequences of alcoholism and venereal diseases, and attributed criminal behaviour and sexual perversions (including homosexuality) to hereditary biological damage.

French psychiatrists continued to address topics of acute cultural sensitivity in the last decades of the century. The Salpêtrière hospital became the venue of strongly sexualised medical spectacles of hysteria – the neurologist Jean-Martin Charcot's now infamous Tuesday lessons of the 1880s. His research generated an extensive photographic iconography of hysterical crisis. In a lengthy dispute during the 1890s, the rival neurologist Hippolyte Bernheim alleged that Charcot was creating a 'culture of hysteria' through hypnotic suggestion, rather than documenting an objective malady. Fascination with processes that bypassed rational agency was also evident in research on the psychology of crowds by Gustave Le Bon. Still another strand of research splintered into the new field of sexology, and, by the *fin de siècle*, exotic phobias, perversions, and fetishes were flourishing. Whilst there was some opposition to alienism, including an emergent anti-alienist movement, the psychiatric profession gained considerable social and symbolic power in the course of the century. The period also saw the emergence of experimental psychology and the immediate prehistory of psychoanalysis, which would place greater importance on patients' experiences and voices. The latter was shaped by Freud's visit to Paris to study under Charcot in 1885–6, together with Pierre Janet's pioneering analyses of trauma.

What role did social power play in encounters between medical professionals and those labelled insane? Some scholars have proposed that psychiatric judgements about sanity were determined by gender norms, particularly the perception that women were intrinsically unstable and prone to hysteria, and men 'naturally' stoical and self-sufficient. There is a need for caution in constructing grand narratives, given the existence of, for instance, important strands of medical and literary discourse about male hysteria and frailty. Nonetheless, unconscious assumptions about gender, class, and race clearly influenced medical and legal attitudes. The history of medicine has typically been written from an institutional point of view. Whilst historians and critics have increasingly emphasised the need to reconstruct the voices of those diagnosed with mental illnesses, much remains to be done.

Vocabularies of madness

Literary critics have tended to focus on representations of madness and neurosis (often vaguely defined) within literary texts, leaving analysis of medical documents to historians of medicine, who in turn are often wary of rhetorical analysis. This disciplinary division is unhelpful for a number of reasons. Nineteenth-century scientific discourse was far more accessible to an educated reader than is now the case, and there were many popularisers; alienists' attitudes were profoundly shaped by broader cultural tropes; and writers and journalists were often sensitive to, and interested in, contemporaneous medical developments. Writers and doctors could both claim authority in unravelling the deeper significance of unconventional mental states, leading to potential symbolic struggles.

As Juan Rigoli has shown in his detailed account of the rhetoric of nineteenth-century alienism, French doctors developed complex strategies to bolster their claims to expertise in 'reading' and 'deciphering' madness, marshalling metaphors, dramatic scenarios, narrative patterns, and literary citations and allusions to this end.[1] Cultural historians have also demonstrated that alienists reproduced cultural stereotypes in their case histories, which often resemble the kernels of short stories and novels ('unnatural' women who reject the feminine vocations of marriage and motherhood, for example, are diagnosed with moral insanity; the victims and perpetrators in *crimes passionnels* are modelled on the stock types of the stage melodrama).

Writers, in turn, constructed powerful narratives and images of mental affliction. At times, alienists and the asylum figure explicitly in literary plots, as in Honoré de Balzac's *Louis Lambert* (1832), Charles Nodier's *La Fée aux miettes* (1832), and Eugène Sue's *Le Juif errant* (1844–5). Medical sources could more discreetly inform artistic depictions: Flaubert based many of his descriptions of Emma Bovary's hysteria in *Madame Bovary* (1857) on the entry on this topic in the *Dictionnaire des sciences médicales*. Other accounts of madness were partially autobiographical, including Nerval's *Aurélia* (1855) and August Strindberg's *Inferno*, first published in French in 1897. Still others portray mad fictional characters or narrators, such as Nerval's 'Pandora' (1853) and Baudelaire's 'Mademoiselle Bistouri' (1869). Nodier elaborated the deliberately eccentric concept of the 'Bibliographie des fous' (1835) at a time when the writings of the insane were of growing interest to the reading public.

But the scope of reciprocal influence between literature and alienism was simultaneously more diffuse and more pervasive than these examples suggest, owing partly to the porous nature of language. The term 'folie' was not completely medicalised; it had other associations dating back to antiquity, including creative frenzy and passionate love. It was inflected with still

---

1 See J. Rigoli, *Lire le délire: aliénisme, rhétorique et littérature en France au XIXe siècle* (Paris: Fayard, 2001).

further layers of (often highly personal) significance in the writing of figures such as Stendhal, Rimbaud, and Lautréamont. Despite their efforts to purify scientific terminology, alienists continued to be influenced by these semantic associations, for they too formed part of the reading public.

Just as the diagnoses of autism and attention-deficit disorder have generated public debate in recent decades, certain psychiatric categories captured the public imagination in nineteenth-century France. This process left many traces in literary and journalistic texts during a period of lexical expansion. Though most critical attention has been devoted thus far to depictions of hysteria, there were lively investigations into other mental states researched by contemporaneous alienists, including hashish intoxication (explored by Nerval, Gautier, and Baudelaire, and the unconventional alienist Jean-Jacques Moreau), and the *phénomènes du sommeil*, a category encompassing hallucinations, catalepsy, and somnambulism as well as dreams. Monomania was portrayed in Parisian journalism, fiction by Balzac, essays by Nodier, and lesser-known works such as Boucher de Perthes's 1853 novel *Emma, ou quelques lettres de femme*, written in the first-person voice of a woman afflicted with homicidal monomania. Eccentricity was associated with the motley and 'half-mad' characters of the Parisian underworld sketched by Champfleury, Nerval, Jules Vallès, and Victor Fournel. Hypochondria, which together with neurasthenia was perhaps the closest male equivalent of hysteria, was thought to afflict sensitive male artists and intellectuals. *Théomanie*, a form of religious madness, had evident affinities with the mystical and occult obsessions of writers such as Victor Hugo and Nerval (himself diagnosed with this malady). Of the plethora of categories which emerged in the latter part of the century, some were destined to rapid oblivion, including an epidemic of 'mad travellers',[2] and others to fame (*la folie circulaire*, introduced in 1854 by Jules Falret, evolved into bipolar disorder, whilst the categories of persecution mania and erotomania gradually coalesced, with others, into paranoia). As this stream of disorders implies, the history of madness offers a lens through which to reflect on broader issues of cultural periodisation and shared 'structures of feeling'.[3]

Maladies and movements in vogue

Psychological acuity was highly prized in neo-classical French culture of the seventeenth and eighteenth centuries. By the early nineteenth century the

---

2 See I. Hacking, *Mad Travelers: Reflections on the Reality of Transient Mental Illnesses* (Charlottesville: University Press of Virginia, 1998).
3 Raymond Williams's term.

roman d'analyse was ceding ground, but a strong cultural interest in mental processes remained, fracturing into new constellations of genres and forms.

Shaped by the legacy of Rousseau and the literary trope of sensibility, French Romanticism privileged nervous disorders as a sign of superiority. The *mal du siècle*, the French equivalent of the German *Weltschmerz*, had a range of near synonyms including 'ennui', 'mélancolie', and 'spleen'; the last of these, later popularised by Baudelaire, had its roots in English medical debates on humour, and was seen as a serious malady that could result in suicide. Male victims of melancholia were portrayed in confessional novels such as Chateaubriand's *René* (1805) and Senancour's *Obermann* (1804), though in Vigny's philosophical novel *Stello* (1832) the cheerful Doctor Noir enjoins the poet Stello to renounce his 'blue devils'. Women writers, often stereotyped as excessively emotional by hostile critics, tended to avoid the topic; Claire de Duras's *Ourika* (1823) and George Sand's *Lélia* (1833) constitute remarkable exceptions. Melancholia continued to shape literary culture of the Second Empire, an era of bitter disillusionment in the cultural elite.

With their roots in the Gothic novel, the genres of melodrama and sensation permeated nineteenth-century fiction. Sue, Hugo, Balzac, and Jules Barbey d'Aurevilly, amongst others, depicted violent and extreme mental states in order to generate dramatic suspense. The related genre of the fantastic, associated with such figures as Théophile Gautier, Edgar Allan Poe, and Maupassant, uses madness as a central narrative device. Fantastic narratives create irresolvable uncertainty in readers about whether mysterious events have a supernatural explanation or are the delusions of a deranged mind. Indeed, the genre overlapped significantly in its subject matter with the research of early French alienists. The writing of Maupassant, who dramatised madness in disturbing narratives such as 'Lettre d'un fou' (1885) and 'Le Horla' (1887), has generated particular biographical speculation; he attended Charcot's lectures around the same period, and later died insane.

Proponents of literary realism drew on medical and scientific rhetoric to bolster their epistemological claims. By the 1850s, when realism became a fully fledged movement, Champfleury and Flaubert emphasised the centrality of mental and physical pathology to the mimetic enterprise, to the disgust of some contemporaneous critics. 'Experimentalism' was simultaneously an artistic *and* a medical concept, associated with a 'virile' attitude of risk-taking and the desire for mastery. The novel was repeatedly framed as a case history; the male novelist posed as a natural historian or surgeon, wielding his pen as a scalpel. This performative tendency intensified with the rise of naturalism, reaching its peak in Émile Zola's incorporation of degeneration theory into the twenty novels of the Rougon-Macquart cycle, an ideology dramatised in *Le Docteur Pascal* (1893) and justified in *Le Roman expérimental* (1880). The series charts the decline of a family during the Second Empire, owing to a hereditary taint that is traced back to their convulsive and cataleptic ancestor Adélaïde Fouque. Readers are presented with an astonishing array of socially disruptive maladies, from addictions, dementia, and hysteria to compulsive homicide.

During the *fin de siècle*, a body of now neglected fiction drew on naturalist and sensationalist techniques to portray these and other maladies for wide audiences. In a more elevated register, Paul Bourget proposed in his *Essais de psychologie contemporaine* (1883) that literature and psychology were intimately linked. Yet writers and doctors typically harnessed their shared preoccupations to ideologically divergent ends. Writers broadly associated with the Decadent movement turned to the theme of pathology for counter-cultural purposes. Rachilde, Auguste Villiers de l'Isle-Adam, Octave Mirbeau, and Joris-Karl Huysmans, amongst others, exploited the seductive literary appeal of sadism, masochism, and neurasthenia – the very traits being denounced by contemporaneous psychiatrists intent on eradicating abnormality from society. Artists and poets who identified with the similarly loose cultural configuration of Symbolism sought to evoke trance-like mystical and aesthetic states in readers and viewers. Together with the often extreme religious experiences fostered by Catholic revivalism, much *fin-de-siècle* artistic production thus undermined the hegemony of rationality, setting the scene for the earliest medical theories of the unconscious.

One other persistent link between literature and medicine reached its zenith at the turn of the twentieth century: the association of artistic innovation with neurosis and madness, a tendency with roots in eighteenth-century English culture. With their deliberately subversive self-stylisation, French Romantics and Bohemians of the 1830s appeared to confirm the association of originality with social and mental eccentricity. Around the same time, French alienists began to medicalise genius. Not content with diagnosing their contemporaries, they projected the latest psychiatric categories onto the writers and thinkers of the past, inaugurating a dubious tradition of 'retrospective medicine' which persists today. Gautier's narrative 'Elias Wildmanstadius' (1833) probes the line between anti-bourgeois nonconformism and full-blown madness. The most widely commented 'case' of madness in a Bohemian writer was, of course, that of Gérard de Nerval, who suffered from intermittent episodes of insanity and spent periods in private clinics before committing suicide in 1855. Nerval used complex rhetorical strategies to contest his pathologisation and attributed profound mystical insight to his 'malady'. His preface

'À Alexandre Dumas' (1854) proposes bold analogies between madness and the everyday practices of reading and imaginary identification. Despite the subtlety of his own writing about madness and eccentricity, his fate was taken as evidence of the link between pathology and creativity in studies such as Jean-Jacques Moreau's *La Psychologie morbide* (1859), which influenced Cesare Lombroso's analyses of artistic degeneration. The tormented demise of Vincent van Gogh appeared perfectly to illustrate medical theories of 'mad genius'; it also echoed literary depictions of catastrophic mental collapse in visionary artists, from Balzac's *Le Chef d'œuvre inconnu* (1831) to Zola's *L'Œuvre* (1886).

Nineteenth-century French representations of madness were an important influence on the surrealist movement, which was fascinated by the disruptive and creative potential of the unconscious. Their legacy has also been felt on the writing of post-war French psychoanalytic and poststructuralist critics.[4] Polemical appropriations of the past are necessarily present-centred, and these accounts have not paid close attention to the embedding of nineteenth-century writing about madness within the types of historical and ideological context I have outlined. Future research on madness within French studies will no doubt combine rhetorical analysis with greater emphasis on historical specificity and social power. It may also draw increasingly on the 'popular' and discursive writings of the period; for these testify quite as forcefully as their canonical counterparts to French culture's ambivalent relationship to madness and its many hinterlands.

4 See, e.g., Shoshana Felman, *La Folie et la chose littéraire* (Paris: Seuil, 1978), and Julia Kristeva, *Soleil noir: Dépression et mélancolie* (Paris: Gallimard, 1987).

55

Literature and the city in the nineteenth century

CHRISTOPHER PRENDERGAST

Paris, capital of the nineteenth century, is a trope that now trips so easily off the tongue that we have almost forgotten both its nature and origins as trope. Although it is commonly attributed to Walter Benjamin, he himself did not invent the label but found it almost everywhere, along with a multitude of cognates ('capital of Europe', 'capital of the world', 'capital of the universe', in ascending order of grandiloquence), during his excavations of the vast archive of nineteenth-century representations and descriptions of the city. They belong in the stock of what, from the 1830s, came to be called *parisianismes*. The latter are almost endless and are to be found routinely in that subgenre of Paris-writing, the *physiologie*, storehouse of a whole urban doxology (Curmer's *Les Français peints par eux-mêmes* was the most widely known). But the doxa also travelled to the major literary genres, both popular and highbrow, on a spectrum from the unselfconscious to the ironic. At one end of this spectrum stands Balzac, his exuberant creative genius able to forge single-handedly from a cornucopia of clichés a whole myth of the city, as at once mysterious yet masterable. One such from the ample reservoir of lapidary Balzacian apothegms is the unfathomable utterance, in *Le Père Goriot*, by the policeman at the moment of arresting the grandest criminal of nineteenth-century fiction (Vautrin): 'Paris est Paris, voyez-vous' ('Paris is Paris'), articulating an 'insider's' knowledge that can take only the impenetrable form of a tautology.[1] Another – the narrator's – explicitly stresses the unfathomable as a property of the city itself: Paris is an 'océan', into which the diver can plunge but never touch bottom 'Paris est un océan. Jetez-y la sonde, vous n'en connaîtrez jamais la profondeur' ('Paris is an ocean. Cast the sounding line if you will, you will never fathom its depth').[2] As so often

---

1 H. de Balzac, *Le Père Goriot* (1835), in *La Comédie humaine*, 12 vols. (Paris: Gallimard, 1951–65), II, p. 1005. All references to *La Comédie humaine* are to this edition. Translations are mine.
2 Ibid., p. 856.

in Balzac, the dividing line here between aperçu and platitude is thin. Viewed in the latter aspect, they are plausible candidates for inclusion in Flaubert's *Dictionnaire des idées reçues*. But Flaubert, ever attentive to the unavoidable grip of cliché on all human discourse, also locked in the issue of city platitudes at both ends, with his own entry on the subject of Paris in the same text: 'Ne plus aimer Paris, marque de décadence. Ne pouvoir s'en passer, marque de bêtise' ('No longer in love with Paris, a mark of decadence; being unable to do without her, a mark of stupidity').[3] Both propositions are fatuous; both are true.

As an artist, Balzac certainly 'loved' Paris, and to make the point will often allegorise the capital as an irresistibly seductive woman. Relatedly, it is also seen as a 'fecund' body (we find a similar stress in Baudelaire in connection with poetry: the city is 'féconde en sujets poétiques et merveilleux' ['fertile in poetic and marvellous subjects'], although in the final poem of *Le Spleen de Paris* the city woman has become a jaded whore).[4] Its fecundity consists primarily in giving birth to narrative, and it is no accident that the age of the modern city is also the period that sees the consolidation of the novel as a literary form. The city is a narrative playground writ large. Paris, writes Balzac, is 'la ville aux cent mille romans' ('the city of a hundred thousand novels'),[5] the gargantuan *Comédie humaine* but a footnote to the repertoire of actual and possible stories the city is capable of generating. This was hyperbole but also connected to reality. The urban historian Lewis Mumford wrote: 'Living by the record and for the record became one of the great stigmata of urban existence, indeed life as recorded – with all its temptations to overdramatisation, illusory inflation and deliberate falsification – tended often to become more important than life as lived'.[6] If life modelled fiction (the theoretical bedrock of literary 'realism'), the converse also held, in turn spawning further, more self-conscious fictions that reflected the extent to which the city had become, in both imagination and experience, a 'narrativised' entity. When the two young heroes of Flaubert's *L'Education sentimentale*, Moreau and Deslauriers, muse on the lives Paris prospectively offers them, their first port of call is the precedent of Balzac's *Le Père Goriot*: 'Rappelle-toi Rastignac dans *La Comédie humaine*! Tu réussiras, j'en suis sûr' ('Remember Rastignac in *The Human Comedy*! You will succeed,

3 G. Flaubert, *Carnets de travail*, ed. P.-M. de Biasi (Paris: Balland, 1988), p. 548.
4 C. Baudelaire, *Salon de 1846*, in *Écrits esthétiques* (Paris: Christian Bourgeois Editeur, 1986), p. 186.
5 H. de Balzac, *Ferragus, Histoire des treize*, in *La Comédie humaine*, v, p. 19.
6 L. Mumford, *The City in History, its Origins, its Transformations, and its Prospects* (New York: Harcourt, Brace and World, 1961), p. 97.

I'm sure').[7] What of course they get is the antithesis of the conquering, if tawdry, epic of Rastignac's 'success'. Flaubert's novel spells the dead-end of story-induced 'inflationary' expectation, though the latter does not give up without a fight, and will return very late in the century, with the example of Rastignac once more to the fore, in, for example, Barrès's *roman de l'énergie nationale*.

The social basis of this imbrication of life and fiction was the phenomenon of *arrivisme*: the young man from nowhere who takes the world by storm, a new type thrown up by the turbulence of the French Revolution, the most spectacular historical example being Napoleon Bonaparte, whose memory haunts nineteenth-century French fiction from Stendhal to Barrès. The city was the natural magnet for these buccaneering individuals, as a space of new and highly fluid social and economic transactions, in turn based on the material transformation of the city (of which 'Haussmanisation' was the most dramatically accelerated phase) which underlay the conversion of Paris from capital of a nation state to imperial metropolis. The three main axes of transformation were those on which, if in varying combinations and degrees, all the great nineteenth-century cities expanded: production, circulation, and migration. To be sure, on certain measures Paris could not rival its cross-Channel neighbour, London. Where London was the epicentre of the Industrial Revolution, throughout most of the nineteenth century production in Paris was rooted in small-scale artisanal enterprises, the workshop rather than the factory, although by the end of the century much of this traditional economic structure had been destroyed by the 'rationalising' power of big finance capital. Relatedly, the population of London was much larger. On the other hand, in the first half of the century the population of Paris doubled, furnishing the demographic base for new relations of exchange and massively speeded-up modalities of circulation.

Modernised infrastructure – streets, boulevards, buildings, transport systems (roads, river, and railways) – was both cause and effect of these transformations, and was to supply writers, photographers, and painters with myriad objects of fascinated attention (not for nothing has nineteenth-century Paris been described as a vast canvas of pure 'exposition', or as the origin of the *société du spectacle*). Nadar's shots from an air balloon capture perfectly these new forms of interest and ways of seeing, but the photographer was not alone; the mobile panoramic view sweeping across the cityscape became a

---

7 G. Flaubert, *L'Education sentimentale* (1869), ed. Edouard Maynial (Paris: Classiques Garnier, 1964), p. 17.

stock literary and artistic device, a signature-motif in the novel from Balzac to Zola, as well as an endlessly repeated device of Impressionist painting from Manet to Van Gogh. The productive and circulatory potential of material infrastructure was nevertheless as nothing compared to population, the city's people, the sheer density of bodies in movement. If in certain imaginings a death-haunted ghost town, for nineteenth-century French literature as a whole Paris remained overwhelmingly a place for the young and a focus of youthful energy and aspiration. In the novel the hero arrives from the provinces and his itineraries through and across the capital provide the structural pivot of the narrative. The paradigm is Lucien de Rubempré in Balzac's *Illusions perdues*, whose first week in Paris is a giddying spin within 'la rapidité du tournoiement parisien' ('the speed of the Parisian swirl'): boulevards, carriage rides, cheap restaurants, glamorous salons, the unforgettable Palais-Royal.[8] Speed and noise are the organising motifs, a veritable urban cacophony orchestrated by the self-seeking imperative 'ôte-toi de là que je m'y mette' ('move over, my turn'). At one level this experience of the city produces exhilaration, at another the threat of a loss of control, a helplessly overwhelmed sensorium along with a disintegration of the moral self whence the typical modes of narrative resolution: capitulation in the case of Eugène de Rastignac, suicide for Lucien de Rubempré, withdrawal (effectively itself a form of suicide) for Stendhal's Julien Sorel, and fade-out for Flaubert's Frédéric Moreau. The city as opportunity and challenge invariably ends as disillusion and defeat.

But the literary place where the impact of the city's turbulence on the human sensorium and nervous system was most sensitively registered was in the genre of poetry, in ways that transformed the genre itself. Baudelaire is the key figure, single-handedly reorienting many of the directions modern poetry was to take. Baudelaire subscribed to the traditional view of lyric as a system for reintegrating the disordered fragments of experience into a harmonious whole (the musical analogy with 'harmony' is fundamental to the Baudelairian aesthetic, above all in the synaesthetic and metaphor-making of *correspondances*, based primarily on the generative power of the olfactory ['Parfum exotique', 'La Chevelure']). The lyric representation of Baudelaire's urban wanderings tries to slow down and master input from the environment, distinctively via the figures of the strolling *flâneur* and the impassive dandy, 'sniffing' rhymes on street corners ('Le Soleil', a poem from the 'Tableaux parisiens' section of *Les Fleurs du Mal*), appropriating novel stimulus and random encounter as a source of poetic nourishment.

8 H. de Balzac, *Illusions perdues*, in *La Comédie humaine*, IV, p. 62.

But more often than not the leisurely pace of the *flâneur* is overtaken by the frenetic self-abandonings of what Baudelaire called 'l'homme de la foule', permanently vulnerable to the shock experience. In 'Le Soleil' we also find the characteristic Baudelairian image of the 'fencer', using the resources of poetry to ward off an aggressive threat to the psyche. On many occasions the parrying gesture proves useless. In the sonnet 'À une passante', dissonance (the noise of the city, 'la rue assourdissante') shatters the harmonies of lyric, while framing the erotic–traumatic shock of fixation on the unknown passerby (the subject is 'crispé comme un extravagant' ['tense as in a delirium'], the term 'extravagant' to be taken in the strong sense of close to breakdown). Draped in the attire of mourning, the woman herself signifies grief and loss, an experience comprehensively transposed to Baudelaire's greatest city poem, 'Le Cygne', an extended allegory of identities, of both person and city, subjective integrity and social community, informed by the themes of exile, ruins, and irrecoverability.

The very forms of poetry were altered by these new registrations of urban dissonance and spasmodic happenstance. The metrically ordered rhythms of regular verse will cohabit with the metrical unpredictabilities of *vers libre*, open to all manner of strange prosodic turns, suggestive ellipses and unexpected rhymes, so many 'poem events' attuned to the thronging circulations of the city itself. There was also the new, more free-wheeling and surprise-laden form of the prose poem, initially in Baudelaire, then in the fragmented, estranging cityscapes of Rimbaud's *Illuminations* and the 'prose blanche' of Laforgue's 'Grande complainte de la ville de Paris', an ironic collage of the fast-moving, commercialised space of the city in which the elements of the poem itself 'circulate' as a set of derailments and deformations, wrenching all sense of settled identities into the unrecognisable.

Baudelaire's passerby is unknown and unnamed, a figure in the anonymous crowd. The paradox of proximity, even a kind of intimacy, and anonymity was grounded in the social and demographic realities of migration. The young man from the provinces who provides the novel with its basic convention is a migrant. But this phenomenon has also to be seen on a mass scale. This was the army of people from the countryside in search of work, from day labourers to vagrants, subject to the wheel of fortune of the labour market, some settling in the traditional artisan quarters, but in large measure a floating, amorphous population on the fringes and margins of the city's economy, denizens of the *bohème* (to which many radical writers and painters were drawn) and the *banlieue*. The ragpicker became their emblematic type, attracting the attention of Baudelaire and Lautréamont among others. It was a world of immiseration, disease, and danger, the juncture at which crime and poverty met, and generating, in literature and social thought, both a fascination with the 'underworld' and a fear (more rarely, a welcoming) of revolution. In *Les Mystères de Paris*, Eugène Sue recast the forms of popular fiction, with its focus on the *bas-fonds* of society, while at the same time forging through narrative a symbolic machine for managing the intractable and threatening; the blurred line between 'dangerous classes' and 'labouring classes' called for systems of surveillance and control, of which the embryonic form of the detective novel, in which the policeman or his surrogate enables a reading of the otherwise unreadable, was one example. The masterpiece of the genre was Hugo's *Les Misérables*. These were the zones of the city's waste, literal as well as metaphorical. The ragpicker lived off the detritus of the city's commodity economy. Waste matter, including the body's waste and the body itself as waste, became a central preoccupation, reflected notably in an obsession with the link between the underground city and ancient mythologies of the 'telluric' – Hugo's sewers in *Les Misérables*; Nadar's photos once more, this time of the catacombs and their arrayed display of skulls and skeletal remains; the spectral presences of Baudelaire's urban crowd in *Les Fleurs du Mal*; the excremental world of Lautréamont's *Les Chants de Maldoror* cancelling the brightly illuminated image of the overground city.

Many of these migrant outcasts were women. The parvenu heroes of the novel were male. Emma Bovary, trapped in provincial life, can only dream of 'Paris' (in part via novels by Balzac). To the extent that they entered the private and public circuits of the city, women did so principally as domestic servants or prostitutes. Controlling the latter ranked with controlling waste matter (the urban sociologist Parent-Duchâtelet wrote surveys of both prostitution and the sewers). In the collective imaginary, the prostitute circulated as both object of sale and instrument of havoc. In an earlier incarnation (Balzac's Esther in *Splendeurs et misères des courtisanes*, for example), she was the harlot with a golden heart. But in the plays of Dumas *fils*, she is more often a scourge, a source of contamination, both physical and moral. Zola's Nana erupted shockingly onto the stage of literature, as both occasion of terror and avenging angel, bent on humiliating and destroying her buyers. But there is also Zola's Denise Baudu in his novel of the modern department store, *Au Bonheur des Dames*, who, in partnership with the ruthless Octave Mouret, learns both how to master him and to exploit the female fantasies of an expanding consumer culture. From the point of view of the formal history of the novel, what is especially striking is the story's remarkable *incipit*, where we have not only the first female character to arrive in the city from the provinces at the novel's own point of departure, but also the first to do so by train. Denise's disembarkation at the Gare Saint-Lazare (lovingly painted by Monet) joins technology and gender at a crossroads of new narrative possibility.

When Paris was repeatedly represented as 'capital of the nineteenth century', all of these developments along the triple axis of production, circulation, and migration fed into sustaining the trope. But in an important sense, by the later nineteenth century, the city was no longer just a capital in the traditional sense of the centralised nation-state that had taken the better part of two centuries to evolve, from the administrative rationality imposed by Louis XIV through the Jacobin dictatorship of the French Revolution to Louis-Napoléon. By the time of the Second Empire, Paris had become an imperial metropolis, the heartland of a vast network of trade and conquest stretching well beyond the shores of the Hexagon. The great World Exhibitions were its triumphal public face, the city as pure display on a grand scale, further enhanced as fairyland by the use of illuminations made possible by the invention of electric light. Yet, as metropolis, the city was experienced as increasingly abstract, subject to the impersonal law of exchange and with a corresponding loss of felt connection with a knowable community and a civic identity. Auguste Cochin summed it up when he wrote: 'il y a encore à Paris des habitants, il n'y a plus de citoyens' ('there are still inhabitants of Paris, there are no more citizens').[9] In conservative circles, this created yet another anxiety associated with migration: the fear of deracination and the loathing of cosmopolitanism, both symptoms of decline and decay.

Barrès's novel *Les Déracinés* was one expression of this, as was Paul Bourget's *Cosmopolis*. The 'other' from elsewhere was no longer just the migrant worker from the provinces or the impoverished street girl. It also came to include the Jew (notoriously in the Dreyfus Affair) and, though this was to be more a twentieth-century concern, the alien from the imperial beyond. But if there was here an attempted closing of the city to the unwanted, there were also the first indications of an opening. Both the novel and poetry had sought to cross the line of demarcation separating high literary culture and the idioms of urban demotic: in their diverse ways, the vocabularies of Zola, Vallès, Hugo, Baudelaire, Rimbaud, Corbière, and Laforgue would reach across this divide, inaugurating a 'democratising' literary tendency that would come to full fruition with the work of Céline, Queneau, and Prévert. But if crossing the linguistic boundaries of class was one of the distinctive features of the literature of the city, empire eventually installed an even broader horizon

---

9 A. Cochin, *Paris, sa population, son industrie* (1864), quoted in L. Chevalier, *La Formation de la population parisienne au xixe siècle, 1809–1880* (Paris: Presses Universitaires de France, 1950), p. 241.

(today we call it going global). The appearance of African motifs in the scattered sensory and cultural world of Rimbaud's prose poems is not just a reprise of the nineteenth-century 'orientalist' topos; it is an early sign that the migrant *in* literature was to herald the migration *of* literature, its very forms and languages decisively altered as, on the back of colonialism, it would eventually make contact with the wider world of *francophonie*, in ways that challenged and re-directed nothing less than the identity of 'literature' itself, severing the bond that tied letters to nation, *patrimoine* to *patrie*. Paris, finally, became a 'world city', though not without generating a powerful strain of reactive nostalgic fantasy. At the close of the nineteenth century, the World Exhibition of 1900 invited the spectator–consumer to turn the clock back, even as it solicited admiration for the trophies of modernity. One of the exhibits – a colossal exercise in kitsch – was a simulacrum of *vieux Paris* in which to wander, as if transported back to the world of Balzac and Hugo – definitive proof that the age of *flânerie*, if it had ever really existed at all, was over.

56

Nineteenth-century travel writing

WENDELIN GUENTNER

The 'long' nineteenth century (1789–1914) inherited a rich tradition of travel writing, both narratives resulting from actual voyages and fictional works inspired by travel, including imaginary voyages and novels. The baron de Montesquieu's claim that human values and institutions are not universal, but rather are influenced by outside factors such as climate, placed new emphasis on travel to foreign lands. Through the identification of national 'préjugés' ('false preconceptions') travel writers fostered a sense of relativism, which challenged central political and religious authority. The French Revolution of 1789 was the culmination of this cultural shift, and the upheavals in the political and social status quo that it initiated continued to be felt throughout the following century in a series of ideological, social, and political aftershocks. This instability helped bring questions of individual and national identity to the forefront of private and public consciousness. In the cultural arena, the static worldview that subtended Classical values was likewise questioned. As a result, universality gave way to relativity, generality to the particular, the collectivity to the individual, the eternal to the momentary.

Classical literary tradition insisted upon the rigid separation of the 'noble' genres – tragedy, epic, and poetry – both from each other through the respect of immutable rules, and from prose genres perceived as being inferior. Writers with the new sensibility, however, sought discursive forms that allowed the free expression of individual sensations, thoughts and feelings. Prose genres which had traditionally been considered minor – the novel and the travel narrative – and literary forms often associated with private life and orality – the journal and the letter – found new favour.

Prose fiction

It was during the nineteenth century that the novel passed from the generic periphery to its centre. One of the most popular subtypes, the apprenticeship novel, draws on the age-old allegorical topos of the journey to express human life as it progresses through time. Stendhal's *Le Rouge et le noir* (1830), Honoré de Balzac's *Le Père Goriot* (1835) and *Illusions perdues* (1837), and Gustave Flaubert's *L'Education sentimentale* (1869) each follow a young protagonist's move from the provinces to Paris and from the margins of society to the seats of economic, social, and political power. Joris-Karl Huysmans unravels this tradition of travel as motif and narrative structure in his Decadent novel, *À rebours* (1884). The book's protagonist, Des Esseintes, withdraws from society, rejecting the conventional teleology of a life story articulated by movement through space and social class, in favour of interior voyages artificially provoked through sensation.

Other authors sought to explore questions of identity – both individual and national – through confrontations with the racial or cultural other. In order to assuage the anguished melancholy of a deracinated ego, often called the '*mal du siècle*', fictional characters are depicted searching in foreign lands for the meaning that a restructured and politically unstable French society seemed incapable of providing. François-René de Chateaubriand's *Atala* (1801), in which the luxuriant nature of North America serves as backdrop to a contrastive and often ambiguous presentation of indigenous and European values and social structures, and his *René* (1802), in which the eponymous character seeks relief from his melancholy in journeys to countries of both the 'North' and the 'Midi', are foundational texts in this regard. In this post-revolutionary privileging of alterity, the cultures of countries and regions which were considered primitive, including those in Europe, incited particular curiosity. Italy, Spain, and Corsica frequently served as settings for fictional works, as Germaine de Staël's *Corinne, ou l'Italie* (1807), Alfred de Musset's *Contes d'Espagne et d'Italie* (1829), Stendhal's *La Chartreuse de Parme* (1839), and Prosper Mérimée's *Colomba* (1840) and *Carmen* (1847) all attest. Geographical remoteness enhanced by natural barriers, such as the Alpine region and Scotland, inspired curiosity. In this vein, the mountainous landscape of the Jura and the primitive mores of its inhabitants provides a privileged setting in which the narrator of Étienne Pivert de Senancour's epistolary novel, *Obermann* (1804), recounts his solitary contemplations and rêveries.

In Musset's *La Confession d'un enfant du siècle* (1836) the hero-narrator cites Napoleon Bonaparte's military campaigns, especially that in Egypt, to explain the existential dissatisfaction felt by many in the post-revolutionary generations, as well as their fascination with oriental exoticism. He argues that this and other military exploits of the Imperial army had fired the imaginations of many young Frenchmen with dreams of heroic adventure in foreign lands.

Succeeding political regimes, however, appeared to offer only restricted horizons. This opening of France beyond its borders would soon be expressed in its colonial aspirations, first in the Mediterranean basin and, later in the century, in sub-Saharan Africa, the South Seas and the Far East. This literary Orientalism is reflected in prose fiction, including the stories Alphonse Daudet wrote after his stay in Algeria in 1860–1, and Gustave Flaubert's Carthage-based novel, *Salammbô* (1862). Pierre Loti's autobiographical and confessional fiction from the final decades of the period, inspired by his travels from Turkey to Japan and from Egypt to China, India, and the South Pacific, reflects France's colonial experience through a *fin-de-siècle* sensibility. Jules Verne's often visionary novels, which combine the mythic quality of the quest narrative and the imaginary voyage with an initiation into the modern world of technology and scientific discovery, introduced readers to all corners of the world and even to its very centre.

While Chateaubriand, Flaubert, and Loti actually travelled to the countries that formed the picturesque backdrop to their narratives, this was not always the case. Unable to verify the conventional images of foreign lands and cultures many writers simply reproduced them. Moreover, writers who travelled abroad, whether in search of 'local colour' or simply to flee the quotidian quality of life at home, often experienced the unfamiliar via topographical and cultural stereotypes: in the collective imagination Germany was an idyllic and charming country, while Spaniards and Italians were passionate and often violent. The Orient took on the power of myth, especially for French travellers who used it to project their fantasies of individual pleasure and national superiority. By the end of the century, Loti was less concerned with national stereotypes than with the homogenisation of foreign cultures – their mores, as well as their distinctive landscapes and architecture – through the double impact of industrial development and European colonial expansion.

Poetry

In poetry, the enhanced interest in subjectivity of writers with Romantic affinities often found expression through the travel motif. In 1845 Théophile Gautier writes in his poem 'Départ': 'Je sentais le désir d'être absent de moi-même' ('I felt the desire to be absent from myself').[1] However, he predicts that the discovery of new dimensions of subjectivity during his travels would

---

1 T. Gautier, *España* in *Poésies complètes*, 2 vols. (Paris: G. Charpentier, 1890), II, p. 90. Translations are mine.

compensate for the loss of his present sense of identity. In the wake of Napoleon's invasion of Egypt, the French increased their travel to countries in which Islam was the dominant religion. Moreover, during the 1820s Greece's war of independence against the occupying Ottoman Turks provoked widespread sympathy in Europe. The French colonisation of Algeria in 1830 expanded interest to North Africa as well. The Islamic Orient provided Romantic and art-for-art's-sake poets with new topographical tropes, such as the desert and the oasis, as well as decorative, architectural, and cultural ones, such as the harem and the bazaar. It also created a literary arena in which to explore and develop a new poetics free from the constraints of the French tradition. If Victor Hugo wrote *Les Orientales* (1829) without ever travelling to the Near East, Théophile Gautier's *España* (1843) appeared several years after his travels in Spain, and the publication of Gérard de Nerval's hermetic poems, *Les Chimères*, in 1854 came long after his trip to Beirut and Cairo in the early 1840s. Thus the exotic poems of the French Romantics result as much from reverie as from reading, from imagination as from memory. The Parnassians, Leconte de Lisle (*Poèmes barbares*, 1862) and José-Maria de Heredia (*Les Trophées*, 1893), continued the tradition of depicting the exotic singularity of foreign lands, while de-emphasising human subjectivity, a theme at the core of the Romantic ethos.

Charles Baudelaire was the century's greatest poet of the voyage theme, for this literary trope is intrinsic to his collection, *Les Fleurs du Mal* (1857). Some poems are informed by his memories of the exotic sensations he had experienced during his youthful travels in the Indian Ocean. However, the voyage is also the structuring ontological principle of the collection as the melancholy poet explores various paths – both spiritual and sensual – in his search for deliverance from the spleen that haunts him. The long closing poem of the collection, 'Le Voyage', brilliantly lays bare the illusion that travel to anywhere in this world, however unfamiliar and exotic, is capable of eradicating the suffering inherent in the human condition.

For poets associated with the Symbolist movement, such as Arthur Rimbaud and Stéphane Mallarmé, the voyage motif was used primarily to recount an internal – psychological and metaphysical – undertaking and experience. On a more quotidian level, Paul Verlaine's poems inspired by train travel through the industrial landscapes of northern Europe reflect the disorientation many experienced as long-held habits of visual perception were disturbed by the accelerated speed of rail travel. The extension of France's national interests into the Far East resulted in two innovative volumes of prose poetry inspired by China, Paul Claudel's *Connaissance de l'Est* (1900) and Victor Ségalen's *Stèles*

(1912). Claudel's poetic voice is often descriptive as it records the discovery of an exotic landscape that is both physical and cultural. In contrast, Ségalen attempts to translate China from the inside by presenting his poems as traditional texts or imperial decrees that have been inscribed in stone.

The travel narrative

New theories in epistemology developed during the eighteenth century changed how the experience of travel, and indeed of its writing, were conceived. Following British empiricists, French sensualists rejected the notion that knowledge was acquired through the universal deductive powers of reason. Rather, they maintained that it came through sensation and by induction. Thus in *Promenades de Dieppe aux montagnes d'Écosse* (1821) Charles Nodier cites his ignorance of Scottish history and mores as proof that he would recount only his personal sensations rather than repeating what he might have read. Similarly, Stendhal writes in his *Rome, Naples et Florence* (1826): 'Je ne prétends pas dire ce que *sont* les choses, je raconte la *sensation* qu'elles me firent, ('I don't claim to say what things *are*, I recount the *sensation* that they give me').[2] With his *Voyage en Italie* (1866) the French positivist, Hippolyte Taine, would continue this sensation-based vein well into the following century.

This rejection of a priori ideas in favour of individual sensation meant that self-knowledge and discovery of the world were concomitant endeavours. As Romantic individualism found an expressive outlet in travel writing it took on an autobiographical dimension. Thus Chateaubriand states in the preface to his *Itinéraire de Paris à Jérusalem* (1811) that in what followed 'je parle éternellement de moi' ('I speak of myself eternally'). He therefore asks readers to consider his work less a travel narrative than memoirs based upon one year in his life. Often, preoccupations with the self are projected onto – or expressed through – the descriptions of places seen. Thus in his *Voyage en Italie* (1827) the profuse growth of vegetation covering Roman ruins reminds Chateaubriand not only of the death of civilisations but also of his own mortality. He communicates his distress in dolorous outpourings in poetic prose.

The realist reaction to this inclination towards introspection resulted in a certain waning of the travel genre around mid-century. Gustave Flaubert chose not to publish the notes taken during his Egyptian travels. However, they evidence a move towards his personal ideal of 'impassibility', that is,

---

2 Stendhal, *Rome, Naples et Florence* (1826), in *Voyages en Italie*, ed. V. Del Litto (Paris: Gallimard, 1973), p. 360.

an attitude of disengaged observation, one to which successive realist and naturalist writers would aspire. In the opening to his 1892 *Sensations d'Italie*, Paul Bourget feels obliged to strike an apologetic note, wondering if readers would forgive his choice of such an old-fashioned genre, one in which a sensation-based experience of a painting or statue is conveyed in a subjective and literary manner, rather than in a putatively objective one. In the notes that Victor Segalen wrote between 1904 and 1918 in preparation for his projected 'Essay on Exoticism. An Aesthetic of the Diverse', the author has another concern. Segalen defines exoticism as a 'sensation' of 'differentness' and bemoans the degradation of the exotic. He asserts that instead of privileging and protecting the unique and distinct traits of unfamiliar places, modern societies were rendering the borders between the domestic and the unfamiliar ever more permeable. His condemnation of this ever-increasing homogenisation of culture resulted from his belief that the 'intensity of sensation' was what determined the quality of human life.[3]

The spirit of relativism nascent in the eighteenth century stimulated, in turn, an interest in the particularities of history. The notions of progress and infinite perfectibility, foundational myths of the French Revolution, created a new understanding of history as something dynamic rather than static. As a result, the French came to the belief that the study of their own history was as valid as that of Graeco-Roman antiquity. The French re-discovery of their national past during the post-revolutionary period was reflected in their travel writing. In fact, according to Théophile Gautier, it was historicism that often motivated travel: 'la fièvre du *moyen âge* . . . a engendré la *couleur locale*, qui a engendré les voyages' ('the fever of the *Middle Ages* . . . engendered *local colour*, which engendered voyages').[4] The twenty-one volumes of the *Voyage pittoresque et romantique de l'ancienne France* (1820–78) by Charles Nodier and le Baron Taylor is replete with both lithographs and verbal descriptions of monuments and ruins, witnesses to France's cultural heritage, which helped the nation recover its past.

Recording the present as future history

Many travellers considered their written accounts to be contributions to the historical record. The accuracy of their descriptions and anecdotes was therefore considered paramount. In the preface to his *Itinéraire de Paris à*

---

3 V. Segalen, *Essai sur l'exotisme* (Paris: Livre de Poche, 1986), p. 77.
4 T. Gautier, 'Voyages littéraires', in *Fusains et eaux-fortes* (Paris: Charpentier, 1880), p. 35.

Jérusalem, Chateaubriand asserts that a traveller is a kind of historian whose task is to faithfully record what he saw and heard, inventing nothing and omitting nothing. Citing the changes both in culture and in the natural landscape that the Industrial Revolution was bringing about, some attributed this historical function to narratives of travel in France itself. For example, in *Nouveaux souvenirs de voyage: Franche Comté* (1845), Xavier Marmier states that modern means of transportation – canals and railways – were threatening regional identities by extending the reach of Parisian values as never before. Marmier claims that it was the duty of all who loved the provinces 'd'en dire la beauté, d'en dépeindre les monuments et les mœurs primitifs' ('to recount their beauty, to depict their monuments and primitive mores').[5] In France less accessible or seemingly backward-looking regions – Brittany, the Vendée, and the Pyrenees – tended to be seen through this primitivist lens.[6]

Comments made by travellers of the period reveal a shared belief both in the referentiality of language and in the linguistic and discursive challenges inherent in travel writing. In relating their experiences, travellers have recourse to many discursive tools, but description is generally the most important one. In the last chapter of his *Voyage à l'Île-de-France* (1773), Jacques-Henri Bernardin de Saint-Pierre drew attention to the constraints that Classical aesthetics, with its stress on the general and universal, had placed upon travellers intent on accurately rendering the particular characteristics of the unfamiliar natural environments that they encountered. In succeeding decades, travellers began to describe distinctive vegetation and landscapes in detail instead of using vague terms or euphemisms. This expansion of the French lexicon was yet another manifestation of the post-revolutionary belief in individuality. Moreover, the names of exotic fauna and flora often acquired the power to transport readers in imagination far from everyday life, thereby stimulating interest in foreign travel.

The poet and historian Alphonse de Lamartine recognised the challenge of transforming travel experiences into discourse. In the preface to his *Voyage en Orient* (1835) he writes that a translation is the most difficult book to write and that the travel narrative was essentially that: writers were expected to translate to the eyes, the mind, and the soul of their readers the places, colours, impressions, and feelings to which the scenes of nature or humanity had given rise in themselves. Travel writers often have recourse to the rhetorical trope

---

5 X. Marmier, *Nouveaux souvenirs de voyages: Franche-Comté* (Paris: Charpentier, 1845), pp. ii–iv.
6 For an early example, see R. de Carbonnières, *Voyage dans les Pyrénées, pour servir de suite à des observations sur les Alpes* (1789).

of analogy as they confront the challenge of rendering the unfamiliar both visible and comprehensible.

As well-known authors began travelling for the express purpose of writing a publishable account of their experiences, the travel narrative became a literary vogue. Frequently these appeared first as serials in the periodic press before being brought out in book form. Some, like Nerval, related their travels in newspaper articles as a strategy for breaking into the literary marketplace.

Since travel narratives were often seen as a historical record in the making, it is understandable that writers were preoccupied with issues of sincerity and credibility. Flora Tristan asserts early on in *Pérégrinations d'une paria* (1838) that she was, above all, an 'être de foi' ('being of faith'), and that as such she was incapable of not telling the full truth. As proof that they had given a faithful account of their journey, many (such as Astolphe de Custine in the foreword to his *La Russie en 1839*) denied the role memory played in the writing of their narratives, asserting that they had been drafted in situ. Travellers often stressed the spontaneity of their writing practice itself and the fact that the resulting prose had been only slightly revised, if at all. This refusal to recognise a travel account's 'literariness' becomes, in fact, a generic convention.

Truthfulness was also connoted by literary style and form and writers consciously attempted to give their works a natural air. The journal and letter forms were popular because their association with orality and private life allowed a certain artlessness which connoted sincerity. Particularly at the century's end travellers sometimes went so far as to publish accounts in a fragmentary prose style, Edmond de Goncourt's *L'Italie d'hier* (1894) and André Gide's *Le Renoncement au voyage* (1906) being two examples.

As the steam engine accelerated the pace at which land and water could be traversed, the farthest reaches of the Earth became more accessible to the ordinary traveller. The notion of arduous travel (voyage) to places of 'otherness' eventually gives way to voluntary displacement for pleasure. But the development of mass tourism in the nineteenth century had perhaps less of an impact on travel writing than did the introduction of new modalities of representation. By the 1820s, lithography had greatly reduced the cost of illustrating travel books, but from the 1840s photography was on its way to becoming the documentary medium of choice. As early as 1842 Noël Lerebours would publish his *Excursions daguerriennes* and already the following year Gautier would characterise his *Voyage en Espagne* as fulfilling the 'humble mission de touriste descripteur et de daguerréotype littéraire' ('humble mission of a describing tourist and a literary daguerreotype').[7] In his 1939 'Discours du centenaire de la photographie', Paul Valéry describes how the photographic image had replaced verbal description as the dominant mode of visual representation. However, use of the photograph in illustrating travel narratives only became economically feasible in the 1880s, with the development of the photo-gravure process.

Recent trends in literary criticism have opened up travel writing to new readings. Feminism and other identity-focused perspectives have enlarged the corpus of travel writing. By drawing attention to narratives that lie outside the traditional literary canon they often contest the interpretative assumptions of travel conceptualised only as conquest and domination. Poststructuralist theory has questioned the notion of individual identity and offers another lens through which to view the instability of the travelling self as it confronts the other. The formal dissolution of the French Empire, brought about by the independence movements of the twentieth century, has given birth to new theories shedding fresh light on the travel writing of earlier centuries. Postcolonial theories have questioned the validity of a whole series of binary oppositions: home and abroad, seeing subjects and seen objects, centres and peripheries and dynamic and static identities, both individual and cultural. Increasing globalisation has led to new models of human culture such as 'hybridity'.[8] Mimetic theory proposes a comprehensive anthropological account of human evolution and history.[9] With concepts such as 'interdividuality' it invites new understandings of travel accounts, especially those which describe how the self responds when the stability of its symbolic universe is threatened by encounters with unfamiliar ways of being human. Finally, emerging environmentalist literary criticism explores modalities of perceiving and engaging with another kind of alterity, that of the non-human world, that transcend the impulse to anthropomorphise or exploit.

7 T. Gautier, *Voyage en Espagne* (Paris: Charpentier, 1859), p. 149.
8 See H. K. Bhabha, *The Location of Culture* (London: Routledge, 1994).
9 See R. Girard, *Things Hidden since the Foundation of the World* (London: Athlone, 1987).

57

Philosophy and ideology in nineteenth-century France

SUZANNE GUERLAC

There is nothing neutral about philosophy at the turn of the nineteenth century in France. Traditionalists such as Joseph de Maistre see a 'fight to the death between Christianity and the spirit of philosophy [le philosophisme]';[1] they hold Enlightenment *philosophes* responsible for the 'satanic' events of the French Revolution and consider philosophy a dissolving force that threatens the social fabric, rendering the establishment of enduring social or political institutions impossible.[2] On their view divine providence governs human history; God will restore order and counter-revolution will return the French, chastened and purified, to the values and institutions of the past. This is the perspective Stendhal so vividly represented in *Le Rouge et le noir* when Julien Sorel finds himself implicated in a conspiracy of the Ultras. It never quite disappears. Monarchists still have a strong voice when the Third Republic is finally established after the fall of the Second Empire in 1870.

At the turn of the century, however, others believe that there can be no return to the past. If philosophy precipitated the Revolution that evolved into the Terror, the remedy for revolutionary violence is to be found 'in the very source of the evil/suffering [du mal], in philosophy'.[3] One can only look to the future and since, at this post-revolutionary juncture, 'the future has no precursor',[4] it will be necessary for men and women to invent it. 'To found a government on philosophical grounds', writes Germaine de Staël, 'there is no more beautiful thought.'[5] This is the liberal position that will continue to inform social thinkers throughout the century.

There were two main cultural sites of philosophy throughout the nineteenth century: official institutions of learning such as universities or

---

1 J. de Maistre, *Considérations sur la France*, in *Œuvres choisies de Joseph de Maistre*, 4 vols. (Paris: R. Roger et F. Chernoviz), IV, p. 52. (Translations from French are mine.)
2 Ibid., p. 47.
3 G. de Staël, *Des circonstances actuelles qui peuvent terminer la Révolution et des principes qui doivent fonder la République en France* (Paris: Librairie Fischbacher, 1906), p. 184.
4 Ibid., p. 2.   5 Ibid, p. 183.

academies on the one hand and journalism on the other. Not surprisingly, the very notion of what philosophy is, or should be, shifts from one site to the other. On the official side, the Ideologues (Destutt de Tracy, Cabanis, Volney) hold sway until the Restoration. Inheritors of Enlightenment thinking in the traditions of Montesquieu and Condillac, they emphasise direct contact with the real through sensation, examining how we pass from sensation to knowledge and moral judgement, and how we unify the knowledge produced by various mental faculties. Ousted from the Institut de France by Napoleon because they turned against the First Consul's imperialist aspirations, the Ideologues are superseded during the Restoration by the Spiritualists, who, as their name suggests, rebel against the materialism of the Ideologues and return to metaphysical speculation. This academic perspective, advanced by Paul Royard-Collard at the Sorbonne, becomes the official 'doctrine of the university' during the Restoration; it remains so throughout the July Monarchy, thanks to the teachings of Eclectic Spiritualism presented by Victor Cousin, professor at the Sorbonne, director of the École Normale and eventually Ministre de l'Instruction Publique.[6]

Prompted by Staël's romantic evocation of German philosophy in *De l'Allemagne*, Cousin made several trips to Germany where he studied Kant, Schelling, and Hegel before undertaking to produce a distinctly French synthesis: a new philosophical system that aspired to reconcile elements borrowed from Scottish empiricists, German idealists, Plato, and Descartes. Cousin's philosophy included an aesthetics and was compatible with an emerging spirit of Romanticism that affected historians, philosophers, and social thinkers, as well as literary writers and painters. Balzac, Delacroix, and Hugo all found inspiration in Cousin, whose popular lectures at the Sorbonne during the Restoration were published in book form as *Du vrai, du beau, du bien* (1837).

Although Staël's *De l'Allemagne* inspired the metaphysical and romantic aspect of this academic philosophy (its evocations, for example, of the infinite, the ideal, and *l'esprit impersonnel*, a version of Hegelian *Geist* or spirit), Staël herself not only recognised the importance of the journalistic site of philosophy, she privileged it. At the turn of the century she wrote that Enlightenment philosophy had been too caught up in abstract ideas and that the philosopher must now yield to the writer – the *écrivain philosophe* – whose philosophical practice was both enabled, and rendered necessary, by new advances in print media and by the post-revolutionary political fact of freedom. The task of

---

6 E. Bréhier, *Histoire de la philosophie*, vol. III, *XIXe–XXe siècles* (Paris: Presses Universitaires de France, 1994), p. 578.

the *écrivain philosophe* is to bring ideas to bear on actual circumstances and to mould public opinion. In answer to Maistre's concern about the social bond, Staël writes: 'Only writers [*écrivains philosophes*] can . . . find the point that reconciles interests and principles'. Social and political institutions will be founded on this basis, she argues, for 'when an idea is lodged in everyone's heads . . . people demand the institution that consecrates it'.[7]

Staël's *De la littérature* (1800), which introduced a Romantic literary aesthetic to the French, was not merely a work of literary criticism, as it has often been characterised. Its chief task was to examine the figure of the *écrivain philosophe* historically, to trace 'the work of thought in writing' from Homer to the French Revolution, and, even more importantly perhaps, to explore the future possibilities of 'the perfectibility of the human species'.[8] To Enlightenment philosophers, Staël writes, perfectibility was merely a metaphysical idea. Modern print technology in an era of freedom of the press, however, enables the *écrivain philosophe* to actively fashion 'the perfectibility of the spirit'.[9] Here Staël launches a concept that will orient the thought and the politics of the entire century: civilisation.

Between 1828 and 1830, François Guizot (historian, leader of the liberal opposition party and subsequently prime minister during the July Monarchy) presented a series of lectures on the history of European civilisation in which he theorised this concept and insisted upon its 'fundamental idea': progress.[10] One of the virtues of Guizot's theory (influenced by Spiritualist thought concerning the intervention of spirit within history) was that it held together notions of material progress and moral or social progress in a philosophy of history that also proposed a dialectical relation between individual and social advancement. To this extent his theory served the liberal ideology of the opposition party (the Doctrinaires), which supported restricting electoral participation to an elite public of (male) property holders, even as it opposed the legitimist monarchy of Charles X; the Doctrinaires were influential in the eventual overthrow of Charles X and the establishment of a constitutional monarchy under Louis Philippe in 1830. The discourse of civilisation enabled the leaders of the July Monarchy to appear to hold values of social reform, while at the same time ignoring these values. Equality before the law was

---

7 Staël, *Des circonstances actuelles*, pp. 188–9.
8 G. de Staël, *De la littérature, considérée dans ses rapports avec les institutions sociales* (Paris: Flammarion, 1991), p. 87.
9 Staël, *Des circonstances actuelles*, p. 191.
10 F. Guizot, *Histoire de la civilisation en Europe depuis la chute de l'empire romain jusqu'à la révolution française* (Paris: Didier et Cie, 1875), p. 15.

considered a fundamental right, for example, but this juridical fact did not extend to political or social realms – a fuller realisation of the ideal would be reserved for a more advanced stage of civilisation.

Claude Henri de Rouvroy, comte de Saint-Simon, a thinker who operated outside the university system as a journalist or *publiciste*, embraced the notion of progress in a quite different way during the Restoration. To him progress meant above all advances in industry and the applied sciences; he argued that society should be reorganised on this basis. Philosophy was not a speculative endeavour but a pragmatic one. As such, as 'the thought that embraces all modes of human activity and solves all social and individual problems', it belongs not in the university but in the newspaper.[11] To Saint-Simon, Restoration society was a 'world upside down', in which non-productive or 'incapable' men, the parasitic members of the *noblesse*, had power over the 'capable' or useful members of society: manufacturers, artisans, and workers, whom he called the Industrialists.[12] From his perspective, the march of civilisation calls for a radical reorganisation of society according to criteria of social utility and productivity in view of greater social prosperity for all. There is no need for political conflict or revolutionary violence to effect the reforms he proposes, such as reorganising the governing administration under the leadership of a minister of finance taken from the industrialist class, and replacing the Chamber of Deputies with a chamber of industry – 'the king can execute the political plan I propose simply by decree'.[13] In the last year of his life, Saint-Simon published *Un Nouveau Christianisme* in which he linked his idea of social progress to Christian moral teachings. The aim of social reorganisation, he suggests here, is not just to maximise productivity, but also to protect the very poorest members of society and to realise the political and ethical value of *fraternité*.

One legacy of Saint-Simon is what Engels called the Utopian Socialist current of thought (Leroux, Tristan, Proudhon, but also Fourier, Louis Blanc, Prosper Enfantin, and Victor Considérant, among others): visionaries and social reformers whose ideas, activism, and social experiments precipitated the Revolution of 1848.[14] During the July Monarchy, disciples of Saint-Simon rephrased the discourse of civilisation and progress in a language of

---

11 H. de Saint-Simon, in *Doctrine de Saint-Simon*, ed. Bourglé and Halévy (1926), p. 126 (cited in Bréhier, *Histoire de la philosophie*, III, p. 560).
12 H. de Saint-Simon, *Écrits économiques et politiques: anthologie critique* (Paris: Pocket, 2005), p. 234.
13 Ibid., p. 372.
14 F. Engels, 'Socialism Utopian and Scientific', in *Marx/Engels Selected Works*, 3 vols. (Moscow, Progress Publishers, 1970), III.

emancipation that emphasised class and gender. Pierre Leroux, for example (breaking with the Saint-Simonians after the Revolution of 1830), rephrased the terms of class conflict: 'the People', he writes, is now 'composed of two Classes, with distinct conditions and distinct interests: the Proletarians and the Bourgeois'.[15] Because the interests of the dominant class went unchallenged, thanks to a political system that restricted electoral participation to male property owners, Leroux concentrated his attention on electoral reform. Like Saint-Simon, he gave a religious cast to the narrative of civilisation, even as he politicised it. Progress becomes a divine force and the body politic a *corps mystique*.[16] The march of civilisation implies the realisation of a figure of Humanity, a quasi-messianic principle of reconciliation that would mark the end of class struggle and of the tension between the revolutionary values of freedom on the one hand and equality on the other. (We find these values at play in the social novels of George Sand.)

Other thinkers take up the language of class struggle and devote themselves to this messianic ideal. Flora Tristan, writer and militant, refashioned Leroux's discussion of class interest into a discourse of political rights, emphasising that a right to be alive implies a right to work. She attempted to organise workers on the basis of their class interest and struggled just as forcefully for the rights of women of all classes, since they were all excluded from electoral participation. Attacking electoral restrictions formulated in terms of property ownership, Joseph Proudhon famously declared that property is theft, since it implies economic value obtained without work.[17] Railing against 'professors of pure philosophy' such as Cousin, who 'make it their job . . . to market the absolute', Proudhon sought an economic approach to social reform, promoting the idea of a national bank that would make interest-free loans to workers, even as he advanced an anarchist politics.[18]

Another legacy of Saint-Simon was positivism, an epistemological perspective advanced by Auguste Comte (student and collaborator of Saint-Simon for many years), which would become the dominant philosophical discourse during the Second Empire and remain so throughout the Third Republic. Because of this success (which Flaubert parodied in the famous Comices Agricoles scene of *Madame Bovary* and mocked through the character of M Homais) we tend to forget that initially positivism served as an

15 P. Leroux, *Aux philosophes, aux artistes, aux politiques: trois discours et autres textes* (Paris: Éditions Payot, 1994), p. 226.
16 Ibid., p. 250.
17 P. J. Proudhon, *Textes choisis*, ed. J. Lajugie (Paris: Libraire Dalloz, 1953), p. 270.
18 Cited in Bréhier, *Histoire de la philosophie*, III, p. 779.

epistemological foundation for social reform. Given that public education was a crucial requirement for social progress, Comte believed that an intellectual, or epistemological, revolution – an 'alliance of proletarians and philosophers' – was required before social change could occur.[19] The first step was to determine a foundation for knowledge that would be accessible to all. His solution was an epistemology of direct observation of fact, one that provided the basis for the discourses of the social sciences that emerged during the nineteenth century when philosophers became sociologists (like Comte, who invented the term), historians, psychologists, anthropologists, archaeologists, and philologists.

Comte made a firm distinction between positivism (which seeks laws on the basis of observed facts) and empiricism (which merely collects facts), a distinction the physiologist Claude Bernard insisted upon even more emphatically in his account of scientific method in *Introduction à l'étude de la médecine expérimentale*. This work reached a broad audience, including Emile Zola, who made it the cornerstone of his programme of literary naturalism. Bernard (whose experiments on the human body applied positivist methods beyond the precinct of observable fact) elevated the experimental scientist (whose obligation is to 'force nature to reveal herself') to quasi-divine status.[20]

Readers of *L'Avenir de la science*, published in 1890, would approach Ernest Renan's humanist discourse, which attributes 'divine action' to human reason, with this figure of the experimental scientist in mind.[21] Actually, Renan wrote this work in 1848–9 (in a moment of enthusiasm for socialist ideals) and then delayed its publication; his chief interlocutors are Auguste Comte and Victor Cousin and, of course, the traditionalists his secular humanism directly challenges. Whereas Comte, working within a Kantian critical framework, limited the reach of positivism for which he made no claim to absolute knowledge, Renan's faith in human reason is unlimited. He anticipates the day when reason 'will know the metaphysical and moral world as it already knows the physical world'.[22] He is not speaking here about a transcendental horizon (about the infinite and the ideal that the Spiritualists invoked), but rather about human culture. Influenced by Herder and Humboldt, Renan's interests have shifted from Comtian sociology to philology, 'exact science of things of the spirit', with an emphasis on comparative analyses of language, literature, and religion.[23]

---

19 A. Comte, *Philosophie des sciences* (Paris: Gallimard, 1996), p. 125.
20 C. Bernard, *Introduction à l'étude de la médecine expérimentale* (Paris: Flammarion, 1993), p. 53.
21 E. Renan, *L'Avenir de la science* (Paris: Flammarion, 1995), p. 102.
22 Ibid., p. 151.   23 Ibid., p. 200.

This shift has consequences for the narrative of civilisation, which, as we have seen, drives philosophical reflection during this century. To the extent that Renan's study of comparative religion engaged with non-European civilisations, it encouraged reflection about nationality and race – compelling issues during the Third Republic. To restore national pride after the wounding defeat in the Franco-Prussian War, which resulted in the territorial losses of Alsace and Lorraine, leaders of the Third Republic intensified colonial activity, justifying it as a gift of civilisation. Author of the celebrated essay 'Qu'est-ce qu'une nation?', Renan is known for the emphasis he placed on shared history and cultural experience as the foundation for national identity. He also insisted on linguistic community as the principle of ethnic identity. And yet, as Aimé Césaire reminds us in his *Discours sur le colonialisme*, Renan also repeated the racist stereotypes theorised by Gobineau, whose analysis of racial inequality he vindicated in his 1890 preface to *L'Avenir de la science*.[24]

Universalist claims associated with the notions of 'civilisation' and 'humanity' were undermined from the start in France, when the Rights of Man, proclaimed during the French Revolution, were not extended to colonial subjects. They were challenged in debates concerning the slave trade, which was not definitively abolished until 1848. By then, Alphonse de Toussenel had already published his anti-Semitic account of modernity, *Les Juifs, rois de l'époque: histoire de la féodalité financière* (1847) a work followed by Edouard Drumont's even more toxic *La France juive*, published eight years before the Dreyfus Affair. Here Jewish identity is no longer based on religion, but upon race. Arthur, comte de Gobineau's *Essai sur l'inégalité des races humaines* (1854) marks a turning point in discussions of race in France. Gobineau systemised the findings of French anthropologists who had defined race in terms of physical traits. Although Victor Schoelcher, leader of the anti-slavery movement, had repudiated such theories, Gobineau gives them philosophical authority in an explicit challenge to the Enlightenment universalist principle of human perfectibility, a repudiation fuelled by anxieties about cultural decline that he lays at the door of ethnic mixing. Gobineau insisted not only that the white race is superior to all others but that 'a part of humanity' (he specifically names 'African negroes') 'intrinsically lacks the power to ever become civilised', indeed 'will always be' incapable of taking 'even a first step toward civilisation'.[25] Mme de Staël and Guizot had both invoked a notion of universal civilisation that, as we have seen, nourished emancipatory projects. In

24 A. Césaire, *Discours sur le colonialisme* (Paris: Présence Africaine, 2000).
25 Arthur, comte de Gobineau, *Introduction à l'Essai sur l'inégalité des races humaines* (Paris: Nouvel Office d'Édition, 1963), p. 26.

the second half of the century, however, the discourse of civilisation shifts increasingly towards an imperial discourse on the one hand (colonisation is characterised as a civilising mission by Republican leader Jules Ferry and by the socialist leader, Jean Jaurès) and a nationalist discourse on the other (as in the writings of the monarchist Charles Maurras whose *Avenir de l'intelligence* [1905] rephrased Renan's title in a nationalist key).

As the myth of universal civilisation recedes, a determinist myth of science takes its place. A mechanistic worldview holds that everything can be explained in terms of determining material causes and effects. In the course of the nineteenth century this perspective, grounded in the physical sciences (especially Newton's laws of nature), is gradually extended to the sciences of man. Thanks to important developments in experimental physiology and psychology (in 1861, for example, Pierre Paul Broca proved that aphasia could be linked to lesions in specific areas of the brain), by the end of the nineteenth century determinism began to impinge on discussions of human subjectivity, which, up to this point, had been considered a locus of freedom and associated with religious, ethical, or aesthetic practices and ideals.

Hippolyte Taine, for example, explained literary invention in terms of contextual factors such as race, milieu, and historical moment. Psychology, for Taine, becomes 'a science of facts' – 'one can speak with precision and detail of a sensation, an idea, a memory', he argues, 'as well as of . . . a physical movement'.[26] Émile Littré sums up this deterministic perspective when he writes: 'Things are determined, that is certain: there is no exception to the natural laws and we are all marionettes [*pantins*] subjected to these laws.'[27] If the myth of science takes over from the myth of civilisation it is perhaps because Herbert Spencer had declared that 'mechanistic science . . . represents the last stage' of the evolutionary process of human adaptation to external reality.[28] There is no future left to invent. It is simply a question of extending the range of our certainty, of subjecting, as Taine put it, not only inanimate things, but also 'every living thing' to 'the steel pincers of necessity'.[29] As Foucault argued, by the end of the nineteenth century man had become both the 'foundation of all positivities' (as subject of positive knowledge) and 'present, in a way we cannot even claim is privileged, in the element of empirical things' (as object of knowledge). Foucault concludes his analysis of

---

26 Cited by S. Guerlac in *Thinking in Time: An Introduction to Henri Bergson* (Ithaca, NY: Cornell University Press, 2006), p. 24.
27 E. Littré, *Les Limites du connaissable* (1903), cited in Bréhier, *Histoire de la philosophie*, III, p. 811.
28 Cited in Guerlac, *Thinking in Time*, p. 26.   29 Ibid.

the nineteenth century by evoking this paradox of finitude with the figure of the 'end of man'.[30]

At the end of the nineteenth century Bergson challenged the application of the scientific paradigm to subjectivity. Ideally suited to give us knowledge about inanimate things, he argued, positivism cannot give us knowledge about living beings because these exist in, and through, time in a modality of real duration that cannot be quantified or measured. In his most celebrated work, *L'Évolution créatrice*, Bergson challenged Herbert Spencer's deterministic view of evolution. He proposed that human rational intelligence is not a transcendental foundation of positive knowledge but rather a product of evolutionary adaptation toward instrumental ends. He relativised scientific reason in relation to other modes of knowing such as philosophical intuition that opens directly onto the experience of time and life. What made Bergson's challenge to determinism so compelling was that he himself was a mathematician and well informed about the most cutting-edge developments in modern science (thermodynamics, spectral analysis, and radiation, for example). These developments were in the process of undermining the very mechanistic model of classical science that had begun to infiltrate into the study of man, even as they prepared the way for the scientific revolution to come: relativity and quantum mechanics.

Remarkably popular at the turn of the twentieth century, Bergson's thought was appropriated by a range of Bergsonisms that reshaped it to fit the needs of various (and often conflicting) cultural agendas, ultimately contaminating its philosophical force. His influence was superseded by a renewed interest in Hegel (and Marx) in the 1930s. His legacy in the twentieth century will be felt in the contexts of existentialism, on the one hand, and French phenomenology, on the other.

---

30 M. Foucault, *Les Mots et les choses, une archéologie des sciences humaines* (Paris: Gallimard, 1966), p. 355. Foucault evokes 'the end of man' on p. 396 and p. 398.

58

Naturalism

NICHOLAS WHITE

Rise and fall

Naturalism was a literary movement of particular social urgency that flourished during the first decades of the Third Republic, its outstanding gift being the twenty novels of the Rougon-Macquart cycle (1871–93) by Émile Zola (1840–1902), though its ramifications can also be traced by reference to those writers referred to, both affectionately and disparagingly, as *les petits naturalistes*. Its lineaments were already visible in Second Empire fiction, not least in responses to the ambivalent realism of *Madame Bovary*, which are legible in three texts of the 1860s: first, *Germinie Lacerteux* (1864) by Edmond and Jules de Goncourt; second, Zola's *Thérèse Raquin* (1867); and third, Flaubert's own *L'Éducation sentimentale* (1869). Indeed, it was in the 1860s that Zola first borrowed the term 'naturalism' to denote a longer realist literary heritage typified by that rival modern epic, Balzac's *La Comédie humaine*.

Naturalist fiction is characterised by two plot shapes: first, the rise and fall of modern tragedy, in which ignoble protagonists are pushed down the slope towards their nemesis by supra-individual forces, explained in materialist rather than theological terms (naturalism seeing myth itself as a social fact); and, second, the pessimistic anti-plot which is in a double sense platitudinous, given its flat narrative trajectory and listless characters. The first of these forms is exemplified by Zola's study of physiology, *Thérèse Raquin*, which follows the path from wifely adultery via the murder of Thérèse's husband, Camille, at the hands of her bull-like lover, Laurent, to the lovers' eventual suicide. Just as subsequent readers of Zola might rearticulate Zola's language of temperament in terms of 'drives', so he too echoes the classical language of the humours: Thérèse is nervous (hence typical of the hysteria associated with transgressive female desire by the voyeuristic male gaze of nineteenth-century medicine and literature); Laurent is sanguine, blood coursing through his veins; and the lymphatic Camille is as calm as camomile tea! In response to

Louis Ulbach and Sainte-Beuve, Zola's preface defends the novel against the criticism that his writing was contaminated by the degeneracy of its subject matter. To a modern ear, Zola's invocation of science sounds bombastic, but his backgrounding of 'caractère' and 'âme' hoped to redefine identity by demystifying earlier theological assumptions (the materialist philosophy of Enlightenment figures such as Diderot providing an intellectual model).[1] Between the achievements of Diderot and Zola stand modernity's practical enactment of scientific discoveries, and the philosophical assertiveness of positivism, translated into literary criticism by Hippolyte Taine (1828–93). To replace theology with science is perhaps simply to rearrange the deck chairs of metadiscourse. But in the Enlightenment tradition, science represented not bombast but one of its contraries, scepticism.

Visible in this defence is the strategic nature of scientific rhetoric, which reappears in the multitudinous literary criticism Zola wrote for the newspapers. Indeed, Zola's dual career as novelist and journalist reflects the particular vision he had of the role of the publicly visible intellectual. This role came fully to fruition with the most famous newspaper article in the history of the French press, *J'accuse* (1898), and Zola's intervention in the Dreyfus Affair in which he defended a Jewish officer in the French army who had been falsely accused of betraying the country to the Germans. No longer an angry young man by the 1890s, Zola's heroic defence pitted this cultural heavyweight against the interests of the army and the Catholic church (the very incarnations of what the Marxist philosopher Louis Althusser would term ideological state apparatuses three-quarters of a century later). In stressing the disparity between Zola's scientific rhetoric and fictional practice, it is worth noting that his theory of naturalism, inspired by Claude Bernard's *Introduction à l'étude de la médecine expérimentale* (1865), appeared in book form as late as 1880, as if to provide academic credentials for this most scandalous social melodrama.

The pessimistic anti-plot of *L'Éducation sentimentale* points forwards more accurately than any other nineteenth-century novel to the self-immolatory impulse of much twentieth-century art. Rather than merely designate in mimetic fashion the disappointments of modern social tragedy, it performs such disappointment in the very experience of reading. How, Flaubert answers in his twin tale of failed romance and failed politics, is it possible to write an interesting novel about futile lives? Huysmans celebrates this text rather than *L'Assommoir* (1877) in his farewell to naturalism, *À rebours* (1884). In fact,

---

1 É. Zola, *Œuvres complètes*, ed. H. Mitterand *et al.*, 20 vols. (Paris: Nouveau Monde, 2002–), III, p. 27.

naturalist fiction of the non-event is already to be found in Henry Céard's tale of failed seduction *Une belle journée* (1881). Indeed, one might well argue that naturalism in general is characterised by a privileging of description at the expense of plot.

Naturalism stands out as a literature defined by its relationship to history, neither the Romantic historical novel's auratic mysteries of distant times and places, nor the disavowal of modernity witnessed in Decadent fiction's disdain for the here and now. Although literary critics keen to defend naturalism from the naïvety of its referential claims have often stressed the creative distortions afforded by the mediating effects of its fiction, readers of Romanticism and Decadence could not fail to notice the disturbing immanence of recent and contemporary French history barely concealed in much naturalist literature. As the Second Empire came to a close, Zola was planning the Rougon-Macquart cycle, its subtitle 'Histoire naturelle et sociale d'une famille sous le Second Empire' pointing towards the new scientific authorities of genetics and sociology, which reflected Taine's explanatory categories, 'race' and 'milieu'. Henceforth Zola attempted to establish clear water between realism and naturalism, defining the latter as a scientifically rigorous systematisation of the observational realism practised, actually in radically different ways, by Balzac, Stendhal, Champfleury, Duranty, and Flaubert. By the time the first volume, *La Fortune des Rougon*, appeared in book form (1871), the Second Empire had been replaced by the Third Republic, with this transition marked traumatically by defeat in the Franco-Prussian War and the civil war of the Commune ('moment', or the pressures of historical actuality, being Taine's third category). In the preface Zola explains how history has intervened to impose political and aesthetic closure: 'la chute des Bonaparte, dont j'avais besoin comme artiste, et que toujours je trouvais fatalement au bout du drame, sans oser l'espérer si prochaine . . . [Mon œuvre] est, dès aujourd'hui, complète . . . elle devient le tableau d'un règne mort, d'une étrange époque de folie et de honte' ('the fall of the Bonapartes, which I needed as an artist, and which I saw fatally at the end of the drama, without daring to hope that it might be so close . . . [My work] is, from today, complete . . . it becomes the depiction of a dead regime, of a strange era of madness and shame').[2] The preface advertises an epic family romance: 'comment une famille, un petit groupe d'êtres, se comporte dans une société, en s'épanouissant pour donner naissance à dix, à vingt individus qui paraissent, au premier coup d'œil, profondément dissemblables, mais que l'analyse montre intimement liés les

---

2 Ibid., IV, p. 21. Translations are mine.

uns aux autres' ('how a family, a little group of beings, behaves in a society, blossoming to give birth to ten or twenty individuals who, at first glance, seem profoundly dissimilar, but whom analysis shows to be intimately connected to each other').[3] This genealogical fiction pursues the legitimate (Rougon) and illegitimate (Macquart) strands of the family and thereby criticises the excesses of Napoleon III's Empire: 'la famille que je me propose d'étudier, a pour caractéristique le débordement des appétits, le large soulèvement de notre âge, qui se rue aux jouissances' ('the characteristic of the family I plan to study is the excess of appetites, the vast uprising of our age, hell-bent on pleasure').[4]

For all Zola's liberal sympathies, it says much for the underlying conservatism of his work that the most famous (and melodramatic) of his novels emanate from the pathology of the illegitimate line. Zola was more of a reformist than a revolutionary, and in this he embodies many of the compromises of the Third Republic, unwilling to return to monarchy or empire, but traumatised by the memory of the Commune. As such, he is to be contrasted with Jules Vallès (1832–85), a novelist more formally and politically radical, who recounts events in Paris in 1870–1 in the diary format of *L'Insurgé* (1886). Vallès writes his own *romans du peuple* from the unstable vantage point of the street and refuses to adopt the 'bad faith' inherent in the high view of naturalist omniscience. Indeed, left-wing criticism (most famously from György Lukács) has retained an ambivalent relationship with the *maître de Médan* – so-called because of the followers Zola gathered at the house bought on the proceeds from his *succès de scandale*, *L'Assommoir*, which brought naturalist writing to the attention of a mass public (of which more below). Although one should not exaggerate their subservience, this group of young writers associated with the project of post-Flaubertian social realism, took the strategic decision to publish alongside Zola a collection of short stories about the Franco-Prussian War, *Les Soirées de Médan* (1880). These writers included: Henry Céard (1851–1924), Léon Hennique (1851–1935), and Paul Alexis (1847–1901), best remembered for their novels of adultery, *Une belle journée*, *L'Accident de M. Hébert* (1883) and *Madame Meuriot* (1890); but most notably Guy de Maupassant (1850–93), who penned not only scores of much-loved short stories but also a handful of novels including *Bel-Ami* (1885); and J.-K. Huysmans (1840–1907), whose first novel, *Marthe, histoire d'une fille* (1876), marked out the naturalist fascination for female transgression in the form of the prostitute, not just in the motif of wifely adultery.

3 Ibid.   4 Ibid.

The exponential force of Zola's heteronormative family history rapidly turned the projected ten volumes of the Rougon-Macquart cycle into twenty, completed in 1893 by *Le Docteur Pascal*. By then, naturalism was no longer in the cultural vanguard, and here Zola's writing turns inwards in a gesture of reflexive self-justification, as its scientifically minded hero collects the genealogical data that would make possible the writing of the previous nineteen novels. As well as criticism from conservatives such as Brunetière, the 1880s saw dissent from within, not just in *À rebours* but also in the *Manifeste des cinq*, where young writers poured vitriol on the bestiality of *La Terre* (1887), a rural tale about the twin desires for sexual and territorial possession. Even Maupassant's timely defence was proffered in the preface to an 'étude psychologique' (*Pierre et Jean* [1887]), and thus in a rival novelistic tradition soon to be dominated by Paul Bourget (1852–1935). In reply to Jules Huret's *Enquête sur l'évolution littéraire* (1891), Alexis famously sent the desperate telegram: 'Naturalisme pas mort. Lettre suit.'

Voice and class in *L'Assommoir*

Rather than taking language for granted, *L'Assommoir* highlights its capacity to stage the tensions between polite society and the *peuple*. Hence this supposedly archetypal naturalist novel second-guesses the referential fallibility of the naturalist aesthetic. What can language best imitate if not language itself? Although the narrative voice of mimetic fiction wishes to pass itself off as natural and unbiased, it displays ideological specificity in terms of gender, race, and class. The middle-class language of the Frenchman in much naturalist fiction ensures the readability of these *textes de plaisir*. Yet naturalism promises anti-conservative critique rather than ideological affirmation. The Goncourts' tale of the secret life of the servant, Germinie Lacerteux, had already dramatised the way in which dominant social classes had in no small degree remained culturally blind to the realities of working-class life. In *L'Assommoir* the mismatch between radical ideas and mainstream expression is addressed in Zola's attempt to transcribe the popular language of the urban working class (the *argot* of *la langue verte*). So effective was such cross-class defamiliarisation that contemporary readers and critics complained immediately of the unreadability of Zola's prose. To this day, editions include a glossary of terms, thereby confirming the foreignness of this margin at the heart of the Hexagon. For Zola, the danger in an account such as Hugo's *Les Misérables* (1862) would be the verbal reinforcement of class boundaries, as the narrator leads his readers around the urban zoo, speaking of but not via the *peuple*. How, then, to stop liberal empathy from patronising? Must critical distance reinforce social difference?

Zola borrows, most clearly from Flaubert, the technique of free indirect discourse, referred to as *style indirect libre*. Rather than passively conveying the facts of the story as if in some caricature of naturalism, the narrator borrows the perspectives, and indeed language, of his characters. The blurring of first- and third-person viewpoints allows the narrator to inhabit their mindset momentarily. This slippage between quotation and narration foregrounds the common verbal wealth of representative politics (in other words, democracy) and fictional representation (*la voix* meaning voice as well as vote). Though it is tempting to gloss *Germinal* (1885) as Zola's political answer to the questions left hanging in the alcohol-scented air of his social novel *L'Assommoir*, one could read *L'Assommoir* as the novel of *le politique* (the political in its broadest adjectival sense), whereas *Germinal* addresses the literalism of explicit political ideologies, *la politique*. The anti-democratic politics of Napoleon III denies the inhabitants of the Goutte-d'or a political voice. One response to this is the idle *flânerie* of Gervaise's lover, Lantier, who likes few things more than 'pub talk' with his mates about the irrelevance of such elite subjects as politics. It is, they conclude, 'not for the likes of us'. Apparently trivial conversations between Lantier's associates give voice to the political alienation of the *peuple* in the wake of 1848. As an affront to the reactionary geopolitics of Napoleon III's Paris (and the neo-classical clarity of Baron Haussmann's redesign of the city), Zola's quotations without quotation marks remove from popular language those speech marks which cling like handcuffs to the popular language of Eugène Sue's *Les Mystères de Paris* (1842–3) or *Les Misérables*. Zola's cross-class gesture of free indirect speech repunctuates the sentences to which class identity habitually condemns us. It is easy to draw a dogmatic distinction between the prescriptive idealism of George Sand and the descriptive pessimism of mimetic fiction. The naturalist imperative of describing things as they are rather than as they ought to be undercuts the idealism that Goujet offers Gervaise. But the power of verbal play allows Zola to renegotiate the 'is/ought' philosophical problem, describing the status quo in a transgressive narrative mode. His manipulation of voice symbolically imposes on the genre of the novel a social porosity unthinkable in the class structure Gervaise actually inhabits.

In borrowing the voice from the body and nevertheless returning the voice to a proletarian body both repressed and fantasmatically resurgent in bourgeois fiction, Zola contributes to what might be termed a cult of presence in Third Republic writing. So rapid does the acceleration of modern society appear to be, that the responsibility to capture the immediacy of the present moment of any linguistic utterance imposes itself not just on *L'Assommoir* but on sometimes strange bedfellows: the 'zutisme' of Rimbaud (1854–91), the dialogue novels of Gyp (1849–1932), and, beyond language, Impressionism's seizure of evanescence. We might even dimly intuit the modernist desire to capture in solid print form the stream of human consciousness, anticipated in the interior monologue of Edouard Dujardin's *Les Lauriers sont coupés* (1888). In Zola's case, however, this desire to conflate *mots* and *paroles* must be set against the dead hand of imperious narrative surveillance and its past historic diktats. The written word can barely manage to keep up with the immediacy and authenticity of speech, and it is little surprise that Zola was criticised for his failure to capture the rapidly changing nuances of *la langue verte*, if, in some general sense, the written word alienates language from the body.

The pitfalls of mimetic referentiality are accommodated by the dual reflexivity of *L'Assommoir*. Not only does language in this novel refer generally to language, as we have seen, but cross-class cultural politics are foregrounded specifically by the *mise en abyme* of the visit to the Louvre in Chapter 3. Short of activities to entertain guests after the wedding of Coupeau and Gervaise, Madinier suggests that everyone visit the Louvre. This comedy of snobbery, both haughty and inverted, emblematises the gesture of allowing the *peuple* right of entry into the places of high culture, which is precisely the grand project of *L'Assommoir* as a whole. More disturbing still, the Louvre scene overturns the social logic of the novel as a spectacle. Whereas *L'Assommoir* takes the novel-reading class of the Third Republic on a tour of Second Empire proletarian culture, Madinier takes the *peuple* on a tour of the elite culture of fine art. At moments, the *peuple* seem capable of deriding and desublimating the idealising force of classic art, hence the knowing glances at Mme Gaudron's pregnant belly before one of Murillo's early modern Spanish paintings of the Virgin Mary, whose theological force depends on her willingness and Joseph's to embrace the *invraisemblable*. Indeed, naturalism in general brings back to life two bodies repressed by the wider society of middle-class Frenchmen with whom its narrators identify: the working-class body and the female body. In spite of such carnivalesque derision, the visitors to the Louvre are seen to be bereft of the cultural vocabulary needed to make proper sense of the tableaux before them. In a literal as well as figurative sense, they lack a map to guide them, and in the end they need to be shown the door at closing time by the museum guards.

High and low

The social critique inherent in the naturalist project produced largely dystopian plots, which provided narrative enactments of the philosophy of pessimism associated with Schopenhauer, and of the theory of entropy articulated earlier in the century by the second law of thermodynamics, following the work of the physicist Sadi Carnot (1796–1832). As lives (and their material contexts) fray at the edges and fall apart, a lexis of decomposition informs Zola's texts, not least in the critique of bourgeois sexual hypocrisy offered by Juillerat and Mauduit in *Pot-Bouille* (1882), following his tale of the courtesan, *Nana* (1880), whose career culminates in the desublimation of theatrical and classical myth: 'Vénus se décomposait' ('Venus was decomposing').[5] Counter to this pessimistic diagnosis of dystopia, entropy, and decomposition, stands the sheer energy of Zola's enterprise, which finds an analogue in the vital force of a protagonist such as Octave Mouret. He graduates from the sexual seduction of the married women who live behind the crumbling, kitsch architectural facade of Haussmannised Paris in the apartments of the building on the rue de Choiseul which houses the plot of *Pot-Bouille*, to the commercial seduction of similar women in the vast department store which gives its name to the next novel, *Au Bonheur des Dames* (1883). The explicit critique of pessimism in Chapter 3, in Octave's argument with his world-weary old schoolfriend Vallagnosc, is echoed in that rare naturalist trope: a romantic happy ending, as the shop assistant Denise tames her voracious boss and offers an enlightened communitarian alternative to his rabid capitalism. The final decade of Zola's career saw him pursue such utopian idealism in the ensuing novel series, *Les Trois Villes* (1894–8), and the unfinished *Les Quatre Evangiles* (1899–1903).

It is one of the characteristics of Zola's fiction that it has attracted the empathy of other practitioners of fiction more than the admiration of academic critics. It is also true that French naturalism was particularly influential outside France, not least in North and South America as well as Germany and Spain. Indeed, the critical ignominy heaped upon naturalism means that any account of such writing must appear defensive in the present company, lodged, as all Zola scholarship must be, somewhere between accounts of Flaubert and Proust. The teleology that encourages subsequent readers to analyse the nineteenth century in light of twentieth- and twenty-first-century concerns is bound to disadvantage Zola. For, on the high road to modernism and

---

5 Ibid., IX, p. 277.

then to postmodernism, naturalism looks like a wrong turning, or, worse still, an intellectual cul-de-sac. Rather than judging naturalism in terms of the objectivity it advertises, and then dismissing such terms of reference, it makes more sense to view it as a reaction to early modern and then Romantic intellectual culture. From a purely aesthetic standpoint, it is hard to miss naturalism's flaws; but from the perspective of cultural historians of literature, naturalism appears to be doubly symptomatic. Keen as it was to depict the pathological symptoms of modernity, it now lends itself to particularly rich readings of the ideological symptoms shared by this literature of the body and the attendant discourses of nineteenth-century medicine. To apply the models of social and cultural history to naturalism is to understand it in cognate terms, if not on its own terms.

In one sense, naturalism was a literature that fantasised about not being literature at all, and part of the difficulty in the critical assimilation of naturalism lies in its Janus-like insistence on a dual relationship to popular culture as well as literary history. Ever since the success of L'Assommoir, Zola's writing has been popular as well as populist. As such, his fiction loomed large in the marketplace it describes, not least in Le Ventre de Paris (1873) and Au Bonheur des Dames. As Charles Bernheimer reminds us in the 'headline' to his piece on Zola and the novel of prostitution, in another kind of literary history: 'Forty-five Thousand Copies of Emile Zola's Nana Are Sold on its Publication Day.'[6] Zola remains to this day the most popular of all French writers in that most popularising of publications, the Livre de Poche series – his sales only bettered by one foreign author, Agatha Christie. Zola's fiction has been habitually popular with undergraduates, sometimes, it seems, almost to the mild irritation of sober academics. However, the limits of the scientific analogy and the gap between Zola's theory and practice, initially used to undermine the referential claims of the naturalist project, have in recent decades allowed critics to identify the mythopoeic and symbolic qualities of such writing, and thus assert its literariness. Indeed, to read the fiction against its own theory is to assert the properly 'literary' qualities of a kind of writing that has rarely sat easily with la critique universitaire. Moreover, for all the aesthetic flaws of naturalism, the ethos of J'accuse persists: authenticity, sincerity, and social morality.

6 C. Bernheimer, 'Prostitution in the Novel', in D. Hollier (ed.), A New History of French Literature (Cambridge MA: Harvard University Press, 1989), p. 780.

59

Impressionism: art, literature, and history, 1870–1914

ROBERT LETHBRIDGE

A Studio in the Batignolles Quarter, by Henri Fantin-Latour (1836–1904), is an emblematic picture. It was produced in 1870, and immediately caricatured as 'Jesus Painting among the Disciples, or the Divine School of Manet'. That response anticipates hostile contemporary critical reaction to the new avant-garde. It groups around Édouard Manet (1832–83) younger men we think of as the Impressionists, notably Auguste Renoir (1841–1919), Frédéric Bazille (1841–70), and Claude Monet (1840–1926). And it includes Émile Zola (1840–1902), the first of whose twenty-volume Rougon-Macquart series had just been started and who would dominate French literature (or at least the novel genre) until its completion in 1892. All those dates are telling, speaking of a particular artistic generation and the intersections of pictorial, textual, and political history.

The latter, in particular, is too seldom evoked in this context. Shortly after this apparently optimistic statement of aesthetic solidarity, France suffered a catastrophic defeat in the Franco-Prussian War (1870–1), leading directly to the civil war of the Commune and the burning of Paris. The resulting disruption meant that it was only in February 1871, for example, that Manet discovered that Bazille, who had volunteered for military duty early in the conflict, had been killed in action on 28 November 1870. Renoir survived in spite of being called up. Manet and Edgar Degas (1834–1917) enlisted in the National Guard. Zola found refuge in Marseille and Bordeaux. Camille Pissarro (1830–1903) left his paintings in his studio at Louveciennes and fled to Brittany before seeking exile in London, being joined there by Alfred Sisley (1839–99) whose own rural studio, at Bougival, had also been sacked by the invading German armies. Monet too spent this period in England. And this hiatus in French cultural life meant that there would be no annual Salon exhibition in Paris until 1872.

The luminous and tranquil images of Impressionism have obscured for posterity the terrible circumstances of the movement's emergence. The exact relation between this art and history remains a matter of debate. Although an exhibition in London in March 1871, at which Pissarro showed his *Effect of Snow*, has been termed the "'pre-première" Impressionist exhibition',[1] it was not until the spring of 1874 that the first Impressionist exhibition, organised as such by the painters, took place and that the term itself was established in the public domain. The Fantin-Latour collective portrait of 1870 is thus both proleptic and misleading to the extent that Manet himself never explicitly allowed himself to be thought of as the leader of a 'school'. It was also partly retrospective. For, at this stage, his own controversial status (achieved as a result of paintings as notorious as *Olympia* [1863] and *Le Déjeuner sur l'herbe* [1865]) was simply a rallying point for painters who had been experimenting, and flouting convention, since the mid-1860s. That they were bold enough to do so is arguably linked to the liberalising terminal period of the Second Empire (1852–70), during which the ad hoc creation of the Salon des Refusés (1863) neatly symbolises attempts by the authorities of a repressive regime to accommodate marginal expressions of protest. There is less consensus in respect of the immediate consequences of the events of 1870–1 for the development of Impressionism. The most persuasive account is Jane Roos's contention that, rather than being a response to the recent collapse of institutional constraints, the catalyst for the painters' organisation of an artistic movement in its own subversive right was political: the return of conservative forces in the shape of the 'Ordre Moral' presidency of General MacMahon, and specifically the new Salon des Refusés of 1873 indicating the exclusion of modernist tendencies.[2] When they put on their own exhibition the next year, the painters deliberately pre-empted the official Salon to which, for the first time, they did not submit works, not least in scheduling it (15 April – 15 May) immediately before it. This was a 'thoughtfully conceived counter-exhibition', as Roos puts it. And, by holding it in Nadar's former studio, Albert Boime adds that it was freighted not only with the urban intensity captured from its window in Monet's *Boulevard des Capucines* (1873) but also surrounded with a 'political aura' by virtue of the photographer having famously concealed there two prominent escapees of the Commune.[3] As John House has more plausibly and more generally demonstrated, the political dimensions of Impressionism extend beyond groupings and exhibition strategies to issues of legibility and the rule-breaking brushwork of its exponents.[4]

1 M. Melot, *The Impressionist Print* (New Haven, CT: Yale University Press, 1996), p. 100.
2 J. Roos, *Early Impressionism and the French State (1866–1874)* (Cambridge: Cambridge University Press, 1996), pp. 182–99.
3 A. Boime, *Art in an Age of Civil Struggle, 1848–1871* (Chicago: University of Chicago Press, 2007), p. 753.
4 J. House, *Impressionism: Paint and Politics* (New Haven, CT: Yale University Press, 2004), p. 8.

The other sets of histories encoded, or occluded, in the iconic 1870 Fantin-Latour picture which decorates so many catalogues and book-covers, are personal and literary. Zola's presence there testifies to overlapping friendships and to his pioneering role as an art critic. He had been the first to defend Manet in the press, polemically, if not without self-interest, predicting his profile in our narratives of modern art. As a result, the writer was on uniquely familiar terms with the painters who frequented the Café Guerbois (located in the 'Batignolles Quarter' of Fantin-Latour's title), which became the energising meeting point of a self-appointed avant-garde. To this he would in due course introduce Paul Cézanne (1839–1906), having encouraged him to come up to Paris from Aix-en-Provence where the two had enjoyed childhood and schooldays together. But the biographical cross-references are only part of the story. For if Zola's inclusion in these networks is explicable, his actual positioning in the Fantin-Latour picture is perhaps revealing. Turned away from Manet at his easel, he seems as awkwardly misplaced as in Bazille's *The Artist's Studio, Rue de la Condamine*, also of 1870 and picturing Manet, Monet, and Renoir, in which he is spatially and discursively disengaged from the work in progress. The same can be said of Manet's *Portrait of Emile Zola* (1868). Often cited as a celebratory statement of shared aims and aesthetic values grounded in a pattern of creative interchanges, it may speak as much of the tensions and rivalries between literature and the visual arts during the whole of this period.[5]

Manet would remain Zola's favourite painter. This is brought into sharper relief by the fact that, over three decades, from his first writing on painting in 1866 up until 1896 (when he does so for the last time), there are only passing mentions of Cézanne, with not a single one of his works subject to analysis or detailed appreciation. By comparison, there are over 100 references to Manet, and almost thirty to Monet. Yet Manet's privileged status also illuminates Zola's shifting attitude to Impressionism. His initial enthusiasm for it is predicated on the assumption that it is a realist mode, its practitioners 'voués à l'étude de la nature' ('devoted to the study of nature'),[6] exemplified in landscapes liberated from the inauthenticities of academic practice and studio conditions, and in properly modern subjects of the kind to be found in his own novels. In the 1870s, Zola would dismiss the negative connotations of 'impressionistic' which had been crystallised (if not invented) in

5 R. Lethbridge, 'Manet's Textual Frames', in P. Collier and R. Lethbridge (eds.), *Artistic Relations: Literature and the Visual Arts in Nineteenth-Century France* (New Haven, CT: Yale University Press, 1994), pp. 153–7.
6 É. Zola, *Ecrits sur l'art*, ed. J.-P. Leduc-Adine (Paris: Gallimard, 1991), p. 419.

Louis Leroy's satirical response (in *Le Charivari* of 25 April 1874) to the inaugural exhibition and identified since as the movement's baptismal moment. As the pictures themselves gradually became sketchier, leaving behind the compositional and tonal structures that Zola continued to admire in Manet, he found himself adopting the lexicon of Impressionism's original critics, castigating its mimetic insufficiencies and incompletions. And this increasingly unsympathetic commentary would culminate in the writing of *L'Œuvre* (1886), in which Zola's composite portrait of the painters of his time resulted in Cézanne breaking off a forty-year friendship, and in a notorious dinner-party, attended by Pissarro, Monet, and others, at which it was determined that Joris-Karl Huysmans (1848–1907) should be substituted as their champion, given the perception of his more sensitive understanding of modern painting.

Literary Impressionism

But Zola's approach to Impressionist painting is as instructive as it has been influential. His militant assimilation of Impressionism and naturalism does not survive scrutiny (even without recourse to his own progressive disenchantment). There remain equations less easy to dismiss, at the level of subject and theme, between the painting of the period and the work of the majority of contemporary novelists: stations, steam-engines and railways; the suburbs; river settings west of the capital; scenes from peasant or working-class life; laundresses; cafés and carriages; absinthe drinkers; strolling Parisian crowds; markets and shops; prostitutes and brothels. There are also analogies of perspective in innumerable panoramic views from windows, balconies, or other elevated sites (such as Montmartre) overlooking the bustle of the modern city. And so precise are the correlations of descriptive fabric, with a similar emphasis on the unfocused and the play of light and shade at different times of day according to the weather, that temptations of transpositional identification are hard to resist. There are clearly specific instances when such a critical move is justified: Manet's painting *Nana* (1877), for example, is almost certainly inspired in part by the apprenticeship of the Nana who appears in the second half of Zola's *L'Assommoir* (serialised in the autumn of 1876) prior to her re-presentation in the scene in *Nana* (1880), in which the courtesan transfixes Count Muffat's obsessive gaze while admiring herself in the mirror. In *Une Page d'amour* (1878), Zola inserts into its five parts successive extended views of Paris, differentiated only by time and tonality, which seem to correspond to the series of paintings by Monet and Pissarro: the former's twenty versions of Rouen Cathedral (exhibited together in 1895) look back to his multiple paintings of the Gare Saint-Lazare in the mid-1870s; the latter's repeated re-workings of Parisian vistas (the Pont-Neuf, the Boulevard Montmartre, and more than fifty images of the Tuileries) can be read back against Zola's preface to the illustrated edition of the novel in 1884. And there are countless passages, also in the writing of Gustave Flaubert (1821–80), Alphonse Daudet (1840–97), the Goncourt brothers (Jules, 1830–70; Edmond, 1822–96) and Guy de Maupassant (1850–93), to cite only the best known, that can be juxtaposed to pictorial equivalents. Even when this is no more than coincidence in terms of detail, such intersections point to a newly expanded focus on the prosaic texture of the modern world and new ways of seeing it.

An attempted codification of these parallels is to be found in 'L'Impressionnisme dans le roman', published in the *Revue des deux mondes* on 15 November 1879 by the doyen of conservative critics, Ferdinand Brunetière (1849–1906). Supposedly a review of one of Daudet's novels, this essay both laments and systematises the literary techniques corresponding to those of contemporary painting: the prevalence of synecdoche and the descriptive imperfect; grammatical dislocation; the absence of a stable narrative point of view, the suppression of conjunctions and the accumulation of superimposed notations, all in the interests of visual immediacy; a stress on the language of the senses, with nominative constructions and adjectival nouns replacing qualifying epithets. What is often equated with (and defying translation) *l'écriture artiste* is as characteristic of the stylistic particularities of Flaubert's *L'Education sentimentale* (1869) as it is of Daudet's *Le Nabab* (1877) and the Goncourt brothers' writing, from *Charles Demailly* (1860) onwards. For if many of Zola's novels also gesture towards this kind of literary Impressionism, Philippe Hamon's seminal essay shows that, in more fundamental ways, his prose remains paradoxically clear even when referring to blur, suggesting the extent to which a traditional rhetoric informs what may ultimately be superficial descriptive experimentation.[7] But it is also true, more generally, that necessarily sequential reading is at odds with the illusion of undirected optical experience available to the painter. And even the most striking of textual effects remain linguistically and syntactically anchored by the imperatives of rhythm, cadence, and harmony, in which the potential extremes of dislocation and repetition are subordinate to the priorities of a sense-making verbal contract. The limits of the seductive analogy between the arts, in

---

7 P. Hamon, 'À propos de l'impressionnisme de Zola', *Les Cahiers naturalistes*, 34 (1967), pp. 139–47.

this period, are evident in Zola's *L'Œuvre*. On the one hand, the repeated translations of his fictional (and failed) painter's gaze into virtuoso word-paintings seem to confirm Degas's reported remark that Zola had written the entire novel 'pour prouver la grande supériorité de l'homme de lettres sur l'artiste' ('to demonstrate the clear superiority of the writer over the painter').[8] On the other, impressionistic effects are not only framed by the delineations, perspectival coordinates, and geometry Impressionism had erased, but also editorially corrected in the recuperative signalling of the material realities it seemed to have lost sight of.

The work of the Goncourts provides an alternative argument whereby the descriptive effects of literary Impressionism do not so much evoke an external reality as foreground their own linguistic substance. This is certainly one of Brunetière's principal objections to it, likening verbal superimposition to the sensation of glutinous and all-too-visible paint in Impressionist pictures approached too closely, effectively obscuring the object of intended focus. Edmond de Goncourt's definition of *l'écriture artiste*, in the preface to *Les Frères Zemganno* (1879), lays claim to its capacity to penetrate beneath the surfaces of external reality. In trying to capture its palpitating and fleeting nuances, however, this kind of writing too often degenerates into inanimate linguistic inventory and a frenetic vertigo of synonym and substitution. It is ironic that while the Goncourts aimed to explore the possibility of representing the temporality which the visual arts could not, Impressionism itself adopts that challenge more effectively. Nor is it beside the point that it should be Brunetière, as the spokesman of stable cultural values, who criticised Edmond de Goncourt for being 'plus attentif aux mots qu'aux choses' ('more attentive to words than things'), thereby inadvertently anticipating Stéphane Mallarmé's (1842–98) radical poetic principle: 'Peindre non la chose mais l'effet qu'elle produit' ('Depict not the thing but the sensation it produces').

Mallarmé had himself written a penetrating essay entititled 'The Impressionists and Edouard Manet' (published in English translation in the *Art Monthly Review* in 1876), and he was among the guests at that dinner-party, mentioned earlier, at which it was decided that Zola was no longer qualified to write on the painters' behalf. But to bring so prominent a poet into the discussion is also to suggest that it is perhaps in contemporary poetry – rather than in the novel as a genre – that Impressionism finds a more valid equivalence. To read the verbal sketches of London by Paul Verlaine (1844–96) as virtual

8 Cited by T. Reff, 'Degas and the Literature of his Time', in U. Finke (ed.), *French Nineteenth-Century Painting and Literature* (Manchester: Manchester University Press, 1972), p. 203.

commentaries on Monet's views of the Thames is to risk falling back to the level of analogy. It is more profitable to interpret his 'recueillir des impressions' ('capture impressions') within a similar effort to locate the poetic essence behind prosaic surfaces, outlined in the third verse of his 'L'Art poétique' (1874), with its emphasis on nuance and the inderterminacies of optical experience. The visual semantics of Arthur Rimbaud's (1854–91) significantly entitled *Les Illuminations* (1874) are even more rewarding in this respect. His landscapes and city scapes often dissolve in a fragmentation of colour freed from reference, as his shadows and clouds become subjects rather than objects of reflection. His 'Fleurs', to take a single example, with its illogically euphoric colorations, looks precociously forward to the dazzling indistinctions of Monet's Giverny paintings at the turn of the century, forcing us to resist clarity of focus in the dynamic process of stepping forward to, and back from, the canvas. Such poetry, like Mallarmé's own, seeks out the vestigial and the non-recognisable. It operates on the margins of legibility and privileges the undefined and the syntactically ambiguous, its impact inseparable from the discontinuities and paradoxes it illuminates. Indeed, if the essentially non-referential qualities of poetic language make it akin to modes characteristic of painting after 1880, it is not perverse to argue that it is only with music (as in the modulations of Claude Debussy's [1862–1918] *La Mer*, 1903–5) that Impressionism's pretexts and practices can be genuinely compared.

The end of Impressionism

While the above heading instantly evokes Richard Shiff's authoritative book on the subject,[9] consideration of where it 'ends up' begs the prior question of Impressionism's original directions. Both Zola's initial celebration of its apparently realist ambitions and his ensuing disappointment remind us that such painting's current popularity may also be based on partially false assumptions. To track its development, from the quasi-photographic works of the 1860s to Pissarro's *Applepicking* (1888) is to problematise, in hindsight, the conceptual framework through which Impressionism is habitually viewed. For even an early work such as Monet's *Impression: Sunrise* (1872) (such titles afforded Leroy his satirical licence), when viewed up close, is less the dawn over Le Havre than fractured pigment prefiguring the increasingly *pointilliste* technique associated with neo-Impressionism (coined as a term in

---

9 R. Shiff, *Cézanne and the End of Impressionism: A Study of the Theory, Technique, and Critical Evaluation of Modern Art* (Chicago: University of Chicago Press, 1984).

1887) and the work of Georges Seurat (1859–91) and Paul Signac (1863–1935). Impressionist preference for evanescent subjects (water, rain, snow, shifting patterns of light, reflections of boats and bridges), capturing the instantaneous, may itself be seen less as realist endeavour than symptomatic of a more profound shift towards the primacy of subjectivity, locating the perceptual construction of the external world in the projections of the perceiving self. As in Rimbaud, vision is no longer synonymous with visuality. Such changes of emphasis need to take account of factors as diverse as advances in contemporary philosophy, psychology, and the science of optics.

Those wider contexts have literary consequences too, whether in the shape of what is known as 'la crise du roman'[10] or in the musings of Mallarmé's 'Crise de vers'. Novelists such as Paul Bourget (1852–1935), Huysmans, or even the later Maupassant, leave behind the explanations of material determinants to explore the inner life. Impressionism's own so-called 'crisis' is also situated in the 1880s, with the break-up of artistic groupings confirmed in the eighth, and last, of its exhibitions in 1886: the year of Seurat's friend and admirer, Jean Moréas's (1856–1910) Symbolist manifesto (Le Figaro, 18 September), Zola's L'Œuvre (with its autobiographical irritation at the loss of, and nostalgia for, the heroic certainties of the 1860s), and the emergence of the vitriolic critical rejection of naturalism itself (Le Manifeste des Cinq, 1887). In practice, strategic unity had always masked both individual sensibilities and agendas, from the moment that more than thirty artists assembled 165 works in Nadar's former studio twelve years earlier. And within apparently coherent developments an artist such as Degas reflects the ambivalence of, on the one hand, inspiration in the gritty realism of Zola's early novels and, on the other, the self-reflexivity of art in performance.[11]

It remains true that, from the 1880s onwards, the directions of Impressionism are less in doubt, theorised in fin-de-siècle Symbolist theory (in the writings of Gustave Khan [1859–1936], Jules Laforgue [1860–87], and others associated with painting and painters). The function of art, both textual and pictorial, is now to objectify the subjective impression as a symbol, or idea, of universal significance. As early as 1874, however, a critic as intelligent as Jules Castagnary (1830–88) had already noted of the first exhibition that 'they are impressionists in the sense that they render not the landscape, but the sensation produced by the landscape'; 'leaving reality', as he goes on, 'to enter into full idealism', and thereby revealing permanent truths as well as particularised and

---

10 M. Raimond, La Crise du roman (Paris: Corti, 1966).
11 D. Kelley, 'Degas: Naturalist Novelist or Symbolist Poet?', French Studies, 38.3 (1984), pp. 306–18.

transient ones. The Impressionists no longer record the individuation of community, or of town and country. Social history, at least, is relegated to factory chimneys on the skyline (in Pissarro) or registered in the anonymous dots of urban crowds. Instead, the fullest expression of Impressionism is arguably to be found in Monet's *Water-Lilies* (1899–1904), in the appropriately narcissistic reflections of reflection.

Zola's confrontations with Symbolist art reject such paintings' incursion into the literary domain. In the work of Gustave Moreau (1826–98) he detects a return to an intellectualism akin to a latter-day Romanticism. More generally, he is disorientated by the disintegration of 'schools' and hierarchies, referring as early as 1875 to 'l'anarchie complète des tendances' ('the complete anarchy of tendencies') and repeating this word-for-word six years later.[12] But he is certainly right in identifying transitional disorder. Cézanne is not depicting their native Provence but abstracting Mont Saint-Victoire into pre-Cubist patterns which would effect a radical break in the history of art. Gustave Caillebotte (1848–94) moves from views from a balcony to its iron lacework through which Parisian shapes are seen. Vincent van Gogh (1853–90), whether reworking Zola's evocation of working-class famine (*The Potato Eaters*, 1885), Jean-François Millet's (1814–75) tropes or making still-lives of novels scattered across a table (*The Yellow Books, Parisian Novels*, 1887), Paul Gauguin (1848–1903) (exploring the archetypal and irrational), and Odilon Redon (1840–1916) (mythology and the occult) are so distinct from each other that labels and 'movements' seem arbitrary. The Société des Artistes Indépendants was founded in 1884 by Seurat, Signac, and Henri-Edmond Cross (1856–1910). But the first two of these were invited to participate in the final Impressionist exhibition two years later. And Cross, who began his career under the aegis of Monet, went on to become one of the principal exponents of neo-Impressionism, and spent his *pointilliste* period in Signac's camp in 1904 and his Fauvist one under the influence of Henri Matisse (1869–1954). The 'post-Impressionist' Henri Toulouse-Lautrec (1864–1901) is inseparable from the earlier work of Degas. Decadents, Nabis, Fauvists, and Expressionists are all indebted, however awkwardly, to the freedoms enacted by Impressionism. It would be equally tendentious to straighten the jagged relations between Rimbaud's spatial projections on the page and the typographical effects of Guillaume Apollinaire's (1880–1918) posthumously published *Calligrammes* (1918).

On the eve of the First World War, Roger Fry and Clive Bell 'justified the Symbolists and post-Impressionist aesthetics with a set of universal concepts

12 Zola, *Écrits*, pp. 285, 443.

which legitimised them for the art-buying elite'.[13] It is at least as important to bring together the indirections of 'cultural crisis' and the historical vicissitudes of these final decades of the century (and of the Third Republic), which were marked by massive social unrest in France. Decomposition is not merely safely pictorial and literary. Anarchism, in its other (violent 1892–4) sense, is a bomb thrown into the Chamber of Deputies and the assassination of President Carnot. This reminds us that the imaginative geographies of the neo-Impressionists are as ideologically constructed as their commitment to landscape is shared by Piotr Kropotkin (1842–1921). Through their association of traditional (and even much Impressionist) landscape with tourist leisure and luxurious consumption by the urban viewer, they consciously restore the social tensions and commodification evacuated from idealised sites of harmony between nature and human experience. The admixture of the picturesque and industrial refashioned in Seurat's Asnières and *La Grande Jatte* (1884–6) can be traced back to Pissarro. Maximilien Luce's (1858–1941) *Site in Montmartre, Rue Championnet* (1887), his post-1896 pictures of manual workers, and Signac's dystopian views of Clichy are all as oppositional as conjuring up, in the latter's 1894–5 mural, *In the Time of Harmony*, a medievalised vision of social cohesion. In the shadow of the Dreyfus Affair (ranging lifelong artist friends against each other after 1893), such imaginings were more urgent than ever. As France returns to the nationalist right, political history informs the end of Impressionism as much as it did its beginnings.

13 A. Boime, *Revelation of Modernism: Responses to Cultural Crisis in Fin-de-Siècle Painting* (Columbia: University of Missouri Press, 2008), p. 221.

60

Decadence

HANNAH THOMPSON

As a manifestation of a set of intellectual and artistic preoccupations, elements of decadence exist throughout French literature in writers as diverse as Sade (*Justine* [1791]; republished 1884), Flaubert (*Salammbô* [1862]), Barbey d'Aurevilly (*Les Diaboliques* [1874]), Gautier (*Mademoiselle de Maupin* [1835]), Villiers de l'Isle-Adam (*L'Eve future* [1886]), and Baudelaire (*Les Fleurs du Mal* [1857]). An interest in decadence was not a uniquely French phenomenon but occurred in the work of writers and artists throughout Western Europe in the latter years of the nineteenth century. However, this chapter focuses primarily on the movement known as Decadence which flourished in France in the years between the catastrophic French defeat at Sedan (1870) and the Dreyfus Affair (1898–9). Decadence, which is related to, but not the same as, terms like 'modernism', 'fin-de-siècle', and 'avant-garde', is used to describe a disparate and often contradictory group of writers who were drawn together by a specific combination of historical events, intellectual attitudes, and social and scientific circumstances. The characteristics of Decadence are notoriously difficult to define, and detailed discussions of various critical definitions can be found elsewhere.[1] This chapter will begin by investigating the state of post-Second Empire France, before examining the most significant thematic and aesthetic concerns which developed in this specific historical context, and united (however tenuously) the Decadent writers J.-K. Huysmans, Rachilde (the pseudonym of Marguerite Eymery), Octave Mirbeau, Joséphin Péladan, Jean Lorrain, Rémy de Gourmont, and Pierre Louÿs as well as the artist Gustave Moreau.

The positivism that characterises much Balzacian realism is an accurate reflection of the prevailing mood in the second half of the nineteenth century. France's confident belief in social, economic, and scientific progress coupled

1 See David Weir's important discussion of the various ways in which decadence can be defined in *Decadence and the Making of Modernity* (Amherst: University of Massachusetts Press, 1995), pp. 1–22.

with advances in medicine, the advent of consumer culture, a belated Industrial Revolution, the modernisation of Paris and the creation of a new class of affluent and ambitious bourgeois workers all contributed to an optimistic and self-confident nation. This optimism reached its peak during the hedonistic excesses of the Second Empire (1852–70), known as the 'fête impériale'.[2] Napoleon III's France, particularly his newly 'Haussmannised' Paris, was greedy, selfish, and corrupt. Money and pleasure were the twin idols of the regime and they were worshipped by all those who had the means to do so. The frivolous and jubilant consumption of the Second Empire was widely held responsible for France's defeat by the Prussians at the decisive battle of Sedan which marked the end of the Franco-Prussian War and the subsequent collapse of Napoleon III's Second Empire. France's fall also signalled the end of the country's status as the dominant European power brought about at the beginning of the century by the triumphant achievements of Napoleon III's much more successful great-uncle and namesake. After Sedan, France became a weak and diminished nation, threatened on all sides by the might of Germany, Italy, Russia, and Great Britain. In addition, France was hit by a population crisis which further diminished the nation's already deflated self-confidence. It was felt that the moral depravity of the Second Empire – grippingly illustrated in Émile Zola's novels of Second Empire excess *La Curée* (1872) and *Nana* (1880) – was responsible for the catastrophic defeat at Sedan. Like the Roman and Byzantine Empires, the Second Empire was seen to fall when moral decay led to military weakness. Perverse – that is, pleasurable rather than procreative – sexuality was hailed as the most pernicious reason for France's perceived degeneration. The new (pre-Freudian) science of sexology, which flourished in France in the 1880s and 1890s, revealed, and more importantly explained, a range of sexual behaviours – such as fetishism, hysteria, and male and female homosexuality – which had hitherto only been suspected. By disclosing the array of human sexual perversions which were being engaged in at the time, as well as their perceived effects on the physical, mental, and emotional health of their perpetrators, such studies – of which Krafft-Ebing's *Psychopathia Sexualis* (1886) is the most significant – suggested, however spuriously, that sexual perversion contributed to the degeneration of the nation.

This view was widely held by the Parisian intellectual elite and Zola's twenty-volume Rougon-Macquart novel series (1871–93) is an example of a

2 For an intelligent and insightful examination of the excesses of the Second Empire see David Baguley, *Napoleon III and his Regime: An Extravaganza* (Baton Rouge: Louisiana State University Press, 2000).

fictional work that reacted to the historical moment in which it was produced by illustrating the perceived impact of this degeneracy on the French nation. Maxime Saccard (*La Curée* [1872] and *L'Argent* [1891]) is both physically and morally degenerate. His physical weakness, manifested through his effeminacy, is echoed in his sexual promiscuity, adulterous and semi-incestuous liaisons, and taste for expensive and indulgent pleasures. Ultimately the premature death of his young haemophiliac son Charles (*Le Docteur Pascal* [1893]) signals the fate of a family whose degenerate heredity inevitably leads to its own destruction. Charles's death is an allegorical representation of France's weakened state: France's strength is draining away as degeneracy leads to both physical and moral weakness. Zola's condemnation of nineteenth-century degeneracy is not absolute. Indeed there are elements of his novel series that celebrate the exuberant excesses of the *fin-de-siècle*. We should remember that Decadence and naturalism are closely related and cannot always be distinguished. Naturalist writers such as Zola and Maupassant show an interest in the themes and motifs of Decadent literature whilst Decadent writers frequently employ naturalist techniques in their work. Indeed J.-K. Huysmans started out as a disciple of Zola's and wrote the resolutely naturalist texts *Les Sœurs Vatard* (1879) and *En ménage* (1881) before his seminal Decadent text *À rebours* (1884) made of him the putative leader of the Decadent movement. On the whole, however, naturalism condemned the pleasure-seeking ethos of the age. The Decadents, on the other hand, deliberately embraced, indeed knowingly celebrated, the very degeneracy that was criticised by the rest of France.

À rebours represents the culmination of a set of aesthetic concerns which were first clearly articulated in the work of Théophile Gautier and Charles Baudelaire. Gautier's preface to the 1868 Calmann-Lévy edition of *Les Fleurs du Mal* and Baudelaire's essay *Le Peintre de la vie moderne* (1863), especially the passages in praise of make-up and jewellery, epitomise the rejection of the natural, the concomitant celebration of the artificial, and the related investment in aestheticism characteristic of Decadent literature. Unlike the Romantics – with whom the Decadents share certain concerns such as an introverted interest in the cult of the individual, the association of Beauty and Death and an erotic sensibility – the Decadents saw an investment in the artificial as arrogant proof of man's superiority: unlike other mammals, man is not dependent on nature but in control of it, able to manipulate the natural order of things and to change the way the world works. The title of Huysmans's masterpiece, which can mean 'Against Nature', 'The Wrong Way Round', or 'Against the Grain', gestures towards this rejection of the natural order which is illustrated throughout the novel. *À rebours* is the story of Decadent anti-hero Jean des Floressas Des Esseintes. Like Maxime's son Charles, Des Esseintes is the last in his aristocratic family line. His effeminacy, refined tastes, hypochondria, and dandyism – all archetypal Decadent traits – testify to his degenerate heredity. In his quest for aesthetic and intellectual perfection, and as a reaction against the horrors of everyday existence, Des Esseintes retreats from Paris to the solitude of his house in Fontenay. He closes himself away in a completely artificial world, which he has had specially designed and decorated, and engages in a quest for ideal beauty in which his imagination is charged with creating the kind of perfection impossible in reality. The novel is less a story of events than a list of Des Esseintes's tastes in art, literature, perfumes, and flowers; as such it quickly became the reference point for the Decadent movement and the primary articulation of the Decadent aesthetic.

There were other attempts to define literary Decadence: Paul Bourget produced a significant discussion of the Decadent aesthetic in *Essais de psychologie contemporaine* (1883), and after the publication of *À rebours*, Anatole Baju published a review, *Le Décadent* (1886–9), which showcased Decadent literature. But *À rebours*'s particular combination of the intellectual discussion of the Decadent aesthetic and its representation in fiction, along with its distinctive Decadent hero, and its idiosyncratic style which combines various registers, elevated it to the status of Decadent manifesto. *À rebours* is the archetypal Decadent novel because, unlike other novels of the time (Decadent or otherwise), it focuses on style rather than content. Not only does its absence of plot in the realist or naturalist sense foreground its own distinctive style, but its thematic concerns are all centred on the hero's particular tastes in all manner of things, from women to food. As a consequence, it brilliantly illustrates the Decadents' belief in artistic refinement known as 'l'art pour l'art': art is valued for its own sake, and purposeless beauty – along with the pleasure it affords – is celebrated above all else. One such example of Des Esseintes's – and indeed the Decadents' – fascination with art and artifice, and related repulsion with, and gleeful manipulation of, nature, is the artificial flower episode in the eighth chapter when Des Esseintes decides to decorate his house with flowers. Des Esseintes's Decadence is made manifest in his floral preferences: 'Autrefois, à Paris, son penchant naturel vers l'artifice l'avait conduit à délaisser la véritable fleur pour son image fidèlement exécutée, grâce aux miracles des caoutchoucs et des fils, des percalines et des taffetas, des papiers et des velours' ('Previously, in Paris, his natural penchant for the artificial had encouraged him to reject the real flower in favour of an image faithfully reproduced with the help of the miracles worked by rubber, wire, percaline, taffeta, paper and velvet').[3] As his aesthetic refinement grows, so his tastes evolve, and he becomes fascinated with the perverse possibility that the function of nature might in fact be to imitate the artificial: 'Après les fleurs factices singeant les véritables fleurs, il voulait des fleurs naturelles imitant des fleurs fausses' (p. 187) ('After fake flowers mimicking real flowers, he wanted natural flowers to imitate artificial ones'). Des Esseintes's fascination with the artificial flowers' ability to change perceived reality reveals his revulsion when faced with the mundane business of existence.

This horror of base reality is a feature common to a number of Decadent writers. Decadent literature is best understood as a quest – reminiscent of that undertaken by Baudelaire in *Les Fleurs du Mal* – for an existence untarnished by the petty concerns and disappointments of everyday existence. Like Baudelaire before them, the Decadents employ a range of means to distance themselves from the trivialities and banalities of the mundane. Imaginative forays back in time are common and many Decadent novels use a nostalgic attachment to classical, medieval, or biblical settings in order to escape the torments of the present. Gourmont's *Sixtine* (1890) and Péladan's epic fourteen-volume cycle *La Décadence latine* (1884–1900) are examples of works that refuse any overt references to the present day. The Decadents' dissatisfaction with the here-and-now occasioned a related fascination with spiritual forms of escapism such as mysticism, occultism, and rosicrucianism, as well as a renewed investment in the masochistic repressions and guilty secrets of Catholicism. In addition, the Decadents favoured geographical as well as temporal exoticism. By setting their novels in the glamorous and mysterious realms of Asia and the Middle East, the Decadents created another means of distancing themselves – in their imagination if not in reality – from the actuality of late nineteenth-century Paris. By resurrecting myths and legends from various traditions, the Decadents created an otherworldly literature rich in dreams, hallucinations, and drug- and sex-induced states of ecstasy.

Notwithstanding the vast spatial and temporal scope of Decadent litera-ture, two features of the Decadent text remain remarkably constant. First, the Decadents' understanding of the figure of the hero, and, second, this hero's (and thus the Decadents' own) relationship to women. In male-authored Decadent fiction – and with one notable exception to which we will return, all Decadent fiction was written by and for men – the dandy-hero is

---

3 J.-K. Huysmans, *À rebours* (Paris: Gallimard, 1977), p. 186. Page references will be given subse-quently in the text. Translations are mine.

represented as a refined, highly educated, aristocratic, and effete artist who, like Pygmalion, creates ideal beauty in the form of woman. Unlike Pygmalion, however, the Decadent hero is at once the creator and the victim of the female idol. The Decadent heroine is almost invariably represented as a dangerous, even deadly, creature who wields an attractive yet terrifying power over the submissive, frequently masochistic hero. This dangerous attraction manifests itself in a number of ways, from Pierre Louÿs's self-indulgent and semi-pornographic attack on lesbianism in *Aphrodite* (1896) to Gourmont's blasphemous and vicious *Lilith* (1892), with its panoply of sexual perversions – from sodomy to bestiality – played out in the Garden of Eden, to Péladan's display of female cruelty in *Le Vice suprême* (1884). Like monstrous women such as Medusa, Messalina, and Lilith, Salomé is an archetypal Decadent figure who encapsulates the male Decadents' ambivalent attitude to the related female attributes of beauty and crime. Flaubert's short story 'Hérodias', the last of the *Trois Contes* (1877), recounts the story of Salomé, as do Oscar Wilde's play (first written in French as *Salomé* [1893] and premiered in Paris in 1896) and Gustave Moreau's painting of the same name (1876). Salomé, daughter of Hérodias, danced so seductively for her stepfather Herod that he promised to give her anything she desired. Salomé asked for the head of John the Baptist on a platter and, against his will, Herod was forced to have John beheaded. Des Esseintes's reaction to Moreau's painting of Salomé, whilst demonstrating the Decadents' tendency to refer to each other in their work, also epitomises this late nineteenth-century fascination with Salomé, here representative of Woman more generally. For him:

> Elle devenait, en quelque sorte, la déité symbolique de l'indestructible Luxure, la déesse de l'immortelle Hystérie, la Beauté maudite, élue entre toutes . . . la Bête monstrueuse, indifférente, irresponsable, insensible, empoisonnant, de même que l'Hélène antique, tout ce qui l'approche, tout ce qui la voit, tout ce qu'elle touche. (*À rebours*, pp. 144–5)

> (She became, in a way, the symbolic deity of Lust, Goddess of immortal hysteria, accursed Beauty, chosen amongst all women . . . she was the monstrous Beast, indifferent, irresponsible, insensitive, poisoning, like Helen of Troy, all who approach her, all who see her, all who touch her.)

One explanation for the Decadents' fascination with Salomé is the fact that she represents a problem with what were perceived to be natural gender roles. Far from subscribing to the traditional feminine qualities of weakness and pliability, Salomé is represented by the Decadents as undermining them; she is seductive and feminine yet also assertive and masculine. Des Esseintes's erotic relationships with women illustrate this Decadent fascination with sex roles that depart from the naturalist norm. In the ninth chapter of *À rebours*, Des Esseintes remembers his obsession with the American acrobat Miss Urania. What attracts him to this woman is her masculinity. She represents all that he is not: she is strong, healthy, capable. In contrast Des Esseintes casts himself in the role of weak, feminised lover.

The relationship between Des Esseintes and Miss Urania illustrates the Decadents' emphasis on the unnatural nature of perverse sexual relationships and non-normative gender designations. The female Decadent writer Rachilde embraces – in both her life and her work – the reversal of sex and gender norms fantasised in the male-authored Decadent texts. Her early works, particularly *Monsieur Vénus* (1884) and *La Marquise de Sade* (1887), although stylistically more related to realism or naturalism than Decadence, foreground masculine heroines Raoule de la Vénérade and Mary Barbe who trouble societal norms by taking pleasure in dominating, both socially and sexually, their weaker emasculated partners. Although Rachilde's acceptance into the literary and artistic circles that the Decadents frequented (such as Le Chat Noir and the Club des Hydropathes) suggests that her male counterparts were less ambiguous about powerful women in the flesh than in their fictional fantasies, a number of Decadent works – notably Joséphin Péladan's androgyny novels of which *La Gynandre* (1891) is the best known – sketch out a make-believe world of gender breakdown and misogynistically warn of what might happen if sexual difference dissolves completely. The Decadents are without exception both fascinated by and terrified of the powerful women who populate their fictions. This contradictory approach to women, desire, sex, and sexuality is the most interesting and abiding legacy left to modern readers by the Decadents and it is the main reason why they are still read and taught today.

If Salomé is an emblem of the Decadents' indecisive relationship with perverse eroticism, the prevalence of reference to her in Decadent literature and art also reveals that the Decadents' fascination with the beautiful corruption of women is part of a wider interest in death found throughout their works. Baudelaire's demonstration in 'Une charogne' of how the ugly can be made beautiful by art heralds the Decadents' more sustained preoccupation with morbidity, sickness, and decay. In Octave Mirbeau's 1898 novel *Le Jardin des supplices*, the narrator – another effeminate male emulating Des Esseintes – lists, in disturbing amounts of detail, the sadistic punishments inflicted on prisoners in a Chinese Torture Garden. His lover Clara (who might well have been modelled on Rachilde) shows him round the garden – which is full of mutilated, dying, and decaying bodies – and takes sado-masochistic delight in each cruel method of torture they encounter. The sadism of the garden is a terrifying magnification of the couple's perverted erotic relationship. Mirbeau's garden, like Baudelaire's flowers of evil and Huysmans's artificial blooms, represents nature tainted by humanity's inevitable degeneration and subsequent immorality. As such it crystallises the Decadent fascination with pain and murder which is found in a number of texts, namely Rachilde's *La Marquise de Sade*, with its sadistic, crime-obsessed heroine, and novels by Jean Lorrain such as his catalogue of the excesses of contemporary crime, *Buveurs d'âmes* (1893), and his picture of violence and transgression in society, *Monsieur de Phocas* (1901).

Late nineteenth-century French Decadence was a short-lived but significant moment in French literary history. By the beginning of the twentieth century, the Decadents' impact and enthusiasm was waning and France was becoming more outward-looking and less morbidly concerned with her own shortcomings. In addition, the Dreyfus Affair had become the central focus of Parisian intellectual life. Decadence did not disappear completely, however, and diluted elements of its foremost concerns – such as an abiding fascination with questions of non-normative gender, sex, and sexuality and an interest in a self-conscious aestheticism, can be found in much twentieth- and twenty-first-century literature.

61

Avant-garde: text and image

KATHARINE CONLEY

Since its origin French verse has allied text and image through the way words look as well as how they sound. For example, how each poetic verse scans depends at times on a visible but silent feminine 'e' that completes the requisite syllable count and rhyme scheme, a letter that must be seen to be understood. Only in the mid-nineteenth century with his sonnet 'Correspondances' from *Les Fleurs du Mal* (1857) did Charles Baudelaire make this blending of seeing and hearing clear with his invocation of synaesthesia as a peak experience, emphasising the importance of the ways in which all the senses blend and bleed into one another. Yet it was not until the turn of the century that Stéphane Mallarmé created a poem that explicitly linked seeing with reading, image with text: the metaphors within it are underscored by the visual arrangement of words on the page. In 'Un Coup de dés jamais n'abolira le hazard' ('A Throw of the Dice Never Will Abolish Chance', 1897)[1] words on the page mirror the poem's narrative of shipwreck under a constellated sky, allowing the reader to visualise mentally the images conjured by the poetic verses. Furthermore, Mallarmé's poem closely followed the coinage of the noun *visualisation* (1892), preceded by the verb *visualiser* (1887), to render visible something that is not, to put an idea into images. As the century turned, France was ready for the separate domains of words and images to cross over into the other's territory.

By the time Guillaume Apollinaire declared in 'Zone' from 1911 that *la poésie ce matin*, 'poetry this morning', was to be found on the advertising posters adorning the walls of Paris, the concept of visualisation had been internalised and the idea that poster art could convey poetry and vie with it as a high art was clearly communicated by this telegraphic reference. Mallarmé's fostering of painters, photographers, and newspaper reporters writing on politics and fashion had become the norm, as had a crossing of boundaries from one discipline to another. Apollinaire's circle similarly involved poets and painters

---

1 Translations are mine unless otherwise stated.

such as Pablo Picasso who, coming from the direction of painting in 1912, began to link words with images irrevocably through his use of collage. Like Apollinaire he vaunted modest materials; Picasso pasted and painted words from advertisements and newspapers onto his canvases, mixing low and high art, including the emblematic word *jour*, from the word for newspaper, *journal*, thus signalling and launching the twentieth century's fascination with the everyday.

Apollinaire made two more key contributions to the blending of words and images: the creation of image-poems he called *calligrammes* in 1914 and the coinage of the word *sur-réalisme* in the programme notes he wrote for the avant-garde ballet *Parade* in 1917, a word which would become synonymous with shifting visual and verbal taxonomies. His image-poems, published in *Calligrammes* in 1918, feature letters handwritten into shapes that mirror the dominant verbal image, such as the ocean liner in 'Lettre-Océan'. These calligram-poems explore everyday objects and phenomena: a tie, a fountain, a cigar, a star, a mirror, a crown, and rain. The one in the shape of a heart also looks like a reversed flame – an old metaphor for ardour here doubly *visible* in the image as well. As we follow the letters curving around in a heart shape, we discover the metaphorical link between heart and flame: *Mon cœur pareil à une flamme renversée* ('My heart like an upside-down flame').

By 1917 the Dada group was well underway in Zurich, Switzerland, having been founded the previous spring by Tristan Tzara, Hugo Ball, Hans Arp, Marcel Janco, and Richard Huelsenbeck at the Cabaret Voltaire. Its anti-war zeal and zany inventiveness quickly took hold in Germany, Paris, and New York; its popularity was furthered by the multiple manifestos penned by Tzara, including the 'Manifeste 1918', in which he took aim at all distinctions between high and low art and again proclaimed advertising to be a poetic element. Dada was the most prominent avant-garde movement to arrive in Paris, perhaps partly because Tzara wrote in French. The most adept Dada practitioner of the incorporation of words into images was Marcel Duchamp, working first in New York then in Paris. Textual and visual puns proliferate in his *ready-mades* – objects renamed in a way that repositions them culturally so that they take on new meaning while retaining a ghost of their previous incarnation. His famous *Fountain* from 1917, a renamed industrial urinal signed R. Mutt and displayed in the first Society of Independent Artists' show, makes sense only when the viewer understands that water flowing in a urinal indeed constitutes a kind of everyman's fountain, a conclusion linked to the name *mutt*, a term that refers to a dog of no particular breed. Without the title and signature the work would be only provocative; with the addition of text it becomes a social commentary about the expectations visitors bring to an art gallery.

Words like *fountain*, which can designate an artistic creation as well as a common urinal, are distinguished by a flexibility that also characterises Duchamp's pseudonym Rrose Sélavy, adopted in 1920 as an alter ego that is feminine and also possibly Jewish. An ordinary name for a woman, Rose, with the addition of an extra letter R, becomes *éros* in spoken French and her surname, which sounds like the name Levy, works as a pun for *c'est la vie* – eros or love is life. Duchamp signed ready-mades and punning poems Rrose Selavy, as well. The poems were published in *Littérature* in 1922 by three Dada admirers of Apollinaire – André Breton, Philippe Soupault, and Louis Aragon. These one-line poems like *Sa robe est noire dit Sarah Bernhardt* ('Her dress is black, said Sarah Bernhardt'), *sound* like what they say, in a variation on Duchamp's visual transpositions: the phrase *sa robe est noire* sounds something like the proper name *Sarah Bernhardt*, who may also have been a wearer of black dresses. Two months later *Littérature* published a new set of poems entitled (not signed) 'Rrose Sélavy', by the poet Robert Desnos.

By September 1922 Breton, Soupault, Aragon, and Desnos had begun to use Apollinaire's term *surrealism* as a way of describing 'a certain psychic automatism that corresponds quite well to the dreamstate' and to conduct experiments with psychic automatism in Breton's Paris apartment.[2] Of all of them Desnos was the most adept at going into a trance and performing automatically both orally and in writing. Francis Picabia, who had spent time with the New York Dada group, challenged Desnos to create an Rrose Sélavy-type poem, which Desnos promptly did. The first one, *Dans un temple en stuc de pomme le pasteur distillait le suc des psaumes* ('In an apple-stucco temple, a pastor distilled the sap of psalms'), turns on the aural and visual resemblances between words and syllables to make sense. He used what Aragon would call word mirrors in *Le Paysan de Paris* (*Paris Peasant*, 1926) in order to make sense out of what sounded at first like spontaneous gibberish. A pastor in an apple-stucco temple who distils the sap of psalms only makes sense if we accept that pastors, in addition to exegesis of the Bible, might enjoy Calvados, the preferred apple liqueur of the Desnos family's native Normandy. It also helps to allow the visual elements of the letters and sounds to move in our minds into shapes resembling Apollinaire's calligrams – a movement encouraged by the graphic resemblances between words and syllables such as *pomme,*

---

2 A. Breton, 'The Mediums Enter', in *The Lost Steps*, trans. M. Polizzotti (Lincoln: University of Nebraska Press, 1996).

psaumes as well as *stuc* and *suc* – so that *psaumes* blends with *pommes* just as *stuc* overlaps with *suc*. It is these resemblances that prompted Breton to exclaim in admiration that with Desnos's pen and tongue 'words make love', because of the way they stimulate attractions that mix up syllables and lead to the procreation of new words and meanings – all initiated by automatic inspiration whereby the *voice* prompting these word-image games comes from within. In Paul Eluard's extended metaphor for the automatic voice in the poem 'La Parole' ('The Word', 1926), words slide as smoothly as silk on a mirror, both ancient and beautiful, and, like shadows at sunset, envelop the human being receptive to them at the moment of falling asleep.

Fellow surrealist Joan Miró took up Desnos's challenge to see as well as hear in one word a possible link to another word. Painting in Paris in the mid-1920s as a new arrival from Spain, Miró saw French words as visual elements, the way his countryman Picasso had done with *jour*. This phenomenon becomes clear in his series of works from 1925, which the poet-critic Jacques Dupin calls 'dream' paintings because of their washed backgrounds and the way that Miró used random blotches, produced as though automatically, as points of departure for images he then doubled with painted words that mirrored them. *Ceci est la couleur de mes rêves* (*This is the Colour of my Dreams*) and *Étoiles en des sexes d'escargots* (*Stars in the Shape of the Sex of Snails*) take their titles from the words he painted on the canvas. The first one draws the viewer's eye to a blue blob and then to what appears to be a textual explanation for it – that this vivid blue is the color of Miró's dreams. The second one also marries text and image through the dominant shape generated by the background wash that looks like snails's tracks; furthermore, the words for stars and snail – *étoiles* and *escargot* – joined by the noun *sexes* (a literalisation of Breton's suggestion that words that look or sound alike can 'make love') – together emphasise their visual link through the curves of the repeated letters, in the manner of Desnos's Rrose Sélavy poems. The words at either end of the phrase *look* similar with their shared e's, t's, and s's that could be interchangeable, reminding the viewer that snails can change sex and seeming to ask whether a snail could also be visualised as a star or a word as an image?

Miró and Desnos make sense out of nonsense through automatic word play and build on the emblematic title 'La Glace sans tain' ('The Unsilvered Mirror') of the first section of the first surrealist automatic text, *Les Champs magnétiques* (*The Magnetic Fields*), written by Breton and Soupault in 1918 and published first in segments in 1919 and then as a whole in 1920. The two-way mirror of this first 'magnetic field' anticipates the equally emblematic window from the first 'Manifesto of Surrealism', published by Breton in the autumn of 1924. This window appears in the first sentence ever to occur automatically to Breton one night as he was falling asleep: *Il y a un homme coupé en deux par la fenêtre* ('There is a man cut in two by the window').[3] Breton explains that this phrase was accompanied by the faint mental image of a man walking with a window around his torso, which, had Breton been an artist, would doubtless have been more dominant than the words. To underscore this interchangeability between words and images he refers to automatic drawings created by Desnos as a part of a hoax, pretending they were made by mentally ill patients according a category of drawing later championed by the surrealists as *art brut*.[4] The mirror and window emblematise and materialise the importance of the liminal space separating consciousness from the unconscious in surrealism, waking from dream reality, day from night, writing or drawing from hearing, seeing, or thinking.

The permeability of images and texts that began with Dada and became incorporated into surrealism was again highlighted in René Magritte's *La Trahison des images* (*Treason of Images*, 1928–9), which juxtaposes the image of a pipe with the text *Ceci n'est pas une pipe*, 'This is not a pipe'. One thing does not turn into a double of another here, except to the extent that *both* painted image and text are exposed as not the thing itself.[5] Neither text nor image can dominate the other; Magritte levels the playing field of representational sign systems. For Pierre Alechinsky, a painter of the following generation, Magritte's work points to what *almost* exists – the viewer can *almost* imagine having seen a pipe – whereas Miró's *Ceci est la couleur de mes rêves* points to what almost does *not* exist, in a reference to the ephemerality of dreams in relation to the materiality of a pipe.[6] Both paintings push image *and* text to the edge of representational logic through juxtaposition.

In *Challenge to Painting* (*La Peinture au défi*, 1930), Aragon questions painting's superiority as an art form by extolling collage – a technique that defines the mechanism of the surrealist image (coined by Pierre Reverdy and repeated in the 'Manifesto') as a phenomenon that could not come from a metaphoric comparison but only from the collage-like juxtaposition of two more or less distant realities. Any one image or word can hide within it another, possibly dissonant, one, according to what Tzara identified as Max Ernst's skill with

3 A. Breton, 'Manifesto of Surrealism', in *Manifestoes of Surrealism*, trans. Richard Seaver and Helen R. Lane (Ann Arbor: University of Michigan, 1972), pp. 21–2.
4 Desnos also made rebus drawings like the one he drew of an *apple in air*, in honor of Apollinaire.
5 For Michel Foucault, painting always told stories that functioned partly through the exclusion of narrative. See *Ceci n'est pas une pipe* (Paris: Éditions Fata Morgana, 1973).
6 P. Alechinsky, 'Ceci n'est pas une pipe', in *Baluchons et richochets* (Paris: Gallimard, 1994), p. 94.

images réversibles. This skill is evident in the punning homonyms for 100 – *cent* (one hundred) and *sans* (without) – in the title of Ernst's collage novel *La femme 100 têtes* (*The Hundred Headless Woman*, 1929), which transforms the title's 100 women into one headless one. The technique of collage took many forms, from Ernst's collage novels which invite us to *read* the images and *visualise* the narrative with only intermittent titles for text, to Claude Cahun's self-portraits mixed with words in the photo-collages published in *Aveux non avenus* (*Unrealised Avowals*, 1930). Cahun's final photo-collage displays a series of self-portraits in an array of disguises piled on top of each another, around which curves a sentence of commentary: *Sous ce masque un autre masque, Je n'en finirai pas de soulever tous ces visages* ('Under this mask another one, I will never finish lifting all these faces'). Not unlike Miró's later challenge, Cahun uses words to ask the question posed by her images: does automatic truth lie in the plain photographed face or in the masked visage which, through disguise, might paradoxically reveal more about personal identity than a snapshot, as though through a window, a *glace sans tain*, onto the unconscious.

With surrealism Breton laid the ground for new avant-gardes, including the short-lived CoBrA group that emerged out of 'Le Surréalisme révolutionnaire' in 1948. For automatism CoBrA substituted spontaneity and relaunched their predecessors' admiration for *art brut*, children's drawings, and popular art. Even though the new name identified the non-Parisian origins of the founders – Copenhagen (Asger Jorn); Brussels (Christian Dotremont, Joseph Noiret, and later Alechinsky); and Amsterdam (Karl Appel, Constant Nieuwenhuys, and Guillaume Corneille) – their journal, *Cobra*, was dominated by French, thanks to Dotremont. French was also the language of Dotremont's *dessins-mots* and *peintures-mots* (drawing- and painting-words), created with friends like Jorn and Alechinsky, begun during his involvement with CoBrA (1948–51) and continued until his death in 1979. Dotremont, who admired Miró, also proposed seeing letters as visual elements in 'Signification et sinification' (1950), a meditation on writing as a visual form. Twelve years later, in 1962, he created the logogram, which Alechinsky called an exaggeration of writing and the poet Yves Bonnefoy, who, like Dotremont, had begun his career close to surrealism, called a *véritable yoga* in writing, because of its nature as a *practice*.[7] These word-paintings performed a simpler version of Miró's and Magritte's challenge to seeing and reading at the same time, understanding *both* efforts as aspects of one another like seeing a surrealist reversible

7 P. Alechinsky, 'Dotremont et l'exagération', in *Des deux mains* (Paris: Mercure de France, 2004), pp. 67, 72; Y. Bonnefoy, 'Preface', in *Christian Dotremont: Œuvres poétiques complètes* (Paris: Mercure de France, 1998), p. 44.

image or looking at something one way and then the other through a two-way mirror. Their titles often identify the verbal key to the sensual shapes of the brushed ink flurries. One of them, *À côté du dessous s'imagine le reste du dessus* (*Next to what's underneath may be imagined what remains above*, 1977), even explains how we are meant to read them, as though seen backwards through a glass painted on from the opposite side. For Dotremont one sign system acts as the mirror image of, a window onto, the other (see Figure 1).

All the avant-gardes worked at the edge of the representable and demonstrated this effort by developing images and texts about to melt into one another along the edges of each sign system's legibility, practising eclectic mixing of genres in their journals. Jacqueline Chénieux-Gendron identifies this phenomenon as surrealism's fascination with the inside-outside, right-side-up/upside-down experience of automatism, the thin distinction between the sayable and the unsayable, the textual and the material, delimited by the window-word *langue*, meaning both language and tongue.[8] Crossing boundaries between the textual and the visual became commonplace after Dada and surrealism, as did painters writing about poets and vice versa – Alechinsky writing about Dotremont, for example, and poets like Dupin, Bonnefoy, and André du Bouchet writing about artists and art. By the end of the twentieth century the resolution of oppositions – what Breton had called the 'old antinomies' in the 'Second Manifesto' – had become internalised by avant-gardistes born after the war such as Annette Messager and Sophie Calle. These artists shared the influence of earlier movements and the left-wing and sexual politics of the 1960s and 1970s that had already been anticipated and threaded through the surrealist movement by its female participants.

Recent work has shown the continuity between pre- and post-war surrealism in the commitment of the group to politics as well as to a subversive spirit linked to eroticism.[9] Women artists such as Cahun early in the movement and Messager and Calle in the post-surrealist era embraced the avant-garde tendency to turn the female body into a social commentary. In her albums from the 1980s Messager integrates words in the form of personal notes, newspaper cuttings, drawings, and marked-up photographs into her art. She shows how familiar the combination of text and image has become through the popular media, using her work as a bridge between the everyday and the world of

---

8 See J. Chénieux-Gendron, 'L'Envers du monde, l'envers de la langue: un "travail" surréaliste', in W. Spies (ed.), *La Révolution surréaliste* (Paris: Centre Pompidou, 2002), pp. 349–59.
9 See A. Mahon, *Surrealism and the Politics of Eros, 1938–1968* (London: Thames and Hudson, 2005), and J. Eburne, 'Antihumanism and Terror: Surrealism, Theory, and the Postwar Left', *Yale French Studies*, 109 (Summer 2006), pp. 39–51.

Figure 1 Christian Dotremont, *Logogramme*, 1977. Reproduced by kind permission of the artist.

art. She plays with her persona as a woman, like Cahun emphasising the ways in which young women are encouraged to learn femininity through the activities they are expected to perform, such as wearing make-up, collecting, and tallying household costs, which she then pointedly exaggerates.

For Messager the personal is political, as the women's movement argued in the 1970s, and before that as Cahun had suggested in her sly short stories from the 1920s, the *Heroines*. Yet, through Messager's humorous insertion of herself into the public domain, pasting her own photograph onto newspaper portraits of newlyweds, for example, she succeeds in politicising and universalising the personal. Calle also stages aspects of her life in photographic poses that are paradoxically revealing, like Cahun's photo-collages, even as they superficially mask her inner reality. Textual elements are part of Messager's art, just as art, for Calle, has a textual dimension. Calle's sequences of photographs involve text and also have a textual nature. Often subversively founded on cultural assumptions about women's romantic desires, a visualised narrative links the images in such works as *Suite Vénitienne* from 1980, the story-in-pictures of her pursuit of a man to Venice. We see images and imagine text; we read text and see art. Like Duchamp's *Boîte en valise* from 1934 Messager and Calle's work is at once transposable – from text to image, everyday object to art – and transportable – works created more for notebooks than frames, the significance of the artist's touch translated into the homemade, from the public realm to the domestic and back again. Dada's inherent levelling applies to the broader levelling of hierarchical distinctions between text and image by the beginning of the twenty-first century. Text and image have fallen out of the hands of elite theorisers of the everyday and into those of countless technologically adept operators who cross over effortlessly, fluently, from one language, one sign system, to another, every day.

62

Autobiography

CLAIRE BOYLE

Perhaps the place to start when thinking about the development of French autobiography since the beginning of the twentieth century is with a work published early on in the century which is not usually considered to belong to the literary genre of autobiography at all, despite possessing certain structural features that suggest otherwise. Marcel Proust's mammoth *À la recherche du temps perdu* (1913–27) is a multi-volume work taking the form of a first-person narrative. It traces in writing the lengthy, intricate voyage which the narrator, eventually named as Marcel, makes as he embarks upon a journey into his recollections of the past, prompted by the experience of re-living a taste sensation from his childhood as he eats a small cake called a *madeleine*. Although not considered an autobiography, despite a clear autobiographical dimension, Proust's work showcases many of the recurrent issues and themes of modern French autobiography. Grappling with the nature of perception, memory and remembering, self-consciously attentive to writing as an act of representation, blurring the boundary between fiction and autobiography, *À la recherche* alerts us to a number of persistent and knotty conundrums that would beset French literary autobiographers writing later in the twentieth century, and indeed into the twenty-first. The purpose of this chapter is to give an account of those recurrent preoccupations which come to characterise the genre of autobiography, and of the evolution autobiography has undergone since Proust's time.

The foremost of these conundrums is the thorny and still vexed question of where the dividing line is between what is autobiography and what is not: a matter that would dog would-be writers of autobiography throughout the twentieth century. This question would preoccupy French theorists of autobiography even more, but one of the complexities of modern French autobiography is that the division between a literary autobiographer and a theorist of autobiography is seldom secure: autobiography is very often its own theory. This is never more clearly apparent than in Roland Barthes's

Roland Barthes (1975). Moreover, the theoretical appetite of twentieth-century autobiographies frequently extends beyond the genre, with many, like *Roland Barthes*, offering abstract reflections on the nature of selfhood, life, and writing (the three elements that, etymologically speaking, give 'autobiography' its name). It is for these reasons that the development of French autobiography over the last hundred years or so is inextricably intertwined with that of modern French thought.

The last quarter of the twentieth century saw an explosion in France in the publication of works which at least have affinities with the genre of autobiography, even if autobiography is not the name they claim. (The question of nomenclature is one we will need to return to.) What prompts this upsurge? Among a confluence of factors, including the advent of a consumer society and a commodified self, recent French history and thought supply some important answers.

In autobiography – unlike related modes of first-person writing such as memoirs or the diary form – the writer typically tries to make sense of their relationship with the world. Two developments in French intellectual and literary culture in the post-war years make this endeavour seem particularly vital. The first of these I call the 'testimony imperative', referring to the moral and ethical engagements that stimulate literary responses to particular historical events: the French experience of the Second World War for example, or the ordeal and aftermath of colonial conflict. The second development is 'the crisis of the subject', to which Colin Davis alludes in Chapter 66, and here I refer to the collective insights into the human condition emanating from psychoanalysis, structuralism, and poststructuralism, newly emerging intellectual movements in the mid-twentieth century. The crisis is that of a 'subject' (not a 'self') because, as individuals, we are all subjects: we are subject to constraints that others around us, or society at large, impose on us as the price for being accepted into that society. The 'crisis' stems from the perception that the subject's agency is compromised, along with any possibility of adequately knowing or representing this subject in writing (the task of autobiography).

The testimony imperative is a response to traumatic experiences which writers seek to work through, understand, and come to terms with by producing autobiographical accounts of them. The French experience of Occupation from 1940 to 1945 provides French writers with ample material and stimulus for their autobiographical accounts of personal experiences or those of loved ones. As discussed elsewhere in this volume, the aftermath of the Holocaust brings with it a strong moral imperative to bear witness to what happened through the testimony of an autobiographical narrative. Such ethical impulses lie behind Georges Perec's *W ou le souvenir d'enfance* (1975). Perec's mother was deported to a concentration camp and is presumed to have died at Auschwitz, and it is the traumatic legacy of dispossession inherited by surviving generations of families decimated by the Holocaust that is documented here.

Wartime autobiographical testimony narratives may engage ethics in a still more challenging way, however, contributing to a wider cultural process of confronting and recovering elided, uncomfortable aspects of a collective past. Approaching the war from a rather different angle, Marguerite Duras's *La Douleur* (1985) reveals one woman's implication in dishonourable, even sadistic behaviour towards others, perpetrated in the course of her activities as a member of a French Resistance cell. Through these highly personal glimpses, *La Douleur* provides a powerful account of a dimension of France's wartime experience that for a long time proved resistant to assimilation within the French collective memory of this period of history.

The currency of the testimony imperative circulates beyond these wartime realms, however. Taking the female condition in its darker aspects as its subject, Annie Ernaux's *L'Événement* (2000) shares *La Douleur*'s drive to force out into the open stories about human experience that many would prefer to see swept under the carpet, rather than told. The narrative recounts the author's experience of undergoing a back-street abortion as a result of becoming accidentally pregnant when still a student in 1963, when abortion (and access to contraception) was still illegal in France. *L'Événement* exposes the prevalence of disparaging perspectives on women (not just those who are unmarried and abort) in 1960s French society and its institutions, perspectives rooted in fundamentally misogynist attitudes towards female sexuality. Ernaux's narrator states her purpose as being to bring to literature that for which the world of art has no place: 'Je ne crois pas qu'il existe un *Atelier de la faiseuse d'anges* dans aucun musée du monde' ('I do not believe there exists a [painting called] "Workshop of the Backstreet Abortionist" in any museum in the world').[1]

Ernaux's remark alerts us to a potentially political motive behind autobiographical writing. Autobiographical writing may aspire to contest dominant ideologies; it may be writing for change. The genre of autobiography, sometimes seen as self-indulgent and narcissistic, thus shows its concerns to extend far beyond the individual writing self: self-writing can entail writing for (as well

---

1 A. Ernaux, *L'Événement* (Paris: Gallimard, 2000), p. 82. Translations are mine.

as about) the other. Autobiographers may be inspired to write out of desire to use their own example to educate others or challenge their understanding. Especially where marginalised identities are concerned (i.e. those denigrated due to the subject's gender, ethnic origin, or sexuality), expressions of identity recorded in autobiography can transcend the individual, functioning as collective statements on identity and experience for constituencies of people little understood or respected in wider society. This potential is exploited in Assia Djebar's *L'Amour la fantasia* (1995), which succeeds in writing both the individual and collective colonised Algerian self by interspersing personal reminiscences of an Algerian childhood with fragmentary reconstructions of Algeria's colonial conflict with France.

Another way in which identity in autobiography can be shared between self and other is via a process of identification with the autobiographical self, which enables a wider social grouping to recognise itself in the text. As the author himself anticipated, André Gide's autobiography *Si le grain ne meurt* (1926) is such a text. Amongst much else, this work reveals the narrator's growing realisation of his sexual inclination towards young males, and in correspondence Gide acknowledged the potential for readers sharing his sexual orientation to identify with him and his experiences on the basis of his autobiographical narrative. In this way, autobiography can come to be bound up with identity politics (by this I mean the act of publicly asserting a particular aspect of one's identity, usually one shared by only a minority of people, with a view to raising consciousness and ameliorating society's attitudes to people defined by that personal quality).

However, the identifications between an author and their readers that enable the genre of autobiography to mobilise a politics of identity are very far from unproblematic. For various reasons we, as readers, should consider them with caution. First, not all authors follow Gide in welcoming them. As I have shown elsewhere, autobiographical texts frequently work to prevent their readers from being comfortably able to develop an identification with the autobiographer's self outside the text.[2] Hervé Guibert's *À l'ami qui ne m'a pas sauvé la vie* (1990) is a narrative devoted to recounting the gay male narrator's experience of his terminal decline due to AIDS-related illness. Like Gide's autobiography, it explores minority sexual identities. However, this text disrupts, rather than invites readers' identifications with its author, despite often reading like a faithful and accurate autobiographical account in many

---

2 Claire Boyle, *Consuming Autobiographies: Reading and Writing the Self in Post-War France* (London: Legenda, 2007).

respects. Details – including the narrator's self-conscious and ambiguous use of the *mise-en-abîme* device (one associated with works of fiction) – undercut the representation and draw attention to the elements of fictionality and invention in Guibert's work. This inevitably leads us to wonder how far the autobiographical narrator himself, our gateway to identifying (and identifying with) the flesh-and-blood author, is also a fictional creation.

The mechanism of identification that Guibert disturbs presupposes that the real-life self represented in the autobiographical text corresponds to the self of the author outside of the text: the relationship between the self in writing and the self that writes is understood to be one of mimesis, or imitation. Indeed, this mimetic relationship is precisely the founding structure of the genre of autobiography, according to an influential theory of autobiography developed by Philippe Lejeune.[3] Yet this is the same relationship that many twentieth-century French authors come to refute.

Modern French autobiographers strenuously seek to distance themselves from the notion that their autobiographies offer straightforward representations of the writer's self or life – to the point that this distancing becomes a topos of the genre. Guibert is therefore not unusual in casting doubt on the veracity of his autobiographical narrative by injecting an overtly fictive element into his work. His work represents one of many narratives frequently classed as '*autofiction*', rather than autobiography. Whilst differing conceptualisations of the term exist, all theorists of *autofiction* concur that it is a form of writing that troubles the frontier between autobiography and fiction. For some, such as Serge Doubrovsky (who is credited with inventing the concept), it emerges because it is no longer possible to write autobiography *without* fiction: all autobiographical writing is necessarily a fiction because we lack sufficient insight into ourselves to tell the full truth of who we are. For others, such as Vincent Colonna, *autofiction* is less an admission of defeat than a recognition that the writer's subjectivity is made up not only of their knowledge and experience, but also their imagination, fantasy and desire. The writer's decision to fictionalise in some way his or her self recognises that a more unfettered exploration of the writer's subjectivity can only properly emerge when the imagination is given free play.

Unsurprisingly, given the force of the testimonial imperative in contemporary French literature, the reorientation of autobiographical writing away from representing real events and really existing people towards *autofiction* has attracted controversy, with the characterisation of *autofiction*

3 P. Lejeune, *Le Pacte autobiographique* (Paris: Seuil, 1975).

as 'autobiographie honteuse' ('shameful autobiography') by one eminent French literary theorist illustrating the moral turpitude in which some hold this development.

Yet to see in the restrained ambitions of modern French autobiographical works some kind of voluntary dereliction of duty on the part of their authors would be to miss the point. Even when they do not engage in philosophy itself, the foremost twentieth-century French authors consistently engage with philosophical ideas and critical theories, and, over the course of the twentieth century, a variety of currents within modern French thought have pushed literary autobiographers in France to the conclusion that autobiography cannot be seen as a privileged vehicle for the faithful transmission of the autobiographer's subjectivity or experience to a reader. Psychoanalysis, a discipline whose birth comes only with the twentieth century, yields insights critically important to the autobiographical enterprise. These insights have especially strong currency in autobiography on account of the high incidence of French literary autobiographers undergoing psychoanalysis (Marie Cardinal, Michel Leiris, Perec, and Doubrovsky all fall within this category). Sigmund Freud's work teaches us that our memories can never be complete and that the most significant moments for our psychic development are those that we have forgotten or else mis-remember – an idea integrated into the very narrative structure of Nathalie Sarraute's *Enfance* (1983), in which childhood memories are interspersed with narratorial meditations on the processes of memory and remembering which have generated them. For Freud and his followers, the conscious mind – the instrument of self-examination – will always be inadequate to the task of deriving a full understanding of who the self is. This is because the powerful and yet shadowy workings of the unconscious that stimulate certain impulses within us also repress our knowledge of the deep-seated traumas and desires that drive our actions and responses. The notion that each of us harbours an internal division between what we can and cannot consciously know about ourselves contributes to the sense of a subject in (epistemological) crisis, and leads French psychoanalyst Jacques Lacan to coin the term 'the split subject' to describe the condition of human subjectivity. It is also an explicitly acknowledged impetus behind Doubrovsky's autofictional approach to writing the self.

The work of those poststructuralist thinkers known as deconstructionists has also profoundly influenced autobiography. Deconstruction holds that in language the meaning of utterances is never fixed. The language we use to express ourselves has the endless potential to signify with each use something different and new to its addressee, compared to what it has signified before.

These theories imply for autobiographers an inevitable loss of mastery over the meaning of their autobiographical texts (what Barthes calls the 'death of the author').[4] Additionally, scepticism hangs over language's capacity to act as an invisible mediator of one person's thoughts and observations for another. Language is not merely an instrument for representing an externally existing world, but has an existence and opacity of its own. This recognition of language's materiality, in combination with perspectives on selfhood gleaned from psychoanalysis, decisively alters the face of autobiography. Insistent metanarrative preoccupations with language, memory, and selfhood characterise a distinctive new mode of French autobiography labelled *la nouvelle autobiographie*. Following on the heels of *autofiction* (from which critics do not always distinguish it), the inception of *la nouvelle autobiographie* occurs in the mid-1980s, when a clutch of high-profile writers formerly associated with the *nouveau roman* simultaneously turn to self-writing. Autobiographical writings published in 1983–4 by Nathalie Sarraute, Duras, and Alain Robbe-Grillet are (like their *nouveaux romans*) conspicuously marked by a consciousness of the characteristics and limitations of the medium of language, and of the genre of autobiography more specifically. They all pay pronounced attention to their own acts of self-representation, arising from their narrators' shared conviction that, as Robbe-Grillet writes in his *Le Miroir qui revient* (1984), 'avec des mots et des phrases, je ne peux représenter ni ce que j'ai devant les yeux, ni ce qui se cache dans ma tête, ou dans mon sexe' ('with words and sentences, I cannot represent what I have before my eyes, nor what hides in my head, or in my genitals').[5] The self-reflexive qualities of these works extend to a pronounced awareness of the fallibility in their authors' powers of recall and understanding, and they are expressed at the level of form, as well as narration, as we see in Duras's *L'Amant* (1984). Here, switches between first- and third-person narration render a split subject, whilst gaps in the autobiographical representation are symbolised by repeated references to absent or non-existent photographs.

The postmodern era has sometimes too readily been assumed to coincide with the death of autobiography. Yet there are clearly grounds for a different interpretation. On the one hand, the testimonial imperative, along with the return of the subject (albeit in crisis), has demanded that autobiography should not die. On the other, the notion that autobiography dies at a point in the late twentieth century following a collective realisation of the problems that beset the genre is undermined by the fact that it is unnecessary to await

4 See R. Barthes, 'La Mort de l'auteur' (1968), in *Essais Critiques*, vol. IV: *Le Bruissement de la langue* (Paris: Éditions du Seuil, 1984), pp. 61–7.
5 A. Robbe-Grillet, *Le Miroir qui revient* (Paris: Minuit, 1984), pp. 17–18.

poststructuralism's heyday before finding literary autobiographers in France cognisant of autobiography's inherent limitations as a genre. Preoccupied with the narrator's imaginative and dream life, Leiris's *L'Âge d'homme* (1939) shows especial sensitivity to the unconscious, especially Oedipal, desires driving his being and which he does not fully understand. In a proto-Doubrovskyan gambit, the life chronicled owes more to fantasy, the imagination, and indeed fiction than it does to externally existing reality.

Meanwhile, the recognition that writing one's self is not so much a matter of chronicling a self and its life as it is a question of *creating* or *constructing* a self (and, retrospectively, a destiny for that self) for the reader to encounter can be found in the autobiographies of the French existentialists, and other authors in their intellectual entourage. Jean Genet informs the reader of his autobiographical volume *Journal du voleur* (1949) of his project not to tell who he is, but rather to 'réussir ma légende' ('succeed in creating my legend').[6] Meanwhile, Violette Leduc's *La Bâtarde* (1964) shows from the outset an investment in creating for the reader a narratorial persona marked by various misfortunes. Jean-Paul Sartre's autobiography, *Les Mots* (1964), provides an elaborate deconstruction *avant la lettre* of the idea that life precedes writing (rather than the other way round). Via its ironic treatment of his childhood self's inauspicious attempts to make his mark as a writer, it rejects the idea that the self is born with a character or a destiny susceptible to being chronicled (as opposed to retroactively projected onto it) by writing.

The drama of the self, as played out in twentieth-century French thought and also in autobiography, has been the discovery of how irrevocably the self is estranged from itself. A thematics of self-estrangement and estrangement more broadly is readily discernible in many twentieth-century autobiographies (it is an important thread running through, for example, Duras's *L'Amant*). This need not, however, be a topic approached in melancholic mode (Barthes's autobiographical text joyfully celebrates the non-coincidence of his self with itself). Yet estrangement supplies autobiography with far more than narrative content. Among the most fascinating qualities of modern French autobiography is the virtuosity with which writers such as Perec frequently manipulate form. Estrangement is often the motor behind these formal innovations, as we see in Marie NDiaye's *Autoportrait en vert* (2005), where an uncanny estrangement lies at the heart of both the narrative and its presentation, which is heavily reliant on photographs. In her use of photographs, NDiaye takes up a technique first memorably employed in *Roland Barthes* and

---

6 J. Genet, *Journal du voleur* (Paris: Gallimard, 1949), p. 233.

increasingly used in contemporary self-writings such as Ernaux's *L'Usage de la photo* (2005), co-authored with Marc Marie. Contemporary autobiography increasingly refuses to be confined within the parameters of narrative text, and pushes outwards to embrace photographic and moving images. Thus new media become colonised by autobiography (examples include Agnès Varda's film *Les Glaneurs et la glaneuse* (2000) and Sophie Calle's exhibition 'M'as-tu vue' of 2003–4). Or is it that autobiography loses itself in these new media? For, at the end of the twentieth century, autobiography seemed to desire nothing more than to make itself strange to itself. Autobiography has not so much died as made itself its own uncanny other. Psychoanalysis tells us that the uncanny corresponds to the return of the repressed: that which is part of us, but which we cannot accept and have suppressed. Numerous are the texts that would support the reading that autobiography seems to demand its own suppression (witness the insistence on the death of autobiography). However, psychoanalysis also tells us that what we try to suppress will always come back, albeit in a form we do not recognise.

63

The modern French novel

MARTIN CROWLEY

In his hugely influential 1960 essay 'Modernist Painting', Clement Greenberg famously locates 'the essence of Modernism' in 'the use of the characteristic methods of a discipline to criticise the discipline itself – not in order to subvert it but in order to entrench it more firmly in its area of competence'.[1] Many of the decisive literary works of the early twentieth century are marked by just such a modernist concern with their constitutive formal features: we might typically think of Joyce, for example, working on the encounters between prose narrative, consciousness, social existence, and cultural heritage to form works which are at once densely impacted and vertiginously expansive; or, at the opposite extreme, of Kafka, paring this defining material down to its uncanny minimal elements. This self-consciousness is no less a defining feature of the key French novels of the modernist moment; and, indeed, of the modern French novel per se. Recursivity, here, has little to do with solipsism, however. Rather, an emphasis on the constraints and possibilities of form tends to be part of the enquiry carried out by the works of this period into the ways in which individuals and collectivities register, reflect upon, and act in the world. The following account of these works will, accordingly, be guided by this line (which the twentieth century inherits from the novel as its generic 'area of competence'): the fault-line, or, better perhaps, the membrane which connects and separates self and world, on which the shifts and dramas of their relation are articulated, and which it is the business of any given novel to trace.

Inside out: modernist recursivity, existential commitment

If the early twentieth century is marked notably in Europe by the self-immolation of World War I, this is registered largely outside the French

1 C. Greenberg, 'Modernist Painting', in F. Frascina and C. Harrison (eds.), *Modern Art and Modernism: A Critical Anthology* (London: Harper and Row, 1982), pp. 5–10, at p. 5.

novel. With the significant exceptions of Barbusse's *Le Feu* (1917) and, later, Céline's *Voyage au bout de la nuit* (1932), its devastation is marked principally in Apollinaire's avant-garde lyric poetry, or the convulsive disgust of Dada. The major French novels of the modernist period are characterised much more by that self-referentiality that typifies their moment as a whole. While *À la recherche du temps perdu* (1913–27), Marcel Proust's exhilaratingly mobile multi-volume edifice, does feature memorable references to the war, it spends rather more time telling the story of how someone comes to write a novel, offering along the way considerations of the novelist's craft, the modus operandi of various art forms, and the social settings in which these wither or thrive. The other great work of French novelistic modernism, André Gide's *Les Faux-Monnayeurs* (1925), sets up an extraordinary self-referential spiral, featuring a character called Édouard who is himself working on a novel entitled *Les Faux-Monnayeurs*, and regularly folds into its fabric extracts from Édouard's diary in which he ponders the progress or otherwise of his work, the proper relation between the novel and the world, and other such self-conscious matters. Gide in fact makes great play of the heightened sense of artifice he thus introduces, having his narrator express his interest or otherwise in the development of his characters, or indeed debate theories of the novel with Édouard. Paradox-ically, however, this Gidean artifice is to his mind in the service of a higher form of realism. Just as the natural sciences and philosophy were around this time emphasising the unavoidable presence of an observing consciousness in any account of the world, so for Gide is the fantasy of a third-person, divinely omniscient novelistic narrator just that: an unrealisable, indeed undesirable daydream. Gide makes this insight into the fabric of his prose fiction, in which the distorting presence of a mediating narratorial consciousness is never far away: in his shorter works, which he termed *récits*, the distortions so intro-duced produce an enthralling, if often unforgiving, and irreducibly ironic critical perspective on his characters' often desperate self-justifications.

This insistent mediation is in part a critique of what was perceived as the impossible drive to objectivity of the great nineteenth-century novelists: in his 'farce', *Les Caves du Vatican* (1914), Gide has some fun at the expense of a novelist who glories in the name of Julius de Baraglioul, and whose mechanistic conception of the novel (with the novelist a mere scientific observer) parodies Zola's *Le Roman expérimental* (1880). One could be forgiven for thinking, on the basis of such enthusiastic parricide, that the French novel of the early twentieth century was intent on throwing off the nineteenth-century novel's concern for social history, instead turning inwards to trace the delicate psychology of its now apparently irreducible narrators. And indeed, many writers of the period, with Proust spectacularly pre-eminent amongst them, do delve deeply into this intimate archaeology. In Proust's case, of course, this exceeds by far mere questions of thematisation or narrative structure: at both the micro- and the macro-levels, his novel finds new compelling forms with which to engage the rhythms and textures of lived experience. The architecture of the work as a whole allows its author to explore the development of feelings, relationships, social groupings, psychological and political narratives, and so on, back and forth across a time frame which is both expansive and intensely detailed; and this intensity is largely realised in the breathtaking sinuosity of Proustian syntax, whose sentences wind through the most acute moments of sensory and emotional experience.

It would be a brave reader, however, who would conclude from the rich inwardness of these novels that they had abandoned the world outside in favour of eternal self-scrutiny. On the contrary: for all the intricacy of their internal tracery, what really concerns these works is not the self in isolation, but the permeable membrane between self and world, on which the shocks and delights of the world are registered and negotiated, and from which reverberate the self's often contradictory responses. As in the philosophy of Bergson and then the phenomenology of Husserl, it is the encounter between self and world that is of interest. This interest similarly drives the novels of Colette, where the negotiations of the world by a specifically female self, and the articulation of these in novelistic form, are pioneeringly explored. It also characterises the surrealists' major prose works, notably Breton's *Nadja* (1928) and Aragon's *Le Paysan de Paris* (1926), in which the landscape of the modern city is redrawn by the random, desirous perceptions of the *flâneur's* altered consciousness, along with the work of Mauriac, who gives it a densely psychological and intensely religious inflection; and, as one might expect, it receives detailed attention in the first French novel to feature a demonstrably phenomenological framework, namely Sartre's *La Nausée* (1938). Sartre's triumphant early novel is well supplied with modernist self-referential irony: not only does its narrator, Antoine Roquentin, spend the novel failing to write the biography of a local worthy (concluding at the end of the text that he would be better off trying his luck at a novel), he also punctuates his jottings with regular temporal markers, reminding the reader that this plainly novelistic text is also, supposedly and with arch self-consciousness, his diary. Again, however, this reflexivity works principally to map Roquentin's anguished negotiation of the boundaries between his consciousness and the world around him: questions of form are here part of a broader interrogation of the possibility of meaningful action and human relations in a world of sordid contingency.

In Sartre's subsequent novelistic work, the trilogy *Les Chemins de la liberté* (1945–9) this questioning continues, but within a framework that has become much less local, much more historical. Influenced particularly by the variable panoramic technique of Dos Passos, and moving towards his own conception of literary commitment (*'engagement'*), Sartre sets his characteristic concern for human freedom and authentic action within the France of World War II, moving from the intimate to the world-historical by situating the mobility of subjective choice within the shifting dimensions of its scenery, often shifting narrative perspective to do so. In this, he is also developing the work of Malraux, who, especially in *La Condition humaine* (1933), *Le Temps du mépris* (1935), and *L'Espoir* (1937), had addressed questions of the meaning or otherwise of individual and collective human existence against the backdrop of world-historical events, sharpening individual existential choices by their larger-scale implications. It is a line taken also by Simone de Beauvoir, who builds outwards from the relatively personal concerns of *L'Invitée* (1943), to an existential account of Resistance activity in *Le Sang des autres* (1945), and, subsequently, to the complex intertwining of personal, literary, and political choices in the Goncourt-winning *Les Mandarins* (1954). In all these cases, perhaps pre-eminently in Beauvoir, the demands of political activity are presented as part of the fabric of being in the world, lived intimately as an irreducible element of the self's negotiation with the conditions of its contingent, embodied existence. In more than one sense, here, the personal is always insistently political.

In this respect, it is possible to trace a significant difference between this approach to the novel and that of Camus, a difference which may be seen to prefigure the break that would split Camus from Sartre, Beauvoir, Merleau-Ponty, and the world of their review, *Les Temps modernes*, at the start of the 1950s. Camus's novels tend not to implicate the personal in the political in this way: if the world of history and politics is there as a backdrop, such as the colonial context of *L'Étranger* (1942) or the Holocaust which forms the prehistory to *La Chute* (1956), it remains at one remove from the intimate existence of his protagonists. So when Meursault kills the Arab in *L'Étranger*, the colonial implications of this more or less accidental act remain indeterminable: it is impossible to imagine Malraux, Beauvoir or Sartre allowing such a moment of subjective choice to remain quite so vague. If their characters' actions are never determined by their situation, they are resoundingly developed in close relation to this situation; Camus, on the other hand, seems positively to valorise the margin of indeterminacy by which his characters are allowed to escape the clutches of history. (Precisely the possibility or otherwise of such escape would indeed, as indicated above, form the substance of the break of the early 1950s.) In *La Peste* (1947), Camus's most expansive novelistic work, the high point of fraternal solidarity comes when Tarrou and Rieux symbolically, if briefly, swim freely out into the ocean, away from the constraints of the plague-ridden city. History, for Camus, comes to look increasingly like unstoppable carnage; if in *La Peste* this is no reason not to fight injustice, by *La Chute* the longing for some kind of outside to its procession of terror has imploded into claustrophobia and self-loathing irony. Camus, who arguably got his historical hands rather dirtier than did many of his literary peers, presents throughout his novels – including the unfinished and posthumously published *Le Premier Homme* (1995) – a relation between self and world in which the unremitting hostility of the latter is punctuated by the simple pleasures, generous friendships, and decent actions of selves who refuse to resign themselves to its brutality.

Inwards and outwards, again. And finally, some instructive remnants

By the time of Camus's death at the turn of the 1960s, two of his contemporaries were coming into relatively belated, but increasingly significant prominence. Closely connected since the 1940s, Georges Bataille and Maurice Blanchot set literature at a very different angle to the world than their existentialist peers; in their work, the very existence of something like literature already poses radical questions about the nature and purpose of human activity in general. For Bataille, literature is on the side of an excessive, useless expenditure of energy and resources. Glorying in its shameful refusal of all forms of productivity, it thereby affirms what Bataille valorises as the unemployable negativity at the ruptured heart of human existence. Much of Bataille's fiction dramatises this wasteful sovereignty in the obscene actions of its protagonists; to the extent that they were published at all during his lifetime, these publications were mostly undertaken in an appropriately obscure, if not straightforwardly clandestine way. Unsurprisingly, this position set Bataille at odds with Sartre, whose existential dialectic rejects this excess as so much mysticism. Blanchot similarly insists that the workaday capacity of literature is supplemented by the obscure, intransitive dimension in which it essentially unfolds, and which also indicates an irreducible aspect of our being in the world. This aspect is compellingly developed in Blanchot's fiction, which, taking seriously its own ambivalent ontological and cognitive status, manages to narrate events of considerable existential intensity while simultaneously removing these events from the realm of any certainty whatsoever.

The increased prominence of Bataille and Blanchot throughout the 1950s and at the start of the 1960s was largely due to the interest shown in their work by two emergent tendencies: on the one hand, the thinkers and writers associated with the new combative journal *Tel Quel*, many of whom had also been published in Bataille's journal *Critique*, and who would go on to become the leading figures of their generation; on the other, a new literary grouping which took its lead in part from these two, and, at least in its most fervent self-publicity, distanced itself polemically – and, again, parricidally – from the realist aesthetics and political commitments of existential fiction, and indeed from the realist paradigm per se. Appropriately enough, the work of this grouping came to be known as the *nouveau roman*; grouped principally although not exclusively around the editorial influence of Alain Robbe-Grillet at Minuit (and supported initially by *Tel Quel*), this tendency's characteristic concerns were aired most forcefully in Robbe-Grillet's collection of essays, *Pour un nouveau roman* (1963), for which the ground had to an extent been prepared by Nathalie Sarraute's *L'Ère du soupçon* (1956). Within Robbe-Grillet's own practice, as across the work of the grouping as a whole, an intriguing tension emerges which shows, even at this moment of apparent rupture, the persistence of a defining preoccupation with the relation between the human self and the world of objects and history. On the one hand, especially in Robbe-Grillet's early work, rigorously neutral descriptions of minute objective detail appear to evacuate human consciousness from the field, refusing the anthropocentrism of novelistic practice hitherto. On the other hand, quite quickly in Robbe-Grillet, and throughout the work of Nathalie Sarraute especially, such descriptions emerge as the traces of the outside world registered in the intimate, often pre-conscious recesses of subjective perception, with all the affective distortions this implies. As demonstrated in Robbe-Grillet's tour de force *La Jalousie* (1957), it is thus possible for the distorting consciousness pioneered by Gide, say, to become both maximally present and entirely absent: and the question of the novel becomes the more or less phenomenological question of the relation of human consciousness to the world, particularly as this relation is mediated, vitiated, or evacuated through language.

For all the successful publicity generated by its corporate branding, the *nouveau roman* in fact collected together a diverse bunch of writers, driven by a common commitment to the substantive importance of formal innovation, but developing very different approaches to the novel. If Robbe-Grillet's most significant work holds together rigorous objectivism and obsessive (and increasingly multiple) subjective distortion, Sarraute's heads inwards, deep into the tiniest movements of the pre-subjective. Claude Simon, on the other hand, addresses both the disasters of history and the uncertainties of human experience in allusive, shifting prose, before in the 1970s adopting a more formalistic style; while Michel Butor elaborates complex narratives which seek to disclose the real structures that underpin ordinary experience. Butor is thus close in some ways to Georges Perec, the master technician whose formally playful works are also exercises in committed critical realism; this proximity ought perhaps to encourage us to think of the *nouveaux romanciers* less as the homogeneous school they never really were, and more as part of this ongoing preoccupation throughout the novel of the period with the problematic fault-line between consciousness and the exterior world of objects, other people, and history.

Further evidence of this preoccupation came in the mid-1970s, when many of the *nouveaux romanciers*, and indeed Perec, began to produce works with a markedly autobiographical stamp. It is no coincidence that, at this time, France was beginning to address the traumas of its recent past; first, its role during World War II in the imprisonment and deportation to the Nazi camps of approximately 140,000 people, including 75,000 Jews; later, the violence with which it opposed the decolonisation struggle, most particularly during the Algerian war. Testimonial writing – from Jewish survivors, members of the Resistance, anti-colonial fighters – was becoming much more widely received, with many texts finally making it into print, or being more prominently republished. The effect of this might be measured in the growing convergence between testimonial and novelistic forms: where writers such as Elie Wiesel, Charlotte Delbo, David Rousset, André Schwarz-Bart, and Robert Antelme found in the novel a form (however strained) through which to articulate something of their experiences, these articulations, gaining in prominence from the mid-1970s on, feed back to the novel an interest in the historical less as the context of subjective choice, as it had been for the existential novel, and more as a medium within which to map the flickerings of memory or the complexities of identitarian definition, as seen for example in Marguerite Duras's *L'Amant* (1984) and *La Douleur* (1985). In what is in some respects a more extreme manner, Pierre Guyotat's best-known writings, *Tombeau pour cinq cent mille soldats* (1967) and *Eden, Eden, Eden* (1970), force these self-images through the funnel of a meticulously realised materialism, resulting in an exceptionally intense linguistic encounter with the violence of warfare and sexuality.

This concern with history as mediated through the subjective and the bodily may be seen to have been consistently pioneered by many of the period's most significant female authors. With Colette as the major forerunner, women's writing has here often been characterised by its acute delineation of the boundaries at which the self negotiates the demands of the world. In novels such as *L'Invitée*, but especially in her autobiographical trilogy, and her account of the death of her mother, *Une Mort très douce* (1964), Beauvoir traces these lines with patience, rigour, and generosity. An autobiographical dimension verging on the testimonial also characterises the work of Violette Leduc, Marie Cardinal, and, at the beginning and end of her career, Marguerite Duras; while Christiane Rochefort mordantly and at times fantastically examined sexuality and gender relations, often by scrutinising the social and linguistic structures that serve to regulate individuals' behaviour. With Annie Ernaux, similar concerns lead to a focus both on intimate relationships and, especially in Ernaux's early work, on structures of social class. The writing of women's experiences of this period maps the social and linguistic frames by which it is constrained, articulating these experiences at once through and against these frames – at times, indeed, women writers explode, distort or dismantle such frames, critiquing their violence and suggesting utopian alternatives. In the innovations of Hélène Cixous, Monique Wittig, or mid-period Duras, the multiple politics of women's liberation demand, and find, novelistic forms to match their insurrectional dynamism.

The work of such women writers has been of great importance in the claiming by women of a voice in the French public sphere. In addition, however, their writings allow us to see something of how gendered subjectivity encounters, resists, and is constituted by the external world. These encounters thus emerge as the defining feature of the modern French novel: moving inwards to the self's intimacies, and, in so doing, finding again the various points of abrupt contact between this self and everything it is not. If such a totalising account doubtless has its truth, however, we ought nonetheless to conclude by considering three figures whose resistance to inclusion in the kind of narrative presented here calls us, finally, to consider further the nature of this dynamic: Samuel Beckett, Jean Genet, and Louis-Ferdinand Céline. Plainly, this leftover trio share the defining interest of their time (and of the novel as genre) with the intimate, violent borders on which self meets world. Equally plainly, however, each sits particularly uncomfortably within the broad-brush agglomerations of an account such as this. This discomfort might well be related to their common interest in the messy, perhaps sordid, often comical, sometimes confrontational, almost always shabby detritus of the encounter between the self and what it is not. In Beckett, this is both a generosity and an aesthetics, which sees the novel (and, later, whatever it is that is left after the novel) both speaking a language it knows to be a means of brutal domination, and failing – albeit never quite as completely as in our apocalyptic fantasies – persistently to signify. In Genet, detritus is given social form: Beckett's Molloy, so to speak, is realised in the bodies of specific outlaws, and hymned in a lyrical, sumptuously elegant idiom which perverts that official language whose aim is the removal of these squalid bodies. A whole political and aesthetic history is thus drawn together in Genet's *Un captif amoureux* (1986), in which determinate political commitment and rebel desire meet the world in the beloved body. But this would be far too agreeable a place to conclude.

Accounts of the novel love to stress its inherent heterogeneity, the capacity of its elastic form to embrace social and discursive multitudes. There is no doubting that this anti-totalitarian dynamic does indeed constitute much of the novel's historical significance. But the liberal praise of mess and multiplicity too easily forgets – unlike most of the novelists mentioned here – the antagonisms this dynamic must entail if it is to be other than empty pluralism. Thus it is with Céline, the author of such texts as *Voyage au bout de la nuit* (1932) and *Mort à credit* (1936), that this account will draw to a close. Céline gives voice to the agonies and deceptions of World War I; rips through bourgeois cant with the impatience of a furious materialism; and maps the world-historical clashes of class, race, nation, and gender by which his time is defined in a violently satirical idiom which – embracing vulgarity with a success remarkable even in the supposedly heterogeneous novel – pins the hypocrisy and misery of its world to the spot of its over-inflated, bombastic, flapping signifiers. Céline's hilariously vicious voice is also racist from the start, and moves in an untroubled way into the service of the most shameful anti-Semitism. His example reminds us, finally, that – as all those whose work has been discussed here insistently demonstrate – the permeable membrane between self and world, which the novel is bound to trace, is also the front line of bloody conflict.

64

The contemporary French novel

MICHAEL SHERINGHAM

Since the late 1970s prose fiction in France has continued to flourish, not so much in the guise of a dominant genre – the Novel – concerned with its intrinsic scope and methods, but as an instrument for investigating a wide range of experiences. Whereas Roland Barthes, in the heyday of structuralist 'textuality', the *nouveau roman* and *Tel Quel*, had declared that writing was 'an intransitive verb', fictional writing now becomes transitive again, but not via a return to traditional forms. While popular or 'middlebrow' writing continues to use staple conventions, honed since the mid-nineteenth century, the writers who make a lasting impact in this period (including Modiano, Ernaux, Michon, Djebar, Echenoz, NDiaye, and Quignard) innovate formally by combining narrative fiction with such non-fiction modes as autobiography, biography, testimony, the essay, reportage, and historical or sociological enquiry whilst engaging with different forms of reality – historical, global, social, or personal. The period that saw the rise of autobiography (a key moment being the publication of radically innovative autobiographical texts by Barthes and Georges Perec in 1975), then autobiography's mutation into multiple channels of life-writing with, concurrently, the return of a preoccupation with history (Perec referred to 'l'Histoire avec sa grande hache'),[1] has sometimes been characterised as a period of 'returns'. But if it is legitimate to talk of a 'return' to the human subject, extra-textual reference, and lived experience, the 'real' that comes back is not the same as before but a reality located at another point of the spiral, as Barthes put it, a point where autobiography and history, for example, or fiction and testimony, merge rather than diverging.

Recent historical experience (notably that of two world wars, the Occupation, the Algerian war, and decolonisation) is a central presence in

---

1 G. Perec, *W ou le souvenir d'enfance* (Paris: Denoël, 1975), p. 17.

contemporary French fiction, not via a return to the traditional historical novel, but through the creation of narrative structures, narrating voices, and fusions between genres all tending to maintain focus on the present as much as on the past. Anticipating this trend, Michel Tournier's *Le Roi des Aulnes* (1970) used myth, fable, and epic to explore aspects of the Second World War, a manoeuvre echoed in Jonathan Littell's controversial blockbuster, *Les Bienveillantes* (Goncourt Prize, 2006). In *W ou le souvenir d'enfance* (1975), Perec placed individual autobiographical memory alongside fictional fabulation, declaring that the truth lay in their convergence. Consistently haunted by ancestors who fought in earlier wars, and by his own experience in the cavalry in the Second World War, Claude Simon's novels moved progressively away from the techniques of the *nouveau roman* to lay bare and problematise their autobiographical foundations (*Le Jardin des Plantes*, 1997), bringing questions of memory and testimony to the forefront.

Born after the war, but haunted by his Jewish father's ambiguous role during the Occupation, Patrick Modiano began his career with a trilogy of phantasmagorical novels (including *La Ronde de nuit*, 1969) in which the Occupation became a grotesque charade and a vast echo-chamber of voices. A prolific writer, Modiano continued to write short enigmatic novels, usually involving the interplay between the narrator or protagonist's present and various moments in his or her own past, as well as concern with the period of the Occupation. Often imbued with loss, disorientation, and nostalgia, and marked by consistent ambivalence and ambiguity, Modiano's novels, like many others in the period, often draw on the plot structures of the detective novel in order to foreground themes of disappearance and return, or memory and forgetting. Explicitly autobiographical works such as *Un Pedigree* (2005) embed Modiano's work as a whole in autobiographical space, but he broke new ground with *Dora Bruder* (1997), in which a painstaking attempt to gather information about a young Jewish girl brings together biography, autobiography, archival documentation, and fictive speculation. The starting point for Modiano's biographical quest was a 1941 newspaper where he found an advertisement placed by the desperate parents of a missing girl. Identifying the girl's name in a list of deportees to Auschwitz, Modiano initially wrote a novel, *Voyage de noces* (1990), in which he imagined another fate for the young protagonist. But hours spent imagining and retracing Dora's itineraries led to the project of reconstituting the material traces of her existence in school records, police files, and other archives of the Occupation. *Dora Bruder* quickly achieved the status of a contemporary classic.

The themes of archival questing, and of being haunted by a traumatic past that is not directly one's own but refuses to go away, are central to the interactions between human subjects and historical realities in contemporary French writing. Lydie Salvayre's *La Compagnie des spectres* (1997) features the ravings of an old woman convinced that the Occupation is still going on, with collaborators ruling the roost. Didier Daeninckx has used the idiom of the detective novel to explore both the Occupation and the legacy of the Algerian war (*Meurtres pour mémoire*, 1984). Assia Djebar's *L'Amour la fantasia* (1985) splices together a range of different archives (including letters dating from the period of the French conquest of Algeria in the 1830s, and a 'soundbank' of women's voices from the period of the Algerian war in the 1950s), and in other works, combining fiction, autobiography, and historical record, Djebar explores the joint ramifications of subjectivity and historical reality. With a similar recourse to a polyphony of voices Patrick Chamoiseau, in *Texaco* (Goncourt Prize, 1992) and other works, opens sightlines on how the Caribbean present is haunted by the colonial past. Like those of many writers in this period, Hélène Cixous's novels have come increasingly to focus directly on her own experience, and latterly on her Algerian origins (*Or. Les Lettres de mon père*, 1997). In *Tigre en papier* (2002) Olivier Rolin recounts the *événements* of May 1968, in which he was a participant, to a young teenager as they make repeated circumnavigations of Paris on the *Périphérique* ringroad. A more global history is embraced in his *L'Invention du monde* (1993) in which newspapers dating from the same day all around the world provide the basis for a profusion of stories. Although his work has tended to become more mainstream and commercial since his avant-garde beginnings, the novels of J. M. G. Le Clézio (winner of the Nobel Prize for literature in 2008) reflect a widespread spatial turn in modern literature, and focus on the tensions between European and non-European visions of the world (*Onitsha*, 1991). The global and the political are also central in the 'post-apocalyptic' novels of Antoine Volodine (*Alto Solo*, 1991) where the idiom of sci-fi (mutants, cyborgs) investigates the 'post-human' in the heart of twentieth-century historical horror.

Another way in which engagement with historical reality inspires new fictional or narrative modes is in the tracing out of connections between public and private histories and spaces. The identification of different dimensions of history (and memory) is itself a characteristic feature of contemporary historiography in the work of such historians as Michel de Certeau, Pierre Nora, and Arlette Farge. Family history, genealogy, inheritance, and filiation, along with an interest in archives and other relics of the past (including photographs), figure prominently in works that often combine biography, autobiography, and historical testimony, as well as a strong sense of geographical location. Recognition of the part played by different kinds of otherness in the construction of identities, by the 'transpersonal' as Annie Ernaux calls it, leads to a questioning of the claims of the sovereign individual and hence of the psychological 'territory' of much traditional narrative fiction. Jean Rouaud's *Les Champs d'honneur*, which won the Goncourt Prize in 1985, resurrects his grandfather's participation in the First World War, while subsequent novels have focused in turn on other members of his family. Richard Millet is the author of a series of novels, including *La Gloire des Pythre* (1995) where the 'matter' of his native region, the Corrèze, with its disinherited peasantry and geographical isolation, is transmuted into a mythic universe, as in the novels of Giono or Faulkner. Like Millet, Pierre Bergounioux, also originally from the Limousin, often writes about his geographical region whilst at the same time, as in *Miette* (1995) for example, progressively interrogating his own personal itinerary.

In *Vies minuscules* (1984), a major work of the period, Pierre Michon combined biography, autobiography, and the kind of high-literary stylistic elaboration associated with novels, in a manner that has proved influential, launching a mode of 'biographical fiction' adapted by other writers. *Vies minuscules* draws on the lives of saints and other biographical traditions to 'mythologise' the life histories of eight ordinary individuals, including Michon's grandmother, a boy at his school, an alcoholic country priest, an old girlfriend and a man he met in hospital. Inspired by Michel Foucault's work on the impact of power on the lives of obscure individuals, as revealed by archival traces, Michon's elaborate narratives interweave his own life story with those of others, setting his struggle to realise his literary ambitions in the context of the gulf between rural obscurity and metropolitan sophistication, and between the sublimity of literary language and the incoherence of a disorderly existence. In subsequent works Michon has continued to develop original ways of exploring lives, including those of Rimbaud, Goya, and Van Gogh (via a biography of the postman the artist painted several times).

Having launched her writing career with three autobiographical novels, Annie Ernaux arrived at a combination of autobiography and biography by a different route. Marked by the notions of *habitus* (ingrained social behaviour) and social trajectory in the work of the sociologist Pierre Bourdieu, Ernaux wrote books about her father (*La Place*, 1984) and her mother (*Une femme*, 1989) in which the milieu the author feels she betrayed by becoming middle-class is closely scrutinised, detailed attention being paid to language, gesture, and outlook. This 'ethnographic' perspective (Ernaux uses the term 'ethnotexte') is accentuated in *La Honte* (1997) in which Ernaux focuses on a dramatic incident in her childhood but treats it forensically, as a symptom rather than a trauma, identifying, partly by recourse to archival records, the way her autobiographical experience bears the traces of wider historical forces. In contrast with Michon, Ernaux's way of attending to obscure lives does not involve stylistic richness but a pared-down 'écriture plate' modelled on the idiom of her letters home when she was a student. Yet in its way Ernaux's work is no less literary than Michon's, and despite the strongly factual and representational basis of their writing both authors are central to the evolution of narrative fiction in this period. However referential the ingredients may be, the combination of the biographical, the autobiographical, the ethnographic, and the sociological in Ernaux and Michon makes their works authentically literary, whilst falling outside the ambit of established genres. In *Les Années* (2008), Ernaux chronicles her life history decade by decade, using the first-person plural to merge her own memories and experiences with those of her contemporaries. Although it may involve the exposure of very personal material (as in Ernaux's *L'Usage de la photo*, 2005), and probes the interface of individual and collective history, the work of Michon and Ernaux does not involve the kinds of game-playing associated with the 'autofictions' of Hervé Guibert, Serge Doubrovsky, Christine Angot, or Catherine Millet, which problematise the border between the intimate and the public.

Some of the most significant French fictional writing since 1980 sets out to capture, in stylistically inventive ways, the realities of contemporary social space. Rather than memory and filiation, the concerns here are with the quickly changing immediacies of an increasingly globalised postmodern world. Since *Le Méridien de Greenwich* (1979) Jean Echenoz has been recognised as a writer of true originality who combines the plot conventions of genre fiction (especially detective and spy novels) with a highly articulate and laconic narrating voice which reports, with deadpan humour and seeming impartiality, on the activities of sometimes eccentric characters, and the everyday urban world in which the action takes place. *Je m'en vais* (Goncourt Prize, 1999) concerns a Parisian art-dealer with a weak heart who travels to the Arctic Circle to retrieve some Inuit sculptures and then foils his assistant's attempt to double-cross him. A series of pretty young women flit through his life, including one who panics when she finds him apparently dead in bed one morning, and another who stays long enough to help him recover from heart surgery. The novel abounds in seemingly random descriptions of objects, clothes and gestures, which divert our attention as the narrator shares his surprise at the spectacle of the world around him with the reader. A similar mind-set features in a range of other authors published by the Éditions de Minuit (associated in the 1950s and 1960s with the *nouveau roman*), who are often linked to Echenoz under such labels as 'minimalist' or 'impassive'. But rather than sharing an aesthetic programme, it is more helpful to see such writers, who include Jean-Philippe Toussaint (*La Salle de bain*, 1985), Christian Oster (*Mon Grand Appartement*, 1999), Jean-Christophe Gailly (*Be-bop*, 1995), Tanguy Viel (*L'Absolue Perfection du crime*, 2001), all of considerable interest, as sharing the desire to devise literary styles, often based on pastiche and intertextuality, attuned to the shifting identities of the contemporary world.

Another important writer published by Minuit, François Bon, crosses fact and fiction to cast light on the socio-political realities of the modern world. After writing six novels (including *Sortie d'usine*, 1982) reflecting his professional knowledge of factories and industrial plants, Bon deliberately broke away from narrative to devise ways of engaging more effectively with the social violence of a globalised world that treats human beings like disposable commodities. Drawing on his experience with writing workshops in factories, prisons, and hostels for the homeless, Bon composes hybrid works that incorporate the voices of the dispossessed (*Prison*, 1998), subjecting narrative form to the disruptive immediacy of theatrical performance (*Impatience*, 1998). In *Daewoo* (2004), Bon builds a text out of interviews conducted in the aftermath of a factory closure, while in *Tumulte* (2006), he publishes the accumulated blogs he wrote for a website (the internet plays a central part in his work), as he attempted to capture the multiplicity of events in the space of a year.

Marie NDiaye, whose first novel was published by Éditions de Minuit when she was eighteen, built up a major body of work in the course of the 1990s to emerge as one of the major writers of the period. Drawing on her origins (French mother, absent Senegalese father, French provincial upbringing), NDiaye uses her outstanding ear for linguistic idiom to combine a focus on the family with a sense of the uncanny located in apparently ordinary settings. Inspired by Kafka, her narratives often involve sudden metamorphosis between the human and the animal and situations that are inconsistent with customary logic. In *En famille* (1990) Fanny desperately seeks to be accepted by the family that has repudiated her. Whilst it becomes obvious to the reader that this is owing to her mixed race, the endless equivocations of the family members keep Fanny in the dark. In *Mon cœur à l'étroit* (2008), Nadia, a schoolteacher, has cut off all links with her immigrant family marooned in the poor suburbs of Bordeaux. But when her husband and fellow teacher receives a terrible wound that refuses to heal, Nadia is forced to recognise that only her expulsion from the social body will restore normality. Her flight into exile to join her estranged son (a plot echoed in the earlier *Rosie Carpe*, 2001) offers at least the possibility of moral redemption. In 2009 NDiaye was awarded the Prix Goncourt for her hugely successful *Trois Femmes puissantes*. The elements of the fantastic in NDiaye's novels, and their dystopian tenor, are echoed to some degree in the resolutely dyspeptic works of Michel Houellebecq, who has used the media to court controversy and achieved huge sales for novels (including *Les Particules élémentaires*, 1998, and *Plateforme*, 2001) where key features of the modern world, from corporate sleaze to cloning and terrorism, are reflected with more than a pinch of cynicism.

Along with fashioning new ways of figuring the relations between the self and the historical past, between private and public space, and between individuals and the force fields of postmodernity, contemporary French prose fiction, reflecting key developments in the human sciences, has often become a sounding-board for the profusion of forms of knowledge available in our era. In the prolific output of Pascal Quignard, a writer of unquestionably major stature, the novel is both accompanied and invaded by other genres, such as the essay, the poem, the treatise, and the fable. Quignard's fascination with origins has led him to become expert in a range of fields including ancient, especially Latin, literature, classical music (he was for a long time the organiser of an important music festival), painting and sculpture (he has written an important work on sexuality in Roman art), and the literature of many periods and countries, including seventeenth-century France, which fascinates Quignard partly because of the neo-classical obsession with antiquity. Always teeming with memorable details, his novels range from the relatively mainstream (*Tous les matins du monde*, 1991) to the highly elliptical (*Carus*, 1979), and are often set in the past while betraying timeless preoccupations including sexuality, language, melancholy, and death. Just as the novels may include long disquisitions on abstruse historical and philosophical topics (*Les Tablettes de buis d'Apronenia Avitia* [1984] is the imaginary biography of a Roman matron), Quignard's ostensibly non-fictional works are permeated by storytelling. The series of eight small volumes titled *Petits Traités* he published in 1990, full of unclassifiable and neglected fragments of knowledge, mix fact and fiction in unpredictable doses, creating a universe comparable in some respects to those of Borges, Calvino, and Perec. The originality of Quignard's work lies, however, in his ability to combine critical fictions with treatments of profound human experience, especially love and desire (in this regard Quignard follows in the footsteps of Bataille and Duras). Surprisingly, but symptomatically in view of the evolution we are tracing in the contemporary novel, Quignard was awarded the Goncourt Prize in 2002 for *Les Ombres errantes*, the first volume of a new sequence called *Dernier Royaume* (five volumes thus far), which contains a mixture of autobiographical meditations, little treatises, parables, fables, and erudite expositions of recondite historical fact, often centred on archival materials.

The mixture of erudition, anthropological curiosity, and rejection of conventional historical categorisations to be found in Quignard also features in the work of another important writer, Gérard Macé. The exploration of new biographical forms is a central feature of his *Vies antérieures* (1991) as well as his book-length essay-fictions on Champollion and Proust. Fascinated by the Far East, Macé's medium is essentially the extended prose poem, and he has turned to photography, in theory as well as in practice, to provide a visual extension to his construction of a personal universe embracing materials from numerous cultural locations. If biography has become a central thread in contemporary fictional writing (illustrated by Echenoz's novellas *Ravel* [2006] and *Courir* [2008], based on the Czech athlete, Emil Zatopek), this fascination with the stuff of human lives is often allied with a desire to appropriate new modes of experience and new forms of knowledge for the literary field. In different ways, the works of Marie Darrieussecq and Emmanuel Carrère exemplify what one could call a 'postmodern fantastic', traces of which are to be found in the speculations of Quignard and others. Darrieussecq achieved notoriety for her anti-sexist fable, *Truismes* (1996), in which a woman turns into a sow, but in subsequent works, including *Naissance des fantômes* (1998), her fictional writing has often reflected new models of human consciousness, notably those currently being evolved in the field of the neurosciences. Like Darrieussecq, Carrère is fascinated by situations that place human beings in circumstances that estrange them from the familiar world and expose them to the precariousness of modern identity. In a novel, *La Classe de neige* (1997), and a biographical enquiry, *L'Adversaire* (2000), Carrère explores his fascination with the Romand murder case. Jean-Claude Romand killed his wife and family at the point when the double life he had been leading for over twenty years was on the point of being exposed. What fascinates Carrère is not so much the crime itself as the emptiness of Romand's life in the years when, day after day, he left his home in the morning, claiming to be off to his prestigious job in Geneva, and then roamed the snowy landscapes of the Haute-Savoie in his car, spending hours in lay-bys and service stations. In *La Classe de neige* Carrère uses fiction to explore existential blankness, while *L'Adversaire* records his attendance at Romand's trial and his subsequent exchanges with the murderer, combining biographical accuracy with psychological speculation. As in so much contemporary prose, in Carrère's work the fictional and the factual are both indispensable, and in forging new ways of combining them contemporary writers have produced a fascinating body of work that promises well for the future of French literature.

65

Existentialism

ANDREW LEAK

'Existentialism' refers in the first instance to a mode of philosophical enquiry associated primarily with Martin Heidegger in Germany and Jean-Paul Sartre in France. While critics have pointed to anticipations of existentialist thought in philosophers going as far back as the ancient Greeks, the 'fathers' of existentialism are generally held to be Søren Kierkegaard and Friedrich Nietzsche. Other twentieth-century thinkers associated with the term are Martin Buber, Karl Jaspers, Gabriel Marcel, and Maurice Merleau-Ponty. Existentialism was also a broader cultural phenemenon deriving its force from the notoriety attaching to the literary output, the political stances, and the lifestyle of its two foremost French practitioners, Sartre and Simone de Beauvoir. One would hesitate before referring to existentialism as a 'literary movement': if *nouveau roman* and *nouveau théâtre* were labels which, albeit problematically, designated a set of properly literary concerns shared by groups of writers, the same is not strictly true of 'existentialism'. And yet it was through the literary works – plays, novels, short stories, and memoirs – of Sartre, Beauvoir and, arguably, Albert Camus that existentialism reached an audience beyond the narrow bounds of continental European academic philosophy.

Sartre and Beauvoir were not philosophers who turned to literature in order to 'put their ideas across' to a wider public; neither were they writers who dabbled in philosophy. In France, philosophy and literature had long been seen as complementary. Against that background, Sartre and Beauvoir appear as 'writer-philosophers', that is, as artists who explored what they saw as the most important questions concerning human existence both in theoretical mode (the philosophical article or treatise) and in literary mode (novels, plays, screenplays, etc.). Indeed, both Sartre and Beauvoir saw literature as much more than a means of popularising their philosophies: the disadvantage of philosophical discourse – especially as practised within the academy – is that it must aim at the articulation of a certain truth; literature, on the other hand, because of its constitutive ambiguity, is irreducible to the kinds of truth discovered by science or revealed by religion and is thus capable of suggesting ways in which human experience escapes the normative categories of scientific or religious thought. Camus presents a slightly different case. His ambition to become a professional philosopher had been thwarted by serious illness, so he lacked the thorough philosophical grounding of Sartre and Beauvoir. Nevertheless, his work presents a similar conjugation of philosophical and literary concerns. His early literary works were placed under the sign of his long theoretical meditation on suicide (*Le Mythe de Sisyphe*, 1942) and the later works under that of the concept of revolt that he elaborated in *L'Homme révolté* (1951).

Of course many other writers before and since the mid-twentieth century have demonstrated a preoccupation with the great themes of existentialism that we will shortly discuss. Sartre himself recognised Fyodor Dostoyevsky as an illustrious forebear; certain aspects of the work of André Gide overlap significantly with existentialist preoccupations; even closer to home, the early work of André Malraux – especially *La Condition humaine* (1933) – could be seen as proto-existentialist. Sartre's *Carnets de la drôle de guerre* (1983) present a fascinating picture of the 'anxiety of influence' of the future *chef de file* of existentialism as he attempts to demarcate his own thought *and* literary style from those of prestigious forerunners and contemporaries. What disqualifies the above authors from extended consideration here is that their work lacks the explicit philosophico-literary 'doubling' characteristic of Sartre, Beauvoir, and Camus. A better case for inclusion could be made for Gabriel Marcel. Credited with having coined the term 'existentialism', this Catholic existentialist at first championed the work of the young Sartre, and did much to promote it, before turning on him after the Second World War and denouncing him as a corruptor of youth. Marcel was almost as much a polymath as Sartre: as well as philosophy, he wrote plays and composed music. But very few people today could name a play by Marcel, let alone claim to have seen one performed. Merleau-Ponty, for his part, may be seen by many today as a more substantial philosopher than Sartre, but he wrote no literature.

Existentialism is concerned with a set of problems or issues that arise from a systematic meditation on what it means to exist as a human being. Most of these issues were popularised in slogans which gained wide currency even amongst non-specialist readers. When Sartre delivered a public lecture on the subject 'L'existentialisme, est-il un humanisme?' ('Is existentialism a form of humanism?')[1] on 29 October 1945 at the Club Maintenant, he was

---

1 Translations are mine.

endeavouring to define what had become known in the press as 'existential-ism' in order to defend it against virulent attacks from Catholic right and Communist left: in 1945, at the height of the existentialist vogue, the term was used most often as an insult. In the process, deliberately or not, he created a veritable compendium of existentialist slogans. When Sartre told his audience that 'existence precedes essence' he was encapulating what is most distinctive about existentialist thought. To exist is not to conform to a blueprint of what it is to be a human being: I exist before I exist as anything in particular. Human beings are, to use Heidegger's image, in a state of 'thrownness': they cannot know where they have been thrown from, neither do they know what they are thrown towards, but their 'trajectory' through life will be of their own making; it may well be conditioned or inflected by external circumstances, including the actions of others, but it will never be *determined* by these factors. Arguably the most important systematic working-out of this simple slogan is to be found in Beauvoir's *Le Deuxième Sexe* – destined to become the founda-tional text of modern feminism. In that work Beauvoir demonstrates that, far from being a transcendent essence, 'Woman' is a social, historic, and moral construct: 'on ne naît pas femme, on le devient' ('you are not born a woman, you become one').[2] Antoine Roquentin, the hero of Sartre's 1938 novel *La Nausée*, realises that some things *do* have essences that precede their existence – geometric figures, for example – but, precisely, circles and triangles do not exist in the way that human beings do. Which is not to say that we enter the world devoid of objective qualities. Physical properties (my hair and eye colour, the pigmentation of my skin, deformity, congenital illness, biological sex, etc.), social facts (e.g. the class I am born into), historical facts (such as when and where I was born) are all matters of fact and are not chosen by me. The term 'facticity' is used to refer to all such 'factual' aspects of my being; these elements are also said by existentialists such as Sartre to be 'con-tingent'. This means that they did not have to be as they were: it is entirely necessary that I should have *a* body, but entirely contingent that it should be *this* one rather than that one. Moreover, and this is where an ethical concern starts to appear, although I did not choose any part of my facticity, I must nevertheless 'assume' it as uniquely mine. This means transcending it, by my projects, towards my own possibilities. This idea that consciousness – or 'human reality', as Sartre terms it – surges forth as freedom by negating what *is* in a movement towards what *is not yet* is central to all existentialist thought. Human reality projects itself towards a self-identity that will always

2 S. de Beauvoir, *Le Deuxième Sexe*, 2 vols. (1949) (Paris: Gallimard, 1976), II, p. 13.

elude it; in Sartre's apparently paradoxical expression, human reality is 'un être qui est ce qu'il n'est pas et n'est pas ce qu'il est' ('a being that is what it is not and is not what it is').[3] The idea that we have no substantial being, that our existence is ultimately groundless, is not necessarily one that people find comforting. Indeed, existentialists point to the myriad ways in which human beings seek constantly to abdicate responsibility for the never-ending process of making ourselves anew at every moment. And this is precisely where literature comes into its own as a means of articulating the psychological ruses that people employ to avoid confronting their existential solitude. If facticity can be understood as everything that can be revealed about a person by an 'objective' third-person observer, and transcendence can be likened to the perspective of that person, as a free agent, then literature, and especially the novel, with its capacity to present a given reality from a multiplicity of different subject positions, can be seen as the ideal medium for an exploration of the existential project – including projects of evasion. In the first volume of Sartre's novel trilogy, Les Chemins de la liberté, the protagonist, Mathieu, is faced with the dilemmas raised by the unplanned pregnancy of his long-term partner. His bourgeois older brother presents him with an 'objective' assessment of his situation: Mathieu is a not-so-young state functionary in a supposedly 'free' relationship, which is, in reality, a bourgeois marriage in all but name; he should have the honesty to recognise those 'facts' and marry his partner, says his brother. 'Objectively' true as the assessment may be, it does not imply a necessary course of action: Mathieu is still free to negate or to reaffirm the values on which it resides (the sanctity of life, the bourgeois conception of marriage, etc.). It is only in the climactic scene in the third volume that sees Mathieu firing on the advancing Germans in a desperate last stand, that he finally becomes aware of the implications of his freedom: 'chaque coup de feu le vengeait d'un ancien scrupule ... Un coup sur Marcelle que j'aurais dû plaquer' ('Each shot was revenge for an old scruple ... one shot at Marcelle whom I should have ditched').[4] The 'should' that Mathieu discovers here is clearly not the 'should' of conventional morality, but the first dawning of an 'ought' that corresponds to his authentic becoming or, as Heidegger would put it, his 'ownmost possibilities'.

This dissonance between the perspective of the individual and that of the 'crowd' has antecedents in Kierkegaard (the singular individual who is ultimately irreducible to the Hegelian universal) and in Nietzsche (the Übermensch

---

3 J.-P. Sartre, La Nausée (1943) (Paris: Gallimard, 1976), p. 94.
4 J.-P. Sartre, Les Chemins de la liberté, 3 vols. (Paris: Gallimard, 1949), III, p. 244.

who rises above the common herd by going beyond Good and Evil). It is also there in Heidegger's notion of 'one' (*das Man*) and it gives rise to the archetypal existential hero: the Outsider. This figure is exemplified in two early works of the French existentialist canon: Sartre's *La Nausée* and Camus's *L'Étranger* (1942). As long as we are engaged in practical projects or carried along by habit, the world can appear to be a meaningful place; indeed, the world only comes to 'have' meaning as a function of human projects. When projects fail or collapse, there is a corresponding transformation of the world and the way it appears to us. This is the experience of Roquentin, who, following the collapse of his projects, intuits the nauseating otherness of a world to which he had thought he belonged. It is the realisation that values and meaning are inherently groundless – sustained only by the human freedom that 'chooses' them – that sets Roquentin apart from the bourgeois 'herd' of Bouvillois: they take refuge in what they believe are eternal values, rights, and duties, but the Outsider has nowhere to take cover – he is alone in a world that he now knows to be fundamentally absurd. Camus's Meursault arrives at a similar realisation by a quite different path. It is habit and familiarity that has dulled his sense of the strangeness of the world. The death of his mother, the absurd irruption of violence into his life (he kills a man for reasons he himself cannot fully divine), and the trial that ensues rouse Meursault from his somnambulistic existence. Condemned by society less for his transgression of the moral commandment (thou shalt not kill) than for his failure to do what 'one' is 'supposed' to do in certain circumstances (manifest appropriate grief at his mother's funeral), he falls abruptly into consciousness. The defiant assertion of his singularity over and against the 'crowd' at the end of the novel: 'J'avais eu raison, j'avais encore raison, j'avais toujours raison' ('I had been right, I was still right, I was always right')[5] parallels Roquentin's denunciation of the bourgeois 'salauds' in *La Nausée*.

Individuals who choose to regard facticity as determining, who give greater weight to the world than to their capacity to change it, are said by Sartre to be victims of 'l'esprit de sérieux' ('the spirit of seriousness'). Existential fiction and drama abound with such characters. The 'moral' dilemmas that confront the protagonists of these works are, at heart, existential or ontological dilemmas, but the central notions of freedom, choice, and responsibility have found applications well beyond the realm of individual psychology. For Sartre and Beauvoir, a whole social class – the bourgeoisie – practises and perpetuates a form of collective bad faith sustained by an appeal to illusory rights and

5 A. Camus, *L'Étranger* (1942) (Paris: Gallimard, 1957), p. 185.

duties. And why stop at a mere social class? For a century and a half, successive French governments had justified their colonial exploitation in the name of the 'civilising mission' of France – conveniently overlooking the fact that this 'mission' was not imposed on them as the 'white man's burden' but was the result of a series of historically dated, political, and economic choices.

Values, and their groundlessness, are at the heart of existentialist thought, and it is perhaps here that the influence of Nietzsche is most visible. The most 'Nietzschean' of all existentialist dramas is surely Sartre's 1943 play, *Les Mouches*. In that play, Jupiter is the origin and guarantor of all values, sanctioned as they are by a nature which he created. The significant crime of the play's hero, Oreste, is not the banal murder of the tyrant Egisthe but the unnecessary, and above all unnatural, murder of his own mother. Once Oreste realises that values are constructed by men, not decreed by the gods, he is free to pass beyond good and evil and draw the consequences from the death of God. But the triumphal ending of the play has something of the conjuring trick about it: the properly political problems of Argos have not been resolved; Oreste conquers his freedom but the Argives will most likely continue to be oppressed.

This brings us to another problem of central concern to existentialism: relations between individuals and between individuals and groups. There was significant divergence on this problem between Heidegger and Sartre. The former's notion of 'being-with' (*Mitsein*) was criticised by Sartre who, for his part, saw *conflict* as the defining characteristic of human relations. Drawing inspiration from Hegel's master–slave dialectic, Sartre devoted a whole chapter of *L'Être et le néant* to describing what he called 'Le Regard' (the Look), a notion that was much wider than the perceptual act itself. Put simply, my choice is either to look at (someone), which is to objectify them, or to be looked at (by someone), which is to allow myself to be objectified. Since either attitude is a 'sin' against freedom (I steal that of the other or I abdicate my own), Sartre memorably claims that 'ma chute originelle, c'est l'existence de l'autre' ('the existence of the other is my Fall').[6] But it was existentialist drama that made these somewhat abstruse notions concrete and memorable for a non-specialist public: who has not read, somewhere, the slogan 'L'enfer, c'est les Autres' ('Hell is other people')? Sartre's 1944 play *Huis clos* (from which that quotation is taken) reads almost like a dramatic 'equivalent' of Part 3, chapters 1–3 of *L'Être et le néant*. Yet it is still today the most widely performed of all Sartre's plays – no doubt because the very dialectic of the Look is

6 J.-P. Sartre, *L'Être et le néant* (Paris: Gallimard, 1943), p. 265.

itself inherently theatrical. The conflictual situation the playwright creates for his characters – an aptly named 'eternal triangle' – is indeed insoluble: they are, after all, together for all eternity. Despite Sartre's insistence that human relations are only hellish when people choose to make them so, it is nonetheless true that the dialectic of the Look, as presented in *L'Être et le néant*, offers little indication of how relations between individuals could ever be anything other than infernal. Clearly aware of this, Sartre promised at the end of that treatise that a future work would be devoted to the question of ethics. That work was never written, or at least not by Sartre. It fell to Beauvoir – in *Pyrrhus et Cinéas* (1944) and *Pour une morale de l'ambiguïté* (1947) – to provide the only complete published existentialist ethics. Despite having prefaced her first novel (*L'Invitée*, 1943) with a famous Hegelian dictum to the effect that each consciousness pursues the death of the other, Beauvoir's attitude to self–other relations was rather less conflictual and, some would say, more subtle than Sartre's. For his part, Albert Camus embraced the ambiguities of the human condition if anything even more closely than Beauvoir. His 1947 classic, *La Peste*, explores a range of reactions in the face of moral evil, but the overriding preoccupation is with an exemplary form of *Mitsein*: solidarity. His 1957 collection of short stories, *L'Exil et le royaume*, explores with great subtlety the territory between existential solitude and human solidarity. Each of the stories presents a situation of conflict, but even in those stories where the conflict is resolved through the triumph of common humanity, what emerges above all is the extreme fragility of solidarity: more an aspiration than a firm acquisition.

Already in 1947, Sartre and others around him at *Les Temps modernes* (the journal he had founded in 1945) had tempered their admiration of *La Peste* by pointing out that the struggle against evil would be more problematic when that evil had a human, rather than an animal face (i.e. the rats which carried the plague): the fight against political oppression is not at all the same as the fight against a faceless epidemic. In 1952, it was precisely the question of political efficacy – and a difference of opinion as to the real nature of the Soviet regime – that finally ended the friendship of these two writers who had come, jointly, to embody the figure of the committed writer: Sartre accused Camus of idealism and quietism, Camus reproached Sartre with both cynicism and naïvety in his grasp of politics.

This brings us to the extension of existentialism into the domain of politics and ideology. Some commentators have been puzzled by the 'conversion' of Sartre in the 1950s to a broadly Marxist worldview, arguing that existentialism, with its emphasis on individual freedom, and Marxism, with its view that the 'individual' is little more than a bourgeois-idealist construct, are fundamentally incompatible. This view is based on misconceptions of both existentialism *and* Marxism. It is not as if Sartre, for example, had started as a believer in an unbridled and unconditioned freedom and had only later discovered the 'force of circumstance'. The idea of 'situation' – as we saw in the earlier discussion of facticity and transcendence – had always been central to existentialist thought; both Heidegger and Sartre had insisted on the 'wordly' nature of human reality; an un-situated freedom is properly inconceivable: I always choose myself in a situation that I did not create but which I must assume, and that situation is always, at one level of analysis, social and historical. In choosing (for) me, I choose also for us, and it is the appearance of the 'we' that makes our projects political. In fact, nothing could have been closer to the essence of existentialist thought on man's insertion into the historical process than the remark of Marx in his *Eighteenth Brumaire of Louis-Napoléon* (1852) to the effect that human beings make history but in conditions not of their own choosing. When, in his introduction to *Critique de la raison dialectique* (1960), Sartre referred to Marxism as the unsurpassable philosophy of our time, he did so because he believed that Marxism provided the most thoroughgoing theoretical account of our alienated condition and because the conditions that had given rise to it had still not been 'surpassed'. But which Marxism? Sartre wrote *Critique de la raison dialectique* because he felt that what had been a living philosophy had become frozen into sterile, dogmatic orthodoxy. In that work he sought to re-inject lived experience (*le vécu*) into that tired body of Marxist dogma and thus reinvigorate it. Curiously, in doing so, he was bringing the history of existentialism back full circle to its origins: Kierkegaard's championing of 'subjectivity' against, but also within, the insurpassable philosophy of *his* time: the Hegelian system.

The cultural hegemony of existentialism in France had all but run its course by 1960. Camus was dead; Sartre had abandoned prose fiction in 1949 and devoted the 1950s to theoretical and political writings, producing only two or three plays in that decade; the eclipse of philosophy by the new 'human sciences' in the French universities; the radical literary experimentation of the *nouveau roman* and the *nouveau théâtre* in the 1950s, and the emergence of new *maîtres-à-penser* – Althusser, Barthes, Foucault, Lacan, and Lévi-Strauss – under the banner of the new '-ism' (structuralism) made existentialism appear suddenly outmoded.

Existentialism was above all a philosophy-in-the-world; its works were conceived of as interventions in that world, as appeals to the creative freedom of their readers – as such, it is probably destined to be perpetually 'rediscovered'.

Its spirit is always apt to resurface. In May 1968 at the height of the student unrest a poster appeared in the corridors of the Sorbonne declaring: 'Les structures ne descendent pas dans la rue' ('Structures do not go down onto the streets'). Sartre was the only intellectual of the older generations to be given a platform by the student revolutionaries.

66

Modern French thought

COLIN DAVIS

There is no uniquely right way to mark out the terrain of modern French thought. It might be described as a succession of great or controversial thinkers (Bergson, Sartre, Lévi-Strauss, Foucault, Derrida), as a history of competing movements (vitalism, existentialism, structuralism, poststructuralism), as the rise and fall of key influences (the three Hs, Hegel, Husserl, and Heidegger, giving way to the masters of suspicion, Nietzsche, Marx, and Freud), or as a series of reflections on central issues (freedom, history, justice). There is also no single, stable viewpoint from which to assess what and who mattered most. The philosophical stock of some thinkers has risen and fallen dramatically. In their day Léon Brunschvicg, Lucien Lévy-Bruhl, and André Lalande, for example, were all important figures who are now barely remembered outside the most specialist circles. Even Henri Bergson, probably the most important French philosopher of the first decades of the twentieth century, has declined in influence, despite being championed much later in the century by Gilles Deleuze and others. Louis Althusser, who had a claim to be the world's most prominent Marxist thinker in the 1960s and 1970s, is now better remembered for his private life than for his philosophical work. The best-known French intellectual of the twentieth century was undoubtedly Jean-Paul Sartre; but for most of his life he worked outside academic institutions, and therefore he did not have the direct impact on future generations of professional philosophers that comes from lecturing and supervising doctorates. The view from outside France may also distort the picture. 'Poststructuralism', which in the late twentieth century was sometimes treated as nearly synonymous with contemporary French thought, was largely an Anglo-American invention, grouping together French thinkers who in many respects had little in common. Jacques Derrida in particular was for a period the most famous, even notorious, representative of French philosophy outside France; yet in France for much of his career he was a relatively marginal figure, never holding one of the prestigious established posts that would have enabled him to exert a significant influence on the development of his discipline.

And yet, for all its bewildering diversity, modern French thought is one of the crowning achievements of French culture, eclipsing even the glories of its major artists. The heat of intellectual debate in France has radiated outwards to fuel philosophical and critical developments in the rest of the world. French thought has sometimes been regarded as a valued resource to be avidly drawn upon, sometimes as a source of error and mystification to be angrily refuted. This brief overview picks out some themes that have preoccupied French thinkers in the modern period: subjectivity, gender and sexuality, and ethics. In all of these areas, it is important to stress that there is no natural, absolute divide between creative writers and thinkers. Indeed, a striking feature of French intellectual life is the close collusion of literature and thought. Some authors, such as Sartre, Camus, Beauvoir, Blanchot, Cixous, or Kristeva, wrote both philosophical essays and works conventionally classed as 'literary'. Other notable thinkers, such as Lacan, Foucault, Barthes, Derrida, or Deleuze, accord significant space to the discussion of literature in their work. This is partly because France expects its leading intellectuals to be polymaths, as capable of writing a film script or an article on current events as of explicating a thorny passage in Descartes. It is partly also because of a cultural predisposition to envisage the concerns of philosophy and literature as strictly identical, so that each may learn from the other more than many philosophers working in Anglo-American contexts have been willing to concede. The following sections, therefore, stress some of the important continuities between French literature and thought.

Subjectivity

French philosophy can be said to begin with Descartes's Cogito. The Cogito establishes that, even if I can be sure of nothing else, I can know for certain that I exist as a subject at the moment when I assert 'I think'. This still leaves a lot of important issues in doubt: I do not yet know whether I am awake or dreaming, whether the external world exists, or whether there is a God. Nevertheless, the Cartesian claim against scepticism is that the existence of the thinking subject is assured, and that from this beginning further clarities can be achieved.

Modern French thought can be seen as an ongoing reflection on how Descartes was altogether too optimistic. In the early decades of the twentieth century, Proust's *À la recherche du temps perdu* (1913–27) tells the story of the subject in quest of itself, adrift in time, triviality, and happenstance, unable to recover itself fully through purely intellectual endeavour despite its most strenuous efforts. Proust was indebted to Bergson's critique of the Cartesian subject. In place of Descartes's rational, thinking subject, Bergson envisaged an intuitive subject in immediate contact with the flux of existence. The intellect follows on behind, if at all. For neither Proust nor Bergson is this yet what would later be announced, sometimes euphorically, as the death of the subject. Rather, it entails a discovery within the subject of a constitutive opacity which means that it can never present itself to itself with utter clarity.

Much subsequent French literature and philosophy revolves around the search for the self and the problem of subjectivity. Prolific autobiographers such as Michel Leiris and Simone de Beauvoir sought ways to understand the insertion of the self in history, culture, and language. Authors of auto-fiction explored the boundaries of memory and imagination in the effort of self-narration. At the same time, and often in unison with literary writers, philosophy has continued its long, querulous meditation on the status of subjectivity and related issues, such as freedom, rationality, perception, experience, and determinism. Mid-century Sartrean existentialism represents a highpoint in the subject's self-confidence, as it asserts its power to create itself and its values; yet even this is a far cry from the triumphant celebration of a self-knowing, self-possessing subject. The subject of Sartre's *L'Être et le néant* (1943) is riven, unable to achieve self-coincidence, and thrust outwards into a world of projects which can never be finally realised. Even if, to the disappointment of some, in an infamous lecture of 1945 Sartre would argue that 'existentialism is a humanism', it is a humanism of frustrated desires and failed endeavours.

The anti-humanist impetus of structuralism was in part a reaction against the existentialist retention of the human subject as a free, creative source of value. In *La Pensée sauvage* (1962) Claude Lévi-Strauss insisted, against Sartre, that the ultimate aim of the human sciences 'n'est pas de constituer l'homme, mais de le dissoudre' ('is not to constitute man, but to dissolve him').[1] In *Les Mots et les choses* (1966) Foucault foretold the imminent 'fin de l'homme' ('end of man').[2] So when, in his notorious essay of 1968 'La Mort de l'auteur', Roland Barthes argued against invoking authors as a means of regulating the meaning of literary works, he was merely drawing the consequences for literary criticism of what was by then virtually a philosophical commonplace.

1 C. Lévi-Strauss, *La Pensée sauvage* (Paris: Plon, 1962), p. 294. Translations are mine unless otherwise stated.
2 M. Foucault, *Les Mots et les choses* (Paris: Gallimard, 1966), p. 396.

The human subject, or what at this period was still more often than not called 'l'homme' ('man') despite the gender-specific nature of the term, was regarded as a product of pre-existing psychic, sexual, social, historical, and linguistic structures. Whereas Kant had argued that 'What is the human being?' ('Was ist der Mensch?')[3] was the most fundamental philosophical question of all, the one which contained all others, Foucault concluded *Les Mots et les choses* by dismissing it as outdated. The Cartesian subject, which could proudly assert its existence in the moment of thought, seemed well and truly dead.

In the hothouse of French intellectual exchange, the polemics surrounding the death or decentring of the subject sometimes obscured the actual subtlety of the philosophical positions being adopted. Sartre argued carefully that man both made history and was made by it, never simply upholding the powers of the subject over the obstructions of contingency and facticity. Lévi-Strauss's 'dissolution of man' or Foucault's 'end of man' announced a revolution in our ways of thinking that never entailed denying that human beings are also at least sometimes, if only in ways we do not fully understand, individuated creatures with thoughts, desires, histories, experiences, memories, and personalities that we might think of as our own. The real issue is to understand both why we are not centred, autonomous, free subjects, and why we inevitably think that in some sense we are. So the dissolution, death, decentring, destruction, and deconstruction of the subject is also the story of its resurrection, albeit in altered form. The structuralist assault can now appear as a salutary dismantling of subjectivity into the pre-individual component systems, codes, and discourses that condition and limit its possibilities. Having passed through that trial, more recent thinkers have been willing to talk positively about the constitution of the subject, though they arm themselves with all the necessary precautions that will protect them from the charge of naïvety.

Meanwhile, increasing importance was been accorded to an insight which in part helped advance the assault on the subject and in part required its defence: the subject's embodiment. For thinkers such as Sartre and Merleau-Ponty, whose work developed in large measure out of the phenomenological tradition, the corporeality of the subject cannot be bypassed. This effectively makes the Cartesian thinking subject dependent on the obscure particularities of its body and its desires. Gender and sexuality are thus established as proper topics for philosophical investigation. Moreover gendered, desiring subjects will have a major stake in avoiding their dissolution into anonymous

3 I. Kant, *Kants Werke*, 9 vols. (Berlin: Walter de Gruyter, 1968), IX, p. 25.

structures. Put bluntly, whilst man was facing his imminent end, women and people marginalised because of their sexuality were insisting on being taken seriously as philosophical subjects.

Sexuality and gender

The exploration and analysis of sexuality has traditionally been one of the privileged domains of literature. In the early years of the twentieth century the works, for example, of Proust, Gide, or Colette gave sophisticated, nuanced accounts of the fluctuations and variations of desire. In *Corydon* (published in 1924, but composed some years before that) Gide attempted to write a defence of homosexuality in the form of a philosophical dialogue. Even though Gide hesitated for many years before making the work public, and indeed before openly acknowledging his own homosexuality in his autobiography *Si le grain ne meurt* (1926), the implication was that sexuality in all its forms should be regarded as an intellectual, cultural and historical issue meriting serious philosophical reflection. Sexual preferences that conflicted with heteronormative expectations should not be unthinkingly dismissed as morally aberrant and consigned to the tender mercies of psychopathologists, but understood as variants on the human potential for desire.

Even if *Corydon* itself had little impact on the wider understanding of sexuality, the nature and variety of desire have become central to French intellectual enquiry. Deleuze's *Présentation de Sacher-Masoch* (1967) refuses to dismiss Sacher-Masoch, the man after whom masochism was named, as a sexual deviant; instead, Deleuze analyses the subtle, contractual nature of his sexual preferences. The three volumes of Foucault's *Histoire de la sexualité* (1976–84) show in detail how sexuality is made and nurtured through complex negotiations with the political, medical, and ethical discourses of any given age. Giving his own answer to Kant's 'What is the human being?' Lacan endorses Spinoza in asserting that *'le désir est l'essence de l'homme'* ('*desire is the essence of man*') (emphasis in original),[4] and he spent his career tracking its torsions and contortions. These explorations of multiform sexualities, their consequences, and the social, aesthetic, and ethical issues bound up with the endeavour to give them voice, have constantly been shadowed and often anticipated by the work of literary authors such as Jean Genet, Monique Wittig, and Hervé Guibert.

4 J. Lacan, *Les Quatre Concepts fondamentaux de la psychanalyse* (Paris: Seuil, 1973), p. 306.

The embodied, desiring subject is also a gendered subject, and one of the undoubted achievements of modern French thought has been to give gender its place as a philosophical issue. The foundational work here is Simone de Beauvoir's *Le Deuxième Sexe* (1949). Beauvoir describes how thought and culture have been male-centred. Women have been denigrated as the 'other', wombs to bear future generations, imperfect men lacking rational powers. With the curt aphorism 'On ne naît pas femme: on le devient' ('you are not born woman: you become one),[5] Beauvoir encapsulates an intellectual and political programme. Modern feminism would be (mainly) anti-essentialist, rejecting any sense that women are incarnations of an immutable femininity; it would study the ways in which a culture's science, myths, literature, and thought have constructed women as the 'second sex' behind the dominant male; and it would demand access to education and to the means of producing and disseminating knowledge so that the conditions by which one 'becomes woman' may be improved. It is hard to over-stress the importance of *Le Deuxième Sexe* in empowering women and setting an agenda for ongoing work. Taking up Beauvoir's challenge, Luce Irigaray, Hélène Cixous, and Julia Kristeva became key inspirations in feminist thinking around the world. Even though on the whole the differences between them are often more significant than the similarities, their work has been instrumental in analysing and beginning to overcome the exclusion of women from mainstream thought. Knowledge can no longer appear as disembodied, atemporal and sexless; it is produced by embodied beings who are situated in a history and culture that makes them what they are, but to which they can also contribute. The work of thinkers such as Michèle le Dœuff, Françoise Collin, Sylviane Agacinski, Geneviève Fraisse, and many others shows that female voices are now well established and respected in French intellectual life.

The emergence of sexuality and gender as key issues in French thought indicates that the question 'What is the human being?' is not by any means outdated, despite Foucault's claim to the contrary in the 1960s. The subject has not simply withered away; indeed, the theme of gendered, desiring embodiment suggests rather that aspects of individual, subjective existence are too valuable for us to wish for their abolition. The subject is battered, but still standing. Moreover, the political aims of feminists or gay rights activists require the preservation of a gendered, sexualised subject. So the story of modern French thought is about the necessary survival, not the untimely

---

5 S. de Beauvoir, *Le Deuxième Sexe*, 2 vols. (Paris: Gallimard, 1949), II, p. 13.

death, of the subject. Another related area in which the subject still seems indispensable is ethics.

Ethics

A central concern of modern French thought has been the relation of self and other. How do we recognise and respond to that which is different from ourselves? In a series of massively influential seminars on Hegel held in Paris between 1933 and 1939, the Russian émigré Alexandre Kojève gave a description of this relation which would have a huge influence on subsequent generations of thinkers. With intellectuals such as Georges Bataille, Raymond Aron, André Breton, Jacques Lacan, and Maurice Merleau-Ponty in his audience, Kojève drew out the Marxist implications of the dialectic of master and slave from Hegel's *Phenomenology of Spirit*. Master and slave are locked in a struggle for recognition comparable to class warfare, in which each both needs and seeks to dominate the other. The struggle can easily turn murderous. In a phrase borrowed from Hegel that would resonate through the rest of the twentieth century, 'each seeks the death of the other'.[6] Beauvoir would cite this as the epigraph for her first novel, *L'Invitée* (1943), which culminates in murder. From an ethical point of view this analysis is problematic because, pending the achievement of a classless society, it leaves little prospect of human relations being anything other than a violent struggle for supremacy.

From attendance records it is likely that Sartre was not present at Kojève's seminars, though his account of the relations between self and other in *L'Être et le néant* suggests that he had some knowledge of them. Sartre maintains that the essence of human relations is conflict. The other's freedom robs me of my own, so I must assimilate it or annihilate it. Sartre paints a bleak picture of human reality involving shame, masochism, hatred, indifference, or sadism. And yet Sartre remains optimistic. At the end of his mammoth work, he finally raises the question of morality, but in a famous and teasing final sentence he delays his response to it: 'Nous y consacrerons un prochain ouvrage' ('We will devote a future work to it').[7] Despite several attempts, Sartre never completed the ethics that he promises here. Beauvoir fared better, sketching an existentialist ethics based on freedom and responsibility in *Pyrrhus et Cinéas* (1944) and *Pour une morale de l'ambiguïté* (1947). Beauvoir's analysis allows of no

---

6 G. W. F. Hegel, *Phenomenology of Spirit*, trans. A.V. Miller (Oxford: Oxford University Press, 1977), p. 113.
7 J.-P. Sartre, *L'Être et le néant* (Paris: Gallimard, 1943), p. 692.

moral certainty. Her ethics does not negate the conflictual nature of relations between self and other described by Sartre, but it attempts to work towards an increase in human freedom despite the inevitability of continuing violence and the awareness of ultimate failure.

In the following years ethics slipped from the forefront of philosophical concerns. For Marxists, ethics was a bourgeois mystification, an attempt to give an illusion of universal authority to what were in fact historically rooted values serving the dominant political class. As such, ethics was a distraction from the serious business of politics. For the structuralists, ethics seemed to require the agency of precisely the kind of autonomous, self-determining, rational subject which they had proclaimed to be in its death throes. Meanwhile, a Jewish philosopher of Lithuanian origin named Emmanuel Levinas was patiently working out his ideas. Levinas had established a reputation for himself in philosophical circles in the 1930s and 1940s for his work on Husserl and Heidegger. He published relatively little in the 1950s, but in 1961 his *Totalité et infini* appeared, and, together with his later *Autrement-qu'être ou au-delà de l'essence* (1974), this book would give impetus to the revival of interest in ethics in the latter part of the twentieth century. At the heart of Levinas's work is a description of the encounter with alterity which implicitly rejects the struggle to the death depicted in Kojève's reading of Hegel and in Sartre's *L'Être et le néant*. Levinas's 'other' is utterly alien to me; it cannot be assimilated or understood as a reflection or extension of myself. It throws into doubt both who I am and everything I thought I knew. I can of course respond to the challenge it poses to me with violence, but Levinas's entire endeavour is to develop an ethics in which alterity is welcomed with hospitality rather than eliminated as a threat. Levinas offers no moral maxims or imperatives, no analysis of duties or virtues, only an insatiable demand to learn to live with the otherness that we encounter in others and find within ourselves.

Coming at a time when the Algerian war of independence was still not resolved, when women were becoming more aware of their subordination, and when recognition of the validity of other cultures and religions was becoming more urgent and more difficult, the resonance of Levinas's appeal for peaceful cohabitation with otherness was massive. Derrida was quicker than most to appreciate the importance of *Totalité et infini*. His long article 'Violence et métaphysique: essai sur la pensée d'Emmanuel Levinas' (1964) can be seen as laying the foundation for what would later be described as the ethical turn of poststructuralism palpable in his own work and that of others such as Jean-François Lyotard, Jean-Luc Nancy, and Philippe Lacoue-Labarthe. Whilst some accused poststructuralist thinkers of being morally nihilistic, they could counter that ethics was in fact one of their earliest, abiding and most urgent concerns; and whether or not it was always acknowledged, their ethical engagements were more often than not Levinasian in inspiration.

In the Preface to *Totalité et infini* Levinas describes his book as 'une défense de la subjectivité' ('a defence of subjectivity').[8] In 1961 this was hardly a fashionable position to take; but Levinas's ethics retains a place for the subject, even if that subject is torn apart, inhabited by otherness within and obsessed with an otherness from outside, bereft of self-knowledge and transparency, and never at ease with itself because the ethical demand of the other can never definitively be met. The subject does not quite go away, but it twists and turns in response to its encounters with the world, just as had been discovered in literature by the authors of fiction and of the multiple variants of autobiography, autofiction, and life-writing. Proust's endeavour at the beginning of the twentieth century to refine a language in which to speak of the elusive self has been continued up to the present by his literary and philosophical successors, often questioning, sometimes rejecting, but never entirely losing sight of Kant's deceivingly simple question: 'What is the human being?'

8 E. Levinas, *Totalité et infini* (The Hague: Martinus Nijhoff, 1961), p. 11.

67

French drama in the twentieth century

DAVID BRADBY

The outstanding development in the French theatre of the twentieth century has been its liberation from the dead hand of literary regulation, which had dogged it since the Académie Française first delivered its judgement on Corneille's *Le Cid* in 1638. In the century that runs from the founding of the Théâtre Libre by André Antoine in 1887 to the appointment of Antoine Vitez as head of the Comédie-Française in 1988, theatre (i.e. a live performance given in front of an audience) succeeded in establishing itself as an art form in its own right, and freed itself from dependency on the literary text. Conditions for dramatists in France thus changed more radically in the twentieth century than they had in the preceding four, leading today's writers to develop entirely new strategies.

In addition to this, professional playwrights had to cope with threats coming from other directions as well. First came the threat of the cinema, quickly seen to present a challenge to the drama, especially to the naturalist drama that sought to recreate the conditions of real life, since these could be captured so much better on film. The next challenge came from theatre practitioners themselves: each of the many 'reformers' of theatre, from Jacques Copeau onwards, sought to emphasise the non-verbal means of expression available to theatre, and some explicitly condemned written dialogue. The most prominent of these radical innovators was Antonin Artaud, whose vision came to be seen as prophetic in the years following the Second World War. The near-revolution of 1968 had a powerful effect on theatre; this was when Artaud's repudiation of the French classical tradition in the 1930s was taken up and pushed to its furthest extreme. In the wake of 1968, writers of plays went out of favour completely for a decade, supplanted by collectively devised performances and spectacular productions in which the designer replaced the writer and the image became the privileged bearer of communication.

In some cases, playwrights connived in these developments; in some cases they challenged them; in some cases they served to inspire them. The latter is the case with Paul Claudel, whose unorthodox dramatic texts inspired many directors, notably Jean-Louis Barrault and Antoine Vitez, to develop new ways of thinking about their art. Claudel is perhaps the first major dramatist to appear in the early twentieth century. For Michel Autrand, his plays are 'the quintessence of Symbolist theatre',[1] although his impact was not felt until after the Symbolist movement had run its course, and his plays are quite unlike those of Maurice Maeterlinck. Although Claudel's first collection of dramatic works was published in 1901, they were not produced in significant numbers until the eve of the First World War: *L'Annonce faite à Marie* in 1912, followed by *L'Otage* in 1914 at Lugné-Poë's Théâtre de l'Œuvre and *L'Échange* at Jacques Copeau's Théâtre du Vieux-Colombier. The play often seen as his masterpiece, *Le Soulier de satin* (written 1919–24), was considered unstageable by its author, and it was not until 1943 that it received its first performance, directed by the young Barrault at the Comédie-Française.

Claudel's dramatic output ranges widely from pious morality plays to historical dramas with an epic scope. Firmly embedded in a Catholic vision of the world, his plays sometimes wilfully turn their back on the modern world, while others address it with urgency and relevance. Claudel's great achievement is to have forged a verse form adequate to the task of exploring the major themes of love, liberty, death, and its transcendence while also allowing for humour and playfulness. His reward has been to be regularly represented on the French stage, being taken up by major directors such as Antoine Vitez and Bernard Sobel who were both anti-Catholic left-wingers, as well as by directors and actors more sympathetic to his own outlook. The form elaborated by Claudel is unlike anything before it in the French literary tradition, being based on the rhythm of the breath group rather than the number of feet in the poetic line. He chose large, passionate themes; some of his plays are intense poems to the power of love, such as *Partage de midi* (written 1905), closely based on an episode in his own experience. Others take on larger themes: *Le Soulier de satin* chronicles the events of the sixteenth century, when Catholic missionaries from Spain reached the most distant places, but when Spanish designs on world empire were foiled by the Protestant powers of Britain and northern Europe. Although he proved himself capable of writing concentrated dramas of character that respected the neo-classical unities, still taken for granted in the French dramatic tradition, Claudel also demonstrated the ability to write plays in which the unities were thrown to the winds and in which the different genres – tragedy, comedy, farce, melodrama, music,

1 M. Autrand, *Le Théâtre en France de 1870 à 1914* (Paris: Champion, 2006), p. 288.

clowning – were gloriously combined into an entirely original mix. Although often verbose, his plays were written for the body, and the physical demands they made upon actors introduced something new and exciting into the French tradition.

In contrast, the surrealist playwrights of the 1920s set about gleefully demolishing the theatre as it was then known, and began a movement that was to find its natural conclusion in Samuel Beckett fifty years later. However, they shared Claudel's interest in bodies on stage and in throwing off inherited literary constraints. The founder of the Dada movement, and one of the chief driving forces behind French surrealism, was Tristan Tzara. His plays, as Sarah Bay-Cheng has pointed out, even in their written form, enacted a form of physical disruption of the page, having parallels with Guillaume Apollinaire's *calligrammes* – poems whose subject matter took physical shape through their layout on the page.[2] Plays by Apollinaire, Roger Vitrac, Philippe Soupault, and others employed nonsense tactics, putting together sequences composed entirely of clichés, or of non-sequiturs, and attempting to apply the technique of automatic writing to the stage. These experiments had limited success, since, as Beckett and the 'New Theatre' playwrights were to discover two decades later, an audience will always seek to impose meaning on what is performed on stage, and it is almost impossible to evacuate meaning from a play, however nonsensical the text. Apollinaire's own play *Les Mamelles de Tirésias* (1917) provides a good example, emerging in performance as a passionate plea for repopulating France after the slaughter of the First World War, despite its use of farcical humour and nonsense jokes. Another surrealist writer who gained notoriety by exploiting a rich vein of whimsical nonsense in his early plays was Jean Cocteau. But although he continued writing plays for forty years, his particular vision was more successfully realised through his films and novels and his dramatic output was uneven.

The surrealists did not produce any dramatic literature of lasting greatness; their contribution was far more durable in poetry, fine art, and the cinema. But their new emphasis on performance had long-lasting effects, especially in the case of Antonin Artaud, whose theatre was dedicated to the memory of Alfred Jarry. The corrosive challenge to all established conventions embodied in Artaud's performances was to prove inspirational for the actors and writers of the 'New Theatre' that came into being in the 1950s, as well as to subsequent generations of playwrights.

2 S. Bay-Cheng, 'Translation, Typography, and the Avant-Garde's Impossible Text', *Théâtre Journal* 59 (2007), pp. 467–83.

Artaud was not alone in his passionately prophetic belief that the future of theatre lay in throwing off the tyranny of neatly constructed plots predicated on rational debate. One of the most influential directors of the period, Gaston Baty, mounted a similar attack on *Sire le mot* (*My Lord the Word*). Baty was a partner, along with three great actor-directors, Louis Jouvet, Charles Dullin, and Georges Pitoëff, in forming a 'Cartel', dedicated to raising the prestige of French theatre. Together with Jacques Copeau (who remained an influential figure until his death in 1949), they contributed to the elaboration of a concept of Art Theatre, as distinct from the commercial theatre of the day, which still supported a group of very prolific 'boulevard' playwrights, as well as making a good living for mavericks such as André de Lorde, whose Grand Guignol theatre put on popular horror shows. Although ostensibly dedicated to opening the way for new playwrights, the legacy of Art Theatre was to prove more important in promoting the growth of directors' theatre in the post-war years than to the discovery of new writing talents. In particular, they helped to promote the rediscovery of Shakespeare's oeuvre which was to become a dominant feature of French theatre in the second half of the century. The only major playwrights to emerge in partnership with the 'Cartel' were Jean Giraudoux, whose work was regularly produced by Louis Jouvet, and Jean Anouilh, who began writing for the stage in the 1930s and whose early plays were put on by Pitoëff.

The work of the Cartel had been limited to Paris, but idealists from Antoine and Firmin Gémier to Copeau had attempted to promote a vision of *théâtre populaire* (People's Theatre), that would extend Art Theatre beyond the capital. With the German Occupation of 1940 and the establishment of a French government in Vichy, a youth organisation was created, Jeune France, one of whose achievements was to set up a network of 'Maisons de culture' linking high artistic standards with the democratisation of cultural practice. Jean Yves Guérin comments that this enshrined not only the vision of Copeau, but also that of the post-war innovators Jean Vilar and Ariane Mnouchkine.[3] From 1940 to 1945, theatre throughout France was subject to censorship by the Germans (censorship by the French government had been abolished in 1906). The censors were convinced of German cultural superiority; the role of French theatre, as they saw it, was to provide light entertainment of a frothy kind. They also encouraged the production of Spanish work in order to express their support for General Franco, whose endorsement of the Nazi project for the new Europe was emphasised in the propaganda of the time.

---

3 J. Guérin, *Le Théâtre en France de 1914 à 1950* (Paris: Champion, 2007), p. 299.

This assisted the production of Montherlant's plays set in Spain and probably played its part in allaying the doubts of the Comédie-Française as to the wisdom of attempting Paul Claudel's gigantic epic *Le Soulier de satin*. In Paris, the theatres enjoyed a boom time, despite the difficulties of power cuts and curfew restrictions. The theatre appeared a convivial zone in which French cultural values could still be celebrated. Moreover, after the Allied landings in Normandy, as the Liberation became progressively more certain, plays such as Anouilh's *Antigone* (1943) or Jean-Paul Sartre's *Huis clos* (1944), which had initially seemed quite innocent of political content, came to be seen as carrying an implicit message of resistance to fascist authority.

During the period that followed the Liberation, the audience that had filled the theatres under the Occupation maintained its commitment to new work by authors such as Armand Salacrou and Anouilh, Sartre and Albert Camus, who had emerged from the period as independent spirits and intellectual leaders. The passionate debates dramatised in their plays, weighing up the rival claims of individual freedom and of collective responsibility, reflected the uncertainties of the period of post-war reconstruction and the anxieties induced by the Cold War and by the colonial conflicts in Vietnam and Algeria. A group of existentialist writers, of whom the most prominent were Sartre and Camus, found themselves naturally drawn to dramatic situations in which characters faced stark choices. The theatre suited them as a way of popularising their reflections on the political situation. Their ability to create plausible characters, faced with dilemmas that were not entirely unfamiliar to the lives of their audience, yet also tinged with some of the excitement of the thriller, resulted in a successful subgenre sometimes described as 'philosophical melodramas' that proved very popular with the middle-class audience.

While such plays enjoyed critical success and long runs, an entirely different dramatic form was coming into being. In the decade running from 1950, when the first plays of Adamov and Ionesco were put on with very little success in tiny left-bank theatres, to 1960, when Ionesco's *Rhinocéros* enjoyed the 'consecration' of a production by Jean-Louis Barrault at the Odéon, this new form established itself as the most potent force in French drama, eclipsing the discussion plays of Sartre and his colleagues. Known in Britain and America as 'Theatre of the Absurd' and in France as *le nouveau théâtre* (the New Theatre), this succeeded in harnessing the anarchic energy that had characterised Dada and surrealist performance to the aesthetic rigour of the *nouveau roman* established by such writers as Nathalie Sarraute, Michel Butor, or Alain Robbe-Grillet.

The power of the plays written by Adamov, Ionesco, and Beckett in these years lay in a quality that Adamov named 'literality': they discovered a way of writing not just an action that imitated or depicted a situation, but dramatic action that literally embodied that situation. Although some examples remained locked in the linguistic banalities that had already been explored a generation earlier by the surrealists, others succeeded in creating a form of theatre in which performance as well as spoken words were profoundly integrated. Jean Genet, for example, wrote a sequence of extraordinary theatrical rituals encompassing the major social shifts in twentieth century society and, in *Les Paravents* (1961), denounced the colonial war in Algeria. Beckett provided consummate examples of plays in which the authorial achievement goes beyond writing dialogue and stage directions, to create a whole stage image, complete in itself. In *Oh les beaux jours* (1961), for example, Winnie's situation, buried in the earth up to her waist in the first half and up to her neck in the second has a dramatic impact that is inseparable, in the play's impact, from her stream of verbal comments on her situation, sometimes ecstatic, sometimes bitter.

While the New Theatre triumphed in the capital, and was rapidly exported all over the world, the French provinces were enjoying a theatrical renaissance of a different kind. The decentralisation that had been started by Jeune France acquired new impetus after the Liberation from left-wing cultural groups. A group of charismatic young directors and actors, inspired by the ideals of People's Theatre that had been debated since the turn of the century, set up new permanent companies in the provinces – men such as Jean Dasté and Roger Planchon, encouraged by Jean Vilar's founding of the Avignon festival in 1947. The repertoires of these decentralised companies contained few new plays. They relied more on the classics, especially Molière and Shakespeare, as they initiated new audiences into the pleasures of theatre-going. The modern author most frequently presented by them was Bertolt Brecht, whose dynamic, socialist-inspired humanism matched their own ideological thrust.

The challenge to all institutions entailed in the political upheavals of 1968 was felt in the theatre even more strongly than in other branches of the arts. The passionate discussions that filled the occupied factories and lecture halls up and down the country were concerned to discover new forms of participatory democracy. Nowhere did this project seem more relevant than in the theatre: the power of writers to determine the artistic endeavours of all the other workers in the theatre enterprise was denounced as tyranny and, for several years following 1968, the professional writer suddenly appeared outdated, egocentric, and self-indulgent. Collectively devised shows – *créations collectives* – in which the opinion of every member of the theatre company was as valid as every other became the rule. As a result, playwrights fell on hard times: not only did commissions from directors dry up, but a number of specialist play-publishers went bankrupt and established houses such as Gallimard wound up their theatre collections. The 1970s saw the triumph of directors' theatre: the new stars of the theatre were not the actors or the writers, but directors such as Roger Planchon, Patrice Chéreau, Ariane Mnouchkine, and Antoine Vitez, whose spectacular achievements helped to attract other star directors from all over the world, notably Peter Brook, Bob Wilson, and Tadeusz Kantor.

The playwrights' fortunes began to improve with the election of François Mitterrand in 1981 and the appointment of Jack Lang as his minister of culture. Lang in turn appointed Robert Abirached to be his director of theatre. Abirached was himself a published playwright and was determined to do what he could to reverse the decline of the writer in the theatre. He introduced a number of schemes to aid playwrights and incentives for major theatre companies to commission new work. His efforts bore fruit and the long-term result was that, by the end of the century, France once again had a healthy play-publishing industry and a significant number of writers who were able to earn a living from theatre work.

As theatres began to cast around for new playwrights to commission, many of those chosen were already employed as actors or directors and many of the new plays written in the 1980s and 1990s were the work of 'insiders' who had come to writing from acting or directing, such as Jean-Claude Grumberg, Coline Serreau, or Denise Bonal. The theatre no longer seemed an appropriate or an available form for the 'generalist' writer who also chose to express his ideas through novels, essays, and other literary forms as had been the case earlier in the century (e.g. Gide or Giraudoux in the inter-war years, Sartre or Camus in the post-war years). This tendency continues up to the present day: Jean-Luc Lagarce, Serge Valletti, Joël Jouanneau, Noëlle Renaude, and Olivier Py all came to writing from practical involvement with theatre groups.

The two outstanding dramatists to emerge in this period, however, are exceptions to this general rule. One, Bernard-Marie Koltès, did begin training as a director at the Strasbourg training school, but broke off after a year, and although he put on a few amateur productions of his early works, he spent much of the 1970s travelling rather than participating in dramatic activities. The other, Michel Vinaver, was a successful novelist before turning to the theatre, and always claimed that the theatre, like the mule, is a hybrid creature – designed both for production in public and for reading in private.[4] For many years he combined writing with a successful career as a business executive.

Koltès's plays deal with the large themes concerning Western Europeans in the late twentieth century: the blurring of cultural identities in the aftermath of colonial empires; the disparities between rich and poor; racism, crime, and violence in our cities; fears of things falling apart set against myths of utopian wholeness. His plays present these large themes through studies of families or of small, marginalised communities, often in provincial settings. He saw human relations in the contemporary world as being entirely caught up in a series of 'deals' (he used the English term), giving powerful expression to the deep disillusionment that followed the excitements of 1968 and the sense of capitalism as an uncontrollable monster on a global scale, whose commercial tentacles possess their own secretive life that insinuates itself into every aspect of our existence. Koltès was an admirer of Racine and Marivaux: his plays enact intense dramatic conflicts between individuals, conducted in language that is highly rhetorical without seeming unduly literary or abstruse. For his last play, *Roberto Zucco*, Koltès took a serial killer as his subject, using a real-life case as a springboard for a meditation on identity and criminality. Premiered after his death in 1989, this marked a move towards a more fluid style of dramatic structure, learned from translating Shakespeare.

Vinaver also deals with major subjects, especially the effects of globalised business on the lives of ordinary people. But his methods are diametrically opposed to those of Koltès. Where Koltès sought out the sensational and used a criminal to hold up a mirror to society, Vinaver draws his material from everyday life at its most banal and unsensational. He has described his thematic material as being as vast and shapeless as everyday life, in which the most meaningful experiences rub shoulders with the most banal. Drawing inspiration from composers and painters, Vinaver sees the playwright's task in terms of surprising, stimulating, or questioning his readers and spectators, not in terms of setting up conflicts or conveying lessons. His fragmented, contrapuntal method, learned from T. S. Eliot's early poetry, disrupts traditional or expected patterns of storytelling and of character development. Each of his plays offers insights into how what we conventionally refer to as 'character' is composed of a constantly shifting network of interactions: between people, between groups, between organisations and individuals. Unlike Koltès, whose

---

4 See 'Le Texte de théâtre dans les années quatre-vingt-dix: un statut hybride?' in D. Bradby, *Le Théâtre en France de 1968 à 2000* (Paris: Champion, 2007), pp. 613–60.

characters speak in long passages of uninterrupted monologue, Vinaver's theatre is made up almost entirely of dialogue. Often several dialogues are superimposed one upon the other, so that the audience has to follow several interactions simultaneously and this can make his plays demanding to read or to watch, but also contributes to effects of unexpected humour and irony as unintended echoes or double meanings are thrown into relief.

Noëlle Renaude and Philippe Minyana have both publicly acknowledged their debt to Vinaver's free and musical use of form and his profound exploration of language. Like most other playwrights of their generation, they dismiss theatre of character or plot, attempting instead to create an architecture of words designed to reveal its power only in performance on stage. Mindful of the Artaudian revolution, they aim to rediscover the poetic force of language treated as matter to be manipulated and modelled, rather like the sculptor's clay, not as a means of engaging in *mimesis*. They draw inspiration from the uncompromising work of Didier-Georges Gabily and Jean-Luc Lagarce.[5] These playwrights, among whom one should also include Valère Novarina, prefer to describe their works as 'texts' or 'textual material' rather than as plays. Often they give no directions for staging, not even assigning passages to particular players. In this way they reject the power of the director to step in and insert his own vision between the author's text and the audience's experience of it in performance. They insist instead on the right of the author to be seen as sole creator of the complete work, almost as if it were a three-dimensional concrete poem, resistant to being translated into spectacular images dreamed up by director or designer. By so doing, contemporary French playwrights are seeking to reassert their authority, challenging the right of directors to usurp what had previously been the writers' central role in the enterprise of creating theatre.

5 Lagarce's 1990 play, *Juste la fin du monde*, entered the repertoire of the Comédie-Française in 2008.

68

Twentieth-century poetry

RICHARD STAMELMAN

The history of modern French poetry is the history of spaces and places, real and imaginary. Provinces, cities, villages, streets, fields, meadows, paths, gardens, mountains, rivers, streams, springs, hillsides, ravines, gorges, grottos, rocks, beaches – the geography and geology of France and its colonies offer to many different poets a habitat and a habitation, a sense of rooted identity, and an intense experience of the here-and-now of ordinary life with its momentary joys and sudden sadnesses, its ephemeral beauties and irreversible losses. Poetry, as Heidegger has written, 'is what first brings man onto the earth, making him belong to it, and thus brings him into dwelling'.[1]

Paris

The joy of the new machine age, heralded by the invention of the telegraph, automobile, and airplane, spills over into the streets and boulevards, the cafés and office buildings of the Paris Guillaume Apollinaire (1880–1918) celebrates in his two major works *Alcools* (1912) and *Calligrammes* (1918). Apollinaire sees himself at the intersection of the old and the modern, of order and adventure, of tradition and innovation. Symbol of Apollinaire's metropolitan optimism is the Eiffel Tower; protectively, like a shepherd of Virgil's time, it watches over the Paris cityscape and its 'flocks' of 'bleating', honking cars. The Eiffel Tower's architecture of intersecting girders, its needlepoint spire penetrating the Parisian sky, and its paradoxical juxtaposition of iron solidity and airy openness express the old in terms of the absolutely new. Yet, the modernist beauty and delight of Paris, which Apollinaire joyfully celebrates in 'Zone' – the billboard advertisements crying out for attention, the clocks that 'bark' noon – cannot disguise the melancholy of a lovelorn and loveless poet who,

---

1 M. Heidegger, *Poetry, Language, Thought*, trans. Albert Hofstadter (New York: Harper and Row, 1971), p. 218. Translations from the French are mine.

as he walks through Paris from the dawn of one day to the dawn of the next, revisits his own personal past in a series of cinematic and simultaneous flashbacks. It is no wonder, then, that the sun rising above early morning Paris in the last line of 'Zone' is no longer a sun of hope and joy but rather one of despair and hopelessness. The dazzling modernism of the city is in conflict with the interior darkness of Apollinaire's soul, his unblinking self-scrutiny and self-awareness. Paris may be the centre of the universe towards which all the rivers of France and Europe flow like wine in order to quench the thirst of the drunken Orphic poet, Guillaume Apollinaire, gloriously chanting the 'song of Paris' in which the voices of other European cities join ('Vendémiaire'). And Paris may be the city of love, as permanent as the solid Mirabeau Bridge traversing the Seine. But just as the river flows relentlessly through the city, so love passes away ('Le Pont Mirabeau').

The real streets, boulevards, and bridges of Apollinaire's Paris become in the early 1920s the magical, aleatory spaces of surrealist love and liberty. At street corners, in flea markets, and behind store windows strange, unexpected encounters suddenly surge forth. For the surrealists, poetry is prophecy, dream truth, and desire – the promise of realities to come. With its zigzagging streets, hidden courtyards, and ever-changing light, Paris is the city of *le merveilleux*, the surrealist experience of the marvellous, that can transform an insignificant object lying in a gutter or an accidental meeting with an unknown woman into a life-altering event, as the founder of surrealism, André Breton (1896– 1966), learned first-hand on the evening of 29 May 1934. Having spent the entire night walking from one *quartier* to the next with a woman he had just met – in three months she would become his second wife – Breton realises that nearly every aspect of his journey through the city from Les Halles to the Tour Saint-Jacques had been prefigured in an automatic poem, 'Sunflower' ('Tournesol') – a dream-like text created through free writing and the suspension of consciousness – composed ten years before. Surrealist chance has turned Breton's life toward the rising sun of a marvellous love, which poetry had literally foretold. This poetic prescience is manifest in the works of another surrealist poet, Robert Desnos (1900–45), whose love poems give concrete reality to his erotic yearning for an unattainable woman ('J'ai tant rêvé de toi', 1926). This power of desire to change reality through poetry has a political and global dimension in the poem Desnos published under a pseudonym in the Occupied Paris of 1944, in which the poet standing on the Pont-au-Change, and listening to the imagined voices of marching comrades, calls out to them – in 'a language that has but one word: / Freedom!' ('Le Veilleur du Pont-au-Change') – to come and liberate his beloved city.

Surrealist Paris is, literally, the city dreams are made on, where the imaginary becomes instantaneously real. It is a place of desire actualised, a space of total visibility and of joyful oneness with the beloved that Paul Éluard (1895–1952) celebrates again and again in sensual love poems where landscape and cityscape are raised to the level of an *eroscape*. So intensely is the world reflected in the fertile eyes of lovers (*Les Yeux fertiles*, 1936, *Donner à voir*, 1939) who, looking at each other, see their own reflections superimposed on the images of the world mirrored in their eyes, that sight itself becomes a kind of visual poetry in which world, self, and other merge in an experience of sublime transparence and reciprocity. Eros for the surrealist-inspired Anglo-Egyptian poet Joyce Mansour (1928–86) is, on the other hand, anything but reciprocal; hers is not the idealised desire of (male) surrealists. Her poems express lovemaking in images more violently candid, more physically carnal, more voraciously erotic than do Éluard's and Desnos's. Love is a form of vampiric consummation in which the other is devoured. The female body is pierced, penetrated, torn, broken, wounded, bloodied, its 'back bent under the dreams of men' (*Cris*, 1953). Thanatos and Eros cohabit within a figurative landscape that poem after poem represents in the form of a splayed and besieged body. With a raw intensity unmatched by the poetry of any other surrealist, Mansour conceives of love as a transgressive revolt against bourgeois conventions.

In post-World War II poetry the streets of Paris become less magical, less marvellous, more pedestrian and 'populaire'. Reality, not dreams, is what becomes actual here. Jacques Prévert (1900–77) describes the everyday dramas of the street in a simple, repetitive, often anaphoric language, at once poetically compassionate and politically acerbic. In short poems (*Paroles*, 1946) describing a desperate argument between a man and woman ('Rue de Seine'), or the grinding life of half-dead workers travelling to and from work ('Le Paysage changeur'), or a horse hobbled by an injured leg ('Place du Carrousel'), Paris is the home of the wounded, the underprivileged, the disenfranchised. Prévert's voice is one of harsh social criticism. In 'La Rue de Buci maintenant . . . ' (1943) he uses a once lively, noisy street in the Latin Quarter as the metaphor for the misery of Occupied Paris. Prévert wonders where the street and its colourful Sunday market – 'this street once so happy and proud to be a street / like a girl happy and proud to be naked' – have gone, now that the rue de Buci is nothing more than a 'dismal corridor leading from one dead spot to another'.

While Apollinaire's Mirabeau Bridge and Desnos's Pont-au-Change place the poet above the Seine, several post-war poems see Paris from the level of the river. In 'The Seine Meets Paris', Prévert imagines the river as a person, a cat, a beautiful girl, and a factory. Although its currents sing of youth and love, the Seine is 'scabrous, dangerous, tumultuous'; and yet, when it reflects the Milky Way, it merges joyfully with the cosmos. Similarly, for the poet Francis Ponge (1899–1988) the Seine is more than just a majestic waterway dividing the city into right and left banks. Ponge is interested in the effusive projectiveness of trivial, everyday things – what he calls their object-play *(objeu)*, object-joy *(objoie)*, and ob-jaculation *(ob-jet)* – and in the inherent expressivity of objects such as cigarettes, soap, oranges, blackberries, rain, stones, as well as the words (seen as expressive 'objects' of another kind) that capture the singular difference of these things. Objectively, he offers a description of the Seine in a long text (1947) that ebbs and floods like the river *(Tome premier*, 1965). Ponge's meticulous, nearly scientific, observations of given phenomena, during which all sense of self is suspended, make the objects of study vibrate like the string of a violin; the 'music' emitted provokes verbal associations in the form of words arising automatically in the poet's mind. Consequently, it is the object that expresses itself, since the listening poet merely finds linguistic equivalents to its murmurings. The object is literally a pre-text translated into a text. As regards the Seine, Ponge's writing is a coursing flow of words that corresponds to the coursing of the river (a *cours d'eau*) with the result that the book, *La Seine*, and the river of the same name become, through the fluctuations of Ponge's thoughts and the unending flux of his writing (his *discursus*), synonymous.

More contemporary and more peripatetic as a poetic and adventurous inhabitant of Paris is Jacques Réda (1929–) whose meditations on Paris are inspired by his long peregrinations on foot or by bicycle through some of the least frequented *quartiers* of the city. 'I love train tracks, iron, rust', he writes in *Les Ruines de Paris* (1977), a collection of prose poems exploring the vacant lots, empty factories, deserted squares, ruined houses, discarded bottles, and railway yards that constitute a different kind of Parisian spectacle from the one celebrated by earlier poets. Réda's Paris is a city of obscurity, anonymity, abandonment, and material dissolution. Yet the changing splendour of sky and clouds creates a colourful counterweight to Paris's grey dissoluteness.

Rural France

Not all twentieth-century poets, of course, sing the 'song of Paris'. Many hail from the provinces and have inhabited landscapes that remain the settings for, if not the central presences of, their poems. Carnac, in Brittany, was the birthplace of Eugène Guillevic (1907–97), and his early poetry has the rugged, compressed hardness and the honed concision of the rocky Breton coastline

(*Terraqué*, 1942; *Carnac*, 1961). For the young Guillevic, life was poor and hard in an unyielding, elemental landscape of rocks, marshes, mud, wind, sea, and menhirs; it was a land that only grudgingly accepted the presence of human beings: an earth heavy with the menace of a terrifying and mythic prehistory and dense with the thick substance of indomitable, recalcitrant matter (granite, limestone). In the neighbouring province of Normandy, south of Saint-Malo, Jean Follain (1903–71) was born in the small village of Canisy. His poetry has a Proustian quality of reminiscence. Through precisely remembered details of simple and fleeting childhood events sensually recalled in chiselled, lapidary images – a boy kicking a tin can, the mouldy smell of a book, yellow butterflies in a pear tree – it seeks to find the essence of a lost paradise, once the protective space of a home (*Chants terrestres*, 1937). Further south, in another region of France, the Vaucluse, Jean Tortel (1904–93) poetically cultivates his own garden in the hope that this limited space will reveal secrets about the nature of being and of poetry. The garden is a rectangle of sorts, dug up and dug into first and foremost with a tool – a 'methodical spade' – designed 'to slice, to test, to fragment, to expand' the soil in order to make it ready for seeding: not unlike another 'tool' – namely, the poet's pen – that cuts into another similarly rectangular space, the page, bringing to light all that is hidden beneath the soil of the real ('Critique d'un jardin', in *Relations*, 1968).

Lyrically and aphoristically, René Char (1907–88), a longtime inhabitant of the Vaucluse as well, evokes the countryside around his native Sorgue, the river emerging from the cavern of the Fontaine de Vaucluse to join the Rhône at Avignon. The forward momentum of the Sorgue and the upward thrust of its headwaters become for Char a metaphor for the poem – its 'feverish surge *en avant*', its 'furious ascension', its 'perpetual insomnia' – in a destitute time of war and anguish over the mortality of the human condition. The waters of the Sorgue, murmuring from within Char's fragmentary, laconic, diamond-like verses, are called on to represent the tentative, contradictory nature of poetry: its presence–absence (the poem like the river is always there and always passing away); its refusal of finality ('only through poetry do we live in the place we leave behind, do we create the poem we abandon'); its perpetual incompleteness ('the poet must always leave traces, never proofs, of his passage'); its constant metamorphosis ('the poem is love created from a desire that still remains desire'). Yet, faced with unavoidable death and the ephemerality of all things, the poet strives to preserve 'the infinite faces of living reality' because without the 'dislocating energy of poetry' what, in the end, can reality be?

Around the experience of the ephemeral and around a poetry magazine of the same name (*L'Éphémère*) a group of poets, all of whom had come of poetic age in the late 1940s, joined forces to examine how the writing of poetry might formally simulate and philosophically reflect upon the realities of death, loss, and destruction in a post-Holocaust world for which the certitudes of the first fifty years of the century no longer had value. Yves Bonnefoy (1923–), Jacques Dupin (1927–), and André du Bouchet (1924–2000), along with Louis-René des Forêts (1918–2000), and the German poet Paul Celan (1920–70), served as the editors of *L'Éphémère* during its all too short life (1966–72). While Dupin and du Bouchet, following Mallarmé's example, transform the white page of the text into a poem-landscape on the surface of which fragmented phrases, open spaces, a deconstructed syntax, jagged words, and voiced silences play out the drama of absence and presence, of meanings found and then lost, Bonnefoy privileges geographical spaces that have been marked by change, use, erosion, and oblivion: those overlooked hinterlands (the 'arrière-pays', he calls them) that bear the signatures and signs of loss. He assigns poetry the task of articulating reality at its most elemental, of inviting into the text and texture of poetic language those simple realities that are 'wind, fire, earth, and water': in other words, those particular yet universal building blocks of the physical world that compose life in the here and now and constitute the very language of being which poetry echoes, especially when it calls the distorting illusion (the 'lure') of images into question (*Dans le leurre du seuil*, 1975). Through poems that relentlessly designate their imperfections and question their own will-to-meaning Bonnefoy creates a precarious, imaginary landscape (*Du mouvement et de l'immobilité de Douve*, 1953), open to the movement of clouds, to the cries of birds, and to words as ephemeral as the sky. Whether the landscape is an enigmatic expanse like Douve, or a snowy forest in a corner of Massachusetts, or an abandoned abbey in the south of France, or a painting of the English countryside by Constable, physical space is the crossroads where past and present, self and other, reality and dream, silence and song, life and death become real with the intensity of what Bonnefoy calls *la présence* – a sublime, secular, yet ineffable experience of the absolute that, emerging from an awareness of death, becomes the poem's responsibility to express, although ultimately it is beyond articulation.

A landscape poet who shares many of Bonnefoy's philosophical and poetic feelings regarding the physical reality of the world, although for him what poetry fails to capture is not so much 'presence' as what he calls the 'unseizable' (*l'insaisissable*), is Philippe Jaccottet (1925–). His writings also explore poetry's inadequate response to experiences that transcend expression; no poem, for example, can capture the cry of suffering or the rattle of death, truly inarticulate sounds. Similarly, no poem can fully capture the beauty and plenitude of an almond tree in bloom, or a cluster of grazing sheep, or a pond furrowed by the wind. In his walks around Grignan in south-eastern France, Jaccottet becomes a reader and a questioner of landscapes. But the act of thinking about the land as he contemplates its myriad signs of life meets a greater challenge when the self-deprecating, self-doubting poet sits down to describe, with as light and as hesitant a touch as possible, what his walk has made him see and feel. Jaccottet is continuously challenged by the problem of how to prevent the description of the landscape and the events that make it distinctive from becoming a mimetic representation: of how, in other words, he can compose a poem-landscape perpetually open to the falling and rising of the wind, the soughing of distant pines, the cry of an owl (*L'Effraie*, 1953; *L'Ignorant*, 1958; *Paysages avec figures absentes*, 1970). Jaccottet's poetry looks to these vivid, vibrant, concrete events of the real for 'lessons' on how to live and die in a world where knowledge is limited and transcendence all but absent.

The notion of a poetry refusing to articulate a synthetic or global vision of the world – a poetry of passage and indeterminacy, in other words, that accepts the unseizability and ineffability of life, a poetry 'closer to cinders than to incense' (*Textes pour un poème 1949–1970*) – also takes form in the work of the Egyptian-born poet Andrée Chedid (1920–). Her landscape is not an ordinary space per se, not a geographical locus. Rather, it is landscape figured as the human face, with its changing looks, its expressive movements, its ephemeral immediacy. Indeed, the face is a haven, a site of being, a path through darkness, and a sign of compassionate otherness. Even though the contemplation of this 'landscape' offers no certainty or knowledge, the expanse that is the face evokes the infinite possibilities of life; it calls into being a momentary coalescence, a presence, that in the flash of a smile or the furrowing of a brow reveals the immediacy of being.

Landscapes beyond the sea

Whether they have come to France as exiles or have been born in the French colonies, those poets who bring to their poetry and to their sense of Frenchness the geographical realities of other lands and the languages of other cultures lyrically celebrate the experiences of errancy, wandering, and strangeness through what Saint-John Perse (Alexis Saint-Léger, 1887–1975) calls 'the flashing syntax of lightning . . . the pure language of exile' (*Éloges*, 1911). Born in Guadeloupe, which he left for France at the age of twelve, and as a career diplomat with postings in many different countries, Perse became accustomed not only to living as a foreigner but to turning exile into poetic discourse (*Exil*, 1942). His verses are in continual movement across the page, blowing errantly like the wind (*Vents*, 1946), flowing back and forth like currents (*Amers*, 1957). It is in this last work – an epic ode in homage to an ocean that is raised from the status of mere landscape to that of cosmic myth – that song and sea become one. Over nearly 200 pages the ocean reveals its 'textuality', as the adjectives and epithets describing the sea pile up. The 'nomad', the 'insomniac', the 'loquacious' sea constitutes a universe into which all realities, sensations, and feelings flow. It is a sea of light and delight, of action and tumult, of order and chaos, of strangeness and yet companionship; it is the 'universal spouse'.

Equal to Perse's *Éloges* in its epic scope and its intense evocation of a Caribbean-island childhood, and yet completely different in its political engagement and anti-colonialist rage is *Cahier d'un retour au pays natal* (*Notes on a Return to the Native Land*, 1938) by the Martinique poet Aimé Césaire (1913– 2008), who was, with the Senegalese poet Léopold Sédar Senghor (1906–2001), the founder of the Negritude movement. Césaire came to Paris in 1931 to continue his education and did not return to Martinique for five years. Influenced by Breton's insistence that poetry give voice to unfettered desire and a liberated unconscious, the *Cahier* is an angry, frenzied, and breathless anti-epic: vitriolic in its criticism of French colonisation, acerbic in its attack on traditional forms of French poetry, persuasive in its argument against cultural assimilation, and above all insurrectional in its cry against the misery, poverty, and oppression of the black inhabitants of Martinique and other countries. As in Perse's *Amers*, poetry and landscape coalesce; but in the *Cahier* the powerful, rhythmic orality and emotional intensity of the verses, with their apostrophes, their commands, their injunctions and insults, are like an erupting volcano, spewing a burning lava that flows like the inhabitants' tears of pain. Sickness and stagnation characterise the island's dark, scarred, starving landscape: the ocean is sterile, the wind useless, the sun a misery, the water a wound, the stars dead. Césaire's sea is not the mythic, god-like, creative force it is for Perse; rather, it is a cesspool throwing the world's refuse on shores of 'blackened sand'.

Another landscape of exile, as dry as Césaire's is tropical, is that of Edmond Jabès (1912–91), who until his forced departure from Egypt for Paris in 1957 had lived close to the desert but had never described it in his poetry. Only when lost and distant did the desert appear in Jabès's series of lyrical, philosophical, and enigmatic books (*Le Livre des questions*, *Le Livre des ressemblances*, *Le Livre du dialogue*, etc., written between 1963 and 1991) as if the very writing of the desert could make it reappear. On the blank sheet of paper Jabès places 'footsteps' – the word-traces left by his pen – that are signs of an errant and effaced writing forever wandering like the Jews and the fictional rabbis who throughout his work ask questions, debate points of the Talmud, and remember their centuries-old suffering. Jabès's nearly twenty-five books are caravans, linked one to the other by their constant errancy, their movement towards an unreachable destination. This is because the desert landscape – a place of passage, never a home – and the book – its words in continual, anxious movement – can, like history and language, never come to an end. In Jabès's perpetually open books the landscape of exile and the writing of exile share a common nomadism in which topography and typography coincide.

69

Francophone writing

NICHOLAS HARRISON

'Francophone writing', the French language, and French literature

Taken at face value the term *francophone* may seem to mean merely 'French-speaking', but in practice it tends to be coded and restrictive. Its connotations are shaped by the controversial history of 'official' *francophonie*, the project to promote a notional worldwide community of French speakers, resisted by those who see in it an exercise in neo-colonialism. The boundaries implied in a phrase such as 'French and francophone literature' are blurred and to some extent racialised: thus Assia Djebar, say (whose work I discuss below), will fall under the 'francophone' rubric while Hélène Cixous will not, even though both were born in colonial Algeria, have lived most of their life in France, use French as their main language, and have published in France. In other words, the phrase 'French and francophone literature' at once embraces and marginalises certain writers of French; it appears tautological from one point of view and racist from another.

If the notion of 'francophone writing' nonetheless has a certain currency and validity, this must be understood in relation to the development, from the late eighteenth century onwards, of the idea that each nation has, or should have, its national literature and its national language. In reality, very few countries have ever had anything like a single language spoken by everyone within the country's borders, and outside spoken only by emigrants and language-learners. In France's case, only about two-fifths of the population were native French speakers at the time of the Revolution of 1789, according to Louis-Jean Calvet, but from then on, the need to impose French as a national language became an article of Republican faith.[1] As in other countries the project was at once practical and ideological: on one level it was about spreading social

---

1 L.-J., Calvet, *Linguistique et colonialisme: petit traité de glottophagie* (1974) (Paris: Payot, 1988), pp. 166–78.

glue and promoting a certain intra-national homogeneity, on another about the national genius that language and literature were supposed to embody and convey, and the superiority of France over its European rivals.

For francophone writers in particular, this history, and its extension into France's modern overseas Empire and the *mission civilisatrice*, raises questions about the ideological baggage that the French language brings with it, inherently – in the sense that each language organises the world conceptually in a different way – and/or contingently because it is embroiled in nationalist ideology, which (among other things) associates the French language in particular with rationality and clarity of thought, and which exaggerates the 'Frenchness' and untranslatability of the French language and French literature. From this perspective, when Frantz Fanon wrote in 'The Black Man and Language': 'To speak means . . . above all assuming a culture and bearing the weight of a civilization', his statement could be seen as self-confirming, but the confirmation may rest on questionable assumptions about the extent and nature of the common ground provided by French.[2] Comparable ironies arise in an essay of 1961 by Malek Haddad, when he writes: 'even expressing themselves in French, Algerian writers from an Arabo-Berber background must *translate* thought that is *specifically Algerian*, thought that would have found full expression *if its vehicle had been the Arabic language and Arabic writing* . . . Our *French vocabulary* corresponds only *approximately* to our *Arab thought*'.[3] Again the author's notion of a national language could be seen as decisively shaped by French culture, or a wider European imperial culture. More importantly, in terms of the general scepticism I want to encourage about the notional alignment of language, literature, and national identity, his statement struggles awkwardly with its own internal tensions: implicitly, one might say, in demonstrating that he was able in French to express his views and to be critical of French culture, and more apparently in presenting Arabic as the natural vehicle of specifically Algerian thought, when most Arabic speakers are not Algerian and when a good proportion of Algerians have another language (most often a Berber language) as their mother tongue.

I do not want to deny that to have a language in common is to have something very important in common, or that languages and mindsets are entangled in intricate ways, or that Haddad felt real discomfort in using French. Indeed, one might take Haddad's feelings as exemplary and argue that one

2 F. Fanon, *Peau noire, masques blancs* (Paris: Seuil, 1952), p. 13; *Black Skin, White Masks*, trans. Richard Philcox (New York: Grove Press, 2008), pp. 1–2.
3 M. Haddad, 'Les Zéros tournent en rond', in *Écoute et je t'appelle* (Paris: Maspero, 1961), pp. 7–46, p. 34; Haddad's italics. Translation is mine.

of the principal common denominators of those writers usually grouped as 'francophone' is a self-conscious, often troubled relationship to the French language, especially in its associations with Frenchness. In the next section I will explore this idea through three further francophone texts, hoping also to reveal something of the diversity of contexts, achievements, and ambitions – cultural, generic, historical, and so on – associated with francophone writing, even within the literary realm that is my focus. Before doing so, I should issue some caveats. First, there is greater variety within francophone writing than I can describe here, and I am neglecting major topics including Caribbean cultures and Creole. Second, although geo-historical contexts are crucial to this field and to my own choice of examples, I do not want to exaggerate the extent to which a given background or context determines a particular attitude to language/writing. Examining two different Algerian writers may help clarify this point, and I will try to cast light on it from a different angle in the final section, where I consider how the category 'francophone writing' implies a certain approach on the part of the reader/critic. Finally, I would make the related point that for many purposes it must be unacceptably restrictive to do what I will do here, discussing francophone writers almost entirely in terms of their relationship to the French language, or to think of them exclusively in the context of French imperialism and culture. Nonetheless, those issues seem inevitable, especially if, like me, you are drawn by francophone texts into cultures whose other languages you cannot speak or read.

Three case studies: Tremblay, Kourouma and Djebar

Les Belles Sœurs by Michel Tremblay is a play set in a working-class francophone area of Montreal in 1965.[4] The protagonist, Germaine Lauzon, has won a million savings stamps. Various female family members and friends come round to help her stick them in books and, as it turns out, to steal them. Les Belles Sœurs was first performed in August 1968, at a tense moment in the history of Québécois nationalism. The French language was perceived to be under threat from US cultural imperialism, from the political power of the anglophone minority in Quebec (a factor that subsequent political events have made less important), and from the anglophone majority in Canada.

---

4 I will refer to the 2007 edition (Arles: Actes Sud, and Montreal: Leméac) and the 1988 version of the Scots translation, *The Guid-Sisters*, by William Findlay and Martin Bowman (Toronto: Exile Editions). Page references will be given in the text.

Tremblay's crucial innovation, when nearly all previous theatre in Quebec had used metropolitan French, was to make all his characters speak the dialect known as *joual*. (This initially pejorative term derived from a certain pronunciation of 'cheval' [horse] particularly associated with a working-class dialect of Montreal; it is sometimes applied more elastically to Québécois in general.) Many Québécois critics and theatre-goers disapproved, on linguistic grounds among others (aesthetic, political, religious), and when plans were made to produce the play in Paris, the Québécois Ministry of Cultural Affairs refused funding, which was subsequently provided, in 1973, by the federal government. At the Cinquième biennale de la langue française the same year, in Dakar, reactions were generally hostile.[5]

From the outset, the play's *joual* dialogue would sound exotic to most audiences, even in Quebec, let alone other French-speaking countries. The accent is the main factor, but already in the first line – 'Misère, que c'est ça? Moman!' (p. 7; 'In the name o Christ! Whit's aw this? Maw!', p. 5) – other linguistic particularities are on display: some distinctive syntax, and a religiously inflected expletive.[6] Some of what follows would be incomprehensible to most francophones ('Ben, j'ai mon voyage!', p. 7 – meaning 'well I never!', or, in the Scots translation, simply 'Christ!', p. 5 – or the use of *liqueur* to mean fizzy drink). Conversely, Europeans appear exotic to these characters, admired by some ('À Paris, tout le monde perle bien, c'est du vrai français partout', p. 42; 'In Paris everyone speaks so refined', p. 58), but disdained by others for their dubious personal hygiene ('D'ailleurs, en Urope, le monde se lavent pas', p. 16; 'They don't go in for waashing much either', p. 18) or their dreary classical music ('Beding par icitte, bedang par là', p. 24; 'If thurs wan thing ah cannae staund, it's classical bloody music', p. 29).

A more recent equivalent of Tremblay's language can be found in the animated clips on the internet site *Têtes à claques*,[7] whose dialogue non-Québécois viewers will find hard to follow – which is part of the point, and, as in *Les Belles Sœurs*, a source of humour. In the 'Paris' clip the French waiter cannot understand most of what the Québécois couple say. The one misunderstanding on their side, when he asks for 'des photos de vos gosses' – *gosses* being slang for kids in metropolitan French and testicles in Québécois – is implausible, though funny; there is an asymmetry here, connected with

---

5 R. Killick, *Les Belles Sœurs* (London: Duckworth, 2000), pp. viii–ix. My own understanding of the play is indebted to this excellent edition.
6 'Misère' sits alongside exclamations such as *câlice!* 'chalice', signals of a religiosity of which Tremblay is critical.
7 See www.tetesaclaques.tv/index.php (accessed 9 February 2010).

France's continued centrality, real and imaginary, to the francophone world. Tremblay's writing engages with this asymmetry in various ways, starting with a written rendering of the accent that is only approximately phonetic; anyone who did not already know how *joual* sounds could not work it out from his script, whose idiosyncrasies cannot wholly avoid endorsing tacitly the idea that Québécois falls outside the range of French or Frenches covered by standard spelling. In this sense the gesture of altering standard spelling – as in the Scots version of Tremblay's play – is always double-edged: it points to quirks in the relation between standard spelling and accent, but also reinforces the norm from which the 'dialect' differs. Yet whereas that normative element may be regrettable for some writers, Tremblay, whose stage directions are in standard French, accepted this ambivalence. He saw these working-class women in particular, in their use of *joual*, as upholders and vehicles of a valid national identity but also, in their limited articulacy, as victims and emblems of an undernourished Québécois culture.

My second example, Ahmadou Kourouma's novel *Les Soleils des indépendances*, also appeared in Montreal in 1968, after it had been refused by Parisian publishers.[8] It is set in a fictionalised version of Kourouma's native Ivory Coast, and recounts the downfall of Fama, a Malinke prince. The Malinke language is one of many spoken within the country, which is a complex patchwork linguistically, ethnically, and religiously. Fama, who is out of step with post-independence 'Côte d'Ebène', struggles to reconcile diverse aspects of his own situation and beliefs, which include Islam and animism. The challenge for Kourouma is to translate an oral culture and a worldview not usually expressed in French. Like *Les Belles Sœurs*, *Les Soleils des indépendances* offers French readers a linguistic shock from the very start. The book begins: 'Il y avait une semaine qu'avait fini dans la capitale Koné Ibrahima, de race malinké, ou disons-le en malinké: il n'avait pas soutenu un petit rhume' (p. 9; 'One week had passed since Ibrahima Kone, of the Malinke race, had met his end in the capital city, or to put it in Malinke: he'd been defeated by a mere cold', p. 3). The incongruous use of 'fini' here, a rendering of a Malinke verb, is the first of numerous linguistic peculiarities in Kourouma's riotous text, where neologisms proliferate among literal translations of Malinke idioms and proverbs.[9]

8 References in the text will be to the Seuil edition (Paris: 1970) and the translation, *The Suns of Independence*, by Adrian Adams (London: Heinemann, 1981). Page references will be given in the text.

9 P. O'Flaherty, *Kourouma: Les Soleils des indépendances* (Glasgow: University of Glasgow French and German Publications, 2007), chap. 4; M. Gassama, *La Langue d'Ahmadou Kourouma, ou, Le français sous le soleil d'Afrique* (Paris: Karthala, 1995).

What links Tremblay and Kourouma as 'francophone writers' also separates them: a certain verbal inventiveness, embroiled with different colonial histories and socio-linguistic contexts. Quebec was a settler colony whose precolonial peoples and languages were decimated; French is fundamental and unrivalled in its importance to modern Québécois identity. Despite some stylisation, parts of Tremblay's play, once it is performed, have a mimetic relationship to the speech patterns he wishes to capture; and in other texts Tremblay and other writers explore forms of writing that are closer than *joual* to metropolitan French but are still distinctively Québécois. Kourouma's prose by contrast does not reflect or aspire to a standard Ivorian or Malinke French and must bridge a greater socio-cultural distance: between the writing and the world it represents, and between the represented world and the text's first or imagined audience. Most of Kourouma's characters could not read his stories about them; in many senses, French remains a foreign language in Ivory Coast, even if it is the official language and an accepted lingua franca among the socio-political elite.

The writer I quoted earlier, Malek Haddad, clearly felt that French should not have comparable currency in Algeria, whose government since independence has always distanced itself from *francophonie*. As Haddad's remarks emphasised, a predominantly Muslim and largely arabophone country such as Algeria has in Arabic a written language with its own (not unproblematic) claims to be a national and international language, with its own literature and a particularly close association with the country's main religion – closer than the association of French with Catholicism in Quebec, or even, differently, in Algeria. But if the status of Arabic in these respects is one reason why French felt so inappropriate to Haddad, it also helps explain why his compatriot Assia Djebar feels justified in writing French, and chooses to write provocatively, if tentatively, about Camus and Fromentin (where readers may expect her, as a 'postcolonial' writer, to be more hostile): 'Je suis tentée de les appeler "frères", mes frères en langue en tout cas' ('I am tempted to call them my "brothers", brothers in language, anyway').[10]

On the one hand, Djebar shares with Haddad the view that the fit between the French language and Algerian culture is incomplete; like Tremblay and Kourouma, she makes it clear in her use of French that the standard metropolitan language cannot do the work she wants to do. She studs her writing with untranslatable words from Arabic and uses French words in new contexts

10 A. Djebar, *Ces voix qui m'assiègent . . . en marge de ma francophonie* (Paris: Albin Michel, 1999), p. 218. This untranslated book of essays will be my main point of reference in discussing Djebar. The title could be rendered as 'These voices assailing me . . . on the borders of *francophonie*'.

where their habitual cultural associations are revealed and displaced: so she switches between *Dieu* and *Allah* (in a sense, the first sounds too Christian, the second too Muslim); she uses *maquis* to mean Algerian resistance to the French rather than French resistance to the Nazis; and she uses *faire carême* to mean fasting during Ramadan rather than Lent. Like Kourouma, she wishes to modulate her French rhythmically and syntactically to reflect the other languages she knows, so distancing her writing from spoken French; like Tremblay, Djebar, working across various forms and media, creates work that is generically mixed, incorporating elements of historiography and poetry.

On the other hand, Djebar does not share Haddad's dream of feeling fully at home in written Arabic. Her ethnic background may be significant here – she is part Berber – as is the fact that she has done most of her writing some time after Algerian independence. But three further issues are particularly important. The first is her emphasis on women's marginalisation in Islam and in Algerian nationalist and postcolonial cultures, including its linguistic cultures, which to her appear incapable of accommodating women's perspectives and voices. Second, she presents modern Algerian identities as the hybrid products of a long history of exchange and conquest. This is not to say that she downplays the violence of French colonialism; she writes, for instance, 'la langue française que j'écris s'appuie sur la mort des miens, plonge ses racines dans les cadavres des vaincus de la conquête' ('the French language I write is built on deaths among my own forebears, its roots plunge into the corpses left behind by the conquest').[11] But Djebar accepts that colonialism's effects have been irreversible in many respects; French is woven into its linguistic legacy alongside previous imperial languages including Punic, Latin, Turkish, and – of course – Arabic. More controversially still, she presents at least some aspects of colonialism's impact as actually or potentially positive, both politically – for example in terms of secularism – and personally, in terms of the freedom she has found as a woman and as a writer. This brings us to the third major factor in Djebar's attitude towards French, her understanding of the nature of literary writing as such, which will be central to my final section.

'Francophone writing' as a mode of reading

In an essay entitled 'Être une voix francophone' ('Being a francophone voice'), under the general heading 'Francophonie?', Djebar describes her writing

---

11 Ibid., p. 184.

practice as *'franco-graphie'*.[12] Her awkward, italicised neologism, which draws attention to the gap between writing and speech, is just one of many stylistic and narrative reminders that her work, even when it appears to be about her own life, cannot be read as simply autobiographical. Nor can it be taken as simply representative of Algerian women's experiences; she is explicitly aware of her socio-cultural remoteness from the women for whom she may be taken to 'speak'. She claims to reject any role as *porte-parole* or spokesperson, and describes her task as an *écrivaine* (a feminized *écrivain*, 'writer') not only in terms of gender solidarity but also in terms of the narcissism and futility suggested punningly by the word *vaine*.[13] Comparably, the phrase 'Ces voix qui m'assiègent' (see note 10) on one level suggests her earnest sense of responsibility towards the women about whom she writes, but on another, as an allusion to Beckett's *L'Innommable*, points to her involvement with a cosmopolitan and in some senses placeless literary modernism, and her urge to position her work in a distinctly 'literary' space. She states at one point: 'je vais m'éloigner volontairement d'une certaine critique qui . . . se contente de commentaires ou sociologiques ou biographiques, recréant ainsi à sa manière un harem pseudo-littéraire' ('I will quite deliberately distance myself from a certain sort of criticism which . . . makes do with sociological or biographical commentary, recreating in its way a pseudo-literary harem').[14]

Djebar's immediate point of reference when she made that remark was women's writing, or the idea of 'women's writing', but it applies also to 'francophone writing': it not only groups certain texts in terms of their real or supposed characteristics but also implies a certain approach to reading and criticism, or a certain 'author function'.[15] Viewing a text through the lens of 'francophone writing' tends to mean placing emphasis on socio-cultural material and the political message that the text conveys, or may be taken to convey, and downplaying the singular text's literary, formal, or aesthetic specificity – a tendency one could see writers including Tremblay, Kourouma, and Djebar as resisting through their sophisticated manipulation not only of French vocabulary and syntax but of literary form and voice.

Although these points suggest further reasons to tread warily around 'francophone writing' and its implied hermeneutics, it must be said too that

---

12 Ibid., p. 29.   13 Ibid., pp. 61–8.

14 Ibid., p. 85. In a comparably provocative move, Djebar repeatedly describes French as functioning as a 'veil' for her; e.g. pp. 43, 64. On her relationship to *francophonie* I also recommend her 2006 inaugural speech to the Académie-française: see www.academie-francaise.fr/immortels/index.html (accessed 9 February 2010).

15 On the 'author function' see M. Foucault, 'Qu'est-ce qu'un auteur?', *Bulletin de la Société française de philosophie*, 63e année, 3 (juillet–septembre 1969), pp. 75–104.

historical contextualisation is a legitimate fate for any text, and is invited by the literary texts I have described. In the end, the advice that should be given to the reader of francophone literature might be given to the reader of any literature. I suggested earlier that francophone writing might be defined in terms of its complex, perhaps troubled relationship to the language in which it is written – a definition that could stretch to literature as such. At the risk of lending the idea more consistency than it possesses, I am tempted to argue that 'francophone writing' radicalises and foregrounds demands made ideally by all literary texts, starting with a peculiar balancing act between singularity and representativity. Less abstractly, 'francophone' literature may offer distinctive yet fundamental insights into many of the preoccupations of contemporary criticism and of this Cambridge History, including oral literature, writing in/from the periphery, alterity and alienation, literature and history, women writers, literature and religion, literature and politics, memory, testimony, and autobiography. All of this – alongside political factors including neo-colonialism and other disappointments of the 'postcolonial' world – helps explain why writers such as Haddad or the Tunisian Jewish writer Albert Memmi were wrong in thinking, prior to Algerian independence, that francophone writing from the colonies, in its contributions to nationalist independence movements, would help bring about its own demise.

If francophone writing is thriving, what of 'francophone writing' as a label? In anglophone academic contexts today it is often subsumed under 'postcolonial writing', a term generally treated with suspicion in the French-speaking world and which has similar implications to 'francophone writing' as a hermeneutic framework.[16] More recently 'world literature' has gained a new currency, particularly in North American universities. The manifesto 'Pour une "littérature-monde" en français' of 2007 represented a French variant, declaring that the distribution of numerous major literary awards to 'francophone' writers showed there had been a 'Copernican revolution' such that 'the centre, the point from which the light of Franco-French literature was supposed to radiate, is no longer the centre'.[17] The word 'monde' here signalled two sorts of commitment: to a worldliness declared absent from putatively self-involved metropolitan literature, and to inter- or trans-nationalism. The manifesto thus diverged from the 'world literature' phenomenon seen elsewhere; the latter's proponents rarely place explicit or polemical emphasis on

---

16 See Chapter 70 in the present volume, and C. Forsdick and D. Murphy (eds.), *Francophone Postcolonial Studies: A Critical Introduction* (London: Arnold, 2003).

17 First published in *Le Monde*, 16 March 2007, the whole manifesto can be found at www.fabula. org/actualites/article17941.php (accessed 9 February 2010).

referentiality, and would tend to see the manifesto's restriction of the discussion to literature *in French* as ironically parochial. Yet that restriction was dropped from the title of the volume for which the manifesto was a trailer,[18] and the manifesto itself spoke in its utopian final lines of a borderless language 'freed from its exclusive pact with the nation, and free from all powers except those of poetry and the imagination'. It also proclaimed that *littérature-monde* had killed off *francophonie*, 'the last reincarnation of colonialism'. It is too early to say whether such arguments are really so strong that in coming years 'francophone writing' as a category will die away; there are both good and bad reasons why, for now, it continues to (co)exist uneasily within and outside the borders of a tenacious 'French literature'.

18 M. Le Bris and J. Rouaud (eds.), *Pour une littérature-monde* (Paris: Gallimard, 2007).

70

Writing and postcolonial theory

CELIA BRITTON

Postcolonial theory is a large and contested arena, and its perimeters are difficult to define: which societies count as postcolonial? Are they just those in which the colonised populations have gained power or do they include Canada, for instance? How sharply can 'postcolonial' be distinguished from 'colonial' or 'anti-colonial'? But its central focus is, in contrast, very clear: the dynamic of the colonial encounter and its aftermath – that is, the cultural, psychological, and political repercussions of the contact between colonisers and colonised.

The theory developed largely in the English and Comparative Literature departments of universities in the United States and Australia; this has resulted in an emphasis on literature that has led to its being accused of neglecting the material, economic determinants of postcolonial societies in favour of the textual, the subjective, and the cultural. Within the literary sphere itself, moreover, it has resulted in a strong anglophone bias: despite the significant influence of French theorists such as Michel Foucault and Jacques Derrida on some strands of postcolonial theory, its major works have all, with the exception of Frantz Fanon's *Peau noire, masques blancs* (1952), been produced in English; and whereas a large corpus of what might be regarded as postcolonial literature has been written in French, its analysis in these terms has largely been carried out in universities outside France. Conversely, French scholars who specialise in studying francophone literature have tended to distance themselves from postcolonial theory.[1] The task of connecting francophone literature and overwhelmingly anglophone postcolonial theory has with some exceptions (notably the work of Moura and Bardolph)[2] been undertaken in an English-speaking context.[3]

---

1 *Francophone Postcolonial Studies* 4.2 (2006) contains several articles by French specialists of francophone literature that illustrate these reservations.
2 J.-M. Moura, *Littératures francophones et théorie postcoloniale* (Paris: Presses Universitaires de France, 1999). J. Bardolph, *Études postcoloniales et littérature* (Paris: Champion, 2001).
3 C. Forsdick and D. Murphy (eds.), *Francophone Postcolonial Studies: A Critical Introduction* (London: Arnold, 2003); H. A. Murdoch and A. Donadey (eds.), *Postcolonial Theory and Francophone*

Nevertheless, intellectuals from French-speaking areas of the developing world have written some major works on issues that are central to postcolonial theory – sometimes long before the theory as such existed – and these are now beginning to be recognised as important texts in the postcolonial canon. Thus, for example, Abdelkebir Khatibi's *Maghreb pluriel* (1983) emphasises the cultural hybridity of the area and navigates a course for contemporary North African societies between the metaphysical humanism of the West and the theocratic patriarchal societies of traditional Islam. The Congolese philosopher and novelist V. Y. Mudimbe engages with European poststructuralism in his analysis of Western philosophical and ethnographic discourses on Africa and his work of constructing a new theorisation of African subjectivity.[4] The essays of Edouard Glissant, from the 1960s onwards, explore the experience of French Caribbean subjects in relation to the 'lost' history of transportation and slavery, the conflictual coexistence of French and Creole and the 'mimetic drive' which inhibits the growth of an autonomous culture, while his more recent writings develop an ethic of diversity and 'Relation' which encompasses the postcolonial world as a whole.[5] Also, the Algerian backgrounds of such major French intellectuals as Derrida and Hélène Cixous have recently been considered as a relevant influence on their thought.

One of the tenets of postcolonial theory is that European culture has from at least the eighteenth century been far more profoundly inflected by colonialism than was previously recognised; the study of canonical English writers from this point of view has produced new, less respectful, readings of the work of, for example, Jane Austen and Joseph Conrad. Equivalent studies have been done on major French writers: Edward Said places Flaubert in the context of 'Orientalism'; Conor Cruise O'Brien's book on Albert Camus inaugurated a series of postcolonial analyses of the latter's dehumanising representations of the colonised subjects of Algeria; and similar work has been done on the Indochinese dimension of Marguerite Duras's novels and films.[6]

Literary Studies (Gainesville: University of Florida Press, 2005); C. Britton and M. Syrotinski (eds.), 'Francophone Texts and Postcolonial Theory', special issue of *Paragraph* 24.3 (2001).

4 V. Y. Mudimbe, *L'Odeur du père: essai sur les limites de la science et de la vie en Afrique noire* (Paris: Présence Africaine, 1982), and *The Invention of Africa: Gnosis, Philosophy and the Order of Knowledge* (Bloomington: Indiana University Press, 1994).

5 These essays have been collected in *L'Intention poétique* (Paris: Seuil, 1969); *Le Discours antillais* (Paris: Seuil, 1981); *Poétique de la Relation* (Paris: Gallimard, 1990); and *Introduction à une poétique du divers* (Paris: Gallimard, 1996).

6 E. Said, *Orientalism: Western Conceptions of the Orient* (London: Routledge and Kegan Paul, 1978); C. Cruise O'Brien, *Camus* (London: Fontana, 1970). On Duras, P. Norindr, *Phantasmatic Indochina: French Colonial Ideology in Architecture, Film, and Literature* (Durham, NC: Duke University Press, 1996) and J. Bradley Winston, *Postcolonial Duras: Cultural Memory in Postwar France* (Basingstoke: Palgrave, 2001).

However, it is the authors who are *writing* in or from the periphery of the area whose centre is metropolitan France – i.e. the ex-colonies: mainly African and Caribbean, but also some from Indochina, Lebanon, and the islands of the Indian Ocean – whose work is most relevant to postcolonial theory. In those societies that have achieved full independence, the period leading up to decolonisation was a struggle which, although often complicated and compromised on a practical level, was conceptually very simple: that of the colonised against the French government and its colonial agents. In the postcolonial period, in contrast, this binary opposition gives way to a plurality of conflicts between different sections of the newly independent societies. Decolonisation was (despite the internationalist dimension of the Marxist movements that in some cases led the process) essentially a *nationalist* struggle for independence; and the new states that it created invoked the same nationalist ideology in their efforts to unite their populations. Hence the writers of these 'first generations' aimed to recover – or create – an authentically national culture, free from the alienating European influences to which colonialism had subjected them. But the anticolonial movements had usually been led by members of the Western-educated middle class, who therefore also dominated the governments of the new states; and in these new roles many of them were open to corruption from the neo-colonial economic force of the West. (Aimé Césaire's play *Une Saison au Congo* [1965] shows how Patrice Lumumba fought against but was eventually overthrown by exactly this process.) Therefore the initial wave of literary texts celebrating independence and exalting the unity of the new nation soon gave way to a 'literature of disillusionment' characterised by political satire and irony, in which the ruling nationalist bourgeoisie was shown to be acting just as repressively as the former colonial power. The realisation that independence had not resolved all political conflicts and that the social classes who were still excluded and exploited now had to face new enemies from within their own people is a central issue in postcolonial theory, and is illustrated in many francophone texts: in the case of Algeria, for example, by the novels of Rachid Boudjedra and Tahar Ben Jelloun. One of the best-known sub-Saharan African novels on this theme is Ahmadou Kourouma's *Les Soleils des indépendances* (1970), set in a fictionalised version of the Ivory Coast just after independence and depicting the conflicts between the traditional caste society of the Malinké people and the power structures of the new regime. But whereas Kourouma's melancholy hero is an aristocrat, other novels criticise the new rulers from the point of view of the poor: Ousmane Sembene's *Xala* (1973), for instance, shows the beggars' revenge on a man who had participated selflessly in Senegal's independence movement but has now become a rich and corrupt businessman, and his *Le Dernier de l'empire* (1981) similarly satirises the neo-colonial influences in Senegalese society. Other sub-Saharan African novels concentrate on the figure of the African dictator: Aminata Sow Fall's *L'Ex-père de la nation* (1986) is the ironic pseudo-autobiography of such a dictator, also in Senegal, while the Congolese Sony Labou Tansi's *La Vie et demie* (1979) creates a nightmarish, hallucinatory representation of dictatorship and torture in the fictional state of 'Katamalanasie'. The phenomenon of failed states, warlordism, and child soldiers is treated in a later novel by Kourouma, *Allah n'est pas obligé* (2000); and Tierno Monenembo's *L'Aîné des orphelins* (2000) is based on the Rwandan genocide.

Haiti constitutes a special case within this category of post-independence political disillusionment, in that its main target is the Duvalier regime (1957–86) which came to power long after Haitian independence claiming to represent the poor black population; nevertheless it became just as violently repressive as the worst African dictatorships, and there is a wide literature of protest against it, mainly written by Haitian exiles in France and North America. Typical of these is René Depestre's *Le Mât de cocagne* (1979), in which the impossibility of conventional political opposition is highlighted by the absurdist project of turning the winning of a state-sponsored competition to climb a greasy pole into a gesture of revolt against the regime.

One of the most prominent areas of disillusionment with nationalism is represented by women's writing. Whereas during the anti-colonial campaigns, women had found it difficult to criticise their subordinate role in relation to their male comrades, postcolonial societies are characterised by women asserting their right to an equality that is still denied to them – and in particular, in the case of writers, their right to challenge the patriarchal conventions that imposed silence on them. These are thus novels that could be described as feminist in their aims and their concerns, although many of the writers in question are markedly ambivalent towards Western feminism, seeing it as both too aggressively individualist and too universalist in its prescriptions. Algerian women mainly started writing during the war of independence; and women from Guadeloupe and Martinique also mostly produced their first texts during the 1960s. But it is striking how sub-Saharan African women begin to publish only after the initial euphoria of decolonisation has subsided: Aminata Sow Fall's *Le Revenant* (1976) was the first of a number of novels by Senegalese women, of which the best known is Mariama Bâ's *Une si longue lettre* (1979): the 'letter', written by a newly widowed woman to her friend, describes the 'thirty years of silence' which her marriage has been, her resentment over her husband's second wife, and the wider difficulties of existing as a woman on her own in Senegal.

Francophone women's writing is thus particularly concerned with questions of self-expression and identity; there is a strong autobiographical element in much of it, but it differs from the individualist stance of Western autobiography in its emphasis on the connections between the individual woman and her society. The writing of Assia Djebar, for example, draws on her own experiences of post-revolutionary Algeria, but constantly situates her in relation to all the other Algerian women who, unlike her, have no chance of making their voices heard. The heroine of Maryse Condé's *Hérémakhonon* (1976) is, like her, a middle-class Guadeloupean woman who goes to Africa in search of her roots but discovers a society that denies her any easy foundations on which to build an individual identity. But not all women's novels are based on their own experience: Ananda Devi's *Rue la Poudrière* (1988), for instance, is the first-person narrative of a Mauritian prostitute for whom the act of recounting her tragic life is in itself a conscious means of empowerment.

'Writing in or from the periphery' produces a sense of existing on the margins of a world controlled by its distant centre (which comes across strongly in, for example, Glissant's earlier texts). In this situation, the concepts of *alterity* and *alienation* become crucially relevant: the colonial encounter positions the colonised subject as 'other' to the West's self. For Fanon, and for Tunisian Albert Memmi in his *Portrait du colonisé* (1957), it structures the identities of both colonisers and colonised, but in a way that traps the colonised subject in an alienated desire to identify exclusively with 'white' values. (Homi Bhabha's theorisation of colonial identification is openly indebted to *Peau noire, masques blancs*.[7]) Thus Mayotte Capécia, author of *Je suis Martiniquaise* (1948), is for Fanon an exemplary case of a black woman whose profound alienation produces an overriding desire to marry a white man. But what is more characteristic of francophone writers' representation of alienation is an emphasis on the conscious struggle against it. For example, the hero of Cheikh Hamidou Kane's *L'Aventure ambigüe* (1961) is sent from Senegal to study in France where he struggles to reconcile his African Islamic background with the powerful appeal of European life and Western philosophy. The far less intellectual descendants of plantation slaves in Simone Schwarz-Bart's *Pluie et vent sur Télumée Miracle* (1972) believe that black people are by definition worthless – but the novel is about the heroine's successful psychological fight against this internalised racism.

7 H. Bhabha, *The Location of Culture* (London: Routledge, 1994).

In this sense the motivation for writing is the search for a way for the other to reposition him- or herself as, precisely, self. But this self-expression of an authentic alterity is hampered by the ease with which it can be appropriated by a European readership as a mere exotic commodity (as, for example, in the enthusiastic reception in France of the 'créolité' novels written by Martinicans Patrick Chamoiseau and Raphaël Confiant), and by the social stratification within postcolonial communities whereby authors publishing in French are almost inevitably estranged from more 'authentic' representatives of cultural otherness. (Ananda Devi, for instance, is not a prostitute but an anthropologist who studied in London.) Gayatri Spivak's concept of subalternity, positing the impossibility of recovering the subjectivity of the subaltern other who has no access to discursive agency within the society, is clearly relevant here.[8] Within francophone literature, the writer who has been both most committed to the ideal and most aware of the difficulties of enabling the subaltern to 'speak' is Djebar: her autobiographical and fictional texts demonstrate the necessary delicate mediations involved in translating Arabic to French and oral to written language, and in the opening to *Femmes d'Alger dans leur appartement* (1980) she states her aim as not to speak for, or about, but 'as close as possible' to Algerian women.

The distinction between 'in' and 'from' the periphery is essentially a question of audience: are francophone authors writing *in* the periphery for a local readership, or *from* the periphery *to* the centre? Despite their frequently stated aim of creating a literature for their own people, the fact of writing in French, and in some cases political censorship and/or low levels of literacy, mean that they more often find themselves addressing French readers. But this is not merely a question of expediency: the notion of 'the Empire writing back' is a central theme in postcolonial theory.[9] It implies asserting oneself as a writing *subject*, rather than an object that is written about in the extensive body of exotic and colonial literature produced in France since the eighteenth century. But this implicit ideal of free self-expression or 'coming to voice' is not straightforward, because 'writing back' does not take place in a vacuum: in positioning itself *against* the French literary tradition, it is also necessarily implicated *in* it, however antagonistically.

8 G. Spivak, 'Can the Subaltern Speak?', in C. Nelson and L. Grossberg (eds.), *Marxism and the Interpretation of Culture* (London: Macmillan, 1988), pp. 271–313.
9 The phrase was originally coined by Salman Rushdie, and inspired the title of the first systematic theorisation of postcolonial theory, B. Ashcroft, G. Griffiths, and H. Tiffin, *The Empire Writes Back* (London: Routledge, 1989).

The inescapable influence of French literary models on the first generation of writers in the colonies produced works that were criticised for being
merely second-rate copies of metropolitan originals, so 'writing back' implies
a more active, aggressive *dialogue* with them: using existing forms but also
contesting and transforming them. This ambivalent relation to French literature – as both enabling and constraining – is articulated in Glissant's concept of
'contre-poétique' (in *Le Discours antillais*). One of its consequences is that intertextuality figures strongly in postcolonial writing – from the straightforward
parody of Césaire's rewriting of *The Tempest* with Caliban as the hero (*Une
tempête*, 1969), to complex polyvocal texts such as Werewere Liking's *Elle sera de
jaspe et de corail: journal d'une misovire* (1983), Véronique Tadjo's *À vol d'oiseau*
(1986), or Daniel Maximin's 'Antillean trilogy' (*L'Isolé soleil*, 1981; *Soufrières*,
1987; *L'Île et une nuit*, 1995). To this extent, the *effects* of 'writing back to the
centre' – reappropriation, subversion – ultimately blur the centre–periphery
opposition which originally motivated it: once again, a binary opposition is
replaced by more complex multivalent relationships.

But the centre–periphery structure is more explicitly undermined by the
later emphasis on *métissage* and its quasi-synonyms: hybridity or creolisation.
Some francophone novels stress the problems associated with being a literal
métis – especially being the child of a white father and a non-white mother
whose relationship is seen as a sexual version of colonial exploitation, and
a literalised echo of the anti-colonial trope of the male coloniser invading
and violating the 'female' land. Thus the heroine of Kim Lefèvre's *Métisse
blanche* (1989) and the hero of Henri Lopès's *Le Chercheur d'Afriques* (1990) both
struggle to gain acceptance in their respectively Vietnamese and Congolese
communities. (The situation in the Caribbean is different, because there the
mulattoes have long formed their own powerful social group, and to be light-
skinned was for a long time, and in some circles still is, considered a social
advantage.)

Métissage, however, is as much a feature of communities as of individuals.
The formation of hybrid societies is made possible by migration, especially –
but not exclusively – that which brings former colonial subjects into Europe
and North America. Many francophone texts deal with the experiences of
immigrants and their descendants in France: Calixthe Beyala for sub-Saharan
Africans and Gisèle Pineau for Caribbeans, for example. But it is perhaps those
born in France of North African parentage whose lives have appeared most
frequently in fiction. Leila Sebbar, for instance, sets her 'Shérazade trilogy'
in this community, as does Mehdi Charef in *Le Thé au harem d'Archi Ahmed*
(1983) and Azouz Begag in *Le Gone du Chaâba* (1986). These novels illustrate

the strategies with which their young protagonists navigate their way around French society while creating their own hybrid culture. Condé's novels, in contrast, focus on the actual processes of migration; she herself has lived a nomadic life moving from the Caribbean to Europe, Africa, and the United States, and many of her characters are similarly mobile, lacking any sense of rootedness or belonging to one particular place.

This collective postcolonial *métissage* is seen in a far more positive light than the problematic individual *métis*; and here, moreover, the meaning of the term shifts from the biological register to the cultural: communities composed of different ethnicities that are shaped by a number of diverse cultural influences. The most prominent examples of such communities are in fact not European but in places such as the Caribbean, where European and African traditions mix with those from India, China, and the Middle East. The 'créolité' movement led by Chamoiseau and Confiant proclaims the virtues of mixed or Creole Caribbean societies in their novels and in the manifesto, *Éloge de la créolité* (1989, written together with Jean Bernabé). But Glissant's 'créolisation' takes the Caribbean as a template for a dynamic process now, he claims, operating worldwide; Françoise Lionnet uses anthropologist Jean-Loup Amselle's concept of 'logiques métisses' to theorise postcolonial culture in general as a multiplicity of active negotiations between different traditions;[10] and Khatibi's *Maghreb pluriel* similarly promotes the plurality of historical influences on North Africa.

In this way postcolonial theory's characteristic move away from binary oppositions towards multiplicity and hybridity has also meant a reconceptualisation of both individual and collective identities, which are no longer seen as deriving from one's origins but as constantly (re-)constructed on the basis of one's relations with the different facets of a hybrid community: Glissant defines it as a 'rhizomatic identity' (taking the term from Gilles Deleuze) as opposed to a 'root identity', and sees it as overturning essentialist conceptions of 'pure' being. Sebbar's Shérazade and Maximin's heroine Marie-Gabriel exemplify this ongoing process with particular clarity, as do the characters in Condé's later novels. But it is also perhaps the single most distinctive feature of recent francophone writing in general. The diversity of this literature precludes sweeping generalisations, but I have tried to show how in a variety of ways it is both explicitly and potentially connected to postcolonial theory.

10 F. Lionnet, *Postcolonial Representations: Women, Literature, Identity* (Ithaca, NY: Cornell University Press, 1989).

71

Travel writing, 1914–2010

CHARLES FORSDICK

The outbreak of war has an unfortunate tendency to disrupt the production of travel writing more than it does that of most other literary forms: journeys assume a sudden necessity and an unaccustomed seriousness, and cross-cultural contact is suddenly transformed in ways that the genre is not accustomed to chronicling. This was certainly the case during the First World War. Between 1914 and 1918, the popular exoticism of the *belle époque* and its *fin de siècle* variations, as well as the travel-inspired writing associated with the recently emerged colonial literary school, was suddenly brought to a standstill. This was nevertheless a period of great mobility, as the war triggered the mass movement of a generation of young men, including for the first time many colonial troops who were suddenly faced with a European reality that contrasted starkly with expectations generated by the rhetoric of the 'civilising mission'. The writing to emerge from such journeys, with its extremes of patriotism and pacifism, disrupted the implicit geographical and ethical norms of earlier, especially Romantic, travel writing. Channelled through a range of forms, particularly poetry, novels, and diaries, the literature of 1914–18 tended inevitably to betoken different forms of conceptualising, relating to and finally textualising otherness.

Inter-war journeys

The impact of the conflict on travel, and on the modes of its literary representation, was considerable. New technologies evolved rapidly in the context of war: various forms of mechanised transport, most notably by air; means of information transfer, such as wireless telegraphy and the telephone; modes of capturing and transporting images of elsewhere, in particular lightweight and affordable cameras. Such developments meant that sites deemed inaccessible only decades earlier could not only be visited, but also represented in new ways for a home audience eager for exoticism in the post-war period. These twin shifts permitted the emergence of a new strand of travel writing, *reportage*, associated with the quintessentially inter-war figure of the 'grand reporter'. This new type of traveller was celebrated by Hergé in his 1929 creation Tintin, but whereas the comic-book hero was invariably distracted from the writing that supposedly justified his travel, investigative journalists and *grands reporters* rose to prominence as a result of their travel writing.[1] Celebrated among these were Roland Dorgelès, Joseph Kessel, Albert Londres, and Georges Simenon, several of whom produced significant accounts of colonial abuses following their journeys in sub-Saharan African (most notably Londres's *Terre d'ébène*, 1929). This tradition also permitted, for the first time, the emergence of a significant number of women travel writers, such as Maryse Choisy, Ella Maillart, Titaÿna, and Andrée Viollis, many of whom emerged as proto-feminist icons in the inter-war period. Such travel writing became a genre central to political commentary and ideological debate. Maillart's first two travelogues – *Parmi la jeunesse russe* (1932) and *Des monts célestes aux sables rouges* (1934) – present a positive account of the Soviet Union, whilst other authors – most notably Paul Morand, in *Rien que la terre* (1926), or André Maurois, in *En Amérique* (1933) – offered sympathetic reflections on their journeys through the United States.

The generic indeterminacy of travel writing means that, at any time, very different forms of writing are invariably gathered under its classificatory umbrella. Consequently, the investigative, often journalistic tradition represented by the authors detailed above was accompanied by an alternative literary tradition in the field of travel, closely associated with the clear emergence of modernism as a dominant literary and cultural tendency. Similarly anxious about colonial expansion, without being explicitly anti-colonial, key inter-war literary figures were inspired by their experiences outside France to produce works of travel writing. Although Victor Segalen had died in 1919, his *Équipée* (published posthumously in 1929) outlines a number of the aspects of this tradition, such as the relativisation and even exoticisation of the travelling self, and the elaboration of an imaginary geography that replaces hierarchical understandings of space with more unstable models of cultural fragmentation.[2] Coinciding with the apogee of empire, as epitomised by events such as the colonial exhibition in Vincennes in 1931, travel texts from this period – including André Gide's *Voyage au Congo* (1927), or Henri Michaux's *Ecuador* (1929) and *Un barbare en Asie* (1933) – reveal a growing

---

1 M. Boucharenc, *L'Ecrivain-reporter au cœur des années trente* (Villeneuve d'Ascq: Presses Universitaires du Septentrion, 2004).
2 J. Clifford, *The Predicament of Culture: Twentieth-Century Ethnography, Literature, and Art* (Cambridge, MA: Harvard University Press, 1988).

anxiety regarding assumptions about European cultural superiority and the traditional self-sufficiency of the Western travel writer. Exemplary of this was Michel Leiris's *Afrique fantôme* (1934), the author's personal diary of his experience of the Dakar–Djibouti ethnographic expedition (1931–2), led by Marcel Griaule on behalf of the Musée du Trocadéro. Leiris was secretary to this mission, the aim of which was to carry out ethnographic surveys whilst collecting artefacts to enrich the museum's collections. Leiris's personal account diverges radically from the expedition's official purposes, revealing an anxious narrator frustrated by his persistently European identity, uncomfortable with the ideological underpinnings of the journey and drawn, often despite himself, into an exoticising and eroticising relationship with the cultures and people he encounters.

The travel writing of Gide, Leiris, Michaux, and Segalen reflects a significant shift in the early twentieth-century genre, suggesting a clear break from the previous, predominantly Romantic tradition of describing the mobile self in solipsistic terms, with little reference to cultures visited or to their inhabitants, who are often reduced to the level of mute 'travellees'. Although subsequent authors would be far from immune to Romantic or colonial nostalgia, the possibilities of the travelogue would continue to provide a key opportunity for autobiographical exploration and other early forms of life-writing. Later texts such as Nicolas Bouvier's *L'Usage du monde* (1963) would continue, and on occasion accentuate, the inter-war tradition of exploring the uneven and often uneasy relationship between travellers and those they meet en route, leading even in certain narratives to a progressive effacement of the travel writer. Such self-awareness, and at times open anxiety, is to be read in a more general context characterised by a nascent anti-colonialism (evident in travel texts inspired by the 1931 Exposition coloniale, such as Ousmane Socé's *Mirages de Paris*, 1937) and by a growing sense of the progressive democratisation of travel (a process accelerated by the policies of the Front populaire in 1936, and reflected in texts such as Paul Morand's *Apprendre à se reposer*, 1937).

La fin des voyages?

Just as Paul Fussell described the inter-war years as the golden age of British travel writing, so French production in the same period, although markedly different in its emphases, reveals a similar richness.[3] Again, it was the impact

3 P. Fussell, *Abroad: British Literary Traveling between the Wars* (London: Oxford University Press, 1980).

of a world war on the genre, followed rapidly by an associated and accelerated process of decolonisation, that had major repercussions on the form's short-term visibility as well as its longer-term status. The tendencies underlying much 1930s travel writing, in which authors represent their still privileged access to an elsewhere soon to be subject (it was claimed) to the ever-increasing technologisation and democratisation of the journey, were interrupted by the outbreak of World War II. Travel again assumed very different purposes, not only with the movement of troops but also, in the context of the Holocaust, with newly mechanised means of transport (especially the railways, including those of the SNCF in France) being used to transport interned Jews and other victims to the Nazi concentration and extermination camps. Without the mass transportation made possible by the European rail network, the Final Solution would undoubtedly have been impossible on the same scale, and this is an aspect reflected in a post-war tradition of literary accounts of deportation and the *convois*, produced by authors such as Charlotte Delbo and Jorge Semprun, which adopt certain structures of travel writing to very different ends.[4]

In the immediate aftermath of the war, travel writing was largely eclipsed by the novel as the genre in which social and philosophical questions were explored. The tensions evident in the form at this time are perhaps most apparent in Claude Lévi-Strauss's *Tristes tropiques* (1955), a substantial account of the author's journeys over several decades. The opening chapters outline the post-war desire among many young European men for exoticism and escapism, whilst foretelling at the same time, in anticipation of contemporary globalisation, an imminent 'fin des voyages'. Travel writing nevertheless developed rapidly in the 1950s, often in parallel with the expanding tourist industry, and a number of new subgenres – such as accounts of intercontinental journeys in Citroën 2CVs – achieved considerable popularity. This was, in addition, the period in which a number of travel writers who would come to prominence in the later twentieth century – such as Nicolas Bouvier and Jacques Lacarrière – began their own journeys. Bouvier travelled from Geneva to Japan via Sri Lanka, on an itinerary to whose fragmented textualisation he would devote much of the rest of his life, and Lacarrière spent prolonged periods in Greece, a country whose modern society he would introduce to French-language readers. Additional shifts in the genre, occasioned in particular by imminent decolonisation, were made apparent in texts such

---

4 K. Jones, *Journeys of Remembrance: Memories of the Second World War in French and German Literature, 1960–1980* (Oxford: Legenda, 2007).

as Bernard Dadié's *Un nègre à Paris* (1959), which inaugurated a tradition of postcolonial travel writing and offered a rare voice to a black traveller, disrupting the centre to periphery logic of much colonial travel and bringing an ethnographic gaze to France itself.

In the context of the *nouveau roman* and the emergence of structuralism, travel writing – often dependent on an unspoken pact between reader and narrator regarding the supposed authenticity of events presented – appears in the 1960s to have experienced a marked decline. It is often forgotten, however, that some of the most important and arguably most experimental examples of the genre appeared at this time. Michel Butor, for example, wrote a series of travelogues inspired by his journeys in Europe, North America, and Australia. *Mobile* (1960) represents a road trip around the United States, but eschews fixed itineraries and a clearly identifiable narrative voice in order to present a patchwork of textual fragments inspired by multiple encounters and observations. Whereas Butor suggests that travel remains somehow representable through an accumulation of different textual strategies, Roland Barthes's *L'Empire des signes* (1970) and 'Alors la Chine' (1974) focus on the untranslatability of travel through other cultures and the impossibility of intercultural dialogue.

Pour une littérature voyageuse?

After this period of apparent decline – or, perhaps more accurately, of a growing awareness of the redundancy of an earlier representational tradition of travel literature – a new generation of travel writers came to prominence in the final decades of the twentieth century, progressively forming a coherent group associated with a series of literary phenomena: the increasingly popular 'Étonnants Voyageurs' festival (held annually since 1990 in Saint-Malo), the short-lived journal *Gulliver*, and a manifesto – *Pour une littérature voyageuse* – published in 1992. The key figure in these developments was Michel Le Bris, a former Maoist and editor of *La Cause du peuple*, who was subsequently associated with the *nouveaux philosophes* and recognised for his own travel writing and his scholarship on R. L. Stevenson. Inspired in part by re-evaluation of adventure fiction as defined by earlier authors such as Jacques Rivière, Le Bris was active in the 1980s in attempts by contemporary French novelists to privilege narrative fiction over more postmodern manifestions of the novel. Towards the end of the decade, Le Bris used the Saint-Malo festival and his new journal *Gulliver* to federate the activity of an eclectic group of previously disparate travel writers, most notably Alain Borer, Nicolas Bouvier, Jacques

Lacarrière, Gilles Lapouge, Jacques Meunier, and Kenneth White. The parameters of the movement remain hazy, and the group's slogan of 'une littérature qui dise le monde' provided a category sufficiently flexible to include other subgenres such as detective fiction and postcolonial fiction. Le Bris's argument was that in post-1968 France, ideological uncertainty and increasingly experimental or solipsistic writing had had a deleterious impact on literary production, a tendency that a return to travel writing would counter.

By the early 1990s, travel writing had emerged in France as a real *phénomène d'édition*, with a proliferation of series devoted to the genre and dedicated sections appearing in bookshops. Although partly to be associated with the re-publication of earlier texts and the translation of travel writing from other languages (especially English), this trend was also accompanied by the emergence of new travel writers and the recognition of others – such as Nicolas Bouvier and Ella Maillart – whose work was rediscovered by a new generation of readers. There was also clear evidence of innovation in the form, with the increasing popularity of, for instance, *carnets de voyage*, combining text and image. To focus on *Pour une littérature voyageuse* is, however, to assess only part of the current state of travel writing in the French-speaking world. The choice of contributors to the movement's manifesto (there were no women included, and no non-metropolitan authors) reveals the guild identity that underpinned its conception of travel writing and the policing of generic boundaries this understanding entailed. These issues were partly addressed in the 2007 manifesto relating to *littérature-monde*, in whose formulation Le Bris again played a key role and amongst whose signatories were a number of prominent Francophone postcolonial authors. This document – and other publications relating to it – signalled, however, a shift away from any exclusive emphasis on travel writing and an engagement in more general debates about the decolonisation of traditional binary divisions between 'French' and 'Francophone' literatures.

The future of French-language travel writing in the twenty-first century remains uncertain, especially as the emergence of innovative subgenres dependent on new technologies (e.g. the travel blog) has been accompanied by a recent diversification of the format of more conventional travelogues to intersect with other genres such as the *bande dessinée*. Fear of the genre's imminent collapse – often associated with the decline of cultural diversity, identified most notably by Victor Segalen, as a result of mechanised transport and the entropic forces of globalisation – persists; but this is increasingly complemented by a sense of the periodic reinvention of travel writing and renewal of the gaze and engagement with place on which it depends. At the

same time, a redefinition of the form and an expansion of its generic boundaries – to include work by non-metropolitan and women authors – permits
fresh innovation, with a new generation of travel writers, including figures
such as Antoine Potoski and Brice Bégout, who increasingly eschew traditional exoticism and seek innovation in terms of forms adopted and objects
studied.

Travel writing from beyond metropolitan France

The reluctance of the *Pour une littérature voyageuse* movement to expand
beyond a core consisting primarily of French travel writers in order to include
non-metropolitan authors reflects a more general dominance of the form
throughout the twentieth century (and before) by groups of authors clearly
defined by class, gender, and ethnicity. Despite such restrictions, 'travel'
remains a generalised activity and journey narratives, published and unpublished, are produced by a wide range of authors in forms that are perhaps
not traditionally deemed 'travel writing', but might fit with a more general
category of 'travel literature'. Francophone postcolonial literature, following its emergence in the inter-war period, was heavily reliant on journey
narratives, as key early novels such as Bakary Diallo's *Force-Bonté* (1926) and
Sembene's *Mirages de Paris* (1937) make amply clear.[5] This is also the case with
the foundational texts of Negritude, such as Aimé Césaire's *Cahier d'un retour
au pays natal* (1939) or Léon-Gontran Damas's *Retour de Guyane* (1938), both
of which institute a francophone Caribbean reflection on travel, space, and
displacement that has perhaps reached its most sophisticated recent stage in
the writings of Édouard Glissant.

Glissant's first work, *Soleil de la conscience* (1956), may be read as an early
example of postcolonial travel writing. It recounts its author's experiences as a
Caribbean traveller recently arrived in Paris, exoticising in the process France
itself and reflecting on the transatlantic connections on which its author's
travels depend. The 1950s saw the appearance of other major francophone
travel writing, produced in the context of decolonisation. Bernard Dadié's
epistolary text *Un nègre à Paris* is an ironic and pseudo-ethnographic account
of a West African traveller's journey to Paris presented in the tradition of
Montesquieu's *Lettres persanes*. This was followed by two further travelogues,
Patron de New York (1964) and *La Ville où nul ne meurt* (1968), chronicles of

---

5 M. Mortimer, *Journeys through the French-African Novel* (Portsmouth, NH: Heinemann, 1990).

journeys to the United States and Italy. Dadié is perhaps the most visible non-European travel writer in French, but he is by no means the only one.[6] The Togolese author Tété-Michel Kpomassie published *L'Africain du Groenland* in 1981, disrupting assumptions about the authorship of travel writing and providing a clear indication of the direction the genre might take in the postcolonial period. This potential renewal is not yet widely apparent, not least because much travel writing seems to be persistently associated with the imagery, rhetoric, and assumptions of earlier colonial narratives and seen even as the repository of a certain imperial nostalgia. Travel nevertheless remains a key element of postcolonial literature in French, central to the ambivalent accounts of 'return journeys' – fictional and non-fictional – written by authors of immigrant origin such as Azouz Begag and Kim Lefèvre.

Women's travel writing in French

Just as the guild identity with which travel writing has often been associated suggests exclusion in terms of an author's origin and ethnicity, so the policing of generic boundaries has also often revealed a gendered dimension. In the same way, however, travel writing has remained a consistently permeable form, with women's travelogues constituting an important if often occluded aspect of the genre. The myth of male mobility and female sessility, despite its power as a social regulator and even as a means of oppression, has always been challenged by the existence of travel narratives by female authors. Such a tradition became particularly apparent in the inter-war period, when new technologies of travel and communication were combined with a growing sense of female emancipation. There were prominent women aviators, such as Maryse Bastié, who made a series of record-breaking flights in the 1930s and published her memoirs, *Ailes ouvertes: carnet d'une aviatrice*, in 1937. It was, however, a number of women reporters who made the greatest impact through their travel writing. With two texts, *Un mois chez les filles* (1928) and *Un mois chez les hommes* (1929), Maryse Choisy inaugurated an investigative method dependent on disguise that would influence subsequent travel writing, including the work of more recent authors such as Marc Boulet. Transvestism – a method of facilitating cross-cultural travel already apparent among nineteenth-century travellers such as René Caillé and Isabelle Eberhardt – is central to a number of inter-war travelogues, such as Michel Vieuchange's *Smara* (posthumously

---

6 A. Ní Loingsigh, *Postcolonial Eyes: Intercontinental Travel in Francophone African Literature* (Liverpool: Liverpool University Press, 2009).

published in 1932) and Alexandra David-Neel's *Voyage d'une Parisienne à Lhassa* (1927).

Other women travellers during this period tended to eschew such disguise and rely instead on the credentials provided for them by the newspapers they represented. Titaÿna, author of *La Caravane des morts* (1930), wrote for *Paris-Soir* throughout the 1920s and 1930s, and Andrée Viollis, reporter with *Le Petit Parisien*, travelled throughout the Soviet Union, Afghanistan, India, and Indochina, writing key works combining travelogue and reportage such as *L'Inde contre les Anglais* (1930) and *Indochine S.O.S.* (1935). Ella Maillart worked for a period for the same paper as Viollis, undertaking journeys in China that formed the basis of her best-selling travel narrative, *Oasis interdites* (1937). This journey account – written as a counterpart to Peter Fleming's narrative of the same journey, *News from Tartary* (1936) – brought Maillart to public attention on both sides of the Channel, and she was for several years lionised by the literary establishment. *La Voie cruelle*, the account of a journey made to Afghanistan in 1939 in the company of Annemarie Schwarzenbach, was published only after the Second World War, which Maillart spent in India.

The remaining fifty years of Maillart's life, until her death in 1997, were spent in relative obscurity, and her withdrawal from public life coincided with a decline in the visibility of women travel writers. Very little conventional travel writing was published by women in the decades following the Second World War, although established authors continued to produce travel-related works, often with an openly ideological agenda, such as Simone de Beauvoir's diaries of journeys to the USA (*L'Amérique au jour le jour*, 1948) and China (*La Longue Marche*, 1957). Muriel Cerf's *L'Antivoyage* (1974), a highly personal account of the hippy trail, rapidly became a *livre-culte*, but remained an exception, and it was only with the advent of the *Pour une littérature voyageuse* movement that women's travelogues began to re-emerge, most notably the work of Maillart and Isabelle Eberhardt, re-published after a long period out of print. In the 1990s, important travel narratives appeared by women authors – such as Nicole-Lise Bernheim's accounts of her journeys in Japan and South-East Asia – but were not associated with the mainstream resurgence of travel writing. These divisions along gender lines are slowly being eroded, however, with the emergence of a new generation of women travel writers such as Amandine Roche and Caroline Riegel.

Travel literature remains a key means of exploring modern and contemporary literature in French, not least because it functions as a federating form that brings together a variety of material ranging from the paraliterary to the avant-garde and experimental. Throughout the twentieth century, the genre has regularly been poised between fragmentation and diversification, seen as a glory-hole in which a variety of texts are assembled or as an exclusive category whose boundaries are jealously policed by its principal practitioners. Recent developments – relating to a prising open of both form and potential authorship – suggest that the form is at a stage of evolution rather than decline. Moreover, a renewed interest among travel writers in questions of ethics suggests that the genre continues to play a key role in the literary exploration of the hypercomplexity of a globalised, postcolonial world.

72

French cinema, 1895–2010

T. JEFFERSON KLINE

France is a country that thinks. There is hardly an ideology that we haven't turned into a theory. We have in our libraries enough to talk about for centuries to come. This is why I would like to tell you: Enough thinking, already! Roll up your sleeves! (Christine Lagarde, French minister of finance)[1]

Christine Lagarde's words should come as no surprise to any non-Frenchman who has struggled with that country's cinema. It is, after all, more than geography, language, or even cuisine, that makes the French French (and their cinema so indelibly 'foreign' to Anglo-Saxon audiences). Indeed, what finally separates and defines French cinema from Hollywood and other national cinemas can best be discerned not so much by the totality of films produced and shot on French soil, nor by the various movements and genres that have occupied French filmmakers (such as le Film d'Art, Impressionism, or Poetic Realism), but rather this very Gallic tendency to 'think... to turn ideology into theory' and to write (inject) theory into every cultural artefact they produce. I would like to demonstrate in the following pages, then, the ways in which the 'shadow of theory' guides, problematises and ultimately defines the very charged and intricate existence of the seventh art in France.

Auguste Lumière's report near the end of 1894, that his brother Louis had 'in one night, invented the Cinematographe', founds France's claim to be the cradle of the cinema.[2] The first public demonstration of Lumière's apparatus in Paris on 22 March 1895 was but the first step in the production and promotion of hundreds of short films that were to establish France as the world leader in film exports. And yet the French domination of world production lasted only fifteen years, until about 1910. Despite a rapid organisation of the industry, principally

---

1 Cited in the *Boston Globe*, 22 July 2007, p. A14.
2 Cited in G. Sadoul, *Histoire générale du cinéma*, 6 vols. (Paris: Denoël, 1948), I, p. 210. Translation is mine.

by Léon Gaumont and Georges Pathé, the French grossly underestimated the competition that was to arise from America, and in general failed to appreciate the rapidly evolving art of the medium they felt they had so easily laid sole claim to. This grand failure (exacerbated, of course, by the arrival of World War I and the disastrous collapse of the French industry during the war years) was predicated on three quite symptomatic elements that would haunt the French industry from its inception to the present day: the theoretical assumptions about the medium (immediately articulated by its inventors, ignored by the early practitioners, then embraced enthusiastically by later cineastes); assumptions about the cultural sophistication of film audiences (at first films were too condescending, then overly elitist); and finally demography (which repeatedly bankrupted the major French studios and forced France to turn to its independents).

The Lumières' invention of the cinematograph came at the end of a century whose epistemology Michel Foucault has characterised as being founded in the discovery of history and of evolution, and consequently in the search for an unmediated representation of nature as it evolved.[3] Throughout the nineteenth century, then, as Alan Williams has pointed out, the French behaved as though they were rehearsing for the invention of cinema by pursuing simultaneously the development of photography (J. N. Niépce and Joseph Daguerre), the science of the optical synthesis of motion (Joseph Plateau and Emile Reynaud), and the analysis of movement (Eadweard Muybridge and Jules Marey).[4] The invention of the cinema was never intended to provide mass entertainment, but to perfect a tool for scientific analysis. Louis Lumière would insist that his 'endeavors were the endeavors of technological research, never what they call "mise-en-scene"'. Noel Burch argues that the Lumière brothers saw themselves as scientists whose subjects filmed by the camera could best be compared to 'the behavior of a micro-organism under the biologist's microscope, or the movement of stars at the end of the astronomer's telescope'.[5] Their machine, he claims, belonged to the 'rationalist tradition . . . and it was this tradition that so decisively over-determined films that were to exert a real hegemony over production and consumption internationally for a number of years'.[6] French cinema, in fact, would never

---

3 M. Foucault, *Les Mots et les choses* (Paris: Gallimard, 1966), pp. 229–313.
4 A. Williams, *Republic of Images* (Cambridge, MA: Harvard University Press, 1992), pp. 9–19.
5 N. Burch, *Life to those Shadows*, trans. B. Brewster (Berkeley: University of California Press, 1990), pp. 18–19.
6 Ibid., pp. 16–20 *passim*.

lose this spirit of theoretical inquiry (a trait it shared with all the other arts and human sciences in France throughout the twentieth century). It is not without interest that the Lumières baptised their invention as the *Cinématograph* (*writing* in movement), while Edison, across the Atlantic (where the cinema would by 1914 leap into a position of world dominance it has never relinquished), called his machine the *Vitascope* (a vision of *life*). These two terms perfectly adumbrate the entire set of differences that will come to define and oppose classical Hollywood cinema from its French counterpart. Whereas the early success of the French cinema was due to the fascination exerted by scenes of exotic places, it was soon overtaken and overrun by an American medium satisfying a much more fundamental desire to see stories in which one could lose oneself in an illusion of otherness.

The second symptom of the early failure of the French film industry lay in the assumptions that circulated about the cultural sophistication of this new art. Because of its early successes at fairs, then in vaudeville halls and peep shows settings, the cinema was assumed to appeal to the lower classes (in an extremely class-conscious culture) and the upper-middle classes refused to 'buy into' this kind of lowbrow entertainment. In America, as Burch reports, the medium was quickly aimed at a more affluent, urban, and upwardly mobile social stratum.[7] Because they turned a blind eye to the growing evidence of foreign competition, the French producers did not immediately seek to broaden the cultural and financial appeal of their product. Then, when the industry collapsed during the First World War, the French found themselves on two equally problematic tracks. One had to do with the attempt to reach the urban educated culture by creating Le Film d'Art, a vision of the cinema which limited it to reproducing intellectually acceptable literature and theatre, borrowing the techniques and actors of the Parisian stage. The second even more disastrous track grew out of the misperception that Hollywood's more grandiose approach could be replicated in France. And here we meet the ultimate problematic of French (and other national) cinema(s): demographics. Hollywood could, by the mid-1920s, count on audiences of upwards of 100 million viewers for its most popular films; this meant that it could profitably outspend the French on average by a factor of ten. When Cecil B. De Mille's film *The Cheat* arrived in France in 1915, the French immediately conceded Hollywood's technical superiority (and more spontaneous acting style). What worse way could there have been to react to this

7 Ibid., pp. 17–19.

'colonialisation' by Hollywood than to imitate the classical style, 'a financial adventure with unusually high financial risks'?[8] The result could only have been further economic ruin. The big studios (Pathé, Gaumont, and Éclair) and some of their successors (e.g. Louis Nalpas's Studios Victorine in Nice) went bankrupt trying to make super-productions that might compete. Sadly, their films tended to replicate the very factors that made what David Bordwell has termed the 'classical Hollywood style' so dominant: '(1) rules that set stringent limits on individual innovation; (2) the production of a realistic, comprehensible and unambiguous story; (3) the use of artifice through techniques of continuity and "invisible" storytelling; and (4) a fundamental emotional appeal that transcends class and nation'.[9]

The dissolution of the big studios left the French cinema in the 'happy' position of being able to become itself. The plethora of independent companies that were spawned by this colossal failure brought with them the sensible realisation that France could never compete with Hollywood on its own terms and the certainty that another route had to be pursued: quality films that stressed film's poetic possibilities.

Much of the inspiration for the new alternative cinema had already come from a flurry of journals that were founded to contest the mainstream industrial practice. Henri Diamant-Berger's *Le Film* (1916) from its inception encouraged an independent strain of film criticism that rapidly morphed into a nascent film theory articulated not just by journalists but by the 'new wave' of young film directors that invaded the studios after the First World War. It is in this first joining of theory and practice that French film proper would be born and would, in one form or another, define the French cinema until the present day. The journal *Ciné pour tous* followed in 1919, *Cinéa* in 1920, and *Mon Ciné* in February 1922. In the March 1922 issue of *Cinéa*, Louis Delluc fired the first critical broadside against the Hollywood colonisers: 'Que le cinéma français soit français! Que le cinéma français soit du cinéma!' ('Let the French cinema be French! Let the French cinema be cinematic!') In this call to arms, Delluc summoned his colleagues to reject Charles Pathé's threat that French cinema must become Americanised or disappear,[10] and furthermore to reject a cinema that was, as he put it, merely instinctive and where

8 R. Abel, *French Cinema: The First Wave, 1915–1929* (Princeton, NJ: Princeton University Press, 1984), p. 12.

9 D. Bordwell, J. Staiger, and K. Thompson, *The Classical Hollywood Cinema* (New York: Columbia University Press, 1985), p. 3.

10 Cited in N. Burch, *French Impressionist Cinema* (New York: Arno Press, 1980), p. 75. Translation is mine.

the director was 'secondary to the original authors' intentions'.[11] René Clair would note, disdainfully, 'American technique . . . is completely at the service of the progress of the story. That is also the explanation of the difference in the audience's attitude toward American films, in which the expressions are immediately accessible, and ours, which require an effort of the intelligence alone.'[12] For his part, Pierre Porte saw Hollywood film as merely 'an instrument to convey actions, a machine to recite stories . . . incapable of anything resembling speculations'.[13] Elie Faure would go so far as to call the American film industry 'primitive and at the same time barbarous'.[14] So antagonistic were these theorists that the movement turned into a kind of crusade. Jean Epstein would write, 'Le cinema est à sa période d'apostolat, à une époque qui correspond, pour l'histoire des religions, à leur époque militant . . . [Nous sommes] des missionaires que la Cause envoie pour préparer ses triomphes et pour évangéliser les barbares.' ('Cinema is in its apostolic period, at a moment which, in the history of religions, would be termed its militant period. We are missionaries whom the Cause sends out to prepare the way for victory and to evangelise the barbarians.')[15]

To carry forward this crusade against the invasion of the American barbaric and instinctual pleasure palace, these young French directors began asking the question that was later to animate André Bazin and the entire post-World War II generation of cineastes, 'What is cinema?'[16] Although this question never arises in Hollywood directors' musings on their medium,[17] the French almost immediately begin an attempt to define film as a work of art, '*a Painting and a Sculpture developing in Time*' (original emphasis)[18] which 'translates, develops, explicates or intensifies reality'.[19] Jean Epstein predicts that 'within five years we will compose cinematographic poems'.[20]

From this position it was but a short step to see the cinema as a language, 'a form of ideographic writing',[21] and Jean Epstein set out 'to establish

---

11 Cited in R. Abel, *French Film Theory and Criticism: 1907–1939*, 2 vols. (Princeton, NJ: Princeton University Press, 1988), I, p. 144.

12 Ibid., p. 305.   13 Ibid., p. 385.   14 Ibid., pp. 263.

15 Cited in Bordwell, *French Impressionist Cinema*, p. 52. Translation is mine.

16 A. Bazin, *Qu'est-ce que le cinéma?* (Paris: Cerf, 1958), translated by H. Gray as *What Is Cinema?* (Berkeley: University of California Press, 1967).

17 See E. Bowser, *The Transformation of Cinema, 1907–1918* (Berkeley: University of California Press, 1990), and R. Koszarski, *An Evening's Entertainment: The Age of the Silent Feature Picture, 1915–1928* (Berkeley: University of California Press, 1990).

18 R. Canudo, cited in Abel, *French Film Theory and Criticism: 1907–1939*, I, p. 59.

19 L. Delluc, *Photogénie* (Paris: De Brunhoff, 1920), pp. 11–12.

20 J. Epstein, 'Le Cinéma et les lettres modernes', in J. Epstein, *La Poésie d'aujourd'hui: un nouvel état d'intelligence* (Paris: Éditions de la Sirène, 1921), p. 177.

21 E. Vuillermoz, cited in Abel, *French Film Theory and Criticism: 1907–1939*, I, p. 206.

the premises for a cinematic grammar or rhetoric . . . a grammar peculiar to itself'.[22] This new 'cinégraphie' would become, in Abel Gance's words, 'a new language, a mode of expression of rhythms and truth'.[23]

All of this talk about cinema as poetry with its own language represented a concerted effort to raise the seventh art from the gutter of lower-class entertainment to the salons of Paris's intellectual elite, a concern frequently betrayed by such proclamations as: '[Our films] require an effort of the intelligence alone'[24] and their 'unique specificity'[25] is to be 'a veritable art infused with artistic and intellectual elements',[26] 'a vision we have *intellectually conceived* to transmit to film' (my emphasis),[27] and representing 'an evolution on the intellectual plane'.[28] The cinema director has become 'a poet and scholar-scientist,'[29] working in the 'hope of raising the intellectual level of the cinema'.[30]

We are so far indeed from the Hollywood pleasure palace that throughout this writing in the 1920s (and later) we will encounter the idea that cinema 'must never be a place where the viewer finds pleasure . . . The film must always be something that disturbs . . . it must be completely intolerable for the viewer'.[31] The same theorist who cried 'Let French cinema be French' would go on to assert that the role of the French cinema is to cause *alarm*.[32] In describing the efficacity of the close-up, Jean Epstein would rejoice that 'pain is within reach'.[33] All of which leads one critic to wonder 'might the Latin genius be badly suited to the art of the screen? It's a genius especially well suited to eloquence and conclusive reasoning, but perhaps hostile to the elliptical and silent power of film . . . The French mind', he bemoans, 'may be too rational to possess those qualities of frankness [and] impulsiveness' requisite to good film.[34]

No wonder that *La Passion de Jeanne d'Arc* (1928) is considered the consummate film of the 1920s, for, in its unrelenting insistence on the close-up of Marie Falconetti, Carl Dreyer communicates at once the exquisitely painful

22 J. Epstein, 'L'Elément photogénique', *Ciné-Ciné-pour-tous* no. 12 (1 May 1924), p. 7.
23 A. Gance, 'Images d'hier et voix de demain', *Cinéopse*, no. 125 (January 1930), p. 26.
24 R. Clair cited in Abel, *French Film Theory and Criticism: 1907–1939*, I, p. 305.
25 P. Porte, cited ibid., p. 387.
26 L. Robert, cited in Sadoul, *Histoire générale du cinema*, I, p. 414. Translation is mine.
27 G. Dulac, cited in Abel, *French Film Theory and Criticism: 1907–1939*, I, p. 308.
28 H. Fescourt and J.-L. Bouquet, cited ibid., p. 384.   29 L. Moussinac, cited ibid., p. 250.
30 E. Vuillermoz, cited ibid., p. 225.
31 P. Garrell, cited in J. Forbes, *The Cinema in France after the New Wave* (London: British Film Institute, 1992), pp. 127–8.
32 L. Delluc, cited in Abel, *French Film Theory and Criticism: 1907–1939*, I, p. 285.
33 J. Epstein, cited ibid., I, p. 239.   34 G. Altman, cited ibid., II, p. 82.

beauty accessible to film and suggests the sacrifices necessary for the film's author to bring this experience to light. The film is, however, but one of a series of poetic masterworks of narrative cinema that punctuate the decade, each more experimental than the last.[35] Émile Vuillermoz, the foremost proponent of a cinema that would oppose the Americanisation and regularised aesthetic of Hollywood, saw Abel Gance's *La Roue* (1924) as the very image of what the cinema could be.[36] Jean Epstein agreed, calling it 'la révélation des moyens propres du cinéma et sa capacité d'être un art autonome' ('the revelation of cinema's own means and its capacity to be an autonomous art'), all the while busying himself with producing a series of highly experimental poetic masterpieces such as *La Glace à trois faces* (1927) and *La Chute de la maison d'Usher* (1928).[37]

All of these (and others by L'Herbier *et al.*) maximised the use of lighting, rapid montage, and various tricks of slow motion, superimposition of images, and camera angles to create a series of films that repeatedly tested not only the boundaries of narrative film, but the limits of the audience's ability to comprehend their films. There can be no doubt that letting 'French cinema be French and be cinema' meant a robust dialogue between various theories on the ontology of the cinema coupled with a practice that excited, challenged, and often antagonised audiences. And although Bordwell labels this group of films 'Impressionist cinema', the fact is that the films were produced by individual poet-cineastes who imagined themselves as authors, writing in images against the grain of a tradition they abhorred, more outlaws than participants in a movement. Indeed, the filmmaker as outlaw was to become a favourite signature of French cinema for the next eighty years.[38]

This model of a series of independents awash in film theory and battling the 'imbeciles' (the word is Louis Delluc's)[39] who peopled the major studios in both France and America would become *the* model for French film. In the 1930s the particular slant of the theoretical debates and the persons mobilising them would shift, but the overall pattern persisted of 'a large number

---

35 I have omitted surrealist and other exercises in pure avant-garde film as lying outside the confines of the present essay on narrative cinema, although their excessive side is well known.

36 E. Vuillermoz, cited in Abel, *French Film Theory and Criticism: 1907–1939*, I, pp. 274–5.

37 J. Epstein, cited in J. Mitry, *Histoire du cinéma*, 5 vols. (Paris: Éditions Universitaires, 1969), II, p. 437.

38 Consider the following as exemplars: Lacenaire, the dramatist of Carné's *Les Enfants du paradis* (1945); Antoine Doinel, the bad boy of Truffaut's *Les 400 coups* (1959); Michel Poiccard, the invent-as-you-go hero of Godard's *À bout de souffle* (1960); and Michel the pickpocket in Bresson's *Pickpocket* (1959), to mention but a few.

39 L. Delluc in Abel, *French Film Theory and Criticism: 1907–1939*, I, p. 285.

of small and undercapitalized production companies working in competition and combination with each other',[40] the result of a weak industry and extremely healthy 'subclass' of *'auteurs'*. Of course, the end of the silent era wrought enormous upheaval both in a French industry ill-equipped to make the transition to sound (either in production studios or in France's 4,000 'salles') and in the arena of debates about the significance of sound to 'pure' cinematic practice. Of these two, the theoretical questions, of course, rapidly drowned out the practical ones. (The industry adapted, more slowly than it should have done, but it *did* adapt.[41]) Meanwhile the new theoretical debate centred on the 'dangers' of filmed theatre. On the one hand, Sacha Guitry would trumpet, 'If the French cinema is to be absolutely itself' it must rely on 'French genius, i.e. language, the profound or spiritual words which render beauty lasting'.[42] Guitry's antagonists lamented the dominance of 'bad theatre' and urged the renewal of a cinema based on 'composition, balance, rhythm', and appealing 'to the eyes that see'.[43] And if a certain 'poetic realism' was the dominant movement of the decade because the advent of sound forced many directors back into the studio, the great *auteurs* continued to address the theoretical debates each in his own idiosyncratic way. Cinematic debate entered the political arena as well during this era of the Popular Front. Marcel Carné condemned French cinema for betraying its original hopes and 'ignoring the profound unrest of our time, the urgent problems at hand',[44] and Jean Renoir joined Le Groupe Octobre to produce *La Vie est à nous*, the most directly political film of the entire decade. He would then cap a decade of furious production (fourteen films!) with *La Règle du jeu*, now considered not only a direct cinematic illustration of Bazin's theory of deep focus, but also a blistering satire of the French upper classes. Carné's *Les Enfants du paradis* raises its curtain on a history of the nineteenth-century theatre in such a way as to reopen if not resolve all the debates about filmed theatre. Throughout

40 C. Crisp in M. Temple and M. Witt (eds.), *The French Cinema Book* (London: British Film Institute, 2004), p. 119.

41 One of the more ingenious but ill-fated schemes was to make multilingual films with several casts of actors speaking the same lines on the same sets in as many as eight different languages. See G. Vincendeau, 'Hollywood Babel: The Coming of Sound and the Multiple Language Version', in A. Higson and R. Maltby (eds.), *'Film Europe' and 'Film America': Cinema, Commerce and Cultural Exchange 1920–1939* (New York: Continuum, 1999), pp. 207–24.

42 S. Guitry, in Abel, *French Film Theory and Criticism: 1907–1939*, II, pp. 101–2.

43 M. Bardèche and R. Brasillach, *History of the Film*, trans. I. Barry (London: Allen and Unwin, 1945), p. 411; Le Corbusier, 'Spirit of Truth', in Abel, *French Film Theory and Criticism: 1907–1939*, II, p. 113.

44 M. Carné, 'Cinema and the World', ibid., II, p. 103.

the decade, then, theoretical debate and film production continue hand in hand.

The French film industry experienced a curious renaissance during the German Occupation due primarily to the establishment of Continental Films, financed with German money and encouragement. Following the Occupation, however, and weakened by restrictions imposed by the Vichy government and the Germans, the industry again found itself pitted for its survival against a wave of American films, legitimised by the 1946 Blum–Byrnes accords which opened the door to the immense resources of Hollywood. To survive in the new world market (and with the growing competition from television), French producers went back to the tried and untrue formula of reliance on extravagant costume dramas, adapted for the most part from popular novels. The more successful French films of the late 1940s and early 1950s (e.g. Autant-Lara's adaptation of Stendhal's *The Red and the Black* and Christian-Jacques's adaptation of Zola's *Nana*) resorted to the seamless continuity of classical Hollywood decoupage.

Such films became increasingly stigmatised as 'the tradition of quality' and '*le cinéma de papa*' by a small but extremely vocal group of critics writing for *Les Cahiers du cinéma*, founded in 1951 by Jacques Doniol-Valcroze, Lo Duca, and André Bazin, whose 'Evolution of the Language of Cinema', later anthologised in *What is Cinema?*, set the tone for the journal's aggressive questioning of the nature and language of film. The *Cahiers* group soon grew to include several younger critics, notably François Truffaut, Jean-Luc Godard, Eric Rohmer (the pen name of Maurice Scherer), Claude Chabrol, and Jacques Rivette, all inflamed by passionate debates nourished by Henri Langlois's eclectic programming at the Cinémathèque Française in the rue d'Ulm.

Impatient with a rigidly hierarchical and 'corporatist' industry, these young critics, led by Truffaut, launched a series of vitriolic attacks on what they viewed as the cynical psychological realism of a cinema dominated by mediocre script-writers who were butchering great literature in the service of their own purportedly more cinematic styles. In his now famous 'A Certain Tendency of French Cinema' (*Cahiers*, January 1954), Truffaut argued that film directors should be responsible for the entire process of film production: composition of the scenario, shooting, and editing of the film – should be, in short, sole authors of their films. *La politique des auteurs* quickly became the password at the *Cahiers*, and Truffaut went on to win the *palmes* at Cannes the next year for his quasi-autobiographical, low-budget *The Four Hundred Blows*. Suddenly there was a swarm of new directors storming the walls of the film industry and the term *nouvelle vague* had gained currency as a designation not so much of a specific style or even a group of filmmakers, but of a cultural phenomenon. Measured purely in numbers of new directors, the industry crested in 1958, doubling the number of films made by new directors to thirty-three over the following four years. Because of the proven success of *The Four Hundred Blows*, and Godard's *Breathless*, producers suddenly saw small low-budget films as having significant enough economic potential to gamble on other new directors. Within three years of Truffaut's success at Cannes, *Les Cahiers du cinema* devoted its December 1962 issue to *la nouvelle vague*. In all, *Cahiers* counted 162 new directors of feature films and added numerous 'precursors': Alexandre Astruc, who in 1948 had already argued in 'Le caméra-stylo' that film was a means of writing that was just as flexible and subtle as written language;[45] Agnès Varda, who wanted to 'make a film like one writes a book', had taken up the *cinécriture* torch in *La Pointe courte* (1954), and filmed without authorisation, stars, or respect for union or administrative rules; and Robert Bresson who, well before any of the 'New Wave' directors arrived, had been experimenting with cinematic language in a series of rigorously anti-theatrical and Saussurean films, culminating in his 1959 masterpiece, *Pickpocket*. This list of precursors caused the New Wave to look uncannily like a re-visitation of the 1920s avant-garde spirit of Epstein, L'Herbier, Clair, and Delluc. Thus from the present perspective the 'New Wave' appears riddled with paradoxes: a 'group' which was not one, an insistence on novelty despite an acknowledged debt to earlier theorists and filmmakers, an anti-industry movement which could not have succeeded without significant governmental support, a 'revolution' without any discernible political doctrine, and a disdain for quality by young directors, most of whom rushed to create commercially successful films and thereby hastened a return to the industry's status quo. Nor can the New Wave be said to have reformed mainstream French taste: Hollywood spectacles and traditional French comedies continued to dominate the French box office from 1958 to 1968.

Surely the most significant legacy of the New Wave derives from Godard's and Resnais's radical break with the dominant cinema's illusion of narrative seamlessness and visual continuity. They did not so much invent a practice (that had already had its heyday in the 1920s) as articulate, and thereby expose, cinematic *découpage* as an ontologically fragmented, discontinuous discourse. Godard's jump cuts, self-conscious actors, playful sound track, idiosyncratic

---

45 A. Astruc, 'Naissance d'une nouvelle avant-garde: le caméra stylo', *L'Écran français* 144 (1948). Reprinted and translated as 'The Birth of a New Avant-Garde: Le Caméra-Stylo', in T. Corrigan (ed.), *Film and Literature: An Introduction and Reader* (Saddle River, NJ: Prentice Hall, 1999), pp. 158–62.

use of film grammar, and Renais's experiments with narrative discourse, all foreground a meta-cinematic practice. This renewed emphasis on cinematic language not surprisingly coincided with the emergence of structuralism, semiology, and Lacanian psychoanalysis in France, together creating an aperture in critical thinking that has had a lasting and profound effect on our understanding of the medium itself. Within fifteen years of the emergence of what we must re-baptise the *Next* Wave, a host of theoretical writings emerged which reopened the debates of the 1920s: Christian Metz would re-pose the question of cinematic language in *Langage et cinéma* (1971) and the 1975 issue of *Communications* would fairly bristle with essays such as Jean-Louis Baudry's inquiry into film's relationship to dreams, Metz's semiotic examination of 'le déplaisir filmique' (a French topic if there ever was one), Nick Browne's examination of the rhetoric of cinema, as well as essays by Barthes, Rosolato, Guattari, and Kristeva that examined the nature of the medium from a psychoanalytic point of view. Meanwhile, these same questions were being exposed in such films as Truffaut's *Story of Adèle H.* in which the eponymous heroine literally becomes a figure of the dream; in Agnès Varda's *Sans toit ni loi*, where 'cinécriture' is allowed free play; and in Beineix's *Diva*, 'un cinéma poétique total'[46] reminiscent of Epstein's *Fall of the House of Usher*, but with a postmodern twist.

It is fair to say that over the next quarter of a century French cinema never lost its double articulation of independent auteurism and a self-conscious reliance on theoretical debate. Wave after wave of independent filmmakers worked consistently against the 'classical model of decoupage' to create films that would challenge, provoke and alarm their audiences. Despite yet another spate of 'prestigious big-budget films' such as Arnaud's *Name of the Rose* (1986), Claude Berri's *Jean de Florette* (1986), and Nuttyens / Adjani's *Camille Claudel*, these films, as Phil Powrie notes, did not always bring success in France, and were even less successful abroad.[47] Otherwise, the French independent filmmakers continued in their aberrant ways with films such as Besson's *Subway* (1985) which systematically breaks all the rules of the genre, or Carax's *Mauvais sang* (1986), described by Frederic Jameson as 'schizophrenic experience of isolated, disconnected, discontinuous material signifiers which fail to link up into coherent sequence'.[48] Even the 'cinema du look' which was characterised by

46 Cited in D. Parent, *Jean-Jacques Beineix: version originale* (Paris: Barrault Studio, 1989), p. 256.
47 P. Powrie, *French Cinema in the 1980s: Nostalgia and the Crisis of Masculinity* (Oxford: Oxford University Press, 1997).
48 F. Jameson, 'Postmodernism and Consumer Society', in H. Foster (ed.), *The Anti-Aesthetic: Essays on Postmodern Culture* (London: Pluto, 1985), pp. 111–26, at p. 119.

technical mastery of the medium in service of superficial spectacle would be defended by one of its practitioners as an effort to 'kidnap color [and] dispense with stories' – a very un-American film project. In the 1990s such subversion continued with Chéreau's *La Reine Margot* (1994), which worked constantly to subvert the expectations of the historical costume drama and to break down the comfortable distance usually provided by such historical panoramas. Carax's *Les Amants du Pont-Neuf* (1991), the most expensive production ever mounted in France, could only be described as a combination of grunge film posing as romance and a skein of allusions to other French masterpieces. And the introduction of theory into an otherwise ordinary drama of 'mismatched lovers' makes Benoît Jacquot's *Septième ciel* (1997) perhaps the most emblematic French film of the 1990s. Jacquot's heroine, Mathilde (Sandrine Kiberlain), is caught reading François Roustang's *Qu'est-ce que l'hypnose?* early on, and thereafter seems not only to 'invent' the hypnotist who will save her marriage, but to implement Roustang's theory in such a way that it becomes a double of cinema itself, suggesting that Roustang's title and Bazin's *Qu'est-ce que le cinéma?* be in some mysterious way imbricated in a new version of hypno-cinematography. Indeed, no matter how much the industry (and government subvention of industry) tries to get beyond 'auteurism' it remains paradoxically 'central to French film production and its sense of cultural worth . . . while also being peripheral, since much auteur work defines itself in opposition to mainstream cinema'.[49] As French film entered the twenty-first century, a new aesthetic emerged, labelled 'the cinema of sensation', offering a sense of experimentation, speculation, and renewal around the 'capture and reshaping of pro-filmic reality' which blurs accepted definitions and identities and undermines the very distinction between subject and object. According to Martine Beugnet, the work of Claire Denis, Pascal Ferran, Catherine Breillat, and Bruno Dumont 'always hovers at the edge of pleasure and abjection – between the appeal of a sensuous perception and exploration of the reality portrayed, and the close encounter with the abject'.[50] This new group of filmmakers, then, continues French cinema's struggle with the shadow of theory in the realm of unpleasure, for, as Christine Lagarde says, the French just cannot seem to stop thinking and theorising. It could also be that the two most interesting films of the first decade of the new century are Anne Fontaine's *Comment j'ai tué mon père* which can be read as proposing a very Derridean

---

49 P. Powrie, *French Cinema in the 1990s: Continuity and Difference* (Oxford: Oxford University Press, 1998), p. 1.
50 M. Beugnet, *Cinema and Sensation: French Film and the Art of Transgression* (Edinburgh: Edinburgh University Press, 2007).

notion of cinema as mourning, and Benoît Jacquot's *Princesse Marie* which raises disturbing questions about cinema and seduction. There may be other films in France that escape this Gallic penchant for lucubration and opposition to convention, but they are certainly less interesting than the ones that succomb to it (*pace* Ms Lagarde) and they are definitely less French (as Louis Delluc would happily agree), less complex, and doubtless less intellectually stimulating.

73

Writing, memory, and history

NICHOLAS HEWITT

In 1915, the Action Française journalist Léon Daudet published an essay entitled '*L'Entre-deux-guerres*'. The essay, in fact, was a survey of French politics and literary milieux from 1870 to 1914 from a Royalist and anti-Republican perspective, and, as such, added little to previous Action française polemic. Its significance, however, lies in the title itself, which pre-dates the more common connotation of 'entre-deux-guerres' as the period between the end of the First World War and the beginning of the Second. As such, in the same way that Marshal Foch is alleged to have declared that the Versailles Peace Conference did not usher in peace, but merely a twenty-year armistice, the pre-existence of a term for a period between wars signifies that, for the French, any point between 1918 and 1939 could be viewed, and indeed was viewed, as part of the inevitable progress towards renewed conflict. This consciousness of living through a stay of execution inflects on the processes of French memory in and of the inter-war years and beyond and the writing which translated that memory, not least in terms of the Occupation, the 'guerre franco-française' of 1944–5, and the colonial wars in Indochina and North Africa. This in its turn leads to various overlapping and interlocking conjunctures of memory, history, and writing, initially centred on a number of apparently distinct periods and locations, but which merge and reposition themselves as the memory recedes into the past. Central amongst these are the First World War, the inter-war years – with their evocations of material progress and social conflict – the defeat of 1940, followed by the Occupation, Resistance, and Collaboration, and the Liberation and *Épuration*, and the wars in Indochina and Algeria which dominated the period from the end of the Second World War to the first term of de Gaulle's presidency.

This process of memory involves complex patterns of writing, both fictional and non-fictional, and often written in the form of memoirs. These are typically written during the periods in question, purporting to be eyewitness accounts, or as soon after the period as possible, but if they survive their immediate transient purpose through re-publishing, they take on an afterlife all of their own which can form part of the collective memory of those who took no part in the events whatsoever. The case of Irène Némirovsky is exemplary in this regard: written in 1940–2, before the author's deportation and death, *Suite française* was published over sixty years later, and posthumously awarded the Prix Renaudot in 2004, which resurrected her by then largely forgotten oeuvre, contributing to the memory of the inter-war years and the Occupation, of which all but a minority of French citizens could claim direct experience. The same phenomenon may be identified in the continuing survival of, for example, classic novels from the First World War or accounts of the early period of colonialism in the inter-war years.

In this context, one of the most useful, and most innovative, historical methodologies is Pierre Nora's collective study,[1] which explores the communal construction of French history through two interconnected phenomena: physical monuments, including memorials, especially war-memorials, which are essentially commemorative; and the more extensive 'realms of memory', in the English translation, which may involve significant topography, such as the political significance of the geography of Paris, street names, cathedrals, or gastronomy. It is no coincidence, of course, that books should play a vital role as 'places of memory', from the classic Republican geography primer, *Le Tour de France par deux enfants*, to Proust's *À la recherche du temps perdu*.

The First World War and the inter-war years

The First World War operated both as an experience in itself and as a major dividing point in French, and world, history, to the extent that it is as plausible to date the beginning of the twentieth century from 1914 or 1918 as from 1900. As such, one of its creations was the belle époque, clearly a posthumous concept valid only in subsequent periods and the product of nostalgia for a perceived golden age before the twentieth century began in earnest. In fact, it is difficult to overestimate the importance of the belle époque as a locus of memory and writing in France in the inter-war years. Alain-Fournier's *Le Grand Meaulnes*, for example, although published in 1913, only came of age when the full impact of the war was realised and when its author was dead in the first months of the conflict. In this context the 'lost domain' becomes richly associated with a world of (ambiguous) innocence forever lost, and the 'obstructed path' leading to it becomes the object of a generation of

---

1 P. Nora (ed.), *Les Lieux de mémoire* (Paris: Gallimard, 1984–92).

French historians. A similar iconic status is achieved by Proust's *À la recherche du temps perdu*. Even though the first volume, *Du côté de chez Swann*, was published in 1913, its first section, *Combray*, reads with hindsight like Alain-Fournier's novel, as the prescient eulogy for a lost world. Indeed, the entire novel takes on a powerful afterlife: in spite of the author's death in 1922, the subsequent posthumous publication of the remaining volumes throughout the 1920s provided French readers with a powerful memory of France before and during the war. At the same time, memories of the belle époque in the inter-war years were often used as tools to criticise contemporary society and culture. A case in point is that of Montmartre, the centre of the pre-war avant-garde and locus of a highly romanticised Bohemianism. After the war, many of its most distinguished participants, such as André Warnod, Francis Carco, Roland Dorgelès, and Pierre Mac Orlan, all of whom served with distinction in the conflict, along with a host of more minor figures, produced accounts of a pre-war 'Bohème' which not only idealised the belle époque but served to castigate the post-war world. In this way, Montmartre became not merely a 'lieu de mémoire', but literally a 'lieu de mémoires': a place of memoirs.

Other writers in the inter-war years were less susceptible to the charms of the belle époque: Louis Guilloux's *La Maison du peuple*, of 1926, records the misery of the provincial artisans oppressed by a dominant bourgeoisie and the way in which their attempts at organisation are thwarted by the war in what becomes a pertinent message for the French left in the inter-war years. From another perspective, Louis-Ferdinand Céline's *Mort à crédit*, of 1936, highlights the insecurity and humiliation of the pre-war Parisian petite bourgeoisie, a humiliation that would seek its revenge in the anti-Semitism and right-wing politics of the 1930s.

As would be expected, the narrative of the combats of 1914–18 dominates much of French writing in the inter-war years, both through a cascade of memoirs by *anciens combatants* and in fiction. *Le Feu*, by Henri Barbusse, appeared in 1917, and, in its evocation of the tribulations of an infantry platoon on the Western Front, subsequently helped to determine the nation's memory of the war itself. Dorgelès's *Les Croix de bois*, of 1919, followed the same narrative pattern, but with a significant twist: in his account, the war has already become memory, with the same paradoxical aura of nostalgia as that of the belle époque, leading the narrator to conclude that 'malgré tout, c'était le bon temps'. A similar ambiguity is apparent in his later novel *Le Réveil des morts* (1923), which focuses on a little-recorded but highly significant aspect of the post-war period, the reclamation and reconstruction of the 'lost territories' of northern France, occupied by the Germans and pulverised by shell-fire.

The architect sent to the north to help in its rebuilding falls in love with the widow of a French soldier, only to gradually assume the personality of the dead man: the 'réveil des morts' indicates a post-war France still inhabited and dominated by the ghosts of the one million dead, in the same way that Céline's *Voyage au bout de la nuit* not merely lampoons the conflict in a way that looks forward to Joseph Heller's *Catch-22*, but transforms post-war France into the setting for a vast 'histoire de fantômes'. This subversion and the depiction of the difficulty of reconciling the experience, and mythology, of the war with the reality of post-war civilian existence is also present in two books as different as Roger Vercel's *Capitaine Conan* (1934), which contrasts the heroism of a commando on the Balkan Front and his humdrum post-war existence as a small-town grocer, and Raymond Radiguet's novel of 1922 *Le Diable au corps*, which, from the perspective of a *lycéen* in Paris writing at the beginning of the post-war *années folles*, depicts the conflict as 'de grandes vacances pendant quatre ans'. All of these works become not merely commemorative, like the flood of war-memorials constructed after the conflict, from the grandiose *ossuaire* on the site of the battle of Verdun to the most humble village statue, but also questioning of the public rhetoric in the face of an inevitable second war.

One of the most significant fictional innovations of the inter-war years was the long novel cycle, the *roman-fleuve*, exemplified by Roger Martin du Gard's *Les Thibault* (1922–40), Georges Duhamel's *Chronique des Pasquier* (1933–41), and the twenty-seven-volume *Les Hommes de bonne volonté*, by Jules Romains, which appeared between 1932 and 1944, and taken up by amongst others Henri Troyat from the Occupation period onwards. Although deriving in part from Balzac's *La Comédie humaine* and Zola's Rougon-Macquart cycle, with their recurrent characters, these novel cycles were particularly influenced by Romain Rolland's *Jean-Christophe*, written prior to the war, a multi-volume fictional reflection on Franco-German cultural differences through the character of a French classical composer. In the *romans-fleuve* of the inter-war years, writers used the extended novel form to look back on French society of the belle époque from beyond the watershed of the war, to chart the causes of the conflict. However, as the inter-war years progressed, Daudet's implicit prophecy of a renewed war injected a fierce urgency into the novel cycles' evocation of the Western Front, which became an ultimate warning, and the fact that their final volumes were written in the midst of or following the Second World War gave them an added historical dimension. Once again, these works, only published and distributed widely after the Liberation, take on an additional afterlife.

Interestingly, this form of the novel, in which the broad historical process of French society was explored through the lives of ordinary French men and women, was accompanied by a parallel development in French historiography in the form of the formation of the *Annales* school by Lucien Febvre and Marc Bloch in 1929. As H. Stuart Hughes comments, in a radical departure from traditional historiography, 'Febvre and Bloch made the *Annales* the forum for a broadly-based history that was economic and social, geographical and psychological, all in one. The times were menacing: a review which stressed economics and the historian's concern for his own era fitted the public atmosphere of mounting crisis.'[2] In other words, in both the fiction and history of the inter-war years, the meticulous memory of the past is crucial to the understanding of the present and decoding the omens for the future.

The Second World War: Occupation, Liberation, and *Épuration*

Crucial and traumatic as the First World War was for France, it is subordinate in comparison with the impact of its successor. The slow drift to war from the mid-1930s onwards, punctuated by non-intervention in the Spanish Civil War and the collapse of the democracies at Munich, was chronicled, amongst others, by Sartre in *Les Chemins de la liberté*. Once it came, however, the war was characterised initially by a sense of strangeness: the 'drôle de guerre' of the early period, in a phrase coined by Dorgelès in his reportage of an uncanny quietness on the Western Front, followed by the lightning 'étrange défaite' evoked by Marc Bloch from his experience in the army. Julien Gracq, in *Un balcon en forêt* (1958), and Robert Merle, in *Weekend à Zuydcoote* (1949), translate the strangeness of the defeat in the Ardennes and Flanders into fictional form.

What followed, however, through four years of Occupation, was arguably the most traumatic period of French history since the Revolution, which revealed and opened up fissures in French society which have still not healed – as evidenced by the continuing fascination it exerts on historians, novelists, and general readers. The division of metropolitan France into two zones until 1942, one under direct German rule and the other under the more ambiguous administration of the Vichy regime, which had come to power in what many interpreted as an anti-Republican counter-revolution; the Collaboration, both implicit and explicit, inherent in Vichy itself and prevalent

2 H. S. Hughes, *The Obstructed Path: French Social Thought in the Years of Desperation* (New York: Harper and Row, 1969), p. 39.

in Paris; the resurgence of anti-Semitism, leading to the mass deportation and murder of foreign and French Jews; the Resistance, with its communist and non-communist, Gaullist and non-Gaullist factions, but subject to fierce repression by both German and Vichy authorities, not least through the paramilitary Vichy *milice*; the French citizens who fought in German uniform on the Eastern Front in the Légion des Volontaires Français or the Division Charlemagne of the SS; and the civil war between these various groups in 1944 and 1945 – all contributed to what amounts to a collective psychosis defined by Henry Rousso as *Le Syndrome de Vichy* (1986). In his study, Rousso points to a paradox between the constant reminders of war crimes and Collaboration, with trial reports filling the newspapers until well into the 1950s, and a collective amnesia regarding the reality of French complicity in the Occupation and the full violence of the 'guerre franco-française'. In this sense, the collective response was similar to the official view propounded by de Gaulle in 1944 of the continuity of the Republic under a Vichy regime which technically did not exist, and the minimal role of a small number of traitors and criminals who sided with the occupier while the rest of the nation resisted.

This initial period of amnesia with regard to the complex reality of the Occupation was in part created and reinforced by French writing in the immediate post-war period, both in the form of the huge number of memoirs published by former resistants and, to a certain extent, deportees, and works of fiction, such as Jean-Louis Bory's *Mon village à l'heure allemande*, of 1945, which essentially followed the official view of recent history. Already, however, this view was being contested, and from both sides of the political divide. The communist Roger Vailland's *Drôle de jeu*, of 1945, presents a picture of the Resistance which is far more playful and complex than the stereotype. Marcel Aymé's *Le Chemin des écoliers*, of 1946, consciously echoes Radiguet's *Le Diable au corps* and depicts occupied Paris through the eyes of a *lycéen* who is heavily involved in the black market and charts the progress of his father from vapid liberalism to profiteering. The Hussards, particularly Roger Nimier, Antoine Blondin, and Jacques Laurent, who were heavily indebted to Aymé, similarly proposed an alternative reading of recent history for explicitly right-wing political reasons: Laurent, in *Le Petit Canard* (1954), depicts an adolescent who becomes a collaborator by chance and is executed at the Liberation; Blondin, in *L'Europe buissonnière*, provides a burlesque account of the defeat of 1940, the Resistance, occupied in manufacturing miniature coffins to be sent to suspected collaborators, and conscripted labour in Germany and Austria; Nimier, in *Les Épées* (1945), explores the interchangeable nature of Resistance and Collaboration, and in *Le Hussard bleu* (1946) recounts the exploits of a

French army unit in the invasion of Germany in 1945 and the subsequent occupation, harried by unrepentant former members of the *milice*.

Although joined by the post-war extreme right, such as the revisionist polemicist Maurice Bardèche, the brother-in-law of the executed collaborationist writer and journalist Robert Brasillach, such examples remained relatively rare throughout the Fourth Republic and de Gaulle's presidency, under which the documentary film *Le Chagrin et la pitié* by Marcel Ophuls, which presented a highly variegated portrait of Clermont-Ferrand under the Occupation, was banned from French television. One notable exception, however, was the appearance from 1957 to 1961 of Céline's trilogy, *D'un château l'autre*, *Nord* and *Rigodon*, which chronicled the Vichy government in exile in Sigmaringen and the narrator's hallucinatory journeys through the dying Reich. In fact, it was only after de Gaulle's death that the amnesiac phase of France's collective relationship with its wartime past began to clear, in particular through the novels of Patrick Modiano, such as *Place de l'Étoile* (1968) and *La Ronde de nuit* (1969), and his scenario for Louis Malle's film *Lacombe Lucien*. This re-evaluation of Vichy and the Occupation, however, was not immune from charges of a fashionable and nostalgic *mode rétro*, already present in the writing of the Hussards, and which assimilated the glamour of certain collaborationist milieux to the memory of 1925 and the *années folles*.

The issue was not simply one of historiography, although, following the success of the American Robert Paxton's account of Vichy, a new generation of French historians, including Rousso himself, began to explore the complexities of the Occupation, Liberation, and *Épuration* with an inclusivity and an objectivity that differed sharply from previous semi-official accounts. It was also a question of writing itself, a phenomenon which also emerges in depictions of the Holocaust. In an essay in *Beyond All This Fiddle*, A. Alvarez points to the difficulties inherent in writing what is essentially unwritable and notes the inability of conventional memoirs or narratives to convey the reality of unimaginable experiences. David Rousset's massive three-volume account of his deportation to a concentration camp, *Les Jours de notre mort* (1947), sincere as it undoubtedly is, remains ultimately below the level of the experience, while, on the other hand, Jorge Semprun's fictional account of his deportation in *Le Grand Voyage* (1963), by adopting a range of subversive narrative techniques, conveys more accurately its inherent strangeness. It is undoubtedly for this reason that the literary and political subversion in the accounts of Aymé, the Hussards, and especially Céline, have proved more durable than their more conventional counterparts, and why Sartre's decision to abandon *Les Chemins de la liberté* before its projected fourth volume on the Occupation is due not merely to his own shifting political allegiances but also to his awareness of the aesthetic limitations of a black-and-white account of resistants against Germans and collaborators. It is also why one of the most successful fictional genres for the depiction of the *années noires* should be precisely the *série noire*, from Léo Malet's *120 rue de la Gare* to Didier Daeninckx's *Itinéraire d'un salaud ordinaire* (2006). The hard-boiled detective or the corrupt police officer become more convincing tools for the investigation of a complex and obscure memory than idealised Resistance heroes.

Fin de siècle

If it took the French until the late 1970s to begin to come to terms with the memory of the Occupation, there is every indication that the process has a long way to go in the cases of Indochina and Algeria. In fact, there was barely the briefest of interregnums, let alone an inter-war period, between the end of the Second World War and the Vietminh's campaign for independence in Indochina. Rather, the process is one of almost uninterrupted conflict between 1939 and 1962, although, paradoxically, the wars in Indochina and Algeria are conducted alongside the greatest transformation of French society and its economy in the modern era, the years which Jean Fourastié calls the 'trente glorieuses'.

Daeninckx's 'itinerary' follows the path of an ordinary but ambitious young law graduate through the Paris police during the Occupation into the Fourth and Fifth Republics, during which he participates in counter-terrorism activities in North Africa and the torture and murder of North African citizens in Paris following the pro-FLN demonstration of 18 October 1961, after which the bodies were thrown into the Seine – a 'place of memory' which still remains taboo. In fact, the same amnesia which for so long affected the French collective memory of the Occupation still operates with regard to the post-war period. The long war in Indochina, leading inexorably to the traumatic defeat at Dien Bien Phu in 1954, has received relatively little literary exposure, and the same is true of the Algerian war: indeed, successive French governments showed themselves to be remarkably reluctant to officially label that conflict a 'war', as opposed to a police action. Whilst French writers and intellectuals, often at considerable personal risk, militated against both wars, it can hardly be claimed that either conflict has yet been fully absorbed into the national cultural memory. The major fictional transposition of both conflicts, in fact, is to be found in the popular novels of the journalist Jean Lartéguy, *Les Centurions* (1960) and *Les Prétoriens* (1964), which follow the same paratroop regiment and its charismatic commander from Indochina to Algiers in what is essentially an unambiguous portrayal of French military might. Whilst Modiano, in *Villa triste* (1975), exposes the same dark side of the French handling of the Algerian question, the memory still remains obscured.

74

Holocaust writing and film

LIBBY SAXTON

At the end of *La Question humaine* (2007), a film by Nicolas Klotz and Elisabeth Perceval adapted from a novel by François Emmanuel (1999), the protagonist Simon Kessler (Mathieu Amalric) recounts a dream in which he witnesses a mass of bodies tumbling out of a gas van. The film refuses to visualise this atrocity for us, and as he is speaking the screen turns black. A psychologist working for an international petrochemical corporation with a murky past, Kessler has no ostensible personal connection to the events in his vision, and we never learn whether or not he is Jewish. His excruciatingly graphic account of his dream is a tissue of indirect citations from historical documents, eyewitness testimonies, newspaper articles, and other films, in which the meanings of words are questioned and revised. The neutral, bureaucratic, degraded language of a Nazi memorandum concerning modifications to gas vans is refuted through juxtaposition with the testimonies of Jewish prisoners who worked in the gas chambers at Auschwitz-Birkenau. Moreover, as Kessler names the dead and claims them as his kin, Perceval slips new first names into the list of mainly Hebrew ones in Emmanuel's text, including Robert (Antelme) and Armand (Gatti). *La Question humaine* explores the enduring presence in quotidian reality of traces of the events known in English-speaking countries as 'the Holocaust', but which the French refer to variously as 'la déportation' and 'le génocide' or 'la Shoah'. The film reflects some of the abiding concerns of French-language representations of these events: the referential instability of language, images and sounds in the face of realities that confront representation with exorbitant challenges; the roles of mediation and fantasy in the construction of individual and collective memories; the relationships between different forms of racialised violence in the cultural imagination. As the camps recede into the past, Holocaust writing and film become increasingly palimpsestic; as in Kessler's monologue, traces of the past are layered, over-written and reinterpreted and the meaning of history is perpetually renegotiated.

The title of this essay infers continuities between a wide array of cultural texts which in some other respects have little in common. It groups together representations of the concentration camps and of the smaller network of centres designed solely for the purpose of mass murder, where approximately four-fifths of the Jews deported from France perished (Chelmno, Belzec, Sobibor, Treblinka, and Auschwitz-Birkenau); testimony by survivors of these systems and writing by those who experienced only their after-effects; ostensibly raw, unembellished narratives and formally innovative literary and filmic experiments. This short survey traces the evolving perceptions of testimony, memory, and the Holocaust itself which underpin this varied corpus. Holocaust writing and films are symbiotically connected to some of the broader developments in post-war French culture and thought discussed elsewhere in this volume: the burgeoning interest in personal, retrospective narration and new forms of life-writing such as *autofiction*; psychoanalytic, structuralist, and poststructuralist reconceptualisations of language and subjectivity; philosophical reconsiderations of ethics, alterity, humanity, and community. Authors such as Robert Antelme, Jean Cayrol, Serge Doubrovsky, Georges Perec, and Sarah Kofman are known not only for their Holocaust writing but also for their contributions to wider literary and philosophical debates. Yet they also need to be read in the context of broader cultural narratives about the Holocaust in France, the collective memories which are shaped by and shape individual ones but have often served a bowdlerising or sanitising function.

The Holocaust in French cultural memory

Following cultural historian Henry Rousso, it has become commonplace to describe France's troubled relationship to *les années noires* since the 1980s in terms of an 'obsession' or 'haunting'.[1] Around a quarter of France's Jewish population were murdered during the war, a smaller proportion than those lost by many other European nations, and the killing centres were located a long way from French soil. However, France has struggled to come to terms with revelations of the Vichy regime's implication in the Holocaust through its anti-Semitic legislation and voluntary deportation of Jews. Buried for a couple of decades after the war, these events remain liable to resurface unbidden, as in *La Question humaine*, at unexpected times and in unpredictable configurations.

---

1 H. Rousso, *Le Syndrome de Vichy: de 1944 à nos jours*, 2nd edn (Paris: Seuil, 1990); H. Rousso, *La Hantise du passé*, interview with P. Petit (Paris: Textuel, 1998).

The shifts in the nation's perception of the Holocaust might be marked out in terms of a succession of paradigmatic witnesses and camps. In the first two decades after the war, the privileged witness was a political deportee and the emblematic camp was Buchenwald. This was due in part to the fact that the overwhelming majority (95 per cent) of the survivors who returned to France had been deported for their activities rather than their ethnicity, in part to the efforts of communist organisations and Charles de Gaulle's post-war administration to manage collective memory for political gain, and in part to a reluctance to single out the Jews from the rest of the population. Two of the most influential testimonies from this period, David Rousset's *L'Univers concentrationnaire* (1946) and Antelme's *L'Espèce humaine* (1947), describe in detail the daily struggle to survive in the concentration camps but have comparatively little to say about the particular fate of the Jews, which is also famously a lacuna in Jean-Paul Sartre's *Réflexions sur la question juive* (1954, written in 1946). This virtual silence was perpetuated by Cayrol's commentary for Alain Resnais's *Nuit et brouillard* (1955), a documentary which nevertheless contains a number of photographs relating to the Jewish genocide, including two taken inside the killing zones at Auschwitz-Birkenau, the rarity of which was not recognised at the time when the film was made.

It was not until the early 1960s that the paradigm began to shift. In the wake of the publication of Jewish testimonies such as Elie Wiesel's *La Nuit* (1958) and André Schwarz-Bart's *Le Dernier des justes* (1959), events such as the trial of Adolf Eichmann in 1961, the Six Day War in 1967, the death of de Gaulle in 1969 and a wave of books and films lifting the lid on Vichy's complicity in the genocide, most famously Robert Paxton's *Vichy France: Old Guard and New Order 1940–1944* (1972) and Marcel Ophuls's *Le Chagrin et la pitié* (1971), the plight of the Jews began to assume a more central place in collective memory, and Auschwitz displaced Buchenwald as the representative camp in the cultural imagination. Yet the identity of the 'exemplary' witness remains contested. Discussions about who has authority to speak for the dead have fuelled a fascination with perceived 'limit figures' within the 'limit experience' of the camps. Recent debates have focused on members of the Sonderkommandos, labour details of mainly Jewish prisoners forced to assist with gassings in the death centres, who are presented in Claude Lanzmann's film *Shoah* (1985) as privileged witnesses to the annihilation of their people, but portrayed by witnesses such as Primo Levi as more ambiguous figures. Attention has also centred on the so-called Muselmänner, deportees who had lost their will to live and whose experiences are explored in accounts such as Jorge Semprun's *Le Mort qu'il faut* (2001), yet who, like the Sonderkommandos, were only known in certain camps and represent only one aspect of the Nazis' multifaceted programme of violence.

However, if French cultural memory has fixated on a series of 'model' witnesses, individual authors and filmmakers have proposed more complex understandings of the subject of testimony which have sometimes been at odds with the dominant cultural narratives of the time. Annette Wieviorka argues that the function of testimony has changed over the decades from purveyor of knowledge to vector of memory.[2] Notwithstanding this shift, however, successive generations of witnesses writing in French have questioned the capacity of testimony to present a full and objective account of the past and have drawn attention to the permeability of the boundaries between memory and imagination. The concept of a paradigmatic witness is further troubled in these works by an insistence on the singularity of individual experience and the concomitant impossibility of bearing witness on behalf of others.

Holocaust testimony

At the beginning of the 'Avant-propos' to *L'Espèce humaine*, Antelme attests, on the one hand, to an insatiable desire to speak of his experiences at Buchenwald, Gandersheim, and Dachau, the concentration camps where he was imprisoned for Resistance activities in 1944, and, on the other, to the near insuperable challenges he encounters in attempting to do so.[3] The root of the problem, he explains, is the unbridgeable abyss between the realities of his life in the camps and the language available in which to communicate them. Here, Antelme succinctly formulates an aporia which has since become a central topos – and arguably cliché – in Holocaust writing. Testimony is presented at once as imperative and impossibility; the witness is charged with an obligation which s/he cannot fulfil, since words are not up to the task. For Antelme, Wiesel, Charlotte Delbo, and many other witnesses, the violence of the Holocaust casts doubt on humanist conceptions of language as capable of representing a world outside it. A key preoccupation of structuralist and poststructuralist thinkers, the extent to which the linguistic structures in which we are entangled determine our perceptions of reality, becomes an ethical dilemma for Holocaust survivors attempting to recount the past without betraying it.

2 A. Wieviorka, *Déportation et genocide: entre la mémoire et l'oubli* (Paris: Plon, 1992), pp. 162–3.
3 R. Antelme, *L'Espèce humaine*, 2nd edn (Paris: Gallimard, 1957), p. 9.

French-language Holocaust testimony can be seen as an ongoing endeavour to give a meaningful form to extremes of destitution, privation, and loss which are recurrently described as defying language and yet which are endlessly written about. Berel Lang explains this double-handed gesture in terms of the rhetorical figure of *praeteritio*: 'in these very discourses ... the "unspeakable" and the "ineffable" are pretty clearly spoken (or spoken about), and the "unwritable" is written'.[4] Over the past two decades, discourses of 'ineffability' have met with growing suspicion and been vigorously refuted by witnesses such as Semprun.[5] Antelme's misgivings about language in fact preface a relatively assured first-person retrospective narrative which betrays few signs of linguistic disturbance. The form as much as the content of *L'Espèce humaine* bears witness to a faith in the resilience of the human subject, who remains able to give a more or less coherent account of his or her experiences. For some political deportees such as Antelme, the camps did not signal the collapse of the interpretative frameworks through which we make sense of the world; rather, they could be conceptualised as a product of capitalist and imperialist ideology. However, in other accounts, such sense-making projects threaten to become unsustainable or prompt more self-conscious exploration of aesthetic form. In 'Pour un romanesque lazaréen' (1950, first published in 1949), for instance, Cayrol, a poet and novelist associated with the *nouveau roman* who had been a political prisoner at Mauthausen, envisages a new kind of 'art concentrationnaire' (concentrationary art), anticipated by the work of Albert Camus and Pablo Picasso, capable of evoking the human condition in a post-Holocaust era.

One of the symptoms of the purported insufficiency of language, which at the same time seems to reaffirm its sufficiency, is the frequency with which witnesses revisit, reconsider, or revise occurrences and insights in their own or others' testimonies. Cayrol, Semprun, Delbo, Wiesel, Anna Langfus, and Kofman all produce a series of takes on their wartime experiences in a variety of literary genres which comment directly or indirectly on each other. Kofman, for instance, publishes *Paroles suffoquées* (1987), a discussion of other writers' responses to the camps which engages in particular with *L'Espèce humaine*, before presenting an account of her own experiences as a child in occupied Paris in *Rue Ordener, rue Labat* (1994). The witness may return to an earlier account ostensibly in order to correct an error or clear up a misunderstanding, as when Wiesel, a survivor of Auschwitz and Buchenwald,

---

4 B. Lang, *Holocaust Representation: Art within the Limits of History and Ethics* (Baltimore, MD: Johns Hopkins University Press, 2000), p. 17.
5 J. Semprun, *L'Écriture ou la vie* (Paris: Gallimard, 1994), p. 23.

attempts to clarify incidents depicted in his autobiographical account *La Nuit* in his memoir *Tous les fleuves vont à la mer* (1994). Yet retelling the past may equally serve to cover up the truth, a possibility more openly entertained in Wiesel's novel *Les Portes de la forêt* (1964). The palimpsestic dimension of testimonial writing is more palpably manifested in the work of Semprun, a survivor of Buchenwald, whose texts chart his reappraisal of the meaning of the camps as he loses his faith in communism. In *L'Écriture ou la vie*, Semprun warns that the work of testimony is never finished; what is needed is 'un récit illimité, probablement interminable, illuminé – clôturé aussi, bien entendu – par cette possibilité de se poursuivre à l'infini' ('a boundless and probably never-ending account, illuminated – as well as enclosed, naturally – by that possibility of going on forever').[6] Semprun's remark aptly describes a broader tendency in French-language testimony, in which the past is endlessly rewritten and its significance incessantly renegotiated. Caught up in processes of revision and reinterpretation, these texts are haunted by the disturbing possibility that there is no essential truth or single authoritative understanding of the Holocaust to be reached. This ongoing meditation on the meaning of the camps is simultaneously conducted in cinema, where the testimonial palimpsest acquires distinctive temporal and spatial dimensions.

Holocaust film

In a discussion of the afterlife of the Holocaust on film, Antoine de Baecque contends that modern cinema is born out of the first images of the camps to enter the public domain (those captured by camera operators with the Allied forces), which continue to circulate within the medium. De Baecque proposes a list of 'figures spécifiquement cinématographiques qui témoignent de la présence obsessionelle du palimpseste concentrationnaire' ('specifically cinematographic figures which testify to the obsessive presence of the concentrationary palimpsest'): the to-camera look, the freeze-frame, documentary in fiction, the flashback, montage, contemplation, and malaise.[7] French cinema has borne witness to the Holocaust variously by reassembling indexical traces of the past, through reconstructions, through oral testimony and, as de Baecque suggests, through the use of mnemonically charged, 'traumatised'

6 Ibid., pp. 23–4. Translation by L. Coverdale.
7 A. de Baecque, 'Premières images des camps: quel cinéma après Auschwitz?', *Cahiers du cinéma*, hors série (2000), pp. 62–6, at p. 66.

cinematographic forms which evoke the propensity of this brutal history to intrude upon and impregnate the superficially banal and everyday in the present. All four of these techniques, and most of the figures mentioned by de Baecque, are featured in *Nuit et brouillard*, in which formal experimentation is a marker of ethico-political commitment, and which may be viewed as an example of the 'art concentrationnaire' described by Cayrol. Resnais interpolates black-and-white archive images from the Nazi era and the liberation of the camps with newly shot colour (and occasionally black-and-white) footage where the camera roams around Auschwitz, Birkenau, and Majdanek in search of remnants which might reanimate the past. Investigative tracking shots of the kind that punctuate *Nuit et brouillard* have become a leitmotif in modernist auteur French cinema dealing with the legacy of the deportation and genocide; films such as *Shoah*, *Drancy Avenir* (Arnaud des Pallières, 1996), *Voyages* (Emmanuel Finkiel, 1999), and *La Petite Prairie aux bouleaux* (Marcelline Loridan-Ivens, 2003) continue Resnais's hunt for meaningful remains at different Holocaust sites. Yet each of these films registers doubts about the referential function of the linguistic and visual traces it amasses. Antelme's warning that language is incommensurable with concentrationary experience is reiterated in Cayrol's commentary in *Nuit et brouillard*, which is similarly sceptical about the capacity of images to render the magnitude of the horror of the camps.

Concerns about the representability of the Holocaust are exacerbated in the case of visual culture by two distinct factors which have become entangled in debates in France. The first is the scarcity of photographs or films depicting the 'Final Solution'. As a consequence of Heinrich Himmler's ban on filming activities relating to the murder of the Jews, few images survive from the extermination camps at Chelmno, Belzec, Treblinka, and Sobibor or the killing zones at Auschwitz-Birkenau. Most of the historical images which have come to *symbolise* or *connote* the genocide in the cultural imagination, such as the footage of skeletal prisoners, mass graves, and bulldozers at Bergen-Belsen used in *Nuit et brouillard*, do not actually *document* or *denote* it. The prolonged darkness of the screen at the end of *La Question humaine* constitutes an acknowledgement of both the absence of visual records of the death machines that infiltrate Kessler's dreams and the ongoing conversation about the significance of this absence. The second factor, bearing on debates about the ethics of film as witness, is the prohibition on representation, deriving from the Hebraic proscription of graven images or idols, which has repeatedly been invoked in the context of Holocaust cinema. Both these factors have been linked to Lanzmann's decision to exclude historical footage from his remarkable nine-and-a-half-hour film *Shoah*, which painstakingly reconstructs the Nazis' attempt to assassinate the Jews through interviews with survivors, bystanders, and perpetrators. However, over the past two decades, the validity of interdictions and taboos on representation has been contested by Jacques Rancière, Jean-Luc Nancy, Georges Didi-Huberman, Semprun, and others, and critical emphasis has shifted from prohibition to innovation. In line with this shift, contemporary French filmmakers have repositioned images and texts associated with the Holocaust in new and transformative contexts. In his video-essay *Histoire(s) du cinéma* (1988–98), a vast collage of eclectic aural and visual cultural fragments, Jean-Luc Godard juxtaposes George Stevens's harrowing documentary images of Holocaust victims with shots of Elizabeth Taylor from Stevens's Hollywood film *A Place in the Sun* (1951), a detail from a fresco by Giotto, and a melody by Paul Hindemith. In *Drancy Avenir*, des Pallières weaves an intricate intertextual web of citations from writings by Antelme, Delbo, Perec, Marguerite Duras, Lanzmann, and others. The aim of such reappropriations is not to relativise the Holocaust or individual interpretations of it but to explore the place it occupies within the wider cultural memory and imagination. Unauthorised juxtapositions and imaginative reinterpretations of this kind are also key characteristics of the work of the so-called 'génération d'après' (generation after).

Absent and composite memories

A prominent concern in French literature and film since the 1970s is the predicament of the belated witness who did not experience the camps first-hand yet feels intimately connected to them through memory, whether or not through family history. A series of terms have been coined to describe this form of investment in the past: 'la mémoire trouée' (memory full of holes; Henri Raczymow), 'absent memory' (Ellen Fine) and, perhaps most influentially, 'postmemory' (Marianne Hirsch). In writings by Raczymow, Georges Perec, Patrick Modiano, and others belonging to this later generation of witnesses, the genocide is evoked as an absence or void which resists attempts at textual recuperation. In Perec's *W ou le souvenir d'enfance* (1975), the death of the author's mother at Auschwitz is inscribed obliquely through lacunae and motifs of disappearance, such as the parenthesised ellipsis '(. . .)' at the heart of the text.[8] Modiano's *Dora Bruder* (1997) also revolves around

8 G. Perec, *W ou le souvenir d'enfance* (Paris: Denoël, 1975), p. 85.

a disappearance and the narrator's attempt to reconstruct the life of a Jewish girl deported during the Occupation is replete with signifiers of absence. These autofictional texts narrate endeavours to re-establish links with a past that remains elusive and unassimilable. Photographs, newspapers, letters, and other remnants offer clues to what happened yet prove unable to invest the other's death with meaning. But such traces also serve as catalysts for the imagination; in the new forms of testimonial writing invented by this generation of witnesses the distinctions between memory and fantasy are repeatedly unsettled.

In the final sentence of W, shortly after a quotation from L'Univers concentrationnaire, the narrator draws an implicit parallel between the Nazi camps and the crimes committed by Augusto Pinochet.[9] Rather than proposing an equivalence between two distinct manifestations of inhumanity, Perec's allusion to Chile hints at the propensity of separate histories to impinge upon, inform, and question each other in cultural memory. Similarly, a connection between two forms of racialised violence is established at the end of Nuit et brouillard; the commentary's warning about the persistence of 'la peste concentrationnaire' ('the concentrationary plague') reframes the camps as an allegory for the atrocities perpetrated by the French in Algeria. For Maxim Silverman, the entwining of the legacies of the Holocaust and French imperialism in texts such as W, Dora Bruder, Didier Daeninckx's Meurtres pour mémoire (1984), and films such as Chris Marker's La Jetée (1962) and Michael Haneke's Caché (2005) reveals 'the psychical base of cultural memory' to be 'a genuinely composite affair'.[10] What Silverman calls 'composite memories'[11] are also constructed in La Question humaine, in which depictions of the treatment of immigrants and asylum seekers by the French state today painfully recall the persecution of Algerians and Jews in the past, and the missing images of both events. Holocaust writing and films can create spaces in which the echoes of other – often less thoroughly investigated – crimes reverberate, whether or not these echoes are consciously cultivated, without establishing hierarchies of suffering or denying the specificity of individual atrocities. As the reference to L'Espèce humaine at the end of La Question humaine reminds us, what has been constantly at stake in French culture's engagement with the Holocaust is the question of what it means to be human.

9 Ibid., p. 220.
10 M. Silverman, 'Interconnected Histories: Holocaust and Empire in the Cultural Imaginary', French Studies 62 (2008), pp. 417–28, at p. 426.
11 Ibid., p. 425.

75

Women writers, artists, and filmmakers

EMMA WILSON

Interiors

In Michelle Porte's 1976 documentary, *Les Lieux de Marguerite Duras*, filmed in the novelist's dreamlike house in Neauphle-le-Château, with its draped furniture and trailing flowers, Duras speaks of women's relation to the houses they dwell in: 'Il n'y a que les femmes qui habitent les lieux, pas les hommes' ('Only women inhabit places, not men').[1] Invoking the names of the protagonists of a number of her novels and films, she says that her house has been inhabited by Lol V. Stein, Anne-Marie Stretter, Isabelle Granger, Nathalie Granger. Duras has literally used her house, and its ranging grounds, as the setting for a number of her films; more imaginatively she suggests here that her characters inhabit this location, this material setting, that she has created.

Duras is considered elsewhere in this volume in discussions of the modern novel and of autobiography; she returns here in a chapter which reflects the contribution women have made to French literature and culture through the twentieth century and in the first part of the twenty-first, in particular in those works where they have reflected some difference or specificity of female experience. This grouping of the work of women is not intended to uphold any argument for an *essential* difference between men and women, or indeed between male and female writers. Rather, it is intended to explore ways in which twentieth-century and contemporary works by women have brought into view areas of experience, often affective and corporeal, which have been neglected in previous periods.

Some recent critics, for example Christine Détrez and Anne Simon in an important study, *À leurs corps défendant*, have been sceptical about the return

---

1 M. Duras and M. Porte, *Les Lieux de Marguerite Duras* (Paris: Minuit, 1977), p. 12. Translations are mine.

of what they see as stereotypes of femininity in the work of contemporary women writers in France. My aim here, by contrast, is to re-evaluate the diversity, richness, and unpredictability of such tropes in the twentieth century, and in particular in the contemporary period. In an essential volume,[2] Shirley Jordan speaks of both continuity and change in the work of women writers and isolates returning, transforming themes in their work: 'History and time', 'Wandering and exile', 'Self and other', 'The body and sexuality', 'Writing and telling'. Jordan's critical studies, those of Gill Rye, founder of the Contemporary Women's Writing in French seminar at the Institute of Germanic and Romance Studies in London,[3] and of the scholars who have worked with them, have done much to extend the range of critical interpretations of creative work by women in France. They have found in such work a reinvention of the tropes of femininity, and trenchant, ethically challenging, new representations.

In line with this reinvention, it can be seen that, speaking about houses, Duras is typically sceptical about interpretations that stress the comfort and security of the familial home. She writes: 'Dans une maison, il y a aussi l'horreur de la famille qui est inscrite, le besoin de fuite, toutes les humeurs suicidaires' ('In a house, horror of the family is also inscribed, the need for retreat, a whole set of suicidal feelings').[4] I use the house of Duras's fiction as the point of departure for a discussion of women's writing and filmmaking which argues that the house, family, desire, affect, have all been estranged, reimagined and thought anew in the last century of work.

A point of departure for thinking women's writing in the twentieth century is the work of Colette, named by Hélène Cixous in her manifesto essay 'Le Rire de la méduse' (1975) as one of the three precursor practitioners of an *écriture féminine*. Colette's life and work have since been explored by Julia Kristeva, in a three-volume study of female genius in the twentieth century (her other subjects are Hannah Arendt and Melanie Klein). Colette, like Duras, offers a house of fiction, naming her collection of autobiographical fragments *La Maison de Claudine* (1922), and opening this volume with an evocation of her mother, Sido, and her mother's house, with its spreading gardens and espaliers with ripening apricots. Despite the sensuality of the writing, and the nostalgia that impels it, Colette hints at the reparative function of writing which allows the reimagining of a past world lost in the present. In

---

2 S. Jordan. *Contemporary French Women's Writing: Women's Visions, Women's Voices, Women's Lives* (Oxford: Peter Lang, 2004).
3 http://igrs.sas.ac.uk/events/contemporary-womens-writing-in-french-seminar.html.
4 Duras and Porte, *Les Lieux de Marguerite Duras*, p. 16.

these acts of reparation, her writing incessantly slips between autobiography and fiction, leaving the boundaries of neither secure. In a late novella, *La Lune de pluie* (1940), she invents a character, Madame Colette, a writer, who becomes fascinated by a young woman whom she sees representing the self she might have been. Writing becomes a performative means of testing out identities and refusing to allow any stable sense of a self and its identity to coalesce.

Such unfixing of the self is pursued more radically, at the level of both theme and language, in the work of Hélène Cixous. From an early text such as *Dedans* (1969), with its opening image of a house encircled, the house of her childhood in Oran, Algeria, yet also an image of herself, the interior of her unconscious and of her turn inwards in her act of mourning her father, Cixous works to deconstruct relations between inside and out, between self and other, between psychical and material. Her work, perhaps more than that of any of the other writers discussed here, has been associated with the category of the feminine, yet in her deconstructive moves she keeps any sense of what this might designate strategically uncertain. Her later texts, dream diaries, and meditations on lived moments, shot through with threads referencing multiple intertexts, pursue a cultivation of writing (an *écriture féminine*) as a means of both appropriating language and making it strange. In *L'Amour même dans la boîte à lettres* (2005), she conjures up an image of a glasshouse in which is cultivated an immense garden of words.

Marie NDiaye's *Autoportrait en vert* (2005) likewise conjures up slippage between self and other, unsettling relations of reference. The apparently autobiographical text is interspersed with a series of photographs that have no direct relation to the narrative that unfolds: the images seem to haunt the text, offering it an alternative, phantom narrative thread. In turn, the self-portrait of the title is itself created through a series of unstable moments of identification or recognition between the 'je' of the narrative and a series of 'femmes en vert' (women in green) who return in dream and hallucination near the writer's home on the Garonne. NDiaye, as elsewhere in her writing, lets suggestion and uncertain recognition, a constant shadowing of fantasy and reality, open out the meanings of her text. The opening paragraphs of *Autoportrait en vert* conjure up a moment of waiting, of not knowing whether, this season, the Garonne will flood, water filling the ground floor of the house, its stairwell, or possibly 'la maison entière' ('the whole house').[5]

5 M. NDiaye, *Autoportrait en vert* (Paris: Mercure de France, 2005), p. 7.

Infancy

If the house is no longer secure, harbouring horror and suicide, as well as memory and nostalgia, and is regularly flooded, maternity and the image of the mother is also impeached, in part, in French women's writing of the last hundred years. The association of women with maternity and motherhood again conjures up questions about essentialist identities and female anatomy. Yet even those writings that encourage the association of the female and the feminine with the maternal are cautious about fixing a meaning to this, working rather to embrace its possibilities. Kristeva's influential essay 'Stabat Mater', published in *Histoires d'amour* (1983), offers two parallel, alternative narratives of motherhood: one that explores the iconography of the Virgin Mary and one that offers a more visceral and poetic account of the experience of giving birth. Cixous, again looking towards plurality, has written that, really or virtually mothers (by virtue of anatomy), women have the capacity to hold the other and so to know a nurturing, non-conflictual relation to otherness. Her analysis builds outwards from anatomy to relationality and towards an ethical opening to the other, moving beyond essentialist concerns with reproduction and fertility. While this opening of maternity to embrace an economy of giving and relationality may be encouraging, writings, films, and artworks of the period have not always followed Cixous's idealisation of the mother/child relation and its potential.

Indeed, works by women writers, filmmakers, and artists have worked acutely to testify to the demands of the mother/child relation, from the perspective of both parties. Maternity and maternal subjectivity in the work of French women writers have received excellent attention by critics. More neglected in discussion of recent texts has been the specific interest in infancy also found in the work of women, the claims of infants as they impinge on and interact with their mothers, and the experiences of girlhood which have often escaped representation.

Marie NDiaye draws on images of Medea, on maternal fears for the death of children, and on moves to lose or destroy children. In *Rosie Carpe* (2001) she draws out in extenuating detail the circumstances of Rosie's maltreatment of her child Titi, her inability to respond to his cries or to protect him from the heat in Guadeloupe. Through its evocations of the physical vulnerability of the child, the dampness of his skin, his infinitely fine hair against his scalp, the text conveys the enormity of responsibility in maternity. Marie Darrieussecq, most famous for her novel *Truismes* (1996) about a woman who metamorphoses into a pig, also explores the burden of maternal identity, yet its transformations as well. Her text *Le Bébé* (2002) draws together fragments describing the experience of tending to a baby, moving imperceptibly into broader reflections on the nature and meaning of babyhood and on the ways in which babies have been excluded from literature. The confident voice of the mother within the text allows us to glimpse a lucid, engaged maternity, and to witness a female subject opening to the otherness of the baby, and not being threatened by it.

Darrieussecq's later text, *Tom est mort* (2007), returns to questions of infancy through a narrative about the death of a child. The novel patiently follows its protagonist's processes of mourning for her lost child, her memories of him, and her imaginings of how his and her life might have been. With some drama, the novel leaves until its last page a revelation of how Tom dies. His mother takes a siesta on a hot afternoon and thinking that the flat is secure, and her child safe, she forgets to close the windows on the loggia. Searching for him when she awakes, she looks out in horror to see him lying below the window.

The reception of *Tom est mort* in France at *la rentrée* of 2007 was troubled by claims of 'plagiat psychique' ('psychic plagiarism') from novelist Camille Laurens. Laurens, like Darrieussecq and NDiaye, has offered a searching and sometimes acerbic account of interpersonal relations. Her brief work *Philippe* (1995), and some of her later projects, were inspired by the death of her own infant son; indeed her criticism of *Tom est mort* implied that one could not write about such experience unless it had been lived. *Philippe* stands alongside *Tom est mort* as a contestatory text about the experience of losing a child. Laurens confronts the assumption that women write or speak about their experience of giving birth while men write about war or politics. She recounts that she would never have thought of writing about her experience of childbirth until the day Philippe died, when childbirth became a war. Laurens contests the association of women's writing with particular bodily tropes, yet returns in *Philippe* to turn the meanings of childbirth and maternity inside out. Her project, rooted in personal experience, is, like Simone de Beauvoir's text about the death of her mother, *Une Mort très douce* (1964), a mordant critique of the medical system, making public use of testimony to suffering.

Comparable interweaving of the personal and the political is found in Mariana Otero's documentary *Histoire d'un secret* (2003), where the filmmaker and her sister explore the death of their mother while they were children. Their mother, Clotilde Vautier, an artist, died after trying to abort a foetus. The circumstances of her death were kept hidden from her daughters. The film in memory of Otero's mother becomes a search for truth about her family history and also a statement about abortion. The work pays particular attention to Clotilde's paintings which are restored to the light of day, the film ending with a cathartic scene in a gallery space where the sisters have organised an exhibition of their mother's work. The painstaking hanging of the exhibition reflects the work of editing Otero herself has done, creating a memory portrait of her mother. The film resonates with Agnès Varda's film about the women's movement, with its focus on issues of abortion and female creativity, *L'Une chante, l'autre pas* (1977).

Histoire d'un secret is sensitive in its conjuring of childhood memories of loss. It draws into question children's fantasies of their mother's identity, as does, in a different way, a film such as Diane Kurys's *Coup de foudre* (1983). From Colette's loving re-creation of her childhood persona as dreamed by herself and Sido, to Violette Leduc's explorations of her girlhood sexuality, to Beauvoir's attention to childhood in her discussions of subjectivity and freedom, writing by women has explored the ways in which childhood experience and emotions underlie adult identities. Cixous, in tracing the roots of her family in Europe and North Africa, pictures in *Photos de racines* (1994) their estranged experiences, and shows a photograph of her infant self at a year old, another of her sitting with her cousin against a mantle of wisteria, and another where she is dressed in costume as a poppy. The infant Hélène, whose sensory relation to the Oran of her childhood is addressed elsewhere in her works, is included here in the extending series of identities she explores.

Exploration of the embodied experience of childhood is also particularly rich in work by women directors and artists. The films of Sandrine Veysset, *Y aura-t-il de la neige à Noël?* (1996) and *Martha . . . Martha* (2001), have offered representations of child poverty, with an affecting attention to textures, fabrics, and cloth creatures to summon sensory recall. The installations of artist Annette Messager similarly manipulate the material paraphernalia and debris of childhood. Director Claire Simon offers a painful sense of the rituals of childhood play in her documentary about elementary school breaktimes, *Récréations* (1998). Other directors and writers working on embodiment have been further concerned with body image and its shaping from childhood onwards. This is shown with pathos in the early sequences of Martine Dugowson's *Mina Tannenbaum* (1994). It is also a subject explored at length by novelist Amélie Nothomb, from her virtuoso text of early infancy and the infant subject's relation to the world, *Métaphysique des tubes* (2000), through her volumes which explore girlhood, bodily transformation, and anorexia, notably *Biographie de la faim* (2004).

In their volume *Cinema and the Second Sex*, Carrie Tarr and Brigitte Rollet argue that in focusing on childhood, women directors are drawing on material considered suitable for women, *but* that foregrounding experiences that are normally marginal or marginalised has the potential 'to challenge hegemonic adult modes of seeing'.[6]

Intimacy

Turning from infancy to intimacy, in this section I look at ways in which women's writing, filmmaking, and art has also challenged hegemonic modes of seeing through opening new representations of intimacy (erotic, affective, and traumatic).

Cutting-edge amongst contemporary representations have been those that have embraced the pornographic and in so doing explored new bodily and libidinal configurations in women's writing and filmmaking. Catherine Millet's novel *La Vie sexuelle de Catherine M.* (2001) offered the spectre of a well-known art historian exposing her sexual life. On a less grandiose scale, Catherine Cusset's *Jouir* (1997) exposes its protagonist's sexual history. Christine Angot offers a new voice in French autofiction in her apparently confessional accounts of her incestuous relations with her father and of the relation of this trauma to her adult sexuality, to her family life, and her literary career. Whilst apparently personal, and often cultivating a vigorous first-person diction, Angot's texts are also highly stylised, alluding to intertexts by Guibert, Duras, and others.

Similarly self-conscious, Oulipo member Anne Garréta's *Pas un jour* (2002) opens with a prologue commenting on the tendency towards exposure in contemporary writing: 'Raconter sa vie, on ne fait plus que cela semble-t-il aujourd'hui, et encore, sous l'angle censé depuis plus d'un siècle lui donner sens, en être la clef universelle. Bref, le passé-partout de la subjectivité: le désir' ('It seems that all people do nowadays is narrate their own lives, and furthermore they do it from the perspective which for more than a century has been seen to give it meaning, to be its universal key. In short, the key to subjectivity: desire').[7] While her irony sets her writing at one remove from this trend, the text follows a self-imposed constraint where the writer spends five hours at the computer each day, each time narrating the memory of a different woman who has desired her or whom she has desired.

6 C. Tarr and B. Rollet, *Cinema and the Second Sex: Women's Filmmaking in France in the 1980s and 1990s* (New York: Continuum, 2001), p. 25.
7 A. Garréta, *Pas un jour* (Paris: Grasset, 2002), p. 10.

Garréta references Stendhal in her prologue, and an anecdote about the novelist tracing the initials of the women he loved in the sand. Her text forges connections to former representations of love and yet opens new dimensions to such representations in drawing a series of love affairs between women. Filmmaker Catherine Breillat similarly links contemporary female eroticism and nineteenth-century literature in her 2007 film adaptation of Barbey d'Aurevilly's novel *Une vieille maîtresse* (1851). Her adaptation, pursuing her fascination with masquerade as exemplified in her ethically adventurous films about female sexuality, offers a lavish sensory treatment of the text.

While Claire Denis, like Breillat, has made sexual intimacy her subject, her films more experimentally explore questions of skin, surface, contact, and its failure. Her work has been considered in relation to the philosophical writings of Jean-Luc Nancy, with whom she has collaborated, and whose intimate investigation of openness to the other, *L'Intrus* (2001), inspired Denis's 2004 film of the same title. Nancy's *L'Intrus* is a brief text about immigration which opens out of a narrative of the author's heart transplant operation. Nancy finds language to express the pain of opening to the other and the transformation such opening can offer. Denis, in treating themes such as border crossing and filiation, finds visual modes to reflect on relationality and ethics.

Where the sexual and the ethical have dominated radical work on intimacy in French film and text, there has also been new treatment of romantic love. Nina Bouraoui's *Appelez-moi par mon prénom* (2008) opens with an epigraph from Constant and charts with precision the virtual affair between a French woman writer and a younger man she meets at a book signing in Switzerland. In its references to the internet, to the visual arts – to the body transformations of the photography of Claude Cahun or Cindy Sherman – and to Judith Butler, whose essays are read by the younger lover, the text explores reconfigurations of unrequited love in an era of dissolved gender and spatial fixities.

Photographer and installation artist Sophie Calle also stages and questions heterosexual love in her 2007 installation, *Prenez soin de vous*, where she takes an email apparently sent to her by a lover, ending their affair, and submits it to analysis by 107 women who each interpret the text according to their professional role. Calle's installation explores the possibility of a form of pain management through a relation to the other. As each other women reads, receives, and dissects the email text, its power to bring pain is dissipated. Performance and repetition bring a calibrated form of palliation. Similar strategies are used in Calle's *Douleur exquise* (2003).

In their rethinking of intimacy, women writers, artists, and filmmakers have paid illuminating attention to pain itself, physical and psychic. Such work often intersects with other political histories and discourses, where, for example, Sarah Kofman's writing on the Shoah, Charlotte Delbo's Auschwitz trilogy, or Assia Djebar's works on mourning in Algeria, look outwards beyond the specific situation of gendered experience. Yet an account, such as Chantal Chawaf's novel *Le Manteau noir* (1998), sets its exploration of the archive of memory in the context of a very intimate narrative of the protagonist's traumatic birth and the loss of her mother, and of the mourning of that lost relation through acts of historiographic reconstruction.

Mourning returns as trope in Agnès's Varda's filmic tributes to her husband Jacques Demy, in particular *Jacquot de Nantes* (1991), and in her installation *Les Veuves de Noirmoutier* (2005), in which widows from the island of Noirmoutier speak about the absence of their husbands. From a different perspective, in *Passions d'Annie Leclerc* (2007), Paris-based Canadian writer Nancy Huston mourns the death by cancer of writer Anne Leclerc, the author of such texts of *écriture féminine* as *Parole de femme* (1974). Such writing both testifies to loss and yet in some senses alleviates it too, in an act of symbolisation or an artistic memorial.

Conclusion

In her sculpture *Femme-maison* (1994) artist Louise Bourgeois shows a prone woman's body in white marble, her head replaced by a marble house. Bourgeois's sculpted spider, *Maman* (1999), shows an infant vision of a monstrous maternal figure who is also strangely delicate, precise, with a hanging net of eggs. Bourgeois's various sculptural installations, the 'Cells', are hung with remnants and fetishes, intimate reminders of Bourgeois's past psychic and sexual life. Interiors, infancy and, intimacy return in these forms. Women's writing, art, and filmmaking of the last century has alighted on a nexus of images that in turn are used to reimagine and reinvent the feminine, making it new and making it strange.

76

French popular culture and the case of *bande dessinée*

WENDY MICHALLAT

The French state and popular culture

The French state has sought to harness 'popular cultures' in the form of worker culture, folk culture, and cultural forms communicated by the mass media for political ends since the Revolution.[1] In the 1930s, the Popular Front continued state valorisation of popular cultures with its acknowledgement of working-class entertainment in a new state-sponsored era of leisure.[2] In the 1940s, the Vichy state mobilised pre-1789 folk cultures to construct a mythic anti-Republican 'France éternelle' sharing ancient cultural common-alities with the new leader of a pan-European state, Germany.[3] 'Peuple et Culture', which emerged with the Maquis and Uriage's École des cadres during the Occupation, sought to popularise 'high culture' – literature, theatre, classical music, fine art – by promoting it to the 'people' in a strategy evocative of Popular Front initiatives and anticipatory of Malraux's 'Maisons de Cultures' project of the early 1960s.[4] From the Liberation to the 1980s the state's project to democratise culture was predicated on the assumption of the cultural deprivation of the masses which could be remedied by means of an 'éducation permanente' providing access to erudite culture both inside and outside the formal educational system.[5] However, Jack Lang's first period of tenure as minister of culture in Mitterrand's Socialist government (1981–6) marked a radical change of direction for state policy on culture. Now mass-media driven popular cultures were valorised as authentic culture. Lang's declaration in a 1981 speech to the French National Assembly justifying a

1 M. Ozouf, *La Fête révolutionnaire, 1789–1799* (Paris: Gallimard, 1988).
2 D. Looseley, *The Politics of Fun* (Oxford: Berg, 1995), pp. 22–3.
3 J. Hellman, *The Knight Monks of Vichy France: Uriage 1940–1945* (Montreal and Kingston, Ontario: McGill-Queen's University Press, 1997).
4 Looseley, *The Politics of Fun*, pp. 71–135.
5 B. Rigby, *Popular Culture in Modern France: A Study of Cultural Discourse* (London: Routledge, 1991), pp. 60–4.

doubling of his ministry's budget that, 'Il n'y a pas d'un côté la grande culture, la noble culture, aux mains propres, celle du secteur public et, de l'autre, la culture aux mains sales' ('There is no such thing as a grand culture, a noble culture, an honourable public sector culture on one side and a disreputable culture on the other') signalled the state's incorporation of the popular into cultural policy beginning with its co-option of music and *bande dessinée*.[6] The policy was termed 'décloisonnement' and the state's sponsorship of these erstwhile marginalised forms, although presented as an attempt to break down the barriers between 'high' and 'low' cultures,[7] could be interpreted as a cynical attempt to control potentially disruptive cultural expression. British cultural theorist John Fiske uses the example of jeans to illustrate that popular culture carries within it 'signs of power relations, traces of the forces of domination and subordination' but also that it has the potential to resist these structures. He points to the act of 'tearing one's jeans' as a means of resisting fashion's assimilation of the dissident symbolic value of jeans, thereby making the point that the popular can exist both inside and outside establishment cultural norms.[8] As Jeremy Aherne notes in *Michel de Certeau: Interpretation and its Other*, Certeau (quoted copiously in Fiske) holds that popular cultural expression is merely what one is permitted to consume by a controlling power that suppresses potentially disruptive alterity. 'Tactics' are employed by the disempowered to restore the voice silenced by the 'Strategy' of the controlling power; 'it is manoeuvre "within the enemy's field of vision" . . . and within enemy territory'.[9] However, the notion that popular culture has within it the potential to resist controlling cultural and political authority is contested theoretical territory.

Popular culture theory

Popular culture, described by sociologist Tony Bennett as a useless concept, 'a melting pot of confused and contradictory meanings capable of misdirecting inquiry up any number of theoretical blind alleys', has, nevertheless, been the object of continuous definition and redefinition since Gramsci's elaboration of it as a site of ideological resistance to controlling cultural authority in

6 See www.assemblee-nationale.fr/histoire/lang.asp for the full text of 'un ministère de la culture, pour quoi faire', 17 November 1981.
7 Looseley, *The Politics of Fun*, p. 123.
8 J. Fiske, *Understanding Popular Culture* (London: Routledge, 1989), p. 26.
9 M. de Certeau, *The Practice of Everyday Life*, pp. 36–7 and 60–1 quoted in J. Aherne, *Michel de Certeau: Interpretation and its Other* (Cambridge: Polity Press, 1995), p. 162.

the 1930s.[10] The concept of popular culture as intrinsically oppositional, defined, as John Storey writes, 'in contrast to other conceptual categories: folk culture, mass culture, dominant culture, working class culture etc', dominated thought until the 1980s.[11] Until that time, the predominant perspective had been that of the Frankfurt school which saw in mass-media culture a form of popular culture that was the antithesis of erudite cultural expression and which carried with it a bourgeois, capitalist ethic designed to lull the downtrodden masses into a parallel world of self-delusion and fantasy to consume an illusion of happy self-fulfilment in the form of formulaic entertainment and commodities. The notion of the mass-media form of popular culture as the negative untutored other of an erudite homogeneous culture enjoyed by the economically and culturally privileged can also be seen in the work of theorists generally regarded as having legitimised the intrinsic value of popular culture and the working class 'everyday'. Pierre Bourdieu and Edgar Morin, and the co-founders of the Birmingham Centre for Contemporary Cultural Studies, Richard Hoggart and Stuart Hall, notwithstanding the diversity of their respective methodological approaches, persistently presented mass-media culture as the inferior other of high culture.[12] However, whereas the Frankfurt school thinkers had seen political enlightenment for the masses in radical avant-garde art forms, the British school, in particular, saw in television and comics and in the myriad bifurcations of expressions of youth culture a potential within popular culture for resistance to controlling ideology.[13] In recent years the notion that popular culture necessarily disempowers the consumer masses has lost credibility. Instead, the recipient confronts the culture industry's strategies of control by accepting, rejecting, or subverting what the industry approximates to be their tastes and desires. It is here, where reception combines with participation, that one can find a resonance with a Bakhtinian presentation of popular cultural practice as contestatory. Indeed, Douglas Kellner evokes popular culture's historical associations with protest against the established order and suggests, like Fiske, Storey and Certeau, that the ideological

10 T. Bennett, 'Popular Culture: A Teaching Object', *Screen Education* 34 (1980), pp. 17–29, at p. 18, quoted in J. Storey, *Cultural Theory and Popular Culture* (London: Harvester Wheatsheaf, 1993), p. 1.
11 Storey, *Cultural Theory and Popular Culture*, p. 1.
12 See Rigby, *Popular Culture in Modern France*, p. 127, and Storey, *Cultural Theory and Popular Culture*, p. 62.
13 D. Kellner, 'The Frankfurt School and British Cultural Studies: The Missed Articulation', available at: www.gseis.ucla.edu/faculty/kellner/essays/frankfurtschoolbritishculturalstudies. pdf (accessed 10 February 2010), and in J. T. Nealon, *Rethinking the Frankfurt School: Alternative Legacies of Cultural Critique* (Albany: State University of New York Press, 2002), pp. 31–58.

hegemony vehicled by mass-media-driven popular culture can be challenged by its audience.[14] However, this view is at odds with a turn in theory that has retreated from political concepts of popular culture altogether. Populism holds that there is a false distinction between so-called 'high' and 'low' cultures. Culture is popular simply by the fact of its consumption and, in this sense, all culture, be it opera, theatre, pigeon racing, or video gaming, is popular. The collapsing of the distinction between so-called high and low cultures, lampooned by polemicist Alain Finkelkraut who laments in *La Défaite de la pensée* the attention given to 'l'art du tricot, la mastication du bétel ou l'habitude ancestrale de tremper une tartine grassement beurrée dans le café au lait du matin' ('the art of knitting or tobacco chewing or the time-honoured tradition of dunking a butter-lathered slice of bread into one's morning coffee'), removes popular culture from political consideration.[15] Such an approach, which claims no political or ideological identity for culture, seems unsatisfactory particularly in France, where there has been a formal relationship between politics and culture for much of the twentieth century and where the cultural admissibility of popular cultural expression has been and continues to be a subject of fierce debate. In his article 'The Frankfurt School and British Cultural Studies: The Missed Articulation', Douglas Kellner lobbies for 'a return to critical social theory and political economy' to revitalise cultural studies. A new approach would, he claims, meld an analysis of the political economy of the Frankfurt school with the work done on 'subversive moments of media culture, oppositional subcultures and an active audience' developed by the British school.[16] This approach to discussion of popular culture restores the categories of 'high' and 'low' culture as posited by both schools and allows for a return to an analysis of mass-media-driven popular culture as being a site of ideological and political contestation.

Bande dessinée – case study

Bande dessinée (BD) fits with John Storey's elaboration of the principal characteristics of the popular cultural form. Assessing popularity quantitatively, whilst alone inadequate, can nevertheless assist a definition,[17] and BD, a huge and enduring commercial success in France and highly accessible across social

14 D. Kellner, 'TV, Ideology and Emancipatory Popular Culture', *Socialist Review* 45 (1979), pp. 13–53.
15 A. Finkielkraut, *La Défaite de la pensée* (Paris: Gallimard, 1987), p. 11.
16 Kellner, 'The Frankfurt School and British Cultural Studies'.
17 Storey, *Cultural Theory and Popular* Culture, p. 7.

classes by virtue of its easy intelligibility and relatively low cost, fits this partial interpretation of the popular. BD resonates, also, with the tendency, described by Storey, to view popular culture in terms of its relationship to high culture. Until the late 1960s BD was generally viewed as a low-culture paraliterature for children and adolescents. Somewhat paradoxically, its emergence as a mass-market form in post-war France, when the BD album boom extended its reach from the children's market into the adult market, was, as we will see, accompanied by an acquisition of the traits of high culture. The 'parcours' of what came to be termed the new 'neuvième art' also combines with the view outlined earlier of popular culture carrying within it the potential to disrupt controlling cultural authority. The history of its evolution during the 1960s and 1970s is closely interwoven with that of a young generation increasingly intolerant of state and church control. BD, controlled in large measure by Catholic publishing houses and heavily censored by the state, became a conspicuous target of youth lifestyle rebellion. This case study of *bande dessinée* examines the medium in respect of its emergence as a complex (and ambiguous) popular cultural form in the 1960s and 1970s, drawing on the theoretical approach recommended by Kellner which proposes analysing the dissident possibilities of popular cultural expression from within the political, sociological, and cultural context of its evolution.

BD: ideological control

Under the German Occupation, the Vichy state used comics as a propaganda tool, and Catholic publications that had survived paper shortages, distribution difficulties, and the outright ban imposed on American comics assimilated an ideological discourse that chimed, in many respects, with that of the Occupation government. Although explicit anti-Semitic and anti-communist strips were the preserve of the Paris-based comic *Le Téméraire*, material extolling hero 'chevaliers' in a pre-revolutionary age of ecclesiastical authority, coupled with paternalistic homilies promoting 'bon enfant' conduct in support of the 'révolution nationale', routinely appeared and represented an establishment recuperation of popular folk tradition. From 1940 until 1944 the diminished comics market was subject to an unprecedented dual ideological supervision by both church and state. In the immediate post-war period and early 1950s, ideological control of the market intensified with the introduction of legislation determining what could and could not appear in strips. Left-wing education lobbyists were as zealous as their Vichy forebears in their surveillance of publications. American comics with 'fascist' superheroes were effectively banned by two texts: the 'Loi n° 49.956 du 16 juillet 1949 sur les publications destinées à la jeunesse' and 1953 guidelines issued to the industry that required that comic subject matter should be topical, relevant, and educationally useful to young French readers. American comics, produced overseas but translated and distributed through syndicates in France, could not in general adapt to the new regulations and withdrew from the market as a consequence. Antagonism towards America was provoked by the emerging tensions between the communist bloc and the West in the immediate post-war period as well as by suspicions that dark imperialist designs might lurk behind the US's Marshall Plan beneficence.[18] However, it was the threat posed by emerging American youth culture to the authority that church, state, and family enjoyed over young people that directly inspired legislation imposing restrictions on non-French reading matter for children. So, in the 1950s, while teenage audiences in the United States were enjoying the irreverence of *Mad* magazine and *Tales from the Crypt*, French readers were still being served up boy scout jinks and japes and pirate adventures. BD was, then, very much characterised by control of the church and state. Whilst this was to remain largely the case throughout the 1950s and early 1960s through to the upheaval of 1968, there were two key changes in BD's relationship with the broader media that prompted the emergence of a new style of comic strip that sought to engage an older, wider audience with the contestatory aspects of youth culture. These changes set the scene for a definitive usurpation of formal institutional control of BD in the late 1960s and early 1970s.

BD and radio

In the late 1950s, emerging youth culture prompted tension between market interests and the state and religious ideologies underpinning BD. *Pilote* magazine, launched in October 1959, joined with independent station Radio Luxembourg to capitalise on the new audience of teenage listeners drawn to the radio medium by pop music and the mass availability of the transistor radio. *Pilote* dropped the paternalism and 'bon enfant' moralising characteristic of leading Catholic comics such as *Spirou* and *Tintin*. Instead, the magazine encouraged new teenage readers of BD to express their opinions on what they wanted to see in the magazine. New BD strips such as Astérix and *Les Chevaliers du ciel*, both launched with *Pilote* in 1959, reflected, albeit subtly,

18 B. McKenzie, *Remaking France: Americanization, Public Diplomacy and the Marshall Plan* (New York: Berghahn, 2005).

confrontation with adult authority, and the latter in particular presented more complex narratives in which characters reasoned around moral dilemmas. In establishing a bridge between the nascent adolescent market establishing itself in the broader mass media and BD, *Pilote* opened the medium to a discourse shaped not by the state and religious ideology but by dissident teenager discourse. This accommodation of contestatory discourse would exert a more profound effect on BD towards the end of the 1960s as it acquired a more explicitly political coloration.

The BD book

In the mid-1960s BD publishers, impressed by the phenomenal growth of the Format Poche (FP) book market, copied the FP publishers' strategy of reissuing classic literature and reissued cartoons in album format. The FP's visual impact, its accessibility and desirability as a commodity, which caused it to be derided as the 'livre-objet' by its detractors, was also copied by BD publishers. Like the FP, the BD album was cheap with a colourful cover. Like the FP it was presented as part of a numbered collection to appeal to the collecting instincts of a market of students and young professionals. It used the same distribution networks as the FP and was displayed on the same self-service racks in supermarkets, newspaper kiosks, and 'grands magasins'. This shift of BD from its 'enfantine niche' into a wider market also marked a shift in cultural status for the medium which had effectively moved into the 'literature' market. Its 'low culture' tag as entertainment for children was countered not only by the fact that BD was becoming increasingly populated by references to literature, art, and film, to appeal to an audience of students, but also because the collation of BD into albums and its marketing as a literature prompted the new generation of FP publishers to publish critical work on the BD. Interest in the medium as an art form, as serious literature with a distinctive tradition and aesthetic, came about precisely because BD, old and new, was collated in book form for enthusiasts and nostalgic collectors. Effectively, an archive of comic art was being produced, and critical writing, cheaply produced by the same publishers, further fuelled sales of it. In the late 1960s and early 1970s a francophone genealogy was traced for BD. From the 'images d'Épinal' to Topffer and Christophe, the concern was to attribute to the medium a distinct French/francophone tradition in order to win it legitimacy by setting it up as a 'national literature'. It was during this period of lobbying for 'lauriers' that BD claimed the designation 'le neuvième art'. This move from 'low-culture' disposable comics to the intellectually respectable album book encouraged the medium's articulation of dissident social and political discourses emerging at the end of the 1960s.

The 1960s and 1970s: contestation

From 1968 through to the early 1970s, BD assimilated protest discourses associated with the teenage and student market it had courted from the late 1950s. Upheaval in the BD market was in large measure prompted by the commercialisation and popularisation of the medium as a book form. In the wake of the album boom, BD 'dessinateurs' were authors and media stars and not the jobbing illustrators commissioned to produce to a 'house style' of years past. They were the first generation of BD workers with experience of university or art school, and they saw themselves, like the filmmakers of the *Cahiers du cinéma*, as 'auteurs' with something important to say. Although the artists who at *Pilote* in 1968 threatened to take over the magazine if it remained impervious to the 'events' went on to make careers producing lucrative protest albums, there was, for a brief period at least, a confrontation that challenged the censorship of the state and the commercial prerogatives of the market. The intellectual status of the new literary medium encouraged experimentation that undermined the commercial imperative of saleability (even though experimentation in itself later became a desirable commodity). Artists Philippe Druillet, Fred and Gotlib in particular challenged the formulaic conventions of BD. In their own independent publications they challenged the conventional 'cases' ('frames') and 'bulles' ('bubbles') style of narration with fluid compositional arrangements where shape and colour directed reading. Sexually explicit and politically confrontational content mapping closely the rhetoric of '68 also made an appearance. This graphic experimentation and new style content often took the form of satire characteristic of the tactics of subversion used during 1968. In this respect, BD, emblematic of the control of state, church, and market, was in itself a symbol ripe for subversion that took the form of a dismantling of its formal conventions and a satirisation not only of political and religious figures and media celebrities but also a 'détournement' of cartoons associated with the regime of ideological control.[19] The year 1968 thus marked the first sustained challenge to the ideological and commercial control of the BD market. However, the period between 1968 and 1972 saw an unprecedented seizure of control of youth publishing by its audience.

19 T. Englehart, *The End of Victory Culture: Cold War America and the Disillusioning of a Generation* (New York: Basic Books, 1995).

The underground market

The events of May 1968 saw a second wave of anti-establishment youth publications in France. Protest publications such as *L'Enragé* inspired a wave of auto-publishing which by the early 1970s constituted a market of hundreds of home-produced mimeographed publications. With their own informal networks at universities and *lycées* they mounted, for a brief time, a serious popular challenge to the mainstream youth publication market. Sexually explicit and politically provocative, they were invariably illegal but were impossible to stop; they would simply reappear under a different name and their authors were rarely identifiable. Eventually, the mainstream youth press market responded to the tone and content of these artisanal publications and new publications such as *Actuel* were marketed on an 'alternative' ticket which, in respect of BD, meant an accommodation of the jaundiced sociology of artists such as Robert Crumb. BD thus acquired a new formative component to link with its new culturally legitimate mass-market status. Although quickly recuperated, the French underground movement of the early 1970s nevertheless ensured that authority for the content and style of BD devolved, to an extent, to the 'people'. In this respect, it acquired the profile of popular culture in a traditional pre-mass-media sense of the word as an expression of belief specific to a community and one catalysed by dissident discourse which BD celebrities of that period have since made a career out of recycling.

Twenty-first-century BD – still contestatory?

The arrival of the internet has meant that aspiring BD artists who publish on the web have been able to reassure BD publishers, who would otherwise be reluctant to commit to them, that their work has a market. The process resembles that of the late 1960s and 1970s when publishers began to use BD periodicals to ascertain the popularity of new strips with the public prior to publishing them in book form. Then, as now, the 'pre-publication' platform – essentially a commercial device – did not inspire artists to innovate. The BD blog – accorded its own competition, 'Révélation Blog', at the annual Angoulême BD festival in 2008 – is a showcase for new talent with commercial potential in a BD market that shies away from controversy. In competition with increasingly popular Japanese and American publications, which now account for 40 per cent of the market, French publishers are placing more emphasis than ever on finding strips to appeal to broad popular taste. That, and the fact that the 'spirit of 68', which informed much radical BD throughout the 1970s and 1980s, has been progressively discredited within both BD and politics at large – by 1973, Bretécher was already mocking the earnest 'bo-bo' in 'Les Frustrés' – has meant that the sense of 'BD engagée' has changed. Now, meaningful disruption emanates from artists hitherto excluded from a predominantly white, male, and heterosexual BD milieu. Although relatively scarce, there have been several examples of gay male autobiographical BD. Fabrice Néaud's 'Journal' (1996–2002) drew inspiration from the artist's experience of gay life in provincial France, and Jean-Paul Jennequin's 'Les Folles Nuits de Jonathan', published in 2001, features a gay adolescent who navigates his sexuality alongside his companion and confidante, a talking penis. However, even more scarce is BD by and about women, and feminist-themed BD is practically non-existent. BD artist Chantal Montellier proves the exception. Although her socialist feminism may be dated, its presence in BD is entirely novel. She condemns the sexism and commercialisation of BD both through her work and through public pronouncements published on her website condemning both the poor quality of her peers' output and their complicity with the BD 'industry'. Jacques Tardi's literary adaptations earned him the description 'l'illustrateur besogneux du fasciste Céline et du collabo Géo-Charles Véran' ('the assiduous illustrator of the fascist Céline and collaborator Géo-Charles Véran').[20] Manga and American imports are 'la soupe américano-japonaise industrielle' ('a Yankie–Japanese mass-produced gloup'),[21] the editorial board of *Charlie-Hebdo* is an 'équipe des machos' ('bunch of chauvinists') and Marjane Satrapi is a 'bourgeoisement correcte' ('middle-class pandering') illustrator of 'pictogrammes appliqués mais sans grande imagination ni liberté graphique, sans grand savoir artistique non plus' ('carefully executed but imaginatively barren, graphically contrived and artistically ignorant pictograms'). Whilst Montellier's style of intervention might not be the most delicate, certain of her criticisms, such as those of Satrapi, are not without some justification. Whether Satrapi's 'Persepolis' would have been as commercially successful in the West had it not resonated with Islamophobic discourses post 9/11 is doubtful. As Montellier points out, a BD condemning domestic violence against women in France would be distinctly less marketable.[22] Some fifteen years prior to Despentes' *Baise-moi* (novel 1999, film 2000), Montellier had already published 'Odile et les crocodiles', whose heroine, failed by the legal system, turns vigilante to avenge her rape. In 2006,

20 'Tardi et le Parti Communiste flingués par Chantal "Calamity" Montellier', *Actua-BD*, 12 March 2007, available at: www.actuabd.com/spip.php?breve1935.
21 See www.montellier.org/ (accessed 10 February 2010).
22 Ibid.

she published *Sorcières, mes sœurs* about male demonisation and persecution of free-spirited women in contemporary France. Montellier's contribution is unique. She restores the radical potential of BD by challenging both its androcentrism and the commercialisation that undermines its creative purpose. Engaging with the tradition of dissidence that emerged in the 1960s, Montellier uses cartoons to demand an accommodation and comprehension of a political discourse previously inadmissible in BD.

77

Literature, film, and new media

ISABELLE McNEILL

As the twentieth century became the twenty-first, distinctions between media could no longer be taken for granted. The prevalence of digital media, which convert the signals and traces they record into the same type of numerical code,[1] leads us to reconsider the connections between different forms of representation. It has also, arguably, paved the way for a greater degree of hybridity in art than ever before. From electronic books to interactive films on the internet, new ways of combining and receiving text and images are constantly being proposed and sought, so that it sometimes becomes difficult to know how to refer to, describe, or interpret a particular object. We might think we know what books and films are, but what about Chris Marker's CD-ROM *Immemory* (1997)? Raymond Bellour locates this autobiographical, digital collage in the tradition of the literary self-portrait.[2] Yet the focus on images and juxtaposition also points to cinematic montage and hyperlinks recall internet navigation, creating a 'web' of quotations from other works, textual musings, and digitally processed images. Marker is not the only acclaimed French filmmaker to experiment with different ways of disseminating ideas through images and text. Veterans of the *nouvelle vague*, Jean-Luc Godard and Agnès Varda both held major installation exhibitions in 2006, taking their work into three dimensions, and exploring some of the possibilities of hybridity and interactivity that have become associated with new technologies.[3] If we ever dreamed they were stable, the boundaries between the arts increasingly seem illusory. Of course, these issues extend far beyond the French context, since the media and concepts in question are conditioned by global markets and

1 D. N. Rodowick, *The Virtual Life of Film* (Cambridge, MA: Harvard University Press, 2007), p. 10.
2 R. Bellour and L. Roth, *Qu'est-ce qu'une Madeleine? A Propos du CD-ROM Immemory de Chris Marker*, with English translations by B. Holmes (Paris: Yves Gevaert Éditeur, Centre Georges Pompidou, 1997), p. 74.
3 'Voyages en Utopie', Jean-Luc Godard, Centre Georges Pompidou, Paris, 2006, and *L'Île et elle*, Agnès Varda, Fondation Cartier, Paris, 2006.

delocalised by the transnational communications of cyberspace. Such media and concepts are, however, crucially important aspects of contemporary French culture, forming a context that necessarily frames an understanding of the specifically French examples discussed here.

Arguments about 'newness' should always be treated with caution. 'New media' develop from old media such as books and films, and often recycle their concepts and forms (hence the term 'web page'). Two caveats, in particular, are worth bearing in mind when approaching the hybrid art of the late twentieth and early twenty-first century. The first is that new technology does not automatically guarantee innovation. It is important to avoid what is known as 'technological essentialism', which is the flawed assumption that 'because a technology can do this the medium is indisputably like that'.[4] While technology undoubtedly generates new possibilities, such as the new ways of receiving films created by DVD extras (discussed below), not all possibilities will be realised, and a medium cannot be defined by those that are. The second, related caveat is that what appears new is sometimes just the old in disguise, or at least is part of a continuum rather than constituting a definitive break. Indeed, exploring art that seems obviously hybrid or interactive may make us look differently at the art of the past. Illuminated medieval manuscripts were a complex hybrid of image and text, and, as will be explored below, interactivity may not be as distinct from so-called 'passive' modes of reception as might be thought.

It is nevertheless true that technology has always helped to shape the way art and information are transmitted. In the fifteenth century, the printing press revolutionised the dissemination of literature by rendering it vastly cheaper and easier to reproduce. It can be argued that film distribution has undergone a similarly dramatic transformation at the turn of the twenty-first century, creating new parallels with the book in terms of access and portability, while effecting changes in the way moving images can be 'read'. While cinema was hailed from its birth as an inherently reproducible medium, initially it was hardly comparable to mass-produced books where ease of dissemination was concerned, since numerous heavy cans of film were required to store moving images, and expensive and bulky equipment was needed for projection. Books, in modern times at least, have been both more easily transportable and more accessible to the individual. From the latter part of the nineteenth century smaller formats became more widely commercialised to capitalise on the increase in travel instigated by the development of railway

---

4 M. Lister *et al.* (eds.), *New Media: A Critical Introduction* (London: Routledge, 2003), p. 13.

systems. The publisher Hachette designed the 'Bibliothèque des Chemins de Fer', a collection of books for reading on long train journeys, transporting readers while the locomotive swept them towards their destination.[5] Only towards the end of the twentieth century did film viewing become a way of occupying a journey, thanks to portable supports and devices. The process began with televised broadcasts of films and the subsequent arrival of video tapes, bringing films into the domestic sphere. But it took the explosive commercialisation of information technology during the 1990s to make the moving image as easily transportable as a paperback, if not more so. Theatrical distribution in cinemas continues, for the time being, to form an important means of disseminating film, at least as a marketing strategy to enhance DVD and merchandise sales.[6] Increasingly, however, the experience of cinema has become disconnected from particular locations. Film viewing is often a solitary, rather than collective, activity, and is accessible while on the move.

The digital video disc (DVD), in particular, has become a popular support for the moving image. Though new formats are always being developed and commercialised, notably the high-definition, extra large capacity Blu-Ray disc, DVD dominated from the late 1990s for at least a decade and brought with it potential changes in the viewer's experience. Light, inexpensive to produce, and capable of storing large amounts of data, DVD not only allowed viewers to take films with them on their travels, it also contained enhanced navigability compared to the linear projections of cinema and the laborious rewinding and fast-forwarding required to locate a particular scene on a tape. Viewers were now able to travel more easily through films, returning to and replaying favourite scenes by moving between different 'chapters'. Indeed, in many cases, it is possible to pause with photographic precision on an individual frame. This led film theorist Laura Mulvey to argue compellingly that DVD reacquaints the spectator with the still photographic image at the heart of all cinema, reconfiguring the possibilities of the relationship between spectator and film by allowing us to take possession of and contemplate films in new ways.[7] Certainly, DVD constituted a less bounded experience of film than ever before, delocalising the viewing experience and potentially disrupting linearity with chapter divisions and the pause function. The advent of DVD also troubled the boundary of the film through the inclusion of 'extras' (*les*

5 S. Darricau, *Le Livre* (Paris: Scérén (CNDP); Pyramid, 2004), p. 34.
6 E. Arnoldy, *À perte de vues: images et 'nouvelles technologies' d'hier et d'aujourd'hui* (Paris: Éditions Labor, 2005), p. 28.
7 L. Mulvey, *Death 24 × A Second* (London: Reaktion Books, 2005).

bonus in French, or *les boni*, as Agnès Varda idiosyncratically calls them on the DVDs of her films). Interviews, 'making-of' documentaries (*les making-of*), deleted scenes (*scènes coupées*), and other related material draw into question any clear sense of the limits of the film as text, as our experience of the film potentially includes everything included on the disc. Audio commentaries by the director, cast, or crew of the film bring such supposedly ancillary material into the space of the film itself, as voices overlay the soundtrack, bringing the image track into a direct dialogue with anecdotes surrounding the making of the film or the interpretations and opinions of its makers. With the inclusion of alternative endings and the proliferation of directors' cuts, it has become increasingly difficult to isolate a film as a single, defined object.

An example of the function and significance of DVD extras can be found in the films of Yamina Benguigui, a French filmmaker of Algerian descent whose work addresses questions of memory and identity in North African communities in France. We will see that, as a means of distribution, DVD emphasises the intersections between fiction and documentary, and between filmmaker and film, in Benguigui's work. The inclusion of commentary and interviews offers a variety of openings in the material of the films, a strategy which has a particular relevance for Benguigui's subject matter and political aims. *Inch'Allah dimanche* (2001) is a feature-length fiction film, whose narrative centres on the arrival of Zouina, a young Algerian woman, in France in the 1970s. One woman's journey serves to illustrate the social impact of the *regroupement familial* policy, which allowed immigrant workers to bring their families to France, with the aim of encouraging integration. The women and children often arrived after many years of living away from their husbands, and had to cope not only with adapting to life in a new country but also with an often oppressive family structure dominated by their husbands and mothers-in-law.[8]

Two screens of text at the start of the film situate the fictional tale in the context of real historical events, not only implying an intention of authenticity but also promoting a certain historical seriousness in the way the viewer relates to the film. The DVD extras, which include interviews with Benguigui and the male and female leads, Zinedine Soualem and Fejria Deliba, play a powerful role in conditioning and enriching this relationship for the viewer. Taken together, they serve both to trouble the boundaries between

---

8 For a discussion of the film see C. Tarr, *Reframing Difference:* Beur *and* banlieue *Filmmaking in France* (Manchester: Manchester University Press, 2005) pp. 176–8.

documentary and fiction and to emphasise the 'documentary' aspects of the film. These aspects emerge in two main ways. First, in a filmed interview, Benguigui evokes a personal family history, which has been reimagined through the fictional film in order to fill in the gaps and silences left by memories too overwhelming to articulate. Referring to the affecting opening scene, Benguigui says, 'it's exactly what I'd imagined for my mother's departure. I'm sure she left like that . . . I imagined it because I know she's still unable to talk about it'.[9] The interview thus imbues the film, which might otherwise appear disconnected from the filmmaker's own life, with an autobiographical resonance.

The second key way in which the documentary underpinning of the fictional film emerges is in the director's commentary. Here Benguigui discusses the film as it unfolds, in dialogue with the casting director and acting coach Bouchta Saïdoun. Benguigui recounts the care taken with the *mise-en-scène*, ensuring that the decor, costumes, and fabric were authentic, although the interior of Zouina's home is filmed in a studio. On the one hand this exposes the artificiality of the film's diegetic space, yet at the same time it points to the knowledge drawn from personal experience which makes such re-creation possible. Bouchta Saïdoun observes that most of the cast and crew brought their personal experiences to the film. Perhaps the most striking interweaving of document and artifice is in the casting of the character of Aïcha, Zouina's mother-in-law. The commentary track reveals that Rabbia Mokkedem, who plays Aïcha, is Bouchta Saïdoun's mother. We hear that she found it difficult to distinguish between reality and the fiction of the film and was strongly affected by scenes that brought back memories of her own past. Such oral testimonies, once woven into the viewer's experience of the film, imbue it not only with greater documentary authenticity but also highlight the position of Benguigui's generation, the children of immigration seeking to give voices and images to their parents' stories.

The relationship between documentary and fiction is complex, but this brief example indicates that new modes of viewing can affect the way we interpret and understand a film. If, as Vivian Sobchack argues, 'the generic terms *fiction* and *documentary* designate . . . an experienced difference in our mode of consciousness, our attention toward and our valuation of the cinematic objects we engage',[10] watching certain DVD extras can be seen to alter that consciousness, attention towards, and valuation of a film. Catherine Grant

9 This and all subsequent translations from the French are mine.
10 V. Sobchack, *Carnal Thoughts: Embodiment and Moving Image Culture* (Berkeley: California University Press, 2004), p. 261.

suggests that the director's commentary always functions as a redirection of the fiction film into a documentary, 'one in which the film's existing visual track is employed as a graphic illustration of a teleological story of its own production'.[11] While Grant's argument refers to the commercial exploitation of viewers' concept of an 'auteur' (a director who has artistic control of the film), it is clear from the example of *Inch'Allah dimanche* that ethical aims may also be at stake in these kinds of supplementary viewing experience.

The DVD of *Inch'Allah dimanche* lists its extras under the heading 'interactivité', a term sometimes used generically in French to refer to *les bonus*. Certainly, DVD offers the beginnings of an interaction between the viewer and the materiality of a film, mainly through a limited number of choices that are added to the primary film-watching experience. We have seen that it is possible to choose different audio track(s) such as the director's commentary. One can also choose a narrative order through the chapter options, as for example in Pathé Fox Europa's *Édition Collector* DVD of Christopher Nolan's *Memento* (2000, DVD 2002), whose extras include a 'double chapitrage', allowing a reversible viewing of the famously reversed narrative sequences, as well as a 'montage inversé', taking the reversibility one step further and allowing a chronologically edited viewing. The 'double chapitrage' option is of course one open to any DVD viewer, albeit in a slightly more laborious way where there is no provision of an inversed chapter menu. Gaspar Noé's *Irréversible* (2002) becomes reversible through its DVD chapter menu, and, perhaps more interestingly, the most conventionally linear narratives can be reordered or reversed in sequential 'chapter' blocks. Interactivity in commercially sold DVDs remains relatively limited, however. There may be more options for the viewer than in a cinema projection, but these options remain predetermined and non-manipulable. Moreover, the very term 'chapter' points towards a literary tradition in which a contents page – now called a 'menu' – helped guide the reader through the narrative, a familiar convention which viewers do not necessarily associate with playful intervention. So while DVD opens up a level of interactivity through choice, the active intervention of the viewer remains restricted and secondary. This of course depends on one's understanding of the concept of 'interactivity'. For some scholars, such as Édouard Arnoldy, the contemporary privileging of interactive art objects is based on an obsession with the new, which has a tendency to ignore the full potential of previous modes of interaction:

---

11 C. Grant, 'Auteur Machines?', in J. Bennett and T. Brown (eds.), *Film and Television after DVD* (London: Routledge, 2005), pp. 101–15 at p. 111.

> From a passive being to an active accomplice, the apparent metamorphosis of
> the consumer of images stems undoubtedly from a misunderstanding about
> the possible (in)activity of the 'reader of images'.[12]

Arnoldy goes on to argue that many recent projects whose intention is to break
with the 'passive' traditions of cinema are trapped in a limited understanding
of what cinema is or can be. He takes as an example the internet/television
project *Sens dessus dessous* (2002), created by the television channel ARTE.
These short films by Angelo Cianci, the Coulin sisters, Antoine le Bos, and
Eric Loddé were commissioned to exist both in a linear version, to be shown
on television, and as interactive versions online. On ARTE's website viewers
are invited to use the mouse to participate in the unfolding of the film. For
example, in *Compulsion*, by Antoine le Bos, the mouse pointer becomes a hand,
encouraging the viewer to fondle the bodies of women in the metro, eliciting
a fantasised erotic response, followed by a more realistic angry reaction, all to
the soundtrack of a heightened, masturbatory breathing. The hand allows the
viewer to move through the metro carriage and approach different women
(though not men), but all routes eventually lead inside a woman's sexual
organs, followed by a pseudo-psychoanalytical questioning, where the words
'parlez-moi de votre mère' ('tell me about your mother') crowd both screen
and soundtrack. Arnoldy argues that although the viewer must act to allow
the film to progress and is apparently given choices, the level of interaction
remains limited, coercing the viewer into a predetermined narrative, not to
mention gender and sexuality: 'the spectator's freedom amounts to a forced
"rape" of the female characters encountered'.[13] In other words, the supposedly
liberating or empowering break from the traditional passivity of film viewing
in the end turns the violation uncomfortably back onto the viewer, who is
taken exactly where the filmmaker intends. Arnoldy questions the innovation
in this constrained scenario, when conventional cinema has been well known
for supposedly forcing male and female spectators into the perspective of
the active male hero, while the female characters remain passive objects
of desire. However, it could also be argued that forcing the spectator to
'act' in this predetermined role is in fact a witty parody of such traditional
gender positions, making the viewer aware of them through the frustrations
and discomfort of a compelled participation. Spectators have become used
to the convention of the 'point of view' camera shot, which gives them the
perspective of a particular character. Le Bos uses what one might playfully call
a 'point of hand' device, which is less familiar and therefore more noticeable.

12 Arnoldy, *À perte de vues*, p. 9.   13 Ibid., pp. 46–7.

As Arnoldy suggests, however, it is important to question the idea of a historical 'passivity' in art reception, from which new media would allow us to escape. It is true that the conventional cinematic techniques of 'continuity editing' seek to disguise the apparatus – the material and techniques through which films are constructed – which tends to make spectators forget the artifice of the film's realisation and become immersed in its fictional world. But this is not the only possible way of receiving the film.[14] Nor is it the only way of making films: avant-garde filmmakers have been challenging audiences' passivity since the earliest days of cinema, for example in Luis Buñuel and Salvador Dalí's *L'Âge d'or* (1930), which shocked viewers with its disjointed and bizarre images, hinting at narrative without ever becoming coherent. The reader of literature has always been less prone to accusations of passivity than the film viewer, and once postmodern theorists such as Roland Barthes had questioned the unilateral transmission of meaning through written texts, the reader's active role was difficult to refute. Even a direct intervention in the narrative has long been available to literary texts in the form of the 'livre-jeu', or 'choose your own adventure' book, which allows readers to choose between various plot outcomes at key moments of the story. Raymond Queneau's miniature version *Un conte à votre façon* was written in 1967, while Gildas Sagot's fantasy adventure series were popular in the 1980s and 1990s.[15]

What is perhaps most distinctive about the 'interactive' media of the late twentieth and twenty-first century is the weakening of the barriers between the producers and the consumers of art, rather than any ontological break with so-called passive media of the past. In literature this particularly concerns dissemination, whereas for film production is implicated too. While any literate person has always been able to become an author with the simplest of tools, web logs, or 'blogs', now allow writers to publish their musings for a vast potential audience, without the mediation of publishing houses. As for film, while it is not yet as easy as picking up a pen, cheap digital cameras and editing software packages already make filmmaking an accessible activity, and the results can be posted online on video-sharing websites such as YouTube.com for immediate circulation. Editing software, along with widely available programmes for the extraction of sequences from DVDs, also means that film viewers can now alter the materiality of the film, taking scenes and mixing them with images or soundtrack segments from other films. Mostly this simply means posting favourite sequences on YouTube, sometimes

14 See, for example, J. Mayne, *Cinema and Spectatorship* (London: Routledge, 1993), p. 53.
15 G. Sagot, *Jeux de rôle: tout savoir sur les jeux de rôle et les livres dont vous êtes le héros* (Paris: Gallimard, 1986).

gathered together as 'moments choisis'. However, when the soundtrack is changed, either by adding a favourite song or a humorous reinvention of the dialogues, a new work is created. Likewise, the film may be blended, with varying degrees of editing or technical expertise, with another film or films, resulting in what has become known (even in French) as a 'mashup'. One of the most famous authors of mashups is a skilful French individual who goes by the pseudonym AMDS Films.[16] Best known for *The Terminator Versus Robocop* (2008), combining the science fiction films *Terminator* (James Cameron, 1984) and *Robocop* (Paul Verhoeven, 1987) and their sequels into a dramatic six-minute short, AMDS Films specialises in clever use of the shot–reverse shot formula and smoothly bridged soundtracks to produce persuasive and popular filmic encounters. Some of the most sophisticated mashups use animation technology such as Adobe Flash, going beyond montage and bringing the two films into the same frame, perhaps linked by an animated effect. Whatever the level of technical skill involved, however, two modalities prevail: parody and homage. In both cases, while a new work is undoubtedly created, it contains within it a response to or 'reading' of the source film(s), making the boundary between viewer–reader and author difficult to discern. A high-art precedent can be found in Jean-Luc Godard's extraordinary video series, *Histoire(s) du cinéma* (1989–98), a melancholic yet playful meditation on cinema through a dense collage of music, images, and text.[17] Yet whereas Godard is a professional filmmaker who worked in a special video-editing suite, the practice of recycling and reconfiguring pre-existing images and sounds has now become widely accessible, and indeed popular. Pierre Sorlin suggests, with deep ambivalence, that, 'the "magic of the screen", made accessible to all, will become a banal practical knowledge'.[18] Yet the sheer quantity of postings on video-sharing websites implies that such mystified fascination is being replaced by an equally powerful and irreverent delight in creativity, reappropriation, and self-expression.

To conclude, in recent times dramatic developments in technology have encouraged film and literary scholars to rethink their objects of study. Modes of production, dissemination, and reception have multiplied and are becoming crucial factors in our analysis of the works, which themselves may be hybrid creations that traverse media and genres. Rather like the endless, circuitous information webs of the internet, the art of the twenty-first century tends

16 See http://spiritsnodeal.canalblog.com/ (accessed 1 January 2009).
17 This can be compared with Chris Marker's *Immemory* CD-ROM, mentioned above.
18 P. Sorlin, 'L'Ombre d'un deuil', in 'Où va le cinéma?', special issue of *Cinergon* 15 (2003), pp. 7–15, at p. 11.

to privilege the crossing of boundaries. Literature and film, documentary and fiction, author and reader: no sooner are categories set up, than an experiment comes along to draw them into question. While new technology does not necessarily imply new ways of seeing or understanding the world, new approaches to art are certainly required in order to tackle its proliferating forms.

Select bibliography

The bibliography contains selected works of criticism, literary history, and theory relevant to students and scholars of French and francophone texts. In keeping with the approach taken in the separate chapters, we have included a full range of broader thematic discussions of literature in French. Important and influential studies of single authors are also included. Primary sources are generally not listed, except in the case of recommended critical editions of pre-modern works.

Abel, R. *French Cinema: The First Wave, 1915–1929*, Princeton, NJ: Princeton University Press, 1984
  French Film Theory and Criticism 1907–1939, 2 vols., Princeton, NJ: Princeton University Press, 1988
Adam, A. (ed.), *Romanciers du xviie siècle*, Paris: Gallimard, 1962
  Histoire de la littérature française au xviie siècle, 4 vols., Paris: Editions Mondiales, 1948–56
Adam de la Halle. *Œuvres complètes*, ed. and trans. P.-Y. Badel, Paris: Livre de Poche, 1995
Adamowicz, E. *Surrealist Collage in Text and Image*, Cambridge: Cambridge University Press, 1998
Adenet le Roi, *Berte aus grand pies*, ed. A. Henry, Geneva: Droz, 1982
Adler, A. 'Militia et Amor in the *Roman de Troie*', *Romansche Forschungen*, 72 (1960), pp. 14–29
Agamben, G. *The Idea of Prose*, trans. M. Sullivan and S. Whitsitt, Albany: State University of New York Press, 1995
Agnes (Saint), *see* Denomy, A. J.
Ainsworth, P. 'Conscience littéraire de l'histoire au Moyen Age', in M. Zink and F. Lestringant (eds.), *Histoire de la France littéraire*, vol. i, Paris: Presses Universitaires de France, 2006, pp. 349–419
Akbari. S. and A. A. Iannucci (eds.). *Marco Polo and the Encounter of East and West*, Toronto: University of Toronto Press, 2008
Akehurst, F. R. P. and J. Davis (eds.). *A Handbook of the Troubadours*, Berkeley and Los Angeles: University of California Press, 1995
Aliscans, ed. C. Régnier, Paris: Champion, 1990
Allard, S. *Paris 1820: l'affirmation de la génération romantique*, Berne: Peter Lang, 2005
Allen, V. *On Farting: Language and Laughter in the Middle Ages*, New York: Palgrave Macmillan, 2007

Altfranzösisches Wörterbuch, ed. A. Tobler and E. Lommatzsch, 10 vols. to date, Berlin: Weidmann, 1925–

Altmann, B. K. and D. McGrady. *Christine de Pizan: A Casebook*, New York: Routledge, 2003

Ami et Amile: une chanson de geste, ed. P. Dembowski, Paris: Champion, 1969

Anderson, B. *Imagined Communities: Reflections on the Origin and Spread of Nationalism* (1983), rev. edn London: Verso, 2006

Anderson, L. *Autobiography*, London: Routledge, 2001

Anderson, W. *Diderot's Dream*, Baltimore, MD: Johns Hopkins University Press, 1990

André Le Chapelain, *Andreas Capellanus on Love*, ed. P. G. Walsh, London: Duckworth, 1982

Andrew, D. *Mists of Regret: Culture and Sensibility in Classic French Film*, Princeton, NJ: Princeton University Press, 1995

Andrew, J. D. *The Major Film Theories*, Oxford: Oxford University Press, 1976

Aneau, B. *Alector ou Le Coq: histoire fabuleuse*, ed. Marie-Madeleine Fontaine, 2 vols., Geneva: Droz, 1996

d'Angers, J.-E. *L'Humanisme chrétien au xviie siècle: Saint François de Sales et Yves de Paris*, The Hague: Martinus Nijhoff, 1970

Angold, M. *The Fourth Crusade: Event and Context*, London: Pearson Longman, 2003

Archambault, P. *Seven French Chroniclers: Witnesses to History*, Syracuse, NY: Syracuse University Press, 1974

Ariew, R. *Descartes and the Last Scholastics*, Ithaca, NY: Cornell University Press, 1999

Armogathe, J.-R. *Le Grand Siècle et la Bible*, Paris: Beauchesne, 1989

Arnoldy, E. *À perte de vues: images et 'nouvelles technologies' d'hier et d'aujourd'hui*, Paris: Éditions Labor, 2005

Arnould, J.-C. (ed.). *Marie de Gournay et l'édition de 1595 des 'Essais' de Montaigne*, Paris: Champion, 1996

Aronson, T. *Jean-Paul Sartre: Philosophy in the World*, London: Verso, 1980

Ashcroft, B., G. Griffiths, and H. Tiffin. *The Empire Writes Back*, London and New York: Routledge, 1989

Asher, R. E. *National Myths in Renaissance France: Francus, Samothes, and the Druids*, Edinburgh: Edinburgh University Press, 2003

Ashley, K. A. and W. Hüsken (eds.). *Moving Subjects: Processional Performance in the Middle Ages and the Renaissance*, Amsterdam: Rodopi, 2001

Aslanov, C. *Le Français au Levant, jadis et naguère: à la recherche d'une langue perdue*, Paris: Champion, 2006

Astbury, K. *The Moral Tale in France and Germany 1750–1789*, Oxford: Voltaire Foundation, 2002

Atack, M. *May 68 in French Fiction and Film: Rethinking Society, Rethinking Representation*, Oxford: Oxford University Press, 1999

Atkinson, G. *Les Nouveaux Horizons de la Renaissance française*, Paris: Droz, 1935

L'Âtre périlleux, ed. B. Woledge, Paris: Champion, 1936

Aubignac, F.-H., abbé d'. *Dissertations contre Corneille*, ed. N. Hammond and M. Hawcroft, Exeter: University of Exeter Press, 1995

  La Pratique du théâtre, ed. H. Baby, Paris: Champion, 2001

Aubrit, J.-P. *Le Conte et la nouvelle*, Paris: Colin, 1997

Audé, F. *Ciné-modèles, cinéma d'elles*, Lausanne: L'Âge d'homme, 1981
    Cinéma d'elles 1981–2001, Lausanne: L'Âge d'homme, 2002
Auerbach, E. *Mimesis: The Representation of Reality in Western Literature*, trans. W. R. Trask,
    Princeton, NJ: Princeton University Press, 1953
    'Figura', in *Scenes from the Drama of European Literature: Six Essays*, New York: Meridian
    Books, Inc., 1959; reprinted Gloucester: Peter Smith, 1973
Augustine, *Confessiones*, Turnhout: Brepols, 1983
Aurell, M. *L'Empire des Plantagenêt 1154–1224*, Paris: Perrin, 2003
Austin, J. L. *How to Do Things with Words*, ed. J. O. Urmson and M. Sbisà, 2nd edn,
    Cambridge, MA: Harvard University Press, 1978
Autrand, M. *Le Théâtre en France de 1870 à 1914*, Paris: Champion, 2006
Ayres-Bennett, W. and M. C. Jones (eds.). *The French Language and Questions of Identity*,
    London: MHRA/Legenda, 2007
Azama, M. *De Godot à Zucco: anthologie des auteurs dramatiques de langue française 1950–2000*,
    3 vols., Paris: Éditions Théâtrales, 2003–4
Baby, H. *La Tragi-comédie de Corneille à Quinault*, Paris: Klincksieck, 2001
Baetens, J. and D. Viart (eds.). 'États du roman contemporain', special issue of *La Revue des
    lettres modernes, Ecritures contemporaines*, 2: (1999)
Baguley, D. *Naturalist Fiction: The Entropic Vision*, Cambridge: Cambridge University Press,
    1990
    Napoleon III and his Regime: An Extravaganza, Baton Rouge: Louisiana State University
    Press, 2000
de Baïf, J.-A. *Œuvres complètes*, vol. 1: *Œuvres en rime. Première partie, neuf livres de poemes*, ed.
    J. Vignes with G. Demerson *et al.*, Paris: Champion, 2002
Bakhtin, M. *The Dialogic Imagination: Four Essays*, ed. M. Holquist, trans. C. Emerson and
    M. Holquist, Austin: University of Texas Press, 1981
Balakian, A. *The Symbolist Movement in the Literature of European Languages*, Budapest: John
    Benjamins, 1984
Bales, R. *Persuasion in the French Personal Novel*, Birmingham, AL: Summa Publications, 1997
Barber, R. *The Holy Grail: The History of a Legend*, London: Penguin, 2005
Barchilon, J. *Le Conte merveilleux français de 1690 à 1790*, Paris: Champion, 1975
Bardolph, J. *Études postcoloniales et littérature*, Paris: Champion, 2001
Barnwell, H. T. *Racine and Corneille: An Old Parallel Revisited*, Oxford: Clarendon Press, 1982
Barthes, R. *Nouveaux essais critiques*, Paris: Seuil, 1972
    S/Z, Paris: Seuil, 1970; trans. R. Miller, New York: Hill and Wang, 1974
    'The Reality Effect', in *The Rustle of Language*, trans. R. Howard, Berkeley: University of
    California Press, 1989, pp. 141–8
Bartlett, R. *The Making of Europe: Conquest, Colonization and Cultural Change 950–1350*, Prince-
    ton, NJ: Princeton University Press, 1993
Baumgartner, E. *Le Tristan en prose: essai d'interprétation d'un roman médiéval*, Geneva: Droz,
    1975
    L'Arbre et le pain: essai sur 'La Queste del Saint Graal', Paris: SEDES, 1981
    'Remarques sur la prose du *Lancelot*', *Romania* 105 (1984), pp. 1–15
    De l'histoire de Troie au livre du Graal, Orléans: Paradigme, 1994
    'Le Choix de la prose', *Cahiers des recherches médiévales* 5 (1998), pp. 7–13

'Les Danois dans l'histoire des ducs de Normandie de Benoît de Sainte-Maure', *Le Moyen Age* 107 (2002), pp. 481–95

Bayley, P. J. *French Pulpit Oratory 1598–1650: A Study in Themes and Styles, with a Descriptive Catalogue of Printed Texts*, Cambridge: Cambridge University Press, 1980

Bazin, A. *Qu'est-ce que le cinéma?*, Paris Cerf, 1958. Trans. H. Gray as *What is Cinema?* Berkeley: University of California Press, 1967

Beasley, F. E. *Salons, History, and the Creation of 17th-Century France*, Aldershot and Burlington, VT: Ashgate, 2006

Beaujot, J.-P. 'Le Travail de la définition dans quelques maximes de La Rochefoucauld', in J. Lafond (ed.), *Les Formes brèves de la prose et le discours discontinu (XVIe–XVIIe siècles)*, Paris: Vrin, 1984, pp. 95–101

Beaulieu, J.-P. and D. Desrosiers-Bonin (eds.). *Hélisenne de Crenne: l'écriture et ses doubles*, Paris: Champion, 2004

Beaune, C. *The Birth of an Ideology: Myths and Symbols of Nation in Late-Medieval France*, Berkeley: University of California Press, 1991

Bec, P. *La Lyrique française au moyen-âge (XIIe–XIIIe siècles): contribution à une typologie des genres poétiques médiévaux*, vol. I: *Études*, Paris: Picard, 1977

'*Trobairitz* et chansons de femme: contribution à la connaissance du lyrisme féminin au moyen âge', *Cahiers de Civilisation Médiévale* 22 (1979), pp. 235–62.

'Troubadours, trouvères et espace Plantagenêt', *Cahiers de Civilisation Médiévale* 29 (1986), pp. 9–11.

Becker, C. and A-S. Dufief. *Relecture des 'petits naturalistes'*, Cahiers RITM, Paris: Université de Paris X, 2000

Bédier, J. *Fabliaux: études de littérature populaire et d'histoire littéraire du moyen âge*, Paris: Bouillon: 1893

Les Légendes épiques: recherches sur la formation des chansons de geste, Paris: Champion, 1908

Beer, J. *Early Prose in France: Contexts of Bilingualism and Authority*, Kalamazoo: Western Michigan University Medieval Institute, 1992

Beizer, J. *Ventriloquized Bodies: Narratives of Hysteria in Nineteenth-Century France*, Ithaca, NY: Cornell University Press, 1994

Le Bel Inconnu: roman d'aventures, ed. G. Perrie Williams, Paris: Champion, 1929; reprinted 1991

Bell, D. F. *Models of Power: Politics and Economics in Zola's 'Rougon-Macquart'*, Lincoln: University of Nebraska Press, 1988

Bénassi, S. and A. Cugier (eds.). *Le Montage: état des lieux réel(s) et virtuel(s)*, Paris: L'Harmattan, 2003

Bénichou, P. *Le Sacre de l'écrivain 1750–1830: essai sur l'avènement d'un pouvoir spirituel laïque dans la France moderne*, Paris: Corti, 1973

Benjamin, W. *The Arcades Project*, trans. Howard Eiland and Kevin McLaughlin, Cambridge, MA: Belknap Press of Harvard University Press, 1999

Bennett, J. and T. Brown (eds.). *Film and Television after DVD*, London and New York: Routledge, 2005

Benoît de Sainte-Maure, *Le Roman de Troie*, ed. Léopold Constans, 6 vols., Paris: Société des anciens textes français, 1904–12

Benrekassa, G. *Le Concentrique et l'excentrique: Marges des Lumières*, Paris: Payot, 1980

Bensoussan, G. (ed.). 'La Shoah dans la littérature française', special issue of *Revue d'histoire de la Shoah*, 176 (2002)

Berg, W. *Emile Zola and the Art of his Times*, University Park: Pennsylvania State University Press, 1992
  Imagery and Ideology: Fiction and Painting in Nineteenth-Century France, Newark: University of Delaware Press, 2007

Berger, A.-E. (ed.). *Algeria in Others' Languages*, Ithaca, NY and London: Cornell University Press, 2002

Bérinus, roman en prose du XIVe siècle, ed. R. Bossuat, Paris: Société des anciens textes français, 1931

Berman, M. *All That's Solid Melts into Air: The Experience of Modernity*, London: Verso, 1983

Bernard of Clairvaux, *Liber de diligendo deo*, in *S. Bernardi Opera*, vol. III: *Tractatus et opuscula*, ed. J. Leclercq and H. M. Rochais, Rome: Editiones Cistercienses, 1963, pp. 119–54

Berriot-Salvadore, E. *Les Femmes dans la société française de la Renaissance*, Geneva: Droz, 1990

Bersani, L. *Balzac to Beckett: Center and Circumference in French Fiction*, New York: Oxford University Press, 1970

Berte aus grans pies, *see* Adenet le Roi

Bertrand-Jennings, C. *Un autre mal de siècle*, Toulouse: Presses Universitaires du Mirail, 2005

Best, V. and K. Robson (eds.). 'Memory and Innovation in the Post-Holocaust Generation in France', special issue of *French Studies* 59.1 (2005)

Bettoni, A. 'Claude Colet e *L'Histoire Palladienne*', in *Il romanzo nella Francia del Rinascimento*, Fasano: Schena Editore, 1996, pp. 178–206

Beugnet, M. *Cinema and Sensation: French Film and the Art of Transgression*, Edinburgh: Edinburgh University Press, 2007

Bezzola, R. R. *Les Origines et la formation de la littérature courtoise en Occident (500–1200)*, Paris: Champion, 1963

Bhabha, H. K. *The Location of Culture* (1994), London and New York: Routledge, 2003

Bial, H. (ed.). *The Performance Studies Reader*, 2nd edn, London and New York: Routledge, 2007

Bichard-Thomine, M.-C. *Noel du Fail, conteur*, Paris: Champion, 2001

Biet, C. *La Tragédie*, Paris: Colin, 1997

Billon, F. de. *Le Fort inexpugnable de l'honneur du sexe feminin*, ed. M. A. Screech, Paris: Mouton, 1970

Biot, B. *Barthélemy Aneau, Régent de la Renaissance Lyonnaise*, Paris: Champion, 1996

Birkett, J. *The Sins of the Fathers: Decadence in France 1870–1914*, London: Quartet Books, 1986

Birkett, J. and J. Kearns. *A Guide to French Literature from Early Modern to Postmodern*, Basingstoke and London: Macmillan, 1997

Bishop, M. *Nineteenth-Century French Poetry*, New York: Twayne Publishers, 1993
  Contemporary French Women Poets, Amsterdam: Rodopi, 1995

Blanc, A. *Le Théâtre français du XVIIIe siècle*, Paris: Ellipses, 1998

Blanckeman, B. *Les Fictions singulières: étude sur le roman français contemporain*, Paris: Prétexte éditeur, 2002

Blanckeman, B., A. Mura-Brunel, and M. Dambre, *Le Roman français au tournant du xxie siècle*, Paris: Presses de la Sorbonne Nouvelle, 2004

Blandin de Cornouaille, ed. C. H. M. van der Horst, The Hague and Paris: Mouton, 1974

Blanning, T. C. W. *The Eighteenth Century: Europe 1688–1815*, Oxford: Oxford University Press, 2000

Bloch, R. H. *Medieval French Literature and Law*, Berkeley: University of California Press, 1977

The Anonymous Marie de France, Chicago: Chicago University Press, 2003

Blondel de Néele, see Tarbé, P.

Blumenfeld-Kosinski, R. 'Chrétien de Troyes as a Reader of the *Romans Antiques*', *Philological Quarterly*, 64.3 (1985), pp. 398–405

The Writings of Margaret of Oingt, Newburyport MA: Focus Library of Medieval Women, 1990

(ed.). *The Selected Writings of Christine de Pizan*, trans. R. Blumenfeld-Kosinski and K. Brownlee, New York: Norton, 1997

Bodel, J. *La Chanson des saisnes*, ed. A. Brasseur, 2 vols., Geneva: Droz, 1989.

Bogdanow, F. *The Romance of the Grail: A Study of the Structure and Genesis of a Thirteenth-Century Arthurian Prose Romance*, Manchester: Manchester University Press, 1966

Bogdanow, F. and R. Trachsler. 'Rewriting Prose Romance: The Post-Vulgate *Roman du Graal* and Related Texts', in G. S. Burgess and K. Pratt (eds.), *The Arthur of the French*, Cardiff: University of Wales Press, 2006

Boime, A. *Art and the French Commune. Imagining Paris after War and Revolution*, Princeton, NJ: Princeton University Press, 1995.

Art in an Age of Civil Struggle, 1848–1871, Chicago: University of Chicago Press, 2007.

Revelation of Modernism: Responses to Cultural Crisis in Fin-de-Siècle Painting, Columbia and London: University of Missouri Press, 2008.

Bonaventure des Périers. *Cymbalum Mundi*, ed. Y. Delègue, Paris: Champion, 1995

Bonnel R. and C. Rubinger (eds.). *Femmes savantes et femmes d'esprit: Women Intellectuals of the French Eighteenth Century*, New York: Peter Lang, 1994

Bordwell, D., J. Staiger, and K. Thompson. *The Classical Hollywood Cinema*, New York: Columbia University Press, 1985

Boswell, J. *Christianity, Social Tolerance, and Homosexuality: Gay People in Western Europe from the Beginning of the Christian Era to the Fourteenth Century*, Chicago: University of Chicago Press, 1980

Same-Sex Unions in Premodern Europe, New York: Villard Books, 1994

Bourdieu, P. *The Rules of Art: Genesis and Structure of the Literary Field*, trans. S. Emanuel, Stanford, CA: Stanford University Press, 1995

Bourdin, J.-C. *Les Matérialistes au xviiie siècle*, Paris: Payot, 1996

Boutet, D. *Formes littéraires et conscience historique aux origines de la literature française (1100–1250)*, Paris: Presses Universitaires de France, 1999

Boutière, J. and A. Schutz. *Biographies des troubadours: textes provençaux des XIIIe et XIVe siècles*, Paris: Nizet, 1964

Bowie, M. *Mallarmé and the Art of Being Difficult*, Cambridge: Cambridge University Press, 1978

    Freud, Proust and Lacan, Cambridge: Cambridge University Press, 1987

    Proust Among the Stars, London: Fontana, 1998

Bowman, F. 'Suffering, Madness, and Literary Creation', *French Forum* 1 (1976), pp. 24–48

Bowser, E. *The Transformation of Cinema, 1907–1918*, Berkeley: University of California Press, 1990

Boyer d'Argens, J.-B. de. *Thérèse philosophe*, ed. G. Pigeard de Gurbert, Arles: Actes Sud, 1992

Boyle, C. *Consuming Autobiographies: Reading and Writing the Self in Post-War France*, London: Legenda, 2007

Boyne, R. *Foucault and Derrida: The Other Side of Reason*, London: Routledge, 1990

Bradby, D. *Le Théâtre en France de 1968 à 2000*, Paris: Champion, 2007

Bradby, D. and A. Calder (eds.). *The Cambridge Companion to Molière*, Cambridge: Cambridge University Press, 2006

Bradley Winston, J. *Postcolonial Duras: Cultural Memory in Postwar France*, New York and Basingstoke: Palgrave, 2001

Braudy, L. *The World in a Frame*, New York: Doubleday, 1976

Brecht, B. 'Against Georg Lukács', trans. S. Hood, in *Aesthetics and Politics: Debates between Bloch, Lukács, Brecht, Benjamin, Adorno*, London: Verso, 1980, pp. 68–85

Bréhier, E. *Histoire de la philosophie*, vol. III: *XIXe–XXe siècles*, Paris: Presses Universitaires de France, 1964

Bremond, H. *French Tragic Drama in the Sixteenth and Seventeenth Centuries*, London: Methuen, 1973

    Histoire littéraire du sentiment religieux en France, rev. F. Trémolières, republished in 5 vols., Grenoble: Jérôme Millon, 2006

Brereton, G. *French Comic Drama from the Sixteenth to the Eighteenth Century*, London: Methuen, 1977

Bresson, R. *Notes sur le cinématographe*, Paris: Gallimard, 1975; trans. J. Griffin as *Notes on Cinematography*, New York: Urizen Books, 1975

Britton, C. and M. Syrotinski (eds). *Francophone Texts and Postcolonial Theory*, special issue of *Paragraph* 24.3 (2001)

Brockliss, L. W. B. *French Higher Education in the Seventeenth and Eighteenth Centuries: A Cultural History*, Oxford: Oxford University Press, 1987

Bromilow, P. *Models of Women in Sixteenth-Century French Literature: Female Exemplarity in the 'Histoires tragiques' (1559) and the 'Heptaméron' (1559)*, Lewiston, ME: Edwin Mellen, 2007

Bromwich, R., A. O. H. Jarman, and B. F. Roberts (eds.). *The Arthur of the Welsh: The Arthurian Legend in Medieval Welsh Literature*, Cardiff: University of Wales Press, 1991

Broomhall, S. *Women and the Book Trade in Sixteenth-Century France*, Aldershot: Ashgate, 2002

Brown, C. *Poets, Patrons and Printers: Crisis of Authority in Late Medieval France*, Ithaca, NY: Cornell University Press, 1995

Brownlee, K. and S. Huot. *Rethinking the Romance of the Rose: Text, Image, Reception*, Philadelphia: University of Pennsylvania Press, 1992

Bruckner, M., 'Redefining the Center: Verse and Prose *Charrette*', in Carol Dover (ed.), *Companion to the Lancelot-Grail Cycle*, Cambridge: D. S. Brewer, 2003

Bruckner, M., L. Shepard, and S. White (eds.). *Songs of the Women Troubadours*, New York and London: Garland, 2000

Brunetto Latini. *Li livres dou Tresor*, ed. S. Brown and P. Barrette, Tempe: Arizona Center for Medieval and Renaissance Studies, 2003

Buck Morss, S. *The Dialectics of Seeing: Walter Benjamin and the Arcades Project*, Cambridge, MA: MIT Press, 1989

Burch, N. *French Impressionist Cinema*, New York: Arno Press, 1980
Life to those Shadows, trans. B. Brewster, Berkeley: University of California Press, 1990

Burgess, G. S. *The Lais of Marie de France: Text and Context*, Manchester: University of Manchester Press, 1987

Burgess, G. S. and K. Pratt (eds.). *The Arthur of the French: The Arthurian Legend in Medieval French and Occitan Literature*, Cardiff: University of Wales Press, 2006

Burgwinkle, W. E. *Love for Sale: Materialist Readings of the Troubadour Razo Corpus*, New York and London: Garland, 1997
Sodomy, Masculinity, and Law in Medieval Literature: France and England, 1050–1230, Cambridge: Cambridge University Press, 2004

Burke, P. *Montaigne*, Oxford: Oxford University Press, 1981

Burns, E. J. *Arthurian Fictions: Rereading the Vulgate Cycle*, Columbus: Ohio State University Press, 1985

Burns, E. J., S. Kay, R. L. Krueger, and H. Solterer. 'Feminism and the Discipline of Old French Studies: *Une Bele Disjointure*', in R. H. Bloch and S. G. Nichols (eds.), *Medievalism and the Modernist Temper*, Baltimore, MD: Johns Hopkins University Press, 1995, pp. 225–66

Busby, K. *Codex and Context: Reading Old French Verse Narrative in Manuscript*, 2 vols., Amsterdam: Rodopi, 2002

Cadden, J. '"Nothing Natural is Shameful": Vestiges of a Debate about Sex and Science in a Group of Late-Medieval Manuscripts', *Speculum* 76.1 (2001), pp. 66–89

Cahen, D. *Edmond Jabès*, Paris: Seghers, 2007

Cairns, L. *Lesbian Desire in Post-1968 French Literature*, Lewiston, ME: Edwin Mellen Press, 2002

Calder, A. *Molière: The Theory and Practice of Comedy*, London: Athlone, 1993

Calvet, J. *La Littérature religieuse de François de Sales à Fénelon*, Paris: Del Duca, 1956

Calvet, L.-J. *Linguistique et colonialisme: petit traité de glottophagie* (1974), 2nd edn, Paris: Payot, 1988

Cambis, M. de (trans.). *Épistre consolatoire de Messire Jean Boccacce envoyée au Signeur Pino de Rossi*, ed. C. H. Winn, Paris: Champion, 2003

Cameron, K. and J. Kearns (eds.). *Le Champ littéraire, 1860–1900*, Amsterdam: Rodopi, 1996

Camille, M. *Image on the Edge: The Margins of Medieval Art*, Cambridge, MA: Harvard University Press, 1992

Campbell, E. *Medieval Saints' Lives: The Gift, Kinship and Community in Old French Hagiography*, Woodbridge: Boydell and Brewer, 2008

Campbell, M. B. *Exotic European Travel Writing 400–1600*, Ithaca, NY: Cornell University Press, 1988

Canova, M.-C. *La Comédie*, Paris: Hachette, 1993

Caraion, M. *Photographie, littérature et voyage au milieu du XIXe siècle*, Geneva: Droz, 2003

Cardinal, R. (ed.). *Sensibility and Creation: Studies in Twentieth Century French Poetry*, New York: Barnes and Noble, 1977

Carlat, D. *Témoins de l'inactuel: quatre écrivains contemporains face au deuil*, Paris: Corti, 2007

Carruthers, M. *The Book of Memory*, Cambridge: Cambridge University Press, 1990

Carson, A. *Decreation: Poetry, Essays, Opera*, New York: Knopf, 2005

Carter, A. E. *The Idea of Decadence in French Literature 1830–1900*, Toronto, University of Toronto Press, 1958

Cassan, M. 'La Tragédie *Regulus* (1582) au miroir des Guerres de religion', *Bibliothèque d'Humanisme et Renaissance* 63 (2001), pp. 87–103

Cassirer, E. *The Philosophy of the Enlightenment*, trans. F. Koelln and J. Pettegrove, Princeton, NJ: Princeton University Press, 1951; original title *Philosophie der Aufklärung* (1932)

Castor, G. *Pléiade Poetics: A Study in Sixteenth-Century Thought and Terminology*, Cambridge: Cambridge University Press, 1964

Cave, T. *Devotional Poetry in France c. 1570–1613*, Cambridge: Cambridge University Press, 1969

'Ronsard's Bacchic Poetry: From the *Bacchanales* to the *Hymne de l'autonne*', *L'Esprit créateur* 10 (1970), pp. 104–16

'The Triumph of Bacchus and its Interpretation in the French Renaissance: Ronsard's *Hinne de Bacus*', in A. H. T. Levi (ed.), *Humanism in France at the End of the Middle Ages and in the Early Renaissance*, Manchester: Manchester University Press; New York, Barnes and Noble, 1970, pp. 249–70

The Cornucopian Text: Problems of Writing in the French Renaissance, Oxford: Clarendon Press, 1979

Pré-histoires: textes troublés au seuil de la modernité, Geneva: Droz, 1999

Pré-histoires II: Langues étrangères et troubles économiques au XVIe siècle, Geneva: Droz, 2001

How to Read Montaigne, London: Granta, 2007

Retrospectives: Essays in Literature, Poetics, and Cultural History, ed. N. Kenny and W. Williams, London: Legenda, 2009

Caws, M. A. (ed.). *About French Poetry from Dada to 'Tel Quel': Text and Theory*, Detroit: Wayne State University Press, 1974

Céard, J. *La Nature et les prodiges: l'insolite au XVIe siècle en France*, Geneva: Droz, 1977

'Les transformations du genre du commentaire', in J. Lafond and A. Stegman (eds.), *L'Automne de la Renaissance 1580–1630*, Paris: Vrin, 1981, pp. 101–15

Cerquiglini, B., *La Parole médiévale: discourse, syntaxe, texte*, Paris: Minuit, 1981

In Praise of the Variant: A Critical History of Philology, trans. B. Wing, Baltimore, MD: Johns Hopkins University Press, 1999 (French orig. 1989)

Cerquiglini, J. 'Le Clerc et l'écriture: le *Voir dit* de Guillaume de Machaut et la définition du dit', in H. U. Gumbrecht (ed.), *Literatur in der Gesellschaft des Spätmittelalters*, Heidelberg: Carl Winter, 1980, pp. 151–68

Chambers, E. K. *The Mediaeval Stage*, 2 vols., Oxford: Oxford University Press, 1903

Chambers, F. M. *Old Provençal Versification*, Philadelphia: American Philosophical Society, 1985

Chambers, R. *Mélancolie et opposition: les débuts du modernisme en France*, Paris: Corti, 1987

La Chanson d'Antioche, ed. Jan A. Nelson, Tuscaloosa: University of Alabama Press, 2003

La Chanson de Girart de Roussillon, ed. and trans. M. de Combarieu du Grés and G. Gouiran, Paris: Librairie générale francaise, 1993

La Chanson de Roland, ed. and trans. I. Short, 2nd edn, Paris: Livre de Poche, 1990

La Chanson de Roland / The Song of Roland: The French Corpus, J. J. Duggan (general ed.), with K. Akiyama, I. Short, R. F. Cook, A. C. Rejhon, W. van Emden, W. W. Kibler (eds.), 3 vols., Turnhout: Brepols, 2005

Chaouche, S., *L'Art du comédien: déclamation et jeu scénique en France à l'âge classique (1629–1680)*, Paris: Champion, 2001

Charbonneau, F. *Les silences de l'histoire: les mémoires français du xviie siècle*, Québec: Presses de l'Université de Laval, 2000

Charbonneau, F. and R. Ouellet (eds.). *Nouvelles françaises du xviie siècle*, Quebec: L'instant même, 2000; reprinted Paris: Les 400 coups, 2005

Charlton, D. G. *Positivist Thought in France during the Second Empire 1852–1870*, Oxford: Clarendon Press, 1959

The French Romantics, 2 vols., Cambridge: Cambridge University Press, 1984

Chartier, R. *L'Ordre des livres: lecteurs, auteurs, bibliothèques en Europe entre xive et xviiie siècle*, Aix-en-Provence: Alinéa, 1992

Chaudonneret, M.-C. *L'État et les artistes: de la Restauration à la monarchie de Juillet (1815–1833)*, Paris: Flammarion, 1999

Chauou, A. *L'Idéologie Plantagenêt: royauté arthurienne et monarchie politique dans l'espace Plantagenêt (xiie–xiiie siècles)*, Rennes: Presses Universitaires de Rennes, 2001

Chauveau, J.-P. *Anthologie de la poésie française du xviie siècle*, Paris: Gallimard, 1987

Chaytor, H. J. *From Script to Print: An Introduction to Medieval Literature*, Cambridge: Cambridge University Press, 1945

Cherbuliez, J. *The Place of Exile: Leisure Literature and the Limits of Absolutism*, Lewisburg, PA: Bucknell University Press, 2005

Les Chétifs, ed. Geoffrey M. Myers, Tuscaloosa: University of Alabama Press, 1981

Chevalier, L. *Classes laborieuses et classes dangereuses pendant la première moitié du xixe siècle*, Paris: Plon, 1958

Le Chevalier à l'épée, see *Two Old French Gawain Romances*

Le Chevalier au lion, ed. P. Servet, Paris: Champion, 1996

Li Chevaliers as deus espees, ed. W. Foerster, Halle: Niemeyer, 1877

Chevrel, Y. *Le Naturalisme*, Paris: Presses Universitaires de France, 1982

Cholakian, P. F. and R. C. Cholakian. *Marguerite de Navarre: Mother of the Renaissance*, New York: Columbia University Press, 2006

Chrétien de Troyes, *Les Romans de Chrétien de Troyes*, vols. v and vi, *Le Conte du Graal (Perceval)*, ed. Félix Lecoy, Paris: Champion, 1972–5

Les Romans de Chrétien de Troyes, vol. iii, *Le Chevalier de la Charrette*, ed. Mario Roques, Paris: Champion, 1990

Œuvres complètes, ed. D. Poirion, A. Berthelot, *et al.*, Paris: Gallimard, 1994

Romans, ed. M. Zink, Paris: Livre de Poche, 1994

Christine de Pizan, 'Le Livre de la cité des dames de Christine de Pizan, A Critical Edition 2 vols.', ed. M. Curnow, PhD dissertation, Vanderbilt University, 1975

La Ditié de Jehanne d'Arc, ed. A. J. Kennedy and K. Varty, Oxford: Society for the Study of Medieval Languages and Literatures, 1977

La città delle dame, ed. P. Caraffi and E. J. Richards, Milan: Luni Editrice, 1998

The Book of the City of Ladies, trans. R. Brown-Grant, Harmondsworth: Penguin, 1999

Cixous, H. *'Coming to Writing' and Other Essays*, with an introductory essay by S. Rubin Suleiman, ed. D. Jenson, trans. S. Cornell, Cambridge, MA: Harvard University Press, 1991

Clanchy, M. T. *From Memory to Written Record: England 1066–1307*, 2nd edn, Oxford: Blackwell, 1993; 1st edn 1979

Claris et Laris, ed. Corinne Pierreville, Paris: Champion, 2008

Clark, T. J. *The Painting of Modern Life: Paris in the Art of Manet and his Followers*, London: Thames and Hudson, 1985

Clopper, L. M. *Drama, Play, and Game: English Festive Culture in the Medieval and Early Modern Period*, Chicago: University of Chicago Press, 2001

Cogez, G. *Les Écrivains voyageurs au xxe siècle*, Paris: Seuil, 2004

Cohen, G. *Histoire de la mise en scène dans le théâtre religieux français du moyen-âge*, 2nd edn, Paris: Champion, 1951

Cohen, M. *The Sentimental Education of the Novel*, Princeton, NJ: Princeton University Press, 1999

Coignard, G. de. *Œuvres chrestiennes*, ed. C. H. Winn, Geneva: Droz, 1995

Coldwell, M. '*Jougleresses* and *Trobairitz*: Secular Musicians in Medieval France', in J. Bowers and J. Tick (eds.), *Women Making Music: The Western Tradition, 1150–1950*, Urbana: University of Illinois Press, 1986, pp. 39–61

Coleman, D. *The Gallo-Roman Muse*, Cambridge: Cambridge University Press, 1979

Coleman, J. *Ancient and Medieval Memories: Studies in the Reconstruction of the Past*, Cambridge: Cambridge University Press, 1992.

Public Reading and the Reading Public in Late Medieval England and France, Cambridge: Cambridge University Press, 1996

Collier, P. and R. Lethbridge (eds.). *Artistic Relations: Literature and the Visual Arts in Nineteenth-Century France*, New Haven, CT and London: Yale University Press, 1994

Collot, M. *L'Horizon fabuleux*, vol. ii: *xxe siècle*, Paris: Corti, 1988

Colombat, A. P. *The Holocaust in French Film*, Metuchen, NJ: Scarecrow, 1993

Colonna, V. *Autofiction et autres mythomanies littéraires*, Auch: Tristram, 2004

Compagnon, A. *La Troisième République des lettres: de Flaubert à Proust*, Paris: Seuil, 1983

Proust entre deux siècles, Paris: Seuil, 1989; *Proust between Two Centuries*, trans. R. E. Goodkin, New York: Columbia University Press, 1992

Conesa, G. *La Comédie de l'âge classique (1630–1715)*, Paris: Seuil, 1995

Conley, J. J., SJ. *The Suspicion of Virtue: Women Philosophers in Neoclassical France*, Ithaca, NY and London: Cornell University Press, 2002

Conley, K. *Automatic Woman: The Representation of Woman in Surrealism*, Lincoln and London: University of Nebraska Press, 1996

    Robert Desnos, Surrealism, and The Marvelous in Everyday Life, Lincoln: University of Nebraska Press, 2003

Conley, T. *The Self-Made Map: Cartographic Writing in Early Modern France*, Minneapolis: University of Minnesota Press, 1996

La Conquête de Jérusalem, ed. C. Hippeau, Paris: A. Aubry, 1868

Le Conte du Papegau: roman arthurien du xve siècle, ed. H. Charpentier, Paris: Champion, 2004

The Continuations of the Old French Perceval of Chrétien de Troyes, ed. W. Roach and R. H. Ivy, Philadelphia: University of Pennsylvania Press, 1949–83

Cooper, D. *Existentialism*, Oxford: Blackwell, 1999

Copeland, R. *Rhetoric, Hermeneutics, and Translation in the Middle Ages: Academic Traditions and Vernacular Texts*, Cambridge: Cambridge University Press, 1991

Copenhaver, B. and C. Schmitt. *Renaissance Philosophy*, Oxford and New York: Oxford University Press, 1992

Corcoran, P. *The Cambridge Introduction to Francophone Literature*, Cambridge: Cambridge University Press, 2007

Cornilliat, F. *Or ne mens: couleurs de l'éloge et du blâme chez les 'Grands Rhétoriqueurs'*, Paris: Champion, 1994

    '"J'y mettrai bien remede": Le plaisir du roman d'après *L'Histoire Palladienne* de Claude Colet', in M. Clément and P. Mousnier (eds.), *Le Roman français au xvie siècle*, Strasbourg: Presses Universitaires de Strasbourg, 2005, pp. 189–206

Corvin, M. *Le Théâtre de boulevard*, Paris: Presses Universitaires de France, 1989

    (ed.), *Dictionnaire encyclopédique du théâtre*, 2 vols., 2nd edn, Paris: Larousse-Bordas, 1998

Coudrette, *Le roman de Mélusine ou Histoire de Lusignan*, ed. E. Roach, Paris: Klincksieck, 1982

Coulet, H. *Le Roman jusqu'à la Révolution*, 2 vols., Paris: Colin, 1967

    (ed.). *Nouvelles du xviiie siècle*, Paris: Gallimard, 2002

Crane, S. *The Performance of Self: Ritual, Clothing, and Identity during the Hundred Years War*, Philadelphia: University of Pennsylvania Press, 2002

Crébillon, P. J. de. *Les Égarements du cœur et de l'esprit*, ed. R. Etiemble, Paris: Colin, 1961

Crenne, H. de. *Les Épistres familieres et invectives*, ed. J. C. Nash, Paris: Champion, 1996

    Les Angoysses douloureuses qui precedent d'amours, ed. C. de Buzon, Paris: Champion, 1997

Croizy-Naquet, C. *Écrire l'histoire romaine au début du xiiie siècle*, Paris: Champion, 1999

Crowley, M. *Duras, Writing, and the Ethical: Making the Broken Whole*, Oxford: Oxford University Press, 2000

Crowley, M. and V. Best. *The New Pornographies: Explicit Sex in Recent French Fiction and Film*, Manchester: Manchester University Press, 2007

Cruickshank, J. *Variations on Catastrophe: Some French Responses to the Great War*, Oxford: Oxford University Press, 1982

Cruickshank, R. *Fin de millénaire French Fiction: The Aesthetics of Crisis*, Oxford: Oxford University Press, 2009

Select bibliography

Csúrös, K. *Variétés et vicissitudes du genre épique de Ronsard à Voltaire*, Paris: Champion, 1999

Currie, M. (ed. and intro.). *Metafiction*, New York: Longman, 1995

Curtius, E. R. *European Literature and the Latin Middle Ages*, trans. W. R. Trask, London: Routledge and Kegan Paul, 1979

Cusset, C. (ed.). *Libertinage and Modernity*, special issue of *Yale French Studies* 94 (1998)

Damrosch, D. *What is World Literature?* Princeton, NJ: Princeton University Press, 2003

Dandrey, P. *Molière, ou l'esthétique du ridicule*, Paris: Klincksieck, 1992

Darnton, R. *Mesmerism and the End of the Enlightenment*, Cambridge, MA: Harvard University Press, 1968

  The Literary Underground of the Old Regime, Cambridge, MA: Harvard University Press, 1982

  Bohème littéraire et révolution, Paris: Gallimard, 1983

  'Two Paths through the Social History of Ideas', in H. T. Mason (ed.), *The Darnton Debate: Books and Revolution in the Eighteenth Century*, Oxford: Voltaire Foundation, 1998, pp. 251–94

Darricau, S., *Le Livre*, Paris: Scéren (CNDP); Pyramid, 2004

Daurel et Beton, ed. C. Lee, Parma: Pratiche Editrice, 1991

Davis, C. *Ethical Issues in Twentieth-Century French Fiction: Killing the Other*, Basingstoke: Macmillan, 2000

  After Poststructuralism: Reading, Stories and Theory, New York and London: Routledge, 2004

  Haunted Subjects: Deconstruction, Psychoanalysis and the Return of the Dead, Basingstoke and New York: Palgrave Macmillan, 2007

Davis, C. and E. Fallaize. *French Fiction in the Mitterrand Years: Memory, Narrative, Desire*, Oxford: Oxford University Press, 2000

Davis, J. H. *Tragic Theory and the Eighteenth-Century French Critics*, Chapel Hill: University of North Carolina Press, 1966

De Man, P. *Allegories of Reading: Figural Language in Rousseau, Nietzsche, Rilke, and Proust*, New Haven, CT: Yale University Press, 1982

De Riquer, M. *Los trovadores: historia literaria y textos*, 2 vols., Barcelona: Editorial Planeta, 1975

de Taillemont, C. *Discours des champs faëz*, ed. Jean-Claude Arnould, Geneva: Droz, 1991

Deak, F. *Symbolist Theater: The Formation of an Avant-garde*, Baltimore, MD and London: Johns Hopkins University Press, 1999

Debus, A. G. *Man and Nature in the Renaissance*, Cambridge: Cambridge University Press, 1978

Décaudin, M. *La Crise des valeurs symbolistes*, Toulouse: Privat, 1960

Dédame, R., *Une histoire du livre: De Gutenberg au multimédia*, Pantin: Le Temps des Cérises; Paris: Syndicat Général du Livre et de la Communication Écrite, 2004

DeJean, J. 'Lafayette's Ellipses: The Privilege of Anonymity', *PMLA* 99 (October 1984), pp. 884–902

  Tender Geographies: Women and the Origins of the Novel in France, New York: Columbia University Press, 1991

Delluc, L. *Photogénie*, Paris: De Brunhoff, 1920

Delmas, C. *La Tragédie de l'âge classique 1553–1770*, Paris: Seuil, 1994

Delon, M. *Le Savoir-vivre libertin*, Paris: Hachette Littératures, 2000

Deluz, C. (ed.). *Jean de Mandeville: Le Livre des merveilles du monde*, Paris: CNRS, 2000

Démoris, R. *Le Roman à la première personne: du Classicisme aux Lumières*, Paris: Colin, 1975; reprinted Geneva: Droz, 2002

Denomy, A. J. (ed.). *The Old French Lives of Saint Agnes and Other Vernacular Versions of the Middle Ages*, Cambridge, MA: Harvard University Press, 1938

Denon, V. *Point de lendemain*, ed. Michel Delon, Paris: Gallimard, 1995

Dentière, M. *Epistle to Marguerite de Navarre and Preface to a Sermon by John Calvin*, ed. and trans. M. B. McKinley, Chicago: Chicago University Press, 2004

Derrida, J. *Le Monolinguisme de l'autre ou la prothèse d'origine*, Paris: Galilée, 1996

Des Roches, M. C. *Les Œuvres*, ed. A. R. Larsen, Geneva: Droz, 1993

    Les Secondes Œuvres, ed. A. R. Larsen, Geneva: Droz, 1998

    Les Missives, ed. A. R. Larsen, Geneva: Droz, 1999

Descombes, V. *Le Même et l'autre: quarante-cinq ans de philosophie française (1933–1978)*, Paris: Minuit, 1979

Desrosiers-Bonin, D. *et al.* (eds.). *Actualité de Jeanne Flore*, Paris: Champion, 2004

Détrez, C. and A. Simon. *À leurs corps défendant: Les femmes à l'épreuve du nouvel ordre moral*, Paris: Seuil, 2006

Diaconoff, S. *Through the Reading Glass: Women, Books, and Sex in the French Enlightenment*, Albany: State University of New York Press, 2005

Dictionnaire de l'Académie Françoise, 2 vols., Paris: Coignard, 1694

Dictionnaire universel françois et latin, 3 vols., Trévoux: E. Ganeau, 1704

Didi-Hubermann, G. *Invention de l'hystérie: Charcot et l'iconographie photographique de la Salpêtrière*, Paris: Macula, 1982

Didier, B. *Le Roman français au xviiie siècle*, Paris: Ellipses 1998

The Didot Perceval, according to the manuscripts of Modena and Paris, ed. W. Roach, Philadelphia: University of Pennsylvania Press, 1941

Dinshaw, C. and D. Wallace (eds.). *The Cambridge Companion to Medieval Women's Writing*, Cambridge: Cambridge University Press, 2003

Dipiero, T. *Dangerous Truths and Criminal Passions: The Evolution of the French Novel, 1569–1791*, Stanford, CA: Stanford University Press, 1992

The Donatz Proensals of Uc Faidit, ed. J. H. Marshall, London and New York: Oxford University Press, 1969

Dorra, H. *Symbolist Art Theories*, Berkeley: University of California Press, 1994

Doss-Quinby, E. *The Lyrics of the Trouvères: A Research Guide (1970–1990)*, New York: Garland, 1994

Doss-Quinby, E., J. T. Grimbert, W. Pfeffer, and E. Aubrey (eds.). *Songs of the Women Trouvères*, New Haven, CT and London: Yale University Press, 2001, pp. 7–14

Doubrovsky, S. *Corneille et la dialectique du héros*, Paris: Gallimard, 1963

    Autobiographiques: de Corneille à Sartre, Paris: Presses Universitaires de France, 1988

Doutrepont, G. *Les Mises en proses des épopées et des romans chevaleresques du xive au xvie siècle*, Geneva: Slatkine, 1969

Dover, C. 'Galehot and Lancelot: Matters of the Heart', in K. Karczewska and T. Conley (eds.), *The World and its Rival: Essays on Literary Imagination in Honor of Per Nykrog*, Amsterdam: Rodopi, 1999

Dover C. (ed.). *A Companion to the Lancelot-Grail Cycle*, Cambridge: D. S. Brewer, 2003

Dox, D. *The Idea of the Theater in Latin Christian Thought*, Ann Arbor: University of Michigan Press, 2004

Dragonetti, R. *La Technique poétique des trouvères dans la chanson courtoise: contribution à l'étude de la rhétorique médiévale*, Bruges: De Tempel, 1960

Dronke, P. *Women Writers of the Middle Ages: A Critical Study of Texts from Perpetua (203) to Marguerite Porete (1310)*, Cambridge: Cambridge University Press, 1984

Du Bellay, J. *La Deffence, et illustration de la langue françoyse* (1549), ed. J.-C. Monferran, Geneva: Droz, 2001

Du Camp, M. *Paris, ses organes, ses fonctions et sa vie dans la deuxième moitié du XIXe siècle*, Paris: Hachette, 1883–98

Du Guillet, P. *Rymes*, ed. Victor E. Graham, Geneva: Droz, 1968

Dubois, J. *Les Romanciers du réel de Balzac à Simenon*, Paris: Seuil, 2000

Duché-Gavet, V. (ed.). *L'Amant ressuscité de la mort d'amour*, Geneva: Droz, 1998

(ed.), 'L'Amant ressuscité de la mort d'amours ou comment Nicolas Denisot a écrit son roman', *Nouvelle Revue du XVIe siècle* 19.2 (2001), pp. 33–48

Duchet, M. *Anthropologie et histoire au siècle des Lumières*, Paris: Albin Michel, 1995

Dufournet, J. *Les Écrivains de la Quatrième Croisade: Villehardouin et Clari*, 2 vols., Paris: SEDES, 1973

Dugast-Portes, F. *Annie Ernaux: étude de l'œuvre*, Paris: Bordas, 2008

Duggan, A. E. *Salonnières, Furies, and Fairies: The Politics of Gender and Cultural Change in Absolutist France*, Newark: University of Delaware Press, 2005

Dupront, A. *Qu'est-ce que les Lumières?*, ed. F. Furet, Paris: Gallimard, 1996

Durozoi, G. *History of the Surrealist Movement*, trans. A. Anderson, Chicago: Chicago University Press, 2002

Duvernoy, J. (ed.). *Le Registre d'inquisition de Jacques Fournier, évêque de Pamiers (1318–1325): manuscrit Vat. Latin 4030 de la Bibliothèque Vaticane*, 3 vols., Toulouse, Privat, 1972

Edmiston, W. F. *Hindsight and Insight: Focalization in Four Eighteenth-Century French Novels*, University Park: Pennsylvania State University Press, 1991

Ehrard, J. *L'Idée de nature en France à l'aube des lumières*, Paris: Flammarion, 1970

Enders, J. *Rhetoric and the Origins of Medieval Drama*, Ithaca, NY: Cornell University Press, 1992

The Medieval Theater of Cruelty: Rhetoric, Memory, Violence, Ithaca, NY: Cornell University Press, 1999

Engels, F. 'Socialism Utopian and Scientific', in *Marx/Engels Selected Works*, vol. III, Moscow: Progress Publishers, 1970, pp. 115–33.

Englehart, T. *The End of Victory Culture: Cold War America and the Disillusioning of a Generation*, New York: Basic Books, 1995

Epstein, J. 'Le Cinéma et les lettres modernes', in *La Poésie d'aujourd'hui: un nouvel état d'intelligence*, Paris: Éditions de la Sirène, 1921, pp. 171–7

'Grossissement', in *Bonjour cinema*, Paris: Éditions de la Sirène, 1921, pp. 107–8

Le Cinéma du diable, Paris: Melot, 1947

Fabri, P. *Le Grand et Vrai Art de pleine rhétorique*, ed. A. Héron, 3 vols., Rouen: E. Cagniard, 1889–90; reprinted Geneva: Slatkine, 1969

Fallaize, E. *French Women's Writing: Recent Fiction*, London: Palgrave Macmillan, 1993

Farge, A. *Dire et mal dire: l'opinion publique au xvIIIe siècle*, Paris: Seuil, 1992; trans. R. Morris as *Subversive Words: Public Opinion in Eighteenth-Century France*, Cambridge: Polity Press, 1994

Faure, C. *Le Projet culturel de Vichy folklore et révolution nationale 1940–1944*, Lyon: Presses Universitaires de Lyon, 1989

Fell, A. *Liberty, Equality, Maternity*, Oxford: Legenda, 2003

Felman, S. *La Folie et la chose littéraire*, Paris: Seuil, 1978; *Madness and Writing: Literature/Philosophy/Psychoanalysis*, trans. M. Noel Evans, new edn, Stanford, CA: Stanford University Press, 2003

Felman, S. and D. Laub. *Testimony: Crises of Witnessing in Literature, Psychoanalysis, and History*, New York and London: Routledge, 1992

Ferguson, G. *Queer (Re)Readings in the French Renaissance: Homosexuality, Gender, Culture*, Aldershot: Ashgate, 2008

Ferguson, M., M. Quilligan and N. Vickers (eds.). *Rewriting the Renaissance: The Discourses of Sexual Difference in Early Modern Europe*, Chicago: University of Chicago Press, 1986

Fescourt, H. and J.-L. Bouquet. *L'Idée et l'écran*, Paris: Haberschill and Sergent, 1926

Festugière, A. J. *La Philosophie de l'amour de Marsile Ficin et son influence sur la littérature française du xvIe siècle*, Paris: Vrin, 1941

ffrench, P. *The Time of Theory: A History of Tel Quel (1960–1983)*, Oxford: Oxford University Press, 1995

Finch, A. *Women's Writing in Nineteenth-Century France*, Oxford: Oxford University Press, 2000

Finke, L. A. '"More Than I Fynde Written": Dialogue and Power in the English Translation of *The Mirror of Simple Souls*', in M. Suydam and J. Ziegler (eds.), *Performance and Transformation*, New York: St Martin's, 1999, pp. 47–67

Finke, U. (ed.). *French Nineteenth-Century Painting and Literature*, Manchester: Manchester University Press, 1972

Finkielkraut, A. *La Défaite de la pensée*, Paris: Gallimard, 1987

Finn, M. 'Retrospective Medicine, Hypnosis, Hysteria and French Literature, 1875–1895', in George Rousseau *et al.* (eds.), *Framing and Imagining Disease in Cultural History*, Basingstoke: Palgrave Macmillan, 2003, pp. 173–89

Fiske, J. *Understanding Popular Culture*, London: Routledge, 1989

Fitch, B. T. *Reflections in the Mind's Eye: Reference and its Problematization in Twentieth-Century French Fiction*, Toronto: University of Toronto Press, 1991

Fleischman, S. 'On the Representation of History and Fiction in the Middle Ages', *History and Theory* 22 (1983), pp. 278–310

Fletcher, A. *Allegory: The Theory of a Symbolic Mode*, Ithaca, NY: Cornell University Press, 1964

Flore, J. *Contes amoureux par Madame Jeanne Flore*, ed. G.-A. Pérouse *et al.*, Paris and Lyon: Éditions du CNRS/Presses Universitaires de Lyon, 1980

Florence de Rome: chanson d'aventure du premier quart du xIIIe siècle, ed. A. Wallensköld, 2 vols., Paris: Firmin-Didot, 1907–9

Floriant et Florete, ed. A. Combes and R. Trachsler, Paris: Champion, 2003

Flower, J. E. *Literature and the Left in France: Society, Politics and the Novel since the Late Nineteenth Century*, London: Methuen, 1985

Foley, J. M. *The Theory of Oral Composition: History and Methodology*, Bloomington: Indiana University Press, 1989

Forbes, J. *The Cinema in France after the New Wave*, London: British Film Institute, 1992

Force, P. *Molière ou les prix des choses*, Paris: Nathan, 1994

Forestier, G. *Essai de génétique théâtrale: Corneille à l'œuvre*, Paris: Klincksieck, 1996
  Passions tragiques et règles classiques: essai sur la tragédie française, Paris: Presses Universitaires de France, 2003

Forsdick, C. *Travel in Twentieth-Century French and Francophone Cultures: The Persistence of Diversity*, Oxford: Oxford University Press, 2005

Forsdick, C. and D. Murphy (eds.). *Francophone Postcolonial Studies: A Critical Introduction*, London: Arnold, 2003

Forsdick, C., F. Basu, and S. Shilton. *New Approaches to Twentieth-Century Travel Literature in French: Genre, History, Theory*, New York: Peter Lang, 2006

Foucault, M. *Folie et déraison: histoire de la folie à l'âge classique*, Paris: Plon, 1961
  Les Mots et les choses: une archéologie des sciences humaines, Paris: Gallimard, 1966
  'What Is an Author?', in V. Lambropoulos and D. N. Miller (eds.), *Twentieth-Century Literary Theory*, Albany: State University Press of New York, 1987, pp. 124–42
  Les Anormaux: cours au Collège de France (1974–1975), Paris: Gallimard, 1999

Fourastié, J. *Les Trente Glorieuses: ou, la Révolution invisible de 1946 à 1975*, Paris: Fayard, 1979

Fozzer, G. (intro. and trans.). *Lo specchio delle anime semplici*, Milan: San Paolo, 1994

France, P. *Racine's Rhetoric*, Oxford: Clarendon Press, 1965

France, P. (ed.). *The New Oxford Companion to Literature in French*, Oxford: Oxford University Press, 1995

Franchetti, A. L. *L'Ombre discourante de Marie de Gournay*, Paris: Champion, 2006

Frank, G. *The Medieval French Drama*, Oxford: Clarendon Press, 1954

Frantz P. and F. Jacob (eds.). *Tragédies tardives: actes du colloque de Besançon des 17 et 18 décembre 1998*, Paris: Champion, 2002

Frantzen, A. J., 'Drama and Dialogue in Old English Poetry: The Scene of Cynewulf's *Juliana*', *Theatre Survey* 48.1 (2007), pp. 99–119

Frappier J. and R. Grimm (eds.). *Grundriss der romanischen Literaturen des Mittelalters*, vol. IV, Heidelberg: Carl Winter, 1978, pp. 74–81

Freud, S. *Jokes and their Relation to the Unconscious*, ed. A. Richards, trans. J. Strachey, London: Penguin, 1991

Frick, J.-P. (ed.). *Auguste Comte ou la République positive*, Nancy: Presses Universitaires de Nancy, 1990

Frodon, J.-M. (ed.). *Le Cinéma et la Shoah: un art à l'épreuve de la tragédie du 20e siècle*, Paris: Cahiers du Cinéma, 2007

Froissart, J. *Meliador*, ed. A. Lognon, Paris: Firmin Didot, 1895–9; reprinted New York: Johnson Reprint Corp., 1965

Fumaroli, M. *L'Âge de l'éloquence: rhétorique et 'res literaria'*, Geneva: Droz, 1980
  La Diplomatie de l'esprit: de Montaigne à La Fontaine, Paris: Hermann, 1994

Gaillard, J. *Paris, la ville 1852–1870*, Paris: Champion, 1976

Galand-Hallyn, P. and F. Hallyn. *Poétiques de la Renaissance: le monde italien, le modèle franco-bourguignon et leur héritage en France au XVIe siècle*, Geneva: Droz, 2001

Galderisi, C. 'Vers et prose au Moyen Age', in F. Lestringant and M. Zink (eds.), *Histoire de la France littéraire: naissances, renaissances*, Paris: Presses Universitaires de France, 2006

Galeran de Bretagne, ed. L. Foulet, Paris: Champion, 1981

Gallagher, C. 'George Eliot: Immanent Victorian', *Representations* 90 (Spring 2005), pp. 61–74

   'The Rise of Fictionality', in *The Novel*, vol. 1: *History, Geography, and Culture*, F. Moretti (ed.), Princeton, NJ: Princeton University Press, 2006, pp. 336–63

Gance, A. 'Images d'hier et voix de demain', *Cinéopse* 125 (January 1930), p. 26

Gaposchkin, M. C. *The Making of Saint Louis: Kingship, Sanctity, and Crusade in the Later Middle Ages*, Ithaca, NY: Cornell University Press, 2008

Garber, D. *Descartes's Metaphysical Physics*, Chicago: University of Chicago Press, 1992

Garber, D. and M. Ayers (eds.). *Cambridge History of Seventeenth-Century Philosophy*, 2 vols., Cambridge: Cambridge University Press, 1997

Gasarian, G. *André Breton: une histoire d'eau*, Quebec: Presses Universitaires de Septentrion, 2006

Gaucelm Faidit: see Mouzat, J.

Gaucher, E. *La biographie chevaleresque: typologie d'un genre (XIIIe–XVe siècle)*, Paris: Champion, 1994

Gaullier-Bougassas, C. and L. Harf-Lancner (eds.). *Thomas de Kent: le Roman d'Alexandre ou le Roman de toute chevalerie*, Paris: Champion Classique, 2003

Gaunt, S. *Gender and Genre in Medieval French Literature*, Cambridge: Cambridge University Press, 1995

  Love and Death in Medieval French and Occitan Courtly Literature: Martyrs to Love, Oxford: Oxford University Press, 2006

Gaunt, S. and S. Kay (eds.). *The Troubadours: An Introduction*, Cambridge: Cambridge University Press, 1999

Gautier d'Arras. *Ille et Galeron*, ed. Y. Lefèvre and F. Lecoy, Paris: Champion, 1999

Gay, P. *The Enlightenment: An Interpretation*, New York: Knopf, 1966

Genand, S. *Le Libertinage et l'histoire: politique de la séduction à la fin de l'Ancien Régime*, Oxford: Voltaire Foundation, 2005

Genette, G. 'Vraisemblance et motivation', in *Figures II*, Paris: Seuil, 1969, pp. 71–100

Genova, P. *Symbolist Journals: A Culture of Correspondence*, Aldershot: Ashgate, 2002

Gerald of Wales, *Concerning the Instruction of Princes*, trans. J. Stevenson, Felinfach: J. M. F. Books, 1991

Gethner, P. (ed.) *Femmes dramaturges en France (1650–1750)*, 2 vols., Tübingen: Gunter Narr, 1993–2002

Giacone, F. (ed.). *Le 'Cymbalum Mundi'*, Geneva: Droz, 2003

Gifford, P. and J. Gratton (eds.). *Subject Matters: Subject and Self in French Literature from Descartes to the Present*, Amsterdam: Rodopi, 2000

Gilby, E. *Sublime Worlds: Early Modern French Literature*, London: Legenda, 2006

Gill, M. *Eccentricity and the Cultural Imagination in Nineteenth-Century Paris*, Oxford: Oxford University Press, 2009

Gilot, M. and J. Serroy. *La Comédie à l'âge classique*, Paris: Belin, 1997

Girard, R. *Things Hidden since the Foundation of the World*, London: Athlone, 1987

Girart d'Amiens, *Escanor*, ed. R. Trachsler, Geneva: Droz, 1994

Girou-Giverski, M.-L. 'Profil socio-économique de la femme de lettres française 1740–1780', *Studies on Voltaire and the Eighteenth Century*, 264 (1989), pp. 1159–61

Giuyot, A. and C. Massol (eds.). *Voyager en France au temps du romantisme: poétique, esthétique, idéologie*, Grenoble: ELLUG, 2003

Glissant, É. *Le Discours antillais*, Paris: Seuil, 1981
  Introduction à une poétique du divers, Paris: Gallimard, 1996

Glorieux, P. *La Littérature quodlibétique de 1280–1320*, 2 vols.; vol. I, Kain, Belgium: Le Saulchoir, 1925; vol. II, Paris: Vrin, 1935

Goffman, E. *Frame Analysis: An Essay on the Organization of Experience*, Cambridge, MA: Harvard University Press, 1974

Goldin, F. *Lyrics of the Troubadours and Trouvères*, New York: Anchor/Doubleday, 1973

Goldsmith, E. C. *Publishing Women's Life Stories in France, 1647–1720*, Aldershot and Burlington, VT: Ashgate, 2001

Goldstein, J. *Console and Classify: The French Psychiatric Profession in the Nineteenth Century*, Cambridge: Cambridge University Press, 1987
  'The Uses of Male Hysteria: Medical and Literary Discourse in Nineteenth-Century France', *Representations* 34 (1991), pp. 134–65
  The Post-Revolutionary Self: Politics and Psyche in France, 1750–1850, Cambridge, MA: Harvard University Press, 2005

Goldzink, J. *Comique et comédie au siècle des Lumières*, Paris: L'Harmattan, 2000

Gomez-Géraud, M. C. *Le Crépuscule du grand voyage: les récits des pèlerins à Jérusalem (1458–1612)*, Paris: Champion, 2000

Goodkin, R. *Birth Marks: The Tragedy of Primogeniture in Pierre Corneille, Thomas Corneille, and Jean Racine*, Philadelphia: University of Pennsylvania Press, 2000

Goodman, D. *The Republic of Letters: A Cultural History of the French Enlightenment*, Ithaca, NY: Cornell University Press, 1994

Gordon, D. *Postmodernism and the Enlightenment: New Perspectives on Eighteenth-Century French Intellectual History*, New York and London: Routledge, 2001

Gordon, D. C. *The French Language and National Identity (1930–1975)*, The Hague: Mouton, 1978

Gosman, M. 'Marco Polo's Voyages: The Conflict between Confirmation and Observation', in Z. von Martels (ed.), *Travel Fact and Travel Fiction: Literary Tradition, Scholarly Discovery and Observation in Travel Writing*, Leiden: Brill, 1994
  La Légende d'Alexandre dans la littérature française du 12e siècle, Amsterdam: Rodopi, 1997

Goulbourne, R. *Voltaire Comic Dramatist*, Oxford: Voltaire Foundation, 2006

Goulemot, J.-M. *Adieu les philosophes: Que reste-t-il des Lumières?*, Paris: Seuil, 2001

Gowans, L. 'What Did Robert de Boron Really Write?', in Bonnie Wheeler (ed.), *Arthurian Studies in Honour of P. J. C. Field*, Cambridge: D. S. Brewer, 2004, pp. 15–28

Goyet. F. (ed.). *Traités de poétique et de rhétorique de la Renaissance*, Paris: Livre de Poche, 1990

Graelent and Guingamor: Two Breton Lays, ed. Russell Weingartner, New York: Garland, 1984

Grafton, A. *Commerce with the Classics: Ancient Books and Renaissance Readers*, Ann Arbor: University of Michigan Press, 1997

Grande, N. *Stratégies de romancières: de Clélie à La Princesse de Clèves*, Paris: Champion, 1999

Les Grandes Chroniques de France, vol. I, ed. J. Viard, Paris: Société de l'Histoire de France, 1920

Gravdal, K. *Ravishing Maidens: Writing Rape in Medieval French Literature and Law*, Philadelphia: University of Pennsylvania Press, 1991

Gray, F. 'Jeanne Flore and Erotic Desire: Feminism or Male Fantasy?', in D. LaGuardia and G. Ferguson (eds.), *Narrative Worlds: Essays on the 'Nouvelle' in 15th and 16th Century France*, Tempe: Arizona State University, 2005, pp. 77–95

Greenberg, M. *Corneille, Classicism and the Ruses of Symmetry*, Cambridge: Cambridge University Press, 1986

Greenblatt, S. *Shakespearean Negotiations: The Circulation of Social Energy in Renaissance England*, Berkeley: University of California Press, 1988

   Marvelous Possessions: The Wonder of the New World, Oxford: Oxford University Press, 1991

Greene, R. W. *Six French Poets of Our Time: A Critical and Historical Study*, Princeton, NJ: Princeton University Press, 1979

Greengrass, M. *The French Reformation*, Oxford: Blackwell, 1987

Grey, F. *Anthologie de la poésie française du XVIe siècle*, New York: Appleton–Century-Crofts, 1967 (various reprints)

Griffin, M. *The Object and the Cause in the Vulgate Cycle*, Oxford: Legenda, 2005

Grimod de La Reynière, A. B. L. *Réflexions philosophiques sur le plaisir*, 2nd edn, Neufchâtel: n.p., 1783

Gross, K. *Shakespeare's Noise*, Chicago: University of Chicago Press, 2001

Gudmundsdóttir, G. *Borderlines: Autobiography and Fiction in Postmodern Life-Writing*, Amsterdam: Rodopi, 2003

Guenée, B. *Histoire et culture historique dans l'Occident médiéval*, Paris: Aubier-Montaigne, 1980

Guentner, W. *Esquisses littéraires: rhétorique du spontané et récit de voyage au XIXe siècle*, Saint-Genouph: Nizet, 1997

Guérin, J. *Le Théâtre en France de 1914 à 1950*, Paris: Champion, 2007

Guerlac, S. 'Madame de Staël et le discours (féminin) de la "civilisation universelle"', *Cahiers Staëliens* 57 (2006), pp. 77–87.

   Thinking in Time, An Introduction to Henri Bergson, Ithaca, NY: Cornell University Press, 2006

Guernes de Pont-Sainte-Maxence, *La Vie de Saint Thomas de Canterbury*, ed. and trans. J. T. E. Thomas, Leuven: Peeters, 2002

Guichard, T., *et al. Le Roman français contemporain*, Paris: Culturesfrance, 2007

Guieu, J. M. and A. Hilton (eds.). *Émile Zola and the Arts*, Washington, DC: Georgetown University Press, 1988

Guillaume de Lorris, *Le Roman de la rose*, ed. F. Lecoy, 3 vols., Paris: Champion, 1973–82.

Guillaume de Machaut, *Le Livre du voir dit*, ed. P. Imbs and trans. J. Cerquilini-Toulet, Paris: Livre de Poche, 1999

Guillaume d'Orange, *Les Chansons de geste du cycle de Guillaume d'Orange*, vol. II: *Le Couronnement de Louis, Le Charroi de Nîmes, La Prise d'Orange*, ed. J. Frappier, Paris: Société d'Edition d'Enseignement Supérieur, 1967

Guillaume le Clerc, *Fergus*, ed. E. Martin, Halle: Buchhandlung des Waisenhauses, 1872

Gunn, A. M. *The Mirror of Love: A Reinterpretation of the Roman de la Rose*, Lubbock: Texas Tech Press, 1952

Gusdorf, G. *Le Romantisme*, 2 vols., Paris: Payot, 1993

Gutting, G. *French Philosophy in the Twentieth Century*, Cambridge: Cambridge University Press, 2001

Guynn, N. D. 'Historicizing Shame, Shaming History: Origination and Negativity in the *Eneas*', *Esprit Créateur* 39.4 (1999), pp. 112–27

Allegory and Sexual Ethics in the High Middle Ages, New York: Palgrave Macmillan, 2007

Haddad, E. *Orientalist Poetics: The Islamic Middle East in Nineteenth-Century English and French Poetry*, Aldershot: Ashgate, 2002

Haidu, P. *The Subject of Violence: The Song of Roland and the Birth of the State*, Bloomington and Indianapolis: Indiana University Press, 1993

Hambursin, O. (ed.). *Récits du dernier siècle des voyages: de Victor Segalen à Nicolas Bouvier*, Paris: Presses de l'Université Paris-Sorbonne, 2005

Hammond, N. *Creative Tensions: An Introduction to Seventeenth-Century French Literature*, London: Duckworth, 1997

Hamon, P. 'À propos de l'impressionnisme de Zola', *Les Cahiers naturalistes* 34 (1967), pp. 139–47

Le Personnel du roman: le système des personnages dans 'Les Rougon Macquart', Geneva: Droz, 1983

Expositions: littérature et architecture au xixe siècle, Paris: Corti, 1989

Hampton, T. *Literature and Nation in the Sixteenth Century: Inventing Renaissance France*, Ithaca, NY: Cornell University Press, 2001

Hanning, R. W. 'Arthurian Evangelists: The Language of Truth in Thirteenth-Century French Prose Romances', *Philological Quarterly* 63 (1985), pp. 347–65

Hansen, E. C. *Disaffection and Decadence: A Crisis in French Intellectual Thought 1848–98*, Washington, DC: University Press of America, 1982

Hardison, O. B., Jr. *Christian Rite and Christian Drama in the Middle Ages: Essays in the Origin and Early History of Modern Drama*, Baltimore, MD: Johns Hopkins University Press, 1965

Harris, J. *Hidden Agendas: Cross-Dressing in 17th-Century France*, Tübingen: Biblio 17, 2005

Harris, R. *Murders and Madness: Medicine, Law, and Society in the* Fin de Siècle, Oxford: Oxford University Press, 1989

'The "Unconscious" and Catholicism in France', *Historical Journal* 47 (2004), pp. 331–54

Harrison, N. *Postcolonial Criticism: History, Theory and the Work of Fiction*, Cambridge: Polity, 2003

Harsin, J. 'Gender, Class, and Madness in Nineteenth-Century France', *French Historical Studies* 17 (1992), pp. 1048–70

Harth, E. *Cartesian Women: Versions and Subversions of Rational Discourse in the Old Regime*, Ithaca, NY: Cornell University Press, 1992

Harvey, D. *Consciousness and the Urban Experience: Studies in the History and Theory of Capitalist Urbanization*, Baltimore, MD: Johns Hopkins University Press, 1985

Harvey, H. G. *The Theatre of the Basoche*, Cambridge, MA: Harvard University Press, 1941

Le Haut Livre du Graal: Perlesvaus, ed. W. A. Nitze and T. Atkinson Jenkins, 2 vols., New York: Phaeton, 1932; reprinted 1972

Hayward, S. and G. Vincendeau. *French Film: Texts and Contexts*, 2nd edn, London: Routledge, 2000

Healey, K. J. *The Modernist Traveler: French Detours, 1900–1930*, Lincoln: University of Nebraska Press, 2004

Heldris de Cornüalle, *Le Roman de Silence*, ed. L. Thorpe, Cambridge: Heffer, 1972

Helisenne de Crenne, *Les Angoysses douloureuses qui procedent d'amours (1538)*, Première partie, ed. P. Demats, Paris: Les Belles Lettres, 1968

Hellegouarc'h, J. *Nouvelles françaises du XVIIIᵉ siècle*, 2 vols., Paris: Livre de Poche, 1994
  (ed.), *L'Art de la conversation*, Paris: Dunod, 1997

Heller-Roazen, D. *Fortune's Faces: The 'Roman de la Rose' and the Poetics of Contingency*, Baltimore, MD: Johns Hopkins University Press, 2003

Hellman, J. *The Knight Monks of Vichy France: Uriage 1940–1945*, Montreal and Kingston: McGill-Queen's University Press, 1997

Henry of Huntingdon, *Historia Anglorum: The History of the English*, ed. D. E. Greenaway, Oxford: Clarendon Press, 1996

Hesse, C. 'Reading Signatures: Female Authorship and Revolutionary Law in France, 1750–1850', *Eighteenth Century Studies* 22.3 (Spring 1989), pp. 469–87
  'French Women in Print, 1750–1800: An Essay in Historical Bibliography', In H. T. Mason (ed.), *The Darnton Debate: Books and Revolution in the Eighteenth Century*, Oxford: Voltaire Foundation, 1998, pp. 65–82
  The Other Enlightenment: How French Women Became Modern, Princeton, NJ: Princeton University Press, 2001

Hewitt, N. *Literature and the Right in Postwar France: The Story of the 'Hussards'*, Oxford and Washington, DC: Berg, 1986
  'Images of Montmartre in French writing 1920–1960: 'la Bohème réactionnaire', *French Cultural Studies* 4.11 (1993), pp. 129–43

Hiddleston, J. *Reinventing Community: Identity and Difference in late Twentieth-Century Philosophy and Literature in French*, London: Legenda, 2005

Higgins, I. M. *Writing East: The 'Travels' of Sir John Mandeville*, Philadelphia: University of Pennsylvania Press, 1997

Higgins, L. A. *New Novel, New Wave, New Politics: Fiction and the Representation of History in Postwar France*, Lincoln: University of Nebraska Press, 1996

Higham, N. J. *King Arthur: Myth-Making and History*, London and New York: Routledge, 2002

Hill, L. *Beckett's Fiction: In Different Words*, Cambridge: Cambridge University Press, 1990
  Marguerite Duras: Apocalyptic Desires, London: Routledge, 1993
  Bataille, Klossowski, Blanchot: Writing at the Limit, Oxford: Oxford University Press, 2001

Hipp, M.-T. *Mythes et réalité: enquête sur le roman et les mémoires (1660–1700)*, Paris: Klincksieck, 1976

Histoire ancienne jusqu'à César (Estoires Rogier), ed. M. de Visser-van Terwisga, Orléans: Paradigme, 1999

Hitti, P. K. *An Arab-Syrian Gentleman and Warrior in the Period of the Crusades: Memoirs of Usamah ibn-Munqidh*, trans. P. K. Hitti, Princeton, NJ: Princeton University Press, 1987

Hollier, D. (ed.). *A New History of French Literature*, Cambridge, MA: Harvard University Press, 1989

Hollywood, A. *The Soul As Virgin Wife: Mechtild of Magdeburg, Marguerite Porete, and Meister Eckhart*, Notre Dame, IN: University of Notre Dame Press, 1995

Holmes, D. *French Women's Writing 1848–1994*, London: Athlone Press, 1996

Holt, M. (ed.), *Renaissance and Reformation France, 1500–1648*, Oxford: Oxford University Press, 2002

Honour, H., *Romanticism*, New York: Harper and Row, 1979

Horkheimer, M. and T. Adorno. *Dialectic of Enlightenment*, New York: Herder and Herder, 1972

Houppermans, S. *Jean Echenoz: étude de l'œuvre*, Paris: Bordas, 2008

House, J. *Impressionism: Paint and Politics*, New Haven, CT and London: Yale University Press, 2004

Housley, N. *Contesting the Crusades*, Malden, MA: Blackwell, 2006

Howarth, W. D. *Beaumarchais and the Theatre*, London: Routledge, 1995

Howells, C. (ed.). *The Cambridge Companion to Sartre*, Cambridge: Cambridge University Press, 1992

    French Women Philosophers: A Contemporary Reader, London and New York: Routledge, 2004

Hubert, M.-C. *Le Nouveau Théâtre 1950–1968*, Paris: Champion, 2008

Huchet, J.-C. *Le Roman médiéval*, Paris: Presses Universitaires de France, 1984

    (ed.). *Nouvelles occitanes du Moyen Age*, Paris: Flammarion, 1992

Huchon, M. 'Le Roman, histoire fabuleuse', in M. Clément and P. Mousnier (eds.), *Le Roman au xvie siècle*, Strasbourg: Presses Universitaires de Strasbourg, 2005, pp. 51–67

    Louise Labé, une créature de papier, Geneva: Droz, 2006

Hughes, A. *Heterographies: Sexual Difference in French Autobiography*, Oxford: Berg, 1999

Hughes, E. *Writing Marginality in Modern French Literature: From Loti to Genet*, Cambridge: Cambridge University Press, 2001

Hughes, H. S. *The Obstructed Path: French Social Thought in the Years of Desperation*, New York: Harper and Row, 1969

Hult, D. F. 'Lancelot's Shame', *Romance Philology* 42.1 (1988), pp. 30–50

Huon de Bordeaux, ed. W. W. Kibler and F. Suard, Paris: Champion, 2003

Huon de Méry, *Le Tournoiement de l'Antéchrist*, ed. Prosper Tarbé, Reims: Regnier, 1851; reprinted Geneva: Slatkine, 1977

Huot, S. *From Song to Book: The Poetics of Writing in Old French Lyric and Lyrical Narrative Poetry*, Ithaca, NY: Cornell University Press, 1987

    'Use of Literary Texts as Evidence for Performance Practice', *Musica Disciplina* 43 (1989), pp. 63–113

    The Romance of the Rose and its Medieval Readers: Interpretation, Reception, Manuscript Transmission, Cambridge: Cambridge University Press, 1993

    Postcolonial Fictions in the Roman de Perceforest: Cultural Identities and Hybridities, Cambridge: D. S. Brewer, 2007

Huppert, G. *The Idea of Perfect History: Historical Erudition and Historical Philosophy in Renaissance France*, Urbana and Chicago: University of Illinois Press, 1970

Hutton, J. *Neo-Impressionism and the Search for Solid Ground: Art, Science and Anarchism in Fin-de-Siècle France*, Baton Rouge and London: Louisiana State University Press, 1994

Ilsley, M. H. *A Daughter of the Renaissance. Marie le Jars de Gournay: Her Life and Works*, The Hague: Mouton, 1963

Irwin, R. *The Arabian Nights: A Companion*, London: Allen Lane, 1994

Israel, J. *Radical Enlightenment: Philosophy and the Making of Modernity, 1650–1750*, Oxford: Oxford University Press, 2001

Jacquin, G. *Le Style historique dans les récits français et latins de la Quatrième Croisade*, Paris: Champion-Slatkine, 1986

Jakobson, R. 'On Realism in Art', in L. Matejka and K. Pomorska (eds.), *Readings in Russian Poetics: Formalist and Structuralist Views*, Ann Arbor: University of Michigan Press, 1978, pp. 38–46

James, E. D. 'Scepticism and Positive Values in La Rochefoucauld', *French Studies* 23 (1969), pp. 349–61

James, T. *Dream, Creativity, and Madness in Nineteenth-Century France*, Oxford: Clarendon Press, 1995

Jameson, F. 'Realism and Desire: Balzac and the Problem of the Subject', in *The Political Unconscious: Narrative as a Socially Symbolic Act*, Ithaca, NY: Cornell University Press, 1981, pp. 151–84

Jaufré, ed. Clovis Brunel, 2 vols., Paris: Société des anciens textes français, 1943

Jauss, H. R., *La Genèse de la poésie allégorique en France au XIIIe siècle*, Heidelberg: Carl Winter, 1962

Jean d'Arras. *Mélusine ou la noble histoire de Lusignan*, ed. and trans. J.-J. Vincensini, Paris: Librairie Générale Française, 2003

Jean Froissart, *La Prison amoureuse*, ed. A. Fourrier, Paris: Klincksieck, 1974

Jeanne d'Albret. *Mémoires et poésies de Jeanne d'Albret*, ed. Baron de Ruble, Paris: E. Paul, Huart and Guillemin, 1898; reprinted Geneva: Slatkine, 1970

Jeannelle, J.-L. and C. Viollet (eds.). *Genèse et autofiction*, Louvain-la-Neuve: Academia Bruylant, 2007

Jeanneret, M. *Poésie et tradition biblique au XVIe siècle: les paraphrases des psaumes de Marot à Malherbe*, Paris: Corti, 1969

   La Lettre perdue: écriture et folie dans l'œuvre de Gérard de Nerval, Paris: Flammarion, 1978

   Éros rebelle: littérature et dissidence à l'âge classique, Paris: Seuil, 2003

Jefferson, A. *The Nouveau Roman and the Poetics of Fiction*, Cambridge: Cambridge University Press, 1980

   Biography and the Question of Literature in France, Oxford: Oxford University Press, 2007

Jeffery, B. *French Renaissance Comedy 1552–1630*, Oxford: Clarendon Press, 1969

Jimack, P. (ed.). *A History of the Two Indies: A Translated Selection of Writings from Raynal's* Histoire philosophique et politique des établissements des Européens dans les Deux Indes, Aldershot: Ashgate, 2006

Johnson, B. *A World of Difference*, Baltimore, MD: Johns Hopkins University Press, 1987

   The Feminist Difference: Literature, Psychoanalysis, Race, and Gender, Cambridge, MA: Harvard University Press, 1998

Johnson, J. 'Literary Impressionism in France: A Survey of Criticism', *L'Esprit créateur* 13 (1973), pp. 271–97

Joinville, Jean de. *Vie de Saint Louis*, ed. and trans. J. Monfrin, Paris: Livre de Poche, 1995

Jondorf, G. *French Renaissance Tragedy: The Dramatic Word*, Cambridge: Cambridge University Press, 1990

Jones, C. *Philippe de Vigneulles and the Art of Prose Translation*, Cambridge: D. S. Brewer, 2008

Jones, E. H. *Spaces of Belonging: Home, Culture and Identity in 20th-Century French Autobiography*, Amsterdam: Rodopi, 2007

Jordan, S. *Contemporary French Women's Writing: Women's Visions, Women's Voices, Women's Lives*, Oxford: Peter Lang, 2004

Jung, M.-R. *Études sur le poème allégorique en France au Moyen Age*, Berne: Éditions Francke, 1971

Jussie, J. de. *Le Levain du Calvinisme, ou commencement de l'heresie de Geneve*, Chambéry: Geoffroy du Four, [1611]

Kahn, D. *Alchimie et Paracelsisme en France à la fin de la Renaissance (1567–1625)*, Geneva: Droz, 2007

Kay, S. *Subjectivity in Troubadour Poetry*, Cambridge: Cambridge University Press, 1990

The *Chansons de Geste in the Age of Romance: Political Fictions*, Oxford: Clarendon Press, 1995

Courtly Contradictions: The Emergence of the Literary Object in the Twelfth Century, Stanford, CA: Stanford University Press, 2003

Kay, S., T. Cave, and M. Bowie. *A Short History of French Literature*, Oxford: Oxford University Press, 2003

Kedar, B. Z. 'Latins and Oriental Christians in the Frankish Levant, 1099–1291', in *Franks, Muslims and Oriental Christians in the Latin Levant*, Aldershot: Ashgate, 2006, pp. 209–22

Keefe, T. *French Existentialist Fiction: Changing Moral Perspectives*, London: Croom Helm, 1986

Keller, R. C. *Colonial Madness: Psychiatry in French North Africa*, Chicago: University of Chicago Press, 2007

Kelley, D. 'Degas: Naturalist Novelist or Symbolist Poet', *French Studies* 38 (1984), pp. 306–18

Kelley, D. R. *The Foundations of Modern Historical Scholarship: Language, Law and History in the French Renaissance*, New York: Columbia University Press, 1970

Kelly, D. *Medieval Imagination: Rhetoric and the Poetry of Courtly Love*, Madison: University of Wisconsin Press, 1978

The Art of Medieval French Romance, Madison: University of Wisconsin Press, 1992

Kelly, D. 'Experimenting on Women: Zola's Theory and Practice of the Experimental Novel', in M. Cohen and C. Prendergast (eds.), *Spectacles of Realism: Gender, Body, Genre*, Minneapolis: University of Minnesota Press, 1995, pp. 231–46

Kelly, H. A. *Ideas and Forms of Tragedy from Aristotle to the Middle Ages*, Cambridge: Cambridge University Press, 1993

Kennedy, E. *Lancelot and the Grail*, Oxford: Clarendon Press, 1986

Kennedy, G. A. *Classical Rhetoric and its Christian and Secular Tradition from Ancient to Modern Times*, Chapel Hill: University of North Carolina Press, 1980

Kenny, N. *The Uses of Curiosity in Early Modern France and Germany*, Oxford: Oxford University Press, 2004

An Introduction to Sixteenth-Century French Literature and Thought: Other Times, Other Places, London: Duckworth, 2008

Kibédi Varga, A. *Rhétorique et littérature: études de structures classiques*, Paris: Didier, 1970

(ed.), *Les Poétiques du classicisme*, Paris: Aux Amateurs des Livres, 1990

King, A. *French Women Novelists: Defining a Female Style*, Basingstoke: Macmillan, 1989

Kinoshita, S. *Medieval Boundaries: Rethinking Difference in Old French Literature*, Philadelphia: University of Pennsylvania Press, 2006

'Deprovincializing the Middle Ages', in R. Wilson and C. Leigh Connery (eds.), *The Worlding Project: Doing Cultural Studies in the Era of Globalization*, Santa Cruz, CA: New Pacific Press, 2007

Kittay J. and W. Godzich, *The Emergence of Prose: An Essay in Prosaics*, Minneapolis: University of Minnesota Press, 1987

Kline, T. J. *Screening the Text: Intertexuality in New Wave French Cinema*, Baltimore, MD: Johns Hopkins University Press, 1992

'The French New Wave', in E. Ezra (ed.), *European Cinema*, Oxford: Oxford University Press, 2004, pp. 157–75

'*Last Year at Marienbad*: High Modern and Postmodern', in T. Perry (ed.), *Masterpieces of Modernist Cinema*, Bloomington: Indiana University Press, 2006, pp. 208–35

Unraveling French Cinema, London: Blackwell, 2009

Knight, A. E. *Aspects of Genre in Late Medieval French Drama*, Manchester: Manchester University Press, 1983

Knight, D. *Balzac and the Model of Painting: Artist Stories in* La Comédie Humaine, London: Legenda, 2007

Knowles, D. *French Drama of the Inter-war Years 1918–39*, London: Harrap, 1967

Kocher, S. *Allegories of Love in Marguerite Porete's Mirror of Simple Souls*, Turnhout: Brepols, 2009

Kolakowski, L. *God Owes Us Nothing*, Chicago: University of Chicago Press, 1995

Koszarski, R. *An Evening's Entertainment: The Age of the Silent Feature Picture, 1915–1928*, Berkeley: University of California Press, 1990

Krauss, R. and M. Rowell (eds.). *Joan Miró: Magnetic Fields*, New York: Solomon R. Guggenheim Foundation, 1972

Kreuger, Roberta (ed.). *The Cambridge Companion to Medieval Romance*, Cambridge: Cambridge University Press, 2000

Kristeva, J. *Soleil noir: dépression et mélancolie*, Paris: Gallimard, 1987

Strangers to Ourselves, trans. L. S. Roudiez, New York: Columbia University Press, 1991

Le génie féminin, vol. III: Colette, Paris: Fayard, 2002

Kritzman, L. D. (ed.). *Auschwitz and After: Race, Culture, and 'the Jewish Question' in France*, New York and London: Routledge, 1995

The Columbia History of Twentieth-Century French Thought, New York: Columbia University Press, 2006

Krumenacker, Y. *L'École française de spiritualité*, Paris: Cerf, 1998

La Charité, V. *Twentieth-Century French Poetry*, Lexington, KY: French Forum, 1992

La Garanderie, M.-M. de. *Christianisme et lettres profanes: essai sur l'humanisme français (1515–1535) et sur la pensée de Guillaume Budé*, Paris: Champion, 1995

La Mesnardière, J.-H. Pilet de. *La Poétique*, Geneva: Slatkine, 1972; 1st edn 1639

La Mettrie, J. O. de. *L'Homme machine*, ed. J. Vérain, Paris: Mille et une nuits, 2000

Lacan, J. 'Courtly Love as Anamorphosis', in *The Seminar of Jacques Lacan. Book VII: The Ethics of Psychoanalysis, 1959–1960*, trans. D. Porter, New York: Norton, 1992, pp. 139–154

    'God and Woman's *jouissance*', in *The Seminar of Jacques Lacan. Book XX: Encore 1972–1973*, trans. B. Fink, New York: Norton, 1999, pp. 61–77

LaCapra, D. *A Preface to Sartre*, New York: Cornell University Press, 1978

Lacoue-Labarthe, P. and J.-L. Nancy, *L'Absolu littéraire: théorie de la littérature du romantisme allemand*, Paris: Seuil, 1978

Lacroix, B. *L'Historien au Moyen Age*, Paris: Vrin, 1971

Lacy, N. J. (ed.). *The New Arthurian Encyclopedia*, New York and London: Garland, 1996

Lacy, N. J., G. Ashe, and D. N. Mankoff, *The Arthurian Handbook*, 2nd edn, New York and London: Garland, 1997

Lacy, N. J. and J. Tasker Grimbert (eds.). *A Companion to Chrétien de Troyes*, Cambridge: D. S. Brewer, 2005

Lafay, H. *La Poésie française du premier XVIIe siècle (1598–1630)*, Paris: Nizet, 1975

Lafond, J. (ed.). *Moralistes du XVIIe siècle*, Paris: Robert Laffont, 1992

    L'Homme et son image: morales et littérature de Montaigne à Mandeville, Paris: Champion, 1996

Lafond, R. and J. Picard (eds.). *Les Nouvelles du XVIIe siècle*, Paris: Gallimard, 1997

LaGuardia, D. *The Iconography of Power: The French Nouvelle at the End of the Middle Ages*, Newark: University of Delaware Press, 1999

Lancaster, H. C. *A History of Dramatic Literature in the Seventeenth Century*, Baltimore, MD: Johns Hopkins University Press, 1929

    The French Tragi-comedy: Its Origin and Development from 1552 to 1628, 9 vols., New York: Gordian Press, 1966; 1st edn 1907

Lancelot du Lac, ed. E. Kennedy, preface M. Zink, trans. F. Mosès, Paris: Livre de Poche, 1991

Lancelot du Lac, vol. II, ed. E. Kennedy, trans. M.-L. Chênerie, Paris: Livre de Poche, 1993

Lancelot du Lac, vol. III: *La Fausse Guenièvre*, ed. E. Kennedy, trans. M.-L. Chênerie, Paris: Livre de Poche, 1998

Lancelot-Grail: The Old French Arthurian Vulgate and post-Vulgate in Translation, ed. N. Lacy, 10 vols. New York: Garland, 1993–6

Langer, U. *Vertu du discours, discours de la vertu: littérature et philosophie morale au XVIe siècle en France*, Geneva: Droz, 1999

    (ed.), *The Cambridge: Companion to Montaigne*, Cambridge: Cambridge University Press, 2005

Langlois, Ernest. *Recueil d'arts de seconde rhétorique publié par M. E. Langlois*, Paris: Imprimerie nationale, 1902

Larner, J. *Marco Polo and the Discovery of the World*, New Haven, CT and London: Yale University Press, 1999

Larsen, A. R. '"Un honneste passetems": Strategies of Legitimation in French Renaissance Women's Prefaces', in 'Writing the Feminine in the Renaissance', special issue of *L'Esprit créateur* 30 (1990), pp. 11–22

Laurent, F. *Plaire et édifier: les Récits hagiographiques composés en Angleterre aux XIIe et XIIIe siècles*, Paris: Champion, 1998

Lawler, James R. *René Char: The Myth and the Poem*, Princeton, NJ: Princeton University Press, 1978

Lazar, M. *Amour courtois et fin'amors dans la littérature du xiie siècle*, Paris: Klincksieck, 1964

Le Gendre, M. *L'Exercice de l'âme vertueuse*, ed. C. H. Winn, Paris: Champion, 2001

Le Goff, J. *Medieval Civilization, 400–1500*, trans. J. Barrow, Oxford: Blackwell, 1995

Le Roy Ladurie, E. *Montaillou: Cathars and Catholics in a French Village 1294–1324*, trans. B. Bray, Harmondsworth: Penguin, 1980

Lebrette, F. 'Les Fripiers de la presse', *Valeurs actuelles*, 30 August 1971, pp. 20–1

Lecarme, J. and E. Lecarme-Tabone. *L'Autobiographie*, 2nd edn, Paris: Colin, 1999

Lefranc, A. *Les Navigations de Pantagruel: étude sur la géographie Rabelaisienne*, Paris: Henri LeClerc, 1905

Legge, M. D. 'Anglo-Norman Hagiography and the Romances', *Medievalia et Humanistica* 6 (1975), pp. 41–9

Lehmann, A. G. *The Symbolist Aesthetic in France 1885–1895*, Oxford: Blackwell, 1950

Lejeune, P. *Le Pacte autobiographique*, Paris: Seuil, 1975

Lennon, T. *The Battle of the Gods and Giants: The Legacies of Descartes and Gassendi, 1655–1715*, Princeton, NJ: Princeton University Press, 1993

Lesne, E. *La Poétique des mémoires*, Paris: Champion, 1996

Lestringant, F. *Écrire le monde à la Renaissance: quinze études sur Rabelais, Postel, Bodin et la littérature géographique*, Caen: Paradigme, 1993

  Mapping the Renaissance World, Berkeley: University of California Press, 1994

  Cannibals: The Discovery and Representation of the Cannibal from Columbus to Jules Verne, trans. R. Morris, Cambridge: Cambridge University Press, 1997

  Le Huguenot et le sauvage: L'Amérique et la controverse coloniale, en France, au temps des guerres de Religion (1555–1589), Paris: Aux Amateurs de livres, 1990; Paris: Klincksieck, 1999; Geneva: Droz, 2004

Lestringant, F., J. Rieu and A. Tarrête. *Littérature française du xvie siècle*, Paris: Presses Universitaires de France, 2000

Lethbridge, R. 'Zola, Manet and *Thérèse Raquin*', *French Studies* 34 (1980), pp. 278–99

Lethbridge, R. and T. Keefe (eds.). *Zola and the Craft of Fiction: Essays in Honour of F. W. J. Hemmings*, Leicester: Leicester University Press, 1990

Letzter, J. *Intellectual Tacking: Questions of Education in the Works of Isabelle de Charrière*, Amsterdam: Rodopi, 1998

Leupin, A. *Le Graal et la littérature: étude sur la Vulgate arthurienne en prose*, Lausanne: L'Âge d'homme, 1982

Lever, M. *Romanciers du grand siècle*, Paris: Presses Universitaires de France, 1996

Lévi-Strauss, C. *Tristes tropiques*, trans. J. Russell, New York: Criterion, 1972

Lewis, C. S. *The Allegory of Love: A Study in Medieval Tradition*, Oxford: Oxford University Press, 1936; reprinted 1992

Las Leys d'amor, see Molinier, G.

Liebault, N. [Nicole Estienne]. *Les Misères de la femme mariée où se peuvent voir les peines et tourments qu'elle reçoit durant sa vie*, in I. Zinguer, *Misères et grandeur de la femme au xvie siècle*, Geneva: Slatkine, 1982

Lionnet, F. *Postcolonial Representations: Women, Literature, Identity*, Ithaca, NY: Cornell University Press, 1989

Lister, M. *et al.* (eds.). *New Media: A Critical Introduction*, London: Routledge, 2003

Lloyd, C. *Collaboration and Resistance in Occupied France: Representing Treason and Sacrifice*, Basingstoke: Palgrave Macmillan, 2003

Lloyd, R. *The Land of Lost Content: Children and Childhood in Nineteenth-Century French Literature*, Oxford: Oxford University Press, 1992

   (ed.). *The Cambridge Companion to Baudelaire*, Cambridge: Cambridge University Press, 2005

Lockyer, S. and M. Pickering (eds.). *Beyond a Joke: The Limits of Humour*, Basingstoke and New York: Palgrave Macmillan, 2005

Looseley, D. *The Politics of Fun*, Oxford: Berg, 1995

Looze, Laurence de, *Pseudo-Autobiography in the Fourteenth Century: Juan Ruiz, Guillaume de Machaut, Jean Froissart, and Geoffrey Chaucer*, Gainesville: University of Florida Press, 1997

Lord, A. *The Singer of Tales*, Cambridge, MA: Harvard University Press, 1960

Lowy, V. *L'Histoire infilmable: les camps d'extermination nazis à l'écran*, Paris: L'Harmattan, 2001

Lucey, M. *The Misfit of the Family: Balzac and the Social Forms of Sexuality*, Durham, NC: Duke University Press, 2003

   Never Say I: Sexuality and the First Person in Colette, Gide and Proust, Durham, NC: Duke University Press, 2006

Lukács, G. *Studies in European Realism*, trans. Edith Bone, London: Merlin, 1972

   'Narrate or Describe?', in *Writer and Critic*, trans. Arthur Kahn, London: Merlin, 1978, pp. 110–48

Lusignan, S. *Parler vulgairement: les intellectuels et la langue française aux xiiie et xive siècles*, Paris: Vrin, 1986

Lyon-Caen, J. *La Lecture et la vie: les usages du roman au temps de Balzac*, Paris: Tallandier, 2006

Lyons, J. D. *Kingdom of Disorder: The Theory of Tragedy in Classical France*, West Lafayette, IN: Purdue University Press, 1999

   Before Imagination: Embodied Thought from Montaigne to Rousseau, Stanford, CA: Stanford University Press, 2005

MacEvitt, C. *The Crusades and the Christian World of the East: Rough Tolerance*, Philadelphia: University of Pennsylvania Press, 2008

Maclean, I. *The Renaissance Notion of Woman: A Study in the Fortunes of Scholasticism and Medical Science in European Intellectual Life*, Cambridge: Cambridge University Press, 1980

   Montaigne philosophe, Paris: Presses Universitaires de France, 1996

Maclean, I. and I. D. McFarlane (eds.). *Montaigne: Essays in Memory of Richard Sayce*, Oxford: Clarendon Press, 1982

Macphail, E. *The Voyage to Rome in French Renaissance Literature*, Saratoga, CA: Anma Libri, 1990

Madden, T. F. *The Fourth Crusade: Event, Aftermath, and Perceptions*, London: Ashgate, 2008

Maddox, M. and S. Sturm Maddox (eds.). *The Medieval French Alexander*, Albany: State University of New York Press, 2002

Mahoney, D. B. *The Grail: A Casebook*, New York: Garland, 2000

Mainil, J. 'Ah! quels contes! Idéologies du conte licencieux au siècle des Lumières', in R. A. Francis and J. Mainil (eds.), *L'Abbé Prévost au tournant du siècle*, Oxford: Voltaire Foundation, 2000, pp. 333–43

Maître, M. *Les Précieuses: naissance des femmes de lettres en France au dix-septième siècle*, Paris: Champion, 1999

Malt, J. *Obscure Objects of Desire: Surrealism, Fetishism, and Politics*, Oxford: Oxford University Press, 2004

Mander, J. *Circles of Learning: Narratology and the Eighteenth-Century French Novel*, Oxford: Voltaire Foundation, 1999

    (ed.). *Remapping the Rise of the European Novel*, Oxford: Voltaire Foundation, 2007

Mantero, A. *La Muse théologienne: poésie et théologie en France de 1629 à 1680*, Berlin: Duncker und Humblot, 1995

Marchal, R. *Madame de Lambert et son milieu*, Oxford: Voltaire Foundation, 1991

Marchello-Nizia, C. 'Amour courtois: société masculine et figures du pouvoir', *Annales ESC* 36.6 (1981), pp. 969–82

Margival, Nicole de. *Le Dit de la panthère*, ed. B. Ribémont, Paris: Champion, 2000

Marguerite de Valois. *Mémoires*, ed. P. Bonnefon, Paris: Bossard, 1920

Marguerite d'Oingt, *Oeuvres*, ed. A. Darfour, P. Gardette and P. Durdilly, Paris: Les Belles Lettres, 1965

Marie de France. *Lais*, ed. A. Ewert, Oxford: Blackwell, 1944

    Les Lais, ed. J. Rychner, Paris: Champion, 1966

Marmontel, J.-F. *Œuvres*, 6 vols. Paris: Belin, 1819.

Marnette, S., *Narrateur et points de vue dans la littérature française médiévale: une approche linguistique*, Berne: Peter Lang, 1998

Marotin, F. *La Marge: Actes du colloque de Clermont-Ferrand: Janvier, 1986*, Clermont-Ferrand: Association des publications de la Faculté des lettres et sciences humaines, 1988

Marrou, H.-I. *Les troubadours*, Paris: Seuil, 1971

Marshall, J. H. (ed.). *The Razos de trobar of Raimon Vidal and Associated Texts*, London and New York: Oxford University Press, 1972

Martin, A. (ed.). *Anthologie du conte en France 1750–1799*, Paris: 10/18, 1981

Martin, H.-J., R. Chartier, and J.-P. Vivet (eds.). *Histoire de l'édition française*, vol. 1, Paris: Promodis, 1982

Maskell, D. *Racine: A Theatrical Reading*, Oxford: Clarendon Press, 1991

Mathews, T. *Literature, Art and the Pursuit of Decay in Twentieth-Century France*, Cambridge: Cambridge University Press, 2000

Matlock, J. *Scenes of Seduction: Prostitution, Hysteria, and Reading Difference in Nineteenth-Century France*, New York: Columbia University Press, 1994

    'Novels of Testimony and the "Invention" of the Modern French Novel', in *The Cambridge Companion to the French Novel from 1800 to the Present*, ed. T. Unwin, Cambridge: Cambridge University Press, 1997, pp. 16–35

Maugin, J. *L'Histoire du noble Tristan, prince de Leonnois, chevalier de la Table ronde, et d'Yseulte, princesse d'Yrlande, royne de Cornoüaille*, Paris: N. Bonfons, 1586

May, G. *Le Dilemme du roman au XVIIIe siècle; étude sur les rapports du roman et de la critique, 1715–1761*, New Haven, CT: Yale University Press, 1963

Mayne, J. *Cinema and Spectatorship*, London and New York: Routledge, 1993

McBride, W. (ed.). *The Development and Meaning of Twentieth Century Existentialism*, New York: Garland, 1997

McCracken, P. *The Romance of Adultery*, Philadelphia: University of Pennsylvania Press, 1998

McFarlane, I. D. *A Literary History of France: Renaissance France 1470–1589*, London and Tonbridge: Benn, 1974

McGinn, B. *The Flowering of Mysticism*, New York: Crossroad, 1998

McGowan, M. M. *The Vision of Rome in Late Renaissance France*, New Haven, CT and London: Yale University Press, 2000

McGrady, D. *Controlling Readers: Guillaume de Machaut and his Late Medieval Audience*, Toronto: University of Toronto Press, 2006

McGuinness, P. (ed.). *Symbolism, Decadence and the Fin de Siècle: French and European Perspectives*, Exeter: University of Exeter Press, 2000

(ed.). *Anthologie de la poésie symboliste et décadente*, Paris: Les Belles Lettres, 2001

McKenzie, B. *Remaking France: Americanization, Public Diplomacy and the Marshall Plan*, New York: Berghahn, 2005

McMahon, D. *Enemies of the Enlightenment: The French Counter-Enlightenment and the Making of Modernity*, New York: Oxford University Press, 2001

McNeill, I., 'Agnès Varda's Moving Museums', in P. Collier, A. Elsner, and O. Smith (eds.), *Anamnesia: Private and Public Memory in Modern French Culture*, Berne: Peter Lang, 2009, pp. 283–94

Méchoulan, E. and E. Mortgat (eds.). *Écrire au xviie siècle, une anthologie*, Paris: Presses Pocket, 1992

Melot, M. *The Impressionist Print*, trans. C. Beamish, New Haven, CT and London: Yale University Press, 1996

Melzer, S. and L. Rabine (eds.). *Rebel Daughters: Women and the French Revolution*, New York: Oxford University Press, 1992

Ménard, P. *et al.* (ed.). *Marco Polo: Le Divisement du Monde*, 6 vols., Geneva: Droz, 2001–9

Marco Polo à la découverte du monde, Paris: Glénat, 2007

Méniel, B. *Renaissance de l'épopée: la poésie épique en France de 1572 à 1623*, Geneva: Droz, 2004

Meraugis de Portlesguez: roman arthurien du xiiie siècle, ed. M. Szkilnik, Paris: Champion, 2004

Merlant, J. *Le Roman personnel de Rousseau à Fromentin*, Paris: Hachette, 1905

Merlin-Kajman, H. *Public et littérature en France au xviie siècle*, Paris: Les Belles Lettres, 1994

L'Absolutisme dans les lettres et la théorie des deux corps: passions et politique, Paris: Champion, 2000

Les Mervelles de Rigomer von Jehan: altfranzösischer Artusroman des xiii. Jahrhunderts nach der einzigen Aumale-handschrift in Chantilly, ed. W. Foerster and H. Brauer, 2 vols., Halle: Niemeyer, 1908–15

Met, P., *Formules de la poésie: études sur Ponge, Leiris, Char, et Du Bouchet*. Paris: Presses Universitaires de France, 1999

Meuwese, M. 'Crossing Borders: Text and Image in Arthurian Manuscripts', in B. Besamusca and F. Brandsma (eds.), 'The European Dimensions of Arthurian Literature', special issue of *Arthurian Literature* 24 (2007), 157–77

Micale, M. and R. Porter (eds.). *Discovering the History of Psychiatry*, New York and Oxford: Oxford University Press, 1994

Michallat, W. 'Pilote: Pedagogy, Puberty and Parents', in C. Forsdick, L. Grove, and L. McQuillan (eds.), *The Francophone Bande Dessinée*, Amsterdam: Rodopi, 2005, pp. 83–95

'Modern Life Is Still Rubbish: Houellebecq and the Refiguring of Reactionary Retro', *Journal of European Studies* 37 (2007), pp. 313–31

'*Pilote* Magazine and the Teenager Bande Dessinée', *Modern and Contemporary France* 15 (2007), pp. 277–92

Michaud, G. *Message poétique du Symbolisme*, Paris: Nizet, 1947; reprinted as *Le Symbolisme tel qu'en lui-même*, Paris: Nizet, 1995

Michel, P. *Lamartine, reconnaissance et mémoire*, Lyon: Presses Universitaires de Lyon, 2006

Middleton, R. 'The Manuscripts', in G. S. Burgess and K. Pratt (eds.). *The Arthur of the French: The Arthurian Legend in Medieval French and Occitan Literature*, Cardiff: University of Wales Press, 2006, pp. 8–92

Mieszkowski, G. 'The Prose *Lancelot*'s Galehot, Malory's Lavain, and the Queering of Late Medieval Literature', *Arthuriana* 5.1 (1995), pp. 21–51

Miller, N. K., *Subject to Change: Reading Feminist Writing*, New York: Columbia University Press, 1988

French Dressing: Women, Men, and Ancien Régime Fiction, New York: Routledge, 1995

Milner, J. *Art, War and Revolution in France, 1870–1871: Myth, Reportage and Reality*, New Haven, CT and London: Yale University Press, 2000

Minnis, A. J. *Medieval Theory of Authorship: Scholastic Literary Attitudes in the Later Middle Ages*, London: Scholar Press, 1984

Mirabeau, H. R., comte de. *La Morale des sens, ou l'homme du siècle*, Paris: Phébus, 2000

Mitterand, H. *Zola*, 3 vols., Paris: Fayard, 1999–2002

Moi, T. *Simone de Beauvoir: The Making of an Intellectual Woman*, Oxford: Blackwell, 1994

Molinier, G. *Las Flors del gay saber: estier dichas Las leys d'amors*, trans. M. d'Aguilar, M. d'Escouloubre, and M. Gatien-Arnoult, Toulouse: Bon et Privat, 1841–3

Monicat, B. *Itinéraires de l'écriture au féminin: voyageuses du 19e siècle*, Amsterdam: Rodopi, 1996

Montefiore, A. (ed.). *Philosophy in France Today*, Cambridge: Cambridge University Press, 1983

Montenay, G. de. *Emblèmes ou devises chrestiennes*, ed. J. Horden, Menston: Scholar Press, 1973

Moore, W. G. *Molière, A New Criticism*, Oxford: Clarendon Press, 1949

Moretti, F. *The Way of the World: The Bildungsroman in European Culture*, London: Verso, 1989

Moriarty, M. *Early Modern French Thought*, vol. I: *The Age of Suspicion*, Oxford: Oxford University Press, 2003

Early Modern French Thought, vol. II: *Fallen Nature, Fallen Selves*, Oxford: Oxford University Press, 2006

Mornet, D. *French Thought in the Eighteenth Century*, New York: Prentice-Hall, 1929

Morreall, J. 'Humour and the Conduct of Politics', in S. Lockyer and M. Pickering (eds.), *Beyond a Joke: The Limits of Humour*, Basingstoke and New York: Palgrave Macmillan, 2005, pp. 63–78

Morse, R. *Truth and Conventions in the Middle Ages: Rhetoric, Representation, and Reality*, Cambridge: Cambridge University Press, 1991

Moss, A. *Printed Commonplace-Books and the Structuring of Renaissance Thought*, Oxford: Clarendon Press, 1996

    Renaissance Truth and the Latin Language Turn, Oxford: Oxford University Press, 2003

Motte, W. *Small Worlds: Minimalism in Contemporary French Literature*, Lincoln: University of Nebraska Press, 1999

Moura, J.-M. *Littératures francophones et théorie postcoloniale*, Paris: Presses Universitaires de France, 1999

Mousnier, P. 'Quelques substituts du *roman* au xvie siècle: innovation romanesque et prudence lexicale', in M. Clément and P. Mousnier (eds.), *Le Roman au xvie siècle*, Strasbourg: Presses Universitaires de Strasbourg, 2005, pp. 33–49

    Le Roman humaniste: un genre novateur français, 1532–1564, Paris: Champion, 2007

Mouzat, J. (ed.). *Les Poèmes de Gaucelm Faidit, troubadour du xiie siècle*, Paris: Nizet, 1965

Mudimbe, V. Y. *The Invention of Africa: Gnosis, Philosophy and the Order of Knowledge*, Bloomington: Indiana University Press, 1994

La Mule sans frein, see *Two Old French Gawain Romances*

Müller, A. *La Poésie religieuse catholique de Marot à Malherbe*, Paris: R. Foulon, 1950

Müller, C. *Marguerite Porete et Marguerite d'Oingt de l'autre côté du miroir*, New York: Peter Lang, 1999

Mulvey, L. *Death 24 × A Second*, London: Reaktion Books, 2005

Mumford, L. *The City in History: Its Origins, its Transformations, and its Prospects*, London: Secker and Warburg, 1961

Murdoch, H. A. and A. Donadey (eds.). *Postcolonial Theory and Francophone Literary Studies*, Gainesville: University of Florida Press, 2005

Murphy, J. *Rhetoric in the Middle Ages: A History of Rhetorical Theory from Saint Augustine to the Renaissance* (1974), Berkeley: University of California Press, 1981

Murray, J. (ed.). *Encyclopedia of Modern French Thought*, New York and London: Fitzroy Dearborn, 2004

Musgrove, B. 'Travel and Unsettlement', in S. Clark (ed.), *Travel Writing and Empire: Postcolonial Theory in Transit*, London: Zed Books, 1999, pp. 31–44

Mylne, V. G. *The Eighteenth-Century Novel: Techniques of Illusion*, 2nd edn, Cambridge: Cambridge University Press, 1981

Nadeau, M. *Le Roman français depuis la guerre*, Paris: Gallimard, 1963

Nagy, P. *Libertinage et Révolution*, Paris: Gallimard, 1975

Nancy, J.-L. *L'Intrus*, Paris: Galilée, 2001

Nancy, J.-L. and P. Lacoue-Labarthe. *L'Absolu littéraire: théorie de la littérature du romantisme allemand*, Paris: Seuil, 1978

Naudeix, L. *Dramaturgie de la tragédie en musique (1673–1764)*, Paris: Champion, 2004

Naughton, John T. *The Poetics of Yves Bonnefoy*, Chicago: University of Chicago Press, 1984

Naya, E. '"Ne scepticque, ne dogmatique, et tous les deux ensemble": Rabelais "on phrontistere et escholle des Pyrrhoniens"', *Études Rabelaisiennes* 35 (1998), pp. 81–129

Nelson, B. *Zola and the Bourgeoisie*, London: Macmillan, 1983 (ed.). *The Cambridge Companion to Zola*, Cambridge: Cambridge University Press, 2007

Nelson, R. J. *Immanence and Transcendence: The Theatre of Jean Rotrou*, Columbus: Ohio State University Press, 1969

Newman, B. 'The Mirror and the Rose: Marguerite Porete's Encounter with the *Dieu d'Amours,*' in R. Blumenfeld-Kosinksi, D. Robertson, and N. Bradley Warren (eds.), *The Vernacular Spirit: Essays on Medieval Religious Literature*, New York and Basingstoke: Palgrave Macmillan, 2002, 105–23

Newmark, K. *Beyond Symbolism: Textual History and the Future of Reading*, Ithaca, NY: Cornell University Press, 1991

Ngũgĩwa Thiong'o. *Decolonising the Mind: The Politics of Language in African Literature*, London: Currey, 1986

Nichols, B. *Representing Reality: Issues and Concepts in Documentary*, Bloomington: Indiana University Press, 1991

Niess, R. *Zola, Cézanne and Manet: A Study of 'L'Oeuvre'*, Ann Arbor: University of Michigan Press, 1968

Nochlin, L. *Realism and Tradition in Art 1848–1900: Sources and Documents*, Englewood Cliffs, NJ: Prentice-Hall, 1966

Realism, New York: Penguin, 1971

Nolan, B. *Chaucer and the Tradition of the Roman Antique*, Cambridge: Cambridge University Press, 1992

Nora, P. (ed.). *Les Lieux de mémoire*, Paris: Gallimard, 1992

Norindr, P. *Phantasmatic Indochina: French Colonial Ideology in Architecture, Film, and Literature*, Durham, NC and London: Duke University Press, 1996

Norman, L. F. *The Public Mirror: Molière and the Social Commerce of Depiction*, Chicago: University of Chicago Press, 1999

Nye, R. A. *Crime, Madness and Politics in Modern France: The Medical Concept of National Decline*, Princeton, NJ: Princeton University Press, 1984

O'Brien, C. Cruise. *Camus*, London: Fontana, 1970

O'Brien, J. (ed.), *The Cambridge Companion to Rabelais*, Cambridge: Cambridge University Press, 2010

Odo of Deuil, *De Profectione Ludovici VII in Orientem / The Journey of Louis VII to the East*, ed. and trans. V. Gingerick Berry, New York: Columbia University Press, 1948

Les Œuvres de Guiot de Provins, poète lyrique et satirique, ed. J. Orr, Manchester: Manchester University Press, 1915

Ohayon, A., J. Carroy, and R. Plas. *Histoire de la psychologie en France: xixe–xxe siècles*, Paris: La Découverte, 2006

Olson, G. 'The Medieval Fortunes of 'Theatrica', *Traditio* 4 (1986), pp. 265–86

Ory, P. *Les Collaborateurs: 1940–1945*, Paris: Seuil, 1977

Outram, D. *The Enlightenment*, Cambridge: Cambridge University Press, 2005

Panorama of the Enlightenment, London: Thames and Hudson, 2007

Ozouf, M. *La Fête révolutionnaire, 1789–1799*, Paris: Gallimard, 1988

Paden, W. D. *An Introduction to Old Occitan*, New York: Modern Language Association of America, 1998

Paden, W. D. and F. F. Paden, *Troubadour Poems from the South of France*, Cambridge: D. S. Brewer, 2007

Pagden, A. *European Encounters with the New World: From Renaissance to Romanticism*, New Haven, CT and London: Yale University Press, 1994

Page, C. *The Owl and the Nightingale: Musical Life and Ideas in France 1100–1300*, London: Dent, 1989

Palacio, J. de. *Figures et formes de la décadence*, Paris: Seguier, 1992

Palmer, J. 'Parody and Decorum: Permission to Mock', in S. Lockyer, and M. Pickering, (eds.), *Beyond a Joke: The Limits of Humour*, Basingstoke and New York: Palgrave Macmillan, 2005, pp. 79–97

Palmer, R. B. 'The Metafictional Machaut: Self-Reflexivity and Self-Mediation in the Two Judgment Poems', *Studies in the Literary Imagination* 20 (1987), pp. 23–39

Pantin, I. *La Poésie du ciel en France dans la seconde moitié du xvie siècle*, Geneva: Droz, 1995

Paque, J. *Le Symbolisme belge*, Brussels: Labor, 1989

Paris, G. *Medieval French Literature*, London: Dent, 1903

Parise la Duchesse: chanson de geste, ed. F. Guessard and L. Larchey, Paris: Vieweg, 1860

Paterson, L. M. *The World of the Troubadours: Medieval Occitan society, c. 1100–c. 1300*, Cambridge: Cambridge University Press, 1993

Paton, G. E. C. 'The Comedian as Portrayer of Social Morality', in C. Powell and G. E. C. Paton (eds.), *Humour and Society: Resistance and Control*, Houndmills: Macmillan, 1988, pp. 206–33

Pavel, T. *L'Art de l'éloignement: essai sur l'imagination classique*, Paris: Gallimard, 1996

Pavis, P. *Le Théâtre contemporain: analyses de textes de Sarraute à Vinaver*, Paris: Nathan, 2002

Pearson, R. *Mallarmé and Circumstance: The Translation of Silence*, Oxford: Oxford University Press, 2004

Le Pèlerinage de Charlemagne, ed. G. S. Burgess, Edinburgh: Société Rencesvals, 1998

Perceforest, ed. G. Roussineau, vol. i, Geneva: Droz, 1988

Perchellet, J.-P. *L'Héritage classique: la tragédie entre 1680 et 1814*, Paris: Champion, 2004

Pérouse, G.-A. *Nouvelles françaises du xvie siècle: images de la vie du temps*, Geneva: Droz, 1977

Perret, M., 'De l'espace romanesque à la matérialité du livre: l'espace énonciatif des premiers romans en prose', *Poétique* 50 (1982), pp. 173–82

Peters, E. (ed.). *The First Crusade: The Chronicle of Fulcher of Chartres and Other Source Materials*, Philadelphia: University of Pennsylvania Press, 1971

Petit de Julleville, L. *Historie du théâtre en France*, vols. i and ii: *Les Mystères* (1880), reprinted Geneva: Slatkine, 1968

Petterson, J., *Postwar Figures of 'L'Ephémère'*, Lewisburg, PA: Bucknell University Press, 2000

Philippe de Rémi, *Le Roman de la Manekine*, ed. and trans. B. N. Sargeant-Baur, Amsterdam: Rodopi, 1999

Phillips, H. *Church and Culture in Seventeenth-Century France*, Cambridge: Cambridge University Press, 1997

Pickford, C. E. *L'Évolution du roman arthurien en prose vers la fin du moyen âge d'après le manuscrit 112 du fonds français de la Bibliothèque nationale*, Paris: Nizet, 1960

Pierrot, J. *L'Imaginaire décadent 1880–1900*, Paris: Presses Universitaires de France, 1977

Plagnol-Diéval, M.-E. *Madame de Genlis et le théâtre d'éducation au dix-huitième siècle*, Oxford: Voltaire Foundation, 1997

Le Théâtre de société: un autre théâtre? Paris: Champion, 2003

Platin, C., *L'Hystoire de Giglan, filz de Messire Gauvain qui fut roy de Galles*, Lyons: Claude Nourry, 1532

Plummer, J. F. (ed.). *Vox Feminae: Studies in Medieval Woman's Songs*, Kalamazoo, MI: Medieval Institute, 1981

Poe, E. W. *From Poetry to Prose: The Emergence of the* Vidas, *the* Razos *and the* Razos de Trobar, Birmingham, AL: Summa Publications, 1984

Poirion, D. 'Romans en vers et romans en prose', in J. Frappier and R. R. Grimm (eds.), *Le roman jusqu'à la fin du xiiie siècle*, Heidelberg: Carl Winter, 1978–84

(ed.). *La Littérature française aux xive et xve siècles*, Heidelberg: Carl Winter, 1988

Ponceau, J.-P. *Lestoire del Saint Graal*, Paris: Champion, 1997

Ponnau, G. *La Folie dans la littérature fantastique*, Paris: Presses Universitaires de France, 1997

Popkin, R. H. *The History of Scepticism from Savonarola to Bayle*, New York and Oxford: Oxford University Press, 2003

Porete, M. *Le Mirouer des simples ames/Margeretae Porete Speculum simplicium animarum*, ed. Romana Guarnieri and Paul Verdeyen, Turnhout: Brepols, 1986

The Mirror of Simple Souls, trans. E. Babinsky, Mahwah, NJ: Paulist Press, 1993

Porter, P. *The Enlightenment*, London: Palgrave, 1990

The Creation of the Modern World: The Untold Story of the British Enlightenment, New York: W.W. Norton, 2000

Poster, M. *Existentialist Marxism in Postwar France: From Sartre to Althusser*, Princeton, NJ: Princeton University Press, 1975

Powell, C. and G. E. C. Paton, *Humour and Society: Resistance and Control*, Houndmills: Macmillan, 1988

Powrie, P. *French Cinema in the 1980s: Nostalgia and the Crisis of Masculinity*, Oxford: Oxford University Press, 1997

French Cinema in the 1990s: Continuity and Difference, Oxford: Oxford University Press, 1998

Praz, Mario, *The Romantic Agony*, Oxford: Oxford University Press, 1951; original title: *La Carne, la morte e il diavolo nella letteratura romantica*, Rome, 1930

Prendergast, C. *The Order of Mimesis: Balzac, Stendhal, Nerval, Flaubert*, Cambridge: Cambridge University Press, 1986

(ed.). *Nineteenth-Century Poetry: Introductions to Close Reading*, Cambridge: Cambridge University Press, 1990

Paris and the Nineteenth Century, Oxford: Blackwell, 1992

Prest, J. *Theatre under Louis XIV: Cross-Casting and the Performance of Gender in Drama, Ballet and Opera*, New York: Palgrave Macmillan, 2006

La Prise d'Orange: chanson de geste de la fin du xiie siècle, ed. C. Régnier, Paris: Klincksieck, 1969

Quilligan, M. *The Language of Allegory: Defining the Genre*, Ithaca, NY: Cornell University Press, 1992

Quint, D. *Epic and Empire: Politics and Generic Form from Virgil to Milton*, Princeton, NJ: Princeton University Press, 1993

Rabaté, D. *Marie NDiaye*, Bry-sur-Marne: INA, 2008

Pascal Quignard: étude de l'œuvre, Paris: Bordas, 2008

Raimon Vidal (de Besalú), see Marshall, J. H.

Raimond, M. *La Crise du roman*, Paris: Corti, 1966

Ramm, B. *A Discourse for the Holy Grail in Old French Romance*, Cambridge: D. S. Brewer, 2007

Ramsay, R. L. *The French New Autobiographies: Sarraute, Duras and Robbe-Grillet*, Gainsford: University Press of Florida, 1996

Rancière, J. *The Flesh of Words: The Politics of Writing*, trans. C. Mandel, Stanford, CA: Stanford University Press, 2004

  'Why Emma Bovary Had to Be Killed', *Critical Inquiry* 34.2 (2008), 233–48

Raoul de Cambrai, ed. Sarah Kay, Oxford: Clarendon Press, 1992

Raoul de Houdenc, *La Vengeance Raguidel*, ed. G. Roussineau, Geneva: Droz, 2004

Ravel, J. 'Theater Beyond Privilege: Changes in French Play Publication, 1700–1789', *Studies on Voltaire and the Eighteenth Century* 12 (2001), pp. 299–347

The Razos de trobar of Raimon Vidal and Associated Texts, ed. J. H. Marshall, London: Oxford University Press, 1972

Reader, K. *The Abject Object: Avatars of the Phallus in Contemporary French Theory, Literature and Film*, Amsterdam and New York: Rodopi, 2006

Reeve, M. D. (ed.) and N. Wright (trans.). *Geoffrey of Monmouth: The History of the Kings of Britain*, Woodbridge, Suffolk: Boydell Press, 2007

Régnier-Bohler, D. (ed.). *Splendeurs de la cour de Bourgogne: récits et chroniques*, Paris: Robert Laffont, 1995

Reiss, T. J. *Towards Dramatic Illusion*, New Haven, CT: Yale University Press, 1971

Rémi, P. de. *Le Roman de la Manekine*, ed. and trans. B. N. Sargent-Baur with A. Stones and R. Middleton, Amsterdam and Atlanta, GA: Rodopi, 1999

René d'Anjou, *Le Livre du cœur d'amour espris*, ed. F. Bouchet, Paris: Librairie générale française, 2003

Rewald, J. *The History of Impressionism*, 4th rev. edn, New York: Museum of Modern Art, 1973

Rey, A. 'Le Français dans le monde', in A. Rey (ed.), *Dictionnaire historique de la langue française*, vol. II (1992), Paris: Robert, 1998, 1500–5

Reynolds, D. *Symbolist Aesthetics and Early Abstract Art*, Cambridge: Cambridge University Press, 1995

Reynolds-Cornell, R. (ed.). *Contes amoureux par Madame Jeanne Flore*, Saint-Etienne: Université de Saint-Etienne, 2005

Richard, J.-P. *Onze études sur la poésie moderne*, Paris: Seuil, 1964

Richard de Fournival, *Le Bestiaire d'amour et la response du bestiaire*, ed. and trans. G. Bianciotto, Paris: Champion, 2009

Ridon, J.-X. *Le Voyage en son miroir: essai sur quelques tentatives de réinventions du voyage au 20e siècle*, Paris: Kimé, 2002

Rigby, B. *Popular Culture in Modern France: A Study of Cultural Discourse*, London: Routledge, 1991

Rigoli, J. *Lire le délire: aliénisme, rhétorique et littérature en France au XIXe siècle*, Paris: Fayard, 2001

Rigolot, F. *Louise Labé Lyonnaise, ou la Renaissance au féminin*, Paris: Champion, 1997

  Poésie et Renaissance, Paris: Seuil, 2002

Robert of Clari, *La Conquête de Constantinople*, ed. Peter Noble, Edinburgh: Société Rencesvals British Branch, 2005

Robert von Blois, *Beaudous: Ein altfranzösischer Abenteuerroman des XIII. Jahrhunderts*, ed. Jakob Ulrich, Berlin: Mayer und Müller, 1889; reprinted Geneva: Slatkine, 1978

Robertson, D. *The Medieval Saints' Lives: Spiritual Renewal and Old French Literature*, Lexington, KY: French Forum, 1995

Robertson, D. W. *A Preface to Chaucer: Studies in Medieval Perspectives*, Princeton, NJ: Princeton University Press, 1962

Robreau, Y. *L'Honneur et la honte: leur expression dans les romans en prose du Lancelot-Graal (XIIe–XIIIe siècles)*, Geneva: Droz, 1981

Robson, K. *Writing Wounds: The Inscription of Trauma in Post-1968 French Women's Life-Writing*, Amsterdam: Rodopi, 2004

Rodowick, D. N. *The Virtual Life of Film*, London and Cambridge, MA: Harvard University Press, 2007

Rohou, J. *La Tragédie classique, 1550–1793*, Paris: SEDES, 1996

Le Roman de Brut de Wace, ed. I. D. O. Arnold, Paris: Société des anciens textes français, 1938–40

Le Roman de Flamenca: nouvelle occitane du treizième siècle, 2 vols., ed. U. Gschwind, Berne: Francke, 1976

Le Roman de Gliglois, ed. M.-L. Chênerie, Paris: Champion, 2003

Le Roman de Perceforest, ed. J. H. Taylor and G. Roussineau, Geneva: Droz, 1979–2007

The Roman de Rou, ed. A. J. Holden and G. S. Burgess, St Helier: Société jersiaise, 2002

Roman de Silence: A Thirteenth-Century Arthurian Verse-Romance, ed. L. Thorpe, Cambridge: Heffer, 1972

Le Roman de Tristan en prose, ed. P. Ménard, 9 vols., Geneva: Droz, 1987–97

The Romance of Hunbaut: An Arthurian Poem of the Thirteenth Century, ed. M. Winters, Leiden: Brill, 1984

The Romance of Yder, ed. and trans. Alison Adams, Cambridge: D. S. Brewer, 1983

Li Romans de Durmart le gallois; altfranzösisch Rittergedicht, ed. E. Stengel, Tübingen: Literarischer Verein in Stuttgart, 1873; reprinted Amsterdam: Rodopi, 1969

Romieu, Marie de. *Les Premières Oeuvres poétiques*, ed. A. Winandy, Geneva: Droz, 1972

Ronchi, G. (ed.). *Marco Polo: Milione. Le Divisament dou monde. Il milione delle redazioni toscana e franco-italiana*, Milan: Mondadori, 1982

Roos, J. *Early Impressionism and the French State (1866–1874)*, Cambridge: Cambridge University Press, 1996

Rosario, V. A. *The Erotic Imagination: French Histories of Perversity*, New York: Oxford University Press, 1997

Rosello, M. *Infiltrating Culture: Power and Identity in Contemporary Women's Writing*, Manchester: Manchester University Press, 1996

  Declining the Stereotype: Ethnicity and Representation in French Cultures, Hanover, NH and London: University Press of New England, 1998

  Postcolonial Hospitality: The Immigrant as Guest, Stanford, CA: Stanford University Press, 2001

Rosen, C. and H. Zerner, *Romanticism and Realism. The Mythology of Nineteenth-Century Art*, London: Faber and Faber, 1984

Select bibliography

Rosenberg, S. N., M. Switten, and G. Le Vot (eds.), *Songs of the Troubadours and Trouvères: An Anthology of Poems and Melodies*, New York and London: Garland, 1998
Ross, K. *Fast Cars, Clean Bodies: Decolonization and the Reordering of French Culture*, Cambridge, MA and London: MIT Press, 1995
Rouse, R. H. and M. A. *Manuscripts and their Makers: Commercial Book Producers in Medieval Paris 1200–1500*, 2 vols., London: H. Miller, 2000
Rousso, H. *Le Syndrome de Vichy*, Paris: Seuil, 1987
Rozlak, R. *Neo-Impressionism and Anarchism in Fin-de-Siècle France: Painting, Politics and Landscape*, Aldershot: Ashgate, 2007
Rubin, D. L. *The Knot of Artifice*, Columbus: Ohio State University Press, 1981
Russell, J. S. (ed.). *Allegoresis: The Craft of Allegory in Medieval Literature*, London: Taylor and Francis, 1988; reprinted New York: Garland, 1987
Rustichello da Pisa, *Il romanzo arturiano di Rustichello da Pisa*, ed. and trans. Fabrizio Cigni, intro. Valeria Bertolucci Pizzorusso, Pisa: Cassa di Risparmio di Pisa, Pacini, 1994
Rutebeuf, *Œuvres complètes*, ed. M. Zink, Paris: Livre de Poche, 1990
Rychner, J. *La Chanson de geste: essai sur l'art épique des jongleurs*, Geneva: Droz, 1955
Rye, G. *Narratives of Mothering: Women's Writing in Contemporary France*, Newark: University of Delaware Press, 2009
Rye, G. and C. Tarr (eds.). *Focalizing the Body in Contemporary Women's Writing and Film-making in France*, special issue of *Nottingham French Studies* 45.3 (2006)
Rye, G. and M. Worton (eds.). *Women's Writing in Contemporary France*, Manchester: Manchester University Press, 2002
Sade, D. A. F. de. *Œuvres*, ed. M. Delon, 3 vols., Paris: Gallimard, 1990–8
La Philosophie dans le boudoir, Paris: Flammarion, 2007
Sadoul, G. *Histoire générale du cinéma*, vol. I, Paris: Denoël, 1948
Saenger, P. *Space between Words: The Origins of Silent Reading*, Stanford, CA: Stanford University Press, 1997
Sagot, G. *Jeux de rôle: tout savoir sur les jeux de rôle et les livres dont vous êtes le héros*, Paris: Gallimard, 1986
Said, E. *Orientalism: Western Conceptions of the Orient*, London: Routledge and Kegan Paul, 1978
Sala, P. *Tristan: roman d'aventures du XVIe siècle*, ed. L. Muir, Geneva: Droz, 1958
Sandy, G. (ed.). 'Resources for the Study of Ancient Greek in France', in G. Sandy (ed.), *The Classical Heritage in France*, Leiden: Brill, 2002, pp. 47–78
Sarrazin, *Le Roman du Hem*, ed. A. Henri, Paris: Les Belles Lettres, 1939
Saussy, H. (ed.). *Comparative Literature in an Age of Globalization*, Baltimore, MD: Johns Hopkins University Press, 2006
Saxton, L. *Haunted Images: Film, Ethics, Testimony and the Holocaust*, London: Wallflower, 2008
Scaliger, J. C. *Poetices libri septem / Sieben Bücher über die Dichtkunst*, ed. M. Fuhrmann, L. Deitz, and G. Vogt-Spira, Stuttgart: Frommann-Holzboog, 1994–2003
Schechner, R. *Between Theater and Anthropology*, Philadelphia: University of Pennsylvania Press, 1985
Scherer, J. *La Dramaturgie classique en France*, Paris: Nizet, 1950
Scherer, J. and J. Truchet (eds.). *Théâtre du XVIIe siècle*, 3 vols., Paris: Gallimard, 1975–92

Schmid, M. *Processes of Literary Creation: Flaubert and Proust*, Oxford: Legenda, 1998

Schmidt, A.-M. *La Poésie scientifique en France au xvi siècle*, Paris: Albin Michel, 1938
Poètes du xvie siècle, Paris: Pléiade, 1953

Schmidt, J. *What is Enlightenment? Eighteenth-Century Answers and Twentieth-Century Questions*, Berkeley: University of California Press, 1999

Schmitt, C., Skinner, Q., Kessler, E., and Kraye, J. (eds.). *The Cambridge History of Renaissance Philosophy*, Cambridge: Cambridge University Press, 1988

Schmolke-Hassemann, B. *The Evolution of Arthurian Romance: The Verse Tradition from Chrétien to Froissart*, Cambridge: Cambridge University Press, 1998

Scholar, R. *The je-ne-sais-quoi in Early Modern Europe: Encounters with a Certain Something*, Oxford: Oxford University Press, 2005

Schor, N. *Zola's Crowds*, Baltimore, MD: Johns Hopkins University Press, 1978
George Sand and Idealism, New York: Columbia University Press, 1993

Schrift, A. D. *Twentieth-Century French Philosophy: Key Themes and Thinkers*, Oxford: Blackwell, 2006

Schulte Nordholt, A. *La Génération d'après et la mémoire de la Shoah*, Amsterdam and New York: Rodopi, 2008

Scott, C. *Vers libre: The Emergence of Free Verse in France, 1886–1914*, Oxford: Oxford University Press, 1990

Scott, D. *Semiologies of Travel: From Gautier to Baudrillard*, Cambridge: Cambridge University Press, 2004

Scott, J. W. *Only Paradoxes to Offer: French Feminists and the Rights of Man*, Cambridge, MA: Harvard University Press, 1996

Scott, M. *Baudelaire's* Le Spleen de Paris: *Shifting Perspectives*, Aldershot: Ashgate, 2005

Sébillet, T. *Art poétique françoys*, ed. F. Gaiffe, Geneva: Droz, 1932; reprinted Paris: Nizet, 1988

Segal, N. *Narcissus and Echo: Women in the French récit*, Manchester: Manchester University Press, 1988

Seifert, L. *Fairy Tales, Sexuality and Gender in France, 1690–1715: Nostalgic Utopias*, Cambridge: Cambridge University Press, 1996

Sgard, J. *et al.* (eds.). *Dictionnaire des journaux, 1660–1789*, Paris: Universitas; Oxford: Voltaire Foundation, 1991

Shaw, H. E. *Narrating Reality: Austen, Scott, Eliot*, Ithaca, NY: Cornell University Press, 1999

Sheringham, M. *French Autobiography: Devices and Desires: Rousseau to Perec*, Oxford: Clarendon Press, 1993
Everyday Life: Theories and Practices from Surrealism to the Present, Oxford: Oxford University Press, 2006

Shiff, R. *Cézanne and the End of Impressionism*, Chicago: University of Chicago Press, 1984

Shilton, S. 'Repossessing Travel', in J. Horn and L. Russell-Watts (eds.), *Possessions: Essays in French Literature, Cinema and Theory*, Berne: Peter Lang, 2001, pp. 87–103

Showalter, E. 'Writing off the Stage: Women Authors and Eighteenth-Century Theater', in 'The Politics of Tradition: Placing Women in French Literature', special issue of *Yale French Studies*, 75 (1988), pp. 95–111

Simonin, M. 'La Disgrâce d'Amadis', in *L'Encre et la lumière*, Geneva: Droz, 2004, pp. 189–234

Sinclair, F. E. *Milk and Blood: Gender and Genealogy in the Chansons de Geste*, Oxford: Peter Lang, 2003

Skinner, Q. *The Foundations of Modern Political Thought*, 2 vols., Cambridge: Cambridge University Press, 1978

Smalley, B. *Historians in the Middle Ages*, New York: Charles Scribner's Sons, 1974

Sobchack, V. *Carnal Thoughts: Embodiment and Moving Image Culture*, Berkeley, Los Angeles and London: California University Press, 2004

Sorlin, P. 'L'Ombre d'un deuil', in 'Où va le cinéma?', special issue of *Cinergon* 15 (2003), pp. 7–15

Speake, J. (ed.). *Literature of Travel and Exploration: An Encyclopedia*, 3 vols., New York and London: Fitzroy Dearborn, 2003

Spencer, S. *French Women and the Age of Enlightenment*, Bloomington, IN: Indiana University Press, 1984

Spiegel, G. M. *Romancing the Past: The Rise of Vernacular Prose Historiography in Thirteenth-Century France*, Berkeley: University of California Press, 1993

Spies, W. (ed.). *La Révolution surréaliste*, Paris: Centre Pompidou, 2002

Spitzer, A. W. *The French Generation of 1820*, Princeton, NJ: Princeton University Press, 1987

Spivak, G. 'Can the Subaltern Speak?', in C. Nelson and L. Grossberg (eds.), *Marxism and the Interpretation of Culture*, London: Macmillan, 1988, pp. 271–313

Stahuljak, Z. *Bloodless Genealogies of the French Middle Ages: Translatio, Kinship, and Metaphor*, Gainesville: University Press of Florida, 2005

Stamelman, R. *Lost beyond Telling: Representations of Death and Absence in Modern French Poetry*, Ithaca, NY: Cornell University Press, 1990

Stanesco, M. *Jeux d'errance du chevalier médiéval: aspects ludiques de la fonction guerrière dans la littérature du moyen âge flamboyant*, Leiden: Brill, 1988

'Les Romans en prose au moyen âge', in M. Prigent (ed.), *Histoire de la France littéraire*, vol. I, Paris: Presses Universitaires de France, 2006, pp. 970–83

Stanesco, M. and M. Zink. *Histoire européenne du roman médiéval*, Paris: Presses Universitaires de France, 1992

Stanislavski, C. *An Actor Prepares*, trans. E. R. Hapgood, New York: Theatre Arts, 1936

Starobinski, J. 'La Rochefoucauld et les morales substitutives', *Nouvelle revue française* 14 (1966), pp. 6–34 and 211–29

Montaigne en mouvement, Paris: Gallimard, 1982

Stein, R. M. *Reality Fictions: Romance, History, and Governmental Authority, 1025–1180*, South Bend, IN: University of Notre Dame Press, 2006

Stephens, S. *A History of Women's Writing in France*, Cambridge and New York: Cambridge University Press, 2000

Stephenson, B. *The Power and Patronage of Marguerite de Navarre*, Aldershot: Ashgate, 2004

Stewart, J. H. *Gynographs: French Novels by Women of the late Eighteenth Century*, Lincoln: University of Nebraska Press, 1993

Stewart, P. R. *Imitation and Illusion in the French Memoir-Novel, 1700–1750: The Art of Make Believe*, New Haven, CT and London: Yale University Press, 1969

Stock, B. *Implications of Literacy: Written Language and Models of Interpretation in the Eleventh and Twelfth Centuries*, Princeton, NJ: Princeton University Press, 1983

Stokvis, W. *Cobra: The Last Avant-Garde Movement of the Twentieth Century*, Aldershot: Lund Humphries, 2004

Storey, J. *Cultural Theory and Popular Culture*, London: Harvester Wheatsheaf, 1993

Street, J. S. *French Sacred Drama from Bèze to Corneille*, Cambridge: Cambridge University Press, 1983

Strickland, D. H., *Saracens, Demons and Jews: Making Monsters in Medieval Art*, Princeton, NJ: Princeton University Press, 2003

Strinati, D. *An Introduction to the Theories of Popular Culture*, London and New York: Routledge, 1995

Strubel, A., *La Rose, Renart et le Graal: la littérature allégorique en France au xiiie siècle*, Geneva: Slatkine, 1989

Sturges, R. *Medieval Interpretations: Models of Reading in Literary Narrative, 1100–1500*, Carbondale: Southern Illinois University Press, 1991

Suleiman, S. R. *Crises of Memory and the Second World War*, Cambridge, MA and London: Harvard University Press, 2006

Surand, P. *L'Art d'être Hugo: lecture d'une poésie siècle*, Arles: Actes Sud, 2005

Swart, K. W. *The Sense of Decadence in Nineteenth-Century France*, The Hague: Nijhoff, 1964

Symes, C. *A Common Stage: Theater and Public Life in Medieval Arras*, Ithaca, NY: Cornell University Press, 2007

Szkilnik, M. *Jean de Saintré: une carrière chevaleresque au xve siècle*, Geneva: Droz, 2003

Tarbé, P. (ed.). *Les Œuvres de Blondel de Néele*, Reims: Dubois, 1862

Tarr, C. *Reframing Difference:* Beur and banlieue *filmmaking in France*, Manchester: Manchester University Press, 2005

Tarr, C. and B. Rollet. *Cinema and the Second Sex: Women's Filmmaking in France in the 1980s and 1990s*, New York and London: Continuum, 2001

Taylor, J. *Paths to Contemporary French Literature*, 2 vols., New Brunswick, NJ: Transaction Publishers, 2004–7

Taylor, J. H. M., 'The Fourteenth Century: Context, Text and Intertext', in N. J. Lacy, D. Kelly, and K. Busby (eds.), *The Legacy of Chrétien de Troyes*, vol. 1, Amsterdam: Rodopi, 1987, pp. 267–332

Temple M. and M. Witt (eds.). *The French Cinema Book*, London: British Film Institute, 2004

Tetel, M. *Montaigne et Marie de Gournay*, Paris: Champion, 1997

Thélot, J. *La Poésie précaire*, Paris: Presses Universitaires de France, 1997

Thiher, A. *Revels in Madness: Insanity in Medicine and Literature*, Ann Arbor: University of Michigan Press, 1999

Thomas, J.-J. and S. Winspur. *Poeticized Language: Studies in Contemporary French Poetry*, University Park, PA: Penn State University Press, 1999

Thompson, H. *Naturalism Redressed: Identity and Clothing in the Novels of Emile Zola*, Oxford: Legenda, 2004

Timmermans, L. *L'Accès des femmes à la culture (1598–1715)*, Paris: Champion, 1993

Tinguely, F. *L'Écriture du Levant à la Renaissance: enquête sur les voyageurs français dans l'empire de Soliman le Magnifique*, Geneva: Droz, 2000

Tobin, P. M. O'Hara (ed.). *Les Lais anonymes des xiie et xiiie siècles*, Geneva: Droz, 1976

Todorov, T. *Introduction à la littérature fantastique*, Paris: Seuil, 1970

Poétique de la prose, Paris: Seuil, 1971

Tombs, N. 'Feminist Histories of Psychiatry', in M. Micale and R. Porter (eds.), *Discovering the History of Psychiatry*, New York and Oxford: Oxford University Press, 1994, pp. 348–83

Topping, M. (ed.) *Eastern Voyages, Western Visions: French Writing and Painting of the Orient*, Berne: Peter Lang, 2004

Tristan, F. *Flora Tristan, Utopian Feminist: Her Travel Diaries and Personal Crusade*, ed. P. Beik, trans. D. Beik, Bloomington: Indiana University Press, 1993

Tristan en prose, see Le Roman de Tristan

Tristan et Iseut: les poèmes français, la saga norroise, ed. and trans. P. Walter and D. Lacroix, Paris: Livre de Poche, 1992

Trott, D. *Théâtre du xviiie siècle: jeux, écritures, regards*, Montpellier: Espaces 34, 2000

Trousson, R. (ed.). *Romans libertins du xviiie siècle*, Paris: Robert Laffont, 1993

Romans de femmes du dix-huitième siècle, Paris: Robert Laffont, 1996

Truchet, J. *La Prédication de Bossuet, étude des thèmes*, 2 vols., Paris: Cerf, 1960

La Tragédie classique en France, 3rd edn, Paris: Presses Universitaires de France, 1997

Turner, D. *The Darkness of God: Negativity in Christian Mysticism*, Cambridge: Cambridge University Press, 1995

Turner, V. W. *Dramas, Fields, and Metaphors: Symbolic Action in Human Society*, Ithaca, NY: Cornell University Press, 1974

From Ritual to Theatre: The Human Seriousness of Play (1982); reprinted New York: PAJ, 1992

Tuve, R., *Allegorical Imagery: Some Medieval Books and their Posterity*, Princeton, NJ: Princeton University Press, 1966

Tzanaki, R. *Mandeville's Medieval Audiences: A Study of the Book of Sir John Mandeville (1371–1550)*, Aldershot: Ashgate, 2003.

Unwin, T. *Cambridge Companion to Flaubert*, Cambridge: Cambridge University Press, 2004

Van Delft, L. *Le Moraliste classique: essai de définition et de typologie*, Geneva: Droz, 1982

Van Dyke, C. *The Fiction of Truth: Structures of Meaning in Narrative and Dramatic Allegory*, Ithaca, NY: Cornell University Press, 1985

Van Zuylen, M. *Monomania: The Flight From Everyday Life in Literature and Art*, Ithaca, NY: Cornell University Press, 2005

Vance, E. *Mervelous Signs: Poetics and Sign Theory in the Middle Ages*, Lincoln and London: University of Nebraska Press, 1986

Vernet, M. *Jean-Pierre Camus: théorie de la contre-littérature*, Paris and Quebec: Nizet and Le Griffon d'argile, 1995

Viart, D. *François Bon: étude de l'œuvre*, Paris: Bordas, 2008

Viart, D. and B. Vercier. *La Littérature française au présent: héritage, modernité, mutations*, Paris: Bordas, 2005; 2nd edn, 2008

Vickers, B. '"Words and Things" – or "Words, Concepts, and Things"? Rhetorical and Linguistic Categories in the Renaissance', in Eckhard Kessler and Ian Maclean (eds.), *Res et verba in der Renaissance*, Wiesbaden: Harrassowitz, 2002, pp. 287–335

Vie privée du maréchal de Richelieu, ed. B. Craveri, Paris: Desjonquères, 1993

Voyage de Charlemagne à Jérusalem et à Constantinople, Le Pèlerinage de Charlemagne, ed. G. S. Burgess, Edinburgh: Société Rencesvals British Branch, 1998

The Vulgate Version of the Arthurian Romances, edited from manuscripts in the British Museum, ed. H. O. Sommer, 8 vols., Washington, DC: Carnegie Institution, 1909–16

Wace, *Le Roman de Brut*, ed. I. Arnold, 2 vols., Paris: Société des anciens textes français, 1938–40

Wade, I. *The Intellectual Origins of the French Enlightenment*, Princeton, NJ: Princeton University Press, 1971

Wald Lasowski, P. (ed.). *Romanciers libertins du XVIIIe siècle*, 2 vols., Paris: Gallimard, 2000–5

Waldrop, R. *Lavish Absence: Recalling and Rereading Edmond Jabès*, Middletown, CT: Wesleyan University Press, 2002

Walker, D. *Outrage and Insight: Modern French Writers and the 'fait divers'*, Oxford: Berg, 1995

Waller, M. *The Male Malady*, New Brunswick, NJ: Rutgers University Press, 1993

Wanegffelen, T. (ed.). *La Renaissance*, Paris: Ellipses, 2003

Warner, M., *Monuments and Maidens: The Allegory of the Female Form*, Berkeley: University of California Press, 2001

Warnock, M. *An Existentialist Ethics*, London and Basingstoke: Macmillan, 1967

Warren, M. R., *History on the Edge: Excalibur and the Borders of Britain, 1100–1300*, Minneapolis: University of Minnesota Press, 2000

'Take the World by Prose: Modes of Possession in the *Roman d'Alexandre*', in D. Maddox and S. Sturm-Maddox (eds.), *The Medieval French Alexander*, Albany: State University of New York Press, 2002, pp. 143–60

Watkins, S. *Twentieth-Century Women Novelists: Feminist Theory into Practice*, Basingstoke: Palgrave, 2001

Waugh, P. *Metafiction: The Theory and Practice of Self-Conscious Fiction*, London and New York: Routledge, 1984

Wauquelin, Jean, *Le Roman en prose de Manekine*, in H. Suchier (ed.), *Œuvres poétiques de Philippe de Remi, sire de Beaumanoir*, vol. I, Paris: Firmin Didot, 1884, pp. 267–366

Weir, D. *Decadence and the Making of Modernity*, Amherst: University of Massachusetts Press, 1995

Weiss, D. H. and L. Mahoney (eds.). *France and the Holy Land: Frankish Culture at the End of the Crusades*, Baltimore, MD: The Johns Hopkins University Press, 2004

Wendel, F. *Calvin: The Origins and Development of his Religious Thought*, trans. P. Mairet, London: Collins, 1963; original title, *Calvin: sources et évolution de sa pensée religieuse*, Paris, Presses Universitaires de France, 1950

Wetzel, A. *Partir sans partir: le récit de voyage littéraire au XIXe siècle*, Toronto: Paratexte, 1992

Wheeler B. and J. Carmi Parsons (eds.). *Eleanor of Aquitaine: Lord and Lady*, New York: Palgrave Macmillan, 2003

White, H. *The Content of the Form: Narrative Discourse and Historical Representation*, Baltimore, MD: Johns Hopkins University Press, 1987

White, N. *The Family in Crisis in Late Nineteenth-Century French Fiction*, Cambridge: Cambridge University Press, 1999

Wieviorka, A. *Déportation et génocide: entre la mémoire et l'oubli*, Paris: Plon, 1992

Willard, C. C. *Christine de Pizan: Her Life and Works*, New York: Persea, 1984

William of Malmesbury, *Gesta Regum Anglorum: The History of the English Kings*, ed. R. A. B. Mynors, R. M. Thomson, and M. Winterbottom, 2 vols., Oxford and New York: Clarendon Press, 1998–9

Williams, A. *Republic of Images*, Cambridge, MA: Harvard University Press, 1992

Williams, R. *The Country and the City*, London: Chatto and Windus, 1973

Williams, W. *Pilgrimage and Narrative in the French Renaissance: 'The Undiscovered Country'*, Oxford: Oxford University Press, 1999

   '"Rubbing up Against Others": Montaigne on Pilgrimage', in J. Elsner and J.-P. Rubiés (eds.), *Voyages and Visions: Towards a Cultural History of Travel*, London: Reaktion Books, 1999, pp. 101–23

Wilson, E. *Sexuality and the Reading Encounter: Identity and Desire in Proust, Duras, Tournier and Cixous*, Oxford: Oxford University Press, 1996

Wilson, K. M. and N. Margolis (eds.). *Women in the Middle Ages: An Encyclopedia*, 2 vols., Westport, CT: Greenwood Press, 2004

Winegarten, R. *French Lyric Poetry in the Age of Malherbe*, Manchester: Manchester University Press, 1954

   Accursed Politics: Some Women Writers and Political Life, 1715–1850, Chicago: I. R. Dee, 2003

Wogan-Browne, J. *Saints' Lives and Women's Literary Culture c. 1150–1300: Virginity and its Authorizations*, Oxford: Oxford University Press, 2001

Wokler, R. 'Anthropology and Conjectural History in the Enlightenment', in C. Fox, R. Porter, and R. Wokler (eds.), *Inventing Human Science: Eighteenth-Century Domains*, Berkeley, Los Angeles, and London: University of California Press, 1995, pp. 31–52.

Woledge B. and H. P. Clive. *Répertoire des plus anciens textes en prose française depuis 842 jusqu'aux premières années du XIIIe siècle*, Geneva: Droz, 1964

   Bibliographie des romans et nouvelles en prose française antérieurs à 1500, Geneva: Droz, 1954; *Supplément 1954–1973*, Geneva: Droz, 1975

Wolfgang, A. *Gender and Voice in the French Novel, 1730–1782*, Burlington, VT: Ashgate, 2004

Wolfzettel, F. *Ce désir de vagabondage cosmopolite: Wege und Entwicklung des französischen Reiseberichts im 19. Jahrhundert*, Tübingen: M. Niemeyer, 1986

Woods, Diane S. *Hélisenne de Crenne: At the Crossroads of Renaissance Humanism and Feminism*, Madison, NJ: Fairleigh Dickinson University Press, 2001

Worms, F. *Bergson ou les deux sens de la vie*, Paris: Presses Universitaires de France, 2004

Wright, N. and J. Crick. *The Historia Regum Britannie of Geoffrey of Monmouth*, 5 vols., Cambridge: D. S. Brewer, 1984–95

Yates, F. *The French Academies of the Sixteenth Century*, London: Warburg Institute, 1947, various reprints

   The Art of Memory, Chicago: University of Chicago Press, 1966

Yee, J. *Exotic Subversions in Nineteenth-Century French Fiction*, London: Legenda, 2008

Young, K. *The Drama of the Medieval Church*, 2 vols., Oxford: Clarendon Press, 1933

Zaal, J. W. B. *'A Lei francesca' (sainte Foy, v. 20): étude sur les chansons de saints Gallo-romanes du XIe siècle*, Leiden: Brill, 1962

Zaercher, V. 'La *Mitistoire de Fanfreluche et Gaudichon* de Guillaume des Autels: de l'imitation à la création romanesque', in M. Clément and P. Mousnier (eds.), *Le Roman français*, Strasbourg: Presses Universitaires de Strasbourg, 2005, pp. 281–94

Zink, M. *La Prédication en langue romane*, Paris: Champion, 1976

Les Chansons de toile, Paris: Champion, 1977

Žižek, S. 'Courtly Love, or Woman as Thing', in E. Wright and E. Wright (eds.), *The Žižek Reader*, Oxford: Blackwell, 1999, pp. 148–73

Zumthor, P. *La Lettre et la voix: la 'littérature médiévale'*, Paris: Seuil, 1987

    'De la circularité du chant (à propos des trouvères des xiie et xiiie siècles)', *Poétique* 2 (1970), pp. 129–40

    Essai de poétique médiévale, Paris: Seuil, 1972

Index

French spelling and forms of names are used for French persons., e.g. Henri II (for the King of France) and Henry II (for the King of England), William of Malmesbury, but Guillaume de Lorris. Titles of French works are generally cited in French.